Health
PSYCHOLOGY

SECOND
CANADIAN
EDITION

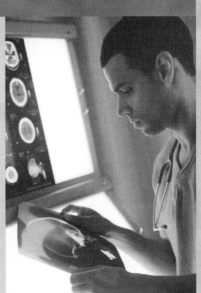

Shelley E. Taylor

Fuschia M. Sirois

Mc Graw Hill **McGraw-Hill Ryerson**
Connect. Learn. Succeed.

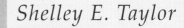

Health Psychology
Second Canadian Edition

ISBN-13: 978-0-07-031979-0

ISBN-10: 0-07-031979-0

2 3 4 5 6 7 8 9 MQ 1 9 8 7 6 5 4 3 2

Printed in Canada

Publisher: *Cara Yarzab*
Marketing Manager: *Margaret Janzen*
Developmental Editor: *Lindsay MacDonald*
Senior Editorial Associate: *Marina Seguin*
Photo/Permissions Editor: *MRM Associates*
Supervising Editor: *Graeme Powell*
Copy Editor: *Evan Turner, Row House Publishing Services*
Production Coordinator: *Emily Hickey*
Cover and Interior Design: *Brett Miller*
Cover Image: *Mother/Daughter (Indeed/Aflo/Getty); Yoga woman (webphotographeer/Getty); Doctor (John Anthony Rizzo/Getty)*
Page Layout: *Aptara®, Inc.*
Printer: *Transcontinental Printing Group*

Library and Archives Canada Cataloguing in Publication

Taylor, Shelley E.
    Health psychology / Shelley E. Taylor, Fuschia M. Sirois.—2nd Canadian ed.

Includes bibliographical references and index.
    ISBN 978-0-07-031979-0

1. Clinical health psychology.   2. Medicine, Psychosomatic.   I. Sirois, Fuschia M., 1961–   II. Title.

R726.7.T39 2012   616.001'9   C2011–905917–7

ABOUT THE AUTHORS

SHELLEY E. TAYLOR is professor of psychology at the University of California, Los Angeles. She received her Ph.D. in social psychology from Yale University. After a visiting professorship at Yale and assistant and associate professorships at Harvard University, she joined the faculty of UCLA in 1979. Her research interests are in health psychology, especially the factors that promote long-term psychological adjustment, and in social cognition. In the former capacity, she is the co-director of the Health Psychology program at UCLA. Professor Taylor is the recipient of a number of awards—most notably, the American Psychological Association's Distinguished Scientific Contribution to Psychology Award, a 10-year Research Scientist Development Award from the National Institute of Mental Health, and an Outstanding Scientific Contribution Award in Health Psychology. She is the author of more than 200 publications in journals and books and is the author of *Social Cognition* and *Positive Illusions.*

FUSCHIA M. SIROIS is an associate professor of psychology at Bishop's University, and a Canada Research Chair in Health and Well-being. While completing an honours degree in biochemistry/nutrition at the University of Ottawa, she took a course in health psychology that inspired her to pursue graduate training in psychology. She received her Ph.D. in social psychology in 2003 from Carleton University. Professor Sirois has a variety of health psychology research interests including self-regulation and health, the role of psychological factors in medical care-seeking and complementary and alternative medicine use in particular, and how individuals adjust to chronic health conditions. Her research is funded by the Social Sciences and Humanities Council of Canada (SSHRC), and the Canadian Foundation for Innovation (CFI), and has been published in several journals including *Social Science and Medicine, Health Psychology, Journal of Alternative and Complementary Medicine,* and *Quality of Life Research.*

CONTENTS

When the first edition of *Health Psychology* was written by Shelley Taylor back in the mid-1980s, health psychology was a relatively new and emerging sub-field within psychology. Since that time it has continued to grow and expand as research and our understanding of the role of human factors in health and illness has advanced. The challenge for me in co-authoring the first Canadian edition of Shelley Taylor's established text was, therefore, to continue her tradition of conveying the increasing sophistication of the field in an accessible, comprehensible, and engaging manner, while at the same time highlighting our uniquely Canadian perspective on health and illness. In this second Canadian edition, I have maintained this stance, including the latest Canadian health-related research and updating content to try to keep current with the ever changing field of health psychology.

Beyond the obvious differences in the health care systems between the United States and Canada, there are other subtle, yet important ways in which the Canadian perspective on health is qualitatively distinct from that of our neighbours to the south. For example, the biopsychosocial model of health, which is prevalent in Canadian health psychology research, has in recent years been augmented by the public health promotion perspective of health. This particular view of the forces and factors that shape health and health-related behaviours evolved from a more social-ecological perspective of health that began back in the 1970s with the Lalonde Report and was continued in the 1980's with the Epp Report. As we explain in Chapter 1, health can be viewed as a product of biological, social or environmental, lifestyle, and health care organizational forces. Thus, the Canadian perspective on health is based on an established tradition that health can best be understood by accounting for the role of not only individual factors but also social factors. It is from this tradition that health is viewed as a capacity that can be attained by all Canadians, rather than simply a state that can only be achieved by the privileged.

I have attempted to address the differences between the U.S. and the Canadian perspectives of health in the presentation of the material in this second Canadian edition in several different ways. For example, I have revised the text to include statistics, current events, and examples of diversity that are relevant to a Canadian context, including increasing the amount of Canadian research presented throughout the text and updating terminology to reflect the Canadian perspective. Relevant international examples of excellent international Health Psychology research are also included. An additional way is through the refocusing and renaming of the feature boxes (presented below), which were first introduced in the first edition and which have been retained for this edition, to reflect themes and research that are more relevant to Canadian readers.

- **Spotlight on Canadian Research:** Although Canadian contributions to the field of health psychology are embedded throughout the text, these feature boxes were added to draw the readers' attention further to specific areas where Canadian researchers are considered as being on the cutting edge or forefront of particular lines of inquiry.

- **Focus on Social Issues:** In addition to several of the original features from the most recent U.S. edition, this second Canadian edition has updated feature content to reflect the idea that health and health-related behaviours from the Canadian perspective are inextricably intertwined with the social context in which they occur.

- **Health Psychology in Action:** Health psychology is both an applied and a basic field. These feature boxes highlight the application of theory to address real world issues that are of particular importance to health psychologists, whether it be changing health behaviours or improving the quality of life for individuals with chronic illness.

- **Measuring Health Psychology Concepts:** The feature boxes from the most recent Canadian and U.S. editions that focused on particular scales have been titled under this common theme to highlight the instruments that are often used in health psychology research for students.

Current understandings of health and health care in Canada and in other parts of the world are just beginning to undergo tremendous change now and in the coming years as our population ages, technology advances, and the balance of chronic versus infectious disease patterns shifts. The coming changes will provide interesting challenges for health psychology and anyone planning to study within this growing and dynamic field. However, health psychology, like any science, is cumulative, and how we respond to the challenges of tomorrow will rely in part on the knowledge and understanding of today. Although some of the updated content for this second Canadian edition is geared toward the already occurring and anticipated changes, some of the important and foundational content from the U.S. edition has been preserved to familiarize students with key advances and theories from health psychology as it has developed since its inception in the early 1980s.

Other features new to this second Canadian edition include the following:

- **Learning objectives as chapter outlines:** To promote enquiry and enhance concept mastery, each chapter's outline is now a series of learning objectives that highlight key concepts. The sections that address each learning objective are indicated throughout the chapter and the learning objectives are then presented with a summary of the relevant content at the end of the chapter. Because multiple presentations of material promotes learning and retention, students can use these learning objectives as a reminder of the key chapter themes and as a study tool for monitoring their learning.

- **Critical Checkpoint:** To challenge the reader to think critically about an important and sometimes controversial topic of issue, a Critical Checkpoint box has been added to each chapter.

- **Updated coverage:** To keep up with the advances in health psychology, many new references from the past one to five years have been added. Older research that is no longer relevant or that does not provide a historical glimpse of the changes within the field have also been removed.

In short, I have attempted to preserve the best from the previous U.S. edition by Professor Taylor, while incorporating changes that reflect and highlight the unique Canadian perspective on the psychology of health.

New to the Second Canadian Edition

In addition to removing U.S. content regarding health and health care and updating it with Canadian content and statistics throughout the text, a number of changes have been made to this latest edition. This section provides examples of some of the key changes to each chapter.

Chapter 1: What Is Health Psychology?

- A new feature box on the day in the life of a health psychologist highlights the diverse ways in which health psychology concepts and principles can be applied in a medical setting.
- A new figure showing a brief timeline has been added to give a broader historical perspective on how our views on the mind–body relationship have changed over time. There is a focus on events relevant to Canada in particular for the recent events.
- The section on current views on the mind–body relationship has been updated to correspond to the new timeline added.
- A section on qualitative research updates the research methods section to feature this increasingly popular method of data collection in health psychology.
- A new table on the allied health professionals outlines the roles and training for the different health-related professions that regularly apply health psychology principles.

Chapter 2: The Systems of the Body

- Content has been reduced throughout this chapter to enhance clarity and ease of reading.
- New section on Alzheimer's disease, a condition that is becoming an increasing concern with the greying of the nation, has been added.
- New research on the psychosocial factors linked to disease development has been included where relevant.

Chapter 3: Health Behaviours

- The section on the transtheoretical model has been streamlined and repositioned within the chapter to co-ordinate better with the sections covering other theories and models.
- New section on the theories and models used for understanding health behaviour change reorganizes theories covered from the first edition along with those new to this edition, including Gollwitzer's implementation intentions. A new sub-section on social cognitive models and Bandura's self-efficacy theory has been added.
- Other new research added covers employee health risk assessments, and the role of affective factors in health behaviour change.

Chapter 4: Preventive and Health-Promoting Behaviours

- New feature box on research addressing the issue of cell phone use related driving accidents has been added.
- Order of chapter sections has been changed to achieve a better flow of topics, starting with preventable injuries, then cancer screening behaviours, then exercise, then diet behaviours, and rest.
- Mammography and other statistics have been updated throughout.
- The section on exercise as stress management has been moved to Chapter 7.

- In response to reviewers' comments, the section on eating disorders has been moved to Chapter 5 as it is a health risk behaviour.
- The section on the set point theory of weight has been removed as it is outdated.

Chapter 5: Health Compromising Behaviours

- New section introduced on illicit drug use plus a figure showing the primary drugs of abuse used by those entering treatment for drug problems in Canada.
- Eating disorders section from Chapter 4 has been moved to end of chapter.

Chapter 6: Stress

- New section on Bullying and Stress features research addressing this important issue in both educational and workplace settings.
- Added new research on the interactive effects of the environment and chronic stress.
- Added Canadian research on the prenatal effects of stress form the ice storm on children.
- Expanded coverage of research supporting the tend-and-befriend model, and research on occupational stress and its impact on health and well-being.

Chapter 7: Moderators of the Stress Experience

- New Table 7.1 outlines the signs and symptoms of stress.
- Expanded coverage of the role of social factors in coping with stress. New research added for dyadic coping, social support and health, attachment and social support, and implicit social support and culture.
- New research from Canadian researchers on the links between perfectionism and health highlights how Canadians are spearheading this emerging topic.

Chapter 8: The Patient in the Treatment Setting

- Revised the section on using health services for emotional disturbances to give more balanced perspective on this issue
- Removed outdated sections on children in the hospital and attentional differences in symptoms.
- Expanded coverage of the issue of culture and seeking medical care, including Canadian research on the role of linguistic barriers in the use of health care services.

Chapter 9: Patient-Provider Relations

- Rearranged sections on non-adherence and the placebo effect for better flow.
- New sections on elderspeak, non-disclosure of complementary and alternative medicine highlight emerging research.
- Expanded coverage of research on physician listening, and holistic health care, with a case study quote added to illustrate the latter.
- Updated coverage of the placebo effect, including current research on the role of personality and placebo responding.

Chapter 10: Pain and Its Management

- New Health Psychology in Action Box 10.4: Can Listening to Your Favourite Music Reduce Pain? features novel research on the role of music in pain management.
- New coping and pain section highlights Canadian research on pain catastrophizing.
- New gender and pain section illustrates the biopsychosocial nature of pain.
- New table summarizes the peripheral nerve fibres involved in nociception.

Chapter 11: Living With Chronic Illness

- Key terms in this chapter–chronic health condition, chronic illness, chronic disease–now described in detail.
- Health Psychology in Action Box revised to focus on online support communities for young adults living with chronic illness.
- New research on cultural differences in quality of life added.
- Feature box on who works with patients with chronic illnesses removed and incorporated into a table in Chapter 1

Chapter 12: Psychological Issues in Advancing and Terminal Illness

- New Spotlight on Canadian Research Box 12.6 on Dignity Therapy
- Research on "assisted suicide" updated to use the less value-laden term "aid in dying".
- Streamlined and clarified Kübler-Ross theory section adding references to new critiques to give a more balanced perspective of this classic model.
- Removed Box 12.1 on the leukemic child to make room for newer content.
- New sections on Caregiver Stress and Home Care, and a "good death" added to reflect current research in this area.

Chapter 13: Heart Disease, Hypertension, Stroke, and Diabetes

- Updated language throughout to conform to new APA style standards.
- Extensive updating of research references to include 2008 – 2011 references where available.
- Expanded coverage of women's heart health issues and women-centred cardiovascular rehabilitation programs.

Chapter 14: Psychoneuroimmunology, AIDS, Cancer, and Arthritis

- New chapter overview statement to help better link chapter topics.
- New sections on employment and HIV issues, depression and cancer, and psychosocial adjustment and coping with rheumatoid arthritis, highlight current research on these important topics.
- Re-organized section on psychosocial factors and cancer to remove redundancies and improve flow.

- Added case study quotes for the section on arthritis to illustrate the effects of this illness on real people.

Chapter 15: Health Psychology: Challenges for the Future

- Added new research on the role of complementary and alternative medicine providers in supporting health behaviour change.
- Expanded coverage of the future of health psychology theory.
- Telehealth description moved to Chapter 8.
- Section headings revised to reflect health psychology priorities not health promotion priorities.

■ SUPPLEMENTS

For Instructors

Online Learning Centre   On the book's Web site, instructors will find the **Instructor's Manual, Test Bank** and **Computerized Test Bank**, and **PowerPoint presentations**, plus an Image Gallery with figures from the book. The Instructor's Manual outlines each chapter and provides detailed learning objectives and suggestions for lectures. Also included are ideas for classroom discussion, student projects, paper topics, and other activities. The extensive Test Bank of true/false, multiple-choice, and essay questions assesses students' recall of material, as well as their ability to comprehend and apply the concepts in the text. The PowerPoint slides focus on key concepts. These materials are available on the password-protected side of the Online Learning Centre (www.mcgrawhill.ca/olc/taylor).

Course Management   McGraw-Hill Ryerson offers a range of flexible integration solutions for Blackboard, WebCT, Desire2Learn, Moodle and other leading learning management platforms. Please contact your local McGraw-Hill Ryerson iLearning Sales Specialist for details.

iLearning Sales Specialist   Your Integrated Learning Sales Specialist is a McGraw-Hill Ryerson representative with the experience, product knowledge, training, and support to help you assess and integrate any of these products, technology, and services into your course for optimum teaching and learning performance. Whether it is using our test bank software, helping your students improve their grades, or putting your entire course online, your *i*Learning Sales Specialist is there to help you do it. Contact your local *i*Learning Sales Specialist today to learn how to maximize all of McGraw-Hill Ryerson's resources.

iLearning Services Program   McGraw-Hill Ryerson offers a unique *i*Learning Services package designed for Canadian faculty. Our mission is to equip providers of higher education with superior tools and resources required for excellence in teaching. For additional information, please visit www.mcgrawhill.ca/highereducation/iservices.

For Students

Online Learning Centre   Students will find a number of study tools on the book's Web site: www.mcgrawhill.ca/olc/taylor. These include learning objectives, chapter outlines, multiple-choice questions, and more.

■ ACKNOWLEDGMENTS

Gratitude is expressed to Stephen Cross and Meaghan Barlow for their invaluable assistance with the preparation of this Canadian edition. I would also like to thank Lindsay MacDonald, my Developmental Editor, and Cara Yarzab at McGraw-Hill, for their supportive and inspiring help throughout the manuscript revision and preparation process. Once again many of the changes to this second edition would not be possible without the detailed, inspiring, and helpful feedback provided by the reviewers. I am appreciative and extremely thankful for their insightful and generous comments which have led to what I believe is a much improved second edition.

Kelly Anthony, *University of Waterloo*

Marcie Balch, *University of New Brunswick*

Cheryl Bereziuk, *Grande Prairie Regional College*

Steven Bray, *McMaster University*

Rory Coughlan, *Trent University*

Gillian Einstein, *University of Toronto*

Anita DeLongis, *University of British Columbia*

Catharine Dishke Hondzel, *King's University College at the University of Western Ontario*

Ken Fowler, *Memorial University of Newfoundland*

Christiane Hoppman, *University of British Columbia*

David Korotkov, *St. Thomas University*

Dr. Barbel Knauper, *McGill University*

Diane LaChapelle, *University of New Brunswick*

Kirsten Madsen, *Sheridan College*

Lachlan McWilliams, *Acadia University*

Anna Nagy, *University of Toronto at Scarborough*

Shelley Delano Parker, *University of New Brunswick*

Wendy Rodgers, *University of Alberta*

Lionel Standing, *Bishop's University*

Stacey Wareham, *Memorial University of Newfoundland*

Fuschia M. Sirois

PART

1

part one

Introduction to Health Psychology

What Is Health Psychology?

After reading this chapter, students will be able to:

(LO1) Describe and define health psychology

(LO2) Understand how our view of the mind–body relationship changed over time

(LO3) Explain the biopsychosocial model of health

(LO4) Identify why the field of health psychology is needed

(LO5) Relate the purpose of health psychology training

Adam arrived at university filled with anticipation. He had gotten into his first-choice school, which he had picked both for the first-rate psychology program and for the opportunities to play basketball and run track.

All his life, Adam had been health conscious. From the time he was young, his parents had made sure that he received regular medical checkups, wore his seat belt, and generally stayed out of circumstances in which he was likely to fall into harm. In elementary school, he had learned about the basic food groups, and his family had reinforced this learning by maintaining a healthy diet.

Because Adam had been active in sports from the time he was seven, regular exercise was an integral part of his life. In high school, he had had an occasional beer because everyone did, but he had avoided smoking cigarettes and taking drugs because he knew he couldn't do as well in sports if he abused his body. He got his eight hours of sleep a night, too, because without them, his concentration in classes lapsed and his coordination on the basketball court fell off.

As he carried in the last of his suitcases and finished unpacking, he wondered what his roommate would be like. "Are you Adam?" a voice asked. Adam turned around to meet his new roommate, Greg. He knew immediately that his roommate wasn't an athlete. A skinny, dissipated-looking person, Greg smelled of stale cigarette smoke.

Over the course of the term, Adam learned more about the ways in which he and his new roommate were not alike. Greg liked to sleep until 10 or 11 in the morning and often stayed up until 4 or 5 A.M. On weekends, he liked to get drunk, which seemed to be his major recreational activity. Residence food was not much to his liking, and he often lived on Doritos and Pepsi for a day or two at a time.

Greg always seemed to be coming down with something, either an upset stomach, a cold, a case of the flu, or just plain fatigue. The medicine cabinet they ostensibly shared was loaded with Greg's over-the-counter medications for every imaginable symptom.

Adam wasn't surprised that Greg was always sick. In high school, Adam had taken a course in psychology and the teacher had taught them about health psychology. Because he was interested in a possible career in sports medicine, he had gotten extra books about the field so that he could learn more about it. Now he had his own case history in health psychology: Greg.

WHAT IS HEALTH PSYCHOLOGY?   (L01)

Health psychology is devoted to understanding psychological influences on how people stay healthy, why they become ill, and how they respond when they do get ill. Health psychologists both study such issues and promote interventions to help people stay well or get

When children leave home for the first time as university students or workers, they often find that the health practices they have taken for granted in their own families are very different than those of their new friends and acquaintances.

over illness. For example, a health psychology researcher might be interested in why people continue to smoke even though they know that smoking increases their risk of cancer and heart disease. Information about why people smoke helps the researcher both understand this poor health habit and design interventions to help people stop smoking.

Fundamental to research and practice in health psychology is the definition of health. In 1948, the World Health Organization defined **health** as "a complete state of physical, mental, and social well-being and not merely the absence of disease or infirmity" (World Health Organization, 1948). This definition, which was very forward-looking for its time, is at the core of health psychologists' conception of health. Rather than defining health as the absence of illness, health is recognized to be an achievement involving balance among physical, mental, and social well-being. Many use the term "wellness" to refer to this optimum state of health.

Health psychology is concerned with all aspects of health and illness across the lifespan (Maddux, Roberts, Sledden, & Wright, 1986). Health psychologists focus on *health promotion and maintenance,* which includes such issues as how to get children to develop good health habits, how to promote regular exercise, and how to design a media campaign to get people to improve their diets.

Health psychologists also study the psychological aspects of the *prevention and treatment of illness.* A health psychologist might teach people in a high-stress occupation how to manage stress effectively so that it will not adversely affect their health. A health psychologist might work with people who are already ill to help them adjust more successfully to their illness or to learn to follow their treatment regimen.

Health psychologists also focus on the *etiology and correlates of health, illness, and dysfunction.* **Etiology** refers to the origins or causes of illness, and health psychologists are especially interested in the behavioural and social factors that contribute to health or illness and dysfunction, factors that can include health habits such as alcohol consumption, smoking, exercise, the wearing of seat belts, and ways of coping with stress.

Finally, health psychologists analyze and attempt to improve *the health care system and the formulation of health policy.* They study the impact of health institutions and health professionals on people's behaviour and develop recommendations for improving health care.

Putting it all together, health psychology represents the educational, scientific, and professional contributions of psychology to the promotion and maintenance of health; the prevention and treatment of illness; the identification of the causes and correlates of health, illness, and related dysfunction; the improvement of the health care system; and health policy formation (Matarazzo, 1980).

In this chapter, we consider why our current state of knowledge about health and health care issues has virtually demanded the field of health psychology. To begin, we consider how philosophers have conceived of the **mind–body relationship** and how we have arrived at our present viewpoint of the mind and body as inextricable influences on health. Next, we consider the dominant clinical and research model in health psychology—the biopsychosocial model—and historical trends that have led to the development of this new way to conceptualize the determinants of health. We then discuss the trends in medicine, psychology, and the health care system that have contributed to the emergence of health psychology.

HOW HAS OUR VIEW OF THE MIND–BODY RELATIONSHIP CHANGED OVER TIME? (L02)

Historically, philosophers have vacillated between the view that the mind and body are part of the same system and the idea that they are two separate ones. When we look at ancient history, it becomes clear that we have come full circle in our beliefs about the mind–body relationship. As Figure 1.1 shows, there have been a variety of critical events throughout history that have played a role in the changing views in Western civilizations and Canada in particular.

In the earliest times, the mind and body were considered a unit. Early cultures believed that disease arose when evil spirits entered the body and that these spirits could be exorcised through the treatment process. Archaeologists have found Stone Age skulls with small holes in them that are believed to have been made intentionally with sharp stone tools. This procedure, called trephination, allowed the evil spirits to leave the body while the "physician," or shaman, performed the treatment ritual (H. I. Kaplan, 1975).

The Greeks were among the earliest civilizations to identify the role of bodily functioning in health and illness. Rather than ascribing illness to evil spirits, they developed a humoral theory of illness, which was first proposed by Hippocrates (ca. 460–ca. 377 B.C.) and later expanded by Galen (A.D. 129–ca. 199). According to this view, disease arises when the four circulating fluids of the body—blood, black bile, yellow bile, and phlegm—are out of balance. The function of treatment

Sophisticated, though not always successful, techniques for the treatment of illness were developed during the Renaissance. This woodcut from the 1570s depicts a surgeon drilling a hole in a patient's skull, with the patient's family and pets looking on.

is to restore balance among the humours. Specific personality types were believed to be associated with bodily temperaments in which one of the four humours predominated. In essence, then, the Greeks ascribed disease states to bodily factors but believed that these factors can also have an impact on the mind.

In the Middle Ages, however, the pendulum swung back toward supernatural explanations of illness. Although Galen's humoral theory was still widely accepted and practised, mysticism and demonology dominated concepts of disease, which were seen as God's punishment for evildoing. Cure often consisted of driving out evil by torturing the body. Prayer and penance along with practices such as bloodletting were viewed as effective "cures" for illness. Throughout this time, the Church was the guardian of medical knowledge; as a result, medical practice took on religious overtones, including religiously based but unscientific generalizations about the body and the mind–body relationship. Not surprisingly, as the functions of the physician were absorbed by the priest, healing and the practice of religion became indistinguishable (H. I. Kaplan, 1975).

During this period and through the early years of the Renaissance, the patients' thoughts and beliefs were viewed as central to changes in physical states. The imagination and emotions were seen as the means through which the individual could connect with God, and therefore implicated in both the genesis and remission of illness. If an individual was ill it was because of a lack of faith and what was required was altering the imagination so as to restore the connection to God. This meant that if the physician was to be successful in curing a particular ailment, then the attack on illness involved not just changing the physical pathologies, but altering the imagination to induce bodily change. Consequently, healing relied heavily upon the patient's unwavering and pure belief in the words and practices of the physician (McMahon, 1975).

Beginning in the Renaissance and continuing up to the present day, great strides have been made in the technological basis of medical practice. Most notable among these were Anton van Leeuwenhoek's (1632–1723) work in microscopy and Giovanni Morgagni's (1682–1771) contributions to autopsy, both of which laid the groundwork for the rejection of the humoral theory of illness. The humoral approach was finally put to rest by growing scientific understanding of cellular pathology (H. I. Kaplan, 1975).

As a result of such advances and Descartes' doctrine of mind–body dualism, medicine looked more and more to the medical laboratory and bodily factors, rather than to the mind, as a basis for medical progress. In an effort to break with the superstitions of the past, the dualistic conception of mind and body was strongly reinforced so that physicians became the guardians of the body while philosophers and theologians became the caretakers of the mind. For the next 300 years, as

FIGURE 1.1 | A Brief Timeline of How Views of the Mind–Body Relationship Have Changed Over Time

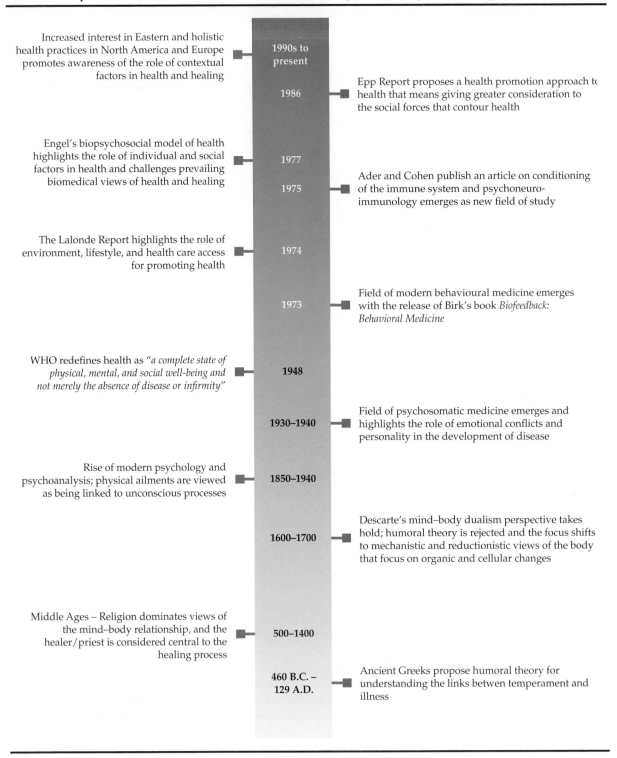

Increased interest in Eastern and holistic health practices in North America and Europe promotes awareness of the role of contextual factors in health and healing

1990s to present

1986
Epp Report proposes a health promotion approach to health that means giving greater consideration to the social forces that contour health

Engel's biopsychosocial model of health highlights the role of individual and social factors in health and challenges prevailing biomedical views of health and healing

1977

1975
Ader and Cohen publish an article on conditioning of the immune system and psychoneuro-immunology emerges as new field of study

The Lalonde Report highlights the role of environment, lifestyle, and health care access for promoting health

1974

1973
Field of modern behavioural medicine emerges with the release of Birk's book *Biofeedback: Behavioral Medicine*

WHO redefines health as *"a complete state of physical, mental, and social well-being and not merely the absence of disease or infirmity"*

1948

1930–1940
Field of psychosomatic medicine emerges and highlights the role of emotional conflicts and personality in the development of disease

Rise of modern psychology and psychoanalysis; physical ailments are viewed as being linked to unconscious processes

1850–1940

1600–1700
Descarte's mind–body dualism perspective takes hold; humoral theory is rejected and the focus shifts to mechanistic and reductionistic views of the body that focus on organic and cellular changes

Middle Ages – Religion dominates views of the mind–body relationship, and the healer/priest is considered central to the healing process

500–1400

460 B.C. – 129 A.D.
Ancient Greeks propose humoral theory for understanding the links betwen temperament and illness

physicians focused primarily on organic and cellular changes and pathology as a basis for their medical inferences, physical evidence became the sole basis for diagnosis and treatment of illness (H. I. Kaplan, 1975).

Psychoanalytic Contributions

This view began to change with the rise of modern psychology, particularly with Sigmund Freud's (1856–1939) early work on **conversion hysteria.** According to Freud, specific unconscious conflicts can produce particular physical disturbances that symbolize the repressed psychological conflicts. In conversion hysteria, the patient converts the conflict into a symptom via the voluntary nervous system; he or she then becomes relatively free of the anxiety the conflict would otherwise produce (N. Cameron, 1963).

Psychosomatic Medicine

Although true conversion hysteria responses are now rarely seen, the idea that specific illnesses are produced by individuals' internal conflicts was perpetuated in the work of Flanders Dunbar in the 1930s (F. Dunbar, 1943) and Franz Alexander in the 1940s (F. Alexander, 1950). Unlike Freud, these researchers linked patterns of personality rather than a single specific conflict to specific illnesses.

Whereas Freud believed that conversion reactions occur via the voluntary nervous system with no necessary physiological changes, Dunbar and Alexander argued that conflicts produce anxiety, which becomes unconscious and takes a physiological toll on the body via the autonomic nervous system, which eventually produces an actual organic disturbance. For example, repressed emotions resulting from frustrated dependency and love-seeking needs were said to increase the secretion of acid in the stomach, eventually eroding the stomach lining and producing ulcers (F. Alexander, 1950).

Dunbar's and Alexander's works helped shape the emerging field of **psychosomatic medicine** by offering profiles of particular disorders believed to be psychosomatic in origin—that is, bodily disorders caused by emotional conflicts: ulcers, hyperthyroidism, rheumatoid arthritis, essential hypertension, colitis, and bronchial asthma. Many of the early ideas generated by the psychosomatic medicine perspective persist today (B. T. Engel, 1986). For example, the idea that there may be a disease-prone personality was resurrected by researchers in the late 1980s, as we will discuss in Chapter 7.

Nonetheless, researchers now believe that a particular conflict or personality type is not sufficient to produce illness. Rather, the onset of disease requires the interaction of a variety of factors; these factors include a possible genetic weakness in the organism, the presence of environmental stressors, early learning experiences and conflicts, current ongoing learning and conflicts, and individual cognitions and coping efforts.

Behavioural Medicine

Although psychosomatic medicine did much to bridge the mind–body gap, it relied on subjective, verbal interventions based on psychodynamic perspectives that did not provide testable hypotheses. With the growing popularity of behaviour modification and cognitive behavioural approaches in the 1960s and 1970s, observable and testable interventions for dealing with health and illness were in demand. **Behavioural medicine** developed, in part, to address this need by focusing on objective and clinically relevant interventions that would demonstrate the connections between body and mind suggested by psychosomatic medicine (Agras, 1982).

In 1973, a book published by Birk titled *Biofeedback: Behavioural Medicine,* formally launched the field of behavioural medicine (Felgoise, 2005). Behavioural medicine is considered the interdisciplinary field concerned with integrating behavioural science and biomedical science for understanding physical health and illness and for developing and applying knowledge and techniques to prevent, diagnose, treat, and rehabilitate (Schwartz & Weiss, 1978).

Current Views of the Mind–Body Relationship

Despite the criticisms of the early psychosomatic movement, it laid the groundwork for a profound change in beliefs about the relation of the mind and the body (B. T. Engel, 1986). It is now known that physical health is inextricably interwoven with the psychological and social environment: All conditions of health and illness, not just the diseases identified by the early psychosomatic theorists, are influenced by psychological and social factors. The treatment of illness and prognosis for recovery are substantially affected by such factors as the relationship between patient and practitioner, and expectations about pain and discomfort. Staying well is heavily determined by good health habits, which are for the most part under one's personal control, and by such socially determined factors as culture, socio-economic status, place, stress, availability of health resources, and social support.

This perspective on the mind–body relationship has also been influenced by the growing interest in more holistic approaches to health and healing in Canada and other Western countries such as the United States, Europe, Australia, and the United Kingdom. For example, Eastern and other alternative medical philosophies emphasize the interrelation of all of the body's systems, and view illness as a disharmony between these systems. Accordingly, healing is accomplished through techniques and treatments that help to restore both physical and psychological balance, such as meditation, massage therapy, acupuncture, herbal remedies, and homeopathy. Increasingly, Western medicine is acknowledging the potential value of these approaches to health, and in some cases integrating them into standard medical care for certain health conditions such as cancer and AIDS. In Canada, the surge of interest in and use of complementary therapies occurred in the late 1990s and continues to grow, with many private health insurance companies now offering partial or full coverage of these therapies. In response to this interest, Health Canada created the Natural Health Products Directorate in 2004 to regulate the safe distribution of over-the-counter natural remedies such as vitamins, homeopathic medicines, herbal remedies, Traditional Chinese Medicines, and

probiotics. We will examine some of the reasons for this growing interest in holistic therapies in Chapter 9.

WHAT IS THE BIOPSYCHOSOCIAL MODEL OF HEALTH? (L03)

The idea that the mind and the body together determine health and illness logically implies a model for studying these issues. This model is called the **biopsychosocial model.** As its name implies, its fundamental assumption is that health and illness are consequences of the interplay of biological, psychological, and social factors (Suls & Rothman, 2004). Because the biopsychosocial model figures so prominently in the research and clinical issues in health psychology, we consider it in some detail here.

The Biopsychosocial Model versus the Biomedical Model

Perhaps the best way to understand the biopsychosocial model is to contrast it with the **biomedical model.** The biomedical model, which governed the thinking of most

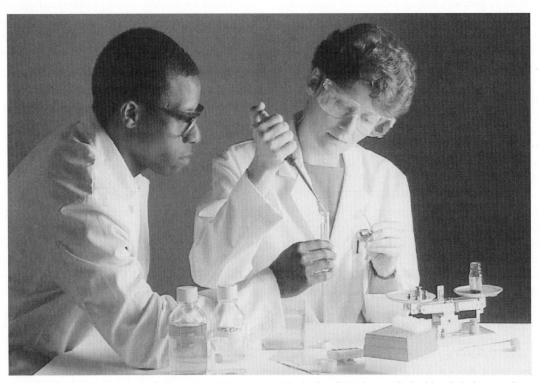

In the 19th and 20th centuries, great strides were made in the technical basis of medicine. As a result, physicians looked more and more to the medical laboratory and less to the mind as a way of understanding the onset and progression of illness.

TABLE 1.1 | A Comparison of the Biomedical and Biopsychosocial Models

Biomedical Model	Biopsychosocial Model
Reductionistic	Macrolevel as well as microlevel
Single causal factor considered	Multiple causal factors considered
Assumes mind–body dualism	Mind and body inseparable
Emphasizes illness over health	Emphasizes both health and illness

health practitioners for the past 300 years, maintains that all illness can be explained on the basis of aberrant somatic processes, such as biochemical imbalances or neurophysiological abnormalities. The biomedical model assumes that psychological and social processes are largely independent of the disease process.

Although the biomedical model has undeniable benefits for studying some diseases, it has several potential liabilities. First, it is a reductionistic model. This means that it reduces illness to low-level processes, such as disordered cells and chemical imbalances, rather than recognizing the role of more general social and psychological processes. The biomedical model is also essentially a single-factor model of illness. That is, it explains illness in terms of a biological malfunction rather than recognizing that a variety of factors, only some of which are biological, may be responsible for the development of illness.

The biomedical model implicitly assumes a mind–body dualism, maintaining that mind and body are separate entities. Finally, the biomedical model clearly emphasizes illness over health. That is, it focuses on aberrations that lead to illness rather than on the conditions that might promote health (see Table 1.1).

The biomedical model also has difficulty accounting for why a particular set of somatic conditions need not inevitably lead to illness. Why, for example, if six people are exposed to measles, do only three develop the disease? There are psychological and social factors that influence the development of illness, and these are ignored by the biomedical model. Whether a treatment will cure a disease is also substantially affected by psychological and social factors, and this cannot be explained by the biomedical model. As a consequence, researchers and practitioners have increasingly adopted a biopsychosocial model.

Advantages of the Biopsychosocial Model

How, then, does the biopsychosocial model of health and illness overcome the disadvantages of the biomedical model? The biopsychosocial model, as previously noted, maintains that biological, psychological, and social factors are all-important determinants of health and illness. As such, both macrolevel processes (such as the existence of social support, the presence of depression) and microlevel processes (such as cellular disorders or chemical imbalances) interact to produce a state of health or illness.

The biopsychosocial model maintains that health and illness are caused by multiple factors and produce multiple effects. The model further maintains that the mind and body cannot be distinguished in matters of health and illness because both so clearly influence an individual's state of health. The biopsychosocial model emphasizes both health and illness rather than regarding illness as a deviation from some steady state. From this viewpoint, health becomes something that one achieves through attention to biological, psychological, and social needs rather than something that is taken for granted.

But how do biological, social, and psychological variables interact, particularly if biological factors are microlevel processes and psychological and social factors are macrolevel processes? To address this question, researchers have adopted a **systems theory** approach to health and illness. Systems theory maintains that all levels of organization in any entity are linked to each other hierarchically and that change in any one level will effect change in all the other levels. This means that the microlevel processes (such as cellular changes) are nested within the macrolevel processes (such as societal values) and that changes on the microlevel can have macrolevel effects (and vice versa). For example, in Canada there is an increasing recognition of the social factors that may determine health, and that changes at the societal level are often needed to improve the health of both communities and individuals.

Consequently, health, illness, and medical care are all interrelated processes involving interacting changes both within the individual and on these various levels. To address these issues impels researchers toward interdisciplinary thinking and collaboration. It also requires researchers to be sophisticated in multivariate approaches to testing problems and to the often complex statistics needed to analyze them (Suls & Rothman, 2004).

Clinical Implications of the Biopsychosocial Model

There are several implications of the biopsychosocial model for clinical practice with patients. First, the biopsychosocial model maintains that the process of diagnosis should always consider the interacting role of biological, psychological, and social factors in assessing an individual's health or illness (Oken, 2000). Therefore, an interdisciplinary team approach may be the best way to make a diagnosis (Suls & Rothman, 2004).

Second, the biopsychosocial model maintains that recommendations for treatment must also examine all three sets of factors. By doing this, it should be possible to target therapy uniquely to a particular individual, consider a person's health status in total, and make treatment recommendations that can deal with more than one problem simultaneously. Again, a team approach may be most appropriate (Suls & Rothman, 2004).

Third, the biopsychosocial model makes explicit the significance of the relationship between patient and practitioner. An effective patient–practitioner relationship can improve a patient's use of services as well as the efficacy of treatment and the rapidity with which illness is resolved (Belar, 1997).

Summary   The biopsychosocial model clearly implies that the practitioner must understand the social and psychological factors that contribute to an illness in order to treat it appropriately. In the case of a healthy individual, the biopsychosocial model suggests that one can understand health habits only in their psychological and social contexts. These contexts may maintain a poor health habit or, with appropriate modifications, can facilitate the development of healthy ones. In the case of the ill individual, biological, psychological, and social factors all contribute to recovery and/or to disease management.

The Biopsychosocial Model: The Case of an Early Heart Attack

To appreciate how the biopsychosocial model can be applied to understanding health and illness, consider the case of a high-powered business owner in her early 50s who has a heart attack. A traditional medical approach to this problem would emphasize possible family history of heart disease, and control of the problem through the regular administration of drugs. The biopsychosocial approach to this woman's problem would consider the

social, cultural, and behavioural factors that may have contributed to the early heart attack. Such an assessment may also consider her status as a recent immigrant from the Caribbean who has been working hard to establish her business over the past two years, while trying to adjust to life in Canada. Treatment efforts might focus on exercise, training in techniques for stress management, and a recommendation to a program to help her stop smoking. In addition, a look at her social environment may reveal that she has been struggling for some time to achieve a healthy balance between her work and family demands, and consequently spends less time than she would like with her family, and less time establishing new friendships and connections within her community. Recommendations for increasing positive social interaction with her family and allowing time to cultivate friendships, while at the same time restricting overtime and the intrusion of other work demands into her personal life, may be an additional goal for her rehabilitation. Finally, providing assistance with her family duties during recovery may be needed to ensure that she completes her rehabilitation program and resists the temptation to return to her caregiver role prematurely. Use of the biopsychosocial model informs these kinds of sophisticated assessments, and health psychologists are at the centre of these developing trends.

WHY IS THE FIELD OF HEALTH PSYCHOLOGY NEEDED?   (L04)

An adequate understanding of what keeps people healthy or makes them get well is impossible without knowledge of the psychological and social context within which health and illness are experienced. The shift toward a biopsychosocial approach to health is one of the many factors that have spawned the rapidly growing field of health psychology. In addition, a number of trends within medicine, psychology, and the health care system have combined to make the emergence of health psychology inevitable. It is safe to say that health psychology is one of the most important developments within the field of psychology in the past 50 years. What factors have led to the development of health psychology?

Changing Patterns of Illness

The most important factor giving rise to health psychology has been the change in illness patterns that has occurred in Canada and other technologically advanced societies.

FIGURE 1.2 | Death Rates for the Leading Causes of Death per 100,000 Population, Canada, 1921–25 and 2004

(*Source:* Statistics Canada, "Mortality, summary list of causes, 2004," Catalogue no. 84F0209XWE, released April 27, 2007, www.statcan.ca/english/freepub/84F0209XIE/2004000/tablesectionlist.htm.)

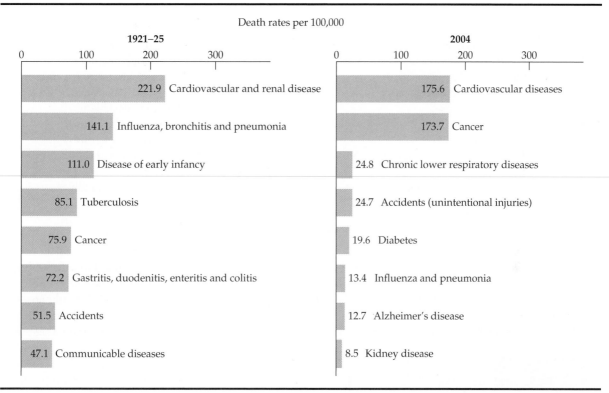

Death rates per 100,000

1921–25	2004
221.9 Cardiovascular and renal disease	175.6 Cardiovascular diseases
141.1 Influenza, bronchitis and pneumonia	173.7 Cancer
111.0 Disease of early infancy	24.8 Chronic lower respiratory diseases
85.1 Tuberculosis	24.7 Accidents (unintentional injuries)
75.9 Cancer	19.6 Diabetes
72.2 Gastritis, duodenitis, enteritis and colitis	13.4 Influenza and pneumonia
51.5 Accidents	12.7 Alzheimer's disease
47.1 Communicable diseases	8.5 Kidney disease

As Figure 1.2 shows, until the 20th century, **acute disorders**—especially tuberculosis, pneumonia, and other infectious diseases—were among the major causes of illness and death in Canada. Acute disorders are short-term medical illnesses, often the result of a viral or bacterial invader and usually amenable to cure.

Now, however, **chronic illnesses**—especially heart disease, cerebrovascular disease, and cancer—are the main contributors to disability and death, especially in industrialized countries. Chronic illnesses are slowly developing diseases with which people live for a long time. Often, chronic illnesses cannot be cured but, rather, only managed by the patient and provider working together. Table 1.2 lists the main diseases worldwide in 2004 compared to those projected for 2030. Note how those causes will change over the next decades.

Why have chronic illnesses helped spawn the field of health psychology? First, these are diseases in which psychological and social factors are implicated as causes. For example, personal health habits, such as diet and

smoking, are implicated in the development of heart disease and cancer, and sexual activity is critically important in the likelihood of developing AIDS (acquired immune deficiency syndrome). Consequently, health psychology has evolved, in part, to explore these causes and to develop ways to modify them.

Second, because people may live with chronic diseases for many years, psychological issues arise in connection with them. Health psychologists help people living with chronic illness adjust psychologically and socially to their changing health state. They help those with chronic illness develop treatment regimens, many of which involve self-care. Some of the ways in which allied health professionals such as social workers, and occupational therapists can help people with chronic illness is summarized in Table 1.3. Chronic illnesses affect family functioning, including relationships with a partner or children, and health psychologists both explore these changes and help ease the problems in family functioning that may result. Many Canadians with chronic illnesses use therapies

TABLE 1.2 | What Are the Worldwide Causes of Death?

The causes of death and disability are expected to change dramatically by the year 2030.

	2004		2030
Rank	Disease or Injury	Projected Rank	Disease or Injury
1	Ischemic heart disease	1	Ischemic heart disease
2	Cerebrovascular disease	2	Cerebrovascular disease
3	Lower respiratory infections	3	Chronic obstructive pulmonary disease
4	Chronic obstructive pulmonary disease	4	Lower respiratory infections
5	Diarrheal diseases	5	Road traffic accidents
6	HIV/AIDS	6	Trachea, bronchus, lung cancers
7	Tuberculosis	7	Diabetes mellitus
8	Trachea, bronchus, lung cancers	8	Hypertensive heart disease
9	Road traffic accidents	9	Stomach cancer
10	Prematurity and low birth weight	10	HIV/AIDS

Source: World Health Organization (2008), "Future trends in global mortality: Major shifts in cause of death patterns." *World Health Statistics 2008,* retrieved April 29, 2011, from http://www.who.int/whosis/whostat/EN_WHS08_Full.pdf

outside formal medicine to help manage their disease symptoms (Fautrel et al., 2002). Understanding what leads people to seek alternative treatments and evaluating the effectiveness of these treatments are also issues on which health psychologists can shed light (Chapter 9).

Critical Checkpoint

Worldwide Causes of Death and Health Psychology

Table 1.2 highlights some of the recent and expected trends in disease patterns and causes of death worldwide. Although the top four causes of death remain essentially unchanged, there are significant changes expected in the remaining causes for the year 2030. What factors might account for these changes and how might health psychology play a role in addressing the projected causes of death for 2030?

Advances in Technology and Research The field of health psychology is changing almost daily because new issues arise that require the input of psychologists. For example, new technologies now make it possible to identify the genes that contribute to many disorders. Just in the past few years, genes contributing to many diseases, including

breast cancer, have been uncovered. How do we help a college student whose mother has just been diagnosed with breast cancer come to terms with her risk, now that the genetic basis of breast cancer is better understood? Should the daughter get tested? And if she does get tested, and if she tests positive for a breast cancer gene, how will this change her life? How will she cope with her risk, and how should she change her behaviour? Health psychologists help answer such questions.

"My father had a heart attack. Should I be making changes in my diet?" asks a student in a health psychology class. Health psychologists conduct research that identifies the risk factors for disease, such as a high-fat diet, and help people learn to change their diet and stick to their resolution. Helping people make informed, appropriate decisions is fundamentally a psychological task.

Advances in genetic research have made it possible to identify carriers of illness and to test a fetus for the presence of particular life-threatening or severely debilitating illnesses. This places some parents in the position of having to decide whether to abort a pregnancy—a wrenching, difficult decision to make.

Certain treatments that may prolong life severely compromise quality of life. Increasingly, patients are asked their preferences regarding life-sustaining measures, and they may require counselling in these matters. These are just a few examples of the increasing role that patients play in fundamental decisions regarding their health and illness and its management and of the help health psychologists can provide in this process.

Role of Epidemiology Changing patterns of illness have been charted and followed by the field of epidemiology, a discipline closely related to health psychology in its goals and interests (N. E. Miller, 1992). **Epidemiology** is the study of the frequency, distribution, and causes of infectious and noninfectious disease in a population, based on an investigation of the physical and social environment. For example, epidemiologists not only study who has what kind of cancer but also address questions such as why some cancers are more prevalent than others in particular geographic areas.

In the context of epidemiologic statistics, we will see the frequent use of two important terms: morbidity and mortality. **Morbidity** refers to the number of cases of a disease that exist at some given point in time. Morbidity may be expressed as the number of new cases (incidence) or as the total number of existing cases (prevalence). Morbidity statistics, then, tell us how many people are suffering from what kinds of illnesses at any given time. **Mortality** refers to numbers of deaths due to particular causes.

In establishing the goals and concerns of health psychology and the health care endeavour more broadly, morbidity and mortality statistics are essential. We need to know the major causes of disease in this country, particularly those diseases that lead to early death, so as to reduce their occurrence. For example, knowing that accidents, especially automobile accidents, have historically been the major cause of death among children, adolescents, and young adults has led to the initiation of a variety of safety measures, including child safety restraint systems and laws, mandatory seat belt laws, and airbags. Knowing that cardiac disease is the major cause of premature death (that is, death that occurs prior to the expected age of death for an individual) has led to programs such as the Canadian Heart Health Initiative, a countrywide strategy to reduce risk factors among those most vulnerable, including smoking reduction efforts, implementation of dietary changes, cholesterol reduction techniques, increased exercise, and weight loss. With innovations such as the healthy heart kit, this initiative has led to Canada being recognized as a worldwide leader in cardiovascular disease prevention (Public Health Agency of Canada, 2003a).

But morbidity is at least as important. What is the use of affecting causes of death if people remain ill but simply do not die? Increasingly, health psychology is concerned not only with biological outcomes but also with health-related quality of life and symptomatic complaints. Consequently, health psychologists are becoming more involved in the effort to improve quality of life among those diagnosed with chronic illnesses so that individuals may live out their remaining years as free from pain, disability, and lifestyle compromise as possible (Stanton, Revenson, & Tennen, 2007).

Changing Perspectives on Health and Health Care

In Canada, the definition of health has continued to evolve since the World Health Organization first introduced the idea that health is a positive state rather than merely the absence of disease. In 1974, the Lalonde Report challenged traditional views of health and suggested that changing lifestyles and physical and social environments would have a greater chance of improving the health of Canadians than simply improving health care delivery systems. Even before the introduction of the biopsychosocial model of health, the Lalonde Report proposed a framework for health that rested on four main cornerstones: human biology, environment, lifestyle, and health care organization. This proposal led to the initiation of several health promotion programs to increase awareness of the importance of healthy behaviours and the risks associated with other behaviours such as smoking and alcohol use.

Since that time, a public health–health promotion perspective of health has continued to shape how we view the factors that contribute to making and keeping Canadians healthy. The Epp Report released in 1986 proposed a health promotion approach to health in Canada that further echoed the need to view health in non-medical terms and give greater consideration to the social factors that contour health (Epp, 1986). According to a public health–health promotion perspective, health is viewed not as a state, but more broadly as a capacity or resource that is linked to the ability to achieve one's goals, to learn, and to grow (Public Health Agency of Canada, 2002). Consequently, a variety of social, economic, and physical environmental factors are recognized as making an important contribution to an individual's health status. (See the Focus on Social Issues box, "Determinants of Health: What Makes Canadians Healthy or Unhealthy?" on page 14.) Under these terms, health is conceptualized as "the capacity of people to adapt to, respond to, or control life's challenges and changes" (Frankish et al., 1996). The public health promotion model that has emerged from these evolving views of health in Canada is aimed at improving the health of both individuals and communities, primarily through highlighting the need for social policy changes

BOX 1.1

Determinants of Health: What Makes Canadians Healthy or Unhealthy?

Similar to the biopsychosocial model, a population health approach to health takes into account a wide range of individual and social factors and how they interact to influence health. Twelve of these key determinants have currently been identified, and it is expected that this list will change as our understanding of what shapes health also changes. For health psychologists, the challenge is to consider not only the individual factors that may influence health but also the larger social context in which the individual lives and works.

1. Income and social status
2. Social support networks
3. Education
4. Employment/working conditions
5. Social environments
6. Physical environments
7. Personal health practices and coping skills
8. Healthy child development
9. Biology and genetic endowment
10. Health services
11. Gender
12. Culture

Consider the following simple, yet revealing story that illustrates how such complex factors can determine the health of Canadians.

> Why is Jason in the hospital?
> Because he has a bad infection in his leg.
> But why does he have an infection?
> Because he has a cut on his leg and it got infected.
> But why does he have a cut on his leg?
> Because he was playing in the junkyard next to his apartment building and there was some sharp, jagged steel there that he fell on.
> But why was he playing in a junk yard?
> Because his neighbourhood is kind of rundown. A lot of kids play there and there is no one to supervise them.
> But why does he live in that neighbourhood?
> Because his parents can't afford a nicer place to live.
> But why can't his parents afford a nicer place to live?
> Because his dad is unemployed and his mom is sick.
> But why is his dad unemployed?
> Because he doesn't have much education and he can't find a job.
> But why . . . ?

Source: Determinants of Health: What Makes Canadians Healthy or Unhealthy? Public Health Agency of Canada, 2008. Reproduced with the permission of the Minister of Health, 2011. www.phac-aspc.gc.ca/ph-sp/phdd/determinants/index.html

and action. This model of health shares many of the same values and assumptions of the biopsychosocial model and views health as resulting from the combined interaction of a multitude of micro- and macrolevel factors, including social context and place (Public Health Agency of Canada, 2002). Thus, health psychologists are in a unique position to understand these determinants of health and to inform health policymakers as they implement changes to help improve the health of Canadians.

Finally, Canada's publicly funded health care system provides access to most basic health care services at no cost to the individual. While this may encourage greater use of these services than if they were pay-per-use, it does not ensure that people will be satisfied with the health care they receive, or that they will in fact make use of these services when they are needed. In addition, the cost of health care expenditures in Canada has increased substantially since the mid-1980s (Canadian Institute for Health Information, 2006a), the burden of which falls mainly on the shoulders of taxpayers. With the rapid aging of Canada's population, the rates of chronic illness are likely to rise, as are the health care costs associated with managing illness.

Health psychology represents an important perspective on these issues for several reasons:

1. Because containing health care costs is so important, health psychology's main emphasis on prevention—namely, modifying people's risky health behaviours before they ever become ill—has the potential to reduce the number of dollars devoted to the management of illness.

2. Health psychologists have done substantial research on what makes people satisfied or dissatisfied with their health care (see Chapters 8 and 9).

Thus, they can help in the design of user friendly health care systems.

3. The health care industry employs thousands of individuals in a variety of jobs. Nearly every individual in the country has direct contact with the health care system as a recipient of services. Thus, its impact on people is enormous.

For all these reasons, then, health has a substantial social and psychological impact on people, an impact that is addressed by health psychologists.

Increased Medical Acceptance

Another reason for the development of health psychology is the increasing acceptance of health psychologists within the medical community (Matarazzo, 1994). Although health psychologists have been employed in health settings for many years, their value is increasingly recognized by physicians and other health care professionals, as is illustrated in Box 1.2, "A Day in the Life of a Health Psychologist," on page 17.

At one time, the role of health psychologists in health care was largely confined to the task of administering tests and interpreting the test results of individuals who were suspected of being psychologically disturbed. Like psychiatrists in health settings, psychologists usually saw only the "problem patients" who were difficult for medical staff to manage or whose physical complaints were believed to be entirely psychological in origin. Now, however, caregivers are increasingly recognizing that psychological and social factors are always important in health and illness. Accordingly, the role of the psychologist in changing patients' health habits and contributing to treatment is increasingly acknowledged.

Demonstrated Contributions to Health

Health psychology has already demonstrated that it can make substantial contributions to health (Melamed, 1995), contributions that form the substance of this book. A few brief examples here can illustrate this point.

Health psychologists have developed a variety of short-term behavioural interventions to address a wide variety of health-related problems, including managing pain; modifying bad health habits, such as smoking; and managing the side effects or treatment effects associated with a range of chronic diseases. Techniques that often take a mere few hours to teach often produce years of benefit. Such interventions, particularly those that

target risk factors such as diet or smoking, have contributed to the actual decline in the incidence of some diseases, especially coronary heart disease (M. McGinnis et al., 1992). As a consequence of these studies, many hospitals and other treatment centres now routinely prepare patients for such procedures. Ultimately, if a discipline is to flourish, it must demonstrate a strong track record, and health psychology has done precisely that.

Methodological Contributions

Many of the issues that arise in medical settings demand rigorous research investigation. Although physicians and nurses receive some methodological and statistical education, their training may be inadequate to conduct research on the issues they wish to address unless they make research their specialty. The health psychologist can be a valuable member of the research team by providing the methodological and statistical expertise that is the hallmark of good training in psychology.

Experiments Much research in health psychology is experimental. In an **experiment**, a researcher creates two or more conditions that differ from each other in exact and predetermined ways. People are then randomly assigned to experience these different conditions, and their reactions are measured. Experiments conducted by health care practitioners to evaluate treatments or interventions and their effectiveness over time are also called **randomized clinical trials**.

What kinds of experiments do health psychologists do? To determine if social support groups improve adjustment to cancer, cancer patients might be randomly assigned to participate in a support group or to participate in a comparison condition, such as an educational intervention, and then evaluated at a subsequent time to pinpoint whether one group of patients is better adjusted to the cancer than the other, or in which ways they differ in their adjustment.

Experiments have been the mainstay of science, because when we manipulate a variable and see its effect, we can more definitively establish a cause–effect relationship. For this reason, experiments and randomized clinical trials have been the mainstays of health psychology research. However, sometimes it is impractical to study issues experimentally. People cannot, for example, be randomly assigned to diseases.

Correlational Studies As a result, other research in health psychology is **correlational research,** in which the health psychologist measures whether a change in one variable corresponds with changes in another variable. A correlational study might identify, for example, that people who are higher in hostility have a higher risk for cardiovascular disease. The disadvantage of correlational studies is that it is impossible to determine the direction of causality unambiguously: It is possible, for example, that cardiovascular risk factors lead people to become more hostile. On the other hand, correlational studies often have advantages over experiments because they are more adaptable, enabling us to study issues when the variables cannot be manipulated experimentally.

Prospective Designs   Moreover, some of the problems with correlational studies can be remedied by using a prospective approach to research. **Prospective research** looks forward in time to see how a group of individuals change, or how a relationship between two variables changes, over time. For example, if we were to find that hostility develops relatively early in life, but other risk factors for heart disease develop later, we might feel more confident that hostility is an independent risk factor for heart disease and recognize that the reverse direction of causality—namely, that heart disease causes hostility—is unlikely.

A particular type of prospective approach is **longitudinal research**, in which we observe the same people over a long period of time. For example, if we wanted to know what factors are associated with early breast cancer in women at risk for it, we might follow a group of young women whose mothers developed breast cancer in an effort to identify which daughters developed breast cancer and whether there are any reliable factors associated with that development, such as diet, smoking, alcohol consumption, or other co-occurring risk factors.

Retrospective Research   Investigators also use **retrospective research**, which looks backward in time, and attempts to reconstruct the conditions that led to a current situation. Retrospective methods, for example, were critical in identifying the initial outbreak and spread of Severe Acute Respiratory Syndrome (SARS) to 30 countries. Through retrospective analysis of patient records, researchers believe that the earliest cases of SARS emerged in mid-November 2002 in the southern Chinese province of Guangdong. The first recorded cases outside China appeared in February 2003 after a medical doctor who had treated patients in Guangdong, and who started suffering respiratory symptoms, stayed at a hotel in Hong Kong. Through presumed contact with others staying or visiting on his hotel floor, he transmitted SARS to at least 16 people who then carried the virus with them as they travelled internationally to Singapore, Vietnam, and Toronto, thus seeding an international outbreak. Because of retrospective studies, researchers were able to calm the fears regarding travel to infected countries such as Canada, as well as highlight the need for all travellers to practise hygienic hand-washing techniques as a way to reduce the risk of infection.

Qualitative Research   An increased focus on quality of life issues has made **qualitative research** a popular choice for many health psychologists. Qualitative research can take many forms including interviews, focus groups, case studies, and open-ended questions on surveys. All of these methods share a common focus of including the individual's voice and perspective to gain a richer understanding of the experiences and factors related to a particular health issue.

Throughout this text, we will refer to a variety of research methods that have developed to address the manifold problems with which health psychologists have been concerned. The previous general introduction to some of the most important research methods serves as context to clarify the more focused methods that are described in subsequent chapters. Suffice it to say at this point that the research training that health psychologists receive in their undergraduate and graduate school experiences makes them valuable parts of the research teams that attempt to understand how we stay healthy and why we get ill.

WHAT IS THE PURPOSE OF HEALTH PSYCHOLOGY TRAINING?   (L05)

Students who are trained in health psychology at the undergraduate level go on to many different occupations in applied settings or research. While some of these careers require graduate training and clinical certification in psychology, others do not. The Canadian Psychological Association accredits a number of clinical health psychology graduate programs in Canada, thereby setting a standard of training that is widely recognized for those seeking professional careers after completing their education. However, students can also complete graduate training in a non-clinical psychology program that focuses on health and receive training for careers in academic, research, or applied health psychology settings.

A Day in the Life of a Health Psychologist

Tobi is a clinical health psychologist working in a cardiac health department in a major academic medical centre. As a member of the cardiac team that includes two other health psychologists and several cardiac physicians, Tobi's responsibilities and duties reflect almost the full spectrum of health psychology practice. Her clinical work is focused on three types of patients: inpatients with heart disease and who are scheduled for heart surgery; outpatients with heart disease or risk factors for heart disease; and, as a member of the heart transplant team, patients who require evaluation for their suitability as heart transplant candidates for whom she also conducts support groups and workshops.

Much of her daily clinical duties are focused on inpatient consultations, which include reviewing patient medical records, making regular visits with patients in the hospital, and interviewing patients to evaluate their health and behaviours to determine their risk factors for cardiac health. Consistent with a biopsychosocial approach she evaluates patients' social support resources (Chapter 7), lifestyle factors, mood, employment situation, and she asks about family health behaviours to understand how their social environment may help or hinder any necessary lifestyle changes (Chapters 3 and 4). She also screens patients for a history of substance abuse (Chapter 5), and mood disorders, asks about their current exercise and diet habits (Chapter 4), and how good they are at taking their medications on time (Chapter 9) and making follow-up medical appointments (Chapter 8). Tobi also asks them about the stressors in their life (Chapter 6), and how well they are coping with everything (Chapter 7), as stress can have a significant impact on cardiac health (Chapter 13). She also discusses their personality and their fears about

their condition that may interfere with them asking for help (Chapter 11).

Based on her assessment, Tobi makes recommendations to the rest of the cardiac team about how to best manage the patient and their needs, as well as possible areas of concern. These recommendations are passed on to nutritionists, social workers, and others who may need to intervene. Thus, her role as a health psychologist also includes facilitating connections with other health professionals, as well as teaching the medical team about how mental health, personality, and psychosocial factors impact health.

Follow-up sessions are also necessary to ensure that the identified issues for a particular patient are being addressed. This involves educating patients about relaxation and the importance of relieving anxiety, and discussing how to change health behaviours and look after their health after being discharged. In a nutshell, her role as a health psychologist is to teach people about how mind–body connections can impact their cardiac health and then help them to make health behaviour changes and manage stress so that they have the best possible health outcomes from treatment.

Finally, working in this setting as a health psychologist is not just about the clinical aspects of cardiac care. About half of Tobi's time is dedicated to research activities such as designing and evaluating interventions for reducing stress in cardiac bypass patients, examining the effects of relaxation exercises on patient health pre and post surgery, and conducting research to assess the quality of life among heart transplant patients. Despite these varied and challenging daily responsibilities, Tobi says that working as a health psychologist in this setting is one of the most rewarding experiences she has ever had.

Careers in Practice

Some health psychology students may go into medicine, becoming physicians and nurses. Because of their experience in health psychology, they are often able to understand and manage the social and psychological aspects of the health problems they treat better than would be the case if their education had included only training in traditional medicine. Thus, for example, they may realize that no amount of education in a self-care plan for a person with a chronic illness will be

successful unless the family members are also brought in and educated in the regimen. Others may work as health psychologists in a clinical research setting in which they apply their breadth of knowledge to deal with a variety of health issues (see Box 1.2).

Other health psychology students go into the allied health professional fields, such as social work, occupational therapy, dietetics, physical therapy, and public health. Table 1.3 summarizes some of the roles of allied health professionals and the areas where they may use

TABLE 1.3 | A Summary of Allied Health Professionals Roles and Areas for the Application of Health Psychology Principles

Allied Health Professional	Training	Work Setting	Roles and Application of Health Psychology
Physiotherapists	• Typically receive their four to five years of training at the undergraduate level • Can have an additional two years in a graduate master's program, both of which lead to required licensure	• Licensed physiotherapists work in hospitals, nursing homes, rehabilitation centres, and schools for children with disabilities • Work primarily with accident victims, children with disabilities, people with chronic illness, and older people	• Responsible for the administration and interpretation of tests of muscle strength, motor development, functional capacity, and respiratory and circulatory efficiency • Develop individualized treatment programs, the goals of which are to increase strength, endurance, coordination, and range of motion • Help patients learn to use adaptive devices and become accustomed to new ways of performing old tasks
Occupational Therapists	• Require four to five years of postgraduate training which consists of a Bachelor of Science degree and 1,000 hours of field work	• Licensed occupational therapists work in schools, hospitals, rehabilitation centres, long-term care facilities, and mental health agencies • Work with individuals who are emotionally and physically disabled, e.g., with people who have mental illness, substance abuse problems, or who have a disabling chronic illness	• Evaluate the existing capacities of patients, help them set goals, and plan a therapy program to improve their occupational abilities and skills for daily living • Help patients regain physical, mental, or emotional stability; relearn daily routines, such as eating, dressing, writing, or using a telephone; and prepare for employment. • Can also teach creative tasks, such as painting, weaving, and other craft activities that help relax patients, provide a creative outlet, and offer some variety to those who are institutionalized
Dietitians	• Must complete a total of five years of post-secondary education, which includes clinically supervised training to be registered with one of the provincial dietetic associations	• Many dietitians are employed as administrators and apply the principles of nutrition and food management to meal planning for hospitals, universities, schools, and other institutions • Others work directly with people who have a chronic illness, e.g., diabetes, coronary heart disease, or obesity-related disorder	• Assess the dietetic needs of patients, supervise the service of meals, instruct patients in the requirements and importance of their diets, and suggest ways of maintaining adherence to diets after discharge • Help plan and manage special diets, and help people control their caloric intake and the types of foods they eat
Social Workers	• Minimum qualification for social work is a bachelor's degree, but for many positions a master's degree (MSW) is required	• Social workers work in hospitals, clinics, community mental health centres, rehabilitation centres, and long-term care facilities • They help individuals and families with the many social problems that can develop during illness and recovery	• Often responsible for assessing where patients go after discharge, decisions that are enlightened by knowledge of the psychosocial needs of individual patients • Help connect patients with resources such as vocational resources, homemaker help, and support groups, which may be led by a social worker • Can help a patient understand his or her illness more fully and deal with emotional responses to illness, such as depression or anxiety, through therapy

health psychology principles to help people within and outside of medical settings.

Careers in Research

Many students go on to conduct research in public health, psychology, and medicine. Public health researchers are involved in research and interventions that have the broad goal of improving the health of the general population. Public health researchers typically work in academic settings, in public agencies (such as regional health departments), Health Canada, family planning clinics, and the Canadian Health Network and its constituent organizations and agencies, as well as in hospitals, clinics, and other health care agencies.

In these settings, public health researchers can be responsible for a variety of tasks. For example, they may be involved in developing educational interventions for the general public to help people practice better health behaviours, or to inform policymakers about changes that would benefit communities. They may formally evaluate programs for improving health-related practices that have already been implemented through the media and through communities. They may chart the progress of particular diseases, monitor health threats in the workplace, and develop interventions to reduce these threats, and conduct research on health issues.

Many undergraduates in health psychology go on to graduate school in psychology, where they learn the research, teaching, and applied skills necessary to research and/or practise health psychology. Many of these health psychologists then work in university departments of psychology, where they conduct research and train new students; others work in medical schools, as independent consultants for health and other agencies, in hospitals and other treatment settings as was illustrated in the example of Tobi, and in industrial or occupational health settings to promote health behaviour and prevent accidents and other job-related morbidity (Quick, 1999; S. Williams & Kohout, 1999).

The remainder of this book focuses on the kind of knowledge, training, research, and interventions that health psychologists undertake, and in the last chapter, Chapter 15, a glimpse of the future trends in this exciting field of psychology. At this point, it is useful to turn to the content of this growing field. ●

SUMMARY

 Describe and define health psychology

- Health psychology is the field within psychology devoted to understanding psychological influences on how people stay healthy, why they become ill, and how they respond when they do get ill. It focuses on health promotion and maintenance; prevention and treatment of illness; the etiology and correlates of health, illness, and dysfunction; and improvement of the health care system and the formulation of health policy.

 Understand how our view of the mind–body relationship changed over time

- The interaction of the mind and the body has concerned philosophers and scientists for centuries. Different models of the relationship have predominated at different times in history, but current emphasis is on the inextricable unity of the two.

Explain the biopsychosocial model of health

- The biomedical model, which dominates medicine, is a reductionistic, single-factor model of illness that regards the mind and body as separate entities and emphasizes illness concerns over health.

- The biomedical model is currently being replaced by the biopsychosocial model, which regards any health or illness outcome as a complex interplay of biological, psychological, and social factors. The biopsychosocial model recognizes the importance of both macrolevel and microlevel processes in producing health and illness and maintains that the mind and body cannot be distinguished in matters of health and illness. Under this model, health is regarded as an active achievement.

- The biopsychosocial model guides health psychologists in their research efforts to uncover factors that predict states of health and illness and in their clinical interventions with patients.

 Identify why the field of health psychology is needed

- The rise of health psychology can be tied to several factors, including the increase in chronic or lifestyle-related illnesses, the changing perspective on the definition of health, the increasing burden of health care expenditures, the realization that psychological and social factors contribute to health and illness, the demonstrated importance of psychological interventions to improving people's health, and the rigorous methodological contributions of expert researchers.

 Relate the purpose of health psychology training

- Health psychologists perform a variety of tasks. They research and examine the interaction of biological, psychological, and social factors in producing health and illness. They help treat patients suffering from a variety of disorders and conduct counselling for the psychosocial problems that illness may create. They develop worksite interventions to improve employees' health habits and work in organizations as consultants to improve health and health care delivery.

KEY TERMS

acute disorders   p. 11
behavioural medicine   p. 7
biomedical model   p. 8
biopsychosocial model   p. 8
chronic illnesses   p. 11
conversion hysteria   p. 7
correlational research   p. 15
dietitian   p. 18
epidemiology   p. 13

etiology   p. 4
experiment   p. 15
health   p. 4
health psychology   p. 3
longitudinal research   p. 16
mind–body relationship   p. 4
morbidity   p. 13
mortality   p. 13
occupational therapist   p. 18

physiotherapist   p. 18
prospective research   p. 16
psychosomatic medicine   p. 7
qualitative research   p. 16
randomized clinical trials   p. 15
retrospective research   p. 16
social worker   p. 18
systems theory   p. 9

The Systems of the Body

LEARNING OBJECTIVES

After reading this chapter, students will be able to:

(LO1) Describe the function of the nervous system

(LO2) Explain how the endocrine system operates

(LO3) Identify how the cardiovascular system works

(LO4) Relate how the respiratory system functions

(LO5) Describe how the digestive system metabolizes food

(LO6) Explain the role of the renal system

(LO7) Understand the importance of the reproductive system and genetics

(LO8) Describe the function of the immune system

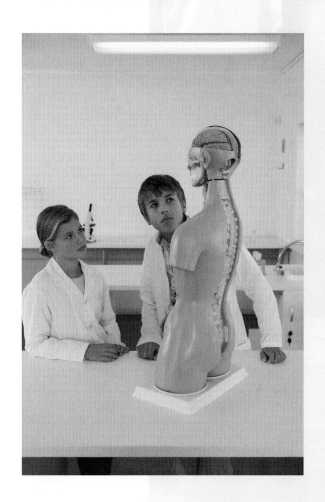

The past two years of Rick's life had been anything but calm. Following the loss of his newborn son to congenital heart defects, and his relocation to a new city shortly thereafter, he had hoped that the recent stress in his life would soon settle down so that he could go back to feeling less fatigued and overwhelmed. What didn't help either was his hour-long commute to work each day to a job near a chemical plant. But when he woke up that Sunday morning with strange bruising around his eyes and blood in his urine, he knew that something was very wrong. After a visit to his family physician who scheduled a visit to a blood specialist, he tried to get back to his normal routine while awaiting the test results. But the call he received at work that week would alter his life forever. "I hope you are sitting down" said his doctor. "You need to go the emergency room and admit yourself to the hospital immediately—you have leukemia." Stunned by the news, Rick drove straight to hospital where he was met by the oncologist who told him that he had acute myelogenous leukemia, and that with chemotherapy and a new treatment derived from vitamin A—all-trans retinoic acid (ATRA)—the success rate for managing his leukemia was excellent.

Rick was relieved that his first course of chemotherapy was uneventful, with little or no side effects. But one day he started having great difficulty breathing, and when he tried to stand up he started to black out and fall over. The doctors were at first perplexed by these seemingly unrelated symptoms, and then recalled that in very rare cases ATRA can cause fluid to build up in the lungs, leading to breathing difficulties, low blood pressure, and blackouts. Rick was then carefully monitored and his dosage of ATRA lowered.

Following this incident, Rick's treatment seemed to be going relatively smoothly. The second course of chemotherapy had its expected side effect of hair loss, but once complete Rick was permitted to go home to his family for two weeks until he was ready for the third course. Less than a week later, Rick woke up with a high fever and extreme pain in his abdomen. He was immediately admitted to the hospital again. But by the time he had arrived back on the cancer ward he was almost incoherent from the pain, and he was immediately admitted into the intensive care unit (ICU). Rick was experiencing sepsis, a serious medical condition caused by a severe infection, which can result in multiple organ failure and potentially death. His oncologist suspected that the cause of the infection was due to an inflammation of Rick's colon, a rare side effect from the chemotherapy that can cause part of his intestinal tract to perforate and leak the infected cells, causing

death. As Rick's body tried to deal with the already spreading infection, his kidneys became overworked and failed. Miraculously, his colon did not rupture, and Rick was placed on dialysis to assist with the work that his overstrained kidneys could no longer do so that they might recover and function again. After several weeks in the ICU, Rick slowly started to gain consciousness as his body began to recover from the near-death experience. Six weeks later, his kidneys regained their functioning, and Rick no longer had to look forward to lifelong dialysis. Today, Rick's leukemia is in remission, his hair has grown back, and other than some lingering pain from nerve damage to his intestines, you would never know to look at him that he had lived through such an ordeal.

An understanding of health requires a working knowledge of human physiology, the study of the body's functioning. This knowledge makes it possible to understand such issues as how good health habits make illness less likely, how stress affects bodily functioning, how repeated stress can lead to hypertension or coronary artery disease, and how cell growth is radically altered by cancer.

The body is made up of many millions of cells that grouped together form tissues, which form organs whose functions overlap to produce the body's systems. In this chapter we consider the major systems of the body, examining how each system functions normally and some of the disorders to which the system may be vulnerable. The body's systems are, however, interconnected, and as was the case with Rick, disruptions in one system can result in problems in other systems.

From a biopsychosocial perspective, a consideration of the role of psychological and social factors in disease development is also important. For example, Rick experienced several major and stressful life events prior to his diagnosis, as well as the chronic strain of a long commute to work in an area with environmental pollutants suspected to be linked to the development of leukemia. Indeed there is mounting evidence for the role of social factors such as lifestyle, family support, and socioeconomic status in physiological changes that lead to the development of a number of diseases and disorders (Bernstein & Shanahan, 2008; Chen, Miller, Walker, Arevalo, Sung, & Cole, 2009; Chen & Schreier, 2008; Miller, Chen, & Cole, 2009). Although the focus of this chapter is understanding the systems of the body, we also highlight some of the links between modifiable psychosocial factors and disease. A full consideration of the implications of psychosocial factors for disease development will be provided in the appropriate chapters throughout the text.

WHAT IS THE FUNCTION OF THE NERVOUS SYSTEM?

Overview

The **nervous system** is a complex network of interconnected nerve fibres that functions to regulate many important bodily functions, including the response to and recovery from stress. The nervous system is made up of the central nervous system and the peripheral nervous system. The central nervous system consists of the brain and the spinal cord. The rest of the nerves in the body, including those that connect to the brain and spinal cord, constitute the peripheral nervous system. The peripheral nervous system is, itself, made up of the somatic nervous system and the autonomic nervous system. The somatic, or voluntary, nervous system connects nerve fibres to voluntary muscles and provides the brain with feedback in the form of sensory information about voluntary movement. The autonomic, or involuntary, nervous system connects the central nervous system with all internal organs over which people do not customarily have control.

Regulation of the autonomic nervous system occurs via the sympathetic nervous system and the parasympathetic nervous system. As will be seen in Chapter 6, the **sympathetic nervous system** plays an important role in reactions to stress. It prepares the body to respond to emergencies; to strong emotions, such as anger or fear; and to strenuous activity. Because it is concerned with the mobilization and exertion of energy, it is called a catabolic system. Activation of the sympathetic nervous system due to stress is often experienced as an increased heart rate and the tensing of muscles.

In contrast, the **parasympathetic nervous system** controls the activities of organs under normal circumstances and acts antagonistically to the sympathetic nervous system. When an emergency has passed, the parasympathetic nervous system restores the body to a normal state. Activation of the parasympathetic nervous system is common during processes such as digestion and can be experienced as a feeling of relaxation and drowsiness such as that which occurs after eating a large, satisfying meal. Because it is concerned with the conservation of body energy, it is called an anabolic system. The components of the nervous system are summarized in Figure 2.1. We now consider several of these components in greater detail.

The Brain

The brain might best be thought of as the command centre of the body. It receives afferent (sensory) impulses from the peripheral nerve endings and sends efferent (motor) impulses to the extremities and to internal organs to carry out necessary movement. The brain consists of three sections: the hindbrain, the midbrain, and the forebrain. The parts of the brain are shown in Figure 2.2.

FIGURE 2.1 | The Components of the Nervous System

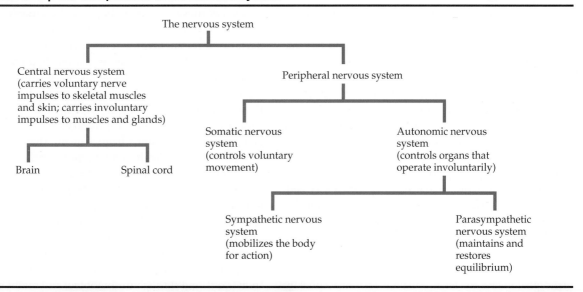

FIGURE 2.2 | The Brain

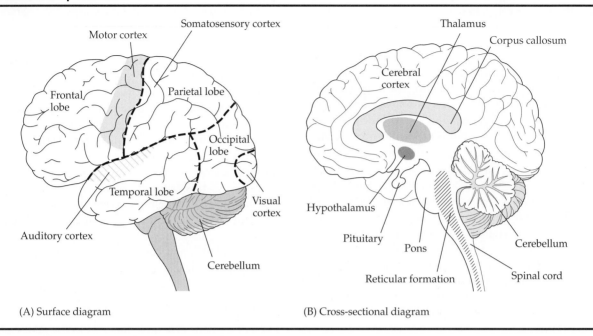

(A) Surface diagram   (B) Cross-sectional diagram

The Hindbrain and the Midbrain   The hindbrain has three main parts: the medulla, the pons, and the cerebellum. The medulla is located just above the point where the spinal cord enters the skull. It is heavily responsible for the regulation of heart rate, blood pressure, and respiration. The **medulla** receives information about the rate at which the heart is contracting, and speeds up or slows down the heart rate as required. The medulla also receives sensory information about blood pressure and the levels of carbon dioxide and oxygen in the body to regulate blood vessel constriction and the rate of breathing. The **pons** serves as a link between the hindbrain and the midbrain. It also helps control respiration.

The **cerebellum** coordinates voluntary muscle movement, the maintenance of balance and equilibrium, and the maintenance of muscle tone and posture. Therefore, damage to this area makes it hard for a person to coordinate muscles effectively; such damage produces lack of muscle tone, tremors, and disturbances in posture or gait.

The midbrain is the major pathway for sensory and motor impulses moving between the forebrain and the hindbrain. It is also responsible for the coordination of visual and auditory reflexes.

The Forebrain   The forebrain has two main sections: the diencephalon and the telencephalon. The diencephalon

is composed of the thalamus and the hypothalamus. The **thalamus** is involved in the recognition of sensory stimuli and the relay of sensory impulses to the cerebral cortex.

The **hypothalamus** helps regulate the centres in the medulla that control cardiac functioning, blood pressure, and respiration. It is also responsible for regulating water balance in the body and for regulating appetites, including hunger and sexual desire. It is an important transition centre between the thoughts generated in the cerebral cortex of the brain and their impact on internal organs. Thus, embarrassment, for example, can lead to blushing via the hypothalamus through the vasomotor centre in the medulla to the blood vessels. Likewise, anxiety may result from secretion of hydrochloric acid in the stomach via signals from the hypothalamus. Together with the pituitary gland, the hypothalamus helps regulate the endocrine system, which releases hormones, influencing functioning in target organs throughout the body.

The other portion of the forebrain, the telencephalon, is composed of the two hemispheres (left and right) of the cerebral cortex. The **cerebral cortex** is the largest portion of the brain and is involved in higher order intelligence, memory, and personality. The sensory impulses that come from the peripheral areas of the body, up the spinal cord, and through the hindbrain and midbrain are received and interpreted in the cerebral cortex. Motor impulses, in turn, pass down from the cortex to the lower portions of the brain and from there to other parts of the body. The cerebral cortex consists of four lobes: frontal, parietal, temporal, and occipital. Each lobe has its own memory storage area or areas of association. Through these complex networks of associations, the brain is able to relate current sensations to past ones, giving the cerebral cortex formidable interpretive capabilities.

The Limbic System   The structures of the limbic system, which border the midline of the brain, play an important role in stress and emotional responses. The amygdala and the hippocampus are involved in the detection of threat and in emotionally charged memories, respectively. The cingulate gyrus, the septum, and areas in the hypothalamus are related to emotional functioning as well. The anterior portion of the thalamus and some nuclei within the hypothalamus are important for socially relevant behaviours.

The Role of Neurotransmitters

The nervous system functions by means of chemicals, called **neurotransmitters,** that regulate nervous system functioning. Stimulation of the sympathetic nervous system prompts the secretion of large quantities of two neurotransmitters, epinephrine and norepinephrine, together termed the **catecholamines.** These substances enter the bloodstream and are carried throughout the body promoting the activity of sympathetic stimulation.

The release of catecholamines prompts a variety of important bodily changes. Heart rate increases, the heart's capillaries dilate, and blood vessels constrict, increasing blood pressure. Blood is diverted into muscle tissue. Respiration rate goes up, and the amount of air flowing into the lungs is increased. Digestion and urination are generally decreased. The pupils of the eyes dilate, and sweat glands are stimulated to produce more sweat. These changes are familiar to anyone who has experienced a highly stressful event or a strong emotion, such as fear or embarrassment. As we will see in Chapter 6, arousal of the sympathetic nervous system and the production and release of catecholamines are critically important in individual responses to stressful circumstances. Repeated arousal of the sympathetic nervous system may have implications for the development of several chronic disorders, such as coronary artery disease and hypertension, which will be discussed in greater detail in Chapter 13.

Disorders of the Nervous System

Approximately one in three Canadians will be affected by a disorder of the nervous system during their lifetime (Neuroscience Canada, 2010). The most common forms of neurological dysfunction are epilepsy and Parkinson's disease. Cerebral palsy, Alzheimer's disease, multiple sclerosis, and Huntington disease also affect a substantial number of people.

Epilepsy   A disease of the central nervous system affecting 1 in every 100 Canadians (Canadian Epilepsy Alliance, 2008), epilepsy is often idiopathic, which means that no specific cause for the symptoms can be identified. Symptomatic epilepsy may be traced to such factors as injury during birth; severe injury to the head; infectious disease, such as meningitis or encephalitis; and metabolic or nutritional disorders. A tendency toward epilepsy may also be inherited.

Epilepsy is marked by seizures, which range from barely noticeable staring or purposeless motor movements (such as chewing and lip smacking) to violent convulsions accompanied by irregular breathing, drooling, and loss of consciousness. Epilepsy cannot be cured, but it can often be successfully controlled through medication and behavioural interventions designed to manage stress (see Chapters 7 and 11).

Cerebral Palsy   Approximately 50,000 children and adults in Canada manifest one or more of the symptoms of cerebral palsy (Ontario Federation for Cerebral Palsy, 2009). Cerebral palsy is a chronic, nonprogressive disorder marked by lack of muscle control. It stems from brain damage caused by an interruption in the brain's oxygen supply, usually during childbirth. In older children, a severe accident or physical abuse can produce the condition. Apart from being unable to control motor functions, those with cerebral palsy may (but need not) also have seizures, spasms, mental handicap, difficulties of sensation and perception, and problems with sight, hearing, or speech.

Alzheimer's Disease   A progressive and degenerative disease of the brain, Alzheimer's disease causes serious impairments to thinking and memory. Due to the aging population, the prevalence of Alzheimer's is on the rise. In 2006, it affected 26.6 million people but it is estimated that by 2050 over 100 million people worldwide, including 1 million Canadians, or 1 in 85 people will be living with Alzheimer's disease (Neuroscience Canada, 2010).

Parkinson's Disease   Patients with Parkinson's disease suffer from progressive degeneration of the basal ganglia, the group of nuclei that controls smooth motor coordination. The result of this deterioration is tremors, rigidity, and slowness of movement. Approximately 100,000 Canadians suffer from Parkinson's disease, which primarily strikes people age 60 and older, and men are more likely than women to develop the disease (Parkinson Society of Canada, 2003). Although the cause of Parkinson's is not fully known, depletion of the neurotransmitter dopamine may be involved.

Multiple Sclerosis   An estimated 55,000 to 75,000 Canadians have multiple sclerosis, and every year 1,000 new cases are diagnosed (Multiple Sclerosis Society of Canada, 2006). This degenerative disease of certain brain tissues can cause paralysis and, occasionally, blindness, deafness, and mental deterioration. Early symptoms include numbness, double vision, dragging of the feet, loss of bladder or bowel control, speech difficulties, and extreme fatigue. Symptoms may appear and disappear over a period of years; after that, deterioration is continuous.

The effects of multiple sclerosis result from the disintegration of myelin, a fatty membrane that surrounds the nerve fibres and facilitates the conduction of nerve impulses. Multiple sclerosis is an autoimmune disorder, so-called because the immune system fails to recognize its own tissue and attacks the myelin sheath surrounding the nerves.

Huntington Disease   A hereditary disorder of the central nervous system, Huntington disease is characterized by chronic physical and mental deterioration. Symptoms include involuntary muscle spasms, loss of motor abilities, personality changes, and other signs of mental disintegration. Because some of the symptoms are similar to those of epilepsy, Huntington disease is sometimes mistaken for epilepsy.

The disease affects men and women alike, occurring at a rate of about 1 in every 10,000 (Huntington Society of Canada, 2008). The gene for Huntington disease has been isolated, and a test is now available that indicates not only if one is a carrier of the gene but also at what age (roughly) a person will succumb to Huntington disease (Morell, 1993). As will be seen later in this chapter, genetic counselling with this group of at-risk individuals is important.

Paraplegia and Quadriplegia   Paraplegia is paralysis of the lower extremities of the body; it results from an injury to the lower portion of the spinal cord. Quadriplegia is paralysis of all four extremities and the trunk of the body; it occurs when the upper portion of the spinal cord is severed. Once the spinal cord has been severed, no motor impulses can descend to tissues below the cut nor can sensory impulses from tissues below the cut ascend to the brain. As a consequence, a person usually loses bladder and bowel control. An estimated 40,000 Canadians live with some form of spinal cord injury (Canadian Paraplegic Association, 2008).

HOW DOES THE ENDOCRINE SYSTEM OPERATE?

(L02)

Overview

The **endocrine system** complements the nervous system in controlling bodily activities. As we will see in Chapter 6, the synergistic interactions of the nervous system and the endocrine system are responsible for the physiological changes that occur in response to stress. The endocrine system is made up of a number of ductless glands, which secrete hormones into the blood, stimulating changes in target organs. The endocrine and nervous systems depend on each other, stimulating and inhibiting each other's activities. The nervous system is chiefly responsible for fast-acting, short-duration responses to changes in the body, whereas the endocrine system mainly governs slow-acting responses of long duration.

The endocrine system is regulated by the hypothalamus and the **pituitary gland.** Located at the base of the brain the pituitary has two lobes. The anterior pituitary lobe of the pituitary gland secretes hormones responsible for growth: somatotropic hormone (STH), which regulates bone, muscle, and other organ development; gonadotropic hormones, which control the growth, development, and secretion of the gonads (testes and ovaries); thyrotropic hormone (TSH), which controls the growth, development, and secretion of the thyroid gland; and adrenocorticotropic hormone (ACTH), which controls the growth and secretions of the cortex region of the adrenal glands (described in the following section, "The Adrenal Glands"). The posterior pituitary lobe produces oxytocin, which controls contractions during labour and lactation, and vasopressin, or antidiuretic hormone (ADH), which controls the water-absorbing ability of the kidneys.

The Adrenal Glands

The **adrenal glands** are two small glands located one on top of each of the kidneys. Each adrenal gland consists

FIGURE 2.3 | Adrenal Gland Activity in Response to Stress

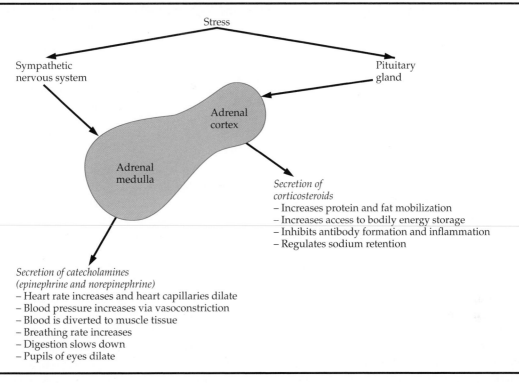

of an adrenal medulla and an adrenal cortex. The hormones of the adrenal medulla are epinephrine and norepinephrine, which were described earlier.

The adrenal cortex is stimulated by adrenocorticotropic hormone (ACTH) from the anterior lobe of the pituitary, and it releases hormones called steroids. These steroids include mineralocorticoids, glucocorticoids, androgens, and estrogens.

As Figure 2.3 implies, the adrenal glands are critically involved in physiological and neuroendocrine reactions to stress. Both catecholamines, secreted in conjunction with sympathetic arousal, and cortico steroids are implicated in biological responses to stress. We will consider stress responses more fully in Chapter 6.

Disorders of the Endocrine System

Diabetes   Diabetes is a chronic endocrine disorder in which the body is not able to manufacture or properly use insulin. Over 2 million Canadians have diabetes, with this number expected to increase to 3 million by the year 2010. In addition, rates of diabetes among Aboriginal Canadians are three to five times higher compared to the general population (Canadian Diabetes Association,

2005). Diabetes consists of two primary forms. Type I diabetes (sometimes called insulin-dependent diabetes) is a severe disorder that typically arises in late childhood or early adolescence. At least partly genetic in origin, Type I diabetes is believed to be an autoimmune disorder, possibly precipitated by an earlier viral infection. The immune system falsely identifies cells in the islets of Langerhans in the pancreas as invaders and destroys those cells, compromising or eliminating their ability to produce insulin.

Type II diabetes typically occurs after age 40 and is the more common form. In Type II diabetes, insulin may be produced by the body but there may not be enough of it, or the body may not be sensitive to it. It is heavily a disease of lifestyle, involving a disturbance in glucose metabolism and the delicate balance between insulin production and insulin responsiveness. This balance appears to be disregulated by such factors as obesity and stress, among other contributing factors.

Diabetes is associated with a thickening of the arteries due to the buildup of wastes in the blood. As a consequence, people with diabetes show high rates of coronary heart disease. Diabetes is also the leading cause of blindness among adults, and it accounts for 50 percent of all the patients who require renal dialysis for kidney failure. Diabetes can also produce nervous system damage, leading to pain and loss of sensation. In severe cases, amputation of the extremities, such as toes and feet, is often required. As a consequence of these manifold complications, people with diabetes have a considerably shortened life expectancy. In Chapter 13, we will consider diabetes and the issues associated with its development and management more fully.

(L03) WHAT IS THE CARDIOVASCULAR SYSTEM?

Overview

The **cardiovascular system** is composed of the heart, blood vessels, and blood, and acts as the transport system of the body. Blood carries oxygen from the lungs to the tissues, and carbon dioxide, excreted as expired air, from the tissues to the lungs. Blood also carries nutrients from the digestive tract to the individual cells so that the cells may extract nutrients for growth and energy. The blood carries waste products from the cells to the kidneys, from which the waste is excreted in the urine. It also carries hormones from the endocrine glands to other organs of the body and transports heat to the surface of the skin to control body temperature.

The arteries carry blood from the heart to other organs and tissues, where oxygen and nutrients are transported through the arterioles (tiny branches of the arteries) and the capillaries (smaller vessels that branch off from the arteries) to individual cells. Veins return the deoxygenated blood to the heart. Together, these vessels control peripheral circulation, dilating or constricting in response to a variety of bodily events.

The Heart

The heart functions as a pump, and its pumping action causes the blood to circulate throughout the body. The left side of the heart, consisting of the left atrium and left ventricle, takes in heavily oxygenated blood from the lungs and pumps it out into the aorta (the major artery leaving the heart), from which the blood passes into the smaller vessels (the arteries, arterioles, and capillaries) to reach the cell tissues. The blood exchanges its oxygen and nutrients for the waste materials of the cells and is then returned to the right side of the heart (right atrium and right ventricle), which pumps it back to the lungs via the pulmonary artery. Once oxygenated, the blood returns to the left side of the heart through the pulmonary veins. The anatomy and functioning of the heart are pictured in Figure 2.4.

FIGURE 2.4 | The Heart

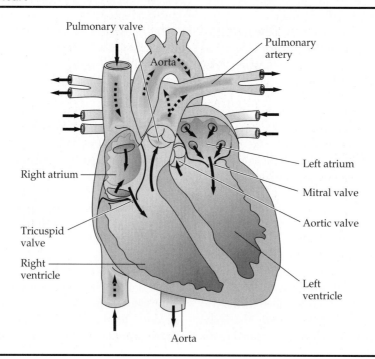

The heart performs these functions through regular rhythmic phases of contraction and relaxation known as the cardiac cycle. There are two phases in the cardiac cycle, systole and diastole. During systole, blood is pumped out of the heart, and blood pressure in the blood vessels increases. As the muscle relaxes during diastole, blood pressure drops and blood is taken into the heart.

A number of factors influence the rate at which the heart contracts and relaxes. During exercise, emotional excitement, or stress, for example, the heart speeds up and the cardiac cycle is completed in a shorter time. Most of this speedup comes out of the diastolic period so that a chronically rapid heart rate reduces overall time for rest. Consequently, a chronically or excessively rapid heart rate can decrease the heart's strength, which may reduce the volume of blood that is pumped. Conversely, heart rate is also regulated by the amount of blood flowing into the veins.

Disorders of the Cardiovascular System

The cardiovascular system is subject to a number of disorders. Some of these are due to congenital defects—that is, defects present at birth, as was the case with Rick's son—others, to infection. By far, however, the major threats to the cardiovascular system are due to damage over the course of life that produces cumulative wear and tear on the cardiovascular system. Lifestyle, in the form of diet, exercise, smoking, and stress exposure, among other factors, heavily affects the development of diseases of the cardiovascular system, as we will see in subsequent chapters.

Atherosclerosis   The major cause of heart disease in this country is atherosclerosis, a problem that becomes worse with age. **Atherosclerosis** is caused by deposits of cholesterol and other substances on the arterial walls, which form plaques that narrow the arteries. The presence of atherosclerotic plaques reduces the flow of blood through the arteries and interferes with the passage of nutrients from the capillaries into the cells—a process that can lead to tissue damage. Damaged arterial walls are also potential sites for the formation of blood clots, which in themselves can completely obstruct a vessel and cut off the flow of blood.

Atherosclerosis is, in part, a disease of lifestyle, as we will see in Chapter 13. It is associated with a number of poor health habits, such as smoking and a high-fat diet. It is also a known risk factor for diabetes. These two factors make it of paramount interest to health psychologists and explain the concern over changing these poor health behaviours.

Atherosclerosis is associated with two primary clinical manifestations:

1. **Angina pectoris,** or chest pain, which occurs because the muscle tissue of the heart must continue its activity without a sufficient supply of oxygen or adequate removal of carbon dioxide and other waste products.

2. **Myocardial infarction (MI),** which is most likely to occur when a clot has developed in a coronary vessel and blocks the flow of blood to the heart. A myocardial infarction, also known as a heart attack, can cause death.

Other related vessel disorders include arteriosclerosis (or hardening of the arteries), aneurysms, and phlebitis. Arteriosclerosis results when calcium, salts, and scar tissue react with the elastic tissue of the arteries. The consequence is to decrease the elasticity of the arteries, making them rigid and hard. Blood pressure then increases because the arteries cannot dilate and constrict to help blood move, and hypertension (high blood pressure) may result. An aneurysm is a bulge in a section of the wall of an artery or a vein; it is the reaction of a weak region to pressure. When an aneurysm ruptures, it can produce instantaneous death from internal hemorrhaging and loss of blood pressure. Phlebitis is an inflammation of a vein wall, often accompanied by water retention and pain. The condition typically results from an infection surrounding the vein, from varicose veins, from pregnancy-related bodily changes, or from the pressure of a tumour on the vein. The chief threat posed by phlebitis is that it can encourage the production of blood clots, which then block circulation.

Blood Pressure

Blood pressure is the force that blood exerts against the blood vessel walls. It is measured as a ratio of the pressure as the heart contracts and pushes blood out (systolic) to the lower pressure when the heart relaxes in between heart beats (diastolic).

Blood pressure is influenced by several factors, the first of which is cardiac output. Pressure against the arterial walls is greater as the volume of blood flow increases. A second factor influencing blood pressure is peripheral resistance, or the resistance to blood flow in the small arteries of the body (arterioles). In addition, blood pressure is influenced by the structure of the arterial walls: If the walls have been damaged, or if they are clogged by deposits of waste, blood pressure will be higher. Chronically high blood pressure, called hypertension, is the consequence of too high a cardiac output or too high a peripheral resistance. The psychosocial issues involved in the management and treatment of hypertension include diet, chronic negative affect, stress levels, and acculturation, which we will more fully discuss in Chapter 13.

The Blood

An adult's body contains approximately five litres of blood, which consists of plasma and cells. Plasma, the fluid portion of blood, occupies approximately 55 percent of the blood volume. The blood cells are suspended in the plasma, which contains plasma proteins and plasma electrolytes (salts) plus the substances that are being transported by the blood (oxygen and nutrients or carbon dioxide and waste materials). The remaining 45 percent of blood volume is made up of cells.

Blood cells are manufactured in the bone marrow, the substance in the hollow cavities of bones. Bone marrow contains five types of blood-forming cells: myeloblasts and monoblasts, both of which produce particular white blood cells; lymphoblasts, which produce lymphocytes; erythroblasts, which produce red blood cells; and megakaryocytes, which produce platelets. Each of these types of blood cells has an important function.

White blood cells play an important role in healing by absorbing and removing foreign substances from the body. They contain granules that secrete digestive enzymes that engulf and act on bacteria and other foreign particles, turning them into a form conducive to excretion.

Lymphocytes also play an important role in combating foreign substances. They produce antibodies—agents that destroy foreign substances through the antigen-antibody reaction. Together, these groups of cells play an important role in fighting infection and disease. We will consider them more fully in our discussion of the immune system.

Red blood cells are chiefly important because they contain hemoglobin, which is needed to carry oxygen and carbon dioxide throughout the body.

Platelets serve several important functions. They clump together to block small holes that develop in blood vessels and play an important role in blood clotting. When an injury occurs and tissues are damaged, platelets help form thromboplastin, which, in turn, acts on a substance in the plasma known as fibrinogen, changing it to fibrin. The formation of fibrin produces clotting.

Disorders Related to White Cell Production

Some blood disorders affect the production of white blood cells; they include leukemia, leukopenia, and leukocytosis. Leukemia, the condition that almost killed Rick in the opening scenario, is a disease of the bone marrow, and is a common form of cancer. It causes the production of an excessive number of white blood cells, thus overloading the blood plasma and reducing the number of red blood cells that can circulate in the plasma. In the short term, anemia (a shortage of red blood cells) will result. In the long term, if left untreated, leukemia will cause death. Although there is no single cause of leukemia, exposure to chemicals such as ethanol and smoking are among the known risk factors (Canadian Cancer Society, 2009).

Leukopenia is a deficiency of white blood cells; it may accompany such diseases as tuberculosis, measles, and viral pneumonia. Leukopenia leaves an individual susceptible to diseases because it reduces the number of white blood cells available to combat infection. Leukocytosis is an excessive number of white blood cells. It is a response to many infections, such as leukemia, appendicitis, and infectious mononucleosis.

Disorders Related to Red Cell Production

Anemia is a condition in which the number of red blood cells or amount of hemoglobin is below normal. A temporary anemic condition experienced by many women is a consequence of menstruation; through loss of blood, much vital iron (essential for the production of hemoglobin) is lost. Iron supplements must sometimes be taken to offset this problem. Other forms of anemia, including aplastic anemia, may occur because the bone marrow is unable to produce a sufficient number of red blood cells. The result is a decrease in the blood's transport capabilities, causing tissues to receive too little oxygen and to be left with too much carbon dioxide. When it is not checked, anemia can cause permanent damage to the nervous system and produce chronic weakness.

Sickle-cell anemia is a genetically transmitted inability to produce normal red blood cells that is found chiefly among those of African and Mediterranean descent, as well as in South and Central America, the Caribbean, and the Middle East. These cells are sickle shaped instead of flattened spheres, and they contain abnormal hemoglobin protein molecules. They are vulnerable to rupture, leaving the individual susceptible to anemia. The sickle cell appears to be a genetic adaptation promoting resistance to malaria. Unfortunately, although these cells are effective in the short term against malaria, the long-term implications are life threatening.

Clotting Disorders A third group of blood disorders involves clotting dysfunctions. Hemophilia affects individuals who are unable to produce thromboplastin and fibrin. Therefore, their blood cannot clot naturally in response to injury, and they may bleed to death unless they receive medication.

As noted earlier, clots (or thromboses) may sometimes develop in the blood vessels, especially if arterial or venous walls have been damaged or roughened because of the buildup of cholesterol. Platelets then adhere to the roughened area, leading to the formation of a clot. A clot formed in this manner may have very serious consequences if it occurs in the blood vessels leading to the heart (coronary thrombosis) or brain (cerebral thrombosis) because it will block the vital flow of blood to these organs. When a clot occurs in a vein, it may become detached and form an embolus, which may finally become lodged in the blood vessels to the lungs, causing pulmonary obstruction. Death is a likely consequence of all these conditions.

HOW DOES THE RESPIRATORY SYSTEM FUNCTION?

LO4

The Structure and Functions of the Respiratory System

Respiration, or breathing, has three main functions: to take in oxygen, to excrete carbon dioxide, and to regulate the composition of the blood.

The body needs oxygen to metabolize food. During the process of metabolism, oxygen combines with carbon atoms in food, producing carbon dioxide (CO_2). The respiratory system brings in air, most notably oxygen, through inspiration; it eliminates carbon dioxide through expiration.

The **respiratory system** involves a number of organs, including the nose, mouth, pharynx, trachea, diaphragm, abdominal muscles, and lungs. Air is inhaled through the nose and mouth and then passes through the pharynx and larynx to the trachea. The trachea, a muscular tube extending downward from the larynx, divides at its lower end into two branches called the primary bronchi. Each bronchus enters a lung, where it then subdivides into secondary bronchi, still-smaller bronchioles, and, finally, microscopic alveolar ducts, which contain many tiny, clustered sacs called alveoli. The alveoli and the capillaries are responsible for the exchange of oxygen and carbon dioxide. A diagram of the respiratory system appears in Figure 2.5.

The inspiration of air is an active process, brought about by the contraction of muscles. Inspiration causes the lungs to expand inside the thorax (the chest wall). Expiration, in contrast, is a passive function, brought about by the relaxation of the lungs, which reduces the volume of the lungs within the thorax. The lungs fill most of the space within the thorax, called the thoracic cavity, and are very elastic, depending on the thoracic

FIGURE 2.5 | The Respiratory System
(*Source:* Lankford, 1979, p. 467)

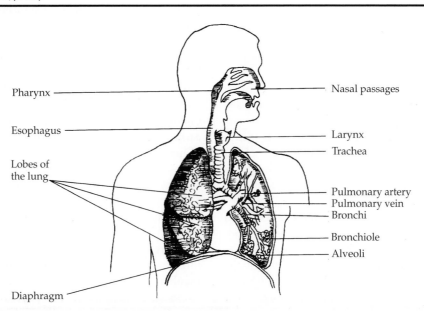

walls for support. Therefore, if air were to get into the space between the thoracic wall and the lungs, one or both lungs would collapse.

Respiratory movements are controlled by a respiratory centre in the medulla of the brain. The functions of this centre depend partly on the chemical composition of the blood. For example, if the blood's carbon dioxide level rises too high, the respiratory centre will be stimulated and respiration will be increased. If the carbon dioxide level falls too low, the respiratory centre will slow down until the carbon dioxide level is back to normal.

The respiratory system is also responsible for coughing. A large amount of dust and other foreign material is inhaled with every breath. Some of these substances are trapped in the mucus of the nose and the air passages and are then conducted back toward the throat, where they are swallowed. When a large amount of mucus collects in the large airways, it is removed by coughing (a forced expiratory effort).

Disorders of the Respiratory System

Asphyxia, Anoxia, and Hyperventilation   Several disorders of the respiratory system—including asphyxia, anoxia, and hyperventilation—have little significance because they are typically short-lived. When they occur on a long-term basis, however, these disorders can have severe effects.

Asphyxia, a condition of oxygen lack and carbon dioxide excess, may occur when there is a respiratory obstruction, when breathing occurs in a confined space so that expired air is reinhaled, or when respiration is insufficient for the body's needs. For example, in Rick's case, the buildup of fluid in his lungs as a side effect from his medication obstructed breathing and resulted in his breathing difficulties.

Anoxia, a shortage of oxygen alone, is more serious. People suffering from anoxia may rapidly become disoriented, lose all sense of danger, and pass into a coma without increasing their breathing. This is a danger to which test pilots are exposed when they take their planes to very high altitudes, so pilots are carefully trained to be alert to the signs of anoxia so that they can take immediate corrective steps.

Another disruption of the carbon dioxide–oxygen balance results from hyperventilation. During periods of intense emotional excitement, people often breathe deeply, reducing the carbon dioxide content of the blood. Because carbon dioxide is a vasodilator (that is, it dilates the blood vessels), a consequence of hyperven-

tilation is constriction of blood vessels and reduced blood flow to the brain. As a result, the individual may experience impaired vision, difficulty in thinking clearly, and dizziness.

Severe problems occur when a person stops breathing and becomes unconscious. If artificial respiration is not initiated within two minutes, brain damage and even death may result.

Asthma   Asthma is a more severe allergic reaction, which can be caused by a variety of foreign substances, including dust, dog or cat dander, pollens, and fungi. An asthma attack can also be touched off by emotional stress or exercise. These attacks may be so serious that they produce bronchial spasms and hyperventilation.

Statistics show a dramatic increase in the prevalence of allergic disorders including asthma in the past 20 to 30 years. Currently, more than 130 million people worldwide have asthma (2.7 million of these are in Canada), and the numbers are increasing, especially in industrialized countries (World Health Organization, 2006a). Consistent with the suggestion that place can have a substantial impact on health, rates are increasing fastest in urban as opposed to rural areas. One intriguing fact that may provide a clue to the increase in allergic sensitization is that children who have a lot of childhood infectious diseases are less likely to develop allergies, suggesting that exposure to infectious agents may actually have a protective effect against allergies. Thus, paradoxically, the improved hygiene of industrialized countries may actually be contributing to high rates of allergic disorders (Yazdanbakhsh, Kremsner, & van Ree, 2002).

There is also emerging evidence that the social environment may play a role not only in the exacerbation of asthma, but also its onset. For example, family factors were found to play a direct role in a youth's asthma symptoms by impacting physiological changes, whereas community factors impacted asthma symptoms by altering health behaviours (Chen & Schreier, 2008).

Viral Infections   The respiratory system is vulnerable to a number of infections and chronic disorders. Perhaps the most familiar of these is the common cold, a viral infection of the upper and sometimes the lower respiratory tract. The infection that results causes discomfort, congestion, and excessive secretion of mucus. The incubation period for a cold—that is, the time between exposure to the virus and onset of symptoms—is

12 to 72 hours, and the typical duration of a cold is a few days. Secondary bacterial infections may complicate the illness. These occur because the primary viral infection causes inflammation of the mucous membranes, reducing their ability to prevent secondary infection.

A more serious viral infection of the respiratory system is influenza, which can occur in epidemic form. Flu viruses attack the lining of the respiratory tract, killing healthy cells. Fever and inflammation of the respiratory tract may result. A common complication is a secondary bacterial infection, such as pneumonia (discussed below).

A third infection, bronchitis, is an inflammation of the mucosal membrane inside the bronchi of the lungs. Large amounts of mucus are produced in bronchitis, leading to persistent coughing.

Bacterial Infections   The respiratory system is also vulnerable to bacterial attack by, for example, strep throat, whooping cough, and diphtheria. Strep throat, an infection of the throat and soft palate, is characterized by edema (swelling) and reddening.

Whooping cough invades the upper respiratory tract and moves down to the trachea and bronchi. The associated bacterial growth leads to the production of a viscous fluid, which the body attempts to expel through violent coughing. For the most part, strep throat and whooping cough do not cause permanent damage to the upper respiratory tract. Their main danger is the possibility of secondary infection, which results from lowered resistance. However, these bacterial infections can cause permanent damage to other tissues, including heart tissue.

Chronic Obstructive Pulmonary Disease (COPD)   Chronic obstructive pulmonary disease is the fourth leading killer of people in Canada. More than 714,000 Canadians have COPD, and although lung cancer is deadlier than COPD, COPD is much more common and nearly as deadly. Chronic bronchitis and emphysema are two of the familiar disorders that comprise COPD.

Pulmonary emphysema involves a persistent obstruction of the flow of air. It occurs when the alveoli become dilated, atrophied, and thin so that they lose their elasticity and cannot constrict during exhalation. As a result, exhalation becomes difficult and forced so that carbon dioxide is not readily eliminated. Emphysema is caused by a variety of factors, including long-term smoking.

Although COPD is not curable, it is highly preventable. Its chief cause is smoking, which accounts for approximately 85 percent of all cases of COPD. Specifically, exposure to toxic substances over a long period leads to inflammation and swelling of the cells lining the lungs. In COPD, this swelling is to a point that it restricts the flow of air, thus sapping energy and producing substantial resulting disability, high medical costs, and costs to the economy (Canadian Lung Association, 2007a).

Pneumonia   There are two main types of pneumonia. Lobar pneumonia is a primary infection of the entire lobe of a lung. The alveoli become inflamed, and the normal oxygen–carbon dioxide exchange between the blood and alveoli can be disrupted. Spread of infection to other organs is also likely. Bronchial pneumonia, which is confined to the bronchi, is typically a secondary infection that may occur as a complication of other disorders, such as a severe cold or flu. It is not as serious as lobar pneumonia.

Tuberculosis   Tuberculosis is an airborne infectious disease caused by bacteria that invade lung tissue, and eventually produce cavities. Such cavities, in turn, can give rise to permanent scar tissue, causing chronic difficulties in oxygen and carbon dioxide exchange between the blood and the alveoli.

Tuberculosis was a major cause of death during the early part of the twentieth century, although the incidence of tuberculosis today has dramatically decreased in developed nations. Increasingly, however, new drug-resistant strains of tuberculosis are being reported worldwide. Tuberculosis claims the lives of approximately 2 million people worldwide each year, with most of these deaths occurring in developing countries (Canadian Lung Association, 2007b). Although tuberculosis is almost eliminated in Canada, most of the newest cases are reported among the foreign-born, or among those who have contact with travellers from other countries (Public Health Agency of Canada, 2005; see also the Focus on Social Issues box, "Portraits of Two Carriers," later in this chapter). Rates are much higher among Aboriginal people compared to other Canadians, with poor living conditions the likely cause (Canadian Lung Association, 2007b).

Lung Cancer   More Canadians die from lung cancer, or carcinoma of the lung, than from any other form of cancer (Canadian Cancer Society, 2008a). It is considered the most preventable form of cancer with smoking as its main cause. Recognition of this and other environmental factors such as air pollution or cancer-causing substances encountered in the workplace (such as asbestos), have led to legislation to reduce exposure to these harmful carcinogens.

The affected cells in the lungs begin to divide in a rapid and unrestricted manner, producing a tumour. Malignant cells grow faster than healthy cells; they crowd out the healthy cells and rob them of nutrients, causing them to die, and then spread into surrounding tissue.

Conclusion

A number of respiratory disorders are tied directly to health problems that can be addressed by health psychologists. For example, smoking is a major health problem that is implicated in both pulmonary emphysema and lung cancer. The spread of tuberculosis can be reduced by encouraging people at risk to obtain regular chest X-rays. Faulty methods of infection control, dangerous substances in the workplace, poor living conditions associated with lower socio-economic status, and air pollution are also factors that contribute to the incidence of respiratory problems.

As we will see in Chapters 3, 4, and 5, health psychologists have addressed many of these problems. In addition, some of the respiratory disorders we have considered are chronic conditions with which an individual may live for some time. Consequently, issues of long-term physical, vocational, social, and psychological rehabilitation become crucial, and we will cover these issues in Chapters 11, 13, and 14.

L05 HOW DOES THE DIGESTIVE SYSTEM METABOLIZE FOOD?

Overview

Food, essential for survival, is converted through the process of metabolism into heat and energy, and it supplies nutrients for growth and the repair of tissues. But before food can be used by cells, it must be changed into a form suitable for absorption into the blood. This conversion process is called digestion.

The Functioning of the Digestive System

Food is first lubricated by saliva in the mouth, where it forms a soft, rounded lump called a bolus. It passes through the esophagus by means of peristalsis, a unidi-rectional muscular movement toward the stomach. The stomach produces various gastric secretions, including pepsin and hydrochloric acid, to further the digestive process. The sight or even the thought of food starts the flow of gastric juices.

As food progresses from the stomach to the duodenum (the intersection of the stomach and lower intestine), the pancreas becomes involved in the digestive process. Pancreatic juices, which are secreted into the duodenum, contain several enzymes that break down proteins, carbohydrates, and fats. A critical function of the pancreas is the production of the hormone insulin, which facilitates the entry of glucose into the bodily tissues. The liver also plays an important role in metabolism by producing bile, which enters the duodenum and helps break down fats. Bile is stored in the gallbladder and is secreted into the duodenum as needed.

Although most metabolic products are water soluble and can be easily transported in the blood, other substances are not soluble in water and therefore must be transported as complex substances in the blood plasma. Known as lipids, these substances include fats, cholesterol, and lecithin. An excess of lipids in the blood is called hyperlipidemia, a condition common in diabetes, some kidney diseases, hyperthyroidism, and alcoholism. It is also a causal factor in heart disease (see Chapters 4 and 13).

The absorption of food primarily takes place in the small intestine, which produces enzymes that complete the breakdown of proteins to amino acids. The motility of the small intestine is under the control of the sympathetic and parasympathetic nervous systems. Parasympathetic activity speeds up metabolism and aids digestion, whereas sympathetic nervous system activity reduces it.

Food then passes into the large intestine (whose successive segments are known as the cecum and the ascending, transverse, descending, and sigmoid colon), which acts largely as a storage organ for the accumulation of food residue and helps in the reabsorption of water. The entry of feces into the rectum then brings about the urge to defecate, or expel, the solid waste from the body via the anus. The organs involved in the metabolism of food are pictured in Figure 2.6.

Disorders of the Digestive System

The digestive system is susceptible to a number of disorders, some of which are only mildly uncomfortable and temporary and others of which are more serious and chronic.

FIGURE 2.6 | The Digestive System

(*Source:* Lankford, 1979, p. 523)

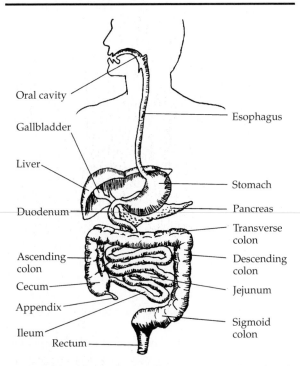

Gastroenteritis, Diarrhea, and Dysentery

Gastroenteritis is an inflammation of the lining of the stomach and small intestine. It may be caused by such factors as excessive amounts of food or drink, contaminated food or water, or food poisoning. Symptoms appear approximately two to four hours after the ingestion of food; symptoms include vomiting, diarrhea, abdominal cramps, and nausea.

Diarrhea, characterized by watery and frequent bowel movements, occurs when the lining of the small and large intestines cannot properly absorb water or digested food. Chronic diarrhea may result in serious disturbances of fluid and electrolyte (sodium, potassium, magnesium, calcium) balance. Dysentery is similar to diarrhea except that mucus, pus, and blood are also excreted. Although these conditions are only rarely life threatening in industrialized countries, in less developed countries, they are common causes of death.

Peptic Ulcer   A peptic ulcer is an open sore in the lining of the stomach or the duodenum. It results from the hypersecretion of hydrochloric acid and occurs when pepsin, a protein-digesting enzyme secreted in the stomach,

digests a portion of the stomach wall or duodenum. Once believed to be primarily caused by stress, evidence suggesting that a bacterium called H. pylori contributes to the development of many ulcers put an end to this view. However, recent studies indicate that stress can still cause peptic ulcers in the absence of H. pylori (Fink, 2011). For example, two studies using data from the Canadian Community Health Survey found that ulcers were more than twice as prevalent among people reporting being physically abused as a child compared to people who had not experienced childhood abuse (Fuller-Thomson, Bottoms, Brennenstuhl, & Hurd, 2011).

Inflammatory Bowel Disease   Crohn's disease and ulcerative colitis are two distinct but similar chronic digestive conditions that are collectively known as inflammatory bowel disease, or IBD. These diseases involve inflammation of the intestinal tissue, which leads to sores and bleeding, and symptoms including abdominal pain, fatigue, cramping, and diarrhea. The main difference between Crohn's disease and ulcerative colitis is where they occur in the digestive tract: the more common Crohn's disease occurs in both the large and small intestines, whereas ulcerative colitis occurs only in the large intestine. Both can be managed with medication and surgery, and in the case of colitis, effectively cured only by surgical removal of the colon (Crohn's and Colitis Foundation of Canada, 2008).

IBD occurs more often in northern areas, and Canada is considered to have the highest incidence of IBD in the world. About one in 350 Canadians suffer from Crohn's disease or ulcerative colitis, with the highest rates found in Alberta and Nova Scotia, and the lowest rates in British Columbia (Bernstein et al., 2006).

The reasons for the IBD rates in Canada are still unknown, but some researchers have speculated about the role of a modern lifestyle, as well as ethnicity, in the epidemiology of IBD. For example, lower rates in British Columbia may be linked to the higher proportion of immigrants in that province who have less likelihood of having IBD (Bernstein et al., 2006). Rates of IBD are also increased among developed and developing nations implicating modern lifestyle factors in the etiology of IBD. Although the exact pathways are not known, the increased incidence of IBD is thought to be linked to sedentary lifestyle and obesity. In addition, advancements such as sanitation and refrigeration, while beneficial overall, also contribute through their impact on the balance and composition of intestinal microbes (Bernstein & Shanahan, 2008), which are implicated as predisposing agents for IBD through their interaction with immune and skin cells in the intestine (Vanderploeg, Panaccione, Ghosh, & Rioux, 2010).

Gallstones   Gallstones are made up of a combination of cholesterol, calcium, bilirubin, and inorganic salts. When gallstones move into the duct of the gallbladder, they may cause painful spasms; such stones must often be removed surgically. Behavioural and sociocultural factors are linked to the formation of gallstones. People who have diabetes, who are overweight, or who lose weight too quickly are particularly at risk, as are women, Aboriginal Canadians, and those over 60. Maintaining a healthy diet and weight (Chapter 4) is one way to lower the risk for gallstones (Dial-A-Dietitian, 2007).

Hepatitis   A common, serious, contagious disease that attacks the liver is hepatitis. "Hepatitis" means inflammation of the liver, and the disease produces swelling, tenderness, and sometimes permanent damage. When the liver is inflamed, bilirubin, a product of the breakdown of hemoglobin, cannot easily pass into the bile ducts. Consequently, it remains in the blood, causing a yellowing of the skin known as jaundice. Other common symptoms are fatigue, fever, muscle or joint aches, nausea, vomiting, loss of appetite, abdominal pain, and sometimes diarrhea.

There are several types of hepatitis, which differ in severity and mode of transmission. Hepatitis A, caused by viruses, is typically transmitted through food and water. It is often spread by poorly cooked seafood or through unsanitary preparation or storage of food. Hepatitis B is a more serious form, with more than 350 million carriers in the world and about 3,000 cases reported each year in Canada (Public Health Agency of Canada, 2008a). Also known as serum hepatitis, it is caused by a virus and is transmitted by the transfusion of infected blood, by improperly sterilized needles, through sexual contact, and through mother-to-infant contact. It is a special risk among intravenous drug users. Its symptoms are similar to those of hepatitis A but are far more serious. Hepatitis C, also spread via blood and needles, is most commonly caused by blood transfusions; more than 240,000 Canadians are carriers. Hepatitis D is found mainly in intravenous drug users who are also carriers of hepatitis B, necessary for the hepatitis D virus to spread. Finally, hepatitis E resembles hepatitis A, but is caused by a different virus (Health Canada, 2003a).

WHAT IS THE ROLE OF THE RENAL SYSTEM?

L06

Overview

The **renal system**—consisting of the kidneys, ureters, urinary bladder, and urethra—is also critically important in metabolism. The kidneys are chiefly responsible for the regulation of the bodily fluids; their principal function is to produce urine. The ureters contain smooth muscle tissue, which contracts, causing peristaltic waves to move urine to the bladder, a muscular bag that acts as a reservoir for urine. The urethra then conducts urine from the bladder out of the body. The anatomy of the renal system is pictured in Figure 2.7.

Urine contains surplus water, surplus electrolytes, waste products from the metabolism of food, and surplus acids or alkalis. By carrying these products out of the body, urine maintains water balance, electrolyte balance, and blood pH. Of the electrolytes, sodium and potassium are especially important because they are involved in the normal chemical reactions of the body, muscular contractions, and the conduction of nerve impulses.

In the case of certain diseases, urinalysis offers important diagnostic clues to many disorders by identifying abnormal levels of certain constituents. For example, an excess of glucose may indicate diabetes, an excess of red blood cells may indicate a kidney disorder, and so on. This is one of the reasons that a medical checkup usually includes a urinalysis.

FIGURE 2.7 | The Renal System
(*Source:* Lankford, 1979, p. 585)

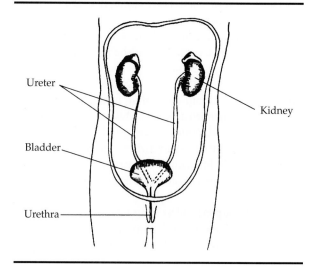

One of the chief functions of the kidneys is to control the water balance in the body. For example, on a hot day when a person has been active and has perspired profusely, relatively little urine will be produced so that the body may retain more water. This is because much water has already been lost through the skin. On the other hand, on a cold day when a person is relatively inactive or a good deal of liquid has been consumed, urine output will be higher, so as to prevent overhydration.

Summary   The renal system regulates bodily fluids by removing surplus water, surplus electrolytes, and the waste products generated by the metabolism of food.

Disorders of the Renal System

The renal system is vulnerable to a number of disorders. Among the most common are urinary tract infections (UTIs), to which women are especially vulnerable and which can result in considerable pain, especially on urination. If untreated, UTIs can lead to more serious infection.

Acute glomerular nephritis is a disease where the glomeruli of the kidneys become markedly inflamed leading to total or partial blockage of a large number of glomeruli, allowing large amounts of protein to leak in. In severe cases, total renal shutdown occurs. Acute glomerular nephritis is usually a secondary response to a streptococcus infection. The infection itself does not damage the kidneys, but leads to problems with the filtering capacity of the glomerular membrane. This infection usually subsides within two weeks.

Nephrons are the basic structural and functional units of the kidneys. In many types of kidney disease, such as that associated with hypertension, large numbers of nephrons are destroyed or damaged so severely that the remaining nephrons cannot perform their normal functions.

Kidney failure is a severe disorder because the inability to produce an adequate amount of urine will cause the waste products of metabolism, as well as surplus inorganic salts and water, to be retained in the body. An artificial kidney, a kidney transplant, or **kidney dialysis** may be required in order to rid the body of its wastes especially if acute kidney failure becomes chronic. In Rick's case (from the scenario at the beginning of this chapter), dialysis allowed his kidneys to recover from his acute kidney failure due to sepsis and return to full functioning without the need for a transplant or lifelong dialysis. Although these technologies can cleanse the blood to remove the excess salts, water, and metabolites, they are highly stressful medical procedures. Kidney transplants carry many health risks, and kidney dialysis can be extremely uncomfortable for patients. Consequently, health psychologists have been involved in addressing the problems experienced by kidney patients.

WHAT IS THE IMPORTANCE OF THE REPRODUCTIVE SYSTEM AND GENETICS?

L07

The development of the reproductive system is controlled by the pituitary gland. The anterior pituitary lobe produces the gonadotropic hormones, which control development of the ovaries in females and the testes in males. A diagrammatic representation of the human reproductive system appears in Figure 2.8.

The Ovaries and Testes

The female has two ovaries located in the pelvis. Each month, one of the ovaries produces an ovum (egg), which is discharged at ovulation into the fallopian tubes. If the ovum is not fertilized (by sperm), it remains in the uterine cavity for about 14 days and is then flushed out of the system with the uterine endometrium and its blood vessels (during menstruation).

The ovaries also produce the hormones estrogen and progesterone. Estrogen leads to the development of secondary sex characteristics in the female, including breasts and the female distribution of both body fat and body hair. Progesterone, which is produced during the second half of the menstrual cycle to prepare the body for pregnancy, declines if pregnancy fails to occur.

In males, testosterone is produced by the interstitial cells of the testes under the control of the anterior pituitary lobe. It brings about the production of sperm and the development of secondary sex characteristics, including growth of the beard, deepening of the voice, male distribution of body hair, and both skeletal and muscular growth.

Fertilization and Gestation

When sexual intercourse takes place and ejaculation occurs, sperm are released into the vagina. These sperm, which have a high degree of motility, proceed upward through the uterus into the fallopian tubes, where one sperm may fertilize an ovum. The fertilized ovum then

FIGURE 2.8 | The Reproductive System

(*Source:* J. H. Green, 1978, p. 122; Lankford, 1979, p. 688)

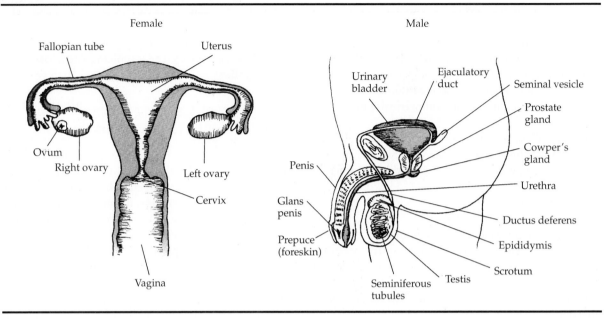

travels down the fallopian tube into the uterine cavity, where it embeds itself in the uterine wall and develops over the next nine months into a human being.

Disorders of the Reproductive System

The reproductive system is vulnerable to a number of diseases and disorders. Among the most common and problematic are sexually transmitted diseases, which occur through sexual intercourse or other forms of sexually intimate activity. These include the human papillomavirus (HPV), herpes, gonorrhea, syphilis, genital warts, chlamydia, and the most serious, AIDS. Of these, HPV is the most common sexually transmitted disease in the world today, and several high-risk types may even lead to the development of cancer (Society of Obstetricians and Gynaecologists of Canada, 2009).

For women, one risk of several sexually transmitted diseases is chronic pelvic inflammatory disease (PID). This may produce a variety of unpleasant symptoms, including severe abdominal pain, and may lead to infections that may compromise fertility. Other gynecologic disorders to which women are vulnerable include vaginitis, endometriosis (in which pieces of the endometrial lining of the uterus move

into the fallopian tubes or abdominal cavity, grow, and spread to other sites), cysts, and fibroids (nonmalignant growths in the uterus).

The reproductive system is also vulnerable to cancer, including prostate cancer in men (see Chapter 4) and gynecologic cancers in women. In Canada, gynecologic cancer, including cancer of the cervix, uterus, and ovaries, accounts for 11 percent of all cancers in women (Duarte-Franco & Franco, 2004). Endometrial cancer is the most common female pelvic malignancy, and ovarian cancer is the most lethal, often because it spreads before it is ever detected.

Women are vulnerable to disorders of the menstrual cycle, including amenorrhea, which is absence of menses, and oligomenorrhea, which is infrequent menstruation. These problems may originate in the hypothalamus, in the anterior pituitary, or in the ovaries or reproductive tract. Location of the cause is essential for correcting the problem, which may include hormone therapy or surgery.

Approximately 7 percent of Canadian couples experience fertility problems, defined as the inability to conceive a pregnancy after one year of regular sexual intercourse without contraception. Once believed to be emotional in origin, researchers have now concluded that there is little evidence for psychogenesis in infertility (Pasch & Dunkel-Schetter, 1997). Infertility, nonetheless, can create substantial psychological distress. Fortunately, over the past two decades, the technology for treating infertility has improved. A variety of drug treatments have been developed, as have more invasive technologies. In vitro fertilization (IVF) is the most widely used method of assistive reproductive technology, and the success rate for IVF is about 24 percent in Canada (Canadian Fertility and Andrology Society, 2006).

Menopause is not a disorder of the reproductive system but, rather, occurs when a woman's reproductive life ends. Because of a variety of unpleasant symptoms that can occur during the transition into menopause, including sleep disorders, hot flashes, joint pain, forgetfulness, and dizziness, many women choose to take hormone therapy (HT), which typically includes estrogen or a combination of estrogen and progesterone. HT was once thought to reduce the symptoms of menopause but also protect against the development of coronary artery disease, osteoporosis, and even Alzheimer's disease. It is now believed that, rather than protecting against these disorders, HT may actually increase some of these risks for some women (Hays et al., 2003; Hodis et al., 2003; Manson et al., 2003). Long-term HT may also increase the risks of breast cancer, especially in women with a family history of breast cancer. As a result of this evidence, many women and their doctors are rethinking the use of HT, especially over the long term.

Genetics and Health

The fetus starts life as a single cell, which contains all the inherited information from both parents that will determine its characteristics. The genetic code regulates such factors as eye and hair colour, as well as behavioural factors. Genetic material for inheritance lies in the nucleus of the cell in the form of 46 chromosomes, 23 from the mother and 23 from the father. Two of these 46 are sex chromosomes, which are an X from the mother and either an X or a Y from the father. If the father provides an X chromosome, a female child will result; if he provides a Y chromosome, a male child will result.

Genetic Studies   The knowledge produced by genetic studies has provided valuable information about the inheritance of susceptibility to disease (Harmon, 2004). Among several methods, scientists have bred

strains of rats, mice, and other laboratory animals that are sensitive or insensitive to the development of particular diseases and then used these strains to study other contributors to illness onset, the course of illness, and so on. For example, a strain of rats that is susceptible to cancer may be used to study the development of this disease and the cofactors that determine its appearance.

In humans, several types of research help demonstrate whether a characteristic is genetically acquired. Studies of families, for example, can reveal whether members of the same family are statistically more likely to develop a disorder, such as heart disease, than are unrelated individuals within a similar environment. If a factor is genetically determined, family members would be expected to show it more frequently than would unrelated individuals.

Twin research is another method for examining the genetic basis of a characteristic. If a characteristic is genetically transmitted, identical twins share it more commonly than fraternal twins or other brothers and sisters. This is because identical twins share the same genetic makeup, whereas other brothers and sisters have only partially overlapping genetic makeup. Examining the characteristics of twins reared together as opposed to twins reared apart is also informative regarding genetics. Attributes that emerge for twins reared apart are suspected to be genetically determined, especially if the rate of occurrence between twins reared together and those reared apart is the same.

Finally, studies of adopted children also help identify which characteristics are genetic and which are environmentally produced. Adopted children should not manifest genetically transmitted characteristics from their adopted parents, but they would very likely manifest environmentally transmitted characteristics.

Consider, for example, obesity, which is a risk factor for a number of disorders, including coronary artery disease and diabetes. If research indicates that twins reared apart show highly similar body weights, then we would suspect that body weight has a genetic component. If, on the other hand, weight within a family is highly related, and adopted children show the same weight as parents and their natural offspring, then we would look to the family diet as a potential cause of obesity. For many attributes, including obesity, both environmental and genetic factors are involved.

Genetic contributions to obesity and alcoholism have emerged in recent years, and even some personality characteristics, such as optimism, which is believed to have protective health effects (Chapter 7), appear to have genetic underpinnings (Sprangers et al., 2010). Continuing advances in the field of genetics will undoubtedly yield much more information about the genetic role in the behavioural factors that contribute to health and illness.

Genetics and Psychology   Psychologists have important roles to play with respect to the genetic contribution to disorders (Shiloh, Gerad, & Goldman, 2006). The first role involves genetic counselling. Prenatal diagnostic tests are currently available that permit the detection of a variety of genetically based disorders, including cystic fibrosis, muscular dystrophy, Huntington disease, and breast cancer (Harmon, 2004). Helping people cope with genetic vulnerabilities of this kind will be an important role for psychologists.

In addition, individuals who have a history of genetic disorders in their family, those who have already given birth to a child with a genetic disorder, or those who have repeated reproductive problems, such as multiple miscarriages, often seek such counselling. In some cases, technological advances have made it possible for some of these problems to be treated before birth. For example, drug therapy can treat some genetically transmitted metabolic defects, and surgery in utero has been performed to correct certain neural problems. However, when a prenatal diagnosis reveals that the fetus has an abnormal condition that cannot be corrected, the parents often must make the difficult decision of whether to have an abortion.

In other cases, individuals may learn of a genetic risk to their health as children, adolescents, or young adults. Breast cancer, for example, runs in families and among young women whose mothers, aunts, or sisters have developed breast cancer, vulnerability is higher. Some of the genes that contribute to the development of breast cancer have been identified, and tests are now available to determine whether a genetic susceptibility is present. Unfortunately, this type of cancer accounts for only 5 percent of breast cancer. Women who carry these genetic susceptibilities are more likely to develop the disease at an earlier age, and thus, these women are at high risk and need careful monitoring and potentially counselling as well (Grady, 2003).

Many scientific investigations attest to the immediate distress and even long-term distress that carriers of genetic disorders may experience (Buckmaster &

Gallagher, 2010; Lobel, Dias, & Myer, 2005; Timman, Roos, Maat- Kievit, & Tibben, 2004). In fact, the reactions to this kind of bad news can be so problematic that many people concerned with ethical issues in medicine question the value of telling people about their genetic risks if nothing can be done to treat them. Growing evidence suggests, however, that people at risk for treatable disorders may benefit from genetic testing and not suffer the same degree of psychological distress (Rimes, Salkovskis, Jones, & Lucassen, 2006; Shiloh & Ilan, 2005).

Moreover, in some cases, genetic risks are magnified because they interact with environmental factors. Such environmental factors include behaviours such as smoking, which increases the risk for those with a genetic susceptibility for cancer. For such individuals, early identification and encouragement to not begin smoking or to stop smoking if they are already smokers may substantially reduce the likelihood of them developing cancer (Lipkus, McBride, Pollack, Lyna, & Bepler, 2004a; Rimes et al., 2006). Recent evidence also suggests that socio-economic status (SES) may interact with genetic risks. For example, researchers at the University of British Columbia found evidence that low SES may actually "get under the skin" by causing changes in gene expression. Among children with asthma, those from a low SES background demonstrated an overexpression of the genes regulating inflammatory processes involved in comparison to children from a high SES background (Chen et al., 2009).

Psychologists have an important role to play in genetic counselling to help people modify their risk status. Knowledge of distress patterns and of who is most likely to be distressed can be helpful for counselling those who learn of their genetic risks (Shiloh et al., 2006). There are not only genetic bases of diseases, there are also genetic bases for fighting diseases. That is, certain genes may act as protective factors against development of a disease. An example is a specific gene that appears to regulate whether the immune system can identify cancer (Carey, 2002). Just as attention to the genetic bases of disease will occupy research attention for decades to come, so the protective genetic factors that keep so many of us so healthy for so long may become better understood as well.

The coming decades will reveal other genetic bases of major diseases, and tests will become available for identifying one's genetic risk. What are the psychosocial ramifications of such technological developments?

These issues are addressed in Chapter 3, and they take on a special urgency by virtue of the ethical issues they raise. For example, if prospective employers are allowed to conduct genetic screening, could an individual's at-risk status be used to deny that individual health insurance or employment (Martin, Greenwood, & Nisker, 2010)? How might one avoid such abuses of the technology?

As yet, our ability to deal intelligently with such important psychological, social, and ethical issues has not kept pace with our scientific capacity to elucidate the role of genetics in illness and risk factors. An emerging discussion is essential if we are to make proper use of these valuable and important technologies. Suffice it to say here that the role of health psychologists in this debate is expanding and will evolve further over the coming decades.

(L08) WHAT IS THE FUNCTION OF THE IMMUNE SYSTEM?

The primary function of the immune system is to protect the body from foreign invaders by distinguishing between what is "self" and what is foreign. However, the immune system can also interact with psychological and neuroendocrine processes to affect health. Psychoneuroimmunology examines these interactions and will be covered in more depth in Chapter 14.

Disease can be caused by a variety of factors, including genetic defects, hormone imbalances, nutritional deficiencies, and infection. In this section, we are primarily concerned with the transmission of disease by infection—that is, the invasion of microbes and their growth in the body. The microbes that cause infection are transmitted to people in four ways: direct transmission, indirect transmission, biological transmission, and mechanical transmission:

- Direct transmission involves bodily contact, such as handshaking, kissing, and sexual intercourse. For example, genital herpes and HPV are generally contracted by direct transmission.
- Indirect transmission (or environmental transmission) occurs when microbes are passed to an individual via airborne particles, dust, water, soil, or food. Influenza is an example of an environmentally transmitted disease.

- Biological transmission occurs when a transmitting agent, such as a mosquito, picks up microbes, changes them into a form conducive to growth in the human body, and passes on the disease to the human. The transmission of yellow fever, for example, occurs by this method.
- Mechanical transmission is the passage of a microbe to an individual by means of a carrier that is not directly involved in the disease process. Transmission of an infection by dirty hands, bad water, rats, mice, or flies are methods of mechanical transmission. For example, hepatitis and H1N1 can be acquired through mechanical transmission. The Focus on Social Issues box, "Portraits of Two Carriers," tells about two people who were carriers of deadly diseases.

Once a microbe has reached the body, it penetrates into bodily tissue via any of several routes. Whether the invading microbes gain a foothold in the body and produce infection depends on three factors: the number of organisms, the virulence of the organisms, and the body's defensive powers. The virulence of an organism is determined by its aggressiveness (that is, its ability to resist the body's defences) and by its toxigenicity (that is, its ability to produce poisons, which invade other parts of the body).

The Course of Infection

Assuming that the invading organism does gain a foothold, the natural history of infection follows a specific course. First, there is an incubation period between the time the infection is contracted and the time the symptoms appear.

Next, there is a period of nonspecific symptoms, such as headaches and general discomfort, which precedes the onset of the disease. During this time, the microbes are actively colonizing and producing toxins.

The next stage is the acute phase, when the disease and its symptoms are at their height. Unless the infection proves fatal, a period of decline follows the acute phase. During this period, the organisms are expelled from the mouth and nose in saliva and respiratory secretions, as well as through the digestive tract and the genitourinary system in feces and urine.

Portraits of Two Carriers

Carriers are people who transmit a disease to others and may or may not actually contract that disease themselves. They are especially dangerous because they may not appear ill, especially if the disease is in its incubation period, and are therefore not removed from society. Thus, it is possible for a carrier to infect dozens, hundreds, or even thousands of individuals while going about the business of everyday life.

Andrew Speaker, the Globetrotting Tuberculosis Carrier

In 2006, Andrew Speaker, a U.S. citizen infected with a contagious and drug-resistant strain of tuberculosis (TB), sparked an international health scare after he flew from Prague to Montreal. TB is a highly contagious disease that is transmitted through the air by an infected person simply coughing, sneezing, or talking. After flying to Montreal, Speaker rented a car and drove back to the U.S. as health officials tried to track him down. Speaker apparently ignored the warnings of health officials not to fly, because he did not believe that he posed a risk to others. True to the characteristics of many carriers, Speaker reported feeling fine and had even been out jogging the week before his flight.

However, for the nine people affected by his decision to fly, Speaker's actions have left them in a state of uncertainty and fear for now and years to come. Five people from Montreal, two from Ottawa, and two from the Czech Republic have filed a US$1.3 million lawsuit against Speaker, alleging that his actions have changed their lives forever. For one 72-year-old Canadian man who has tested positive for TB, the incident has disrupted his closest family relationships. He is now forced to live in a room separate from his wife, and his children will not visit him or allow him any contact with his grandchildren. A social sciences graduate student who sat one row ahead of Speaker has been forced to stay home from

Concordia University as a result of his exposure. The student also fears that his brother who lives with him may also have been affected, and both are involved in the lawsuit. Because it can take years after exposure to TB for the disease to be reactivated, those who came in contact with Speaker face an uncertain future for years to come.

Speaker became the first person to be quarantined by the U.S. government since 1963 (Perreaux, 2007). He has since gone on to file a lawsuit against the Centers for Disease Control and Prevention (CDC) claiming the unwanted attention caused him undue stress.

SARS Hong Kong Index Patient

One of the SARS carriers responsible for the spread of this highly infectious respiratory virus was a semi-retired medical professor who checked into the Metropole Hotel in Hong Kong in late February 2003. Although he had treated patients in Guangdong China with what was later to be known as SARS, his symptoms did not appear until that overnight hotel stay. Contact with several other people at the hotel led to their infection, and they too became carriers of this deadly virus, spreading SARS to several other countries, including Canada. SARS is primarily spread through the saliva of an infected person after coughing or sneezing into the environment.

One 78-year-old woman came in contact with the Hong Kong "index patient" at the hotel and then flew back to Toronto. After manifesting symptoms, she sought care from her doctor, transmitting SARS to both her doctor and her son. When she died March 5, 2003, she became the first SARS patient to die in Canada. Her son also died, only eight short days after taking her to the doctor. Of the over 400 cases of SARS reported in Canada, 44 people died (Health Canada, 2006a).

Source: SARS—Portrait of Two Carriers. Health Canada, 2008. Reproduced with the permission of the Minister of Health, 2011. www.hc-sc.gc.ca/dc-ma/sars-sras/index-e.html.

Infections may be localized, focal, or systemic. Localized infections remain at their original site and do not spread throughout the body. Although a focal infection is confined to a particular area, it sends toxins to other parts of the body, causing other disruptions. Systemic infections, by contrast, affect a number of areas or body systems.

The primary infection initiated by the microbe may also lead to secondary infections. These occur because

the body's resistance is lowered from fighting the primary infection, leaving it susceptible to other invaders. In many cases, secondary infections, such as pneumonia, pose a greater risk than the primary one.

Immunity

Immunity is the body's resistance to injury from invading organisms. It may develop either naturally or artificially.

Some natural immunity is passed from the mother to the child at birth and through breast-feeding, although this type of immunity is only temporary. Natural immunity is also acquired through disease. For example, if you have measles once, it is unlikely that you will develop it a second time; you will have built up immunity to it.

Artificial or acquired immunity is acquired through vaccinations and inoculations. For example, most children and adolescents receive shots for a variety of diseases—among them, diphtheria, whooping cough, smallpox, poliomyelitis, and hepatitis—so that they will not contract them should they ever be exposed.

How does immunity work? The body has a number of responses to invading organisms, some nonspecific and others specific. **Nonspecific immune mechanisms** are a general set of responses to any kind of infection or disorder; **specific immune mechanisms,** which are always acquired after birth, fight particular microorganisms and their toxins.

Nonspecific immunity is mediated in four main ways: through anatomical barriers (e.g., the skin), phagocytosis, antimicrobial substances, and inflammatory response. **Phagocytosis** is the process by which certain white blood cells (called phagocytes) ingest microbes. Phagocytes are usually overproduced when there is a bodily infection so that sufficient numbers can be sent to the site of infection to ingest the foreign particles.

Antimicrobial substances are chemicals mobilized by the body to kill invading microorganisms. One that has received particular attention in cancer research is interferon, an antiviral protein secreted by cells exposed to a viral antigen to protect neighbouring uninfected cells from invasion.

The inflammatory response is a local reaction to infection. At the site of infection, the blood capillaries first enlarge, and a chemical called histamine is released into the area. This chemical causes an increase in capillary permeability, allowing white blood cells and fluids to leave the capillaries and enter the tissues; consequently, the area becomes reddened and fluids accumulate. The white blood cells attack the microbes, resulting in the formation of pus. Usually, a clot then forms around the inflamed area, isolating the microbes and keeping them from spreading to other parts of the body. Familiar examples of the inflammatory response are the reddening, swelling, discharge, and clotting that result when you accidentally lacerate your skin and the sneezing, runny nose, and teary eyes that result from an allergic response to pollen or dust.

Specific immunity is acquired after birth and differs from nonspecific immunity in that it protects against particular microorganisms and their toxins. Specific immunity may be acquired by contracting a disease or through artificial means, such as vaccinations. It operates through the antigen–antibody reaction. Antigens are foreign substances whose presence stimulates the production of antibodies in the cell tissues. Antibodies are proteins produced in response to stimulation by antigens, which then combine chemically with the antigens to overcome their toxic effects.

Humoral Immunity   There are two basic immunologic reactions—humoral and cell mediated. **Humoral immunity** is mediated by B lymphocytes. The functions of B lymphocytes include providing protection against bacteria, neutralizing toxins produced by bacteria, and preventing viral reinfection. B cells confer immunity by the production and secretion of antibodies.

When B cells are activated, they differentiate into two types: (1) mature, antibody-secreting plasma cells and (2) resting, nondividing, memory B cells, which differentiate into antigen-specific plasma cells only when re-exposed to the same antigen. Plasma cells produce antibodies or immunoglobulins, which are the basis of the antigen-specific reactions. Humoral immunity is particularly effective in defending the body against bacterial infections and against viral infections that have not yet invaded the cells.

Cell-mediated immunity, involving T lymphocytes from the thymus gland, is a slower-acting response. Rather than releasing antibodies into the blood, as humoral immunity does, cell-mediated immunity operates at the cellular level. When stimulated by the appropriate antigen, T cells secrete chemicals that kill invading organisms and infected cells.

There are two major types of T lymphocytes: cytotoxic T (Tc cells) and helper T (Th cells). Tc cells respond to specific antigens and kill by producing toxic substances that destroy virally infected cells. Th cells enhance the functioning of Tc cells, B cells, and macrophages by producing cytokines. Th cells also serve a counterregulatory immune function, producing cytokines that suppress certain immune activities. Cell-mediated immunity is particularly effective in defending the body against fungi, viral infections that have invaded the cells, parasites, foreign tissue, and cancer.

What, then, does the integrated immune response look like? When a foreign antigen enters the body, the first line of defence involves mechanistic manoeuvres, such as coughing or sneezing. Once the invader has penetrated the body's surface, the phagocytes, such as the macrophages, attempt to eliminate it by phagocytosis (engulfing and digesting the foreign invader). Macrophages also release interleukin-1 and display part of the antigen material on their surface as a signal to the T_H cells. These, in turn, secrete interleukin-2, which promotes the growth and differentiation of the T_C cells. Other types of T helper cells secrete substances that promote the development of antigen-specific B cells into antibody-producing plasma cells, which then assist in destroying the antigen. T_H cells also secrete gamma-interferon, which enhances the capacities of the macrophages. Macrophages and natural killer (NK) cells also secrete various types of interferon, which enhance the killing potential of the natural killer (NK) cells and inhibit viral reproduction in uninfected cells. In addition, macrophages, NK cells, and T_C cells directly kill infected cells. During this process, the T_H cells down regulate and eventually turn off the immune response.

The Lymphatic System's Role in Immunity

The **lymphatic system,** which is a drainage system of the body, is involved in important ways in immune functioning. There is lymphatic tissue throughout the body, consisting of lymphatic capillaries, vessels, and nodes. Lymphatic capillaries drain water, proteins, microbes, and other foreign materials from spaces between the cells into lymph vessels. This material is then conducted in the lymph vessels to the lymph nodes, which filter out microbes and foreign materials for ingestion by lymphocytes. The lymphatic vessels then drain any remaining substances into the blood.

The spleen, tonsils, and thymus gland are important organs in the lymphatic system. The spleen aids in the production of B cells and T cells and removes worn-out red blood cells from the body. The spleen also helps filter bacteria and is responsible for the storage and release of blood. Tonsils are patches of lymphoid tissue in the pharynx that filter out microorganisms that enter the respiratory tract. Finally, the thymus gland is responsible for helping T cells mature; it also produces a hormone, thymosin, which appears to stimulate T cells and lymph nodes to produce the plasma cells that, in turn, produce antibodies.

Additional discussion of immunity may be found in Chapter 14, where we will consider the rapidly developing field of psychoneuroimmunology and the role of immunity in the development of AIDS (acquired immune deficiency syndrome). As we will see in that context, health psychologists are identifying the importance of social and psychological factors in the functioning of the immune system. Specifically, there is increasing evidence that stressful events can alter immune functioning, in some cases to increase resistance and in other cases to decrease it.

Disorders Related to the Immune System

The immune system and the tissues of the lymphatic system are subject to a number of disorders and diseases. One very important one is AIDS, which is a progressive impairment of immunity. Another is cancer, which is now believed to depend heavily on immunocompromise. We defer extended discussion of AIDS and cancer to Chapter 14.

A number of infections attack lymphatic tissue. Splenomegaly is an enlargement of the spleen that may result from various infectious diseases. It hinders the spleen's ability to produce phagocytes, antibodies, and lymphocytes. Tonsillitis is an inflammation of the tonsils that interferes with their ability to filter out bacteria. Infectious mononucleosis is a viral disorder marked by an unusually large number of monocytes; it can cause enlargement of the spleen and lymph nodes, as well as fever, sore throat, and general lack of energy.

Lymphoma is a tumour of the lymphatic tissue. Hodgkin's disease, a malignant lymphoma, involves the progressive, chronic enlargement of the lymph nodes, spleen, and other lymphatic tissues. As a consequence, the nodes cannot effectively produce antibodies and the phagocytic properties of the nodes are lost. If untreated, Hodgkin's disease can be fatal.

Infectious disorders were at one time thought to be acute problems that ended when their course had run. A major problem in developing countries, infectious disorders were thought to be largely under control in developed nations. Now, however, important developments with respect to infectious diseases merit closer looks (Morens, Folkers, & Fauci, 2004). First, as noted in the discussion of asthma and inflammatory bowel disease earlier in this chapter, the control of at least some infectious disorders through hygiene may have paradoxically increased the rates of these disorders. A second development is that some chronic diseases, once thought to be genetic in origin or unknown in origin, are now being traced back to infections. For example, Alzheimer's disease, multiple sclerosis, and schizophrenia all appear to have infectious triggers, at least in some cases (Jean, Thomas, Tahiri-Alaoui, Shaw, & Vaux, 2007; Kakalacheva, Münz, & Lünemann, 2011; Krause et al., 2010). Increasingly biologists are suggesting that pathogens cause or actively contribute to, many if not most, chronic diseases. Finally, of considerable concern is the development of bacterial strains that are increasingly resistant to treatment. The overuse of antibiotics is thought to be an active contributor to the development of increasingly lethal strains.

The inflammatory response that is so protective against provocations ranging from mosquito bites and sunburn to gastritis in response to spoiled food is now coming under increasing investigation as a potential contributor to chronic disease as well. The destructive potential of inflammatory responses has long been evident in diseases such as rheumatoid arthritis and multiple sclerosis, but researchers are now coming to believe that inflammation underlies many other chronic diseases including athlersclerosis, diabetes, Alzheimer's disease, and osteoporosis. Inflammation is also implicated in asthma, cirrhosis of the liver, bowel disorders such as Crohn's disease cystic fibrosis, possibly even some cancers (Ullman & Itzkowitz, 2011), and in heart disease in men (Edwards et al., 2007; Reilkoff, Bucala, & Herzog, 2011).

The inflammatory response, like stress responses more generally, likely evolved in humans' early prehistory and was selected because it was adaptive. For example, among hunter and gatherer societies, natural selection would have favoured people with vigorous inflammatory responses because life expectancy was fairly short. Few people would have experienced the long-term costs of vigorous inflammatory responses, which now seem to play such an important role in the development of chronic diseases. Essentially an adaptive pattern of earlier times has become maladaptive, as life expectancy has lengthened (Duenwald, 2002).

Autoimmunity is a condition characterized by a specific humoral or cell-mediated immune response that attacks the body's own tissues. Autoimmunity is implicated in certain forms of arthritis, a condition characterized by inflammatory lesions in the joints that produce pain, heat, redness, and swelling. We will discuss arthritis more fully in Chapter 14. Multiple sclerosis is also an autoimmune disorder. One of the most severe autoimmune disorders is systemic lupus erythematosis, a generalized disorder of the connective tissue, which primarily affects women and which in its severe forms can lead to eventual heart or kidney failure, causing death.

In autoimmune disease, the body fails to recognize its own tissue, instead interpreting it as a foreign invader and producing antibodies to fight it. Women are more likely than men to be affected. Although the causes of autoimmune diseases are not fully known, researchers have discovered that a viral or bacterial infection often precedes the onset of an autoimmune disease.

Many of these viral and bacterial pathogens have, over time, developed the ability to fool the body into granting them access by mimicking basic protein sequences in the body. This process of *molecular mimicry* eventually fails but then leads the immune system to attack not only the invader but also the corresponding self-component. Stress may aggravate autoimmune disease. ●

SUMMARY

 LO1 Describe the function of the nervous system

- The nervous system and the endocrine system act as the control systems of the body, mobilizing it in times of threat and otherwise maintaining equilibrium and normal functioning.

- The nervous system operates primarily through the exchange of nerve impulses between the peripheral nerve endings and internal organs and the brain, thereby providing the integration necessary for voluntary and involuntary movement.

 LO2 Explain how the endocrine system operates

- The endocrine system operates chemically via the release of hormones stimulated by centres in the brain. It controls growth and development and augments the functioning of the nervous system.

LO3 Identify how the cardiovascular system works

- The cardiovascular system is the transport system of the body, carrying oxygen and nutrients to cell tissues and taking carbon dioxide and other wastes away from the tissues for expulsion from the body.

- The heart acts as a pump to keep the circulation going and is responsive to regulation via the nervous system and the endocrine system.

- The cardiovascular system is implicated in stress, with cardiac output speeding up during times of stress and slowing down when threat has passed.

- The heart, blood vessels, and blood are vulnerable to a number of problems—most notably, atherosclerosis—which makes diseases of the cardiovascular system the major cause of death in this country.

 LO4 Relate how the respiratory system functions

- The respiratory system is responsible for taking in oxygen, expelling carbon dioxide, and controlling the chemical composition of the blood.

 LO5 Describe how the digestive system metabolizes food

- The digestive system is responsible for producing heat and energy, which—along with essential nutrients—are needed for the growth and repair of cells. Through digestion, food is broken down to be used by the cells for this process.

 LO6 Explain the role of the renal system

- The renal system aids in metabolic processes by regulating water balance, electrolyte balance, and blood acidity-alkalinity. Water-soluble wastes are flushed out of the system in the urine.

 LO7 Understand the importance of the reproductive system and genetics

- The reproductive system, under the control of the endocrine system, leads to the development of primary and secondary sex characteristics. Through this system, the species is reproduced, and genetic material is transmitted from parents to their offspring.

- With advances in genetic technology and the mapping of the genome has come increased understanding of genetic contributions to disease. Health psychologists play important research and counselling roles with respect to these issues.

 LO8 Describe the function of the immune system

- The immune system is responsible for warding off infection from invasion by foreign substances. It does so through the production of infection-fighting cells and chemicals.

KEY TERMS

adrenal glands   p. 26
angina pectoris   p. 29
atherosclerosis   p. 29
autoimmunity   p. 45
blood pressure   p. 29
cardiovascular system   p. 28
catecholamines   p. 25
cell-mediated immunity   p. 43
cerebellum   p. 24
cerebral cortex   p. 24
endocrine system   p. 26
humoral immunity   p. 43

hypothalamus   p. 24
immunity   p. 42
kidney dialysis   p. 37
lymphatic system   p. 44
medulla   p. 24
myocardial infarction (MI)   p. 29
nervous system   p. 23
neurotransmitters   p. 25
nonspecific immune
   mechanisms   p. 43
parasympathetic nervous
   system   p. 23

phagocytosis   p. 43
pituitary gland   p. 26
platelets   p. 30
pons   p. 24
renal system   p. 36
respiratory system   p. 31
specific immune
   mechanisms   p. 43
sympathetic nervous
   system   p. 23
thalamus   p. 24

Health Behaviour and Primary Prevention

CHAPTER

3

Health Behaviours

LEARNING OBJECTIVES

After reading this chapter, students will be able to:

(LO1) Describe and define health promotion

(LO2) Explain why health behaviours are important

(LO3) Know the theories and models used for understanding health behaviour change

(LO4) Describe how cognitive behavioural approaches are used to change health behaviours

(LO5) Relate how social engineering can change health behaviours

(LO6) Identify the venues for health-habit modification

Jill Morgan had just begun her second year in university. Although her first year had been filled with lots of required courses, second year was looking more interesting, giving her the chance to really get into her major, biology. The professor whose work she had so admired had an opening in her lab for a research assistant and offered it to Jill. Jill's boyfriend, Jerry, had just transferred to her school, so instead of seeing each other only one or two weekends a month, they now met for lunch almost every day and studied together in the library at night. Life was looking very good.

Tuesday morning, Jill was awakened by the harsh ring of her telephone. Could she come home right away? Her mother had gone in for a routine mammogram and a malignant lump had been discovered. Surgery was necessary, her father explained, and Jill was needed at home to take care of her younger sister and brother. As soon as her mother was better, her father promised, Jill could go back to school, but she would have to postpone the beginning of her sophomore year for at least a semester.

Jill felt as if her world were falling apart. She had always been very close to her mother and could not imagine this cheerful, outgoing woman with an illness. Moreover, it was cancer. What if her mother died? Her mother's situation was too painful to think about, so Jill began to contemplate her own. She would not be able to take the courses that she was currently enrolled in for another year, and she could forget about the research assistantship. And after all that effort so that she and Jerry could be together, now they would be apart again. Jill lay on her dorm room bed, knowing she needed to pack but unable to move.

"Breast cancer's hereditary, you know," Jill's roommate said. Jill looked at her in amazement, unable to speak. "If your mother has it, the chances are you'll get it too," the roommate went on, seemingly oblivious to the impact her words were having on Jill. Jill realized that she needed to get out of there quickly. As she walked, many thoughts came into her head. Would Jerry still want to date her, now that she might get breast cancer? Should she even think about having children anymore? What if she passed on the risk of breast cancer to her children? Without thinking, she headed for the biology building, which now felt like a second home to her. The professor who had offered her the job was standing in the hall as she went in. The professor could sense that something was wrong and invited Jill in for coffee. Jill told her what happened and broke down crying.

"Jill, you should know that breast cancer can now be treated, particularly when it's caught early. If they detected your mother's breast cancer through a mammogram, it probably means it's a pretty small lump. Cure rates are now 90 percent or better for early breast cancers. On the basis of what your dad has told you so far, your mother's situation looks pretty promising."

"It does?" Jill asked, wiping away tears.

"Not only that, the surgeries they have for breast cancer now are often fairly minimal, just removal of the lump, so you and your father might find that her recovery will be a little quicker than it may look right now. Look, I'm not going to give this research assistantship away. Why don't you go home, find out how things are, and call me in a week or so?"

"My roommate says breast cancer's hereditary," Jill said.

"Heredity is one of the factors that can contribute to breast cancer. The fact that your mother has it does mean you'll have to be aware of your risk and make sure you get screened on a regular basis. But it doesn't mean that you will necessarily get breast cancer. And even if you did, it wouldn't be the end of the world. Early detection and quick treatment mean that most women survive and lead normal lives." The professor paused for a moment. "Jill, my mother had breast cancer, too, about seven years ago. She's doing fine. I have to go in for regular checkups, and so far, everything has been okay. It's not a risk I'm happy to be living with, but it hasn't changed my life. I have a husband, two great kids, and a wonderful career, and the risk of breast cancer is just something I know about. I'm sure that this feels like a tragedy right now, but I think you'll find that the greatest fears you have probably won't materialize."

"Thanks," said Jill. "I think I'd better go home and pack."

In Chapter 3, we take up the important question of health behaviours and risk factors for illness. At the core of this chapter is the idea that good health is achievable through health habits that are practised conscientiously. Health promotion means being aware both of health habits that pose risks for future disease and of already existing risks, such as the vulnerability to breast cancer that Jill and the biology professor have. In the following pages, we consider health habits and risk factors with an eye toward their successful modification before they have a chance to lead to the development of illness.

We first turn to the issue of health behaviours as modifiable risk factors and how and when they can be changed, and next examine psychological theories and interventions that have been used to effect change for people at risk as well as the general population. From a public health promotion perspective it is important to address health behaviour change at the individual, community, and national levels through appropriate education and interventions. Accordingly, we end our discussion by examining the issue of where health behaviour-change interventions may be effective.

L01   WHAT IS HEALTH PROMOTION?

Health promotion is a general philosophy that has at its core the idea that good health, or wellness, is a personal and collective achievement. In 1986, the World Health Organization held the first international conference on health promotion in Ottawa and defined health promotion as "the process of enabling people to increase control over, and to improve, their health" (Ottawa Charter for Health Promotion, 1986). The Epp report also released that year, also stressed the need to view health from a health promotion perspective (Epp, 1986). For the individual, health promotion involves developing a program of good health habits early in life and carrying them through adulthood and old age. For the medical practitioner, health promotion involves teaching people how best to achieve this healthy lifestyle and helping people **at risk** for particular health problems learn behaviours to offset or monitor those risks. For the psychologist, health promotion involves the development of interventions to help people practise healthy behaviours and change poor ones. For community and national policy-makers, health promotion involves a general emphasis on good health, the availability of information to help people develop and maintain healthy lifestyles, and the availability of resources, conditions, and facilities that can help people change poor health habits. The mass media can contribute to health promotion by educating people about health risks posed by certain behaviours, such as smoking or excessive alcohol consumption. Legislation can contribute to health promotion by mandating certain activities that may reduce risks, such as the use of child-restraining seats and seat belts, and banning smoking within indoor public places.

The case for health promotion has grown more clear and urgent with each decade since the Lalonde Report in 1974 first suggested the need for a health promotion approach to keeping Canadians healthy. Accordingly, a number of health promotion initiatives have been successfully launched and continue to be implemented as our understanding of the individual and social factors that play a role in the practice of health behaviours across the lifespan evolves.

WHY ARE HEALTH BEHAVIOURS IMPORTANT?

Role of Behavioural Factors in Disease and Disorder

In the past 70 years, patterns of disease in Canada have changed substantially. The prevalence of acute infectious disorders, such as tuberculosis, influenza, measles, and poliomyelitis, has declined because of treatment innovations and changes in public health standards, such as improvements in waste control and sewage. Simultaneously, there has been an increase in what have been called the "preventable" disorders, including lung cancer, cardiovascular disease, alcohol and other drug abuse, and vehicular accidents (Statistics Canada, 2000b).

The role of behavioural or modifiable risk factors in the development of these disorders is clear (see Table 3.1). It is estimated that nearly half the deaths in Canada are caused by modifiable behaviours, with smoking, poor diet, and physical inactivity as the leading social/behavioural risk factors. Cancer deaths alone could be reduced by 50 percent simply by getting people to avoid smoking, eat more fruits and vegetables, boost their physical activity, protect themselves from the sun, tell their doctor when their health changes, handle hazardous materials carefully, and obtain early screening for breast and cervical cancer (Public Health Agency of Canada, 2007a).

Successful modification of health behaviours, then, will have several beneficial effects. First, it will reduce deaths due to lifestyle-related diseases. Second, it may delay time of death, thereby increasing individual longevity and general life expectancy of the population. Third and more important, the practice of good health behaviours may expand the number of years during which a person may enjoy life free from the complications of chronic disease. Finally, successful modification of health behaviours may begin to make a dent in the more than $191.6 billion that was spent in Canada in 2010 on health services, which is a substantial increase over the past 23 years (Canadian Institute for Health Information, 2010).

TABLE 3.1 | Risk Factors for the Leading Causes of Death in Canada

Disease	Risk Factors
Heart disease	High blood pressure (hypertension), high blood cholesterol, diabetes, being overweight, excessive alcohol consumption, physical inactivity, smoking, stress
Cancer	Smoking, unhealthy diet, physical inactivity, excessive alcohol consumption, excessive exposure to UV light, environmental factors
Stroke	High blood pressure (hypertension), high blood cholesterol, heart disease (atrial fibrillation), diabetes, being overweight, excessive alcohol consumption, physical inactivity, smoking, stress
Accidental injuries	Not buckling up; driving while intoxicated; being unaware of surroundings; not wearing appropriate safety gear; not learning more about how to prevent falls, poisoning, fires, and motor vehicle collisions
Chronic lung disease	Smoking and second-hand smoke, environmental factors (air pollution, aerosol sprays, toxic fumes such as chemicals, solvents, and paints), physical inactivity

Sources: Canadian Cancer Society, 2006; Canadian Lung Association, 2007c; Heart and Stroke Foundation of Canada, 2007a, 2007b; Public Health Agency of Canada, 2007b; Statistics Canada, 2000.

What Are Health Behaviours?

Health behaviours are behaviours undertaken by people to enhance or maintain their health. Poor health behaviours are important not only because they are implicated in illness but also because they may easily become poor health habits.

A **health habit** is a health-related behaviour that is firmly established and often performed automatically, without awareness. These habits usually develop in childhood and begin to stabilize around age 11 or 12 (R. Y. Cohen, Brownell, & Felix, 1990). Wearing a seat belt, brushing one's teeth, and eating a healthy diet are examples of these kinds of behaviours. Although a health habit may have developed initially because it was reinforced by specific positive outcomes, such as parental approval, it eventually becomes independent of the reinforcement process and is maintained by the environmental factors with which it is customarily associated. As such, it can be highly resistant to change. Consequently, it is important to establish good health behaviours and to eliminate poor ones early in life.

A dramatic illustration of the importance of good health habits in maintaining good health is provided by a classic study of people living in Alameda County, California, conducted by Belloc and Breslow (1972). These scientists began by defining seven important good health habits:

- Sleeping seven to eight hours a night
- Not smoking
- Eating breakfast each day
- Having no more than one or two alcoholic drinks each day
- Getting regular exercise
- Not eating between meals
- Being no more than 10 percent overweight

They then asked nearly 7,000 county residents to indicate which of these behaviours they practised. Residents were also asked how many illnesses they had had, which illnesses they had had, how much energy they had had, and how disabled they had been (e.g., how many days of work they had missed) over the previous 6- to 12-month period. The researchers found that the more good health habits people practised, the fewer illnesses they had had, the better they had felt, and the less disabled they had been.

A follow-up of these individuals 9 to 12 years later found that mortality rates were dramatically lower for people practising the seven health habits. Specifically, men following these practices had a mortality rate only 28 percent that of the men following zero to three of the health practices, and women following the seven health habits had a mortality rate 43 percent that of the women following zero to three of the health practices (Breslow & Enstrom, 1980).

Primary Prevention   Instilling good health habits and changing poor ones is the task of **primary prevention.** This means taking measures to combat risk factors for illness before an illness ever has a chance to develop. There are two general strategies of primary prevention. The first and most common strategy has been to employ behaviour-change methods to get people to alter their problematic health behaviours. The many programs that have been developed to help people lose weight are an example of this approach. The second, more recent approach is to keep people from developing poor health habits in the first place. Smoking prevention programs with young adolescents are an example of this approach, which we will consider in Chapter 5. Of the two types of primary prevention, it is obviously far preferable to keep people from developing problematic behaviours than to try to help them stop the behaviours once they are already in place.

What Factors Influence the Practice of Health Behaviours?

Who practises good health behaviours? What are the individual and social factors that lead one person to live a healthy life and another to compromise his or her health? Recall that according to both the biopsychosocial model and the public health promotion model, health and health behaviours result from and are maintained by a complex set of intertwining social and individual factors. Thus, individual health behaviours are influenced by the social, cultural, and physical environments in which they occur.

Socio-economic Factors   As indicated by the 12 determinants of health proposed by the Public Health Agency of Canada (see the Focus on Social Issues box, "Determinants of Health: What Makes Canadians Healthy or Unhealthy?" in Chapter 1), health behaviours differ according to demographic factors. Younger, more affluent, better educated people under low levels of stress with high levels of social support typically practise better health habits than people under higher levels of stress with fewer resources, such as individuals low in social class (Gilmour, 2007).

Age   Health behaviours vary with age and the type of health behaviour. Typically, health habits are good in childhood, deteriorate in adolescence and young adulthood, improve again among retired adults under 73, but then may deteriorate among adults 73 and older (Zanjani, Schaie, & Willis, 2006).

Gender   There are significant gender differences in the practice of health-related behaviours, which may vary by age or developmental stage. For example, among school-aged children, girls tend to eat more nutritious foods than boys, but girls also engage in more unhealthy dieting and meal skipping. Girls are also less likely to engage in sports activities compared to boys (Boyce, 2004). There are also gender differences in the practice of health-compromising behaviours such as smoking, which we will examine more closely in Chapter 5.

Values   Values heavily influence the practice of health habits. For example, exercise for women may be considered desirable in one culture but undesirable in another (Chrisler, McCreary, Gill, & Kamphoff, 2010), with the result that exercise patterns among women will differ greatly between the two cultures (Guilamo-Ramos, Jaccard, Pena, & Goldberg, 2005).

Personal Control   Perceptions that one's health is under personal control also determine health habits. For example, research on the **health locus of control** scale (K. A. Wallston, Wallston, & DeVellis, 1978) measures the degree to which people perceive themselves to be in control of their health, perceive powerful others to be in control of their health, or regard chance as the major determinant of their health. Those people who are predisposed to see health as under personal control may be more likely to practise good health habits than those who regard their health as due to chance factors.

Social Influence   Social influence affects the practice of health habits. Family, friends, and workplace companions can all influence health-related behaviours—sometimes in a beneficial direction, other times in an adverse direction (Broman, 1993; Turbin et al., 2006). For example, peer pressure often leads to smoking in adolescence but may influence people to stop smoking in adulthood. Social influence from indirect sources such as the media (television, magazines, Internet) may also influence health behaviours, for better or worse.

Personal Goals   Health habits are heavily tied to personal goals. If personal fitness or athletic achievement is an important goal that does not interfere with the achievement of other goals such as family goals (Schwartz, Hazen, Leifer, & Heckerling, 2008), the person will be more likely to exercise on a regular basis than if fitness is not a prioritized personal goal.

Perceived Symptoms   Some health habits are controlled by perceived symptoms. For example, smokers may control their smoking on the basis of sensations in their throat. A smoker who wakes up with a smoker's cough and raspy throat may cut back in the belief that he or she is vulnerable to health problems at that time.

Access to Health Care Services   Access to the health services can also influence the practice of health behaviours. Using the tuberculosis screening programs, obtaining a regular Pap smear, obtaining mammograms, and receiving immunizations for childhood diseases are examples of behaviours that are directly tied to the health care delivery system. Other behaviours, such as losing weight and stopping smoking, may be indirectly encouraged by the health care system because many people now receive lifestyle advice from their health care providers.

Place   There is growing evidence that where someone lives can have a significant impact on the practice of health behaviours. Living in a rural area where there is less access to health care services may make it difficult to follow through with intentions to practise preventive health behaviours, such as cancer screening behaviours. There is also some evidence that suggests that those living in rural areas, such as communities in Northern Canada, have less healthy eating habits, lower leisure time physical activity, and higher rates of smoking compared to urban residents (Canadian Institute for Health Information, 2006b), although the reasons for these relations are unclear.

Cognitive Factors   Finally, the practice of health behaviours is tied to cognitive factors, such as the belief that certain health behaviours are beneficial or the sense that one may be vulnerable to an underlying illness if one does not practise a particular health behaviour. Similarly, being less health conscious and thinking less about the future can also lead to unhealthy behavioural choices (Sirois, 2004; Wardle & Steptoe, 2003).

Barriers to Modifying Poor Health Behaviours

The reason that it is important to know the determinants of health habits is because once bad habits are ingrained they are very difficult to change. Researchers still know little about how and when poor health habits develop and exactly when and how one should intervene to change the health habit. For example, young children usually get enough exercise, but as they get older, a sedentary lifestyle may set in. Exactly how and when should one intervene to offset this tendency? The process is gradual, and the decline in exercise is due more to changes in the environment, such as no longer

having to take a compulsory physical education class, than to the motivation to get exercise.

Moreover, people often have little immediate incentive for practising good health behaviour. Health habits develop during childhood and adolescence, when most people are healthy. Smoking, drinking, poor nutrition, and lack of exercise have no apparent effect on health and physical functioning. The cumulative damage that these behaviours cause may not become apparent for years, and few children and adolescents are sufficiently concerned about what their health will be like when they are 40 or 50 years old (R. J. Johnson, McCaul, and Klein, 2002). As a result, bad habits have a chance to make inroads.

Once their bad habits are ingrained, people are not always highly motivated to change them. Unhealthy behaviours can be pleasurable, automatic, addictive, and resistant to change. Consequently, many people find it too difficult to change their health habits because their bad habits are enjoyable. Health habits are only modestly related to each other. Knowing one health habit does not enable one to predict another with great confidence. The person who exercises faithfully does not necessarily wear a seat belt, and the person who controls his or her weight may continue to smoke. It can be difficult to teach people a concerted program of good health behaviour, and health behaviours must often be tackled one at a time.

Instability of Health Behaviours   Another characteristic that contributes to the difficulty of modifying health habits is that they are unstable over time. A person may stop smoking for a year but take it up again during a period of high stress. A dieter may lose 20 kilograms, only to regain them a few years later. Why are health habits relatively independent of each other and unstable?

First, different health habits are controlled by different factors. For example, smoking may be related to stress, whereas exercise may depend on ease of access to sports facilities.

Second, different factors may control the same health behaviour for different people. Thus, one person's overeating may be "social," and she may eat primarily in the presence of other people. In contrast, another individual's overeating may depend on levels of tension, and he may overeat only when under stress.

Third, factors controlling a health behaviour may change over the history of the behaviour (Zanjani, Schaie, & Willis, 2006). The initial instigating factors may no longer be significant, and new maintaining factors may develop to replace them. Although peer group pressure (social factors) is important in initiating the

The foundations for health promotion develop in early childhood, when children are taught to practise good health behaviours.

smoking habit, over time, smoking may be maintained because it reduces craving and feelings of stress. One's peer group in adulthood may actually oppose smoking.

Fourth, factors controlling the health behaviour may change across a person's lifetime. Regular exercise occurs in childhood because it is built into the school curriculum, but in adulthood, this automatic habit must be practised consciously.

Fifth and finally, health behaviour patterns, their developmental course, and the factors that change them across a lifetime will vary substantially between individuals (Zanjani, Schaie, & Willis, 2006). Thus, one individual may have started smoking for social reasons but continue smoking to control stress; the reverse pattern may characterize the smoking of another individual.

Summary Health behaviours are elicited and maintained by different factors for different people, and these factors change over the lifetime as well as during the course of the health habit. Consequently, health habits are very difficult to change. As a result, health habit interventions have focused heavily on those who may be helped the most—namely, the young.

Intervening with Children and Adolescents

Socialization Health habits are strongly affected by early **socialization,** especially the influence of parents as role models (Morrongiello, Corbett, & Bellissimo, 2008). Parents instill certain habits in their children (or

not) that become automatic, such as wearing a seat belt, brushing teeth regularly, and eating breakfast every day. Nonetheless, in many families, even these basic health habits may not be taught, and even in families that conscientiously attempt to teach good health habits there may be gaps.

Moreover, as children move into adolescence, they sometimes backslide or ignore the early training they received from their parents, because they often see little apparent effect on their health or physical functioning. In addition, adolescents are vulnerable to an array of problematic health behaviours, including excessive alcohol consumption, smoking, drug use, and sexual risk taking, particularly if their parents aren't monitoring them very closely and their peers practise these behaviours (Mackey & La Greca, 2007). Adolescents appear to have an incomplete appreciation of the risks they encounter through faulty habits such as smoking and drinking (Henson, Carey, Carey, & Maisto, 2006). Consequently, interventions with children and adolescents are high priority.

Using the Teachable Moment Health promotion efforts capitalize on educational opportunities to prevent poor health habits from developing. The concept of a **teachable moment** refers to the fact that certain times are better than others for teaching particular health practices.

Many teachable moments arise in early childhood. Parents have opportunities to teach their children basic safety behaviours, such as putting on a seat belt in the car or looking both ways before crossing the street, and basic health habits, such as drinking water instead of soda with dinner (L. Peterson & Soldana, 1996). Nonetheless, parents can have a limited understanding of the importance of their role promoting healthy behaviour in their children and may fail to follow up after initially communicating about health-related rules (Hebestreit et al., 2010).

Other teachable moments arise because they are built into the health care delivery system. For example, family physicians often make use of a newborn's early visits to teach motivated new parents the basics of accident prevention and safety in the home. Such visits also ensure that children receive their basic immunizations. Dentists use a child's first visit to teach both the parents and child the importance of correct brushing.

But what can children themselves really learn about health habits? Certainly very young children have cognitive limitations that keep them from fully comprehending the concept of health promotion, yet intervention programs with children clearly indicate that they can develop personal responsibility for aspects of their health. Such behaviours as choosing nutritionally sound foods, brushing teeth regularly, using car seats and seat belts, participating in exercise, crossing the street safely, and behaving appropriately in real or simulated emergencies (such as fire drills) are clearly within the comprehension of children as young as age 3 or 4, as long as the behaviours are explained in concrete terms and the implications for actions are clear (Maddux, Roberts, Sledden, & Wright, 1986).

Teachable moments are not confined to childhood and adolescence. Pregnancy represents a teachable moment for several health habits, especially stopping smoking and eating healthier (Government of Canada, 2008). Adults with newly diagnosed coronary artery disease may also be especially motivated to change their health habits, such as smoking and diet, due to the anxiety their recent diagnosis has caused.

Identifying teachable moments—that is, the crucial point at which a person is ready to modify a health behaviour—is a high priority for primary prevention.

Closing the Window of Vulnerability Junior high school appears to be a particularly important time for the development of several health-related habits. For example, food choices, snacking, and dieting all begin to crystallize around this time (R. Y. Cohen et al., 1990). There is also a **window of vulnerability** for smoking and drug use that occurs in junior high school when students are first exposed to these habits among their peers and older siblings (D'Amico & Fromme, 1997). As we

Adolescence is a window of vulnerability for many poor health habits. Consequently, intervening to prevent health habits from developing is a high priority for children in late elementary and early junior high school.

will see, interventions through the schools may help students avoid the temptations that lead to these health-compromising behaviours.

Adolescent Health Behaviours Influence Adult Health   A final reason for intervening with children and adolescents in the modification of health habits is that, increasingly, research shows that precautions taken in adolescence may be better predictors of disease after age 45 than are adult health behaviours. This means that the health habits people practise as teenagers or college students may well determine the chronic diseases they have and what they ultimately die of in adulthood.

For adults who decide to make changes in their lifestyle, it may already be too late. Research to date suggests that this is true for sun exposure and skin cancer and for calcium consumption for the prevention of osteoporosis. Diet, especially dietary fat intake and protein consumption in adolescence, may also predict adult cancers. Consequently, despite the sense of invulnerability that many adolescents have, adolescence may actually be a highly vulnerable time for a variety of poor health behaviours that lay the groundwork for future problems in adulthood.

Interventions with At-risk People

I'm a walking time bomb.
—37-Year-Old Woman at Risk for Breast Cancer

Children and adolescents are two vulnerable populations toward which health promotion efforts have been heavily directed. Another vulnerable group consists of people who are at risk for particular health problems. For example, a family physician may work with obese parents to control the diet of their offspring in the hopes that obesity in the children can be avoided. If the dietary changes produce the additional consequence of reducing the parents' weight, so much the better. Daughters of women who have had breast cancer are a vulnerable population who need to obtain regular mammograms and monitor themselves for any changes in the breast tissue. As the genetic basis for other disorders is becoming clearer, health promotion efforts with at-risk populations are likely to assume increasing importance.

Benefits of Focusing on At-risk People   There are several advantages to working with people who are at risk for health disorders. Early identification of these people

may prevent or eliminate poor health habits that can exacerbate vulnerability. For example, helping men at risk for heart disease avoid smoking or getting them to stop at a young age may avoid a debilitating chronic illness. Even if no intervention is available to reduce risk, knowledge of risk can provide people with information they need to monitor their situation (Masood, 2008). Women at risk for breast cancer are an example of such a group.

Working with at-risk populations represents an efficient and effective use of health promotion dollars. When a risk factor has implications for only some people, there is little reason to implement a general health intervention for everyone. Instead, it makes sense to target those people for whom the risk factor is relevant.

Finally, focusing on at-risk populations makes it easier to identify other risk factors that may interact with the targeted factor in producing an undesirable outcome. For example, not everyone who has a family history of hypertension will develop hypertension, but by focusing on those people who are at risk, other factors that contribute to its development may be identified.

Problems of Focusing on Risk   Clearly, however, there are difficulties in working with populations at risk. People do not always perceive their risk correctly (Croyle et al., 2006; Rothman & Salovey, 1997). Generally speaking, most people are unrealistically optimistic about their vulnerability to health risks (Albery & Messer, 2005). Sometimes, testing positive for a risk factor leads people into needlessly hypervigilant and restrictive behaviour (e.g., DiLorenzo et al., 2006; G. E. Elmore & Gigerenzer, 2005). For example, women at genetic risk for breast cancer appear to be more physiologically reactive to stressful events, raising the possibility that the chronic stress associated with this familial cancer risk may actually have consequences of its own through changes in psychobiological reactivity (Valdimarsdottir et al., 2002). People may also become defensive and minimize the significance of their risk factor and avoid using appropriate services or monitoring their condition (for example, Brewer, Weinstein, Cuite, & Herrington, 2004). Providing people with feedback about their potential genetic susceptibility to a disorder such as lung cancer can have immediate and strong effects on relevant behaviours—in this case, a reduction in smoking (Lerman et al., 1997).

Ethical Issues   There are important ethical issues in working with at-risk populations. At what point is it appropriate to alarm at-risk people if their personal risk may be low? Among people at risk for a particular disorder, only a certain percentage will develop the problem and, in many cases, only many years later. For example, should daughters of breast cancer patients be alerted to their risk and alarmed even if their risk is low? Given that high levels of cancer-related worry do not match actual genetic contribution to risk, unnecessarily creating distress may not justify instilling risk-reducing behaviours (Quillin, Bodurtha, McClish, & Wilson, 2011).

Some people, such as those predisposed to depression, may react especially badly to the prospect or results of genetic testing for health disorders (S. W. Vernon et al., 1997). These effects may occur primarily just after testing positive for a risk factor and may not be long term (e.g., Tibben, Timman, Bannick, & Duivenvoorden, 1997). In many cases, there is no successful intervention for genetically based risk factors, and in other cases, an intervention may not work (A. Baum, Friedman, & Zakowski, 1997). For example, identifying boys at risk for coronary artery disease and teaching them how to manage stress effectively may be ineffective in changing their risk status.

For other disorders, we may not know what an effective intervention will be. For example, alcoholism is now believed to have a genetic component, particularly among men, and yet exactly how and when we should intervene with the offspring of adult alcoholics is not yet clear.

Finally, emphasizing risks that are inherited can raise complicated issues of family dynamics, potentially pitting parents and children against each other and raising issues of who is to blame for the risk. Daughters of breast cancer patients may suffer considerable stress and behaviour problems, due in part to the enhanced recognition of their risk (Quillin, Bodurtha, McClish, & Wilson, 2011). Matters can be even more complicated when considering that dying family members with cancer who have not received genetic testing literally take their DNA cancer clues with them to the grave. One study of dying cancer patients found that although 23 percent qualified for genetic testing, none had received testing that could have helped identify whether their cancer was hereditary (Quillin, Bodurtha, Siminoff, & Smith, 2010). Intervening with at-risk populations is still a controversial issue.

Critical Checkpoint

Would You Want to Know?

The study by Quilllin and colleagues (2011) highlights some of the challenging and changing issues involved in identifying the hereditary risk for cancer. Should people with terminal cancer be persuaded to undergo genetic testing if they have a cancer that may have a strong hereditary component? Do you believe that the possible benefits from this information would outweigh any potential distress to the surviving relatives?

Health Promotion and the Elderly

Frank Ford, 91, starts each morning with a brisk walk. After a light breakfast of whole wheat toast and orange juice, he gardens for an hour or two. Later, he joins a couple friends for lunch and if he can persuade them to join him, they fish during the early afternoon. Reading a daily paper and always having a good book to read keeps Frank mentally sharp. Asked how he maintains such a busy schedule, Frank says that "exercise, friends, and mental challenge" are the keys to his long and healthy life.

Ford's lifestyle is right on target. One of the chief focuses of recent health promotion efforts has been on the elderly. At one time, prejudiced beliefs that such health promotion efforts would be wasted in old age limited this emphasis. However, policymakers now recognize that a healthy elderly population is essential for increasing the quality of life of this growing group of citizens now and in the years to come. For example, the importance of exercise for the elderly is recognized in the creation of a policy framework by the World Health Organization to promote active aging, which is defined as "the process of optimizing opportunities for health, participation, and security in order to enhance quality of life as people age" (World Health Organization, 2002).

Exercise is one of the most important health behaviours because exercise helps keep people mobile and able to care for themselves. Even just keeping active also has health benefits. Participating in social activities, running errands, and engaging in other normal activities that probably have little effect on overall fitness nonetheless reduce the risk of mortality, perhaps by providing social

Among the elderly, health habits are a major determinant of whether an individual will have a vigorous or an infirmed old age.

support or a general sense of self-efficacy (T. A. Glass, DeLeon, Marottoli, & Berkman, 1999). Among the very old, exercise has particularly beneficial long-term benefits, substantially increasing the likelihood that the elderly can maintain the basic activities of daily living (Kahana et al., 2002), and even reversing age-related cognitive deficits (Erickson & Kramer, 2009).

Controlling alcohol consumption is an important target for good health among the elderly as well. Some elderly people develop drinking problems in response to age-related issues, such as retirement or loneliness (Onen et al., 2005). Others may try to maintain the drinking habits they had throughout their lives, which become more risky in old age. For example, metabolic changes related to age may reduce the capacity for alcohol. Moreover, many older people are on medications that may interact dangerously with alcohol. Alcohol consumption increases the risk of gastrointestinal disorders and accidents, which, in conjunction with osteoporosis, can produce broken bones, which

limit mobility, creating further health problems (Onen et al., 2005). The elderly are at risk for depression, which also compromises health habits leading to accelerated physical decline. Thus, addressing depression, commonly thought of as a mental health problem, can have effects on physical health as well (Wrosch, Schulz, & Heckhausen, 2002).

Vaccinations against influenza are important for several reasons. First, influenza (flu) is a major cause of death among the elderly. Moreover, it increases the risk of heart disease and stroke because it exacerbates other underlying disorders that an elderly person may have (Nichol et al., 2003). Finding ways to ensure that elderly people get their flu vaccinations each fall, then, is an important health priority.

The emphasis on health habits among the elderly is well placed. By age 80, health habits are the major determinant of whether an individual will have a vigorous or an infirmed old age (McClearn et al., 1997). Moreover, current evidence suggests that health habit changes are working. Reports indicate that most Canadian seniors rate their health as excellent, very good, or good (Canadian Institute of Health Research, 2006a).

Ethnic and Gender Differences in Health Risks and Habits

There are ethnic and gender differences in vulnerability to particular health risks, and health promotion programs and guidelines need to take these differences into account. Alcohol consumption is a substantially greater problem among men than women, and smoking is a somewhat greater problem for non-minority men than for other groups. Smoking rates among Aboriginal youth are about triple the rate for Canadians in general. Aboriginal people are also less likely to exercise regularly than non-Aboriginals, and are therefore more likely to be overweight. In fact, the rate of diabetes among Canada's Aboriginal peoples is considered an epidemic, being three times the national rate (Canadian Institute for Health Information, 2004a).

Emerging Canadian research suggests that South Asians and Chinese may have more dangerous abdominal fat than Europeans with the same total amount of body fat, thus putting them at greater risk for cardiovascular disease, hypertension, diabetes, and other related health complications (Lear et al., 2007; Yap et al., 2006). As these findings indicate, the current guidelines for assessing healthy weights may need to change to account for ethnic differences.

Health promotion programs for ethnic groups also need to take account of co-occurring risk factors. The combined effects of low socio-economic status and a biologic predisposition to particular illnesses put certain groups at substantially greater risk. Examples are diabetes among Aboriginal people, which we will consider in more detail in Chapter 14.

 ### WHAT THEORIES AND MODELS ARE USED FOR UNDERSTANDING HEALTH BEHAVIOUR CHANGE?

> Habit is habit, and not to be flung out of the window by any man, but coaxed downstairs a step at a time.
>
> —MARK TWAIN

In the remainder of this chapter, we address the technology of changing poor health habits in people who are and are not at risk for developing disease. In this section we first look at attitudinal approaches to health behaviour change, which assume that if we give people correct information about the implications of their poor health habits, they may be motivated to change those habits in a healthy direction. As will be seen, attitude change campaigns may induce the desire to change behaviour but may not be successful in teaching people exactly how to do so. Next, we turn to a group of similar theories, social cognition models, which specify the role of attitudes and beliefs in changing health behaviours. We finish our discussion of theories and models with a stage-based approach to understanding health behaviour change.

Attitude Change and Health Behaviour

Educational Appeals   Educational appeals make the assumption that people will change their health habits if they have correct information. Research has provided us with the following suggestions of the best ways to persuade people through educational appeals:

1. Communications should be colourful and vivid rather than steeped in statistics and jargon. For example, a vivid account of the health benefits of regular exercise, coupled with a case history of someone who took up bicycling after a heart attack, may be persuasive to someone at risk for heart disease.

2. The communicator should be expert, prestigious, trustworthy, likable, and similar to the audience (W. J. McGuire, 1964). Similarity may be especially important when the appeal is directed towards a particular cultural group and for people whose identity is strongly tied to their cultural group identity (Kreuter & McClure, 2004). For example, a health message targeting eating habits among First Nation peoples will be more persuasive if it comes from a respected, credible Aboriginal public figure rather than from a non-aboriginal expert.

3. Strong arguments should be presented at the beginning and end of a message, not buried in the middle.

4. Messages should be short, clear, and direct.

5. Messages should state conclusions explicitly. For example, a communication extolling the virtues of a low-cholesterol diet should explicitly conclude that the reader should alter his or her diet to lower cholesterol.

6. Extreme messages produce more attitude change, but only up to a point. Very extreme messages are discounted. For example, a message that urges people to exercise for at least half an hour three days a week will be more effective than one that recommends several hours of exercise a day.

7. For illness detection behaviours (such as HIV testing or obtaining a mammogram), emphasizing the problems that may occur if it is not undertaken, i.e., loss-framed messages, will be most effective (O'Keefe & Jensen, 2009). For health promotion behaviours (such as sunscreen use), emphasizing the benefits to be gained may be more effective (Detweiler, Bedell, Salovey, Pronin, & Rothman, 1999).

8. If the audience is receptive to changing a health habit, then the communication should include only favourable points, but if the audience is not inclined to accept the message, the communication should discuss both sides of the issue. For example, messages to smokers ready to stop should emphasize the health risks of smoking. Smokers who have not yet decided to stop may be more persuaded by a communication that points out its risk while acknowledging and rebutting its pleasurable effects.

Providing information does not ensure that people will perceive that information accurately. Sometimes when people receive negative information about risks to their health, they process that information defensively (Kessels, Ruiter, & Jansma, 2010). Instead of making appropriate health behaviour changes, the person may come to view the problem as less serious or more common than he or she had previously believed, particularly if he or she intends to continue the behaviour (Gerrard, Gibbons, Benthin, & Hessling, 1996). Smokers, for example, know that they are at a greater risk for lung cancer than are non-smokers, but they see lung cancer as less likely or problematic and smoking as more common than do non-smokers.

Fear Appeals   In part because of these issues, attitudinal approaches to changing health habits often make use of **fear appeals.** This approach assumes that if people are fearful that a particular habit is hurting their health, they will change their behaviour to reduce their fear. Common sense suggests that the relationship between fear and behaviour change should be direct: The more fearful an individual is, the more likely he or she will be to change the relevant behaviour. However, persuasive messages that elicit too much fear may actually undermine health behaviour change (Witte & Allen, 2000). Moreover, research suggests that fear alone may not be sufficient to change behaviour. Strong fear appeals coupled with recommendations for action or information about the efficacy of the health behaviour may be needed to produce the greatest behaviour changes (Witte & Allen, 2000). In Chapter 5, we will revisit the issue of fear appeals for changing people's smoking behaviour.

Message Framing   Any health message can be phrased in positive or negative terms, but matching the framing of the message with the health behaviour can impact the effectiveness of the message. According to **prospect theory** (Kahneman & Tversky, 1979), different presentations of risk information will change people's perspectives and actions. Messages that emphasize potential problems (loss-framed) should work better for behaviours that have uncertain outcomes (high risk), whereas messages that stress benefits (gain-framed) may be more persuasive for behaviours with certain outcomes (low risk). For example, messages focusing on the relationship threat (high risk) associated with not using condoms were rated as more convincing by university students when they were loss-framed versus gain-framed, whereas messages that focused on disease prevention (low risk) were seen as more convincing when they were gain-framed rather than loss-framed (Kiene, Barta, Zelenski, & Cothran, 2005).

The effectiveness of the type of message framing may also depend on how congruent the message is with the individual's own motivation (Mann, Sherman, & Updegraff, 2004). People who are approach-oriented or who seek to maximize rewards are more influenced by messages that are gain-framed (e.g., "great breath, healthy gums are only a floss away"), whereas people who are avoidance-oriented or who seek to minimize losses are influenced by messages that are loss-framed (e.g., "floss now and avoid bad breath and gum disease"). One reason for the effectiveness of congruency-framed messages is that they increase feelings of self-efficacy for engaging in the behaviour (Sherman, Mann, & Updegraff, 2006). However, the effectiveness of the health message framing may also depend on matching the message to the current emotional state of the message recipient (Gerend & Maner, 2011).

Social Cognition Models of Health Behaviour Change

In addition to attitudes, **social cognition models** suggest that the beliefs that people hold about particular health behaviour motivate their decision to change that behaviour. These models are based on the core assumptions of

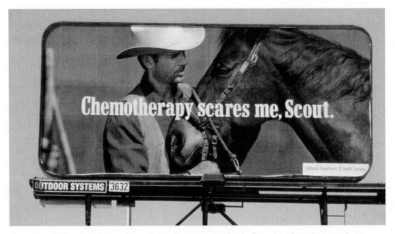

Fear appeals, such as those pictured on tobacco packaging in Canada, often alert people to a health problem but do not necessarily change behaviour.

the **expectancy-value theory,** which suggests that people will choose to engage in behaviours that they expect to succeed in and that have outcomes that they value (Feather, 1982; Fishbein, 1967). For example, people are more likely to engage in behaviours such as disposing of old medications and keeping walkways free of tripping hazards if they believe that household safety is important and that these behaviours will help make their home a safer place (Sirois, 2007a). Accordingly, outcome expectancies figure prominently in these models.

The Health Belief Model   Formerly one of the most influential social cognition models of why people practise health behaviours, the **health belief model** (Hochbaum, 1958; Rosenstock, 1966) states that whether a person practises a particular health behaviour can be understood by knowing two factors: whether the person perceives a personal health threat and whether the person believes that a particular health practice will be effective in reducing that threat.

Perception of Health Threat   The perception of a personal health threat is influenced by at least three factors: general health values, which include interest and concern about health; specific beliefs about personal vulnerability to a particular disorder; and beliefs about the consequences of the disorder, such as whether they are serious. Thus, for example, people may change

their diet to include low-cholesterol foods if they value health, feel threatened by the possibility of heart disease, and perceive that the threat of heart disease is severe.

Perceived Threat Reduction   Whether a person believes a health measure will reduce threat has two subcomponents: whether the individual thinks a health practice will be effective and whether the cost of undertaking that measure exceeds the benefits of the measure (Rosenstock, 1974). For example, the man who feels vulnerable to a heart attack and is considering changing his diet may believe that dietary change alone would not reduce the risk of a heart attack and that changing his diet would interfere with his enjoyment of life too much to justify taking the action. Thus, although his belief in his personal vulnerability to heart disease may be great, if he lacks faith that a change of diet would reduce his risk, he would probably not make any changes. A diagram of the health belief model applied to smoking is presented in Figure 3.1.

Support for the Health Belief Model   The health belief model explains people's practice of health habits quite well. For example, it predicts preventive dental care (Buglar, White, & Robinson, 2010), breast self-examination (Norman & Brain, 2005), AIDS risk-related behaviours (Aspinwall, Kemeny, Taylor, Schneider, & Dudley, 1991), sexual risk-taking among college students

FIGURE 3.1 | The Health Belief Model Applied to the Health Behaviour of Stopping Smoking

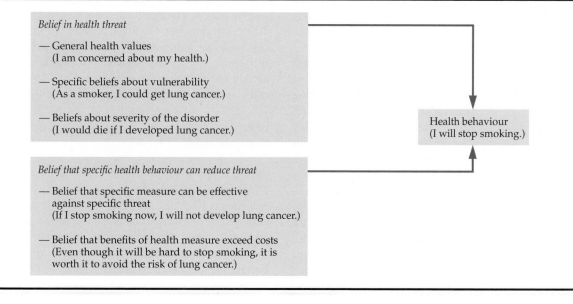

Belief in health threat

— General health values
  (I am concerned about my health.)

— Specific beliefs about vulnerability
  (As a smoker, I could get lung cancer.)

— Beliefs about severity of the disorder
  (I would die if I developed lung cancer.)

Belief that specific health behaviour can reduce threat

— Belief that specific measure can be effective against specific threat
  (If I stop smoking now, I will not develop lung cancer.)

— Belief that benefits of health measure exceed costs
  (Even though it will be hard to stop smoking, it is worth it to avoid the risk of lung cancer.)

Health behaviour
(I will stop smoking.)

(Downing-Matibag & Geisinger, 2009), and drinking and smoking intentions among adolescents (Goldberg, Halpern-Felsher, & Millstein, 2002). Typically, health beliefs are a modest determinant of intentions to take these health measures.

Changing Health Behaviour Using the Health Belief Model   The health belief model also predicts some of the circumstances under which people's health behaviours will change. A good illustration of this point comes from the experience of a student in a psychology class a few years ago. This student (call him Bob) was the only person in the class who smoked, and he was the object of some pressure from his fellow students to quit. He was familiar with the health risks of smoking. Although he knew that smoking contributes to lung cancer and heart disease, he believed the relationships were weak. Moreover, because he was in very good health and played a number of sports, his feelings of vulnerability were quite low.

Over Thanksgiving vacation, Bob went home to a large family gathering and discovered to his shock that his favourite uncle, a chain smoker all his adult life, had lung cancer and was not expected to live more than a few months. Suddenly, health became a more salient value for Bob because it had now struck his own family. Bob's perceived susceptibility to the illness changed both because a member of his own family had been struck down and because the link between smoking and cancer had been graphically illustrated. Bob's perceptions of stopping smoking changed as well. He concluded that this step might suffice to ward off the threat of the disease and that the costs of quitting smoking were not as great as he had thought. When Bob returned from Thanksgiving vacation, he had stopped smoking, cold turkey.

Interventions that draw on the health belief model have generally supported its predictions. Highlighting perceived vulnerability and simultaneously increasing the perception that a particular health behaviour will reduce the threat are somewhat successful in changing behaviour, whether the behaviour is smoking (Goldberg, Halpern-Felsher, & Millstein, 2002), preventive dental behaviour (Buglar, White, & Robinson, 2010), or osteoporosis prevention measures (Hazavehei, Taghdisi, & Saidi, 2007), for example. However, the health belief model focuses mainly on beliefs regarding risk rather than the emotional responses to perceived risk which are known to predict behaviour (Lawton, Conner, & Parker, 2007; Peters, Slovic, Hibbard, & Tusler, 2006; Weinstein et al., 2007). In addition, the health belief model leaves out an important component of health behaviour change: the perception that one will be able to engage in the health behaviour. Although the Health Belief Model continues to be used as means for understanding and effecting health behaviour change, several other social cognitive models have gained popularity among researchers.

Self-efficacy and Health Behaviours   An important determinant of the practice of health behaviours is a sense of **self-efficacy:** the belief that one is able to control one's practice of a particular behaviour (Bandura, 1991). Self-efficacy is a core concept in Bandura's Social Cognitive theory (1986) which states that behaviour results from efficacy expectancies, the confidence that one can successfully engage in a behaviour to produce desired outcomes, and outcome expectancies, the belief that a given behaviour will result in a particular outcome. Outcome expectancies can motivate behaviour change by linking behaviours to outcomes and are, therefore, most important for the development of intentions to engage in behaviours. Efficacy expectancies play a critical role once intentions are formed by providing motivation to initiate and maintain behaviour change. For example, smokers who believe that using the patch will help them quit and believe that they will be able to break their habit are more likely to try to quit.

Self-efficacy can be a powerful determinant of behaviour by promoting persistence in the face of difficulties as well as a strong conviction to follow through with behaviour. Self-efficacy affects health behaviours as varied as quitting smoking (Schnoll et al., 2011), weight control (Linde, Rothman, Baldwin, & Jeffery, 2006), condom use (Wulfert & Wan, 1993), exercise (McAuley & Courneya, 1992), dietary change (Schwarzer & Renner, 2000), and a variety of health behaviours among older adults (Grembowski et al., 1993). Typically, research finds a strong relationship between perceptions of self-efficacy and both initial health behaviour change and long-term maintenance of that behaviour change.

The Theory of Planned Behaviour   Although health beliefs go some distance in helping us understand when people will change their health habits, increasingly health psychologists are turning their attention to the analysis of action. A theory that attempts to link health attitudes directly to behaviour is Ajzen's **theory of planned behaviour** (Ajzen & Madden, 1986; M. Fishbein & Ajzen, 1975).

FIGURE 3.2 | The Theory of Planned Behaviour Applied to the Health Behaviour of Dieting

(*Sources:* Ajzen & Fishbein, 1980; Ajzen & Madden, 1986)

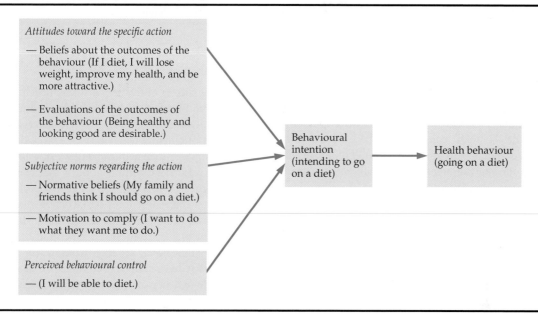

According to this theory, a health behaviour is the direct result of a behavioural intention. Behavioural intentions are themselves made up of three components: attitudes toward the specific action, subjective norms regarding the action, and perceived behavioural control (see Figure 3.2). Attitudes toward the action are based on beliefs about the likely outcomes of the action and evaluations of those outcomes. Subjective norms are what a person believes *others* think that person should do (normative beliefs) and the motivation to comply with those normative references. Perceived behavioural control is when an individual needs to feel that he or she is capable of performing the action contemplated and that the action undertaken will have the intended effect; this component of the model is very similar to self-efficacy. These factors combine to produce a behavioural intention and, ultimately, behaviour change.

To take a simple example, smokers who believe that smoking causes serious health outcomes, who believe that other people think they should stop smoking, who are motivated to comply with those normative beliefs, and who believe that they are capable of stopping smoking will be more likely to intend to stop smoking than individuals who do not hold these beliefs.

Benefits of the Theory of Planned Behaviour The theory of planned behaviour is a useful addition to understanding health behaviour–change processes for two reasons. First, it provides a model that links beliefs directly to behaviour. Second, it provides a fine-grained picture of people's intentions with respect to a particular health habit.

Evidence for the Theory of Planned Behaviour The theory of planned behaviour predicts a broad array of health behaviours, including condom use among injection drug users (Gu et al., 2009), sunbathing and sunscreen use (Myers & Horswill, 2006), use of oral contraceptives (J. Doll & Orth, 1993), consumption of soft drinks by adolescents (Kassem & Lee, 2004), mammography participation (Griva, Anagnostopoulos, & Madoglou, 2009), exercise (Baker, Little, & Brownell, 2003), participation in cancer screening programs (Sieverding, Matterne, & Ciccarello, 2010), smoking (Norman, Conner, & Bell, 1999), healthy eating (Baker, Little, & Brownell, 2003), medication adherence for people with tuberculosis or HIV/AIDS (Munro, Lewin, Swart, & Volmink, 2007), follow-up appointments for abnormal cervical screening results (Orbell & Hagger, 2006), and intentions to perform several health protective behaviours, including getting enough sleep and taking vitamins (Sirois, 2004).

Implementation Intentions and Health Behaviour Change   Despite the utility of social cognitive theories for understanding the factors that may strengthen intentions to make health behaviour changes, having good intentions is often not enough to ensure such changes are successful. One approach that can help bridge the intention–behaviour gap is forming **implementation intentions.** An implementation intention (Gollwitzer, 1993, 1999) is a specific behavioural intention that highlights the *how, when, and where* of a behaviour, and also includes "if-then" contingency plans to deal with anticipated barriers to the behaviour. For example, instead of the general intention of "I will exercise more" an implementation intention would be "I will go jogging in my neighbourhood on Monday, Wednesday, and Friday evenings this week from 4 to 5 p.m.". It might also include an if–then plan to deal with social invitations that might derail exercise intentions such as: "If my friend asks me to go out I will reschedule to a night that I am not exercising."

This more specific type of intention provides a clear plan of how the intention can be carried out even in less-than-ideal circumstances, and accordingly has a stronger influence on behaviour than more general intentions for behaviour (Gollwitzer & Sheeran, 2006). Implementation intentions have been found to be an effective way to shield ongoing dieting and exercise goals from interfering states such as cravings and disruptive thoughts (Achtziger, Gollwitzer, & Sheeran, 2008). When used as an intervention strategy, implementation intentions are an effective way to increase fruit consumption (Armitage, 2007), especially when paired with mental imagery (Knauper et al., 2011). Moreover, implementation intentions can be especially effective for those with strong unhealthy snacking habits when the implementation intentions are framed in a manner that is congruent with personal approach or avoidance tendencies (Tam, Bagozzi, & Spanjol, 2010).

Summary   Social cognitive theories of health behaviour change suggest that whether a person practices a particular health behaviour depends on several beliefs, attitudes, and values: the magnitude of a health threat, the degree to which that person believes he or she is personally vulnerable to that threat, the degree to which that person believes he or she can perform the response necessary to reduce the threat (self-efficacy), and the degree to which the particular health measure advocated is effective, desirable, and easy to implement. Sometimes, though, good intentions are not enough, and forming implementation intentions about the specifics of behaviour change is necessary to ensure that intentions translate into actual behaviour.

Attitudes, Social Cognition, and Changing Health Behaviours: Some Caveats

Despite the success of theories that link beliefs to behaviour and modification of health habits, attitudinal and social cognitive approaches are not very successful for explaining spontaneous behaviour change, nor do they predict long-term behaviour change very well (Kirscht, 1983). An additional complication is that communications designed to change people's attitudes about their health behaviours sometimes evoke defensive or irrational processes: People may perceive a health threat to be less relevant than it really is (A. Liberman & Chaiken, 1992), they may falsely see themselves as less vulnerable than others (Clarke, Lovegrove, Williams, & Machperson, 2000), and they may see themselves as dissimilar to those who have succumbed to a particular health risk (Thornton, Gibbons, & Gerrard, 2002). Continued practice of a risky behaviour may itself lead to changes in perception of a person's degree of risk, inducing a false sense of complacency (Halpern-Felsher et al., 2001).

Moreover, thinking about disease can produce a negative mood (Millar & Millar, 1995), which may, in turn, lead people to ignore or defensively interpret their risk. Although some studies have found that inaccurate risk perception can be modified by information and educational interventions (Kreuter & Strecher, 1995), other reports suggest that simple interventions such as self-affirmation can be effective for increasing intentions to engage in health protective behaviours (Klein et al., 2010).

Social cognitive models view health behaviour change as largely a rational process and can therefore neglect to consider other important factors such as the role of affective variables. One study found that feeling positive about physical activity was a better predictor of the actual physical activity engaged in than attitudes, perceived control, and other beliefs about staying active (Kiviniemi, Voss-Humke, & Seifert, 2007). Moreover, affective responses explained the link between attitudes and behaviour, suggesting that affective associations may be an important consideration when understanding health behaviour change.

Because health habits are often deeply ingrained and difficult to modify, attitude change procedures may not go far enough in simply providing the informational base for altering health habits (Ogden, 2003). The attitude-change procedures may instill the motivation to change a health habit but not provide the preliminary steps or skills necessary to actually alter behaviour and maintain behaviour change (Bryan, Fisher, & Fisher, 2002). Consequently, health psychologists have also turned to identifying when such interventions might be most effective.

The Transtheoretical Model of Behaviour Change

In contrast to social cognitive models and attitudinal approaches which examine the factors that predict behaviour change, the **transtheoretical model of behaviour change** acknowledges that changing a bad health habit may not take place all at once by addressing the process or stages of behaviour change (J. O. Prochaska, 1994; J. O. Prochaska, DiClemente, & Norcross, 1992). This model accounts for and analyzes the stages of change that people go through as they attempt to change a health behaviour, and suggests treatment goals and interventions for each stage.

Originally developed to treat addictive disorders, such as smoking, drug use, and alcohol addiction, the transtheoretical model of behaviour change (or stages of change model, as it is often referred to) has now been applied to other health habits, such as exercising and obtaining regular mammograms (Rakowski, Fulton, & Feldman, 1993).

Precontemplation   The precontemplation stage occurs when a person has no intention of changing his or her behaviour. Many individuals in this stage are not even aware that they have a problem, although families, friends, neighbours, or co-workers may well be. An example is the problem drinker who is largely oblivious to the problems he or she creates for his or her family. Sometimes people in the precontemplation phase seek treatment, but typically they do so only if they have been pressured by others and feel themselves coerced into changing their behaviour.

Contemplation   Contemplation is the stage in which people are aware that a problem exists and are thinking about it but have not yet made a commitment to take action. Many individuals remain in the contemplation stage for years, such as the smoker who knows he or she should stop but has not yet made the commitment to do so. Individuals in the contemplation stage are typically still weighing the pros and cons of changing their behaviour, continuing to find the positive aspects of the

Readiness to change a health habit is an important prerequisite to health habit change.

behaviour enjoyable. Those who do decide to change their behaviour have typically formed favourable expectations about their ability to do so and the rewards that will result (Rothman, 2000).

Preparation   In the preparation stage, individuals intend to change their behaviour but may not yet have begun to do so. In some cases, it is because they have been unsuccessful in the past, or they may simply be delaying action until they can get through a certain event or stressful period of time. In some cases, individuals in the preparation stage have already modified the target behaviour somewhat, such as smoking fewer cigarettes than usual, but have not yet made the commitment to eliminate the behaviour altogether.

Action   The action stage is the one in which individuals modify their behaviour to overcome the problem. Action requires the commitment of time and energy to making real behaviour change. It includes stopping the behaviour and modifying one's lifestyle and environment so as to rid one's life of cues associated with the behaviour.

Maintenance   Maintenance is the stage in which people work to prevent relapse and to consolidate the gains they have made. Typically, if a person is able to remain free of the addictive behaviour for more than six months, he or she is assumed to be in the maintenance stage (Wing, 2000).

Because relapse is the rule rather than the exception with addictive behaviours, this stage model is conceptualized as a spiral. As Figure 3.3 indicates, individuals may take action, attempt maintenance, relapse, return to the precontemplation phase, cycle through the subsequent stages to action, repeat the cycle again, and do so several times until they have successfully eliminated the behaviour (see J. O. Prochaska et al., 1992).

Importance of the Stages of Change Model

The stage model of health behaviour change is potentially important for several reasons. It captures the processes that people actually go through while they are attempting to change their behaviour, it illustrates that successful change may not occur on the first try or all at once, and it also explicates why many people are unsuccessful in changing their behaviour. Specifically, people who are in the precontemplation stage or the contemplation stage are not ready to be thrust into action. For example, a study of smokers revealed that 10 to 15 percent were prepared for action, 30 to 40 percent were in the contemplation stage, and 50 to 60 percent were in the precontemplation stage (J. O. Prochaska et al., 1992). These statistics help explain why so many interventions show dismal rates of success. When success rates are recalculated to include only individuals who are ready to change their behaviour—namely, those people in the action or preparation stage—most of these programs look more successful.

Using the Stages of Change Model

Applications of the spiral stage model of health behaviour change have shown mixed success. The model has been used with many different health behaviours, including smoking cessation, quitting cocaine use, weight control, modification of a high-fat diet, adolescent delinquent behaviour, practice of safe sex, condom use, sunscreen use, control of radon gas exposure, exercise acquisition, and regular mammograms (J. O. Prochaska et al., 1994). In some cases, interventions matched to the particular stage a person is in have been successful (for example, Park et al., 2003); in other cases, not (N. D. Weinstein, Rothman, & Sutton, 1998). Specific applications of the stages of change model will be examined in Chapter 4. In the next section we discuss some of the types of interventions that may be used to help people change their health behaviours across the various stages of change.

FIGURE 3.3 | A Spiral Model of the Stages of Change
(*Source:* J.O. Prochaska et al., 1992)

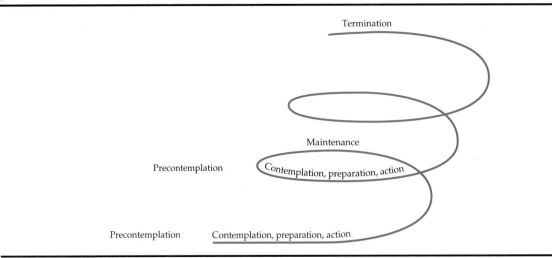

HOW ARE COGNITIVE BEHAVIOURAL APPROACHES USED TO CHANGE HEALTH BEHAVIOURS?

Attitudinal approaches to the modification of health behaviours appear to be most useful in predicting when people will be motivated to change a health behaviour. **Cognitive behaviour therapy (CBT)** approaches to health habit modification change the focus to the target behaviour itself—the conditions that elicit and maintain it and the factors that reinforce it (Hobbis & Sutton, 2005). Cognitive behaviour therapy also focuses heavily on the beliefs that people hold about their health habits and therefore it may be an effective way to support health behaviour change especially when used in the context of social cognitive models that highlight the role of beliefs about health behaviours (Hobbis & Sutton, 2005). For example, a person who wishes to give up smoking may derail the quitting process by generating self-doubts ("I will never be able to give up smoking"; "I'm one of those people who simply depend on cigarettes"; "I've tried before, and I've never been successful"). Unless these internal monologues are modified, cognitive behavioural therapists argue, the person will be unlikely to change a health habit and maintain that change over time.

Recognition that people's cognitions about their health habits are important in producing behaviour change has led to another insight: the importance of involving the patient as a co-therapist in the behaviour-change intervention. Most behaviour-change programs begin with the client as the object of behaviour-change efforts, but in the therapeutic process, control over behaviour change shifts gradually from the therapist to the client. By the end of the formal intervention stage, clients are monitoring their own behaviours, applying the techniques of cognitive behavioural interventions to their behaviour, and rewarding themselves, or not, appropriately. Cognitive behavioural interventions draw on a variety of behaviour-change techniques including some of the following strategies.

Self-observation and Self-monitoring

Many programs of cognitive behavioural modification use **self-observation** and **self-monitoring** as the first steps toward behaviour change. The rationale is that a person must understand the dimensions of a target behaviour before change can be initiated. Self-observation and self-monitoring assess the frequency of a target behaviour and the antecedents and consequences of that behaviour (Lootens & Nelson-Gray, 2010). This process also sets the stage for enlisting the patient's joint participation early in the effort to modify health behaviours.

The first step in self-observation is to learn to discriminate the target behaviour. Although for some behaviours such as smoking, this step is easy, for others such as the urge to smoke, discrimination may be more difficult. A second stage in self-observation is recording and charting the behaviour. Techniques range from very simple counters for recording the behaviour each time it occurs to complex records documenting the circumstances under which the behaviour was enacted as well as the feelings it aroused. For example, a smoker may be trained to keep a detailed behavioural record of all smoking events such as each time she smokes a cigarette, the time of day, the situation in which the smoking occurred, and whether or not anyone else was present. She may also record the subjective feelings of craving that were present when lighting the cigarette, In this way, she can begin to get a sense of the circumstances in which she is most likely to smoke and can then initiate a structured behaviour-change program that deals with these contingencies.

Although self-observation is usually only a beginning step in behaviour change, it may itself produce behaviour change. Typically, however, behaviour change that is produced by self-monitoring is short-lived and needs to be coupled with other techniques (for example, McCaul, Glasgow, & O'Neill, 1992).

Classical Conditioning

First described by Russian physiologist Ivan Pavlov in the early twentieth century, **classical conditioning** was one of the earliest principles of behaviour change identified by researchers. The essence of classical conditioning is the pairing of an unconditioned reflex with a new stimulus, producing a conditioned reflex. Classical conditioning is represented diagrammatically in Figure 3.4.

Classical conditioning was one of the first methods used for health behaviour change. For example, consider its use in the treatment of alcoholism. Antabuse (unconditioned stimulus) is a drug that produces extreme nausea, gagging, and vomiting (unconditioned response) when it is taken in conjunction with alcohol. Over time, the alcohol will become associated with the nausea and vomiting caused by the Antabuse and elicit the same nausea, gagging, and vomiting response (conditioned response).

Classical conditioning approaches to health-habit modification do work, but clients know why they work. Alcoholics, for example, know that if they do not take

FIGURE 3.4 | A Classical Conditioning Approach to the Treatment of Alcoholism

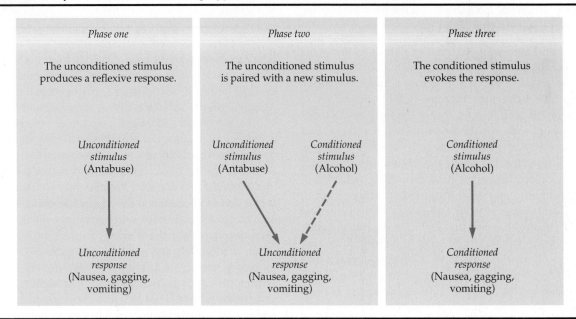

the drug, they will not vomit when they consume alcohol. Thus, even if classical conditioning has successfully produced a conditioned response, it is heavily dependent on the client's willing participation. Procedures like these produce health risks as well, and as a result, they are no longer as widely used.

Operant Conditioning

In contrast to classical conditioning, which pairs an automatic response with a new stimulus, operant conditioning pairs a voluntary behaviour with systematic consequences. The key to **operant conditioning** is reinforcement. When an individual performs a behaviour and that behaviour is followed by positive reinforcement, the behaviour is more likely to occur again. Similarly, if an individual performs a behaviour and reinforcement is withdrawn or the behaviour is punished, the behaviour is less likely to be repeated. Over time, these contingencies build up those behaviours paired with positive reinforcement, and behaviours that are punished or not rewarded decline.

Many health habits can be thought of as operant responses. For example, drinking may be maintained because mood is improved by alcohol, or smoking may occur because peer companionship is associated with it. In both of these cases, reinforcement maintains the poor health behaviour. Thus, using this principle to change behaviour requires altering the reinforcement or its schedule.

Operant Conditioning to Change Health Behaviours   Operant conditioning is often used to modify health behaviours. At the beginning of an effort to change a faulty health habit, people typically will be positively reinforced for any action that moves them closer to their goal. As progress is made toward reducing or modifying the health habit, greater behaviour change may be required for the same reinforcement. For example, suppose Mary smokes 20 cigarettes a day. She might first define a set of reinforcers that can be administered when particular smoking-reduction targets are met—reinforcements such as going out to dinner or seeing a movie. Mary may then set a particular reduction in her smoking behaviour as a target (such as 15 cigarettes a day). When that target is reached, she would administer a reinforcement (the movie or dinner out). The next step might be reducing smoking to 10 cigarettes a day, at which time she would receive another reinforcement. The target then might be cut progressively to 5, 4, 3, 1, and none. Through this process, the target behaviour of abstinence would eventually be reached.

Modelling

Modelling is learning that occurs by virtue of witnessing another person perform a behaviour (Bandura, 1969). Observation and subsequent modelling can be effective approaches to changing health habits. For example, high school students who observed others donating blood were more likely to do so themselves (I. G. Sarason, Sarason, Pierce, Shearin, & Sayers, 1991).

Modelling can be an important long-term behaviour-change technique. For example, the principle of modelling is implicit in some self-help programs that treat destructive health habits, such as alcoholism (Alcoholics Anonymous) or drug addiction. In these programs, a person who is newly committed to changing an addictive behaviour joins individuals who have had the same problem and who have had at least some success in solving it. In meetings, people often share the methods that helped them overcome their health problem. By listening to these accounts, the new convert can learn how to do likewise and model effective techniques in his or her own rehabilitation.

Modelling can also be used as a technique for reducing the anxiety that can give rise to some bad habits or the fears that arise when going through some preventive health behaviours, such as receiving inoculations. When modelling is used to reduce fear or anxiety, it is better to observe models who are also fearful but are able to control their distress rather than models who are demonstrating no fear in the situation because fearful models provide a realistic portrayal of the experience. Modelling, or imitative learning, has an important role in the modification of health habits because it exposes an individual to other people who have successfully modified the health habit. Modelling may be most successful when it shows the realistic difficulties that people encounter in making these changes.

Stimulus Control

The successful modification of health behaviour involves understanding the antecedents as well as the consequences of a target behaviour. Individuals who practise poor health habits, such as smoking, drinking, and overeating, develop ties between those behaviours and stimuli in their environments. Each of these stimuli can come to act as a **discriminative stimulus** that is capable of eliciting the target behaviour. For example, the sight and smell of food act as discriminative stimuli for eating. The discriminative stimulus is important because it signals that a positive reinforcement will subsequently occur.

Stimulus-control interventions with patients who are attempting to alter their health habits take two approaches: ridding the environment of discriminative stimuli that evoke the problem behaviour and creating new discriminative stimuli signalling that a new response will be reinforced. For example, to reduce overeating one could remove rewarding but unhealthy foods from their home, not eat while engaged in other activities such as watching television, and introduce other reinforcers such as reminders of the rewards that will come from not overeating.

The Self-control of Behaviour

Cognitive behaviour therapy, including that used to modify health habits, has increasingly moved toward a therapeutic model that emphasizes **self-control.** In this approach, the individual who is the target of the intervention acts, at least in part, as his or her own therapist and, together with outside guidance, learns to control the antecedents and consequences of the target behaviour to be modified.

Self-reinforcement   **Self-reinforcement** involves systematically rewarding the self to increase or decrease the occurrence of a target behaviour (Thoresen & Mahoney, 1974). Positive self-reward involves reinforcing oneself with something desirable after successful modification of a target behaviour. An example of positive self-reward is allowing oneself to go to a movie following successful weight loss. Negative self-reward involves removing an aversive factor in the environment after successful modification of the target behaviour. An example of negative self-reward is taking the picture of the *Biggest Loser* star from the beginning of the season off the refrigerator once regular controlled eating has been achieved. When used in the context of other lifestyle interventions, self-reinforcement can be effective for helping overweight youth achieve better weight-related outcomes (Dalton & Kitzmann, 2011).

Like self-reward, self-punishment is of two types. Positive self-punishment involves the administration of an unpleasant stimulus to punish an undesirable behaviour, such as a smoker making himself do 20 push-ups every time he smokes. Negative self-punishment consists of withdrawing a positive reinforcer in the environment each time an undesirable behaviour is performed, such as a smoker reducing the time he plays video games every time he smokes. Studies that have evaluated the success of self-punishment suggest two conclusions: (1) positive self-punishment works somewhat better than negative self-punishment, and (2) self-punishment works better if it is also coupled with self-rewarding techniques.

Contingency Contracting   Self-punishment is effective only if people actually perform the punishing activities. When self-punishment becomes too aversive, people often abandon their efforts. However, one form of self-punishment that works well and has been used widely in behaviour modification is **contingency contracting** (Turk & Meichenbaum, 1991). In contingency contracting, an individual forms a contract with another person, such as a therapist, detailing what rewards or punishments are contingent on the performance or non-performance of a behaviour. For example, a person who wanted to stop drinking might deposit a sum of money with a therapist and arrange to be fined each time he or she had a drink and to be rewarded each day that he or she abstained.

Covert Self-control   As noted earlier, poor health habits and their modification are often accompanied by internal monologues, such as self-criticism or self-praise. **Covert self-control** trains individuals to recognize and modify these internal monologues to promote health behaviour change (Hollon & Beck, 1986). Sometimes the modified cognitions are antecedents to a target behaviour. For example, if a smoker's urge to smoke is preceded by an internal monologue that he is weak and unable to control his smoking urges, these beliefs are targeted for change. The smoker would be trained to develop antecedent cognitions that would help him stop smoking (e.g., "I can do this" or "I'll be so much healthier").

Cognitions themselves may be the targets for modification. **Cognitive restructuring,** developed by Meichenbaum (Meichenbaum & Cameron, 1974), is a method for modifying internal monologues that has been widely used in the treatment of stress disorders. In a typical intervention, clients are first trained to monitor their monologues in stress-producing situations so that they learn to recognize what they say to themselves during times of stress. They are then taught to modify their self-instructions to include more constructive cognitions.

Frequently, modelling is used to train a client in cognitive restructuring. The therapist may first demonstrate adaptive **self-talk.** She may identify a target stress-producing situation and then self-administer positive instructions (such as "Relax, you're doing great"). The client then attempts to deal with his stressful situation while the therapist teaches him positive self-instruction. In the next phase of training, the client attempts to cope with the stress-producing situation, instructing himself out loud. Following this phase, self-instruction may become a whisper, and finally the client performs the anxiety-reducing self-instruction internally.

Behavioural Assignments   Another technique for increasing client involvement is **behavioural assignments,** home practice activities that support the goals of a therapeutic intervention (Shelton & Levy, 1981). Behavioural assignments are designed to provide continuity in the treatment of a behaviour problem, and typically, these assignments follow up points in the therapeutic session. For example, if an early therapy session with an obese client involved training in self-monitoring, the client would be encouraged to keep a log of his or her eating behaviour, including the circumstances in which it occurred. This log could then be used by the therapist and the patient at the next session to plan future behavioural interventions. Figure 3.5 gives an example of the behavioural assignment technique.

The value of systematic homework assignments is widely recognized in the treatment of behaviours. A survey of programs for the treatment of health problems indicated that 75 percent of obesity programs, 71 percent of physical illness and rehabilitation programs, and 54 percent of smoking programs included behavioural assignments (Shelton & Levy, 1981).

Skills Training   Psychologists have realized that some poor health habits develop in response to or are maintained by the anxiety that people experience in social

FIGURE 3.5 | Example of a Systematic Behavioural Assignment for an Obese Client
(*Source:* Shelton & Levy, 1981, p. 6)

Homework for Tom [client]

Using the counter, count bites taken.

Record number of bites, time, location, and what you ate.

Record everything eaten for 1 week.

Call for an appointment.

Bring your record.

Homework for John [therapist]

Reread articles on obesity.

situations. For example, adolescents often begin to smoke in order to reduce their social anxiety by communicating a cool, sophisticated image. Social anxiety then can act as a cue for the maladaptive habit, necessitating an alternative way of coping with the anxiety.

A number of programs designed to alter health habits include either **social skills training** or **assertiveness training,** or both, as part of the intervention package. The goals of social skills programs as an ancillary technique in a program of health behaviour change are (1) to reduce anxiety that occurs in social situations, (2) to introduce new skills for dealing with situations that previously aroused anxiety, and (3) to provide an alternative behaviour for the poor health habit that arose in response to social anxiety.

Motivational Interviewing   Motivational interviewing is increasingly used in the battle for health promotion. Originally developed to treat addiction (W. R. Miller & Rollnick, 1991), the techniques have been adapted to target smoking, dietary improvements, exercise, cancer screening, and sexual behaviour, among other habits (Lundahl, Kunz, Brownell, Tollefson, & Burke, 2010; Resnicow et al., 2002).

Motivational interviewing is an amalgam of principles and techniques drawn from psychotherapy and behaviour-change theory that draws on many of the principles just discussed. It is a client-centred counselling style designed to get people to work through whatever ambivalence they may be experiencing about changing their health behaviours. It appears to be especially effective for those who are initially wary about whether or not to change their behaviours (Resnicow et al., 2002; Resnicow et al., 2005).

In motivational interviewing, there is no effort to dismantle the denial often associated with the practice of bad health behaviours or to confront irrational beliefs or even to persuade a client to stop drinking, stop smoking, or otherwise improve health. Rather, the goal is to get the client to think through and express some of his or her own reasons for and against change and for the interviewer to listen and provide encouragement in absence of giving advice.

Relaxation Training   In 1958, psychologist Joseph Wolpe (1958) developed a procedure known as systematic desensitization for the treatment of anxiety. The procedure involved training clients to substitute relaxation in the presence of circumstances that usually produced anxiety. To induce relaxation, Wolpe taught patients how to engage in deep breathing and progressive muscle relaxation (**relaxation training**).

In deep breathing, a person takes deep, controlled breaths, which produce a number of physiological changes, such as decreased heart rate and blood pressure and increased oxygenation of the blood. People typically engage in this kind of breathing spontaneously when they are relaxed. In progressive muscle relaxation, an individual learns to relax all the muscles in the body to discharge tension or stress, a technique that can be effectively used for stress reduction (discussed further in Chapter 7). As just noted, many deleterious health habits, such as smoking and drinking, represent ways of coping with social anxiety. Thus, in addition to social skills training or assertiveness training, people may learn relaxation procedures to cope more effectively with their anxiety.

Broad-spectrum Cognitive Behaviour Therapy

The most effective approach to health-habit modification often comes from combining multiple behaviour-change techniques. This eclectic approach has been termed **broad-spectrum cognitive behaviour therapy,** sometimes known as multimodal cognitive behaviour therapy (A. A. Lazarus, 1971). From an array of available techniques, a therapist selects several complementary methods to intervene in the modification of a target problem and its context.

The advantages of a broad-spectrum approach to health behaviour change are several. First, a carefully selected set of techniques can deal with all aspects of a problem: Self-observation and self-monitoring define the dimensions of a problem; stimulus control enables a person to modify antecedents of behaviour; self-reinforcement controls the consequences of a behaviour; and social skills training may be added to replace the maladaptive behaviour once it has been brought under some degree of control. An example of the application of this kind of therapy to the treatment of alcoholism appears in the Health Psychology in Action box, "Cognitive Behaviour Therapy in the Treatment of Alcoholism." A second advantage is that the therapeutic plan can be tailored to each individual's problem. Each person's faulty health habit and personality is different, so, for example, the particular package identified for one obese client will not be the same as that developed for another obese client. Third, multi-modal interventions impart a broad range of skills that can be used to modify not one but several health habits (e.g., diet and exercise) at the same time (Persky, Spring, Vander Wal, Pagoto, & Hedeker, 2005; J. J. Prochaska & Sallis, 2004).

Cognitive Behaviour Therapy in the Treatment of Alcoholism

Mary was a 32-year-old executive who came in for treatment, saying she thought she was an alcoholic. She had a demanding, challenging job, which she handled very conscientiously. Although her husband, Don, was supportive of her career, he felt it was important that evenings be spent in shared activities. They had had several arguments recently because Mary was drinking before coming home and had been hiding liquor around the house. Don was threatening to leave if she did not stop drinking altogether, and Mary was feeling alarmed by her behaviour. Mary was seen over a three-month period, with follow-up contact over the following year.

Mary's first week's assignment was to complete an autobiography of the history and development of her drinking problem—her parents' drinking behaviour, her first drinking experience and first "drunk," the role of drinking in her adult life, her self-image, any problems associated with her drinking, and her attempts to control her drinking. She also self-monitored her drinking for two weeks, noting the exact amounts of alcohol consumed each day, the time, and the antecedents and consequences.

At the third session, the following patterns were identified. Mary started work at 8:30, typically had a rushed business lunch, and often did not leave work until 6:00, by which time she was tense and wound up. Because she knew Don did not approve of her drinking, she had begun to pick up a pint of vodka after work and to drink half of it during the 20-minute drive home, so that she could get relaxed for the evening. She had also begun stashing liquor away in the house just in case she wanted a drink. She realized that drinking while driving was dangerous, that she was drinking too much too quickly, and that she was feeling very guilty and out of control. Her husband's anger seemed to increase her urges to drink.

Mary agreed to abstain from any drinking during the third and fourth weeks of treatment. During this period, it became apparent that drinking was her only means of reducing the tension that had built up during the day and represented the one indulgence she allowed herself in a daily routine of obligations to external job demands and commitments to her husband and friends. A plan to modify her general lifestyle was worked out that included alternative ways of relaxing and indulging that were not destructive.

Mary joined a local health club and began going for a swim and a sauna every morning on the way to work. She also set aside two days a week to have lunch alone or with a friend. She learned a meditation technique, which she began using at the end of the day after getting home from work. She negotiated with Don to spend one evening a week doing separate activities so that she could resume her old hobby of painting.

Mary also decided that she wanted to continue drinking in a moderate way and that Don's support was essential so that she could drink openly. Don attended the sixth session with Mary, the treatment plan was explained to him, his feelings and concerns were explored, and he agreed to support Mary in her efforts to alter her lifestyle as well as to be more accepting of her drinking.

During the next few sessions, Mary learned a number of controlled drinking techniques, including setting limits for herself and pacing her drinking by alternating liquor with soft drinks. She also developed strategies for dealing with high-risk situations, which for her were primarily the buildup of tension at work and feelings of guilt or anger toward Don. She learned to become more aware of these situations as they were developing and began to practise more direct ways of communicating with Don. She also was instructed to use any urges to return to old drinking patterns as cues to pay attention to situational factors and use alternative responses rather than to interpret them as signs that she was an alcoholic.

The final two sessions were spent planning and rehearsing what to do if a relapse occurred. Strategies included the process of slowing herself down, cognitive restructuring, a decision-making exercise to review the consequences and relative merits and liabilities of drinking according to both the old and the new pattern, an analysis of the situation that led to the relapse, problem solving to come up with a better coping response to use next time, and the possibility of scheduling a booster session with her therapist.

At the final follow-up a year later, Mary reported that she was feeling better about herself and more in control, was drinking moderately on social occasions, and was communicating better with Don. She had had a couple of slips but had managed to retrieve the situation, in one case by being more assertive with a superior and in the other by simply deciding that she could accept some mistakes on her part without having to punish herself by continuing the mistake.

Source: J. R. Gordon and G. A. Marlatt, 1981, "Addictive Behaviors," in J. L. Shelton and R. L. Levy (eds.). *Behavioral Assignments and Treatment Compliance*, pp. 167–186, Champaign, IL: Research Press. Used with permission from Dr. J. L. Shelton.

Relapse

One of the biggest problems faced in health-habit modification is the tendency for people to relapse to their previous behaviour following initial successful behaviour change (for example, McCaul et al., 1992). This problem occurs both for people who make health-habit changes on their own and for those who join formal programs to alter their behaviour.

What do we mean by "relapse"? A single cigarette smoked at a cocktail party or the consumption of a pint of ice cream on a lonely Saturday night does not necessarily lead to permanent relapse. However, over time, initial vigilance may fade and relapse may set in. Research suggests that relapse rates tend to stabilize at about three months, which initially led researchers to believe that most people who are going to relapse will do so within the first three months. However, subsequent research suggests that, although relapse rates may remain constant, the particular people who are abstaining from a bad health habit at one point in time are not necessarily the same people who are abstaining at another point in time. Some people go from abstinence to relapse; others, from relapse back to abstinence.

Why Do People Relapse?   Our knowledge of who relapses is limited. Genetic factors may be implicated in alcoholism, smoking, and obesity (Wang et al., 2008). Withdrawal effects occur in response to abstinence from alcohol and cigarettes and may prompt a relapse, especially shortly after efforts to change behaviour. Conditioned associations between cues and physiological responses may lead to urges or cravings to engage in the habit (Lubman et al., 2009). For example, people may find themselves in a situation in which they used to smoke, such as at a party, and relapse at that vulnerable moment.

Relapse is more likely when people are depressed, anxious, or under stress (Rose, 2010). For example, when people are moving, breaking off a relationship, or encountering difficulties at work, they may have greater need for their addictive habits than is true at less stressful times. Relapse occurs when motivation flags or goals for maintaining the health behaviour have not been established. Relapse is less likely if a person has social support from family and friends to maintain the behaviour change, but it is more likely to occur if the person lacks social support or is involved in a conflictual interpersonal situation.

A particular moment that makes people vulnerable to relapse is when they have one lapse in vigilance. The **abstinence violation effect**—that is, a feeling of loss of control that results when a person has violated self-imposed rules—can result when someone dieting who is trying to avoid sweets has a bad day and eats a whole pint of ice cream, or a smoker trying to quit has a single cigarette to calm her nerves. The result is that a more serious relapse is then likely to occur as the individual sees his or her resolve falter. This may be especially true for addictive behaviours because the person must cope with the reinforcing impact of the substance itself. Figure 3.6 illustrates the relapse process.

Consequences of Relapse   What are the consequences of relapse? Clearly, relapse produces negative emotions, such as disappointment, frustration, unhappiness, or anger. Even a single lapse can lead a person to experience profound disappointment, a reduced sense of self-efficacy, and a shift in attributions for controlling the health behaviour from the self to uncontrollable external forces. A relapse could also lead people to feel that they can never control the habit that it is simply beyond their efforts.

In some cases, however, relapse may have paradoxical effects, leading people to perceive that they can control their habits, at least to a degree. With smoking, for example, multiple efforts to stop often take place before people succeed suggesting that initial experiences with stopping smoking may prepare people for later success. The person who relapses may nonetheless have acquired useful information about the habit and have learned ways to prevent relapse in the future.

Reducing Relapse   Because of the high risk of relapse, behavioural interventions build in techniques to try to reduce its likelihood. Typically, such interventions have centred on three techniques. Booster sessions following the termination of the initial treatment phase have been one method. Several weeks or months after the end of a formal intervention, smokers may have an additional smoking-prevention session or dieters may return to their group situation to be weighed in and to brush up on their weight-control techniques. Although booster sessions were originally thought to be ineffective, recent evidence suggests that booster sessions may be successful at reducing relapse but that their effects may not emerge immediately following the session (Gwaltney et al., 2011).

Another approach to relapse prevention is to consider abstinence a lifelong treatment process, as is done in such programs as Alcoholics Anonymous and other

FIGURE 3.6 | A Cognitive Behavioural Model of the Relapse Process

This figure shows what happens when a person is trying to change a poor health habit and faces a high-risk situation. With adequate coping responses, the individual may be able to resist temptation, leading to a low likelihood of relapse. Without adequate coping responses, however, perceptions of self-efficacy may decline and perceptions of the rewarding effects of the substance may increase, leading to an increased likelihood of relapse.

(*Source:* From Marlatt, G. A., & Gordon, J. R. (1985). "A Cognitive Behavioural Model of the Relapse Process," from *Relapse Prevention: Maintenance Strategies in the Treatment of Addictive Behaviors.* New York: Guilford Press. Used by permission of Guilford Publications, Inc.)

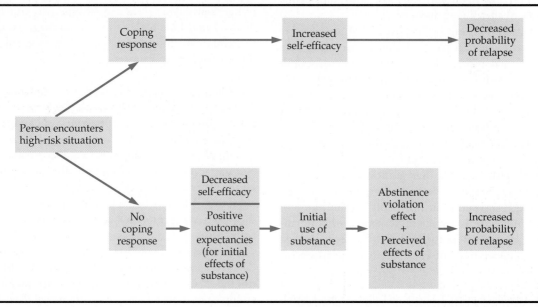

well-established lay treatment programs. Although this approach can be successful, it also has certain disadvantages. The philosophy can leave people with the perception that they are constantly vulnerable to relapse, potentially creating the expectation of relapse when vigilance wanes. Moreover, the approach implies that people are not in control of their habit, and research on health-habit modification suggests that self-efficacy is an important component in initiating and maintaining behaviour change (Bandura, 1986).

Relapse Prevention   Researchers have argued that **relapse prevention** must be integrated into treatment programs from the outset. Changing a health habit is not a simple action, but it is a process that may occur in stages (J. O. Prochaska & DiClemente, 1984a), and relapse prevention efforts can be built in at all stages.

Some factors are especially relevant when people first join a treatment program. Those people who are initially highly committed to the program and motivated to engage in behaviour change are less likely to relapse. These observations imply that one important focus of

programs must be to increase motivation and maintain commitment. For example, programs may create a contingency management procedure in which people are required to deposit money, which is returned if they successfully attend meetings or change their behaviour.

Once motivation and commitment to follow through have been instilled, techniques must be developed in the behaviour-change program itself to maintain behaviour change and act as relapse prevention skills once the program terminates. One such strategy involves having people identify the situations that are likely to promote a relapse and then develop coping skills that will enable them to manage that stressful event successfully. This strategy draws on the fact that successful adherence promotes feelings of self-control and that having available coping techniques can enhance feelings of control still further (Kearney, Rosal, Ockene, & Churchill, 2002). In addition, the mental rehearsal of coping responses in a high-risk situation can promote feelings of self-efficacy, decreasing the likelihood of relapse.

Cue elimination, or restructuring the environments to avoid situations that evoke the target behaviour, can be used (Bouton, 2000). The alcoholic who drank exclusively in bars can avoid bars. For other habits, however, cue elimination is impossible. For example, smokers are usually unable to eliminate completely the circumstances in their lives that led them to smoke. Consequently, some relapse-prevention programs deliberately expose people to the situations likely to evoke the old behaviour to give them practice in using their coping skills. The power of the situation may be extinguished over time if the behaviour does not follow (Marlatt, 1990). Moreover, such exposure can increase feelings of self-efficacy and decrease the positive expectations associated with the addictive behaviour. Making sure that the new habit (such as exercise or alcohol abstinence) is practised in as broad an array of new contexts is important as well for ensuring that it endures (Bouton, 2000).

Lifestyle Rebalancing   Finally, long-term maintenance of behaviour change can be promoted by leading the person to make other health-oriented changes in lifestyle, a technique termed **lifestyle rebalancing** (Marlatt & George, 1988). Making lifestyle changes, such as adding an exercise program or learning stress-management techniques, may promote a healthy lifestyle more generally and help reduce the likelihood of relapse. Returning to smoking or excessive alcohol consumption may come to feel inappropriate in the context of a generally healthier lifestyle.

Overall, at present, relapse prevention seems to be most successful when people perceive their successful behaviour change to be a long-term goal, develop coping techniques for managing high-risk situations, and integrate behaviour change into a generally healthy lifestyle.

(L05) HOW CAN SOCIAL ENGINEERING CHANGE HEALTH BEHAVIOURS?

Much behaviour change occurs not through behaviour-change programs but through social engineering. **Social engineering** involves modifying the environment in ways that affect people's ability to practise a particular health behaviour. These measures are called passive because they do not require an individual to take personal action. For example, wearing seat belts is an active measure that an individual must take to control possible injury from an automobile accident, whereas airbags, which inflate automatically on impact, represent a passive measure.

Many health behaviours are already determined by social engineering. Banning the use of certain drugs,

such as heroin and cocaine, and regulating the disposal of toxic wastes are examples of health measures that have been mandated by legislation. Alcohol consumption is legally restricted to particular circumstances and age groups. As of the beginning of 2010, all Canadian provinces and territories have legislated smoke-free indoor work environments, and nine banned smoking in indoor public spaces. Requiring vaccinations for school entry in some provinces has led to more than 98 percent of children receiving most of the vaccinations they need (Health Canada, 2004a).

Many times, social engineering solutions to health problems are more successful than individual ones. We could urge parents to have their children vaccinated against the major childhood disorders of measles, influenza, hepatitis, diphtheria, and tetanus, but requiring immunizations for school entry has been very successful. We could intervene with parents to get them to reduce accident risks in the home, but approaches such as using safety containers for medications and making children's clothing with fire-retardant fabrics are more successful (Fielding, 1978). Lowering the speed limit has had far more impact on death and disability from motor vehicle accidents than interventions to get people to change their driving habits (Fielding, 1978). The move toward a smoke-free Canada through banning smoking in the workplace and in indoor public places will help to reduce non-smokers' exposure to second-hand smoke, and has helped motivate many smokers to quit (Health Canada, 2007a; Shields, 2007). The recent introduction of regulations to eliminate the amount of trans fat allowed in foods by the Canadian government has also led to reductions in the amount of this harmful saturated fat, especially in fast food, and should help combat the rising rates of obesity in Canada.

The prospects for continued use of social engineering to change health habits are great. Controlling what is contained in vending machines at schools, putting a surcharge on foods high in fat and low in nutritional value, and controlling advertising of high-fat and high-cholesterol products should be considered to combat the enormous rise in obesity that has occurred over the past two decades (M. F. Jacobson & Brownell, 2000). Indeed, as the contributions of diet and obesity to poor health and early death become increasingly evident, social engineering solutions with respect to food sales and advertising may well emerge.

A relatively new method of social engineering to improve health habits involves using the entertainment media to illustrate good practices. Soap operas have been found to influence people in many countries more successfully than lectures and pamphlets on health habits, especially in developing countries. Research shows that when people watch the stars of their favourite TV dramas practise good health habits, they have been more inclined to change (C. J. Williams, 2001). There are limits, of course, on just how much one can use the media to this end, but to combat such problems as teen pregnancy and AIDS, television drama shows some potential success.

There are limits on social engineering more generally. Even though smoking has been banned in public areas, it is still not illegal to smoke; if this were to occur, most smokers and a substantial number of non-smokers would find such mandatory measures unacceptable interference with civil liberties. Even when the health advantages of social engineering can be dramatically illustrated, the sacrifice in personal liberty may be considered too great. Thus, many health habits will remain at the discretion of the individual. It is to such behaviours that psychological interventions speak most persuasively.

(L06) WHAT ARE THE VENUES FOR HEALTH-HABIT MODIFICATION?

What is the best venue for changing health habits? There are several possibilities: the private therapist's office, the physician's office, the family, self-help groups, schools, the workplace, the community setting, and the mass media. Each has its particular advantages and disadvantages, and some may be more or less effective depending on the target population (World Health Organization, 2009b).

The Private Therapist's Office

Some health-habit modification is conducted by psychologists, psychiatrists, and other clinicians privately on a one-to-one basis. These professionals are carefully trained in the techniques of cognitive behavioural modification that seem to work best in altering health habits.

There are two striking advantages of the one-to-one therapeutic experience for the modification of health habits:

1. Precisely because it is one-to-one, the extensive individual treatment a person receives may make success more likely.
2. Because of the individual nature of the experience, the therapist can tailor the behaviour-change package to the needs of the individual.

However, there is a major disadvantage. Only one individual's behaviour can be changed at a time. If the modification of health habits is to make any dent in rates of disease, we must find ways of modifying health behaviours that do not require expensive one-to-one attention.

The Health Practitioner's Office

Health-habit modification can be undertaken in the health practitioner's office. Many people have regular contact with a physician or another health care professional who knows their medical history and can help them modify their health habits. Among the advantages of intervening in the physician's office is that physicians are highly credible sources for instituting health-habit change, and their recommendations have the force of their expertise behind them. Nonetheless, as in the case of private therapy, the one-to-one approach reduces only one person's risk status at a time.

The Family

Increasingly, health practitioners are recognizing the value of intervening with the family to improve health (Fisher et al., 1998). There are several reasons for this emphasis. First and most obviously, children learn their health habits from their parents, so making sure the entire family is committed to a healthy lifestyle gives children the best chance at a healthy start in life.

Second, families, especially those in which there are children and one or more adults who work, typically have more organized, routinized lifestyles than single people do, so family life often builds in healthy behaviours, such as getting three meals a day, sleeping eight hours, brushing teeth, and using seat belts. The health-promoting aspects of family life are evident in the fact that married men have far better health habits than single men, in part because wives often run the home life that builds in these healthy habits (for example, Hampson, Andrews, Barckley, Lichtenstein, & Lee, 2000). Single and married women have equally healthy lifestyles, with the exception of single women with children who are disadvantaged with respect to health (Hughes & Waite, 2002).

A third reason for intervening with families is that multiple family members are affected by any one member's health habits. A clear example is second-hand smoke, which harms not only the smoker but also those around him or her.

A stable family life is health promoting, and increasingly, interventions are being targeted to families rather than individuals to ensure the greatest likelihood of behaviour change.

Finally and most important, if behaviour change is introduced at the family level—such as a low-cholesterol diet or stopping smoking—all family members are on board, ensuring greater commitment to the behaviour-change program and providing social support for the person whose behaviour is the target (D. K. Wilson & Ampey-Thornhill, 2001). Evidence suggests that the involvement of family members can increase the effectiveness of an intervention substantially (Wing & Jeffery, 1999).

As we'll see shortly, the emphasis on individual behaviour change is a culturally limited approach that may not be a useful intervention strategy for Aboriginal, Asian, or southern European cultures; people in these latter cultures may be more persuaded to engage in behaviour change when the good of the family is at stake (Han & Shavitt, 1994; Klonoff & Landrine, 1999; Willows, 2005). Consequently, the emphasis on family health behaviour change is especially well placed for people from cultures that emphasize family ties.

Self-help Groups

Thousands of people in Canada attempt to modify their health habits through self-help groups. These self-help groups bring together individuals with the same health-habit problem, either in person or on-line and, often with the help of a counsellor, they attempt to solve their problem collectively. Some prominent self-help groups include Overeaters Anonymous for obesity, Alcoholics Anonymous for alcoholics, and Smokenders for smokers. Many of the leaders of these groups employ cognitive-behavioural principles in their programs. The social support and understanding of mutual sufferers are also important factors in producing successful outcomes. At the present time, self-help groups constitute a major venue for health-habit modification in this country. We will examine the self-help group experience further in Chapters 4 and 5.

Schools

Interventions to encourage health behaviours can be implemented through the school system (Public Health Agency of Canada, 2004a; Health Canada, 2002a). A number of factors make schools a desirable venue for health-habit modification. First, most children go to school; therefore, virtually the entire population can be reached, at least in their early years. Second, the school population is young. Consequently, we can intervene before children have developed poor health habits. Chapter 5 provides examples of smoking-prevention programs that are initiated with schoolchildren before they begin smoking. Moreover, when young people are taught good health behaviours early, these behaviours may become habitual and stay with them their whole lives. Third, schools have a natural intervention vehicle—namely, classes of approximately an hour's duration; many health interventions can fit into this format. Finally, certain sanctions can be used in the school environment to promote health behaviours. For example, school systems in three provinces now require that children receive a series of inoculations before they attend school.

For these reasons, then, the schools are often used as a venue for influencing health habits. For example, interventions in elementary schools targeted to increasing exercise and knowledge about proper nutrition have documented improvements in diet and exercise patterns that have especially benefited unfit and obese children (Health Canada, 2002a).

Work-site Interventions

Very young children and the elderly can be reached through the health care system to promote healthy behaviour. Children and adolescents can be contacted through the schools. The bulk of the adult population, however, is often difficult to reach. They do not use medical services regularly, and it is difficult to reach

them through other organizational means. Because a substantial proportion of the adult population is employed, the workplace can be utilized to reach this large percentage of the population (S. G. Haynes, Odenkirchen, & Heimendinger, 1990).

There are at least three ways in which the work site has typically dealt with employees' health habits. The first is the provision of on-the-job health promotion programs that help employees practise better health behaviours. In Canada, most employers offer some form of wellness initiative to help promote the health of their employees, although relatively few are comprehensive (Public Health Agency of Canada, 2000). These programs include smoking cessation, stress management, weight control, physical fitness, nutrition awareness, cardiovascular health and diabetes awareness, CPR and first aid training, and back care (Bachmann, 2002; see Figure 3.7). Often such programs begin with a **health risk assessment** (HRA) to identify employees' specific risks based on current age, family history, and lifestyle factors. These HRAs provide employers with a general view of their employees'

FIGURE 3.7 | Specific Wellness Initiatives Offered in the Workplace

(*Source:* Public Health Agency of Canada, 2000, *National Wellness Survey Report 2000,* reproduced with the permission of the Minister of Public Works and Government Services Canada, 2008, www.phac-aspc.gc.ca/pau-uap/fitness/work/trends_e.html.)

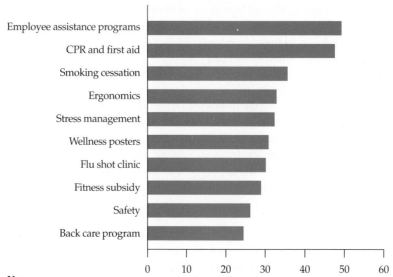

Notes:
- 422 businesses representing 716,885 employees responded to the survey.
- 17.5% of companies are offering comprehensive worksite wellness programs.
- 64% are offering some wellness initiatives.

health and more importantly to help identify specific areas for employees' health behaviour improvement before they undertake wellness interventions. Participation in wellness initiatives may be supplemented by individual health coaching, which can be delivered in person or online.

A second way in which industry has promoted good health habits is by structuring the environment to help people engage in healthy activities. For example, many companies provide health clubs for employee use or restaurant facilities that serve meals that are low in fat, sugar, and cholesterol. Third, some industries provide special incentives, such as reduced insurance premiums for individuals who successfully modify their health habits (e.g., individuals who stop smoking, or lose weight). Health psychologists have also been involved in the creation of general wellness programs designed to address multiple health habits.

In addition to being the main venue through which the adult population can be contacted, the work site has other advantages for intervention. First, large numbers of individuals can be educated simultaneously. Second, the work site can provide sanctions for participating in a program. For example, workers may get time off if they agree to take part. Third, the work site has a built-in social support system of fellow employees who can provide encouragement for the modification of health habits. Finally, because people spend so much of their lives at work, changing the reinforcements and discriminative stimuli in the environment can help maintain good health habits instead of poor ones.

How successful are worksite interventions? A review of 16 worksite health-promotion programs aimed at improving employee diets suggest that they may be moderately successful (Ni Mhurchu, Aston, & Jebb, 2010). However, interventions often reach those with jobs of higher rather than lower occupational prestige (Dobbins, Simpson, Oldenburg, Owen, & Harris, 1998). More efforts need to be made to recruit those in less prestigious occupations and positions. Formal evaluation and high rates of success will be critical in the continuation of such programs as implementing such programs involve the use of valuable resources by the employer. For example, employers cite lack of resources and staffing as the two main reasons why they do not have a comprehensive wellness program (Public Health Agency of Canada, 2000). If corporations can see reductions in absenteeism, insurance costs, accidents, and other indicators that these programs are successful, they will be more likely to continue to support them. Future research should, therefore, include concurrent measures of these more objective indicators of the benefits of worksite health-promotion programs to demonstrate their practical benefits (Ni Mhurchu, Aston, & Jebb, 2010).

Community-based Interventions

Community-based interventions have the potential to reach large numbers of individuals. The term encompasses a variety of specific approaches. A community-based intervention could be a door-to-door campaign informing people of the availability of a breast cancer screening program, a media blitz alerting people to the risks of smoking, a diet-modification program that recruits through community institutions, or a mixed intervention involving both media and interventions directed to high-risk community members.

There are several potential advantages of community-based interventions. First, such interventions reach more people than individually based interventions or interventions in limited environments, such as a single workplace or classroom. Second, community-based interventions can build on social support for reinforcing compliance with recommended health changes. For example, if all your neighbours have agreed to switch to a low-cholesterol diet, you are more likely to do so as well. Third, community-based interventions can potentially address the problem of behaviour-change maintenance by restructuring the community environment to reduce or eliminate cues and reinforcers of risky behaviour and replace them with cues and reinforcements for healthy behaviours.

Several prominent community-based interventions have been developed to reduce risk factors associated with heart disease. For example, the Multiple Risk Factor Intervention Trial (MRFIT) in the USA, the North Karelia project in Finland, and the Canadian Heart Health Initiative (CHHI) were all designed to modify cardiovascular risk factors such as smoking, dietary cholesterol level, and blood pressure through a combination of media interventions and behaviour-change efforts targeted to high-risk groups (see also Alexandrov et al., 1988).

Community interventions have been controversial. Some researchers have argued that these interventions show good success rates. For example, the North Karelia project appears to have produced declines in

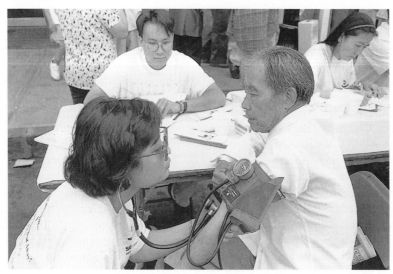

To reach the largest number of people most effectively, researchers are increasingly designing interventions to be implemented on a community basis through existing community resources.

cardiovascular mortality (Tuomilehto et al., 1986), and the MRFIT program brought about reductions in cigarette smoking, reductions in blood pressure, and improvements in dietary knowledge (M. Sexton et al., 1987). Other researchers have argued, however, that these interventions are too expensive for the modest changes they bring about (H. Leventhal et al., 2008). Moreover, behaviour change may not be maintained over time (Klepp, Kelder, & Perry, 1995), and program effectiveness may vary widely depending on whether the community is urban, suburban, or rural. For example, the Quebec Heart Health Demonstration Project, part of the CHHI, targeted three different communities in the Montreal area over a five-year period with an intervention program to change smoking, diet, and physical activity. Although the program was based on several well-established health-education strategies including Bandura's (1986) social learning theory, the theory of planned behaviour, the suburban and urban sites showed dietary improvement while dietary behaviours deteriorated for the rural site (Huot, Paradis, & Ledoux, 2004). Although large-scale and expensive intervention studies that involve individualized behaviour therapy for those at high risk are unlikely to be sustainable in the future on the basis of expense, more modest efforts to integrate healthy lifestyle programs into existing community outreach programs are likely to continue.

The Mass Media

One of the goals of health promotion efforts is to reach as many people as possible, and consequently, the mass media has great potential. Evaluations of the effectiveness of health appeals in the mass media suggest some qualifications regarding their success (Lau, Kane, Berry, Ware, & Roy, 1980). Generally, mass media campaigns bring about modest attitude change but less long-term behaviour change.

The mass media appears to be most effective in alerting people to health risks that they would not otherwise know about (Lau et al., 1980). For example, the media campaign on the health risks of second-hand smoke as illustrated by the story of Heather, a waitress who never smoked but who was dying of lung cancer, alerted thousands of Canadians to the problem of second-hand smoke (Health Canada, 2003), and helped fuel support for the nationwide smoke-free legislation. We will examine Heather's story more closely in Chapter 5.

By presenting a consistent media message over time, the mass media can also have a cumulative effect in changing the values associated with health practices. (See the Health Psychology in Action box, "ParticipAC-TION: Portrait of a Media Campaign to Promote Healthy Living and Physical Fitness.") For example, the cumulative effects of antismoking mass media messages have been substantial, and the climate of public opinion

ParticipACTION: Portrait of a Media Campaign to Promote Healthy Living and Physical Fitness

For more than three decades, ParticipACTION has been associated with healthy living and physical fitness for many Canadians. Originally launched in 1972 as a non-profit government program to encourage Canadians to get fit and practise other healthy living habits, ParticipACTION is perhaps the most well-known health-related media campaign in Canada's history. Although the program is probably best remembered for its television and media ads, the ParticipACTION program involved a number of pioneering initiatives to help raise the fitness levels of Canadians. These included community fitness programs, the first of which started in Saskatoon; joint initiatives with sponsor organizations to build activity trails across 100 communities (1976); information booklets about the growing problems of childhood obesity (1979); and information campaigns to promote employee fitness (1981), to name a few.

In the early years, a variety of television and other media ads were used to make Canadians aware of their poor fitness and inactivity. For example, a 1976 television ad suggesting that a 60-year-old Swede was as fit as the average 30-year-old Canadian provided a provocative and powerful message about the need for Canadians to get fit. For the 1980s, ParticipACTION tackled the issue of getting started becoming physically fit with the popular media message, "Don't Just Think About It—Do It!" in its television, radio, and print media campaigns. In the early 1990s, the Body Break campaign emerged with its hosts Hal Johnson and Joanne McLeod who focused on promoting simple physical activities that anyone could do while at work, on the road, or at home with the message, "Keep fit and have fun." In its final years during the late 1990s, the focus of the ParticipACTION campaigns shifted to prevention of chronic illnesses and other health and social issues through physical activity. These ads were considered particularly influential as they featured real people sharing their stories of the positive impact of physical activity on their lives, modelling the benefits of staying active.

Over the years ParticipACTION was funded by a number of sources including Health Canada, the private sector, provincial/territorial governments, and mass media partners who provided free media exposure of the popular ParticipACTION ads. However, by 1999 funding sources became scarce and ParticipACTION stopped producing new national public service announcement campaign material. Soon after, in 2001, all government funding was cut and the ParticipACTION program was officially closed.

After a six-year absence, ParticipACTION is back. Recognizing the need to deal with Canada's rising obesity levels and declining rates of physical activity, the Canadian government announced in early 2007 that it would provide $5 million to support the renewal of ParticipACTION. The newly revived program was launched October 2007 and includes a new Web site (www.participaction.com) as an interactive community designed to help Canadians "get up and get moving." Through a combination of active living tips, information about community resources, and interactive tools, the new ParticipACTION aims to continue to be the voice of physical activity in Canada. Although the effectiveness of this media campaign to change Canadians' fitness behaviours has not been formally evaluated, the revival of ParticipACTION offers an opportunity for researchers to examine this in the coming years.

Source: The ParticipACTION Archive Project, 2004.

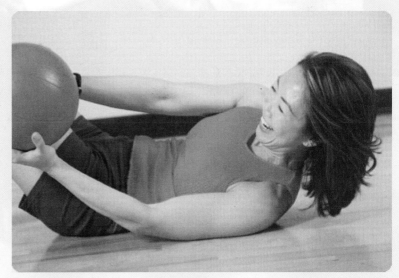

Mass media appeals, such as those featured in the ParticipACTION campaigns, can change the attitudes of the general public toward particular health behaviours, such as exercise.

is now clearly on the side of the non-smoker. In conjunction with other techniques for behaviour change, such as community interventions, the mass media can also reinforce and underscore elements in existing behaviour-change programs.

The Internet

A promising yet underutilized tool for modifying health habits is the Internet. It provides low-cost access to health messages for millions of people who can potentially benefit from the information, suggestions, and techniques offered on Web sites. For example, Health Canada has launched two Internet-based programs to help people quit smoking. "On the Road to Quitting" is a self-help online program designed to help smokers understand their smoking motivations, find the right ways to quit, and use the tools to deal with their cravings and stress as they quit smoking. "Quit 4 Life" is a similar four-step program designed specifically to assist teenage smokers kick the habit. The Internet also enables researchers to recruit a large number of partici-

pants for studies at relatively low cost, thus enabling data collection related to health habits as well (Lenert & Skoczen, 2002).

Conclusions

The choice of venue for health-habit change is an important issue. We need to understand the particular strengths and disadvantages of each venue and continue to seek methods that reach the most people for the least expense possible. By making use of the distinct advantages associated with each venue, we may most successfully modify health habits. Our primary challenge for the future will be to integrate our rapidly accumulating knowledge of how individuals alter their health habits with broader macrolevel policies of federal, and provincial health care agencies to create a truly integrative approach to building healthy lifestyles. The manifold evidence for the effectiveness of interventions is ultimately successful only if it is translated into practice (Glasgow, Klesges, Dzewaltowski, Bull, & Estabrooks, 2004). ●

SUMMARY

 Describe and define health promotion

- Health promotion is the process of enabling people to increase control over and improve their health. It involves the practice of good health behaviours and the avoidance of health-compromising ones. The impetus for health promotion has come from recognizing the impact of lifestyle factors, such as smoking, drinking, and controlling weight, on chronic health disorders.

 Explain why health behaviours are important

- Health habits are determined by socio-economic factors, social factors (such as early socialization in the family), gender, values and cultural background, perceived symptoms, access to medical care, place, and cognitive factors (such as health beliefs). Health habits are only modestly related to each other and are highly unstable over time.

- Health promotion efforts target children and adolescents before bad health habits are in place. They also focus on individuals and groups at risk for particular disorders to prevent those disorders from occurring. An increasing focus on health promotion among the elderly may help contain the soaring costs of health care at the end of life.

 Know the theories and models used for understanding health behaviour change

- Attitudinal approaches to health behaviour change can instill knowledge and motivation. But approaches such as fear appeals and information appeals have had limited effects on behaviour change, and may be most effective when combined with other motivational factors.

- Research using the health belief model, the self-efficacy principle, and the theory of planned behaviour have identified the attitudes most directly related to health-habit modification. These attitudes are the belief that a threat to health is severe, that one is personally vulnerable to the threat, that one is able to perform the response needed to reduce the threat (self-efficacy), that the response will be effective in overcoming the threat (response efficacy), and that social norms support one's practice of the behaviour. Behavioural intentions are also important determinants of behaviour.

- Successful modification of health habits does not occur all at once. Individuals go through stages, which they may cycle through several times: precontemplation, contemplation, preparation, action, and maintenance. When interventions are targeted to the stage an individual is in, they may be more successful.

 Describe how cognitive behavioural approaches are used to change health behaviours

- Cognitive behavioural approaches to health habit change use principles of self-monitoring, classical conditioning, operant conditioning, modelling, and stimulus control to modify the antecedents and consequences of a target behaviour. Cognitive-behaviour therapy brings patients into the treatment process by teaching them principles of self-control and self-reinforcement.

- Social skills training and relaxation training methods are often incorporated into broad-spectrum, or multimodal, cognitive behavioural interventions to deal with the anxiety or social deficits that underlie some health problems.

- Increasingly, interventions focus on relapse prevention, which is the training of clients in methods to avoid the temptation to relapse. Learning coping techniques for high-risk-for-relapse situations is a major component of such interventions.

 Relate how social engineering can change health behaviours

- Some health habits are best changed through social engineering, such as mandated childhood immunizations or banning smoking in the workplace and indoor public places.

 Identify the venues for health-habit modification

- The venues for intervening in health habits are changing. Expensive methods that reach one individual at a time are giving way to group methods that may be cheaper, including self-help groups and school, work-site, and community interventions. The mass media can reinforce health campaigns implemented via other means and can alert people to health risks.

KEY TERMS

abstinence violation effect   p. 75
assertiveness training   p. 73
at risk   p. 52
behavioural assignments   p. 72
broad-spectrum cognitive-
   behaviour therapy   p. 73
classical conditioning   p. 69
cognitive behaviour
   therapy (CBT)   p. 69
cognitive restructuring   p. 72
contingency contracting   p. 72
covert self-control   p. 72
discriminative stimulus   p. 71
expectancy-value theory   p. 63
fear appeals   p. 62
health behaviours   p. 53

health belief model   p. 63
health habit   p. 53
health locus of control   p. 54
health promotion   p. 52
health risk assessment   p. 80
implementation intentions   p. 66
lifestyle rebalancing   p. 77
modelling   p. 70
operant conditioning   p. 70
primary prevention   p. 53
prospect theory   p. 62
relapse prevention   p. 76
relaxation training   p. 73
self-control   p. 71
self-efficacy   p. 64
self-monitoring   p. 69

self-observation   p. 69
self-reinforcement   p. 71
self-talk   p. 72
social engineering   p. 77
socialization   p. 56
social cognition models   p. 62
social skills training   p. 73
stimulus-control
   interventions   p. 71
teachable moment   p. 56
theory of planned
   behaviour   p. 64
transtheoretical model of behaviour
   change   p. 67
window of vulnerability   p. 57

CHAPTER
4

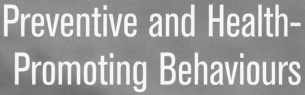

Preventive and Health-Promoting Behaviours

After reading this chapter, students will be able to:

(LO1) Identify preventable injuries

(LO2) Describe cancer-related health behaviours

(LO3) Understand how exercise enhances health

(LO4) Explain why maintaining a healthy diet is important

(LO5) Know how weight control is related to health

(LO6) Describe how sleep is related to health

(LO7) Explain why rest, renewal, and savouring are important for health

Every New Year's morning, Chitra sat down and took stock of what she wanted to accomplish during the next year. This year's list was like many other New Years' lists. It began with "lose five pounds" and included "get exercise every day" and "eat better (cut out junk food and soda)." After making the list, Chitra promptly went out running and returned 45 minutes later with a plan to consume a healthy lunch of steamed vegetables.

The phone rang. It was a friend inviting her to a last-minute New Year's Day brunch. The brunch sounded like a lot more fun than what Chitra had in mind, so off she went. Several hours later, after eggs Benedict and an afternoon of televised football games, soda, and potato chips, Chitra had already broken her New Year's resolve.

Chitra is very much like most of us. We know what we should do to preserve and maintain our health, and we want very much to do it. Given a moment of private reflection, most of us would make decisions similar to Chitra's. In fact, surveys show that the most common New Year's resolutions, in addition to saving money, are losing weight and getting exercise. Although most of us manage to pursue our New Year's resolutions longer than the few hours that Chitra lasted, rarely do we get more than a few weeks into the year before we lapse back to our more sedentary, less healthy lifestyle. Yet these health habits are important, and changing or maintaining our behaviour in the direction of good health habits should be a high priority for all of us.

Chapter 4 employs the attitudinal and behavioural principles identified in Chapter 3 and examines how they apply to several preventive and self-enhancing behaviours such as accident prevention, cancer prevention, exercise, weight control, and eating a healthy diet. Although the focus of these behaviours is preventing disease and injury and promoting health, we will also discuss the subsequent problems that may arise when these behaviours are not practised to underscore their importance. These behaviours are important because each has been systematically related to at least one major cause of illness, disability, and death in industrialized countries. As people in less-developed countries adopt the lifestyle of people in industrialized nations, these health habits will assume increasing importance throughout the world.

(L01) **WHAT ARE PREVENTABLE INJURIES?**

> No wonder that so many cars collide;
> Their drivers are accident prone,
> When one hand is holding a coffee cup,
> And the other a cellular phone.
>
> —Art Buck

Despite the jocular nature of this bit of doggerel, it captures an important point. Unintentional injuries represent one of the major causes of preventable death in this country. Worldwide, 1.2 million people died as a result of road-traffic injuries, and the estimated economic cost of unintentional injuries is $518 billion per year (World Health Organization, 2007). Of particular concern are traffic accidents, which represent one of the largest causes of death among children, adolescents, and young adults.

Several million people are injured each year in Canada, and falls are the leading cause of serious injury (Wilkins & Park, 2004). Bicycle accidents were responsible for more than 4,300 hospitalizations between 2009 and 2010, and constitute the major cause of head injury, thereby making helmet use an important issue (Canadian Institute for Health Information, 2011a). Indeed, over a four-year period, child and youth head injury rates were 25 percent lower in provinces with bicycle helmet legislation compared to provinces without such legislation (Macpherson et al., 2002). However, to date, six provinces have introduced legislation for mandatory bicycle helmet use, but only four of these provinces have legislation that applies to all ages (Safe Kids Canada, 2010). Not surprisingly, rates of helmet use are highest in all but one of the provinces that has helmet legislation (Statistics Canada, 2010).

Preventable injuries at work and their resulting impact on disability are a particular health risk for working men. Consequently, strategies to reduce unintentional injuries have increasingly been a focus of health psychology research and interventions.

Home and Workplace Unintentional Injuries

Unintentional injuries in the home, such as accidental poisonings and falls, are the most common causes of death and disability among children under age 5. Interventions to reduce preventable injuries at home are typically conducted with parents because they have control over the child's environment. Parents are most likely to undertake injury prevention activities if they believe that the recommended steps really will avoid injuries, if they feel knowledgeable and competent to teach safety skills to their children, and if they have a realistic sense of how much time will actually be involved in doing so (L. Peterson, Farmer, & Kashani, 1990).

Providing education and resources about how to keep the home safe is key to preventing accidents in the home. For example, family physicians can incorporate such training into their interactions with new parents, and parenting classes can be used to teach parents to identify the most common poisons in their household

FIGURE 4.1 | Injury-Related Deaths in Canada, 1980–1997

(*Source:* Health Canada, 1999, *Injury in Canada: Statistics and trends,* Ottawa, ON: Health Canada, reproduced with the permission of the Minister of Public Works and Government Services Canada, 2008, www.injurypreventionsstrategy.ca/downloads/HC_stat.pdf.)

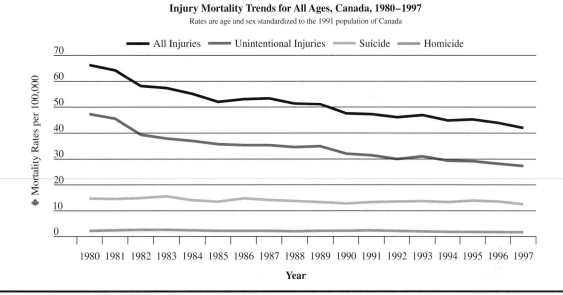

Injury Mortality Trends for All Ages, Canada, 1980–1997

Rates are age and sex standardized to the 1991 population of Canada

and how to keep these safeguarded or out of reach of young children. A study evaluating training on how to childproof a home suggested that such interventions can be successful (J. R. Matthews, Friman, Barone, Ross, & Christophersen, 1987). In addition, home safety information and resources are now readily available on the Internet through the Public Health Agency of Canada Web site. Parents can learn ways of keeping their home and children safe and can find a wealth of information on topics ranging from the dangers of poisons and baby walkers, to balloon injuries and unsafe toys.

Statistics suggest that, overall, deaths due to unintentional injuries in the home and in the workplace have declined (see Figure 4.1). This decline may be due, in part, to better safety precautions by employers in the workplace and by parents in the home. Social engineering solutions, such as safety caps on medications and strict guidelines for occupational safety, have added to the decline. Home and workplace preventable injuries, then, represent a domain in which interventions have been fairly successful in reducing mortality.

Motorcycle and Automobile Unintentional Injuries

You know what I call a motorcyclist who doesn't wear a helmet? An organ donor.

—EMERGENCY ROOM PHYSICIAN

The single greatest cause of death from unintentional injury is motorcycle and automobile accidents (Statistics Canada, 2004a). To date, little psychological research has gone into helping people avoid vehicular traffic accidents. Instead, efforts have concentrated on such factors as the maintenance of roadways, the volume of travel, and safety standards in automobiles. However, psychological research can address factors associated with

Automobile accidents represent a major cause of death, especially among the young. Legislation requiring child safety restraint devices has reduced fatalities dramatically.

Distracted to Death?

Although it is well known that impaired driving increases risk for vehicular accidents and fatalities, we usually associate impairment with alcohol consumption. But there is increasing evidence that using common technological devices such as cell phones and PDAs while driving can be just as impairing and dangerous. Although conversations on the phone while driving may be viewed as not much different from those with passengers, research says otherwise. One study comparing performance during a driving simulation with no conversation, conversation with a passenger, and conversation on a cell phone found that cell phone conversations were more distracting and consumed more attention resources than conversations with passengers (Hunton & Rose, 2005). Estimates from a national survey suggest that 5.9 percent of urban drivers use a handheld cell phone while driving, with rates highest in Ontario (7.4 percent) and Alberta (11.7 percent), and lowest in Nova Scotia (2.2 percent) (Transport Canada, 2008).

Despite what many people believe, hands-free is not risk free. A review conducted by researchers from Dalhousie University suggests that talking on the phone while driving, whether it is a cell phone or a hands-free phone, negatively impacts driving performance (Ishigami & Klein, 2009). Detecting and identifying events were particularly compromised, and drivers compensated for the effects of cell phone use but not hands-free phones despite the fact that performance deficits for each were roughly the same.

So why do people continue to use cell phones even though the risk is known? One study of university students suggests that positive illusions and high illusory control may partly explain why. After predicting their driving performance with and without a cell phone, students completed a driving simulation task (Schlehofer, Thompson, Ting, Ostreman, Nierman, & Skenderian, 2010). Cell phone use negatively impacted driving performance, and perceiving oneself as being able to compensate for driving distractions and overestimating driving simulator performance while using the cell phone predicted greater cell phone use while driving.

Joining more than 50 countries worldwide, most provinces in Canada have distracted driving legislation in place that bans talking, texting, typing, or dialling while driving, with legislation to take effect in fall 2010 in Manitoba. However, at the time of this writing, Alberta and the Yukon have yet to finalize legislation banning the use of handheld electronic devices while driving.

---

accidents, including driving distractions (see the Focus on Social Issues box, "Distracted to Death?"), the way people drive, the speed at which they drive, and the use of preventive measures to increase safety.

It is clear that safety measures such as reducing highway driving speeds, requiring seat belts, and placing young children in safety restraint seats have reduced the number of severe injuries and vehicular fatalities (Canada Safety Council, 2004). Making themselves visible through reflective or fluorescent clothing and the use of helmets among bicycle and motorcycle riders has reduced the severity of accidents by a substantial degree, especially preventing serious head injury (Canada Safety Council, 2004; Wells et al., 2004).

However, getting people to follow these safety measures is difficult. Although the rate of seat belt use in Canada is generally high, younger drivers tend to wear seat belts less (Transport Canada, 2004). To promote the use of seat belts, a combination of social engineering, health education, and psychological intervention may be most appropriate. For example, Transport Canada now requires that infants and toddlers up to age 3 or 4 or about 18 kilograms (40 lbs.), be restrained in safety seats. Guidelines for the use of booster seats vary slightly across the provinces and territories (8–10 years old, 36–45kg), although most recommend that children are at least the recommended height of 145cm (or 4 feet, 9 inches) for wearing seat belts alone before they can ride in a car without a booster seat (Safe Kids Canada, 2008).

Interventions to increase seat belt use have involved social influence and social engineering principles. For example, a study in Norway found that signs reminding drivers of "seat belt enforcement" were somewhat effective in increasing driver's intentions to wear seat belts (Høye & Vaa, 2010). Whether this simple approach actually translates into increased seat belt use behaviour is however, difficult to assess. On the whole, however, social engineering solutions may be more effective— specifically, penalizing people for not using seat belts. Enforcement of penalties is also essential, as decreases in seat belt use are known to correspond with decreases in enforcement of fines for nonuse (Canadian Council of Motor Transport Administrators, 2001).

(L02) WHAT ARE CANCER-RELATED HEALTH BEHAVIOURS?

Cancer continues to be a major cause of death in Canada, and it is estimated that approximately one out of four Canadians will die from cancer (Canadian Cancer Society/National Cancer Institute of Canada, 2007). Promoting the practice of cancer-related health behaviours, such as screening and other preventative behaviours, is therefore essential to help reduce the future incidence of cancer and loss of life to this disease. Chapter 14 covers cancer and its consequences more fully. Here, we focus on understanding the individual and social factors that either deter or promote the practice of these important behaviours and the role of health behaviour change theory for designing interventions and public health programs to promote cancer protective behaviours.

Breast Cancer Screening

Although breast cancer is the most common cancer in women in Canada and worldwide, recent figures indicate that the death rate from breast cancer in Canada has dropped 25 percent since the time that breast screening programs were initiated across Canada in 1986 (Canadian Cancer Society/National Cancer Institute of Canada, 2007). Still, breast cancer remains one of the leading causes of cancer deaths among Canadian women and the most common cause of cancer death in women under 50 (Canadian Cancer Society/National Cancer Institute of Canada, 2007), striking one out of every nine women at some point during her life (Public Health Agency of Canada, 2007a).

The Canadian Cancer Society (2008b) recommends different screening activities for women in different age and risk groups. It is recommended that women ages 40 to 49 receive a clinical breast exam performed by a trained health professional at least once every two years, whereas women ages 50 to 69 should have a mammogram every two years in addition to the clinical breast exam. Although breast self exams (BSE) were once commonly used for screening, current evidence suggesting that the BSE is not an effective method of screening has led the World Health Organization (2008a) to recommend that national cancer screening programs should not recommend BSE as a screening activity, and instead indicate that the clinical breast exam and mammogram are the most effective screening activities.

Mammograms are an important way of detecting breast cancer in women over 50. Finding ways to reach older women to ensure that they obtain mammograms is a high priority for health scientists.

Clinical Breast Exam

A **clinical breast exam (CBE)** involves a thorough physical examination of the breast by a health care professional, such as a family physician, to detect changes or abnormalities that could indicate the early signs of breast cancer. If any problems are found, a referral for further tests such as mammography or a breast ultrasound may be required.

Like the mammogram and other cancer screening tests, educating women about the importance of having a regular CBE can be difficult and often depends on beliefs about vulnerability, perceived barriers, and self-efficacy for getting the screening. Such beliefs and misperceptions about the CBE and breast cancer may be especially problematic when cultural barriers are involved. To address these issues, a team of researchers from the Women's Health Program at the University of Toronto developed and tested a socio-culturally tailored intervention to improve health beliefs, knowledge, and the practice of CBE among South Asian immigrant women (Ahmad, Cameron, & Stewart, 2005). Applying the principles of the health belief model (Chapter 3), a series of articles were published in Hindi and Urdu community newspapers, and featured information about the benefits of screening, encouragement to discuss breast health concerns with family members and health care providers to increase efficacy, and details about the procedure to help dispel any fears and misperceptions. The benefits of screening were also framed in a culturally sensitive manner by highlighting how the screening would improve the quality of family life in addition to the quality of the woman's life. The series of 10 articles were mailed to participants over a five-month period, and follow-up interviews were conducted to evaluate the effects on CBE knowledge, beliefs, and practice. Consistent with the prediction of the health belief model, misperceptions about vulnerability and perceived barriers to CBE decreased, and CBE self-efficacy and uptake of CBE increased after the socio-culturally tailored intervention. The change in perceived barriers to CBE was also the most significant predictor of getting a CBE. In addition to providing promising support for an intervention to increase cancer screening behaviour, this study suggests that it may be possible to tailor Western theoretical models of behaviour change to address health behaviour change issues among non-Western immigrant populations.

Mammograms

The recent decrease in breast cancer mortality has been linked in part to better screening. Although the number of women who are screened is increasing in Canada, many women still do not get screened. Results from the 2008 Canadian Community Health Survey (CCHS) indicate that mammography rates among women 50 to 69 have reached 72 percent, up from only 40 percent in 1990 (Shields & Wilkins, 2009). Nonetheless, there are certain segments of the population that are not participating in mammography screening

Why is screening through mammography so important for older and high-risk women? The reasons are several:

1. The prevalence of breast cancer in this country remains high, with approximately 22,000 Canadian women being diagnosed each year.

2. The majority of breast cancers continue to be detected in women over age 40, so screening this age group is cost effective. However, mammography is usually only warranted in women under 50 if recommended by a nurse or doctor as the benefits of mammography for this age group remain unclear.

3. Most important, early detection, as through mammograms, can improve survival rates.

Getting Women to Obtain Mammograms   Unfortunately, compliance with mammography recommendations is low among certain groups. For example, there remain significant gaps in participation between women in the highest and lowest income groups and these gaps have increased since 2001. Women who are immigrants, who smoke, and who do not have a regular family doctor are less likely to get screened (Shields & Wilkins, 2009). Although rates of time-appropriate mammography were highest in British Columbia previously (Maxwell, Bancej, & Snider, 2001), in 2008, non-use was highest in British Columbia, Prince Edward Island, and Nunavut (Shields & Wilkins, 2009). Increases in the immigrant population in British Columbia may be one reason for the shift in rates. Fear of radiation, embarrassment over the procedure, anticipated pain, anxiety, fear of cancer (Gurevich et al., 2004; M. D. Schwartz, Taylor, & Willard, 2003), and, most important, perception of need, act as deterrents to getting regular mammograms (Maxwell, Bancej, & Snider, 2001; Shields & Wilkins, 2009). Lack of awareness, time, incentive, and availability are also important.

Consequently, research has focused on how to increase women's use of mammographic services. One study found that repeat mammography use among women aged 50 and over increased substantially with an intervention that included the mailing of a "mammogram due soon" postcard and two follow-up automated phone calls (Feldstein et al., 2009). Counselling and mailed materials promoting mammography are also effective at increasing the use of this important screening procedure (Champion et al., 2002).

However, it may be necessary to tailor this material to women's readiness to adopt mammography as part of their regular preventive health behaviours. Using longitudinal data from the Canadian National Population Health Survey, researchers applied Prochaska's transtheoretical model of behaviour change (see Chapter 3) to predict mammogram use (Maxwell, Onysko, Bancej, Nichol, & Rakowski, 2006). Using responses to questions about intentions to get a mammogram and previous history of using mammography, researchers established the women's stage of change to examine if it predicted getting a mammogram at the two-year follow-up. Consistent with the stages of change model, women in precontemplation, relapse, contemplation, and action stages were significantly less likely to report a recent mammogram during follow-up compared to those in the maintenance stage. These findings support the suggestions of other researchers that interventions for increasing mammography behaviour may be more successful if they are geared to the stage of readiness of prospective participants (Champion et al., 2003; Lauver, Henriques, Settersten, & Bumann, 2003).

Changing attitudes toward mammography may increase the likelihood of obtaining a mammogram. In particular, the health belief model, especially the attitudes of perceiving benefits of mammograms and encountering few barriers to obtaining one, has been associated with a greater likelihood of obtaining a mammogram (Champion & Springston, 1999; McCaul, Branstetter, Schroeder, & Glasgow, 1996). However, educational programs designed to raise awareness of the need for mammography also need to be culturally sensitive, and consider the cultural beliefs, attitudes and practices of certain minority groups, such as Aboriginal women and South Asian immigrants, who are less likely to have regular cancer screening (Gupta, Kumar, & Stewart, 2002; Steven et al., 2004).

The theory of planned behaviour has also been used as a framework to predict the likelihood of obtaining regular mammograms: Although perceived behaviour control may be most important for predicting mammography use (Tolma, Reininger, Evans, & Ureda, 2006), the addition of other factors such as optimism and risk perception may also enhance the effectiveness of this model for explaining mammography use (Griva, Anagnostopoulos, & Madoglou, 2009). Social support also predicts getting a mammogram and may be especially important for low-income and older women (Messina et al., 2004).

But interventions with women alone will not substantially alter rates of participation in mammography screening programs if the health care system is not also changed. Mammograms have not been well integrated into standard care for older women. Instead of receiving all necessary diagnostic tests and checkups from one physician, as adult men do, many older women must make multiple appointments, such as with their general practitioner and with a mammography centre. Minority women and older women, and those living in rural areas, especially fall through the cracks, because often they do not have a regular source of health care (Maxwell, Bancej, & Snider, 2001; Shields & Wilkins, 2009). Indeed, a meta-analysis of mammography screening behaviour among ethnic minority women over 50 found lower mammography rates compared to non-minority women, with evidence suggesting that socio-economic status played a role (Purc-Stephenson & Gorey, 2008). Interventions need to be directed to health professionals to ensure that physicians routinely refer their older and minority women patients to mammography centres, and health care delivery services need to be established so that mammography is more accessible to older and rural-dwelling women, as well as women from ethnic-minority groups (Maxwell, Bancej, & Snider, 2001; Purc-Stephenson & Gorey, 2008).

Prostate Cancer Screening

In Canada, prostate cancer is the most common cancer among men, with one in eight men likely to develop prostate cancer during their lifetime (Canadian Cancer Society/National Cancer Institute of Canada, 2007). Risk for prostate cancer increases with age, and men over 50 are encouraged to discuss screening options with their family doctor. Although there are two recommended screening tests for early detection of prostate cancer, there is some controversy over their effectiveness. The digital rectal exam (DRE) is the most common screening method, and the prostate specific antigen test (PSE) involves a blood test to screen for prostate problems. However, both are susceptible to false positives, detecting cancer that is not present, and false negatives, missing cancer that is present. As such, recommendations for screening depend on the presence of risk factors such as age, family history, and African ethnicity (Canadian Cancer Society, 2008c).

Colorectal Cancer Screening

In Western countries, colorectal cancer is the second highest cause of cancerous deaths, and in Canada it is the fourth most common cancer for men and women. In addition, colorectal cancer is increasing at higher rates among Canada's Aboriginal population than among the general public, and may surpass the levels found among non-aboriginal Canadians if preventive measures are not taken (Canadian Cancer Society, 2008d). In recent years, medical guidelines have increasingly recommended routine colorectal screening for older adults (Wardle, Williamson, McCaffery, et al., 2003). Colorectal screening is distinctive for the fact that people often learn that they have polyps (a benign condition that can increase risk for colorectal cancer) but not detected malignancies. The Canadian Cancer Society (2008d) recommends screening for colorectal cancer with a fecal occult blood test at least once every two years for men and women over 50 with normal risk, and more frequently for those at high risk.

Factors that predict the practice of other cancer-related health behaviours also predict participation in colorectal cancer screening, specifically self-efficacy, perceived benefits of the procedure, a physician's recommendation to participate, and low perceived barriers to taking advantage of the screening program (Hays et al., 2003). Community-based programs that employ such strategies as mass media, community-based education, use of social networks, interventions through churches, health care provider recommendations, and reminder notices promote participation in cancer screening programs, including colorectal cancer, and indicate that community-based interventions can attract older populations to engage in appropriate screening behaviours (M. K. Campbell et al., 2004; Curbow et al., 2004). An intervention aimed at a hard-to-reach group of older adults that provided reassuring information regarding colorectal screening was effective in modifying initially negative attitudes and increasing rates of screening attendance (Wardle, Williamson, McCaffery, et al., 2003).

Sun Safety Practices

Each year in Canada there are more than 69,000 new cases of skin cancer diagnosed, and the rates have been rising steadily since 1992. Although common basal cell and squamous cell carcinomas do not typically kill, malignant melanoma takes nearly 900 lives each year in Canada (Health Canada, 2006b). Moreover, these cancers are among the most preventable cancers we have. The chief risk factor for skin cancer is well known: excessive exposure to ultraviolet radiation. Living or vacationing in southern latitudes, participating in outdoor activities, and using tanning salons all contribute to dangerous sun exposure (J. L. Jones & Leary, 1994). Women are more likely than men to practise

sun protective behaviours, although about half of Canadian adults report being sunburned each year, and 45 percent of children have been sunburned at least once. Sun safety behaviours do increase with age, but rates of sun exposure and lack of sun protective practices are lowest among those ages 15 to 24 (Canadian Cancer Society, 2005). As a result, health psychologists have increased their efforts to promote safe sun practices. Typically, these efforts have included educational interventions designed to alert people to the risks of skin cancer and to the effectiveness of sunscreen use for reducing risk (for example, Abar et al., 2010). There is some debate as to whether individualized or generic materials are more effective for changing sun safety behaviours. At least one study suggests that both are equally effective with generic materials having the advantage of reaching a greater number of people (E. Lewis et al., 2005).

Despite the risks of exposure to the sun, millions of people each year continue to sunbathe.

Problems with getting people to engage in safe sun practices stem from the fact that tans are perceived to be attractive. Young adults who are especially concerned with their physical appearance and who believe that tanning enhances their attractiveness are most likely to expose themselves to ultraviolet radiation through tanning (Jackson & Aiken, 2000). Even people who are persuaded of the importance of safe sun habits often practise them incompletely. Many of us use an inadequate sun protection factor (SPF), and few of us apply sunscreen as often as we should during outdoor activities (Wichstrom, 1994). Nonetheless, the type of skin one has—burn only, burn then tan, or tan without burning—is the strongest influence on likelihood of using sun protection (Clarke, Williams, & Arthey, 1997), suggesting that people are beginning to develop some understanding of their risk.

Effective sunscreen use is influenced by a number of factors, including perceived need for sunscreen, perceived efficacy of sunscreen as protection against skin cancer, and social norms regarding sunscreen use and attitudes towards the appearance related benefits of tanning, among other factors (Hillhouse, Turrisi, Stapleton, & Robinson, 2008; Jackson & Aiken, 2000). Consistent with the tenets of the health belief model, increasing perceived self-efficacy and reducing perceived barriers have been found to be important for encouraging sun safe behaviours (K. D. Reynolds, Buller, Yaroch, Maloy, & Cutler, 2006). Health communications that enhance these perceptions may be helpful in increasing the practice (Abar et al., 2010; Hillhouse et al., 2008).

Communications to adolescents and young adults that stress the gains that sunscreen use will bring them, such as freedom from concern about skin cancers, appear to be more successful than those that emphasize the risks (Detweiler, Bedell, Salovey, Pronin, & Rothman, 1999; Jackson & Aiken, 2006). When the risks are emphasized, it is important to stress the immediate adverse effects of poor health habits rather than the long-term risks of chronic illness, since adolescents and young adults are especially influenced by immediate concerns. In one clever investigation, beachgoers were given a photo-aging intervention that showed premature wrinkling and age spots; a second group received a novel ultraviolet photo intervention that made negative consequences of UV exposure very salient; a third group received both interventions; and a fourth group was assigned to a control condition. Those beachgoers who received the UV photo information engaged in more

protective behaviours for incidental sun exposure, and the combination of the UV photo with the photo-aging information led to substantially less sunbathing over the long term (Mahler, Kulik, Gibbons, Gerrard, & Harrell, 2003; Mahler, Kulik, Gerrard, & Gibbons, 2007). Similar interventions may be effective in reducing the use of tanning salons (Gibbons, Gerrard, Lane, Mahler, & Kulik 2005). Communications drawing on the stages of change model, which aim to move the tanning public from a precontemplation to a contemplation stage and subsequently to implementation of sun protective behaviours, may also be successful (Pagoto, McChargue, & Fuqua, 2003).

Social engineering solutions to the sun exposure problem may be needed as well. Few schools have sun protection policies that encourage children and teens to use sunscreen. However, programs such as Health Canada's Children's UV Index Sun Awareness Program encourage high school and elementary school teachers to register their schools and make use of available resources, educate students on sun safe practices, and initiate their own sun savvy policies for their school. Although this program is voluntary, it offers the potential of intervening in the school to address this important health issue.

In addition to behaviours that prevent injury and disease, behaviours that promote health such as regular exercise, healthy eating, and adequate sleep are an equally important part of a healthy lifestyle. We now turn our discussion to these issues.

HOW DOES EXERCISE ENHANCE HEALTH?   (L03)

In recent years, health psychologists have examined the role of aerobic exercise in maintaining mental and physical health. **Aerobic exercise** is sustained exercise that stimulates and strengthens the heart and lungs, improving the body's utilization of oxygen. All aerobic exercise is marked by its high intensity, long duration, and requisite high endurance. Among the forms of exercise that meet these criteria are jogging, bicycling, rope jumping, running, and swimming. Other forms of exercise—such as isokinetic exercises (weightlifting, for example) or high-intensity, short-duration, low-endurance exercises (such as sprinting)—may be satisfying and build up specific parts of the body but have less effect on overall fitness because they draw on short-term stores of glycogen rather than on the long-term energy conversion system associated with aerobics.

TABLE 4.1 | Health Benefits of Regular Exercise

- Increases maximum oxygen consumption.
- Decreases resting heart rate.
- Decreases blood pressure (in some).
- Increases strength and efficiency of heart (pumps more blood per beat).
- Decreases use of energy sources, such as glutamine.
- Increases slow wave sleep.
- Increases HDL, unchanged total cholesterol.
- Decreases cardiovascular disease.
- Decreases obesity.
- Increases longevity.
- Decreases menstrual cycle length, decreases estrogen and progesterone.
- Decreases risk of some cancers.
- Increases immune system functions.
- Decreases negative mood.
- Improves cognitive functioning

Benefits of Exercise

The health benefits of aerobic exercise are substantial (see Table 4.1). Regular exercise can decrease the risk of chronic disease including heart disease and some cancers including breast cancer. Exercise, coupled with dietary change, can cut the risk of Type II diabetes in high-risk adults significantly. However, only 49 percent of Canadians are at least moderately active during their leisure time (Canadian Fitness and Lifestyle Research Institute, 2004). Moreover, results from the Canadian Health Measures Survey suggest that fitness levels among Canadian adults and children have declined significantly between 1981 and 2007–9 (Shields, Tremblay, Laviolette, Craig, Janssen, & Gorber, 2010; Tremblay, Shields, Laviolette, Craig, Janssen, & Gorber, 2010). Exercise also accelerates wound healing (Emery, Kiecolt-Glaser, Glaser, Malarkey, & Frid, 2005). Physical inactivity is more common among women than men, among older than younger adults, among those with lower versus higher incomes and education levels (Canadian Fitness and Lifestyle Research Institute, 2004), and among Aboriginal versus non-Aboriginal Canadians (Public Health Agency of Canada, 2003c).

Perhaps more surprising is the fact that health practitioners do not uniformly recommend physical exercise, even to their patients who could especially benefit from it, such as their elderly patients (Leveille et al., 1998); yet studies show that a physician's recommendation is an effective way to get people to increase their exercise (Ortega-Sanchez et al., 2004).

Aerobic exercise has been tied to increases in cardiovascular fitness and endurance and to reduced risk for heart attack (Alderman, Arent, Landers, & Rogers, 2007). Exercise is considered to be the most important health habit for the elderly, and cardiovascular benefits of exercise have been found even for preschoolers (B. Alpert et al., 1990). Other health benefits of exercise include increased efficiency of the cardiorespiratory system, improved physical work capacity, the optimization of body weight, the improvement or maintenance of muscle tone and strength, an increase in soft tissue and joint flexibility, the reduction or control of hypertension, improved cholesterol level, improved glucose tolerance, improved tolerance of stress, and reduction in poor health habits, including cigarette smoking, alcohol consumption, and poor diet (Warburton, Nicol, & Bredin, 2006). Strenuous exercise in adolescents and moderate exercise in postmenopausal women may even reduce the risk of breast cancer (Suzuki et al., 2010; Suzuki et al., 2011).

The effects of exercise translate directly into increased longevity. Even a single weekly exercise session of moderate to high intensity can reduce all-cause and cardiovascular mortality in both women and men (Moholdt, Wisløff, Nilsen, & Slørdahl, 2008).

Regular exercise can also have cognitive benefits, which may be especially important for older adults. A review of studies examining the effects of exercise on cognitive functioning found that engaging in moderate levels of aerobic exercise for as little as six months can significantly improve cognitive functioning in adults aged 60 to 75 (Erickson & Kramer, 2009). However, the effects of exercise on cognitive functioning and performance are not isolated to older adults. Another review examining the effects on people of different ages suggests that regular cardiovascular exercise can improve academic performance and cognitive functioning for children, and adults as well (Hillman, Erickson, & Kramer, 2008).

How Much Exercise?   The typical exercise prescription for a normal adult is to accumulate 60 minutes of physical activity every day to stay healthy, and 30 minutes of moderate-intensity activity four days a week (Public Health Agency of Canada, 2003c). However, recent revisions to these recommendations have been made to better harmonize Canadian recommendations with those of other countries such as Australia, the United Kingdom, and the United States. The new recommendations are that adults should strive to engage in at least 150 minutes per week of moderate-to-vigorous physical activity, which can be accumulated in bouts lasting at least 10 minutes each (Colley et al., 2011). For example, exercising 5 days per week for 30 minutes would satisfy this new recommendation. Recent findings indicate that only 15.4 percent of Canadians achieve the recommended 150 minutes per week, suggesting that educational interventions may be necessary to improve awareness about how much exercise is enough (Colley et al., 2011).

A person with low cardiopulmonary fitness may derive benefits with even less exercise each week. Even short walks, often recommended for older individuals or those with some infirmities, may have benefits for both physical and psychological health (Schectman & Ory, 2001; Ekkekakis, Hall, VanLanduyt & Petruzzello, 2000). Lifestyle interventions designed to increase activity levels more generally may eventually lead to a commitment to exercise as well (Heesch, Mâsse, Dunn, Frankowski & Mullen, 2003). Because it is difficult to get sedentary adults committed to a full-fledged exercise program, a lifestyle intervention aimed at increasing physical activity may represent a good start for aging sedentary adults (Conn, Valentin, & Cooper, 2002) and for the obese (Levine et al., 2005).

Effects on Psychological Health   Researchers have examined the effect of aerobic exercise on psychological states, such as mood, anxiety, depression, and tension, and have found a beneficial role of exercise on both mental and physical health. Regular exercise improves mood and feelings of well-being immediately after a workout; there may also be some improvement in general mood and well-being as a result of long-term participation in an exercise program (Motl, Konopack et al., 2005). But how much exercise is needed to improve psychological well-being? One study on the effects of exercise duration on mood state noted mood improvements after just 10 minutes of exercise building up to 20 minutes, but no additional improvements over longer duration (Hansen, Stevens, & Coast, 2001). However, another study found that even a single 30-minute bout of moderate intensity exercise had beneficial effects on the mood of people with Major Depressive Disorder (Bartholomew, Morrison, & Ciccolo, 2005). Thus, even acute exercise may provide beneficial psychological effects.

At least some of the positive effects of exercise on mood may stem from factors associated with exercise, such as social activity and a feeling of involvement with others. For example, the group cohesion and social sup-

Regular aerobic exercise produces many physical and emotional benefits, including reduced risk for cardiovascular disease.

port arising from shared exercise classes can increase both positive mood and self-efficacy to exercise (U. Christensen et al., 2006). The increased self-efficacy associated with social support during exercise also increases the likelihood that people will maintain their exercise programs (Resnick, Orwig, Magaziner, & Wynne, 2002).

An improved sense of self-efficacy can also underlie some of the mood effects of exercise (Annesi, 2009; McAuley, Jerome, Marquez, Elavasky, & Blissmer, 2003). In one study researchers recruited participants for an exercise group and manipulated the experience of self-efficacy during the program by providing contrived feedback to the participants about how well or poorly they were doing. Results indicated that, compared with a control group, people in the efficacy condition had significantly higher levels of perceived self-efficacy, and these perceptions were associated with improvements in mood and psychological well-being (Motl, Dishman et al., 2005; Rhodes & Plotnikoff, 2006).

Because of its beneficial effects on mood and self-esteem (Annesi, 2009) exercise has been used as a treatment for depression (Herman et al., 2002) and for symptoms of stress, anxiety, and depression associated with menopause (Nelsom et al., 2008). One study assigned depressed women to an exercise condition, a drug treatment session, or a combined treatment. The exercise group improved their mood significantly and as much as those who received only the drug or the combined treatment. More important, once treatment was discontinued, those who continued to exercise were less likely to become depressed again when compared with those who had been on the drug treatment (Babyak et al., 2000). Thus, an increase in symptoms of depression is one of the risks of stopping exercise (Berlin, Kop, & Deuster, 2006).

The impact of exercise on well-being should not be overstated, however. The effects are often small, and the expectation that exercise has positive effects on mood may be one reason that people so widely report the experience. Despite these cautions, the positive effect of exercise on well-being is now quite well established.

Determinants of Regular Exercise

Although the health benefits of exercise are well established, most people's participation in exercise programs is erratic. Many children get regular exercise through required physical education classes in school. However, by adolescence, the practice of regular exercise has declined substantially, especially among girls and among boys not involved in formal athletics (Crosnoe, 2002). Smoking, being overweight, and teen pregnancy also account for some of the decline in physical activity (Kimm et al., 2002). Adults cite lack of time and other stressors in their lives as factors that undermine their good intentions (R. S. Myers & Roth, 1997). As humorist Erma Bombeck noted, "The only reason I would take up jogging is so that I could hear heavy breathing again."

Many people seem to share this attitude toward exercise. Participation levels for exercise programs tends to vary with the type of exercise engaged in as well as individual factors such as the level and location of current pain among people with chronic pain conditions (Dobkin et al., 2006), and whether exercise is engaged in for its own sake or for achieving a specific outcome (Wilson & Brookfield, 2009). People may begin an exercise program but find it difficult to make exercise a regular activity. Paradoxically, although exercise seems to be a stress buster, stress itself is one of the most common reasons that people fail to adhere to their exercise regimens (Stetson, Rahn, Dubbert, Wilner, & Mercury, 1997), especially if they have not reached the maintenance stage in their exercise behaviour (Lutz, Stults-Kolehmainen, & Bartholomew, 2010). Accordingly, research has attempted to identify the factors that lead people to participate in exercise programs over the long term (B. H. Marcus et al., 2000).

Individual Characteristics   Who is most likely to exercise? People who perceive themselves as athletic or as the type of person who exercises (Salmon, Owen, Crawford, Bauman, & Sallis, 2003), who enjoy their form of exercise (Kiviniemi, Voss-Humke, & Seifert, 2007), and

who have positive attitudes towards physical activity, a strong sense of self-efficacy for exercising, and social support from friends to exercise (Marquez & McAuley, 2006), are more likely to get involved in exercise programs initially than people who do not have these attitudes. However, these factors do not predict participation in exercise programs over the long term.

Gender predicts who exercises. From an early age, boys get more exercise than girls (Boyce, 2004). Despite the known benefits of exercise for middle-aged and older women (Kamijo & Murakami, 2009), there are several reasons why these groups of women are especially unlikely to get exercise. The lifestyles of older women may not afford opportunities for regular exercise (Cody & Lee, 1999). Women also report significant barriers to getting exercise, including caregiving responsibilities and concomitant lack of energy (A. C. King et al., 2000).

Race also predicts who is more likely to exercise. Findings from the 2005 Canadian Community Health Survey indicate that compared to non-Aboriginal Canadians, First Nations (people off reserve) and Métis people are more likely to have physically active lifestyles (Findley, 2011).

Social support predicts exercise. Among people who participate in group exercise programs such as running groups or walking groups, a sense of support and group cohesion contributes to participation (Christensen et al., 2006). One reason may be that engaging in exercise with others serves to reinforce social norms, which, according to the theory of planned behaviour, contribute to the performance of health behaviours.

People who are high in self-efficacy with respect to exercise (that is, believing that one will be able to perform exercise regularly) are more likely to practise it and more likely to perceive that they are benefiting from it than those people low in self-efficacy (Marquez & McAuley, 2006). In one study of sedentary, middle-aged adults, those with high self-efficacy beliefs with respect to their exercise plan perceived themselves to expend less effort and reported more positive mood during exercise than did those with low beliefs in self-efficacy. The positive emotions experienced during exercise, in turn, predicted subsequent self-efficacy beliefs, suggesting that positive effect may help maintain the practice of exercise (LePage & Crowther, 2010). The converse is also true: Those individuals with low self-efficacy beliefs with respect to exercise are less likely to engage in it. Those who do not exercise regularly may have little confidence in their ability to exercise and may regard exercise as entailing nearly as many costs as benefits (Marquez &

McAuley, 2006; Motl et al., 2002). Consequently, interventions aimed at modifying attitudes about the importance of exercise, especially for improving age-related cognitive deficits (Erickson & Kramer, 2009), and one's ability to perform it might be successful for increasing exercise in older adults (S. Wilcox & Storandt, 1996).

Characteristics of the Setting Which characteristics of exercise programs promote its practice? Convenient and easily accessible exercise settings lead to higher rates of adherence (for example, Humpel, Marshall, Leslie, Bauman, & Owen, 2004). If your exercise program is vigorous walking that can be undertaken near your home, you are more likely to do it than if your source of exercise is an aerobics program in a crowded health club five miles from your home. Lack of resources for physical activity may be a particular barrier for regular exercise among those low in socio-economic status, or SES (Estabrooks, Lee, & Gyurcsik, 2003; Feldman & Steptoe, 2004).

Perhaps the best predictor of regular exercise is regular exercise. Studies that have assessed attitudinal and motivational predictors of exercise have found that, although exercise intentions are influenced by attitudes, long-term practice of regular exercise is heavily determined by habit (McAuley, 1992). Developing a regular exercise program, embedding it firmly in regular activities, and practising it regularly for a period of time means that it begins to become automatic and habitual. However, habit has its limits. Unlike such habitual behaviours as wearing a seat belt or not lighting a cigarette, exercise requires additional thoughtfulness and planning, especially regarding its long-term benefits. Exercising takes willpower to overlook the initial short-term costs (see the Spotlight on Canadian Research box, "Does Time Perspective Influence Exercise Behaviour?"), the recognition that hard work is involved, and a belief in personal responsibility in order to be enacted on a regular basis (Wilson & Brookfield, 2009).

Characteristics of Interventions

Strategies The theory of planned behaviour can also be used to explain participation exercise programs. For example, a study of 94 people newly enrolled at a gym found that participation was predicted from initial perceived behavioural control, and stable exercise habits developed during exercise participation further increased perceptions of behavioural control over the ability to exercise, which in turn contributed to successful maintenance of exercise behaviour (Armitage,

2005). Cognitive behavioural strategies—including contingency contracting, self-reinforcement, self-monitoring, and goal setting—have also been employed in exercise interventions and appear to promote adherence (Dalle Grave, Calugi, Centis, El Ghoch, & Marchesini, 2011). With older adults, even simple telephone or mail reminders may help maintain adherence to a physical activity program (C. M. Castro, King, & Brassington, 2001).

Stages of change identified by the transtheoretical model of behaviour change suggest that different interventions should be targeted to people at different stages of readiness to exercise. For example, people who are contemplating starting an exercise program may perceive practical barriers to it (R. S. Myers & Roth, 1997), which can be attacked through persuasive communications. Those people already engaged in exercise, however, face the problem of maintenance and relapse to a sedentary lifestyle, so interventions that provide successful techniques for not abandoning an exercise program may be more useful for them (Nigg, 2001). Groups at particular risk for not exercising can be especially well served by stages of change interventions designed to increase exercise. These include sedentary mothers of young children (Fahrenwald, Atwood, Walker, Johnson, & Berg, 2004) and the frail elderly (Leveille et al., 1998).

Several studies confirm the efficacy of the transtheoretical model of behavioural change (that is, the stages of change model) as successful in producing self-efficacy with respect to physical activity and higher levels of physical activity. Generally speaking, interventions designed to increase physical activity that are matched to the stage of readiness of the sample are more successful than interventions that do not have this focus (Blissmer & McAuley, 2002; Litt, Kleppinger, & Judge, 2002; A. L. Marshall et al., 2003).

Even minimal interventions to promote exercise are showing some success. In an intervention that mailed stage-targeted printed materials encouraging physical exercise to older adults, those who reported receiving and reading the intervention materials were significantly more likely to be exercising six months later. The advantage of such an intervention, of course, is its low cost and ease of implementation (A. L. Marshall et al., 2003). One study of middle-aged and older adults found that a regular exercise program improved feelings of physical self-worth, physical condition, and health as long as 37 weeks later (Taylor & Fox, 2005).

Incorporating exercise into a more general program of healthy lifestyle change can be successful as well. For example, among adults at risk for coronary heart disease,

Does Time Perspective Influence Exercise Behaviour?

Getting people to initiate and maintain an exercise program is a formidable task, despite the fact that there are clear long-term benefits to staying physically active. For many people the short-term costs of exercise (such as initial discomfort and time commitment) outweigh the down-the-road advantages, and consequently commitment to maintaining an exercise regimen is low. Recognizing these potential obstacles, which may be especially important for people just beginning an exercise routine, researchers at the University of Waterloo designed a unique intervention to increase physical activity that targets people's time perspective (Hall & Fong, 2003).

Across two studies, university students who had signed up for fitness classes at the university recreation centre were randomly assigned to one of three conditions (time-perspective intervention, goal-setting control, no intervention control) that preceded their scheduled fitness class. The time-perspective intervention included education and activities designed to make the participants more aware of the fact that a short-term time perspective inevitably highlights the immediate costs of exercise, whereas a long-term time perspective favours recognizing the obvious benefits of exercise. In addition, the researchers posited that simply making these observations would not be enough to change behaviour and therefore included activities that would help connect and reinforce the future consequences of the participants' present behaviour. For example, in one exercise participants generated lists of the immediate costs and benefits of exercise and then contrasted them to the long-term costs of benefits in order to recognize that the long-term benefits outweigh the short-term costs. Those who received the goal-setting intervention engaged in activities similar to the time-perspective intervention (e.g., goal setting, cost and benefits of exercise) but without any short- or long-term time perspectives imposed. Finally, those in the no intervention group attended their fitness class as usual without any special intervention.

In the first study, all students completed measures of physical activity levels and time perspective for exercise before starting the program and then at three and seven weeks later. Controlling for pre-intervention levels of physical activity, those who received the time-perspective intervention increased their monthly physical activity by almost 11 hours, compared to an increase of less than three hours reported by those who received the goal-setting intervention, and an increase of less than one hour reported by those who received no intervention. In addition, participants who received the time intervention experienced an increase in their long-term thinking about exercise. In the second study, participants were followed up six months after the intervention and similar increases in exercise behaviour were found, although long-term thinking about exercise did not change. However, those who initially had a tendency to think long term about exercise reported higher levels of physical activity six months later, suggesting that individual differences in time perspective can influence exercise behaviour even without any intervention (Hall & Fong, 2003).

Thus, interventions that target an individual's time perspective, such as goal setting and focusing on the long-term benefits of exercise before an exercise program is started, may be one way to help encourage long-term exercise participation.

Source: From "The Effects of a Brief Time Perspective Intervention for Increasing Physical Activity Among Young Adults" by Hall, P. A. and Fong, G.T. (2003). *Psychology and Health,* Volume 18:6, pp. 685–706. Reprinted by permission of the publisher (Taylor & Francis Ltd.), www.informaworld.com.

brief behavioural counselling matched to stage of readiness showed success in achieving maintenance to physical activity, as well as smoking reduction and reduction in fat intake (Steptoe, Kerry, Rink, & Hilton, 2001). Although interventions targeted to multiple behaviours are sometimes less easy to undertake because of their complexity, linking health habits to each other in a concerted effort to address risk can be successful, as this intervention study showed.

Individualized Exercise Programs Because research has identified few individual differences, exercise-setting characteristics, or intervention strategies that promote long-term adherence, perhaps the best approach is to individualize exercise programs. Understanding an individual's motivation and attitudes with respect to exercise provides the underpinnings for developing an individualized exercise program that fits the person well. If people participate in activities that they like, for which they can develop goals, and that they are motivated to pursue for the pleasure of exercising rather than for just achieving a specific outcome, exercise adherence will be greater (Wilson & Brookfield, 2009). Ensuring that people have realistic expectations for their exercise programs may also improve long-term adherence (Sears & Stanton, 2001).

There may be unintended negative effects of interventions to increase exercise that need to be guarded against in the design of any intervention program. For example, one study (Zabinsky, Calfas, Gehrman, Wilfley, & Sallis, 2001) found that an intervention program directed to university men and women inadvertently promoted an increase in the desire to be thin, despite warnings about dieting. Such pressures can promote eating disorders. Otherwise, exercise interventions do not appear to have negative side effects.

Physical activity Internet sites would seem to hold promise for inducing people to participate in regular exercise (Napolitano et al., 2003). Of course, if one is on the Internet, one is by definition not exercising. Indeed, thus far, there is little evidence that physical activity Internet sites provide the kind of individually tailored program that is needed to get people to participate on a regular basis (Doshi, Patrick, Sallis, & Calfas, 2003). To date, then, using the Internet to modify physical activity levels has demonstrated mixed success.

Despite the problems psychologists have encountered in getting people to exercise, to stay active, and to do so faithfully, the exercise level in the Canadian population has been rising. For example, the proportion of Canadians in the 10 provinces who were moderately active in their leisure time rose from 43 percent to 52 percent from 1996–97 to 2005 (Gilmour, 2007), and to 52.5 percent in 2009 (Colley, Garriguet, Janssen, Craig, Clarke, & Tremblay, 2011). This appears to be part of a larger trend toward increased physical activity among Canadians, as levels have been increasing since 1981 (Craig, Russell, Cameron, & Bauman, 2004). To be able to sustain and build on these changes in the future suggests that although the population may be aging, it may be doing so in a healthier way than in any previous generation.

(L04) **WHY IS MAINTAINING A HEALTHY DIET IMPORTANT?**

Developing and maintaining a healthy diet should be a goal for everyone. The dramatic rise in obesity in Canada has added urgency to this recommendation.

Diet is an important and controllable risk factor for many of the leading causes of death and contributes substantially to risk factors for disease as well. However, in 2009 only 45.6 percent of Canadians over 12 consumed the recommended minimum five servings of fruits and vegetables each day (Statistics Canada, 2011b). Experts estimate that the economic burden of a poor diet to be $6.3 billion annually, which includes $1.8 billion in direct health care costs (McAmmond, 2000). Dietary change is often critical for people at risk for or already diagnosed with chronic diseases, such as coronary artery disease, hypertension, diabetes, and cancer (Chronic Disease Prevention Alliance of Canada, 2007). These are diseases for which low-SES people are more at risk, and diet may explain some of the relation between low SES and these disorders. Research consistently shows that supermarkets in high-SES neighbourhoods carry more health-oriented food products than do supermarkets in low-income areas. Thus, even if the motivation to change one's diet is there, the food products may not be (Conis, 2003a).

Dietary factors have been implicated in a broad array of diseases and risks for disease. Perhaps the best known is the relation of dietary factors to total serum cholesterol level and to low-density lipid proteins in particular (McCaffery et al., 2001). Although diet is only one determinant of a person's lipid profile, it can be an important one because it is controllable and because elevated total serum cholesterol and low density lipid proteins are risk factors for the development of coronary heart disease (CHD) and hypertension. Of dietary recommendations, switching from trans fats (as are used for fried and fast foods) and saturated fats (from meat and dairy products) to polyunsaturated fats and monounsaturated fats is one of the most widely recommended courses of action (Marsh, 2002).

Dietary habits have also been implicated in the development of several cancers. Findings from a large multinational prospective study conducted in Europe suggest links between a variety of different foods and increased and decreased risks of several cancers including colorectal, stomach, prostrate, and breast (Gonzalez & Riboli, 2010). Dietary modification is also important for polyp prevention among individuals at risk for colorectal cancers, specifically a low-fat, high-fibre diet (Corle et al., 2001). Estimates of the degree to which diet contributes to the incidence of cancer exceed 20 percent (Chronic Disease Prevention Alliance of Canada, 2007).

The good news is that changing one's diet can improve health. For example, a diet high in fibre may protect against obesity and cardiovascular disease by lowering insulin levels (Ludwig et al., 1999). A diet high in fruits, vegetables, whole grains, peas and beans, poultry, and fish and low in refined grains, potatoes, and red and processed meats has been shown to lower the risk of coronary heart disease in women (Fung, Willett, Stampfer, Manson, & Hu, 2001). Modifications in diet can lower blood cholesterol level and these modifications may, in turn, reduce the risk for atherosclerosis (Heart & Stroke Foundation, 2011). A class of drugs, called statins, substantially reduces cholesterol in conjunction with dietary modification. In fact, the effects of statins are so rapid that low-density lipoprotein (LDL) cholesterol is lower within the first month after beginning use. Together, diet modification and a statin regimen appear to be highly successful for lowering cholesterol.

A controversial issue about diet that promises to occupy attention over the next decade concerns reduced-calorie diets (Spinney, 2006). In several organisms, caloric restriction or reduced-calorie diets have increased life span. It is not yet known if caloric restriction increases life span in humans, but experiments with primates suggests that it may. There is already evidence that caloric restriction is associated with biomarkers that predict longevity in humans (G. S. Roth et al., 2002). Thus, in addition to changing specific patterns of food consumption in the future, we may also all be urged to reduce our caloric intake overall (Lee & Ruvkun, 2002).

Resistance to Modifying Diet

It is difficult to get people to modify their diet, even when they are at high risk for CHD or when they are under the instruction of a physician. Recall from Chapter 3 that health behaviours, including eating habits, become established by age 11 or 12. Dietary preferences may be therefore resistant to change, especially if the choice is not self-motivated (Pelletier, Dion, Slovinec-D'Angelo & Reid, 2004). In addition, the typical reason that people switch to a diet low in cholesterol, fats, calories, and additives and high in fibre, fruits, and vegetables is to improve appearance, not to improve health.

Another difficulty with modifying diet is the problem of maintaining change. Adherence to a new diet may be high at first, but falls off over time. One reason is because of the factors that plague all efforts to change poor health habits: insufficient attention to the needs for long-term monitoring and relapse prevention techniques. In the case of diet, other factors are implicated as well: Self-management is essential because dietary recommendations may be monitored only indirectly by medical authorities, such as physicians. A strong sense of self-efficacy, motivation, and the perception that dietary change has important health benefits are critical to successfully making dietary change (Madlensky et al., 2008; Steptoe, Doherty, Carey, Rink, & Hilton, 2000).

Some dietary recommendations are restrictive, monotonous, expensive, and hard to find and prepare. Drastic changes in shopping, meal planning, cooking methods, and eating habits may be required. In addition, tastes are hard to alter. So-called comfort foods, many of which are high in fat and sugars, may help to turn off stress hormones, such as cortisol, thus contributing to eating things that are not good for us (Dallman et al., 2003). Preferences for high-fat foods are so well established that people will consume more of a food they have been told is high in fat than one low in fat, even when that information is false (Bowen, Tomoyasu, Anderson, Carney, & Kristal, 1992). People who are high in conscientiousness and intelligence also seem to do a better job of adhering to a cholesterol-lowering diet, and people high in depression or anxiety are less likely to do so (Stilley, Sereika, Muldoon, Ryan, & Dunbar-Jacob, 2004).

Stress has a direct effect on eating, especially in adolescence. Greater stress is tied to consuming more fatty foods and less fruit and vegetables and to the lesser likelihood of eating breakfast with more snacking between meals (Cartwright et al., 2003). Thus, stress may contribute to long-term risk for disease by steering the adolescents' and young adults' diet in an unhealthy direction. A lower status job, high workload, and lack of control at work are also associated with less healthful diets, although scientists do not yet know exactly why (Devine, Connors, Sobal, & Bisogni, 2003). It may be that these factors enhance stress and that an unhealthy diet marked by comfort foods reduces it.

Interventions to Modify Diet

Many efforts to modify diet are done on an individual basis in response to a specific health problem or health risk. Physicians, nurses, dieticians, and other experts work with patients to modify a diet-responsive risk, such as obesity, diabetes, CHD, or hypertension. As with any health-habit change, the motivation to pursue dietary change and commitment to long-term health are essential ingredients for success (Kearney, Rosal, Ockene, & Churchill, 2002). Any effort to change diet needs to begin with education and self-monitoring training because many people have a poor idea of the importance of particular nutrients and how much of them their diet actually includes; estimation of fat intake appears to be poor, for example (O'Brien, Fries, & Bowen, 2000).

Much dietary change has been implemented through cognitive behavioural interventions. These include self-monitoring, stimulus control, and contingency contracting, coupled with relapse-prevention techniques for high-risk-for-relapse situations, such as parties or other occasions where high-fat foods are readily available. Motivational interviewing can also be successfully used to get people to increase their fruit and vegetable intake (Ahluwalia et al., 2007; Carels et al., 2007).

Another method of dietary change adopts Prochaska's transtheoretical stages of change model (Chapter 3), which assumes that different interventions are required for people at different stages. Research shows that, among people given blood cholesterol tests and a questionnaire assessing diet, those already contemplating dietary change were more likely to enroll in an intervention than those at the stage of precontemplation (B. S. McCann et al., 1996).

Family Interventions Recently, efforts to intervene in the dietary habits of high-risk individuals have focused on the family group. There are several good reasons for focusing interventions on the family. When all family members are committed to and participate in dietary change, it is easier for the target family member to do so as well (D. K. Wilson & Ampey-Thornhill, 2001). Moreover, different aspects of diet are influenced by different family members. Regardless of whether wives do the shopping and food preparation, husbands' food preferences can be a more powerful determinant of what the family eats if the couple does not have an egalitarian relationship style (Brown & Miller, 2002).

In family interventions, family members typically meet with a dietary counsellor to discuss the need to change the family diet and ways for doing so. Although such family interventions were originally developed over 25 years ago, a recent study comparing outcomes of earlier programs to current programs suggest that they are just as effective, despite the fact that obesity rates have increased and the environment has become more obesogenic (Epstein, Paluch, Roemmich, & Beecher, 2007).

Community Interventions Many interventions have been implemented on the community level, and specifically within the school system. One study (Veugelers & Fitzgerald, 2005) compared the nutrition programs among 282 schools in Nova Scotia and assessed the height, weight, and dietary intake of more than 5,000 grade 5 students to evaluate their potential effectiveness. Schools were categorized as not having a nutrition program, having a healthy-menu nutrition program, or having an intensive, multifaceted nutrition program. The students from the schools with the intensive program showed lower rates of obesity, healthier diets, and higher levels of physical activity than those from schools with or without a healthy menu. In fact, there were no differences between the latter two groups suggesting that simply offering a healthy menu at school may not be sufficient to help reduce childhood obesity.

A more recent approach to modifying diet has involved targeting particular groups for which dietary change may be especially important and designing interventions specifically directed to these groups. For example, the Kahnawake Schools Diabetes Prevention Project included both school-based and community-based activities to improve diet and lower the risk for diabetes among elementary school children in a Mohawk community near Montreal. One of the outcomes of this program was the development of a school nutrition policy that includes offering healthy foods in the school cafeteria and requiring students to bring healthy lunches and snacks to school (Macaulay et al., 1997).

Change can come from social engineering solutions to the problem, as well as from individual efforts to alter diet. Factors such as banning snack foods from schools, making school lunch programs more nutritious, and making snack foods more expensive and healthy foods less so will all make some inroads into promoting healthy food choices (Horgen & Brownell, 2002).

HOW IS WEIGHT CONTROL RELATED TO HEALTH?

Maintaining a proper diet and getting enough exercise jointly contribute to weight control, the issue to which we now turn. This issue has become especially urgent in recent years because of the galloping levels of obesity in the population. Consequently, our discussion on health promoting and preventive behaviours will begin to cross the line into the area of health-compromising behaviours, as we will look at interventions both for normal, healthy adults to practise weight control and for the obese, who may need to control their weight to promote their health.

The Regulation of Eating

All animals, including people, have sensitive and complex systems for regulating food. Taste has been called the chemical gatekeeper of eating. It is the most ancient of sensory systems and plays an important role in selecting certain foods and rejecting others.

Although the molecular pathways that govern weight gain and loss are not completely understood, scientists have a fairly good idea what some of these pathways are. A number of hormones control eating. Leptin and insulin, in particular, circulate in the blood in concentrations that are proportionate to body fat mass. They decrease appetite by inhibiting neurons that produce the molecules neuropeptide Y (NPY) and agouti-related peptide (AgRP), peptides that would otherwise stimulate eating. They also stimulate melacortin-producing neurons in the hypothalamus, which inhibit eating.

As may be evident, an important player in weight control is the protein leptin, which is secreted by fat cells. Leptin appears to signal the neurons of the hypothalamus as to whether the body has sufficient energy stores of fat or whether it needs additional energy. The brain's eating control centre reacts to the signals sent from the hypothalamus to increase or decrease appetite. As noted, leptin inhibits the neurons that stimulate appetite and activates those that suppress appetite. These effects of leptin have made scientists optimistic that leptin may have promise as a weight-control agent, although thus far the promise of leptin as a pharmacological method of weight control has remained elusive (Morton, Cummings, Baskin, Barsh, & Schwartz, 2006).

Ghrelin may also play an important role particularly in why dieters who lose weight often gain it back so quickly. Ghrelin stimulates the appetite by activating the NPY-AgRP-expressing neurons. It is secreted by specialized cells in the stomach, spiking just before meals and dropping afterward. When people are given ghrelin injections, they feel extremely hungry. Therefore blocking ghrelin levels or the action of ghrelin may help people lose weight and keep it off (Grady, 2002).

Studies with rats have suggested a possible brain mechanism for the control of at least some eating and its regulation. Rats who have a damaged ventromedial hypothalamus behave like obese humans do: They eat excessive amounts of food, show little sensitivity to internal cues related to hunger (e.g., how long it has been since they last ate), and respond to food-related external cues, such as the presence of food. This evidence implies that at least some obese humans have a malfunctioning ventromedial hypothalamus, which interferes with normal eating habits.

Why Obesity Is a Health Risk

What is obesity? **Obesity** is an excessive accumulation of body fat. Generally speaking, fat should constitute about 20 percent to 27 percent of body tissue in women and about 15 percent to 22 percent in men. Figure 4.2 presents guidelines from Health Canada for calculating your body mass index and determining whether or not you are overweight or obese.

The World Health Organization estimates that 400 million people worldwide are obese and a further 1.6 billion are overweight, including 20 million children under 5 (World Health Organization, 2006b). The global epidemic of obesity stems from a combination of genetic susceptibility, the increasing availability of high-fat and high-energy foods, and low levels of physical activity (Kopelman, 2000).

Although obesity is a worldwide problem, it is becoming a problem of increasing concern in Canada. Over the past three decades, the median body mass index (BMI) of adults rose from 24.4 to 26.1. Approximately 36 percent of the Canadian population is overweight, and an additional 23 percent is obese (Garriguet, 2004), with women somewhat more likely to be overweight or obese than men (see Figure 4.3). Considering that in Canada, 5 in 10 women and 7 in 10 men consume more calories than what they need (Health Canada, 2010), these statistics are not surprising.

There is no mystery as to why people in Canada have become so heavy. The food industry spends

FIGURE 4.2 | Body Mass Index (BMI) Nomogram

(*Source:* Health Canada, Canadian Guidelines for Body Weight Classification in Adults, 2003; and National Heart, Lung & Blood Institute, 2004.)

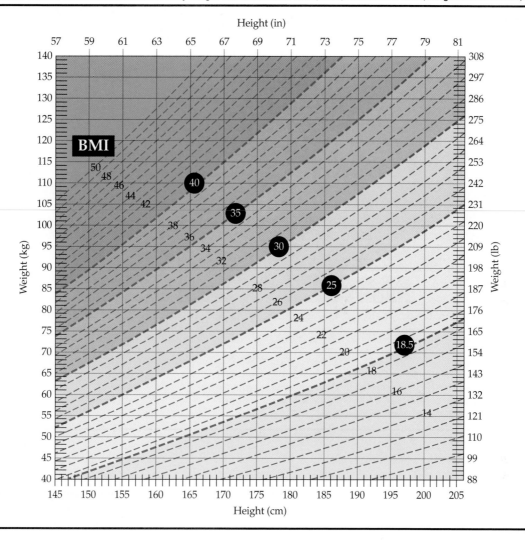

approximately $600 million per year on ads and promotion for food. Portion sizes have increased, and healthful foods are often not available. The average Canadian's food intake rose from 2,356 calories a day in 1976 to 2,788 by 2002, an 18 percent increase. Similarly, carbohydrate and fat consumption has increased 18 percent over the same time span. In addition, many Canadians get more calories from their snacks and beverages consumed between meals than from their meals. A recent survey also suggests that one in four Canadians eats at a fast-food outlet daily (Garriguet, 2004). So-called supersize portions are very high in calories. Thus, even

those people who are not dieting for obesity should be attentive to their portion sizes, and among dieters, this concern is critical (Nielsen & Popkin, 2003).

Risks of Obesity   Obesity is a risk factor for many disorders, both in its own right and because it affects other risk factors, such as blood pressure and plasma cholesterol level (Kopelman, 2000). Estimates suggest that more than 4,000 deaths annually in Canada can be directly attributed to overweight and obesity (Katzmarzyk & Ardern, 2004). This number increases dramatically when deaths attributed to obesity causing diabetes,

FIGURE 4.3 | Percent of Canadian Population Obese

Obese is BMI over 30.

(*Source:* Statistics Canada, "Adult Obesity," *Health Reports,* Catalogue 82-003, Volume 17, Issue 3, released August 22, 2006, www.statcan.ca/ english/studies/82-003/archive/2006/17-3-a.pdf.)

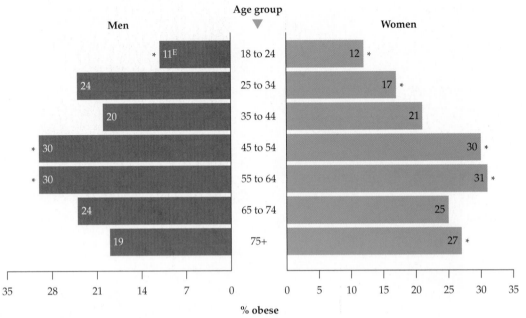

Data source: 2004 Canadian Community Health Survey: Nutrition
* Significantly different from overall estimate for same sex (p < 0.05)
E Coefficient of variation 16.6% to 33.3% (interpret with caution)
Health Reports, Vol. 17, No. 3, August 2006

cardiovascular disease, and certain cancers are included (Chronic Disease Prevention Alliance of Canada, 2007). Obesity has been associated with atherosclerosis, hypertension, diabetes, gallbladder disease, and arthritis; obesity is a risk for heart failure (Kenchaiah et al., 2002). Increased body weight contributes to increased death rates for all cancers combined and for the specific cancers of colon, rectal, liver, gallbladder, pancreas, kidney, esophagus, non-Hodgkin's lymphoma, and multiple myeloma. Obesity also increases risks in surgery, anesthesia administration, and childbearing (Brownell & Wadden, 1992), as well as increasing the risk of stroke during and after pregnancy (Kuklina, Tong, Bansil, George, & Callaghan, 2011). One study found that women who were 30 percent overweight were more than three times as likely to develop heart disease as women who were of normal or slightly under normal weight (Manson et al., 1990). This risk increased to five times

that of normal-weight women among the overweight women who were also smokers (Manson et al., 1990).

As a consequence of its links to chronic disease (especially cardiovascular disease, kidney disease, and diabetes), obesity is associated with early mortality (Adams et al., 2006). As a ballpark statistic, people who are overweight at age 40 are likely to die three years earlier than those who are thin (Peeters et al., 2003). Even mildly overweight women sustain an increased risk for heart disease and heart attack compared with women who are underweight (Manson et al., 1990). In addition, many of the treatments for overweight that people undertake on their own, such as use of diet pills and other medications, fad diets, fasting, and anorexia or bulimia, create substantial risks of their own.

Often ignored among the risks of obesity is the psychological distress that can result. Although there is a robust stereotype of overweight people as more "jolly," studies suggest that the obese are worse off in terms of

More than one-third of the adult population in Canada is overweight, and an additional 23 percent are obese, putting almost 60 percent of this population at risk for heart disease, kidney disease, hypertension, diabetes, and other health problems.

Critical Checkpoint

Exercise or Eating Regulation to Lose Weight?

It is widely recognized that maintaining a healthy weight ideally involves lifestyle changes that include both regulating eating habits and being physically active. If you or a friend needed to lose some weight to get back into a healthy weight range and could only use one of these options to lose weight in a healthy manner, which would you choose or recommend—changing eating habits or exercising more—and why would you choose that option?

psychological functioning, especially depression (de Wit et al., 2010; Rydén, Karlsson, Sullivan, Torgerson, & Taft, 2003). Depression may be maintained by increasing recognition that the world is not designed for overweight people. One may have to pay for two seats on an airplane, have little luck finding clothes, endure others' derision and rude comments, and experience other reminders that the obese, quite literally, do not fit. The stigmas and stereotypes that obese people are subject to may further reduce their psychological health (Carr & Friedman, 2005; see the Focus on Social Issues box, "The Stigma of Obesity: Comments on the Obese," on page 112).

As just noted, obesity increases the risk for a number of diseases and disorders, yet the obese often avoid the trips to the physician that might help them. For example, getting in and out of a car and in and out of a doctor's office presents challenges for the morbidly obese. The obese may not fit in standard chairs or in standard wheelchairs. X-rays may not penetrate far enough to give accurate readings, blood pressure cuffs are not big enough, and hospital gowns do not cover them (Pérez-Peña & Glickson, 2003). If an obese person increasingly withdraws into a reclusive life, by the time he or she seeks treatment, the complications of diabetes, heart disease, and other disorders may be out of control.

Obesity in Childhood

The prevalence of overweight children has substantially increased over the past 20 years among children 2 to 11 years of age and more than doubled among those ages 12 to 17. In 2009, 17 percent of children and youth age 6 and over had BMIs in the overweight range and another 9 percent had BMIs in the obese category (Statistics Canada, 2010). Aboriginal children and adolescents are disproportionately affected, with obesity rates that are two-and-a-half times that of the national average (Shields, 2006a). Young women are at particular risk for substantial weight gain during their teens and twenties, especially if they have a child during this time (Gore, Brown, & West, 2003).

Obesity in childhood is one of the fastest growing health concerns in Canada.

In Canada, approximately 26 percent of children are overweight and 8 percent are obese. Childhood obesity is becoming a global epidemic. Being overweight in childhood must now be considered a major health problem rather than merely a problem in appearance (Dietz, 2004). Specifically, 60 percent of overweight children and adolescents are already showing risk factors for cardiovascular disease, such as elevated blood pressure, elevated lipid levels, or hyperinsulemia (Sinha et al., 2002). Obesity can also have significant negative psychological consequences for the children's self-esteem. Results from the Canadian National Longitudinal Survey of Children and Youth found that obese children were about twice as likely as normal weight children to report low self-esteem four years later after controlling for baseline self-esteem (Wang, Wild, Kipp, Kuhle, and Veugelers, 2009).

What is leading to childhood obesity? A number of factors are indicated in this epidemic. One important factor is an increasingly sedentary lifestyle among children and adolescents, involving television and video games (Dietz & Gortmaker, 2001). Exercise and obesity are clearly related. Children are less likely to be obese when they participate in organized sports or physical activity. The link between inactivity and obesity is stronger for boys than for girls (Carrière, 2003). Parental behaviours are also related to their children's obesity. Simply having an obese parent greatly increases the odds that a child will be obese (Carrière, 2003). Figure 4.4 illustrates the high rates of obesity among Canadian children.

Where the Fat Is   Recent epidemiologic evidence suggests that abdominally localized fat, as opposed to excessive fat in the hips, buttocks, or thighs, is an especially potent risk factor for cardiovascular disease, diabetes, hypertension, and cancer. Sometimes called "stress weight," abdominal fat increases especially in

FIGURE 4.4 | Overweight and Obesity Rates for Canadian Children Ages 2 to 17, 1978–79 and 2004

Overweight is defined as greater than or equal to the 95th percentile of the age- and sex-specific BMI.

(*Source:* Statistics Canada, "Measured Obesity," *Nutrition: Findings from the Canadian Community Health Survey,* Catalogue 82-620, released July 6, 2005, www.statcan.ca/english/research/82-620-MIE/2005001/articles/child/obesity.htm and www.statcan.ca/english/research/82-620-MIE/2005001/charts/child/chart2.htm.)

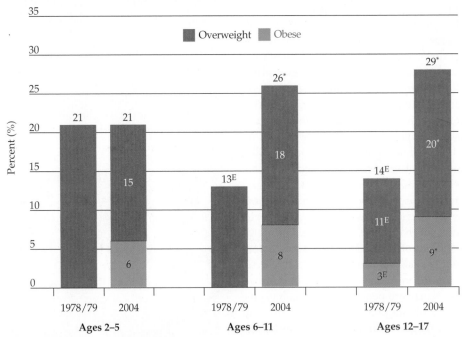

Data source: 2004 Canadian Community Health Survey: Nutrition; Canada Health Survey 1978/79
Note: The obesity rates for the 2–5 and 6–11 age groups from the 1978/79 Canada Health Survey have coefficients of variation greater than 33.3%; therefore, the estimates are not releasable.
E Coefficient of variation between 16.6% to 33.3% (interpret with caution)
* Significantly different from estimate for 1978/79 (p < 0.05)

response to stress (Donoho, Weigensberg, Emken, Hsu, & Spruijt-Metz, 2011). People with excessive central weight (sometimes called "apples," in contrast to "pears," who carry their weight on their hips) are more psychologically reactive to stress and show greater cardiovascular reactivity (M. C. Davis, Twamley, Hamilton, & Swan, 1999) and neuroendocrine reactivity to stress (Epel et al., 2000). This reactivity to stress may be the link between centrally deposited fat and increased risk for diseases. Inasmuch as uncontrollable stress may contribute to mortality risk from such diseases as hypertension, cancer, diabetes, and cardiovascular disease, abdominally localized fat may represent a sign that health is eroding in response to stress.

Factors Associated with Obesity

Obesity depends on both the number and the size of an individual's fat cells. Among moderately obese people, fat cells are typically large, but there is not an unusual number of them. Among the severely obese, there is a large number of fat cells, and the fat cells themselves are exceptionally large (Brownell, 1982).

What determines the number and size of fat cells and the propensity to be obese? Childhood constitutes a window of vulnerability for obesity for a number of reasons. One reason is that the number of fat cells an individual has is typically determined in the first few years of life, as by genetic factors or by early eating habits. A high number of fat cells leads to a marked propensity for fat storage, thus promoting obesity in adulthood. In contrast, poor eating habits in adolescence and adulthood are more likely to affect the size of fat cells but not their number.

Our style of eating has changed in ways that promote overweight and obesity. Most obvious is a rise in calorie consumption. In addition, many Canadians get more calories from their snacks and beverages consumed between meals than from their meals (Garriguet, 2004). The time involved in preparing food because of microwave ovens and advances in food processing and packaging has led to greater convenience for preparing food (Koretz, 2003b).

Family History and Obesity   Family history is clearly implicated in obesity. Overweight parents are more likely to have overweight children than are normal-weight parents. This relationship appears to be due to both genetic and lifestyle factors, although genetic factors are believed to explain at least 50 percent of the vari-

ance in individual differences in BMI (Hebebrand & Hinney, 2009). Evidence for genetic factors comes from twin studies, demonstrating that twins reared apart show a tendency toward obesity when both natural parents were obese, even when the twins' environments are very different. There also appear to be genetically based tendencies to store energy as either fat or lean tissue (Hebebrand & Hinney, 2009). Identifying the role of genetics in obesity is important because it helps identify individuals for whom weight management interventions are especially important.

Whether or not one diets is also influenced by family environment. More than two-thirds of the population say they are dieting at any given point in time. Efforts to lose weight among daughters are influenced heavily by perceived criticism of parents, whereas sons' weight-loss efforts (or lack of them) seem to be more related to fathers' attitudes toward eating (Baker, Whisman, & Brownell, 2000).

SES, Culture, and Obesity   Additional risk factors for obesity include social class and culture. In Canada, women of low socio-economic status tend to be heavier than high-SES women, and Aboriginal women, in particular, appear to be vulnerable to obesity (Tjepkema, 2005). A recent national survey suggests though that the relationship between SES and obesity is changing in Canada, with only women in the highest household income groups maintaining low rates of obesity from 1986 to 2004. For men over the same time period, the link between low income and obesity disappeared, with the highest rates of obesity found in men with the highest incomes (Shields & Tjepkema, 2006). Interestingly, in developing countries, obesity among men, women, and children is rare, possibly because of insufficient food; in these countries, the prevalence of obesity rises with SES and increasing wealth.

Place is also implicated in childhood obesity. For example, a national longitudinal survey of Canadian children from 1994 to 2002 found that as the income level of the neighbourhood rose, obesity rates declined (Oliver & Hayes, 2008). In the poorest neighbourhoods, rates of obesity were the highest at 40 percent, compared to only 27 percent in the richest neighbourhoods. In addition, the associations between neighbourhood and obesity were not present initially when the children were 2 to 3 years old, but were evident eight years later when the children were 10 and 11 years old. These effects were present after controlling for family structure and other socio-demographic factors, suggesting that weight gain was associated with living in a poor neighbourhood. Although the aspects of the neighbourhoods that may have contributed to obesity were not examined, lack of access to high-energy sports such as hockey and soccer, which are expensive to participate in, as well as restricted access to healthy food choices are possible explanations.

Values are implicated in obesity. Thinness is valued in women from high SES levels and developed countries, which in turn leads to a cultural emphasis on dieting and on physical activity (Wardle et al., 2004). Although these social norms can prompt women, not just those who are obese, to be discontented with their bodies (Foster, Wadden, & Vogt, 1997), according to researchers from the University of Ottawa, women who are intrinsically motivated may be less vulnerable to these thin ideals (Mask & Blanchard, in press).

Stress and Eating

Stress affects eating, although in different ways for different people. About half of people eat more when they are under stress, and half eat less (Wardle & Gibson, 2007). For nondieting and nonobese normal eaters, the experience of stress or anxiety may suppress physiological cues suggesting hunger, leading to lower consumption of food. Stress and anxiety, however, can disinhibit the dieter, removing the self-control that usually guards against eating, thus leading to an increase in food intake both among dieters and the obese (Heatherton, Herman, & Polivy, 1991, 1992).

Stress also influences what food is consumed. People who eat in response to stress are usually dieters who change their food choices from low-calorie, low-fat foods to more high-caloric and high-fat foods when they are stressed (Zellner et al., 2006). Anxiety and depression appear to figure into **stress eating** as well, which in turn can contribute to weight gain. One study found that susceptibility to overeating in response to emotional distress was significantly associated with weight gain in women over a 20-year period (Hays & Roberts, 2007). Those who eat in response to negative emotions show a preference for sweet and high-fat foods (Oliver, Wardle, & Gibson, 2000). It is not surprising then that stress eating is one factor that may contribute to obesity.

Treatment of Obesity

Some people attempt to lose weight because they perceive obesity to be a health risk. Others seek treatment because their obesity is coupled with binge eating and other symptoms of psychological distress (Fitzgibbon, Stolley, & Kirschenbaum, 1993). However, most people are motivated by the fact that being overweight is considered to be unattractive and that it carries a social stigma (Hayes & Ross, 1987; see the Focus on Social Issues box, "The Stigma of Obesity: Comments on the Obese"). British model Kate Moss' self-confessed mantra throughout her career—"Nothing tastes as good as skinny feels"—captures the importance that society places on physical appearance and, in particular, on a thin appearance.

Dieting   Treating obesity through dieting has historically been the most common approach, and most weight-loss programs still begin with dietary treatment. People are trained to restrict their caloric and/or carbohydrate intake through education about the caloric values and dietary characteristics of foods. Generally, weight losses produced through dietary methods are small and rarely maintained for long (Agras et al., 1996). Weight losses achieved through dieting rarely match the expectations of clients, whose disappointment may contribute to regaining the lost weight (Foster, Wadden, Vogt, & Brewer, 1997). However, even when the diet is self-set, adherence and success rates can be low. Researcher's from McGill University followed women who were dieting over a two month period using their own self-set dieting rules. Although some were successful at reducing the amount they ate and losing weight the majority were not successful at adhering to their own dieting rules (Knäuper, Cheema, Rabiau, & Borten, 2005).

Very low-carbohydrate or low-fat diets do the best job in helping people lose weight initially, but these diets are the hardest to maintain, and people commonly revert to their old habits. As already noted, repeated dieting, especially yo-yo dieting, may increasingly predispose the dieter to put on weight. Weight gain following reduced calorie intake or even fasting does not result from overeating following food restriction; rather weight gain following restrictive eating likely results from changes in metabolic rate induced by the restrictive eating (Levitsky & DeRosimo, 2010). Recently popular, low-carbohydrate diets claim to allow people to lose large amounts of weight. However, formal investigation of low-carbohydrate diets does not suggest that they are necessarily more effective than other kinds of diets (D. Butler, 2004). Instead, reducing caloric intake to recommended levels, increasing exercise, and sticking with an eating plan over the long term are the only factors reliably related to staying slim.

Surgery Surgical procedures, especially gastric surgeries, represent a radical way of controlling extreme obesity. In the most common surgical procedure, the stomach literally is stapled up to reduce its capacity to hold food so that the overweight individual must restrict his or her intake. As with all surgeries, there is some risk, and side effects, such as gastric and intestinal distress, are common. Consequently, this procedure is usually reserved for people who are at least 100 percent overweight, who have failed repeatedly to lose weight through other methods, and who have complicating health problems that make weight loss urgent.

Appetite-suppressing Drugs Drugs, both prescription and over-the-counter types, are often used to reduce appetite and restrict food consumption (Bray & Tartaglia, 2000). In some weight-loss programs, drugs may be employed in conjunction with a cognitive behavioural intervention. Such programs often produce substantial weight loss, but participants can regain the weight quickly, particularly if they attribute the weight loss to the drug rather than to their own efforts (J. Rodin, Elias, Silberstein, & Wagner, 1988). This point underscores the importance of perceived self-efficacy in any weight-loss program.

The Multimodal Approach Many current interventions with the obese use a multimodal approach to maladaptive eating behaviour.

Screening
Some programs begin with screening applicants for their readiness and their motivation to lose weight. Unsuccessful prior dieting attempts, weight lost and regained, high body dissatisfaction, and low self-esteem are all associated with less weight loss for behavioural weight reduction programs, and these criteria can be used to screen individuals before treatment or be used to provide a better match between a particular treatment program and a client (Teixeira et al., 2002).

Self-monitoring
Obese clients are trained in self-monitoring and are taught to keep careful records of what they eat, when they eat it, how much they eat, where they eat it, and other dimensions of eating. This kind of record-keeping simultaneously defines the behaviour and makes clients more aware of their eating patterns which can lead to successful weight loss in both adults and children (Germann, Kirschenbaum, & Rich, 2007). Many patients are surprised to discover what,

when, and how much they actually eat. This kind of monitoring is always important for weight loss, but it becomes especially so at high-risk times, such as during the holidays, when weight gain reliably occurs (Boutelle, Kirschenbaum, Baker, & Mitchell, 1999).

Behavioural analysis then focuses on influencing the antecedents of the target behaviour—namely, the stimuli that affect eating. Clients are trained to modify the stimuli in their environment that have previously elicited and maintained overeating. Such steps include purchasing low-calorie foods (such as raw vegetables), making access to them easy, and limiting the high-calorie foods kept in the house. Behavioural control techniques are also used to train patients to change the circumstances of eating. Clients are taught to confine eating to one place at particular times of day. They may also be trained to develop new discriminative stimuli that will be associated with eating. For example, they may be encouraged to use a particular place setting, such as a special place mat or napkin, and to eat only when those stimuli are present. When such environmental cues are used to prime dieting goals they may be especially effective for promoting self-regulation of eating, especially in the presence of tempting eating situations (Papies & Hamstra, 2010).

Control over Eating
The next step in a multimodal behavioural intervention is to train clients to gain control over the eating process itself. For example, clients may be urged to count each mouthful of food, each chew, or each swallow. They may be told to put down eating utensils after every few mouthfuls until the food in their mouths is chewed and swallowed.

Thousands of Canadians participate in organized weight reduction programs. Many of these programs now include exercise.

The Stigma of Obesity: Comments on the Obese

Obese people are often the target of insensitive comments about their weight. They are teased by their peers as children, and called names such as whale or fatty. The teasing endures into adulthood, where, while in public, they encounter people staring at them, whispering behind their back about their weight, and calling them names.

Family life for obese people can be even more traumatic than public life. Receiving criticism and comments about their weight from loved ones can irreparably damage family relationships. Lack of family acceptance can remove the home as a buffer against peer cruelty. Some parents push their overweight children to lose weight, using techniques that shame their children into weight loss, such as by withdrawing affection.

The resulting effect of repeated exposure to others' judgments about their weight can be social alienation and low self-esteem. From a young age, overweight children may recognize that they are different from other children. Childhood activities, such as swimming and athletics, when children must wear a swimsuit or change in a locker room, may involve uncomfortable exposure that leads to more teasing. Unfortunately, obese children learn from a young age to avoid interaction with their peers and may thereby compromise their ability to develop close relationships.

Obese people are one of very few disabled groups to endure public criticism for their disability. Obesity is stigmatized as a disability whose fault lies with obese people (Carr & Friedman, 2005; Puhl, Schwartz, & Brownell, 2005; Wang, Houshyar, & Prinstein, 2006). This stigma fuels public sentiments that obese people are responsible for being obese, that they are lazy or gluttonous. Public comments to obese people, such as "Why don't you lose some weight?" may often be to this effect.

Coping with public views of their weight is difficult for obese people as well. To address teasing directly, especially when the comments are simply a stated fact, such as "That person is fat," is to admit that being fat is a bad thing. Increasingly, our society will need to accommodate not only the physical needs of obese people but also their emotional needs.

Marcia Millman. From Such a Pretty Face: Being Fat in America by Marcia Millman. Copyright © 1980 Marcia Millman. Used by permission of W. W. Norton & Company, Inc.

Longer and longer delays are introduced between mouthfuls so as to encourage slow eating (which tends to reduce intake). Such delays are first introduced at the end of the meal, when the client is already satiated, and progressively moved closer to the beginning of the meal. Finally, clients are urged to enjoy and savour their food and to make a conscious effort to appreciate it while they are eating.

Clients are also trained to gain control over the consequences of the target behaviour and are trained to reward themselves for activities they carry out successfully. For example, keeping records, counting chews, pausing during the meal, or eating only in a specific place might be reinforced by a tangible positive reinforcement, such as going to a movie or spending time with friends. Developing a sense of self-control over eating is an important part of behavioural treatments of obesity. Training in self-control can help people override the impact of urges or temptations.

Adding Exercise   Exercise is a critical component of any weight-loss program. In fact, as people age, increasing exercise is essential just to maintain weight and avoid gaining it (Jameson, 2004). High levels of physical activity are associated with initial successful weight loss, better eating self-regulation, and the maintenance of that weight loss (Andrade et al., 2010).

Controlling Self-talk   Cognitive restructuring is an important part of weight-reduction programs. As noted in Chapter 3, poor health habits can be maintained through dysfunctional monologues (e.g., "I'll never lose weight—I've tried before and failed so many times"). Participants in many weight-loss programs are urged to identify the maladaptive thoughts they have regarding weight loss and its maintenance and to substitute positive self-instruction. Having a strong sense of self-efficacy, that is, believing that one can lose weight, also predicts weight loss (Linde, Rothman, Baldwin, & Jeffrey, 2006).

Social Support   Another factor that consistently predicts successfully maintained weight loss is the presence of social support. Because clients with high degrees of social support are more successful than those with little social support, programs that include training in eliciting effective support from families, friends, and co-workers are more successful at promoting weight loss and maintenance of weight loss compared to programs without social support strategies (Wing &

Jeffery, 1999). Even supportive messages from a behavioural therapist over the Internet seem to help people lose weight more successfully (Oleck, 2001).

Relapse Prevention   Relapse-prevention techniques are incorporated into many treatment programs. As noted earlier, initial relapse prevention begins with effective screening of applicants to weight-loss programs. In addition, relapse-prevention techniques include matching treatments to the eating problems of particular clients, restructuring the environment to remove temptation, rehearsing high-risk situations for relapse (such as holidays), and developing coping strategies to deal with high-risk situations. Taken together, these components of weight-loss treatment programs are designed to address all aspects of weight loss and its maintenance.

Relapse prevention is important not only for diet control but also for the self-recrimination that occurs when people are unsuccessful. Such negative consequences may fall more heavily on women than men. When their diets fail, women are more likely to blame their own lack of self-discipline, whereas men are more likely to blame external factors, such as work (*New York Times,* 2000). Often weight-loss efforts fail simply because the process of maintaining behaviours needed for weight control is so arduous and there are few long-term rewards for so doing (Jeffrey, Kelly, Rothman, Sherwood, & Boutelle, 2004).

There is also some evidence that some people may undo their dieting efforts by justifying their relapse, and focusing on the future healthy behaviours that will balance out an occasional slip. Researchers at McGill University have proposed that these compensatory health beliefs are aimed at neutralizing the negative feelings that come from giving in to a desire or craving that interferes with one's health goals (Knäuper, Rabiau, Cohen, & Patriciu, 2004; Rabiau, Knäuper, & Miquelon, 2006). For example, if someone on a diet has a craving for chocolate cake, his or her compensatory health belief may be "I can eat this piece of cake now because I will exercise this evening." Although such beliefs may help minimize any guilt from giving into this craving, research suggests these compensatory health beliefs interfere with successful adherence to health behaviour-change programs such as dieting (Rabiau, Knäuper, & Miquelon, 2006). Thus, interventions that target and minimize these beliefs may be useful for preventing relapse and promoting dietary adherence.

Where Are Weight-loss Programs Implemented?

Work-site Weight-loss Interventions A number of weight-loss programs have been initiated through the work site, and a technique that has proven especially effective has been competition between work groups to find out which group can lose the most weight and keep it off.

Commercial Weight-loss Programs Thousands of people each week are exposed to behavioural methods of controlling obesity through commercial clinics such as Herbal Magic, Weight Watchers, and Jenny Craig. Many of these programs incorporate the behaviour-change principles described in this chapter. Because of the sheer number of people affected by these programs, formal evaluation of their effectiveness is important; yet rarely have such organizations opened their doors to formal program evaluation.

Evaluation of Cognitive Behavioural Weight-loss Techniques

Early evaluations of cognitive behavioural programs for obesity suggest that modest weight losses, of perhaps a pound a week for up to 20 weeks, could be achieved and maintained for up to a year (Brownell, 1982). More recent research suggests that cognitive behavioural interventions can be successful for helping people lose weight and maintain weight loss up to 3 years later whether they are administered on an individual or group basis (Cresci et al., 2007). Table 4.2 describes some of the promising leads that current research suggests for enhancing long-term weight loss in cognitive behavioural programs.

Overall, though, efforts to treat obesity have been only somewhat successful. And because unsuccessful dieting can exacerbate the problem, many health psychologists have come to the conclusion that obesity might also be treated by urging people to develop the healthiest

TABLE 4.2 | Weight Management Tips

Increasing awareness	**Exercise**
Keep track of what you eat.	Track your exercise progress: what do you enjoy doing?
Keep track of your weight.	Incorporate exercise into your lifestyle—become more active in all areas of life.
Write down when you eat and why.	
While you're eating	**Attitudes**
Pace yourself—eat slowly.	Think about your weight-loss goals—make them realistic.
Pay attention to your eating process.	Remember that any progress is beneficial and not reaching your goal does not mean you failed.
Pay attention to how full you are.	Think about your desire for foods—manage and work through cravings.
Eat at the same place and at the same time.	
Eat one portion and serve yourself before beginning the meal.	
Shopping for food	**Working with others**
Structure your shopping so that you know what you are buying beforehand.	Incorporate friends and family into your goals and your new lifestyle, including meal preparation and exercise routines.
Limit the number of already prepared items.	Communicate to them what they can do to help you reach your goals.
Don't shop when you are hungry.	
The eating environment	**Knowing nutrition**
Make healthy foods more available than unhealthy ones.	Be informed about nutrition.
Do your best to stick to your eating routine when dining out.	Know your recommended daily intake of calories, vitamins, and minerals.
Think about the limitations and possible adjustments to your eating routine before dining out or eating with other people.	Know which foods are good sources of vitamins, minerals, proteins, carbohydrates, and healthy fats.
	Eat a balanced diet.
	Prepare foods that are both healthy and taste good.

lifestyle they can, involving sensible eating and exercise, rather than specific weight-reduction techniques.

Taking a Public Health Approach

In Canada, and worldwide, the obesity epidemic threatens to overwhelm health care systems, as rates continue to soar. It is estimated that the direct and indirect costs of obesity are over $4.3 billion annually (Katzmarzyk & Janssen, 2004). Trends in the rise of obesity in Canada suggest that this cost will also continue to rise. For example, the obesity rate in 1974 was only 10 percent compared to 23 percent in 2004, and is expected to increase even more in the future (Luo et al., 2007). The increasing prevalence of obesity makes it essential to combat this growing problem in Canada by viewing it from a public health lens that emphasizes prevention. Programs that take into account the social and environmental determinants of obesity in addition to the individual and behavioural determinants are therefore needed to address this growing public health issue.

Prevention with families at risk for producing obese children is one important strategy. If parents can be trained early to adopt sensible meal planning and eating habits that they can convey to their children, the incidence of obesity may ultimately decline. Using nutrition labels to help motivate consumers to make healthy food choices is another strategy that can help families in making healthy food choices that would help prevent the development of obesity. The Heart and Stroke Foundation of Canada's Health Check program is an example of a point-of-choice nutrition education program that helps promote healthy eating (Raine, 2004).

Another approach to obesity that emphasizes prevention concerns weight-gain prevention programs for normal-weight adults. If exercise can be increased, diet altered in a healthy direction, and good eating habits developed, the weight gains that often accompany the aging process may be prevented (L. H. Epstein, Valoski, Wing, & McCurley, 1994). This approach may be particularly successful for women during menopause, as weight gain is very common during this time (Simkin-Silverman, Wing, Boraz, & Kuller, 2003). Canada's ParticipACTION program (see the Health Psychology in Action box in Chapter 3, p. 83) is an example of a media-based public health program aimed at promoting healthy living and therefore preventing the development of obesity.

Like many health habits, social engineering strategies may become part of the attack on this growing problem. The World Health Organization has argued for several changes, which include food labels that contain more nutrition and serving size information, a special tax on foods that are high in sugar and fat (the so-called "junk food" tax), and restriction of advertising to children or requiring health warnings (Arnst, 2004). As of December 2005, Health Canada introduced mandatory nutrition labelling on all prepackaged food in Canada, a measure that will help better educate Canadians about the nutritional value of the food they consume.

HOW IS SLEEP RELATED TO HEALTH?

(L06)

> Eighteen-year-old honours student Elliot Long and three friends were returning from an end-of-summer camping trip before starting their first year at the University of Waterloo. All straight-A students, they were eager to begin university life. But as they travelled along North Easthope Road in Kitchener, their vehicle began weaving back and forth on the road—the driver had fallen asleep. Their car veered into the path of an oncoming transport truck, killing Elliot. The driver lost his leg in the accident, one friend has not been able to talk about the accident since it happened, and the truck driver was left traumatized and had to take time off work to recover.
>
> HAMILTON SPECTATOR, MAY 25, 2007

As illustrated in the story above, sleep can have important implications for health. Sleep is a health practice all of us engage in, but many of us abuse our sleep. Sleep consists of five stages. The lightest and earliest stage of sleep (stage 1) is marked by theta waves, when we begin to tune out the sounds around us, although we are easily awakened by any loud sound. In stage 2, breathing and heart rates even out, body temperature drops, and brain waves alternate between short bursts called sleep spindles and large K-complex waves. In stages 3 and 4, known as deep sleep, blood pressure falls, breathing slows, and body temperature drops even lower. These are the phases most important for restoring energy, strengthening the immune system, and prompting the body to release growth hormone. These phases are marked by delta waves. In REM (rapid eye-movement) sleep, eyes dart back and forth, breathing and heart rate flutter, and we often dream vividly. This stage of sleep (stage 5) is marked by beta waves, and it is believed to be important for consolidating memories, solving problems from the previous day, and turning knowledge into long-term memories (Weintraub, 2004). All of these phases of sleep are essential.

Scientists have begun to identify the health risks associated with little or poor-quality sleep.

Sleep and Health

About one in every seven Canadians has trouble going to sleep or staying asleep. Those who suffer from insomnia report sleeping on average 6.5 hours compared to the 7.5 hours that people get who do not have this sleeping order (Tjepkema, 2005). For women, sleep disorders may be tied to hormonal levels related to menopause (Manber, Kuo, Cataldo, & Colrain, 2003).

It has long been known that insufficient sleep (less than seven hours a night) affects cognitive functioning, mood, performance in work, and quality of life (Altena, Van Der Werf, Strijers, & Van Someren, 2008; Pressman & Orr, 1997). Any of us who has spent a sleepless night tossing and turning over some problem knows how unpleasant the following day can be. Poor sleep can be a particular problem in certain high-risk occupations, with nightmares as one of the most common symptoms. This is especially true for occupations such as police work, in which police officers are exposed to traumatic events (Neylen et al., 2002).

Increasingly, we are also recognizing the health risks of inadequate sleep. Chronic partial sleep can compromise the ability to secrete and respond to insulin as well as adversely affect appetite regulation suggesting links between sleep loss, obesity, and diabetes (Knutson & Van Cauter, 2008). It can also increase the risk of developing coronary heart disease (Ekstedt, Akerstedt, & Söderström, 2004), it is linked to poorer vagal tone (Irwin, Cole, & Nicassio, 2006), and it can reduce the efficacy of flu shots, among its other detrimental effects (Weintraub, 2004). Each year more than 400 Canadians are killed in automobile crashes attributed to sleepy drivers, and a recent survey suggests that

in Ontario almost 167,000 drivers may have been involved in a drowsy driving collision (Traffic Injury Research Foundation, 2007). In one study of healthy older adults, sleep disturbances predicted all-cause mortality over the next 4 to 19 years of follow-up (Dew et al., 2003). Even just six nights of poor sleep in a row can impair metabolic and hormonal function, and over time, chronic sleep loss can reduce pain tolerance (Kundermann, Spernal, Huber, Krieg, & Lautenbacher, 2004), and aggravate the severity of hypertension and Type II diabetes (Hamilton, Catley, & Karlson, 2007).

Sleep deprivation has a number of adverse effects on immune functioning. For example, it reduces natural killer cell activity, which may, in turn, lead to greater receptivity to infection (Irwin et al., 1994), and it leads to reduced counts of other immune cells as well (Savard, Laroche, Simard, Ivers, & Morin, 2003). Poor sleep compromises human antibody response to hepatitis A vaccination (Lange, Perras, Fehm, & Born, 2003). Shift workers, who commonly experience disordered sleep when they change from one shift to another, have a high rate of respiratory tract infections and show depressed cellular immune function. Even modest sleep disturbance seems to have these adverse effects, although after a night of good sleep, immune functioning quickly recovers (Irwin et al., 1994). Poor sleep can also lead to elevated cytokines, which in turn can further compromise sleep. Elevated cytokines are also linked to several chronic illnesses, suggesting that this may be a possible pathway through which poor sleep can increase risk for negative health outcomes (Motivala & Irwin, 2007).

Sleep may have particular significance for those low in SES. In particular, the strong relationship between socio-economic status and health may be partly explained by the poorer sleep quality that people low in SES routinely have (Moore, Adler, Williams, & Jackson, 2002).

Poor sleep can also interfere with appetite regulation, and may therefore indirectly contribute to obesity. In one study, sleep-deprived adults were found to have increased levels of ghrelin, the hormone that promotes appetite, and decreased levels of leptin, the hormone that signals fullness, as well as experiencing the expected increases in appetite and hunger (Spiegel, Tasali, Penev, & Van Cauter, 2004). However, a prospective study of the links between sleep duration and body mass index among British civil servants did not find that shorter sleep duration was associated with obesity six years later (Stranges et al., 2007). For children, there is some evidence that lack of sleep is indeed related to later obesity. One study found that the less sleep children had in third grade, the more likely they were to be obese in sixth grade (Lumeng et al., 2007). In addition to changes in appetite hormones, it may be that children who get less sleep are also less likely to want to stay active and exercise. Thus, one approach to preventing obesity may be to ensure that children get enough sleep.

People who are going through major stressful life events or who are suffering from major depression especially report sleep disturbances (Tjepkema, 2005). Particularly when stressful events have been appraised as uncontrollable, insomnia may be the result (Morin, Rodrigue, & Ivers, 2003).

Although the health risks of insufficient sleep are now well known, less well known is the fact that people who habitually sleep more than seven hours every night, other than children and adolescents, also incur health risks. Long sleepers, like short sleepers, have more symptoms of psychopathology, including chronic worrying (Fichten, Libman, Creti, Balles, & Sabourin, 2004; Grandner & Kripke, 2004).

Apnea

Many of the problems related to sleep disruption have to do with amount of sleep, but in other cases, quality of sleep is the culprit. Recently, researchers have recognized that **sleep apnea,** an air pipe blockage that disrupts sleep, can compromise health. Each time that apnea occurs, the sleeper stops breathing, sometimes for as long as three minutes, until he or she suddenly wakes up, gasping for air. Some people are awakened dozens, even hundreds, of times each night without realizing it. Researchers now believe that sleep apnea triggers thousands of nighttime deaths, including heart attacks. Apnea also contributes to high rates of accidents in the workplace and on the road and to irritability, anxiety, and depression. Sleep apnea is difficult to diagnose because the symptoms, such as grouchiness, are so diffuse, but fitful, harsh snoring is one signal that a person may be experiencing apnea.

The next years promise to enlighten us more fully as to the health benefits of sleep and liabilities of disordered sleeping. For those with persistent sleep problems, a variety of cognitive behavioural interventions are available that typically make use of relaxation therapies (Perlis et al., 2000; Perlis, Sharpe, Smith, Greenblatt, & Giles, 2001). Such programs also recommend better sleep habits, many of which can be undertaken on one's own (Gorman, 1999; S. L. Murphy, 2000). How can we sleep better? See Table 4.3.

TABLE 4.3 | A Good Night's Sleep

- Get regular exercise, at least three times a week.
- Keep the bedroom cool at night.
- Sleep in a comfortable bed that is big enough.
- Establish a regular schedule for awakening and going to bed.
- Develop nightly rituals that can get one ready for bed, such as taking a shower.
- Use a fan or other noise generator to mask background sound.
- Don't consume too much alcohol or smoke.
- Don't eat too much or too little at night.
- Don't have strong smells in the room, as from incense, candles, or lotions.
- Don't nap after 3 p.m.
- Cut back on caffeine, especially in the afternoon or evening.
- If awakened, get up and read quietly in another place, to associate the bed with sleep, not sleeplessness.

Source: Gorman, 1999; S. L. Murphy, 2000.

WHY ARE REST, RENEWAL, AND SAVOURING IMPORTANT FOR HEALTH?

(L07)

An important set of health behaviours that is only beginning to be understood involves processes of relaxation and renewal, the restorative activities that help people reduce stress and restore their personal balance. The ability to savour the positive aspects of life may also have health benefits. We know, for example, that not taking a vacation can be a risk factor for heart attack among people with heart disease (Gump & Matthews, 1998; Steptoe, Roy, & Evans, 1996). Unfortunately, little other than intuition currently guides our thinking about restorative processes. Nonetheless, health psychologists suspect that rest, renewal, and savouring—involving such activities such as going home for the holidays, relaxing after exams, enjoying a beautiful hiking path or sunset and similar activities—will be shown to have health benefits.

This point underscores the fact that an understanding of health-enhancing behaviours is a work in progress. As new health risks are uncovered or the benefits of particular behaviours become known, the application of what we already know to these new behaviours will take on increasing importance. ●

SUMMARY

 Identify preventable injuries

- Unintentional injuries are a major cause of preventable death, especially among children. Recent years have seen increases in the use of accident prevention measures, especially car safety restraint devices for children, and bicycle helmets. These changes have been credited to publicity in the mass media, legislation favouring accident prevention measures, and training of parents by physicians and through interventions to promote safety measures for children.

 Describe cancer-related health behaviours

- Breast canacer is the most common cancer among Canadian women. The clinical breast exam (CBE) and the mammogram are the two recommended screening tests for this cancer. Yet national screening rates are still well below the national target of 70 percent.

- Factors associated with lack of CBE and mammography uptake include perceived barriers, lack of self-efficacy, fear, embarrassment, and lack of knowledge about breast cancer or the need for screening. Older women, women living in rural areas, and women from an ethnic- minority group may be less likely to participate in screening and therefore interventions need to be sensitive to their diverse needs.

- Screening for colorectal cancer and sun safe practices are predicted by the factors that predict other preventive cancer behaviours (e.g., perceived barriers and self-efficacy).

 Understand how exercise enhances health

- Aerobic exercise reduces risk for heart attack and improves other aspects of bodily functioning. Exercise also improves cognitive functioning and mood, and reduces stress.

- Few people adhere regularly to the standard exercise prescription of aerobic exercise for at least 30 minutes at least three times a week. People are more likely to exercise when the form of exercise is convenient and they like it. If their attitudes favour exercise and they come from families in which exercise is practised, they are also more likely to exercise.

- Cognitive behavioural interventions including relapse-prevention components have been at least somewhat successful in helping people adhere to regular exercise programs.

 Explain why maintaining a healthy diet is important

- Obesity is a health risk that has been linked to cardiovascular disease, kidney disease, diabetes, and other chronic conditions.

- Factors associated with obesity include genetic predisposition, early diet, family history of obesity, low SES, living in a poor neighbourhood, little exercise, and cultural values. Ironically, dieting may contribute to the propensity for obesity.

LO5 Know how weight control is related to health

- Weight may also be regulated by prior caloric consumption. Some individuals eat in response to stress, and stress eating may exacerbate existing weight problems.

- Obesity has been treated through diets, surgical procedures, drugs, and more recently cognitive-behavioural approaches. Most interventions use a multimodal approach that includes monitoring eating behaviour, modifying the environmental stimuli that control eating, gaining control over the eating process, and reinforcing new eating habits. Relapse-prevention skills training helps in long-term maintenance.

- Some success in weight loss has been found in the work site using work-group competition techniques and in commercial weight-loss programs that employ cognitive behavioural techniques.

- With the rates of obesity continuing to rise, a public health approach to treatment and intervention may be necessary to minimize the burden of the costs of obesity on the health care system. Social engineering interventions such as nutritional labelling and education, and media fitness campaigns, can assist families and individuals to make health promoting food choices.

- Dietary interventions through the mass media and community resources have promise as intervention techniques. Intervening with the family unit also appears to be useful for promoting and maintaining dietary change.

 LO6   **Describe how sleep is related to health**

- Although it is well known that insufficient sleep affects mood and well-being, the health risks of inadequate sleep are increasingly being recognized. Poor or inadequate sleep can have adverse effects on immune functioning and exacerbate hypertension and Type II diabetes.

 LO7   **Explain why rest, renewal, and savouring are important for health**

- Although there is little research on the health benefits of rest, renewal, and savouring, health psychologists believe that these restorative activities may have their influence through stress reduction and restoring personal balance.

KEY TERMS

aerobic exercise p. 95
clinical breast exam (CBE) p. 91

obesity p. 104
sleep apnea p. 117

stress eating p. 110

CHAPTER 5

Health-Compromising Behaviours

LEARNING OBJECTIVES

After reading this chapter, students will be able to:

(LO1) Identify the characteristics of health-compromising behaviours

(LO2) Describe and define substance dependence

(LO3) Understand how alcoholism and problem drinking compromise health

(LO4) Explain how smoking is harmful for health and what factors influence smoking

(LO5) Describe eating disorders

Several decades ago, my father went for his annual physical and his doctor told him, as the doctor did each year, that he had to stop smoking. As usual, my father told his doctor that he would stop when he was ready. He had already tried several times and had been unsuccessful. My father had begun smoking at age 14, long before the health risks of smoking were known, and it was now an integrated part of his lifestyle, which included a couple of cocktails before a dinner high in fat and cholesterol and a hectic life that provided few opportunities for regular exercise. Smoking was part of who he was. His doctor then said, "Let me put it this way. If you expect to see your daughter graduate from university, stop smoking now." That warning did the trick. My father threw his cigarettes in the wastebasket and never had another one. Over the years, as he read more about health, he began to change his lifestyle in other ways. He began to swim regularly for exercise, and he pared down his diet to one of mostly fish, chicken, vegetables, fruit, and cereal. Despite the fact that he once had many of the risk factors for early heart disease, he lived to age 83.

In this chapter, we turn our attention to health-compromising behaviours—behaviours practised by people that undermine or harm their current or future health. My father's problems with stopping smoking illustrate several important points about these behaviours. Many health-compromising behaviours are habitual, and several, including smoking, are addictive, making them very difficult habits to break. On the other hand, with proper incentive and help, even the most intractable health habit can be modified. When a person succeeds in changing a health behaviour for the better, often he or she will make other lifestyle changes in the direction of a healthier way of living. The end result is that risk declines, and a disease-free middle and old age becomes a possibility.

—*AUTHOR SHELLEY TAYLOR*

(L01) ## WHAT ARE THE CHARACTERISTICS OF HEALTH-COMPROMISING BEHAVIOURS?

Many health-compromising behaviours share several additional important characteristics. First, there is a window of vulnerability in adolescence. Drinking to excess, smoking, illicit drug use, over-controlled eating, unsafe sex, and risk-taking behaviour that can lead to accidents or early death all begin in early adolescence and sometimes cluster together as part of a problem behaviour syndrome (Lam, Stewart, & Ho, 2001; Public Health Agency of Canada, 2004b).

This is not to suggest that all health-compromising behaviours evolve and are firmly implanted during adolescence. Several health problems, such as obesity, begin early in childhood and others, such as alcoholism, may be special risks for older adults. These exceptions notwithstanding, there is an unnerving similarity in the factors that elicit and maintain many of these health-compromising behaviours.

Many of these behaviours are heavily tied to the peer culture, as children learn from and imitate the peers they like and admire (Gaughan, 2006). Wanting to be attractive to others becomes very important in adolescence, and this factor is significant in the development of eating disorders, alcohol consumption, tobacco and drug use, tanning, unsafe sexual encounters, and vulnerability to injury, among other behaviours (for example, Shadel, Niaura, & Abrams, 2004).

Several health-compromising behaviours are also intimately bound up in the self-presentation process—that is, in the adolescent's or young adult's efforts to appear sophisticated, cool, tough, or savvy in his or her social environment (Evans, Powers, Hersey, & Renaud, 2006). The image conveyed by these behaviours, then, is another shared characteristic that must be considered in their modification.

A third similarity is that many of these behaviours are pleasurable, enhancing the adolescent's ability to cope with stressful situations, and some represent thrill-seeking, which can be rewarding in its own right. However, each of these behaviours is also highly dangerous. Each has been tied to at least one major cause of death in this country, and several, especially smoking, are risk factors for more than one major chronic disease.

Fourth, development of all these behaviours occurs gradually, as the individual is exposed to and becomes susceptible to the behaviour, experiments with it, and later engages in its regular use (Wills, Pierce, & Evans, 1996). As such, these health-compromising behaviours are not acquired all at once, but through a process that may make different interventions important at the different stages of vulnerability, experimentation, and regular use.

Fifth, substance abuse of all kinds, whether cigarettes, alcohol, or drugs, are predicted by some of the same factors. Those adolescents who get involved in such risky behaviours often have high levels of conflict with their parents and poor self-control, suggesting that these behaviours may function in part as coping mechanisms to manage a stressful life (M. L. Cooper, Wood,

Orcutt, & Albino, 2003; Wills, Gibbons, Gerrard, & Brody, 2000).

Common to the abuse of many substances, including cigarettes, alcohol, and marijuana, is the profile of those who use these substances. Adolescents with a penchant for deviant behaviour, with low self-esteem, and with problematic family relationships often show higher levels of these behaviours (Duncan, Duncan, Strycker, & Chaumeton, 2002; Wagner et al., 2010). Combining long hours of employment with school increases the risk of alcohol, cigarette, and marijuana abuse among adolescents, although this may be truer for non-minority rather than minority students (M. K. Johnson, 2004). Those who abuse substances typically do poorly in school. Family problems, deviance, and low self-esteem appear to explain this relationship (Andrews & Duncan, 1997). Likewise, difficult temperament, poor self-control, and deviance-prone attitudes are related to peer and adolescent substance use of tobacco, alcohol, and marijuana (Repetti, Taylor, & Seeman, 2002).

Finally, problem behaviours are related to the larger social structure in which they occur (Latkin, Williams, Wang, & Curry, 2005). Most of these problem behaviours are more common in lower social class individuals, and are associated with attitudes toward health (e.g., less health consciousness, beliefs that health is a matter of chance) that may develop from exposure to hardships and poor health (Wardle & Steptoe, 2003). In some cases, these social class differences occur because of greater exposure to the problem behaviour and, in other cases, because lower social class provides more stressful circumstances with which the adolescent may need to cope. Practice of these health-compromising behaviours is thought to be one reason that social class is so strongly related to most causes of disease and death (Denton, Prus, & Walter, 2004).

In this chapter, we are especially concerned with two of the most common and commonly treated health-compromising behaviours—alcohol abuse and smoking. Many of the points raised, however, will be relevant to other health-compromising behaviours, such as illicit drug use, which we will examine briefly. In particular, many of these health-compromising behaviours involve addiction.

(L02) WHAT IS SUBSTANCE DEPENDENCE?

A person is said to be dependent on a substance when he or she has repeatedly self-administered it, resulting in tolerance, withdrawal, and compulsive behaviour (American Psychiatric Association, 2000). Substance dependence can include **physical dependence,** the state that occurs when the body has adjusted to the substance

and incorporates the use of that substance into the normal functioning of the body's tissues. Physical dependence often involves **tolerance,** the process by which the body increasingly adapts to the use of a substance, requiring larger and larger doses of it to obtain the same effects, eventually reaching a plateau. **Craving** is a strong desire to engage in a behaviour or consume a substance. It seems to result from physical dependence and from a conditioning process: As the substance is paired with many environmental cues, the presence of those cues triggers an intense desire for the substance. **Addiction** occurs when a person has become physically or psychologically dependent on a substance following use over time. **Withdrawal** refers to the unpleasant symptoms, both physical and psychological, that people experience when they stop using a substance on which they have become dependent. Although the symptoms vary, they include anxiety, irritability, intense cravings for the substance, nausea, headaches, shaking, and hallucinations. All these characteristics are common to substance abuse involving addiction, which includes smoking, alcohol consumption, and drug abuse.

The costs of substance abuse in Canada are substantial. The burden to health care resources, law enforcement, and loss of productivity at work and home due to death and disability from substance abuse was $39.8 billion in 2002. Smoking accounted for most of this cost (43 percent), alcohol for about 37 percent, and the remaining 20 percent of the social costs of substance abuse was accounted for by illegal drug use (Rehm et al., 2006).

Although there are different approaches to treating substance dependence, one approach that has been increasingly used as an intervention strategy for dealing with substance abuse is **harm reduction.** Described as a public health response to the substance abuse problem, harm reduction is defined as an "approach that focuses on the risks and consequences of substance use rather than on the use itself" (Poulin, 2006). In Canada, harm reduction has been adopted as the model guiding our national drug strategy, and has similarly been adopted as a treatment strategy in other countries including the United Kingdom, Australia, and Germany (Ogborne, Carver, & Wiebe, 2001). At the heart of harm reduction is the philosophy that completely eliminating substance use in society is an unrealistic goal, and therefore it is preferable to focus on reducing substance use to help minimize the social and physical harm associated with substance abuse. From a practical standpoint, harm reduction may also be an effective strategy to initially promote safe substance use before moving to interventions directed at complete cessation (Health

Canada, 2005a). Accordingly, use of substances is not judged as something that is good or bad, and strategies like abstinence that are promoted by organization such as Alcoholics Anonymous (see the Focus on Social Issues box, "A Profile of Alcoholics Anonymous," on page 129) are viewed as only one of many possible strategies for dealing with substance abuse (Poulin, 2006).

Harm reduction is most often implemented at the community level with community-based programs that focus on facilitating safe use of substances (Health Canada, 2005a). Methadone maintenance and needle exchange programs are examples of community-based harm-reduction strategies for dealing with illicit injection drug use (e.g., heroin use). Injection drug use is associated with a host of social and health problems including increased crime and the spread of HIV/AIDS, tuberculosis, and infectious hepatitis. Needle sharing is often the main route for the spread of these infectious diseases. Needle exchange programs recognize that not all injection drug users want to or are able to stop using drugs and accordingly offer the means (sterile needles) and knowledge (education about how to prevent the spread of infection) for them to change the behaviours that put them most at risk for contracting and spreading infections (Riley, 1993).

Because injection drug use is especially problematic in large cities, harm-reduction initiatives have been implemented in several Canadian urban centres, including Toronto, Montreal, Ottawa, and Vancouver. One harm-reduction strategy (Insite) was launched in 2003 in Vancouver's downtown east side, where the concentration of injection drug users was particularly high, and rates of HIV, hepatitis, and death from drug overdose were soaring. Based on a harm-reduction philosophy, Insite was Canada's first safe-injection site, offering users a disposable injection kit and other sterile drug-use tools to prepare and inject under the supervision of medical staff. Initial response to this intervention program was mixed as many believed that it would convey the wrong message and actually increase injection drug use. However, initial evaluations of the effectiveness of Insite are promising. People who use this facility are 70 percent less likely to share needles than those who do not visit Insite or do so infrequently, and needle-sharing rates in the community have also decreased since Insite was opened (Vancouver Coastal Health, n.d.).

Building on the success of the Insite program, Vancouver Coastal Health plans to launch a new pilot program for distributing clean, unused crack pipes to drug users by the end of 2011. This new program will be an upgrade to the previous program, which only distributed the pipe mouthpieces in an effort to reduce the

spread of HIV and hepatitis, which are common among crack cocaine smokers.

Although injection drug use is perhaps one of the more harmful health-compromising behaviours, concerns are increasing about other types of substance abuse, such as marijuana use, which is now the most common illegal drug used by young people in the world (see the Focus on Social Issues box, "Toker Nation?").

Illicit Drug Use

According to the United Nations Office on Drugs and Crime, the use of illicit drugs is a global problem, with an estimated 155 to 250 million people worldwide having used an illicit drug in 2008 (United Nations, 2010). In Canada, approximately 12 percent had used at least one form of illicit drug in 2008 (Health Canada, 2009a). There are four main classes of illicit drugs that are of particular concern because of their addictive and harmful properties: opiates (e.g., heroin), cocaine, cannabis (e.g., marijuana), and the amphetamine type stimulants (ATS; e.g., ecstasy). Like alcohol, drugs are considered to be **psychoactive substances,** that is they impact cognitive and affective processes and alter the way a person behaves when ingested (World Health Organization, 2010).

In addition to these four drug types, use of psychoactive prescription drugs has become a growing concern worldwide (United Nations, 2010) and in Canada (Haydon, Rehm, Fischer, Monga, & Adlaf, 2005), as they become diverted into the illicit drug market. Non-medical use of prescription drugs including sedatives and tranquilizers (such as valium), opioid pain killers (such as Oxycontin and Demorol), and stimulants (such as Ritalin) is on the increase among young adults and youth. For example, a recent survey of Ontario students aged 12 to 19 found that 21 percent had used prescription drugs in the past year, with the majority obtaining the drugs from home (Brands, Paglia-Boak, Sproule, Leslie, & Adlaf, 2010). Not surprisingly, students who were frequent users of alcohol, other illicit drugs, and daily smokers were more likely to use prescription drugs without medical supervision.

What are the consequences of illicit drug use? In addition to legal and economic problems, use of illicit drugs and prescription drugs taken without medical guidance can result in a variety of physical, mental and social problems. Physical problems can include lung damage from smoking marijuana, damage to the inside of the nose from sniffing cocaine, and risk for HIV and other infections from use of injection drugs. Moreover, stimulant drugs such as cocaine, ecstasy and metamphetamines can

FIGURE 5.1 | Primary Drugs of Abuse Among People Treated For Drug Problems, Canada 2008
(*Source:* Adapted from United Nations Office on Drugs and Crime (UNODC), World Drug Report 2011 (United Nations publication, Sales No.E.10.XI.13), Retrieved July 6, 2011 from www.unodc.org/unodc/en/data-and-analysis/WDR-2011.htm

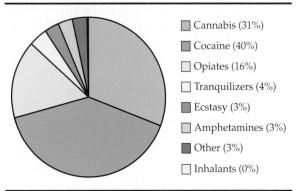

- Cannabis (31%)
- Cocaine (40%)
- Opiates (16%)
- Tranquilizers (4%)
- Ecstasy (3%)
- Amphetamines (3%)
- Other (3%)
- Inhalants (0%)

increase heart rate and blood pressure to a degree that increases risk for strokes and even death. Even prescription drugs when used under medical guidance can have unpleasant physical side effects such as digestive upset and headaches. When they are used without guidance or in combination with other drugs the risk for these side effects increases considerably. As with any substance, continued use can lead to physical dependence and addiction. Mental health problems include short-term anxiety and confusion from having a "bad trip," and long-term memory and personality changes if drug use becomes habitual. Finally, drugs can lower inhibitions and affect judgment resulting in decisions and behaviours that might normally not be undertaken. Risky sexual behaviours, driving while impaired, and engaging in other risky behaviours are more likely when someone is under the influence of drugs (Health Canada, 2009a). Thankfully, there are treatment programs available to deal with the spectrum of problems that result from using illicit drugs (see Figure 5.1).

(LO3) HOW DO ALCOHOLISM AND PROBLEM DRINKING COMPROMISE HEALTH?

Scope of the Problem

Alcohol is responsible for more than 8,000 deaths each year (Rehm et al., 2006), making it one of the leading causes of preventable death after tobacco and improper diet and exercise. Nearly 20 percent of Canadians

drink at levels that exceed government recommendations (Adlaf, Begin, & Sawka, 2005). Originally characterized as a social ill, alcoholism was officially recognized as a disease by the American Medical Association in 1957.

As a health issue, alcohol consumption has been linked to a number of disorders, including high blood pressure, stroke, cirrhosis of the liver, some forms of cancer, and fetal alcohol syndrome—a condition of retardation and physiological abnormalities that arises in the offspring of heavy-drinking mothers (Higgins-Biddle, Babor, Mullahyl, Daniels, & McRee, 1997). Alcoholics can show major sleep disorders; disordered sleep may contribute to immune alterations that elevate risk for infection among alcoholics (Redwine, Dang, Hall, & Irwin, 2003). Excessive drinking also accounts for substantial cognitive impairments, many of them irreversible. Almost 1,000 road fatalities are attributed to drinking and driving annually, and approximately 80,000 incidents of impaired driving are reported annually. Although the rate of impaired driving offences in Canada has been slowly declining over the past decade, (Collin, 2006), there have been three consecutive increases in the number of impaired driving offences in Canada since 2007 (Dauvergne & Turner, 2010).

Economically, alcohol abuse is estimated to cost Canada $14.6 billion, which includes approximately $7 billion in lost productivity, $3.3 billion in treatment costs for alcohol misuse and related disorders, and almost $1 billion in other costs, including motor vehicle accidents, fire, and crime (Rehm et al., 2006). This translates into a cost of $463 per every living Canadian per year to cover the economic burden of alcohol abuse. In addition to the direct costs of alcoholism through illness, accidents, and economic costs, alcohol abuse contributes to other health problems. For example, alcohol disinhibits aggression, so a substantial percentage of homicides, suicides, and assaults occur under the influence of alcohol. Alcohol can also facilitate other risky behaviours such as more impulsive sexual behaviour (Bryan, Ray, & Cooper, 2007) and poorer skills for negotiating condom use, relative to those who were more sober (Anstey et al., 2006).

Overall, though, it has been difficult to define the scope of alcoholism. Many problem drinkers keep their problem successfully hidden, at least for a time. By drinking at particular times of day or at particular places and by restricting contact with other people during these times, the alcoholic may be able

Toker Nation?

According to the 2007 World Drug Report by the United Nations Office on Drugs and Crime, Canada leads the industrialized world in marijuana use. Approximately 16.8 percent of the Canadian population between the ages of 15 and 64 reported to have consumed marijuana during 2006. Compared to rates in Australia and New Zealand (13.4), the United States (12.6 percent), Britain (8.7 percent), France (8.6 percent), Germany (6.9 percent), and the Netherlands (6.1 percent), where marijuana use is decriminalized, Canada has the unfortunate distinction of being number one when it comes using this illegal drug. Although the proportion of Canadians who consume marijuana dropped to 13.6 in 2008, Canada remains in first place for consumption among industrialized countries according to the 2009 World Drug Report.

Besides being somewhat embarrassing internationally, the use of marijuana by a large number of Canadians raises concerns about the health and social issues associated with its use, especially among young adults. The proportion of adolescents who use marijuana is much higher than the national rates found in the World Drug Report. A Canadian survey suggests that 40 percent of girls and 50 percent of boys in grade 10 have tried marijuana, and another one-quarter of girls and one-third of boys use marijuana three or more times a year. Similar to other types of substance use, marijuana use is related to a variety of health-compromising and risky health behaviours, as well as other social and psychological issues. Marijuana use among adolescents is associated with smoking, frequent and excessive drinking, having unprotected sex, and other risky sexual behaviours. In addition, those who "toke up" are more likely to be dissatisfied with life, have negative attitudes towards school, and have poor relationships with their parents (Public Health Agency of Canada, 2004b).

Marijuana use appears to increase after high school also, with nearly 70 percent of those between 18 and 24 reporting having tried marijuana (Patton & Adlaf, 2005).

Why is marijuana so popular among adolescents and young adults? Some researchers suggest that its acceptance as a social drug among adults (and therefore its greater use and availability) has contributed to the perception that marijuana is a safe recreational drug (Tonkin, 2002). Indeed, marijuana is the most commonly used illegal substance in Canada. However, the misperceptions about its safe use are not well founded. In fact, marijuana contains more tar than cigarettes, and has higher levels of some cancer-causing chemicals than that found in tobacco smoke. In addition, long-term use can lead to cognitive impairments and early development of schizophrenia among those at high risk. And, like cigarettes and other substances, marijuana is addictive (Centre for Addiction and Mental Health, 2007).

Source: CBC News, July 6, 2007.

to drink without noticeable disruption in his or her daily activities.

What Are Alcoholism and Problem Drinking?

Exactly what constitutes alcoholism and problem drinking is fuzzy. **Problem drinking** and **alcoholism** encompass a variety of specific patterns (Adlaf, Demers, & Gilksman, 2005). The term "alcoholic" is usually reserved for someone who is physically addicted to alcohol. Alcoholics show withdrawal symptoms when they attempt to stop drinking, they have a high tolerance for alcohol, and they have little ability to control their drinking. Problem drinkers may not have these symptoms, but they may have substantial social, psychological, and medical problems resulting from alcohol.

Problem drinking and alcoholism have been defined by a variety of specific behaviours, which range from the milder ones associated with problem drinking to the severe ones associated with alcoholism. These patterns include the need for daily use of alcohol, the inability to cut down on drinking, repeated efforts to control drinking through temporary abstinence or restriction of alcohol to certain times of the day, binge drinking, occasional consumptions of large quantities of alcohol, loss of memory while intoxicated, continued drinking despite known health problems, and drinking of nonbeverage alcohol.

Origins of Alcoholism and Problem Drinking

The origins of alcoholism and problem drinking are complex. Based on twin studies and on the frequency of alcoholism in sons of alcoholic fathers, genetic factors appear to be implicated in 50 percent of the vulnerabilities that lead to alcoholism (Schuckit, 2009). Men have traditionally been at greater risk for alcoholism than women (Kalaydjian et al., 2009), although with changing norms, younger women and women employed outside the home are beginning to catch up (D. R. Williams, 2002). Socio-demographic factors, such as low income, also predict alcoholism, although only modestly.

Drinking and Stress   Drinking clearly occurs, in part, as an effort to buffer the impact of stress (Mulia, Schmidt, Bond, Jacobs, & Korcha, 2008; Sayette et al., 2007). Many people begin drinking to enhance positive emotions and reduce negative ones (Repetto, Caldwell, & Zimmerman, 2005). People who are experiencing a lot of negative life events, chronic stressors, and little social support are more likely to become problem drinkers than are people without these problems (Mulia, Schmidt, Bond, Jacobs, & Korcha, 2008; Sadava & Pak, 1994). For example, alcohol abuse rises among people who have been laid off from their jobs (Catalano, Dooley, Wilson, & Hough, 1993). Alienation from work, low job autonomy, little use of one's abilities, and lack of participation in decision making at work are associated with heavy drinking (E. S. Greenberg & Grunberg, 1995). Financial strain, especially to the degree that it produces depression, leads to drinking in order to cope (Mulia, Schmidt, Bond, Jacobs, & Korcha, 2008).

Social Origins of Drinking   Alcoholism is tied to the social and cultural environment of the drinker. Many people who eventually become problem drinkers or alcoholics learn early in life to associate drinking with pleasant social occasions. They may develop a social life centred on drinking, such as going to bars or attending parties

where alcohol consumption is prominent. In contrast, those people who marry and become parents reduce their risk of developing alcohol-related disorders in part because marriage predicts decreased involvement in social activities, which in turn leads to decreased heavy drinking. (Lee, Chassin, & MacKinnon, 2010).

There appear to be two windows of vulnerability for alcohol use and abuse. The first, when chemical dependence generally starts, is during adolescence when the developing adolescent brain is more vulnerable to the effects of alcohol on the brain's reward circuitry, which in turn can diminish the ability to control alcohol consumption (Nixon & McClain, 2010). The other window of vulnerability is in late middle age, in which problem drinking may act as a coping method for managing stress (Brennan, Schutte, & Moos, 2010). Late-onset problem drinkers are more likely to control their drinking on their own or be successfully treated, compared with individuals with more long-term drinking problems (Moos, Brennan, & Moos, 1991).

Depression and alcoholism may be linked. Alcoholism may represent untreated symptoms of depression, or depression may act as an impetus for drinking in an effort to improve mood. Thus, in some cases, symptoms of both disorders must be treated simultaneously (Gopalakrishnan, Ross, O'Brien, & Oslin, 2009; Oslin et al., 2003). Social isolation and lack of employment can exacerbate these problems. For women who are survivors of violence, trauma, or abuse, substance abuse and mental health problems frequently co-occur (Canadian Women's Health Network, 2006). Drinking among older adults may be confounded by the fact that tolerance for alcohol reliably decreases with age, leaving an older person vulnerable to alcohol-related accidents such as falls.

Treatment of Alcohol Abuse

For years, alcohol abuse was regarded as an intractable problem, but substantial evidence indicates that it can be modified successfully, for example with cognitive behavioural interventions (Loeber et al., 2007). There is also a "maturing out" of alcoholism, which is especially likely in the later years of life (Brennan, Schutte, & Moos, 2010).

Earlier, we noted that alcohol consumption is heavily dependent on the social environment in which it occurs, and this fact is prominent in understanding the recovery process as well. Alcoholics who come from high socio-economic backgrounds and who are in highly socially stable environments (that is, who have a regular job, an intact family, and a circle of friends) do very well in treatment programs, achieving success rates as high as 68 percent,

Adolescence and young adulthood represent a window of vulnerability to problem drinking and alcoholism. Successful intervention with this age group may reduce the scope of the alcoholism problem.

whereas alcoholics of low socio-economic status (SES) with low social stability often have success rates of 18 percent or less. No treatment program will be highly successful unless it takes account of the alcoholic's environment. Without employment and social support, the prospects for recovery are dim (MedicineNet.com, 2002). The Health Psychology in Action box, "After the Fall of the Berlin Wall," presents an example of these problems.

Treatment Programs

In addition to private treatment facilities for alcoholism, there are a limited number of provincially licensed residential care facilities in Canada that offer treatment for alcoholism. However, with only 6,000 beds available and a decline in the number available over the past few years (Dell & Garabedian, 2003), many people are forced to seek other options for treatment. A self-help group, especially Alcoholics Anonymous (AA), is often the most commonly sought source of help for alcohol-related problems (see the Focus on Social Issues box, "A Profile of Alcoholics Anonymous").

Treatment programs for alcoholism and problem drinking typically use broad-spectrum cognitive behavioural therapy to treat the biological and environmental factors involved in alcoholism simultaneously (National Institute on Alcohol Abuse and Alcoholism [NIAAA], 2000a). The goals of the approach are to decrease the reinforcing properties of alcohol, to teach people new behaviours inconsistent with alcohol abuse, and to modify the environment to include reinforcements for activities that do not involve alcohol. These approaches also attempt to instill coping techniques for dealing with stress and relapse-prevention methods to enhance long-term maintenance.

For hard-core alcoholics, the first phase of treatment is **detoxification.** Because this can produce severe symptoms and health problems, detoxification is typically conducted in a carefully supervised and medically monitored setting.

Once the alcoholic has at least partly dried out, therapy is initiated. The typical program begins with a short-term, intensive inpatient treatment followed by a period of continuing treatment on an outpatient basis (NIAAA, 2000b). Typically, inpatient programs last

After the Fall of the Berlin Wall

When the Berlin Wall came down in 1989, there were celebrations worldwide. In the midst of the jubilation, few fully anticipated the problems that might arise in its wake. Hundreds of thousands of East Germans, who had lived for decades under a totalitarian regime with a relatively poor standard of living, were now free to stream across the border into West Germany, which enjoyed prosperity, employment, and a high standard of living. But for many people, the promise of new opportunities failed to materialize. Employment was less plentiful than had been assumed, and the East Germans were less qualified for the jobs that did exist. Discrimination and hostility toward the East Germans was higher than expected, and many migrating East Germans found themselves unemployed.

Unemployment is a severe stressor that has pervasive negative implications for one's entire life. It produces chronic tension, anxiety, and a sense of discouragement. Because alcohol is known to reduce tension and anxiety and can stimulate a good mood, the potential for drinking to alleviate stress among the unemployed is high. Several studies document the fact that alcohol intake often rises among the unemployed (for example, Catalano, Dooley, Wilson, & Houph, 1993). But not everyone responds to the stress of unemployment by drinking.

Two German researchers, Mittag and Schwarzer (1993), examined alcohol consumption among men who had found employment in West Germany and those who had remained unemployed. In addition, they measured self-efficacy with respect to coping with life's problems through such items as "When I am in trouble, I can rely on my ability to deal with the problem effectively." Presumably, individuals who have high feelings of self-efficacy are less vulnerable to stress, and thus they may be less likely to consume alcohol under stressful circumstances than are those with a low sense of self-efficacy.

The researchers found that men with a high sense of self-efficacy were less likely to consume high levels of alcohol. Self-efficacy appeared to be especially important in responding to the stress of unemployment. Those men who were unemployed and had a low sense of self-efficacy were drinking more than any other group. Thus, being male, being unemployed for a long time, and not believing in a sense of personal agency led to heavy drinking.

Although psychologists cannot provide jobs to the unemployed, perhaps they can empower individuals to develop more optimistic self-beliefs. If one believes that one can control one's behaviour, cope effectively with life, and solve one's problems, one may be able to deal effectively with setbacks (Mittag & Schwarzer, 1993).

---

between 10 and 60 days, with an average of approximately 28 days (R. K. Fuller & Hiller-Strumhöfel, 1999). After discharge, some patients attend follow-up sessions, whereas others are discharged to supervised living arrangements.

Cognitive Behavioural Treatments   A variety of behaviour modification techniques have been incorporated into alcohol treatment programs (NIAAA, 2000b). Many programs include a self-monitoring phase, in which the alcoholic or problem drinker begins to understand the situations that give rise to and maintain drinking. Contingency contracting is frequently employed, in which the person agrees to a psychologically or financially costly outcome in the event of failure. Motivational enhancement procedures have also been included in many cognitive behavioural interventions with alcoholics and problem drinkers, because the responsibility and the

capacity to change rely entirely on the client. Consequently, working to provide individualized feedback about the patient's drinking and the effectiveness of his or her efforts can get the client motivated and on board to continue a program of treatment that may be more resistant to the inevitable temptations to relapse (NIAAA, 2000b).

Some programs have included medications for blocking the alcohol-brain interactions that may contribute to alcoholism. One such medication is naltrexone, which is used as an aid to prevent relapse among alcoholics. It blocks the opioid receptors in the brain, thereby weakening the rewarding effects of alcohol. Although drugs have shown some success in reducing alcohol consumption in conjunction with cognitive-behavioural interventions, successful maintenance requires patients to continue taking the drugs on their own, and if they choose not to do so, they reduce the effectiveness of the chemical treatment.

A Profile of Alcoholics Anonymous

No one knows exactly when Alcoholics Anonymous (AA) began, but it is believed that the organization was formed around 1935 in Akron, Ohio. The first meetings were attended by a few acquaintances who discovered that they could remain sober by attending services of a local religious group and sharing with other alcoholics their problems and efforts to remain sober. In 1936, weekly AA meetings were taking place around the country.

Who participates in AA? Currently, its membership is estimated to be more than 2 million individuals worldwide, with over 95,000 members in Canada (Alcoholics Anonymous, 2011). The sole requirement for participation in AA is a desire to stop drinking. Originally, the organization attracted hardened drinkers who turned to it as a last resort; more recently, however, it has attracted many people who are experiencing drinking problems but whose lives are otherwise intact. Members come from all walks of life, including all socio-economic levels, races, cultures, sexual preferences, and ages.

The philosophy of Alcoholics Anonymous is a commitment to the concept of self-help. Members believe that the person who is best able to reach an alcoholic is a recovered alcoholic. In addition, members are encouraged to immerse themselves in the culture of AA—to attend "90 meetings in 90 days." At these meetings, AA members speak about the drinking experiences that prompted them to seek out AA and what sobriety has meant to them. Time is set aside for prospective members to talk informally with long-time members so that they can learn and imitate the coping techniques that recovered alcoholics have used.

AA has a firm policy regarding alcohol consumption. It maintains that alcoholism is a disease that can be managed but never cured. Recovery means that an individual must acknowledge that he or she has a disease, that it is incurable, and that alcohol can play no part in future life. Recovery depends completely on staying sober.

Is Alcoholics Anonymous successful in getting people to stop drinking? AA's dropout rate is unknown, and success over the long term has not been carefully chronicled. Moreover, because the organization keeps no membership lists (it is anonymous), it is difficult to evaluate its success. However, AA itself maintains that two out of three individuals who wish to stop drinking have been able to do so through its program.

Evaluations of alcohol treatment programs have found that people do better if they participate in AA while participating in a medically based formal treatment program, than they would in the formal treatment program alone (Timko, Finney, Moos, & Moos, 1995). A study that compared AA participation with more formal treatment found comparable effects, a striking finding because the AA attendees had lower incomes and less education initially and thus had somewhat worse prospects for improving.

Researchers attempting to understand the effectiveness of AA programs have pointed to several important elements. AA is like a religious conversion experience in which an individual adopts a totally new way of life; such experiences can be powerful in bringing about behaviour change. Also, a member who shares his or her experiences develops a commitment to other members. The process of giving up alcohol contributes to a sense of emotional maturity and responsibility: helping the alcoholic accept responsibility for his or her life. AA may also provide a sense of meaning and purpose in the individual's life—most chapters have a strong spiritual or religious bent and urge members to commit themselves to a power greater than themselves. The group can also provide affection and satisfying personal relationships and thus help people overcome the isolation that many alcoholics experience.

AA is significant as an organization for several reasons. First, it was one of the earliest self-help programs for individuals suffering from a health problem; therefore, it has provided a model for self-help organizations whose members have other addictive problems, such as Overeaters Anonymous and Gamblers Anonymous, among many others. Second, in having successfully treated alcoholics for decades, AA has demonstrated that the problem of alcoholism is not as intractable as had been widely assumed.

Many successful treatment programs have attempted to provide alcoholics with stress management techniques that they can substitute for drinking because, as noted earlier, alcohol is sometimes used as a method of coping with stress. For example, relaxation training, assertiveness training, and training in social skills help the alcoholic or problem drinker deal with problem situations without resorting to alcohol.

Relapse Prevention   Relapse is a major difficulty in treating alcohol abuse. Authoritative studies report relapse rates of 50 percent or more at two to four years after treatment. One recent meta-analysis of past alcohol treatment outcome studies estimates that more than 50 percent of treated patients relapse within the first three months after treatment (NIAAA, 2000b). Practising coping skills or social skills in high-risk-for-relapse situations is a mainstay of relapse-prevention interventions. In addition, the recognition that people often stop and restart an addictive behaviour several times before they are successful has led to the development of techniques for managing relapses. Understanding that an occasional relapse is normal helps the problem drinker realize that any given lapse does not signify failure or a lack of control. Drink-refusal skills and the substitution of nonalcoholic beverages in high-risk social situations are also important components of relapse-prevention skills. Interventions with heavy-drinking university students have made use of these approaches (see the Focus on Social Issues box, "The Drinking University Students").

Evaluation of Alcohol Treatment Programs   Surveys of alcohol treatment programs suggest several factors that are consistently associated with success: identifying factors in the environment that control drinking and modifying those factors or instilling coping skills to manage them, a moderate length of participation (about six to eight weeks), outpatient aftercare, inclusion of a stress management component, and active involvement of relatives and employers in the treatment process (Health Canada, 1999).

Minimal Interventions   Even minimal interventions can make a dent in drinking-related problems. In one study (Oslin et al., 2003), veterans with depression or who were at risk for problem drinking received either usual care or a telephone alcoholism and depression management program in which a behavioural health specialist provided information and support over a four-month period. Compared with usual care, the telephone-implemented intervention produced beneficial changes, suggesting that telephone interventions can be a viable, low-cost approach to this problem (Oslin et al., 2003).

The biggest problem facing treatment for alcoholism is that most alcoholics (approximately 85 percent) do not receive any formal treatment. In response, many health psychologists have suggested that social engineering represents the best attack on the problem. Banning alcohol advertising, raising the legal drinking age, and strictly enforcing the penalties for drunk driving may be the best approaches for reaching this untreated majority.

Critical Checkpoint

Addressing the Culture of Drinking in University

Box 5.4 highlights some of the issues and problems associated with alcohol use among university students. Given events like "frosh week" and the stress that many first-year students experience as they transition to a new environment, what role, if any, should universities play in helping to reduce the risk of binge drinking and/or problem drinking among students?

Can Recovered Alcoholics Ever Drink Again?

A controversial issue in the treatment of alcohol abuse is whether alcoholics and problem drinkers can learn to drink in moderation. For decades, research and self-help treatment programs for alcoholism, such as Alcoholics Anonymous, have argued that the alcoholic is an alcoholic for life and must abstain from all drinking.

It does appear that a narrow group of problem drinkers may be able to drink in moderation—namely, those who are young and employed, who have not been drinking long, and who live in a supportive environment (Marlatt, Larimer, Baer, & Quigley, 1993). Drinking in moderation has some advantages for these problem drinkers. First, moderate drinking represents a realistic social behaviour for the environments that a recovered problem drinker may encounter. For example, as the Focus on Social Issues box, "The Drinking University Students," indicated, moderating drinking may be a more realistic goal than total abstinence for university students, who are often in heavy-drinking environments. Second, traditional therapeutic programs that emphasize total abstinence often have high dropout rates. Programs for problem drinkers that emphasize moderation may be better able to hold on to these participants.

Preventive Approaches to Alcohol Abuse

Because alcoholism is a serious health problem, many researchers have felt that a prudent approach is to appeal

The Drinking University Students

Most Canadian university students drink alcohol, and as many as 16 percent of them are heavy drinkers (Adlaf, Demers, & Gilksman, 2005). A survey of more than 6,000 undergraduate students from 40 Canadian universities suggests that a significant proportion of students engage in patterns of harmful or hazardous drinking. According to the Canadian Campus Survey 2004, about 41 percent of university students overall appear to be involved in occasional binge drinking, defined as having five or more drinks on one occasion (Adlaf, Demers, & Gilksman, 2005). Moreover, binge drinking and other harmful drinking patterns appear to be increasing in women (see Table 5.1).

Many universities have tried to deal with the heavy drinking problem by providing educational materials about the harmful effects of alcohol. However, dogmatic alcohol-prevention messages may actually enhance intentions to drink in those who already have unhealthy attitudes towards drinking (Campo & Cameron, 2006). Moreover, the information conflicts markedly with the personal experiences of many university students who find drinking in a party situation to be satisfying, even exhilarating, behaviour. Many university students do not see drinking as a problem (Baer, Kivlahan, Fromme, & Marlatt, 1991), and others mistakenly assume that they are alone in their discomfort with campus alcohol practices (Suls & Green, 2003). Those students who would normally be a target for interventions may regard their drinking as a natural outgrowth of their social environment. Consequently, motivating students even to

attend alcohol abuse programs, much less to follow their recommendations, is difficult.

Therefore, some of the more successful efforts to modify university students' drinking have encouraged students to gain self-control over drinking rather than explicitly trying to get them to reduce or eliminate alcohol consumption altogether. A program developed by Lang and Marlatt (Baer et al., 1991; Lang & Marlatt, 1982) incorporates techniques derived from attitude-change research and from cognitive behavioural therapy in a total program to help university students gain such control. The program includes information about the risks of alcohol consumption, the acquisition of skills to moderate alcohol consumption, the use of drinking limits, relaxation training and lifestyle rebalancing, nutritional information, aerobic exercise, relapse-prevention skills designed to help students cope with high-risk situations, assertiveness training, and drink-refusal training.

Such programs typically begin by getting students to monitor their drinking and to understand what blood-alcohol levels mean and what their effects are. Often, merely monitoring drinking and recording the circumstances in which it occurs actually leads to a reduction in drinking.

The consumption of alcohol among students is heavily under the control of peer influence, the need to relax in social situations, and the need for approval (Turrisi, Wiersma, & Hughes, 2000). Thus, many intervention programs include training in cognitive behavioural alcohol skills designed to get students to find alternative ways to relax and have fun in social situations without abusing alcohol. Such skills training has proven to be an important component of successful alcohol abuse programs with university students (Kivlahan, Marlatt, Fromme, Coppel, & Williams, 1990). What are some of these skills?

To gain personal control over drinking, students are taught to identify the circumstances in which they are most likely to drink, and especially to drink to excess. For example, attendance at special events on campus may actually encourage binge drinking (see Table 5.2). Then students are taught specific coping skills so that they can moderate their alcohol consumption. For example, one technique for controlling alcohol consumption in high-risk situations, such as a party, is **placebo**

TABLE 5.1 | Patterns of Hazardous or Harmful Drinking among Canadian Undergraduates

	1998	2004
All students	30.0%	32.0%
Men	36.9	37.6
Women	24.3	27.5
Living on campus	—	53.0
Living off campus without family	—	44.0
Living off campus with family	—	34.1

Source: Adlaf, Demers, & Gilksman, (2005).

The Drinking University Students (continued)

Despite the success of such programs, interest has shifted from treatment to prevention, because so many students get into a heavy drinking lifestyle. Alan Marlatt and colleagues (Marlatt et al., 1998) enrolled 348 students in an intervention during their senior year of high school and randomly assigned half to an individualized motivational brief intervention in their first year of university or to a no-treatment control condition. The intervention, conducted individually with each student, consisted of guiding the students through their drinking patterns and risks and their knowledge about alcohol's effects. Their rates of drinking were compared with university averages and their risks for current and future problems, such as potential decline in grades, blackouts, and accidents, were identified (see Table 5.3).

The interviewers were careful not to confront the students but did ask them questions such as "What do you make of this?" and "Are you surprised?" Each student was urged, but not forced, to come up with specific goals that might lead them to change their behaviour, an intentional low-key effort to place responsibility for this change on the student. Over a two-year follow-up period, students in the intervention showed significant reductions in both their drinking rates and the harmful consequences that frequently accompany heavy drinking. Interventions like these emphasize the importance of coming up with effective prevention strategies before problems have a chance to take root (Baer et al., 1991; see also Baer et al., 1992).

drinking. This involves either the consumption of non-alcoholic beverages while others are drinking or the alternation of an alcoholic with a nonalcoholic beverage to reduce the total volume of alcohol consumed.

TABLE 5.2 | Percentage of Students Who Reported Binge Drinking at a Campus Event during a One-Month Period

Campus Event Attended	%
Happy hours	78.4
Low-priced promotions at bar	83.2
Special promotions by beer company	86.1
Cover charge for unlimited drinks at bar	84.5

Source: Adlaf, Demers, & Gilksman, (2005).

TABLE 5.3 | Alcohol-Related Problems of University Students Who Had a Drink during a One-Year Period

Alcohol-Related Problem	Drinkers Who Reported Problems
Had a hangover	53.4%
Memory loss	25.4
Missed class	18.8
Engaged in unplanned sexual activity	14.1
Drank while driving	7.4
Got hurt or injured	6.5
Engaged in unsafe sexual activity	6.4

Source: Adlaf, Demers, & Gilksman, (2005).

to adolescents to avoid drinking altogether or to control their drinking before the problems of alcohol abuse set in. Social influence programs mounted through high schools are one approach to teaching young adolescents drink-refusal techniques and coping methods for dealing with high-risk situations so that they will not end up in situations in which drinking is difficult to avoid. Media campaigns are another approach that may be effective in preventing alcohol abuse. For example, the Manitoba Liquor Control Commission has launched a unique media campaign consisting of television ads and a Web site (www.beundrunk.com) to help promote responsible drinking. In addition to providing resources and information about the consequences of irresponsible drinking, the video clips on the Web site illustrate the negative consequences of not drinking responsibly, and challenge young adults to resist social pressures and be "undrunk."

In addition to interventions with children and adolescents, social engineering solutions hold promise for managing alcohol. These include increasing taxes on alcohol, restricting alcohol advertising and promotion that especially targets young people, cracking down on misleading health claims for alcohol, supporting education programs in schools and media, and strengthening the federal government's focus on alcohol as a major youth problem. As long as alcohol remains the substance of choice for abuse among young people, its prevention will be a high priority (Chenier, 2001).

Drinking and Driving

Thousands of vehicular fatalities each year result from drunk driving. This aspect of alcohol consumption is probably the one that most mobilizes the general public against alcohol abuse. Programs such as MADD (Mothers Against Drunk Driving) have been founded and staffed by the parents and friends of those killed by drunk drivers. Increasingly, the political impact of these and related groups is being felt, as they pressure provincial and municipal governments for tougher alcohol control measures and stiffer penalties for convicted drunk drivers.

Moreover, hosts and hostesses are now pressured to assume responsibility for the alcohol consumption of their guests and for friends to intervene when they recognize that their friends are too drunk to drive. But this can be a difficult task to undertake. How do you know when to tell a friend that he or she is too drunk to drive and to intervene so that the drunk individual will not drive? Knowing the driver well, perceiving that he or she really needs help, feeling able to intervene, and having

had conversations in the past that encouraged intervention all enhance the likelihood that an individual will intervene in a situation when a peer is drunk (Newcomb, Rabow, Monto, & Hernandez, 1991). However, the norms to control others' drinking, though growing stronger, still fly in the face of beliefs in individual liberty and personal responsibility. Consequently, many drunk drivers remain on the road.

With increased media attention on the problem of drunk driving, drinkers seem to be developing self-regulatory techniques to avoid driving while drunk. Such techniques involve limiting drinking to a prescribed number, arranging for a designated driver, getting a taxi, or delaying or avoiding driving after consuming alcohol (S. L. Brown, 1997). Thus, although prevention in the form of eliminating drinking altogether is unlikely to occur, the rising popularity of self-regulation to avoid drunk driving may help reduce in this serious problem.

Is Modest Alcohol Consumption a Health Behaviour?

Despite the fact that problem drinking and alcoholism remain major health risks and contribute to overall mortality, modest alcohol intake actually adds to a long life. Moderate drinking is associated with reduced risk of a heart attack, lower blood pressure, lower risk of dying after a heart attack, decreased risk of heart failure, less thickening of the arteries with age, an increase in high-density lipoprotein (HDL) cholesterol (the so-called "good" cholesterol), and fewer strokes among the elderly (Britton & Marmot, 2004; Goatcher, 2002). However, moderate drinking in younger populations may actually enhance risk of death, probably through alcohol-related injuries (Goatcher, 2002).

Debate has centred on whether a particular type of alcohol consumption shows more benefits than others. Some researchers have suggested that red wine is healthier because of pigments called polyphenols that may inhibit hardening of the arteries (Magrone & Jirillo, 2011), and may have immuno-modulating properties that are protective against a variety of diseases (Magrone & Jirillo, 2010). But other studies have suggested that white wine may be equally beneficial (Heart and Stroke Foundation, 2001). The evidence from one Canadian study suggests that modest consumption of any alcoholic beverage—beer, wine, or spirits—may produce beneficial effects as the body absorbs equally effective amounts of protective molecules from alcoholic drinks (Prickett et al., 2004).

Postscript

Despite the fact that moderate drinking is now being recognized as a potential health behaviour, the benefits appear to occur at fairly low levels. For example, women who drink an average of half a drink a day reduce their risk for high blood pressure, but those who have more than one and a half drinks a day can actually raise it (Goatcher, 2002). The World Health Organization has warned that the message that moderate drinking promotes health may encourage people to continue or increase alcohol consumption to dangerous levels. Overall, the number of deaths attributable to alcohol consumption continues to increase worldwide (Pearson, 2004).

 ## HOW IS SMOKING HARMFUL FOR HEALTH AND WHAT FACTORS INFLUENCE SMOKING?

Smoking is the single greatest cause of preventable death. In Canada, smoking accounts for at least 45,000 deaths each year—with a large portion of these deaths cardiovascular related. Smoking also accounts for at least 30 percent of all cancer deaths (Physicians for a Smoke-Free Canada, 2002; see Table 5.4).

In addition to the risks for heart disease and lung cancer, smoking increases the risks for chronic bronchitis, emphysema, respiratory disorders, damage and injuries due to fires and accidents, lower birth weight in offspring, and retarded fetal development (Physicians for a Smoke-Free Canada, 2002).

Cigarette smokers also appear to be generally less health conscious and are more likely to engage in other unhealthy behaviours than are non-smokers (Public Health Agency of Canada, 2004). In particular, smoking and drinking often go together, and drinking seems to cue smoking and to make it more difficult to give up smoking (Shiffman, Fischer, et al., 1994). Smokers also

TABLE 5.4 | Cigarette Smoking–Related Mortality among Canadians

Disease	Deaths
Cancer of the lung, oral cavity, esophagus, pancreas, etc.	17,700
Cardiovascular conditions, including ischemic heart disease and stroke	17,600
Respiratory conditions, including chronic obstructive pulmonary disease (COPD)	9,500

Source: Physicians for a Smoke-Free Canada, 2002, www.smoke-free.ca/Health/pscissues_health.htm.

have more accidents and injuries at work, take off more sick time, and use more health benefits than non-smokers, thereby representing substantial costs to employers (Rehm et al., 2006). Not surprisingly, a prospective study of smokers that followed smokers over a five-year period found that current smokers were spent more than twice as many days in the hospital than did people who had never smoked (Wilkins, Sheilds, & Rotermann, 2009).

Although it was once thought that smoking and alcohol served as entry-level drugs in childhood and adolescence for subsequent substance use and abuse, a recent cross-national study involving 17 countries calls this "gateway" theory into question. Although marijuana use was often preceded by smoking and alcohol use, this sequence of drug use initiation was not constant across different cultures and contexts (Degenhardt et al., 2010). The dangers of smoking are not confined to the smoker. Studies of second-hand smoke reveal that spouses, family members of smokers, and co-workers are at risk for a variety of health disorders (Health Canada, 2004b). Parental cigarette smoking may lower cognitive performance in adolescents by reducing blood oxygen capacity and increasing carbon monoxide levels (Bauman, Koch, & Fisher, 1989).

Synergistic Effects of Smoking

Smoking has a synergistic effect on other health-related risk factors; that is, it enhances the detrimental effects of other risk factors in compromising health. For example, smoking and cholesterol interact to produce higher rates of morbidity and mortality due to heart disease than would be expected from simply adding together the risk of smoking and high cholesterol (Perkins, 1985). Because nicotine stimulates the release of free fatty acids, it may increase the synthesis of triglycerides, which in turn decreases HDL production. Reducing smoking and modifying diet for people with both risk factors, then, is a high priority for intervention.

Stress and smoking can also interact in dangerous ways. For men, nicotine can increase the magnitude of heart rate reactivity to stress. For women, smoking can reduce heart rate but increase blood pressure responses, also an adverse reactivity pattern (Girdler, Jamner, Jarvik, Soles, & Shapiro, 1997). The stimulating effects of nicotine on the cardiovascular system may put smokers at risk for a sudden cardiac crisis, and the long-term effects on reactivity in response to stress may aggravate coronary heart disease risk factors. Smoking also acts synergistically with low socio-economic status, with greater harm caused to disadvantaged groups than more advantaged groups, perhaps due to the stressful life circumstances of those in lower socio-economic groups (Pampel & Rogers, 2004).

Smoking also appears to interact with exercise and the motives for exercising. Smokers engage in less physical activity as long as they continue smoking, while people who engage in exercise for friendship, stress relief, and health benefits are less likely to smoke (Verkooijen, Nielsen, & Kremers, 2009). Because physical exercise is so important to a variety of health outcomes, the fact that smoking reduces its likelihood represents a further indirect contribution of smoking to ill health.

Smoking is related to a substantial increase in women's risk of developing breast cancer after menopause. An expert review panel comprised of four Canadian health agencies found that both active and passive smoking (i.e., exposure to second-hand smoke) increased the risk for breast cancer. The review also found up to a 50 percent greater chance for women who smoke and are carriers of genes that restrict the breakdown of certain chemicals in cigarette smoke and therefore carry more of those chemicals in their bloodstream (Johnson et al., 2011). Shockingly, there was also evidence for a 65 percent increased risk for breast cancer among premenopausal women who had never smoked but who had been exposed to second-hand smoke. Cigarette smoking interacts synergistically with depression such that a depressed person who smokes is at substantially greater risk for cancer. Immune alterations associated with major depression interact with smoking to elevate white blood cell count and to produce a decline in natural killer cell activity. Natural killer cells are thought to serve a surveillance function in detecting and responding to early cancers (Jung & Irwin, 1999). Smoking is also considered to be a potential cause of depression. Findings from a 26-year population-based study in Denmark found clear links between daily smoking in women and men and subsequent development of depression (Flensborg-Madsen et al., 2011). Thus, the concern about the synergistic impact of smoking and depression on health is even more alarming.

The synergistic health risks of smoking are extremely important and may be responsible for a substantial percentage of smoking-related deaths. However, research suggests that the public is largely unaware of the synergistic adverse effects of smoking in conjunction with other risk factors (Hermand, Mullet, & Lavieville, 1997). Nonetheless, the direct effects of smoking on poor health are well established, and its synergistic effects are increasingly being uncovered. Moreover, stopping smoking clearly has beneficial health effects. The risks for coronary heart disease (CHD) and lung cancer are substantially lowered by stopping smoking, which makes smoking the most important health-compromising behaviour in existence.

The risks of smoking are not confined to the smoker. Co-workers, spouses, and other family members of smokers are at continued risk for many smoking-related disorders.

A Brief History of the Smoking Problem

For years, smoking was considered to be a sophisticated and manly habit. Characterizations of 19th- and 20th-century gentry, for example, often depicted men retiring to the drawing room after dinner for cigars and brandy. Cigarette advertisements of the early 20th century built on this image, and by 1965, 61 percent of the adult male population in Canada was smoking (Physicians for a Smoke-Free Canada, 2007).

In 1962, a report of the Royal College of Physicians of the United Kingdom concluded that cigarette smoke may be an important cause of lung cancer. Soon after, in June 1963, the Minister of Health announced in the Canadian House of Commons that smoking was linked to cancer (Wyckam, 1997). After the 1964 Surgeon General's report concluding that smoking was a cause of cancer in men (U.S. Department of Health, Education, and Welfare and U.S. Public Health Service, 1964), and an extensive publicity campaign to highlight the dangers of smoking, male smoking subsequently declined in Canada (to 51 percent by 1975). However, women's smoking actually remained stable during the same period, from 38 percent in 1965 to 39 percent by 1974. More frightening still, by 1975 the percentage of female teenage smokers had increased to 48 percent from 37 percent in 1965. The advantage in life expectancy that women usually enjoy compared with men is shrinking noticeably, and a large part of this decline in women's longevity advantage is due to smoking (Koretz, 2003a). Despite dawning awareness of the threat of smoking, then, smoking continues to be a formidable problem.

FIGURE 5.2 | Percentage of Canadian Men, Women, and Teenagers Who Smoke (2009)

Source: Physicians for a Smoke-Free Canada, 2007, www.smokefree.ca/factsheets/pdf/prevalence.pdf.

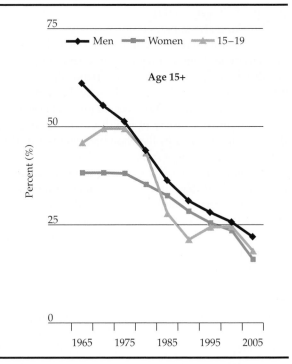

The good news is that, in Canada, the number of adults who smoke has fallen substantially since 1975 (see Figure 5.2). Nonetheless, smoking continues to be a major health problem. Critics have argued that the

Smoking has been represented by the tobacco industry as a glamorous habit, and one task of interventions has been to change attitudes about smoking.

TABLE 5.5 | Smoking Prevalence by Age and Sex

	Percentage of Population	
Age	Males	Females
Total	22.6%	17.7%
12–19	12.2	9.8
20–34	29.9	23.0
35–44	25.3	19.9
45–64	24.8	20.3
65+	10.9	8.6

Source: 2002 Youth Smoking Survey. Health Canada, 2007. Reproduced with the permission of the Minister of Health, 2011.

tobacco industry has disproportionately targeted minority groups and teens for smoking, and indeed, the rates among certain low-SES minority groups, such as First Nations female youth, are especially high (Assembly of First Nations, 2003). In 1994, about 27 percent of teenagers smoked regularly but by 2001 that figure was 22.5 percent; as of 2009, it has once again declined to 20.1 percent (Statistics Canada, 2010). Table 5.5 presents current figures on the prevalence of smoking.

Why Do People Smoke?

Decades of research on smoking have revealed how difficult smoking is to modify. This is in large part because smoking is determined by multiple physiological, psychological, and social factors. Smoking runs in families, and some twin and adoption studies suggest that there may be some genetic influences on smoking (Piasecki, 2006).

Genes that regulate dopamine functioning are likely candidates for heritable influences on cigarette smoking (Timberlake et al., 2006; Wang & Li, 2009), particularly whether people are able to stop smoking and resist relapse during the treatment phase (Lerman et al., 2003). Should smokers be told if they have a genetic risk for smoking? This feedback may heighten a sense of vulnerability and promote distress, and it does not appear to enhance quitting in most smokers. Consequently, the value of providing such information is questionable.

Factors Associated with Smoking in Adolescents Smoking begins early. The 2006 Canadian Tobacco Use Monitoring Survey from Health Canada (2007b) indicates that almost 15 percent of the adolescent population between the ages of 15 and 19 already smokes cigarettes regularly and consider themselves to be smokers; if anything, these statistics probably underestimate the adolescent smoking rate. However, smoking does not start all at once. There is a period of initial experimentation, during which an individual tries out cigarettes, experiences peer pressure to smoke, and develops attitudes about what a smoker is like. Following experimentation, only some adolescents go on to become heavy smokers (Maggi, Hertzman, & Vaillancourt, 2007; see Figure 5.3).

FIGURE 5.3 | Teenage Smoking

Smoking among Canadian youth, in grades 5 to 9, continues to be a problem as experimental and occasional smoking remains high. (*Source:* Health Canada, 2007c, www.phac-aspc.gc.ca/dca-dea/publications/hbsc-2004/chapter_6_e.html#6-1 and www.hc-sc.gc.ca/hl-vs/ tobac-tabac/research-recherche/stat/survey-sondage/2004–2005/chart-image_e.html, reproduced with the permission of the Minister of Public Works and Government Services Canada, 2011.)

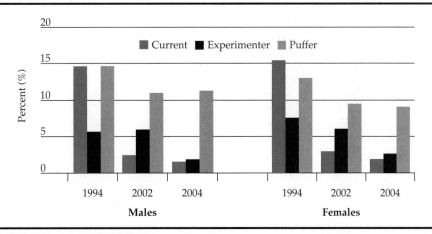

Peer and Family Influences   Peer influence is one of the most important factors in beginning smoking in adolescence. Starting to smoke results from a social contagion process, whereby non-smokers have contact with others who are trying out smoking or with regular smokers and then try smoking themselves (Presti, Ary, & Lichtenstein, 1992). Having a best friend who smokes is strongly associated with also being a smoker among adolescents (Youth Smoking Survey, 2010). The presence of peers and family members who smoke can encourage smoking by reducing the perception that smoking is harmful (Rodriguez, Romer, & Audrain-McGovern, 2007).

Adolescents are also more likely to start smoking if their parents smoke, if they are lower class, if they feel social pressure to smoke, and if there has been a major stressor in the family (for example, Unger, Hamilton, & Sussman, 2004). These effects are partly due to the increase in stress and depression that may result (Kirby, 2002; Unger, Hamilton, & Sussman, 2004).

There are also different types of smokers depending on whether they have ever experimented or tried smoking. "Puffers" refers to those who have tried a few puffs of a cigarette smoking but have never smoked a whole cigarette (Health Canada, 2007c). "Chippers," or experimental smokers, on the other hand, are light smokers who consume five or fewer cigarettes a day. Researchers have been interested in what distinguishes them from people who go on to be addicted heavy smokers. Chippers appear to share several risk factors with heavy smokers, including tolerance for deviance, and attitudes and health beliefs that are similar to those of smokers (see Table 5.6 and Figure 5.3). But they also

have more protective factors such as high value placed on academic success, supportive relationships at home, and little smoking among peers and parents. Chippers may be informative regarding tobacco control efforts generally and for theories regarding addiction as well (Zhu, Sun, Hawkins, Pierce, & Cummins, 2003).

Finally, peers and family may also influence smoking through their effects on adolescents' smoking-related attitudes and beliefs. For example, a recent national survey of smoking among Canadian youth in grades 5 to 9 suggests that adolescent smokers have more positive beliefs about smoking and are also less likely to see smoking as something that can be immediately harmful (Health Canada, 2007c; see Table 5.6). The only exception is that smokers and non-smokers alike believed that smoking is addictive and harmful to others. The latter belief in particular may be attributable to media campaigns raising awareness about the harmful effects of second-hand smoke (see the Focus on Social Issues box, "Can Non-smokers Be Harmed by Second-hand Smoke?" on pages 146–147).

Weight Control and Smoking   There is also some evidence that smoking for some individuals may be tied to a belief that smoking helps to maintain or reduce one's weight, perhaps through controlling appetite (Copeland and Carney, 2003). This may be especially true for women who are worried about staying thin and who are trying to live up to cultural norms regarding thinness. For example, one study examined how self-objectification was related to smoking motives among female undergraduates at the University of Windsor (Fiissel & Lafreniere, 2006). Results suggested that women

TABLE 5.6 | Health Beliefs and Attitudes by Smoking Status, Youth Grades 5 to 9, Canada 2004–05

Smoking-related Attitude	Belief/Smokers	Chippers/ Experimental Smokers	Puffers	Non-smokers
Tobacco is addictive.	85.5%	89.5%	89.4%	88.2%
Smoke can harm nonsmokers health.	86.4	91.3	90.8	86.6
Smoking helps to stay thin.	32.0	25.1	23.2	16.2
Smoking helps when bored.	46.5	30.1	15.3	10.4
Must smoke many years to hurt health.	27.2	22.5	18.9	13.4
Occasional smoking endangers health.	46.4	46.8	54.9	68.2
Quitting reduces damage to health.	56.8	47.5	46.2	41.0
Smoking helps to relax.	75.7	65.7	39.6	25.7
Smoking is cool.	18.0	12.3	4.0	1.1

Source: Health Beliefs and Attitudes by Smoking Status. Health Canada, 2007c, www.hc-sc.gc.ca/hl-vs/tobac-tabac/research-recherche/stat/_survey-sondage_2004-2005/table-13_e.html. Reproduced with the permission of the Minister of Health, 2011.

who internalized the prescribed cultural standards of thinness for the female body were also more likely to report that they smoked to control their appetite and weight.

Self-image and Smoking   The image of the smoker is a significant factor in beginning smoking. Consistent with this point, teenagers whose ideal self-image is congruent with that of a typical smoker are most likely to smoke (Chang, 2007). Appearance-related evaluations that do not involve weight issues are also associated with smoking in both men and women, suggesting that interventions for quitting smoking that target negative appearance concerns in addition to weight control concerns may be especially effective (Grogan, Hartley, Conner, Fry, & Gough, 2010).

Mood and Smoking   Smoking among adolescents is also tied to aggressive tendencies and depressive episodes (Repetto, Caldwell, & Zimmerman, 2005; Rodriguez, Moss, & Audrain-McGovern, 2005). Feelings of being hassled, angry, or sad increase the likelihood of smoking (Whalen, Jammer, Henker, & Delfino, 2001). One study found that experimentally induced sadness among smokers resulted in smoking longer and taking more puffs compared to a control group of smokers (Fucito & Juliano, 2009) In studies that examine smoking over time for adolescents, feelings of stress and psychological distress were clearly tied to the increase in smoking (Wills, Sandy, & Yaeger, 2002). Schools that look the other way or have poor levels of discipline may inadvertently facilitate a student moving from experimentation to regular cigarette use (Novak & Clayton, 2001). As the prevalence of smoking goes up at a particular school, so does the likelihood that additional students will start smoking. Maladaptive coping styles, especially those that involve withdrawal or repressive coping, and lower levels of exercise may contribute to the depression seen among some teen tobacco users (Vickers et al., 2003).

At one time it was thought that the primary window during which young people are vulnerable to smoking was adolescence, specifically late elementary school. Now, however, it appears that there is a new window of opportunity when students make the transition to university. Smoking rates among university students have increased substantially over the past few years, and so far little is known about the factors that predict this disturbing trend. As is true in adolescence, peer behaviour may be one influential factor. Overall, little is known about the determinants of smoking among university students, although it appears to be more common among those who doubt the health significance of smoking and those who expect smoking will help control their mood (Wetter et al., 2004). Exposure to peers that smoke may have an effect as well (Ellickson, Bird, Orlando, Klein, & McCaffrey, 2003). Clearly, increased efforts need to be undertaken to include university students in smoking prevention and cessation programs (Choi, Harris, Okuyemi, & Ahluwalia, 2003).

The Nature of Addiction in Smoking   Smoking is an addiction, reported to be harder to stop than heroin addiction or alcoholism by many who suffer from multiple addictions. Only experimental smokers are able to smoke casually without showing signs of addiction. Despite the fact that nicotine is known to be a powerfully addictive drug, the possible mechanisms underlying nicotine addiction are only just being uncovered (Hinrichs et al., in press).

Nicotine Addiction   Theories that stress the role of nicotine addiction and the persistence of smoking argue that people smoke to maintain blood levels of nicotine and to prevent the withdrawal symptoms that occur when a person stops smoking. In essence, smoking regulates the level of nicotine in the body, and when plasma levels of nicotine depart from the ideal levels, smoking occurs.

Nicotine alters levels of active neuroregulators, including acetylcholine, norepinephrine, dopamine, endogenous opioids, and vasopressin. Nicotine may be used by smokers to engage these neuroregulators because they produce temporary improvements in performance or affect. Specifically, acetylcholine, norepinephrine, and vasopressin appear to enhance memory; acetylcholine and beta endorphins can reduce anxiety and tension. Alterations in dopamine, norepinephrine, and opioids improve mood, and people find that their performance of basic tasks is often improved when levels of acetylcholine and norepinephrine are high. Consequently, smoking among habitual smokers increases concentration, recall, alertness, arousal, psychomotor performance, and the ability to screen out irrelevant stimuli.

Consistent with this point, habitual smokers who stop smoking report that their concentration is reduced; their attention becomes unfocused; they show memory impairments; and they experience increases in anxiety, tension, irritability, craving, and moodiness.

Summary   People smoke for a number of reasons. Genetic influences may contribute to smoking; smoking typically begins in early adolescence, when youth may have little idea of the problems they face as a result of smoking; smoking clearly has an addictive component related to nicotine; and smoking regulates moods and responses to stressful circumstances. As a consequence, it has been a very difficult problem to treat.

Interventions to Reduce Smoking

Interventions to reduce smoking can be focused on either preventing people, especially young Canadians, from ever starting to smoke, or encouraging smoking cessation among current smokers. Although both approaches are equally important, the immediate versus long-term impacts on tobacco-related mortality differ. For example, reducing the current number of smokers will produce a much larger decrease in the number of tobacco related deaths by the year 2050 than by reducing the number of new smokers (Jha, 2009). In contrast, preventing young adults from ever smoking will only have effects on tobacco related deaths after the year 2050 (Peto & Lopez, 2001).

Changing Attitudes toward Smoking   Following the media releases in the mid-1960s regarding the harmful health effects of smoking, the mass media engaged in a campaign to warn the public about the hazards of smoking. In a short period of time, the Canadian public came to acknowledge these risks. Attitudes toward smoking changed substantially. Even adolescents now view smoking as addictive and as having negative social consequences (Health Canada, 2007c).

Media campaigns, thus, can be extremely effective for providing information about health habits. Media campaigns against smoking have helped instill antismoking attitudes in the general population. These attitudes have also been very effective in discouraging adults from beginning to smoke as well as persuading them to remain non-smokers (Hershey et al., 2005), and for discouraging youth from ever starting to smoke (see the Spotlight on Canadian Research box, "How Effective Are Health Warnings on Cigarette Packages?"). In essence, then, antismoking messages in the media set the stage for efforts to quit smoking.

The Therapeutic Approach to the Smoking Problem   Attitude-change campaigns alone do not help smokers stop smoking, so psychologists have increasingly adopted a therapeutic approach to the smoking problem.

Nicotine Replacement Therapy   Many therapies begin with some form of nicotine replacement. Nicotine gum was originally used to help motivated smokers with quitting. However, smokers do not like chewing nicotine gum, in part because nicotine is absorbed rather slowly through this method. More recently, therapeutic efforts have made use of transdermal nicotine patches, which are worn by individuals motivated to stop smoking. These patches release nicotine in steady doses into the bloodstream. Evaluations show that nicotine replacement therapy produces significant smoking cessation (Cepeda-Benito, 1993; J. R. Hughes, 1993). Although nicotine replacement therapy is not recommended for use among youth smokers in Canada, results from the 2006–7 Youth Smoking Survey suggest that more than 20 percent of current and former youth smokers use this smoking cessation tool (Lane, Leatherdale, & Ahmed, in press).

Multimodal Intervention   Treatments for smoking generally adopt a multimodal approach. This focus incorporates a variety of specific interventions geared to the stage of readiness that an individual experiences with respect to his or her smoking. In addition, as is true in all multimodal interventions, the goal is to engage the smoker's sense of self-control and to enlist active participation in the intervention process (Wittchen, Hoch, Klotsche, & Muehlig, 2011).

Many smoking intervention programs have used the stages model of change as a basis for intervening. Interventions to move people from the precontemplation to the contemplation stage centre on attitudes: emphasizing the adverse health consequences of smoking and the negative social attitudes that most people hold about smoking. Motivating a readiness to quit may, in turn, increase a sense of self-efficacy that one will be able to do so, contributing further to readiness to quit (Baldwin et al., 2006). Moving people from contemplation to action requires that the smoker develop a timetable for quitting, a program for how to quit, and an awareness of the difficulties associated with quitting. Moving people to the action phase would employ many of the cognitive behavioural techniques that have been used in the modification of other health habits.

As this account suggests, smoking would seem to be a good example of how the stages model might be applied. However, interventions matched to the stage of smoking are inconsistent in their effects and do not, at present, provide strong support for a stage approach to helping people stop smoking (Quinlan & McCaul, 2000; Stotts, DiClemente, Carbonari, & Mullen, 2000; Segan, Borland, & Greenwood, 2004).

How Effective Are Health Warnings on Cigarette Packages?

In Chapter 3, we examined the possible merits of fear appeals for changing attitudes about health behaviours. But does warning people about the risks associated with a behaviour using fear-invoking messages and images actually lead to changing unhealthy behaviours such as smoking? One group of Canadian researchers attempted to answer this question by examining the effect of reading the cigarette package warning labels on smokers' behaviour over a three-month period (Hammond, Fong, McDonald, Cameron, & Brown, 2003).

More than 600 smokers took part in a phone survey in which they reported whether they had read the graphic warning labels, and the extent to which they had cognitively processed their content (thought about or discussed the messages). Not surprisingly, over 90 percent stated that they had read the labels. Smokers also reported their current intentions to quit smoking or reduce their smoking frequency. When the smokers were contacted again in three months, 23 percent had attempted or successfully quit smoking, and nearly 25 percent had reduced the number of cigarettes they smoked daily. Perhaps most significantly, those who had read, thought about, and discussed the warning labels in greater depth at baseline were more likely to have quit, attempted to quit, or reduced their smoking three months later. Although these findings provide compelling evidence for the effectiveness of cigarette warning labels in changing smoking behaviour, the direction of the relationships are not entirely clear. It

is possible that smokers who already have high intentions to quit are more likely to read the labels as a means of reinforcing their intentions. The researchers suggest that the relationship between intentions to quit and reading the labels is likely reciprocal in nature, with the labels strengthening quitting intentions, which then make the smokers more likely to read and discuss the labels as they prepare to quit.

Canada is not the only country to use health warning labels as an intervention to curb smoking behaviour. The United States, Australia, and the United Kingdom also use health warning labels that contain text and/or graphic images to convey the dangers of smoking. However, one international study suggests that the Canadian warnings, which contain both graphic images and text, are among the most effective, especially when it comes to making smokers think about the health risks of smoking (Hammond et al., 2007).

Social Support and Stress Management As is true for other health-habit interventions, those who wish to quit are urged to enlist social support from their spouse, friends, and co-workers in their resolution to stop. Ex-smokers are more likely to be successful over the short term if they have a supportive partner and if they have non-smoking supportive friends. Social support from a partner appears to be more helpful for men attempting to stop smoking than for women (Westmaas, Wild, & Ferrence, 2002).

Because smoking seems to be relaxing for so many people, relaxation training has also been incorporated into some smoking cessation programs. Teaching former smokers to relax in situations in which they might have been tempted to smoke provides an alternative method for coping with stress or anxiety (Manning, Catley, Harris, Mayo, & Ahluwalia, 2005).

Lifestyle rebalancing, through changes in diet and exercise, may also help people cut down on smoking or maintain abstinence after quitting. Image is also important in helping people stop. Specifically, research suggests that people who have a strong sense of themselves as non-smokers may do better in treatment than those who have a strong sense of themselves as smokers (Gibbons & Eggleston, 1996; Shadel & Mermelstein, 1996).

Maintenance   To bridge the transition from action to maintenance, relapse-prevention techniques are typically incorporated into smoking-cessation programs (Piasecki, 2006). Relapse prevention is important because the ability to remain abstinent shows a steady month-by-month decline, such that within two years after a smoking cessation program, even the best program does not exceed a 50 percent abstinence rate (Piasecki, 2006).

Like most addictive health habits, smoking shows an abstinence-violation effect, whereby a single lapse reduces perceptions of self-efficacy, increases negative mood, and reduces beliefs that one will be successful in stopping smoking. Stress-triggered lapses appear to lead to relapse more quickly than other kinds (Shiffman et al., 1996). Consequently, smokers are urged to remind themselves that a single lapse is not necessarily worrisome, because many people lapse on the road to quitting.

Relapse Prevention   Relapse-prevention techniques often begin by preparing people for the management of withdrawal, including cardiovascular changes, increases in appetite, variations in the urge to smoke, increases in coughing and discharge of phlegm, and the like. These problems may occur intermittently during the first 7 to 11 days. In addition, relapse prevention focuses on the long-term, high-risk situations that lead to a craving for cigarettes, such as drinking coffee or alcohol (Piasecki, 2006). As just noted, relapse prevention may especially need to focus on teaching people coping techniques for dealing with stressful interpersonal situations. Successful relapse prevention may also rely on being satisfied with one's physical emotional state following quitting (Baldwin et al., 2006).

Self-efficacy is a strong predictor of success in smoking cessation; research has found that, when a sense of self-efficacy wanes, vulnerability to relapse is high, so interventions that address the dynamics of self-efficacy over time may well improve maintenance rates (Shiffman et al., 2000). Self-efficacy during attempts to quit smoking is also sensitive to external contexts such as seeing others smoking, stressful events, and caffeine and alcohol consumption, suggesting that these may be additional areas for interventions to target (Van Zundert, Engels, & Kuntsche, 2011). Unhappily too, after they relapse, new smokers may increase their positive beliefs about smoking (Chassin, Pressen, Sherman, & Kim, 2002; Dijkstra & Borland, 2003). Over the long term, simply remaining vigilant about not smoking predicts abstinence best.

Evaluation of Multimodal Interventions   How successful have multimodal approaches to smoking been? Virtually every imaginable combination of therapies for getting people to stop has been tested. Typically, these programs show high initial success rates for quitting, followed by high rates of return to smoking, sometimes as high as 90 percent. Those who relapse are more likely to be young, have a high degree of nicotine dependence, a low sense of self-efficacy, greater concerns about gaining weight after stopping smoking, more previous quit attempts, and more slips (occasions when they used one or more cigarettes; Ockene et al., 2000).

Although the rates of relapse suggest some pessimism with respect to smoking, it is important to consider the cumulative effects of smoking-cessation programs, not just each program in isolation (Baer & Marlatt, 1991). Any given effort to stop smoking may yield only a 20 percent success rate, but with multiple efforts to quit, eventually the smoker may be successful in becoming an ex-smoker. In fact, hundreds of thousands of former smokers have successfully stopped, albeit, not necessarily the first time they tried. Factors that predict the ability to maintain abstinence include educational attainment, contemplating quitting smoking, being ready to quit at the beginning of an intervention, and having a sense of self-efficacy (Rosal et al., 1998). Formal smoking-cessation programs may look less successful than they actually are because, over time, the individual may amass enough successful techniques and motivation to persist.

Who Is Best Able to Induce People to Stop Smoking?   Is any particular change agent more able to induce people to stop smoking? For example, is a person more likely to stop smoking if a psychotherapist or physician induces that person to do so?

Although advice about stopping smoking coming from a physician or other health care professional may help with controlling relapse, such advice is rarely given (Ockene et al., 2000). Physician advice is known to increase quit rates among adults up to 3 percent over and above unassisted quit rates, and can also improve smoking attitudes quitting intentions, and quitting behaviour in adolescents (Hum, Robinson, Jackson, & Ali, in press). Health care professionals' perceptions about the role they can play in smoking cessation may be important for improving outcomes. For example, a survey of pharmacists in four provinces (Ontario, Quebec, Saskatchewan, and Prince Edward Island) regarding attitudes toward their role in smoking cessation found that while most had positive attitudes about stopping smoking, just over 50 percent believed that pharmacists could play an important role in motivating people to cut down or quit smoking (Ashley, Victor, & Brewster, 2007). Despite these positive beliefs, less than 40 percent had actually taken steps to intervene by offering advice about nicotine-replacement therapy or giving other motivating suggestions.

Commercial Programs and Self-help Commercial stop-smoking clinics, which make use of cognitive-behavioural techniques, enjoy fairly wide attendance. Although cure rates are often advertised to be high, these assessments may be based only on misleading statistics about the short-term, but not long-term, effects. Continued evaluation of these popular programs is essential.

A variety of **self-help aids** and programs have been developed for smokers to quit on their own. These include nicotine gum and nicotine patches, as well as more intensive self-help programs that provide specific instruction for quitting. Although it is difficult to evaluate self-help programs formally, studies suggest that self-help programs' initial quit rates are lower, but long-term maintenance is just as high as more intensive behavioural interventions. Because self-help programs are less expensive, they represent an important attack on the smoking problem (Lipkus et al., 2004).

Public Health Approach Public health approaches to reducing smoking have included community interventions combining media blitzes with behavioural interventions directed especially at high-risk individuals, such as people who have other risk factors for CHD. Incentive-based community cessation programs have also been used with some success. For example, Ontario implemented a quit smoking contest in 2002 that challenged people to quit and win (Ashbury et al., 2006). An evaluation of the effectiveness of the program one year later revealed that approximately one-third of the smokers who participated in the contest had quit and remained abstinent.

Why Is Smoking So Hard to Change? As we have seen, smoking is a deeply entrenched behaviour pattern. Although many people are able to stop initially, relapse rates are very high. Several problems contribute to the difficulty of modifying smoking. Initially, smokers are resistant to interventions because of their lack of knowledge and their health-compromising attitudes. Because tobacco addiction typically begins in adolescence, adolescents may use tobacco in ways and in social situations that make it particularly difficult to modify, because it comes to be associated with a broad array of pleasurable activities (Gibson, 1997). In addition, because smoking patterns are highly individualized (Chassin, Presson, Pitts, & Sherman, 2000), it is sometimes difficult for group interventions to address all the factors that may influence and maintain any particular smoker's smoking.

People Who Stop on Their Own Despite the difficulties of stopping smoking, more than half a million Canadians successfully quit smoking each year (Physicians for a Smoke-Free Canada, 2004). The impetus for stopping smoking on one's own typically comes from health concerns (for example, McBride et al., 2001).

People who successfully quit on their own have good self-control skills, self-confidence in their ability to stop, and a perception that the health benefits of stopping are substantial. Stopping on one's own is easier if one has a supportive social network that does not smoke (Gerrard, Gibbons, Lane, & Stock, 2005). People who stop smoking on their own, however, have no magical solution to the smoking problem. After several efforts to stop, however, many quitters who stop on their own are successful. A list of guidelines for people who wish to stop on their own appears in Table 5.7.

Smoking Prevention

Because smoking is so resistant to intervention and because, increasingly, we have come to understand how and why young people begin to smoke, the war on smoking has shifted from getting smokers to stop to keeping potential smokers from starting (Chassin, Presson, Rose, & Sherman, 1996). These **smoking-prevention programs** are aimed to catch potential smokers early and attack the underlying motivations that lead people to smoke.

Advantages of Smoking-prevention Programs The advantages of smoking-prevention programs are several. They represent a potentially effective and cost-effective assault on the smoking problem that avoids the many factors that make it so difficult for habitual smokers to stop. Smoking-prevention programs can be easily implemented through the school system. Little class time is needed and no training of school personnel is required. How do researchers try to prevent smoking before it starts?

Social Influence Interventions An early program to keep adolescents from smoking was developed by Richard Evans and his colleagues in the Houston School District (Evans, Dratt, Raines, & Rosenberg, 1988). Two theoretical principles were central in the design of Evans's **social influence intervention.** First, the fact that parental smoking and peer pressure promote smoking in adolescents indicates that children acquire smoking at least partly through the modelling of others. By observing

TABLE 5.7 | Quitting Smoking

Here are some steps to help you prepare for your quit day:

- Select a date within the next three weeks.
- Complete your pledge to quit smoking.
- Delay your first cigarette of the day by 30 minutes to an hour.
- Develop a strict schedule for smoking.
- Avoid activities that trigger smoking for you, such as drinking, socializing, and celebrating with friends who smoke.

On the day before your quit day:

- Throw away your cigarettes. Put away your ashtrays, lighters, and matches.
- Tell a trusted friend that you are quitting and ask for support. Arrange to call your friend at least once a day for your first week as a non-smoker. Look for a support group in your community.
- Feel good about having the courage to try—and the commitment to succeed.
- If you have decided to use a nicotine-replacement therapy or medication, make sure you have everything you need.

On your quit day, follow these suggestions:

- Do not smoke.
- Apply your self-talk to trigger situations.
- Call a trusted friend and tell the tactics you are using to remain smoke-free.
- Drink less coffee and cola.
- If you aren't using medication to help with nicotine withdrawal, remind yourself that nicotine will be flushed out of your system in three to five days.
- Practise relaxation activities.
- Reward yourself with a treat.
- Avoid as many triggers as you can and change your responses to the ones you can't.
- Review your schedule for tomorrow and decide how you will cope with triggers.
- Put the money you save by not smoking in a glass jar where you can see it.

Source: Canadian Cancer Society, 2007a.

models who are apparently enjoying a behaviour they know to be risky, the children's fears of negative consequences are reduced and their expectation of positive consequences is enhanced. Thus, Evans reasoned, a successful intervention program with adolescents must include the potential for modelling high-status non-smokers.

A second theoretical principle on which the social influence intervention is based is the concept of behavioural inoculation developed by W. J. McGuire (1964, 1973). **Behavioural inoculation** is similar in rationale to inoculation against disease. If one can expose an individual to a weak dose of some germ, one may prevent infection because antibodies against that germ will develop. Likewise, if one can expose individuals to a weak version of a persuasive message, they may develop counterarguments against that message, so that they can successfully resist it if they encounter it in a stronger form.

The following are the three components of the social influence intervention program:

1. Information about the negative effects of smoking is carefully constructed so as to appeal to adolescents.

2. Materials are developed to convey a positive image of the non-smoker (rather than the smoker) as an independent, self-reliant individual.

3. The peer group is used to facilitate not smoking rather than smoking.

Let us consider each component in turn.

Most adolescents know that smoking is a risky behaviour. However, the fact that they continue to smoke suggests that they ignore much of what they know. Therefore, selection of appropriate antismoking materials for this group is critical. Typically, the adolescent's time frame does not include concern about health risks that are 20 to

30 years away. Therefore, antismoking materials must highlight the disadvantages of smoking now, including adverse effects on health, the financial costs of smoking, and negative social consequences of smoking (such as rejection by others), rather than long-term health risks.

The image of the non-smoker is also addressed in the social influence materials. Specifically, films and posters are developed to appeal to adolescents' need for independence, conveying such messages as "You can decide for yourself" and "Here are the facts so you can make a decision." These messages also show how cigarette advertisers use subtle techniques to try to get people to smoke in the hopes that the students will resist cigarette advertising when they encounter it. Simultaneously, these messages also convey an image of the smoker as someone who is vulnerable to advertising gimmicks.

These interventions address the significance of the peer group in several ways. First, high-status, slightly older peer leaders are typically featured in the films and posters as the primary agents delivering the interventions. They demonstrate through role playing how to resist peer pressure and maintain the decision not to smoke. The films convey techniques that adolescents can use to combat pressure, such as stalling for time or using counter-pressure (for example, telling the smoker that she is a fool for ruining her health). In some cases, these messages are reinforced by contact with a peer leader in a small-group interaction after exposure to the filmed material.

Evaluation of Social Influence Programs Do these programs work? This question has been hard to answer for several reasons. Students may learn how to turn down cigarettes, but this may not lead them to do so (Elder, Sallis, Woodruff, & Wildey, 1993). Smoking prevention programs sometimes delay smoking but may not reduce overall rates when assessed several years later. Validating self-reports of smoking is difficult and often is only successfully accomplished through tests such as saliva thiocyanate and expired air carbon monoxide. Despite the fact that school-based anti-smoking programs may be rated as compelling and viewed positively, there is evidence that this may not necessarily translate into changes in smoking behaviour (Primack, Fine, Yang, Wickett, & Zickmund, 2009).

The Life–skills-training Approach Another effort to prevent smoking in the adolescent population is called the **life–skills-training approach** (G. J. Botvin et al., 1992). Interestingly enough, this approach to smoking prevention deals with cigarette smoking per se in only a small

way. Rather, the rationale for the intervention is that if adolescents are trained in self-esteem and coping enhancement as well as social skills, they will not feel as much need to smoke to bolster their self-image: The skills will enhance the adolescent's sense of being an efficacious person. The results of these programs to date are encouraging as they have also been successfully implemented with different cultural groups (e.g., Seal, 2006). These programs also show some success in the reduction of smoking onset over time (G. J. Botvin et al., 1992).

Smoking-prevention programs are relatively expensive and logistically difficult to implement, so researchers have looked for easier ways to bring about the same positive messages. An interactive CD-ROM program designed to reduce adolescent substance use was developed and made use of several of the same principles on which both the social influence and the life–skills-training programs are based. Directed primarily to marijuana use, students were presented with vignettes that illustrated refusal skills and socially acceptable responses to substance use situations that created temptations—specifically, offers of marijuana. In a randomized experiment with 74 public schools, significant changes were found on adolescents' abilities to refuse an offer of marijuana, their intentions to refuse it, and their perceptions of the social norms that surround it (T. E. Duncan, Duncan, Beauchamp, Wells, & Ary, 2000). These findings present promising prospects for the development of low-cost interventions that may promote substance abuse prevention.

Social Engineering and Smoking

> Since smoking might injure your health, let's be careful not to smoke too much.
> —Warning Label on Cigarette Packages in Japan
> (*Time*, June 25, 2001)

Ultimately, smoking may be more successfully modified by social engineering than by techniques of behavioural change (Heishman, Kozlowski, & Henningfield, 1997; R. M. Kaplan, Orleans, Perkins, & Pierce, 1995). Although it is unlikely that cigarettes will be outlawed altogether, a number of social engineering alternatives may force people to reduce their smoking.

One possibility that has been particularly successful in Canada is to restrict smoking to certain places because of the known harm that can be done to nonsmokers by second-hand smoke (see the Focus on Social Issues box, "Can Non-smokers Be Harmed by Second-hand Smoke?"). As of the end of 2006, nine provinces and territories had implemented 100 percent smoke-free

Can Non-smokers Be Harmed by Second-hand Smoke?

Heather's Story (told in the winter of 2003)

"My name is Heather Crowe. I'm 58 years old, and I'm dying from lung cancer caused by second-hand smoke in the workplace. I was a waitress for over 40 years.

"I worked in the hospitality industry because it let me earn a decent living for myself and my daughter. I worked long hours, sometimes more than 60 hours every week. The air was blue with smoke where I worked, but until recently nobody did or said anything about the smoke in our workplaces. Until last year, I had no idea that second-hand smoke was dangerous. People would say, 'Do you mind if I smoke?' and I said, 'I really don't care.' I didn't have any idea that the smoke in the restaurants could do me harm. I just wasn't protected. I just wasn't told.

"My cancer was diagnosed last year. My health had usually been good, but last spring I noticed some lumps on my neck that didn't go away. Even though I wasn't feeling sick, my daughter encouraged me to visit the doctor. My doctor measured the lumps and sent me for some X-rays and tests. When she told me that results showed a cancerous tumour on my lung that was as big as my hand, I had trouble believing it. 'Are you sure it's not tuberculosis?' I asked. 'I've never smoked a day in my life.'

"The first thing I did was to hire a lawyer to help me make a claim with the Workers Compensation Board. I figured by going forward with a workers compensation claim it would help give other workers financial support as well as helping change the way workers in the hospitality sector are treated. Then I began to ask for letters to support my claim. I got some letters from my doctor, from the politicians, like the mayor and former mayor, and the medical officer of health for Ottawa, and from some Members of Parliament and councillors. To my surprise, the board accepted my claim within eight weeks. I learned that mine was the first claim accepted for illness caused by second-hand smoke in restaurants.

"On the day after I had a biopsy of my lung, one of my regular clients asked me why I was favouring my left arm. I told him I had lung cancer from second-hand smoke. He worked at Health Canada and asked me if they could use me in an advertisement about second-hand smoke. This would help people learn about the need to protect workers, and I said yes.

"By coincidence, the advertisement started the same day that I learned that my claim for compensation had been accepted. My phone began ringing off the hook, there were so many newspapers and television stations interested in the claim.

"Since then I have been across Canada talking to politicians, to schools, and to communities about the need to protect workers from smoke. I think I help because I put a face to cancer. There are lots of statistics out there, but I am a person, and I think that helps people understand that this is a real problem. I just want people to become a little more aware of what second-hand smoke can do.

"My goal is to be the last person to die from second-hand smoke." Heather died at 8:00 p.m. on May 22, 2006 (Physicians for a Smoke-Free Canada, 2006, www.smoke-free.ca/heathercrowe).

As suggested by Heather's story and other increasing evidence, the answer to whether people exposed to smokers' smoke are also harmed is a resounding yes. This so-called **passive smoking,** or **second-hand smoke,** which involves inhaling smoke and smoky air produced by smokers, has been tied to higher levels of carbon monoxide in the blood, reduced pulmonary functioning, and higher rates of lung cancer.

Second-hand smoke is a growing cause of preventable death in the Canada, killing up to 1,000 non-smokers every year (see Table 5.8). Although prolonged

TABLE 5.8 | The Toll of Second-hand Smoke

Disease	Annual Canadian Deaths or Cases
Lung cancer	Over 300 deaths
Heart disease	700 deaths
Sudden infant death syndrome (SIDS)	60 percent of deaths from SIDS may be attributed to parental smoking before or after birth
Low-birth-weight babies	Babies with parental exposure to second-hand have a reduced birth weight
Cognitive difficulties	Exposure to second-hand smoke prenatally can affect children's behaviour, attention, and ability to reason and understand
Asthma and bronchitis in children	Children exposed to second-hand smoke on a regular basis are at least 50 percent more likely to suffer damage to their lungs and breathing problems such as asthma and bronchitis

Source: Health Canada, 2004. Reproduced with the permission of the Minister of Health, 2011; Ontario Medical Association 2004.

Can Non-smokers Be Harmed by Second-hand Smoke? (continued)

exposure to second-hand smoke poses the greatest threat to health, exposure for as little as 8 to 20 minutes can cause heart rate increases, depletion of the heart's oxygen supply, constriction of the blood vessels, and increased blood pressure, all reactions which are known to cause heart disease and stroke (Health Canada, 2004b)

The exposure of children to second-hand smoke is particularly disturbing as their higher metabolism means that they absorb higher amounts of smoke than adults. Thankfully, recent estimates suggest that rates of children under 12 who are regularly exposed to second-hand smoke in the home have dropped to only 6 percent in 2008 compared to 26 percent in 1999 (Health Canada, 2009b). Adolescents are also at risk for second-hand smoke exposure with about 11 percent of non-smokers ages 12 to 17 being regularly exposed to second-hand smoke (Statistics Canada, 2009).

In addition to children, spouses and even pets of smokers may be at particular risk. A study conducted in Japan (Hirayama, 1981) followed 540 non-smoking wives of smoking or non-smoking husbands for 14 years and examined mortality due to lung cancer. The wives of heavy smokers had a higher rate of lung cancer than did the wives of husbands who smoked little or not at all. Moreover, these women's risk of dying from lung cancer was between one-third and one-half of what they would have faced had they been smokers themselves. Even dogs whose owners smoke are at 50 percent greater risk of developing lung cancer than are dogs whose owners are non-smokers (Reif, Dunn, Ogilvie, & Harris, 1992).

The importance of protecting people from passive smoking has led to legislation across Canada to make the indoor public and workplaces smoke-free. In addition, the majority of Canadian provinces now have legislature in place to ban smoking in cars with children. In December 2007, Nova Scotia became the first province to adopt legislation banning smoking in cars with children under the age of 19, and, as of this writing, all provinces

except Newfoundland and Labrador, Alberta, Quebec, and the Northwest Territories have banned smoking in cars in which there are children passengers. However, Newfoundland Labrador is expected to amend its Smoke Free Environment Act to include a ban on smoking in cars with children (CBC News, 2011). Although Canada is moving toward a smoke-free society, there is still some way to go before Heather Crowe's vision is realized.

Source: Physicians for a Smoke-Free Canada, 2008.

As a spokesperson for the harmful effects of second-hand smoking, Heather Crowe became a powerful advocate for making workplaces in Canada smoke-free.

legislation banning smoking in enclosed workplaces and public places. An evaluation of the effectiveness of these laws in reducing smoking is promising, with the percentage of Canadians who smoked decreasing from 24 percent to 18 percent between 2000 and 2006. During this period, the number of smoke-free homes and workplaces increased, while cigarette consumption

decreased among those smokers who lived or worked in smoke-restricted environments. In addition, smokers living and working in smoke-free areas were more likely to be in the later stages of change and less likely to be in the early planning and contemplation stages than those smokers who did not encounter such work and home smoking restrictions (Shields, 2007).

Actions such as increasing taxes on cigarettes are most likely to influence smoking among teenagers and young adults with little disposable income. A total ban on tobacco advertising is not out of the question, and at the very least, where and how companies may advertise has come under increasing regulation in Canada since the first tobacco advertising laws were introduced in 1988. Although there have been several changes and updates to these laws since they were introduced, including the required health warning notices and now graphic images in ads, some advocates suggest that our current laws are still not sufficiently stringent to prevent tobacco companies from targeting vulnerable populations (Physicians for a Smoke-Free Canada, 2003).

With the movement toward a smoke-free Canada in full swing through workplace and indoor public place smoking bans in most provinces and territories, and bans on smoking in cars with children growing in acceptance, the next social engineering efforts will likely involve tighter restrictions on tobacco advertising to protect those who are vulnerable from ever becoming smokers.

(L05) WHAT ARE EATING DISORDERS?

In Chapter 4 we examined the benefits of eating a healthy diet for enhancing health and avoiding obesity. However, with the heightened public awareness about the risks associated with obesity, for some people the goal of avoiding weight gain can go to extremes and become a health risk rather than a health enhancing behaviour. Cultural standards of beauty and even fitness may motivate some people's eating behaviour to become disordered and harmful (see the Focus on Social Issues box, "The Barbie Beauty Battle").

In pursuit of the elusive perfect body, numerous women and an increasing number of men chronically restrict their diet and engage in other weight-loss efforts, such as laxative use, cigarette smoking, and chronic use of diet pills. Eating disorders typically start during adolescence or young adulthood, and occur more frequently among women than in men (Health Canada, 2002).

The epidemic of eating disorders suggests that the pursuit of thinness is a growing social problem and public health threat of major proportions. Recent years have seen a dramatic increase in the incidence of eating disorders in the adolescent female population of Western countries. Indeed, more than 500,000 Canadians reported suffering from some form of eating disorder in 2005 (Canadian Mental Health Association, 2005). Chief among these are anorexia nervosa and bulimia.

Anorexia Nervosa

Anorexia nervosa is an obsessive disorder amounting to self-starvation, in which an individual diets and exercises to the point that body weight is grossly below optimum level, threatening health and potentially leading to death. Most sufferers are young women.

Developing Anorexia Nervosa   Several factors have been identified in the development of the illness. Genetic factors play a role, especially genes involved in the serotonin, dopamine, and estrogen systems. These systems, which are implicated in both anxiety and food intake, appear to be disrupted in eating disorders (Klump & Culbert, 2007; Striegel-Moore & Bulik, 2007). Genetic factors may also interact with environmental risks, such as stress, in the development of anorexia (Striegel-Moore & Bulik, 2007). A hyperactive HPA axis may also be involved in both anorexia and bulimia (Gluck, Geliebter, Hung, & Yang, 2004). Researchers are therefore increasingly viewing eating disorders as types of behavioural manifestations of efforts to cope with stress (Rojo, Conesa, Bermudez, & Livianos, 2006).

Women who have eating disorders, as well as those who have tendencies toward eating disorders, show high blood pressure and heart rate reactivity to stress and high urinary cortisol, suggesting that they may chronically overreact to stress. In addition, women with eating disorders or tendencies toward them are more likely to be depressed, anxious, and low in self-esteem and to have a poor sense of mastery. The fact that this profile is seen in women with eating disorder tendencies, as well as those women with full-blown eating disorders, suggests that they may be precipitating factors rather than consequences of eating disorders (Koo-Loeb, Costello, Light, & Girdler, 2000).

Body image distortions are also common among anorexic girls, although it is not clear whether this distortion is a consequence or a cause of the disorder. For example, these girls see themselves as still overweight when they have long since dropped below their ideal weight.

Treating Anorexia   Initially, the chief target of therapy is to bring the patient's weight back up to a safe level, a goal that must often be undertaken in a residential treatment setting, such as a hospital. To achieve weight gain, most therapies use behavioural approaches. However, motivation is particularly important, and the anorexic must want to change her behaviour and take an active, collaborative approach to regaining weight if treatment is to be successful (G. T. Wilson, Grilo, & Vitousek, 2007).

The Barbie Beauty Battle

Many health psychologists have criticized the media and the products they popularize for perpetuating false images of feminine beauty (J. K. Thompson & Heinberg, 1999). These images include unhealthily thin models and actresses, as well as children's fashion dolls. Indeed, emerging research indicates that exposure to images of thin-ideal women in advertisements increases negative mood, body dissatisfaction, levels of depression, and lowers self-esteem (Bessenoff, 2006), all factors known to be associated with unhealthy dieting behaviours and eating disorders. The Barbie doll has come under particular criticism because researchers believe that its widespread popularity with young girls may contribute to excessive dieting and the development of eating disorders. Using hip measurement as a constant, researchers have made calculations to determine the changes that would be necessary for a young, healthy woman to attain the same body proportions as the Barbie doll. She would have to increase her bust by five inches, her neck length by more than three inches, and her height by more than two feet while decreasing her waist by six inches (Brownell & Napolitano, 1995). This clearly unattainable standard may contribute to the false expectations that girls and women develop for their bodies.

Nevertheless, Barbie remains one of the most popular dolls worldwide.

The Barbie Beauty Battle

Because of the health risks of anorexia nervosa, research has increasingly moved toward prevention. Some interventions have tried to address social norms regarding thinness directly (for example, Neumark-Sztainer et al., 2003). For example, one study gave women information about other women's weight and body type, on the grounds that women with eating disorders often wrongly believe that other women are smaller and thinner than they actually are (Sanderson, Darley, & Messinger, 2002). The intervention succeeded in increasing women's estimates of their actual and ideal weight (Mutterperl & Sanderson, 2002).

Bulimia

Bulimia is an eating syndrome characterized by alternating cycles of binge eating and purging through such techniques as vomiting, laxative abuse, extreme dieting or fasting, and drug or alcohol abuse (M. K. Hamilton, Gelwick, & Meade, 1984). A related eating disorder, termed binge eating disorder, describes the many individuals who engage in recurrent binge eating but do not engage in the compensatory purging behaviour to avoid weight gain (Spitzer et al., 1993). Binge eating usually occurs when the individual is alone; bingeing may be triggered by negative emotions produced by stressful experiences (Telch & Agras, 1996). About half the people diagnosed with anorexia are also bulimic.

Who Develops Bulimia? Whereas many anorexics are thin, bulimics are typically of normal weight or overweight, especially through the hips. The binge phase has been interpreted as an out-of-control reaction of the body to restore weight; the purge phase, an effort to regain control over weight. When a person goes on a diet, the association between physiological cues of hunger and eating break down. Dropping below the set point for her personal weight, the individual reacts as if she may starve. Metabolism slows, and she begins to respond to external food cues instead of internal cues, such as hunger.

Food can become a constant thought. Restrained eating, then, sets the stage for a binge. The control of eating shifts from internal sensations and is replaced by decisions about when and what to eat, which is called a cognitively based regulatory system. This regulatory system is easily disrupted by stress or distraction, and when it is, the dieter is vulnerable to bingeing (Polivy & Herman, 1985). Overvaluing body appearance, a larger body mass than is desired, dieting, and symptoms of depression appear to be especially implicated in triggering binge episodes (Stice, Presnell, & Spangler, 2002).

Stress, especially conflict with others, appears to be implicated in the onset of binge-purge cycles, because the cues that normally are used to restrain eating are less salient in times of stress. One study of women in college found that their bulimia worsened in response to stress or to any experience that led to a feeling of being unattractive, overweight, or ineffectual (Striegel-Moore, Silberstein, Frensch, & Rodin, 1989). Their disordered eating symptoms grew worse over the course of the school year, presumably because their level of stress also increased.

Treating Bulimia   The first barrier to treating bulimia is the fact that many women do not go in for treatment. Either they do not believe that their problem is a serious one, or they do not believe that any medical intervention will overcome it. Accordingly, one of the first steps for helping bulimics get treatment is to convince them that the disorder threatens their health and that medical and psychological interventions can help them overcome the disorder (Smalec & Klingle, 2000).

A number of therapies have been developed to treat bulimia. Overall, a combination of medication and cognitive behavioural therapy appears to be the most effective treatment for bulimia (G. T. Wilson et al., 2007). Typically, this treatment begins by instructing the patient to keep a diary of eating habits, including time, place, type of food consumed, and emotions experienced. Simple self-monitoring can produce decreases in binge-purge behaviour. Monitoring is also often combined with other behavioural treatments in an individualized effort to bring eating under control (Agras, Schneider, Arnow, Raeburn, & Telch, 1989; Kirkley, Agras, & Weiss, 1985).

The increasing prevalence of eating disorders, coupled with the difficulty of treating them effectively, suggests that health psychologists must begin to think about ways to prevent eating disorders from developing rather than exclusively treating them after they occur (Battle & Brownell, 1996). ●

SUMMARY

 Identify the characteristics of health-compromising behaviours

- Health-compromising behaviours are those that threaten or undermine good health, either in the present or in the future. Many of these behaviours cluster and first emerge in adolescence.

 Describe and define substance dependence

- Substance dependence involves the repeated self-administration of a substance that results in tolerance, withdrawal, and compulsive behaviour.

- Harm reduction is an approach to dealing with substance abuse that aims to reduce but not necessarily eliminate substance abuse to help minimize the associated health and social harms.

- Psychoactive substances such as illicit drugs result in cognitive and affective changes when ingested that can alter behaviour in ways that can result in a variety of physical, mental and social problems.

 Understand how alcoholism and problem drinking compromise health

- Alcoholism accounts for thousands of deaths each year through cirrhosis, cancer, fetal alcohol syndrome, and accidents connected with drunk driving.

- Alcoholism and problem drinking encompass a wide range of specific behaviour problems with associated physiological and psychological needs.

- Alcoholism has a genetic component and is tied to socio-demographic factors, such as low socio-economic status. Drinking also arises in an effort to buffer the impact of stress and appears to peak between ages 18 and 25.

- Most treatment programs for alcoholism use broad-spectrum cognitive behavioural approaches. Many begin with an inpatient "drying-out" period, followed by the use of cognitive behavioural change methods, such as aversion therapy and relapse-prevention techniques.

- The best predictor of success is the patient. Alcoholics with mild drinking problems, little abuse of other drugs, and a supportive, financially secure environment do better than those without such supports.

 Explain how smoking is harmful for health and what factors influence smoking

- Smoking accounts for more than 45,000 deaths annually in Canada due to heart disease, cancer, and lung disorders. Smoking adds to and may even exacerbate other risk factors associated with CHD.

- Several theories have attempted to explain the addictive nature of smoking, including theories of nicotine regulation and those that emphasize nicotine's role as a neuroregulator.

- In the past few decades, attitudes toward smoking have changed dramatically for the negative, largely due to the mass media. Attitude change has kept some people from beginning smoking, motivated many to try to stop, and kept some former smokers from relapsing.

- Many programs for stopping smoking begin with some form of nicotine replacement, such as nicotine gum or transdermal nicotine patches. Many multimodal programs include social skills training programs or relaxation therapies. Relapse prevention is an important component of these programs.

- No particular venue for changing smoking behaviour appears to be especially effective. However, physicians and other health care professionals working directly with patients at risk may achieve greater success than other change agents.

- Smoking is highly resistant to change. Even after successfully stopping for a short period of time, most people relapse. Factors that contribute to relapse include addiction and the loss of an effective coping technique for dealing with social situations, among other factors.

- Smoking-prevention programs have been developed to keep youth from beginning to smoke. Many of these programs use a social influence approach and teach how to resist peer pressure to smoke. Others help adolescents improve their coping skills and self-image.

- Social engineering approaches to control smoking have also been employed by banning smoking in indoor public and workplaces, the rationale being that second-hand smoke harms others in the smoker's environment.

 Describe eating disorders

- The obsession with weight control has induced many people to diet, and may contribute to the epidemic of eating disorders in the adolescent female population of Western countries.

- Anorexia nervosa is an obsessive disorder amounting to self-starvation, in which an individual diets and exercises to the point that body weight is grossly below optimum level.

- Bulimia is characterized by alternating cycles of binge eating and purging through such techniques as vomiting, laxative abuse, extreme dieting or fasting, and drug or alcohol abuse.

KEY TERMS

addiction   p. 122
alcoholism   p. 125
anorexia nervosa   p. 148
behavioural inoculation   p. 144
bulimia   p. 149
craving   p. 122
detoxification   p. 127
harm reduction   p. 122

life–skills-training approach   p. 145
passive smoking   p. 146
physical dependence   p. 122
placebo drinking   p. 131
problem drinking   p. 125
psychoactive substances   p. 123
second-hand smoke   p. 146

self-help aids   p. 143
smoking-prevention
   programs   p. 143
social influence intervention
   p. 143
tolerance   p. 122
withdrawal   p. 122

PART

3

Stress and Coping

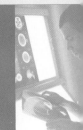

CHAPTER

6

Stress

The night before her biology final, Lisa confidently set her alarm and went to sleep. A power outage occurred during the night, and her alarm, along with most of the others in the dorm, failed to go off. At 8:45, Lisa was abruptly awakened by a friend banging on the door to tell her that her final started in 15 minutes. Lisa threw on some clothes, grabbed a muffin and a cup of coffee from the machines in her dorm, and raced to the exam room. Ten minutes late, she spent the first half-hour frantically searching through the multiple-choice questions, trying to find ones she knew the answers to, as her heart continued to race.

WHAT IS STRESS?

Most of us have more firsthand experience with stress than we care to remember. Stress is being stopped by a police officer after accidentally running a red light. Stress is waiting to take an exam when we are not sure that we have prepared well enough or studied the right material. Stress is missing a bus on a rainy day full of important appointments.

Psychologists have been studying stress and its impact on psychological and physical health for several decades. **Stress** is a negative emotional experience accompanied by predictable biochemical, physiological, cognitive, and behavioural changes that are directed either toward altering the stressful event or accommodating to its effects (see A. Baum, 1990). Research on stress, including causes and consequences, provides one of the best illustrations of the mind-body relationship and how individual perceptions, behaviours, and predispositions are intertwined with the social and environmental context in which they occur to influence health. In this chapter we will examine the factors that influence the experience of stress, and then we will turn to the internal and external factors that may moderate the experience of stress in Chapter 7.

What Is a Stressor?

Initially, researchers focused on stressful events themselves, called **stressors.** Such events include noise, crowding, a bad relationship, a round of job interviews, or the commute to work. The study of stressors has helped define some conditions that are more likely to produce stress than others, but a focus on stressful events cannot fully explain the experience of stress. A stressful experience may be stressful to some people but not to others. If the "noise" is your radio playing the latest rock music,

then it will probably not be stressful to you, although it may be to your neighbour. Whereas one person might find the loss of a job highly stressful, another might see it as an opportunity to try a new field, as a challenge rather than a threat. How a potential stressor is perceived determines whether it will be experienced as stressful.

Person–Environment Fit

Stress is the consequence of a person's appraisal processes: the assessment of whether personal resources are sufficient to meet the demands of the environment. Stress, then, is determined by **person–environment fit** (R. S. Lazarus & Folkman, 1984b; R. S. Lazarus & Launier, 1978).

When a person's resources are more than adequate to deal with a difficult situation, he or she may feel little stress and experience a sense of challenge instead. When the individual perceives that his or her resources will probably be sufficient to deal with the event but only at the cost of great effort, he or she may feel a moderate amount of stress. When the individual perceives that his or her resources will probably not suffice to meet an environmental stressor, he or she may experience a great deal of stress.

Stress, then, results from the process of appraising events (as harmful, threatening, or challenging), of assessing potential responses, and of responding to those events. To see how stress researchers have arrived at our current understanding of stress, it is useful to consider some of the early contributions to the field.

WHAT THEORIES AND MODELS ARE USED TO STUDY STRESS?

Fight-or-Flight

One of the earliest contributions to stress research was Walter Cannon's (1932) description of the **fight-or-flight response.** Cannon proposed that, when an organism perceives a threat, the body is rapidly aroused and motivated via the sympathetic nervous system and the endocrine system. This concerted physiological response mobilizes the organism to attack the threat or to flee; hence, it is called the fight-or-flight response (Kemeny, 2003).

At one time, fight-or-flight literally referred to fighting or fleeing in response to stressful events such as attack by a predator. Now more commonly *fight* refers to aggressive responses to stress, whereas *flight* may be seen in social withdrawal or withdrawal through substance use such as alcohol or drugs.

On the one hand, the fight-or-flight response is adaptive because it enables the organism to respond quickly to threat. On the other hand, it can be harmful because stress disrupts emotional and physiological functioning, and when stress continues unabated, it lays the groundwork for health problems.

Selye's General Adaptation Syndrome

Another important early contribution to the field of stress is Hans Selye's (1956, 1976) work on the **general adaptation syndrome.** Selye, a Hungarian-born Canadian physician and the first director of the Institute of Experimental Medicine and Surgery at the Université de Montréal (1945–76), is considered to be the "father" of the field of stress research. Although Selye initially intended to explore the effects of sex hormones on physiological functioning, he became interested in the stressful impact his interventions seemed to have. Accordingly, he exposed rats to a variety of stressors—such as extreme cold and fatigue—and observed their physiological responses. To his surprise, all stressors, regardless of type, produced essentially the same pattern of physiological responding. In particular, they all led to an enlarged adrenal cortex, shrinking of the thymus and lymph glands, and ulceration of the stomach and duodenum. Thus, whereas Cannon's work explored adrenomedullary responses to stress—specifically, catecholamine secretion—Selye's work more closely explored adrenocortical responses to stress.

From these observations, Selye (1956) developed his concept of the general adaptation syndrome. He argued that when an organism confronts a stressor, it mobilizes itself for action. The response itself is nonspecific with respect to the stressor; that is, regardless of the cause of the threat, the individual will respond with the same physiological pattern of reactions. Over time, with repeated or prolonged exposure to stress, there will be wear and tear on the system.

The general adaptation syndrome consists of three phases. In the first phase, *alarm,* the organism becomes mobilized to meet the threat. In the second phase, *resistance,* the organism makes efforts to cope with the threat, as through confrontation. The third phase, *exhaustion,* occurs if the organism fails to overcome the threat and depletes its physiological resources in the process of trying. These phases are pictured in Figure 6.1.

Selye's model continues to influence the field of stress today. One reason is that it offers a general theory of reactions to a wide variety of stressors over time. As such, it provides a way of thinking about the interplay of physiological and environmental factors. Second, it posits a physiological mechanism for the stress-illness relationship. Specifically, Selye believed that repeated or prolonged exhaustion of resources, the third phase of the syndrome, is responsible for the physiological damage that lays the groundwork for disease. In fact, prolonged or repeated stress has been implicated in a broad array of disorders, such as cardiovascular disease, arthritis, hypertension, and immune-related deficiencies, as we will see in Chapters 13 and 14.

Criticisms of the General Adaptation Syndrome   Selye's model has also been criticized on several grounds. First, it assigns a very limited role to psychological factors, and researchers now believe that the psychological appraisal of events is important in the determination of stress (R. S. Lazarus & Folkman, 1984b). This limitation is not surprising given that all of Selye's research was conducted

FIGURE 6.1 | The Three Phases of Selye's (1974) General Adaptation Syndrome

Phase A is the alarm response, in which the body first reacts to a stressor. At this time, resistance is diminished. Phase B, the stage of resistance, occurs with continued exposure to a stressor. The bodily signs associated with an alarm reaction disappear and resistance rises above normal. Phase C is the stage of exhaustion that results from long-term exposure to the same stressor. At this point, resistance may again fall to below normal.

(*Source:* From "The General Adaptation Syndrome" from Stress Without Distress by Hans Selye, M.D., Fig. 3, p. 39. Copyright © 1974 by Hans Selye, M.D. Reprinted by permission of HarperCollins Publishers, Inc.

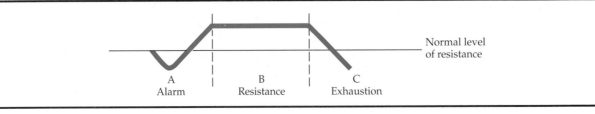

with animals and not humans. A second criticism concerns the assumption that responses to stress are uniform (Hobfoll, 1989). There is evidence that not all stressors produce the same endocrinological responses (Kemeny, 2003). Moreover, how people respond to stress is substantially influenced by their personalities, perceptions, and biological constitutions. A third criticism concerns the fact that Selye assessed stress as an outcome, such that stress is evident only when the general adaptation syndrome has run its course. In fact, people experience many of the debilitating effects of stress while a stressful event is going on and even in anticipation of its occurrence. Despite these limitations and reservations, Selye's model remains a cornerstone of the field of stress, and has led to the development of other conceptualizations of the physiological effects of stress that have attempted to improve upon the shortcomings of Selye's model.

Tend-and-Befriend

Animals, whether nonhuman or human, do not merely fight, flee, and grow exhausted in response to stress. They also affiliate with each other, whether it is the herding behaviour of deer in response to stress, the huddling one sees among female rats, or the coordinated responses to a stressor that a community shows when it is under the threat of flood, tornado, or other natural disaster.

To address this issue, Taylor and colleagues (S. E. Taylor, Klein, et al., 2000) developed a theory of responses to stress termed **tend-and-befriend.** The theory maintains that in addition to fight-or-flight, humans respond to stress with social and nurturant behaviour. These responses may be especially true of women.

During the time that responses to stress evolved, males and females faced somewhat different adaptive challenges. Whereas men were responsible for hunting and protection, women were responsible for foraging and child care. These activities were largely segregated, with the result that women's responses to stress would have evolved so as to protect not only the self but offspring as well. These responses would be characteristic not only of humans. The offspring of most species are immature and would be unable to survive were it not for the attention of adults. In most species, that attention is provided by the mother.

Because tending to offspring, particularly in times of stress, is a complex task, the tend-and-befriend theory maintains that *befriending*—that is, affiliating with others and seeking social contact during stress—may be especially characteristic of females and may help in self-preservation and the protection of offspring.

Like the fight-or-flight mechanism, tend-and-befriend may depend on underlying biological mechanisms. In particular, the hormone oxytocin may have significance for female responses to stress. Oxytocin is a stress hormone, rapidly released in response to at least some stressful events, and its effects are especially influenced by estrogen, suggesting a role in the responses of women to stress (S. E. Taylor, Gonzaga, et al., 2006). The potential contribution of oxytocin to stress responses is to act as an impetus for affiliation. Numerous animal and human studies show that oxytocin increases affiliative behaviours of all kinds, including mothering (S. E. Taylor, 2002), and warm touching between couples (Holt-Lunstad, Birmingham, & Light, 2008). In addition, animals and humans with high levels of oxytocin are calmer and more relaxed, which may contribute to social and nurturant behaviour (McCarthy, 1995; Ross & Young, 2009). Opioids may also contribute to affiliative responses to stress in females (S. E. Taylor, Klein, et al., 2000).

In support of the theory, there is evidence that women are consistently more likely than men to respond to stress by turning to others (Luckow, Reifman, & McIntosh, 1998; Tamres, Janicki, & Helgeson, 2002). Tend and befriend responses have also been noted in female university students (Turton & Carol, 2005). Mothers' responses to offspring during stress also appear to be different from those of fathers in ways encompassed by the tend-and-befriend theory. Nonetheless, men, too, show social responses to stress, and at present, less is known about men's social responses to stress than women's. There is also some evidence that male and female infants responding differently to parental stress. One study observed mother-infant dyads for maternal frightening behaviour and found that as mother's frightening behaviour increased, female infants approached their mothers for comfort more than male infants did (David & Lyons-Ruth, 2005).

In addition to offering a biobehavioural approach to differences in male and female responses to stress, the tend-and-befriend theory brings social behaviour into stress processes. We are affiliative creatures who respond to stress collectively, as well as individually, and these responses are characteristic of men as well as women.

Psychological Appraisal and the Experience of Stress

In humans, psychological appraisals are an important determinant of whether an event is responded to as stressful.

FIGURE 6.2 | The Experience of Stress

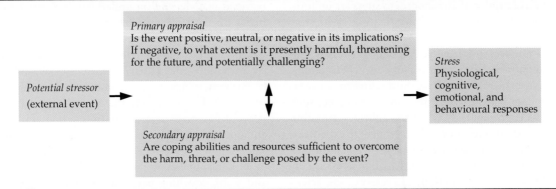

Primary appraisal
Is the event positive, neutral, or negative in its implications?
If negative, to what extent is it presently harmful, threatening
for the future, and potentially challenging?

Potential stressor
(external event)

Stress
Physiological,
cognitive,
emotional, and
behavioural responses

Secondary appraisal
Are coping abilities and resources sufficient to overcome
the harm, threat, or challenge posed by the event?

Primary Appraisal Processes   Lazarus, a chief proponent of the psychological view of stress (R. S. Lazarus, 1968; R. S. Lazarus & Folkman, 1984b), maintains that when individuals confront a new or changing environment, they engage in a process of **primary appraisal** to determine the meaning of the event (see Figure 6.2).

Events may be perceived as positive, neutral, or negative in their consequences. Negative or potentially negative events are further appraised for their possible harm, threat, or challenge. *Harm* is the assessment of the damage that has already been done by an event. Thus, for example, a man who has just been fired from his job may perceive present harm in terms of his own loss of self-esteem and his embarrassment as his coworkers silently watch him pack up his desk.

Threat is the assessment of possible future damage that may be brought about by the event. Thus, the man who has just lost his job may anticipate the problems that loss of income will create for him and his family in the future. Primary appraisals of events as threats have important effects on physiological responses to stress. For example, blood pressure is higher when threat is higher or when threat is high and challenge is low (Maier et al., 2003).

Finally, events may be appraised in terms of their *challenge,* the potential to overcome and even profit from the event. For example, the man who has lost his job may perceive that a certain amount of harm and threat exists, but he may also see his unemployment as an opportunity to try something new. Challenge appraisals are associated with more confident expectations of the ability to cope with the stressful event, more favourable emotional reactions to the event, and lower blood pressure (Maier et al., 2003; N. Skinner & Brewer, 2002).

The importance of primary appraisal in the experience of stress is illustrated in a classic study of stress by Speisman, Lazarus, Mordkoff, and Davidson (1964). University students viewed a gruesome film depicting unpleasant tribal initiation rites that included genital surgery. Before viewing the film, they were exposed to one of four experimental conditions. One group listened to an anthropological account about the meaning of the rites. Another group heard a lecture that de-emphasized the pain the initiates were experiencing and emphasized their excitement over the events. A third group heard a description that emphasized the pain and trauma that the initiates were undergoing. A fourth group was given no introductory information, and the film they viewed had no soundtrack. Measures of autonomic arousal (skin conductance, heart rate) and self-reports suggested that the first two groups experienced considerably less stress than did the group whose attention was focused on the trauma and pain. Thus, this study illustrated that stress not only was intrinsic to the gruesome film itself but also depended on the viewer's appraisal of it.

Secondary Appraisal Processes   At the same time that primary appraisals of stressful circumstances are occurring, secondary appraisal is initiated. **Secondary appraisal** is the assessment of one's coping abilities and resources and whether they will be sufficient to meet the harm, threat, and challenge of the event. Ultimately, the subjective experience of stress is a balance between primary and secondary appraisal. When harm and threat are high and coping ability is low, substantial stress is felt. When coping ability is high, stress may be minimal. Potential responses to stress are many and include physiological, cognitive, emotional, and behavioural consequences. Some of these responses are involuntary reactions to stress, whereas others are voluntarily initiated in a conscious effort to cope.

Cognitive responses to stress include beliefs about the harm or threat an event poses and beliefs about its causes or controllability. They also include involuntary responses, such as distractability and inability to concentrate; performance disruptions on cognitive tasks (e.g., Shaham, Singer, & Schaeffer, 1992); and intrusive, repetitive, or morbid thoughts. Cognitive responses are also involved in the initiation of coping activities, as we will see in Chapter 7.

Potential emotional reactions to stressful events range widely; they include fear, anxiety, excitement, embarrassment, anger, depression, and even stoicism or denial. Emotional responses can be quite insistent, prompting rumination over a stressful event, which in turn, may keep biological stress responses elevated (Glynn, Christenfeld, & Gerin, 2002).

Potential behavioural responses are virtually limitless, depending on the nature of the stressful event.

Confrontative action against the stressor ("fight") and withdrawal from the threatening event ("flight") constitute two general categories of behavioural responses. We will examine others in the course of our discussion.

The Physiology of Stress

> Stress-related disease emerges, predominantly, out of the fact that we so often activate a physiological system that has evolved for responding to acute physical emergencies, but we turn it on for months on end, worrying about mortgages, relationships, and promotions.
>
> SAPOLSKY (1998, P. 7)

Stress is important, both because it causes psychological distress and because it leads to changes in the body that may have short- or long-term consequences for health. Two interrelated systems are heavily involved in the stress response. They are the sympathetic-adrenomedullary (SAM) system and the hypothalamic-pituitary-adrenocortical (HPA) axis. These components of the stress response are illustrated in Figure 6.3.

FIGURE 6.3 | The Body's Stress Systems

Stressful events result in sympathetic activation (solid lines) and the release of catecholamines, and HPA activation (dashed lines) and the release of CRF.

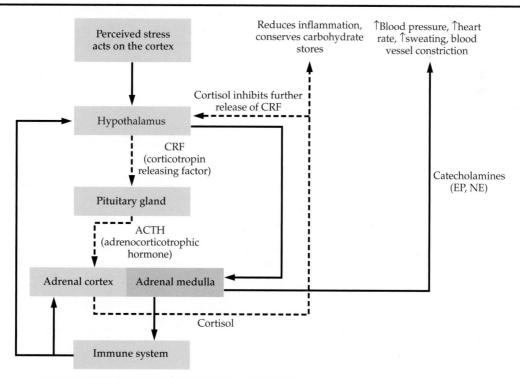

Sympathetic Activation   When events are encountered that are perceived as harmful or threatening, they are labelled as such by the cerebral cortex, which in turn sets off a chain of reactions mediated by these appraisals. Information from the cortex is transmitted to the hypothalamus, which initiates one of the earliest responses to stress—namely, sympathetic nervous system arousal, or the fight-or-flight response first described by Walter Cannon.

Sympathetic arousal stimulates the medulla of the adrenal glands, which in turn secrete the catecholamines, epinephrine and norepinephrine. These effects result in the cranked-up feeling we usually experience in response to stress. Sympathetic arousal leads to increased blood pressure, increased heart rate, increased sweating, and constriction of peripheral blood vessels, among other changes. As can be seen in Figure 6.3, the catecholamines have effects on a variety of tissues and are believed to lead to modulation of the immune system as well.

HPA Activation   In addition to the activation of the sympathetic nervous system, the HPA system is activated. Hans Selye provided the basis for understanding the effects of stress on the HPA in his general adaptation syndrome, the nonspecific physiological reaction that occurs in response to stress and involves the three phases of alarm, resistance, and exhaustion.

The hypothalamus releases corticotrophin-releasing factor (CRF), which stimulates the pituitary gland to secrete adrenocorticotropic hormone (ACTH), which in turn stimulates the adrenal cortex to release glucocor-

ticoids. Of these, cortisol is especially significant. It acts to conserve stores of carbohydrates and helps reduce inflammation in the case of an injury. It also helps the body return to its steady state following stress by inhibiting release of CRF from the hypothalamus.

Repeated activation of the HPA axis in response to chronic or recurring stress can ultimately compromise its functioning. When the HPA axis becomes dysregulated in response to stress, several things may happen. Daily cortisol patterns may be altered. That is, normally cortisol is high upon wakening in the morning, decreases over the day (although peaking following lunch) until it flattens out at low levels in the afternoon. People under chronic stress, however, can show elevated cortisol levels long into the afternoon or evening (for example, Powell et al., 2002), a general flattening of the diurnal rhythms (McEwen, 1998), an exaggerated cortisol response to a challenge, a protracted cortisol response following a stressor, or alternatively no response at all. Any of these patterns is suggestive of compromised ability of the HPA axis to respond to and recover from stress (McEwen, 1998; Pruessner, Hellhammer, Pruessner, & Lupien, 2003). When researchers study physiological and neuroendocrine stress responses, they look for signs like these (see Figure 6.4).

Effects of Long-term Stress   We have just examined some of the major physiological changes that occur in response to the perception of stress. What do these changes mean? Although the short-term mobilization that occurs in

FIGURE 6.4 | Routes by Which Stress May Produce Disease

The text describes how direct physiological effects may result from sympathetic and/or HPA activation. In addition, as this figure shows, stress may affect health via behaviours—first, by influencing health habits directly and second, by interfering with treatment and the use of services.

(*Source:* A. Baum, 1994)

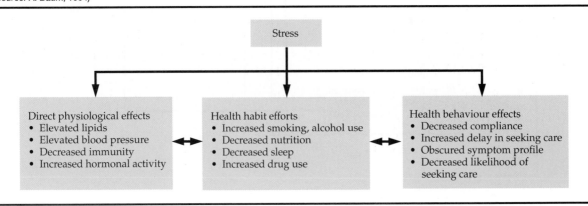

response to stress originally prepared humans to fight or flee, rarely do stressful events require these kinds of adjustments. Consequently, in response to stress, we often experience the effects of sudden elevations of circulating stress hormones that, in certain respects, do not serve the purpose for which they were originally intended.

Over the long term, excessive discharge of the catecholamines, epinephrine and norepinephrine, can lead to suppression of immune functions; produce changes such as increased blood pressure and heart rate; provoke variations in normal heart rhythms, which may be a precursor to sudden death; and produce neurochemical imbalances that may contribute to the development of psychiatric disorders. The catecholamines may also have effects on lipid levels and free fatty acids, all of which may be important in the development of atherosclerosis and cardiovascular disease.

Corticosteroids can compromise the functioning of the immune system, and prolonged cortisol secretion can lead to problems in verbal functioning, memory, and concentration because of its detrimental effects on the hippocampus (Starkman, Giordani, Brenent, Schork, & Schteingart, 2001) Pronounced HPA activation is common in depression, with episodes of cortisol secretion being more frequent and of longer duration among depressed than nondepressed people, although it is not entirely clear whether HPA activation is a cause or an effect of these disorders. Another long-term consequence from chronic HPA activation is the storage of fat in the abdominal areas rather than to the hips. This accumulation leads to a high waist-to-hip ratio, which is used by some researchers as a marker for chronic stress (Bjorntorp, 1996), and is associated with depression (Rivenes, Harvey, & Mykletun, 2009).

Which of these responses to stress have implications for disease? Several researchers (Dienstbier, 1989; Frankenhaeuser, 1991) have suggested that the health consequences of HPA axis activation are more significant than those of sympathetic activation. Sympathetic adrenal activation in response to stress may not be a pathway for disease; HPA activation may be required as well. Some researchers have suggested that this reasoning explains why exercise, which produces sympathetic arousal but not HPA activation, is protective for health rather than health compromising. In essence, then, exercise may engage different neurobiological and emotional systems and patterns of activation than those engaged by stress.

Stress may also impair the immune system's capacity to respond to hormonal signals that terminate

Stressful events, such as writing a final exam, produce agitation and physiological arousal.

inflammation. A study that demonstrates this point compared 50 healthy adults, half of whom were parents of cancer patients and, the other half, parents of healthy children. Childhood cancer is known to be one of the most stressful events that parents encounter. The parents of the cancer patients reported more stress and had flatter daily slopes of cortisol secretion than was true for the parents of healthy children. Moreover, the ability to suppress production of a proinflammatory cytokine called IL-6 was diminished among parents of the cancer patients. Because proinflammatory cytokines are implicated in a broad array of diseases including coronary artery disease, these findings suggest that the impaired ability to terminate inflammation may be another pathway by which stress affects illness outcomes (G. E. Miller, Cohen, & Ritchey, 2002).

Researchers are increasingly focusing on poor sleep quality as both an indicator of chronic stress and a consequence of chronic stress. It has long been suspected that chronic insomnia can result from stressful events. Evidence suggests that the combination of emotional arousal and neuroendocrine activation due to chronic stress may indeed underlie chronic insomnia (Shaver, Johnston, Lentz, & Landis, 2002). Because sleep represents a vital restorative activity, this mechanism, too, may represent an important pathway to disease (S. Edwards, Hucklebridge, Clow, & Evans, 2003). The coming years will help clarify the important psychobiological pathways from stress to disease.

Individual Differences in Stress Reactivity   People vary in their reactivity to stress. **Reactivity** is the degree of change that occurs in autonomic, neuroendocrine, and/or immune responses as a result of stress. Reactivity is, in part, a genetic predisposition to respond physiologically to environmental threats or challenges (Jacobs et al., 2006) that may be implicated in both short- and long-term health complications due to stress. Some people show very small reactions to stressful circumstances, whereas others show large responses. These differences may be genetic in origin or develop prenatally or in early life.

Reactivity to stress can affect vulnerability to illness. For example, in one study, a group of children ranging in age from 3 to 5 years old were tested for their cardiovascular reactivity (change in heart rate and blood pressure) or their immune response to a vaccine challenge following a stressful task. Parents were then asked to report on the number of family stressors during a 12-week period, and illness rates were charted during this period. The results indicated that stress was associated with increased rates of illness only among the children who had previously shown strong immune or cardiovascular reactions. The less reactive children did not experience any change in illness under stressful circumstances (Boyce, Alkon, Tschann, Chesney, & Alpert, 1995).

Do changes like this actually lead to illness? S. Cohen and colleagues (2002) found that people who reacted to laboratory stressors with high cortisol responses and who also had a high level of negative life events were especially vulnerable to upper respiratory infections. People who reacted to laboratory stressors with low immune responses were especially vulnerable to upper respiratory infection if they were also under high stress. High immune reactors, in contrast, did not show differences in upper respiratory illness as a function of the stress they experienced, perhaps because their immune systems were quick to respond to the threat that a potential infection posed.

Studies like these suggest that psychobiological reactivity to stress is an important factor that influences the effects that stress has on the body and the likelihood that it will contribute to distress or disease. As will be seen in Chapter 13, differences in reactivity are believed to contribute especially to the development of hypertension and coronary artery disease.

Physiological Recovery Processes   Recovery processes following stress are also important in the physiology of the stress response (Rutledge, Linden, & Paul, 2000). In particular, the inability to recover quickly from a stressful event may be a marker for the cumulative damage that stress has caused. Researchers have paid special attention to the cortisol response—particularly prolonged cortisol responses that occur under conditions of high stress.

In one intriguing study (Perna & McDowell, 1995), elite athletes were divided into groups that were experiencing a high versus a low amount of stress in their lives, and their cortisol response was measured following vigorous training. Those athletes under higher degrees of stress showed a longer cortisol recovery. Because elevated cortisol affects the immune system, the researchers suggested that stress may widen the window of susceptibility for illness and injury among competitive athletes by virtue of its impact on cortisol recovery.

As the research on recovery processes implies, the long-term effects of stress on the body are of great importance when understanding the mechanisms by which physiological changes in response to stress may promote illness.

Allostatic Load   As Selye noted, the initial response of the body to stressful circumstances may be arousal, but over time this response may give way to exhaustion, leading to cumulative damage to the organism. Building on Selye's ideas and Cannon's notion of homeostasis, researchers have developed the concept of **allostatic load** (McEwen & Stellar, 1993). This concept refers to the fact that physiological systems within the body fluctuate to meet demands from stress, a state called allostasis. Over time, allostatic load builds up, which is defined as the physiological costs of chronic exposure to fluctuating or heightened neural or neuroendocrine response that results from repeated or chronic stress.

This buildup of allostatic load—that is, the long-term costs of chronic or repeated stress—can be assessed by a number of indicators (Juster, McEwen, & Lupien, 2010). These include decreases in cell-mediated immunity, the inability to shut off cortisol in response to stress, lowered heart rate variability, elevated epinephrine levels, a high waist-to-hip ratio, volume of the hippocampus (which is believed to decrease with repeated stimulation of the HPA), problems with memory (an indirect measure of hippocampal functioning), high plasma fibrinogen, and elevated blood pressure. Many of these changes occur normally with age, so to the extent that they occur early, allostatic load may be thought of as accelerated aging of the organism in response to stress. Over time, this kind of wear and tear can lead to illness (Karlamanga, Singer, & Seeman, 2006). These effects may be exacerbated by the poor health habits practised by people under chronic stress. The damage due to chronic or repeated stress is only made worse if people also cope with stress via a higher fat diet, less frequent exercise, and smoking, all of which stress can encourage (Ng & Jeffery, 2003).

The physiology of stress and, in particular, the recent research on the cumulative adverse effects of stress are important because they suggest the pathways by which stress exerts adverse effects on the body, ultimately contributing to the likelihood of disease. The relationship of stress, both short and long term, to both acute disorders such as infection, and chronic diseases is now so well established that stress is implicated in most diseases, either in their etiology, their course, or both. We explore these processes more fully when we address different diseases such as heart disease and hypertension in Chapter 13 and cancer and arthritis in Chapter 14. At this point, suffice it to say, stress is one of the major risk factors for disease that humans encounter.

(L03) WHAT MAKES EVENTS STRESSFUL?

Assessing Stress

Given that stress can produce a variety of responses, what is the best way to measure it? Researchers have used many indicators of stress. These include self-reports of perceived stress, life change, and emotional distress; behavioural measures, such as task performance under stress; physiological measures of arousal, such as heart rate and blood pressure; and biochemical markers (or indicators), especially elevated catecholamines and alterations in the diurnal rhythm of cortisol or cortisol responses to stress. In each case, these measures have proven to be useful indicators.

However, each type of measurement has its own associated problems. For example, catecholamine secretion is enhanced by a number of factors other than stress. Self-report measures are subject to a variety of biases, because individuals may want to present themselves in as desirable a light as possible. Behavioural measures are subject to multiple interpretations. For example, performance declines can be due to declining motivation, fatigue, cognitive strain, or other factors. Consequently, stress researchers have called for the use of multiple measures (A. Baum et al., 1982). With several measures, the possibility of obtaining a good model of the stress experience is increased.

Dimensions of Stressful Events

As we have just noted, events themselves are not inherently stressful. Rather, whether they are stressful depends on how they are appraised by an individual. What are some characteristics of potential stressors that make them more likely to be appraised as stressful?

Negative Events   Negative events are more likely to produce stress than are positive events. Many events have the potential to be stressful because they present people with extra work or special problems that may tax or exceed their resources. Shopping for the holidays, planning a party, coping with an unexpected job promotion, and getting married are all positive events that draw off substantial time and energy. Nonetheless, these positive experiences are less likely to be reported as stressful than are undesirable events, such as getting a traffic ticket, trying to find a job, coping with a death in the family, or getting divorced.

Negative events show a stronger relationship to both psychological distress and physical symptoms than do positive ones. This may be because negative stressful events have implications for the self-concept producing loss of self-esteem or erosion of a sense of mastery or identity.

Uncontrollable Events   Uncontrollable or unpredictable events are more stressful than controllable or predictable ones. When people feel that they can predict, modify, or terminate an aversive event, or feel they have access to someone who can influence it, they experience it as less stressful, even if they actually do nothing about it (Koolhaas et al., 2011).

Feelings of control not only mute the subjective experience of stress but also influence biochemical reactions to it. Believing that one can control a stressor, such as noise level or crowding, is associated with lower cortisol levels than believing that one has no control over the stressor (Dickerson & Kemeny, 2004). Uncontrollable stress has been tied to immunosuppressive effects as well (Brosschot et al., 1998; Peters et al., 1999).

Ambiguous Events   Ambiguous events are often perceived as more stressful than are clear-cut events. When a potential stressor is ambiguous, a person has no opportunity to take action. He or she must instead devote energy to trying to understand the stressor, which can be a time-consuming, resource-sapping task.

Events such as crowding are experienced as stressful only to the extent that they are appraised that way. Some situations of crowding make people feel happy, whereas other crowding situations are experienced as aversive.

Overload   Overloaded people are more stressed and have poorer health than are people with fewer tasks to perform (Shultz, Wang, & Olson, 2010). People who have too many tasks in their lives report higher levels of stress than do those who have fewer tasks. For example, one of the main sources of work-related stress is job overload, the perception that one is responsible for doing too much in too short a period of time.

Which Stressors?   People may be more vulnerable to stress in central life domains than in peripheral ones because important aspects of the self are overly invested in central life domains (Swindle & Moos, 1992). For example, among working women for whom parental identity was very salient, role strains associated with the parent role, such as feeling that their children did not get the attention they needed, took a toll (R. W. Simon, 1992).

Summary   Events that are negative, uncontrollable, ambiguous, or overwhelming or that involve central life tasks are perceived as more stressful than are events that are positive, controllable, clear-cut, or manageable or that involve peripheral life tasks.

Must Stress Be Perceived as Such to Be Stressful?

The preceding points suggest that stress is both a subjective and objective experience. In fact, both of these aspects of stress affect the likelihood of resulting health

problems. Repetti (1993b) studied air traffic controllers and assessed their subjective perceptions of stress on various days, and she also gathered objective measures of daily stress, including the weather conditions and the amount of air traffic. She found that both subjective and objective measures of stress independently predicted psychological distress and health complaints.

Similarly, S. Cohen, Tyrrell, and Smith (1993) recruited 394 healthy people for a study of the common cold. Participants completed questionnaires designed to obtain objective information about the stressful life events they had encountered, and they completed a measure of perceived stress. The researchers then exposed participants to a common cold virus and found that both objectively assessed stressful life events and perceived stress predicted whether or not the people developed a cold.

These kinds of studies suggest that, although the perception of stress is important to the physical and psychological symptoms it causes, objectively defined stress also shows a relation to adverse psychological and physiological changes.

Can People Adapt to Stress?

If a stressful event becomes a permanent or chronic part of their environment, will people eventually habituate to it or will they develop **chronic strain?** Will it no longer cause them distress, drain psychological resources, or lead to symptoms of illness? The answer to this question depends on the type of stressor, the subjective experience of stress, and which indicator of stress is considered.

Psychological Adaptation   Most people are able to adapt psychologically to moderate or predictable stressors. At first, any novel, threatening situation can produce stress, but such reactions often subside over time. However, particularly vulnerable populations—especially children, the elderly, and poor people—do seem to be adversely affected by environmental stressors (Maschke, 2011); they may show signs of helplessness and difficulty in performing tasks. One study found that children exposed to chronic environmental noise demonstrated low increases in blood pressure to a variety of different stressors—not just noise—suggesting that chronic exposure results in more than just habituation to noise (Lepore, Shejwal, Kim, & Evans, 2010). One possible reason is that these groups already experience little control over their environments and accordingly may already be exposed to high levels of stress; the addition of an environmental stressor, such as noise or crowding, may push their resources to the limits. Similarly, one study of the effects of stress on the mortality of Canadian seniors found that for senior women financial stress was a predictor of death eight years later, even after controlling for education and other factors (Wilkins, 2005). This suggests that this population may be particularly vulnerable to stress from lack of resources.

Thus, the answer to the question of whether people can adapt to chronic stress might best be summarized as follows: People (and animals) show signs of both long-term strain and habituation to chronically stressful events. Most people can adapt moderately well to mildly stressful events; however, it may be difficult or impossible for them to adapt to highly stressful events, and already-stressed people may be unable to adapt to even moderate stressors. Moreover, even when psychological adaptation may have occurred, physiological changes in response to stress may persist.

Physiological Adaptation   In terms of physiological adaptation, animal models of stress suggest evidence for both habituation and chronic strain. For example, rats exposed to relatively low-level stressors tend to show initial physiological responsiveness followed by habituation. When the stimuli employed to induce stress are intense, however, the animal may show no habituation (Pitman, Ottenweller, & Natelson, 1988). Physiological evidence from studies of humans also suggests evidence for both habituation and chronic strain. Low-level stress may produce habituation in most people, but with more intense stress damage from chronic stress can accumulate across multiple organ systems as the allostatic load model suggests. Habituation is more likely for HPA responses to stress than for sympathetic responses to stress (Schommer, Hellhammer, & Kirschbaum, 2003). But chronic stress can also impair cardiovascular and neuroendocrine recovery from stressors and through such effects, contribute to an increased risk for diseases, such as cardiovascular disorders, in midlife (K. A. Matthews, Gump, & Owens, 2001).

Researchers have looked at immune responses that are associated with long-term stressful events to address the question of habituation. Wright and colleagues (2004) found that exposure to a long-term stressful event was significantly related to poorer immune functioning. What this research suggests is that physiological habituation may not occur or may not be complete when stressors are long-term and that the immune system may be compromised by long-term stress.

Must a Stressor Be Ongoing to Be Stressful?

Does the stress response occur only while a stressful event is happening, or can stress result in anticipation of or as an after-effect of exposure to a stressor? One of the wonders and curses of human beings' symbolic capacities is their ability to conceptualize things before they materialize. We owe our abilities to plan, invent, and reason abstractly to this skill, but we also get from it our ability to worry. Unlike lower animals, human beings do not have to be exposed to a stressor to suffer stress.

Anticipating Stress   The anticipation of a stressor can be at least as stressful as its actual occurrence, and often more so (e.g., Wirtz et al., 2006). Consider the strain of anticipating a confrontation with a boyfriend or girlfriend or worrying about a test that will occur the next day. Sleepless nights and days of distracting anxiety testify to the human being's capacity for anticipatory distress.

One study that illustrates the importance of anticipatory stress made use of ambulatory blood pressure monitors to assess natural fluctuations in blood pressure during daily activities. In this study, medical students wore the pressure monitors on an unstressful lecture day, the day before an important examination, and during the examination itself. Although the lecture day was characterized by stable patterns of cardiovascular activity, cardiovascular activity on the pre-examination day when the students were worrying about the exam was as high as that seen during the examination (Sausen, Lovallo, Pincomb, & Wilson, 1992). Thus, in this instance, the anticipation of the stressful event taxed the cardiovascular system as much as the stressful event itself. In addition to examinations, students have to deal with a number of stressors as they adapt to university life (see the Spotlight on Canadian Research box, "The Stress of University Life," on page 168).

After-effects of Stress   Adverse **after-effects of stress,** such as decreases in performance and attention span, are also well documented. In fact, one of the reasons that stress presents both a health hazard and a challenge to the health psychology researcher is that the effects of

Post-Traumatic Stress Disorder

Following the Vietnam War, a number of unnerving events were reported in the media regarding American veterans who, as civilians, apparently relived some of the experiences they had undergone during battle. In one especially distressing case, a man took charge of a shopping mall, believing that it was under attack by the North Vietnamese, and shot and wounded several police officers before he was shot in an effort to subdue him.

When a person has been the victim of a highly stressful event, symptoms of the stress experience may persist long after the event is over. The after-effects of stress can include physiological arousal, distractability, and other negative side effects that last for hours after a stressful event has occurred. In the case of major traumas, these stressful after-effects may go on intermittently for months or even years. For example, among World War II prisoners of war and combat veterans from Canada who lived through the Dieppe raid, many were found to still be experiencing symptoms of extreme stress over 50 years later (Beal, 1995).

The term **post-traumatic stress disorder (PTSD)** has been developed to explain these effects. The person suffering from PTSD has typically undergone a stressor of extreme magnitude (Lamprecht & Sack, 2002). One of the reactions to this stressful event is a psychic numbing, such as reduced interest in activities that were once enjoyable, detachment from friends, or constriction in emotions. In addition, the person often relives aspects of the trauma, as some Vietnam veterans did. Other symptoms include excessive vigilance, sleep disturbances, feelings of guilt, impaired memory or concentration, avoidance of the experience, and an exaggerated startle response to loud noise (D. Mohr, Bendantham, et al., 2003). PTSD is often accompanied by other physical symptoms, including chest pain, gastrointestinal problems, and immune system impairments (Canadian Mental Health Association, 2007).

Such long-term stress reactions have been especially documented in the wake of violent wars, such as occurred in Vietnam and the Gulf War (Ford et al., 2001; D. W. King, King, Gudanowski, & Vreven, 1995). But they may also occur in response to assault, rape, domestic abuse, a violent encounter with nature (such as an earthquake or flood; Ironson et al., 1997), a disaster (such as 9/11; Fagan et al., 2003), and being a hostage (Vila, Porche, & Mouren-Simeoni, 1999). There is also some evidence that simply being exposed to certain events or crises and not necessarily being a victim of them is associated with the development of PTSD. For example, being in the forefront of a public health crisis, such as the SARS outbreak, has been linked to PTSD. Among Torontonians who were quarantined during the SARS crisis but did not have SARS, almost 30 percent reported symptoms of PTSD. Rates were higher among those who had been quarantined for longer periods of time, and for those who knew or had direct exposure with someone infected with SARS (Hawryluck et al., 2004). Simply witnessing domestic abuse between one's parents, or interparental violence, may also result in PTSD in some children. Researchers from Simon Fraser University and the University of British Columbia found that about one-third of adolescent boys and girls who had been exposed to interparental violence met PTSD criteria, and those with PTSD were also more likely to engage in aggressive behaviours towards friends and peers (Moretti, Obsuth, Odgers, & Reebye, 2006).

Occupations such as employment as an urban police officer (Fagan et al., 2003; D. Mohr et al., 2003) or having responsibility for clearing up remains following war, disaster, or mass death (McCarroll, Ursano, Fullerton, Liu, & Lundy, 2002) increase the risk of traumatic stress exposure and resulting PTSD. For example, researchers from Dalhousie University examined the

stress often persist long after the stressful event itself is no longer present. After-effects of stress have been observed in response to a wide range of stressors, including noise, high task load, electric shock, bureaucratic stress, crowding, and laboratory-induced stress (S. Cohen, 1980). The Health Psychology in Action box, "Post-

Traumatic Stress Disorder," profiles that particular kind of after-effect of stress.

In a series of studies, D. C. Glass and Singer (1972) put university students to work on a simple task and exposed them to an uncontrollable, unpredictable stressor in the form of random, intermittent bursts of

Post-Traumatic Stress Disorder (continued)

effects of the 1998 Swissair Flight 111 crash in Nova Scotia on the volunteer disaster workers. The rate of PTSD among the disaster volunteers was estimated at 46 percent, and largely resulted from their exposure to a variety of disaster-related stressors including airplane debris and personal effects, human remains, and emergency personnel and equipment (Mitchell, Griffin, Stewart, & Loba, 2004).

PTSD has been tied to temporary and permanent changes in stress regulatory systems as well. Research suggests that people suffering from PTSD may experience permanent changes in the brain involving the amygdala and the hypothalamic-pituitary-adrenal (HPA) axis (Nemeroff et al., 2006). Those suffering from PTSD show substantial variability in cortisol patterns (Mason et al., 2002) as well as higher levels of norepinephrine, epinephrine, testosterone, and thyroxin functioning. In one study of victims of the ice storm of 1998 from the Ottawa area, cortisol levels one month following the storm were more variable among those who showed symptoms of PTSD compared to others

without PTSD symptoms (Anisman, Griffiths, Matheson, Ravindran, & Merali, 2001).

These hormonal alterations can last a long time (Lindauer et al., 2006; O'Donnell, Creamer, Elliott, & Bryant, 2007). Studies have also reported alterations in natural killer cell cytotoxicity following a natural disaster (Hurricane Andrew; Ironson et al., 1997) and chronically elevated T cell counts among those with combat-related PTSD (Boscarino & Chang, 1999). PTSD is also prognostic of poor health (Lauterbach, Vora, & Rakow, 2005), and may interact with pre-existing health risks to increase health-related problems. For example, among peacekeeping veterans from the Canadian forces with existing health problems, PTSD was associated with greater use of medical services in the previous year (Elhai, Richardson, & Pedlar, 2007).

Who is most likely to develop PTSD? In several studies of wartime experiences, researchers have found that men who had more combat experience, who were exposed to potentially traumatizing events, such as being deployed to a 'forward' area in close contact with the enemy, were most likely to experience PTSD (Iversen et al., 2008). People who develop the symptoms of PTSD may also have had a pre-existing vulnerability to emotional distress as well, inasmuch as many PTSD sufferers have had a prior emotional disorder (Keane & Wolfe, 1990). Avoidant coping, low levels of social support, a history of chronic stress, and general negativity may also predict who will develop PTSD in the wake of a traumatic stressor (L. D. Butler, Koopman, Classen, & Spiegel, 1999; Widows et al., 2000).

Can PTSD be alleviated? Cognitive behavioural therapies are often used to treat PTSD (Nemeroff et al., 2006). Combining pharmacologic, psychological, and psychosocial treatments into a multimodal intervention program is thought to be the best way of treating PTSD (Shalev, Bonne, & Eth, 1996).

noise over a 25-minute period. After the noise period was over, these participants were given additional tasks to perform, including solvable and unsolvable puzzles and a proofreading task. The participants who had been exposed to the noise consistently performed more poorly on these tasks.

The fact that stressful events produce after-effects should not be surprising. Exposure to a stressor over a longer period of time may have cumulative adverse effects so that reserves are drained and resistance breaks down when a person has to cope with a new stressful event.

The Stress of University Life

University life presents a host of challenges for most students, which may lead to feelings of being overwhelmed. Keeping on top of deadlines and frequent examinations, and balancing academic life, social life, and financial or work demands can all take a toll on well-being. This stress from university life can have a variety of academic and health consequences that may further add to existing stress. For some first-year students simply trying to adjust to university life after high school, or being away from friends and family for the first time in a strange city, may also contribute to feelings of stress. For example, a longitudinal study of first-year undergraduates at the University of Calgary found that self-reported stress increased significantly across the academic year (Arthur, 1998).

The stress of adjusting to the first year of university can have important implications for overall and academic well-being. First-year students at York University were followed from the fall to winter term over a 10-week period to examine the effects of stress and social support on adjustment to their first year (Friedlander, Reid, Shupak, & Cribbie, 2007). Better adjustment was predicted by increased social support from friends but not family, and students with lower stress initially reported improved academic, personal, and social adjustment 10 weeks later. Clearly, the experience of stress has important consequences for student life.

For some students the demands of academic life may be further exacerbated by social and individual factors outside of their control. For example, a survey of undergraduates at the University of Regina found that students who reported greater financial stress and stress from trying to balance work, school, and social life had poorer academic performance (Chow, 2007). Academic stress was also linked to poor psychological well-being. Students who have fewer financial resources and therefore greater demands on their time to work to keep up financially may therefore be particularly vulnerable to the stress from university life.

Perceptions of stress and what can be done to reduce that stress may also differ among students depending on their age and gender. One study of 457 undergraduate students at the University of Alberta found that the majority reported that their lives were stressful, and women in particular were more likely than men to report high stress (R. L. Campbell, Svenson, & Jarvis, 1992). In addition, mature women reported experiencing higher stress than younger women, perhaps because of having to balance academic life with family life and responsibilities. The reverse was true for older men compared to younger men, with mature men reporting less stress. Not surprisingly, most of the students were in their first year of university. When asked about what they believed could be done to reduce stress, women were more likely than men to report that they needed to learn to limit their commitments, learn to relax and worry less, and exercise more. Men were however more likely to believe that their current levels of stress were acceptable and that nothing needed to change. Perceived barriers to reducing stress also differed according to gender. Women were more likely to report that lack of time and lack of self-discipline prevented them from taking steps to reduce their stress. These results make it clear that the stress of university life can affect students differently, and that being aware of strategies that may help reduce stress does not ensure that they will be used.

HOW HAS STRESS BEEN STUDIED?

We now turn to the methods that health psychologists have used for measuring stress and assessing its effects on psychological and physical health.

Studying Stress in the Laboratory

Imagine that you have arrived at a lab to participate in an experiment and you are told that the research assistant is missing and that the experimenter needs you to give an impromptu speech to the other participants. Or you are asked to count as quickly as you can, backwards by 7's. These types of short-term stressful events are often used in an experimental setting to study the impact of that stress on physiological, neuroendocrine, and psychological responses. This **acute stress paradigm** consistently finds that when people are induced to perform stressful tasks they show both short-term psychological distress and strong indications of sympathetic activity and neuroendocrine responses (Kirschbaum, Klauer, Filipp, & Hellhammer, 1995; Ritz & Steptoe, 2000).

Use of the acute stress paradigm has proven invaluable for understanding what kinds of events produce stress and how reactions to stress are influenced by factors such as personality, social support, and the presence of chronic stress in a person's life. For example, responses to acute stress among those who are also chronically stressed tend to be more exaggerated than among those not going through chronic stress as well (J. Pike et al., 1997). Acute stress studies have also elucidated physiological profiles that may be indicative of the development of heart disease (Gregg, Matyas, & James, 2005).

The acute stress paradigm has also been proven useful for elucidating the kinds of individual differences that contribute to stress. For example, people who are high in hostility show heightened blood pressure and cardiovascular responsivity to laboratory stress, compared with people who are not as hostile (M. Davis, Matthews, & McGrath, 2000). As we will see in Chapter 14, hostile individuals' tendency to respond to interpersonal stressors in a hostile manner and with strong sympathetic responses may contribute to the higher incidence of coronary heart disease in hostile individuals.

The acute stress paradigm has also provided insight into the factors that may ameliorate the experience of stress. For example, when people go through these acute laboratory stressors in the presence of a supportive other person, even a stranger, their stress responses may be reduced (for example, Ditzen et al., 2007; C. M. Stoney & Finney, 2000). We will explore this phenomenon of social support more fully in Chapter 7.

Overall, the acute stress paradigm has proven to be very useful in identifying how biological, psychological, and social factors change and influence each other in situations of short-term stress.

Inducing Disease

An intriguing way of studying the effects of stress on disease processes has involved intentionally exposing people to viruses and then assessing whether they get ill and how ill they get. For example, S. Cohen, Doyle, and Skoner (1999) measured levels of psychological stress in a group of adults, infected them with an influenza virus by swabbing their nose with a swab soaked in a viral culture, and measured their respiratory symptoms, the amount of mucus they produced, and interleukin-6 (IL-6), a pro-inflammatory cytokine that may link stress through the immune system to illness. They found, as predicted, that psychological stress led to a greater evidence of illness and an increased production of IL-6 in

response to the viral challenge than was true of people exposed to the virus whose lives were less stressful.

Stressful Life Events

Another line of stress research has focused more heavily on the psychological experience of stress. One such line of work measures **stressful life events.** These range from cataclysmic events, such as the death of one's spouse or being fired from a job, to more mundane but still problematic events, such as moving to a new home.

Two pioneers in stress research, T. H. Holmes and Rahe (1967) argued that, when an organism must make a substantial adjustment to the environment, the likelihood of stress is high. They developed an inventory of stressful life events in an attempt to measure stress, the Social Readjustment Rating Scale (SRRS; see Table 6.1). Specifically, they identified which events force people to make the most changes in their lives and then assigned point values to those events to reflect the amount of change that must be made. Thus, for example, if one's spouse dies, virtually every aspect of life is disrupted. On the other hand, getting a traffic ticket may be upsetting and annoying but is unlikely to produce much change in one's life. To obtain a stress score, one totals up the point values associated with the events a person has experienced over the past year. Although all people experience at least some stressful events, some will experience a lot, and it is this group, according to Holmes and Rahe, that is most vulnerable to illness.

Recognizing that the impact of certain life events may change as social and societal values change, the original SRRS was rescaled first in 1975, and then again in 1995. The revised Recent Life Changes Questionnaire (RLCQ)

Work strains, like the argument between these co-workers, are common sources of stress that compromise well-being and physical health.

TABLE 6.1 | Changes in Life Events Scaling across 30 Years

Life Event	1965 Rank	1965 LCU	1995 Rank	1995 LCU
Death of spouse	1.	100	1.	119
Divorce	2.	73	2.	98
Marital separation from mate	3.	65	4.	79
Detention in jail or other institution	4.	63	7.	75
Death of a close family member	5.	63	3.	92
Major personal injury or illness	6.	53	6.	77
Marriage	7.	50	19.	50
Being fired at work	8.	47	5.	79
Marital reconciliation with mate	9.	45	13.	57
Retirement from work	10.	45	16.	54
Major change in the health or behaviour of a family member	11.	44	14.	56
Pregnancy	12.	40	9.	66
Sexual difficulties	13.	39	21.	45
Gaining a new family member (e.g., through birth, adoption, oldster moving in, etc.)	14.	39	12.	57
Major business readjustment (e.g., merger, reorganization, bankruptcy, etc.)	15.	39	10.	62
Major change in financial state (e.g., a lot worse off or a lot better off than usual)	16.	38	15.	56
Death of a close friend	17.	37	8.	70
Changing to a different line of work	18.	36	17.	51
Major change in the number of arguments with spouse (e.g., either a lot more or a lot less than usual regarding child rearing, personal habits, etc.)	19.	35	18.	51
Taking out a mortgage or loan for a major purchase (e.g., for a home, business, etc.)	20.	31	23.	44
Foreclosure on a mortgage or loan	21.	30	11.	61
Major change in responsibilities at work (e.g., promotion, demotion, lateral transfer)	22.	29	24.	43
Son or daughter leaving home (e.g., marriage, attending university, etc.)	23.	29	22.	44
Trouble with in-laws	24.	29	28.	38
Outstanding personal achievement	25.	28	29.	37
Spouse beginning or ceasing work outside the home	26.	26	20.	46
Beginning or ceasing formal schooling	27.	26	27.	38
Major change in living conditions (e.g., building a new home, remodelling, deterioration of home or neighbourhood)	28.	25	25.	42
Revision of personal habits (dress, manners, associations, etc.)	29.	24	36.	27
Trouble with the boss	30.	23	33.	29
Major change in working hours or conditions	31.	20	30.	36
Change in residence	32.	20	26.	41
Changing to a new school	33.	20	31.	35
Major change in usual type and/or amount of recreation	34.	19	34.	29
Major change in church activities (e.g., a lot more or a lot less than usual)	35.	19	42.	22
Major change in social activities (e.g., clubs, dancing, movies, visiting, etc.)	36.	18	38.	27
Taking out a mortgage or loan for a lesser purchase (e.g., for a car, television, freezer, etc.)	37.	17	35.	28
Major change in sleeping habits (a lot more or a lot less sleep, or change in part of day when asleep)	38.	16	40.	26
Major change in number of family get-togethers (e.g., a lot more or a lot less than usual)	39.	15	39.	26
Major change in eating habits (a lot more or a lot less food intake, or very different meal hours or surroundings)	40.	15	37.	27
Vacation	41.	13	41.	25
Christmas	42.	12	32.	30
Minor violations of the law (e.g., traffic tickets, jaywalking, disturbing the peace, etc.)	43.	11	43.	22

LCU = Life change units

Source: "The Social Readjustment Rating Scale," reprinted from *Journal of Psychosomatic Research,* 11, pp. 213–218. Copyright © 1967, with permission from Elsevier.

was administered to a group of people with characteristics that were closely matched to the original sample used to develop the rankings for the original SRRS, and *life change units* (LCU) were calculated to estimate the amount of impact of each stressful event. A comparison of the rankings and impact of the events from the original SRRS and the revised RLCQ are presented in Table 6.1. Surprisingly, the stressfulness of many of the life events did not change that dramatically over the 30 years.

Several studies demonstrate the links between stressful live events and both acute and chronic illness. In one study, people who had a greater stress reactivity to a laboratory-based stress induction were more likely to develop a cold in the 12 weeks that followed if they had experienced one or more stressful life events (S. Cohen et al., 2002). A recent review of over 150 studies examining the effects of psychosocial factors including stressful life events found that experiencing stressful life events was linked to cancer prognosis (Chida & Steptoe, 2008).

Problems Measuring Stressful Life Events   What are some of the problems of using a stressful life event inventory? First, some of the items on the list are vague; for example, "personal injury or illness" could mean anything from the flu to a heart attack. Second, because events have preassigned point values, individual differences in the way events are experienced are not taken into account (Schroeder & Costa, 1984). For example, a divorce may mean welcome freedom to one partner but a collapse in living standard or self-esteem to the other.

Third, inventories usually include both positive and negative events. They include events that individuals choose, such as getting married, as well as events that simply happen, such as the death of a close friend. As we have seen, sudden, negative, unexpected, and uncontrollable events predict illness. Fourth, researchers typically do not assess whether those events have been successfully resolved or not (Thoits, 1994), and stressful events that have been successfully resolved do not produce adverse effects for an individual. Consequently, this evidence, too, weakens the ability of life event inventories to predict adverse health consequences (R. J. Turner & Avison, 1992).

Another problem is that assessing specific stressful events may also tap ongoing life strain, that is, chronic stress that is part of everyday life. Chronic strain may also produce psychological distress and physical illness, but it needs to be measured separately from specific life events. Additional concerns are that some people may just be prone to report more stress in their lives or to experience it more intensely (S. Epstein & Katz, 1992). Life event

measures may be unreliable because people forget what stressful events they have experienced, especially if the events occurred more than a few weeks earlier (Kessler & Wethington, 1991). Many people have theories about what kinds of events cause illness, so they may distort their reports of stress and reports of illness to correspond with each other.

A final difficulty in trying to estimate the stress-illness relationship concerns the time period between the two. Usually, stress over a one-year period is related to the most recent six months of illness bouts, yet is it reasonable to assume that January's crisis caused June's cold or that last month's financial problems produced a malignancy detected this month? After all, malignancies can grow undetected for 10 or 20 years. Obviously, these cases are extreme, but they illustrate some of the problems in studying the stress-illness relationship over time. For all these reasons, stressful life event inventories are no longer used as much. Some researchers, as a result, have turned to perceived stress to assess the degree of stress people experience (see the Measuring Health Psychology Concepts box, "A Measure of Perceived Stress").

Critical Checkpoint

Life Events Update

The revised Recent Life Changes Questionnaire provides an updated list of life events considered to be stressful in 1995. Explain how and why would you update this list of events so that is relevant for the current year?

Daily Stress

In addition to studies on major stressful life events and past stressors, researchers have also studied minor stressful events, or **daily hassles,** and their cumulative impact on health and illness. Such hassles include being stuck in a traffic jam, waiting in line, doing household chores, and having difficulty making a small decision. Daily minor problems reduce psychological well-being over the short term and produce physical symptoms (Bolger, DeLongis, Kessler, & Schilling, 1989; Brantley et al., 2005).

Lazarus and his associates (Kanner, Coyne, Schaeffer, & Lazarus, 1981) developed a measure of minor stressful life events termed the hassles scale. Research has also tied daily hassles to declines in physical health (DeLongis, Coyne, Dakof, Folkman, & Lazarus, 1982)

A Measure of Perceived Stress

Because people vary so much in what they consider to be stressful, many researchers feel that **perceived stress** is a better measure of stress than are instruments that measure whether people have been exposed to particular events. To address this issue, S. Cohen, Karmarck, and Mermelstein (1983) developed a measure of perceived stress, some items of which follow. Higher scores on the perceived stress scale indicate greater perceptions of stress. Note the differences between this measure of stress and the items on the social readjustment rating scale in Table 6.1. Research suggests that perceived stress predicts a broad array of health outcomes (Kojima et al., 2005; Young, He, Genkinger, Sapun, Mabry, & Jehn, 2004).

ITEMS AND INSTRUCTIONS FOR THE PERCEIVED STRESS SCALE

The questions in this scale ask you about your feelings and thoughts during the last month. In each case, you will be asked to indicate how often you felt or thought a certain way. Although some of the questions are similar, there are differences between them, and you should treat each one as a separate question. The best approach is to answer each question fairly quickly. That is, don't try to count up the number of times you felt a particular way, but, rather, indicate the alternative that seems like a reasonable estimate.

For each question, choose from the following alternatives:

0 never
1 almost never
2 sometimes
3 fairly often
4 very often

1. In the last month, how often have you been upset because of something that happened unexpectedly?

2. In the last month, how often have you felt nervous and stressed?

3. In the last month, how often have you found that you could not cope with all the things that you had to do?

4. In the last month, how often have you been angered because of things that happened that were outside your control?

5. In the last month, how often have you found yourself thinking about things that you had to accomplish?

6. In the last month, how often have you felt difficulties were piling up so high that you could not overcome them?

and to a worsening of symptoms in those already suffering from illnesses (e.g., Peralta-Ramírez, Jiménez-Alonso, Godoy-García, & Pérez-García, 2004). Recent research also indicates that daily hassles are associated with unhealthy eating and that this may be an additional route through which hassles influence health (O'Connor, Jones, Conner, McMillan, & Ferguson, 2008). An example of how daily hassles can be measured is shown in the Measuring Health Psychology Concepts box, "The Measurement of Daily Strain."

Minor hassles can conceivably produce stress and aggravate physical and psychological health in several ways. First, the cumulative impact of small stressors may wear down an individual, predisposing him or her to become ill. Second, such events may influence the relationship between major life events and illnesses. For example, psychological distress may be exacerbated by daily hassles if they occur in conjunction with chronic stress (Serido, Almeida, & Wethington, 2004). However, it is also possible that chronic stress may mute the impact of daily hassles, which may be barely noticeable against the backdrop of ongoing stress (McGonagle & Kessler, 1990).

Unfortunately, the measurement of daily hassles is subject to some of the same problems as the measurement of major stressful life events. The tendency to report hassles may be linked to pre-existing anxiety levels that may also magnify the psychological distress reported as an outcome.

WHAT ARE THE SOURCES OF CHRONIC STRESS?

(L05)

Earlier we posed the question: Can people adapt to chronically stressful events? The answer was that people can adapt to a degree but continue to show signs of stress in response to severe chronic strains in their lives. Ongoing stress can exacerbate the impact of life events by straining the person's coping capacities when he or she is confronted with yet another problem to manage (Kristenson, Eriksen, Sluiter, Starke, & Ursin, 2004).

The Measurement of Daily Strain

Psychologists have examined the role of minor stresses and strains in the development of illness. The following are some examples of how psychologists measure these stresses and strains.

INSTRUCTIONS

Each day we can experience minor annoyances as well as major problems or difficulties. Listed are a number of irritations that can produce daily strain. Indicate how much of a strain each of these annoyances has been for you in the past month.

Severity

0	Did not occur
1	Mild strain
2	Somewhat of a strain
3	Moderate strain
4	Extreme strain

Hassles

1.	A quarrel or problems with a neighbour	0	1	2	3	4
2.	Traffic congestion	0	1	2	3	4
3.	Thoughts of poor health	0	1	2	3	4
4.	Argument with romantic partner	0	1	2	3	4
5.	Concerns about money	0	1	2	3	4
6.	Getting a parking ticket	0	1	2	3	4
7.	Preparing meals	0	1	2	3	4

Increasingly, stress researchers are coming to the conclusion that the chronic stressors of life may be more important than major life events in the development of illness. There are several kinds of chronic strain, and how they differ in terms of their psychological and physical effects is not yet known.

Post-traumatic Stress Disorder

One type of chronic strain results from severely traumatic or stressful events whose residual effects may remain with the individual for years. Post-traumatic stress disorder, described in the Health Psychology in Action box on pages 166–167, is an example of this kind of chronic stress, as is the response to the Westray mine disaster detailed in the Spotlight on Canadian Research box, "Stress and Human-made Disasters: The Case of the Westray Mine Disaster."

Childhood sexual abuse, rape, and exposure to natural and human-made disasters, such as the Westray Mine disaster, may produce chronic mental health and physical health effects that maintain the virulence of the initial experience (for example, A. Baum, Cohen, & Hall, 1993; Downey, Silver, & Wortman, 1990). In the case of the World Trade Center attacks on September 11, 2001, the stress of this event has been tied to inflammatory processes potentially enhancing risk for illness (S. Melamed, Shirom, Toker, Berliner, & Shapira, 2004).

Long-term Effects of Early Stressful Life Experiences

Recent research has focused on the long-term effects of early stressors, including those experienced in early childhood, on disease later in life (Repetti, Taylor, & Seeman, 2002). Some of this work has been prompted by the allostatic load view of stress, which argues that major, chronic, or recurrent stress dysregulates stress systems, which, over time, can produce accumulating risk for disease.

Chronic physical or sexual abuse in childhood or adulthood has long been known to increase a broad array of health risks because it results in intense, chronic stress that taxes physiological systems (Leserman, 2005; Sachs-Ericsson, Blazer, Plant, & Arnow, 2005). It is now clear that even more modest family stress can increase risk for disease as well. Repetti, Taylor, & Seeman (2002) reported that "risky families"—that is, families that are high in conflict or abuse and low in warmth and nurturance—produce offspring with problems in stress-regulatory systems. By virtue of having to cope with a chronically stressful family environment, children from such families may develop heightened sympathetic reactivity to stressors and exaggerated cortisol responses. Moreover, by virtue of exposure to chronic stress early in life, the developing stress systems themselves may become dysregulated, such that physiological and neuroendocrine stress responses across the life span are

Stress and Human-made Disasters: The Case of the Westray Mine Disaster

Increasingly, stress researchers are examining how people cope with human-made disasters, such as the threats posed by nuclear contamination or toxic wastes, or even unsafe mines. Although in many ways reactions to human-made disasters are similar to reactions to natural disasters, such as fire, tornado, or flood, there are important differences. Natural catastrophes are usually time limited, and they dissipate over time. Also, governments have programs ready to move in almost immediately to ameliorate the effects of natural disasters. And finally, they are random acts of nature for which no one can be blamed. In contrast, the threat posed by human made disasters can linger depending on the nature of the disaster and how it is handled by those perceived to be responsible, and can be more difficult to deal with if the disaster was something that was perceived as avoidable. Such was the case with the Westray Mine disaster.

On September 11, 1991, the Westray Mine opened in Plymouth, Pictou County, Nova Scotia. Miners initially complained about poor working conditions, and a local union official upon inspecting the mines stated in a safety report that he suspected someone might be killed in the mines in the near future because of these conditions.

Nine months later at 5:18 on the morning of May 9, 1992, a methane gas explosion blew up the mine killing all 26 men working underground. So strong was the explosion that the top of the mine entrance more than a mile above was blown off, as well as the steel roof supports throughout the mine. The explosion shattered windows and shook houses in nearby towns. Despite rescue efforts the bodies of 11 miners were never recovered.

However, the tragedy and shock of this senseless disaster was further aggravated by the response of the mining company and the Government of Nova Scotia, which claimed that the explosion was an accident. This naturally outraged the families who had heard their loved ones complain about the bad working conditions and even filed complaints with the Nova Scotia Department of Labour. They argued that it was clear case of criminal negligence and demanded justice. A highly publicized inquiry followed and Justice K. Peter Richard concluded:

> *"The Westray Story is a complex mosaic of actions, omissions, mistakes, incompetence, apathy, cynicism, stupidity, and neglect. Some well-intentioned but misguided blunders were also added to the mix. It was clear from the outset that the loss of 26 lives at Plymouth, Pictou County, in the early morning hours of 9 May 1992 was not the result of a single definable event or misstep. Only the serenely uninformed (the wilfully blind) or the cynically self-serving could be satisfied with such an explanation."*

Despite this finding no one was ever held accountable for the 26 deaths.

Researchers Christopher Davis (now at Carleton University) and Norine Verberg of St. Francis Xavier University have studied the psychological impact of the Westray Mine disaster on the families of the deceased miners. Specifically they have tried to understand how the

affected by these early experiences. Because these stress systems and their dysfunctions are implicated in a broad array of diseases, it should not be surprising that an early major stressful event would produce damage later in life. The evidence for this position is quite substantial (for example, Luecken, Rodriguez, & Appelhans, 2005; Repetti et al., 2002; Wickrama, Conger, Wallace, & Elder, 2003).

For example, in a retrospective study, Felitti and colleagues (1998) asked adults to complete a questionnaire regarding their early family environment that inquired, among other things, how warm and supportive the environment was versus how cold, critical, hostile, or conflict-ridden it was. The more of these problems these adults reported from their childhood, the more vulnerable they were in adulthood to an array of disorders, including depression, lung disease, cancer, heart disease, and diabetes. At least some of the risk may have occurred not only because of stress-related biological dysregulations but also because of poor health habits, such as smoking, poor diet, and lack of exercise that these early stressful environments prompted.

Of course, there are potential problems with retrospective accounts. People who are depressed or ill, for example, may be especially likely to regard their childhoods as traumatic or stressful. However, substantial evidence from prospective longitudinal investigations supports many of these conclusions (see Repetti et al., 2002, for a review), and consequently distortions in reconstructions of one's childhood family environment may not account for the results.

Stress and Human-made Disasters: The Case of the Westray Mine Disaster (continued)

Westray families coped with this tragic event, especially in light of evidence that it could have been prevented. They interviewed 52 relatives from 16 of the families involved eight years after Westray and assessed their psychological adjustment as well as asked about any upsetting thoughts, dreams, or memories they had experienced. They found that 80 percent reported having thoughts or dreams about their lost loved one, and that half of these individuals described these thoughts and dreams as upsetting. Overall, the researchers found that about a third of those interviewed had not gotten over Westray.

Most of the family members (85 percent) felt that someone was to blame and many described their predominant feeling from the whole experience as "anger," "frustration," or "bitterness."

> "I guess I never thought that anything like this could ever happen. I never thought that we would be made a mockery of in public, and I never thought anybody could kill somebody and get away with it, so publicly."

Some family members were able to find meaning in the experience:

> "I met a lot of wonderful people and really saw how a community can be really really good. I admire a lot of the community, I lost a lot of admiration for the so-called upper and gained a lot for the lower."

However, others were unable to make sense of their loss:

> "Well there is no purpose, it was a waste, just a waste of people's lives is all it was"

In a subsequent analysis of the interview data, Davis and colleagues found that the families' responses could be viewed as reflecting one of three distinct ways of coping with the ordeal. Nearly half were able to find meaning in their loss and experienced some personal growth, whereas others could not find any meaning or purpose from the tragedy and subsequently felt that nothing positive had come from the Westray disaster.

Unlike recovery from other natural and human-made disasters, the Westray Mine disaster presents an unnerving spectre for stress researchers. In addition to the immediate aftermath and shock of losing loved ones, the explosion at Westray reverberated throughout the community, and indeed throughout the province, as people had to come to terms with the prospect that it could have been prevented but wasn't, and that the justice system had failed them. Thus, the initial stress from this unfortunate event became a source of continuing stress for those who felt that justice was and never would be served. Understanding how people deal with these challenges to their belief systems in addition to the loss of loved ones may be key for helping people adjust to such senseless human-made disasters.

Sources: Davis & Vergerg, 2003; Davis, Wohl, & Verberg, 2007; Richard, 1997a, 1997b.

In addition to stressful childhood experiences, stressful life events experienced prenatally may have serious long term repercussions for health. In a prospective study led by researchers from McGill University, women who were pregnant and living in Quebec during the ice storm of January 1998 were assessed in June 1998 for both objective (exposure to the ice storm) and subjective measures of stress (King & Laplante, 2005; Laplante, Brunet, Schmitz, Ciampi, & King, 2008). The researchers assessed the children's cognitive and language skills at two follow-ups when they were two and five and half years old. After controlling for maternal personality, they found that the greater the extent to which the mother was exposed to stress from the ice storm according to objective measures, the poorer the child's cognitive

and language development was at age two (King & Laplante, 2005). At five and half years old, these effects persisted. Children who were exposed in utero to a high level of stress from the ice storm scoring lower on IQ and language tests compared to children who were exposed in utero to moderate or low levels of stress (Laplante et al., 2008).

Chronic Stressful Conditions

Sometimes chronic stress is of the long-term, grinding kind, such as living in poverty, being in a bad relationship, being bullied at school or work, or remaining in a high-stress job. In a survey of Toronto residents, R. J. Turner and Lloyd (1999) found that

FIGURE 6.5 | Stress Can Compromise Both Mental and Physical Health
This figure shows some of the routes by which these effects may occur.
(*Source:* After S. Cohen, Kessler, & Gordon, 1995)

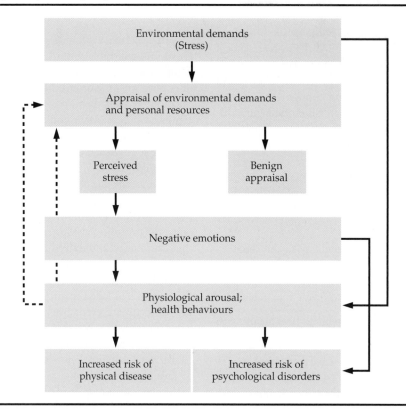

the depression that was associated with lower socio-economic status was completely explained by the increasing stress exposure of those individuals further down the SES ladder. Chronic stress is an important contributor to psychological distress and physical illness (Kahn & Pearlin, 2006; see Figure 6.5).

Chronic childhood stress from living in a "risky family" environment can have significant impact on later health and well-being. For example, a review of several studies found that children who grow up in a family environment that is cold, unsupportive, neglectful, with exposure to frequent episodes of anger and aggressive, are at increased risk for mental health issues, chronic disease and even early mortality (Repetti, Taylor, & Seeman, 2002).

Chronic strain may influence the relationship between specific stressors and adverse physical or psychological effects. Jennifer Pike and colleagues (J. Pike et al., 1997) found that people who were undergoing chronic life stress showed exaggerated sympathetic reactivity and corresponding decrements in natural killer

cell activity in response to an acute stress in the laboratory, as compared with people who had fewer background stressors (see also Lepore, Miles, & Levy, 1997).

Bullying and Stress

Another common form of chronic stress that is being increasingly recognized as having negative consequences for psychological and physical well-being is bullying. Whether it takes place in the schoolyard or the workplace, **bullying** involves acts intended to harm which are repeated over time and often occur in a relationship where there is an imbalance of power (Pepler & Craig, 2000). Bullying can take the form of physical, verbal or social acts which are directed at the victim either directly (face-to-face) or indirectly such as through social exclusion, gossip, and the Internet.

The stress from being bullied can have both immediate and long lasting effects on well-being. For example, both boys and girls who have been bullied are more likely to experience depression (David & Michael, 2000). Employees who experience bullying in the form of verbal abuse and belittlement, and having work undermined are more likely to experience burnout and physical health symptoms (Lee & Brotheridge, 2006). In one study, researchers tested a variety of physiological responses to an acute stressor among adults with and without a history of being bullied as adolescents (Hamilton, Newman, Delville, & Delville, 2008). They found that although there were no differences on the measures between women who had and had not been bullied, men with a history of frequent bullying had altered sympathetic responses to stress, as well as some evidence for long term effects of bullying on the HPA axis. The different ways in which boys and girls are bullied may explain this finding, as boys tend to experience physical and direct bullying , whereas girls tend experience verbal and social bullying in a an indirect manner (van der Wal, de Wit, & Hirasing, 2003).

Chronic Stress and Health

Research relating chronic stress to mental and physical health outcomes is difficult to conduct, because it is often hard to demonstrate that a particular chronic stressor is the factor contributing to illness. A second problem is that chronic stress is often assessed subjectively on the basis of self-reports. Unlike life events, which can often be assessed objectively, chronic stress may be more difficult to measure objectively because it can be more difficult to determine objectively whether particular chronic strains are actually going on. Third, as in the measurement of life events, inventories that attempt to assess chronic strain may also tap psychological distress and neuroticism rather than the objective existence of stressful conditions. Finally, assessment of stressful life events may also pick up the effects of chronic strain so that the impact of chronic strain on psychological and physical health is obscured. Nonetheless, a wealth of evidence supports the idea that chronic stress is related to illness.

Consistent with the biopsychosocial and public health approaches to health, research showing social class differences in death from all causes and in rates of specific diseases, such as most cancers and cardiovascular disease, is evidence suggestive of a relationship (Grzywacz, Almeida, Neupert, & Ettner, 2004). For example, poverty, exposure to crime, and other chronic stressors vary with social class (Lantz, House, Mero, & Williams, 2005). Even children of low SES experience greater risks than those from families with more resources (Chen, Matthews, & Boyce, 2002). In addition,

many psychological disorders, such as depression, may show the same gradient (Wilkins, 2005). For example, people who are low in SES typically have low-prestige occupations, which may expose them to greater interpersonal conflict and arousal at work; the consequences can include psychological distress and changes in cardiovascular indicators, among other stress-related outcomes (K. A. Matthews et al., 2000). Low SES is also linked to living in disadvantaged neighbourhoods which can be an ongoing source of stress that take a toll on psychological health (Santiago, Wadsworth, & Stump, 2011). Chronic stress has been related to a variety of adverse health-related outcomes, including alterations in catecholamines and cortisol patterns (S. Cohen, Doyle, & Baum, 2006; S. Cohen, Alper et al., 2006; Vlachopoulos et al., 2006) and the likelihood of developing coronary artery disease (see Chapter 13). In addition, some of the health risks linked to financial adversity may be reversible if circumstances improve (Steptoe, Brydon, & Kunz-Ebrecht, 2005).

Chronic stress can also interactive other environmental factors to affect health. In one study led by researchers at the University of British Columbia, children with asthma who experienced chronic life stress and were exposed to traffic-related air pollution experienced significant increases in both clinical and biological measures of asthma symptoms over time (Chen, Schreier, Strunk, & Brauer, 2008). What's more, the stress from the social environment interacted with the physical environment to exacerbate their asthma symptoms, such that interactive effects were stronger than the effects of either stressor alone.

As we will next see, the chronic stress of particular jobs, especially those jobs that are high in demands and low in control, has been reliably tied to stress and illness.

Stress in the Workplace

A large body of literature has examined the causes and consequences of work-related stress. Studies of occupational stress are important for several reasons:

1. They help identify some of the most common stressors of everyday life.

2. They provide additional evidence for the stress-illness relationship.

3. Work stress may be one of our preventable stressors and thereby provide possibilities for intervention (Sauter, Murphy, & Hurrell, 1990).

In addition, work-related stress is estimated to have an enormous cost to the Canadian economy through sick pay, absenteeism, lost productivity, and health care costs (Park, 2007). Although not all occupational stress can be avoided, knowledge of job factors that are stressful raises the possibility of redesigning jobs and implementing stress-management interventions. As is the case with stress research in general, contextual factors such as gender and socio-economic status may confer additional risk for work-related stress. For example, a large national survey found that low income and low education were associated with high levels of work stress, and that women in particular were more likely to report experiencing work stress even after controlling for sociodemographic and employment factors (Park, 2007). Interventions designed to help reduce work stress should therefore consider the other social factors that may be involved.

Physical Hazards   Many workers are exposed as a matter of course to physical, chemical, and biological hazards (G.W. Evans & Kantrowitz, 2001). In addition, work place injuries can result from being exposed to physical hazards or to an overwhelming workload (Breslin et al., 2007). Even noise can produce elevated catecholamines (Center for the Advancement of Health, September, 2003). Recently, workplace stress studies have also focused on such disorders as repetitive stress injuries, including carpal tunnel syndrome, which are a product of our sedentary, computerized way of life.

In addition, the changing patterns of work may erode certain health benefits of work that used to occur

Research shows that workers with high levels of job strain and low levels of control over their work are under great stress and may be at risk for coronary heart disease.

as a matter of course. For example, the most common work that people undertook before the Industrial Revolution involved agricultural production, in which people engaged in physical exercise as they were going about their work tasks. More people today are working in jobs that require more sitting and less physical activity. Because activity level is related to health, this change in the nature of work creates the possibility of vulnerability to illness.

Overload   Work overload is a chief factor producing high levels of occupational stress. Workers who feel required to work too long and too hard at too many tasks feel more stressed, practise poorer health habits, and sustain more health risks than do workers not suffering from overload (Repetti, 1993a). Research suggests that the chronic neuroendocrine activation and cardiovascular activation associated with over-commitment can contribute to cardiovascular disease (Steptoe, Siegrist, Kirschbaum, & Marmot, 2004).

An old rock song states, "Monday, Monday, can't trust that day." Increasingly, research suggests that this may be true. Monday appears to be one of the most stressful days of the week. Weekdays are generally associated with more worry and chronic work overload than weekends, resulting in altered cortisol patterns that may be risky for health (Schlotz, Hellhammer, Schulz, & Stone, 2004). However, people do not often take the weekends to recover from the demands of the week or may find that their stress from the week carries over making it difficult to relax. Such incomplete recovery from work may contribute to death from cardiovascular disease (Kivimäki et al., 2006).

So well established is the relation between work overload and poor health that in Japan, a country notorious for its long working hours, long work weeks, little sleep, and lack of vacations, there is a term, *karoshi,* that refers to death from overwork. One study found that men who worked more than 61 hours a week experienced twice the risk of a heart attack as those working 40 hours or less; sleeping 5 hours or less at least 2 days a week increased this risk by two to three times (Liu & Tanaka, 2002). Under Japanese law, families are entitled to compensation if they can prove that the breadwinner died of *karoshi* (*Los Angeles Times,* 1993).

Work overload is a subjective as well as an objective experience. The sheer amount of work that a person does—that is, how many hours he or she works each week—is not consistently related to poor health and compromised psychological well-being (A. R. Herzog, House, & Morgan, 1991). The *perception of* work overload shows a stronger relationship to physical health complaints and psychological distress. As we will see in Chapter 8 work overload combined with a stressful, demanding job can lead to emotional exhaustion and burnout.

Ambiguity and Role Conflict Role conflict and role ambiguity are also associated with stress. As noted earlier, role ambiguity occurs when a person has few clear ideas of what is to be done and no idea of the standards used for evaluating work. **Role conflict** occurs when a person receives conflicting information about work tasks or standards from different individuals. For example, if a university professor is told by one colleague to publish more articles, is advised by another colleague to publish fewer papers but of higher quality, and is told by a third to work on improving teaching ratings, the professor will experience role ambiguity and conflict.

Social Relationships The inability to develop satisfying social relationships at work has been tied to psychological distress at work (B. P. Buunk, Doosje, Jans, & Hopstaken, 1993), and to poor physical and mental health (Landsbergis, Schnall, Deitz, Friedman, & Pickering, 1992; Repetti, 1993a). Having supportive work relationships may therefore be protective against the development of depression among stressed workers. For example, one national survey of employed workers found that those who reported high stress and low support from co-workers were more likely to develop depression two years later (Shields, 2006b).

Having a poor relationship with one's supervisor appears to be especially related to job distress and may also increase a worker's risk for coronary heart disease (M. C. Davis, Matthews, Meilahn, & Kiss, 1995; Repetti, 1993a). Conversely, men and women who are satisfied with their relationships at work have enhanced well-being (Simon, Judge, & Halvorsen-Ganepola, 2010). Similarly, one study of Canadian nurses found that satisfying relationships with one's co-workers and managers was a key determinant of remaining employed despite the stressors associated with the profession (Tourangeau, Cummings, Cranley, Ferron, & Harvey, 2010).

Social relationships may not only be important in combatting stress in their own right; they may also buffer other job stressors. Social support may help to buffer

against having low control over work or anger towards co-workers (S. T. Fitzgerald, Haythornthwaite, Suchday, & Ewart, 2003; Park, 2007). In one study of accountants, higher trust in management buffered the negative effects of work overload on psychological strain, burnout, and degree of interference of work with family life (Harvey, Kelloway, & Duncan-Leiper, 2003).

Control Lack of control over work has been related to a number of stress and illness indicators, including heightened catecholamine secretion, job dissatisfaction, absenteeism, and the development of coronary artery disease in particular (Bosma et al., 1997), as well as the risk of death from all causes (Amick et al., 2002).

Karasek and his associates (1981) developed a model of job strain that is based on the relation between a worker and the job environment. They hypothesized that high psychological demands on the job with little decision latitude (such as low job control) causes job strain, which, in turn, can lead to the development of coronary artery disease. Research generally supports this idea (Cesana et al., 2003; Kivimäki et al., 2006). The chronic anger that can result from these jobs may further contribute to coronary artery disease risk (S. T. Fitzgerald et al., 2003). When high demands and low control are combined with little social support at work, what has been termed as the demand-control-support model, risk for coronary artery disease may be even greater (Muhonen & Torkelson, 2003).

The exact mechanisms whereby work stress contributes to coronary heart disease are unknown, but potentially a broad array of processes are implicated. High levels of work stress can lead to impaired fibrolytic capacity, which may be a result of the impact of chronic stress on insulin resistance (Steptoe, Kunz-Ebrecht, Owen, Feldman, Rumley, et al., 2003). Overinvolvement in work is associated with higher cortisol levels in the morning and across the workday, as well as high blood pressure (Steptoe et al., 2004). Longer-term stress lipid activity may well have significance for the development of coronary artery disease (Stoney, Niaura, Bausserman, & Matacin, 1999). Increases in blood pressure prognostic for cardiovascular disease have also been tied to work stress.

Job Insecurity Job insecurity, the uncertainty about one's employment future, whether one is employed or not, is also associated with higher levels of stress. In one study of employed and unemployed high-technology workers across Canada (Mantler, Matejicek, Matheson,

& Anisman, 2005), those who had been laid off work reported more stress than those who were currently employed. However, the relationship between employment status and stress was largely accounted for by appraisals of employment uncertainty. Individuals who appraised their employment future as less secure and more uncertain experienced levels of stress similar to those who were unemployed.

Employment security has been identified as one of the key determinants of health by the Public Health Agency of Canada. Consistent with this idea, uncertainty over one's continuing employment and unstable employment have also been tied to poor physical health (László et al., 2010). For example, a study found that men who had held a series of unrelated jobs were at greater risk of dying over a follow-up period than men who had remained in the same job or in the same type of job over a longer period of time (Pavalko, Elder, & Clipp, 1993). Generally speaking, being stably employed is protective of health (Rushing, Ritter, & Burton, 1992).

Unemployment   A final source of stress related to work concerns the impact of unemployment on psychological distress and health. Unemployment can produce a variety of adverse outcomes, including psychological distress (J. R. Reynolds, 1997), physical symptoms, physical illness (V. L. Hamilton, Broman, Hoffman, & Renner, 1990), alcohol abuse (Catalano, Dooley, Wilson, & Hough, 1993), difficulty achieving sexual arousal, low birth weight of offspring (Catalano, Hansen, & Hartig, 1999), and compromised immune functioning (F. Cohen et al., 2007; Segerstrom & Miller, 2004). However, a large study of workers in the United States found that although unemployment contributes to feelings of job insecurity, unemployment alone does not explain the link between job insecurity and health (Burgard, Brand, & House, 2009).

Other Occupational Outcomes   Stress also shows up in ways other than illness that may be extremely costly to an organization. Many of these factors may represent workers' efforts to control or to offset stress before it ever gets to the point of causing illness. For example, workers who cannot participate actively in decisions about their jobs show higher rates of absenteeism, job turnover, tardiness, job dissatisfaction, sabotage, and poor performance on the job. Indeed, high work stress among Canadian workers was strongly related to taking a disability day in the previous two weeks (Shields,

2006b). In essence, workers have taken stress into their own hands and have reduced it by not working as long, as hard, or as well as their employers apparently expect (Kivimäki, Vahtera, Ellovainio, Lillirank, & Kevin, 2002). A stressful work environment, that is one where demands are high and support and control are low, is also linked to higher rates of workplace bullying, which can be a source of chronic strain especially for employees who have little power (Tuckey, Dollard, Hosking, & Winefield, 2009).

Reducing Occupational Stress   What are some solutions to these workplace stresses? A blueprint for change has been offered by several organizational stress researchers (for example, Kahn, 1981; McGregor, 1967):

1. Physical work stressors, such as noise, harsh lighting, crowding, or temperature extremes, should be reduced as much as possible.

2. An effort to minimize unpredictability and ambiguity in expected tasks and standards of performance reduces stress. When workers know what they are expected to do and at what level, they are less distressed.

3. Involving workers as much as possible in the decisions that affect their work life reduces stress. Some corporations have given workers control over certain facets of their jobs, including working hours, the rate at which a task is performed, and the order in which tasks are performed, with corresponding increases in productivity and drops in absenteeism and tardiness.

4. Making jobs as interesting as possible may contribute to the reduction of stress. In some plants, workers who previously worked on an assembly line and were responsible for assembling a small part of a product were retrained to perform several tasks or even to assemble the entire product. These "job enlargement" or "job enrichment" programs have produced increases in productivity and product quality and increases in job satisfaction.

5. Providing workers with opportunities to develop or promote meaningful social relationships can reduce stress or buffer its impact (B. Buunk, 1989; Moos, 1988). Providing social and recreational facilities for break times, lunch time, and after-hours free time can improve social relations on the job. Extending facilities to workers' families for afterhours and weekend events have all been used

to try to bring families into corporations (C. J. Cooper & Marshall, 1976), inasmuch as family support can buffer the impact of work-related stress (Revicki & May, 1985).

6. Rewarding workers for good work, rather than focusing on punishment for poor work, improves morale and provides incentives for better future work (Kahn, 1981).

7. People who are in a supervisory position in work settings can look for signs of stress before stress has an opportunity to do significant damage. For example, supervisors can watch for negative affect, such as boredom, apathy, and hostility, among workers because these affective reactions often precede more severe reactions to stress, such as poor health or absenteeism.

A workplace intervention that addresses some of these issues was conducted by Rahe and colleagues (2002). They randomly assigned 500 participants to one of three groups: an intervention that included assessment for stress-related problems, personalized feedback, and six small group face-to-face counselling sessions; a self-help group that received personalized feedback and assessment by mail; and a wait-list control. Although all three groups experienced less stress and anxiety over the course of the study, the participants in the first intervention showed a more rapid reduction in their stress responses, fewer days of illness, and a large reduction in their health care utilization, suggesting that even a relatively short-term intervention that includes stress management and social support can reduce workplace stress.

Combining Work and Family Roles

So far, our discussion of chronic stress has considered only factors related to employment. But much of the stress that people experience results not from one role in their lives but from the combination of several roles. As adults, most of us will be workers, partners, and parents, and each of these roles entails heavy obligations. Accordingly, recent work has focused on the stress that can result when one is attempting to combine multiple roles simultaneously, and trying to maintain a **work–life balance.**

Women and Multiple Roles These problems have been particularly acute for women. A survey of Canadian families found that employed mothers with young children spend twice the amount of time on personal child care than men, and still take on the management role of domestic work (Hunsley, 2006). Concern has grown over the psychological and health implications of combining demanding family roles and work roles.

The task of balancing multiple roles is great when both work and family responsibilities are heavy. Because concessions to working parents are rarely made at work and because mothers tend bear the larger burden of domestic responsibilities, home and work responsibilities may conflict with each other, enhancing stress. Balancing the demands of multiple roles may be especially difficult for ethnic minority women who often have to deal with additional cultural, community, or religious responsibilities (Kamenou, 2008). One study suggests that as many as 50 percent of Canadian workers may experience stress due to work–life imbalance (Duxbury & Higgins, 2001). Studies of neuroendocrine responses to stress support this conclusion as well, with working women who have children at home showing higher amounts of cortisol, higher cardiovascular reactivity, and more home strain than those without children at home (Luecken et al., 1997). Single women raising children on their own are most at risk for health problems (M. E. Hughes & Waite, 2002). An imbalance between work and home responsibilities can also have other health consequences. Those who experience role overload are three times more likely to suffer from infections, injuries, heart problems, back pain and mental health problems, and five times as likely to suffer from certain cancers (Hunsley, 2006).

Many women hold multiple roles, such as worker, homemaker, and parent. Although these multiple roles can provide much satisfaction, they also make women vulnerable to role conflict and role overload.

Protective Effects of Multiple Roles Despite the potential for women to suffer role conflict and role overload by combining work and the homemaker role, some researchers suggest that there are positive effects of combining home and work responsibilities (Waldron, Weiss, & Hughes, 1998).

On the one hand, juggling heavy responsibilities at work with heavy responsibilities at home reduces the enjoyment of both sets of tasks and may leave women vulnerable to depression (Hunsley, 2006). Combining employment with the family role has also been tied to better health, including lower levels of coronary risk factors (Weidner, Boughal, Connor, Pieper, & Mendell, 1997). Nonetheless, a review of three decades of research found inconsistent support for either the role strain or the role enhancement hypotheses, and instead suggested that the beneficial psychological effects of maternal employment may be largely due to becoming over absorbed in one role (Elgar & Chester, 2007).

As we will see in Chapter 7, whether the effects of combining employment and child rearing are positive or negative can depend heavily on resources that are available. Having control and flexibility over one's work environment (Lennon & Rosenfield, 1992), having a good income (Rosenfield, 1992), and having a helpful and supportive partner (Klumb, Hoppmann, & Staats, 2006; Tobe et al., 2005; Tobe et al., 2007) can all reduce the likelihood that juggling multiple role demands will lead to stress and its psychological and physical costs.

Men and Multiple Roles That so much research on combining home and work responsibilities is conducted on women suggests that these issues are not important for men, but this suggestion is not true. To be sure, men and women are distressed by different kinds of events. Evidence suggests that men are more distressed by financial strain and work stress, whereas women are more distressed by adverse changes in the home (Barnett, Raudenbusch, Brennan, Pleck, & Marshall, 1995; Conger, Lorenz, Elder, Simons, & Ge, 1993). But increasingly, studies suggest that satisfaction in the parent role is also important to men (Barnett & Marshall, 1993).

Combining employment and marriage is protective for men with respect to health and mental health (Burton, 1998), just as it seems to be for women who

have enough help. But multiple roles can take their toll on men as well. Repetti (1989) studied workload and interpersonal strain and how they affected fathers' interactions with the family at the end of the day. She found that after a demanding day at work (high workload strain), fathers were more behaviourally and emotionally withdrawn in their interactions with their children. After stressful interpersonal events at work (high interpersonal strain), conflict with children increased. In addition, some of the factors that may ameliorate the stress of multiple roles for women may create more stress for men. One study found that as a woman's employment increased her share of the family's income and increased her husband's share in the domestic labours, her mental health and well-being increased, but her husband's mental health and well-being declined (Rosenfield, 1992).

For both men and women, the research on multiple roles and work–life balance is converging on the idea that stress is lower when one finds meaning in one's life. The protective effects of employment, marriage, and parenting on psychological distress and the beneficial effects of social support on health are all testimony to the salutary effects of social roles (Burton, 1998). When these potential sources of meaning and pleasure in life are challenged, as through a demanding and unrewarding work life or stressful close relationships, the effects on health can be devastating (Stansfield, Bosma, Hemingway, & Marmot, 1998).

Children Children and adolescents have their own sources of stress that can make home life stressful. One study found that social and academic failure experiences at school, such as being rejected by a peer or having difficulty with schoolwork, significantly increased a child's demanding and aversive behaviour at home—specifically, acting out and making demands for attention (Repetti & Pollina, 1994). As was discussed earlier, bullying can be a source of stress for children. Not surprisingly, children are affected by their parents' work and family stressors as well, and the strains their parents are under have consequences both for the children's academic achievement and the likelihood that they will act out their problems in adolescence (Menaghan, Kowaleski-Jones, & Mott, 1997). Such findings make it clear that, in fully understanding the impact of multiple roles, it is important to study not just working parents but also children. ●

SUMMARY

 Describe and define stress

- Events are perceived as stressful when people believe that their resources (such as time, money, and energy) may not be sufficient to meet the harm, threat, or challenge in the environment. Stress produces many changes, including adverse emotional reactions, cognitive responses, physiological changes, and performance decrements.

 Know what theories are used to study stress

- Early research on stress examined how the organism mobilizes its resources to fight or flee from threatening stimuli (the fight-or-flight response). Building on this model, Selye proposed the general adaptation syndrome, arguing that reactions to stress go through three phases: alarm, resistance, and exhaustion. More recent efforts have focused on the neuroendocrine bases of social responses to stress—that is, the ways in which people tend-and-befriend others in times of stress.

- The physiology of stress implicates the sympathetic adrenomedullary (SAM) system and the hypothalamic-pituitary-adrenocortical (HPA) axis. Over the long term, repeated activation of these systems can lead to cumulative damage, termed allostatic load, which represents the premature physiological aging that stress produces.

 Understand what makes events stressful

- Whether an event is stressful depends on how it is appraised. Events that are negative, uncontrollable or unpredictable, ambiguous, overwhelming, and threatening to central life tasks are likely to be perceived as stressful.

- Usually, people can adapt to mild stressors, but severe stressors may cause chronic problems for health and mental health. Stress can have disruptive after-effects, including persistent physiological arousal, psychological distress, reduced task performance, and over time, declines in cognitive capabilities. Vulnerable populations—such as children, the elderly, and the poor—may be particularly adversely affected by stress.

 Explain how stress has been studied

- Research on stressful life events indicates that any event that forces a person to make a change increases stress and the likelihood of illness. The daily hassles of life can also affect health adversely, as can chronic exposure to stress.

LO5 **Describe the sources of chronic stress**

- Stress researchers are coming to the conclusion that the chronic stressors of life may be more important than major life events in the development of illness. Such stressors can take many forms.

- Studies of occupational stress suggest that work hazards, work overload, work pressure, role conflict and ambiguity, inability to develop satisfying job relationships, inadequate career development, inability to exert control in one's job, job insecurity, work–life imbalance, and unemployment can produce increased illness, job dissatisfaction, absenteeism, tardiness, and turnover. Some of these job stresses can be prevented or offset through intervention.

- Combining multiple roles, such as those related to work and home life, can create work–life imbalance, producing psychological distress and poor health. On the other hand, such role combinations may also enhance self-esteem and well-being. Which of these effects occurs depends, in large part, on available resources, such as time, money, social support, and help.

KEY TERMS

acute stress paradigm   p. 168
after-effects of stress   p. 165
allostatic load   p. 162
bullying   p. 176
chronic strain   p. 164
daily hassles   p. 171
fight-or-flight response   p. 155

general adaptation syndrome   p. 156
perceived stress   p. 172
person–environment fit   p. 155
post-traumatic stress disorder
    (PTSD)   p. 166
primary appraisal   p. 158
reactivity   p. 161

role conflict   p. 179
secondary appraisal   p. 158
stress   p. 155
stressful life events   p. 169
stressors   p. 155
tend-and-befriend   p. 157
work–life balance   p. 181

CHAPTER 7

Moderators of the Stress Experience

After reading this chapter, students will be able to:

(LO1) Describe and define coping

(LO2) Know the role of external coping resources

(LO3) List coping outcomes

(LO4) Explain how social support affects stress

(LO5) Describe coping interventions

In January 1998 a massive ice storm wreaked havoc across Ontario, Quebec, New Brunswick, and Nova Scotia, covering trees and power lines in a thick sheet of ice, and leaving over a million households without power for hours, and in some cases, days. The ice storm, which has been described by Environment Canada as directly affecting more people than any other weather event in Canadian history, left more than 30 people dead, nearly a thousand injured, and forced nearly 600,000 out of their homes.

Eastern Ontario was one the areas that was most severely hit by the storm. I was living in Ottawa at the time and had the opportunity to witness first-hand both the storm and the different effects it had on people. Some people, who were overcome with fear and panic, not knowing when power would be restored or when the roads would be safe, were afraid to leave their homes. Others were overcome with curiosity and wonder, never having seen so much glistening ice coating every physical surface outside. I recall stepping cautiously outside after the freezing rain had stopped and being surprised to see a few other people inspecting the surreal and icy world that the storm created. My family experienced a near mishap when a large branch from the 100-year-old oak tree in our backyard came crashing down, just barely missing the side of our house and our adjoining neighbour's house. Although our power was not affected by the storm, the huge branch knocked out our phone lines. Our concerns then turned to the well-being of our 82-year-old neighbour who lived alone. Fortunately, she had family members who were equally concerned about her and who braved the treacherous road conditions to check in on her shortly after we had.

Although we were lucky that our home did not sustain any damage from the storm, many others were not so lucky and were left homeless. What became clear from this experience was that how people dealt with the storm and its aftermath depended not just on individual differences in how they viewed and coped with the storm, but also on differences in their individual circumstances, including their financial and social support resources. Whether the stressor is an ice storm or extreme flooding like that experienced in Quebec's Richelieu Valley in 2011 which lasted weeks and left over 2,000 homes flooded, these factors are considered **stress moderators** because they modify how stress is experienced and the effects it has. Moderators of the stress experience may have an impact on stress itself, on the relation between stress and psychological responses, on the relation between stress and illness, or on the degree to which a stressful experience intrudes into other aspects of life.

—author Fuschia Sirois

WHAT IS COPING?   LO1

People respond very differently to stress. We all know people who throw up their hands in despair when the slightest thing goes wrong with their plans, yet we know others who seem able to meet setbacks and challenges with equanimity, bringing their personal and social resources to bear on the problem at hand. The impact of any potentially stressful event is substantially influenced by how a person appraises it. Accordingly, **coping** is defined as the thoughts and behaviours used to manage the internal and external demands of situations that are appraised as stressful (Folkman & Moskowitz, 2004; Taylor & Stanton, 2007).

This definition of coping has several important aspects. First, the relationship between coping and a stressful event is a dynamic process. Coping is a series of transactions between a person, who has a set of resources, values, and commitments, and a particular environment with its own resources, demands, and constraints (Folkman & Moskowitz, 2004). Thus, coping is not a one-time action that someone takes; rather, it is a set of responses, occurring over time, by which the environment and the person influence each other. For example, the impending breakup of a romantic relationship can produce a variety of reactions, ranging from emotional responses, such as sadness or indignation, to actions, such as efforts at reconciliation or attempts to find engrossing, distracting activities. These coping efforts will, in turn, be influenced by the way the partner in the relationship responds. With encouragement from the partner, the person may make renewed efforts at reconciliation, whereas anger or rejection may drive the person further away.

A second important aspect of the definition of coping is its breadth. The definition clearly encompasses a great many actions and reactions to stressful circumstances. Viewed within this definition, then, emotional reactions, including anger or depression, can be thought of as part of the coping process, as can actions that are voluntarily undertaken to confront the event. In turn, coping efforts are moderated by the resources that the individual has available. Figure 7.1 presents a diagram of the coping process.

Personality and Coping

The personality that each individual brings to a stressful event influences how he or she will cope with that event. These enduring characteristics can be a result of both genes (e.g., Kozak, Strelau, & Miles, 2005), and

FIGURE 7.1 | The Coping Process

(*Sources:* F. Cohen & Lazarus, 1979; D. A. Hamburg & Adams, 1967; R. S. Lazarus & Folkman, 1984b; Moos, 1988; S. E. Taylor, 1983)

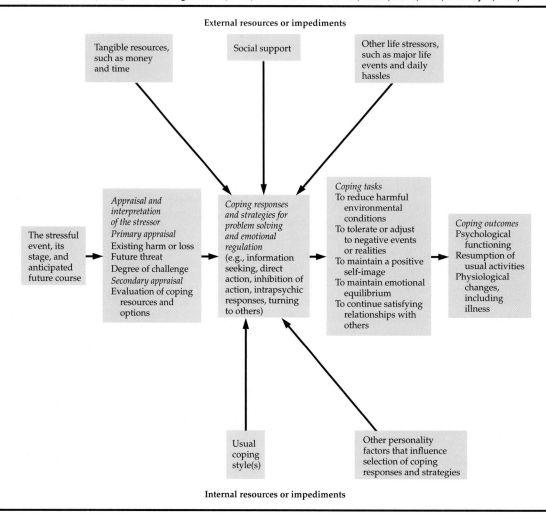

environmental factors (Repetti et al., 2002). Some personality characteristics make stressful situations worse, whereas others improve them.

Negativity, Stress, and Illness   Certain people are predisposed by their personalities to experience stressful events more powerfully, which may, in turn, affect their psychological distress, their physical symptoms, and/or their rates of illness. This line of research has focused on a psychological state called **negative affectivity** (Watson & Clark, 1984), a pervasive negative mood marked by anxiety, depression, and hostility.

Individuals high in negative affectivity (or neuroticism) express distress, discomfort, and dissatisfaction across a wide range of situations (Gunthert, Cohen, & Armeli, 1999). People who are high in negative affectivity are more prone to have genetic markers linked to alcohol dependence (Grabe et al., 2011), to be depressed (Uliaszek et al., 2010), and to have an increased risk for suicide (Roy, 2002).

Neuroticism is related to poor health. For example, people high in neuroticism were found to have an increased risk for diabetes, arthritis, kidney or liver disease, stomach or gallbladder problems and ulcers in one study (Goodwin, Cox, & Clara, 2006). In a review of literature relating personality factors to five diseases—asthma, arthritis, ulcers, headaches, and coronary artery disease—H. S. Friedman and Booth-Kewley (1987) found weak but consistent evidence of a relationship between these disorders and negative emotions. They suggested that psychological distress involving depression, anger, hostility, and anxiety may constitute the basis of a "disease-prone" personality that predisposes people to these disorders. Although their hypotheses were based on correlational studies, recent longitudinal evidence suggests a role for negative affectivity in increasing risk of disease among those who have a family history of certain illnesses. A longitudinal study of twins found that levels of negative affectivity (as assessed by neuroticism) in 1973 predicted greater risk for one of 13 chronic health conditions over 25 years later (Charles, Gatz, Kato, & Pedersen, 2008).

Negative affectivity can be associated with elevated cortisol secretion, and this increased adrenocortical activity may provide a possible biopsychosocial pathway linking negative affectivity to adverse health outcomes (Polk, Cohen, Doyle, Skoner, & Kirschbaum, 2005). Particular behavioural styles that have negative affectivity as a central feature may also be more prone to health issues for this reason (see the Spotlight on Canadian Research box, "Can Procrastination Be Bad for Your Health?"). Negative affectivity can also affect adjustment to treatment. One study (Duits, Boeke, Taams, Passchier, & Erdman, 1997) found that people who were very anxious or depressed prior to coronary artery bypass graft surgery were more likely to adjust badly during surgical recovery (see also P. G. Williams et al., 2002). Negative affectivity has also been directly linked to a higher risk for mortality in old age (R. S. Wilson et al., 2005).

Although it's true that negativity may compromise health, it is also clear that negativity can sometimes create a false impression of poor health when none exists. People who are high in negative affectivity report higher levels of distressing physical symptoms, such as headaches, stomach aches, and other pains, especially under stress (Watson & Pennebaker, 1989), but in many cases, there is no evidence of an underlying physical disorder (Diefenbach, Leventhal, Leventhal, & Patrick-Miller, 1996). For example, Cohen and his associates (S. Cohen, Doyle, Turner, Alper, & Skoner, 2003) obtained both subjective complaints (runny nose and congestion) and objective measures (for example, mucus secretion) of illness from people who had been exposed to a respiratory virus. Negative affectivity was associated with a higher number of complaints but not with more objective measures of disease.

People high in negative affectivity also often appear more vulnerable to illness because they are more likely to use health services during stressful times than are people low in negative affectivity (S. Cohen & Williamson, 1991). Thus, individuals who are chronically high in negative affect may be more likely to get sick, but they also show distress, physical symptoms, and illness behaviour even when they are not getting sick.

Pessimism Individuals who habitually appraise their circumstances in a negative, unhopeful way, may also be prone to poor health outcomes. Some researchers have described **pessimism** as a relatively stable dispositional characteristic to expect negative outcomes in the future (Scheier & Carver, 1985), whereas others view it as an explanatory style that can be learned (C. Peterson, Seligman, & Vaillant, 1988). People with a **pessimistic explanatory style** characteristically explain the negative events of their lives in terms of internal, stable, global qualities of themselves. In so doing, they may lay the groundwork for poor health.

In one study (C. Peterson et al., 1988), interviews completed by graduates of the Harvard University classes of 1942 to 1944 when they were 25 years old were analyzed to find out how the men habitually explained the negative events in their lives. Their health was then assessed 20 to 30 years later. Those men who explained bad events by referring to their own internal, stable, global negative qualities had significantly poorer health between ages 45 and 60. This was true even when physical and mental health at age 25 were taken into account. Thus, pessimism in early adulthood seems to be a risk factor for poor health in middle and late adulthood (Maruta, Colligan, Malinchoc, & Offord, 2002).

There is also some evidence that people marked by this personality characteristic may have reduced immunocompetence. In a study of post-menopausal women, those who showed the pessimistic explanatory style were found to have poorer functioning cell-mediated immunity (O'Donovan et al., 2009). This study is important, because it shows a direct relationship between pessimistic explanatory style and a biological pathway that can have health implications.

Dispositional pessimism may also compromise coping efforts and the use of coping resources such as social support in response to threatening health events. In one study, breast cancer patients were followed after surgery and throughout the following year. Pessimism after surgery predicted greater distress and disruptions in social and recreational activities at the three-month and nine-month follow-ups (Carver, Lehman, & Antoni, 2003).

Finally, having a pessimistic outlook may be linked to one's larger social and economic circumstances. Several studies have shown that people from a lower socio-economic status (SES) have a greater expectancy that negative events will occur in the future compared to those from a higher SES (Finkelstein, Kubzansky, Capitman, & Goodman, 2007; S. E. Taylor, 1998), suggesting that socio-economic factors may contribute to pessimistic appraisals of resources, and consequently increase risks for poor health.

Perfectionism   Although the negative consequences of **perfectionism** for mental health have long been recognized, it is only recently that researchers have acknowledged the links between perfectionism and physical health. Perfectionism has been described as a tendency to experience frequent cognitions about the attainment of ideal standards (Flett, Hewitt, Blankstein, & Gray, 1998), and is generally recognized as a multidimensional construct which can take several forms (Hewitt & Flett, 1991). Early research, which viewed perfectionism as a unidimensional construct, found perfectionism was linked to several negative health outcomes including migraines (Stout, 1984), chronic pain (Van Houdenhove, 1986), and asthma (Morris, 1961).

Emerging research examining the links between the different dimensions of perfectionism suggests that only certain forms increase risk for poor health outcomes. For example, socially prescribed perfectionism, the belief that others hold unrealistically high standards for their behaviour (Hewitt & Flett, 1991), is consistently linked to a variety of negative health outcomes, whereas self-oriented perfectionism, the tendency to set high personal standards which motivate achievement, is not. For example, socially prescribed or maladaptive perfectionism, is associated with high stress (Chang, Ivezaj, Downey, Kashima, & Morady, 2008; Flett, Madorsky, Hewitt, & Heisel, 2002), physical health symptoms (Chang et al., 2008; Martin, Flett, Hewitt, Krames, & Szanto, 1996; Molnar, 2006; Saboonchi & Lundh, 2003), and even greater risk for mortality among older adults (Fry & Debats, 2009). Maladaptive perfectionism is also associated with practising fewer wellness promoting behaviours (Sirois, 2010a).

One study found that the link between socially prescribed perfectionism and health was explained by stress (Molnar & Sadava, 2010), suggesting that this may be why this particular type of perfectionism poses a risk for poor health. Given the known links between perfectionism and procrastination (Chabaud, Ferrand, & Maury,

2010), it is possible that similar pathways involving stress and health behaviours may also explain how perfectionism poses a risk for health (see Box 7.1).

Coping Resources

Although characteristics such as negative affect or pessimism may increase stress and therefore risks for poor health, other psychological resources may contribute to effective coping and thereby reduce the risk of poor mental and physical health.

Optimism   An optimistic nature can also lead people to cope more effectively with stress and thereby reduce their risk for illness (Scheier & Carver, 1985). **Dispositional optimism** is a general expectancy that good things, not bad, will happen in the future. Scheier and Carver developed a measure of dispositional optimism aimed at identifying generalized expectations that outcomes will be positive. The Measuring Health Psychology Concepts box, "The Measurement of Optimism," lists the items on this measure, the Life Orientation Test (LOT). As can be seen from the items, some measure optimism, whereas others assess pessimism.

In one study, university students completed measures of optimism, perceived stress, depression, and social stress at the beginning of university and again at the end of first semester. Optimism was associated with less stress and depression and with an increase in social support. The optimists were more likely to seek out social support and to reinterpret positively the stressful circumstances they encountered, which was why they coped with the transition to university better (Brissete, Scheier, & Carver, 2002).

Exactly how might optimism exert a positive impact on symptom expression, psychological adjustment, and health outcomes? Optimists have a more positive mood, which itself may lead to a state of physiological resilience. Positive emotional states are associated with better mental and physical health (Cohen & Pressman, 2006; Pressman & Cohen, 2005). For example, the tendency to experience positive emotional states has itself been tied to greater resistance to illness following exposure to a flu virus (Cohen Alper, Doyle, Treanor, & Turner, 2006), and predicts lower risk of mortality among seniors with diabetes (Moskowitz, Epel, & Acree, 2008). Optimism also promotes more active and persistent coping efforts, which may improve long-term prospects for psychological adjustment and health (Segerstrom, Castañeda, & Spencer, 2003). Scheier,

Can Procrastination Be Bad for Your Health?

Nothing is so fatiguing as the eternal hanging on of an uncompleted task.

—WILLIAM JAMES

For some people procrastination is a familiar way of dealing with stressful or unpleasant tasks. Indeed, for many students dealing with academic demands and deadlines, procrastinating on preparing term papers and studying for exams can be an all-too-common occurrence. Current estimates suggest that 80 percent to 95 percent of students procrastinate, and 50 percent do so consistently (Steel, 2007). But can this avoidant behavioural style actually be bad for your health? According to several Canadian researchers, the answer is yes.

In a large meta-analysis and review of the procrastination literature, Piers Steel from the University of Calgary noted that procrastination was consistently and significantly associated with negative affectivity, impulsiveness, and depression across several studies (Steel, 2007), all characteristics that are known to be linked to poor health outcomes. Procrastination was also noted to be associated with stress and poor health in a handful of studies. For example, researchers from York University and the University of Toronto found links between procrastination and depression, as well as life stress, and suggested that these relations may be explained by procrastinators' tendency to negatively evaluate themselves (Flett, Blankstein, & Martin, 1995). By putting off important tasks, procrastinators may therefore increase their own stress levels, which in turn are exacerbated by negative attribution styles and poor self-esteem.

But how then does procrastination put one at risk for poor health? Current theories on the links between personality and health suggest both direct and indirect routes to explain how behavioural patterns such as procrastination may exert a negative effect on health outcomes (Suls & Rittenhouse, 1990). The direct route involves a tendency to experience stress, which is well known to negatively impact health through altering adrenocortical and endocrine activity. The indirect route involves behavioural paths and the interaction of personality with the environment, which can result in the delay of health-protective and health-promoting behaviours and the practice of unhealthy behaviours, as well as creating stressful circumstances. In addition, stress and health behaviours are known to be inversely related and may have a combined negative effect on health.

To test this proposition, researchers examined the relations among stress, acute health problems, and health-promoting behaviours in a sample of undergraduates at Carleton University (Sirois, Melia-Gordon, & Pychyl, 2003). Students were asked about recent health problems and whether they had sought care, delayed care, or not done anything to deal with their health issue. Chronic procrastinators reported higher levels of stress, poor wellness behaviours (e.g., healthy eating habits, exercise, etc.), delays in seeking medical care, and a greater number of health problems including headaches, insomnia, and digestive problems compared to those who did not habitually procrastinate. Moreover, the procrastinators' poor health was partly accounted for by their high stress and the tendency to delay going to the doctor, but not wellness behaviours, supporting the notion that both stress and certain health behaviours may make procrastinators vulnerable to poor health.

Given the correlational nature of these findings, the researchers followed the students across the academic year, assessing their ongoing levels of stress, health behaviours, and health at two subsequent intervals to examine the possible causal relations suggested by the first study (Sirois & Pychyl, 2002). They found that procrastination at interval one was again related to higher stress, poor health behaviours, and more health problems at intervals two and three. In addition, student procrastinators were also more likely to engage in health-compromising behaviours, such as higher alcohol consumption and recreational drug use, and were more likely to be smokers. It appears then that, for students, procrastination may indeed be bad for health.

However, the stress from procrastinating in university life may have different effects than the stress of day-to-day life. To replicate the findings from the student study, the relationships among procrastination, stress, health behaviours, and health were examined in a community sample of adults (Sirois, 2007a). Consistent with the previous study, chronic procrastination was associated with higher stress, more acute health problems, and the practice of fewer wellness behaviours, including less frequent dental and medical check-ups. Moreover, the procrastinators' poor health was fully explained by their higher stress, which was further exacerbated by their tendency to not engage in health-promoting behaviours.

Together, these studies suggest that, in addition to hindering a variety of health promoting behaviours and negatively impacting well-being, procrastination may confer additional risk for increased stress, and consequently more health problems.

The Measurement of Optimism

People vary in whether they are fundamentally optimistic or pessimistic about life. Scheier and Carver (1985) developed a scale of dispositional optimism to measure this pervasive individual difference. Items from the Life Orientation Test are as follows (for each item, answer "true" or "false"):

1. In uncertain times, I usually expect the best.

2. It's easy for me to relax.

3. If something can go wrong for me, it will.

4. I'm always optimistic about my future.

5. I enjoy my friends a lot.

6. It's important for me to keep busy.

7. I hardly ever expect things to go my way.

8. I don't get upset too easily.

9. I rarely count on good things happening to me.

10. Overall, I expect more good things to happen to me than bad.

Scoring:

1. Reverse code items 3, 7, and 9 prior to scoring (0 5 4) (1 5 3) (2 5 2) (3 5 1) (4 5 0)

2. Sum items 1, 3, 4, 7, 9, and 10 to obtain an overall score.

Note: Items 2, 5, 6, and 8 are filler items only. They are not scored as part of the revised scale.

The revised scale was constructed in order to eliminate two items from the original scale, which dealt more with coping style than with positive expectations for future outcomes. The correlation between the revised scale and the original scale is 95.

_____

Source: Scheier, M.F. Carver, C.S. and Bridges, M.W. (1994). "Distinguishing optimism from neuroticism (and trait anxiety, self-mastery, and self-esteem): A re-evaluation of the Life Orientation Test", Table 6 (adapted) pp. 1073, Journal of Personality and Social Psychology, 67(6), 1063–1078. (c) 1994 by the American Psychological Association. reproduced with permission.

Weintraub, and Carver (1986) examined the coping strategies typically associated with dispositional optimism and pessimism. In studies conducted with undergraduates given both the LOT and a measure of coping, the researchers found that optimism was associated with more use of problem-focused coping, seeking of social support, and emphasizing the positive aspects of a stressful situation. In a study with coronary artery bypass patients (Scheier et al., 1989), optimism was also an important predictor of coping efforts in recovery from surgery. Specifically, optimists used more problem-focused coping and made less use of denial. They had a faster rate of recovery during hospitalization and of returning to normal life activities after discharge. Optimists also had a higher post-surgical quality of life six months later (see also Carver et al., 1993; T. E. Fitzgerald, Tennen, Affleck, & Pransky, 1993).

Optimism has clear health benefits (Segerstrom, 2006). To begin with, optimists and pessimists differ in their physiological functioning. Pessimistic and anxious adults not only feel more negative but also have higher blood pressures than more optimistic, less anxious adolescents (Räikkönen & Matthews, 2008). An optimist style appears to be protective against the risk of coronary heart disease in older men (Kubzansky, Sparrow, Vokonas, & Kawachi, 2001), side effects of cancer treatments (de Moor et al., 2006), depression in middle age (Bromberger & Matthews, 1996), lung cancer mortality (Novotny et al., 2010), loss of pulmonary function in older men (Kubzansky et al., 2002), and illness-related disruption of social and recreational activities among breast cancer patients (Carver, Lehman, & Antoni, 2003).

In short, optimism is a potent and valuable resource. It may help people deal with stressful events by getting them to use their resources more effectively (Segerstrom, 2006). Optimists also appear to size up stressful situations more positively and seem especially prone to making favourable appraisals that their resources will be sufficient to overcome the threat (Chang, 1998).

Optimism may not always be beneficial. Because they are more persistent in pursuing goals, optimists sometimes experience short-term physiological costs (Segerstrom, 2001). When trying to cope with particularly difficult stressors, optimists' expectations for good outcomes may not be met, despite their persistent efforts. And as a result they may experience stress and compromised immune functioning (Segerstrom, 2006).

Critical Checkpoint

Personality and Stress Interventions

From the previous discussion it is clear that personality traits such as optimisms, perfectionism, and procrastination influence coping and stress, and therefore health. Yet most interventions targeting stress are designed to deal with modifiable factors such as perceptions, beliefs, and behaviours. Given the relative stability of personality, why should we study personality as it relates to stress and coping outcomes?

Psychological Control   Feelings that one can exert control over stressful events have long been known to help people cope effectively with stress (S. E. Taylor, Helgeson, Reed, & Skokan, 1991; S. C. Thompson, 1981). **Psychological control** is the belief that one can determine one's own behaviour, influence one's environment, and bring about desired outcomes. As may be apparent, perceived control is closely related to self- efficacy, which is a more narrow perception that one has the ability to enact the necessary actions to obtain a specific outcome in a specific situation (Bandura, 1977). Both types of cognitions appear to help people cope with a wide variety of stressful events (Wrosch, Schulz, Miller, Lupien, & Dunn, 2007). For example, as we noted in Chapter 5, East German migrants to West Germany who found themselves unemployed often turned to alcohol for solace unless they had high feelings of self-efficacy; those migrants with high feelings of self-efficacy, which appeared to buffer them against the stress of unemployment, did not abuse alcohol.

Perceptions of control in one's work life and in the general tasks of living may be especially protective against adopting a risky lifestyle that involves health-compromising behaviours (Wickrama, Conger, & Lorenz, 1995). Across a wide variety of investigations, a feeling that one can control stressful events has been related to emotional well-being, successful coping with a stressful event, good health, behaviour change that may promote good health, and improved performance on cognitive tasks (S. C. Thompson & Spacapan, 1991).

Control is important for most people going through stressful events or who live with the ongoing stress from chronic health conditions (Sirois, Davis, & Morgan, 2006). For example, among adolescents with asthma, beliefs in personal control are associated with better immune responses related to their disease (E. Chen, Fisher, Bacharier, & Strunk, 2003). A sense of control may be especially important for vulnerable populations, such as medical patients, children, and the elderly, who are at risk for health problems (Wrosch, Schulz, Miller, Lupien, & Dunne, 2007). Because control may be problematic for individuals who already have little opportunity to exercise control (S. C. Thompson & Spacapan, 1991), anything that enhances perceptions of control may benefit such individuals.

So powerful are the effects of psychological control that they have been used extensively in interventions to promote good health habits and to help people cope successfully with stressful events, such as surgery and noxious medical procedures. For example, in Chapters 4 and 5, we saw how self-efficacy influences a wide variety of health behaviours, including obtaining exercise and stopping smoking. When people are able to perceive events in their environment as controllable, or regard their coping efforts as likely to be successful, the stress they experience is lessened, their distress is lower, and their physiological responses to stress are reduced.

Additional Coping Resources

High self-esteem may moderate the stress-illness relationship. In one study of students facing exams, those with high self-esteem were less likely to become upset in response to stress (Shimizu & Pelham, 2004). However, self-esteem seems to be more protective at low levels of stress; at higher levels of stress, the stressful events themselves can overwhelm differences in self-esteem (Whisman & Kwon, 1993). In a study of the elderly, high self-esteem was associated with lower levels of cortisol and ACTH in response to a challenge task— namely, an automobile-driving simulation task (T. E. Seeman et al., 1995)—suggesting a biopsychosocial route whereby self-esteem may affect illness.

Given the suggested buffering effects of self-esteem against stress, it is not surprising that interventions designed to enhance a sense of self may improve responses to stressful events. For example, one experimental study assigned some people to think and write about values that were important to them, whereas others wrote about values that were less important (Creswell et al., 2005).

All participants were then exposed to stressors such as challenging mental arithmetic tasks and public speaking to an unresponsive audience. Those who had affirmed important personal values had significantly lower cortisol responses to stress and also reported experiencing less psychological stress.

A cluster of personal qualities called ego strength—dependability, trust, and lack of impulsivity—appear to have health benefits. In a longitudinal investigation (H. S. Friedman, Tucker, Schwartz, Tomlinson-Keasey, et al., 1995), researchers studied children who had first been interviewed in 1947. Some were impulsive and undercontrolled personalities, whereas others showed signs of ego strength. Those who were high in ego strength as children lived longer as adults. One reason was that those high in ego strength were somewhat less likely to smoke and use alcohol to excess.

Being self-confident and having an easygoing disposition also mute the likelihood that stressful events will lead to psychological distress (Holahan & Moos, 1990, 1991), perhaps because self-confident and easygoing individuals cope with stressful events more actively (Holahan & Moos, 1990). However, cheerful people die somewhat sooner than people who are not cheerful (H. S. Friedman et al., 1993). It appears that cheerful people may grow up being more careless about their health and as a result encounter health risks (L. R. Martin et al., 2002).

A sense of coherence about one's life (Jorgensen, Frankowski, & Carey, 1999), a sense of purpose or meaning in one's life (Krause, 2007), a sense of humour (Bennett & Lengacher, 2008), trust in others (Barefoot et al., 1998), and religion (Folkman & Moskowitz, 2004) are internal resources that promote effective coping.

Conscientiousness also moderates the stress-illness relationship. One study (H. S. Friedman et al., 1993) looked at ratings of personality that had been made about youngsters in 1921 and 1922 to find out whether personality would predict who lived longer. The researchers found that those children who scored high on conscientiousness were more likely to live to an old age (H. S. Friedman, Tucker, Schwartz, Tomlinson-Keasey, et al., 1995; see also Chapman, Lyness, & Duberstein, 2007). It may be that conscientious people are more successful in avoiding situations that could harm them or they may be more reliable in their practice of good health habits (Hampson, Goldberg, Vogt, & Dubanoski, 2006).

Coping resources are important because they enable people to manage the demands of job, neighbour-hood stress, financial strain, and other daily stressful events. People who deal with chronic stress in the absence of protective psychosocial resources have a higher risk of emotional distress, greater health risks, and impaired quality of life, and they show more biological risk factors predictive of coronary heart disease (Steptoe & Marmot, 2003). Just as some people appear to have an illness-prone personality, then, other people may possess a health-prone personality, characterized by a sense of control, self-esteem, optimism, and resilience.

Coping Style

In addition to personality traits, which are general ways of responding across situations, coping style represents a more specific individual difference in how people respond to stress. **Coping style** is a general propensity to deal with stressful events in a particular way. As an example, we all know people who deal with stress by talking a lot about it, whereas other people keep their problems to themselves. Coping styles, then, are thought to be like personality traits in that they characterize an individual's way of behaving in a general fashion, but they are more specific than personality traits because they are thought to come into play primarily when events become stressful.

Approach versus Avoidance   Some people cope with a threatening event by using an **avoidant (minimizing) coping style,** whereas others use an **approach (confrontative, or vigilant) coping style** by gathering information or taking direct action. Neither style is necessarily more effective in managing stress; each seems to have its advantages and liabilities. Approach-related coping is most successful if one can focus on the information present in the situation rather than on one's emotions, and if there are actions that can be taken to reduce the stressor (Taylor & Stanton, 2007).

People who cope with threatening events through approach-related methods may engage in the cognitive and emotional efforts needed to deal with long-term threats. In the short term, however, they may pay a price in anxiety and physiological reactivity (T. W. Smith, Ruiz, & Uchino, 2000). Thus, the avoider or minimizer may cope well with a trip to the dentist but cope poorly with ongoing job stress. In contrast, the vigilant coper may fret over the visit to the dentist but make efforts to reduce stress on the job.

Whether avoidant or confrontative strategies are successful also depends on how long term the stressor is.

Religion promotes psychological well-being, and those people with religious faith may be better able to cope with aversive events.

People who cope with stress by minimizing or avoiding threatening events seem to cope effectively with short-term threats (Krause, 2007). However, if the threat is repeated or persists over time, a strategy of avoidance may not be so successful. For example, people who reported post-traumatic stress symptoms in the wake of the World Trade Center attack on September 11, 2001, and who used avoidant strategies to cope with their distress over the long term, fared worse psychologically than those who used more active strategies to cope with their distress (Silver, Holman, McIntosh, Poulin, & Gil-Rivas, 2002). One explanation is that people who cope using avoidance may not make enough cognitive and emotional efforts to anticipate and manage long-term problems (Taylor & Stanton, 2007).

Studies of short-term threats may have underestimated how unsuccessful avoidant coping strategies are. A number of studies now confirms that approach coping is associated with beneficial outcomes in general, including less psychological distress and lower stress-related physiological responses. In contrast, avoidance coping is associated with adverse psychological and health-related outcomes (for a review, see Taylor & Stanton, 2007).

Problem-focused versus Emotion-focused Coping

Coping strategies can also be distinguished according to the target of the coping efforts (Folkman, Schaefer, & Lazarus, 1979; Pearlin & Schooler, 1978). **Problem-focused coping** involves attempts to do something constructive about the stressful conditions that are harming, threatening, or challenging an individual. **Emotion-focused coping** involves efforts to regulate emotions experienced because of the stressful event. Problem-focused coping appears to emerge during childhood; emotion-focused coping skills develop somewhat later in late childhood or early adolescence (Compas et al., 1991). Typically, people use both problem-focused and emotion-focused coping in their stressful episodes, suggesting that both types of coping are useful for most stressful events (Folkman & Lazarus, 1980).

However, the nature of the event also contributes to what coping strategies will be used (for example, Vitaliano et al., 1990). For example, work-related problems lead people most commonly to attempt problem-focused coping efforts, such as taking direct action or seeking help from others. Health problems, in contrast, lead to more emotion-focused coping, perhaps because a threat to one's health is an event that must be tolerated but is not necessarily amenable to direct action. When health problems are amenable to active coping efforts, however, problem-focused coping is beneficial (Penley, Tomaka, & Wiebe, 2002). These findings suggest that situations in which something constructive can be done will favour problem-focused coping, whereas those situations that simply must be accepted favour emotion-focused coping (Zakowski, Hall, Klein, & Baum, 2001).

Emotion-focused coping includes coping of two kinds. One involves emotional distress as may be experienced in rumination. Ruminating, that is, negative recurrent thoughts, is detrimental to health. Among other outcomes, rumination has been tied to several indicators of compromised immune functioning in both young and elderly samples (Thomsen et al., 2004).

The other type of emotion-focused coping involves emotional-approach coping, which involves clarifying, focusing on, and working through the emotions experienced in conjunction with a stressor (Austenfeld & Stanton, 2004; Stanton, Danoff-Burg, Cameron, & Ellis, 1994). This type of coping has benefits for a broad array of stressful situations. Emotional-approach coping improves adjustment to many chronic conditions, including chronic pain (J. A. Smith, Lumley, & Longo, 2002) and medical conditions such as pregnancy (Huizink, Robles de Medina, Mulder, Visser, & Buitelaar, 2002) and breast cancer (Stanton, Kirk, Cameron, & Danoff-Burg, 2000). Even managing the stressors of daily life can be benefited by emotional-approach coping (Stanton et al., 2000). For example, both emotion-focused coping and problem-focused coping predicted well-being across the first year of medical school in a study of medical students (Park & Adler, 2003). Coping via emotional approach appears to be especially beneficial for women (Stanton et al., 2000).

Why is emotion-focused coping so successful? One reason may be that it has a soothing effect on stress regulatory systems (e.g., Epstein, Sloan, & Marx, 2005). Another reason is that it promotes affirmation of important aspects of the self and identity which can result in health benefits (Low, Stanton, & Danoff-Burg, 2006; Creswell, Lam, Stanton, Taylor et al., 2007).

Specific Coping Strategies

A seriously ill cancer patient was asked how she managed to cope with her disease so well. She responded, "I try to have cracked crab and raspberries every week." Although her particular choice of coping strategy may be somewhat unusual, her answer illustrates the importance of personal coping strategies for dealing with stressful events.

Research has also focused on more specific coping strategies as well as general coping strategies. This shift has occurred in part because research has ques-

Coping researchers have found that direct action often leads to better adjustment to a stressful event than do coping efforts aimed at avoidance of the issue or denial.

tioned whether general coping styles measured at the trait level really predict how people behave in specific situations (J. E. Schwartz, Neale, Marco, Shiffman, & Stone, 1999). Such an approach also provides a more fine-grained analysis of exactly how people manage the myriad stressful events they confront each day. Carver, Scheier, and Weintraub (1989) developed a measure called the COPE to assess the specific coping strategies people employ to deal with stressful events. Examples from this widely used instrument appear in the Measuring Health Psychology Concepts box, "The Brief Cope."

Some researchers prefer to look at coping in a more microscopic fashion. A. A. Stone and Neale (1984) developed a measure of daily coping designed for use in studies to find out how changes in coping on a day-today basis influence psychological and health outcomes (A. A. Stone, Kennedy-Moore, & Neale, 1995). Examples of the coping strategies used to manage the daily challenge of living with

The Brief Cope

The Brief Cope is a measure of coping that relies on two items to tap each of a broad array of commonly used coping styles for managing stressful events. People rate how they are coping with a stressful event by answering each of these items on a scale from 0 ("I haven't been doing this at all") to 3 ("I've been doing this a lot").

Think of a stressful event that you are currently going through (e.g., a problem with your family, a roommate difficulty, problems in a course) and find out which coping methods you use.

1. Active coping

   I've been concentrating my efforts on doing something about the situation I'm in.

   I've been taking action to try to make the situation better.

2. Planning

   I've been trying to come up with a strategy about what to do.

   I've been thinking hard about what steps to take.

3. Positive reframing

   I've been trying to see it in a different light, to make it seem more positive.

   I've been looking for something good in what is happening.

4. Acceptance

   I've been accepting the reality of the fact that it has happened.

   I've been learning to live with it.

5. Humour

   I've been making jokes about it.

   I've been making fun of the situation.

6. Religion

   I've been trying to find comfort in my religion or spiritual beliefs.

   I've been praying or meditating.

7. Using emotional support

   I've been getting emotional support from others.

   I've been getting comfort and understanding from someone.

8. Using instrumental support

   I've been trying to get advice or help from other people about what to do.

   I've been getting help and advice from other people.

9. Self-distraction

   I've been turning to work or other activities to take my mind off things.

   I've been doing something to think about it less, such as going to movies, watching TV, reading, daydreaming, sleeping, or shopping.

10. Denial

    I've been saying to myself, "This isn't real."

    I've been refusing to believe that it has happened.

11. Venting

    I've been saying things to let my unpleasant feelings escape.

    I've been expressing my negative feelings.

12. Substance use

    I've been using alcohol or other drugs to make myself feel better.

    I've been using alcohol or other drugs to help me get through it.

13. Behavioural disengagement

    I've been giving up trying to deal with it.

    I've been giving up the attempt to cope.

14. Self-blame

    I've been criticizing myself.

    I've been blaming myself for things that happened.

Source: With kind permission from Springer Science+Business Media: International Journal of Behavioral Medicine, "You Want to Measure Coping but Your Protocol's too Long: Consider the Brief COPE." vol. 4 pp. 92–100. C.S. Carver., DOI: 10.1207/s15327558ijbm0401_6

Coping with Inflammatory Bowel Disease

With over 10,000 new cases diagnosed each year, the rates of inflammatory bowel disease (Crohn's disease and ulcerative colitis; IBD) in Canada are considered the highest in the world. For many people, living with this painful, invisible, and potentially embarrassing chronic condition is a daily challenge that elicits a variety of different coping strategies, some of which are illustrated in the following excerpts given by people with IBD in response to this question:

> "Different people have different things that they do to cope with their IBD when it is most bothersome. What do you do to cope with it?"

SOCIAL SUPPORT OR SEEKING INFORMATION

I do a lot of research about IBD. I also have been getting a lot of different opinions from a lot of different doctors.

My husband is a wonderful source of support. I also think about the other people with IBD that I have talked to and realize that there are people out there who are a lot more ill than I am, and that helps me not to feel sorry for myself.

I turn to my faith for spiritual encouragement. I go on the Internet, the Crohn's and colitis message board, for understanding and support and to learn more about how to cope. I sometimes get help and support from my family and boyfriend.

DIRECT ACTION

Try to stay home if I can, avoid meetings away from the office, always carry emergency kit (toilet paper, spare underpants, moist wipes), go to sleep earlier, avoid restaurants and movies, first find the toilet wherever I go, never forget to go to toilet before leaving a place, avoid buses, avoid traffic rush-hour, have TP in the car, travel alone, not take passengers in the car, not eat or drink coffee before long drives.

I make changes to my diet that may include eliminating certain foods, reducing food intake, or even fasting when necessary. (I have found that by going a day or two without any food and giving my system a rest, I can lessen the severity of, or even completely stop, a flareup.) I also will spend extra time doing meditation or yoga practices to try to become more relaxed. I also may take some extra dietary supplements that I have found helpful in the past, such as slippery elm root powder. I guess my coping strategies mostly focus on dealing directly with my symptoms to try to reduce them and their interference with my life.

I've made my bathroom very luxurious so that it's a comfortable and soothing place to spend time when necessary. I keep a stack of books to read next to the bed for bad days. I have amassed a large collection of DVDs so that I can rest quietly and have interesting things to watch.

STRATEGIES OF DISTRACTION, ESCAPE, OR AVOIDANCE

I try very hard to ignore it, living as far as possible into the centre of denial.

I try to keep my mind off of it by reading, taking part in an online support group, watching movies, spending time with my new granddaughter.

---

inflammatory bowel disease appear in the Health Psychology in Action box, "Coping with Inflammatory Bowel Disease."

People who are able to shift their coping strategies to meet the demands of a situation cope better with stress than those who do not. This point is of course suggested by the fact that the problem-solving and emotional approaches may work better for different stressors. Overall, research suggests that people who are flexible copers may cope especially well with stress (Cheng, 2003).

WHAT ARE EXTERNAL COPING RESOURCES?

L02

Coping is influenced not only by the internal resources that an individual has, such as personality traits and coping methods, but also by external resources. These include time, money, education, a decent job, children, friends, family, standard of living, the presence of positive life events, and the absence of other life stressors (Hobfoll, 1989).

In addition to shaping perceptions about future outcomes, having greater resources provides people with the

Coping with Inflammatory Bowel Disease (continued)

I surround myself with friends and family. . . . I like to keep my mind busy to try to forget about it.

I use drugs! Cannabis.

EMOTIONAL REGULATION/ VENTILATION

Diet, pray, scream, curse mean people who don't understand the pain of it all, and that you are not being a hypochondriac.

Cry. Honestly, I have a good crying jag then I get mad. After that I sit down, either by myself or with someone in my support network (friends, or mom—she has CD too) and figure out how to get past any specific problem I'm having to face at that time.

I have always kept a journal. Yet, now that I have Crohn's I have started to write down when I felt like people didn't understand and it helps me to get my feelings out. I also try to surround myself with my friends whenever I am feeling low.

PERSONAL GROWTH

I remember how lucky I am to have a chronic disease that is treatable. Colitis, I think, has changed my life in a positive way. . . . I appreciate life more and I don't take it for granted.

I take some time out and say to myself, "Hey, this isn't my fault and I can't do anything about it so let's just chill until it passes." I try yoga as well as it helps me to relax.

I try not to think about it. I'm not letting something like this get the better of me. I'm stronger than some stupid disorder.

I love my job. I am a registered nurse in an ICU unit. I enjoy going to work and helping others who are so sick. It puts my life into perspective and always makes me realize that I have much to be thankful for.

POSITIVE THINKING AND RESTRUCTURING

I always try to have a sense of humour and to stay positive. If I didn't do that, I would be depressed and crusty all the time, and who wants to be friends, or hang around someone who's no fun to be with? (Of course, you can always have your times to cry and complain—that's only human.)

I tend to remind myself about my general good fortune; that my health could be worse (quadriplegic, dying of cancer) and that I could live in a war-torn or poor country. I should consider myself lucky compared to many people in the world.

I have several coping mechanisms. First of all, I have a support board on the Internet, which is a source of commiseration, sympathy, listening, understanding, and valuable patient-to-patient information. I also use humour, including the self-deprecating variety, to help myself feel better about my situation. A good fart joke can go a long way, and it's easier for me to talk about the gross details of my disease when I can sort of laugh them off—that way, I don't make the listener feel too uncomfortable.

Source: Wolfe & Sirois, 2008.

---

opportunity to cope with stressful events better because time, money, friends, and other resources simply provide more ways of dealing with a stressful event. For example, divorce is, generally speaking, an extremely stressful experience. However, men and women with higher income, higher educational achievement, and a greater number of close friends experience less distress (Booth & Amato, 1991). In Chapter 6, we saw another example of the moderation of stress by resources. Relative to nonworking women, working women who had adequate child care and whose husbands shared in homemaking tasks bene-

fited psychologically from their work, whereas women without these resources showed higher levels of distress.

Consistent with a public health perspective, one of the most potent external resources with respect to health is socio-economic status (SES). People who are higher in SES are less likely to have most medical and psychiatric disorders, and they show lower mortality from all causes of death and from a variety of specific causes, including several cancers and cardiovascular disease. So strong is this relationship that, even in animals, higher-status animals are less vulnerable to infection than lower-status animals

FIGURE 7.2 | Mortality Rate by Socio-economic Status

Annual death rate per 1,000 males.

(*Source:* J. Feldman, Makuc, Kleinman, & Corononi-Huntley, 1989)

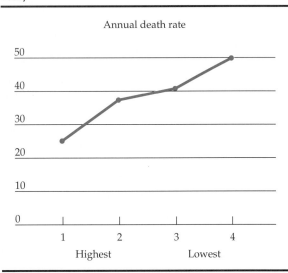

Annual death rate

(for example, S. Cohen, Line, Manuck, et al., 1997). Figure 7.2 illustrates the relation between social class and mortality (see N. E. Adler, Boyce, Chesney, Folkmann, & Syme, 1993).

The presence of other life stressors also moderates coping responses, acting, in essence, as a resource depleter. People who must simultaneously deal with several sources of stress in their lives—such as a failing marriage, financial difficulties, or health problems—will have fewer resources left to use for coping with a new stressor than will people who do not have to deal with other life stressors (F. Cohen & Lazarus, 1979).

Sources of Resilience

Positive life events, good mood, and opportunities for rest, relaxation, and renewal may help people cope more effectively with life stressors and/or prevent stressful events from taking a toll on health (Ong, Bergeman, Bisconti, & Wallace, 2006; Ryff & Singer, 2000). Experiencing positive events and having the opportunity to describe them or celebrate them with others affects both immediate mood and long-term well-being (Langston, 1994). Thus, being engaged in life has positive mental and physical health consequences (Ryff et al., 2006).

Whether such activities also have beneficial effects on health has not yet been widely studied. One restful event, however—taking a vacation—is now known to be beneficial for the health of one group—middle-aged men at risk for heart disease (Gump & Matthews, 2000). Whether similar positive experiences are beneficial for other people remains to be seen.

Resilience also comes from individual differences in how people cope with stressful events. Some people seem to recover from stressful events quickly, whereas others do not. Psychological resilience is characterized by the ability to bounce back from negative emotional experiences and by adapting flexibly to the changing demands of stressful experiences (B. L. Fredrickson, Tugade, Waugh, & Larkin, 2003). Being able to experience positive emotions, even in the context of otherwise intensely stressful events, appears to be one of the methods of coping that resilient people draw on (Tugade & Fredrickson, 2004). For example, being able to experience positive emotions, such as gratitude or love, following the Westray Mine disaster (see Chapter 6) enabled many people to cope with these distressing events and to experience post-traumatic growth (Davis, Wohl, & Verberg, 2007).

Being resilient to the stress of a traumatic event may rely not just on internal resources but also on the presence of external resources and the socio-contextual factors that may limit their availability. For example, a large survey of people in New York after the September 11, 2001, terrorist attack found that women, people who suffered financial loss after the attacks, people who had a chronic illness, those who reported less perceived social support, or those with the presence of other life stressors were significantly less likely to be resilient to the harmful mental health effects of this stressful event (Bonanno, Galea, Bucciareli, & Vlahov, 2007).

WHAT ARE COPING OUTCOMES?   (L03)

Throughout our discussion, we have referred several times to successful coping. But how does a person know when coping efforts are successful? Coping efforts centre on five main tasks (F. Cohen & Lazarus, 1979):

1. To reduce harmful environmental conditions and enhance the prospects of recovery.
2. To tolerate or adjust to negative events or realities.
3. To maintain a positive self-image.
4. To maintain emotional equilibrium.
5. To continue satisfying relationships with others.

A person may be said to have coped successfully to the extent that these tasks are successfully addressed.

To assess successful coping, researchers have also looked at a variety of specific outcomes. One set of **coping outcomes** has included measures of physiological and biochemical functioning. Coping efforts are generally judged to be more successful if they reduce arousal and its indicators, such as heart rate, pulse, and skin conductivity. If blood or urine levels of catecholamines and corticosteroids are reduced, coping is judged to be more successful.

A second criterion of successful coping is whether and how quickly people can return to their pre-stress activities. Many stressors—especially severe ones, such as the death of a spouse, or chronic ones, such as excessive noise—interfere with the conduct of daily life activities. To the extent that people's coping efforts enable them to resume usual activities, coping may be judged to be successful. In some cases though, life may be perceived as improved following a stressful event. In such cases, a re-evaluation of priorities may lead to new way of living.

Third, and most commonly, researchers judge coping according to its effectiveness in reducing psychological distress. When a person's anxiety or depression is reduced, the coping response is judged to be successful. Finally, coping can be judged in terms of whether it terminates, lessens, or shortens the duration of the stressful event itself (Harnish, Aseltine, & Gore, 2000).

(L04) HOW DOES SOCIAL SUPPORT AFFECT STRESS?

The most vital of all resources against stress is social support. Social ties and relationships with others have long been regarded as emotionally satisfying aspects of life. They can also mute the effects of stress, help an individual cope with stressful events, and reduce the likelihood that stress will lead to poor health.

What Is Social Support?

Social support has been defined as information from others that one is loved and cared for, esteemed and valued, and part of a network of communication and mutual obligations from parents, a spouse or lover, other relatives, friends, social and community contacts (such as churches or clubs; Rietschlin, 1998), or even a devoted pet (Allen, 2003). People with high levels of social support may experience less stress when they confront a stressful experience, and they may cope with it more successfully (S. E. Taylor, 2007).

Social support can take several forms. **Tangible assistance** or support, involves the provision of material support, such as services, financial assistance, or goods. For example, the gifts of food that often arrive after a death in a family mean that the bereaved family members will not have to cook for themselves and visiting relatives at a time when their energy and enthusiasm for such tasks is low.

Family and friends can provide **informational support** about stressful events. Information may help an individual understand a stressful event better and determine what resources and coping strategies may be mustered to deal with it. With information, the individual facing a stressful event can determine how threatening the stressful event is likely to be and can profit from suggestions about how to manage the event. For example, if an individual is facing an uncomfortable medical test, a friend who went through the same thing could provide information about the exact procedures, how long the discomfort will last, and the like.

During times of stress, people often suffer emotionally and may experience bouts of depression, sadness, anxiety, and loss of self-esteem. Supportive friends and family can provide **emotional support** by reassuring the person that he or she is a valuable individual who is cared for. The warmth and nurturance provided by other people can enable a person under stress to approach it with greater assurance.

The types of social support just discussed involve the actual provision of help and solace by one person to another. But in fact, many of the benefits of social support may actually come from the perception that social support is available. Actually receiving social support from another person can have several potential costs. First, one is using up another's time and attention, which can produce a sense of guilt. Needing to draw on others can also threaten self-esteem because it suggests a need to be dependent on others (Bolger, Zuckerman, & Kessler, 2000). These potential adverse costs of receiving social support can compromise the ability of social support to otherwise ameliorate psychological distress and health.

Indeed, research suggests that when one receives help from another, but is unaware of it, that help is most likely to benefit the self (Bolger & Amarel, 2007). This kind of support is called **invisible support.** Consistent with the idea that implicit or invisible aspects of social support most benefit others, researchers have increasingly uncovered evidence that merely perceiving that one has social support goes considerable distance in providing the health and mental health benefits of social support (Bolger et al., 2000).

Humour has long been thought to be an effective defence against stress. Writer Norman Cousins referred to laughter as "inner jogging" (Cousins, 1979). Now research supports that intuition. In one research investigation, a group of university students was shown a silent but highly stressful movie. Half the students were given an opportunity to generate a humorous monologue while watching the stressful film, whereas the other half generated a serious monologue. Compared with the students who produced a serious narrative, the students who produced the humorous narrative had better mood, less tension, and reduced psychophysiological reactivity in response to the stressful movie.

Implicit versus Explicit Social Support   In addition to taking different forms, social support has also been described in terms of its focus. Social support that is designed to target a specific problem or is meant for a specific purpose has been termed explicit social support. This type of support usually takes one of the three different forms of tangible, informational, or emotional support described above. However, when social support originates from implicit social networks without being directly targeted at a specific problem, it is considered **implicit social support** (S. E. Taylor, Welch, Kim, & Sherman, 2007). Implicit social support includes simply knowing that you have a social network that you can rely upon if there were a stressful event, and receiving support from that network without actively having to seek out that support.

Cultural context may also play a role in who benefits the most from each type of social support. For example, compared to European Americans, Asians and Asian Americans are less likely to seek out or benefit from explicit social support because of concerns regarding the potential negative relationship implications of explicitly seeking social support and actively disclosing about stressors (Kim, Sherman, Ko, & Taylor, 2006). In addition, Asians and Asian Americans are more likely to experience psychologically and biologically

benefits from implicit but not explicit social support, whereas the reverse is true for European Americans (S. E. Taylor et al., 2007).

Effect of Social Support on Psychological Distress

Lack of social support during times of need can itself be very stressful, especially for people with high needs for social support but insufficient opportunities to obtain it. Such people may include the elderly, the recently widowed, and victims of sudden, severe, uncontrollable life events (for example, Sorkin, Rook, & Lu, 2002). Loneliness clearly leads to health risks, in large part because lonely people appear to have more trouble sleeping and show more cardiovascular activation (Hawkley, Burleson, Bentson, & Cacioppo, 2003; Cacioppo et al., 2002). People who have difficulty with social relationships, such as those who are chronically shy (Naliboff et al., 2004) or who anticipate rejection by others (Cole, Kemeny, Fahey, Zack, & Naliboff, 2003), are at risk for isolating themselves socially, with the result that they experience more psychological distress and are at greater risk for health problems. Social support reduces psychological distress (e.g., depression, anxiety) during times of stress (for a review, see S. E. Taylor, 2007).

Effects of Social Support on Physiological and Neuroendocrine Responses to Stress

Social support can reduce physiological and neuroendocrine responses to stress under a broad array of conditions. Psychologists often study these conditions using the acute stress paradigm—that is, by taking people into the laboratory, putting them through stressful tasks (such as counting backwards quickly by 13s or giving an impromptu speech to an unresponsive audience), and then measuring their sympathetic and HPA axis responses to stress. Quite consistently, these biologic responses to stress are more subdued when a supportive companion is present than when no companion is present (Christenfeld et al., 1997). One reason may be that supportive social contact is associated with the release of oxytocin, which is important for lowering the stress response (Grewen, Girdler, Amico, & Light, 2005). Even just believing that support is available (Uchino & Garvey, 1997) or contemplating the sources of support one typically has in life (Broadwell & Light, 1999) can yield these beneficial effects.

These calming effects are greater when support comes from a friend than from a stranger (Christenfeld et al., 1997). Both men and women seem to benefit somewhat more when the support provider is female than male (Glynn, Christenfeld, & Gerin, 1999). In fact, when women perform stressful tasks in the presence of a partner, especially their male partner, they sometimes appear to be more stressed than when they complete stressful tasks alone (Kirschbaum et al., 1995), unless their partner is actively supportive.

Going through a stressful event in the presence of a pet can keep heart rate and blood pressure lower during that event and lead to faster physiological recovery (K. Allen, Blascovich, & Mendes, 2002). Dogs are somewhat better at providing social support than are other pets. Even a short encounter with a friendly dog has been found to increase opioid functioning and other hormones associated with companionship and to decrease levels of stress-related hormones such as cortisol; interestingly, the dogs experienced many of these benefits as well (Odendaal & Meintjes, 2002). Exceptions notwithstanding, on the whole, social support lessens cardiovascular and cortisol responses to short-term stressful events.

Effect of Social Support on Illness and Health Habits

Social support can lower the likelihood of illness, speed recovery from illness or treatment (Krohne & Slangen, 2005), and reduce the risk of mortality due to serious disease (Rutledge, Matthews, Lui, Stone, & Cavley, 2003). Studies that control for initial health status show that people with a high quantity and sometimes a high quality of social relationships have lower mortality rates (J. S. House et al., 1988). Poor social relationships, and in particular poor social integration, are major risk factors for death (Holt-Lunstad, Smith, & Layton, 2010). Thus, the evidence linking social support to a reduced risk of mortality is substantial.

In a study of the common cold, healthy volunteers reported their social ties, such as whether they had a spouse, living parents, friends, or workmates, and whether they were members of social groups, such as clubs. The volunteers were then given nasal drops containing one of two viruses and were followed for the development of the common cold. Those people with larger social networks were less likely to develop colds, and those who did, had less severe colds (S. Cohen, Doyle, Skoner, Rabin, & Gwaltney, 1997). Social support appears to help people hold off or minimize complications from more serious medical conditions and disorders as well.

People with high levels of social support have fewer complications during pregnancy and childbirth (N. L.

In addition to being an enjoyable aspect of life, social support from family and friends helps keep people healthy and may help them recover faster when they are ill.

Collins, Dunkel-Schetter, Lobel, & Scrimshaw, 1993); report less pain (J. L. Brown, Sheffield, Leary, & Robinson, 2003); have lower rates of myocardial (Mookadam & Arthur, 2004); are less susceptible to the development of new brain lesions if they have multiple sclerosis (Mohr, Goodkin, Nelson, Cox, & Weiner, 2002); are less likely to show age-related cognitive decline (Seeman, Lusignolo, Albert, & Berkman, 2001); and are more likely to show better adjustment to coronary artery disease (Holahan, Moos, Holahan, & Brennan, 1997), diabetes, lung disease, cardiac disease, arthritis, and cancer (Penninx et al., 1998; Stone, Mezzacappa, Donatone, & Gonder, 1999).

Not surprisingly, the advantages of social support during times of stress can be cumulative. Research has found that reoccurring positive social experiences affect a range of biological systems resulting in cumulative differences in risks for a broad array of chronic diseases later in life (Seeman, Singer, Ryff, Love, & Levy-Storms, 2002).

Social support, and especially the quality of one's social bonds, may also have a cumulative effect on health through its links to self-esteem. Researchers at the University of Waterloo and the University of Manitoba found that low self-esteem prospectively predicted health problems, and that poor-quality social bonds explained this association (Stinson et al., 2008). In a second longitudinal study, poor quality social bonds predicted decreases in self-esteem, which in turn led to poorer quality of social bonds and increases in health problems.

Although social support has an impact on health independent of any influence on health habits, it also appears to affect health habits directly (Allgöwer, Wardle, & Steptoe, 2001; M. A. Lewis & Rook, 1999).

People with high levels of social support typically adhere more to their medical regimens (DiMatteo, 2004). Social influences may adversely affect some health habits, however, as when much social contact is coupled with high levels of stress; under these circumstances, risk of minor illnesses such as colds or flus may actually increase (Hamrick, Cohen, & Rodriguez, 2002).

Biopsychosocial Pathways   The frontier of social support research is to identify the biopsychosocial pathways by which social support exerts beneficial or health-compromising effects. Studies suggest that social support has beneficial effects on the cardiovascular, endocrine, and immune systems (S. E. Taylor, 2007). For example, one study found that the perception of social support was associated with lower systolic blood pressure in working women, suggesting that the presence of or the perception of social support may have enabled these women to go through a stressful workday without experiencing as much sympathetic arousal as was true for women who felt they lacked support (Linden, Chambers, Maurice, & Lenz, 1993). Other studies report similar beneficial effects of social support on blood pressure (for example, Carels, Blumenthal, & Sherwood, 1998). In fact, just thinking about supportive ties can reduce cardiovascular reactivity in response to stress (T. W. Smith, Ruiz, & Uchino, 2004).

Social support also affects endocrine functioning in response to stress. Studies have found that social support is associated with reduced cortisol responses to stress, which can have beneficial effects on a broad array of diseases, including heart disease and cancer (Turner-Cobb, Sephton, Koopman, Blake-Mortimer, & Spiegel, 2000). Generally speaking, social support is associated with better immune functioning (Miyazaki et al., 2003), and with better health (Rutledge et al., 2004).

These biopsychosocial pathways, then, provide the links between illness and social support. These links are important because they play critical roles in the leading causes of death—namely, cardiovascular disease, cancer, and respiratory illness.

Genetic Bases of Social Support?   Researchers have questioned exactly why social support is so helpful during times of stress. Certainly, some of these effects are due to benefits that one's close friends, family, and community ties can provide, but there are also advantages to perceiving that social support is available. Research using twin study methodology has discovered genetic underpinnings either in the ability to construe social support as available or in the ability to pick supportive networks (Kessler, Kendler, Heath, Neale, & Eaves, 1992). During periods of high stress, genetic predispositions to draw on social support networks may be activated, leading to the perception that support will be available to mute stress.

Moderation of Stress by Social Support

What is the role of social support in moderating the effects of stress? Two possibilities have been extensively explored. One hypothesis maintains that social support is generally beneficial during nonstressful times as well as during highly stressful times (the **direct effects hypothesis**). The other hypothesis, known as the **buffering hypothesis,** maintains that the health and mental health benefits of social support are chiefly evident during periods of high stress; when there is little stress, social support may have few physical or mental health benefits. According to this hypothesis, social support acts as a reserve and resource that blunts the effects of stress or enables the individual to cope with stress more effectively when it is at high levels.

Results from a study examining the effects of social support on physical and mental health eight months after the 2008 Wenchuan earthquake in China provide a good illustration of the buffering effects of social support during times of need. The 8.0 magnitude earthquake which struck South China claimed almost 70,000 lives and left thousands more missing or injured across a widespread area. Researchers examined the self-reported social support and health of earthquake survivors from a variety of regions affected by the earthquake. They found that those who reported having a greater degree of social support scored higher on measures of physical and mental well-being (Ke, Liu, & Li, 2010), supporting the buffering model of social support.

Evidence suggests both direct effects and buffering effects of social support amassed (S. Cohen & Hoberman, 1983; S. Cohen & McKay, 1984; Penninx et al., 1998). Generally, when researchers have looked at social support in social integration terms, such as the number of people one identifies as friends or the number of organizations one belongs to, direct effects of social support on health have been found. When social support has been assessed more qualitatively, such as the degree to which a person feels that there are other people available who will provide help if it is needed, then buffering effects of social support have been found (J. S. House et al., 1988).

Extracting Support   The effectiveness of social support depends on how an individual uses a social support network. Some people are better than others in extracting the support they need. To examine this hypothesis, S. Cohen, Sherrod, and Clark (1986) assessed incoming first-year university students as to their social competence, social anxiety, and self-disclosure skills. The researchers wanted to see if these skills influenced whether the students were able to develop and use social support effectively and whether the same skills could account for the positive effects of social support in combatting stress. Those students with greater social competence, lower social anxiety, and better self-disclosure skills did develop more effective social support and were more likely to form friendships, lending credence to the idea that the use of social support as a coping technique reflects, in part, a difference in personality, social skills, or competence, rather than an external resource (for example, Kessler et al., 1992).

One factor that may affect how well an individual is able to extract, use, and benefit from social support is attachment. Attachment styles develop from early emotional relationships which can be secure or insecure (anxious or avoidance promoting) and which serve as working models of what to expect from others in times of need (Bowlby, 1977). Attachment styles may operate as lenses which predispose individuals to perceive their support experiences in ways that are consistent with their particular attachment style, especially if the support given is ambiguous (Collins & Feeney, 2004). Some researchers have suggested that the perceived social support is simply an offshoot of attachment style and that those with an insecure attachment style are less likely to perceive and experience the benefits from social support (Moreira et al., 2003). For example, researchers from Carleton University found that among women with inflammatory bowel disease, those with an insecure attachment style

Social support can come not only from family and friends but also from a loved pet. Research suggests that dogs are better at providing social support than cats and other animals.

(anxious or avoidant) reported lower perceived social support, coped less effectively with their disease, and experienced greater disease activity and higher levels of negative affectivity (Gick & Sirois, 2010a). However, the effects of insecure attachment on perceived social support and well-being may be more pronounced for older than for younger adults (Kafetsios & Sirideris, 2006).

What Kinds of Support Are Most Effective?

Not all aspects of social support are equally protective against stress. Too much or overly intrusive social support may actually exacerbate stress. When social support is controlling or directive, it may have some benefits on health behaviours but produce psychological distress (M. A. Lewis & Rook, 1999). For example, a study of breast cancer patients found that receiving unwanted support was associated with worse psychological adjustment (Reynolds & Perrin, 2004). People who belong to "dense" social networks (friendship or family groups that are highly interactive and in which everyone knows everyone else) may find themselves besieged by advice and interference in times of stress.

Certain types of social support may take time before their beneficial effects are noticed. Researchers for Memorial University and St. John's University examined the effects of different types of social support on depressive symptoms in a large sample of Canadian adults (Wareham, Fowler, and Pike, 2007). They found that emotional and informational support was associated with increases in the severity of depressive symptoms, whereas positive social interaction was linked to decreases in symptom severity. However, when the duration of depressive symptoms was examined, emotional and informational support predicted decreases in the duration of these symptoms. Talking to others about one's depressive symptoms may make one acutely aware of these symptoms initially, but then having this type of support may help to reduce how long one feels depressed.

Dyadic Coping Social support can also come in the form of support from a partner or spouse and impact outcome for better or worse. **Dyadic coping,** the interplay of the stress experienced and expressed by one partner and the coping reactions of the other, can have important implications for the outcomes of both. When both members of the couple respond empathetically to each other's needs during stress, this empathetic responding can help to reduce daily stress (O'Brien, DeLongis, Pomaki, Puterman, & Zwicker, 2009). However, in the context of a chronic health condition, such as a woman diagnosed with breast cancer, negative dyadic coping can increase distress for both the patient and her partner (Badr, Carmack, Kashy, Cristofanilli, & Revenson, 2010). Similarly, partners of patients with high negative affectivity can also increase distress for patients after heart surgery (Ruiz, Matthews, Scheier, & Schulz, 2006).

Simply approaching and describing the joint experience of a stressful event in terms of "we" instead of "I" may also have beneficial effects. One study of heart failure patients and their spouses found that more frequent use of the term "we" rather than I among spouses when discussing how they coped predicted improved heart failure symptoms and overall health six months later (Rohrbaugh, Mehl, Shoham, Reilly, & Ewy, 2008).

Matching Support to the Stressor Different kinds of stressful events create different needs, and social support should be most effective when it meets those needs. The hypothesis that a match between one's needs and what one receives from others in one's social network is called the **matching hypothesis** (S. Cohen & McKay, 1984; S. Cohen & Wills, 1985). For example, if a person has someone he or she can talk to about problems but actually needs only to borrow a car, the presence of a confidant is useless. But if a person is upset about how a relationship is going and needs to talk it through with a friend, then the availability of a confidant is a very helpful resource.

Empathetic understanding helps support providers sense what kinds of support will be most helpful to a person going through a particularly stressful event. People who need support, in turn, may be most effectively helped by others when they are able to communicate that they need support and what particular kind of support they need.

Some kinds of support are useful with most kinds of stressors. Having someone to talk to about problems and having a person who makes one feel better about oneself may be especially helpful because these are issues that arise with most stressful events.

Support from Whom? Providing effective social support is not always easy for the support network. It requires skill. When it is provided by the wrong person, support may be unhelpful or even rejected, as when a stranger tries to comfort a lost child.

Social support may also be ineffective if the type of support provided is not the kind that is needed. Emotional support is most important from intimate others, whereas information and advice may be more valuable from

experts. Thus, a person who desires solace from a family member but receives advice instead may find that rather than being supportive, the family member actually makes the stressful situation worse (Dakof & Taylor, 1990).

Support from a partner, usually a spouse, is very protective of health, especially for men (Janicki et al., 2005; Kiecolt-Glaser & Newton, 2001). For example, a large prospective Canadian survey of seniors' mortality found that senior men who were widowed had a higher likelihood of dying over an eight-year period compared to men who were married or living with a partner (Wilkins, 2005). On average, men's health is substantially benefited from marriage. Women's health is only slightly benefited by marriage. The quality of marital relationship influences these outcomes as well. Exiting a marriage, being unmarried, or being in an unsatisfying marriage all entail health risks (Umberson, Williams, Powers, Liu, & Needham, 2006; D. R. Williams, 2003).

Support from family is important as well. Social support from one's parents in early life and/or living in a stable and supportive environment as a child has long-term effects on coping and on health (Repetti et al., 2002). Experiencing the divorce of one's parents in childhood can predict premature death in midlife (H. S. Friedman, Tucker, Schwartz, Martin, et al., 1995); however feeling satisfied with one's life at midlife may attenuate the link between divorce and mortality risk (Martin, Friedman, Clark, & Tucker, 2005). A study of university students (Valentiner, Holahan, & Moos, 1994) found that students who perceived themselves as having a lot of support from their parents were more likely to make favourable appraisals of potentially stressful events and were more likely to cope actively with those stressful events when they occurred. When faced with uncontrollable events, parental support enabled these students to cope well emotionally, even when they could not take direct action to reduce the stressor (see also Maunder & Hunter, 2001). Similarly, a long-term study of undergraduate men at Harvard revealed that those men who perceived themselves to have had warm, close relationships with their parents were healthier 35 years later (Russek & Schwartz, 1997). Those men in childhood who did not report a warm relationship with their parents were more likely to be diagnosed in midlife with coronary artery disease, hypertension, ulcers, and alcoholism (see also Russek, Schwartz, Bell, & Baldwin, 1998).

Threats to Social Support Stressful events can interfere with the ability to use potential social support effectively. People who are under extreme stress may continually express distress to others and drive those others away, thus making a bad situation even worse (for example, G. E. Matt & Dean, 1993; McLeod, Kessler, & Landis, 1992). For example, depressed or ill people can repel their friends and family instead of using them effectively for social support (Alferi, Carver, Antoni, Weiss, & Duran, 2001).

Effects of Stress on Support Providers   When a close friend, family member, or partner is going through a stressful event, the event also has an impact on close family members who may themselves have resulting needs for social support that go unmet (for example, Aneshensel, Pearlin, & Schuler, 1993). To the extent that family members and friends are adversely affected by the stressful event, they may be less able to provide social support to the person in greatest need (G. R. Smith, Williamson, Miller, & Schulz, 2011). For example, long-term caregiving for another has been tied to both psychological distress—including anxiety and depression—and compromised health (Schulz, O'Brien, Bookwala, & Fleissner, 1995), a topic covered more extensively in Chapter 11.

On the whole, though, the evidence suggests that giving social support to others has beneficial effects on mental health and health (Li & Ferraro, 2005; C. Schwartz, Meisenhelder, Ma, & Reed, 2003). For example, one study assessed giving and receiving social support in older married people and related both to mortality rates over a five-year period (Brown, Nesse, Vinokur, & Smith, 2003). Death was significantly less likely for those people who reported providing instrumental support to friends, relatives, and neighbours and to those who reported providing emotional support to their spouses. Receiving support did not affect mortality. This study, then, provides important evidence that the giving of support can promote health and retard illness progression.

These findings are especially important because social support and helping have long been thought to benefit the beneficiary of the help while taxing the resources of those that provide it. The fact that helping, altruism, and support lead to health and mental health benefits for both the giver and the receiver make social support that much more important. Feeling that one matters to another person improves well-being, especially for women (J. Taylor & Turner, 2001).

Enhancing Social Support

Health psychologists need to view social support as an important resource in primary prevention. Patterns in social support are, however, shifting. More and more Canadians are living alone, and family sizes have been decreasing steadily over the past few decades. For example, in 1941, families with five or more members comprised over 38 percent of all Canadian households and only 6 percent of households consisted of only one person. But by 2006 a reverse family pattern was observed: Almost 27 percent of all households were one-person households whereas just over 8 percent of households had five or more members. What's more, for the first time in recent history there were more Canadian adults who were unmarried (never married, separated, divorced, or widowed) than there were legally married Canadians (Milan, Vézina, & Hall, 2007). Given the benefits of marriage for men's health in particular, this trend is alarming.

Seniors are another group that may be at risk for social isolation and not having sufficient social support resources. According to the 2002 General Social Survey, seniors who report not having close or other friends were less likely to be in excellent or good health and also less likely to report that they were happy (Turcotte & Schellenberg, 2007). Activities such as joining community groups, volunteering, and maintaining contact with family members and neighbours may help reduce feelings of isolation for some. Ensuring that seniors have the skills to recognize, build, and effectively use the potential sources of social support in their environment is clearly an important priority for improving the physical and mental well-being of this growing population of Canadians.

Increasingly people are getting "connected" to others through the use of information and communication technologies such as e-mail and the Internet. For example, MySpace, Facebook, and other social networking Web sites have more than 90 million members (McPherson, Smith-Lovin, & Brashears, 2006; Hulbert, 2006). In addition, Internet-based support groups are a popular form of social support for people with specialized support needs, such as single mothers, and those living with chronic illness or addictions. Such virtual communities and communication technologies offer new possibilities for the delivery of social support and the formation of social ties that could have important implications for how we define social support in the future.

WHAT ARE COPING INTERVENTIONS?   (L05)

Because not everyone can find ways to successfully cope with stressors on their own, a variety of interventions for coping with stress have been developed.

Mindfulness Training

Mindfulness-based stress reduction (MBSR) refers to systematic training in meditation to assist people in self-regulating their reactions to stress and any negative emotions that may result (K. W. Brown & Ryan, 2003). It is based on the practice of mindfulness of moment or moment awareness, which enables people to become more aware of the present moment and less distracted by distressing thoughts and feelings that arise in response to a stressor. Mindfulness training incorporates several tools, including relaxation, body scanning, yoga, and meditation. The primary goal of MBSR is to approach situations mindfully rather than react to them automatically (S. R. Bishop, 2002).

Initial studies into the effectiveness of MBSR for reducing stress and its harmful effects are promising (Carlson & Garland, 2005; Carlson, Speca, Patel, & Goodey, 2003). For example, researchers at the University of Calgary investigated the effects of an eight-week MBSR program on the quality of life, stress, mood, and immune parameters of breast cancer and prostate cancer patients (Carlson, Speca, Patel, & Goodey, 2003). Significant improvements were found in quality of life and sleep quality, and stress symptoms were reduced. There were also significant shifts in the immune parameters, which suggested a change from a profile associated with depression to one that was non-depressed. There is also some evidence that the effects of MBSR may be long-lasting. A one-year follow-up of the same patients found that the initial improvements in stress symptoms and mood were maintained, and that there were also significant reductions in cortisol levels, blood pressure, and pro- inflammatory cytokines (Carlson, Speca, Patel, & Faris, 2007). Similarly, a recent review comparing the effects of a yoga—a common mindfulness-based practice—to exercise found that it was equal if not superior to exercise across a variety of health outcomes (Ross & Thomas, 2010).

Engaging in mindfulness promoting activities such as meditation and yoga may be especially important for individuals with behavioural styles that create more stress. Unfortunately, these are the very individuals who are less likely to get involved in mindfulness activities on their own. For example, one study found that students who chronically procrastinated were also less likely to engage in a variety of mindfulness-based practices (Sirois & Tosti, 2011 online). Not surprisingly, these same students also scored very low on several measures of mindfulness, and this low mindfulness explained their higher levels of stress and lower self-reported health.

Disclosure and Coping

Considerable research has examined disclosure of emotional experiences and its beneficial effects on health. The rationale for the benefits of disclosure stems, in part, from the research just discussed that shows the benefits of emotional-approach coping. For many years, researchers have suspected that when people undergo traumatic events and cannot or do not communicate about them, those events may fester inside them. This inhibition of traumatic events involves physiological work, and the more people are forced to inhibit their thoughts, emotions, and behaviours, the more their physiological activity may increase (Pennebaker, 1997). Consequently, the ability to confide in others or to consciously confront their feelings and perceptions may reduce the physiological activity associated with the event.

To examine this hypothesis, Pennebaker and Beall (1986) had 46 undergraduates write either about the most traumatic and stressful event ever in their lives or about trivial topics. Although the individuals writing about traumas were more upset immediately after they wrote their essays (see also Pennebaker, Colder, & Sharp, 1990), they were less likely to visit the student health centre for illness during the following six months.

A subsequent study (Pennebaker, Hughes, & O'Heeron, 1987) found that when people talked about traumatic events, their skin conductance, heart rate, and systolic and diastolic blood pressure all decreased. Emotional disclosure can also have beneficial long-term effects on immune functioning (for example, A. J. Christensen et al., 1996; Petrie, Booth, Pennebaker, Davison, & Thomas, 1995), and cancer-related pain (Cepeda et al., 2008). In another study, people who wrote about traumatic life experiences not only experienced less distress three months later but also had changed their self-perceptions in directions reflecting mastery, personal growth, and self-acceptance, suggesting that such interventions may actually lead to a more resilient self-concept (Hemenover, 2003). Together, these changes may influence the long-term positive effects on health that have been found in studies of disclosure.

Drawing on the value of this method, interventions have employed written exercises designed to encourage emotional expression. There is also some evidence that written disclosure via email can be just as effective as traditional pen and paper disclosure (Sheese, Brown, & Graziano, 2004). Such interventions have led to improved health among AIDS patients (Petrie, Fontanilla, Thomas, Booth, & Pennebaker, 2004), breast cancer patients (Stanton et al., 2002), and asthma and rheumatoid arthritis patients, among other conditions (Norman, Lumley, Booley, & Diamond, 2004). Even writing about emotional topics via e-mail can promote health (Sheese, Brown, & Graziano, 2004). Writing may also help people cope with debilitating treatments. For example, a writing exercise also led to a more beneficial, post-operative course in surgery patients (Solano, Donati, Pecci, Persichetti, & Colaci, 2003); those who wrote about their experience, on average, left the hospital several days earlier with lower psychological distress.

There are many reasons why talking or writing about a stressful event or confiding in others may be useful for coping. Talking with others allows one to gain information about the event or about effective coping; it may also elicit positive reinforcement and emotional support from others. In addition, there may be reliable cognitive effects associated with talking about or writing about a traumatic event, such as organizing one's thoughts and being able to find meaning in the experience (Lepore, Ragan, & Jones, 2000). Finally, the benefits of emotional disclosure have increasingly been uncovered. Talking or writing about traumatic or stressful events provides an opportunity for emotional approach coping (Lepore & Smyth, 2002), and for affirming personal values (Creswell et al., 2007; Langens & Schuler, 2007).

Stress Management

Many coping interventions focus on stress management. Because people so obviously have difficulty managing stress themselves, health psychologists have increasingly turned their attention to developing techniques of **stress management** that can be taught. Who participates in stress-management programs? Some people obtain help in stress management through private therapists in a one-to-one psychotherapeutic experience.

More commonly, stress management is taught through workshops. For example, increasingly, stress-management courses are offered in the workplace. Stress-related disorders are estimated to drain as much as $33 billion a year from Canada's economy. Roughly 20 percent of a typical company's payroll is allocated towards costs associated with stress-related problems such as employee turnover, absenteeism, disability leaves, counselling, and health care. Increasingly, costs are also incurred through "presenteeism"—employees showing up for work in body but not in spirit due to increased work-related stress (Riga, 2006). Consequently, organizations have been motivated to help their workers identify and cope with the variety of stressful events that they experience in

their lives and on the job. Chapter 5 points out that the treatment of alcohol abuse also frequently incorporates stress-management skills (Health Canada, 1999).

Basic stress-management techniques can help people reduce their risk for a variety of different health problems ranging from tension headaches to heart disease (Kirby, Williams, Hocking, Lane, & Williams, 2006).

Basic Techniques of Stress Management

Stress-management programs typically involve three phases. In the first phase, participants learn what stress is and how to identify the stressors in their own lives. In the second phase, they acquire and practise skills for coping with stress. In the final phase, participants practise these stress-management techniques in the targeted stressful situations and monitor their effectiveness (Meichenbaum & Jaremko, 1983).

As an example, university can be an extremely stressful experience for many students. For some students, it is the first time away from home, and they must cope with the problems of living in a residence surrounded by strangers. They may have to share a room with a person of a very different background with very different personal habits. High noise levels, communal bathrooms, institutional food, and rigorous academic schedules may all be trying experiences to new students. In addition, academic life may prove to be more difficult than they had expected.

If the student sees little prospect for improvement, he or she may become increasingly anxious, find that the university environment is too stressful, and drop out. Recognizing that these pressures exist, university administrators have increasingly made stress-management programs available to their students.

An Interactive Stress-management Program

One university responded to these problems by developing an online stress-management program that reaches troubled students before the stresses of academic life lead them to flunk out or drop out. The program, called "Students and Stress: How to Get Your Degree without Losing Your Mind," from the University of Alberta, makes use of an interactive software program to help students learn about stress, discover effective ways to cope, and self-assess their own stress levels and stressors. Students navigate through each section of the program (described below), and their progress through each phase is recorded. The self-guided program is directed specifically at the types of stressors that students may

There are many stressful aspects of university life, such as speaking in front of large groups. Stress-management programs can help students master these experiences.

face and can be downloaded for free from the University of Alberta's Web site.

Identifying Stressors   In the first part of the Students and Stress program, participants learn what stress is and how it creates physical wear and tear. Relevant examples of stressors commonly experienced in university life are presented to help reassure students that in fact many other students experience stressors similar to their own. Students are then presented with the idea that some stress may enhance performance, but that too much stress may compromise the ability to cope effectively, leading to exhaustion and poor performance.

Warning Signs of Stress   In the self-monitoring phase of the Students and Stress program, students are made aware of the possible warning signs that their stress is getting out of hand. An interactive checklist presents 53 different symptoms, and students identify which they have experienced. Table 7.1 gives some examples of the signs and symptoms of stress that may signal stress overload.

TABLE 7.1 | Stress Warning Signs and Symptoms

Cognitive Symptoms	Emotional Symptoms
• Memory problems	• Moodiness
• Inability to concentrate	• Irritability or short temper
• Poor judgment	• Agitation, inability to relax
• Seeing only the negative	• Feeling overwhelmed
• Anxious or racing thoughts	• Sense of loneliness and isolation
• Constant worrying	• Depression or general unhappiness
Physical Symptoms	**Behavioural Symptoms**
• Aches and pains	• Eating more or less
• Diarrhea or constipation	• Sleeping too much or too little
• Nausea, dizziness	• Isolating yourself from others
• Chest pain, rapid heartbeat	• Procrastinating or neglecting responsibilities
• Loss of sex drive	• Using alcohol, cigarettes, or drugs to relax
• Frequent colds	• Nervous habits (e.g. nail biting, pacing)

Source: From article, "Understanding Stress: Signs, Symptoms, Causes, and Effects", "http://www.helpguide.org/mental/stress_signs.htm"www. helpguide.org/mental/stress_signs.htm. Reprinted with permission from "http://Helpguide.org"Helpguide.org © 2001–2010. All rights reserved. For more information, visit HYPERLINK "http://www.Helpguide.org"www.Helpguide.org.

Identifying Stress Antecedents Next, the students are prompted to identify the possible sources of stress in their lives, and differentiate between controllable and uncontrollable stressors. An interactive screen prompts them to check off stressors that they may be able to change, such as over-commitment, unhealthy relationships, and procrastination, and reminds them that they may be able to change or reduce the influence of each of these stressors. The next screen provides a checklist of stressors that may be out of their control, such as illness, financial problems, and being away from home. Once the stressors have been identified, students can then learn how to deal with them.

Stress Self-assessment At this point, students complete a 17-item lifestyle quiz to assess how the stress in their lives may be affecting their overall well-being. Areas include general health, healthy behaviours such as eating and exercise, social support, taking time to relax and have fun, and spirituality. After completing the self-test, areas where students are doing great, are doing well with room for improvement, and need improvement are highlighted on the screen. In addition, clicking on each of the areas provides an overview of why it is important for managing stress along with specific suggestions on how to make improvements in that area of life.

Stress-management Tips The next section of the Students and Stress program presents a variety of coping skills that can be used for managing stressors that may have been identified. Examples include reducing exposure to stressful world events, using positive self-talk, altering perceptions and attitudes to gain perspective on problems, writing and journaling about one's feelings, building a social support network, and using humour, to name a few.

Relaxation In addition to the stress-management tips, students in the Students and Stress program are made aware of how relaxation can help them return to a calm, balanced state by reducing heart and respiration rates. This section highlights the importance of deep breathing, meditation, yoga, Tai Chi, and visualization to help achieve a relaxed state. One screen actually includes a mini-guided visualization complete with the sound of crashing waves to help students picture themselves in a calm relaxation setting.

Test-taking Tips Students are provided with a variety of different tips specifically designed to help them mini-mize the stress from this common academic stressor, such getting a good night's sleep the night before and eating healthy foods such as complex carbohydrates to help keep their blood sugar levels balanced.

Time Management In the final section, students are reminded of the importance of managing their time so that they can effectively meet their academic demands. Suggestions include making to-do lists, breaking larger unmanageable projects into smaller more manageable ones to increase self-efficacy and successful completion, prioritizing, and learning not to overcommit.

Most stress-management programs include this cafeteria-like array of techniques so that people have a broad set of skills from which to choose. The interactive, online format of the Students and Stress program offers a quick and easy way for people to learn about these techniques, although without the opportunity to fully acquire and test the effectiveness of each skill. Nonetheless, it helps students discover the skills that may work best for them, and invites them to apply each toward reducing the stress in their lives. In these ways, individuals can "inoculate" themselves against stress (Meichenbaum & Turk, 1982). This **stress inoculation** training, as Meichenbaum and Turk called it, enables people to confront stressful events with a clear plan in mind and an array of potential measures that they can take before the stressful event becomes overwhelming.

Relaxation Training and Stress Management

Relaxation training techniques, like the ones suggested in the Students and Stress program, are designed to affect the physiological experience of stress by reducing arousal.

Relaxation training therapies include progressive muscle relaxation training, guided imagery, transcendental meditation, and other forms of meditation, including yoga and hypnosis. These techniques can reduce heart rate, skin conductance, muscle tension, blood pressure, inflammatory processes, lipid levels, energy utilization, self-reports of anxiety, and tension (Barnes, Davis, Murzynowski, & Treiber, 2004; Lutgendorf, Anderson, Sorosky, Butler, & Lubaroff, 2000; Scheufele, 2000; R. H. Schneider et al., 1998; Speca, Carlson, Goodey, & Angen, 2000).

Because of the value of relaxation for health and mental health, students in a stress-management program are often trained in relaxation therapy. First, they learn how to control their breathing, taking no more than six to eight breaths per minute. They are trained to relax the muscles in each part of the body progressively, until they experience no tension (progressive muscle relaxation). They are urged to identify the particular spots that tense up during times of stress, such as a jaw that clamps shut or fists that tighten up. By becoming especially aware of these reactions, they can relax these parts of the body as well. Thus, for example, when students find that the stress of university life is catching up with them, they can take a 5- or 10-minute break in which they breathe deeply and relax completely. They can return to their tasks free of some of their previous tensions.

Exercise as Stress Management   The fact that exercise improves well-being suggests that it might be an effective way of managing stress. Research suggests that this intuition is well placed. One study of post-menopausal women found that those who were sedentary reported more stress and had a greater chance of having shorter telomeres at the end of their chromosomes—a reliable marker of chronic stress—compared to women who exercised regularly (Puterman et al., 2010). Thus, exercise may be a useful resource for combating the adverse health effects of stress (for example, C. M Castro, Wilcox, O'Sullivan, Baumann, & King, 2002). Exercise improves self-concept, and self concept in turn improves the likelihood of continuing exercise (Dishman et al, 2006; Marsh, Papaionnou, & Theodorakis, 2006).

One possible mechanism whereby exercise may buffer certain adverse health effects of stress involves its beneficial impact on immune functioning (Friedrich, 2008). An increase in endogenous opioids (natural pain inhibitors; see Chapter 10) stimulated by exercise may also play a role in the modulation of immune activity during periods of psychological stress.

Supplementary Stress-management Skills

In addition to the basic cognitive and relaxation skills of stress management, many programs also include training in supplementary skills. In many cases, the experience of stress depends heavily on feeling that one has too much to do in too little time. Recall the research from Box 7.1 highlighting the links between procrastination and stress. Consequently, many stress-management programs include training in **time management** and planning. This training helps students

set specific work goals for each day, establish priorities, avoid time wasters, and learn what to ignore altogether. Similar to making implementation intentions, a student may learn to set aside two hours for a particularly important task, such as studying for a test. In this way, the student has a particular goal and particular time period in which to pursue it and therefore is less subject to interruption. Simple how-to manuals effectively illustrate the time-management approach to stress management.

Like the Students and Stress program, many stress-management programs emphasize good health habits and social skills as additional techniques for the control of stress. These include good eating habits, exercise, assertiveness in social situations, and using social support. Stress often affects eating habits adversely: People under stress consume too many stimulants (such as coffee), too much sugar, and too much junk food. By learning to control dietary habits effectively and by eating three balanced meals a day, the student can ameliorate physiological reactions to stress. Likewise, regular exercise reduces stress.

Assertiveness training is sometimes incorporated into stress management. Often, people experience stress because they are unable to confront the people who contribute to their stress. For example, students who have identified other individuals in their environment as causing them special stress (called **stress carriers**) may help one another practise dealing with these individuals. One student may practise approaching a professor with whom he is having difficulty communicating; another student may practise dealing tactfully with a roommate who constantly brags about how well she is doing in her classes.

As we have already seen, social support can buffer the adverse effects of stress. Unfortunately, people under stress sometimes alienate rather than effectively engage those people who might provide social support. A harried executive snaps at his wife and children, or a student facing a threatening exam angrily rejects a friend's well-intentioned advice. Students in a stress-management program are trained to recognize the important functions that social support can serve in helping them manage stress. They are urged to confide in close friends, to seek advice from people who can help them, and to use their relationships with other people as sources of positive reinforcement after successfully meeting their goals. ●

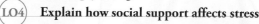

SUMMARY

LO1 Describe and define coping

- Coping is the process of managing demands that tax or exceed a person's resources. Coping is influenced by primary appraisals ("Is the event harmful, threatening, or challenging?") and by secondary appraisals ("What are my coping resources and how adequate are they?").

- Selection of coping efforts is guided by internal and external resources. Internal resources include preferred coping style and other personality factors, such as negativity, hardiness, optimism, and control.

- Coping styles consist of predispositions to cope with stressful situations in particular ways. Avoidance versus confrontation is one prominently studied coping style. Research has explored the value of emotional disclosure.

LO2 Know the role of external coping resources

- External resources include time, money, the presence of other simultaneous life stressors, and social support.

- Coping efforts may be directed at solving problems or at regulating emotions. Most stressful events evoke both types of coping, as well as more specific strategies.

LO3 List coping outcomes

- The tasks toward which coping efforts are typically directed include reducing harmful

environmental conditions and enhancing the adjustment process, tolerating and adjusting to negative events and realities, maintaining a positive self-image, maintaining emotional equilibrium, and continuing satisfying relations with others.

- Coping efforts are judged to be successful when they reduce physiological indicators of arousal, enable the person to return to prestress activities, and free the individual from psychological distress.

LO4 Explain how social support affects stress

- Social support can be an effective resource in times of stress. It reduces psychological distress and the likelihood of illness. However, some events can undermine or threaten social support resources.

LO5 Describe coping interventions

- Because not everyone can find ways to successfully cope with stressors on their own, a variety of interventions for coping with stress have been developed. These include mindfulness-based stress reduction (MBSR) programs, disclosure, and basic stress-management techniques. Each of these approaches offers coping tools to help people respond to stress in less harmful ways.

KEY TERMS

approach (confrontative, or vigilant) coping style   p. 192
avoidant (minimizing) coping style   p. 192
buffering hypothesis   p. 202
coping   p. 185
coping outcomes   p. 199
coping style   p. 192
direct effects hypothesis   p. 202
dispositional optimism   p. 188
dyadic coping   p. 203
emotional support   p. 199

emotion-focused coping   p. 193
implicit social support   p. 200
informational support   p. 199
invisible support   p. 199
matching hypothesis   p. 204
mindfulness-based stress reduction (MBSR)   p. 206
negative affectivity   p. 186
perfectionism   p. 188
pessimism   p. 187
pessimistic explanatory style   p. 187

problem-focused coping   p. 193
psychological control   p. 191
social support   p. 199
stress carriers   p. 210
stress inoculation   p. 209
stress management   p. 207
stress moderators   p. 185
tangible assistance   p. 199
time management   p. 210

part *four*

The Patient in the Treatment Setting

Using Health Services

LEARNING OBJECTIVES

After reading this chapter, students will be able to:

(LO1) Explain how people recognize and interpret symptoms

(LO2) Know what predicts the use of health services

(LO3) Describe how health services are misused

(LO4) Understand how hospitalization impacts the patient

(LO5) Describe how control can be increased in hospital settings

Some years ago, creative puppeteer Jim Henson died abruptly in his mid-50s from an apparent cold or flu that coursed rapidly through his system. Henson had been working long hours and was run down from heavy business and travel commitments, and although he knew he should see a doctor—his symptoms were getting worse—he put it off. When he finally did check into a hospital, the infection had spread so far that doctors could not save him. Generations of children and parents who had grown up with *Sesame Street* and who had come to love Kermit the Frog, Oscar, and the other endearing inventions of Henson's mind were stunned, not only by the abrupt ending to his outstanding career but by the form it took.

A few days later, my young son developed a cold and low-grade fever that proved to be surprisingly intractable to his usual medication. I took him to the medical centre immediately and was informed by the overworked but patient physician that my son was just fine, the infection was viral in origin, and there was nothing to do but keep him at home, give him lots of rest and fluids, and continue to administer medication on a regular basis. I felt silly and told the doctor that I had probably been a bit overzealous in coming to see him because the Jim Henson account had alarmed me so much. He smiled wearily and said, "Dr. Taylor, you are probably the 30th 'Jim Henson' mother we have seen here this week."

—*Author Shelley Taylor*

On the surface, the questions of who uses health services and why would seem to be a medical issue. That is, the decision to seek medical care for a health problem would appear to be the logical outcome of feeling sick. If this was true, then everyone who felt ill would flock to the doctor's office. And conversely, everyone who visited their physician would indeed have a physical illness. But not everyone who feels sick or is sick seeks medical care from a professional, and not everyone who seeks medical care is sick with a physical illness. Clearly, psychological, social, and cultural factors are also involved in the decision to seek medical care. So the question then becomes when and how does a person decide that he or she is sick? When are symptoms dismissed as inconsequential or acknowledged as something serious that requires immediate medical attention? When does a person decide that a symptom requires treatment by a professional, and when do chicken soup, fluids, and bed rest seem to be all that is needed?

HOW DO WE RECOGNIZE AND INTERPRET SYMPTOMS? L01

Although people have some awareness of what is going on in their bodies, that awareness may be limited. This limitation leaves a great deal of room for social and psychological factors to operate in the recognition of symptoms and the interpretation of illness (Petrie & Weinman, 1997). Recognizing and then interpreting symptoms as reflecting an illness are the necessary first steps before decisions to seek medical care can be made.

Recognition of a Symptom

> I have a tumor in my head the size of a basketball. I can feel it when I blink.
>
> —Woody Allen, *Hannah and Her Sisters*

Common observation reveals that some individuals maintain their normal activities in the face of what would seem to be overwhelming symptoms, whereas others take to their beds the moment they detect any minor bodily disturbance.

Individual Differences and Personality   Some of these individual differences are stable. That is, some people are consistently more likely to notice a symptom than other people are. Hypochondriacs, like characters that Woody Allen has played, are people who are preoccupied and worried that normal bodily symptoms are indicators of illness. Although hypochondriacs are only 4 percent to 5 percent of the population, because these individuals make such extensive use of medical care services, understanding who experiences symptoms more intensely is an important goal of health psychologists (Lecci & Cohen, 2002).

The most frequent symptoms that show up among patients who convert their distress into physical symptoms are back pain, joint pain, pain in the extremities, headache, abdominal symptoms such as bloating, "allergies" to particular foods, and cardiovascular symptoms such as palpitations (Carmin, Weigartz, Hoff, & Kondos, 2003; Rief, Hessel, & Braehler, 2001). Contrary to stereotypes, women are not more likely than men to report these symptoms. There are pronounced age effects with older people reporting more symptoms than young people.

Neuroticism also affects the perception of symptoms. Neuroticism is a pervasive dimension of personality marked by negative emotions, self-consciousness, and a concern with bodily processes. According to the symptom perception hypothesis (Watson & Pennebaker, 1989), people who are high in neuroticism or trait negative affectivity recognize their symptoms more quickly, report their symptoms more quickly, or both (P. Feldman, Cohen, Doyle, Skoner, & Gwaltney, 1999). It may be that neurotic, anxious people exaggerate their symptoms, or they may simply be more attentive to real symptoms (Gramling, Clawson, & McDonald, 1996; S. Ward & Leventhal, 1993).

A recent update of the symptom perception hypothesis proposes that anxiety and depression, two different forms of negative affectivity, have distinct roles in the experience of physical symptoms (Howren & Suls, 2011). Across several studies, depression was linked to increased physical symptom reporting but only when symptoms were recalled retrospectively. However, anxiety increased reports of physical symptoms only for concurrent or momentary physical symptoms. These differential associations are consistent with the notion that encoding and retrieval processes are distinct for anxious and depressed individuals, with depression linked to better retrieval of past symptoms, whereas anxiety heightens encoding of current symptoms.

Cultural Differences   There are reliable cultural differences in how quickly and what kind of symptoms are recognized (Kirmayer & Young, 1998). Cultural differences in symptom experience and reporting have been known about for decades (Zola, 1966), but the reasons underlying these differences are not fully understood. One possible explanation is that cultural variations in the emotional responses associated with the experience of troubling symptoms are partly responsible for the observed differences (Ots, 1990). Even symptoms arising from the same problem can be experienced differently as illustrated in the following example described by German physician Thomas Ots during his travels in China:

> "While riding a train, a Chinese friend and I had eaten a lot of snacks that did not mix well. I suddenly suffered from nausea and realized that I was pressing the epigastric region with one hand. I was sure that I had strained my stomach. At the same moment, my Chinese friend said that he was suffering from vertigo and he seemed very concerned about it. I inquired about his perception several times. He insisted that he was suffering from vertigo and only after some time he remarked that something was wrong with his stomach. I tried also to experience vertigo, and actually found it was not very difficult because the nausea was associated with a feeling of unclarity or confusion in my head."

(Ots, 1990, p. 39)

A comparative study of menopause symptom reporting among Canadian, American, and Japanese women provides an intriguing perspective on the possible reasons for cultural differences in symptom experiences. Compared to the North American women, the rates of multiple symptom reporting were significantly lower among the Japanese women, who were also more likely to report no menopause symptoms (Lock, 2002). In particular, hot flushes, a commonly reported symptom among North American women, were reported less frequently among the Japanese women. One explanation is that the Japanese word, *konenki,* which translates approximately to the English term menopause, has a very different meaning, which may influence whether symptoms are recognized as being part of menopause. However, Japanese women are among the healthiest in the world, engaging in healthy eating and activity, and have few chronic health conditions compared to women in North America. Soy beans and certain teas consumed by Japanese women are well known to reduce hot flushes (Lock, 1993). Thus, it would appear that cultural differences in symptom reporting may be accounted for not only by socio-cultural differences in language and meaning but also perhaps by biological variations in the experience of symptoms associated with different lifestyles (Lock, 2002).

Situational Factors   Situational factors influence whether a person will recognize a symptom. A boring situation makes people more attentive to symptoms than an interesting situation does. For example, people are more likely to notice itching or tickling in their throats and to cough in response to the sensations during boring parts of movies than during interesting parts (Pennebaker, 1980). A symptom is more likely to be perceived on a day when a person is at home than on a day full of frenzied activity. Intense physical activity takes attention away from symptoms, whereas quiescence increases the likelihood of their recognition.

Any situational factor that makes illness or symptoms especially salient promotes their recognition. For example, a common phenomenon in medical school is **medical students' disease.** As they study each illness, many members of the class imagine that they have it. Studying the symptoms leads students to focus on their own fatigue and other internal states; as a consequence, symptoms consistent with the illness under study seem to emerge (Mechanic, 1972). Interestingly, as students learn more about the different diseases, the distress from, but not the perceptions of, apparent symptoms tends to decrease. This suggests that medical students' disease may be a normal process rather than hypochondriasis (Moss-Morris & Petrie, 2001).

Stress   Stress can precipitate or aggravate the experience of symptoms. People who are under stress may believe that they are more vulnerable to illness and so attend more closely to their bodies. Financial strain, disruptions in personal relationships, and other stressors can lead people to believe that they are ill (Alonso & Coe, 2001; Angel, Frisco, Angel, & Ciraboga, 2003), perhaps because they experience stress-related physiological changes, such as accelerated heartbeat or breathing, and interpret these changes as symptoms of illness (L. Cameron, Leventhal, & Leventhal, 1995). In other instances, the symptoms people experience are real but their perception and interpretation of the meaning of the symptoms may be exaggerated if they are under stress. For certain disorders, such as arthritis and inflammatory bowel disease, stress may trigger symptoms or flare-ups of existing health problems.

Mood   Mood influences self-appraised health. People who are in a positive mood rate themselves as more healthy, report fewer illness-related memories, and report fewer symptoms. People in a negative mood, however, report more symptoms, are more pessimistic that any actions they might take would relieve their symptoms, and perceive themselves as more vulnerable to future illness than do people in positive moods (E. A. Leventhal, Hansell, Diefenbach, Leventhal, & Glass, 1996; Salovey, O'Leary, Stretton, Fishkin, & Drake, 1991). Even people who have diagnosed illnesses report fewer or less serious symptoms when they are in a positive mood (Gil et al., 2004).

Summary   Symptom recognition is determined both by individual differences in attention to one's body and by transitory situational factors that influence the direction of one's attention. When attention is directed outward, as by vigorous physical activity or a highly distracting environment, symptoms are less likely to be noticed. When attention is directed toward the body, on the other hand, as by cues that suggest illness, symptoms are more likely to be detected.

Interpretation of Symptoms

Any time someone sneezes or coughs these days, nobody says "Bless you" anymore. They just say, "SARS!"
—A TORONTO NURSE SHORTLY AFTER THE SARS OUTBREAK (EVENSON, 2003)

The interpretation of symptoms is also a heavily psychological process. As the above quote illustrates, understanding the contextual factors surrounding the symptom can often provide valuable clues about how it may be interpreted. Consider the following incident. At a large metropolitan hospital, a man in his late twenties came to the emergency room with the sole symptom of a sore throat. He brought with him six of his relatives: his mother, father, sister, aunt, and two cousins. Because patients usually go to an emergency room with only one other person and because a sore throat is virtually never seen in the emergency room, the staff were understandably curious about the reason for his visit. There was much chuckling about how Italian families stick together and how they panic at any sign of a disturbance in health. But one particularly sensitive medical student reasoned that something more must have caused the man to come to the emergency room with his entire family in tow, so he probed cautiously but persistently during the intake interview with the patient. Gradually, it emerged that the young man's brother had died a year earlier of Hodgkin's disease, a form of cancer that involves the progressive infection and enlargement of the lymph nodes. The brother's first symptom had been a sore throat, which he and the family had allowed to go untreated.

This poignant incident illustrates how important social and psychological factors can be in understanding people's interpretations of their symptoms and their decisions to seek treatment (Frostholm et al., 2005). To this family, the symptom "sore throat" had special significance. It had a history for them that overrode its usual association with the beginnings of a cold (which is, in fact, what the young man turned out to have). Moreover, it symbolized for them a past failure of the family to respond adequately to an emergency, a failure that they were determined not to repeat. What this incident also illustrates, albeit in a less direct way, is that individual, historical, cultural, and social factors all conspire to produce an interpretation of the symptom experience.

Prior Experience   As the preceding incident attests, the interpretation of symptoms is heavily influenced by prior experience. People who have experience with a medical condition estimate the prevalence of their symptoms to be greater and often regard the condition as less serious than do people with no history of the condition (Jemmott, Croyle, & Ditto, 1988). A symptom's meaning is also influenced by how common it is within a person's range of acquaintances or culture (for example,

Croyle & Hunt, 1991). Highly prevalent risk factors and disorders are generally regarded as less serious than are rare or distinctive risk factors and disorders (Croyle & Ditto, 1990). The very fact that the symptom or condition is widespread may be seen as a reason for attaching little significance to it.

Expectations   Expectations play a role in the experience and interpretation of symptoms. For example, neuroimaging techniques have revealed that simply expecting symptoms activates brain areas associated with the experience of symptoms, whereas distracting oneself from symptoms reduces brain activity in the symptom perception areas (Rief & Broadbent, 2007).

Seriousness of the Symptoms   Symptoms that affect highly valued parts of the body are usually interpreted as more serious and as more likely to require attention than are symptoms that affect less valued organs. For example, people are especially anxious when their eyes or face are affected, rather than if the symptom involves part of the trunk. A symptom will be regarded as more serious and will be more likely to prompt the seeking of treatment if it limits mobility or if it affects a highly valued organ, such as chest discomfort thought to be indicative of heart disease (Eifert, Hodson, Tracey, Seville, & Gunawardane, 1996). Indeed, believing that a symptom has a profound impact on one's life, such as hand pain that limits daily activities, can prompt seeking medical care and/or taking medication (Hill, Dziedzic, Thomas, Baker, & Croft, 2007). Above all, if a symptom causes pain, it will lead a person to seek treatment more promptly than if it does not cause pain.

Cognitive Representations of Illness

Illness Schemas   People have concepts of health and illness that influence how they react to symptoms (Henderson, Hagger, & Orbell, 2007; Leventhal, Weinman, Leventhal, & Philips, 2008). Termed **illness representations** (or **schemas**), these organized conceptions of illness are acquired through the media (see the Spotlight on Canadian Research box, "Do People Recognize the Symptoms of Serious Illness?"), through personal experience, and from family and friends who have had experience with particular disorders (for a review, see Croyle & Barger, 1993).

Illness schemas range from being quite sketchy and inaccurate to being extensive, technical, and complete. Their importance stems from the fact that they lend coherence to

a person's comprehension of the illness experience (e.g., Hall, Weinman, & Marteau, 2004). Accordingly, they can influence people's preventive health behaviours, their reactions when they experience symptoms or are diagnosed with illness, their adherence to treatment recommendations, and their expectations for their health in the future (e.g., Rabin, Leventhal, & Goodin, 2004).

According to the self-regulatory model of illness cognitions (Leventhal et al., 2008), illness schemas have five distinct components that include basic information about an illness. The *identity,* or label, for an illness is its name; its *consequences* are its symptoms and treatments that result, as well as the extent to which the person believes the illness has ramifications for his or her life; its *causes* are the factors that the person believes gave rise to the illness, such as environmental or behavioural factors; *duration* refers to the expected length of time the illness is expected to last; and *cure* identifies whether the person believes the illness can be cured through appropriate treatment. The characteristics of illness cognitions accordingly guide decisions about the types of actions that may need to be taken to help cope with the perceived illness.

These illness conceptions appear to develop quite early in life (S. L. Goldman, Whitney-Saltiel, Granger, & Rodin, 1991). Most people have at least three models of illness (Leventhal et al., 2008):

- *Acute illness* is believed to be caused by specific viral or bacterial agents and is short in duration with no long-term consequences. An example is the flu.
- *Chronic illness* is caused by several factors, including health habits, and is long in duration, often with severe consequences. An example is heart disease.
- *Cyclic illness* is marked by alternating periods during which there are either no symptoms or many symptoms. An example is herpes.

There is considerable variability in the disease models that people hold for their disorders, and the disease model a person holds can greatly influence their behaviour related to that disease. For example, diabetes may be seen by one individual as an acute condition caused by a diet high in sugar, whereas another person with the same disease may see it as a genetic condition lasting for the rest of his or her life with potentially catastrophic consequences. Not surprisingly, these people will treat their disorders differently, maintain different levels of vigilance toward symptoms, and show different patterns of seeking treatment (Lange & Piette, 2006; Weinman, Petrie, Moss-Morris, & Horne, 1996). People's conceptions

Do People Recognize the Symptoms of Serious Illness?

For certain life-threatening illnesses, such as heart disease or stroke, recognizing that certain symptoms may reflect a serious health problem that requires immediate medical care is critical for survival. But recognizing the symptoms of a serious health problem depends on having an accurate illness schema. Misinterpreting symptoms, or not attributing them to something potentially life threatening, can have harmful if not fatal consequences. One way to avoid these problems is to help people develop accurate illness schemas through public awareness campaigns.

The Heart and Stroke Foundation of Ontario did exactly this with their campaign, "Recognize the signs of stroke when you see them." This public education media campaign, which included 30-second television ads that aired in Ontario, spread a simple but important message:

> "Vision problems . . . Headache . . . Weakness . . . Trouble speaking . . . Dizziness
>
> "The sudden appearance of any of these symptoms can mean that you are having a stroke. Get immediate medical attention. Call 911 or your local emergency number."

But was this ad effective in influencing illness schemas for stroke and subsequent medical care seeking? To answer this question, researchers used the Ontario stroke registry to examine emergency room (ER) visits for stroke and ER visits for which a diagnosis of stroke was made, and also conducted brief telephone polls with 1,000 Ontario residents to find out how many of the warning signs of stroke they could spontaneously name (Hodgson, Lindsay, & Rubini, 2007). The two ad campaigns were run from late 2003 to mid-2004, and again from late 2004 to mid-2005. There were also two blackout periods, one in-between the two campaigns and again after the second campaign, in which the ads did not run. Six polls were conducted: two during and right after each of the two campaigns, one before the campaign, and one five months after the campaign during the second blackout. Over the study period there was a significant increase in the public's awareness of the warning signs of stroke. However, awareness decreased slightly after the final five-month blackout period. More importantly, the number of ER visits for stroke increased significantly during the campaign, suggesting that the increased awareness about the warning signs for stroke created by the campaign may have led more people to seek medical attention for suspected stroke.

Despite the promising results from this media campaign, a recent survey by the Heart and Stroke Foundation of Canada (2011a) found that stroke awareness is alarmingly low among women, and among women of Chinese and South Asian descent in particular. When asked to correctly identify at least two of the five warning signs of stroke, only 53 percent of South Asian women were able to do so. This compares to the national average of 62 percent of women.

To address this and other stroke awareness issues, the Heart and Stroke Foundation has released two free smart phone apps to help Canadians reduce their risk of stroke. Clearly, more work is needed to increase awareness among Canadian women of the signs and symptoms of stroke.

Source: The Heart and Stroke Foundation, 2007c.

---

of disease give them a basis for interpreting new information, influence their treatment-seeking decisions, lead them to alter or fail to adhere to their medication regimens (Coutu, Dupuis, D'Antono, & Rochon-Goyer, 2003), and influence expectations about future health (G. D. Bishop & Converse, 1986). The conception of disease an individual holds, then, determines health behaviours in important ways.

The Lay Referral Network

The meaning of a symptom ultimately blends into diagnosis, a process that begins not in the physician's office but in an individual's conversations with friends, neighbours, and relatives. Sociologists have written at length about the **lay referral network,** an informal network of family and friends who offer their own interpretations of symptoms well before any medical treatment is sought (Freidson, 1960). This lay referral network offers advice and support for the individual experiencing troubling symptoms, and reflects a network of social contacts starting from the more intimate nuclear family through to successively more informed and authoritative lay people. The patient may mention the symptoms to a family member or co-worker, who may then respond with personal views of what the symptom is likely to mean

("George had that, and it turned out to be nothing at all"; cf. Croyle & Hunt, 1991). The friend or relative may offer advice about the advisability of seeking medical treatment ("All he got for going to see the doctor was a wasted afternoon in the waiting room") and recommendations for various home remedies ("Honey, lemon juice, and a little brandy will clear that right up").

In many communities, the lay referral network is the preferred mode of treatment. One study found that 70 percent of people engage in conversation with people in their lay referral networks about whether to seek medical care for new symptoms that they experience (Cornford & Cornford, 1999). These lay referral networks often recommend home remedies and other alternative forms of medicine as more appropriate or more effective than traditional medicine. For example, many people who use alternative and complementary therapies do so because of the recommendation of friends and family members (Caspi, Koithan, & Criddle, 2004; Robinson & Cooper, 2007).

Nonetheless, the use of alternative forms of medicine is on the rise, and as a consequence, the United Nation's World Health Organization has taken the unprecedented step of evaluating the efficacy of these treatments (McNeil, 2002). For example, the Chinese herb ma huang helps breathing problems that can cause heart attacks and stroke in some individuals. Ginkgo biloba stimulates circulation but can also enhance bleeding, which is risky during surgery. The goal of the World Health Organization's effort is to catalogue all alternative remedies to identify those that are both successful and not risky and to reduce or eliminate use of those that are unsuccessful or risky.

In Canada, complementary and alternative therapies are gaining popularity and acceptance, and are less likely to be viewed as simply unconventional or folk medicine. Complementary and alternative therapies can take many forms and can be self-administered or delivered by a practitioner. **Natural health products (NHP),** for example, include vitamins, minerals, herbal remedies and teas, and plant products, with 71 percent of Canadian reporting trying NHPs, and about 38 percent reporting daily use (Health Canada, 2005b). Use of complementary and alternative health care is less widespread with about one in five Canadians consulting a complementary and alternative therapy provider, such as a chiropractor or acupuncturist, over the course of a year (Park, 2005). The reasons why people may choose to use complementary therapies to treat their health problems will be examined in more depth in Chapter 9.

What therapies are people using? Most commonly, Canadians consult chiropractors, massage therapists, and acupuncturists, and use vitamins, echinacea, and herbal remedies as NHPs (Health Canada, 2005b; Park, 2005). However, complementary therapies can also include relaxation techniques, imagery, spiritual healing, energy healing, biofeedback, hypnosis, homeopathy, and reflexology. As the name suggests, these therapies are used mainly to complement rather than to replace conventional treatment. However, health care providers are typically unaware that their patients are supplementing their care with complementary therapy, which can increase the risk of treatment conflicts.

The Internet

The Internet may well constitute a lay referral network of its own. On a typical day, almost 4 million Canadians will seek health information online. Indeed, there has been a dramatic 262 percent increase in the number of households in Canada looking for health information online between 1998 and 2002 (Earl, 2004). Seeking health information online is a common activity with almost six out of every ten Internet users reporting that they have used the Internet to find health information (Underhill & McKeown, 2008). Who is most likely to use the Internet for health information? Women are twice as likely as men to try and find answers to health questions on the Internet, and households with children are far more likely than those without children (Earl, 2004; Underhill & McKeown, 2008). Young men, ages 15 to 24, are the least likely to search out health information on the Web (Stevenson, 2002).

What types of health information are Internet users looking for? The most common information searched for is related to specific diseases and health conditions, with nearly 5 million Canadians using the Internet for this purpose. Lifestyle information, including diet, nutrition, and exercise, is the next most frequent searchedfor health topic. The remaining topics include information about specific symptoms, drugs and medications, complementary and alternative therapies, and the health care system (Underhill & McKeown, 2008). Among those with chronic health conditions, the Internet is used mainly for information about possible treatments and the application of treatments, with scientific websites being visited most often (Khechine, Pascot, & Premont, 2008).

Are these trends worrisome? According to a recent study of physicians, 96 percent said that they believe that the Internet will affect health care positively, and many turn to the Internet themselves for the most up-to-date information on illnesses, treatments, and the healthy lifestyle tips. One excellent source of health-related issues is the Health Canada Web site (www.hc-sc.gc.ca). However, some of what is seen on the Internet is not accurate (Kalichman et al., 2006), and some health-related Internet sites want you to pick up a shopping cart and buy their products. Nonetheless, it is evident the Internet is playing an increasingly major role in providing the information that people get about symptoms, illnesses, and their treatment.

Critical Checkpoint

Getting Help to Determine the Seriousness of Symptoms

Whether someone seeks medical care for symptoms depends upon a variety of factors including whether the symptom is perceived to be serious or not. People may seek the advice of friends and family members or even the Internet to guide their choice to seek care. What are the advantages and disadvantages of using such advice for serious and not so serious symptoms?

(LO2) WHAT PREDICTS THE USE OF HEALTH SERVICES?

Canada's publicly funded health care system provides universal access to several key health care services, including physicians and hospitals. Compared to Americans, whose health care is mainly funded through private insurance, somewhat fewer Canadians report difficulties accessing health care when needed. Wait times tend to be the main reason for not getting care when needed in Canada, whereas cost is the main barrier in the United States (Sanmartin, Ng, Blackwell, Gentleman, Martinez, & Simile, 2004). Despite these differences, the apparent advantages of Canada's health care system do not ensure that all Canadians will use health care services when they are needed or that they will always be used in the best way.

Recall from Chapter 1 that from a public health perspective, health services are a key social determinant of health. Accordingly, it is important to understand the factors that predict whether and how someone uses health care services, as well as the type of services used.

Symptom perception and interpretation is central to appraising whether one is ill and if medical care should be sought (Anderson, Cacioppo, & Roberts, 1995; L. Cameron, Leventhal, & Leventhal, 1995). The presence of atypical or numerous symptoms, a serious illness, or disability are common reasons that people seek help (L. Cameron, Leventhal, & Leventhal, 1993; Gick & Thompson, 1997). However, other individual and social factors also play a role in the use of health services.

Age

Age influences the use of health care services, with the very young and the elderly using health care services most frequently (Meara, White, & Cutler, 2004). Young children develop a number of infectious childhood diseases as they are acquiring their immunities and therefore they frequently require the care of a physician. Young children are also more likely to experience unintentional injuries such as falls and poisonings. In 2006 and 2007, children under 5 accounted for more emergency department visits than any other age group (Canadian Institute for Health Information, 2008a). Both illness and unintentional accident frequency and the use of services decline in adolescence and throughout young adulthood. Use of health services increases again in late adulthood, when people begin to develop chronic conditions and diseases, and continues to increase as people age. A national study found that among Canadian seniors, advancing age was associated with consulting a physician and making multiple consultations even after controlling for chronic health conditions and other factors (Nabalamba & Millar, 2007). Given the greying of the Canadian population, the increase in health service use associated with aging and the burden this will place on the health care system in the future is an important issue that will soon have to be dealt with.

Gender

Women use the health care system more than men do. For example, women are more likely to consult a physician and make multiple consultations than men (Statistics Canada, 2001a; Nabalamba & Millar, 2007). Pregnancy and childbirth account for much of the gender difference in health services use, but not all. Various explanations have been offered, including, for example, that women have better homeostatic mechanisms than men do: They report pain earlier, experience temperature changes more rapidly, and detect new smells faster.

Thus, they may also be more sensitive to bodily disruptions, especially minor ones (for example, H. Leventhal, Diefenbach, & Leventhal, 1992). However, as women age their use of some health care services becomes more similar to men's use. Among Canadian seniors, rates of making single and multiple visits to their family doctor did not differ from men after controlling for chronic health conditions and self-reported health status (Nabalamba & Millar, 2007).

Another possible explanation stems from the different social norms for men and women regarding the expression of pain and discomfort. Men are expected to project a tough, macho image, which includes being able to ignore pain and not give in to illness, whereas women are not subject to these same pressures (Klonoff & Landrine, 1992).

Economic factors may also be important. Because more women are part-time workers and nonworkers, they do not have to take time off from work to seek treatment and they do not lose income when they are ill. However, the same factors—namely, that women are less likely to be employed, are more likely to work part-time, and experience more economic hardship—also contribute to women's poorer health (C. E. Ross & Bird, 1994).

Research suggests that women use health care services more often because their medical care is more fragmented. Medical care for most men occurs through a trip to a general practitioner for a physical examination that includes all preventive care. But women may visit a general practitioner for a general physical, a gynecologist for Pap tests, and a breast cancer specialist or mammography service for breast examinations and mammograms. Thus, women may use services more than men in part because medical care is not particularly well structured to meet their basic needs.

Socio-economic Status

Although Canada's universal health care system was intended to provide equitable access to needed medical services for people from all socio-economic groups, this is not always the case. Income, education, and culture are associated with how and when health services are used.

Differences in the use of health care services based on socio-economic status (SES) are somewhat paradoxical. On the one hand, people in the lowest-income households and with less than high school education

Women use medical services more than men, they may be sick more than men, and their routine care requires more visits than men. It is often easier for women to use services, and they require services for such gender-related needs as maternity care.

are less likely to have visited a family physician or a specialist in a year compared to those in the highest income groups or with post-secondary education. On the other hand, people with lower incomes and education who do consult a family physician are more likely to make four or more visits to physicians in a given year compared to those with a higher SES (Nabalamba & Millar, 2007). They also make more emergency room visits, and have more hospital admissions than those with higher incomes (Johansen & Millar, 1999). A similar pattern of health service use is seen for rural-dwelling Canadians. People who live in rural areas have less access to health services, and specialists in particular, and are also more likely to have a lower SES than urban dwelling Canadians (Canadian Institute for Health Information, 2006b). Differences in access to health services and how they are used may be one explanation for this paradoxical pattern of health care use among Canadians with low SES.

However, when it comes to health services not covered by Canada's medical insurance, people living in low income situations are less likely to have dental and prescription drug coverage (Johansen & Millar, 1999).

Culture

Cultural factors influence the types of medical and health services that people use. In 2001, a large national survey found that the use of health services varied considerably by ethnicity in Canada. After accounting for differences in socio-demographic and health characteristics, members of ethnic minority groups were more likely to visit a physician but not a specialist, than Caucasians. Minority groups also used cancer screening services such as having a mammogram, Pap test, or prostate screening less often (Quan et al., 2006). However, a national survey suggests a slightly different pattern of use. According to the 2005 Canadian Community Health Survey, Aboriginal peoples, those of African or Caribbean origin, and members of other ethnic minorities were no more likely to have consulted a physician in the previous year than Caucasians, after accounting for differences in health and demographic factors. Those from an ethnic minority were much more likely to make four or more visits to the doctor compared to non-minority Canadians. And consistent with the 2001 survey, those from an ethnic minority were also less likely to visit a specialist (Nabalamba & Millar, 2007). Because specialist referrals are usually made through the primary health care provider (e.g., family physician), cultural differences in how symptoms are expressed or even disclosed, may partially explain why people from ethnic minorities make fewer specialist visits.

Linguistic barriers may also influence the use of health care services. For example, researchers at Bishop's University found that Anglophones living in the Quebec Eastern Townships not only perceived that there were fewer health care services in English available to them than there actually were, but they were more dissatisfied with the services offered and therefore less likely to want to use these services in the future (Charpentier, Stout, Benoit, Poulin, & Philip, 2011). What's more, the perception of not having readily available health care in English impacted Anglophone's future perceptions of their health, with Anglophones rating their future health as significantly poorer than that of Francophones if they remained living in Quebec (Stout, Charpentier, Chiasson, & Fillion, 2009). Such misperceptions about the availability of health services can contribute to low use among members of a socially cohesive minority group. Using data from three cycles of the Canadian National Population Health Survey, one study found that health care service utilization by immigrants was related to the number of doctors in their neighbourhood who spoke their first language (Deri, 2005). Providing linguistic minorities with language appropriate health care services is therefore one important way to increase the appropriate use of health services.

Social Psychological Factors

Social psychological factors—that is, an individual's attitudes and beliefs about symptoms and health services, influence who uses health service. As we saw in Chapter 3, the health belief model maintains that whether a person seeks treatment for a symptom can be predicted from two factors: (1) the extent to which the person perceives a threat to health, and (2) the degree to which he or she believes that a particular health measure will be effective in reducing that threat.

A large number of studies suggest that the health belief model explains people's use of services quite well. The health belief model does a better job of explaining the treatment-seeking behaviour of people who access to health care services than of people who do not.

The use of health care services is influenced by socialization, chiefly by the actions of one's parents. Just as children and adolescents learn other behaviours from their parents, they also learn when and how to use health care services. For example, someone who was raised in a family where scheduling a visit to the family doctor was the norm whenever a troubling symptom was experienced will similarly be inclined to visit the doctor for their symptoms. And conversely, someone growing up in a family that only used health care services for serious medical emergencies may rarely visit their family doctor unless symptoms are viewed as being serious.

Health services, then, are used by people who have the need, time, prior experience, beliefs that favour the use of services, and access to services (R. M. Andersen, 1995).

HOW ARE HEALTH SERVICES MISUSED? (L03)

Health services may be misused as well as used. In this section, we consider several types of misuse. One type of misuse occurs when people seek out health services for problems that are not medically significant, overloading the medical system. Another significant type of misuse involves delay, when people should seek health care for a problem but do not. Similar to the factors that influence the use of health care services in general, symptom interpretation and meaning, cultural values and norms, attitudes towards health care, and accessibility to health care are implicated in the misuse of health services.

Using Health Services for Emotional Disturbances

Physicians estimate that as much as two-thirds of their time is taken up by patients whose complaints are psychological rather than medical. This problem is more common for general practitioners than for specialists, although no branch of medicine is immune. (University health services periodically experience a version of this phenomenon during exam time; see the Health Psychology in Action box, "University Students' Disease.") These nonmedical complaints typically stem from anxiety and depression, both of which, unfortunately, are widespread (e.g., Franko et al., 2005). Sometimes, however, these symptoms may be due to an independent physical problem the symptoms of which are difficult to disentangle from those more directly linked to the psychological disorder. Further complicating the issue is the possibility that the symptoms may be medically unexplainable but not attributable to mental health issues (see Box 11.2 in Chapter 11), suggesting that, in some cases, what can appear as misuse may in fact be appropriate use of medical services. These occasions aside, using health services to deal with problems associated with mental health issues either mistakenly or purposely is potentially problematic.

Why do people seek a physician's care when their complaints should be addressed by a mental health specialist? There are several reasons (Rief, Martin, Klaiberg, & Brahler, 2005). Stress and the emotional responses to it create a number of physical symptoms and so during stressful times people use health services more. Anxiety, depression, and other psychological disorders are accompanied by a number of physical symptoms. Anxiety can produce diarrhea, upset stomach, sweaty hands, shortness of breath, difficulty in sleeping, poor concentration, and general agitation. Depression can lead to fatigue, difficulty in performing everyday activities, listlessness, loss of appetite, and sleep disturbances. Indeed, Canadians who make emergency room visits are also more likely to have consulted mental health professionals (Carrière, 2004). People may mistake the symptoms of their mood disorder for a legitimate medical problem and thus seek a physician's care (Goodwin, Lewinsohn, & Seeley, 2004; Haug, Mykletum, & Dahl; Smith et al., 2005). Anxiety and depression may not only influence the likelihood of seeking contact initially but also lead to recurrent visits and prolong hospital stays as well (De Jonge, Latour, & Huyse, 2003; Rubin, Cleare, & Hotopf, 2004). Finally, limited access to mental health specialists may mean that seeking help from a medical doctor is the only available option for those who do not enjoy the benefits of extended health care coverage.

Who are these people? One group is the **worried well.** These people are concerned about physical and mental health, inclined to perceive minor symptoms as serious, and believe that they should take care of their own health. Paradoxically, their commitment to self-care actually leads them to use health services more (Wagner & Curran, 1984). The emphasis that our culture places on living a healthy lifestyle and media attention to new health problems and technologies may inadvertently have increased the number of worried well people who use health services inappropriately (Petrie & Wessely, 2002).

Another group of inappropriate users are **somaticizers** —that is, individuals who express distress and conflict through bodily symptoms (Miranda, Perez- Stable, Munoz, Hargreaves, & Heike, 1991). When they have experienced a threat to self-esteem or to their accomplishments, such individuals are especially likely to somaticize, convince themselves they are physically ill, and seek treatment. This issue is so problematic that a study in the *Annals of Internal Medicine* suggested that physicians begin all their patient interviews with the direct questions "Are you currently sad or depressed?" and "Are the things that previously brought you pleasure no longer bringing you pleasure?" Positive answers to these questions would suggest that a patient may need treatment for depression as well as, or even instead of, medical treatment (Means-Christensen, Arnau, Tonidandel, Bramson, & Meagher, 2005; Pignone et al., 2002; Rhee, Holditch-Davis, & Miles, 2005). Unfortunately, psychiatric disorders continue to be underrecognized and therefore undertreated in primary care (Jackson, Passamonti, & Kroenke, 2007).

Often patients present with multiple physical symptoms that are chronic, unresponsive to treatment, and unexplained by any medical diagnosis; these patients are *polysymptomatic somaticizers* (Interian et al., 2004). Although a number of psychosocial interventions have been attempted with this group, so far these interventions have not had a lasting impact or reduced the psychiatric problems associated with the physical complaints of these somaticizers (L. A. Allen, Escobar, et al., 2002).

There is some evidence that somaticization and related hypochondriasis is more of an interpersonal disorder than a vigilance to or misinterpretation of low-level symptoms. Thus, people with interpersonal problems may seek reassurance by gaining medical attention (Noyes, Stuart, et al., 2003).

University Students' Disease

Visit the health service of any college or university just before exams begin and you will see a unit bracing itself for an onslaught. Admissions to health services can double or even triple as papers become due and examinations begin. Why does this influx occur?

Some of the increase in health service visits is due to an actual increase in illness. Students who are under pressure to do well work long hours and eat and sleep poorly. Others with fewer financial resources may be struggling to balance academic and work demands and find themselves with little time to take care of themselves. Some students who procrastinate by leaving their term work and studying to the last minute may be particularly stressed. As they run themselves down, their vulnerability to many common disorders can increase. For example, any one individual who develops an infectious disorder can give it to others who live in close proximity.

Some students may not actually be sick, but they think they are. Stressors, such as exams, can produce a variety of symptoms—such as inability to concentrate, sleeplessness, and upset stomach—which may be mistaken for illness. Moreover, exam time may preclude other activities that would provide distraction, so students may be more aware of these symptoms than they would otherwise be. In addition, the "symptoms" may make it hard for students to study, and disruption in important activities often acts as an impetus for seeking treatment.

Finally, there is the self-handicapper with four papers due but enough time to complete only two of them because of poor time management. What better excuse than illness for failure to meet one's obligations? Illness legitimizes procrastination, lack of motivation, lack of activity, and a host of other personal failures.

Another reason that people use health services for psychological complaints is that medical disorders are perceived as more legitimate than psychological ones. For example, a man who is depressed by his job and who stays home to avoid it will find that his behaviour is more acceptable to both his boss and his wife if he says he is ill than if he admits he is depressed. Many people are even unwilling to admit to themselves that they have a psychological problem, believing that it is shameful to see a mental health specialist or to have mental problems. Cultural differences can also play a role. For example, in Chinese society expressing emotional distress as a physical complaint is seen as more culturally acceptable, as mental health issues carry with them considerable stigma (Lee, Rodin, Devins, & Weiss, 2001). Some Chinese-Canadians may therefore feel more comfortable seeking medical help for psychological complaints (Mok & Morishita, 2002).

Illness brings benefits, termed **secondary gains,** including the ability to rest, to be freed from unpleasant tasks, to be cared for by others, and to take time off from work. These reinforcements can interfere with the process of returning to good health. Finally, the inappropriate use of health services can represent true malingering. A person who does not want to go to work may know all too well that the only acceptable excuse that will prevent dismissal for absenteeism is illness. Moreover, workers may be required to document their absences in order to collect wages or disability payments and may thus have to keep looking until they find a physician who is willing to "treat" the "disorder."

Unfortunately, the worried well and those who seek treatment for psychological symptoms or to meet other needs can be hard to discriminate from patients with legitimate medical complaints (Bombardier, Gorayeb, Jordan, Brooks, & Divine, 1991). Sometimes this differentiation means that patients are put through many tests and evaluations before it is concluded that there may be a psychological basis rather than a physical one for their discomfort. And given that visits to physicians are covered under Canada's publicly funded health care system whereas visits to mental health care professionals are not, seeking care from a medical professional may be the only option for those without extended health care insurance or the means to pay for mental health care services.

But because of this difficulty, errors can be made in the opposite direction as well: Individuals with legitimate medical problems may be falsely assumed to be psychologically disturbed. Research suggests that physicians are more likely to reach this conclusion about their female patients than their male patients (Redman, Webb, Hennrikus, Gordon, & Sanson-Fisher, 1991), even when objective measures suggest equivalent rates of psychological disturbance between men and women. Discriminating the truly physically ill from those who use health services to meet other needs can be a very tricky business, complicated by physician bias as well as patient misuse of the system.

Delay Behaviour

One morning, while Monica was taking a shower, she discovered a small lump in her left breast. She felt it a couple of times to make sure she wasn't just imagining it, but it was definitely there. A shudder of alarm passed through her, and she thought that she should go in and get it checked.

After she dried herself off and got dressed, she realized that that week would be a busy one and next week was no better. She had exams the following week, so she couldn't find any time in the next two to three weeks when she could get to the doctor to have it checked out.

"I'll have to wait until next month," she thought, "when things settle down a bit."

A very different misuse of health services occurs when an individual should seek treatment for a symptom but puts off doing so. A lump, chronic shortness of breath, blackouts, skin discoloration, radiating chest pain, seizures, and severe stomach pains are serious symptoms for which people should seek treatment promptly, yet an individual may live with one or more of these potentially serious symptoms for months without seeking care. This behaviour is called **delay behaviour.** For example, a major problem contributing to the high rate of death and disability from heart attacks is the fact that patients so often delay seeking treatment for its symptoms, instead normalizing them as gastric distress, muscle pain, and other, less severe disorders.

Delay is defined as the time between when a person recognizes a symptom and when the person obtains treatment. Delay is composed of several time periods, diagrammed in Figure 8.1: **appraisal delay,** which is the time it takes an individual to decide that a symptom is serious; **illness delay,** which is the time between the recognition that a symptom implies an illness and the decision to seek treatment; **behavioural delay,** which is the time between actually deciding to seek treatment and actually doing so (Safer, Tharps, Jackson, & Leventhal, 1979); and **medical delay** (scheduling and treatment), which is the time that elapses between the person's making an appointment and receiving appropriate medical care. Obviously, delay in seeking treatment for some symptoms is appropriate. For example, usually a runny nose or a mild sore throat will clear up on its own. However, in other cases, symptoms may be debilitating for weeks or months, and to delay seeking treatment is inappropriate.

Who Delays?   The reasons for delay have been extensively explored. Not surprisingly, the portrait of the delayer generally bears strong similarities to the portrait of the nonuser of services. The elderly appear to delay less than middle-aged individuals, particularly if they experience symptoms judged to be potentially serious (E. A. Leventhal, Easterling, Leventhal, & Cameron, 1995). Delay is common among people who do not have a regular physician, no doubt because in addition to seeking treatment, such individuals have the extra burden of finding someone from whom to seek it. In Canada, about 3.5 million adults do not have a regular family physician, and are therefore also less likely to visit a doctor (Nabalamba & Millar, 2007).

Delay, like nonuse of services in general, is also more common among people who seek treatment primarily in response to pain or social pressure. People who are fearful of doctors, examinations, surgery, and medical facilities generally delay longer than do people who are not fearful. People with generally good medical habits are less likely to delay, and they seek attention quickly for a condition that is unusual or potentially serious.

Because the delayer looks so much like the nonuser of services, one might expect the health belief model to predict delay behaviour as well as use of services. In fact, it does explain some delay behaviour. For example, people who fail to seek treatment for symptoms that may indicate cancer are more likely to believe that treatments will be extremely painful (high perceived barriers to, or "costs" of, treatment) and to believe that nothing can be done to cure cancer (low perceived efficacy of treatment; Safer et al., 1979).

Symptoms and Delaying   Another factor that predicts delay is the nature of the symptoms. When a symptom is similar to one that previously turned out to be minor, the individual will seek treatment less quickly than if the symptom is new (see, for example, Safer et al., 1979). For example, women with a history of benign breast lumps may be less likely to have a new suspicious lump checked out than women with no such history. Highly visible symptoms, symptoms that do not hurt, symptoms that do not change quickly, and symptoms that are not incapacitating are less likely than their opposites to prompt a person to seek medical treatment (Safer et al., 1979).

FIGURE 8.1 | **Stages of Delay in Seeking Treatment for Symptoms**

Source: B. L. Anderson, J. T. Cacioppo, & D. C. Roberts. "Delay in seeking a cancer diagnosis: Delay stages and psychophysiological comparison processes." *British Journal of Social Psychology* 34, 1995, Fig.1, p. 35. Used with permission by The British Psychological Society.

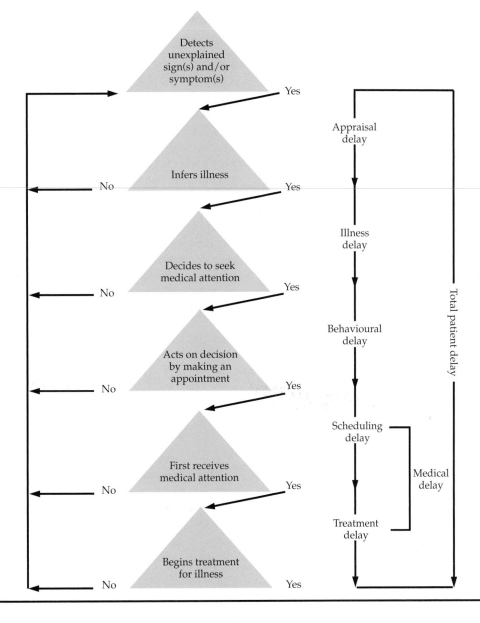

Any time a symptom is easily accommodated and does not provoke alarm, treatment may be delayed. For example, if the primary symptom is a breast problem or a lump suggestive of breast cancer, women are more likely to be treated promptly than if the primary symptom is atypical (Meechan, Collins, & Petrie, 2003).

Treatment Delay   Surprisingly, delay does not end with the first treatment visit. Even after a consultation, up to 25 percent of patients delay taking recommended treatments, put off getting tests, or postpone acting on referrals. In some cases, patients have had their curiosity satisfied by the first visit and no longer feel any urgency about their condition. In other cases, precisely the opposite occurs: Patients become truly alarmed by the symptoms and, to avoid thinking about them, take no further action.

Provider Delay   Delay on the part of the health care practitioner is also a significant factor, accounting for at least 15 percent of all delay behaviour (Cassileth et al., 1988). Medical delay occurs when an appropriate test or treatment is not undertaken with a patient until some time after it has become warranted. In most cases, health care providers delay as a result of honest mistakes. For example, a symptom such as blackouts can indicate any of many disorders ranging from heat prostration or overzealous dieting to diabetes or a brain tumour. A provider may choose to rule out the more common causes of the symptom before proceeding to the more invasive tests needed to rule out a less probable cause. Thus, when the more serious diagnosis is found to apply, the appearance of unwarranted delay exists.

Medical delay is more likely when a patient deviates from the profile of the average person with a given disease. For example, because breast cancer is most common among women age 45 or older, a 25-year-old with a breast lump might be sent home with a diagnosis of fibrocystic disease (a noncancerous condition) without being given a biopsy to test for possible malignancy. When a patient's symptom departs from the standard profile for a particular disorder, medical delay is more likely.

HOW DOES HOSPITALIZATION IMPACT THE PATIENT?   (L04)

About 2.8 million people are admitted yearly to the more than 800 hospitals in this country (Canadian Institute for Health Information, 2008a). As recently as 60 or 70 years ago, hospitals were thought of primarily as places where people went to die (for example, Noyes et al., 2000). Our grandparents may still think of hospitals in terms of dying. And in some cultures, such as Chinese culture, being admitted to the hospital is viewed as inevitably resulting in death (Waxler-Morrison, 2005). Now, however, as we will see, the hospital has assumed many treatment functions. As a consequence, there has been a gradual downward trend in the number of hospitalizations over the past few decades, as Figure 8.2 illustrates. Compared to 1995–1996, when 11 out of 100 Canadians were hospitalized,

FIGURE 8.2 | Inpatient Hospitalizations and Age–Sex Standardized Inpatient Hospitalization Rates (per 100,000 Population) for Canada, 1995–1996 to 2006–2007

Source: Reprinted with permission from Canadian Institute for Health Information, 2008.

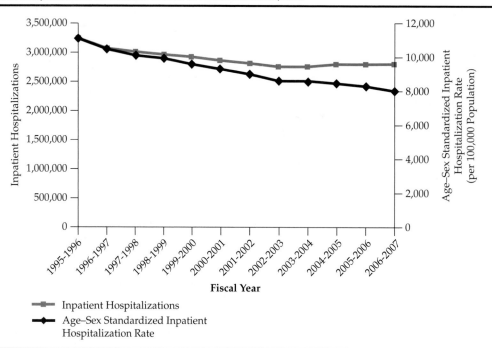

only 8 out of every 100 Canadians were hospitalized in 2006–2007. This has occurred largely because outpatient visits have increased, and there has been a 31 percent increase in the number of patients who have same day surgery as opposed to being admitted for inpatient surgery (Canadian Institute for Health Information, 2008a). The hospital has always fascinated social scientists because its functions are so many and varied. It is a custodial unit, a treatment centre, a teaching institution, a research centre, and a laboratory. Because of the diversity of treatment needs, many kinds of skills are needed in hospitals.

Structure of the Hospital

To understand the psychological impact of hospitalization, it is useful to have a working knowledge of its structure and functions. Because of Canada's publicly funded health care system, or "medicare," hospitals are funded through annual budgets that have been negotiated with either the provincial and territorial ministries of health, or the regional health board or authority. Thus, the operation of Canadian hospitals comes under the direction of community boards of trustees, voluntary organizations, or municipalities (Health Canada, 2005c). Consequently, the hospital structure is organized very much as any other hierarchically organized bureaucracy, with administration at the top and physicians, nurses, and technicians as employees.

Many Canadian hospitals have adopted a new organizational model based on the John Hopkins Model. Central to this model is the structuring of specialty areas within the hospital as functional units that are headed by a physician chief. This physician chief reports to the chief executive officer of the hospital, who in turn reports to the hospital's board of trustees. The nursing directors and administrators of each unit report to the physician chief, thus placing the physician at the top of the medical line of authority in the hospital. Physicians are therefore afforded high status because they are chiefly responsible for the treatment of patients. However, critics of this model suggest that it maintains an environment of subordination rather than fostering teamwork, and leaves nurses and other health professionals with little power in health care decisions (Storch, 2007)

Functioning of the Hospital

Conditions change rapidly in the hospital, and because of these fluctuating demands, the social order in which patient care is delivered is constantly being negotiated. Although each person involved in patient care, whether nurse, physician, or orderly, has general ideas about his or her functions, it is understood that, under conditions of emergency, each must perform the tasks that he or she knows best while remaining flexible to respond effectively to the changing situation. Television programs such as *ER* and *Grey's Anatomy* capture this aspect of the hospital quite effectively and demonstrate how medical personnel must often grab anyone qualified who is available to help in an emergency situation.

The different goals of different professionals in the hospital setting are reflected in hospital workers' communication patterns. Occupational segregation in the hospital is high: Nurses talk to other nurses, physicians to other physicians, and administrators to other administrators. Physicians have access to some information that nurses may not see, whereas nurses interact with patients daily and know a great deal about their day-to-day progress, yet often their notes on charts go unread by physicians.

An example of the problems associated with lack of communication is provided by a study on **nosocomial infection**—that is, infection that results from exposure to disease in the hospital setting (Inweregbu, Dave, & Pittard, 2005). As is illustrated in the Focus on Social Issues box, "Can Going to the Hospital Kill You?" these hospital-based infections are a serious issue that affect a quarter of a million Canadians each year and result in death for several thousands. Many of these infections result from not following the strict guidelines for handwashing, sterilization, and waste control. Of all hospital workers, physicians are the most likely to commit such infractions, and the least likely to be corrected by those under them. If staff members felt free to communicate across the different levels of the hospital hierarchy and felt free to point out violations to others in a constructive way, better infection control might result.

The discussion in the Focus on Social Issues box below has emphasized potential sources of conflict, ambiguity, and confusion in the hospital structure. Burnout, a problem that can result in part from these ambiguities, is described in the Spotlight on Canadian Research box, "Burnout among Canadian Nurses." However, this description presents an incomplete picture. In many respects, hospital functioning is remarkably effective, given the changing realities to which it must accommodate at any given time. Thus,

Can Going to the Hospital Kill You?

When most of us go to the hospital we do so to seek acute care for a troubling health issue, or perhaps to have day surgery. But a recent study suggests that every year about 250,000 Canadians, or one in every nine who are admitted, pick up an infection unrelated to their original health complaint when they visit the hospital. The cost of treating those who are infected is estimated to be about $1 billion a year. What's more, between 8,000 and 12,000 Canadians every year die from a nosocomial infection, an infection acquired from exposure to disease in the hospital. Nosocomial infections account for more deaths per year in Canada than breast cancer, AIDS, and car accidents combined.

How do these infections occur? One of the main ways is when strict infection-control measures, including handwashing and sterilization of equipment, are not practised. The likelihood of patients experiencing infected surgical wounds, blood infections, and the transfer of antibiotic resistant organisms could all be prevented if such guidelines were strictly adhered to. Following the SARS outbreak in 2003, hand sanitizers have become a common fixture among many hospitals in an effort to prevent the spread of hospital infections. However, even simple precautions like handwashing is often forgotten when physicians and health care staff are in a rush to care for their patients. In fact, a CBC investigation found that doctors often walk right by the hand sanitizers, even when moving from patient to patient, with many washing their hands only about 10 percent to 20 percent of the time.

Who is most likely to become infected? Particularly susceptible are those with weakened immune systems, including newborn and premature infants and the elderly. This is especially true if they are exposed to one of the "superbugs," microbes that are resistant to antibiotic treatment. For example, Toronto's Mount Sinai Hospital closed its neo-natal intensive care unit in May 2007 after a premature baby died from bacteraemia, a nosocomial blood poisoning caused by exposure to a resistant strain of bacteria.

Anyone who has an open wound or who undergoes a surgical procedure is also at risk. For one woman who went into the hospital for day surgery on her hand, the staph infection that she picked up was more than she bargained for. "I was in emergency at 2:00 in the morning having an IV started and antibiotics and having to call my family to come and pick me up." Years later, the scar and pain from the ordeal are constant reminders of her shaken faith in the sanitary conditions of hospitals.

Even more concerning is that sharing a hospital room with one or more people increases the risk of acquiring a nosocomial infection. A study conducted by researchers at Queen's University that tracked the rates of infection over a five-year period in one Ontario hospital found that the risk of getting infected with a hospital-acquired infection increased by 10 percent with each new roommate (Hamel, Zoutman, & O'Callaghan, 2010).

A survey conducted in 2000 suggests that Canadian hospitals still have a long way to go to tighten up their infection-control measures. Of the 73 percent of the hospitals in this country, only 53 percent were found to have met the minimum recommendations for infection-control staff (Zoutman et al., 2003).

What's being done to address this issue? In 2005, the World Health Organization launched a global challenge campaign called *Clean Care Is Safer Care,* to raise awareness of the importance of handwashing for patient safety. Canada joined the challenge and in late 2007 launched the *STOP! Clean Your Hands* campaign to promote hand hygiene among health care professionals, patients, and visitor in health care settings.

Source: CBC News, 2003, 2007; Canadian Patient Safety Institute, 2007.

the ambiguities in structure, potential conflicts in goals, and problems of communication occur within a system that generally functions quite well.

Changes in Hospitalization

Over the past few decades, the delivery of health care services has changed from relying mainly on hospitals and doctors to alternatives to traditional hospital care. Walk-in and urgent care clinics, for example, can deal with less serious complaints and routine surgeries that used to require hospitalization. Clinics, including urgent care clinics, handle a large proportion of the smaller emergencies that historically have filled the hospital emergency room. More community primary health centres are providing services around the clock to relieve some of the demand for emergency room care. Other hospital alternatives include providing post–acute care services in the home and the community to help lessen the time spent in the hospital. In addition, home care services and hospices provide services for the chronically and terminally ill who require primarily palliative and custodial care rather than active medical intervention. Hospital consolidation has helped to reduce redundancies in the types of services offered in acute-care facilities located within the same area (Health Canada, 2005c). A shift from inpatient to day surgeries has also contributed to changes in the types of services offered through the hospital. And a greater emphasis on promoting health, preventing disease, and managing chronic illness through public health initiatives has been introduced to improve health among Canadians and therefore reduce the need for hospitalization. Many of these health care reforms have come about in response to government fiscal restraints, the increasing costs of technology, and the greying of the nation. Given that these concerns are expected to continue in the future, changes to the health care system will also continue (Health Canada, 2005c).

In addition to general acute care hospitals, there are also 16 children's hospitals in Canada that focus exclusively on the treatment of childhood disease, injury, and illness. Although only two remain as free-standing children's hospitals not associated with an adult hospital or maternal care centre, each provides specialized services and health care for children. Several of these specialized hospitals also include unique programs that address changes in the way health and health care is viewed. For example, Stollery Children's Hospital in Edmonton includes an Aboriginal Child Health Program that employs workers from the Aboriginal community to assist with language interpretation and emotional support, as well as to act as cultural liaisons with health care staff who are dealing with First Nations patients.

Role of Psychologists   Among the important developments in hospital care has been the increasing involvement of psychologists. The number of psychologists in hospital settings has continued to increase in recent years and their roles have expanded. In 1982 there was one full-time psychologist for every 131 hospital beds in Canada; in 1999 there was one psychologist for every 51 beds. In addition, psychologists have become more autonomous since the 1980s, with more

hospitals including independent department of psychology (Humbke et al., 2004). Psychologists participate in the diagnosis of patients, particularly through the use of personality, intellectual, and neuropsychological tests. Psychologists also determine patients' general level of functioning, as well as patients' strengths and weaknesses that can help form the basis for therapeutic intervention.

Psychologists are also involved in pre-surgery and post-surgery preparation, pain control, interventions to increase medication and treatment compliance, and behavioural programs to teach appropriate self-care following discharge (Enright, Resnick, DeLeon, Sciara, & Tanney, 1990). They also diagnose and treat psychological problems that can complicate patient care. What areas are psychologists most likely to be involved in? A 1999 survey of Canadian hospitals found that pain, eating disorders, and cancer were the top three clinics/units in which psychologists were involved (Humbke et al., 2004). However, as the incidence of many chronic illnesses such as diabetes and heart disease continues to rise in this country, these areas are likely to change in the coming years.

Impact of Hospitalization on the Patient

> The patient comes unbidden to a large organization which awes and irritates him, even as it also nurtures and cares. As he strips off his clothing so he strips off, too, his favored costume of social roles, his favored style, his customary identity in the world. He becomes subject to a time schedule and a pattern of activity not of his own making. (R. Wilson, 1963, p. 70)

Patients arrive at the hospital with anxiety over their illness or disorder, confusion and anxiety over the prospect of hospitalization, and concern over all the role obligations they must leave behind unfulfilled. The hospital does little, if anything, to calm anxiety and in many cases exacerbates it. The admission process is often long and impersonal, and once admitted the patient is ushered into a strange room, given strange clothes, provided with an unfamiliar roommate, and subjected to peculiar tests. The patient must entrust himself or herself completely to strangers in an uncertain environment in which all procedures are new. The patient is expected to be cooperative, dependent, and helpful without demanding excessive attention. The patient quickly learns that the hospital is organized for the convenience of

Burnout among Canadian Nurses

Burnout is an occupational risk for anyone who works with needy people (Maslach, 2003). It is a particular problem for physicians, nurses, and other medical personnel who work with sick and dying people. As a syndrome, burnout is marked by three components: emotional exhaustion, cynicism, and a low sense of efficacy in one's job. Staff members suffering from burnout show a cynical and seemingly callous attitude toward those whom they serve. Their view of clients is more negative than that of other staff members, and they treat clients in more detached ways (Maslach, 2003).

For Canadian nurses, burnout is a growing concern that may be the result and perhaps even the cause of several factors. An aging nursing population, high job turnover, workplace injuries, and high absenteeism are fuelling the critical nursing shortage in Canada (O'Brien-Pallas, 2007). And with hospital restructuring in recent years, job insecurities only add to these problems, prompting many to go south of the border. Combined, these issues may add to the nursing shortage, which in turn contributes to workplace stress as fewer nurses take on more responsibilities. And because burnout is known to be linked to increased on-the-job injuries and a higher rate of mistakes (Cameron, Horsburgh, & Armstrong- Strassen, 1994), this can create a potentially vicious cycle with increased burnout as the result.

A 2005 national survey of Canadian nurses' health and work found that the demands and tolls that nurses experience are overwhelming. Two-thirds of nurses in Canada believed that they were given too much work for one person, 45 percent reported that they were not given enough time to do what was expected of them, and nearly 60 percent felt that because of these issues they could not do everything well (Shields & Wilkins, 2006). Not surprisingly, more than half said that they arrived earlier or stayed later than their required shift time to try and get everything done, and nearly two-thirds said that they worked through their breaks. The physical tolls reported by nurses were also alarming. Over 60 percent of both male and female nurses re-ported that they experienced high physical demands from their job, and that they had to take time off work in the previous year for health reasons. Compared to the other working Canadians, nurses reported higher rates of depression and a greater number of chronic health conditions, including pain. Of those who reported pain, and that it interfered with their ability to perform their job, most believed that it was a result of work-related activities. Add to this the emotional abuse that many nurses report at the hand of patients, visitors, physicians, and even other nurses (Shields & Wilkins, 2006), and it is clear the demands experienced by Canadian nurses can only lead to further burnout.

The job stress is a particular challenge for young nurses and those who work in a hospital setting. A survey conducted by researchers at the University of Western Ontario of junior Ontario nurses who had been on the job for less than two years found that two-thirds reported experiencing symptoms of burnout such as depression and emotional exhaustion. One junior nurse who has been nursing for three years found that her training did not prepare her for the emotional demands of the job. "The emotional stress is the most. I wasn't prepared that well for how emotionally draining it is to work 12-hour shifts with a heavy workload." She also knew of two nurses who left the hospital to work in personal-care homes because they were so stressed and overwhelmed by their jobs (CBC News, 2006).

Such role strain and physical demands are experienced more often by nurses in a hospital setting. Working within a larger organizational setting can reduce autonomy and increase the potential for strained working relations, as well as involve more physical tasks. However, across all working situations nurses who experienced job strain, low supervisor/co-worker support, low autonomy, poor nurse-physician working relations, high physical demands, and job insecurity were twice as likely to experience poor or fair physical and mental health compared to nurses who did not experience these demands (Shields & Wilkins, 2006). The low job

staff rather than patients. He or she is also physically confined, making adjustment to the new situation that much more difficult.

Hospital patients may show a variety of problematic psychological symptoms, especially anxiety and depression. Nervousness over tests or surgery and their results can produce insomnia and nightmares. Procedures that isolate or immobilize patients are particularly likely to produce psychological distress. Hospital care can be highly fragmented, with many as 30 different

Burnout among Canadian Nurses (continued)

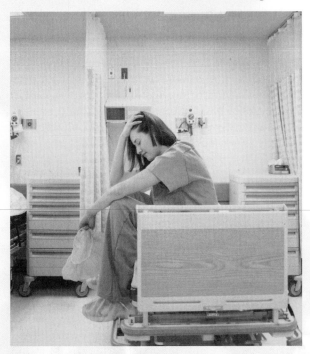

satisfaction and distress experienced by nurses in these conditions can have additional implications. A recent update suggests that nurses who report low job satisfaction, lack of respect in their workplace, and feel less control over their job are much more likely to have higher rates of absenteeism (Canadian Institute of Health Information, 2008a).

Although each of these demands may be challenging for nurses, researchers from York University found that workload in particular was strongly linked to emotional exhaustion, a key symptom of burnout (Greenglass & Burke, 2000). The results from a large survey of Canadian nurses found that the greater the nurses' workload, the more emotional exhaustion, depression, anxiety, and cynicism they experienced. What's more, emotional exhaustion was directly linked to the amount of cynicism reported, and that this distancing and detaching from their patients was likely a response to feeling emotionally drained by their job (Greenglass & Burke, 2001).

Not surprisingly, since burnout results from stress, it is associated with alterations in physiological and neuroendocrine functioning. There is evidence that burnout influences endocrine and immune functioning, such that people with burnout show elevated cytokine levels (Fukuda et al., 2008; Mommersteeg, Heijnen, Kavelaars, & van Doornen, 2006). However, there is some evidence that particular coping styles may offset or increase this job related stress, which in turn can buffer against these harmful immunological changes. In one study, nurses who used control-based coping and self-efficacy reported less jobrelated distress and greater satisfaction with their job, whereas those who used more avoidant coping methods greater distress and more feelings of job insecurity (Greenglass & Burke, 2000).

How can burnout be avoided? Given the link between burnout and workload, dealing with the shortage of nurses at a national level may help to alleviate some of the strain on nurses. However, the continuing nursing shortage in Canada is not a unique one, as many other countries are experiencing a similar nursing workforce crisis, and therefore it may be some time before the workload issues are solved. In the meantime, interventions designed to help nurses manage their demanding workloads and cope with their distress may be necessary. For example, an institutionalized support group can provide nurses working in hospital settings with an opportunity to meet informally with others to deal with the problems they face. These groups can give nurses the opportunity to obtain emotional support, reduce their feelings of being alone, and share feelings of emotional distress about their workplace demands. In so doing, they can reduce distress and emotional exhaustion both immediately and for several months after (Günüşen & Üstün, 2010).

staff people passing through a patient's room each day, conducting tests, taking blood, bringing food, or cleaning up. Often, the staff members have little time to spend with the patient beyond exchanging greetings, which can be a very alienating experience.

Although patients are now typically given information about the procedures they can expect to go through and what they may experience as a result, many may be too ill to fully understand what lies ahead. Moreover, whereas once patients' hospital stays were long, now

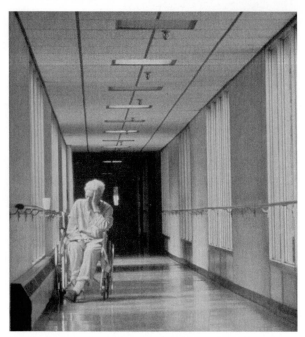

The hospital can be a lonely and frightening place for many patients, leading to feelings of helplessness, anxiety, or depression.

people are typically hospitalized primarily on a short-term basis for specific treatments. Often prepared for those treatments in advance, the patient may be discharged shortly after they are over.

HOW CAN CONTROL BE INCREASED IN HOSPITAL SETTINGS?

In part because of the issues just noted, many hospitals now provide interventions that help prepare patients generally for hospitalization and, more specifically, for the procedures that they will undergo. Something as simple as providing information about medical procedures can help to improve patients' perceptions of control. Accordingly, many hospitals now provide extensive information about the admitting process, day surgeries, and other medical procedures performed in the hospital to help increase psychological control among patients and their families. In this section we turn to how interventions that increase perceptions of control have been used to help the hospitalized patient cope with procedures such as surgery.

Interventions to Increase Information in Hospital Settings

In 1958, psychologist Irving Janis conducted a landmark study that would forever change the preparation of patients for surgery. Janis was asked by a hospital to study its surgery patients to find out whether something could be done to reduce the stress that many of them experienced both before and after operations. One of Janis's earliest observations was that, without some anticipatory worry that he termed the "work of worrying," patients were not able to cope well with surgery.

To get a clearer idea of the relationship between worry and adjustment, Janis first grouped patients according to the level of fear they experienced before the operation (high, medium, and low). Then he studied how well they understood and used the information that the hospital staff gave them to help them cope with the after-effects of surgery. Highly fearful patients generally remained fearful and anxious after surgery and showed many negative side effects, such as vomiting, pain, urinary retention, and inability to eat. Patients who initially had little fear also showed unfavourable reactions after surgery, becoming angry or upset or complaining. Of the three groups, the moderately fearful patients coped with post-operative stress most effectively, as determined by both interviews and staff reports.

In interpreting these results, Janis reasoned that very fearful patients had been too absorbed with their own fears pre-operatively to process the preparatory information adequately and that patients with little fear were insufficiently vigilant to understand and process the information effectively. Patients with moderate levels of fear, in contrast, were vigilant enough but not overwhelmed by their fears, so they were able to develop realistic expectations of what their post-surgery reactions would be; when they later encountered these sensations and reactions, they expected them and were ready to deal with them.

Subsequent studies have borne out some but not all of Janis's observations. Researchers now believe that the effect is primarily determined by the informational value of the preparatory communication itself (J. E. Johnson, Lauver, & Nail, 1989). That is, patients who are carefully prepared for surgery and its after-effects will show good post-operative adjustment; patients who are not well prepared for the after-effects of surgery will show poor post-operative adjustment.

Research on the role of preparatory information in adjustment to surgery overwhelmingly shows that such

Social Support and Distress from Surgery

Patients who are hospitalized for serious illnesses or surgery often experience anxiety. From our discussion of social support, we know that emotional support from others can reduce distress when people are undergoing stressful events. Researchers have made use of these observations in developing interventions for hospitalized patients. Kulik and Mahler (1987) developed a social support intervention for patients about to undergo cardiac surgery. Some of the patients were assigned a roommate who was also waiting for surgery (pre-operative condition), whereas others were assigned a roommate who had already had surgery (post-operative condition). In addition, patients were placed with a roommate undergoing surgery that was either similar or dissimilar to their own.

The results suggested that patients who had a post-operative roommate profited from this contact (see also Kulik, Moore, & Mahler, 1993). Patients with a postoperative roommate were less anxious before surgery, were more ambulatory after surgery, and were released more quickly from the hospital than were patients who had been paired with a roommate who was also awaiting surgery. Similarity versus dissimilarity of the type of surgery made no difference, only whether the roommate's surgery had already taken place.

Why exactly did rooming with a post-operative surgical patient improve the adjustment of those awaiting surgery? It may be that post-operative patients were able to provide relevant information to patients about the post-operative period by telling them how they felt and what the patient might expect (Thoits, Harvey, Hohmann, & Fletcher, 2000). Post-operative roommates may also have acted as role models for how one might feel and react post-operatively. Alternatively, those awaiting surgery may simply have been relieved to see that somebody who had undergone surgery had come out all right.

Whatever the specific explanation, the social contact produced by the presence of the post-operative roommate clearly had a positive impact on the pre-operative and post-operative adjustment of these surgery patients. These results have intriguing implications and may well be used to design future interventions to improve the adjustment of those awaiting unpleasant medical procedures, such as surgery (Kulik & Mahler, 1993; Kulik, Moore, & Mahler, 1993).

preparation has beneficial effects on patients. Most surgical preparation interventions provide information about the procedures and sensations that can be expected. Patients who have been prepared in these ways are typically less emotionally distressed, regain their functioning more quickly, and are often able to leave the hospital sooner. One study (Kulik & Mahler, 1989) even found that the person who becomes your post-operative roommate can influence how you cope with the aftermath of surgery, because of the information a roommate conveys (see the Health Psychology in Action box, "Social Support and Distress from Surgery").

Preparation for patients is so beneficial that many hospitals show videotapes to patients to prepare them for upcoming procedures. In another study by Mahler and Kulik (1998), patients awaiting coronary artery bypass graft (CABG) were exposed to one of three preparatory videotapes or to no preparation. One videotape conveyed information via a health care expert; the second featured the health care expert but also included clips of interviews with patients who reported on their progress; and the third presented information from a health care expert plus interviews with patients who reported their recovery consisting of "ups and downs." Compared with patients who did not receive videotaped preparation, patients who saw a videotape—any videotape—felt significantly better prepared for the recovery period, reported higher self-efficacy during the recovery period, were more adherent to recommended dietary and exercise changes during their recovery, and were released sooner from the hospital. Similar interventions have been employed successfully for patients awaiting other medical procedures (for example, Doering et al., 2000). ●

SUMMARY

 LO1 **Explain how people recognize and interpret symptoms**

- The detection of symptoms, their interpretation, and use of health services are all heavily influenced by psychological processes.
- Personality and culture, focus of attention, the presence of distracting or involving activities, mood, the salience of illness or symptoms, and individual differences in the tendency to monitor threat influence whether a symptom is noticed. The interpretation of symptoms is influenced by prior experience and expectations about their likelihood and meaning.
- Illness schemas (which identify the type of disease, its consequences, causes, duration, and cure) and disease prototypes (conceptions of specific diseases) influence how people interpret their symptoms and whether they act on them by seeking medical attention.
- Social factors, such as the lay referral network, can act as a go-between for the patient and the medical care system.

 LO2 **Know what predicts the use of health services**

- Health services are used disproportionately by the very young and very old, by women, and by middle- to upper-class people.
- The health belief model, which ascertains whether a person perceives a threat to health and whether a person believes that a particular health measure can overcome the

disorder, influences use of health services. Other social psychological factors include an individual's social location in a community and social pressures to seek treatment.

 LO3 **Describe how health services are misused**

- Health services may also be abused. A large percentage of patients who seek medical attention are depressed or anxious and not physically ill. People commonly ignore symptoms that are serious, resulting in dangerous delay behaviour.

 LO4 **Understand how hospitalization impacts the patient**

- The hospital is a complex organizational system buffeted by changing medical, organizational, and financial climates. Different groups in the hospital develop different goals, such as cure, care, or core, which may occasionally conflict. Such problems are exacerbated by communication barriers.
- Hospitalization can be a frightening and depersonalizing experience for patients. Nosocomial infections are a serious issue that some patients may also need to deal with.

 LO5 **Describe how control can be increased in hospital settings**

- Control-restoring and control-enhancing interventions improve adjustment to hospitalization and to stressful medical procedures in both adults and children. The benefits of information, relaxation training, and coping skills training are well documented.

KEY TERMS

appraisal delay   p. 226
behavioural delay   p. 226
delay behaviour   p. 226
illness delay   p. 226
illness representations
    (schemas)   p. 218

lay referral network   p. 219
medical delay   p. 226
medical students' disease   p. 216
natural health products
    (NHP)   p. 220

nosocomial infection   p. 229
secondary gains   p. 225
somaticizers   p. 224
worried well   p. 224

Patient–Provider Relations

LEARNING OBJECTIVES

After reading this chapter, students will be able to:

(LO1) Define health care provider

(LO2) Explain why patient–provider communication is important

(LO3) Understand the consequences of poor patient–provider communication

(LO4) Define non-adherence and how it can be reduced

(LO5) Describe how to improve patient–provider communication

(LO6) Understand the placebo effect

"I've had this cold for two weeks, so finally I went to the Student Health Services to get something for it. I waited more than an hour—can you believe it? And when I finally saw a doctor, he spent a whole five minutes with me, told me what I had was viral, not bacterial, and that he couldn't do anything for it. He sent me home and told me to get a lot of rest, drink fluids, and take over-the-counter medications for the stuffiness and the pain. Why did I even bother?!" (Student account of a trip to the health services)

Nearly everyone has a horror story about a visit to a physician. Long waits, insensitivity, apparently faulty diagnoses, and treatments that have no effect are the stuff of these indignant stories (Pescosolido, Tuch, & Martin, 2001), yet in the same breath, the storyteller may expound on the virtues of his or her latest physician with an enthusiasm bordering on worship. To what do we attribute this seemingly contradictory attitude toward health care practitioners?

Health ranks among the values we hold most dear. Good health is a prerequisite to nearly every other activity, and poor health can interfere with nearly all one's goals. Moreover, illness is usually uncomfortable, so people want to be treated quickly and successfully. Perhaps, then, it is no wonder that physicians and other health care professionals are alternately praised and vilified: Their craft is fundamental to the enjoyment of life.

In this chapter, we take up the complex issue of patient–provider interaction. First, we consider why patient–provider communication is important. Next, we look at the nature of patient–provider communication and the factors that erode it. Then, we consider some of the consequences of poor communication, including noncompliance with treatment regimens and use of complementary and alternative health care. Finally, we consider efforts to improve patient–provider communication.

(L01) WHAT IS A HEALTH CARE PROVIDER?

In the following pages, we refer to the "provider" rather than to the "physician." Although physicians continue to be the main providers of health care, Canadians are increasingly receiving much of their primary care from individuals other than physicians, including nurse practitioners and complementary and alternative medicine providers (Canadian Institute for Health Information, 2005).

Nurses as Providers

Advanced-practice nursing is an umbrella term given to registered nurses who have gone beyond the typical two to four years of basic nursing education and who have many responsibilities for patients. For example, a **nurse practitioner** is a registered nurse (RN) who has additional education in health assessment, diagnoses, and management of injuries and illness, and who can therefore order tests and prescribe drugs. Nurse practitioners are affiliated with physicians in private practice, but also provide care across diverse settings such as community clinics, health centres in hospitals, nursing homes, and home care settings. Their practice emphasizes health promotion and illness prevention (Canadian Institute for Health Information/Canadian Nurses Association, 2006). As a consequence, they must often explain disorders and their origins, diagnoses, prognoses, and treatments. Even in medical practices that do not employ nurse practitioners, much patient education falls to nurses. Nurses frequently give treatment instructions or screen patients before they are seen by a physician.

Advanced-practice nurses work both autonomously and collaboratively with other health care providers in nursing outposts, community health centres, emergency departments, clinics, specialty units, and long–term-care facilities. Despite the additional functions performed by nurse practitioners, their role as professional nurses is to complement rather than replace other health care providers (Health Canada, 2006c).

Nurses may also deliver advice remotely via telehealth services. **Telehealth** includes a variety of services that use communication technology to connect people with health services. These services can include the delivery of advice and information from a nurse via telephone, as well as consultation, diagnoses, treatment, and family visiting using audiovideo conferencing (Health Council of Canada, 2006).

Physician Assistants as Providers

Physician assistants are skilled health care team members who perform a wide range of medical services. Physician assistants are supervised by physicians as part of a physician/physician assistant team to complement existing health care services. The scope of their duties is usually outlined in a practice agreement with the supervising physician, and also with the facility where the physician assistant works. Their exact duties often vary by clinical setting but can include taking medical histories, conducting physical examinations, diagnoses and treatment of illness, ordering and interpreting tests, writing prescriptions, and assisting in surgery. Although these duties sound extensive and very similar to those of a physician, physician assistants are taught to know their limits and seek guidance from their supervising physician as necessary. Until recently, the main employer of physician assistants in Canada has been the Canadian Forces, although some remotely located industries often hire ex-military physician assistants to provide health care to their work force (Canadian Association of Physician Assistants, 2006).

However, physician assistants may become more common in Canadian health care settings in the near future. Pilot programs introducing physician assistants into select health care facilities in Ontario are underway, and their evaluation will inform how physician assistants will be integrated into the province's health care delivery. Physician Assistant Education Master's degree programs were launched in the fall of 2008 at the University of Manitoba and McMaster University, and were aimed at providing training to increase the number of physician assistants to help alleviate some of the strain on the health care system due to physician shortages. Indeed, at the time of this writing some of the 21 graduates from the inaugural McMaster program class had already started to work in the emergency room (ER) at the Oakville-Trafalgar Memorial Hospital to improve ER care and wait times. The two-year program includes seminar-driven education in the first year followed by a second year of clinically based training. These were the first programs of their kind in Canada and are expected to herald the launch of similar programs at other universities, such as the University of Toronto, which launched its Physician Assistant program in January 2010.

As medical practice has become increasingly complex, other professionals, such as physiotherapists, social workers, nutritionists, occupational therapists, and psychologists, have also become involved in specialized care, and are now commonly members of inter-professional teams that deliver health care in a more comprehensive manner. Consequently, issues of communication—especially poor communication—that arise in medical settings are not the exclusive concern of the physician.

L02   WHY IS PATIENT–PROVIDER COMMUNICATION IMPORTANT?

Criticisms of providers usually centre on volumes of jargon, little feedback, and depersonalized care. Clearly, the quality of communication with a provider is important to patients, but does good communication do anything more than produce a vague sense of satisfaction or dissatisfaction in the patient's mind? The answer is yes. Poor patient–provider communication has been tied to outcomes as problematic as non-adherence to treatment recommendations and failing to disclose the concurrent use of alternative treatments and therapies.

Judging Quality of Care

People often judge the adequacy of their care by criteria that are irrelevant to its technical quality (Yarnold, Michelson, Thompson, & Adams, 1998). Although we might be able to discern a case of blatant incompetence, most of us are insufficiently knowledgeable about medicine and standards of practice to know whether we have been treated well. Consequently, we often judge technical quality on the basis of the manner in which care is delivered (Ben-Sira, 1980). A warm, confident, friendly provider is often judged to be both nice and competent, whereas a cool, aloof provider may be judged less favourably, as both unfriendly and incompetent (for example, Bogart, 2001). Moreover, if a physician expresses uncertainty about the nature of the patient's condition, patient satisfaction declines (C. G. Johnson, Levenkron, Suchman, & Manchester, 1988). In reality, technical quality of care and the manner in which care is delivered are unrelated.

Patient Consumerism

Another factor that may heavily influence patient–provider interaction is patients' increasing desire and need to be involved in the decisions that affect their health. This does not necessarily mean that patients wish to be completely autonomous in their health-related decisions or that they necessarily want to have to pay to get better treatments. But against the backdrop of a publicly funded health care system, as consumers of health-related information and self-care products, Canadians wish to take a more active and less passive role in the decisions that affect their health. Whereas at one time the physician's authority was accepted without question or complaint (Parsons, 1954), increasingly patients have adopted consumerist attitudes toward their health care. Indeed it has been noted that Canadians often choose the combination of conventional and alternative health care practitioners or products that they feel will best treat their health issue

(Kelner & Wellman, 1997). This change has come from several factors.

The increasing emphasis on maintaining and achieving good health in Western society has contributed to patient consumerism in recent years (Kelner & Wellman, 1997). Patients have therefore become more proactive in managing their health. However, to induce a patient to follow a treatment regimen, one must have the patient's full cooperation and participation in the treatment plan. Giving the patient a role in the development of the plan and how it will be enacted can help ensure such commitment. Moreover, as we have seen, lifestyle is a major cause of disability and illness. Modifying lifestyle factors such as diet, smoking, and alcohol consumption must be done with the patient's full initiative and cooperation if change is to be achieved. In fact, patients who regard their behaviour as under the control of providers instead of themselves are less likely to adhere to lifestyle change (Lynch et al., 1992).

The Internet has also contributed to patients taking a more active role in their treatment. Recall from Chapter 8 that the majority of Internet users search for information about health. Among Canadians who use the Internet for health information, more than a third (38 percent) discuss what they find with a health care provider. Information about surgery and alternative therapies are the most commonly discussed types of health information (Underhill & McKeown, 2008). The Internet can provide patients with a relatively easy and accessible way to get a second opinion about their health.

In addition, patients often have considerable expertise about their illness, especially if it is a recurring or chronic problem. A patient will do better if this expertise is tapped and integrated into the treatment program. For example, a diabetic may have a better sense of how to control his or her own blood glucose level than does a physician unfamiliar with the particular case. Clearly, then, the relationship between patient and provider is changing in ways that make better communication essential. The factors that erode communication include aspects of the office setting itself, the changing nature of the health care delivery system, provider behaviours, patient behaviours, and qualities of the interaction. We will consider each in turn.

Setting

On the surface of it, the medical office is an unlikely setting for effective communication. The average visit only lasts 12 to 15 minutes, and when you are trying to explain your symptoms to the physician, he or she will, on average, interrupt you before you get 23 seconds into your comments (N. Simon, 2003). Moreover, if you are ill, you must communicate that fact to another person, often a stranger; you must respond to specific and direct questions and then be content to be poked and prodded while the diagnostic process goes on. At the very least, it is difficult to present one's complaints effectively when one is in pain or has a fever, and a patient's ability to be articulate may be reduced further by any anxiety or embarrassment about the symptoms or the examination.

The provider, on the other hand, has the task of extracting significant information as quickly as possible from the patient. The provider is often on a tight schedule, with other patients backing up in the waiting room. The difficulties presented by the patient may have been made more complex by the use of various over-the-counter remedies so that symptoms are masked and distorted. Moreover, the patient's ideas of which symptoms are important may not correspond to the provider's knowledge, so important signs may be overlooked. With the patient seeking solace and the provider trying to maximize the effective use of time, it is clear that there are many potential sources of strain.

Structure of Health Care Delivery System

In Canada, primary health care providers, including physicians, are usually the first point of entry for

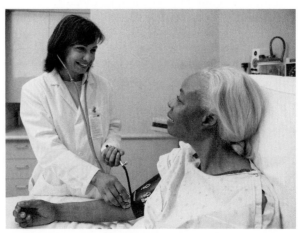

When physicians treat patients in a warm, friendly, confident manner, they are judged to be competent as well as nice.

individuals into our publicly funded health care system. Primary health care facilitates and coordinates the provision of the services that are delivered to ensure continuity of care if more specialized services such as specialists or hospitalization are required. When secondary health care services are required, records of any necessary tests or procedures are passed along to the referring primary care physician (Health Canada, 2005c).

One difficulty with this gatekeeper system is that receiving specialized care or tests necessarily requires an initial referral from a physician. But for the estimated 3.5 million Canadians who do not have a regular family physician (Nabalamba & Millar, 2007), moving through the health care system can become problematic. However, even having a regular family physician does not always ensure that needed medical care will be received in a timely manner due to the high demand on the few physicians available. For example, Ontario has one of the lowest physician-to-patient ratios in the country, and among those family physicians available, fewer than 10 percent are even accepting new patients. In some regions, such as eastern and southwestern Ontario, only about 4 percent of physicians are available to accept new patients (College of Physicians and Surgeons of Ontario, 2007), leaving many Canadians to rely on walk-in clinics and emergency rooms for their primary care.

The long wait times to receive an initial consultation can be frustrating and stressful for patients. Almost a quarter of Canadians report that they cannot get in to see a doctor on the same day when they were sick or needed medical attention, and more than a third report having to wait six or more days to get an appointment with a doctor (Canadian Institute for Health Information, 2007b). And compared to five other industrialized nations, access to primary health care in Canada is by far the lowest (see Figure 9.1). Among those who report having to wait for care, 21 percent felt the wait time was unacceptable, and about 12 percent said that the wait affected them negatively; over a third experienced pain while waiting, and almost three-quarters said they experienced worry, anxiety, and stress (Canadian Institute for Health Information, 2007b). Add to this the even longer wait times to receive certain types of specialized care, such as cardiac and cancer care, and you have a possible formula for dissatisfaction that may drive people to consider seeking alternative means of dealing with their

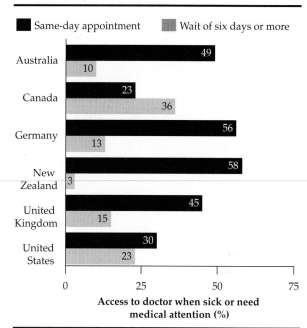

FIGURE 9.1 | Access to Health Care in Canada and Other Developed Countries, 2005

Source: Reprinted by permission of Canadian Institute for Health Information (CIHI).

health issues (see the Spotlight on Canadian Research box, "Why Do People Use Complementary and Alternative Medicine?").

One study of primary care users in southwestern Ontario, a particularly underserved region, found that although the majority had a family physician, almost half experienced difficulty getting an appointment with their doctor in the past year (Sirois & Purc-Stephenson, 2008b). When asked if they would consider consulting with a complementary and alternative medicine (CAM) practitioner the next time they experienced difficulties seeing a physician, over 90 percent of those who had previously used CAM said yes. What is perhaps more telling though is that almost 60 percent of those who had never used CAM before said they would consider consulting a CAM provider should they have difficulty getting an appointment with a doctor in the future. Despite our universal access health care system, many Canadians cannot access care when needed and may therefore decide to use other treatment options.

Why Do People Use Complementary and Alternative Medicine?

Complementary and alternative medicine (CAM) includes a diverse group of healing therapies (e.g., chiropractic, massage therapy, homeopathy, and acupuncture) not currently considered an integral part of conventional medical practice (National Center for Complementary and Alternative Medicine, 2007). It is estimated that there are up to 300 different types of CAM (Public Health Agency of Canada, 2006a), some of which are delivered by a health care provider and others that involve self-care. The interest and use CAM has continued to rise in recent decades in Canada and other developed nations, such as the United States, the United Kingdom, Europe, and Australia. According to one large national survey in 2006, almost three-quarters of Canadians had used at least one CAM in their lifetime, and just over half (54 percent) had used CAM within the past year (Esmail, 2007). The proportion of the general Canadian population that consult CAM providers is, however, much lower (20 percent; Park, 2005; see Figure 9.2), whereas it is just as high among breast cancer patients (57 percent; Boon, Olatunde, & Zick, 2007).

Understanding the motivations for CAM use has been of particular interest to researchers in Canada, especially given our universal health care system, which does not cover the costs of CAM consultations. So why do people choose to use CAM when in most cases it involves an additional cost? Part of the answer may lie in the socio-demographic and health factors associated with CAM use. For the most part people who use CAM tend to be female, middle-aged, and highly educated, and they have a greater number of health complaints that are chronic in nature compared to those who do not use CAM (Foltz et al., 2005; Park, 2005; Sirois & Gick, 2002, Sirois & Purc-Stephenson, 2008a).

This profile suggests that people who use CAM take a more consumerist and proactive approach to managing their health and may not be satisfied with simply accepting the physician's authority. This may

FIGURE 9.2 | Percentage of Canadians Reporting Alternative Health Care Consultations in the Past Year, by Sex

Source: Use of alternative health care, "Health Reports," Catalogue 82-003, Volume 16, Issue 2, released March 15, 2005, www.statcan.ca/english/ studies/82-003/archive/2005/16-2-e.pdf.

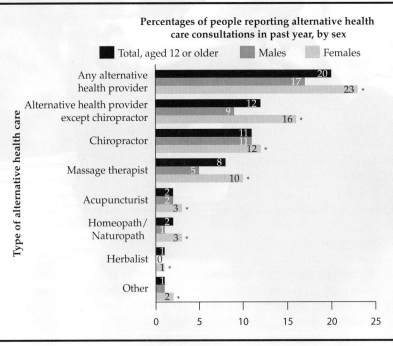

Why Do People Use Complementary and Alternative Medicine? (continued)

reflect a desire to maintain good health and avoid illness (Sirois & Gick, 2002). However, given the poor health status of many CAM users, this approach may also indicate a need to find effective and satisfying treatment to manage their health issues. Most chronic illnesses can only be managed, not cured, and physicians typically do not prefer to deal with the issues involved in treating a chronically ill patient. People who turn to CAM may therefore do so to achieve the best combination of treatments, conventional and alternative, to maximize their treatment benefits (Balneaves, Truant, Kelly, Verhoef, & Davison, 2007; Sirois, 2008). Research on the health care use of people who do and do not visit CAM providers supports this notion. Among general medical and chronic illness populations, people who consulted CAM providers also used a greater number and variety of conventional health services compared to those who did not use CAM (Sirois, 2002; Sirois, 2008). Relative to CAM non-users, CAM clients report significantly more consultations with general practitioners, nutritionists, physiotherapists, and psychologists, independent of their greater number of health problems (Sirois, 2008).

Consultations with CAM providers tend to be longer, and more in depth than those with physicians (Busato & Kunzi, 2010), and can often involve an extensive consideration of the psychosocial aspects of the individual's life, which may be contributing to their health issue. Many conventional treatments involve unpleasant side effects that can be worse than the symptoms of the ailment being treated. Patients who are dissatisfied with aspects of conventional medical care for managing a chronic health issue, and those who wish to feel more in control of their health and their treatment decisions may therefore turn to CAM.

The benefits patients report from CAM treatments also tend to focus on outcomes that go beyond symptom relief (Verhoef, Vanderheyden, Dryden,

Mallory, & Ware, 2006). For example, one study found that patients who used CAM treatments reported symptom relief and improved physical functioning, as well as psychological benefits such as improved coping, empowerment, increased hope, and advocacy and support from their CAM provider (Greene, Walsh, Sirois, & McCaffrey, 2009). In addition, patients who used CAM in this study also reported that they made healthy lifestyle changes such as eating better and becoming more physically active, which they attributed to their use of CAM.

The motivations for CAM use are complex, and may vary depending on the type of CAM used (Kelner & Wellman, 1997), the health condition it is used for (Sirois, 2008), and whether it is initial or continued CAM use (Sirois & Gick, 2002; Sirois & Purc-Stephenson, 2008a). For example, dissatisfaction with aspects of conventional care may be more important for initial use, whereas beliefs in a more holistic and empowering approach to health may become important to sustain CAM use over time (Sirois & Gick, 2002; Sirois & Purc-Stephenson, 2008a). Such beliefs may emerge and be strengthened from repeated interactions with CAM providers, as patients become exposed to a different philosophy of health care, which in turn may reinforce these health beliefs. However, the increased uptake of CAM in the past two decades also means that some people may be born into a culture of CAM use—that is, they were raised in a family where CAM use was the norm (Sirois, 2010b). For this next generation of CAM users the reasons suggested by current CAM research may have little to do with their motivations to use CAM. Understanding the factors that influence their decision to continue to use CAM as they become independent adults will be more important. Future research on the reasons for CAM use will need to address these issues in order to disentangle the products from the precursors of CAM use.

Changes in the Philosophy of Health Care Delivery

A number of changes underlying the philosophy of health care delivery are altering the face of health care delivery. The physician's role is changing. The increasing acceptance and use of complementary and alternative

therapies and the rising number of women in the medical profession have changed what was once a very clear physician role characterized by dominance and authority. Although these changes promote more egalitarian attitudes among physicians, they also challenge the physician's dominance, autonomy, and authority (Kelner,

Wellman, Boon, & Welsh, 2004). Responsibilities that once fell exclusively to physicians are now shared with other authorities, including other health care providers and patients (Conrad, 2005).

Holistic Health Movement and Health Care   Western medicine is increasingly incorporating Eastern approaches to medicine and nontraditional therapies, such as meditation and biofeedback. The philosophy of **holistic health,** the idea that health is a positive state to be actively achieved, not merely the absence of disease, has gained a strong foothold in Western medicine. This viewpoint acknowledges psychological and spiritual influences on achieving health, and it gives patients responsibility for both achieving health and curing illness through their behaviours, attitudes, and spiritual beliefs. Holistic health emphasizes health education, self-help, and self-healing. Natural, low-technology interventions and non-Western techniques of medical practice may be substituted for or added to traditional care and include herbal medicine, acupuncture, acupressure, massage, homeopathy, reiki, spiritual healing, and dance therapy. Collectively referred to as complementary and alternative medicine (CAM), these therapies are gaining popularity among Canadians as treatment options, and increasing the demand for acceptance among conventional medicine providers.

As illustrated in the following quote, the biopsychosocial approach to health advocated by CAM use provides patients with a very different way of viewing their health:

> It isn't so much for me a symptom and treatment as much as it has been a very different way of life and looking at my body and my health and having alternative methods to support that. To think not about so much the cause and affect [sic] symptoms but to think more about my overall wellness. It is more about bringing the whole system into balance and that is a real . . . not so much [the] cause/effect [of] these symptoms. Anyway this idea of coming back into balance and shifting my thinking about my body and what wellness is and what balance is. That, in itself I think, is very healing.
>
> (Greene, Walsh, Sirois, & McCaffrey, 2009)

These changes alter the relationship between provider and patient, making it more open, equal, and reciprocal and potentially bringing emotional contact into the relationship between patient and provider (Astin, 1998; Bann, Sirois, & Walsh, 2010). Indeed, CAM patients rate the quality of the interpersonal care and communication higher than do patients of conventional medicine physicians (Busato & Kunzi, 2010). This shift to a more egalitarian relationship between patient and provider may also have additional benefits that can directly and indirectly impact outcomes. In one study, the degree to which patients felt supported and cared for *by their CAM providers* was significantly associated with feeling empowered, which in turn was linked to greater symptom relief (Bann et al., 2010).

Provider Behaviours That Contribute to Faulty Communication

"I believe you understand what you think I said, but I'm not sure you realize that what you heard is not what I meant ... "

—Anonymous, from blackboard in Weagamow Lake Band Office

Not Listening   Communication between the patient and physician can be eroded by certain provider behaviours. One problematic provider behaviour is not listening. In a study of physicians' initial responses to patient-initiated visits, Beckman and Frankel (1984) studied 74 office visits. In only 23 percent of the cases did patients have the opportunity to finish their explanation of concerns before the provider began the process of diagnosis. In 69 percent of the visits, the physician interrupted, directing the patient toward a particular disorder. On an average, physicians interrupted after their patients had spoken for only 18 to 22 seconds. Because physicians knew their behaviour was being recorded during the office visits, the study may have actually underestimated the extent of this problem.

The consequence of provider efforts to manage the interaction not only prevents patients from discussing their concerns but may also lead to loss of important information. Such information may be valuable not just for addressing the patients' needs but also for helping to identify when the patient may be experiencing adverse reactions to certain prescribed drugs, information which may help improve the safety monitoring of new drugs. For example one study of over a thousand patient records examined the agreement rates between physicians' documentation of symptoms and patients self-reported symptoms. Although there was some degree of concordance, 31 percent of patients with chest pain, 38 percent with shortness of breath, and 45 percent with cough did not have their symptoms mentioned in the physicians' notes (Pakhomov, Jacobsen, Chute, & Roger, 2008). Accordingly, some physicians are suggesting that less attention should be given to physicians' impressions of patient symptoms, and more attention be given to patients' firsthand experience of their symptoms (Basch, 2010).

Use of Jargon   The use of jargon and technical language is another important factor in poor communication. Studies reveal that patients understand relatively few of the complex terms that providers often use. Why do providers use complex, hard-to-understand language? In some cases, jargon-filled explanations may be used to keep the patient from asking too many questions or from discovering that the provider is not certain what the patient's problem is.

Physicians have long used medical jargon to impress gullible laymen. As far back as the thirteenth century, the medieval physician Arnold of Villanova urged colleagues to seek refuge behind impressive-sounding language when they could not explain a patient ailment. "Say that he has an obstruction of the liver," Arnold wrote, "and particularly use the word obstruction because patients do not understand what it means" (*Time,* 1970, p. 35). One physician explained, with great amusement, that if the term "*itis*" (meaning "inflammation of") was connected to whatever organ was troubled (for example, "stomachitis"), this would usually forestall any additional questions from the patient.

More commonly, however, providers' use of jargon may be a carryover from their technical training. Providers learn a complex vocabulary for understanding illnesses and communicating about them to other professionals; they often find it hard to remember that the patient does not share this expertise. The use of jargon may also stem from an inability to gauge what the patient will understand and an inability to figure out the appropriate non-technical explanation. How much should one tell a patient? Does the patient need to know how the disorder developed? If so, how should that explanation be provided?

Baby Talk   Because practitioners may underestimate what their patients will understand about an illness and its treatment, they may resort to baby talk and simplistic explanations.

"Nurse, would you just pop off her things for me? I want to examine her." In the hospital, everything is "popped" on or off, slipped in or out. I don't think I met a single doctor who, in dealing with patients, didn't resort to this sort of nursery talk. I once heard one saying to a patient, an elderly man, "We're just going to pop you into the operating theater to have a little peep into your tummy." Nurses, too, had people "popping" all over the place—in and out of lavatories, dressing gowns, beds, scales, wheelchairs, bandages. (Toynbee, 1977)

As these remarks indicate, overly simple explanations coupled with infantilizing baby talk can make the patient feel like a helpless child. Moreover, such behaviour can forestall questions. The tendency to lapse into simple explanations with a patient may become almost automatic. One woman, who is both a cancer researcher and a cancer patient, reports that when she goes to see her cancer specialist, he talks to her in a very complex and technical manner until the examination starts. Once she is on the examining table, he shifts to very simple sentences and explanations. She is now a patient and no longer a colleague.

Elderspeak   Equally problematic is elderspeak, a communication issue that is unfortunately common between health care workers and their patients. It includes using overly familiar terms such as "dear" and "sweetie" to address elderly strangers, and altering pronouns such as "Are we ready for our bath?" Similar to baby talk, **elderspeak** is an overly caring and infantilizing communication issue that sends the message that elderly people are incompetent (K. N. Williams et al., 2009).

Aside from being potentially demeaning, there is some evidence that elderspeak can negatively impact health. One study used videotapes of actual interactions between nursing staff and nursing home residents with Alzheimer's, coding them for normal or elderspeak staff communication and cooperative or resistant patient behaviour. Elderspeak was linked to an increased probability of patients resisting care compared to normal communication, suggesting that elderspeak may create barriers to delivering needed health care (K. N. Williams et al., 2009). Elderspeak also reinforces negative age-related stereotypes both for the person using elderspeak and for the older person being targeted. Not only can this impact how older adults think about themselves which in turn can negatively impact health (Levy, 2003), but it may also have long-range health consequences for the person using elderspeak. One longitudinal study following adults for 38 years found that those who held negative age stereotypes as younger adults had an increased risk of having a cardiac event in their later life (Levy, Zonderman, Slade, & Ferrucci, 2009). Communication training may be one way to effectively reduce this problem and its consequences for both the patient and the provider (K. N. Williams et al., 2009). Education and interventions designed to target ageism among health care workers may also be necessary to help address this widespread issue, as one recent review suggests that physicians' attitudes towards the elderly tend to be more negative than not (Meisner, 2011).

Nonperson Treatment   Depersonalization of the patient is another problem that impairs the quality of the patient–provider relationship (Kaufman, 1970). This nonperson treatment may be employed intentionally to try to keep the patient quiet while an examination, a procedure, or a test is being conducted, or it may be used unintentionally because the patient (as object) has become the focus of the provider's attention.

> When I was being given emergency treatment for an eye laceration, the resident surgeon abruptly terminated his conversation with me as soon as I lay down on the operating table. Although I had had no sedative, or anesthesia, he acted as if I were no longer conscious, directing all his questions to a friend of mine—questions such as, "What's his name? What occupation is he in? Is he a real doctor?" etc. As I lay there, these two men were speaking about me as if I were not there at all. The moment I got off the table and was no longer a cut to be stitched, the surgeon resumed his conversation with me, and existence was conferred upon me again. (Zimbardo, 1969, p. 298)

To understand the phenomenon of non person treatment, consider what a nuisance it can be for a provider to have the patient actually there during a treatment—fussing, giving unhelpful suggestions, and asking questions. If the patients could drop their bodies off, as they do their cars, and pick them up later, it would save both the provider and the patient a lot of trouble and anxiety. As it is, the provider is like an auto mechanic who has the misfortune of having the car's owner following him or her around, creating trouble, while he or she is trying to fix the car (E. Goffman, 1961).

The emotion communicated by a provider in interaction with a patient can have a substantial impact on the patient's attitude toward the provider, the visit, and his or her condition (J. A. Hall, Epstein, DeCiantis, & McNeil, 1993). One study, for example, found that women getting their mammogram results from a seemingly worried physician recalled less information, perceived their situation to be more severe, showed higher levels of anxiety, and had significantly higher pulse rates than women receiving mammogram results from a non-worried physician (D. E. Shapiro, Boggs, Melamed, & Graham-Pole, 1992).

Stereotypes of Patients   Negative stereotypes of patients may contribute to problems in communication and subsequent treatment. For example, First Nations people are often stereotyped as being "quiet and passive" or "angry" or even "drunk" by health care providers (Browne, 2007). This can lead to social distancing in health care encounters as illustrated in the following excerpt from a hospital nurse dealing with a First Nations woman:

> This woman . . . She wouldn't look at me. She wouldn't answer anything. She would nod occasionally. She really didn't know what was going on . . . so I got the Native Support Worker. I mean, it's a cultural thing. (Browne, 2007, p. 2169)

When a person is seen by a provider of the same race or ethnicity, satisfaction with treatment tends to be higher, underscoring the importance of increasing the number of minority physicians (Laveist & Nuru-Jeter, 2002). Another way to deal with potential problems due to cultural differences is to ensure that health care is delivered in a culturally appropriate way. The province of Nova Scotia has done just that through its initiative called "Diversity and Social Inclusion in Health Care," which is a set of provincial cultural competency guidelines to help ensure the delivery of culturally appropriate primary health care. The first of its kind in Canada, these guidelines have been designed to help health care professionals tailor health care so that it better meets the social, cultural, and linguistic needs of patients (Province of Nova Scotia, 2008).

Sexism is a problem in medical practice as well. For example, in three experimental studies that attributed reported chest pain and stress to either a male or female patient, medical intervention was perceived to be less important for the female patient (R. Martin & Lemos, 2002). Male physicians and female patients do not always communicate well with each other. Research suggests that in comparison with male physicians, female physicians generally conduct longer visits, ask more

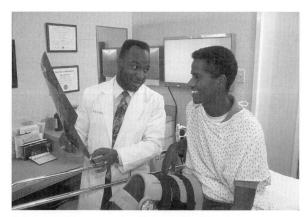

Patients are often most comfortable interacting with a physician who is similar to themselves.

questions, make more positive comments during a visit, and show more nonverbal support, such as smiling and nodding (J. A. Hall, Irish, Roter, Ehrlich, & Miller, 1994). Female physicians are also more likely to discuss preventive health behaviours than male physicians (Ramirez et al., 2009).

Patients' Contributions to Faulty Communication

Certain patients may not clearly understand their diagnoses and this can affect adherence to prescribed treatment especially after they are discharged from the hospital. One study found that although 72 percent of patients being discharged felt that they had a good understanding of their diagnoses, older patients and those with cognitive impairments were less likely to have a clear understanding (Ní Chróinín, Syed Farooq, Burke, & Kyne, 2011). Identifying the characteristics of patients that increase the risk for poor communication is therefore important for finding solutions to improve communication and ultimately the quality of their care.

Patient Characteristics   Several factors on the patient's part contribute to poor patient–provider communications. Patients scoring high in neuroticism often present an exaggerated picture of their symptoms (for example, Ellington & Wiebe, 1999). This style can, unfortunately, compromise a physician's ability to gauge effectively the seriousness of a patient's condition. When patients are anxious, their learning can be impaired (Graugaard & Finset, 2000). Anxiety makes it difficult to focus attention and process incoming information and even harder to retain it. Because anxiety is often

high during a visit to a provider, it is not surprising that patients retain so little information. Focusing directly on the patient's concerns can alleviate this barrier to effective communication (Graugaard & Finset, 2000).

Patient Knowledge   Some patients are unable to understand even simple information about their case. Linguistic barriers can contribute to this problem and further complicate communication (Stout, Charpentier, Chiasson, & Fillion, 2009). Although the use of the Internet for medical and health-related information is becoming increasingly common, patients who do not have easy access to the Internet or are less skilled at using the Internet may fall on the wrong side of the so-called "digital divide" and may not be able to make use of this resource (Underhill & McKeown, 2008).

Patient Attitudes toward Symptoms   Patients respond to different cues about their illness than do practitioners (R. Martin & Lemos, 2002). Patients place considerable emphasis on pain and on symptoms that interfere with their activities. But providers are more concerned with the underlying illness—its severity and treatment. Patients may misunderstand the provider's emphasis on factors that they consider to be incidental, they may pay little attention when vital information is being communicated, or they may believe that the provider has made an incorrect diagnosis.

Patients sometimes give providers misleading information about their medical history or their current concerns. Patients may be embarrassed about their health history (such as having had an abortion) or their health practices (such as being a smoker) and often do not report these important pieces of information to the physician (L. Smith, Adler, & Tschann, 1999).

Patients may fear asking questions because they do not think they will receive straight answers, and providers may erroneously assume that because no questions have been asked, the patient does not want any information. The following episode illustrates the lengths to which such misconceptions can be carried:

> At the age of 59, [Mr. Tischler] suffered progressive discomfort from a growing lump in his groin. He did not discuss it with his wife or anyone else until six weeks prior to his admission to the hospital, when he began to fear that it was cancer. When Mrs. Tischler heard about it, she, too, was fearful of cancer, but she did not mention this to her husband. She did, however, discuss his condition with a close friend who was the secretary of a local

surgeon. Through this friend, Mr. Tischler was introduced to the surgeon who examined him, made a diagnosis of a hernia, and recommended hospitalization for repair of the hernia. Both Mr. and Mrs. Tischler thought the surgeon was trying to be kind to them since Mr. Tischler, in their fearful fantasies, was afflicted with cancer. The surgeon scheduled admission to the hospital for elective repair of the hernia. After the surgery, the hernia disappeared, the incision healed normally, and there were no complications. Mr. Tischler then realized that the surgeon had been accurate in his diagnosis and prognosis. He returned to work in three weeks, free from pain and all disability. (Duff & Hollingshead, 1968, p. 300)

Interactive Aspects of the Communication Problem

Qualities of the interaction between practitioner and patient may perpetuate faulty communication. A major problem is that the patient–provider interaction does not provide the opportunity for feedback to the provider. Providers rarely know whether information was communicated effectively because they rarely learn about the results of the communications (Sicotte, Pineault, Tilquin, & Contandriopoulos, 1996).

Specifically, the provider sees the patient, the patient is diagnosed, treatment is recommended, and the patient leaves. When the patient does not return, any number of things may have happened: The treatment may have cured the disorder; the patient may have gotten worse and decided to seek treatment elsewhere; the treatment may have failed, but the disorder may have cleared up anyway; or the patient may have died. Not knowing which of these alternatives has actually occurred, the provider does not know the impact and success rate of the advice given. Obviously, it is to the provider's psychological advantage to believe that the diagnosis was correct, that the patient followed the advice, and that the patient's disorder was cured by the recommended treatment, but the provider may never find out for certain.

The provider may also find it hard to know when a satisfactory personal relationship has been established with a patient. Many patients are relatively cautious with providers. If they are dissatisfied, rather than complain about it directly, they may simply change providers, or supplement their care with alternative therapies to meet their needs. The provider who finds that a patient has stopped coming does not know if the patient has moved out of the area or switched to another practice. When providers do get feedback, it is more likely to be negative than positive: And for those who live in areas where it may be difficult to change providers and who are dissatisfied with aspects of their care, they may nonetheless return out of necessity rather than choice.

Two points are important here. First, learning is fostered more by positive than by negative feedback; positive feedback tells one what one is doing right, whereas negative feedback may tell one what to stop doing but not necessarily what to do instead. Because providers get more negative than positive feedback, this situation is not conducive to learning. Second, learning occurs only with feedback, but in the provider's case, lack of feedback is the rule. Clearly, it is extremely difficult for the provider to know if communication is adequate and, if not, how to change it. It is no wonder, then, that when social scientists display their statistics on poor patient–provider communication, each provider can say with confidence, "Not me," because he or she indeed has no basis for self-recrimination.

Critical Checkpoint

Improving Patient-Provider Communication

As noted, maximizing patient-provider communication can have a variety of benefits, mainly for the quality of care for the patient. But should the onus for good communication be on the patient or on the provider? Should patients be better prepared before engaging in the medical encounter with their health care providers? Or should physicians take more time and care in their encounters with patients, and is this even possible given Canada's already overburdened health care system?

WHAT ARE THE CONSEQUENCES OF POOR PATIENT–PROVIDER COMMUNICATION?

(L03)

The patient–provider communication problems would be little more than an unfortunate casualty of medical treatment were it not for the toll they take on health. For example, researchers surveyed hospital admissions from 20 randomly chosen hospitals in Quebec for adverse events such as experiencing constipation from taking drugs to control irritable bowel syndrome or suicidal thoughts while taking antidepressants. They found that patients with communication problems in the delivery of their care were at greater risk for experiencing multiple preventable adverse events compared to those who did not experience communication problems (Bartlett, Blais, Tamblyn, Clermont, & MacGibbon, 2008). Dissatisfied patients are also less likely to use medical services in the future (Stout et al., 2009). They are more likely to turn to CAM to supplement their conventional medical care (Sirois & Gick, 2002), and less likely to disclose the use of CAM treatments and therapies to their physicians (Barraco et al., 2005).

Thus, it appears that patient dissatisfaction with patient–provider interaction not only fosters health risks by leading patients to avoid using services in the future but also engenders more communication problems and more fragmented health care for patients.

Patient–Provider Communication and Complementary and Alternative Medicine Use

When patients are dissatisfied with aspects of conventional medical care, including patient–provider interactions, they may be more likely to consider consulting CAM providers to fulfill their unmet needs. In particular, people who use CAM expect a collaborative and caring interaction with their health care provider and may find that the brief 10 minutes that they spend with their doctor does not satisfy this need (Busato & Kunzi, 2010). For example, the lack of a caring therapeutic relationship with conventional doctors has been noted as a reason for using CAM (Luff & Thomas, 2000). CAM users also expect to have their treatment delivered in a caring and empathetic manner (Richardson, 2004). In one Canadian study the preference for a collaborative and more egalitarian relationship with one's health care provider as opposed to one where the provider assumes an authoritative and directive role, was associated with consulting CAM providers (Sirois & Purc-Stephenson, 2008).

Non-disclosure of Complementary and Alternative Medicine Use

One important and potentially problematic consequence of poor patient–provider communication is that patients will be less likely to disclose their use of CAM treatments or natural health products to their primary health care provider. Physician awareness of concurrent CAM treatments

and natural health product (NHP) use is crucial for preventing harmful treatment interactions and adverse drug reactions. Disclosure is especially important in the context of ongoing life-threatening conditions such as cardiac problems and cancer. Despite the high use of CAM in conjunction with conventional treatment, disclosure of CAM use to physicians is low ranging from only 22 to 36 percent (Barraco et al., 2005; Robinson & McGrail, 2004). Similar low rates of disclosure have been found regarding the use of natural health products (Walji et al., 2010).

Why do patients not disclose their use of CAM to their physicians? The main reasons include expecting a negative response from their physician, not feeling comfortable enough to discuss this with their physician, believing that their physician did not need to know about their use of CAM, and because their physician did not explicitly ask them about CAM or NHP use (Robinson & McGrail, 2004; Walji et al., 2010). Improving communication between patients and providers is one way to build trust and increase CAM disclosure rates, which in turn can prevent potentially serious treatment interactions.

In the next section we consider another common problem that arises from poor patient–provider communication, namely patient non-adherence, and the factors that contribute to this issue.

WHAT IS TREATMENT NON-ADHERENCE AND HOW CAN IT BE REDUCED?   (L04)

Chapters 3, 4, and 5 examined **adherence** to treatment regimens in the context of health behaviours and noted how difficult it can be to modify or eliminate poor health habits, such as smoking, or to achieve a healthy lifestyle. In this section we examine the role of health institutions, and particularly the role of the provider, in promoting adherence.

A 17th-century French playwright, Moliere, aptly described the relationship that physicians and patients often have with respect to treatment recommendations:

> The King: You have a physician. What does he do?
> Moliere: Sire, we converse. He gives me advice which I do not follow and I get better. (Treue, 1958, as cited in Koltun & Stone, 1986)

When patients do not adopt the behaviours and treatments their providers recommend, the result is termed **non-adherence** (DiMatteo, 2004). Estimates of non-adherence vary from a low of 15 percent to a staggering high of 93 percent. On average, non-adherence is about 26 percent (DiMatteo, Giordani, Lepper, & Croghan, 2002). For short-term antibiotic regimens, one of the most common prescriptions, it is estimated that at least one-third of all patients fail to comply adequately. As many as 80 percent of patients drop out of lifestyle change programs designed to treat obesity (Grossi et al., 2006). Adherence is typically so poor that researchers believe that the benefits of many medications cannot be realized at the current levels of adherence that patients achieve (R. B. Haynes, McKibbon, & Kanani, 1996). Adherence is highest in HIV disease, arthritis, gastrointestinal disorders, and cancer, and lowest among patients with pulmonary disease, diabetes, and sleep disorders (DiMatteo et al., 2002).

Measuring Adherence   Obtaining reliable indications of non-adherence is not an easy matter (Turk & Meichenbaum, 1991). One study that attempted to assess use of the drug theophylline for patients suffering from chronic obstructive pulmonary disease (COPD) found that physicians reported that 78 percent of their COPD patients were on the medication, chart audit revealed 62 percent of the patients were on the medication, videotaped observation of patient visits produced an estimate of 69 percent, and only 59 percent of the patients reported they were on theophylline (Gerbert, Stone, Stulbarg, Gullion, & Greenfield, 1988). And the study did not even assess whether theophylline was administered correctly, only if it was prescribed at all.

Asking patients about their adherence yields unreliable and artificially high estimates (for example, R. M. Kaplan & Simon, 1990; Turk & Meichenbaum, 1991). Because most patients know they are supposed to adhere, they may bias their answers to appear more cooperative than they really are (Turk & Meichenbaum, 1991). As a consequence, researchers draw on indirect measures of adherence, such as the number of follow-up or referral appointments kept, but even these measures can be biased. Treatment outcome might be a way to assess non-adherence, but there is little evidence of a clear relationship between the extent of adherence and health outcomes. In short, many factors obscure the relationship between adherence and recovery (Turk & Meichenbaum, 1991). The unnerving conclusion is that, if anything, the research statistics underestimate the amount of non-adherence that is actually going on.

Creative Non-adherence   One especially interesting form of non-adherence is termed **creative non-adherence,** or intelligent non-adherence, because it involves modifying and supplementing a prescribed treatment regimen. For example, a poor patient may change the dosage level of required medication to make the medicine last as

long as possible or may keep some medication in reserve in case another family member comes down with the same disorder. Creative non-adherence may also be a response to concerns or confusion over the treatment regimen. Not understanding the dosage level may lead some people not to take any at all in the fear that they will overmedicate. Others may stop a medication because of unpleasant side effects.

Creative non-adherence can also result from private theories about a disorder and its treatment (Wroe, 2001). For example, patients may decide that particular symptoms that merit treatment were ignored by the provider; they may then supplement the treatment regimen with over-the-counter preparations or home remedies that interact with prescribed drugs in unpredictable, even dangerous ways. Alternatively, the patient may alter the dosage requirement, reasoning, for example, that if four pills a day for ten days will clear up the problem, then eight pills a day for five days will do it twice as quickly. One motive for this potentially risky behaviour may be to overcome the sense of loss of control that illness and its treatment brings (Turk & Meichenbaum, 1991).

Causes of Adherence and Non-adherance

When asked to explain non-adherence, physicians usually attribute it to patients' uncooperative personalities, to their ignorance, to lack of motivation, or to their forgetfulness (W. C. House, Pendelton, & Parker, 1986). In fact, efforts to identify the types of patients that are most likely to be non-adherent have been unsuccessful (R. M. Kaplan & Simon, 1990). Non-adherence, then, is a widespread and complex behaviour. Some of the contributing factors are listed in Table 9.1. Nonetheless, the greatest cause of non-adherence is poor communication.

Good Communication   Good communication fosters adherence. The patient must understand the treatment regimen, be satisfied with the relationship and treatment regimen, and decide to adhere. Accordingly, adherence is highest when a patient receives a clear, jargon-free explanation of the etiology, diagnosis, and treatment recommendations. The Health Psychology in Action box ("Improving Adherence to Treatment," p. 255) presents several recommendations for increasing adherence through good communication.

Satisfaction with the patient–provider relationship also predicts adherence. When patients perceive the provider as warm and caring, they are more compliant; providers who show anger or impatience toward their

TABLE 9.1 | Some Determinants of Adherence to Treatment Regimens and Care

	Following Prescribed Regimen	Staying in Treatment
Social Characteristics		
Age	0	+
Sex	0	0
Education	0	0
Income	0	0
Psychological Dispositions		
Beliefs about threat to health	+	+
Beliefs about efficacy of action	+	+
Knowledge of recommendation and purpose	+	+
General attitudes toward medical care	0	0
General knowledge about health and illness	0	0
Intelligence	0	0
Anxiety	–?	–
Internal control	0?	0
Psychic disturbance	–	2
Social Context		
Social support	+	+
Social isolation	–	–
Primary group stability	+	+
Situational Demands		
Symptoms	+	+
Complexity of action	–	–
Duration of action	–	–
Interference with other actions	–	–
Interactions with Health Care System		
Convenience factors	+	+
Continuity of care	+	+
Personal source of care	+	+
General satisfaction	0	0
Supportive interaction	+	+

Table entries indicate whether a factor encourages compliance (+), works against it (–), has no impact (0), or has uncertain impact (?).
Source: Adapted from Kirscht & Rosenstock, 1979, p. 215.

patients, or who just seem busier, have more non-adherent patients (Sherbourne, Hays, Ordway, DiMatteo, & Kravitz, 1992). On the other hand, providers who answer patients' questions have more adherent patients (DiMatteo et al., 1993). Providers who show respect for patients also foster greater patient satisfaction and adherence to treatment (Clucas & St Claire, 2010).

The final step in adherence, one that is frequently overlooked, involves the patient's decision to adhere to a prescribed medical regimen. Many providers simply assume that patients will follow their advice, without realizing that the patients must first decide to do so.

Treatment Regimen   Qualities of the treatment regimen also influence the degree of adherence a patient will exhibit. Treatment regimens that must be followed over a long period of time, that are highly complex, and that interfere with other desirable behaviours in a person's life all show low levels of adherence (Turk & Meichenbaum, 1991). As the Health Psychology in Action box, "Protease Inhibitors: An Adherence Nightmare?" illustrates, sometimes these can be the very treatment regimens on which survival depends.

Adherence is high (about 90 percent) when the advice is perceived as "medical" (for example, taking medication), but lower (76 percent) if the advice is vocational (for example, taking time off from work), and lower still (66 percent) if the advice is social or psychological (for example, avoiding stressful social situations; Turk & Meichenbaum, 1991). Adherence is higher for treatment recommendations that seem like medicine (taking pills), but much lower when the treatment seems nonmedical (such as instructions to rest). Adherence is very poor (20 percent to 50 percent) when people are asked to change personal habits, such as smoking or drinking (DiMatteo & DiNicola, 1982).

Complex self-care regimens show the lowest level of overall adherence (Blumenthal & Emery, 1988). People with diabetes, for example, must often take injections of insulin, monitor their blood glucose fluctuations, strictly control their dietary intake, and in some programs, engage in prescribed exercise programs and efforts at stress management. Even with the best of intentions, it is difficult to engage in all the required behaviours, which take up several hours a day (Turk & Meichenbaum, 1991).

Avoidant coping strategies on the part of patients are associated with poor adherence to treatment recommendations. In a longitudinal study of patients with a variety of chronic disorders, patients who relied on avoidant coping strategies were less likely to follow their doctors' specific recommendations and to adhere to treatment goals in general (Sherbourne et al., 1992). Consistent with our analysis of avoidant coping in Chapter 7, it may be that patients who cope with stressful events via avoidance are less attentive or responsive to information about threatening events, such as health problems.

Another patient factor that influences adherence is the presence of life stressors. Non-adherent patients cite lack of time, no money, or distracting problems at home, such as instability and conflict, as impediments to adherence. In contrast, people who enjoy the activities in their lives are more motivated to adhere to treatment (Irvine et al., 1999). Adherence is substantially higher in patients who live in cohesive families but lower with patients whose families are in conflict (DiMatteo, 2004). Likewise, people who are depressed show poor adherence to treatment medication (DiMatteo, Lepper, & Croghan, 2000).

Reducing Non-adherence

Reducing non-adherence is important, made all the more so as research increasingly reveals the importance of lifestyle change to promote health and avoid illness.

Counselling patients on issues related to health promotion and health habit modification are activities physicians have traditionally not had to undertaken. Because lifestyle changes are the very behaviours that show low levels of adherence, teaching physicians to communicate effectively to increase treatment adherence has become a critical goal. A review of reviews of the effectiveness of adherence enhancing interventions found that many interventions lacked a clear theoretical framework (van Dulmen et al., 2007). Nonetheless interventions that were found to be effective fell into one of four different categories: technical, behavioural, educational, and multi-faceted or complex interventions. Among these technical interventions such as simplifying the treatment regimen were often found to be the most effective.

Treatment Presentation Interventions   The presentation of the treatment regimen can also influence adherence. Treatment recommendations should be written down and the patient should be tested for understanding and

When physicians present concrete advice about lifestyle change, patients are more likely to adhere.

Protease Inhibitors: An Adherence Nightmare?

People living with AIDS who once believed they were at death's doorstep now have a life-prolonging treatment available to them in the form of protease inhibitors. Protease is an HIV enzyme that is required for HIV replication. Protease inhibitors prevent the protease enzyme from cleaving the virus-complex into pathogenic virions (the infective form of a virus). Taken regularly, protease inhibitors not only stop the spread of HIV but also in some cases, following treatment, people once diagnosed with AIDS show no trace of the virus in their bloodstreams.

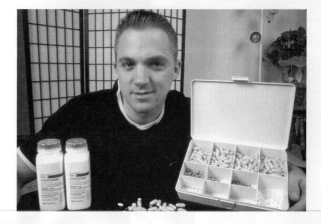

But taking protease inhibitors regularly is the trick. Protease inhibitors have several qualities that make adherence problematic. First, many protease inhibitors must be taken four times a day. Most people can barely remember to take one tablet a day, and estimates of levels of compliance with antibiotic regimens requiring two tablets a day put adherence at less than one-third. Moreover, on these other regimens, a skipped date does not mean failure, whereas with protease inhibitors, missing even one dose may make the medication permanently unsuccessful. Many protease inhibitors require refrigeration, and consequently, the patient must remain close to the refrigerated drug throughout the day so as to take the medication on time. This factor is impractical for some people with AIDS.

For middle-class people with stable lives, regular employment, and socially supportive networks, adherence may be likely. However, for the poor, the homeless, and the unemployed, who may lack even a refrigerator for keeping protease inhibitors cold, much less the stable life that promotes their regular use, adherence is a difficult task. Moreover, drug use, chronic anxiety, and other affective or psychotic disorders interfere with the ability to use the drugs properly, and these states characterize some of the people who are eligible for protease inhibitors. Protease inhibitors have unpleasant side effects, including diarrhea and nausea. Unpleasant side effects often produce high levels of non-adherence.

In short, although protease inhibitors represent a life-saving discovery, they have many features that make their faithful use problematic. Integrating medication into busy, often chaotic and changing lives is difficult, yet adherence holds the key to survival, so psychologists will be heavily involved in the effort to help people with AIDS adhere faithfully to the medication regimen.

recall. Giving the patient a medication information sheet that describes the treatment, the dosage level of medication, and possible side effects can also improve compliance (Peck & King, 1982). Such interventions are now commonly used by pharmacies to better inform patients about the medications they are prescribed by physicians, and to promote adherence.

Probing for Barriers The provider can also probe for potential barriers to adherence. Patients are remarkably good at predicting how compliant they will be with treatment regimens (R. M. Kaplan & Simon, 1990). By making use of this personal knowledge, the physician may discover what some of the barriers to

adherence will be. For example, if the patient has been told to avoid stressful situations but anticipates several high-pressure meetings the following week at work, the patient and provider together might consider how to resolve this dilemma—one option may be to have a coworker take the patient's place at some of the meetings.

For the vocational and social advice on which non-adherence rates are known to be high, special measures are needed. The health care provider can begin by explaining why these seemingly nonmedical aspects of the treatment regimen are, in fact, important to health. For example, the benefits of regular exercise can be concretely explained. Finally, because of the face-to-face nature of patient–provider interaction, the provider may be in a good position to extract a commitment from the patient—that is, a promise that the recommendations will be undertaken and followed through. Such verbal commitments are associated with increased adherence (Kulik & Carlino, 1987).

Consistent with self-efficacy theory (Bandura, 1977, 1986), breaking advice down into manageable subgoals that can be more easily achieved by the patient and monitored by the provider is another way to increase adherence. With the success of each subgoal, the patient's confidence and motivation for achieving the next subgoal increases, resulting in better adherence. For example, if patients have been told to alter their diet and lose weight, intermediate weight-loss goals that can be checked at successive appointments might be established (for example, "Try to lose three pounds this week").

In short, then, adherence is a formidable issue that can be attacked on several fronts simultaneously. Modifying institutional procedures for following patients, presenting the treatment regimen clearly, and increasing the skill of the practitioner in communicating with the patient all have potential for increasing adherence.

(L05) HOW CAN WE IMPROVE PATIENT–PROVIDER COMMUNICATION?

The fact that poor patient-provider communication appears to be so widespread and tied to problematic outcomes, such as nonadherance, suggests that improving the communication process should be a high priority. One attack on the problem is to teach providers how to communicate more effectively.

Patient-centred Communication

Providers have known for some time that the course of medical treatment can be affected by communication (see, for example, Shattuck, 1907), yet many may see communication as a knack that some people have and others do not. However, efforts to identify the personalities of physicians who communicate effectively have revealed only one reliable predictor of physician sensitivity: the physician's reported interest in people. This fact suggests that provider sensitivity is more a matter of motivation than skill; hence, anyone, given the desire, has the potential to be an effective communicator.

Training Providers   Talking to patients takes time. With pressures toward cost-effective treatment in mind, what constitutes realistic training in communication skills? **Patient-centred communication** is an important way to improve the patient–provider dialogue and also improve patient outcomes (Stewart, 1995). As an essential component of patient-centred care (Stewart et al., 2000), this type of communication enlists the patient directly in decisions about medical care: Physicians try to see the disorder and the treatment as the patient does, and in so doing enlist the patient's cooperation in the diagnostic and treatment process. Not only is this approach successful in improving doctor–patient communication, it also seems to be especially effective with "difficult" patients, such as those who are high in anxiety (M. Sharpe et al., 1994; Langewitz, Eich, Kiss, & Wossmer, 1998). Interventions designed to enhance patient-centred communication may also be particularly well-suited for working with patients with more advanced communication deficits such as stroke survivors who have speech and language impairments (McGilton et al., 2010).

Any communication program should teach skills that can be learned easily, that can be incorporated in medical routines easily, and that, over time, come to be automatic. Such interventions often take the form of cognitive (teaching providers about effective communication), behavioural (including bedside practices), and psychological (providing individual feedback) interventions (McGilton et al., 2009). Communication courses should also be taught in settings that mirror the situations in which the skills will later be used.

Training Patients   Interventions to improve patient–provider interaction include teaching patients skills for eliciting information from physicians (Greenfield, Kaplan, Ware, Yano, & Frank, 1988). For example, a study by S. C. Thompson, Nanni, and Schwankovsky (1990) instructed women to list three questions they wanted to ask their physician during their visit. Compared with a control group, women who listed questions in advance asked more questions during the visit and were less anxious. In a second study, Thompson and her colleagues added a third condition: Some women received a message from their physician encouraging question asking. These women, too, asked more of the questions they wanted to, had greater feelings of personal control, and were more satisfied with the office visit. This pair of studies suggests that either thinking up one's own questions ahead of time or

Improving Adherence to Treatment

Non-adherence to treatment is a formidable medical problem, and many of the reasons can be traced directly to poor communication between the provider and the patient. The following are some guidelines generated by research findings that can help improve adherence.

1. Listen to the patient.

2. Repeat things, where feasible, and ask the patient to repeat what has to be done.

3. Give clear instructions on the exact treatment regimen, preferably in writing.

4. Make use of special reminder pill containers and calendars.

5. Call the patient if an appointment is missed.

6. Prescribe a self-care regimen in concert with the patient's daily schedule.

7. Emphasize at each visit the importance of adherence and acknowledge the patient's efforts to adhere.

8. Involve the patient's spouse or other partner.

9. Whenever possible, provide patients with instructions and advice at the start of the information to be presented, and stress how important they are.

10. Use short words and short sentences, and avoid medical jargon.

11. Use explicit categorization where possible (for example, divide information clearly into categories of etiology, treatment, or prognosis).

12. When giving advice, make it as specific, detailed, and concrete as possible.

13. Find out what the patient's worries are. Do not confine yourself merely to gathering objective medical information.

14. Find out what the patient's expectations are. If they cannot be met, explain why.

15. Provide information about the diagnosis and the cause of the illness.

16. Adopt a friendly rather than a businesslike attitude.

17. Spend some time in conversation about nonmedical topics.

Source: Based on R. B. Haynes, Wang, & da-Mota-Gomes, 1987; Ley, 1977; DiMatteo, 2004.

perceiving that the physician is open to questions improves communication during medical office visits, leading to greater patient satisfaction.

Skills Training As has been noted, poor provider communication skills are also tied to non-adherence. The Health Psychology in Action box, "Improving Adherence to Treatment," summarizes the specific steps that should be incorporated into communication efforts to help patients adhere to medical advice. Providers, especially physicians, are high-status figures for most patients, and what they say is generally accepted as valid. The provider is in a position to underscore the patient's personal vulnerability to the disorder: He or she has intimate personal knowledge of the patient. The provider can help the patient decide to adhere to a medical treatment regimen by highlighting its advantages, downplaying attendant disadvantages, and stressing the disadvantages of non-adherence (J. H. Brown & Raven, 1994). Reasons for how a provider can change patients' health behaviours are listed in Table 9.2.

TABLE 9.2 | Why the Health Practitioner Can Be an Effective Agent of Behaviour Change

- The health practitioner is a highly credible source with knowledge of medical issues.
- The health practitioner can make health messages simple and tailor them to the individual needs and vulnerabilities of each patient.
- The practitioner can help the patient decide to adhere by highlighting the advantages of treatment and the disadvantages of non-adherence.
- The private face-to-face nature of the interaction provides an effective setting for holding attention, repeating and clarifying instructions, extracting commitments from a patient, and assessing sources of resistance to adherence.
- The personal nature of the interaction enables a practitioner to establish referent power by communicating warmth and caring.
- The health practitioner can enlist the cooperation of other family members in promoting adherence.
- The health practitioner has the patient under at least partial surveillance and can monitor progress during subsequent visits.

(LO6) WHAT IS THE PLACEBO EFFECT?

Placebos are the ghosts that haunt our house of biomedical objectivity, the creatures that rise up from the dark and expose the paradoxes and fissures in our own self-created definitions of the real and active factors in treatment. (Harrington, 1997, p. 1)

- Inhaling a useless drug improved lung function in children with asthma by 33 percent.
- People exposed to fake poison ivy develop rashes.
- Forty-two percent of balding men taking a placebo maintained or increased their hair growth.
- Sham knee surgery reduces pain as much as real surgery. (Blakeslee, 1998)

All of these astonishing facts are due to one effect—the placebo. The placebo effect is a phenomenon that has both intrigued and confused medical and psychological researchers over the last half-century. The attitudes toward placebos have followed the trends of psychological and medical research, with placebos once being referred to as pseudo-medicine (Kurland, 1957), and more recently as the forgotten drug (Bostrom, 1997). Others have proposed that the placebo effect represents a true instance of belief becoming biology (Cousins, 1989). Today technological advances have provided researchers the opportunity to get a closer glimpse of the possible mechanisms involved in placebo effects.

This 16th-century woodcut shows the preparation of theriac, a supposed antidote to poison. If theriac was a successful treatment, it was entirely due to the placebo effect.

Historical Perspective

In the early days of medicine, few drugs or treatments gave any real physical benefit. As a consequence, patients were treated with a variety of bizarre, largely ineffective therapies. Egyptian patients were medicated with "lizard's blood, crocodile dung, the teeth of a swine, the hoof of an ass, putrid meat, and fly specks" (T. Findley, 1953), concoctions that were not only ineffective but dangerous. If the patient did not succumb to the disease, he or she had a good chance of dying from the treatment. Medical treatments of the Middle Ages were somewhat less lethal, but not much more effective. These European patients were treated with ground-up "unicorn's horn" (actually, ground ivory); bezoar stones (supposedly a "crystallized tear from the eye of a deer bitten by a snake" but actually an animal gallstone or other intestinal piece); theriac (made from ground-up snake and between 37 and 63 equally exotic ingredients); and, for healing wounds, powdered Egyptian mummy (A. K. Shapiro, 1960). As late as the seventeenth and eighteenth centuries, patients were subjected to bloodletting, freezing, and repeatedly induced vomiting to bring about a cure (A. K. Shapiro, 1960).

Such accounts make it seem miraculous that anyone survived these early medical treatments. But people did; moreover, they often seemed to get relief from these peculiar and largely ineffective remedies. Physicians have, for centuries, been objects of great veneration and respect, and this was no less true when few remedies were actually effective. To what can one attribute the success that these treatments provided? The most likely answer is that these treatments are examples of the **placebo effect.** Placebo effects continue to be powerful today, even though medicine now boasts a large number of truly effective treatments.

What Is a Placebo?

A **placebo** is "any medical procedure that produces an effect in a patient because of its therapeutic intent and not its specific nature, whether chemical or physical" (R. Liberman, 1962, p. 761). The word comes originally from Latin, meaning "I will please." Any medical procedure, ranging from drugs to surgery to psychotherapy, can have a placebo effect. The role of placebos in reducing pain and discomfort is substantial. Many patients who ingest useless substances or who undergo useless procedures find that, as a result, their symptoms disappear and their health improves. For example, in previous decades some physicians would prescribe antibiotics to patients who complained of suffering from the common cold. If the patient subsequently got better as a result of taking the antibiotics, this would be considered a placebo effect. Why? Because colds are caused by viruses that cannot be effectively treated by antibiotics that are, in fact, only effective for treating bacterial infections.

Moreover, placebo effects extend well beyond the beneficial results of ineffective substances. Much of the effectiveness of active treatments that produce real cures on their own include a placebo component. For example, in one study (Beecher, 1959), patients complaining of pain were injected with either morphine or a placebo. Although morphine was substantially more effective in reducing pain than was the placebo, the placebo was a successful painkiller in 35 percent of the cases. Another study demonstrated that morphine loses as much as 25 percent of its effectiveness in reducing pain when patients do not know they have been injected with a painkiller and are therefore not preset to experience the drug's effects.

How does a placebo work? The placebo effect is not purely psychological, as stereotypes would have us believe. That is, people do not get better only because they think they are going to get better, although expectations of success play an important role (Stewart-Williams, 2004), as does having hope that the treatment will work (Kaptchuk et al., 2009). The placebo response is a complex, psychologically mediated chain of events that often has physiological effects. For example, if the placebo reduces anxiety, then activation of stress systems may be reduced, thus increasing the body's ability to recover from illness. Placebos may also work in part by stimulating the release of opioids, the body's natural pain killers. Exciting new research that examines brain activity using functional magnetic resonance imaging (fMRI) technology reveals that when patients report reduced pain after taking a placebo, they also show decreased activity in pain-sensitive regions of the brain (Wager et al., 2004). Evidence like this suggests that placebos may work via some of the same biological pathways that account for the effects of "real" treatments (Lieberman et al., 2004; Petrovic, Kalso, Peterson, & Ingvar, 2002). Neurobiological studies have also started to uncover some of the potential underlying neurobiological mechanisms of placebos (Pacheco-López, Engler, Niemi, & Schedlowski, 2006).

For ethical reasons, placebos are not knowingly used as part of medical care, but in some countries they may be administered as part of a clinical trial to test the efficacy of a new pharmaceutical treatment. In some cases, a placebo produces an apparently successful recovery, whereas in other cases it has no effect. What factors determine when placebos are most effective?

Provider Behaviour and Placebo Effects

The effectiveness of a placebo varies, depending on how a provider interacts with the patient and how much the provider seems to believe in the curative powers of the treatment being offered. Providers who exude warmth, confidence, and empathy get stronger placebo effects than do more remote and formal providers (Kelley et al., 2009). Placebo effects are also strengthened when the provider radiates competence and provides reassurance to the patient that the condition will improve.

The provider's faith in the treatment increases the effectiveness of placebos (A. H. Roberts, Kewman, Mercier, & Hovell, 1993). Signs of doubt or scepticism may be communicated subtly, even nonverbally, to a patient, and these signs will reduce the effect. Even clearly effective drugs will lose much of their effectiveness when providers express doubt over their effectiveness. In one classic study, for example, patients were given chlorpromazine (a tranquilizer commonly used with psychiatric patients) by a provider who either expressed great confidence in its effectiveness or who voiced some doubt as to its ability to reduce symptoms. This usually effective drug's actual effectiveness dropped from 77 percent to 10 percent when the provider was doubtful regarding its effectiveness (P. E. Feldman, 1956).

Patient–Provider Communication and Placebo Effects

As noted in this chapter, good communication between provider and patient is essential if patients are to follow through successfully on their prescribed treatment regimens. This point is no less true for placebo responses. For patients to show a placebo response, they must understand what the treatment is supposed to do and what they need to do. When the patient–provider relationship is based on effective communication, placebo effects will be stronger.

Another aspect of the patient–provider relationship that enhances the placebo effect is the symbolic value the placebo may have for the patient. When patients seek medical treatment, they want an expert to tell them what is wrong and what to do about it. The placebo response may therefore depend on a shift in meaning regarding the illness that occurs through interaction with the provider. When a provider explains the illness in a way that is understandable and satisfying, and shows support and concern, this may restore the patient's sense of control over their symptoms, and facilitate healing (Brody, 1997).

Patient Characteristics and Placebo Effects

Although there is no placebo-prone personality, there is some evidence to suggest that individual characteristics may play a role in the degree to which placebo effects are experienced. That is, certain people may show stronger or weaker placebo effects in some but not necessarily all situations, depending on whether other factors which contribute to placebo effects are present. For example, one study found that when the characteristics of the treatment matched patients' dispositional characteristics such as spirituality, placebo effects were enhanced (Hyland, Whalley, & Geraghty, 2007). Similarly, placebo responses may be enhanced when the expectation of the nature of the placebo response is matched with the patient's personality. For example, optimists show greater placebo responding to placebos that produce positive physical effects, whereas pessimists respond best to placebos that produce negative side effects (Geers, Helfer, Kosbab, Weiland, & Landry, 2005; Geers, Kosbab, Helfer, Weiland, & Wellman, 2007). From this interactionist perspective then both the qualities of the treatment environment and of the placebo itself are key considerations when evaluating whether or not certain people will respond to placebos.

Anxious people show stronger placebo effects. This effect seems to result less from personality, however, than from the fact that anxiety produces physical symptoms, including distractibility, racing heart, sweaty palms, nervousness, and difficulty sleeping. When a placebo is administered, anxiety may be reduced, and this overlay of anxiety-related symptoms may disappear (T. R. Sharpe, Smith, & Barbre, 1985).

Renewed interest in recent years into the role of personality in placebo effects has led to more rigorous research into which characteristics may make some people more or less responsive to placebos. One study examined the relation of the Big Five factors of personality to placebo responding among people with irritable bowel syndrome and found that people scoring high in agreeableness, openness, or extraversion were more likely to experience placebo effects (Kelley et al., 2009). Of the three factors,

extraversion was the only one to uniquely predict placebo responding. Because reward sensitivity is a central feature of extraversion (Ashton, Lee, & Paunonen, 2002), and the dopamine reward system in the brain is linked to placebo responding (Schweinhardt, Seminowicz, Jaeger, Duncan, & Bushnell, 2009), extraversion may be one trait that can predict placebo responsiveness.

Contextual Determinants of Placebo Effects

The characteristics of the placebo itself, and the setting in which it is administered influence the strength of the placebo response. A setting that has the trappings of medical formality (medications, machines, uniformed personnel) will induce stronger placebo effects than will a less formal setting. If all the staff radiate as much faith in the treatment as the physician, placebo effects will be heightened. The importance of the setting in the placebo response has prompted some researchers to suggest that the placebo effect should be considered as resulting primarily from the context in which it occurs, and accordingly should be renamed "contextual healing" (Miller & Kaptchuk, 2008).

The shape, size, colour, taste, and quantity of the placebo also influence its effectiveness: The more a drug seems like medicine, the more effective it will be (see the Health Psychology in Action box, "Medication Expectations and the Placebo Effect"). Similarly, treatment regimens that seem medical and include precise instructions, medications, and the like will produce stronger placebo effects than will regimens that do not seem very medical; for example, exercise prescriptions and dietary restrictions show weaker placebo effects than do pills and other medications.

Social Norms and Placebo Effects

The placebo effect is facilitated by norms that surround treatment regimens—that is, the expected way in which treatment will be enacted. In Canada, people spend more than $25 billion each year on prescription drugs and over-the-counter medications (Canadian Institute for Health Information, 2007a). Clearly, there is enormous faith in medications, and the psychological if not the physical benefits can be quite substantial. Thus, placebos are effective in part because people believe that drugs work and because people have a great deal of experience in drug taking (A. H. Roberts et al., 1993).

Medication Expectations and the Placebo Effect

Consider the accompanying picture of various pills. Which would be most effective for treating a bad headache? Which would help you relax or fall asleep? And which pill would be a potent decongestant? According to research on the physical characteristics of placebos, your choices are likely very similar to what other people would choose and would also probably enhance any placebo effect you experienced when taking these pills.

Responses to both active medication and placebo may be altered just by changing the colour or form of the drug, and most likely by altering the perceptions of its specificity and efficacy. Owing to social norms and previous experiences, we develop specific expectations about the properties of the medications we take, which can influence treatment responses. For example, the colour, size, shape, and form of a pill have been shown to alter treatment response. Green and blue pills are associated with having a sedative effect, whereas yellow and red pills are associated with having a stimulant placebo effect. White pills are perceived to be better at painkilling (Jacobs & Nordan, 1979; Schapira, McClelland, Griffiths, & Newells, 1970). Capsules are also perceived to be more effective than tablets (Buckalew and Coffield, 1982), presumably because they resemble medications that can be obtained only by prescription rather than over the counter. Quantity effects have also been noted for placebos. More pills administered per day result in better placebo improvement than taking

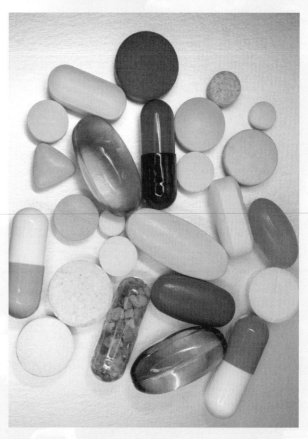

fewer pills (Rickels, Hesbaucher, Weise, Gray, & Feldman, 1970).

Generalizability of Placebo Effects

As noted earlier, virtually any medical procedure can have placebo effects (Sirois, 2009). For example, many surgical patients show improvement simply as a function of having had surgery and not as a result of the actual procedure employed (Stolberg, 1999a). Psychiatry and clinical psychology also show placebo effects; some patients feel better simply knowing that a psychiatrist or psychologist has found a cause for their problems, even if this cause is not the real one. Adherence to a placebo can even be associated with lower death rates due to illness (Irvine et al., 1999).

The efficacy of the placebo should not be thought of as either a medical trick or a purely psychological response on the part of the patient. Placebo effects merit respect. The placebo achieves success in the absence of truly effective therapy (A. H. Roberts et al., 1993). It increases the efficacy of a therapy that has only modest effects of its own. It reduces substantial pain and discomfort. It is the foundation of most of early medicine's effectiveness, and it continues to account for many of medicine's effects today. The efficacy of the placebo is becoming so well recognized that some researchers have gone so far to suggest that it be used as an effective, drug-free treatment for certain conditions. For example, one study demonstrated that using a placebo without deception—that is telling patients that they were receiving a placebo pill instead of an active drug—provided significant symptom relief in comparison to a no-treatment control for individuals with irritable bowel syndrome (Kaptchuk et al., 2010). Although the efficacy of placebo treatments for other conditions remains to be tested, this one controversial study indicates that placebos warrant future research to determine their full potential across different treatment settings.

Placebo as a Methodological Tool

The placebo response is so powerful that no drug can be marketed in the United States unless it has been evaluated against a placebo. In Canada, the *Tri-Council Policy Statement* on the ethics of conducting research with human subjects prohibits the regular use of placebos in drug trials, except under certain circumstances. The standard method for so doing is termed a **double-blind experiment.** In such a test, a researcher gives half a group of patients a drug that is supposed to cure a disease or alleviate symptoms; the other half receives a placebo. The procedure is called double-blind because neither the researcher nor the patient knows whether the patient received the drug or the placebo; both are "blind" to the procedure. Once the effectiveness of the treatment has been measured, the researcher looks in the coded records to see which treatment the patient got. The difference between the effectiveness of the drug and the effectiveness of the placebo is considered to be a measure of the drug's effectiveness. Comparison of a drug against a placebo is essential for accurate measurement of a drug's success. Drugs may look four or five times more successful than they really are if there is no effort to evaluate them against a placebo (N. E. Miller, 1989). ●

SUMMARY

 Define health care provider

- Although physicians are the main health care providers, Canadians are increasingly receiving health care from other types of health care providers, including nurse practitioners and complementary and alternative medicine practitioners.

 Explain why patient–provider communication is important

- Patients evaluate their health care based more on the quality of the interaction they have with the provider than on the technical quality of care.

- Many factors impede effective patient–provider communication. The office setting and the structure of the health care delivery system are often designed for efficient rather than warm and supportive health care. Pressures toward more humane health care treatment are fuelled by movements toward holistic health and wellness.

- Providers contribute to poor communication by not listening, using jargon-filled explanations, alternating between overly technical explanations and infantilizing baby talk and elderspeak, communicating negative mood or expectations, and depersonalizing the patient.

- Patients contribute to poor communication by failing to learn details of their disorder and treatment, failing to give providers correct information, and failing to follow through on treatment recommendations. Patient anxiety, lack of education, lack of experience with the disorder, and incomplete information about symptoms interfere with effective communication as well.

- Because the provider usually receives little feedback about whether the patient followed instructions or if the treatments were successful, it is difficult to identify and correct these problems in communication.

 Understand the consequences of poor patient–provider communication

- Communication is one of the main factors leading to high rates of non-adherence to treatment and dissatisfaction with medical care. This dissatisfaction is one of the reasons why patients may seek alternative forms of care such as using complementary and alternative medicine and natural health products. Poor communication has also been related to failure to disclose the use of other treatments that may interfere with prescribed treatments.

 Define non-adherence and how it can be reduced

- Adherence is lower when recommendations do not seem medical, when lifestyle modification is needed, when complex self-care regimens are required, and when patients have private and conflicting theories about the nature of their illness or treatment.

- Adherence is increased when patients have decided to adhere; when they feel the provider cares about them; when they understand what to do; and when they have received clear, written instructions.

 Describe how to improve patient–provider communication

- Efforts to improve communication have included training in communication skills and taking full advantage of the provider's potent professional role, a movement termed patient-centred communication. Face-to-face communication with a physician can enhance adherence to treatment because of the personalized relationship that exists.

 Understand the placebo effect

- A placebo is any medical procedure or treatment that produces an effect in a patient because of its therapeutic intent and not its actual nature. Virtually every medical treatment shows some degree of placebo effect.

- Placebo effects are enhanced when the physician shows faith in a treatment, the patient is preset to believe it will work, these expectations are successfully communicated, and the trappings of medical treatment are in place.

- Placebos are also a useful methodological tool in evaluating drugs and other treatments.

KEY TERMS

adherence   p. 249

complementary and alternative
    medicine (CAM)   p. 242

creative non-adherence   p. 250

double-blind experiment   p. 260

elderspeak   p. 245

holistic health   p. 244

non-adherence   p. 249

nurse practitioner   p. 238

patient-centred
    communication   p. 254

physician assistants   p. 238

placebo   p. 256

placebo effect   p. 256

telehealth   p. 238

Pain and Its Management

At the end of this chapter, students will be able to:

(LO1) Understand the significance of pain

(LO2) Explain why pain is difficult to study

(LO3) Identify the clinical issues in pain management

(LO4) Describe the techniques used to control pain

(LO5) Explain how chronic pain is managed

Jesse woke up to the sun streaming in through the windows of his new home. It was his first apartment and, with a sigh of contentment, he revelled in the experience of finally being on his own. Yesterday had been a busy day. He and several of his friends had moved all the stuff he had accumulated from university up two flights of narrow stairs to his small but cozy new place. It had been a lot of work, but it had been fun. They'd had a few beers and some pizza afterward, and everyone went home tired and sore but contented.

As Jesse rolled over to admire his apartment, he experienced a sharp pain. Muttering an unprintable epithet to himself, he realized that his back had gone out on him. It must have been from carrying all those boxes. Slowly and carefully, he eased himself into a sitting, and then a standing, position. He was definitely stiff, probably aggravated by the injuries he had acquired during years of football. It was not the first time he had had this experience, and he knew that over-the-counter painkillers and moving around would help him feel better as long as he did not exert himself too much that day.

Jesse is fortunate because he is young and his pain is only short term in response to the exertion of carrying boxes and using muscles not accustomed to regular use. For many people, though, the kind of experience that Jesse has is a chronic one—that is, long term, painful, and difficult to treat. In fact, chronic back pain is one of the most common causes of disability in this country, and large numbers of middle-aged and older Canadians deal with back pain on a daily or intermittent basis. Even his short-term experience leads Jesse to realize that he has to moderate his physical activity the following day.

No introduction to pain would be complete without a consideration of its prevalence and cost. Chronic pain, that is pain lasting longer than six months or long after an injury has healed, has been called a silent epidemic in Canada (LaChapelle, 2004) affecting 1 in 10 Canadians (1.5 million), with rates even higher among those 65 and over (Ramage-Morin, 2008) and among women (Ramage-Morin & Gilmore, 2010). Many Canadians who suffer from chronic pain also have one or more other chronic health conditions. Women are more likely than men to have chronic pain, with back pain, migraine headaches, and arthritis the most common chronic conditions (Ramage-Morin & Gilmore, 2010). One large survey of southeastern Ontario residents found that being unmarried, having a lower income, and living in a rural area were additional factors associated with reporting higher chronic pain intensity and interference (Tripp, Vandenkherkoff, & MacAlister, 2006). Results from the

Pain is a valuable cue that tissue damage has occurred and activities must be curtailed.

2007–8 Canadian Community Health Survey also found that chronic pain rates were highest among those with a lower level of education and among Aboriginal populations (Ramage-Morin & Gilmore, 2010).

Costs in health care utilization and lost productivity add up to about $10 billion annually (Canadian Pain Society, 2006). Indeed, pain typically leads people to change their activity level and other aspects of their behaviour, and chronic pain in particular is the most prevalent form of disability among Canadians. Over $4 billion is spent annually on over-the-counter medications, with much of this spent on medication used for the relief of pain (Canadian Institute of Health Information, 2007a). Indeed, those with chronic pain use pain relievers, tranquilizers, and sleeping pills at rates that are two to four times higher than those without chronic pain (Meana, Cho, & DesMeules, 2003).

As this chapter explains, such pain behaviours are an important component of the pain experience. Jesse is annoyed with himself for not taking basic precautions in lifting and carrying that might have spared him this agony. For people who experience chronic pain, the emotional reactions are more likely to be anxiety and depression. As we will see, emotional reactions to pain are also integral to the pain experience (Severeijns, Vlaeyen, van den Hout, & Picavet, 2004).

WHAT IS THE SIGNIFICANCE OF PAIN?   (L01)

On the surface, the significance of pain would seem to be obvious. Pain hurts, and it can be so insistent that it overwhelms other, basic needs. But the significance of pain goes far beyond the disruption it produces. Pain is significant for managing daily activities. Although we normally think of pain as an unusual occurrence, we live with minor pains all the time. These pains are critical for survival because they provide low-level feedback about the functioning of our bodily systems, feedback that we then use, often unconsciously, as a basis for making minor adjustments, such as shifting our posture, rolling over while asleep, or crossing and uncrossing our legs.

Pain also has important medical consequences. It is the symptom most likely to lead an individual to seek treatment (see Chapter 8). It exacerbates illness and hampers recovery from medical procedures (L. McGuire et al., 2006). Unfortunately, though, the relationship between pain and the severity of an underlying problem can be weak. For example, a cancerous lump rarely produces pain, at least in its early stages, yet it is of great medical importance.

Pain has psychological as well as medical significance (Keefe et al., 2002). For example, both depression and anxiety worsen the experience of pain (for example, Vowles, Zvolensky, Gross, & Sperry, 2004). When patients are asked what they fear most about illness and its treatment, the common response is pain. The dread of not being able to reduce one's own suffering arouses more anxiety than the prospect of surgery, the loss of a limb, or even death. In fact, inadequate relief from pain is the most common reason for patients' requests for euthanasia or aid in dying (Cherny, 1996).

(L02) WHY IS PAIN DIFFICULT TO STUDY?

> Pain is a personal, subjective experience, influenced by cultural learning, the meaning of the situation, attention paid to the situation and other psychological variables. Pain that does not arise from physical injury is no less real than pain that does. (Dr. Ronald Melzack, in *McGill University Health Centre Journal*, 2002)

Pain has been one of the more mysterious and elusive aspects of illness and its treatment. It is fundamentally a psychological experience, and the degree to which it is felt and how incapacitating it is depend in large part on how it is interpreted. Howard Beecher, a physician, was one of the first to recognize this (1959). During World War II, Beecher served in the medical corps, where he observed many wartime injuries. In treating the soldiers, he noticed a curious fact: Only one-quarter of them requested morphine (a widely used painkiller) for what were often severe and very likely to be painful wounds. When Beecher returned to his civilian practice, he often treated patients who sustained comparable injuries from surgery.

In Canada, millions of dollars are spent annually on over-the-counter remedies to reduce the temporary pain of minor disorders.

However, in contrast to the soldiers, 80 percent of the civilians appeared to be in substantial pain and demanded painkillers. To make sense of this apparent discrepancy, Beecher concluded that the meaning attached to pain substantially determines how it is experienced. For the soldier, an injury meant that he was alive and was likely to be sent home. For the civilian, the injury represented an unwelcome interruption of valued activities.

A variety of factors including culture, gender, and coping styles can impact how pain is interpreted and contribute to the challenges of studying pain. Pain is also heavily influenced by the context in which it is experienced. Sports lore is full of accounts of athletes who have injured themselves on the playing field but stayed in the game, apparently oblivious to their pain. Such action may occur because sympathetic arousal, as it occurs in response to vigorous sports, seems to diminish pain sensitivity (Schlereth & Birklein, 2008). In contrast, stress and psychological distress may aggravate the experience of pain.

Culture and Pain   Pain has a substantial cultural component. Although there are no ethnic or racial differences in the ability to discriminate painful stimuli, members of some cultures report pain sooner and react more intensely to it than individuals of other cultures (Hernandez & Sachs-Ericsson, 2006). For example, one study found that compared to European Canadians, Chinese students reported lower pain tolerance for experimentally induced pain (Hsieh, Tripp, Ji, & Sullivan, 2010). These ethnic and cultural differences may derive both from differences in cultural norms regarding the expression of pain and in some cases from different pain mechanisms (Mechlin,

Maixner, Light, Fisher, & Girdler, 2005; Sheffield, Biles, Orom, Maixner, & Sheps, 2000).

Gender and Pain   There are gender differences in the experience of pain as well. Although women typically showing greater sensitivity to pain (Lowery, Fillingim, & Wright, 2003), there can be a great deal of variation in these gender differences depending on the type of pain and when the pain is assessed (Berkley, Zalcman, & Simon, 2006). For example, hormonal fluctuations across the menstrual cycle are known to influence pain perception in women (Aloisi, 2003). One study found that although women who had lost a limb were more likely to report phantom limb pain and greater average pain intensity than men who lost a limb, there were no sex differences in the pain specific to the limb loss (Hirsh, Dillworth, Ehde, & Jensen, 2010). One explanation is that these differences may arise in part from the differences in the ways that men and women experience and emotionally process pain, as there is some evidence that women may respond to threatening stimuli with greater negative affect which in turn can amplify the response to pain (Rhudy & Williams, 2005). The gender difference in the experience of pain is a complex issue that demonstrates the biopsychosocial nature of pain.

Coping Styles and Pain   Certain ways of coping with pain can influence how pain is interpreted and therefore affect how individuals experience and report pain. Pain catastrophizing is one such way of coping with pain that has been studied extensively. People who catastrophize about pain tend to ruminate about it, magnify it, and feel helpless about how to manage their pain (Sullivan, Bishop, & Pivik, 1995). This particular way of coping with pain leads to more dramatic pain reports and has also been established as a risk factor for prolonged pain and disability (Campbell & Edwards, 2009). For example, pain catastrophizing predicts greater post-surgical pain (Pavlin, Sullivan, Freund, & Roesen, 2005), more intense labour pain, and poorer physical recovery after childbirth (Flink, Mroczek, Sullivan, & Linton, 2009), and longer post-injury work absence (Sullivan & Stanish, 2003). In contrast, resilience appears to be protective for pain catastrophizing, as individuals who are resilient are able to bounce back from moments of intense pain by experiencing positive emotions (Ong, Zautra, & Reid, 2010).

Interestingly, individuals who typically react to pain by catastrophizing are also more likely to attend more to and estimate greater pain from the pain behaviours

displayed by other people (Sullivan, Martel, Tripp, Savard, & Crombez, 2006). This and recent neuroimaging evidence suggest that pain castrophizing may reflect a relatively enduring way of perceiving pain that has both social and psychobiological underpinnings.

Measuring Pain

One barrier to the treatment of pain is the difficulty people have describing it objectively. If you have a lump, you can point to it, or if a bone is broken, it can be seen in an X-ray. Pain does not have these objective referents. This is a particularly important issue when assessing pain in children, as discussed in the Spotlight on Canadian Research box, "Children's Experience and Reporting of Pain."

Verbal Reports   One solution to measuring pain is to draw on the large, informal vocabulary that people use for describing pain. Medical practitioners usually use this source of information when trying to understand patients' complaints. A throbbing pain, for example, has different implications than does a shooting pain or a constant, dull ache.

Other researchers have developed pain questionnaires. For example, the McGill Pain Questionnaire (MPQ; Melzack, 1975) was created by Ronald Melzack from McGill University (see Figure 10.1 to review a portion of the MPQ). Measures like the MPQ typically provide indications of the nature of pain, such as whether it is throbbing or shooting, as well as its intensity (Dar, Leventhal, & Leventhal, 1993; Fernandez & Turk, 1992). Measures have also been developed to address the psychosocial components of pain, such as the fear it causes or the degree to which it has been catastrophized. One such measure, the Pain Catastrophizing Scale (Sullivan et al., 1995), was created by a team of Canadian researchers, and has become one of the most widely used measures of pain-related catastrophic thinking. Combinations of measures like these can help those who treat pain patients get a full picture of all the dimensions of a patient's pain.

Pain Behaviour   Other measures of pain have focused on **pain behaviours.** Pain behaviours are observable behaviours that arise as manifestations of chronic pain. Four basic types of pain behaviours have been identified: (1) facial and audible expressions of distress; (2) distortions in posture or gait; (3) negative affect; and (4) avoidance of activity (Turk, Wack, & Kerns, 1995).

FIGURE 10.1 | The McGill Pain Questionnaire

Patient's name _____   Date _____   Time _____ A.M./P.M.

1 Flickering — Quivering — Pulsing — Throbbing — Beating — Pounding —	**11** Tiring — Exhausting —
2 Jumping — Flashing — Shooting —	**12** Sickening — Suffocating —
3 Pricking — Boring — Drilling — Stabbing — Lancinating —	**13** Fearful — Frightful — Terrifying —
4 Sharp — Cutting — Lacerating —	**14** Punishing — Grueling — Cruel — Vicious — Killing —
5 Pinching — Pressing — Gnawing — Cramping — Crushing —	**15** Wretched — Blinding —
6 Tugging — Pulling — Wrenching —	**16** Annoying — Troublesome — Miserable — Intense — Unbearable —
7 Hot — Burning — Scalding — Searing —	**17** Spreading — Radiating — Penetrating — Piercing —
8 Tingling — Itchy — Smarting — Stinging —	**18** Tight — Numb — Drawing — Squeezing — Tearing —
9 Dull — Sore — Hurting — Aching — Heavy —	**19** Cool — Cold — Freezing —
10 Tender — Taut — Rasping — Splitting —	**20** Nagging — Nauseating — Agonizing — Dreadful — Torturing —

PPI
0 No pain —
1 Mild —
2 Discomforting —
3 Distressing —
4 Horrible —
5 Excruciating —

Brief — Momentary — Transient —	Rhythmic — Periodic — Intermittent —	Continuous — Steady — Constant —

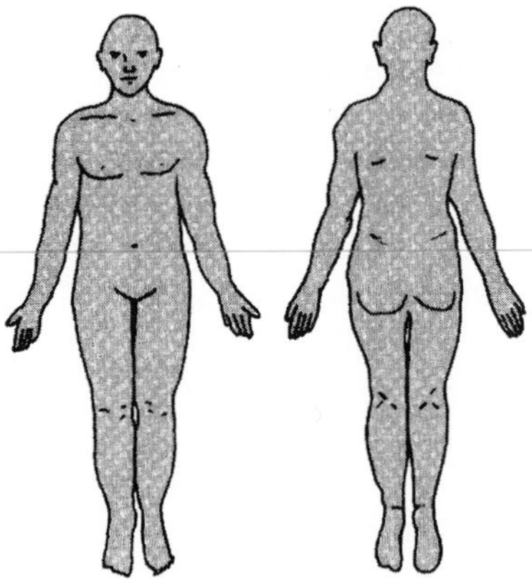

E = External
I = Internal

Comments:

Analyses of pain behaviours provide a basis for assessing how pain has disrupted the life of particular patients or groups of patients, distinguishing, for example, between how people manage lower back pain versus chronic headaches.

Because pain behaviour is observable and measurable, the focus on pain behaviours has helped define the characteristics of different kinds of pain syndromes. Pain is now viewed as a complex biopsychosocial event involving psychological, behavioural, and physiological components.

Children's Experience and Reporting of Pain

Think back to when you were a young child, when you had one of your first painful experiences. Perhaps it was when you scraped your knees or elbows taking a fall while running. Or maybe it was after you had a painful needle for an immunization. How did your parents know you were in pain? And did their reaction to you impact your pain experience? Understanding how children express pain and the role of parental factors in their pain experience are just some of the issues that Canadian pediatric pain researchers have addressed.

Assessing pain in children is an important but challenging task that often relies on behavioural and self-report measures. For example, in a clinical setting, children may be asked to describe their pain and its intensity so that decisions about pain management can be made. But the language they use may vary depending on their age and on whether their pain expressions are made spontaneously (Stanford, Chambers, Craig, McGrath, & Cassidy, 2005). Yet until recently little was known about the relationship of children's spontaneous expressions of pain and their relation to experienced pain. To address this issue, researchers from the University of British Columbia and Dalhousie University examined children's spontaneous pain verbalizations during immunization. The children, who were 4 to 8 years old, were video-recorded while receiving an immunization injection with their parents present. Afterwards they then indicated the level of pain they experienced using a visual scale of faces with expressions ranging from no pain to extreme pain. Interestingly, just less than half of the children spontaneously verbalized their pain, with the majority exclaiming "Ow!" Children who spontaneously expressed their pain verbally also displayed more painful facial reactions, and rated their pain as being more intense than children who did not verbalize their pain. The tendency to make pain verbalizations was also associated with age, with older children less likely to make spontaneous pain verbalizations (Stanford et al., 2005).

There is also evidence that parents may play a role in their children's pain experience. For example, reassurance, distraction, or the use of humour by parents has been differentially associated with children's pain experiences. But few studies have tested the direct impact of parental behaviour on children's pain. Using an experimental design, researchers from Dalhousie University and the University of British Columbia examined how maternal behaviours impacted their child's pain experience (Chambers, Craig, & Bennett, 2002). Mothers were randomly assigned to one of three conditions in which they were first trained to interact with their child in particular way: (1) a pain-promoting interaction in which mothers tried to be reassuring, (2) a pain-reducing interaction in which mothers used strategies such as distraction and humour, and (3) a no-training control group where mothers were not given any particular instructions about how to act. For each mother and child dyad, the child submerged his or her hand into ice cold water for four minutes to induce pain. Afterwards children self-reported the intensity of their pain experience. As expected, children whose mothers interacted with them in a pain-promoting manner reported more pain than those children from the control group, and the control-group children reported more pain than the children whose mothers interacted with them in a pain-reducing manner. However, the influence of maternal behaviour was found only for girls, but not for boys (Chambers, Craig, & Bennett, 2002). Although the popular notion that parents can influence how their children respond to pain may be accurate, it may be most true for daughters, whose pain reporting may be directly influenced and shaped by their mothers' behaviour towards them.

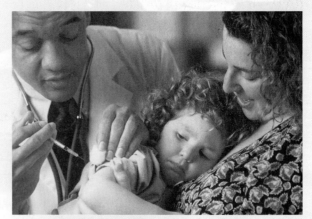

How children experience and report their pain can be influenced by factors such as their age and by how parents respond to their pain.

Physiology of Pain

The experience of pain is a protective mechanism to bring into consciousness the awareness of tissue damage. At the time of the pain experience, however, it is unlikely to feel very protective. Unlike other bodily sensations, the experience of pain is accompanied by motivational and behavioural responses, such as withdrawal and intense emotional reactions, such as crying or fear. These experiences are an integral part of the pain experience and thus become important in its diagnosis and treatment.

Scientists have distinguished among three kinds of pain perception. The first is mechanical **nociception** (pain perception) that results from mechanical damage to the tissue of the body. The second is **thermal damage,** or the experience of pain due to temperature exposure. The third is referred to as **polymodal nociception,** a general category referring to pain that triggers chemical reactions from tissue damage.

Nociceptors in the peripheral nerves first sense injury and, in response, release chemical messengers, which are conducted to the spinal cord, where they are passed directly to the reticular formation and thalamus and into the cerebral cortex. These regions of the brain, in turn, identify the site of the injury and send messages back down the spinal column, which lead to muscle contractions, which can help block the pain and changes in other bodily functions, such as breathing.

Nociception occurs through the activity of several major types of peripheral nerve fibres: the A-delta fibres which respond especially to mechanical or thermal pain, the C-fibres, and the A-delta fibres which respond to pressure and vibration. The function of each fibre is summarized in Table 10.1. For example,

the incision from a surgical scalpel would produce a quick, sharp pain due to activity in the A-delta fibres if an anesthetic was not used to dull the pain. Post surgery the long lasting and burning pain from the surgical wound would be transmitted by the C-fibres. Rubbing the painful area would reduce the pain temporarily by activating the A-beta fibres, which can have a suppressing effect on the aching pain transmitted by the C-fibres. As will be outlined in the following section on the gate control theory, the experience of pain depends not only on the activity in these fibres, but on the complex interplay of several biological and psychological factors including the release of endogenous opioids, emotional states, and beliefs about pain.

Theories of Pain

Arguably, one of the most influential theories for understanding pain is the **gate control theory,** developed by Canadian psychologist Ronald Melzack and British physiologist Patrick Wall (1965). Before the gate control theory, traditional models suggested that pain resulted from the transmission of pain signals from the site of injury to the brain, and that the amount of pain experienced was directly proportional to the amount of tissue damage. Melzack and Wall challenged the idea that pain resulted solely from a linear process from nerve stimulation to brain reception, and instead proposed that psychological factors play a significant role in the experience of pain.

According to the gate control theory, there is a neural "pain gate" that can open and close to modulate pain signals to the brain. Modulation can occur at the spinal column level by the dorsal horn, through

TABLE 10.1 | Summary of Peripheral Nerve Fibres Involved in Nociception and Their Function in the Experience of Pain

Peripheral nerve fibre	Description	Type of pain	Function	Pain Gate Modulation
A-delta fibre	Small, myelinated fibres	Transmit first pain and sharp pain rapidly	Affects sensory aspects of pain	Opens gate
C-fibres	Unmyelinated fibres	Transmit secondary dull or aching pain	Affects motivational and affective elements of pain	Opens gate
A-beta fibres	Large diameter myelinated fibres	Transmit information about vibration and position	Concurrent stimulation can suppress pain transmitted by C-fibres	Closes gate

TABLE 10.2 | Factors That Open or Close the Pain Gate

Type of Factor	Factors That Open the Gate	Factors That Close the Gate
Physical	Extent of injury Inappropriate activity level	Medications Counter stimulation (e.g., massage, heat)
Emotional	Anxiety or worry Tension Depression	Positive emotions (e.g., joy, interest) Relaxation
Cognitive	Focusing on pain Boredom	Distraction or intense concentration on other things Involvement and interest in life activities

the activity of the A-delta and C-fibres, which tend to open the gate. A-beta fibres are also involved in the closing of the gate. However, signals descending from the brain can also modulate pain through a central control trigger, a system of large-diameter, rapidly conducting fibres that activate cognitive processes. According to this view of pain, physical, emotional, and cognitive factors can make substantial contributions to the experience of pain by either opening or closing the gate. Some of these factors are presented in Table 10.2.

The significance of psychological process in the experience of pain suggested by the gate control theory forced researchers to view pain and the role of the brain and other central nervous system regions in the pain experience in a vastly different way. For example, the brain could now be viewed as actively selecting, filtering, and modulating signals rather than simply passively receiving them. Similarly, the dorsal horns, which were originally seen as being passive transmission stations, were now viewed as dynamic sites involved in the inhibition and amplification of neural transmission (Melzack, 1999).

Subsequent research based on this new perspective on pain has led to the acknowledgement of other regions of the brain that are involved in the modulation of pain. The periductal gray, a structure in the midbrain, has been tied to pain relief when it is stimulated. Processes in the cerebral cortex are involved in cognitive judgments about pain, including the evaluation of its meaning. The psychological and neural mechanisms of the affective dimension of pain are a critical aspect of the pain experience. The affective dimension of pain is made up of feelings of unpleasantness and negative emotions associated with future

concerns. Researchers call these concerns secondary affect (Price, 2000).

Pain sensation, intensity, and duration interact to influence pain, its perceived unpleasantness, and related emotions. Nociceptive input is integrated with contextual information about the painful experience, which contributes to the strong emotions often experienced during pain and which can themselves exacerbate pain (Meagher, Arnau, & Rhudy, 2001). As suggested by the gate control theory, the overall experience of pain is a complex outcome of the interaction of these elements of the pain experience (see Figure 10.2).

The gate control theory has contributed to the understanding of pain by providing a conceptual framework from which to explain several pain-related phenomena, such as injury without pain, and the role of emotions in the pain experience. Rather than simply being dismissed as part of the reactions to pain, this theory suggests that psychological processes are central to the experience of pain, and has opened the doorway to new methods of pain control (Melzack, 1993). We will review some of these interventions later in this chapter.

Despite it usefulness, the gate control theory has limitations. For example, it cannot explain several types of chronic pain, including **phantom limb pain** (see the Health Psychology in Action box, "Phantom Limb Pain and Immersive Virtual Reality"). In phantom limb pain, a phenomenon that occurs commonly among amputees, an individual experiences pain in a limb that is not there. But without a limb present to generate nerve impulses, then how is phantom limb pain generated?

To address these issues, Melzack has suggested an extension to the gate control theory, the **neuromatrix**

FIGURE 10.2 | The Experience of Pain

The signal goes to the spinal cord, where it passes immediately to a motor nerve (1) connected to a muscle, in this case, in the arm. This causes a reflex action that does not involve the brain. But the signal also goes up the spinal cord to the thalamus (2), where the pain is perceived.

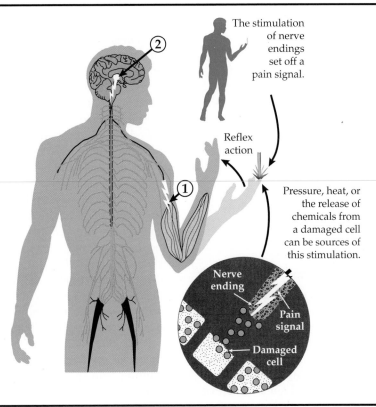

The stimulation of nerve endings set off a pain signal.

Reflex action

Pressure, heat, or the release of chemicals from a damaged cell can be sources of this stimulation.

Nerve ending

Pain signal

Damaged cell

theory (Melzack, 1990, 2001). According to this theory, there is a network of neurons that extends throughout areas of the brain to create the felt representation of a unified physical self, called the body-self *neuromatrix*. The neuromatrix is genetically determined initially but open to changes from sensory inputs from experience. The neuromatrix generates nerve impulses that are continuously and cyclically processed and synthesized into a characteristic pattern called the *neurosignature*. Thus, for each pain experience a neurosignature is created that reflects the multitude of sensory, cognitive, and emotional factors that are unique to that particular experience of pain (Melzack, 2001). It is this neurosignature, generated from the body-self neuromatrix, then, and not sensory inputs, that give rise to pain and accordingly explain phenomena like phantom limb pain:

The absence of inputs does not stop the networks from generating messages about missing body parts; they continue to produce such messages throughout life. In short, phantom limbs are a mystery only if we assume the body sends sensory messages to a passively receiving brain. Phantoms become comprehensible once we recognize that the brain generates the experience of the body. Sensory inputs merely modulate that experience; they do not directly cause it. (Melzack, 1992)

Like the gate control theory, the neuromatrix theory suggests that pain is a multidimensional experience that results from multiple determinants and not sensory factors alone (Melzack, 2001). As such, it opens up possibilities for treatment interventions that researchers will no doubt continue to explore in years to come.

Critical Checkpoint

Experiencing the Pain of Others

One of the major issues in the study of pain is the reliance on pain self-reports and the individual and contextual factors that can influence these self-reports. Imagine a time in the future when technology has advanced to the point that there is a device that clinicians can wear so that they can neurally experience the pain of their patients for just a moment. Would such a device increase the accuracy of measuring pain? Why or why not?

Neurochemical Bases of Pain and Its Inhibition

The brain can control the amount of pain an individual experiences by transmitting messages back down the spinal cord to block the transmission of pain signals. One landmark study that confirmed this hypothesis was conducted by D. V. Reynolds (1969). He demonstrated that by electrically stimulating a portion of the rat brain, one could produce such a high level of analgesia that the animal would not feel the pain of abdominal surgery, a phenomenon termed stimulation produced analgesia (SPA). Reynolds's findings prompted researchers to look for the neurochemical basis of this effect, and in 1972, Akil, Mayer, and Liebeskind (1972, 1976) uncovered the existence of endogenous opioid peptides.

What are endogenous opioid peptides? Opiates, including heroin and morphine, are drugs manufactured from plants that help control pain. Opioids are opiate-like substances produced within the body that constitute a neurochemically based, internal pain-regulation system. Opioids are produced in many parts of the brain and glands of the body, and they project onto specific selective receptor sites in various parts of the body.

The **endogenous opioid peptides** fall into three general families:

1. Beta-endorphins, which produce peptides that project to the limbic system and brain stem, among other places.

2. Proenkephalin, which are peptides that have widespread neuronal, endocrine, and central nervous system distributions.

3. Prodynorphins, found in the gut, the posterior pituitary, and the brain (Jonsdottir, 2000).

Each of these families of opioids has several forms with differing potencies, pharmacological profiles, and receptor selectivities (Jonsdottir, 2000). For example, one opioid receptor may be receptive to beta-endorphins but not to proenkephalin or prodynorphins. Thus, the system of endogenous opioid peptides in the body is highly complex.

Endogenous opioid peptides, then, are important in the natural pain suppression system of the body. Clearly, however, this pain-suppression system is not always in operation. Particular factors must trigger its arousal. Research on animals suggests that stress is one such factor. Acute stress reduces sensitivity to pain. This phenomenon is called stress-induced analgesia (SIA). As we saw in Chapter 6, endogenous opioid peptides are secreted in response to stress in humans as well as animals. Physical activity is another factor that can trigger the release of endogenous opioids, which in turn can enhance immune functioning and account for the beneficial effects of exercise on health (Jonsdottir, 2000) discussed in Chapter 4.

Researchers do not yet know all the functions of endogenous opioid peptides. They are one method of inhibiting pain, particularly under stressful circumstances. Because the endogenous opioid peptides can be found in the adrenal glands, the pituitary gland, and the hypothalamus, they are clearly involved in responses to stress. Opioid peptides have been implicated in immune functioning (Jonsdottir, 2000), and thus, release of opioid peptides may represent one route by which stress depresses immune functioning (see Chapter 14).

WHAT ARE THE CLINICAL ISSUES IN PAIN MANAGEMENT? (L03)

The World Health Organization has suggested that pain is a "disease in its own right" and that effective pain management is a global health patient issue that needs to be addressed (World Health Organization, 2004, October 11). So how can pain best be managed? Historically, pain has been managed by physicians and other health care workers. Traditional pain-management techniques include pharmacological, surgical, and sensory techniques. Increasingly, psychologists have become involved in pain management, and as a result, techniques that include a heavily psychological component have been used to

Phantom Limb Pain and Immersive Virtual Reality

The perception of an amputated limb being intact is common among people who have had a limb amputated. This perception is so strong that amputees will often describe the phantom limb as moving through space in a manner similar to a normal and present limb. Thus, the phantom limb is perceived as an integral part of oneself (Melzack, 1990). Many amputees experience pain in the phantom limbs, which can be transient or enduring. Phantom limb pain can interfere with adjustment to amputation over time (Horgan & MacLachlan, 2004). Finding effective treatment interventions for dealing with this unusual type of pain are, therefore, an important part of rehabilitation.

Several unique treatment approaches for phantom limb pain have been developed in recent years. For example, using a mirror box to reflect movements from the intact limb and effectively create the illusion of the amputated limb has shown some success in reducing phantom limb pain (Ramachandran & Rogers-Ramachandran, 1996; MacLachlan, McDonald, & Waloch, 2004). The treatment is believed to work by increasing feelings of control over the phantom limb and creating a coherent body image, which in turn reduces phantom limb pain. However, this procedure can be restrictive and requires shifting attention from the intact limb to its reflection, while sitting in a position that maintains the illusion. To address these limitations, researchers have suggested immersive virtual reality (IVR) as an alternative intervention for phantom limb pain (Murray, Patchick, Pettifer, Cailette, & Howard, 2006). Instead of using mirrors to transpose the amputees' intact limb, the IVR system creates a virtual limb to occupy the phenomenal space where the phantom limb is perceived to be. The overall experience involves a full virtual body representation, and engaging in several virtual tasks such as kicking or batting a virtual ball

with the virtual/phantom limb. IVR sessions usually last about 15 minutes and are delivered over several weeks (Murray, Pettifer, Howard, et al., 2007).

The following case study of PK, a 63-year-old male left-upper-limb amputee, illustrates the potential effectiveness of IVR for managing phantom limb pain (PLP).

> He had been an amputee for 12 years and 10 months, as the result of a swimming accident, and he did not use a prosthetic limb. PK suffered with severe PLP "twenty-four seven—I'm never ever out of pain." His phantom limb was shorter than his anatomical limb in a fixed position with the elbow bent at roughly right angles and the fingers in a cupped position. PK suffered with intense flashes of pain attacks in his phantom which could be very severe; he would often find himself immobilized by the pain.
>
> During each period of IVR use PK reported a decrease in his phantom limb pain. . . .During the third session, PK reported vivid sensations of movement in his phantom arm: "During it, I actually felt as if it was my left arm that was doing the work and chasing the ball. My actual phantom arm rather than my right . . . and that was more like reality than virtual reality." PK commented that "If I could harness that (the movement in his phantom limb) maybe I could open my fingers and ease the cramping pain a little."
>
> Self-reported evidence from PK suggested a positive change in his sleep patterns after the first session of IVR which has continued throughout the 3-week period: "I've actually been sleeping a little better over the last few days . . . I'm getting about 5–6 [hours] of uninterrupted sleep as opposed to 2–3 [hours] and I'm doing nothing else different in my life except coming here."

Source: Murray et al., 2007

combat pain. These techniques include biofeedback, relaxation, hypnosis, acupuncture, distraction, guided imagery, and other cognitive techniques. As these methods have gained centrality in the treatment of pain, the importance of patients' self-management, involving responsibility for and commitment to the course of pain treatment, has assumed centrality in the management of chronic pain (Glenn & Burns, 2003).

Acute and Chronic Pain

There are two main kinds of clinical pain: acute and chronic. **Acute pain** typically results from a specific injury that produces tissue damage, such as a wound or broken limb. As such, it is self-limiting and typically disappears when the tissue damage is repaired. Jesse's pain, from moving into his new apartment, is an example of acute pain. Acute pain is usually short in duration and is defined as pain that goes on for six months or less. This type of pain can produce substantial anxiety and prompts its sufferer to engage in an urgent search for relief. Anxiety, however, usually decreases after pain-killers are administered or the injury begins to heal.

Types of Chronic Pain   **Chronic pain** typically begins with an acute episode, but unlike acute pain, it does not decrease with treatment and the passage of time. There are several different kinds of chronic pain. **Chronic benign pain** typically persists for longer than six months and is relatively intractable to treatment. The pain varies in severity and may involve any of a number of muscle groups. Chronic low back pain and myofascial pain syndrome are examples.

Recurrent acute pain involves a series of intermittent episodes of pain that are acute in character but chronic inasmuch as the condition persists for more than six months. Migraine headaches, temporomandibular disorder (involving the jaw), and trigeminal neuralgia (involving spasms of the facial muscles) are examples.

Chronic progressive pain persists longer than six months and increases in severity over time. Typically, it is associated with malignancies or degenerative disorders, such as cancer or rheumatoid arthritis.

It is estimated that about one-third of Canadians suffer from chronic pain at any given time (Canadian Pain Society, 2006). Such pain is not necessarily present every moment, but the fact that it is chronic virtually forces sufferers to organize their lives around it.

Acute versus Chronic Pain   The distinction between acute and chronic pain is important in clinical management for several reasons. First, acute and chronic pain present different psychological profiles because chronic pain often carries an overlay of psychological distress, which complicates diagnosis and treatment. The realization that pain is interfering with desired activities and the perception that one has little control over that fact often produce depression in pain patients (Maxwell, Gatchel, & Mayer, 1998). One study found that pain is present in two-thirds of patients who seek care from physicians with primary symptoms of depression (Bair et al., 2004). Thus, pain and depression appear to be heavily intertwined.

Some chronic pain patients develop maladaptive coping strategies, such as catastrophizing their illness, engaging in wishful thinking, or social withdrawal, which can further complicate treatment and enhance care-seeking (Severeijns et al., 2004). When patients

have endured their pain for long periods of time without any apparent relief, it is easy to imagine that the pain will go on forever, only get worse, and be a constant part of the rest of their life—beliefs that magnify the distress of chronic pain and feed back into the pain itself (Tennen, Affleck, & Zautra, 2006). When these psychological issues are effectively treated, this fact may in itself reduce chronic pain (Fishbain, Cutler, Rosomoff, & Rosomoff, 1998). The sheer duration of chronic pain can account for the fact that many chronic pain patients become nearly completely disabled over the course of their pain treatment (Groth-Marnat & Fletcher, 2000).

A second reason to distinguish between acute and chronic pain is that most of the pain control techniques presented in this chapter work well to control acute pain but are less successful with chronic pain, which requires individualized multiple techniques for its management.

Third, chronic pain involves the complex interaction of physiological, psychological, social, and behavioural components, more than is the case with acute pain. For example, chronic pain patients often experience social rewards from the attention they receive from family members, friends, or even employers; these social rewards, or secondary gains, of pain can help maintain pain behaviours (Osterhaus, Lange, Linssen, & Passchier, 1997).

Lastly, chronic pain more so than acute pain can have widespread effects on not just the individual, but their families, and society itself (Breivik, Collett, Ventafridda, Cohen, & Gallacher, 2006; Ramage-Morin & Gilmore, 2010). Findings from the Canadian Community Health Survey indicate that those with chronic pain are more likely to view their lives as stressful, be less satisfied with their lives, and report feeling a lower sense of community belonging (Ramage-Morin & Gilmore, 2010). Families in which there is a child with chronic pain function more poorly than those without a family member with chronic pain (Lewandowski, Palermo, Stinson, Handley, & Chambers, 2010). In addition, individuals who experience chronic pain report restrictions in their day to day activities (Karoly & Ruehlman, 2007), and chronic pain can restrict work activities and contribute to absenteeism at work (Ramage-Morin & Gilmore, 2010).

The psychological and social components of pain are important in part because they are an integral aspect of the experience of pain and they influence the likelihood of successful pain programs (for example, J. Burns, 2000). As such, chronic pain management is complicated and must be thought of not as a particular pain that simply goes on for a long period of time but as an unfolding physiological, psychological, and behavioural experience that evolves over time into a syndrome (Flor, Birbaumer, & Turk, 1990).

Who Becomes a Chronic Pain Patient?   Of course, all chronic pain patients were once acute pain patients. What determines who makes the transition to chronic pain? One might assume that pain intensity determines making the transition into chronic pain, but, in fact, functional disability appears to play a more important role (Young Casey, Greenberg, Nicassio, Harpin, & Hubbard, 2008). Patients for whom pain interferes with life activities make the transition into the chronic pain experience (Epping-Jordan et al., 1998). Chronic pain patients may experience pain especially acutely because of high sensitivity to noxious stimulation, impairment in pain regulatory systems, and an overlay of psychological distress (Hassinger, Semenchuk, & O'Brien, 1999; Maixner et al., 1997).

Although on a case by case basis it may be difficult to determine the exact factors involved, the transition from acute to chronic pain is likely facilitated by a complex interplay of predisposing and contextual factors. For example, one study found that depressed mood and beliefs that pain was permanent in the context of an accumulation of traumatic life events predicted the transition from acute to chronic back pain several months later (Young, Casey, et al., 2008). However, experiencing higher levels of pain at baseline were also related to depression scores at follow up highlighting the interactive nature of depression and pain and the difficulty in disentangling their effects.

The Focus on Social Issues box, "Chronic Pain in Canadian Seniors: A Silent Epidemic," examines the growth of chronic pain as a health issue for elderly Canadians.

Lifestyle of Chronic Pain   By the time a pain patient is adequately treated, this complex, dynamic interaction of physiological, psychological, social, and behavioural components is often tightly integrated, making it difficult to modify (Flor et al., 1990). The following case history suggests the disruption and agony that can be experienced by the chronic pain sufferer:

> The pain started 20 years ago, after Larry Cross was checked from behind playing hockey and ruptured a disc. Doctors repaired his spine in a dozen separate operations, eventually reinforcing it with steel, but the pain grew so intense he could barely cope.

Millions of Canadians, many of them elderly, suffer from chronic pain.

> Morphine or other drugs only worked if he took them in doses so high he felt comatose. He was bedridden, depressed and shunning the people who loved him the most: "I was on the verge of suicide. I did not want to wake up the next morning."
>
> In 2001, his doctor recommended he travel to the United States to have a morphine pump surgically implanted in his abdomen that would send the drug through a catheter to his spine. He was lucky to be wealthy—the surgery cost $35,000—and lucky that it worked.
>
> "It felt wonderful," said the 66-year-old retiree, who lives near Guelph, Ontario, and once owned several plants that manufactured auto parts. His pain dropped from 10 out of 10 to a 5 on his good days, a level he can live with. "I cannot tell you how much it gives you your life back." (McIlroy, 2006)

As this case history suggests, chronic pain can entirely disrupt a person's life. Many such sufferers have left their jobs, abandoned their leisure activities, withdrawn

Chronic Pain among Canadian Seniors: A Silent Epidemic

The distress and disability associated with chronic pain underscore its importance as a public health issue. Chronic pain is a particularly concerning issue for seniors for several reasons. The risk for experiencing chronic pain increases with age, as does the likelihood of having other chronic health conditions, cognitive changes, and activity limitations. Chronic pain and the limitations it can impose significantly impact the mobility, dependence, and energy levels of seniors who are already at risk for deficits in these areas. According to results from the National Population Health Survey and the Canadian Community Health Survey, chronic pain is more common among seniors than it is among adults age 64 and under: 27 percent of seniors living in private households experience chronic pain compared to only 17 percent of other adults. What's more, the rates are even higher among seniors living in long-term health care institutions, with 38 percent of seniors reporting some form of chronic pain. In fact, the rates of chronic pain in seniors may actually be underestimated, as many do not report their pain, believing that it is just a normal part of aging. With the proportion of seniors projected to skyrocket in coming years, chronic pain may reach crisis levels within Canada. In 2005, 13 percent of the population was over 65, and by 2031 this proportion is expected to skyrocket to nearly 25 percent, with an estimated 9 million seniors in Canada.

Chronic pain among seniors is also associated with gender, socio-economic, and other health factors. Women, those with less than secondary education, and those with lower household incomes are more likely to experience chronic pain. Seniors with arthritis, heart disease, and diabetes are more likely to report chronic pain, as are those with two or more chronic conditions. Thus, chronic pain is a concern among particular groups of Canadians who are already at risk for poor quality of life.

The impact of chronic pain on Canada's senior population is clear. Pain interferes with daily activities, and as pain severity increases so does the number of activities that are affected. Seniors who experience chronic pain are more likely to be unhappy and have lower self-perceived health compared to seniors without chronic pain, even after accounting for differences in socio-economic status and the number of health conditions.

Unfortunately, pain treatment and intervention trials have primarily been conducted with younger adults (Gibson, 2006), despite the high prevalence of chronic pain among seniors. The challenge in coming years will be to develop effective strategies and interventions to help manage and reduce the chronic pain of Canadian seniors so that their quality of life can be maximized.

Source: Adapted from Statistics Canada, "Chronic pain in Canadian seniors," *Health Reports,* catalogue no. 82-003-XIE, volume no. 19, issue no. 1, released on March 19, 2008, www.statcan.ca/english/freepub/82-003-XIE/2008001/article/10514-en.pdf

---

from their families and friends, and evolved an entire lifestyle around pain. Typically, chronic pain sufferers have little social or recreational life and may even have difficulty performing simple tasks of self-care. Because their income is often reduced, their standard of living may decline. Their lifestyle becomes oriented around the experience of pain and its treatment. A good night's sleep is often elusive for months or years at a time (Currie, Wilson, & Curran, 2002). Work-related aspirations and personal goals may be set aside because life has become dominated by chronic pain (Karoly & Ruehlman, 1996). Therefore, the loss of self-esteem that is experienced by these patients can be substantial.

Some patients receive compensation for their pain because it has resulted from an injury, such as an automobile accident. Compensation can actually increase the perceived severity of pain, the amount of disability experienced, the degree to which pain interferes with life activities, and the amount of distress that is reported (Ciccone, Just, & Bandilla, 1999; Groth-Marnat & Fletcher, 2000) because it provides an incentive for being in pain.

The Toll of Pain on Relationships   Chronic pain can take a special toll on marriage and other family relationships. Chronic pain patients often do not communicate well with their families, and sexual relationships almost always deteriorate. Ironically, among those chronic pain patients whose spouses remain supportive, such positive attention may inadvertently maintain or increase expression of pain and the experience of disability (Ciccone et al., 1999).

Social relationships, in addition to the marital relationship, can be threatened by chronic pain as well. The resulting reduction in social contact that pain patients experience may contribute to their tendency to turn inward and become self-absorbed. Neurotic behaviour, including preoccupation with physical and emotional symptoms, can result. Many chronic pain patients are clinically depressed; a large number have also contemplated or attempted suicide.

Pain and Personality

Because psychological factors are so clearly implicated in the experience of pain and because at least some pain serves clear functions for the chronic pain sufferer, researchers have examined the role of personality traits in the experience of chronic pain. Although previous hypotheses of a pain-prone personality have been dismissed as being too simplistic, certain personality correlates are reliably associated with chronic pain, including neuroticism, introversion, and the use of passive coping strategies (Ramírez-Maestre, López Martinez, & Zarazaga, 2004). Because findings like these provide clues to the treatment of pain, researchers have continued to refine their understanding of profiles of pain patients.

Pain Profiles   Developing psychological profiles of different groups of pain patients has proven to be helpful for treatment and in specifying problems that patients with particular types of pain have or may develop. To examine these issues, researchers have drawn on a variety of personality instruments, especially the Minnesota Multiphasic Personality Inventory (MMPI; Johansson & Lindberg, 2000). Chronic pain patients typically show elevated scores on three MMPI subscales: hypochondriasis, hysteria, and depression. This constellation of three factors is commonly referred to as the "neurotic triad" because it frequently shows up in the personality profiles of patients with neurotic disorders as well.

Depression reflects the feelings of despair or hopelessness that can often accompany long-term experience with unsuccessfully treated pain. Pain does not appear to be a sufficient condition for the development of depression but, rather, leads to a reduction in activity level and in perceptions of personal control or mastery, which, in turn, can lead to depression (Nicassio, Radojevic, Schoenfeld-Smith, & Dwyer, 1995). Depression itself increases perceptions of pain (Dickens, McGowan, &

Dale, 2003). Depression can, then, feed back into the total pain experience, both aggravating the pain itself and increasing the likelihood of debilitating pain behaviours, such as leaving work. Depression associated with chronic pain can also interfere with returning to work after injury. One team of Canadian researchers assessed the role of depression in worker's return to work after being enrolled in a rehabilitation intervention to minimize disability (Corbière, Sullivan, Stanish, & Adams, 2007). Individuals with a profile of severe to moderate depression and high levels of affective pain were less likely to return to work compared to those with a profile of mild depression and affective pain. This profile has implications for the treatment of pain because interventions with depressed pain patients must address chronic depression and the thought disorders that result, in addition to the pain itself (Jann & Slade, 2007).

Chronic pain is also associated with psychopathology including depression and anxiety disorders, substance use disorders, and other psychiatric problems (Vowles, Zvolensky, Gross, & Sperry, 2004; Nash, Williams, Nicholson, & Trask, 2006). The reason chronic pain and psychopathology are so frequently associated is not fully known. One possibility is that chronic pain activates and exacerbates a latent psychological vulnerability that was not previously recognized, leading to diagnosable psychopathology (Dersh, Polatin, & Gatchel, 2002).

WHAT TECHNIQUES ARE USED TO CONTROL PAIN?

LO4

We now turn to pain control techniques, examining individual techniques that have been used to reduce or control pain. What exactly is pain control? **Pain control** can mean that a patient no longer feels anything in an area that once hurt. It can mean that the person feels sensation but not pain. It can mean that he or she feels pain but is no longer concerned about it. Or it can mean that he or she is still hurting but is now able to stand it.

Some pain control techniques work because they eliminate feeling altogether (for example, spinal blocking agents), whereas others may succeed because they reduce pain to sensation (such as sensory control techniques), and still others succeed because they enable patients to tolerate pain more successfully (such as the more psychological approaches). It will be useful to bear these distinctions in mind as we evaluate the success of individual techniques in the control of pain.

Pharmacological Control of Pain

The traditional and most common method of controlling pain is through the administration of drugs. In particular, morphine (named after Morpheus, the Greek god of sleep) has been the most popular painkiller for decades (Melzack & Wall, 1982). A highly effective painkiller, morphine does have the disadvantage of addiction, and patients may become tolerant to it. Nonetheless, it is a mainstay of pain control, especially in the case of severe pain. It is typically the first line of defence against pain, and it is often sufficient and successful in the management of acute pain. In addition, for chronic patients it may be employed in conjunction with other techniques.

Any drug that can influence neural transmission is a candidate for pain relief. Some drugs, such as local anesthetics, can influence transmission of pain impulses from the peripheral receptors to the spinal cord. The application of an analgesic to a wounded area is an example of this approach. The injection of drugs, such as spinal blocking agents that block the transmission of pain impulses up the spinal cord, is another method.

Pharmacological relief from pain may also be provided by drugs that act directly on higher brain regions involved in pain. Antidepressants, for example, combat pain not only by reducing anxiety and improving mood but also by affecting the downward pathways from the brain that modulate pain. As such, antidepressant administration is often a successful pain reduction technique for depressed pain patients, as well as for pain patients not showing clinical signs of depression.

Over the long term, however, analgesic medications have limitations. Sometimes these treatments make the pain worse rather than better. Patients may consume large quantities of painkillers, which are only partially effective, and they have a variety of undesirable side effects, including inability to concentrate and addiction.

The main concern practitioners have about the pharmacological control of pain is addiction. However, it now appears that this threat is less than was once thought to be the case. One estimate is that about 15 percent of patients with cancer-related pain and as much as 80 percent with non-cancer chronic pain do not receive sufficient pain medication, leading to a cycle of stress, distress, and disability (Chapman & Gavrin, 1999). In three studies involving 25,000 patients treated with opioids who had no history of drug abuse, only

seven cases of addiction were reported (Brody, January 2002), suggesting that the concern over addiction is indeed exaggerated. Even long-term use of prescription pain drugs for such conditions as arthritis appears to produce very low rates of addiction.

However, concerns of potential addiction are so great that patients with legitimate complaints requiring pain medication are often undermedicated. At present, this issue is one of the most controversial and significant ones faced by researchers and practitioners concerned with pain management.

Surgical Control of Pain

The surgical control of pain also has an extensive history. Surgical treatment involves cutting or creating lesions in the so-called pain fibres at various points in the body so that pain sensations can no longer be conducted. Some surgical techniques attempt to disrupt the conduct of pain from the periphery to the spinal cord, whereas others are designed to interrupt the flow of pain sensations from the spinal cord upward to the brain.

Although these surgical techniques are sometimes successful in reducing pain temporarily, the effects are often short-lived. It is now believed that the nervous system has substantial regenerative powers and that blocked pain impulses find their way to the brain via different neural pathways. Moreover, there is some indication that surgery can ultimately worsen the problem because it damages the nervous system, and this damage can itself be a chief cause of chronic pain. Hence, whereas surgical treatment for pain was once relatively common, researchers and practitioners are increasingly doubtful of its value, even as a treatment of last resort.

Sensory Control of Pain

One of the oldest known techniques of pain control is counterirritation, a sensory method. **Counterirritation** involves inhibiting pain in one part of the body by stimulating or mildly irritating another area. The next time you hurt yourself, you can demonstrate this technique on your own (and may have done so already) by pinching or scratching an area of your body near the part that hurts. Typically, the counterirritation produced when you do this will suppress the pain to some extent.

This common observation has been increasingly incorporated into the pain treatment process. An example of a pain control technique that uses this principle is dorsal column stimulation (Nashold & Friedman, 1972). A set of small electrodes is placed or implanted near the point at which the nerve fibres from the painful area enter the spinal cord. When the patient experiences pain, he or she activates a radio signal, which delivers a mild electrical stimulus to that area of the spine, thus inhibiting pain.

In recent years, pain management experts have turned increasingly to exercise and other ways of increasing mobility to help the chronic pain patient. At one time, it was felt that the less activity, the better, and patients with problems ranging from back trouble to nerve problems (such as sciatica) and other disorders were urged to take it easy and not to put too much strain on those parts of the body. Exactly the opposite philosophy has become increasingly popular, and patients are urged to stay active in the hopes of keeping as much of their functioning as possible. This approach has been especially successful with older people in helping manage the discomfort of musculoskeletal disorders (Avlund, Osler, Damsgaard, Christensen, & Schroll, 2000). As was discussed previously, exercise also has the added benefit of triggering the release of endogenous opioids, the body's own natural pain killers which can further provide pain relief.

We now turn to psychological techniques for the management of pain. Unlike the pharmacological, surgical, and sensory pain management techniques considered so far, these more psychological techniques require active participation and learning on the part of the patient and demonstrate the importance of psychological factors in the experience and treatment of pain. Therefore, they are more effective for managing slow-rising pains, which can be anticipated and prepared for, than sudden, intense, or unexpected pains.

Biofeedback

Biofeedback, a method of achieving control over a bodily process, has been used to treat a variety of health problems, including stress (see Chapter 6) and hypertension (see Chapter 13). It has also been used as a pain control technique.

Biofeedback comprises a wide variety of techniques that provide biophysiological feedback to a patient about some bodily process of which the patient is usually unaware. Biofeedback training can be thought of as an operant learning process. First, a target body function to be brought under control, such as blood pressure

or heart rate, is identified. This function is then tracked by a machine, and information about the function is passed on to the patient. For example, heart rate might be converted into a tone, so the patient can hear how fast or slowly his or her heart is beating. The patient then makes efforts to change the bodily process. Through trial and error and continuous feedback from the machine, the patient learns what thoughts or behaviours will modify the bodily function.

Biofeedback has been used to treat several chronic disorders, including Reynaud's disease (a disorder of the cardiovascular system in which the small arteries in the extremities constrict, limiting blood flow and producing a cold, numb aching), hypertension (Glaros & Burton, 2004), and temporomandibular joint pain (Mishra, Gatchel, & Gardea, 2000).

Success of Biofeedback   How successful is biofeedback in treating pain patients? Despite widely touted claims for the efficacy of biofeedback, there is only modest evidence that it is effective in reducing pain in general (Gatchel, Robinson, Pulliam, & Maddrey, 2003). However, for certain types of pain, such as migraine headaches, the evidence suggests that biofeedback may be effective for reducing the frequency of attacks and increasing self-efficacy for pain management (Yvonne & Alexandra, 2007). Even when biofeedback is effective, it may be no more so than less expensive, more easily used techniques, such as relaxation (Mullally, Hall, & Goldstein, 2009).

Relaxation Techniques

Relaxation training has been employed with pain patients extensively, either alone or in concert with other pain control techniques. Originally developed to treat anxiety-related disorders (E. Jacobson, 1938), relaxation is known as an effective means of coping with stress (see Chapter 6). One rationale for teaching pain patients relaxation techniques, then, is that it enables them to cope more successfully with stress and anxiety, which may also ameliorate pain.

Relaxation may also affect pain directly. For example, the reduction of muscle tension or the diversion of blood flow induced by relaxation may reduce pains that are tied to these physiological processes.

What Is Relaxation?   In relaxation, an individual shifts his or her body into a state of low arousal by progressively relaxing different parts of the body. Controlled

Can Listening to Your Favourite Music Reduce Pain?

Increasing interest in non-analgesic forms of pain control has led researchers to consider some interesting alternatives. One accessible and potentially effective method of pain reduction that has received increasing attention is listening to music. Recent research provides some compelling support for the use of "audio-analgesia" as an effective means of managing pain. Moreover, researchers from Glasgow Caledonian University have conducted a number of studies which suggest that it is not any music, but listening to your favourite music in particular that may have pain reducing benefits. A survey of over 318 chronic pain sufferers found that those who self-imitated using music as a means to manage pain were more likely to rate music as being personally important, and also report higher quality of life scores (Mitchell, MacDonald, Knussen, & Serpell, 2007).

Why might music help to reduce pain perception? Although the exact mechanisms are not clear, researchers believe that music may serve both cognitive and emotional functions consistent with the tenets of the gate control theory of pain. Listening to one's preferred music may facilitate emotional changes, decreasing anxiety and also enhancing positive mood states, thereby closing the pain gate. Becoming absorbed in listening to favourite music can also distract one from pain sensations, enhancing perceptions of control over pain and closing the pain gate (Mitchell et al., 2007). Recent brain imaging studies using fMRI have demonstrated that perceiving control over pain is associated with less activity in neural areas associated with the processing of pain (Salomons, Johnstone, Backonja, & Davidson, 2004).

The effects of music on pain management have been tested both experimentally and in hospital settings following minor surgery. In one study of patients undergoing minor foot surgery patients in a no music control group and a listening to preferred music experimental group were assessed just at two times points after baseline post-surgery (Macdonald et al., 2003). Those who listened to music reported less anxiety but no less pain compared to the control group. However, patients indicated that their pain levels initially were very low, suggesting that there may have been little room for significant effects.

To test the relative effectiveness of music versus other forms of distraction, Mitchell and colleagues (2006) used a standard cold pressor methodology for assessing pain tolerance and intensity. The **cold pressor test** involves participants submerging their hands to the wrist in frigid water and keeping it there as long as they can. Each participant had three cold pressor trials, one per condition: listening to music of their choice, listening to audio recordings of popular comedy shows, and completing a distracting verbally delivered serial addition task. Preferred music listening was significantly more effective in increasing pain tolerance than the arithmetic task but not more than listening to humour. Music listening did increase perceptions of control significantly more than listening to humour. None of the distraction conditions had an effect on ratings of pain intensity. However, in a follow-up study, listening to preferred music was more effective in increasing pain tolerance and reducing pain intensity than either a no distraction control condition or an art viewing condition (Mitchell, MacDonald, & Knussen, 2007). So whether it's Pink or Eminem, or Bryan Adams or Vivaldi, this research suggests that listening to favourite music is an easy-to-use and effective means of managing pain.

Listening to your favourite music may reduce pain by decreasing anxiety and enhancing positive mood states.

breathing is another component of relaxation, in which breathing shifts from relatively short, shallow breaths to deeper, longer breaths. Anyone who has been trained in prepared childbirth techniques will recognize that these procedures are used for pain management during early labour.

An alternative method of inducing relaxation is through meditation. In this process, a person attempts to focus attention fully on some very simple and usually unchanging stimulus. For example, one may repeat a very simple syllable (such as "Om") slowly over and over again; this process is used in transcendental meditation, and the syllable is called a mantra.

Success of Relaxation   How successful have relaxation strategies been in the management of pain? Relaxation is modestly successful with some acute pains and may be of value in treating chronic pain when used in conjunction with other methods of pain control. Some of the beneficial physiological effects of relaxation training may be due to the release of endogenous opioid mechanisms.

Hypnosis

Hypnosis is one of the oldest techniques for managing pain, and it is one of the most misunderstood. Its mere mention conjures up visions of Svengalilike power seekers forcing others to do their bidding by inducing a hypnotic trance. In one of his most troublesome cases, Sherlock Holmes was nearly assassinated by a young man ordered to kill him while under the hypnotic control of a bewitching woman.

The use of hypnosis for decreasing sensitivity to pain has been termed hypno-analgesia and has been gaining wider acceptance as a strategy for pain management in clinical settings due in part to evidence from well-controlled studies supporting its effectiveness (Montgomery, DuHamel, & Redd, 2000).

How Does Hypnosis Work?   As an intervention, hypnosis relies on several pain reduction techniques. First, a state of relaxation is brought about so that the trance can be induced; relaxation alone can, of course, help reduce pain. Next, patients are explicitly told that the hypnosis will reduce pain; the suggestion that pain will decline is also sufficient to reduce pain. Hypnosis is itself a distraction from the pain experience, and distraction can reduce the experience of pain.

In the hypnotic trance, the patient is usually instructed to think about the pain differently; as noted earlier in this chapter, the meaning attached to pain influences its occurrence. And finally, patients undergoing painful procedures with hypnosis are often given painkillers. The beneficial effects of hypnosis in reducing pain are due at least in part to the composite effects of relaxation, reinterpretation, distraction, and drugs. Debate has centred on whether hypnosis is merely the sum of these other methods or whether it adds an altered state of consciousness to the experience. Although this issue has not yet been resolved a recent review of controlled clinical trials suggests that hypnosis results in significantly greater pain reduction than non-hypnotic interventions such attention control, physical therapy, and education (Stoelb, Molton, Jensen, & Patterson, 2009).

In a study that made use of hypnotherapy, 28 patients with irritable bowel syndrome were randomly assigned either to receive hypnotherapy directed to modifying gastric experiences or a supportive verbal therapy as a control group. The hypnotherapy was found to reduce discomfort associated with the gastric, colonic response to their syndrome, suggesting that hypnotherapy may have clinical benefits for this patient group (Simrén, Ringström, Björnsson, & Abrahamsson, 2004).

Regardless of the exact mechanism by which it works, the efficacy of hypnosis for the management of some acute procedural pain and chronic pain conditions is now established (Elkins, Jensen, & Patterson, 2007; Patterson & Jensen, 2003). It has been used successfully to control acute pain due to surgery, childbirth, dental procedures, burns, painful medical procedures, and headaches, as well as pain due to a variety of laboratory procedures (Stoelb, Molton, Jensen, & Patterson, 2009). It has also been used with success in the treatment of chronic pain, such as that due to cancer, arthritis, sickle cell disease, fibromyalgia (Elkins et al., 2007) and multiple sclerosis (Jensen et al., 2009).

Acupuncture

Acupuncture has been in existence in China for more than 2,000 years. In acupuncture treatment, long, thin needles are inserted into specially designated areas of the body that theoretically influence the areas in which a patient is experiencing a disorder. Although the main goal of acupuncture is to cure illness, it is also used in pain management because it appears to have an analgesic effect. In fact, in China, a substantial percentage of patients are able to undergo surgery with only the analgesia of acupuncture. During surgery, these patients are typically conscious, fully alert, and able to converse while the procedures are going on.

How Does Acupuncture Work?   How acupuncture controls pain is not fully known. It is possible that acupuncture functions partly as a sensory method of controlling pain. Researchers also believe that acupuncture may work because it is associated with other psychologically based techniques for pain control. In particular, patients believe that acupuncture will work, and their expectations may help reduce pain. The belief that acupuncture will reduce pain can reduce anxiety, inducing a state of relaxation. Thus, the effects of acupuncture may be largely non-specific and/or placebo like in nature (Langevin et al., 2011).

Before acupuncture begins, patients are usually fully prepared for it and are told what the sensations of the needles will be and how to tolerate them. Such informed preparation often reduces fear and increases tolerance of pain (see Chapter 9). Acupuncture needles and the process of inserting them are distracting; accordingly, attention may be directed away from pain. Patients undergoing acupuncture often receive analgesic drugs of various kinds, which also reduce the pain experience.

Overall, is acupuncture an effective method of pain control? A review of the literature suggests that it can help reduce some kinds of short-term pain (Trinh, Phillips, Ho, & Damsma, 2004), but it may not be as effective for chronic pain. With an increase in controlled clinical trials testing the efficacy of acupuncture evidence greater acceptance of this ancient pain control method for chronic pain will likely increase in coming years (see the

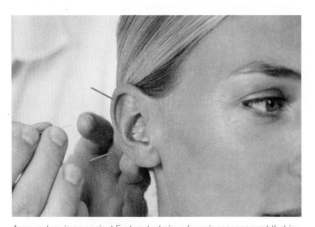

Acupuncture is an ancient Eastern technique for pain management that is gaining increasing acceptance in Western medicine.

Health Psychology in Action box, "East Meets West to Combat Pain").

Distraction

Individuals who are involved in intense activities, such as sports or military manoeuvres, can be oblivious to painful injuries. These are extreme examples of a commonly employed pain technique: **distraction.** By focusing attention on an irrelevant and attention-getting stimulus or by distracting oneself with a high level of activity, one can turn attention away from pain.

There are two quite different mental strategies for controlling discomfort. One is to distract oneself by focusing on another activity. The other kind of mental strategy for controlling stressful events is to focus directly on the events but to reinterpret the experience. The following is a description from an 8-year-old boy who confronted a painful event directly:

> As soon as I get in the dentist's chair, I pretend he's the enemy and I'm a secret agent, and he's torturing me to get secrets, and if I make one sound, I'm telling him secret information, so I never do. I'm going to be a secret agent when I grow up, so this is good practice.

According to Albert Bandura (1991), who reported this story, occasionally the boy "got carried away with his fantasy role-playing. One time the dentist asked him to rinse his mouth. Much to the child's own surprise, he snarled, "I won't tell you a damned thing," which momentarily stunned the dentist.

Does Distraction Work?   Distraction appears to be a successful technique of pain control, especially with acute pain (for example, L. Cohen, Cohen, Blount, Schaen, & Zaff, 1999). As discussed in the Health Psychology in Action Box, "Can Listening to Your Favourite Music Reduce Pain?" listening to preferred music can be an effective pain management strategy in part because the music serves a as distraction from the pain.

New advances in technology have led researchers to consider other alternate means of creating distraction for pain management. For example, several researchers have now investigated the effectiveness of using immersive virtual reality as a distraction technique for managing experimental pain induced by the cold-presser test (Gutiérrez-Maldonado et al., 2011; Malloy & Milling, 2010), and pain-related burn injury care (Malloy & Milling, 2010). However, the practical significance of

East Meets West to Combat Pain

Traditional Chinese Medicine merged with Western medicine when McMaster University started training health care professionals in the use of contemporary acupuncture in 1998. Although the McMaster Acupuncture/Pain Clinic has been in operation since 1985, it is only in the past decade that professionals such as doctors, physiotherapists, and chiropractors have been able to receive training in this ancient technique through the McMaster Contemporary Medical Acupuncture program. More than 500 health care professionals from Canada and around the world have received training in this gentle analgesic therapy since the program began.

Electro-acupuncture (which involves applying pulsating electrical current to acupuncture needles) has also been used successfully for minor surgical procedures by staff anesthesiologists at McMaster University Medical Centre for a number of years, and has been especially beneficial for patients who have adverse reactions to the usual anesthetics administered for surgery. For one woman, who formerly had severe reactions to anesthetics, including lingering numbness in her legs months after a procedure, electro-acupuncture has become her analgesic therapy of choice. This technique has been used for three separate biopsies, and each time she has come out of the procedure feeling alert, happy, and most importantly, pain-free.

In addition to surgical procedures such as biopsies, electro-acupuncture has also been used for postoperative pain relief from breast reduction surgery, to assist women in labour, and as treatment to help increase the rate of pregnancy during in vitro fertilization procedures.

Source: Nandagopal, Fargas-Babjak, & Claraco, 2006.

distraction for chronic pain is limited by the fact that such patients cannot distract themselves indefinitely. Thus, while effective, distraction may be most useful when used in conjunction with other pain control techniques.

Coping Techniques

Coping skills training has been increasingly used for helping chronic pain patients manage pain. For example, one study with burn patients found that brief training in cognitive coping skills, including distraction and focusing on the sensory aspects of pain instead of their painful qualities, led to reduced reported pain, increased satisfaction with pain control, and better pain coping skills (Haythornthwaite, Lawrence, & Fauerbach, 2001). Active coping skills have been found to reduce pain in patients with a variety of chronic pains (Mercado, Carroll, Cassidy, & Cote, 2000; S. R. Bishop & Warr, 2003). Emotional disclosure through expressive writing has also been found to reduce pain in people with cancer (Cepeda et al., 2008), and fibromyalgia (Junghaenel, Schwartz, & Broderick, 2008).

In contrast, for chronic pain patients, attending directly to the pain, rather than avoiding it, was more adaptive, enabling these chronic pain patients to mobilize their resources for reducing or controlling the pain (J. A. Holmes & Stevenson, 1990). Such studies suggest that pain patients might be trained in different coping strategies, avoidant versus attentive, depending on the actual or expected duration of their pain (J. A. Holmes & Stevenson, 1990).

Patients' assessments of their own coping techniques may be useful information for planning interventions with chronic pain patients. One study found that patients who appraised their problem-solving abilities as poor suffered increased pain, depression, and disability whereas those with a more favourable assessment of their problem-solving competence did better (Kerns, Rosenberg, & Otis, 2002).

Guided Imagery

Guided imagery has been used to control some acute pain and discomfort. In **guided imagery,** a patient is instructed to conjure up a picture that he or she holds in mind during the painful experience. The patient is encouraged to visualize a peaceful, relatively unchanging scene, to hold it in mind, and to focus on it fully. This process brings on a relaxed state, concentrates attention, and distracts the patient from the pain or discomfort—all techniques that have been shown to reduce pain.

The use of guided imagery to induce relaxation can control slow-rising pains, which can be anticipated and prepared for, or it can be used to control the discomfort of a painful medical procedure. As an example of the former use, advocates of prepared childbirth encourage a woman in labour to develop a focal point—a real or an imagined picture that she can focus on fully when labour pains begin. An example of using guided imagery to control the discomfort of a medical procedure is provided by a patient undergoing radiation therapy:

> When I was taking the radiation treatment, I imagined I was looking out my window and watching the trees and seeing the leaves go back and forth in the wind. Or, I would think of the ocean and watch the waves come in over and over again, and I would hope, "Maybe this will take it all away."

A very different kind of visualization technique may be used by patients trying to take a more personally aggressive stance toward pain. Instead of using imagery to calm and soothe themselves, these patients use it to rouse themselves into a confrontative stance by imagining a combative, action-filled scene. The following examples are from patients who used aggressive imagery in conjunction with their chemotherapy treatment:

> I happened to see something my husband was watching on TV. It was on World War II and the Nazis were in it. They were ruthless. They killed everything. I visualized my white blood cells were the German Army, and that helped me get through chemotherapy.
>
> I imagined that the cancer was this large dragon and the chemotherapy was a cannon, and when I was taking the chemotherapy, I would imagine it blasting the dragon, piece by piece.

What Does Guided Imagery Do?   Aggressive imagery may improve coping with the uncomfortable effects of illness or treatment by enhancing perceptions of control over the pain. When the body is in a state of excitement or arousal, pain can be inhibited. Moreover, aggressive imagery can serve as a distraction to pain, and it gives the patient something to focus on.

It is interesting to note that these two virtually opposite forms of imagery may actually achieve some beneficial effects in controlling pain through the same means. Both may induce a positive mood state (relaxation or excitement), which contributes to the reduction of pain, and both focus attention and provide a distraction from pain—one by concentrating attention on a single, unchanging or repetitive stimulus, the other by diverting attention to the drama of an active scene.

How effective is guided imagery in controlling pain? Evidence from at least one randomized controlled

Visualizing a calming image such as the waves rolling onto a beach can help to control pain by inducing a state of relaxation and/or focus attention away from pain.

trial suggests that guided imagery is more effective than some pharmacologic interventions such as amitriptyline for reducing pain associated with fibromyalgia (Fors, Sexton, & Götestam, 2002). However, because guided imagery is typically used in conjunction with other pain control techniques, its unique contribution to pain reduction relative to other psychological techniques is as yet, unknown.

Additional Cognitive Techniques to Control Pain

In recent years, psychologists have attempted to expand the arsenal of cognitive behavioural techniques for controlling pain. These have several objective approaches. They encourage patients to reconceptualize the problem from overwhelming to manageable. The rationale is that the pain problem must be seen as modifiable for cognitive behavioural methods to have any impact. Clients are also encouraged to reconceptualize their own role in the pain management process, from being passive recipients of pain to being active, resourceful, and competent individuals who can aid in the control of pain. These cognitions are important in the pain experience and may promote feelings of self-efficacy. Encouraging clients to attribute their success to their own efforts can help patients come to see themselves as efficacious agents of change and who may therefore be in a better position to monitor subsequent changes in the pain and bring about successful pain modification.

Similarly clients need to learn how to monitor their thoughts, feelings, and behaviours to break up maladaptive cognitions that may have resulted in response to pain. As we noted in Chapter 3, patients often inadvertently undermine behaviour change by engaging in discouraging self-talk. Leading pain patients to develop more upbeat monologues increases the likelihood that cognitive behavioural techniques will be successful.

Do Cognitive Behavioural Interventions Work?   Those techniques that enhance perceptions of self-efficacy may be especially successful. Self-efficacy is important, both because it leads patients to undertake steps to control their pain and because perceptions of efficacy may offset the potential for depression that is so often seen in chronic pain patients.

Cognitive behavioural interventions may also be useful for helping children manage the pain and distress associated with medical procedures such as injections. Researchers from Dalhousie University conducted a review of 28 clinical trials on the effectiveness of cognitive behavioural interventions for the management of needle pain in children and adolescents (Uman, Chambers, McGrath, & Kisely, 2006). Distraction, hypnosis, and combined cognitive behavioural interventions were among the most effective interventions for reducing pain.

L05   HOW IS CHRONIC PAIN MANAGED?

As we noted in our previous discussion, no single pain control technique has been clearly effective in modifying chronic pain. Thus, a combination of techniques is usually recommended and recognized as the most effective way to manage this type of pain.

At one time, the patient who suffered from chronic pain had few treatment avenues available, save the tragedy of addiction to morphine or other painkillers and rounds of only temporarily successful operations. Now, however, a coordinated form of treatment has developed to treat chronic pain. These interventions are termed **pain management programs,** and they make available to patients all that is known about pain control.

Some of the earliest pain clinics in Canada appeared in Halifax, Kingston, and Saskatoon (Merskey, 1998). At present, there are such publicly funded clinics around the country. However, wait times can be long with a recent survey indicating that the average wait time for admission was six months (Peng et al., 2007). Typically, these programs are interdisciplinary efforts, bringing together neurological, cognitive, behavioural, and psychological expertise concerning pain (Peng et al., 2007). As such, they involve the expertise of physicians, clinical

psychologists or psychiatrists, and physical therapists, with consultation from neurology, rheumatology, orthopedic surgery, internal medicine, and physical medicine. The goals of programs in pain management are to enable patients to reduce their pain as much as possible, to increase their levels of activity, to reduce perceptions of disability, to return to work, and to lead meaningful and rewarding lives, even if the pain cannot be entirely eliminated (Peng et al., 2007; Vendrig, 1999).

Initial Evaluation

Initially, all patients are evaluated with respect to their pain and pain behaviours. Typically, such evaluation begins with a qualitative and quantitative assessment of the pain, including its location, sensory qualities, severity, and duration, as well as its onset and history. Functional status is then assessed, with patients providing information about the degree to which their work and family lives have been impaired.

Exploring how the patient has coped with the pain in the past helps establish treatment goals for the future. For example, patients who withdraw from social activities in response to their pain may need to increase their participation in social activities or their family life. Most patients are evaluated for their emotional and mental functioning as well, since many can be very distressed and may suffer significant emotional and cognitive disruption in their lives (Iezzi, Archibald, Barnett, Klinck, & Duckworth, 1999).

Individualized Treatment

Individualized programs of management are developed following completion of the profile of the patient's pain and how it has affected their lives. Such programs are typically structured and time limited, and they provide concrete aims, rules, and endpoints so that each patient has specific goals to achieve. Goals include decreasing the intensity of the pain, increasing physical activity, decreasing reliance on medications, improving psychosocial functioning, reducing perception of disability, returning to full work status, and reducing the need to use health care services. An overarching goal has been to get patients to adopt a self-management approach for dealing with their pain. As we saw earlier in a discussion of self-efficacy, accepting the role of self-management for controlling pain may be helpful in reducing pain severity and interference with lifestyle (Glenn & Burns, 2003).

Components of Chronic Pain Management Programs

Pain management programs include several common features. The first is patient education. All patients are provided with complete information about the nature of their condition. Often conducted in a group setting, the educational component of the intervention may include discussions of medications; assertiveness or social skills training; ways of dealing with sleep disturbance; depression as a consequence of pain; nonpharmacological measures for pain control, such as relaxation skills and distraction; posture, weight management, and nutrition; and other topics related to the day-to-day management of pain.

Most patients are then trained in a variety of measures to reduce pain. Typically, such programs include relaxation training and exercise and may include other components, such as temperature biofeedback for muscle-contraction headaches or stretching exercise for back pain patients. Because many pain patients are emotionally distressed and suffer from some degree of depression, anxiety, or irritability, group therapy is often conducted to help patients gain control of their emotional responses.

Pain management programs also target the maladaptive cognitions that may arise in response to chronic pain. Given what has often been a history of unsuccessful treatment of their pain, patients often catastrophize, and so interventions are aimed at the distorted negative perceptions patients hold about their pain and their ability to overcome and live with it. Such cognitive interventions have also been shown to enhance the effectiveness of physiotherapy interventions alone (Sullivan & Adams, 2010).

Relapse prevention and follow-up activities are typically initiated in pain management programs so that patients will not backslide once they are discharged from the outpatient program. The incidence of relapse following initially successful treatment of persistent pain appears to range from about 30 percent to 60 percent (Turk & Rudy, 1991), and it appears that, for at least some pains, relapse is directly related to non-adherence to treatment.

Involvement of Family

Many pain management programs intervene at the family level, combining family therapy with other interventions. On the one hand, chronic pain patients often withdraw from their families, but on the other hand, efforts by the family to be supportive can sometimes inadvertently reinforce pain behaviours. Working with the family to reduce such counterproductive behaviours may be necessary.

Despite these potential problems, certain types of family support can help those with chronic pain cope. In a study conducted by researchers at the University of British Columbia, married people with rheumatoid arthritis were followed for one week with daily interviews to assess their pain, catastrophizing, negative affect, and satisfaction with their spouses' responses (Holtzman & DeLongis, 2007). As expected, catastrophizing was associated with reports of increased pain and negative affect. However, a synergistic effect between satisfaction with spousal responses, pain, and catastrophizing was found. The more individuals were satisfied with their spouses' responses, the less impact catastrophizing had on pain and negative affect. This suggests that positive responses from family members may act as a coping resource, which can attenuate the harmful effects of maladaptive coping for people with chronic pain (Holtzman & DeLongis, 2007). Interventions that help a family respond positively to a family member's chronic pain may be one way to provide aid.

Evaluation of Pain Management Programs

Pain management programs appear to be successful in helping control chronic pain. A review of studies of the efficacy of comprehensive chronic pain treatment programs indicate that they are the most consistently effective and cost-effective means for managing chronic pain (Robert & Akiko, 2006). As the importance, complexity, and costs of pain have become increasingly clear, pain is now taken more seriously in the medical management of patients and is recognized as an important medical issue in its own right rather than the inconvenient symptom it was once regarded to be (Turk, 1994). Originally directed largely to the alleviation of pain itself, programs designed to manage chronic pain now acknowledge the complex interplay of physiological, psychological, behavioural, and social factors, representing a truly biopsychosocial approach to pain management.

Pain management programs extend a promise of relief to thousands of sufferers who previously had little to aid them. These programs offer not only the possibility of a pain-free existence but also the dignity that comes from self-control of pain management and freedom from a life of pain, addiction, and depression. ●

SUMMARY

Understand the significance of pain

- Pain is a significant aspect of illness because it is the symptom of chief concern to patients and leads them to seek medical attention. However, pain is often considered of secondary importance to practitioners.

Explain why pain is difficult to study

- Pain is intensely subjective and, consequently, has been difficult to study. It is heavily influenced by the context in which it is experienced. To objectify the experience of pain, pain researchers have developed questionnaires that assess its dimensions and methods to assess pain behaviours.

- According to the gate control theory, the experience of pain results from a combination of physical, emotional, and cognitive factors which modulate the intensity of pain by closing or opening the pain gate.

- A-delta fibres conduct fast, sharp, localized pain; C-fibres conduct slow, aching, burning, and long-lasting pain; higher-order brain processes influence the experience of pain through the central control mechanism.

- Neurochemical advances in the understanding of pain centre around endogenous opioid peptides, which regulate the pain experience.

Identify the clinical issues in pain management

- Acute pain is short term and specific to a particular injury or disease, whereas chronic pain does not decrease with treatment and time. An estimated 20 to 40 percent of the Canadian population suffers from chronic pain, which

may lead them to disrupt their entire lives in an effort to cure it. Chronic pain is complicated to treat because it has a functional and psychological overlay.

- Developing psychological profiles of different groups of pain patients has proven to be helpful for treatment and in specifying problems that patients with particular types of pain have or may develop. The presence of depression is an important consideration for such profiles.

Describe the techniques used to control pain

- Pharmacologic (for example, morphine), surgical, and sensory stimulation techniques (for example, dorsal column stimulator) have been the mainstays of pain control. Increasingly, treatments with psychological components, including biofeedback, relaxation, hypnosis, acupuncture, distraction, and guided imagery, have been added to the pain control arsenal. Although all these techniques show at least some success, the exact mechanisms by which they do so are still elusive.

- Most recently, cognitive behavioural techniques that help instill a sense of self-efficacy have been used successfully in the treatment of pain.

Explain how chronic pain is managed

- Chronic pain is often treated through coordinated pain management programs oriented toward managing the pain, extinguishing pain behaviour, and re-establishing a viable lifestyle. These programs employ a mix of technologies in an effort to develop an individualized treatment program for each patient—a truly biopsychosocial approach to pain.

KEY TERMS

Management of Chronic and Terminal Illness

CHAPTER 11

Living with Chronic Illness

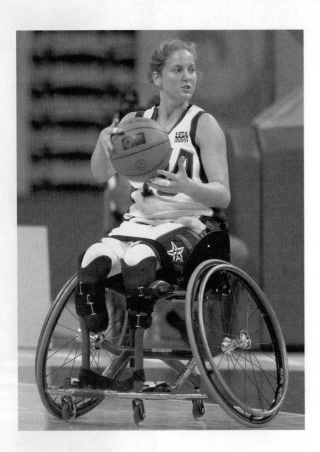

After reading this chapter, students will be able to:

(LO1) Define quality of life

(LO2) Understand the emotional responses to chronic illness

(LO3) Describe how the self is changed by chronic illness

(LO4) Explain how people cope with chronic illness

(LO5) Explain how people manage chronic illness

(LO6) Identify the psychological interventions used to manage chronic illness

During a race at a high school track meet, a young runner stumbled and fell to the ground, caught in the grips of an asthma attack. As her mother frantically clawed through her backpack, looking for the inhaler, three other girls on the track team offered theirs. As this account implies, asthma rates have skyrocketed in recent years, particularly among children and adolescents. Nearly 3 million Canadians over the age of 12 have asthma, with the rates highest among children and teens (Chen, Johansen, Thillaiampalam, & Sambell, 2005; Public Health Agency of Canada, 2007c). In fact, there has been a fourfold increase in the rates of asthma among children in the past 20 years, with 20 percent of boys and 15 percent of girls, ages 8 to 11, diagnosed with asthma in Canada. Although scientists are not entirely sure why asthma is on the increase, exposure to environmental and air pollutants are believed to play a role, with children living in southern Ontario and in poor urban neighbourhoods being particularly vulnerable to developing asthma (Commission for Environmental Cooperation, 2006). The complications that asthma creates for children and young adults are evident (Gregerson, 2000). Caution in activities, medication, and inhalers become a part of daily life. In addition to social and environmental determinants, psychosocial factors are clearly an important part of this adjustment, helping us answer such questions as "What factors precipitate an asthma attack?" and "What does it mean to have a chronic disease so early in life?"

In this chapter we will examine the impact of living with one or more chronic health conditions and the factors that affect management of the condition for better or worse. Broadly speaking, chronic health conditions are those which can impact day to day physical, emotional, and even social functioning, and therefore take a toll on quality of life. For this reason we will consider some of the challenges and issues involved in living with a chronic condition that are common to many chronic health issues such as physical limitations, quality of life, and coping with the many challenges of a chronic health condition. In later chapters (13 and 14) issues and research that are specific to some of the more common chronic illnesses such as cardiovascular disease, diabetes, cancer, and arthritis will be examined in detail.

Many chronic health conditions such as arthritis, diabetes, coronary heart disease, and multiple sclerosis involve disease processes and are often referred to as a chronic disease or more commonly chronic illness. Other chronic health conditions may be the result of injury or prolonged strain, such as chronic back pain or chronic tinnitus (a persistent ringing in the ears), and do not necessary involve a disease process. Similarly chronic conditions such as irritable bowel syndrome and chronic fatigue syndrome are not fully understood and therefore no clear disease process has been established. Yet regardless of whether a disease process is identified, chronic health conditions present a challenge to daily living, functioning and even self-image that can require special management and coping skills. For this reason the terms chronic (health) condition, chronic illness, and chronic disease will be used interchangeably, with the understanding that chronic condition may sometimes refer to conditions that do not involve a disease process.

At any given time, 58 percent of the Canadian population, and 81 percent of the community-dwelling senior population, has a chronic condition, and these rates may increase in years to come. Taken together, the medical management of these chronic disorders accounts for about two-thirds of the nation's health spending. Care for people with chronic illnesses accounts for 67 percent of all the health care costs incurred in Canada. As the opening example implies, these conditions are not confined to the elderly. More than one-third of young adults, age 18 to 44, have at least one chronic condition (Schultz & Kopec, 2003). Nonetheless, chronic conditions are much more common among women, lower-income Canadians, seniors (see Figure 11.1), and certain ethnic groups, such as Aboriginal peoples (Health Council of Canada, 2007a). For example, the rates of arthritis, hypertension, asthma, diabetes, and heart disease are higher among First Nations women than among Canadian women in general (Assembly of First Nations, 2007).

Chronic conditions range from relatively mild, such as partial hearing loss, to severe and life-threatening disorders, such as cancer, coronary artery disease, and diabetes. For example, in Canada, arthritis in its various forms afflicts 4 million people (The Arthritis Society, 2010); over 145,000 new cases of cancer are diagnosed each year (Canadian Cancer Society, 2011); diabetes afflicts over 1.7 million people (Statistics Canada, 2010); more than 500,000 people are living with the effects of a stroke (Heart and Stroke Foundation, 2011a); and thousands of people have a history of heart attack and/or chest pain. Five million people have diagnosed hypertension (Canadian Institute for Health Research, 2005).

A more startling statistic is that most of us will eventually develop at least one chronic disability or

FIGURE 11.1 | Chronic Conditions Are More Common among Lower-Income Canadians, Women, and Seniors

Source: Health Council of Canada (2007). *Why Health Care Renewal Matters: Learning from Canadians with Chronic Health Conditions.*
Toronto: Health Council. ISBN 978-1-897463-10-9. (Data source: Statistics Canada. Canadian Community Health Survey (Cycle 3.1) 2005)
Graph shows crude prevalence for people aged 12 and over. Income data are not adjusted for age or gender differences. Numbers
may not sum to 100% due to rounding.

* Select chronic health conditions include arthritis, cancer, chronic obstructive pulmonary disease, diabetes, heart disease,
high blood pressure, and mood disorders.

† Income quintiles divide all Canadians into five equal-sized groups based on household income. People in quintile 1 have the
lowest incomes; the highest in quintile 5.

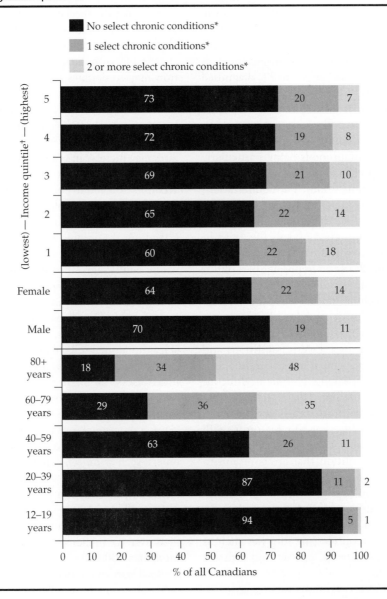

disease, which may ultimately be the cause of our death. Thus, it is likely that, at some time, each of us will hear a physician say that our condition is chronic and cannot be cured; it can only be managed.

The impacts of chronic disease are serious and multiple. Also referred to as non-communicable diseases, chronic diseases cause premature death. More than 63 percent of deaths globally were due to chronic disease in 2008, amounting to an estimated 36 million people (World Health Organization, 2011). Although the largest number of these deaths occurred in low- and middle-income countries, in relative terms the prevalence rates were highest among developed countries like Canada. Chronic disease can seriously compromise the quality of life of individuals, and present an enormous economic and social burden to families, communities, and society in general. For example, the estimated total direct (e.g., health care) and indirect (e.g., disability and premature mortality) health care costs of chronic diseases in Canada are staggering: nearly $10 billion for diabetes; almost $18 billion for cancer; over $20 billion for arthritis; over $26 billion for cardiovascular disease, hypertension, and stroke (Patra et al., 2007).

In this chapter, we consider some of the problems posed by chronic illness. We begin with a consideration of quality of life and how it may be assessed. Next, we consider patients' psychological reactions to chronic illness. We consider patients' spontaneous efforts to deal with the problems and emotional reactions posed by illness, their individual coping efforts, and their illness

In the past decade, researchers have begun to consider psychosocial functioning as an important aspect of quality of life among those with a chronic illness or disability.

related cognitions. We then turn to the specific issues of rehabilitation posed by chronic illness, including physical management, vocational problems, and problems in social functioning, and examine some general strategies for comprehensive rehabilitation programs. The vital importance of **self-management** by those with chronic illnesses is a central concept that guides this discussion (Lorig & Holman, 2003; Glasgow et al., 2002). Self-management refers to involvement of the patient in all aspects of a chronic illness and its implications, including medical management, changes in social and vocational roles, and coping.

WHAT IS QUALITY OF LIFE?   (L01)

Until recently, quality of life was not considered an issue of psychological importance. For many years, it was measured solely in terms of length of survival and signs of presence of disease, with virtually no consideration of the psychosocial consequences of illness and treatments (S. E. Taylor & Aspinwall, 1990).

However, medical measures are only weakly related to patients' or relatives' assessments of quality of life. In fact, one classic study of hypertension (Jachuck, Brierley, Jachuck, & Willcox, 1982) found that although 100 percent of the physicians reported that their patients' quality of life had improved with the regular use of hypertensive medication, only half the patients agreed and virtually none of the relatives did (see also Brissette, Leventhal, & Leventhal, 2003; Gorbatenko-Roth, Levin, Altmaier, & Doebbeling, 2001). Moreover, some illnesses and treatments are perceived by patients to be "fates worse than death" because they threaten valued life activities so completely (Ditto, Druley, Moore, Danks, & Smucker, 1996).

One important aspect of quality of life is people's perceptions of their own health. Self-reports of health status (e.g., "Would you rate your health as poor, fair, good, very good, or excellent?") have found to predict morbidity and mortality beyond medical and psychological factors (Frankenberg & Jones, 2004; McCullough & Laurenceau, 2004). Clearly self-reported health is an important aspect of quality of life.

Perhaps the most important impetus for evaluating quality of life stems from the psychological distress patients with a chronic illness often experience. Those with a chronic illness are more likely to suffer from depression, anxiety, and distress (for example, De Graaf & Bijl, 2002; Mittermaier et al., 2004). Depression, psychological distress, and neuroticism contribute to substantially increased risks for mortality from chronic conditions (Christensen, Moran, Wiebe, Ehlers, & Lawton, 2002). Stress exacerbates the symptoms and course of many chronic illnesses, and since depression and anxiety are common consequences of stress, reducing stress levels and managing those stressors that cannot be eliminated are paramount for the management of chronic illness.

Because of findings like these, quality of life is now given attention in the management of chronic illness. **Quality of life** has several components, specifically physical functioning, psychological status, social functioning, and disease- or treatment-related symptomatology (Kahn & Juster, 2002; Power, Bullinger, Harper, & The World Health Organization Quality of Life Group, 1999; see Table 11.1). Quality of life among people with chronic illnesses is now assessed with emphasis especially placed on how much the disease and its treatment interferes with the activities of daily living, such as sleeping, eating, going to work, and engaging in recreational and social activities. For patients with more advanced diseases, such assessments focus on the functional aspects of daily living and include whether the patient is able to bathe, dress, use the toilet, be mobile, be continent, and eat without assistance. Essentially then, quality of life assessments gauge the extent to which a patient's normal life activities have been compromised by disease and treatment.

Evaluating Quality of Life

A broad array of measures is now available for evaluating quality of life in both adults (for example, Hazuda, Gerety, Lee, Mulrow, & Lichtenstein, 2002; Logsdon, Gibbons, McCurry, & Teri, 2002), and children (Varni, Burwinkle, Rapoff, Kamps, & Olson, 2004). In addition, there are not only generic measures that can be used across a variety of different health conditions and chronic diseases but also disease-specific measures to help understand how a particular chronic illness may impact an individual's quality of life. An example of the areas that are assessed by a generic measure of quality of life, the SF-36, is presented in Table 11.1.

One way of understanding how chronic illness may impact quality of life is by examining how the quality of life of people living with a chronic disease or condition compares to that of the general population. This is usually accomplished by establishing population norms for a country that can be used as a comparison standard for evaluating individual or group quality of life scores within the population. These same norms can also be used to compare the quality of life across different countries. For example, one large national survey assessed the quality of life of Canadians using the SF-36 to establish population norms, and then compared the scores to those of Americans and people living in the United Kingdom (see Figure 11.2). Canadians scored higher

---

TABLE 11.1 | The Eight Health Concepts and Two Summary Domains Assessed by the Short Form Health Survey (SF-36)

The SF-36 yields an 8-scale profile of functional status and well-being. It has been translated for use in more than 40 countries and is considered one of the most widely used generic measures of quality of life in the world.

Summary Domains	Health Concept	Description
Physical Health Overall	Physical functioning	Limitations in physical activities because of physical health problems
	Role physical	Limitations in usual role activities because of physical health problems
	Bodily pain	Pain magnitude and interference
	General health	General health perceptions
Mental Health Overall	Vitality	Energy and fatigue
	Social functioning	Limitations in social activities because of physical or emotional problems
	Role social	Limitations in usual role activities because of emotional problems
	Mental health	Psychological distress and well-being

Source: Ware & Sherbourne, 1992

FIGURE 11.2 | Quality of Life Assessment: Canada, the United States, and the United Kingdom

Mean age- and sex-standardized scores for the eight domains of the Medical Outcomes Study 36-item Short Form (SF-36) and for the two summary scales (physical component and mental component) for Canada (dark blue bars), the United States (light blue bars), and the United Kingdom (medium grey bars)

Source: From Hopman, W. M., Towheed, T., Anastassiades, T., Tenenhouse, A., Poliquin, S., Berger, C., et al. (2000). "Canadian normative data for the SF-36 health survey." Reprinted from CMAJ-Aug-00; 163(3), pages 265–271 by permission of the publisher. ©2000 Canadian Medical Association.

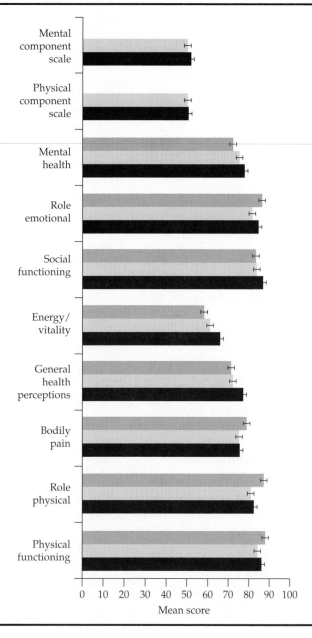

than Americans on all eight dimensions of quality of life and on both the physical and mental health components. Compared to people in the U.K., Canadians scored somewhat higher on general health perceptions, vitality, social functioning, and mental health. However, within Canada, men had quality of life scores that were substantially higher than women across all of the eight domains and summary scores (Hopman et al., 2000).

For Canadian women then, living with a chronic illness further compromises quality of life.

Quality of life may also fluctuate depending on the characteristics of the illness, acute changes in symptoms, and age-related changes in health over time (Sacco et al., 2005). An assessment of quality of life during an acute phase of a chronic illness when symptoms are flaring will therefore be very different from an assessment made when symptoms are less active. Certain illnesses such as multiple sclerosis and rheumatoid arthritis, for example, are progressive, and quality of life may rapidly decline over a short period of time depending upon the natural course of the illness and how well the person can adjust to these changing demands. Developmental changes can also impact quality of life. A five-year population study of quality of life among Canadian adults found that although quality of life remained relatively stable overall, for certain groups quality of life improved while for others it deteriorated. For younger Canadians under 35, there were significant improvements in mental health scores over the five years, whereas for Canadians who were over 65 or who had a chronic illness, psychiatric condition or both, quality of life declined (Hopman et al., 2006).

Culture can also play a role in how a chronic illness impacts quality of life. For example, one study examining quality of life in people with irritable bowel syndrome in Greece and Sweden found notable differences across different quality of life domains even after controlling for age, gender, education level, and comorbidity. Women from Greece scored much lower on both general health related quality of life and mental health than women from Sweden suggesting that differences in cultural environments may impact how people experience the same chronic health condition. (Faresjö et al., 2006).

Why Study Quality of Life?

Why should we study quality of life among those with chronic illnesses? There are several reasons:

1. Documentation of exactly how illness affects vocational, social, and personal activities, as well as the general activities of daily living, provides an important basis for interventions designed to improve quality of life (Maes, Leventhal, & DeRidder, 1996).

2. Quality of life measures can help pinpoint which problems are likely to emerge for patients with diseases and be helpful in anticipating the interventions that are required. Such a measure, for example, might indicate that sexual functioning is a problem for patients with certain kinds of cancer but that depression is a more common problem for patients with other kinds of cancer.

3. Such measures assess the impact of treatments on quality of life. For example, if a cancer treatment has disappointing survival rates and produces adverse side effects, the treatment may be more harmful than the disease itself (Aaronson et al., 1986). Quality of life measures have made it possible to assess the impact of unpleasant therapies and to identify some of the determinants of poor adherence to those therapies.

4. Quality of life information can be used to compare therapies. For example, if two therapies produce approximately equivalent survival rates but one lowers quality of life substantially, one would be inclined to go with the treatments that keep quality of life at a higher level (S. E. Taylor & Aspinwall, 1990).

5. Quality of life information can inform decision makers about care that will maximize long-term survival with the highest quality of life possible. Such information enables policy makers to compare the impact of different chronic diseases on health care costs and to assess the cost effectiveness of different interventions, given quality of life information (Lubeck & Yelin, 1988).

A final point to consider when examining quality of life is the presence of multiple chronic physical or mental health conditions. Most chronic disease management programs are designed to target one chronic condition. Yet many people live with multiple chronic conditions that can have an additive impact on quality of life, and introduce a greater level of complexity into the self-management of their chronic conditions. For example, the symptoms or treatment of one condition may aggravate the symptoms of other conditions, and there is a greater risk for conflicting care recommendations, medication interactions, and feeling overwhelmed by the combined conditions (Broemeling, Watson, & Black, 2005). In Canada, of those who live with a chronic illness, one-third has more than one chronic health condition. For example, estimates from a national survey suggest that over half of Canadians living with arthritis or high blood pressure, and three-quarters of Canadians with heart disease or diabetes, have at least one other chronic health condition (Health Council of Canada, 2007b).

The impact of chronic illness and especially multiple chronic conditions on quality of life is clear. Whereas Canadians with no chronic health conditions report the highest levels of quality of life, more than a third of those with one chronic illness, and more than half of those with two or more chronic conditions, report having moderate to severe disability (Health Council of Canada, 2007b). Similarly, one national study found that Canadians who had both diabetes and cancer had significantly poorer quality of life than those who had either cancer or diabetes alone (Bowker, Pohar, & Johnson, 2006). Thus those who live with multiple chronic health conditions may require specialized treatment and management strategies to address their quality of life deficits.

Attention to quality of life issues has been useful in pinpointing some of the areas that require particular attention and interventions following the diagnosis of a chronic disease to which we now turn.

(L02) WHAT ARE THE EMOTIONAL RESPONSES TO CHRONIC ILLNESS?

Many chronic diseases affect all aspects of a patient's life (Maes et al., 1996; Stanton, Revenson, & Tennen, 2007). As in acute diseases, there is a temporary first phase, when all life activities are disrupted. Chronic disease, however, may also carry the need to make intermittent or permanent changes in physical, vocational, and social activities. In addition, people with chronic illnesses must integrate the patient role into their lives psychologically if they are to adapt to their disorders.

Immediately after a chronic disease is diagnosed, patients can be in a state of crisis marked by physical, social, and psychological disequilibrium. They find that their habitual ways of coping with problems do not work. If the problems associated with a chronic disease fail to respond to coping efforts, the result can be an exaggeration of symptoms and their meaning, indiscriminate efforts to cope, and worsening health (Drossman et al., 2000; Stanton, Revenson, & Tennen, 2007). Anxiety, fear, and depression may temporarily take over.

Eventually, the crisis phase of chronic illness passes, and patients begin to develop a sense of how the chronic illness will alter their lives. At this point, more long-term difficulties that require ongoing rehabilitative attention may set in. These problems and issues fall into the general categories of physical rehabilitation, vocational rehabilitation, social rehabilitation, and psychological issues. In the next sections, we first consider emotional issues and coping with chronic illness and then turn to more general issues of rehabilitation.

Denial

Denial is a defence mechanism by which people avoid the implications of an illness. It is a common reaction to chronic illness that has been observed among chronic illness patients (Livneh, 2009a). Patients may act as if the illness were not severe, as if it will shortly go away, or as if it will have few long-term implications. However, immediately after the diagnosis of illness, during the acute phase of illness, denial can serve a protective function. It can keep the patient from having to come to terms with the full range of problems posed by the illness at a time when he or she may be least able to do so (Livneh, 2009a). One study of patients with myocardial infarction (MI) found that high initial denial was associated with fewer days in intensive care and fewer signs of cardiac dysfunction (M. N. Levine et al., 1988). Denial can mask the fear associated with a chronic disease until the patient is more accustomed to the diagnosis and better able to sort out realistically the restrictions that it will pose. During the rehabilitative phase of illness, denial may have adverse effects if it interferes with the ability to take in necessary information that will be part of the patient's treatment or self-management program (Livneh, 2009b).

Overall, then, denial may be useful in helping patients control their emotional reactions to illness, but it may interfere with their ability to monitor their conditions, to take the initiative in seeking treatment, or to follow through when they must act as responsible co-managers of their illness.

Anxiety

Following the diagnosis of a chronic illness, anxiety is common. Many patients become overwhelmed by the potential changes in their lives and, in some cases, by the prospect of death. Every twinge of chest pain may raise concern over another heart attack for the patient recuperating from MI. Many cancer patients are constantly vigilant to changes in their physical condition, and each minor ache or pain may prompt fear of a possible recurrence. Anxiety is especially high when people are waiting for test results, receiving diagnoses, awaiting invasive medical procedures, and anticipating or experiencing adverse side effects of treatment (for example, Rabin, Ward, Leventhal, & Schmitz, 2001; P. B. Jacobsen et al., 1995). It is also high when people expect substantial lifestyle changes to result from an illness or its treatment, when they feel dependent on health professionals, when they experience concern over recurrence (S. E. Taylor & Aspinwall, 1990), and when they lack information about the nature of the illness and its treatment (Marks, Sliwinski, & Gordon, 1993).

Anxiety is a problem not only because it is intrinsically distressing but also because it can interfere with good functioning. Anxious patients may be debilitated by their emotional distress even before therapy begins (Stauder & Kovacs, 2003; P. B. Jacobsen et al., 1995). Anxious diabetic patients report poor glucose control and increased symptoms (Lustman, 1988). Anxiety can increase the risk of subsequent heart attacks among patients with heart disease (Janszky, Ahnve, Lundberg, & Hemmingsson, 2010), increase the frequency of attacks of Raynaud's disease (K. M. Brown, Middaugh, Haythornthwaite & Pillory, 2001), and lead to hyperreactivity in the gut for patients suffering from irritable bowel syndrome (Blomhoff, Spetalen, Jacobsen, & Malt, 2001). Anxiety is especially prevalent among people with asthma and pulmonary disorders, and not surprisingly, anxiety compromises quality of life (Katon, Richardson, Lozano, & McCauley, 2004). Symptoms of anxiety can also be mistaken for symptoms of the underlying disease and therefore interfere with assessments of severity of the disease and its treatment (Chen, Hermann, Rodgers, Oliver-Welker, & Strunk, 2006).

Both assessment and treatment of anxiety may be needed, an issue we turn to later in this chapter.

Depression

Depression is a common and often debilitating reaction to chronic illness. Up to one-third of all medical inpatients with chronic disease report at least moderate symptoms of depression, and up to one-quarter suffer from severe depression (L. Moody, McCormick, & Williams, 1990). Indeed, a population survey found that the incidence of depression was highest among Canadians who had at least one chronic illness (Patten, 2005). Although there is evidence that depression may occur somewhat later in the adjustment process than does de-

nial or severe anxiety, it can also occur intermittently. Depression is common among stroke patients, cancer patients, and heart disease patients, as well as for those suffering from many other chronic diseases (Egede, 2005; S. E. Taylor & Aspinwall, 1990). For other conditions such as multiple sclerosis (MS), which can have an unpredictable and progressive course, depression is especially common. For example, results from a large-scale national study suggest that the rates of depression are higher in Canadians with MS than those without MS or those with other chronic health conditions (Patten, Beck, Williams, Barbui, & Metz, 2003). There is also some evidence that depression may be more likely among certain chronic health conditions. Among Canadians living with chronic illness, the likelihood of having clinical depression is highest for people with chronic fatigue syndrome (seven times more likely), and fibromyalgia (almost three and a half times more likely), and lower for people with diabetes, heart disease, hypertension, and thyroid disease (Patten, Beck, Kassam, Williams, Barbui, & Metz, 2005). Although having a chronic illness is an important risk factor for developing depression, people with certain health conditions are at particular risk.

At one time, depression was treated as an unfortunate psychological result of chronic illness, but its medical significance is increasingly being recognized. Depression can be a sign of impending physical decline, especially among elderly men (Anstey & Luszcz, 2002). Depression exacerbates the risk and course of several chronic disorders, most notably coronary heart disease. Depression complicates treatment adherence and medical decision making. It interferes with patients adopting a co-managerial role, and it confers enhanced risk of mortality from a broad array of chronic diseases (Anstey & Luszcz, 2002). For all these reasons, the assessment and management of depression in chronic illness has become of paramount importance to health care providers and health psychologists.

Depression is sometimes a delayed reaction to chronic illness because it often takes time for patients to understand the full implications of their condition. During the acute phase and immediately after diagnosis, the patient may be hospitalized, be awaiting treatments, and have other immediate decisions to make. There may be little time to reflect fully on the implications of the illness. Once the acute phase of chronic illness has ended, the full implications of the disorder may begin to sink in.

Significance of Depression   Depression is important not only for the distress it produces but also because it has an impact on the symptoms experienced and on the overall prospects for rehabilitation or recovery (J. J. W. Schaeffer et al., 1999). Depression is very common among patients with a variety of different chronic health conditions and significantly worsens health and quality of life (Moussavi et al., 2007). It is common among people with irritable bowel syndrome, an emotional overlay that can complicate treatment (Trikas et al., 1999). Rheumatoid arthritis patients with high levels of depression are more likely to catastrophize, overgeneralize, and negatively interpret their situation (T. W. Smith, Peck, Milano, & Ward, 1988). Depression can exacerbate the symptoms and complicate the treatment of major chronic diseases, including diabetes (de Groot, Anderson, Freedland, Clouse, & Lustman, 2001), cancer, coronary heart disease, and hypertension.

Depression over illness and treatment has also been linked to suicide among those with a chronic illness (Goodwin, Kroenke, Hoven, & Spitzer, 2003; Rollman & Shear, 2003). Perhaps most important, depression is a potent risk factor for death among the individuals with chronic illness (Herrmann et al., 1998; Wulsin, Vaillant, & Wells, 1999).Unlike anxiety, which ebbs and flows during the course of a chronic illness, depression can be a long-term reaction.

Assessing Depression   Assessing depression in people with a chronic illness can be problematic. Many of the physical signs of depression, such as fatigue, sleeplessness, or weight loss, may also be symptoms of disease or side effects of a treatment. If depressive symptoms are attributed to aspects of illness or treatment, their significance may be less apparent, and, consequently, depression may go untreated (Ziegelstein et al., 2005). Depression, as well as anxiety, is so prevalent among patients with a chronic illness that many experts recommend routine screening for these symptoms during medical visits (for example, Löwe et al., 2003).

Who Gets Depressed?   Depression increases with the severity of the illness (for example, Moussavi et al., 2007). The experiences of pain and disability, in particular, lead to depression (for example, Wulsin et al., 1999), which, in turn, increases pain and disability.

In recent years, a variety of effective cognitive and behavioural interventions have been developed to deal with the depression that so frequently accompanies chronic illness. Treatment for depression may not only alleviate psychological distress but also improve functioning by reducing symptoms associated with the illness (Mohr, Hart, & Goldberg, 2003).

HOW IS THE SELF CHANGED BY CHRONIC DISEASE?

L03

There are two of me. One "before" and one "after" RA. The before was a healthy, active, outgoing and confident person. The after focuses on how to get through the day. Has concerns about how long I will be able to maintain my job full-time. The "after" me has to plan to do anything outside of my workday. I have to get extra rest, plan what to shop for by weight (too much at one time or large packages are out of the question), and prepare myself for social outings (self talk—I know you're tired and in pain, but you have to smile and participate. No complaining—no one really wants to hear it.)

—41-Year-Old Woman with Rheumatoid Arthritis

To fully understand changes in response to chronic illness requires a consideration of the self, its sources of resilience, and its vulnerabilities. The self is one of the central concepts in psychology. Psychologists refer to the **self-concept** as a stable set of beliefs about one's qualities and attributes. **Self-esteem** refers to the general evaluation of the self-concept—namely, whether one feels good or bad about personal qualities and attributes.

A chronic illness can produce drastic changes in self-concept and self-esteem. Many of these changes will be temporary, but some may be permanent and may have a significant impact on future goals and aspirations (see the Health Psychology in Action box, "Future of Fear, Future of Hope"). The self-concept is a composite of self-evaluations regarding many aspects of one's life, which include body image, achievement, social functioning, and the private self.

The Physical Self

Body image is the perception and evaluation of one's physical functioning and appearance. Studies of hospitalized patients indicate that body image plummets during illness. Not only is the affected part of the body evaluated negatively but also the whole body image may take on a negative aura (Clarke, Griffin, & Team, 2008). For acutely ill patients, changes in body image are short lived; however, for those with a chronic illness, negative evaluations may last. For several reasons, body image is importantly implicated in chronic illness. First, a poor body image is related to low self-esteem and an increased likelihood of depression and anxiety. Second, body image may influence how adherent a person is to the course of treatment and how willing he or she is to

Future of Fear, Future of Hope

The uncertainty that living with a chronic illness brings can take a toll on the hopes and aspirations for the future. Certain goals may have to be altered or even abandoned, and with this fears may arise about what the future may bring. Despite this uncertainty many people use their hopes and vision for the future to guide them through the daily challenges of life with a chronic illness.

Possible selves are visions of the self for the future, which can help to motivate, organize, and direct an individual's current goals and aspirations (Markus & Nurius, 1986). These future selves embody the hopes and fears for the future that may preoccupy someone adjusting to life with a chronic illness. Although they are not yet real, such future visions may play an important role in the current tasks and goals that someone living with a chronic illness chooses to put their limited energy towards. Hoped-for possible selves can reflect current strivings and motivate efforts to continue with one's goals in the face of obstacles. However, they may also reflect a wish to return to life before chronic illness. Feared possible selves may motivate necessary actions to be taken in order to avoid a feared future from becoming reality.

The following excerpts are from people living with inflammatory bowel disease (Crohn's disease and ulcerative colitis) who were asked about their hoped-for and feared possible selves. They illustrate how these possible selves embody the hopes and fears for the future, and highlight the issues that many people with chronic illness struggle with as they try to renegotiate their sense of self and their goals for the future.

Feared possible selves:

A person whose Crohn's disease rules his life. Someone who can't achieve his goals because of his illness. A drain on the resources of his family because of Crohn's. Hospitalized and useless.

—36-YEAR-OLD MALE WITH CROHN'S DISEASE

Not being able to finish school and become an RN, not being able to ride or be physically fit, not being able to support myself and/or my health problem, being a burden on my husband and children.

—48-YEAR-OLD FEMALE WITH CROHN'S DISEASE

That I might give up dreaming and striving because it all seems too hard with UC, uncontrolled disease, perhaps leading to surgery, being alone.

—22-YEAR-OLD FEMALE WITH ULCERATIVE COLITIS

Hoped-for possible selves:

I want to be someone who can travel, without worrying. Someone who doesn't have to frantically search for bathrooms wherever they go. Someone who can go for long car rides in the country. Those are the things I miss.

—38-YEAR-OLD MALE WITH CROHN'S DISEASE

I just want to be happy, HEALTHY, able to enjoy my family and friends, look after my son properly and enjoy my granddaughter to the full. I want to be a full and proper wife to my husband and to fully embrace our new home and life in the sun.

—50-YEAR-OLD FEMALE WITH ULCERATIVE COLITIS

I'd be happy being the person I was before getting IBD. Being self-reliant, being in control of my health and feeling like I have a purpose and to be able to help others with their problems instead of having the ones that I have.

—34-YEAR-OLD FEMALE WITH CROHN'S DISEASE

(*Source:* Sirois, F. M. (2008, June). What is and what may never be: Possible selves and adjustment to inflammatory bowel disease. In F.M. Sirois (chair), *Guts, gumption, and go-ahead: Psychological adjustment to inflammatory bowel disease.* Paper presented at the 69th Annual Convention of the Canadian Psychological Association, Halifax, NS.

adopt a comanagement role. Finally, body image is important because it can be improved through psychological and educational interventions (Wenninger, Weiss, Wahn, & Staab, 2003). Many chronic disorders, including cancers, cystic fibrosis, multiple sclerosis, and other disabling conditions, have adverse effects on body image. In most cases, body image can be restored to a degree, although it may take time (Wenninger et al, 2003).

Two exceptions are patients with facial disfigurements or with extensive burns (for example, Hagedoorn & Molleman, 2006). Patients whose faces have been scarred or disfigured may never truly accept their altered appearance. There appear to be two reasons that facial disfigurements produce chronic alterations in body image. First, the face is often associated with personality, and, when the face is deformed, both patients themselves and others reacting to them may see the individual's

Chronic disease or disability can interfere with some life activities, but a sense of self that is based on broader interests and abilities will sustain self-esteem.

whole nature as tainted (S. A. Richardson, Goodman, Hastorf, & Dornbusch, 1961). Second, facial disfigurements cannot be masked; they are apparent to all passersby, who may act with involuntary disgust or withdrawal. An example of the potent impact of facial disfigurement is the case of Mrs. Dover:

> Before her disfigurement (amputation of half of her nose), Mrs. Dover, who lived with one of her two married daughters, had been an independent, warm, and friendly woman who enjoyed travelling, shopping, and visiting her many relatives. The disfigurement of her face, however, resulted in a definite alteration in her way of living. The first two or three years she seldom left her daughter's home, preferring to remain in her room or to sit in the backyard. "I was heartsick," she said, "The door had been shut on my life." (E. Goffman, 1963, p. 12)

When illness threatens sexual functioning—as it does for stroke, paralysis, and some cancers and heart conditions—body image may be affected. Disease severity and the presence of debilitating symptoms also clearly affect body image and overall quality of life (L. Moody et al., 1990).

Body image can be improved by stressing other aspects of appearance and health. Researchers have sometimes noted spontaneous increases in physical exercise and improvement of other aspects of physical appearance or health as a reaction to illness (Graham, Kremer, & Wheeler, 2008). Feelings of social self-efficacy may also lessen the effects of disfigurement on social isolation (Hagedoorn & Molleman, 2006).

The Achieving Self

Achievement through vocational activities is also an important aspect of self-esteem and self-concept. Many people derive their primary satisfaction from their job or career; others take great pleasure in their hobbies and leisure activities. If chronic illness threatens these valued aspects of the self, the self-concept may be damaged, as illustrated in the following quote from a woman with arthritis when asked to describe herself.

> About me? I'm not sure yet who I am anymore. . . . I was a national sales manager for a large company; loved my position and got to travel a lot. I've had to leave my career. I've gained 60 pounds in prednisone weight that I'm unable to "work" off because I hurt too hard to do anything. My husband and I don't go out socially anymore because I can't walk very far—can't wear any shoes other than sneakers, can't even have a cocktail because of all the drugs. I used to be out socially all the time three to four times per week. Now I'm lucky if it's three to four times in a year. I don't know how to answer you because I don't know myself. (Sirois, 2007b)

However, when work and hobbies are not threatened or curtailed by illness, the patient has these sources of satisfaction from which to derive self-esteem and they can come to take on new meaning.

The Social Self

As we have already seen, rebuilding the social self is an important aspect of readjustment after chronic illness. Interactions with family and friends can be a critical source of self-esteem. Social resources provide patients with a chronic illness with badly needed information, help, and emotional support. On the other hand, a breakdown in the support system has implications for all aspects of life. Perhaps for these reasons, fears about withdrawal of support are among the most common worries of patients with a chronic illness. Consequently, family participation in the rehabilitation process is widely encouraged. Providing all family members, even young children, with at least some information about the disorder, its course, and its treatment can offset the potential for confusion and miscommunication (P. D. Williams et al., 2002).

The Private Self

The private self may be severely strained by chronic illness. Many illnesses create the need to be dependent on others; the resulting loss of independence and the strain of imposing on others represent major threats to the self (van Lankveld, Naring, van der Staak, van't Pad Bosch, & van de Putte, 1993).

The residual core of a patient's identity—ambitions, goals, and desires for the future—are also affected by chronic illness. Occasionally, adjustment to chronic illness may be impeded because the patient has an unrealized secret dream, which is now out of reach, or at least appears to be. Encouraging the patient to discuss this difficulty may reveal alternative paths to fulfillment and awaken the ability to establish new ambitions, goals, and plans for the future.

(LO4) HOW DO INDIVIDUALS COPE WITH CHRONIC ILLNESS?

Despite the fact that most patients with chronic illness suffer at least some adverse psychological reactions as a result of the disease, most do not seek formal or informal psychological treatment for their symptoms. Instead, they draw on their internal and social resources for solving problems and alleviating psychological distress. How do they cope so well?

Coping Strategies and Chronic Illness

The appraisal of a chronic disease as threatening or challenging leads to the initiation of coping efforts (see Chapter 7; R. S. Lazarus & Folkman, 1984a, 1984b). Chronic illness can be thought of as a chronic stressor that elicits the use of coping strategies to manage its challenges for better or worse. In addition to the stressors directly associated with living with a chronic illness, people with chronic illness are vulnerable to other stressors unrelated to their illness which can exacerbate symptoms.

In one study (Dunkel-Schetter, Feinstein, Taylor, & Falke, 1992), cancer patients were asked to identify the aspect of their cancer they found to be the most stressful. The results indicated that fear and uncertainty about the future were most common (41 percent); followed by limitations in physical abilities, appearance, and lifestyle (24 percent); followed by pain management (12 percent). Patients were then asked to indicate the coping strategies they had used to deal with these problems. The five identified strategies were social support/direct problem solving (for example, "I talked to someone to find out more about the situation"), distancing (for example, "I didn't let it get to me"), positive focus (for example, "I came out of the experience better than I went in"), cognitive escape/avoidance (for example, "I wished that the situation

would go away"), and behavioural escape/avoidance (for example, efforts to avoid the situation by eating, drinking, or sleeping; cf. Felton & Revenson, 1984).

The strategies identified in this investigation are not substantially different from those employed to deal with other stressful events (see Chapter 7). One notable difference, though, is that those with a chronic illness report fewer active coping methods, such as planning, problem solving, or confrontative coping, and more passive coping strategies, such as positive focus and escape/avoidant strategies. This discrepancy may reflect the fact that some chronic diseases, such as cancer, raise many uncontrollable concerns that active coping strategies cannot directly address. One might find that in coping with the aftermath of MI, for example, confrontative coping and problem solving would emerge as people attempt to modify their health habits and lifestyle, with the hope of reducing subsequent risk. For other conditions, such as Crohn's disease or ulcerative colitis where symptoms can be unpredictable and uncontrollable, active coping efforts may be less frequently used because they lead to frustration and lower overall quality of life (Petrak et al., 2001; Wolfe & Sirois, 2008, June).

Which Coping Strategies Work?   Do any particular coping strategies facilitate psychological adjustment among people with chronic illness? As is true for coping with other stressful events, the use of avoidant coping is associated with increased psychological distress and thereby may be a risk factor for adverse responses to illness (for example, Heim, Valach, & Schaffner, 1997). It may also exacerbate the disease process itself. For example, avoidant coping has also been related to poor adjustment among people with inflammatory bowel disease (Voth & Sirois, 2009).

Active coping, in contrast, has been found to predict good adjustment to multiple sclerosis (Pakenham, 1999) and spinal chord injury (Miller Smedema, Catalano, & Ebener, 2010). Also, those patients who actively solicit health-related information about their condition may cope better with it (for example, A. J. Christensen, Ehlers, Raichle, Bertolatus, & Lawton, 2000). Research has also found lower psychological distress when patients cope by using positive, confrontative responses to stress; and with beliefs that one can personally direct control over an illness or its symptoms (Sirois, Davis, & Morgan, 2006; S. E. Taylor, Helgeson, Reed, & Skokan, 1991).

Illness duration is another important factor to consider when assessing the use of coping strategies. For example, one study of people with chronic fatigue syndrome found that those who with a shorter illness duration tended to use behavioural disengagement and other avoidant coping strategies, whereas those with a longer duration of illness used strategies such as active coping, positive reframing, and acceptance (Brown, Brown, & Jason, 2010). Thus, the development of more adaptive coping strategies may take time as the individual learns to adjust to her or his illness.

Research suggests that the types of coping strategies used and how effective they are may also depend upon the social context in which they occur (Holtzman, Newth, & DeLongis, 2004; Revenson, 2003). For example, researchers from the University of British Columbia followed the pain, coping, and use of social support of people with rheumatoid arthritis over a one-week period using a daily process methodology (Holtzman, Newth, & DeLongis, 2004). Patients recorded their pain severity, coping strategies used, support received, and their satisfaction with that support twice daily (morning and evening). Results indicated that social support influenced both pain reports and the choice of coping strategies used. For example, patients who were more satisfied with the support they received tended to use more cognitive reframing strategies, which in turn when used in the morning were linked to decreased pain severity in the evening. Similarly, satisfaction with support predicted greater use of active problem solving in the evening; however, this form of coping was not particularly adaptive for dealing with daily pain. A consideration of how social support and coping strategies are dynamically linked may therefore be important for understanding why certain strategies may or may not be chosen or effective.

Because of the diversity of problems that chronic diseases pose, people who are flexible copers may cope better with the stress of chronic disease than do those who engage in a predominant coping style. Coping strategies may be most effective when they are matched to the particular problem for which they are most useful. If people have available to them multiple coping strategies, they may be more able to engage in this matching process than those who have a predominant coping style (for example, Cheng, Hui, & Lam, 2004).

Patients' Beliefs about Chronic Illness

If patients are to adjust to chronic illness satisfactorily, they must somehow integrate their illness into their lives. Virtually all chronic illnesses require some alteration in activities and some degree of management. For example, diabetic patients must control their diet and perhaps take daily injections of insulin. Cancer patients, even those whose cancer is not currently active, must remain vigilant to possible signs of recurrence. Both stroke and heart patients must make substantial alterations in their daily activities as a consequence of their physical and psychological impairments.

Patients who are unable to incorporate chronic illness into their lives may fail to follow their treatment regimen and be nonadherent. They may be improperly attuned to possible signs of recurrent or worsening disease. They may engage in inappropriate behaviours that pose a risk to their health, or they may fail to practise important health behaviours that could reduce the possibility of recurrence or other complicating illnesses. Thus, developing a realistic sense of one's illness, the restrictions it imposes, and the regimen that is required is an important process of coping with chronic illness. Beliefs that allow the patient to find meaning in their illness are also important for psychosocial adjustment (Kocaman, Kutlu, Ozkan, & Ozkan, 2007).

Beliefs about the Nature of the Illness   One of the problems that often arises in adjustment to chronic illness is that patients adopt an inappropriate model for their disorder—most notably, the acute model (see Chapter 8). Thus, it is often important for health care providers to probe patients' beliefs about their illness to check for significant gaps and misunderstandings in their knowledge that may interfere with self-management (Guzman & Nicassio, 2003).

Beliefs about the Cause of the Illness   People suffering from both acute and chronic illness often develop theories about where their illness came from (Affleck, Tennen, Croog, & Levine, 1987; A. Ali et al., 2000). These theories include stress, physical injury, disease-causing bacteria, and God's will. Of perhaps greater significance is where patients ultimately place the blame for their illness. Do they blame themselves, another person, the environment, or a quirk of fate?

Self-blame for chronic illness is widespread. Patients frequently perceive themselves as having brought on their illness through their own actions. In some cases, these perceptions are to some extent correct. Poor health habits, such as smoking, improper diet, or lack of exercise, can produce heart disease, stroke, or cancer. Nonetheless, in illness such as chronic obstructive pulmonary disease, feelings of self-blame combined with perceptions of being exiled from society can take a toll on coping and well-being (Halding, Heggdal, & Wahl, 2011). But in many cases, the patient's self-blame is ill placed, as when a disease is caused by a genetically based defect or by the complex interplay of multiple factors.

What are the consequences of self-blame? Unfortunately, a definitive answer to this question is not available. Some researchers have found that self-blame can lead to guilt, depression, and decreased psychological well-being (Bennett, Compas, Beckjord, Glinder, 2005; Sirois, Davis, & Morgan, 2006; Voth & Sirois, 2009), but perceiving the cause of one's illness as self-generated may represent an effort to assume control over the disorder; such feelings can be adaptive in coping with and coming to terms with the disorder. It may be that self-blame is adaptive under certain conditions but not others (Schulz & Decker, 1985; S. E. Taylor et al., 1984a).

Research uniformly suggests that blaming another person for one's disorder is maladaptive (Affleck, Tennen, Croog, & Levine, 1987). For example, some patients believe that their disorder was brought about by stress caused by family members, ex-spouses, or colleagues at work. Blame of this other person or persons may be tied to unresolved hostility, which can interfere with adjustment to the disease, whereas forgiveness is tied to fewer health complaints (Lawler et al., 2005).

Beliefs about the Controllability of the Illness   Researchers have also examined whether patients who believe they can control their illness are better off than those who do not see their illness as under their control. Patients develop a number of control-related beliefs with respect to chronic illness. They may believe, as do many cancer patients, that they can prevent a recurrence of the disease through good health habits or even sheer force of will. They may believe that by complying with treatments and physicians' recommendations, they achieve vicarious control over their illness (Helgeson, 1992). They may believe that they personally have direct control over the illness through self-administration of a treatment regimen. These control-related beliefs may or may not be accurate. For example, if patients do maintain a treatment regimen, they may very well be exercising real control over the possibility of recurrence or exacerbation of their illness. On the other hand, the belief that one's illness can be controlled through a positive attitude may or may not be correct.

Recall from earlier chapters that feelings of psychological control are generally beneficial for good mental functioning. As noted in Chapter 8, interventions that attempt to instill feelings of control are often highly successful in promoting good adjustment and in reducing physiological arousal and emotional distress caused by illness and its treatment. However, people who live with a chronic illness often learn on their own to develop a sense of control over aspects of their condition that may be controllable.

Belief in control and a sense of self-efficacy with respect to the disease and its treatment are generally adaptive. For example, cancer patients who believed that they had control over their illness were better adjusted to their cancer and experienced less distress over times than were patients without such beliefs (Bárez, Blasco, Fernández-Castro, & Viladrich, 2009). A sense of control or self-efficacy has been found to lead to improved adjustment among people with rheumatoid arthritis (Tennen, Affleck, Urrows, Higgins, & Mendola, 1992), sickle-cell diseases (R. Edwards, Telfair, Cecil, & Lenoci, 2001), chronic obstructive pulmonary disease (Kohler, Fish, & Greene, 2002), AIDS (S. E. Taylor et al., 1991), multiple sclerosis (Bishop, Frain, & Tschopp, 2008), and patients recovering from angioplasty (Helgeson & Fritz, 1999), among many others. Even for patients who are physically or psychosocially badly off, adjustment is facilitated by high perceptions of control (McQuillen, Licht, & Licht, 2003). Thus, control appears to be helpful not only in coping with acute disorders and treatments but also with the long-term management of chronic illness (Kaptein, Klok, Moss-Morris, & Brand, 2010).

Children with chronic illness may also benefit from perceived control. Researchers from the University of British Columbia examined the role of perceived control in children with asthma (Griffin & Chen, 2006). After taking baseline measures of control perceptions, pulmonary functioning and immune markers associated with asthma were assessed over a two-week period. Control perceptions were found to be significantly associated with better pulmonary and immune outcomes, after controlling for demographics, asthma, and other medical factors. Interventions to increase control perceptions for children with chronic conditions may therefore be beneficial for health outcomes in this growing chronic illness group.

The experience of control or self-efficacy may prolong life. A study of patients with chronic obstructive pulmonary disease found that those with high self-efficacy expectations lived longer than those without such expectations (R. M. Kaplan, Ries, Prewitt, & Eakin, 1994). When real control is low, efforts to induce it or exert it may be unsuccessful and backfire (Tennen et al., 1992).

Instead, focusing on aspects of the chronic condition that are controllable such as symptoms, may help patients experience a shift in their control perceptions that can facilitate better adjustment (Sirois, Davis, & Morgan, 2006).

L05   HOW DO PEOPLE MANAGE CHRONIC ILLNESS?

Chronic illness raises specific problem-solving tasks that patients encounter on the road to recovery. These tasks include physical problems associated with the illness, vocational problems, problems with social relationships, and personal issues concerned with chronic illness. Even more than acute illness, chronic illness depends critically on patient co-management of the disorder (for example, Goldring, Taylor, Kemeny, & Anton, 2002). Patients are effective collaborators in managing their chronic conditions because they have personal knowledge of its development, symptoms, and course over a period of time. They are vital to effective treatment because the often complex and long-term treatment regimens that are recommended may require the active, committed participation of the patient (Health Council of Canada, 2007a). We next turn to these issues.

Physical Problems Associated with Chronic Illness

Physical rehabilitation is an important aspect of chronic illness. Chronic disability leads to anxiety, depression, and even thoughts of suicide. Consequently, any measures that can be taken to improve activity level, physical independence, and the ability to manage the tasks of daily living will have positive effects, not only on daily functioning but also on psychosocial adjustment (Zautra, Maxwell, & Reich, 1989).

Goals of Physical Rehabilitation   **Physical rehabilitation** of patients with chronic illness or disabled patients typically involves several goals: to learn how to use one's body as much as possible, to learn how to sense changes in the environment in order to make the appropriate physical accommodations, to learn new physical management skills, to learn a necessary treatment regimen, and to learn how to control the expenditure of energy.

Patients must develop the capacity to read bodily signs that signal the onset of a crisis, know how to respond to that crisis, and maintain whatever treatment regimen is required. Even general exercise goes a long way in reducing the symptoms of many chronic disorders, in-

Physical rehabilitation concentrates on enabling people to use their bodies as much as possible, to learn new physical management skills if necessary, and to pursue an integrated treatment regimen.

cluding diabetes, chronic obstructive pulmonary disease (Emery, Schein, Hauck, & MacIntyre, 1998), cancer (Stevinson et al., 2007), and arthritis. For heart patients, exercise is a critical component of recovery programs.

Many patients who require physical rehabilitation have problems resulting from prior injuries or participation in athletic activities earlier in life, including knee problems, shoulder injuries, and the like. Many of these problems simply worsen with age. Functional decline in the frail elderly who live alone is a particular problem (Gill et al., 2002). Physical therapy can ameliorate these age-related aches and pains and can also help patients recover from treatments designed to alleviate them, such as surgery (Stephens, Druley, & Zautra, 2002). Studies have suggested that group cognitive behavioural interventions may be successful in getting people to adhere to physical activity than individual therapy (Rejeski et al., 2003). Regular exercise is also critical because it may not only affect physical functioning but also beneficially affect cognitive and psychological functioning (Emery, Shermer, Hauck, Hsaio, & MacIntyre, 2003).

Chronic Fatigue Syndrome and Other Functional Disorders

In recent years, health psychologists have become increasingly interested in **functional somatic syndromes** characterized by an intriguing pattern: These syndromes are marked by the symptoms, suffering, and disability they cause rather than by any demonstrable tissue abnormality. In fact they are often referred to as **medically unexplained physical symptoms (MUPS),** simply because we don't know why people have these disorders.

Functional somatic syndromes include chronic fatigue syndrome, irritable bowel syndrome, and fibromyalgia, as well as chemical sensitivity, sick building syndrome, repetitive stress injury, complications from silicone breast implants, Gulf War syndrome, and chronic whiplash.

Chronic fatigue syndrome (CFS), also known as myalgic encephalomyelitis, is a disorder of uncertain etiology marked by debilitating fatigue present for at least six months. Approximately 1.3 percent of Canadians have this disorder, which is more common among women and those living in low-income households (Park & Knudson, 2007). It is largely a diagnosis of exclusion. That is, a patient is diagnosed with CFS only after other conditions with similar medical symptoms have been ruled out. The onset of CFS may be related to a prior viral condition, muscle abnormalities, and/or immunological or neurological changes. To date, though, no clear distinguishing biological cause has been found (Moss-Morris & Petrie, 2001). Twin studies of chronic fatigue syndrome suggest that there may be genetic underpinnings (Buchwald et al., 2001). A history of childhood maltreatment and abuse may also be implicated.

Fibromyalgia is a syndrome involving widespread pain with particular tenderness in multiple sites. It is estimated that almost 400,000 Canadians, or 1.5 percent of the population suffer from this disorder (Park & Knudson, 2007). As with chronic fatigue syndrome the pathogenesis of fibromyalgia remains unclear, but the disorder is associated with sleep disturbance, disability, and psychological distress (Thieme, Turk, & Flor, 2004; Zautra et al., 2005). People with a body mass index (BMI) over 30 are also twice as likely to have fibromyalgia compared to those with lower BMI (McNally, Matheson, & Bakowsky, 2006), suggesting that obesity may be a risk factor. Sympathetic and HPA axis system stress responses may also show alterations (Peckerman et al., 2003; Buske-Kirschbaum et al., 2003; Gaab et al., 2002; LaManca et al., 2001). Results from the Canadian

Community Health Survey (CCHS) suggest that people with fibromyalgia are three times more likely to also have major depression than the general population, and report restrictions in a variety of work and personal activities (Kassam & Patten, 2006). Fibromyalgia is also six times more common among women than men (McNally, Matheson, & Bakowsky, 2006), and both women and men from the poorest households are more likely to suffer from fibromyalgia (McNally, Matheson, & Bakowsky, 2006; (Park & Knudson, 2007). Interestingly, rates are lowest in Quebec compared to the rest of Canada. Although cultural and regional differences are suspected, the reasons for this difference are not fully understood (McNally, Matheson, & Bakowsky, 2006).

Functional disorders have proven to be extremely difficult to treat inasmuch as their etiology is not well understood. Because of their insidious way of eroding quality of life, the functional syndromes are typically accompanied by a great deal of psychological distress, including depression (Park & Knudson, 2007), and the symptoms of the illness have sometimes been misdiagnosed as depression. Consequently, people with medically unexplained symptoms use both conventional and complementary/alternative health care at much higher rates than those without these symptoms or those with other chronic health conditions (Park & Knudson, 2007; see Figure 11.3).

Substantial overlap exists among the individual syndromes in terms of symptoms and consequences (Ciccone & Natelson, 2003; Schmaling, Fiedelak, Katon, Bader, & Buchwald, 2003). Many of the disorders are marked by abdominal distention, headache, fatigue, and disturbances in the HPA axis, for example (Di Giorgio, Hudson, Jerjes, & Cleare, 2005; Gaab et al., 2002). Among the common factors implicated in their development are a pre-existing viral or bacterial infection and a high number of stressful life events (for example, Theorell, Blomkvist, Lindh, & Evengard, 1999; Fink, Toft, Hansen, Ornbol, & Olesen, 2007). Regardless of the cause, functional somatic syndromes have a negative impact on the lives and well-being of people who live with one of these conditions (Park & Knudson, 2007).

The similarity among the functional symptoms should not be interpreted to mean that these disorders are psychiatric in origin or that the care of patients suffering from them should be shifted to psychology and psychiatry. Rather, the similarity among these disorders suggests

Chronic Fatigue Syndrome and Other Functional Disorders (continued)

FIGURE 11.3 | Percentage of People Who Consulted Health Care Providers in the Past Year, by Presence of Medically Unexplained Physical Symptoms (MUPS), Canada, 2003

Source: Adapted from Statistics Canada, "Medically unexplained physical symptoms," *Health Reports,* catalogue no. 82-003-XIE, volume no. 18, issue no. 1, released on February 21, 2007, www.statcan.ca/english/freepub/82-003-XIE/2006001/articles/symptoms/82-003-XIE2006002.pdf.

Percentage who consulted health care providers in past year, by presence of medically unexplained physical symptoms (MUPS), household population aged 12 or older, Canada, 2003

* *Significantly different from estimate for no MUPS (p < 0.05)*

† *Significantly different from estimate for total MUPS (p < 0.05)*

Source: *2003 Canadian Community Health Survey, cycle 2.1*

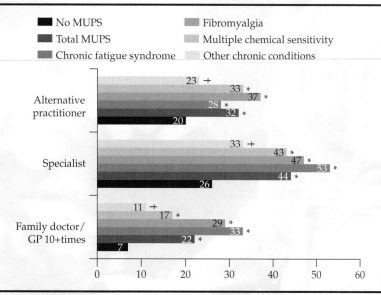

that breakthroughs in understanding the etiology and treatment of these disorders may be made by pooling knowledge from the study of all these functional syndromes rather than by treating them as completely separate disorders (Fink et al., 2007). For example, among Canadians who have fibromyalgia, chronic fatigue syndrome, or multiple chemical sensitivity, 14 percent report having at least two of these three syndromes, suggesting that similar etiological pathways may be involved (Park & Knudson, 2007). Although each disorder has distinctive features (Moss-Morris & Spence, 2006), the core symptoms of fatigue, pain, sick-role behaviour, and negative affect are all symptoms of chronic, low-level inflammatory processes, and it is possible that this sustained or recurrent immune response is what ties these disorders together. Given the socio-economic determinants common among these disorders, exposure to uncontrollable environmental stressors may also be involved.

What helps people cope with these debilitating disorders? Although social support is helpful to those with functional somatic syndromes, particularly solicitous behaviour from significant others may actually aggravate the disorder by increasing sick-role behaviour (Schmaling, Smith, & Buchwald, 2000). As is true for most chronic disorders, positive reinterpretation and a sense of self-efficacy predict good psychological adjustment to the disorder, whereas avoidant coping strategies and emotional venting are associated with greater disability and poorer psychological wellbeing (J. C. Findley, Kerns, Weinberg, & Rosenberg, 1998; Moss-Morris, Petrie, & Weinman, 1996).

How are these disorders treated? Generally speaking, medical practitioners have combined pharmacological interventions for such symptoms as sleep deprivation and pain with behavioural interventions, including exercise and cognitive behavioural therapy, efforts

Chronic Fatigue Syndrome and Other Functional Disorders (continued)

that appear to achieve some success (for example, Rossy et al., 1999). Coping interventions such as written emotional expression can produce health benefits in these patient groups also (Broderick, Junghaenel, & Schwartz, 2005). The specific treatment recommended for functional disorders varies, of course, with the particular nature of the problem (Hamilton, Karoly, & Zautra, 2005). Those whose chronic fatigue developed in the wake of an infectious disorder may require different treatments than those whose chronic fatigue is unrelated to a prior infection; the latter group may require more psychological counselling (Masuda, Munemoto, Yamanaka, Takei, & Tei, 2002).

Overall, functional somatic syndromes are common, persistent, disabling, and costly. Simultaneous attention to the medical symptoms and the psychosocial distress generated by these disorders is essential for successful treatment.

Some physical problems are produced by the disease itself. They include physical pain, such as the chest pain experienced by heart patients; the discomfort associated with cancer; and the chronic pain of rheumatoid arthritis (van Lankveld et al., 1993). Breathlessness associated with respiratory disorders, metabolic changes associated with diabetes and cancer, and motor difficulties produced by spinal cord injuries are also important physical problems Cognitive impairments may occur, such as the language, memory, and learning deficits associated with stroke. In many cases, then, the physical consequences of a chronic disorder place severe restrictions on an individual's life.

Treatment of primary symptoms and the underlying disease can also produce difficulties in physical functioning. Cancer patients receiving chemotherapy sometimes face nausea, vomiting, hair loss, skin discoloration, and other unattractive and uncomfortable bodily changes. Medications for hypertension can produce a variety of unpleasant side effects, including drowsiness, weight gain, and impotence. Restrictions on the activities of patients who have had a heart attack—including dietary changes, elimination of smoking, and exercise requirements—may pervade their entire way of life. (A disease for which this is the case is profiled in the Health Psychology in Action box, "Chronic Fatigue Syndrome and Other Functional Disorders"). In many cases, patients may feel that in terms of the discomfort and restrictions they impose, the treatments are as bad as the disease.

Developing a Comprehensive Program Comprehensive physical rehabilitation must take into account all the illness- and treatment-related factors. Patients may need a pain management program for the alleviation of discomfort. They may require prosthetic devices, such as an artificial limb after amputation related to diabetes.

They may need training in the use of adaptive devices; for example, a patient with multiple sclerosis or severe arthritis may need to learn how to use a cane or a wheelchair. Certain cancer patients may elect cosmetic surgery, such as breast reconstruction after a mastectomy or the insertion of a synthetic jaw after head and neck surgery. Parkinson's disease patients may require behavioural interventions to improve their motor skills and reduce their tremors. Disorders such as stroke, diabetes, and high blood pressure may compromise cognitive functioning, requiring active intervention (Zelinski, Crimmins, Reynolds, & Seeman, 1998).

As these examples indicate, chronic illness often creates a need for assistive technologies—namely, those aids and types of training that enable people with disabilities to perform the daily tasks of independent living. Unfortunately, access to such technologies remains uneven. Patients with good medical care, good insurance, and access to technology receive such assistance; those with fewer resources, no insurance, and little access to high-quality care are less likely to receive them (Seelman, 1993). Thus, one of the tasks facing those who work in physical rehabilitation is making assistive technologies more generally available to those patients who need them.

In addition to physical rehabilitation, a program for identifying and controlling factors that contribute to recurrence or that exacerbate the disease may be required. For example, stress has been implicated in the course of diabetes (Surwit, Schneider, & Feinglos, 1992), heart disease (see Krantz, 1980), hypertension (Harrell, 1980), multiple sclerosis (Ackerman et al., 2002), cancer (Visintainer, Volpicelli, & Seligman, 1982), and Crohn's disease (Garrett, Brantley, Jones, & McKnight, 1991). As a consequence, stress management programs are increasingly incorporated into the physical treatment regimens of many patients with chronic illness.

Adherence   Physical rehabilitation must also tackle the very complex and serious problem of adherence to a long-term medical regimen. Unfortunately, the features that characterize the treatment regimens of patients with chronic illness are those typically associated with high levels of nonadherence. As will be recalled from Chapter 9, treatment regimens that must be followed over a long time period, that are complex, that interfere with other desirable life activities, and that involve lifestyle change show very low levels of adherence (Turk & Meichenbaum, 1991).

An important first step in ensuring adherence to a treatment regimen is appropriate education. Some patients fail to realize that aspects of their treatment regimen are important to their successful functioning. For example, some patients may believe that exercise is a discretionary lifestyle decision rather than an essential ingredient in the restoration of physical functioning.

Sometimes patients with chronic illness employ creative nonadherence. Such actions may occur because they know their disease extremely well, perhaps even better than some medical personnel, and so they make adjustments in their treatment in response to internal feedback. Nonetheless, creative nonadherence can lead to mistakes. For example, the use of natural health products or complementary therapies is very common among those with chronic illness (Sirois, 2008). However, they may produce problematic interactions with prescribed medications, especially if their use is not disclosed. For a full consideration of adherence, refer to Chapter 9. On the whole, though, cognitive behavioural interventions that explain therapies to people with chronic illness or disability and enlist their cooperation as co-managers achieve considerable success in adherence (Christensen et al., 2002).

Summary   Effective physical rehabilitation requires consideration of all the illness- and treatment-related factors that may influence a patient's level of functioning. It requires pooling the skills of many specialists, including physical therapists and health psychologists, to make sure that the most effective methods of meeting treatment goals are employed. An eclectic collection of physical, behavioural, and cognitive interventions may be needed to develop the ideal physical management program that is individually tailored to each patient to control disabilities and treatment-related side effects, as well as to promote adherence. Such a program should be initiated early in the patient's recovery, with provision for alterations in training as illness and treatment goals

change. This kind of programmatic assistance, when effective, can be of enormous benefit to patients with chronic illness. Not only can it help them resume the activities of daily living, but it may also contribute to a reduction in illness-related emotional disturbances as well (Emery et al., 1998). A crucial element in all such programs is the patient's active role as a co-manager in rehabilitation. That is, rehabilitation is not something that is done to a patient. It is done with his or her full cooperation and participation.

Vocational Issues in Chronic Illness

Many chronic illnesses create problems for patients' vocational activities and work status. Some patients may need to restrict or change their work activities. For example, a salesman who previously conducted his work from his car but is now newly diagnosed with Crohn's disease may need to switch to a job where he will have convenient access to a washroom. Patients with spinal cord injuries who previously held positions that required physical activity will need to acquire skills that will let them work from a seated position. Others may have to find ways to cope with working conditions that are not ideal but necessary to stay employed. Such work-related issues can create job strain for people with a chronic health condition in addition to other illness-related stress (Gignac, Sutton, & Badley, 2007). Some of the challenges faced by people with a chronic illness are illustrated in the Focus on Canadian Research box, "Work-Related Problems for People with Arthritis: The Patients' Perspective."

Discrimination against Patients with Chronic Illness   Many patients with chronic illness, such as heart patients, cancer patients, and AIDS patients, face job discrimination (for example, Heckman, 2003). One survey, reported in *Time,* indicated that employees with cancer are fired or laid off five times as often as other workers. When these patients return to their jobs, they may be moved into less demanding positions, and they may be promoted less quickly because the organization believes that they have a poor prognosis and are not worth the investment of time and resources required to train them for more advanced work (*Time,* 1996).

Because of these potential problems, any job difficulties that the patient may encounter should be assessed early in the recovery process. Job counselling, retraining programs, and advice on how to avoid or combat discrimination can then be initiated promptly.

Work-related Problems for People with Arthritis: The Patients' Perspective

Working with a painful, chronic health condition such as arthritis can introduce difficult challenges that may not be visible or understood by those who do not live with a chronic illness. The added stress from these challenges may exacerbate symptoms and further contribute to work-related issues. To better understand the problems that people with arthritis face at work because of their chronic illness, researchers from the University of Toronto, the University of British Columbia, and the Arthritis Research Centre of Canada conducted focus groups with 36 employed people with arthritis. Specifically they asked, "What makes it difficult for you to continue working while having arthritis?"

A qualitative analysis of the responses to this question revealed four broad categories of problems that affected work: (1) symptoms and characteristics of arthritis, (2) working conditions, (3) interpersonal difficulties at work, and (4) emotional challenges.

Fatigue was the most limiting symptom of arthritis that created problems at work, often because of its invisibility.

I think the fatigue goes outside the work environment. I use all of the energy I have for my work and there is nothing left for my family or my friends. I have no life.

And I don't think they understand the tiredness aspect of it because you look fine. You look well, and that is part of the problem at work and everywhere. People look at me and I am sure they are thinking: What is she complaining about? She looks fine, she's not sick.

Job satisfaction, aspirations for advancement, and salary were often sacrificed for working conditions that were better suited to having arthritis.

The other financial difficulty is having to take a job of lesser stature that doesn't allow you to fulfill your life goals . . . . It was pretty brainless and I just didn't have it in me to do anything more. Even though I had goals that were much higher, I had to compromise with the kind of work that I was doing.

For several people, interpersonal difficulties at work due to arthritis were a source of stress. Lack of understanding and misattributing fatigue for laziness or lack of motivation by co-workers and employers contributed to these difficulties.

My boss will come up to me and say, "Okay, you have been working at home too many days; people are saying something."

And it is known as an illness for old people for some reason. So in my case when I tell someone I have arthritis they will look at me like—yeah right. We don't feel trust. It seems like you are lying all the time and you are coming up with excuses.

Along with depression, people often reported experiencing feelings of guilt and inadequacy from not being able to meet their own performance standards.

I find that fatigue brings on guilt. I am not a good employee, why would they keep me hired?

This account of employment issues from the patients' perspective highlights key areas for developing employment interventions. For example, having flexible work arrangements and ergonomic modifications in the work environment were strategies identified by the patients as being useful to address some of these issues. However, having health professionals and programs to assist and support people with arthritis in the work environment may be necessary to help people with arthritis cope with these issues.

Source: Lacaille, D., White, M. A., Backman, C. L., & Gignac, M. A. (2007). "Problems faced at work due to inflammatory arthritis: New insights gained from understanding patients' perspective." *Arthritis and Rheumatism*, 15(7), 1269–1279. Reprinted with permission on Wiley-Liss, Inc., a subsidiary of John Wiley & Sons, Inc.

Financial Impact of Chronic Illness   A difficulty related to the vocational problems of chronic illness concerns the enormous financial impact that chronic illness can have on the patient and the family. Many people do not have a private insurance plan to cover their prescription medications. In other cases, patients who must cut back on their work or stop working altogether will lose this insurance coverage, which is often only available to full-time employees. This can add enormous financial costs to the burden of their care. In this sense, then, the threat to vocation that chronic illness sometimes raises can be a double whammy: The patient with chronic illness capacity to earn income may be reduced, and simultaneously, the benefits that would have helped shoulder the costs of expensive medications may be cut back.

Social Interaction Issues in Chronic Illness

The development of a chronic illness can create problems of social interaction for the patient. After diagnosis, patients may have trouble re-establishing normal social relations. They may complain of others' pity or rejection but behave in ways that inadvertently elicit these behaviours. They may withdraw from other people altogether or may thrust themselves into social activities before they are ready.

Negative Responses from Others   Patients are not solely responsible for whatever difficulties and awkwardness arise in interaction with others. Acquaintances, friends, and relatives may have problems of their own adjusting to the patient's altered condition. Many people hold pejorative stereotypes about certain groups of patients with chronic illness, including those with cancer or AIDS (Fife & Wright, 2000).

Intimate others may themselves be distressed by the loved one's condition (for example, P. N. Stein, Gordon, Hibbard, & Sliwinski, 1992) or may be worn down by the constant pain, disability, and dependency of the partner (S. L. Manne & Zautra, 1990). Moreover, they may be ineffective in providing support because their own support needs are unmet (for example, Horwitz, Reinhard, & Howell-White, 1996).

Patients with chronic illness may need to think through whether they want to disclose the fact of their illness to those outside their immediate family. If they decide to do so, they may need to consider the best approach because certain illnesses—particularly cancer, AIDS, and inflammatory bowel disease—may elicit negative responses from others.

Working through problems with family members often helps patients lay the groundwork for reestablishing other social contacts. As the first social group with whom the patient interacts, the family can be a social microcosm on whom the patient tries out his or her coping efforts and who react to him or her in turn. By developing effective ways of dealing with family members and friends in various contexts, the patient simultaneously builds skills for dealing with other people in a variety of social situations.

Impact on Family   It has been said that individuals do not develop chronic diseases; families do. The reason for

this belief is that the family is a social system and disruption in the life of one family member invariably affects the lives of others (for example, P. D. Williams et al., 2002). One of the chief changes brought about by chronic illness is an increased dependency of the individual with a chronic illness on other family members. If the patient is married, the illness inevitably places increased responsibilities on the spouse.

Simultaneously, other responsibilities may fall to children and other family members living at home. Consequently, the patient's family may feel that their lives have gone out of control and may have difficulty coping with the changes (Compas, Worsham, Ey, & Howell, 1996). Role strains of all kinds can emerge as family members find themselves assuming new roles and simultaneously realize that their time to pursue recreational and other leisure-time activities has declined (Pavalko & Woodbury, 2000; Quittner et al., 1998; Williamson, Shaffer, & Schulz, 1998). Increased responsibilities may be difficult to handle. If family members' resources are already stretched to the limit, accommodating new tasks is very difficult.

Despite the clear sources of strain that develop when a member of a family has a chronic illness, there is no evidence that such strains are catastrophic. There is no higher divorce rate among families with a chronic illness, nor do such families show less cohesion.

Caregiving Role   Nonetheless, substantial strains may fall on family members, as just seen. In no case is this strain more evident than in the case of the primary caregiver.

Care for the people with chronic illness is notoriously irregular (Stolberg, 1999b). Consequently, the burden often falls on a family member to provide this often intense, unrelenting care for another. Both men and women may be involved in caregiving, although on the whole, the role more commonly falls to women. The typical caregiver is a woman in her sixties caring for an elderly spouse, but caregivers also provide help for their own parents and for disabled or children with a chronic illness.

Caregiving may be intermittent or supplementary in the case of patients who can contribute actively to their own disease management; many cancer and heart patients fall into this category. In other cases, it may be intense for a period until recovery progresses; some stroke patients fall into this category. In other cases, caregiving needs increase, as the disease progresses to the point where the caregiver has responsibility for virtually every activity the patient must undertake, including brushing their teeth, feeding them, cleaning them, and the like; progressive cancers, Alzheimer's disease, Parkinson's disease, and advanced multiple sclerosis are among the illnesses that may create this need for intense caregiving.

Not surprisingly, family members who provide caregiving are at risk for distress, depression, and declining health (Bigatti & Cronan, 2002; O'Rourke, Cappeliez, & Neufeld, 2007). To begin with, caregivers are often elderly, and, consequently, their own health may be threatened when caregiving begins. Many studies attest to the risks that caregiving poses to immune functioning (Glaser, Sheridan, Malarkey, MacCallum, & Kiecolt-Glaser, 2000; Redwine, Mills, Sada, Dimsdale, Patterson, & Grant, 2004), endocrine functioning (Mausbach et al., 2005), poor quality of sleep (Brummett et al., 2006), declines in health over time (O'Rourke, Cappeliez, & Neufeld, 2007; von Kaenel, Dimsdale, Patterson, & Grant, 2003), long-term changes in stress responses (Grant, Adler, Patterson, & Irwin, 2002), an increased risk of infectious disease, and even death (Schulz & Beach, 1999).

Why does caregiving compromise the health of the caregiver? Findings from a national study of depression and health among dementia patient caregivers conducted over a ten-year period suggest that elevated levels of depression may explain this worrisome finding. Researchers from Simon Fraser University and the University of Ottawa assessed depression symptoms and health at three different time points across a decade in family members who were providing care for dementia patients living in the same household (O'Rourke, Cappeliez, & Neufeld, 2007). Caregivers who reported higher levels of depressive symptoms at multiple points reported poorer and worsening health over time. The researchers suggested that in addition to immune alterations associated with depression, the caregivers health may have also been compromised because of a decline in health-protective behaviours and self-care, which is well known to occur with depression.

Caregiving can also strain the relationship between patient and caregiver (Martire, Stephens, Druley, & Wojno, 2002). Patients are not always appreciative of the help they receive and may resent the fact that they need help. Their expression of resentment can contribute to the depression and distress so often seen in caregivers. Caregivers fare better when they have a high sense of personal mastery and active coping strategies (for example, Aschbacher et al., 2005).

Given the toll that caregiving takes on the caregivers themselves, and especially those involving social sup-

port, interventions may be needed because the demands of caregiving may tie them to the home and give them little free time. Recently, the possibility that the Internet can be used to provide support to caregivers has been explored. One study (Czaja & Rubert, 2002) found that caregivers who were able to communicate online with other family members, a therapist, and members of an online discussion group found the services to be extremely valuable, suggesting that this intervention has substantial promise for caregivers who might otherwise be isolated from others. Interventions to help caregivers accept and find meaning in the caregiving experience can also reduce psychological distress (Kim, Schulz, & Carver, 2007).

Impact on Sexuality   Many chronic illnesses—including heart disease, stroke, and cancer—lead to a decrease in sexual activity. In some cases, the condition itself prompts temporary restrictions on sexual activity; more commonly, however, the decline can be traced to psychological origins (such as loss of desire, fears about aggravating the chronic condition, or impotence). For example, people with Crohn's disease or ulcerative colitis may feel apprehensive about becoming sexually intimate because of the stigma and fear of losing bowel control. The ability to continue physically intimate relations can be protective of mental health and relationship satisfaction among people with chronic illness but attention to issues of physical intimacy can improve emotional adjustment to chronic illness and quality of life (Perez, Skinner, & Meyerowitz, 2002).

Gender and the Impact of Chronic Illness   Women who have a chronic illness may experience more deficits in social support than do men with chronic illness. Even when women with a chronic illness are married, they are more frequently institutionalized for their illnesses than are husbands. Married men spend fewer days in nursing homes than married women (Freedman, 1993). It may be that husbands feel less capable providing care than wives, or, because husbands are older than wives, they may be more disabled than are wives of husbands with a chronic illness. Despite the fact that institutionalization can reduce the strain of caregiving, hospitalization of one's spouse also increases risk of death for both husbands and wives (Christakis & Allison, 2006). Women with chronic illness also experience more distress than men (Hagedoorn, Sanderman, Bolks, Tuinstra, & Coyne, 2008).

Following the diagnosis of a chronic illness, women may nevertheless continue to carry a disproportionate burden of household responsibilities and activities, a burden that may pose a threat for progressive illness (J. S. Rose et al., 1996). Gender differences in the availability and effects of social support among people with chronic illness clearly merit concern.

Positive Changes in Response to Chronic Illness

At the beginning of this chapter, we considered quality of life, and throughout the chapter, we have focused on many of the adverse changes that chronic illness creates and what can be done to ameliorate them. This focus tends to obscure an important point, however—namely, that chronic illness can confer positive outcomes as well as negative ones (S. E. Taylor, 1983, 1989).

Research has focused disproportionately on the negative emotions that are produced by chronic illness. However, many people experience positive reactions (Ryff & Singer, 1996), such as joy (S. M. Levy, Lee, Bagley, & Lippman, 1988) and optimism (Cordova, Cunningham, Carlson & Andrykowski, 2001). These reactions may occur because people who have a chronic illness perceive that they have narrowly escaped death or because they have reordered their priorities in a more satisfying way. They may also find meaning in the daily activities of life in response to the illness (McFarland & Alvaro, 2000).

In one study (R. L. Collins, Taylor, & Skokan, 1990), more than 90 percent of cancer patients reported at least some beneficial changes in their lives as a result of the cancer, including an increased ability to appreciate each day and the inspiration to do things now in life rather than postponing them. These patients reported that they were putting more effort into their relationships and believed they had acquired more awareness of others' feelings and more empathy and compassion for others. They reported feeling stronger and more self-assured as well. This **benefit finding,** acknowledgement of the positive affects of illness in one's life, is an important indicator of adjustment to chronic illness. Benefit finding has been found for several different chronic health conditions including multiple sclerosis (Pakenham & Cox, 2009) and has been linked not only to psychological adjustment but to better social functioning and health as well (Aspinwall & MacNamara, 2005; Danoff-Burg & Revenson, 2005; Low, Stanton, & Danoff-Burg, 2006).

A study of patients who had had a heart attack found that 46 percent reported that their lives were unchanged by the disease, 21 percent reported that it had worsened, but 33 percent felt that their lives had improved overall (Mohr et al., 1999). Half of the patients reported increased joy in life and increased value in families, hobbies, and health. A study of people with multiple sclerosis found that many had experienced a deepening of their relationships, an enhanced appreciation of life, and an increase in spiritual interests (Pakenham, 2008). Two studies compared the quality of life experienced by cancer patients with a normal sample free of chronic disease, and both found the quality of life experienced by the cancer sample to be higher than that of the non-ill sample (Danoff, Kramer, Irwin, & Gottlieb, 1983; Tempelaar et al., 1989).

The ability to reappraise one's situation positively has been tied to a more positive mood (Pakenham, 2005) and to posttraumatic growth in women with breast cancer (Manne et al., 2004; Sears, Stanton, & Danoff-Burg, 2003), and people with coronary artery disease (Leung et al., 2010). Finding meaning in a chronic illness and coping through religion can also improve adjustment to chronic illness (Calhoun, Cann, Tedeschi, & McMillan, 2000; Schanowitz & Nicassio, 2006).

How do people with chronic disease so often manage to achieve such a high quality of life? Many people perceive control over what happens to them, they have positive expectations about the future, and they have a positive view of themselves. These kinds of beliefs are adaptive for mental and physical health much of the time (S. E. Taylor & Brown, 1988) but become especially important when a person faces a chronic illness. In a recent investigation, Helgeson (2003) examined these beliefs in men and women treated for coronary artery disease with an angioplasty and then followed them over four years. These beliefs not only predicted positive adjustment to disease but also were associated with a reduced likelihood of sustaining a repeat cardiac event.

Finding benefits in illness is often, but not invariably, associated with good adjustment (Tomich & Helgeson, 2004). Regardless of why they occur, these positive reactions usually serve a beneficial function in recovery from illness and imply that health psychologists should be attentive to this fact (for example, O'Carroll, Ayling, O'Reilly, & North, 2003). In short, people rearrange their priorities and their beliefs in such a way that they are able to extract benefit and meaning from the event (J. A. Schaefer & Moos, 1992), as Figure 11.4 reveals.

FIGURE 11.4 | This figure shows the positive life changes experienced by MI patients and cancer patients in response to their illness. An interesting point is that most of the benefits reported by MI patients involve lifestyle changes, perhaps reflecting the fact that the course of heart disease is amenable to changes in personal health habits. Cancer patients, in contrast, report more changes in their social relationships and meaning attached to life, perhaps because cancer may not be as directly influenced by health habits as heart disease but may be amenable to finding greater purpose or meaning in other life activities

(*Source:* Petrie, Buick, Weinman, & Booth, 1997)

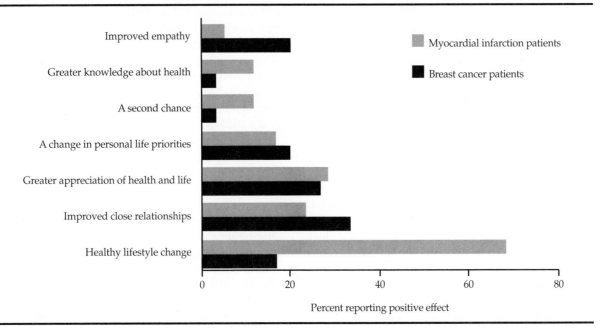

Critical Checkpoint

Finding Benefits from Chronic Illness

Research across a variety of chronic health conditions indicates that some individuals will perceive one or more benefits from their experience of living with a chronic illness. What might account for this phenomenon? Do people's lives actually get better after being diagnosed with a chronic illness or are their perceptions biased? Is it even important to understand the reasons why benefit finding occurs?

When the Patient with a Chronic Illness Is a Child

Chronic illness can be especially problematic when the patient is a child. First, children may not fully understand the nature of their diagnosis and treatment and thus ex-perience confusion as they are trying to cope with illness and treatment (Strube, Smith, Rothbaum, & Sotelo, 1991). Second, because children with a chronic illness often cannot follow their treatment regimen by themselves, the family must participate in the illness and treatment process even more than is the case with an adult with a chronic illness. Such interdependence can lead to tension between parent and child (for example, S. L. Manne, Jacobsen, Gorfinkle, Gerstein, & Redd, 1993). Sometimes, children must be exposed to isolating and terrifying procedures to treat their condition. All these factors can create problems of adjustment for both children and parents (E. J. Silver, Bauman, & Ireys, 1995).

Although many children adjust to these radical changes in their lives successfully, others do not. Children suffering from chronic illness exhibit a variety of behavioural problems, including rebellion and withdrawal from others (Alati et al., 2005). They may suffer low self-esteem, either because they believe that the chronic illness is a punishment for bad behaviour or because they feel cheated because their peers are healthy. Nonadherence to treatment, underachievement in school, and regressive behaviour,

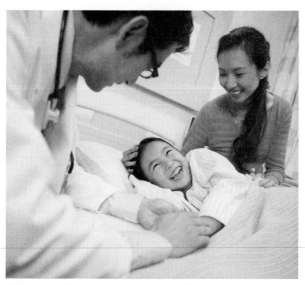

Children's needs to be informed about their illness and to exert control over illness-related activities and over their lives have prompted interventions to involve children in their own care.

such as bedwetting or throwing temper tantrums, are not uncommon. These problems can be aggravated if families do not have adequate styles of communicating with each other and of resolving conflict (for example, S. L. Manne et al., 1993). In addition, children with a chronic illness may develop maladaptive coping styles involving repression, which may interfere with their understanding of and ability to co-manage their disorders (Phipps & Steele, 2002). They are also at risk for developing anxiety disorders (Pao & Bosk, 2011). Like other chronic diseases, childhood chronic diseases can be exacerbated by stress. For example, among children with asthma, number of hospitalizations was associated with family conflict and strain and with the strain experienced by caregivers as well (E. Chen, Bloomberg, Fisher, & Strunk, 2003).

Improving Coping   Several factors can improve a child's ability to cope with chronic illness. Parents with realistic attitudes toward the disorder and its treatment can soothe the child emotionally and provide an informed basis for care. If the parents are free of depression, have a sense of mastery over the child's illness, and can avoid expressing distress, especially during treatments (DuHamel et al., 2004), this may also aid adjustment (Timko, Stovel, Moos, & Miller, 1992). If children are encouraged to engage in self-care as much as possible and only realistic restrictions are placed on their lives, adjustment will be better. Encouraging regular school

attendance and reasonable physical activities is particularly beneficial. If the parent can learn to remain calm in crisis situations, maintain emotional control, and become familiar with the child's illness, these factors can contribute positively to the child's functioning.

WHAT PSYCHOLOGICAL INTERVENTIONS ARE USED TO MANAGE CHRONIC ILLNESS?

LO6

As we have seen, the majority of patients with chronic illness appear to achieve a relatively high quality of life after diagnosis and treatment for their illness. In fact, many who are free from pain or advancing disease achieve at least as high, if not higher, a quality of life than before the illness, by their self-reports. However, as we have also seen, there are reliable adverse effects of chronic disease, such as anxiety, depression, and disturbances in interpersonal relations. Increasingly, depression, psychological distress, and neuroticism are being targeted for intervention to reduce risk for mortality from chronic conditions (Christensen, Ehlers, Wiebe, et al., 2002). In addition, because stress aggravates so many chronic diseases and conditions (for example, Ackerman et al., 2002), assistance in managing the demands of daily life may be required. Consequently, health psychologists have increasingly focused on ways to ameliorate these problems.

The fact that anxiety and depression are intermittently high among patients with chronic illness suggests that evaluation for these problems should be a standard part of chronic care. Researchers and clinicians need to develop ways to identify people who are at high risk for emotional disorders. A variety of interventions have been developed to deal with these and other problems associated with chronic illness.

Individual Therapy

Individual therapy is one of the most common interventions for patients who have psychosocial complications due to chronic illness (Mago, Gomez, Gupta, & Kunkel, 2006). But there are important differences between psychotherapy with medical patients.

First, therapy with medical patients is more likely to be episodic than continuous. Chronic illness raises crises and issues intermittently that may require help. Recurrence or worsening of a condition may present a crisis that needs to be addressed with a therapist, as for a heart patient who has had a second heart attack or a cancer patient who has developed a new malignancy.

Second, collaboration with the patient's physician and family members is critical in therapy with medical patients. The physician can inform the psychologist or other counsellor of a patient's current physical status. Problems experienced by the patient will have implications for other family members' activities; accordingly, family members are almost inevitably involved in the problems created by illness.

Third, therapy with medical patients more frequently requires respect for patients' defences than does traditional psychotherapy. In traditional psychotherapy, one of the therapist's goals may be to challenge a patient's defences that may interfere with an adequate understanding of his or her problems. However, in the case of patients with a chronic illness, the same defences may serve a benign function in protecting them from the full realization of the ramifications of their disease.

Fourth and finally, the therapist working with a medical patient must have a comprehensive understanding of the patient's illness and its modes of treatment. Because many of the issues are centred around particular aspects of illness and treatment, the therapist who is uninformed about the illness will not be able to provide adequate help. Moreover, illness and treatments themselves produce psychological problems (for example, depression due to chemotherapy), and a therapist who is ignorant of this fact may make incorrect interpretations.

Brief Psychotherapeutic Interventions

Several short-term interventions ranging from informal communication with a health care professional to brief psychotherapy are available to alleviate emotional distress in patients with a chronic illness. Some brief informational interventions can be accomplished on a preventive basis within the medical setting (for example, Dobkin et al, 2002). Simply telling patients that anxiety is a normal response to the stress of chronic illness (Welch-McCaffrey, 1985) or that depression is a common consequence of certain disorders, such as stroke (R. G. Robinson, 1986), may alleviate patients' and family members' concerns over whether the patient is reacting normally to illness.

Increasingly, psychologists have made use of short-term, structured therapeutic interventions to help the most people in the shortest period of time (for example, van Dulmen, Fennis, & Bleijenberg, 1996). Even brief therapies, such as those conducted over the telephone, have been shown to benefit patients, enhancing a sense of personal control (Sandgren & McCaul, 2003).

Although many interventions focus on coping skills, others have made use of more novel techniques for attempting to improve a patient's emotional and behavioural responses to chronic illness. These include music, art, and dance therapies (see, for example, Pacchetti et al., 2000).

Patient Education

Patient education programs that include coping skills training relative to particular disorders have been found to improve functioning for a broad variety of chronic diseases. Such programs can increase knowledge about the disease, reduce anxiety, increase patients' feelings of purpose and meaning in life (Brantley, Mosley, Bruce, McKnight, & Jones, 1990), reduce pain and depression (Lorig, Chastain, Ung, Shoor, & Holman, 1989), improve coping (Lacroix, Martin, Avendano, & Goldstein, 1991), increase adherence to treatment (Greenfield, Kaplan, Ware, Yano & Frank, 1988), and increase confidence in the ability to manage pain and other side effects (J. C. Parker et al., 1988), relative to waitlist patients who have not yet participated in the program or to patients who did not participate at all (Helgeson, Cohen, Shulz, & Yasko, 2001).

Internet The Internet poses exciting possibilities for providing interventions in a cost-effective manner. Information about illnesses can be presented in a clear and simple way, and even information about skills for coping with common illness-related problems or side effects of treatment can be posted at appropriate Web sites for use by patients and their families (Budman, 2000). Many Web sites now offer information to a broad array of patients with chronic illnesses. In one study, breast cancer patients who used the Internet for medical information were surveyed, and the results showed that they experienced greater social support and less loneliness than those who did not use the Internet for information. Moreover, the time involved was less than an hour a week, suggesting that these psychological benefits may result from only a minimal time commitment (Fogel, Albert, Schnabel, Ditkoff, & Neugut, 2002).

Expressive Writing In Chapter 7, we discussed the benefits of expressive writing for coping with stress, a technique pioneered by James Pennebaker (1997; Pennebaker & Beall, 1986). These interventions have been especially beneficial to patients with chronic illness (Sheese, Brown, & Graziano, 2004). A study of metastatic renal cell carcinoma patients, for example, found that those who wrote about their cancer (versus those who wrote about a neutral topic) had less sleep disturbance and better sleep quality and duration and fewer problems with activities of daily life, suggesting that expressive writing has benefits for terminally ill patients (de Moor et al., 2002). Expressive writing has also been demonstrated to reduce pain and enhance well-being in cancer patients (Cepeda et al., 2008).

Relaxation, Stress Management, and Exercise

Relaxation training is a widely used intervention with people who have a chronic illness. Along with other stress management techniques, it can reduce the likelihood that asthmatics will have an asthma attack for example (Lehrer, Feldman, Giardino, Song, & Schmaling, 2002). It can decrease anxiety and increase energy and vigour in multiple sclerosis patients (Sutherland, Andersen, & Morris, 2005). Combinations of relaxation training with stress management and blood pressure monitoring have proven useful in the treatment of essential hypertension (Agras, Taylor, Kraemer, Southam, & Schneider, 1987) and asthma (Smyth, Soefer, Hurewitz, & Stone, 1999). Relaxation training has also been shown to be more effective than lifestyle modification in reducing blood pressure in the elderly (Dusek et al., 2008).

In recent years, mindfulness-based stress reduction has been used to improve adjustment to medical illness. Mindfulness-based stress reduction (MBSR) refers to systematic training in meditation to enable people to self-regulate their reactions to stress and the negative emotions that may result (K. W. Brown & Ryan, 2003). Mindfulness meditation teaches people to strive for a state of mind in which one is highly aware and focused on the reality of the present moment, accepting and acknowledging it without becoming distracted or distressed by stress. Thus, the goal is to induce people to approach stressful situations mindfully rather than reacting to them automatically (S. R. Bishop, 2002). Research supporting the long-term efficacy of this approach is emerging, with several Canadian studies indicating that MBSR may be effective in reducing stress, anxiety, and distress among people with chronic illness (Carlson & Garland, 2005; Carlson, Speca, Patel, & Goodey, 2003; Carlson, Speca, Patel, & Faris, 2007).

Exercise interventions are becoming increasingly common among various chronic health conditions, including cancer and coronary artery disease. Results from a randomized controlled trial with breast cancer patients receiving chemotherapy conducted by a team of Cana-

dian researchers suggests that exercise may be useful for improving not only physical but also mental health. Over a two-year period, breast cancer patients were assigned to receive either the standard treatment of chemotherapy alone, or combined with supervised resistance exercise or supervised aerobic exercise. Both resistance and aerobic exercise significantly improved fitness levels and self-esteem compared to the no- exercise condition. There were also improvements noted in quality of life, fatigue, depression, and anxiety, which although not statistically significant were nonetheless clinically meaningful (Courneya et al., 2007). Exercise training programs are also very effective for reducing anxiety and improving quality of life among heart disease patients (Lavie & Milani, 2004). In addition, a recent review suggests that exercise training can help manage the anxiety associated with a number of chronic health conditions including cancer, cardiovascular disease, multiple sclerosis, fibromyalgia, and other chronic pain disorders (Graham et al., 2008; Herring, O'Connor, & Dishman, 2010). Overall, exercise training programs that are no longer than 12 weeks and include sessions of 30 minutes are effective for managing chronic illness related anxiety.

Social Support Interventions

As we noted in Chapter 7 and earlier in this chapter, social support is an important resource for people suffering from chronic disease. Patients with a chronic illness who report good social relationships are more likely to be positively adjusted to their illness. Indeed a study of 700,000 working age Canadian women living with a disability found that having two or more friends to confide in or spending time visiting with friends or family was associated with greater life satisfaction (Crompton, 2010). The importance of social support for adjustment has been found with cancer patients (Neuling & Winefield, 1988), and arthritis patients (Holtzman, Newth, & DeLongis, 2004), among others.

Social **support groups** are one type of social support intervention that may be particularly beneficial for someone living with a chronic illness. Such groups are available for many patients with chronic illnesses, including stroke patients, patients recovering from myocardial infarction, and cancer patients. Some of these groups are initiated by a therapist, or are patient-led, but increasingly the Internet provides manifold opportunities for giving and receiving social support and information (see the Health Psychology in Action box, "Social Support on the Web").

These support groups discuss issues of mutual concern that arise as a consequence of illness. They often provide specific information about how others have successfully dealt with the problems raised by the illness and provide people with an opportunity to share their emotional responses with others facing the same problems (Sirois & Purc-Stephenson, 2006). Social support groups can satisfy unmet needs for social support from family and caregivers, or they may act as an additional source of support provided by those going through the same event.

Studies that have evaluated the efficacy of social support groups vis-à-vis people waiting to participate or nonparticipants have found beneficial results. Social support groups have been shown to be beneficial for rheumatoid arthritis patients (for example, Bradley et al., 1987), men with prostate cancer (Lepore, Helgeson, Eton, & Schulz, 2003), and MI patients (for example, Dracup, 1985), among others. Self-help groups may help victims especially cope with the stigma associated with certain disorders, such as cancer or epilepsy (Droge, Arntson, & Norton, 1986), and such groups may help patients develop the motivation and techniques to adhere to complicated treatment regimens (Storer, Frate, Johnson, & Greenberg, 1987).

Support groups may encourage adherence for several reasons:

1. People must commit themselves to change their behaviour in front of other individuals. Commitment to a decisional course can frequently improve adherence (Janis, 1983).

2. In the course of interacting with others, people may also learn techniques that others have used successfully to maintain adherence and adopt them to combat their own problems.

3. The emotional support and encouragement that others with similar problems provide can also encourage adherence.

Participation in social support groups may even promote better health and long-term survival. One study of patients in a weekly cancer support group found that participants survived longer than nonparticipants (Spiegel & Bloom, 1983). Increasingly self-help groups are becoming a general resource for the people with chronic illness. Indeed, as more Canadians become regular Internet users, Internet-based support groups may provide the needed support for those who are not able to access traditional support groups due to physical or disease-related limitations. Although they lack the personal qualities of face to face support groups, they do offer convenient 24/7 access to a large and diverse group of people who can offer support (Sirois & Purc-Stephenson, 2006).

Family Support

Family support of patients with a chronic illness is especially important, not only because it enhances the patient's physical and emotional functioning but also because it can promote adherence to treatment. Family members may not only remind the patient about activities that need to be undertaken but also tie treatment to already existing activities in the family so that adherence is more likely. For example, the family may undertake a daily jog through the neighbourhood just before breakfast or dinner.

Sometimes family members also need guidance in the well-intentioned actions they should nonetheless avoid because such actions actually make things worse (for

Social support groups can satisfy unmet needs for social support from family and friends and can enable people to share their personal experiences with others like themselves.

Social Support on the Web

One of the problems of living with a chronic health condition is that fatigue and physical limitations can impede daily functioning so much that even getting out of the house to attend a support group can be an insurmountable challenge for some. In addition, there may not be available support group resources nearby, or existing groups may not be suitable when the person who has the chronic illness does not fit the stereotypical middle-age or older adult demographic profile, or has a less common chronic health condition. Fortunately an increasing number of online support communities have sprung up to answer these needs and ensure that 24/7 support is just a few clicks away for the person living with a chronic illness and their families.

Although there are a number of disease specific support sites, sites such as ButYouDon'tLookSick.com are very popular in part because they provide support for a broad range of chronic health conditions including less common conditions. The ButYouDon'tLookSick.com blog site was established in 2003 by Christine Miserandino after she had to give up her career dreams of being a dancer on Broadway and the debilitating pain and fatigue from lupus forced her to leave college. The online community which includes tips on how to cope with stress and unsympathetic strangers, and healthy eating tips, boasts one of the largest online message boards for people with chronic illness with over 6,500 members and includes a Facebook page to help keep their readers stay connected. As the name implies many chronic health conditions are invisible and providing support and in-

formation to those who might not otherwise receive it is a key mandate of this site.

Because people tend to associate chronic illness with middle-aged or older adults, young women with chronic illness may be particularly disadvantaged when it comes to finding and receiving appropriate support. Sites such as ChronicBabe.com have sprung up specifically to meet the needs of younger women who live with one or more chronic health conditions by offering information about managing illness and staying healthy, a weekly newsletter, podcasts, a blog, and an online support forum. Founded by freelance writer Jenni Prokopy in 2005 who lives with several chronic health conditions including fibromyalgia and asthma, ChronicBabe is "for Babes, who just happen to have a chronic illness." Frustrated by the disbelief she encountered when explaining her health conditions to others, Jenni set out to create a support community where "sick chicks" could find like-minded others who wanted to live well despite of their illness and live like babes instead of patients. In short, ChronicBabe.com is a place where young women can share their success stories and offer hope to those who may be struggling with the identity issues associated with being young and having a chronic illness.

Online communities have created opportunities for patients diagnosed with a chronic illness and their families to obtain information and gain social support that never existed before, bringing together people who were once isolated, so that they can solve their problems collectively.

---

example, Martin, Davis, et al., 1994). For example, many family members think they should encourage a patient with a chronic illness to be relentlessly cheerful, which can have the unintended adverse effect of making the patient feel unable to share distress or concern with others.

Summary Several psychotherapeutic interventions are available to patients with a chronic illness who are trying to cope with complex problems. These interventions include crisis intervention, family therapy, individual therapy, group therapy, and support groups. Each has distinctive features and benefits, and different options may be better suited to some problems than others. Evaluations of these kinds of interventions suggest consistent beneficial effects.

Despite these advances in care for those with chronic illnesses and our expanded understanding of the psychosocial issues that they face, medical and psychosocial care for these patients is still irregular, as the burden on caregivers clearly attests. Consequently, managed care may need to assume responsibility for broader-based behavioural and psychological approaches to improving health among people with a chronic illness. Physicians and other health practitioners need better training in behavioural and psychosocial approaches to chronic disorders. Techniques for teaching self-management of chronic illness need to be refined, and educational interventions for communicating them to patients need to be undertaken; monitoring the success of programs like these will be important as well. ●

S U M M A R Y

 Define quality of life

- At any given time, almost 60 percent of the population has a chronic condition that requires medical management, yet only recently has attention turned to the psychosocial aspects of quality of life. Quality-of-life measures pinpoint problems associated with diseases and treatments and help in policy decision making about the effectiveness and cost effectiveness of interventions.

 Understand the emotional responses to chronic illness

- Patients with a chronic illness often experience denial, intermittent anxiety, and long-term depression. But too often, these reactions, especially anxiety and depression, are underdiagnosed, confused with symptoms of disease or treatment, or presumed to be normal and therefore not appropriate for intervention.

- Anxiety is reliably tied to illness events, such as awaiting test results or obtaining regular checkups. Depression increases with the severity of disease, pain, and disability.

 Describe how the self is changed by chronic illness

- Chronic illness can produce drastic changes in self-concept and self-esteem. Many of these changes will be temporary, but some may be permanent and have a significant impact on future goals and aspirations.

LO4 Explain how people cope with chronic illness

- Despite problems, most patients cope with chronic illness as they cope with other stressful events in life. Active coping and multiple coping efforts may be more successful than avoidance, passive coping, or use of one predominant coping strategy.

- Patients also develop concepts of their illness, its cause, and its controllability that relate to their coping. Perceived personal control over illness and/or treatment is associated with good adjustment.

 Explain how people manage chronic illness

- Rehabilitation centres around physical problems, especially recovering functioning and adherence to treatment; vocational retraining, job discrimination, financial loss, and loss of insurance; gaps and problems in social support; and personal losses, such as the threat that disease poses for long-term goals.

- The majority of patients appear to achieve some positive outcomes of chronic illness as well as negative ones. These positive outcomes may occur because patients compensate for losses in some areas of their lives, with value placed on other aspects of life.

 Identify the psychological interventions used to manage chronic illness

- Interventions with patients who have a chronic illness include pharmacological interventions, individual therapy, brief psychotherapeutic interventions oriented toward solving crises or providing information, relaxation and exercise, social support interventions, and support groups. Traditional face-to-face support groups appear to be an underused but potentially helpful resource for people with chronic illnesses, although Internet support groups may provide many of the same advantages with much more convenience.

K E Y   T E R M S

benefit finding   p. 313
body image   p. 299
denial   p. 297
depression   p. 298
functional somatic
    syndromes   p. 306

medically unexplained physical
    symptoms (MUPS)   p. 306
patient education   p. 316
physical rehabilitation   p. 305
possible selves   p. 300
quality of life   p. 294

self-concept   p. 299
self-esteem   p. 299
self-management   p. 293
support groups   p. 317

Psychological Issues in Advancing and Terminal Illness

LEARNING OBJECTIVES

After reading this chapter, students will be able to:

(LO1) Describe how death differs across the life span

(LO2) Know the psychological issues in advancing illness

(LO3) Identify the stages in adjustment to dying

(LO4) Understand the concerns in the psychological management of the terminally ill

(LO5) Describe the alternatives to hospital care for the terminally ill

(LO6) Explain the issues survivors face

At the first assembly of the first-year students in a suburban high school, the principal opened his remarks by telling the assembled students, "Look around you. Look to your left, look to your right, look in front of you, and look in back of you. Four years from now, one of you will be dead." Most of the students were stunned by this remark, but one boy in the back feigned a death rattle and slumped to the floor in a mock display of the principal's prophecy. He was the one. Two weeks after he got his driver's license, he crashed his car into a stone wall, when the car spun out of control at high speed.

The principal, of course, had not peered into the future but had simply drawn on the statistics showing that even adolescents die, especially from accidents. By the time most of us are 18, we will have known at least one person who has died, whether it be a classmate from high school, a grandparent, or a family friend. Many of these causes of death are preventable as we will see. Many children die from unintentional injuries in the home. Adolescents, as well as children, die in car crashes often related to risky driving, drugs, alcohol, or a combination of factors. Even death in middle and old age is most commonly due to the cumulative effects of bad health habits, such as smoking, poor eating, lack of exercise, and accompanying obesity (Mokdad, Marks, Stroup, & Gerberding, 2004).

(L01) HOW DOES DEATH DIFFER ACROSS THE LIFE SPAN?

Comedian Woody Allen is said to have remarked on his 40th birthday, "I shall gain immortality not through my work but by not dying." Many of us would echo this desire to live forever, but life inevitably ends in death. A mere 100 years ago, people died primarily from infectious diseases, such as tuberculosis, influenza, or pneumonia. Now those illnesses are much less widespread because of substantial advances in public health and preventive medical technologies that developed in the twentieth century. On average, people in Canada can now expect to live 81 years, longer than the average for most developed countries (World Health Organization, 2011c). When death does come, it will probably stem from a chronic illness or non-communicable disease, such as heart disease or cancer, rather than from an acute disorder as Tables 12.1 and 12.2 indicate. This fact means that, instead of facing a rapid, unanticipated death, the average Canadian may know what he or she will probably die from for 5, 10, or even more years.

TABLE 12.1 | Deaths: Leading Causes in Canada, All Ages, 2007

Rank and Cause	Number of Deaths
1. Malignant neoplasms (cancer)	69,595
2. Diseases of heart (heart disease)	50,499
3. Cerebrovascular diseases (stroke)	13,981
4. Chronic lower respiratory diseases	10,659
5. Accidents (unintentional injuries)	9,951
6. Diabetes mellitus (diabetes)	7,394
7. Alzheimer's disease	5,903
8. Influenza and pneumonia	5,452
9. Nephritis, nephrotic syndrome and nephrosis (kidney disease)	3,803
10. Intentional self-harm (suicide)	3,803

Source: Statistics Canada. Leading Causes of deaths in Canada, 2007, CANSIM Table 102–0561, http://www.statcan.gc.ca/pub/84-215-x/2010001/table-tableau/tbl001-eng.htm. Reproduced with the permission of the Minister of Public Works and Government Services Canada, 2010.

Understanding the psychological issues associated with death and dying first requires a tour, a rather grim tour, of death itself. What is the most likely cause of death for a person of any given age, and what kind of death will it be?

Death in Infancy or Childhood

Although Canada is one of the most technologically developed countries in the world, our **infant mortality rate** is still high (5.1 per 1,000; Statistics Canada, 2010a), relative to some Western European nations. In fact, Canada's reputation for low infant mortality has dropped from 6th to 24th place among other countries, falling well below countries such as Sweden, Japan, France, and Greece and ranking just above Poland and Hungary with the 2007 rate of 5.1 (Organization for Economic Co-operation and Development, 2011). Despite the reduction in infant mortality from the rate of 5.4 in 2005, there remains significant disparity in the rates of infant deaths across different socio-economic status groups and locations. For example, in 1996 the rates of infant mortality in Canada's richest neighbourhoods were closer to the Swedish rates of 4.0 per 1,000. However, the rates of infant mortality in Canada's poorest neighbourhoods were much higher at 6.5 per 1,000 (Statistics Canada, 1999). Mortality rates among First Nations infants are

TABLE 12.2 | Leading Causes of Mortality among Adults, Worldwide and in High Income Countries, 2004

Mortality—Adults, Worldwide			Mortality—Adults, high income countries		
Rank	Cause	Deaths	Rank	Cause	Deaths
1	Coronary heart disease	7,200,000	1	Coronary heart disease	1,33,000
2	Stroke and other cerebrovascular diseases	5,710,000	2	Stroke and other cerebrovascular diseases	760,000
3	Lower respiratory infections	4,180,000	3	Trachea, bronchus, lung cancers	480,000
4	Chronic obstructive pulmonary disease	3,020,000	4	Lower respiratory infections	310,000
5	Diarrhoeal diseases	2,160,000	5	Chronic obstructive pulmonary disease	290,000
6	HIV/AIDS	2,040,000	6	Alzheimer and other dementias	280,000
7	Tuberculosis	1,460,000	7	Colon and rectum cancers	270,000
8	Trachea, bronchus, lung cancers	1,320,000	8	Diabetes mellitus	220,000
9	Road traffic accidents	1,270,000	9	Breast cancer	160,000
10	Prematurity and low birth weight	1,180,000	10	Stomach cancer	140,000

Source: World Health Organization, 2008.

also higher than those for non–First Nations people, although the gap has been shrinking dramatically since the 1980s. At first glance it may appear that this disparity may be due to differences in neighbourhood socio-economic status. But the gap in risks of infant mortality from rich to poor neighbourhoods among First Nations peoples parallels the gap noted for other Canadians, suggesting that this disparity may be unrelated to socio-economic status (Statistics Canada, 2004, November 9).

During the first year of life, the main causes of death are congenital abnormalities and **sudden infant death syndrome (SIDS),** with three babies dying of SIDS each week in Canada (Health Canada, 2005d). Rates of SIDS are also higher among Aboriginal children (Canadian Foundation for the Study of Infant Deaths, n.d.). The causes of SIDS are not entirely known—the infant simply stops breathing—but epidemiologic studies reveal that it is more likely to occur in lower-class urban environments, when the mother smoked during her pregnancy, and when the baby is put to sleep on its stomach or side (Canadian Foundation for the Study of Infant Deaths, 2007). Mercifully, SIDS appears to be a gentle death for the child, although not for parents: The confusion, self-blame, and suspicion of others who do not understand this phenomenon can take an enormous psychological toll on the parents (Davis, Lehman, Wortman, Silver, & Thompson, 1995). News stories detailing how some infant deaths blamed on SIDS were, in fact, murders

has not helped parents of SIDS babies cope well, either. SIDS may be confused with homicide and vice versa, leading to substantial legal and emotional complications (Nowack, 1992). For mothers of SIDS infants, adjustment seems to be better if they do not blame themselves for the death by trying to mentally undo the events (Davis et al., 1995).

The fact that sleeping position has now been reliably related to SIDS is a great breakthrough in its reduction. The initial recommendations regarding sleeping position from the Canadian Institute of Child Health, Health Canada, and the SIDS Foundation in 1993, and the update from the Back to Sleep campaign in 1999, resulted in a reduction of almost 50 percent in the number of infant deaths due to SIDS in Canada between 1999 and 2004 (Public Health Agency of Canada, 2010). A survey of parents and caregivers suggests that the substantial decrease in the number of SIDS deaths in Canada can be attributed to the success of this campaign. Before the campaign only 40 percent reported placing infants on their backs to sleep; after the campaign 71 percent reported doing so.

After the first year, external causes are the main cause of death among children under age 15, which account for 42 percent of all deaths in this group. In early childhood, deaths from external causes are most frequently due to motor vehicle accidents, accidental drowning, poisoning, injuries, or falls in the home. In later years, automobile accidents take over as the chief external cause of accidental death. The good news is that both accidental deaths in the home and automobile deaths have declined in recent years, in part because of the increasing attention to these causes of childhood death and the preventive technologies, such as infant car seats, that have resulted.

Cancer, especially leukemia, is the second leading cause of death in youngsters between ages 1 and 15, and its incidence is rising. Leukemia accounts for approximately 25 percent of new cancer cases in children in this age group, and 29 percent of deaths due to cancer (Canadian Cancer Society/National Cancer Institute of Canada, 2007). Leukemia is a form of cancer that strikes the bone marrow, producing an excessive number of white blood cells and leading to severe anemia and other complications. As recently as 50 years ago, a diagnosis of leukemia was a virtual death sentence for a child. Now, because of advances in treatment, including chemotherapy and bone marrow transplants, more than 80 percent of its victims survive the disease (Canadian Cancer Society/National Cancer Institute of Canada, 2007). Unfortunately, these procedures, especially bone marrow transplants, can be very painful and produce a variety of unpleasant side effects. But they have given leukemia sufferers and their families hope when there used to be none. Overall, the mortality rates for most causes of death in infants and children have declined.

Children's Understanding of Death   A discussion of death in childhood is incomplete without some understanding of how children develop a concept of death. The child's idea of death appears to develop quite slowly. Up to age 5 or 6, most children think of death as a great sleep. Children at this age are often curious about death rather than frightened or saddened by it, partly because they may not understand that death is final and irreversible (Slaughter, 2005).

Between ages 5 and 9, the idea that death is final may develop, although most children of this age do not have a biological understanding of death. For some of these children, death is personified into a shadowy figure, such as a ghost or the devil. They may, for example, believe that death occurs because a supernatural being comes to take the person away. The idea that death is universal and inevitable may not develop until age 9 or 10. At this point, the child typically has some understanding of the processes involved in death (such as burial and cremation), knows that the body decomposes, and realizes that the person who has died will not return (Slaughter, 2005).

Death in Young Adulthood

When asked their view of death, most young adults envision a trauma or fiery accident. This perception is somewhat realistic. Although the death rate in adolescence is low (about 2,450 per 100,000 for youths ages 15 to 24), the major cause of death in this age group is unintentional injury, mainly involving automobiles (Statistics Canada, 2007). In this age group, suicide is the second leading cause of death, cancer is the third leading cause, and homicide the fourth. Heart disease, respiratory diseases, and congenital abnormalities account for most of the remaining mortality in this age group.

Reactions to Young Adult Death   Next to the death of a child, the death of a young adult is considered the most tragic. Young adults are products of years of socialization and education and are on the verge of starting their own families and careers. Their deaths are tragic both because of the seeming waste of life and because they are robbed of the chance to develop and mature.

Not surprisingly, when young adults do receive a diagnosis of a terminal illness, such as cancer, they may feel shock, outrage, and an acute sense of injustice. Partly for these reasons, medical staff often find it difficult to work with these patients. They are likely to be angry much of the time and, precisely because they are otherwise in good health, may face a long and drawn-out period of dying. For them, unlike older people, there are simply fewer biological competitors for death, so they do not quickly succumb to complications, such as pneumonia or kidney failure. Of particular concern is the terminally ill parent of young children. These parents feel cheated of the chance to see their children grow up and develop and concerned over what will happen to their children without them.

Death in Middle Age

In middle age, death begins to assume more realistic and, in some cases, fearful proportions, both because it is more common and because people develop the chronic health problems that may ultimately kill them. Interestingly, fear of death is more prominent during middle-age more so than in later adulthood (Fountoulakis, Siamouli, Magiria, & Kaprinis, 2008). The much popularized midlife crisis that may occur in the forties or early fifties is believed to stem partly from the gradual realization of impending death. It

One of the chief causes of death among adolescents and young adults is vehicle accidents.

may be touched off by the death of a parent, an acquaintance, or a friend or by clear bodily signs that one is aging. The fear of death may be symbolically acted out as a fear of loss of physical appearance, sexual prowess, or athletic ability. Or it may be focused on one's work: the realization that one's work may be meaningless and that many youthful ambitions will never be realized. The Focus on Social Issues box, "A Confrontation with Mortality," offers a poignant example of such an experience.

Premature Death The main cause of **premature death** in adulthood—that is, death that occurs before the projected age of 79—is sudden death due to heart attack or stroke. Members of a cancer conference some years ago were startled to hear the keynote speaker say that he wished everyone would die of a heart attack. What he meant is that, compared with a slow and painful death, such as that caused by cancer, sudden death is quick and relatively painless. When asked, most people reply that they would prefer a sudden, painless, and nonmutilating death. Although sudden death has the disadvantage of not allowing people to prepare their exit, in some ways it facilitates a more graceful departure, because the dying person does not have to cope with physical deterioration, pain, and loss of mental faculties. Sudden death is, in some ways, kinder to family members as

well. The family does not have to go through the emotional torment of watching the patient's worsening condition, and finances and other resources are not as severely taxed. A risk is that families may be poorly prepared financially to cope with the loss, or family members may be estranged, with reconciliation now impossible.

Apart from having a family history of heart attack or stroke, there is some evidence that environmental factors may also contribute to the risk for premature death. One study found that the likelihood of a family member dying before the age of 65 was increased for those who experienced a variety of different adverse childhood events including neglect, abuse, domestic violence in the home, and criminal acts by a family member (Anda et al., 2009). These findings echo the message from Chapter 6 about the toll of chronic stress on health and highlight the importance of managing and addressing these important social issues.

Overall, death rates in the middle-aged group have declined, although the rates of decrease have shown distinct gender differences. For example, the decline in death rates due to lung cancer has been more dramatic for men than for women, owing to corresponding changes in smoking rates over the past few decades. Recall from Chapter 5 that smoking became popular earlier for men than for women, and that as smoking

A Confrontation with Mortality

Personal contact with death can prompt a person to re-evaluate the course of his or her life and, sometimes, to make radical life changes. In the following excerpt from *Passages,* writer Gail Sheehy (1974, pp. 2–3, 5) describes the circumstances that led to her own personal crisis:

> Without warning, in the middle of my thirties, I had a breakdown of nerve. It never occurred to me that while winging along in my happiest and most productive stage, all of a sudden simply staying afloat would require a massive exertion of will. Or of some power greater than will.
>
> I was talking to a young boy in Northern Ireland where I was on assignment for a magazine when a bullet blew his face off. That was how fast it all changed. We were standing side by side in the sun, relaxed and triumphant after a civil rights march by the Catholics of Derry. We had been met by soldiers at the barricade; we had vomited tear gas and dragged those dented by rubber bullets back to safety. Now we were surveying the crowd from a balcony. "How do the paratroopers fire those gas canisters so far?" I asked.
>
> "See them jammin' their rifle butts against the ground?" the boy was saying when the steel slug tore

into his mouth and ripped up the bridge of his nose and left of his face nothing but ground bone meal.

> "My God," I said dumbly, "they're real bullets." I tried to think how to put his face back together again. Up to that moment in my life I thought everything could be mended . . . When I flew home from Ireland, I couldn't write the story, could not confront the fact of my own mortality . . .
>
> Some intruder shook me by the psyche and shouted: Take stock! Half your life has been spent. What about the part of you that wants a home and talks about a second child? Before I could answer, the intruder pointed to something else I had postponed: What about the side of you that wants to contribute to the world? Words, books, demonstrations, donations—is this enough? You have been a performer, not a full participant. And now you are 35.
>
> To be confronted for the first time with the arithmetic of life was, quite simply, terrifying.

Source: From *Passages* by Gail Sheehy. Copyright © 1974, 1976 by Gail Sheehy. Used by permission of Dutton, a division of Penguin Group, USA, Inc. and International Creative Management, Inc.

rates started declining for men, they were rising for women. The rates of heart disease and stroke have also declined over the past decade, although the rates of decline have been similar for men and women (Statistics Canada, 2001).

Death in Old Age

In olden times, as was the custom, an elderly woman went out of sight of others to become young again. She swam off a little way and discarded her aged skin, but on her return she was not recognized by her granddaughter, who became frightened and drove her away. The aged woman recovered her old skin from the water and resumed it. From then on, this power was lost to man; aging and death was inevitable. (Melanesian folk tale, Hinton, 1967, p. 36)

Dying is not easy at any time during the life cycle, but it may be easier in old age. The elderly are generally more prepared to face death than are the young. They may have thought about their death and have made some initial preparations. The elderly have seen friends and relatives die and often express readiness to die themselves. They may have come to terms with issues associated with death, such as loss of appearance and failure to meet all the goals they once had for themselves, and may have withdrawn from activities because of their now limited energy.

Typically, the elderly die of degenerative diseases, such as cancer, stroke, heart failure, or just general physical decline that predisposes them to infectious disease or organ failure. The terminal phase of illness is generally shorter for them because there is often more than one biological competitor for death. As an age group, the elderly may have a greater chance to achieve death with dignity.

Health psychologists have begun to investigate the factors that predict mortality in the elderly age group. Why do some individuals live into their seventies, whereas others live into their nineties or longer? Obviously, new illnesses and the worsening of pre-existing conditions account for many of these differences. But changes in psychosocial factors also appear to be important. Psychological distress predicts declines in health and even increased risk for mortality among the elderly in Canada (Wilkins, 2006). Again there are gender differences in these risks. For men, much of the association between distress and mortality can be accounted for by socio-demographic differences and the presence of chronic diseases. For women, however, the link between distress and risk of death persists even after accounting for these factors. What's more, experiencing greater financial distress was also linked to a greater risk of death in elderly women, but not in men. For elderly men, lower education and widowhood are associated with a greater likelihood of death (Wilkins, 2006). Clearly, psychosocial factors play an important role in health and illness throughout the life course.

In part because of such findings, health goals for the elderly now focus less on the reduction of mortal-ity than on improving quality of life. In Canada, older people age 65 and up now experience less morbidity and fewer restricted activity days than was true 15 years ago. However, the worldwide picture is quite different. People are living longer, averaging 64 years in non-industrialized countries, but the prevalence of chronic diseases in those countries, especially those caused by smoking, bad diet, sedentary lifestyle, and alcohol abuse, means that many older people are living poor-quality lives.

As our emphasis on morbidity and the importance of enhancing quality of life takes precedence in health policy concerns, we may see improvement in these figures. With the baby boom generation moving into old age in the next few years, the need to reduce morbidity and improve quality of life still further will assume a special urgency so that the baby boomers do not completely consume health care resources.

One curious fact about the elderly is that typically women live longer than men, women to age 82, men only to age 77 (St-Arnaud, Beaudet, & Tully, 2005; see Figure 12.1). The Focus on Social Issues box, "Why Do Women Live Longer Than Men?" explores some of the reasons for this difference in mortality rates. Table 12.3 provides a formula for roughly calculating personal longevity.

FIGURE 12.1 | Life Expectancy at Birth, by Sex, Canada, 1991–2004

Source: Adapted from the Statistics Canada CANSIM database, cansim2.statcan.ca.

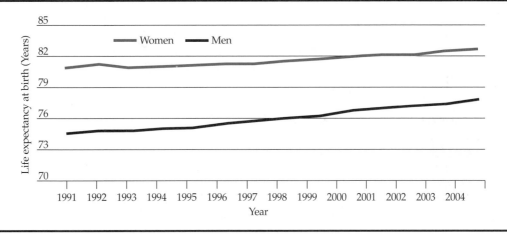

TABLE 12.3 | How Long Will You Live?

This is a rough guide for calculating your personal longevity. The basic life expectancy for males in Canada is 77.2 and for females is 82.1 (St-Arnaud, Beaudet, & Tully, 2005). Write down your basic life expectancy. If you are in your fifties or sixties, you should add 10 years to the basic figure because you have already proven yourself to be quite durable. If you are over age 60 and active, add another 2 years.

Basic Life Expectancy
Describe how each item below applies to you and add or subtract the appropriate number of years from your basic life expectancy.

1. **Family history**
    Add 5 years if 2 or more of your grandparents lived to 80 or beyond. _____
    Subtract 4 years if any parent, grandparent, sister, or brother died of a heart attack or
       stroke before 50; subtract 2 years if anyone died from these diseases before 60. _____
    Subtract 3 years for each case of diabetes, thyroid disorders, breast cancer, cancer of the
       digestive system, asthma, or chronic bronchitis among parents or grandparents _____

2. **Marital status**
    If you are married and male, add 10 years; if married and female, add 4 years.
    If you are over 25 and not married, subtract 1 year for every unwedded decade. _____

3. **Economic status**
    Subtract 2 years if your family income is over $400,000 per year.
    Subtract 3 years if you have been poor for the greater part of your life. _____

4. **Physique**
    Subtract 1 year for every 10 pounds you are overweight.
    For each inch your girth measurement exceeds your chest measurement deduct 2 years.
    Add 3 years if you are over 40 and not overweight. _____

5. **Exercise**
    Regular and moderate (jogging 3 times a week), add 3 years.
    Regular and vigorous (long-distance running 3 times a week), add 5 years.
    Subtract 3 years if your job is sedentary. Add 3 years if it is active. _____

6. **Alcohol***
    Add 2 years if you are a light drinker (1–3 drinks a day).
    Subtract 5 to 10 years if you are a heavy drinker (more than 4 drinks a day).
    Subtract 1 year if you are a teetotaller. _____

7. **Smoking**
    Two or more packs of cigarettes per day, subtract 8 years.
    One to two packs per day, subtract 4 years.
    Less than one pack, subtract 2 years.
    Subtract 2 years if you regularly smoke a pipe or cigars. _____

8. **Disposition**
    Add 2 years if you are a reasoned, practical person.
    Subtract 2 years if you are aggressive, intense, and competitive.
    Add 1–5 years if you are basically happy and content with your life. _____

9. **Education**
    Less than high school, subtract 2 years.
    Four years of school beyond high school, add 1 year.
    Five or more years beyond high school, add 3 years. _____

10. **Environment**
    If you have lived most of your life in a rural environment, add 4 years.
    Subtract 2 years if you have lived most of your life in an urban environment. _____

11. **Sleep**
    More than 9 hours a day, subtract 5 years. _____

12. **Temperature**
    Add 2 years if your home's thermostat is set at no more than 20°C (68°F). _____

13. **Health care**
    Regular medical checkups and regular dental care, add 3 years. _____
    Frequently ill, subtract 2 years. _____

*It should be noted that these calculations for alcohol consumption are controversial and require additional evidence. It is not clear that moderate drinking is healthful relative to teetotaling, and indeed the reverse may be true.

Sources: R. Schulz, *Psychology of Death, Dying, and Bereavement*, © 1978 by the McGraw-Hill Companies. Reproduced with permission of the McGraw-Hill Companies.

WHAT ARE THE PSYCHOLOGICAL ISSUES IN ADVANCING ILLNESS?

Although many people die suddenly, most of the terminally ill know that they are going to die for some time before their death. As a consequence, a variety of medical and psychological issues arise for the patient.

Continued Treatment and Advancing Illness

Advancing and terminal illness frequently brings the need for continued treatments with debilitating and unpleasant side effects. For example, radiation therapy and chemotherapy for cancer may produce discomfort, nausea and vomiting, chronic diarrhea, hair loss, skin discoloration, fatigue, and loss of energy. The patient with advancing diabetes may require amputation of extremities, such as fingers or toes. The patient with advancing cancer may require removal of an organ to which the illness has now spread, such as a lung or part of the liver. The patient with degenerative kidney disease may be given a transplant, in the hope that it will forestall further deterioration.

Many patients find themselves repeated objects of surgical or chemical therapy in a desperate effort to save their lives; after several such efforts, the patient may resist any further intervention. Patients who have undergone repeated surgery may feel that they are being disassembled bit by bit. Or the person who has had several rounds of chemotherapy may feel despair over the apparent uselessness of any new treatment. Each procedure raises anew the threat of death and underscores the fact that the disease has not been arrested, and in many cases, the sheer number of treatments can lead to exhaustion, discomfort, and depression. Thus, there comes a time when the question of whether to continue treatments becomes an issue. In some cases, refusal of treatment may indicate depression and hopelessness, but in many cases, the patient's decision may be supported by thoughtful choice. For example, a recent study of patients with end-stage renal disease who decided to discontinue kidney dialysis found that the decision was not influenced by a major depressive disorder or by ordinary suicidal thought, but rather represented a decision to forego aggressive painful therapy (L. M. Cohen, Dobscha, Hails, Pekow, & Chochinov, 2002).

What is a Good Death?   An increasing focus on improving end-of-life care has led researchers and clinicians to consider what constitutes a "good death." According to the Institute of Medicine (1997), a good death is defined as "one that is free from avoidable suffering for patients, families, and caregivers in general accordance with the patients' and families' wishes." As ideal as this sounds, how does one achieve a good death? One qualitative study of health care providers, patients, and their families identified six components that enhance the quality of dying: pain and symptom management, clear decision making, preparation for death, completion, contributing to others, and affirmation of the whole person (Steinhauser et al., 2000). Rather than being a prescriptive framework these qualities may provide a glimpse of what patients, families, and their caregivers see as valuable at the end of life.

Other approaches have focused on assessing a good death using a self-report scale. The Good Death Inventory (Miyashita et al., 2008), for example, assesses 10 dimensions associated with quality of death outcomes for patients. Included are several psychological and social dimensions such as not being a burden to others; having physical, psychological, and spiritual comfort; good relationships with family and caregivers; and having a sense of control over the future. The nature of a good death may, however, depend upon the nature of the terminal illness. A study of lung cancer patients' perceptions of a good death found that patients focused on themes reflecting a need for a death free from physical suffering (Hughes, Schumacher, Jacobs-Lawson, & Arnold, 2008).

Although there may be several key qualities that contribute to experiencing a good death, they may need to be considered within the context of the unique challenges and course of each illness. For some conditions, attaining the ideal of the good death may be difficult or impossible. In such cases aid in dying may be seen as the only option to die with dignity.

Is There a Right to Die?   In recent years, the right to die has assumed importance due to several legislative and social trends. An important social trend affecting terminal care is the right-to-die movement, which maintains that dying should become more a matter of personal choice and personal control. Derek Humphry's book *Final Exit* virtually leaped off bookstore shelves when it appeared in 1991. A manual of how to assist dying (formerly termed assisted suicide), it was perceived to give back to dying people the means for achieving a dignified death at a time of one's choice.

In 1992, the right-to-die issue became highly debated in Canada after Sue Rodriguez, a woman suffering

Why Do Women Live Longer Than Men?

Women live an average of 4 years longer than men in Canada (World Health Organization, 2011c), a difference that has doubled since 1921. By 2031, this gap is expected to stay the same or narrow with the average life expectancy expected to rise to 86 for women, and 81.9 for men (Statistics Canada, 2010a). This difference also exists in most other industrialized countries. Only in underdeveloped countries, in which childbirth technology is poorly developed or in countries where women are denied access to health care, do men live longer. What are the reasons that women typically live longer than men?

One theory maintains that women are biologically more fit than men. Although more male than female fetuses are conceived, more males are stillborn or miscarried than are females. This trend persists in infancy with more male than female babies dying. In fact, the male death rate is higher at all ages of life. Thus, although more males than females are born, there will be more females than males left alive by the time young people reach their 20s. Exactly what biological mechanisms might make females more fit are still unknown. Some factors may be genetic; others may be hormonal. For example, males are more prone to infectious disease and parasites (I. P. F. Owens, 2002).

Another reason that men die in greater numbers at all ages than do women is that men engage in more risky behaviours (D. R. Williams, 2003). Chief among these is smoking, which accounts for as much as 40 percent of the mortality difference between men and women. Men are typically exposed to more occupational hazards and more hold hazardous jobs, such as construction work, police work, or firefighting. Men's

alcohol consumption is greater than women's, exposing them to liver damage, and they consume more drugs than do women. Men also use automobiles and motorcycles more than women, contributing to their high death rate from accidents. Men's tendencies to cope with stress through fight (aggression)-or-flight (social withdrawal or withdrawal through drugs and alcohol) may thus, also account for their shorter life span.

A third theory maintains that social support may be more protective for women than for men. On the one hand, being married benefits men more than women in terms of increased life span. In fact, marriage for women seems to serve little or no protective function. However, women report having more close friends and participating in more group activities, such as church, that may offer support. Social support keeps stress systems at a low ebb and thus may prevent some of the wear and tear that men, especially unattached men, sustain (S. E. Taylor, Kemeny, Reed, Bower, & Gruenewald, 2000). Thus, women's tendencies to tend-and-befriend in response to stress may account for part of their longevity as well (S. E. Taylor, 2002).

Which of these theories is correct? Although the exact causes are still not clear, the current evidence suggests the sex difference in mortality is likely due to a complex interplay of biological, behavioural, and social causes (Oksuzyan, Brønnum-Hansen, & Jeune, 2010). Whether the factors that have protected women from early mortality in the past will continue to do so is unknown. The next decades will elucidate further whether the changes in men's and women's roles that expose them to similar activities and risks will eventually produce similar mortality rates.

from amyotrophic lateral sclerosis, or Lou Gehrig's disease, challenged the legislated ban against aid in dying by arguing for her right to die. The 42-year-old woman from Victoria, British Columbia, took her case to the Supreme Court of Canada and lost by a narrow 5-to-4 vote, but later opted for aid in dying in 1994 in the presence of an unknown physician (CBC News, 2007, June 11). Following her death, the Special Senate Committee on Euthanasia and Assisted Suicide was launched with recommendations of less severe penalties for certain forms of aid in dying.

Following the publicity surrounding cases such as that of Sue Rodriguez, receptivity to such ideas as aid in dying for the terminally ill has increased in the Canadian population. In a 1995 survey of terminally ill cancer patients, physicians, and members of the general public, only 50 percent of the public and 60 percent of cancer patients believed that euthanasia and aid in dying should be legalized in Canada, whereas 60 percent to 80 percent of physicians opposed changing the laws. Over a decade later, a nationwide survey of cancer patients receiving palliative care suggests acceptance of aid in dying may be growing among patients. Results from the Canadian National Palliative Care Survey indicate that 63 percent of cancer patients believe that euthanasia and/or aid in dying should be legal, and 40 percent said that they would consider requesting aid in dying in the future should their situation deteriorate (K. G. Wilson et al., 2007). Interestingly, patients who supported the right to die were not in more pain or closer to death. Instead, feeling more fatigued, depressed, and more of a burden to others was associated with considering aid in dying.

However, there is by no means agreement on the criteria under which requests for assisted suicide might be honoured (Pfeifer & Brigham, 1996), and many people have regarded the aid in dying movement with concern (for example, Byock, 1991). Until genuine access to comprehensive hospice and

"If I cannot give consent to my own death, whose body is this? Who owns my life?" Sue Rodriguez. In Canada's most famous case of fighting for the right to aid in dying, Sue Rodriguez took her case all the way to the Supreme Court of Canada, but lost.

quality care becomes a reality for dying patients and their families, aid in dying may result from unmet needs rather than a genuine choice (see the Focus on Social Issues box, "A Letter to My Physician Concerning My Decision about Physician Assisted Aid-in-Dying").

Moral and Legal Issues Increasingly, our culture must struggle with the issue of **euthanasia,** that is, ending the life of a person who is suffering from a painful terminal illness. "Euthanasia" comes from the Greek word meaning "good death" (Pfeifer & Brigham, 1996). Terminally ill patients most commonly request euthanasia or aid in dying when they are experiencing distress, fatigue, and suffering, and when they feel that they are a burden to their family members (K. G. Wilson et al., 2007).

For the most part, euthanasia has polarized attitudes among the public and health care providers in Canada. For obvious reasons physicians feel that aid in dying conflicts with their oath to "do no harm," and goes against the basic principle of respecting the sanctity of life and accordingly doing all that can be done to either heal or make their patients as comfortable as possible during their last few days. Canadian physicians also fear that legalizing euthanasia will actually reduce rather than support patients' autonomy, by putting the decision of whether to assist with dying not in the patients' hands but in those of the medical profession. The power to make this decision could lead to patients being killed or coerced into taking aid in dying against their will, as well as causing profound change in society's attitudes towards illness and disability (Raabe et al., 2005). As of 2011, euthanasia is only legal in the Netherlands, Belgium, and Luxemburg, and physician-aid in dying (PAD) is legal in the Netherlands, Switzerland, and in the states of Oregon, Washington, and Montana. But with the growing acceptance of legalizing aid in dying and PAD in the Canadian public, especially after the Sue Rodriguez case, this debate on whether Canadians should have the right to die will likely continue to stir controversy in years to come.

More passive measures to terminate life have also received attention. Advance directives (also referred to as **living wills**) are also advocated by those who believe that people should have choice in dying. Advance directives can request that extraordinary life-sustaining procedures not be used if they are unable to make this decision on their own. The will, which is signed in front of witnesses, is usually developed

A Letter to My Physician Concerning My Decision about Physician Aid-in-Dying

Dear Dr. _____ ,

It is important to me to have excellent and compassionate medical care—to keep me healthy and alive and, at the end of my life, to alleviate suffering and ensure that I have a peaceful and dignified death. When there are measures available to extend my life, I would like to know their chances of success and how they will impact my quality of life.

I would like the reassurance:

- That if I am able to speak for myself, my requests will be honoured; if I am not, the requests from my health care proxy and advance directives will be honoured.

- That you will make an appropriate referral to hospice should I request it.

- That you will support my desire to die with dignity and in peace if the burdens of an incurable condition became too great.

I believe in physician aid-in-dying as one option at the end of life. If the end is inevitable, the quality of my life is more important than the quantity. My dignity, comfort and the burden I may be to those I love are critical considerations for me.

Thank you.

_____   _____
Signature   Date

_____

Source: "A Letter to My Physician." From Compassion & Choices. For more information, visit www.compassionandchoices.org. Used with permission.

---

when the person is diagnosed as having a terminal illness. It provides instructions and legal protection for the physician so that life-prolonging interventions, such as respirators, will not be indefinitely undertaken in a vain effort to keep the patient alive. This kind of document also helps to ensure that the patient's preferences, rather than a surrogate's (such as a relative) preferences are respected (Ditto & Hawkins, 2005; see the Focus on Social Issues box, "Letting Go with Compassion"). However, some right-to-die organizations, such as Dying with Dignity, suggest that having such a document does not necessarily ensure that the wishes outlined will be honoured, and suggest that more proactive means of choice at the end of life (e.g., aid in dying) are important considerations that all Canadians should have the freedom to choose.

Unfortunately, research suggests that many physicians ignore the wishes of their dying patients and needlessly prolong pain and suffering. One study (Seneff, Wagner, Wagner, Zimmerman, & Knaus, 1995) found that although one-third of the patients had asked not to be revived with cardiopulmonary resuscitation, half the time this request was never indicated on their charts. Thus, at present, the living will

and related tools available to patients are not completely successful in allowing patients to express their wishes and ensure that they are met. The Focus on Social Issues box, "Death: A Daughter's Perspective," presents a daughter's perspective on some of these issues with regard to her dying father.

The complex moral, legal, and ethical issues surrounding death are relatively new to our society, prompted in large part by substantial advances in health care technologies. Life-sustaining drugs, cardiopulmonary resuscitation, advanced cardiac life support, renal dialysis, nutritional support and hydration, mechanical ventilation, organ transplantation, antibiotics, and other interventions that prolong life were unheard of as recently as 30 years ago. Our understanding of how to make appropriate use of these technologies has not kept up with their increasing sophistication. Our society has yet to achieve consensus on the appropriate role that the individual may play in choosing the time and means of his or her own death and the roles that health care practitioners may or may not play in assisting this process. These issues will assume increasing importance in the coming decades with the aging of the population.

Letting Go with Compassion

When Mom was diagnosed with pancreatic cancer at age 71, the news was a complete shock to all of us—6 children and 15 grandchildren. Her choices for treatment were simple; she chose quality of life over time, refusing those few options which would have, perhaps, given her a month or two more, but would have diminished the woman she was. She clearly knew what she wanted and she helped us understand her wishes. Though we all had our own thoughts about what would be best for Mom, we knew in our hearts it was her journey, not ours.

One evening, a pain management specialist made a recommendation to change my mother's meds in order to relieve the suffering she was enduring but advised that it could also slow her respiration and she could pass away. We knew that at this point, pain management, along with love and comfort, was all we could do for her. Upon hearing this, my teenaged nephew was quite upset. "Why would we give Grandma something that might kill her?" he choked. We explained to him how much grandma loved life, but that she was ready to go. We explained that, as a family, we were ready to let her go as peacefully and painlessly as possible.

He processed this, and then wondered, "Then why can't we give her more? If she's ready to go and it will help her pass peacefully like she wants?" The family and healthcare providers could only respond, "We're not allowed to." My young nephew helped us realize that it's not just about dying with dignity; it's about letting go with compassion. It's about respecting the wishes of our loved ones and about talking with our families about these issues so that the next generation can be free to choose and let go with compassion.

Source: Dying with Dignity Canada, *The Voice, 27*(1), p. 3, (2011, February), "Youth: A Fountain of Hope" by Anonymous. Accessed October 1, 2011 from http://www.dyingwithdignity.ca/database/rte/files/Feb%202011.pdf.

Critical Checkpoint

Assisted Suicide versus Aid in Dying
The death with dignity movement and the continued media attention on terminally ill patients choosing to use life-ending medication has led to recommendations to avoid using the term physician-assisted suicide in favour of the more neutral term physician-aid in dying or simply aid in dying. What, if any, impact will this change in terms have for patients? Their families? Medical professionals? Or the general public?

Psychological and Social Issues Related to Dying

Changes in the Patient's Self-concept   Just as patients with a chronic illness must engage in new health-related activities and continued monitoring of their physical condition, so must patients with advancing illness adjust their expectations and activities according to the stage of their disorder. The difference is that for patients with progressive diseases such as cancer or severe diabetes, life is a constant act of readjusting expectations and activities to accommodate an ever-expanding patient role.

Advancing illness can threaten the self-concept. It may become difficult for them to maintain control of biological and social functioning. They may be incontinent (unable to control urination or bowel movements); they may drool, have distorted facial expressions, or shake uncontrollably. None of this is attractive either to the patient or to others.

These patients may also be in intermittent pain; may suffer from uncontrollable retching or vomiting; and may experience a shocking deterioration in appearance due to weight loss, the stress of treatments, or the sheer drain of illness. Even more threatening to some patients is mental regression and inability to concentrate. Cognitive decline accelerates in the years before death (Wilson, Beck, Bienias, & Bennett, 2007). Such losses may be due either to the progressive nature of the disease itself or to the tranquilizing and disorienting effects of painkillers.

Death

A DAUGHTER'S PERSPECTIVE

My father sleeps, I sit writing . . . trying to get something on paper I know is there, but which is as elusive and slippery as the life that's ending before me.

My father has cancer. Cancer of the sinuses, and as the autopsy will show later, of the left occipital lobe, mastoid, cerebellum. . . .

I have not seen my father for nine months, when the lump was still a secret below his ear. A few months later I heard about it and headaches, and then from time to time all the diagnoses of arthritis, a cyst, sinusitis . . . even senility. Then finally—the lump now a painful burden to be carried—he was subjected to nine days of tests of bowels, bladder, blood. And on the last day a hollow needle was inserted into the growth; the cells gathered, magnified, interpreted, and pronounced cancer. Immediate surgery and/or cobalt treatment indicated. . . .

And after the trauma of no dentures, no hearing aid, and one unexpected cobalt treatment, triumphant that his mind functioned and his voice was firm, he stated unfalteringly: "Let me alone. No more treatments. I am 75. I have had an excellent life. It is time for me to die in my own way." His decision was not to be met with approval. . . .

Death is not easy under any circumstances, but at least he did not suffer tubes and IVs and false hope, and we did not suffer the play-acting, the helpless agonies of watching a loved one suffer to no purpose, finally growing inured to it all or even becoming irritated with a dying vegetable that one cannot relate to any longer. In the end, I have learned, death is a very personal matter between parents and offspring, husbands and wives, loving neighbors and friends, and between God or symbols of belief and the dying ones and all who care about them.

Source: Carol K. Littlebrant. Selected excerpts from "Death is a Personal Matter," an essay originally published in *Newsweek,* January 12, 1976, under the name of Carol K. Gross. Used with permission of the author.

Issues of Social Interaction The threats to the self-concept that stem from loss of mental and physical functioning spill over into threats to social interaction. Although terminally ill patients often want and need social contact, they may be afraid that their obvious mental and physical deterioration will upset visitors. Family and friends can help make this withdrawal less extreme: They can prepare visitors in advance for the patient's state so that the visitor's reaction can be controlled; they can also screen out some visitors who cannot keep their emotions in check.

Some disengagement from the social world is normal and may represent the grieving process through which the final loss of family and friends is anticipated. This period of anticipatory grieving may exacerbate communication difficulties because it is hard for the patient to express affection for others while simultaneously preparing to leave them.

In other cases, withdrawal may be caused by fear of depressing others and becoming an emotional burden. The family may mistakenly believe that the patient wishes to be left alone and may therefore respect these wishes. Instead, family and friends may need to make a strong and concerted effort to draw out the patient, in part because depression appears to precipitate death (Herrmann et al., 1998; Wulsin, Vaillant, & Wells, 1999). Yet another cause of withdrawal may be the patient's bitterness over impending death and resentment of the living. In such cases, the family may need to understand that such bitterness is normal and that it usually passes.

Social interactions during the terminal phase of illness, then, are complex and often marked by the patient's gradual or intermittent withdrawal. In determining how to respond to this withdrawal, one must try to understand which of several reasons may be producing the behaviour.

Communication Issues As long as a patient's prognosis is favourable, communication is usually open; however, as the prognosis worsens and therapy becomes more drastic, communication may start to break down. Medical staff may become evasive when questioned about the patient's status. Family members may be cheerfully optimistic with the patient but confused and frightened when they try to elicit information from medical staff. The potential for a breakdown in communication as illness advances can be traced to several factors.

First, death itself is still a taboo topic in our society. The issue is generally avoided in polite conversation; little research is conducted on death; and even when death strikes within a family, the survivors often try to bear their grief alone. The proper thing to do, many people feel, is not to bring it up.

A second reason that communication may break down in terminal illness is because each of the participants—medical staff, patient, and family—may believe that others do not want to talk about the death. Moreover, each of the participants may have personal reasons for not wanting to discuss death as well. Some patients do not want to hear the answers to their un-asked questions because they know the answers and fear having to cope with the finality of having them confirmed. Family members may wish to avoid con-fronting any lingering guilt they have over whether they urged the patient to see a doctor soon enough or whether they did everything possible. Medical staff

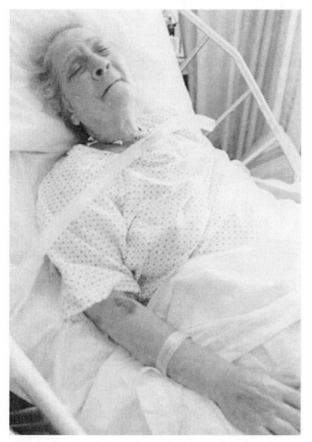

Many terminally ill patients who find themselves repeated objects of intervention become worn out and eventually refuse additional treatment.

may fear having to cope with the upset or angry re-proaches of family members or the patient over whether enough was done.

ARE THERE STAGES IN ADJUSTMENT TO DYING?

Do people pass through a predictable series of **stages of dying?**

Kübler-Ross's Five-stage Theory

More than forty years ago, psychiatrist Elisabeth Kübler-Ross (1969) suggested that people pass through five pre-dictable stages as they adjust to the prospect of death: denial, anger, bargaining, depression, and acceptance. Although this stage model has dominated the literature on death and dying, a lack of empirical support for the five-stage model has led some researchers to call into question its validity. By suggesting that adjustment to death follows a regimented process some suggest that the knowledge of the five-stage model may actually cre-ate more anxiety and fear about the process of dying (Konigsberg, 2011).

Nonetheless, the popularity of this model persists and it is still widely used in many end-of-life care set-tings. Accordingly, the next sections provide a very brief overview of this stage model of dying and grief as several of the stages are relevant for understanding the psycho-logical states of people who are dying regardless of their meaning within Kübler-Ross' model.

Denial   The first stage, *denial,* is thought to be a person's initial reaction on learning of the diagnosis of terminal illness. The diagnosis of a terminal illness can come as a shock to a person. And denial is a defence mechanism by which people avoid the implications of an illness. They may act as if the illness were not severe, as if it will shortly go away, or as if it will have few long-term implications. In extreme cases, the patient may even deny that he or she has the illness, despite having been given clear infor-mation about the diagnosis (Ditto et al., 2003). Denial, then, is the subconscious blocking out of the full realiza-tion of the reality and implications of the disorder.

Denial early on in adjustment to life-threatening illness is both normal and useful because it can protect a patient from the full realization of impending death (R. S. Lazarus, 1983). However, long-term denial of one's illness is a defensive pattern from which a patient should be coaxed through therapeutic intervention.

Anger   Denial usually abates because the illness itself creates circumstances that must be met. Decisions must be made regarding future treatments, if any, where the patient will be cared for, and by whom. At this point, according to Kübler-Ross, the second stage, *anger*, may set in. The angry patient is asking the question "Why me?" Considering all the other people who could have gotten the illness, all the people who had the same symptoms but got a favourable diagnosis, and all the people who are older, dumber, more bad-tempered, less productive, or just plain evil, why should the patient be the one who is dying?

Anger is one of the harder responses for family and friends to manage. They may feel they are being blamed by the patient for being well. The family may need to work together with a therapist to understand that the patient is not really angry with them but at fate; they need to see that this anger will be directed at anyone who is nearby, especially toward people with whom the patient feels no obligation to be polite and well-behaved. Unfortunately, family members often fall into this category.

Bargaining   *Bargaining* is the third stage of Kübler-Ross's formulation. At this point, the patient abandons anger in favour of a different strategy: trading good behaviour for good health. Bargaining frequently takes the form of a pact with God, in which the patient agrees to engage in good works or at least to abandon selfish ways in exchange for health or more time. A sudden rush of charitable activity or uncharacteristically pleasant behaviour may be a sign that the patient is trying to strike such a bargain.

Depression   *Depression,* the fourth stage in Kübler-Ross's model, may be viewed as coming to terms with lack of control. Recall from Chapter 6 the links between helplessness and depression. The patient acknowledges that little can now be done to stay the course of illness. This realization may be coincident with a worsening of symptoms, tangible evidence that the illness is not going to be cured. At this stage, patients may feel nauseated, breathless, and tired. They may find it hard to eat, to control elimination, to focus attention, and to escape pain or discomfort.

Kübler-Ross refers to the stage of depression as a time for "anticipatory grief," when patients mourn the prospect of their own deaths. The stage of depression, though far from pleasant, can be functional in that patients begin to prepare for what will come in the future. As a consequence, it may sometimes be wise not to intervene immediately with depression but, rather, to let it run its course, at least for a brief time. However, this advice obviously does not extend to clear cases of pathological depression, in which the patient is continually morose, unresponsive to friends and family, unable to eat, and basically uninterested in activity. In these cases, a therapist may have to intervene. In so doing, however, it is important that depression be distinguished from further physical deterioration. In advanced illness, patients often have so little energy that they cannot discharge activities on their own. Disentangling end-of-life depression from behaviours associated with a deteriorating physical state is therefore particularly challenging.

Acceptance   The fifth stage in Kübler-Ross's theory is *acceptance.* At this point, the patient may be too weak to be angry and too accustomed to the idea of dying to be depressed. Instead, a tired, peaceful, though not necessarily pleasant calm may descend. Some patients use this time to make preparations, deciding how to divide up their last personal possessions and saying goodbye to old friends and family members. At one point, researchers believed that "giving up" might actually hasten death. But research suggests that this is not the case (Skala & Freedland, 2004; G. Smith, 2006). In addition, "holding on" to survive through a holiday or other important event does not appear to occur reliably either (G. Smith, 2004).

Evaluation of Kübler-Ross's Theory

How good of an account of the process of dying is Kübler-Ross's stage theory? As a description of the reactions of dying patients, her work has been invaluable. Her work has also been useful for pointing out the counselling needs of the dying. Along with other researchers, she has broken through the silence and taboos surrounding death, making them objects of both scientific study and sensitive concern. As a stage theory, however, the work has several limitations. There is little if any empirical evidence to support the proposition that patients go through five stages at all or in a predetermined order (Konigsberg, 2011). Kübler-Ross's stage theory also does not fully acknowledge the importance of anxiety, which can be present throughout the dying process.

Is Kübler-Ross's stage theory wrong and some other stage theory correct, or is it simply inappropriate to talk about stages of dying? The answer is that no stage model can be infallibly applied to the process of dying. Dying is a complex and individual process, subject to no rules and few regularities.

WHAT ARE THE CONCERNS IN THE PSYCHOLOGICAL MANAGEMENT OF THE TERMINALLY ILL?

Medical Staff and the Terminally Ill Patient

Approximately 67 percent of Canadians die in hospitals each year (Statistics Canada, 2004a), a proportion that has increased significantly since the 1950s when just over half of Canadian deaths occurred in hospitals (D. M. Wilson et al., 2001). Unfortunately, death in the institutional environment can be depersonalized and fragmented. Wards may be understaffed, so the staff may be unable to provide the kind of emotional support the patient needs. Hospital regulations may restrict the number of visitors or the length of time that they can stay, thereby reducing the availability of support from family and friends. Pain is one of the chief symptoms in terminal illness, and in the busy hospital setting, the ability of patients to get the kind and amount of pain medication that they need may be compromised. Moreover, as we saw in Chapter 10, prejudices against drug treatments for pain still exist, so terminal patients run the risk of being undermedicated for their pain (Turk & Feldman, 1992a, 1992b). Death in an institution can be a long, lonely, mechanized, painful, and dehumanizing experience.

The Significance of Hospital Staff to the Patient   Hospital staff can come to be very significant to a patient. Physical dependence on hospital staff is great because the patient may need help for even the smallest thing, such as brushing teeth or turning over in bed. Patients are entirely dependent on medical staff for amelioration of their pain. Frequently, staff are the only people to see a dying patient on a regular basis if he or she has no friends or family who can visit regularly.

Moreover, staff can also be the only people who know the patient's actual physical state; hence, they are the patient's only source of realistic information. They may also know the patient's true feelings when others do not; often, patients put up a cheerful front for family and friends so as not to upset them. The patient, then, may welcome communication with staff because he or she can be fully candid with them. Finally, staff are important because they are privy to one of the patient's most personal and private acts, the act of dying.

Risk of Terminal Care for Staff   Terminal care is hard on hospital staff. It is the least interesting physical care be-

cause it is often **palliative care**—that is, care designed to make the patient feel comfortable—rather than **curative care**—that is, care designed to cure the patient's disease. **Terminal care** involves a lot of unpleasant custodial work, such as feeding, changing, and bathing the patient. Even more important is the emotional strain that terminal care places on staff. The staff may burn out from watching patient after patient die, despite their efforts.

Staff may be tempted to withdraw into a crisply efficient manner rather than a warm and supportive one so as to minimize their personal pain. Physicians, in particular, want to reserve their time for patients who can most profit from it. Consequently, they may spend little time with a terminally ill patient, yet terminally ill patients may interpret such behaviour as abandonment and take it very hard. Accordingly, a continued role for the physician in the patient's terminal care in the form of brief but frequent visits is desirable. The physician can interpret new and confusing physical changes and allay anxiety by providing information and a realistic timetable of events. The patient and the physician may also make decisions about subsequent medical interventions, such as the use of life support systems and the living will, as noted earlier.

One of the most controversial issues regarding patient–staff interaction during the terminal phase of illness concerns what information patients should be told about their illness. At one time, it was widely believed that patients did not want to know if they were terminally ill, although research subsequently proved that belief groundless. Nonetheless, great disparities remain regarding perceived preferences for information and beliefs about the amount of information that patients should have. For example, one study compared the perceptions of Canadian, European, and South American physicians' beliefs about the information that terminally ill cancer patients want. Almost all (93 percent) of the Canadian physicians believed that the majority of patients wanted to know if the prognosis was terminal, whereas only 26 percent of European physicians and 18 percent of South American physicians believed this. There were similar differences in perceptions regarding whether family members wanted to know the patients' stage of illness. However, all physicians agreed that they would want to be told if they had cancer and it was terminal (Bruera, Neumann, Mazzocato, Stiefel, & Sala, 2000).

Medical staff can be very significant to a dying patient because they see the patient on a regular basis, provide realistic information, and are privy to the patient's last personal thoughts and wishes.

Achieving an Appropriate Death Psychiatrist Avery Weisman (1972, 1977), who worked with dying patients for many years, outlined a useful set of goals for medical staff in their work with the dying:

1. *Informed consent*—Patients should be told the nature of their condition and treatment and, to some extent, be involved in their own treatment.

2. *Safe conduct*—The physician and other staff should act as helpful guides for the patient through this new and frightening stage of life.

3. *Significant survival*—The physician and other medical staff should help the patient use his or her remaining time as well as possible.

4. *Anticipatory grief*—Both the patient and his or her family members should be aided in working through their anticipatory sense of loss and depression.

5. *Timely and appropriate death*—The patient should be allowed to die when and how he or she wants to, as much as possible. The patient should be allowed to achieve death with dignity.

These guidelines, established many years ago, still provide the goals and means for terminal care. Unfortunately, a "good death" is still not available to all. A recent survey of the survivors of 1,500 people who had died found that dying patients most often did not get enough medication to ease their pain or enough emotional support. Open communication and lack of re-spect from medical staff were also two of the most common complaints (Teno, Fisher, Hamel, Coppola, & Dawson, 2002).

Individual Counselling with the Terminally Ill

Many patients need the chance to talk with someone about how they feel about themselves, their lives, their families, and death, and they need the opportunity to regain a sense of control over their lives. Typically, medical staff cannot devote the kind of time required for this support. Accordingly, therapy for dying patients is an available option.

Therapy with the dying is different from typical psychotherapy in several respects. First, for obvious reasons, it is likely to be short term. The format of therapy with the dying also varies from that of traditional psychotherapy. The nature and timing of visits must depend on the inclination and energy level of the patient, rather than on a fixed schedule of appointments. The agenda should be set at least partly by the patient. If an issue arises that the patient clearly does not wish to discuss, this wish should be respected.

Terminally ill patients may need help in resolving unfinished business. Uncompleted activities may prey on the mind, and preparations may need to be made for survivors, especially dependent children. Some **thanatologists**—that is, those who study death and dying—have suggested that behavioural and cognitive behavioural therapies can be constructively employed with dying patients (Sobel, 1981). For example, progressive muscle relaxation can ameliorate discomfort and instil a renewed sense of control. Positive self-talk, such as focusing on one's life achievements, can undermine the depression that often accompanies dying.

Therapy with the dying is challenging. It can be emotionally exhausting to become intimately involved with people who have only a short time to live. Few guidelines are available for **clinical thanatology**—that is, therapy with the dying. Nonetheless, such efforts can be important in that they can help the dying place their lives into perspective prior to death. Many people find meaning in **symbolic immortality,** a sense that one is leaving behind a legacy through one's children or one's work or that one is joining the afterlife and becoming one with God (Lifton, 1977). Thus, the last weeks of life can crystallize the meaning of a lifetime.

Dignity Therapy

Maintaining dignity at the end of life is an important issue that can be difficult to achieve for those receiving palliative care at home, in a hospice setting, or in a nursing home. Older people living in a nursing home often have multiple health problems, which means that they depend that much more on staff for their care. In addition, not being able to find the meaning in one's life as it nears its end is associated with a loss of dignity (Chochinov et al., 2002a).

Researchers at the University of Manitoba have addressed this issue by developing a unique brief psychotherapy intervention called "dignity therapy" to help enhance feelings of dignity and reduce distress for those in the final phase of life (Chochinov et al., 2005). Based on a model of dignity that was developed from interviews with hospice patients (Chochinov, Hack, McClement, Kristjanson, & Harlos, 2002b), **dignity therapy** involves a trained therapist such as a nurse or other health care worker recording an interview with the patient that invites them to discuss important issues and share anything that they would want remembered about themselves and their lives as death approaches. The interview questions provide a framework for the individual to articulate important personal topics such as one's life history, important life accomplishments and roles, instructions or words of advice to family members to provide them with comfort, and unsaid final words for loved ones. The interview, which can be conducted at the bedside, is then transcribed and edited, and then returned to the patient for their approval. The result of this process is a "generativity" document which forms a permanent record of the individual's life that can be shared with or bequeathed to anyone the patient chooses (Chochinov et al., 2005). This process aims to address concern or distress experienced in physical, psychosocial, spiritual, and existential domains to help rebuild dignity (Hall et al., 2009).

How effective is dignity therapy for resorting dignity among the terminally ill? In one study, terminally ill inpatients and patients receiving in-home palliative care who received dignity therapy reported an increased sense of dignity, meaning, purpose, and will to live (Chochinov et al., 2005). In addition, patients reported less suffering and depression post therapy, and that dignity therapy was useful to their families. In a follow-up study, family members of deceased terminally ill patients who had received dignity therapy provided feedback about the intervention (McClement et al., 2007). Overall, family members confirmed the benefits that patients reported receiving from the dignity therapy, and two-thirds agreed that the therapy was as important as any other part of care that their family member had received. In particular, family members reported that the generativity document provided comfort during their time of grief and that it would continue to be helpful for themselves and other family members.

Although preliminary, these findings indicate that dignity therapy shows promise as a means of addressing the distress and loss of dignity that can occur at the end of life. At the time of this writing, several randomized controlled trials were underway to provide a more rigorous test of the potential benefits of dignity therapy (Hall et al., 2009).

Family Therapy with the Terminally Ill

Sometimes, the preferable therapeutic route with dying patients is through the family. Dying does not happen in a vacuum but is often a family experience. As a consequence, family therapy can be an appropriate way to deal with the most common issues raised by terminal illness: communication, death-related plans and decisions, and the need to find meaning in life while making a loving and appropriate separation. Sometimes, the therapist will need to meet separately with family members as well as with the patient.

Family and patient may be mismatched in their adjustment to the illness. For example, family members may hold out hope, but the patient may be resigned to the prospect of death. Moreover, the needs of the living and the dying can be in conflict, with the living needing to maintain their resources and perform their daily activities at the same time that the patient needs a great deal of support. A therapist can help family members find a balance between their own needs and those of the patient.

Other conflicts may arise that require intervention. If a patient withdraws from some family members but not others, a therapist can anticipate the issues that may arise so that the patient's withdrawal is not misunderstood, becoming a basis for conflict. Both patients and family members may have difficulty saying what they mean to each other. Therapists can interpret what patients and family members are trying to express. For many families, terminal illness can be a time of great closeness and sharing. It may be the only time when the family sets aside time to say what their lives within the family have meant.

The Management of Terminal Illness in Children

Working with terminally ill children is perhaps the most stressful of all terminal care. First, it is often the hardest kind of death to accept. Hospital staff typically serve only limited rotations in units with terminally ill children because they find the work so psychologically painful. Death in childhood can also be physically painful, which adds to the distress it causes. Moreover, one must work not only with a confused and often frightened child but usually also with unhappy, frightened, and confused parents (Whittam, 1993).

It may often be difficult to know what to tell a child. Unlike adults, children may not express their knowledge, concerns, or questions directly. They may communicate the knowledge that they will die only indirectly, as by wanting to have Christmas early so that

they will be around for it. Or they may suddenly stop talking about their future plans:

> One child, who when first diagnosed said he wanted to be a doctor, became quite angry with his doctor when she tried to get him to submit to a procedure by explaining the procedure and telling him, "I thought you would understand, Sandy. You told me once you wanted to be a doctor." He screamed back at her, "I'm not going to be anything," and then threw an empty syringe at her. She said, "OK, Sandy." The nurse standing nearby said, "What are you going to be?" "A ghost," said Sandy, and turned over. (Bluebond-Langner, 1977, p. 59)

Counselling with a terminally ill child can, in certain respects, proceed very much like counselling with a terminally ill adult. The therapist can take cues of what to say directly from the child, talking only when the child feels like talking and only about what the child wants to talk about.

In many cases, it is not just the terminally ill child who requires some kind of counselling but the family as well. Parents may blame themselves for the child's disease, and, even in the best of cases, family dynamics are often severely disrupted by the terminal illness of a child. The needs of other children may go relatively

Hospice care, an alternative to hospital and home care for the terminally ill, is designed to provide personalized palliative treatment without the strains that home care can produce. This photograph shows a 73-year-old woman in a hospice, surrounded by photos of her family.

ignored, and they may come to feel confused and re-sentful about their own position in the family. Parents may have needs for assistance in coping that are getting ignored because of their child's needs. It may be difficult for parents to get good information about the nature of their child's treatment and prognosis. A therapist work-ing with the family can ameliorate these difficulties.

(L05) ## WHAT ARE THE ALTERNATIVES TO HOSPITAL CARE FOR THE TERMINALLY ILL?

Hospital care for the terminally ill is palliative, emotion-ally wrenching, and demanding of personalized atten-tion in ways that often go beyond the resources of the hospital. This has led to the development of treatment alternatives. As a result, two types of care have become increasingly popular: hospice care and home care.

Hospice Care

In the past two decades, **hospice care** has emerged as a type of care for the dying. It is estimated that currently 62 percent of the annual deaths in Canada will require hospice services, and that over the next 40 years this need will increase dramatically as a significant propor-tion of the population ages. The idea behind hospice care is the acceptance of death in a positive manner, em-phasizing the relief of suffering and or improvement of quality of life rather than the cure of illness. Hospice

care is designed to assist patients in gaining more con-trol over their lives, effectively manage pain, and pro-vide palliative care and emotional support to dying patients and their family members. Support for family members continues through the bereavement period (Canadian Hospice Palliative Care Association, 2006; see Figure 12.2).

In medieval Europe, a **hospice** was a place that pro-vided care and comfort for travellers. In keeping with this original goal, hospice care is both a philosophy con-cerning a way of dying and a system of care for the ter-minally ill. Hospice care may be provided in the home, but it is also commonly provided in free-standing or hospital-affiliated units called hospices. Typically, pain-ful or invasive therapies are discontinued. Instead, care is aimed toward managing symptoms, such as reducing pain and controlling nausea.

Most important, the patient's psychological com-fort is stressed. Patients are encouraged to personalize their living areas as much as possible by bringing in their own, familiar things. Thus, in institutional hospice care, each room may look very different, reflecting the personality and interests of its occupant. Patients also wear their own clothes and determine their own activi-ties in an effort to establish the kind of routine they might develop on their own at home.

Hospice care is particularly oriented toward im-proving a patient's social support system. Restrictions on visits from family or friends are removed as much as possible. Family may be encouraged to spend full days

FIGURE 12.2 | The Role of Hospice Palliative Care in End-of-Life-Care
Source: Canadian Hospice Palliative Care Association.

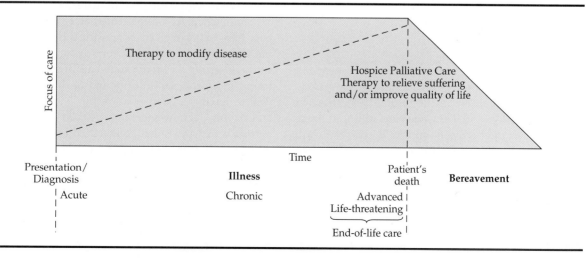

with the patient, to stay over in the hospice if possible, to eat together with the patient. Staff are especially trained to interact with patients in a warm, emotionally caring way. Usually, therapists are made available—either on an individual basis or through family therapy—to deal with such problems as communication difficulties and depression. Other hospices make use of volunteers who provide support to dying patients. Research suggests that patients who receive this type of support from volunteers live significantly longer than those who do not get this type of support (Herbst-Damm & Kulik, 2005).

When hospice care was first initiated, there was some concern that moving a patient to a facility that specialized in death—as hospices, in essence, do—would depress and upset both patients and family members. Such fears have largely proved groundless.

Evaluations of hospice care suggest that it can provide palliative care on a par with that in hospitals—and more emotionally satisfying care for both patients and their families. However, there are sometimes problems attracting trained nursing and medical staff to such units, because palliative care is less technically challenging than other forms of medical care (Sorrentino, 1992).

Although hospices were originally developed to be facilities separate from hospitals, their success as a treatment model has led to their increasingly being incorporated into traditional hospitals. In addition, many hospice programs now involve home care, with residential hospice care as a backup option. In many ways, this flexible program can meet all needs: Patients can remain home as long as the family members are able to manage it and receive professional care, once the patients' needs exceed the families' abilities.

Home Care

In recent years, we have witnessed renewed interest in **home care** for dying patients. And this interest is likely to increase dramatically in the future. It is estimated that by 2046 over 750,000 Canadians will need home care. However, if effective home care is available it will help lower long-term health care costs (Canadian Hospice Palliative Care Association, 2006).

Although home care would solve many logistical difficulties, the important question of quality of care arises. Can patients receive as competent care at home as in the hospital? Researchers who have examined this issue believe that usually they can, provided that there is

regular contact between medical personnel and family members and that the family is adequately trained.

Psychological factors are increasingly raised as legitimate reasons for home care. In contrast to the mechanized and depersonalized environment of the hospital, the home environment is familiar and comfortable. The patient is surrounded by personal items and by loving family rather than by medical staff. The ability to make small decisions, such as what to wear or what to eat, can be maintained. The strongest psychological advantages of home care, then, are the opportunity to maintain personal control and the availability of social support.

Caregiver Stress and Home Care Although home care is often easier on the patient psychologically, it can be very stressful for the family (Stajduhar, Martin, Barwich, & Fyles, 2008). Even if the family is able to afford around-the-clock nursing, often at least one family member's energies must be devoted to the patient on an almost full-time basis. Given work schedules and other daily tasks, it may be difficult for any family member to do this. Such constant contact with the dying person is also stressful. Family members may be torn between wanting to keep the patient alive and wanting the patient's suffering to be over.

Caregiver uncertainty can also contribute to the stress of having a family member die at home. Regardless of whether the uncertainty is medical, practical, psychosocial, or religious/spiritual, receiving clear information delivered in a patient-centred manner by health care professionals is key to managing this uncertainty (Hebert, Schulz, Copeland, & Arnold, 2009). Allowing caregivers time to mentally or emotionally prepare or even assigning behavioural tasks can also be beneficial to reduce caregiver related stress.

Both caregiver and patient characteristics can impact how well caregivers cope with the stress of dealing with a family member who is dying at home. One study of terminal cancer patients in British Columbia found that caregiver security and outlook on life, as well as having a good relationship with the patient and having acknowledgement of their efforts by the patient were factors that contributed to better coping with the stress of home care for a dying family member (Stajduhar, Martin, Barwich, & Fyles, 2008). Home care does, however, give the family an opportunity to share their feelings and to be together at this important time. These benefits may well offset the stresses, and studies often find that families prefer home to hospital care.

WHAT ISSUES DO SURVIVORS FACE?

The death of a family member may be the most upsetting and dreaded event in a person's life. For many people, the death of someone close is a more terrifying prospect than their own death or illness. Even when a death is anticipated and, on some level, actually wished for, it may be very hard for survivors to cope successfully.

We have already discussed several methods of helping families prepare for death. Family therapy, participation in a hospice program, and contact with sensitive medical staff members all help prepare the family. But few such programs can really help the family prepare for life after the death. Nonetheless, it is often at this point that family members need the most help, and it can be when they are least likely to get it (Hebert et al., 2009).

The weeks just before the patient's death are often a period of frenzied activity. Visits to the hospital increase, preliminary legal or funeral preparations may be made, last-minute therapies may be initiated, or the patient may be moved to another facility. Family members are kept busy by the sheer amount of work that must be done. Even after the patient dies, there is typically a great deal of work. Although there are large cultural differences in reactions to death and the formalities that follow (see the Health Psychology in Action box, "Cultural Attitudes toward Death"), typically funeral arrangements must be made, burial and tombstone details must be worked out, family members who have arrived for the services must be housed and fed, and well-intentioned friends who drop by to express their condolences must be talked to. Then, very abruptly, the activities cease. Visitors return home, the patient has been cremated or buried, and the survivor is left alone.

The Adult Survivor

During the period of terminal illness, the survivor's regular routine was probably replaced by illness-related activities. It may be hard to remember what one used to do before the illness began; even if one can remember, one may not feel much like doing it.

The survivor, then, is often left with lots of time and little to do but grieve. Moreover, the typical survivor is a widow in her sixties or older, who may have physical problems of her own. If she has lived in a traditional marriage, she may find herself with tasks to do, such as preparing her income tax return and making household repairs that she has never had to do before. Survivors may be left with few resources to turn to. Increasingly, psychological researchers are turning their attention to the problems experienced by the bereaved (for example, N. Stein, Folkman, Trabasso, & Richards, 1997; R. S. Weiss & Richards, 1997).

Grief, which is the psychological response to bereavement, is a feeling of hollowness, often marked by preoccupation with the image of the deceased person, expressions of hostility toward others, and guilt over the death. Bereaved people often show a restlessness and an inability to concentrate on activities, and experience yearning for their loved one, anger, depression, and other negative emotions, especially during the first six months after the loss (Maciejewski, Zhang, Block, & Prigerson, 2007). They may experience adverse physical symptoms as well (Vahtera et al., 2006).

It may be difficult for outsiders to appreciate the degree of a survivor's grief. They may feel that, especially if the death was a long time in coming, the survivor should be ready for it and thus show signs of recovery shortly after the death. Widows report that often, within a few weeks of their spouse's death, friends are urging them to pull out of their melancholy and get on with life. However, normal grieving may go on for months, and a large percentage of widows and widowers are still deeply troubled by their spouse's death several years later (W. Stroebe & Stroebe, 1987).

The question of whether it is adaptive to grieve or to avoid prolonged grief in response to a death has received research attention recently. In contrast to psychologists' usual caution that the avoidance of unpleasant emotion can be problematic, some emerging evidence suggests that emotional avoidance (Bonanno, Keltner, Holen, & Horowitz, 1995) and positive appraisals (N. Stein et al., 1997) actually lead to better adjustment in the wake of a death. Contrary to the traditional view that loss of a loved can only be a negative experience, recent theory and evidence suggest that the grieving period may also be accompanied by positive changes (Calhoun, Tedeschi, Cann, & Hanks, 2010). The disruption caused by loss may precipitate posttraumatic growth for some individuals as they come to view their relationships with new meaning and gain new spiritual insights as a result of their loss.

Bereaved adults who ruminate on their losses are less likely to have good social support, more likely to have higher levels of stress, and more likely to be

Cultural Attitudes toward Death

Each culture has its own way of coming to terms with death (Pickett, 1993; M. Stroebe, Gergen, Gergen, & Stroebe, 1992). Whereas in some cultures death is feared, in others it is seen as a normal part of life. Each culture, accordingly, has developed death-related ceremonies that reflect these cultural beliefs.

Canada's Aboriginal peoples view death as one of the four stages of the journey of the human spirit through the circle of life. For example, according to Anishnabe (Ojibway) traditions, each person is made up of three parts: spirit, mind, and body. When a person dies, Mother Earth reclaims their physical form, and the Creator takes the spirit and returns it to the place of origin to complete the cycle of life. Accordingly, end-of-life ceremonies and prayers guide the spirit from the physical to the spirit world. These can include pipe ceremonies and the burning of sacred medicines such as sage to purify the dying person and his or her family members. Other supportive ceremonies may also occur outside of the hospital, such as the purification or sweat lodge, and the sacred fire. Offerings of tobacco, cloth, or food are often made in the sacred fire to request a safe journey to the spirit world on behalf of the dying person. Funeral rites are usually performed by elders and spiritual leaders in the ceremonial lodge. Healing ceremonies are often conducted afterwards to help family and clan members let go of the spirit of the deceased (Longboat, 2002).

Within traditional Japanese culture, death is regarded as a process of travelling from one world to another. When someone dies, that person goes to a purer country, a place often described as beautifully decorated with silver, gold, and other precious metals. The function of death rituals is to help the spirit make the journey, and a series of rites and ceremonies takes place, aided by a minister, to achieve this end. The funeral events begin with a bedside service, in which the minister consoles the family. The next service is the Yukan, the bathing of the dead. An appreciation service follows the funeral, with food for all who have travelled long distances to attend. When the mourning period is over, a final party is given for friends and relatives as a way of bringing the mourners back into the community (Kübler-Ross, 1975).

The Andaman Islanders, in the Bay of Bengal, are one of many societies that respond to death with ritual weeping. Friends and relatives gather together with the mourners during the funeral to weep and show other signs of grief. This ritual of weeping is an expression of the bonds among individuals within the society and reaffirms these bonds when they are broken arbitrarily by

---

depressed (Nolen-Hoeksema, McBride, & Larson, 1997). The grief response appears to be more aggravated in men and in those whose loss was sudden and unexpected (Aneshenel, Botticello, & Yamamoto-Mitani, 2004). And it may be especially pronounced in mothers who have lost a child (Li et al., 2005).

Nonetheless, the majority of widows and widowers are resilient in response to their loss, especially if the partner's death had been long and they had had the opportunity to accept its inevitability (Bonnano et al., 2002).

Although many women have short-term difficulties adjusting to widowhood (Vahtera et al., 2006), over the long term the majority do well, with social support being a chief resource from which they draw (Wilcox et al., 2003). In addition, commitment to living is an important factor associated with the well-being of widowed women (O'Rourke, 2004). Among women who are depressed in widowhood, financial strain appears to be the biggest burden. For men, the strains associated with household management can lead to distress (Umberson, Wortman, & Kessler, 1992). As we will see in Chapter 14, the experience of bereavement can lead to adverse changes in immunologic functioning, increasing the risk of disease and even death (Gerra et al., 2003; Goforth et al., 2009). In addition, increases in alcohol and drug abuse are common among survivors (Brent, Melhem, Donohoe, & Walker, 2009). Programs designed to provide counselling to the bereaved have the potential to offset these adverse reactions.

The Child Survivor

Explaining the death of a parent or sibling to a surviving child can be particularly difficult (Brent et al., 2009). As noted earlier, the child's understanding of death may be

death. Mourners are separated from the rest of society for a short time after the death; during this time, they become associated with the world of the dead. At the end of the mourning period, they are reunited with the rest of the community (Radcliffe-Brown, 1964).

In Hinduism, which is the main religion of India, death is not viewed as separate from life or as an ending. Rather, it is considered a continuous, integral part of life. Because Hindus believe in reincarnation, they believe that birth is followed by death and death by rebirth; every moment one is born and dies again. Thus, death is like any transition in life. The Hindus teach that one should meet death with tranquility and meditation. Death is regarded as the chief fact of life and a sign that all earthly desires are in vain. Only when an individual neither longs for nor fears death is that person capable of transcending both life and death and achieving nirvana—merging into unity with the Absolute. In so doing, the individual is freed from the fear of death, and death comes to be seen as a companion to life (Kübler-Ross, 1975).

What would people from another culture think about attitudes toward death in Canada if they were to witness our death practices? First, they would see that the majority of deaths take place in the hospital without the presence of close relatives, and with only nursing services provided. Death is a quiet, often unpainful event with the majority of people in an unconscious state for three days before slipping comfortably away. Once death has occurred, the corpse is promptly removed without the help of the bereaved, who see it again only after morticians have made it acceptable for viewing. In some cases, the corpse is cremated shortly after death and is never again seen by the family. A paid organizer, often a director of a funeral home, takes over much of the direction of the viewing and burial rituals, deciding matters of protocol and the timing of services. In most subcultures within Canada, a time is set aside when the bereaved family accepts condolences from visiting sympathizers. A brief memorial service is then held, after which the bereaved and their friends may travel to the cemetery, where the corpse or ashes are buried. Typically, there are strong social pressures on the friends and relatives of the deceased to show little sign of emotion. The family is expected to establish this pattern, and other visitors are expected to follow suit. A friend or relative who is out of control emotionally will usually withdraw from the death ceremony or will be urged to do so by others. Following the ceremony, there may be a brief get-together at the home of the bereaved, after which the mourners return home (Northcott & Wilson, 2001).

incomplete and as a consequence, the child may keep expecting the dead person to return. This is troubling both to the child and to other family members. Even if the child does understand that the dead person is not going to return, he or she may not understand why. The child may believe either that the parent intended to leave or that the parent left because the child was "bad." It may take counselling to make a child see that this conclusion is not true.

The death of a sibling raises particular complications, because many children have fervently wished, at one time or another, that a sibling were dead. When the sibling actually does die, the child may feel that he or she somehow caused it. The likelihood that this problem will arise may be enhanced if the sibling was ill for some time before death.

As one child remarked on learning of his sibling's death, "Good. Now I can have all his toys" (Bluebond-Langner, 1977, p. 63). Such reactions are typically only temporary and may exacerbate the sorrow or guilt the child feels later on:

> Lars was seven when his sister died of leukemia. He was never told that she was sick and when she did die, he was sent away to a relative. After the funeral he returned home to find his sister gone and his parents in a state of grief. No explanation was offered and Lars was convinced he had done something that caused his sister's death. He carried this burden of guilt with him until he was fifteen. Academically, he had many problems. His math and reading remained at about the second-grade level. His parents were concerned and cooperative, but it was impossible for them to identify the problem. After leukemia was discussed in a health science class, Lars hesitantly told the teacher his story. Lars wanted to believe that he was not responsible for his sister's death, but he needed to hear it directly from his parents. A

Grief involves a feeling of hollowness, a preoccupation with the deceased person, and guilt over the death. Often, outsiders fail to appreciate the depth of a survivor's grief or the length of time it takes to get over the bereavement.

conference was set up, and with the support of his teacher, Lars told his parents his feelings of guilt. The parents were astonished. They had no idea their son felt any responsibility. Through many tears, they told him the entire story and tried to reassure him that in no way was he responsible. In fact, he had been a source of comfort and support to both his sister and his parents. (Spinetta et al., 1976, p. 21)

In leading a child to cope with the death of a parent or a sibling, it is best not to wait until the death has actually occurred. Rather, the child should be prepared for the death, perhaps by drawing on the death of a pet or a flower to aid understanding (Bluebond-Langner, 1977). The child's questions about death should be answered as honestly as possible, but without unwanted detail. Providing only what is asked for when the timing is right is the best course.

Death Education

Some educators and researchers have maintained that one way to make surviving easier is to educate people about death earlier in their lives, before they have had much personal experience with it.

Because death has been a taboo topic, many people have misconceptions about it, including the idea that the dying wish to be left alone, without talking about their situation. Because of these concerns, some courses on dying, which may include volunteer work with dying patients, have been developed for university students. This approach is believed to eliminate myths and to promote realistic perceptions about what can be done to help the dying (Brabant & Kalich, 2008). A potential problem with such courses is that they may attract the occasional suicidal student and provide unintended encouragement for self-destructive leanings. Accordingly, some instructors have recommended confronting such problems head-on, in the hopes that they can be forestalled.

Whether university students are the best and the only population that should receive death education is another concern. Unfortunately, organized means of educating people outside the university system are few, so university courses remain one of the more viable vehicles for death education. Yet a book about death and dying, *Tuesdays with Morrie* (Albom, 1997), was a bestseller in recent years, a fact that underscores how much people want to understand death. Moreover, causes of death, especially diseases with high mortality, dominate the news (Adelman & Verbrugge, 2000). At present, though, the news and a few books are nearly all there is to meet such needs. Through **death education,** it may be possible to develop realistic expectations, both about what modern medicine can achieve and about the kind of care the dying want and need. ●

SUMMARY

Describe how death differs across the life span

- Causes of death vary over the life cycle. In infancy, congenital abnormalities and sudden infant death syndrome (SIDS) account for most deaths. From ages 1 to 15, the causes shift to external ones and childhood leukemia. In young adulthood, death is often due to auto accidents, suicide, cancer, and AIDS. In adulthood, cancer or sudden death due to heart attack is the most common cause of death. Death in old age is usually due to heart attacks, stroke, cancer, and physical degeneration.

- Concepts of death change over the life cycle. In childhood, death is conceived of first as a great sleep and later as a ghostlike figure that takes a person away. Finally, death is seen as an irreversible biological stage. Many believe that middle age is the time when people first begin to come to terms with their own death.

Know the psychological issues in advancing illness

- Advancing disease raises many psychological issues, including treatment-related discomfort and decisions of whether to continue treatment. Increasingly, issues concerning living wills (the patient's directive to withhold extreme life-prolonging measures), aid in dying, and euthanasia have been topics of concern in both medicine and law.

- Patients' self-concepts must continually change in response to the progression of illness, change in appearance, energy level, control over physical processes, and degree of mental alertness. The patient may withdraw from family and friends as a result. Thus, issues of communication are a focal point for intervention.

Identify the stages in adjustment to dying

- Kübler-Ross's theory of dying suggests that people go through a series of predictable stages, progressing through denial, anger, bargaining, depression, and finally acceptance. Research shows, however, that patients do not go through these stages in sequence but that all these phenomena describe reactions of dying people, to a degree.

Understand the concerns in the psychological management of the terminally ill

- Much of the responsibility for psychological management of terminal illness falls on medical staff. Medical staff can provide information, reassurance, and emotional support when others may not.

- Psychological counselling needs to be made available to terminally ill patients, because many need a chance to develop a perspective on their lives. Developing methods for training therapists in clinical thanatology, then, is an educational priority. Family therapy may be needed to soothe the problems of the family and to help the patient and family say goodbye to each other.

- Counselling terminally ill children is especially important because both parents and children may be confused and frightened. Families of dying children may need help in developing effective coping, which can be influenced by the medical environment.

Describe the alternatives to hospital care for the terminally ill

- Hospice care and home care are alternatives to hospital care for the dying. Palliative care in the home or in a homelike environment can have beneficial psychological effects on dying patients and their survivors.

Explain the issues survivors face

- Grief is marked by a feeling of hollowness, preoccupation with an image of the deceased person, guilt over the death, expressions of hostility toward others, and restlessness and inability to concentrate. Many people do not realize how long normal grieving takes.

KEY TERMS

clinical thanatology   p. 338
curative care   p. 337
death education   p. 346
dignity therapy   p. 339
euthanasia   p. 331
grief   p. 343
home care   p. 342

hospice   p. 341
hospice care   p. 341
infant mortality rate   p. 322
living wills   p. 331
palliative care   p. 337
premature death   p. 325
stages of dying   p. 335

sudden infant death syndrome
    (SIDS)   p. 323
symbolic immortality   p. 338
terminal care   p. 337
thanatologists   p. 338

CHAPTER

13

Heart Disease, Hypertension, Stroke, and Diabetes

LEARNING OBJECTIVES

After reading this chapter, students will be able to:

(LO1) Describe coronary heart disease (CHD)

(LO2) Explain hypertension

(LO3) Understand stroke

(LO4) Describe diabetes

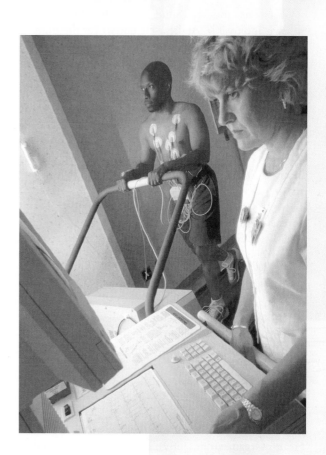

Andrea's father had a heart attack during her junior year in university. It was not entirely a surprise. He was overweight, suffered from hypertension, and had diabetes—all of which are risk factors for heart disease. Fortunately, the heart attack was a mild one, so after a brief hospitalization, he returned home and began a program of cardiac rehabilitation.

Many aspects of his life required change. Although he had always had to watch his diet, dietary intervention now became especially important to his recovery. Previously, he had enjoyed watching sports from his armchair, but he now found that he had to take up physical exercise. And the cigarettes he had always enjoyed were out of the question. On weekends, Andrea called to make sure everything was okay.

First, her mother would get on the phone. "Your father is impossible, Andrea. He doesn't eat the things I fix for him, and he's not doing the exercise he's supposed to be doing. He stops after about five minutes. I think he's even sneaking a cigarette when he goes out to run errands."

Then Andrea's father would get on the phone. "Your mother is driving me crazy. It's like having a spy following me around all the time. I can't do anything without her getting on my case, constantly nagging me about my heart. My blood pressure's going up just having to deal with her."

Unfortunately, Andrea's parents' situation is not unusual. Adjustment to chronic disease, as we have seen, is a difficult process, and one that often requires major changes in lifestyle that are very difficult to make.

In this chapter, we take up four major chronic disorders: heart disease, hypertension, stroke, and diabetes. All four involve the circulatory and/or metabolic system and often represent co-occurring disorders, especially in older adults. For example, heart disease and stroke are two dangerous complications associated with diabetes. Moreover, heart disease and stroke are part of a group of disorders of the heart and blood vessels referred to as cardiovascular disease (CVD), which are now the number one cause of death worldwide (World Health Organization, 2009). From a health psychology perspective, all four conditions involve modifiable risk factors as they are largely diseases of lifestyle that can be prevented by changing health habits such as diet and exercise. As such, the World Health Organization (2011) has termed these and other chronic disorders non-communicable diseases.

WHAT IS CORONARY HEART DISEASE?

(L01)

Coronary heart disease (CHD) is the number two killer in Canada, accounting for more than one out of every five deaths in 2007 (Statistics Canada, 2010b). It was not a major cause of illness and death until the twentieth century; in earlier decades, most people died of infectious diseases, so many people did not live long enough to develop heart disease.

But CHD is also a disease of modernization, due at least in part to the alterations in diet and reduction in activity level that have accompanied modern life. Because of these factors, around the turn of the twentieth century, coronary heart disease began to increase, although it has recently begun to level off. Nonetheless, it is estimated that, in Canada, CHD accounts for about 20 percent of deaths in men and over 22 percent of deaths in women. One of the most significant aspects of CHD is that a number of the deaths that occur each year are premature deaths; that is, they occur well before age 75 (Statistics Canada, 2010b).

In addition to its high death rate, CHD is also a major chronic disease. Thousands of Canadians live with the diagnosis and symptoms. Because of its great frequency and the toll it takes on relatively young people, identifying the biological, individual, and social determinants and cures of heart disease has been a high priority of health research in Canada.

Understanding CHD

Coronary heart disease (CHD) is a general term that refers to illnesses caused by atherosclerosis, the narrowing of the coronary arteries, the vessels that supply the heart with blood. As we saw in Chapter 2, when these vessels become narrowed or closed, the flow of oxygen and nourishment to the heart is partially or completely obstructed. Temporary shortages of oxygen and nourishment frequently cause pain, called angina pectoris, which radiates across the chest and arm. When severe deprivation occurs, a heart attack (myocardial infarction) can result.

A number of factors are involved in the development of coronary artery disease (see Chapter 2). Research has especially implicated inflammatory processes in the development of the disease (Kop & Gottdiener, 2005; Rana et al., 2011). A particular proinflammatory cytokine (IL-6) is thought to play a role in heart disease by stimulating processes that contribute to the buildup of atherosclerotic plaque (Suarez, 2003). Low-grade inflammation appears to underlie many, if not most, cases of cardiovascular disease. A particularly strong predictor of heart disease is the level of C-reactive protein in the bloodstream, which assesses inflammatory activity (Ridker, Rifai, Rose, Buring, & Cook, 2002). C-reactive protein is produced in the liver and released in the bloodstream in the presence of acute or chronic inflammation. Because inflammation can promote damage to the walls of the blood vessels, C-reactive protein is a prognostic sign that this damage may be occurring and that may not be related to other risk factors for heart disease. Recent research also indicates that increased waist circumference and low levels of physical activity, both risk factors for CHD, are associated with elevated levels of C-reactive protein and other inflammatory markers (Rana et al., 2011). As a result of research like this, coronary heart disease is now considered to be a systemic disease rather than a disease of the coronary arteries because it is responsive to inflammatory processes.

Other risk factors for CHD include high blood pressure, diabetes, cigarette smoking, obesity, high serum cholesterol level, and low levels of physical activity (Heart and Stroke Foundation of Canada, 2003). Exposure to air pollution is a recently identified risk factor (e.g., K. A. Miller et al., 2007). Identifying patients with metabolic syndrome also helps predict heart attacks. **Metabolic syndrome** is diagnosed when a person has three or more of the following problems: obesity centred around the waist; high blood pressure; low levels of HDL, the so-called good cholesterol; difficulty metabolizing blood sugar, an indicator of risk for diabetes; and high levels of triglycerides, which are related to bad cholesterol. High cardiovascular reactivity may also be a component of this cluster (Waldstein & Burns, 2003). Routine screening for metabolic syndrome and inflammation (by assessing C-reactive protein) is increasingly recommended for most middle-aged adults.

Heart disease also has a family history component. This component may include a genetically based predisposition to cardiovascular reactivity, which may emerge early in life (Boyce, Alkon, et al., 1995; Yamada et al., 2002) and which is exacerbated by low socio-economic status and a harsh early family environment (Lehman, Taylor, Kiefe, & Seeman, 2005). Exposure to stress and difficulties developing strong relationships may explain why these factors are related to early cardiovascular risk (Gallo & Matthews, 2006; Goodman et al., 2005). For example, in young adolescents and especially those from low socio-economic groups, risk factors for heart disease

cluster by age 14 (Goodman et al., 2005; Lawlor et al., 2005). However, taking all known risk factors together accounts for less than half of all newly diagnosed cases of CHD; accordingly, a number of risk factors remain to be identified that could target people who are at risk for CHD early in the disease process.

Role of Stress

Extensive research links chronic stress to coronary heart disease (Phillips, Carroll, Ling, Sweeting, & West, 2005; Vitaliano et al., 2002). Cardiovascular reactivity contributes to the development of coronary heart disease in part by damaging endothelial cells, which facilitates the deposit of lipids, increases inflammation, and ultimately contributes to the development of atherosclerotic lesions (McDade, Hawkley, & Cacioppo, 2006; T. W. Smith & Ruiz, 2002; Treiber et al., 2003).

Acute stress involving emotional stress, anger, or extreme excitement (Strike & Steptoe, 2005), negative emotions, and sudden bursts of activity can precipitate sudden clinical events, such as a heart attack, angina, or even sudden death (Lane et al., 2006; Nicholson, Fuhrer, & Marmot, 2005). Reactivity to stress or coping with it via hostility may interact with other risk factors, such as elevated cholesterol level, to enhance overall risk (for example, Pradhan, Rifai, & Ridker, 2002).

Heart disease is more common in individuals low in socio-economic status (SES), especially males (see Figure 13.1), and the symptoms and signs of cardiovascular disease develop earlier. These patterns are believed to reflect the higher rates of physical inactivity, smoking, elevated cholesterol, and being overweight among those in the lowest socio-economic groups (Choinière, Lafontaine, & Edwards, 2000).

As already noted, CHD is a disease of modernization and industrialization. As we saw in Chapter 6, occupational stress has been related to its incidence (Chandola et al., 2008). In addition to the direct effects discussed above, there is evidence that the indirect effects of stress may be responsible for the links between work related stress and heart disease. One study found that higher work stress was associated with low physical activity and poor diet which in turn increased risk for experiencing an angina or a heart attack (Chandola et al., 2008). Research has also suggested that the balance of control and demand in daily life more generally (not only at work) is a risk for atherosclerosis. That is, people whose lives are characterized by high levels of demands coupled with low levels of control outside the workplace

FIGURE 13.1 | Number of Cardiovascular Disease Deaths in Canada by Sex, Actual and Projected, 1950–2025

Source: Heart and Stroke Foundation of Canada (2003), *The Growing Burden of Heart Disease and Stroke in Canada 2003*, Ottawa, 1-896242-30-8 (English), www.cvdinfobase.ca/cvdbook/CVD_En03.pdf.

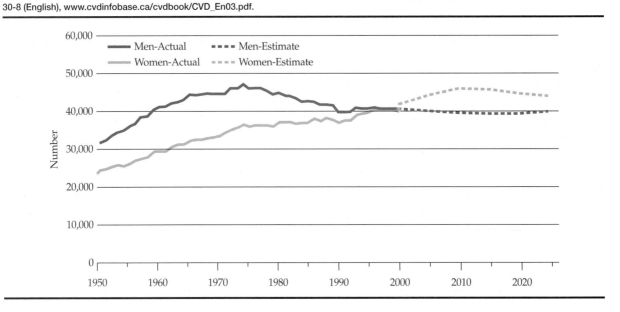

experience a higher risk for atherosclerosis (Kamarck et al., 2004; Kamarck, Muldoon, Shiffman, & Sutton-Tyrrell, 2007).

Stress due to social instability may also be tied to higher rates of CHD. Urban and industrialized countries have a higher incidence of CHD than do underdeveloped countries. Migrants have a higher incidence of CHD than do geographically stable individuals, and acculturation to Western society is a risk factor for high blood pressure. Distress associated with cultural change is linked to increase risk factors for CHD (Steffen, Smith, Larson, & Butler, 2006; Lutsey et al., 2008). And in general, poor social support is associated with increased risk for CHD (Kop & Gottdiener, 2005).

Women and CHD

Coronary heart disease is a leading killer of women in Canada and most other developed countries (World Health Organization, 2011). In 2003, it accounted for 37 percent of all female deaths. Studies of risk factors, diagnosis, prognosis, and rehabilitation have all focused primarily on men. Less is known about patterns of women's heart disease (Burell & Granlund, 2002). Although heart disease typically occurs later for women, it is more dangerous when it does occur, as women are less likely to recover from a cardiac event compared to men

(Heart and Stroke Foundation, 1997). Fewer women are referred to see a cardiologist than men after experiencing a heart attack (32 percent versus 38 percent), and more women (17 percent) die after being admitted to the hospital for heart problems than men (less than 10 percent). Thirty-four percent of women with heart disease are unable to work due to disability, compared with only 28 percent of men (Heart and Stroke Foundation of Canada, 1999; see Figure 13.2). Clearly, women experience a more compromised quality of life from heart disease than do men, and much of this is attributable to existing inequities in socio-economic status.

Women seem to be protected at young ages against coronary disease relative to men. One reason may be their higher levels of high-density lipoprotein (HDL), which appears to be linked to premenopausal women's higher levels of estrogen. Estrogen also diminishes sympathetic nervous system arousal, which may add to the protective effect against heart disease seen in women (K. A. Matthews & Rodin, 1992); in response to stress, premenopausal women show smaller increases in blood pressure, neuroendocrine, and some metabolic responses than do men and older women.

However, women experience a higher risk of cardiovascular disease after menopause (Vaccarino et al., 2011). They typically gain weight during menopause, and this weight gain may partly explain the enhanced

FIGURE 13.2 | Proportion of Canadian Population Aged 35 to 64 with Self-reported Heart Disease Who Have Chronic Pain, Activity Restriction, Disability, or Unemployment, 1996/97

Heart disease significantly impacts quality of life in both men and women, although more women experience these effects.

(*Source:* Heart and Stroke Foundation, 1999. *The changing face of heart disease and stroke in Canada 2000.* Ottawa: Public Health Agency of Canada. ISBN 1-896242-28-6 [English])

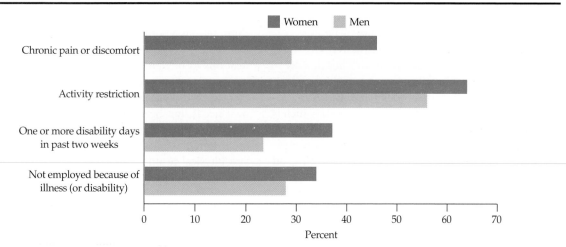

risk; increases in blood pressure, cholesterol, and triglycerides, also risk factors for CHD (Wing, Matthews, Kuller, Meilahn, & Plantinga, 1991), may also occur. However, the belief that estrogen replacement therapy (HRT) following menopause would keep rates of CHD among women low has not been supported by research (Toh, Hernández-Díaz, Logan, Rossouw, & Hernán, 2010). Consequently, the relation of estrogen to heart disease remains unclear.

The fact that women have been so underexamined in research on CHD has meant not only that we know less about women's heart disease and its treatment but also that until recently less information about women's heart disease has been present in the media, leaving women misinformed about their health risks (S. Wilcox & Stefanick, 1999). Women are less likely to receive counselling about heart disease than men or learn about the benefits of exercise, nutrition, and weight reduction in preventing heart disease (Stewart, Abbey, Shnek, Irvine, & Grace, 2004). Women are significantly less likely than men to receive and use drugs for the treatment of heart disease including aspirin, beta blockers, and lipid lowering agents (Vittinghoff et al., 2003), and they are also more likely to not be diagnosed or to be misdiagnosed (Chiaramonte & Friend, 2006).

These disparities may be due in part to inaccurate common sense models of illness that people hold about

how men and women differ in symptom reporting (see Chapter 8). In one study, participants who were presented with separate scenarios of men and women who reported chest pain perceived that medical intervention was less important for the female versus the male patient (Martin & Lemos, 2002). Interestingly, gender differences in the reporting of CHD symptoms do exist with women generally reporting more back pain, palpitations, nausea/vomiting, and loss of appetite during an acute episode than men (Shin et al., 2010).

What research there is suggests that CHD risk factors in women are relatively similar to those in men. As is true of men, social support, especially in the marriage, is associated with less advanced disease in women (Gallo, Troxel, Kuller, et al., 2003a). Hostility is linked to poor cardiovascular recovery from stress (e.g., Neumann et al., 2004), and poor prognosis (Olsen et al., 2005), as is pessimism (Matthews, Räikkönen, Sutton-Tyrrell, & Kuller, 2004). Progression of atherosclerosis in women is also predicted by anger and metabolic syndrome (Räikkönen, Matthews et al., 2004). Among women, depression is a risk factor for metabolic syndrome, a precursor of heart disease (Kinder, Carnethon, Palaniappan, King, & Fortmann, 2004; Rutledge et al., 2006). Some of the job-related factors that predict coronary heart disease in men may also be predictors for women as well (Lallukka et al., 2006). Employment

Can Male and Female Qualities Affect Your Health?

As scientists have explored the risk factors for the development of coronary heart disease, for the most part they have examined factors that may characterize both men and women. However, recently researchers have begun to realize that there may be personality qualities associated with masculine or feminine construals of the world that may be differentially associated with health risks.

In particular, research has focused on *agency*, which is a focus on the self, versus *communion*, which is a focus on others, and on *unmitigated communion*, which is an extreme focus on others to the exclusion of the self. Men typically score higher than women do on measures of agency. Agency has been associated with good physical and mental health outcomes in several studies

(Helgeson, 1993; Helgeson & Fritz, 1999; Helgeson & Lepore, 1997), and it is associated with reduced psychological distress.

Communion, a focus on other people in relationships, reflects a positive caring orientation to others, and it is typically higher in women than in men. It has few relations to mental and physical health outcomes. Unmitigated communion, however, exemplified in a self-sacrificing individual who fails to focus on his or her own needs, has been tied to adverse health outcomes. Like communion, it is higher in women than it is in men, but it is reliably associated with poorer mental and physical health outcomes (Fritz, 2000; Helgeson, Escobar, Siminerio, & Becker, 2007).

---

as a clerical worker as opposed to a white-collar worker enhances risk for coronary artery disease (Gallo, Troxel, Matthews, et al., 2003b). See the Health Psychology in Action box, "Can Male and Female Qualities Affect Your Health?" for a discussion of other factors that may affect men's and women's heart disease rates.

Relatively little is known about the differences in men's and women's responses to treatment. Women do not experience the same quality of life following coronary bypass surgery as men do (Bute et al., 2003). Women experience more anxiety after a heart attack than men do, which may go unrecognized or untreated (Moser et al., 2003). Compared to men, women are more likely to be referred to long-term-care facilities rather than sent home or admitted to a rehabilitation program after a heart attack (Heart and Stroke Foundation, 1997). Not surprisingly, female cardiac patients experience poorer quality of life than men do (Emery et al., 2004; see Figure 13.2).

Much of what we have learned about women's heart disease has come from long-term clinical studies, such as the Nurses' Health Study, and this study presents some basis for cautious optimism regarding women and CHD. The Nurses' Health Study began in 1976, when more than 120,000 female nurses, then between ages 30 and 55, participated in a long-term study of medical history and lifestyle (Nurses' Health Study, 2004). Over the past 25 years, the expected incidence of heart disease in this sample has not appeared—in large part because more older women have stopped smoking and have changed

their diets in healthy directions (C. M. Stoney, Owens, Guzick, & Matthews, 1997). Indeed, among women who have adhered to recommended guidelines involving diet, exercise, and abstinence from smoking, there is a very low risk of coronary heart disease (Stampfer, Hu, Manson, Rimm, & Willett, 2000). As levels of obesity increase in this population, the incidence of heart disease may rise again (Hu et al., 2000), but at present, the study is testimony to the payoffs of good health habits.

Critical Checkpoint

Gender Differences in the Effects of Cardiovascular Disease

As discussed, research suggests that there are differences in how men and women are affected by cardiovascular disease. Notably, women are more likely to die from heart disease and from a heart attack after being admitted to the hospital. They also experience poorer quality of life due to heart disease compared to men. What factors might account for these differences and what, if anything, can be done to address this issue?

Hostility and Cardiovascular Disease

Research has implicated cynical hostility as a psychological culprit in the development of cardiovascular disease. Many studies have employed measures of hostility to look at this association. Some sample items are below:

1. I don't matter much to other people.
2. People in charge often don't really know what they are doing.
3. Most people lie to get ahead in life.
4. People look at me like I'm incompetent.
5. Many of my friends irritate me with the things they do.
6. People who tell me what to do frequently know less than I do.
7. I trust no one; life is easier that way.
8. People who are happy most of the time rub me the wrong way.
9. I am often dissatisfied with others.
10. People often misinterpret my actions.

Cardiovascular Reactivity, Hostility, and CHD

Anger and hostility are implicated as risk factors for CHD (Bleil, McCaffery, Muldoon, Sutton-Tyrrell, & Manuck, 2004; Schum, Jorgensen, Verhaeghen, Sauro, & Thibodeau, 2003). A proneness to the expression of anger has been implicated not only as a potential risk factor for the development of heart disease (Gallacher, Yarnell, Sweetnam, Elwood, & Stansfeld, 1999) but also as a predictor of survival (Boyle et al., 2004), and as a potential trigger for heart attack (Moller et al., 1999). As we will see, anger has also been implicated in hypertension and to a lesser degree in stroke and diabetes as well, suggesting that it may be a general risk factor for coronary heart disease, cardiovascular disease, and their complications. Hostility has been tied to higher levels of proinflammatory cytokines and to the metabolic syndrome, which may explain its relation to coronary heart disease (Niaura et al., 2002).

A particular type of hostility may be especially implicated—namely, cynical hostility, characterized by suspiciousness, resentment, frequent anger, antagonism, and distrust of others. Individuals who have negative beliefs about others, including the perception that other people are being antagonistic or threatening, are often highly verbally aggressive and exhibit subtly antagonistic behaviour. Such individuals may have difficulty extracting (Benotsch, Christensen, & McKelvey, 1997) and making effective use of the social support that they need from their environment (Lepore, 1995; see the Health Psychology in Action box, "Hostility and Cardiovascular Disease"). People high in cynical hostility also appear to have more conflict with others, more negative affect, and more resulting sleep disturbance, which may further contribute to their risk (Brissette & Cohen, 2002).

Hostility combined with defensiveness may be particularly problematic for adverse cardiovascular changes (Guerrero & Palmero, 2010). Specifically, people who are both hostile and defensive (that is, who do not report socially undesirable aspects of themselves) show the greatest association between cardiovascular response under stressful situations (Guerrero & Palmero, 2010).

Who Is Hostile? Overall, men show higher hostility in general relative to women, indicating that hostility may be an important risk factor for men in particular. One large community-based study in the United Kingdom found that hostility was significantly associated with a variety of CHD risk factors including cholesterol levels in white men but was unrelated to CHD risk factors in women (E. D. Williams, Steptoe, Chambers, & Kooner, 2011). Higher hostility is also found among non-whites and those of lower socio-economic status (Barefoot, 1992; Siegman, Townsend, Civelek, & Blumenthal, 2000).

Developmental Antecedents Hostility reflects an oppositional orientation toward people that is developed in childhood, stemming from feelings of insecurity about oneself and negative feelings toward others (Houston & Vavak, 1991). Consistent with this point, research has suggested that particular child-rearing practices may foster hostility—specifically, parental interference, punitiveness, lack of acceptance, conflict, or abuse. Family environments that are nonsupportive, unaccepting, and high in conflict tend to promote the development of hostility in sons (K. A. Matthews, Woodall, Kenyon, & Jacob, 1996). Hostility runs in families and both genetic and environmental factors appear to be implicated

(Weidner et al., 2000). Hyperactivity in childhood may also predict adult risk for hostility (Keltikanagas-Järvinen et al., 2006).

Expressing versus Harbouring Hostility   Is hostility lethal as a psychological state or only in its expression? Research suggests that the expression of hostile emotions, such as anger and cynicism, may be more reliably associated with enhanced cardiovascular reactivity than is the state of anger or hostility (Siegman & Snow, 1997). However, suppressing hostility may be even more detrimental. One study found that among hostile individuals, those who suppressed hostility interpersonally had higher cardiovascular reactivity than those who expressed hostility interpersonally (Kline, Fekete, & Sears, 2008). Although anger suppression and hostile attitudes have been related to atherosclerosis in women (K. A. Matthews, Owens, Kuller, Sutton-Tyrrell, & Jansen-McWilliams, 1998), the relation between hostile style and enhanced cardiovascular reactivity to stress may not be as reliable for women as for men (K. W. Davidson, Hall, & Mac Gregor, 1996).

Hostility and Social Relationships   Hostile individuals have more interpersonal conflict in their lives and less social support, and this fallout may also contribute to their risk for disease. Their reactivity to stress seems especially to be engaged during these episodes of interpersonal conflict. For example, in one study, 60 couples participated in a discussion under conditions of high or low threat of evaluation by others while they were either agreeing or disagreeing with each other. Husbands who were high in hostility showed a greater blood pressure reactivity in response to stressful marital interaction in response to threat; the same relationship was not found for wives, however (T. W. Smith & Gallo, 1999; see also Newton & Sanford, 2003).

Hostile people may produce or seek out more stressful interpersonal encounters in their daily lives and, at the same time, undermine the effectiveness of their social support network (J. Allen, Markovitz, Jacobs, & Knox, 2001). However when hostile individuals receive offers of social support they may view these offers as stressful rather than supportive (Vella, Kamarck, & Shiffman, 2008). Researchers are uncertain whether the enhanced CHD risk of hostile people is caused by the deficits in social support that hostility produces, by the hostile anger itself, or by the underlying cardiovascular reactivity that hostility may reflect.

Hostility and Reactivity   Some health psychologists now suspect that hostility is, at least in part, a social manifestation of cardiovascular reactivity and the likelihood of overresponding sympathetically to stressful circumstances. Among the evidence suggesting this relation are findings that cardiovascular reactivity in social situations explains the relation between hostility and the development of coronary heart disease (Guyll & Contrada, 1998). That is, when a hostile person is provoked in interpersonal situations, the hostility–hyperreactivity relation is seen (Suls & Wan, 1993). Chronically hostile people show more pronounced physiological reactions in response to interpersonal stressors (Guyll & Contrada, 1998).

Hostile individuals appear to exhibit a weak antagonistic response to sympathetic activity in response to stress, suggesting that their reactivity to stress is not only greater initially but also may last longer (Nelson et al., 2005). In response to provocation, hostile individuals have larger and longer-lasting blood pressure responses to anger-arousing situations (B. L. Fredrickson et al., 2000; Suarez et al., 1997). Hostile individuals also show different patterns of immune activation in response to sympathetic activation, which may further contribute to an accelerated development of heart disease (Graham, Robles, Kiecolt-Glaser, Malarkey, Bissell, & Glaser, 2006). When paired with anger and depression, hostility predicts high levels of C-reactive protein (Suarez, 2004).

The fact that hostility may reflect underlying tendencies toward cardiovascular reactivity in stressful circumstances does not undermine or deny the importance of childhood environment in the development of hostility or the significance of the social environment in eliciting it. For example, to the extent that hostility reflects a genetically based underlying physiological reactivity, parents and children predisposed to reactivity may create and respond to the family environment differently. For reactivity to assume the form of hostility, particular environmental circumstances—such as the parental child-rearing practices noted earlier or the interpersonal conflictual stressful circumstances that evoke hostile behaviour—may need to be in place. Consequently, the reactivity–hostility relationship may be thought of as a biopsychosocial process.

Mechanisms Linking Reactivity and Psychological Factors   How might greater physiological and psychological reactivity in conflictive situations promote heart disease? In some individuals, stress causes vasorestriction in peripheral areas of the heart and at the same time accelerates heart rate (Lovallo & Gerin, 2003). Thus, these individuals attempt to transfer more and more blood through ever-shrinking vessels. Presumably, this process produces wear and tear on the coronary arteries, which, in turn, produces atherosclerotic lesions. Blood pressure variability may have adverse effects on the endothelial tissue of the coronary arteries and may promote plaque formation (Sloan, Shapiro, Bagiella, Myers, & Gorman, 1999).

Catecholamines exert a direct chemical effect on blood vessels. The rise and fall of catecholamine levels, as may occur in chronic or recurrent exposure to stress, may prompt continual changes in blood pressure that undermine the resilience of the vessels. Whether the effect of the catecholamines on the endothelial cells that maintain the integrity of the vessels is a mechanism that links psychosocial factors to coronary heart disease is not yet known (K. F. Harris & Matthews, 2004). Sympathetic activation also causes lipids to be shunted into the bloodstream, another possible contributor to atherosclerosis. Low levels of tonic vagal cardiac control may impede recovery from stress and act as another mechanism increasing the risk of cardiovascular disease (Mezzacappa, Kelsey, Katkin, & Sloan, 2001). Hostility is also related to increased lipid profiles (Richards, Hof, & Alvarenga, 2000) and increased platelet activation in coronary heart disease patients, which can precipitate secondary heart disease events (Markovitz, 1998). Cynical hostility does not appear to be linked to inflammatory processes, however (G. E. Miller, Freedland, Carney, Stetler, & Banks, 2003).

Stress and anxiety may be linked to heart disease via changes in blood coagulation and fibrinolytic activity (von Kaenel, Mills, Fainman, & Dimsdale, 2001). Stress can contribute to increased migration and recruitment of immune cells to sites of infection and inflammation. This increase in leukocyte trafficking and consequent increase in inflammatory activity may contribute to endothelial damage and the buildup of plaque (Redwine, Snow, Mills, & Irwin, 2003).

Depression and CHD

Considerable research also suggests a central role for depression in the development and exacerbation of coronary heart disease, so much so that it is generally recommended that patients at high risk be assessed and, if necessary, treated for depression (K. W. Davidson et al., 2006; Barth, Schumacher, & Herrmann-Lingen, 2004; van Melle et al., 2004). Depression is not a psychological

by-product of other risk factors for CHD but an independent risk factor in its own right, environmentally rather than genetically based (Lett et al., 2004). The risk that depression poses with respect to coronary artery disease is greater than that posed by second-hand smoke but sufficiently strong to consider depression a major independent factor in the onset of coronary disease (Wulsin & Singal, 2003).

Research also supports a strong link between depressive symptoms and metabolic syndrome (Kinder et al., 2004), between depression and cardiovascular disease (Elovainio et al., 2005), between depression and the likelihood of a heart attack (Janszky et al., 2010), between depression and heart failure among the elderly (M. A. Williams et al., 2002), between depression and the development of or death from heart disease (Gilmour, 2008), and between hopelessness and heart attack (Everson et al., 1996; see also N. Adler & Matthews, 1994). This additional risk is not explained by health behaviours, social isolation, or work characteristics; this relation is more consistent in men than it is in women (Stansfeld, Fuhrer, Shipley, & Marmot, 2002). The exhaustion and depression characteristic of the phase just before an acute coronary event is thought by some to represent a reactivation of latent viruses and a concomitant inflammation of coronary vessels. Some evidence suggests that the mental state of patients awaiting angioplasty for heart disease is positively associated with blood markers of inflammation (Appels, Bar, Bar, Bruggeman, & DeBaets, 2000). Symptoms of depression before coronary artery bypass graft surgery are an important predictor of long-term mortality (Burg, Benedetto, Rosenberg, & Soufer, 2003).

How does depression relate to heart disease? As is true for hostility, depression has been tied to inflammatory processes. Depression is strongly related to elevated C-reactive protein, a marker of low-grade systemic inflammation. As already noted, atherosclerosis is an inflammatory process, and, because depression promotes inflammation, this may account for the relation between depression and atherosclerosis (K. A. Matthews et al., 2007; G. E. Miller et al. 2003; Suarez, Krishnan, & Lewis, 2003). Inflammatory processes appear to explain the relation of depression to heart failure as well (Pasic, Levy, & Sullivan, 2003). Depressive symptoms are also associated with indicators of the metabolic syndrome, which may represent a related pathway to disease (McCaffrey, Niaura, Todaro, Swann, & Carmelli, 2003). Heart rate turbulence may contribute to the poor survival of depressed patients following a heart attack as well (Carney et al., 2007).

Treatment of depression may improve the prospects of long-term recovery from heart attack. Depression is typically treated by serotonin reuptake inhibitors, which prevent serotonin from attaching to receptors (Bruce & Musselman, 2005). When the receptors in the blood-stream are blocked, it may reduce the formation of clots by preventing the aggregation of platelets in the arteries (Schins, Honig, Crijns, Baur, & Hamukyak, 2003). Essentially, antidepressants may act as blood thinners (S. Gupta, 2002). As yet, whether treatment for depression improves coronary heart disease prevalence and survival remains to be seen (Lett et al., 2004; Naqvi, Naqvi, & Merz, 2005).

Other Psychosocial Risk Factors and CHD

Anxiety has been implicated in sudden cardiac death, perhaps because anxiety appears to reduce vagal control of heart rate (L. L. Watkins, Grossman, Krishnan, & Sherwood, 1998). There is mounting evidence that a composite index of anxiety, hostility, and anger may predict CHD better than considering each factor in isolation (Boyle, Michalek, & Suarez, 2006). Some researchers have therefore suggested that it may more important to consider negative affectivity in general rather than any specific form of negative affect when considering risk factors for CHD (Suls & Bunde, 2005).

Other individual factors such as helplessness, pessimism, and a tendency to ruminate over problems may also contribute to coronary heart disease risk (Kubzansky, Davidson, & Rozanski, 2005). For example, people who ruminate over annoying events may experience sustained blood pressure elevations putting them at greater risk for heart damage (Gerin, Davidson, Christenfeld, Goyal, & Schwartz, 2006).

Researchers have explored whether social dominance contributes to risk for coronary heart disease. Social dominance reflects a pattern of attempting to dominate social interactions through verbal competition, a fast speaking rate, and the tendency to jump on other people's responses before they have had a chance to finish. Evidence suggests that social dominance may be related to all-cause mortality (Houston, Babyak, Chesney, Black, & Ragland, 1997), and it may be especially related to mortality due to coronary heart disease.

Investigators have related vital exhaustion, a mental state characterized by extreme fatigue, a feeling of being dejected or defeated, and enhanced irritability to cardio-vascular disease (Kwaijtaal et al., 2007; Wirtz et al., 2003); vital exhaustion predicts the likelihood of a heart attack and subsequent cardiac events even after controlling for sociodemographic, behavioural, and other biological risk factors (J. E. Williams et al., 2010).

Overall, there is still much to be learned about environmental and social factors that contribute to coronary heart disease, and especially how they differ between the genders and races.

Modification of CHD Risk-related Behaviour

In keeping with the general shift toward prevention and health promotion, interventions have increasingly focused on those at risk for heart disease, as well as reducing risk among the general population. Recall from Chapter 3 that physical inactivity, being overweight, smoking, and a lack of fruits and vegetables in the diet are all modifiable risk factors implicated in the development of CHD. A number of public health promotion initiatives have accordingly been launched to help Canadians alter these lifestyle factors and reduce their risk of developing CHD.

In addition, other interventions target changing these risk-related behaviours at an individual level. People with high cholesterol or poor lipid profiles may be targeted for preventive dietary interventions. Programs to help people stop smoking have been heavily targeted toward those at risk for heart disease. Exercise has been recommended for the modification of coronary-prone behaviour, and numerous studies confirm that it can achieve positive effects in reducing CHD risk factors, psychological well-being, and CHD morbidity and mortality (Lavie, Thomas, Squires, Allison, & Milani, 2009). In addition to the known positive effects for weight management, exercise training programs can also help reduce the anxiety associated with CHD following cardiac events (Lavie & Milani, 2004).

Interventions may be targeted to particular windows of vulnerability, during which time educational interventions to help people control their risk factors may be especially helpful. As we saw earlier, women's risk for heart disease increases after menopause, so targeting diet and exercise interventions at this high-risk group is a promising intervention strategy (Simkin-Silverman et al., 1995).

Management of Heart Disease

Almost 6 percent of Canadians report having heart problems, and it is estimated that almost 30 million physician visits (or 10 percent of all visits) are for cardiovascular diseases (Heart and Stroke Foundation of Canada, 2003). Despite this, many people do not seek care after experiencing a heart attack.

Role of Delay   One of the reasons for high rates of mortality and disability following heart attacks is that patients often delay several hours or even days before seeking treatment. Some patients are simply unable to face the fact that they have had a heart attack. Others interpret the symptoms as more mild disorders and treat themselves. Depression seems to lead to delay as well (Bunde & Martin, 2006).

Older patients appear to delay longer, as do patients who have consulted with a physician or engaged in self-treatment for their symptoms. Experiencing the attack during the daytime, as well as having a family member present, enhances delay, perhaps because the environment is more distracting under these circumstances. Surprisingly, too, a history of angina or diabetes actually increases, rather than decreases, delay (Dracup & Moser, 1991).

One of the psychosocial issues raised by heart attack, then, is how to improve treatment-seeking behaviour and reduce the long delays that patients often demonstrate. At minimum, patients at high risk for an acute coronary event and their family members need to be trained in recognizing the signs of an impending or actual acute event, so as to avoid the delay that can compromise long-term recovery.

Initial Treatment   Coronary heart disease may be managed in several ways depending on the clinical symptoms. Some patients have coronary artery bypass graft (CABG) surgery to treat blockage of major arteries. Although cognitive dysfunction may result from CABG and require intervention (Phillips-Bute et al., 2006), this treatment can lead to improvement in angina and psychological distress if delivered in a timely manner. For example, one prospective study followed 266 patients waiting to have CABG in Montreal from the time they went on the wait list until after they had surgery (Sampalis, Boukas, Liberman, Reid, & Dupuis, 2001). Symptoms and quality of life were measured initially, just before surgery, and six months after surgery. Scores on the physical and social functioning scales of the SF-36 were significantly lower for those who had to wait more than three months for the CAGB, and longer wait times were also associated with an increased number of adverse cardiac events and increased risk for unemployment post surgery.

During the acute phase of illness, the myocardial infarction (MI) patient is typically hospitalized in a coronary care unit in which cardiac functioning is continually monitored. Many MI patients experience anxiety as they cope with the possibility of a recurrence and see their cardiac responses vividly illustrated on the machines before them. Commonly, however, MI patients in the acute phase of the disease cope by using denial and thus may be relatively anxiety-free during this period. Depression or a diagnosis of post-traumatic stress disorder (PTSD), however, predicts longer hospital stays (Oxlad, Stubberfield, Stuklis, Edwards, & Wade, 2006).

Most heart attack victims return home after hospitalization. Therefore, a number of long- and short-term issues of rehabilitation arise. The process of adjusting emotionally to the experience of a heart attack begins almost immediately. A number of heart attack patients experience cardiac arrest during their myocardial infarction and have to be resuscitated through artificial means. Being a victim of cardiac arrest can produce a number of psychological difficulties, including nightmares, chronic anxiety, depression, and low expectations of regaining health and vigour.

Cardiac Rehabilitation   Once the acute phase of illness has passed, patients are encouraged to become more active. At this point, a program of education and intervention begins, covering such topics as medical regimen, health risks, exercise, diet, work, and emotional stress. Heart patients, especially women, report receiving far less information about their disease and treatment than they want from health professionals. Most patients want and expect a shared or autonomous treatment decision-making role with their physician, but very few patients experience this (Stewart, Abbey, Shnek, Irvine, & Grace, 2004). Because adherence to treatment regimens is so much better when patients are actively involved, providing more information to patients and involving them actively in the process is essential. In addition, involvement in treatment can improve self-efficacy, which, in turn, is tied to better coronary health (Sarkar, Ali, & Whooley, 2007).

Cardiac rehabilitation is defined as the active and progressive process by which individuals with heart disease attain their optimal physical, medical, psychological, social, emotional, vocational, and economic status (Dracup, 1985). The goals of rehabilitation are to produce relief from symptoms, to reduce the severity of the disease, to limit further progression of disease, and to promote psychological and social adjustment. Underlying the philosophy of cardiac rehabilitation is the belief that such efforts can stem advancing disease, reduce the likelihood of a repeat myocardial infarction, and reduce the risk of sudden death.

Successful cardiac rehabilitation depends critically on the patient's active participation and full commitment to the behaviour-change efforts that must be undertaken. An underlying goal of such programs is to restore a sense of mastery or self-efficacy. Because a sense of self-efficacy has been related to beneficial outcomes of treatments, in the absence of self-efficacy, adherence to the goals of rehabilitation may be low (for example, Helgeson & Fritz, 1999; Johnston, Johnston, Pollard, Kinmonth, & Mant, 2004).

Although many rehabilitation programs serve both men and women, initiatives such as the Toronto Women's College Hospital's Women's Cardiovascular Health Initiative (WCHI) have been designed to deal specifically with women's needs (Public Health Agency Canada, 2009). This women-only cardiac rehabilitation program offers peer support via small groups with other women, counselling on the pros and cons of using hormone therapies, and personalized fitness training and education sessions on how to manage stress, eat healthy, and stay active. Compared to typical rehabilitation programs, which usually have about a 50 percent completion rate, this one, tailored to women's needs, has an 85 percent completion rate.

It is becoming increasingly clear that the beliefs that patients develop about their disorders are reliably related to successful recovery. Heart patients who respond to their disease and treatment with optimism, efforts to maintain high self-esteem, and sense of mastery over the disorder are at less risk for a new cardiac event and better adjusted (Helgeson, 1999; Helgeson & Fritz, 1999). Cardiac rehabilitation is, thus, most likely to be successful when the patient is fully engaged psychologically.

The components of the typical cardiac rehabilitation program are very similar to the interventions used for people at risk for CHD and include exercise therapy with some psychological counselling, as through support groups, nutritional counselling, and education about coronary heart disease (Lavie et al., 2009).

Treatment by Medication   Treatment for coronary heart disease begins immediately after diagnosis. Much of the drop in deaths from CHD can be attributed to the administration of clot-dissolving drugs and medical procedures such as angioplasty and coronary artery bypass surgery.

Once the acute phase of treatment is over, preparation for the rehabilitation regimen begins. Such a regimen often includes self-administration of beta-adrenergic blocking agents on a regular basis. Beta-blocking agents are drugs that resist the effects of sympathetic nervous system stimulation. Because heightened sympathetic nervous system activity aggravates cardiac arrhythmia, angina, and other conditions associated with heart disease, beta-blocking agents are useful in preventing this kind of stimulation.

Aspirin is commonly prescribed for people recovering from or at risk for heart attacks. Aspirin helps prevent blood clots by blocking one of the enzymes that cause platelets to aggregate. Research on aspirin now shows that men who take half an aspirin a day are at significantly reduced risk for fatal heart attacks (O'Neil, 2003). Women, too, appear to be benefited by aspirin therapy. As with many drugs, adherence is problematic (Vittinghoff et al., 2003).

A relatively new class of drugs called statins are now frequently prescribed for patients following an acute coronary event, particularly if they have elevated lipids. Statins target LDL cholesterol, reducing risk for a repeat event (Cannon et al., 2004). So impressive have statins been that they are now recommended for patients and at-risk individuals as well to lower lipids before any diagnosis of heart disease is made. In fact, statin drugs have surpassed all other drug treatments for reducing the incidence of death, heart attack, and stroke. Not incidentally, statins appear to be protective against a wide range of diseases including multiple sclerosis, neurodegenerative disorders such as Alzheimer's disease, and some types of cancer (Topol, 2004).

Diet and Activity Level   Dietary restrictions may be imposed on the recovering MI patient in an attempt to lower his or her cholesterol level. Instructions to reduce smoking, lose weight, and control alcohol consumption are also frequently given. Exercise appears to improve not only cardiovascular functioning but also psychological recovery so most patients are in a medically supervised exercise program. Adherence to exercise regimens is a problem, and therefore, building in relapse prevention is essential (Kugler, Dimsdale, Hartley, & Sherwood, 1990).

Patients also receive instructions about resumption of their previous activities. Most are urged to return to their prior employment as soon as possible, in part because low economic resources and a decline in income are associated with lower survival (Andersen,

Osler, Petersen, Grønbæk, & Prescott, 2003). Because employment is sometimes affected by heart disease, economic problems may result that require counselling. Twenty percent of MI patients do not return to their previous jobs, thus they often suffer a loss of income. These families may require financial counselling or retraining to help them offset their losses. However, patients in high-stress jobs may be advised to cut back, to work part-time, or to take a position with fewer responsibilities. Unfortunately, adherence is not high in this area of life, typically ranging from 50 to 80 percent. One reason for this low rate of adherence is that advice to cut back on work activities is often phrased in very vague terms, and patients may not understand exactly how they should implement this goal.

Stress Management   Stress management is an important ingredient in cardiac rehabilitation as well, because stress can trigger fatal cardiac events (Jiang et al., 1996). Younger patients, female patients, and those with social support gaps, high social conflict, and negative coping styles appear to be most at risk for high stress levels following a diagnosis of coronary artery heart disease, and therefore might be especially targeted for stress management interventions (Brummett et al., 2004).

Yet at present, stress management with coronary artery disease patients is hit-or-miss and often haphazard. Patients are urged to avoid stressful situations at work and at home, but these comments are often presented as vague treatment goals. Moreover, as many as 50 percent of patients say that they are unable to modify the stress in their lives. These problems are solved by employing methods such as those outlined in Chapter 6—namely, stress management programs.

Recently, stress management interventions have targeted risk factors thought to be especially implicated in cardiovascular disease and MI, including hostility. Hostility ebbs and flows across the life span, and risk factors for coronary heart disease ebb and flow with it. Declines in hostility in midlife, for example, are associated with lower risk (Siegler et al., 2003). Accordingly, one program developed an intervention for modifying hostility and found that eight weekly sessions designed to alter antagonism, cynicism, and anger were somewhat successful in reducing hostility levels (Gidron & Davidson, 1996; Gidron, Davidson, & Bata, 1999). And because PTSD predicts poor disease control, screening for PTSD is also recommended (Shemesh et al., 2004).

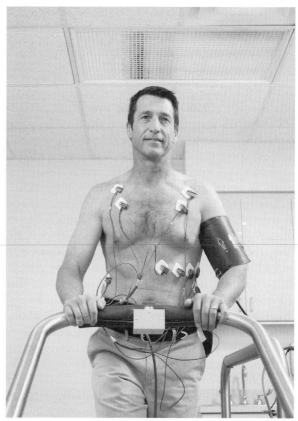

The treadmill test provides a useful indicator of the functional capacity of recovering myocardial infarction patients.

Targeting Depression   Depression is a significant problem during cardiac rehabilitation, as it is throughout the management of CHD (T. W. Smith & Ruiz, 2002). The prevalence is sufficiently great and the relation of depression to reoccurring events is sufficiently strong that depression represents an important target for rehabilitative efforts (Davidson, Rieckmann, & Lesperance, 2004; Freedland et al., 2003). CHD patients with high depression or high anxiety have decreased heart rate variability as compared with the norms, suggesting that they may have sustained alterations in their autonomic nervous system modulation over time (Krittayaphong et al., 1997). Depression and anxiety compromise quality of life (Goyal, Idler, Krause, & Contrada, 2005), as well as responses to drug treatments (Rutledge, Linden, & Davies, 1999). When depressed coronary heart disease patients are treated with cognitive behavioural therapy to reduce depression, it can have beneficial effects on risk factors for advancing disease, including the reduction of heart rate and increases in heart rate variability

(Carney et al., 2000; Lett, Davidson, & Blumenthal, 2005). Even brief counselling interventions delivered by telephone may reduce psychological distress and improve perceived health (Bambauer et al., 2005).

Evaluation of Cardiac Rehabilitation   Cardiac rehabilitation is now a standard part of the aftercare of patients who have had heart attacks or who have been hospitalized for heart disease. More than 130 published studies have evaluated cardiovascular disease management programs. Most of these studies find that interventions targeted to weight, blood pressure reduction, smoking, and, in increasing number, quality of life are successful in reducing patients' standing on risk factors for heart disease and, in some cases, reducing the risk of death from cardiovascular disease. People who are optimistic and who have high levels of social support do significantly better (Barry et al., 2007). Evaluations show that the addition of psychosocial treatments to standard cardiac rehabilitation programs reduces psychological distress and can reduce the likelihood that cardiac patients will experience symptoms, suffer a recurrence, or die following an acute cardiac event (for example, Lisspers et al., 2005; Rozanski, 2005).

As must be evident, a complicating issue in recovery from MI is that many patients need to modify several health habits simultaneously. As we have repeatedly seen, adherence to lifestyle change is often low and may be lower still if several health habits must be modified at the same time. Moreover, the active involvement of the patient is required for successful rehabilitation following MI or another CHD-related event.

Problems of Social Support   As is true for other diseases, social support can help heart patients recover, reducing distress and improving cardiac symptoms, especially in the months just following hospitalization (Lett et al, 2005). Indeed, in one study, heart patients without a spouse or a confidant were twice as likely to die within six months of their first heart attack, compared with those patients who were married or had friends (Case, Moss, Case, McDermott, & Eberly, 1992; see also Collijn, Appels, & Nijhuis, 1995). Social support during hospitalization predicts depressive symptoms during recovery, and depression itself is a risk factor for mortality related to CHD (Gilmour, 2008). So important is social support for long-term prognosis that it is now targeted for intervention during recovery (Burg et al., 2005).

However, many factors may erode the potential for social support. In the home setting, one of the MI patient's chief complaints is loss of independence. MI sharply reduces an individual's physical stamina, and many patients are surprised by the extent of their disability. Feelings of shame, helplessness, and low self-esteem may result. The patient may find it difficult to adhere to dietary restrictions and exercise, whereas the spouse may be highly motivated to help the patient comply. Unfortunately, this support may be interpreted as criticism or controlling behaviour creating further stress (Goldsmith, Lindholm, & Bute, 2006). Stressful interactions over the need to modify daily activities can aggravate the patient's perceptions of dependence and exacerbate already existing depression, as was evident in the example that opened this chapter.

Spouses of recovering heart attack patients tend to see the patient as dependent and irritable, whereas the recovering patient may regard the spouse as meddling and overprotective (Goldsmith, Lindholm, & Bute, 2006). An overly solicitous partner can aggregate severity of symptoms, disability, and symptoms of depression as well (Itkowitz, Kerns, & Otis, 2003). In addition, spouses of heart attack victims often show severe psychological responses to the MI, including nightmares and chronic anxiety over the patient's survival (Moser & Dracup, 2004). Although there is no evidence that heart attacks drive married couples apart, neither does it necessarily bring them closer together. It is a difficult situation for everyone involved. Marital counselling or family therapy may be needed to deal with marital strain.

Cardiac invalidism can be one consequence of MI; that is, patients and their spouses both see the patient's abilities as lower than they actually are (Itkowitz, Kerns, & Otis, 2003). In a study designed to reduce this problem (C. B. Taylor, Bandura, Ewart, Miller, & DeBusk, 1985), wives of recovering MI patients were provided with information about their husbands' cardiovascular capabilities, observed their husbands' performance on a treadmill task, or took part in the treadmill activity personally. Wives who personally experienced the treadmill task increased their perceptions of their husbands' physical and cardiac efficiency after observing their husbands' treadmill attainments. Wives who were simply informed about their husbands' performance or who observed treadmill activity continued to regard their husbands as impaired.

Despite these problems, the family has the potential to play an important role in follow-up care. Both patients and family members should be taught how to recognize the symptoms of an impending heart attack; how to differentiate them from more minor physical complaints, such as heartburn; and how to activate the emergency system. In this way, delay behaviour can be reduced and treatment can be improved in the event of a repeat event.

Family members of the MI patient should also be trained in **cardiopulmonary resuscitation (CPR).** Approximately 80 percent of potential sudden deaths from heart attacks occur in the home rather than the workplace, but relatively few programs have been initiated to train family members in CPR.

As we have repeatedly seen, the beliefs one holds about illness, treatment, and recovery are important determinants of adjustment, and this importance is certainly true for recovering heart patients as well. To the extent that interventions enhance feelings of self-efficacy and personal control, the beneficial contribution that they make to psychological and physical health may go well beyond specific training in diet, exercise, and other components of standard cardiac rehabilitation.

LO2   WHAT IS HYPERTENSION?

Hypertension, or high blood pressure, occurs when the supply of blood through the vessels is excessive. It can occur when cardiac output is too high, which puts pressure on the arterial walls as blood flow increases. It also occurs in response to peripheral resistance—that is, the resistance to blood flow in the small arteries of the body.

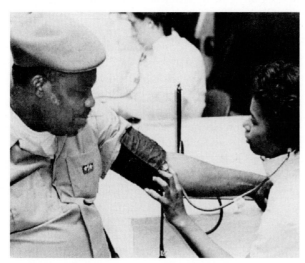

Hypertension is a symptomless disease. As a result, unless they obtain regular physical checkups or participate in hypertension screening programs, many adults are unaware that they have this disorder.

Hypertension is a serious medical problem for several reasons. It is considered an important risk factor for cardiac and cerebrovascular disease (Lawes, Vander, & Rodgers, 2008), and is the leading risk factor for death in the world accounting for 7.5 million deaths per year (World Health Organization, 2009). According to recent estimates from the 2007–9 Canadian Health Measures Survey, about 19 percent of Canadian adults have high blood pressure, and another 20 percent had blood pressure in the pre-hypertension range (Wilkins et al., 2010). But because there are no symptoms, 17 percent of those with hypertension don't know they have it.

Untreated hypertension can also adversely affect cognitive functioning, producing problems in learning, memory, attention, abstract reasoning, mental flexibility, and other cognitive skills (Robbins, Elias, Elias, & Budge, 2005). Even in healthy adults, elevated blood pressure appears to compromise cognitive functioning (Suhr, Stewart, & France, 2004). These problems appear to be particularly significant among young people with hypertension (Gupta, Solanki, & Pathak, 2008). Given the risks and scope of hypertension, early diagnosis and treatment are essential.

How Is Hypertension Measured?

Hypertension is assessed by the levels of systolic and diastolic blood pressure as measured by a sphygmomanometer. As noted in Chapter 2, systolic blood pressure is the greatest force developed during contraction of the heart's ventricles. It is sensitive both to the volume of blood leaving the heart and to the arteries' ability to stretch to accommodate blood (their elasticity). Diastolic pressure is the pressure in the arteries when the heart is relaxed; it is related to resistance of the blood vessels to blood flow.

Of the two, systolic pressure has somewhat greater value in diagnosing hypertension. Mild hypertension is defined by a systolic pressure consistently between 140 and 159; moderate hypertension involves a pressure consistently between 160 and 179; and severe hypertension means a systolic pressure consistently above 180. Keeping systolic blood pressure under 120 is best.

People at risk for hypertension show a less rapid recovery following sympathetic arousal. That is, after blood pressure has been elevated, as in response to a stressful event, it remains so for a significantly longer period of time than is true for people who do not have hypertension or who have no family history of hypertension (Gerin & Pickering, 1995). Hypertension, then, may be characterized both by greater reactivity to stress and by slower recovery. Patients with hypertension also show dampened emotional responses (Pury, McCubbin, Helfer, Galloway, & McMullen, 2004) and reduced pain sensitivity (Al'Absi, France, Harju, France, & Wittmers, 2006).

What Causes Hypertension?

Approximately 5 percent of hypertension is caused by failure of the kidneys to regulate blood pressure. However, almost 90 percent of all hypertension is *essential*— that is, of unknown origin.

Some risk factors have been identified. Blood pressure reactivity in childhood and adolescence predicts later development of hypertension, suggesting a genetic mechanism (Ingelfinger, 2004; K. A. Matthews, Salomon, Brady, & Allen, 2003). Prior to age 50, males are at greater risk for hypertension than are females; above the age 55 however, both men and women living in Canada face a 90 percent chance of developing hypertension in their lifetimes (Heart and Stroke Foundation, 2008). Cardiovascular disease risk factors are higher among minorities than among Caucasians in Canada. This increased risk appears to be due in part largely to low socio-economic status (Kivimäki et al., 2004). For example, compared with Caucasian Canadians, South Asians, First Nations, Aboriginal Peoples or Inuit, and Canadians of African or Caribbean descent have greater rates of high blood pressure (Heart and Stroke Foundation, 2008).

Like many chronic health conditions, behavioural and lifestyle factors play a role in the risk for hypertension. One study suggests that if Canadians cut their salt intake in half, the risk of hypertension would be eliminated in 1 million Canadians, the number of Canadians with adequately controlled hypertension would double, and the health care system would save $430 million a year. Currently, Canadians consume about 35 percent more than the suggested upper intake levels of sodium and about twice the amount recommended for good health. Much of this salt intake comes from consuming processed foods, with only an additional 10 percent to 20 percent of this intake added during cooking and at the table (Heart and Stroke Foundation, 2007). Public health policy and initiatives aimed at reducing the amount of sodium in processed foods and raising the public's awareness about the dangers of high sodium intake may help to reduce this risk factor for hypertension in the future.

Genetic factors clearly also play a role (see Dominiczak & Munroe, 2010): If one parent has high blood pressure, the offspring have a 45 percent chance of developing it; if two parents have high blood pressure, the probability increases to 95 percent. Blood pressure reactivity in childhood and adolescence predicts later development of hypertension, consistent with the possibility of a genetic mechanism (Ingelfinger, 2004; K. A. Matthews, Salomon, Brady, & Allen, 2003). As is true for coronary heart disease more generally, the genetic factor in hypertension may be reactivity, a hereditary predisposition toward elevated sympathetic nervous system activity, especially in response to stressful events (Dominiczak & Munroe, 2010). Further evidence for the importance of a genetically based predisposition to sympathetic nervous system reactivity comes from studies of people with a family history of hypertension but who do not themselves have hypertension. These individuals show reliably greater cardiovascular reactivity in response to stress and in anticipation of stress, despite the fact that they have not yet developed hypertension (Steptoe, 2008).

Emotional factors are also implicated in this constellation of risk. In particular, negative affect and frequent experiences of intense arousal predict increases in blood pressure over time (Jonas & Lando, 2000; S. C. Matthews, Nelesen, & Dimsdale, 2005; Pollard & Schwartz, 2003). A tendency toward anger (Harburg, Julius, Kacirotti, Gleiberman, & Schork, 2003), and cynical distrust (R. B. Williams, 1984), suppressed hostility (Zhang et al., 2005), have all been implicated in the development of hypertension. A family environment that fosters chronic anger may contribute to development of hypertension (Ewart, 1991). In contrast, children and adolescents who develop social competence skills may have a reduced risk for cardiovascular disease (E. Chen, Matthews, Salomon, & Ewart, 2002; Ewart & Jorgensen, 2004). Such observations suggest the importance of intervening early in the family environment to prevent or modify deficits in communication. Although much of the research concerning negative affect and hypertension has focused on men, longitudinal research suggests that anger and other negative emotional states may be related to blood pressure changes over time in women as well (Rutledge & Hogan, 2002).

Relationship between Stress and Hypertension

Stress has been suspected as a contributor to hypertension for many years (Henry & Cassel, 1969). Repeated exposure to stressful events during which heightened blood pressure reactions occur may contribute over the long term to development of chronically high blood pressure (D. Carroll et al., 2001). High blood pressure can result from exposure to chronic social conflict, such as discrimination, and low socioeconomic status, and from job strain—namely, the combination of high demands with little control (Spruill, 2010). Crowded, high-stress, and noisy locales produce higher rates of hypertension. Groups that have migrated from rural to urban areas have higher rates of hypertension. As we noted in Chapter 6, job stress and unemployment have also been tied to higher blood pressure (Spruill, 2010). In women, elevated blood pressure has been related to having extensive family responsibilities, and among white-collar women, the combined impact of large family responsibilities and job strain has been tied to higher blood pressure (Brisson et al., 1999). At present, the suspicion is that hypertension results from high-stress reactivity, possibly genetically based, in conjunction with high-stress exposure (Al'Absi & Wittmers, 2003; Schwartz, Meisenhelder, Ma, & Reed, 2003).

How Do We Study Stress and Hypertension?   To study the effects of stress on hypertension, researchers have adopted several research methods. One method brings people into the laboratory, often people at risk for or already diagnosed with hypertension, to see how they respond to physical or mental challenges that are stressful, such as a difficult arithmetic task. Laboratory studies that expose people to stressors, such as bright lights, or to stressful tasks such as holding one's breath for a long time, reliably show increased blood pressure responses (Girdler et al., 1996). Another line of work identifies stressful circumstances, such shift-work with sleep disruption, and examines the rates of hypertension and how blood pressure ebbs and flows over a 24 hour period (McCubbin, Pilcher, & Moore, 2010).

This last type of research makes use of ambulatory monitoring to examine the relationship between lifestyle factors and blood pressure in natural settings, as people go through their daily lives. That is, a person wears a blood pressure cuff, which assesses blood pressure at intervals throughout the day. This method has the advantage of charting the ebb and flow of blood pressure for each individual in response to different events. It has revealed, among other observations, that variation in blood pressure over the course of a day is considerable (Pickering, Schwartz, & James, 1995). These variations are especially high among people who smoke, who drink heavily, who experience job strain,

and who experience other stressful life conditions, lending support to the idea that blood pressure fluctuations may contribute to the development of essential hypertension (McCubbin, Pilcher, & Moore, 2010).

All of these types of studies provide evidence that links increases in or increased variability in blood pressure to stressful events.

The role of stress in the development and exacerbation of hypertension may be different for people at risk for hypertension than for those who are not, and it may change as hypertension progresses. People without preexisting signs of hypertension show large and reliable blood pressure responses to stressors, primarily when they must make an active behavioural response to that stress (Sherwood, Hinderliter, & Light, 1995). People with borderline hypertension show a similar pattern, although they also show exaggerated stress-induced cardiovascular responses to stress at a relatively young age (K. A. Matthews et al., 1993) and a stronger blood pressure response to laboratory stressors than do people with normal blood pressure (Tuomisto, 1997). The fact that individuals diagnosed with hypertension also show blood pressure responses to a wide array of stressors is consistent with the idea that excessive sympathetic nervous system activity—that is, reactivity in response to stress—may be significant in the development of hypertension (Rutledge & Linden, 2003).

The findings also suggest that factors that usually help people cope successfully with stressful events may not do so with people with hypertension. For example, people who feel they have personal control over stressful events usually show less sympathetic nervous system activity.

Psychosocial Factors and Hypertension

Originally, hypertension was thought to be marked by a constellation of personality factors, dominated by suppressed anger (F. Alexander, 1950; F. Dunbar, 1943). What is the evidence for the role of psychological factors in the development of hypertension? Although personality factors are now known to be insufficient on their own for the development of hypertension, research continues to show that traits such as hostility and defensiveness may play a role (for example, see the Focus on Canadian Research box, "Does Personality Predict Changes in Blood Pressure?").

Research has focused heavily on the experience of anger and its expression. Originally, suppressed hostility was thought to be associated with higher blood pressure levels and hypertension, although evidence for this hypothesis has been mixed. More recently, researchers have suggested that expressed anger and the potential for hostility are associated with exaggerated blood pressure responses, especially under conditions of stress or harassment. Evidence relating anger to hypertension is now quite substantial. Ruminating on the source of one's anger, whether one suppresses or expresses it, is associated with elevated blood pressure (Hogan & Linden, 2004; Schum, Jorgensen, Verhaeghen, Sauro, & Thibodeau, 2003). Conversely, the frequent experience of positive emotions may be protective against hypertension (Ostir, Berges, Markides, & Ottenbacher, 2006).

Social support is a resource for combating most health problems. In the case of people with hypertension, however, those who are also high in hostility can compromise the social support that they receive. Thus, the quality of personal relationships may influence whether social support has a beneficial effect on CVD (Uno, Uchino, & Smith, 2002). People with hypertension who are high in hostility can often drive those who might otherwise be supportive away. Research suggests that hostility may be associated with hypertension via its effects on interpersonal interaction, namely by increasing the number of conflict-ridden or unpleasant interactions in daily life (Brondolo, Rieppi, Erickson et al., 2003). Other evidence suggests that negative emotions, including depression and anxiety, may be prospective risk factors for hypertension as well (Rutledge & Hogan, 2002; Scherrer et al., 2003). Depression and hostility and (lack of) social support are quite closely tied (Räikkönen, Matthews, Flory, & Owens, 1999; Raynor, Pogue-Geile, Kamarck, McCaffery, & Manuck, 2002).

Acculturation and Hypertension among Asian-Canadians   Individuals who immigrate to Canada from non-Western cultures often go through a period of acculturation as they adjust to the new culture and the lifestyle changes that this entails. Such changes can include dietary and activity changes and the adoption of different cultural values. Stress is one of the major outcomes of acculturation that can impact health, independently or in combination with lifestyle factors. One study based on a large national sample of Asian immigrants found that in addition to socio-demographic factors, body mass index (BMI), and psychological distress, hypertension was significantly associated with acculturation. The longer the immigrants had been living in Canada, the

greater the likelihood that they had hypertension. In addition, the chance of having hypertension increased incrementally with the number of years since immigration, and remained after controlling for socio-demographics and distress (Kaplan, Chang, Newsom, & McFarland, 2002). This suggests that acculturation may increase risk for hypertension independent of the effects of stress.

One reason why acculturation may be linked to hypertension apart from stress is that immigrants may find that their traditional lifestyle practices, including diet and activity, are harder to maintain over time as they become influenced by Western cultural values and lifestyle pressures. For example, a study of Canadian- and American-Chinese women found that acculturation was associated with changes in diet (eating less fruits and vegetables) and a belief that cooking traditional Chinese meals was inconvenient (Satia-Abouta, Patterson, Kristal, Teh, & Tu, 2002). Such lifestyle changes combined with the stress of adapting to a new culture may increase risk for hypertension, especially if they are accompanied by increases in weight and sodium intake.

Treatment of Hypertension

Overview   Hypertension has been controlled in a variety of ways. Commonly, patients are put on low-sodium diets, and reduction of alcohol intake is also recommended. Weight reduction in overweight patients is strongly urged, and exercise is recommended for all hypertensive patients.

Caffeine restriction is often included as part of the dietary treatment of hypertension, because caffeine, in conjunction with stress, elevates blood pressure responses among those at risk for or already diagnosed with hypertension (Lovallo et al., 2000). Indeed, caffeine intake may more generally contribute to rising levels of hypertension and thus be considered a strategy for the primary prevention of hypertension as well as its treatment (J. E. James, 2004).

Drug Treatments   Most commonly, hypertension is treated pharmacologically. Diuretics reduce blood volume by promoting the excretion of sodium. Another common treatment is beta-adrenergic blockers, which exert their antihypertensive effects by decreasing cardiac output and decreasing plasma renin activity. Central adrenergic inhibitors are also used to reduce blood pressure by decreasing the sympathetic outflow from the

Does Personality Predict Changes in Blood Pressure?

Given the established links between hostility and cardiovascular disease, researchers at the University of British Columbia set out to answer this question. In addition to hostility they examined how several other personality traits known to be associated with heart disease were linked to blood pressure over time.

In one study of 125 people from the Vancouver area, the links between defensiveness, stress reactivity, and blood pressure were examined initially and three years later to test the potential mediating effects of reactivity (Rutledge & Linden, 2003). Resting blood pressure was measured with different indices, and then after the participants engaged in stressful tasks to assess their stress reactivity. Although there were no differences in baseline blood pressure according to level of defensiveness, individuals who were high in defensiveness had significantly higher blood pressure indices after three years (Rutledge & Linden, 2003).

However, if personality were to play a role in the development of hypertension, and perhaps even heart disease, then the link between personality and health status variables such as blood pressure should be relatively stable over time (Leclerc, Rahn, & Linden, 2006). To test this proposition, the researchers followed a group of 112 people from the Vancouver area over a 10-year period to assess any changes in blood pressure and possible links to several personality dimensions. Participants completed measures of defensiveness, hostility, and depression at time 1, and their baseline blood pressure was recorded. Again, defensiveness was not linked to baseline blood pressure, but hostility and depression were. Ten years later, personality and blood pressure were again assessed, and each proved to be fairly stable over time. However, only hostility was a significant predictor of blood pressure a decade later, and was also the most stable personality trait. Additional analyses revealed that these relations were stronger for those with a family history of hypertension, and that they varied for men and women. For men, high self-defensiveness predicted elevated blood pressure after 10 years, whereas for women it did not (Leclerc, Rahn, & Linden, 2006).

Overall, these studies support the proposition that personality may play a role in the development of hypertension, especially when other factors such as family history are present.

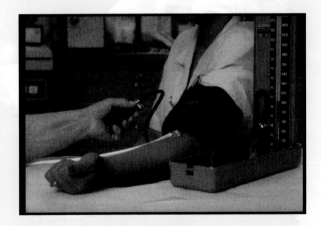

central nervous system. Peripheral adrenergic inhibitors are also used to deplete catecholamines from the brain and the adrenal medulla. Alpha-adrenergic blockers, vasodilators, angiotensin-converting enzyme inhibitors, and calcium channel blockers have also been used in the treatment of hypertension.

Cognitive Behavioural Treatments The fact that antihypertensive medications can actually aggravate sympathetic nervous system activity, coupled with the success of cognitive behavioural therapy in other areas of health psychology, has led to an increasing use of cognitive behavioural modification techniques in the treatment of hypertension.

A variety of behavioural and cognitive behavioural methods have been evaluated for their potential success in lowering blood pressure. Methods that draw on relaxation include biofeedback, progressive muscle relaxation, hypnosis, and meditation, all of which reduce blood pressure via the induction of a state of low arousal. Deep breathing and imagery are often added to accomplish this task. Although there is limited research evaluating the effects of many of these methods, a recent review of the effects of transcendental meditation (TM) for treating hypertension concluded that TM has the potential to make clinically significant reductions in blood pressure (Anderson, Liu, & Kryscio, 2008).

Exercise may also help in blood pressure control, especially for older adults (Cornelissen, Verheyden, Aubert, & Fagard, 2009)). Because obesity is implicated in the development of hypertension, public health interventions to promote healthy weights via exercise and other means may also be successful in reducing hypertension. However, the treatment of obesity itself remains difficult (see Chapter 4), and so a combination of diet, exercise, and behavioural strategies may be most desirable for maintaining weight loss.

The fact that anger has been tied to hypertension implies that teaching people how to manage their anger might be useful. In fact, studies suggest that training hypertensive patients how to manage confrontational scenes through such behavioural techniques as role playing can produce better skills for managing such situations and can lower blood pressure reactivity (Davidson, MacGregor, Stuhr, & Gidron, 1999).

Evaluation of Cognitive Behavioural Interventions   How do behavioural techniques fare comparatively in the treatment of hypertension? Of the nondrug approaches, weight reduction, physical exercise, and cognitive behavioural therapy appear to be quite successful (Linden & Chambers, 1994). Although not all hypertensive patients benefit from such training, many do. Moreover, cognitive behavioural methods have the advantage of being inexpensive as well as easy to implement: They can be used without supervision, and they have no side effects.

Cognitive behavioural interventions may reduce the drug requirements for the treatment of hypertension (D. Shapiro, Hui, Oakley, Pasic, & Jamner, 1997). For some people with hypertension, drug treatments have risks, and may, for example, impair their ability to manage work responsibilities well. Under these circumstances, cognitive behavioural therapies may enable people with hypertension to reduce or replace their drugs (Kristal-Boneh, Melamed, Bernheim, Peled, & Green, 1995). Behavioural treatments appear to be especially successful for individuals with mild or borderline hypertension and, with these groups, may actually substitute for drug control.

Problems in Treating Hypertension

The Hidden Disease   One of the biggest problems in the treatment of hypertension is that so many people who are hypertensive do not know that they are. Hypertension is largely a symptomless disease, so, rather than seeking treatment for hypertension, people are often di-

agnosed when they go in for a standard medical examination. Thus, many thousands of people who do not have regular contact with physicians suffer from hypertension without realizing it.

National campaigns to educate Canadians about hypertension have been fairly successful in getting people diagnosed and treated (Onysko, Maxwell, Eliasziw, Zhang, Johansen, & Campbell, 2006). Early detection is important because, as we have seen, more treatments may be available for individuals with borderline or mild hypertension than for people with more serious forms of the disorder.

Untreated hypertension is related to a lower quality of life, compromised cognitive functioning, and fewer social activities, so, despite the fact that it is symptomless, it nonetheless has adverse effects on daily life (Saxby, Harrington, McKeith, Wesnes, & Ford, 2003).

Increasingly, community interventions enable people to have their blood pressure checked by going to mobile units, their churches or community centres, or even the local drugstore. The widespread availability of these screening programs has helped with early identification of people with hypertension.

Adherence   A second major problem facing the management of hypertension is the high rate of nonadherence to therapy. This, too, is affected by the symptomless nature of the disease. Because hypertensive patients "feel fine," it can be difficult to get them to take medications on a regular basis. Many of us believe that, when we are "cranked up," under stress, or annoyed, our blood pressure is high. In fact, the correlation between beliefs about level of blood pressure and actual blood pressure is low.

What can be done to increase adherence? Clearly, one solution is to educate patients fully about the largely symptomless nature of the disease and the critical importance of treatment for controlling it. It may be necessary, too, to demonstrate to patients that their theories about their blood pressure are wrong. Research testing the effectiveness of patient education interventions has found that they are successful in part because they increase self-efficacy about adhering to medication regimens, (Hacihasanoğlu & Gözüm, 2011).

More recently adherence therapy has been explored as a potential intervention for improving medication adherence therapy with people who have hypertension. Based on the principle that patient beliefs impact adherence, adherence therapy focuses on amplifying personally relevant treatment beliefs, modifying treatment beliefs,

People who have had strokes often must relearn some aspects of cognitive functioning.

and reducing ambivalent feelings about taking medication (Alhalaiqa, Deane, Nawafleh, Clark, & Gray, 2011). Rather than a one size fits all approach, adherence therapy targets specific medication beliefs using techniques such as belief checking and generating discrepancy between the patients' beliefs and their failure to take their medication. An initial investigation suggests that this may be a promising and effective approach for increasing hypertension medication adherence by as much as 3 percent (Alhalaiqa et al., 2011).

L03   WHAT IS A STROKE?

> On Sunday, after supper, our family went to see the movie. As we stood up at the end of the movie, John slipped down between the seats. He was moaning. I thought he had hurt his knee, so Jonathan (16 years old at the time) and I reached under each arm and helped him into the seat. When I saw his face drooping, I realized it was a stroke. Jonathan called 911. The firefighters arrived, then a few minutes later the ambulance. John was taken to emergency. John was 46 years old. (Stroke Survivors Association of Ottawa, 2005)

Stroke, the third leading cause of death in Canada, results from a disturbance in blood flow to the brain, and is responsible for nearly 14,000 Canadian deaths from stroke each year (Heart and Stroke Foundation, 2010). Stroke does not just affect the elderly. Over 10 percent of stroke deaths occur in people under the age of 65 (Public Health Agency of Canada, 2011). Some strokes occur when blood flow to localized areas of the brain is interrupted, a condition that can be due to arteriosclerosis or hypertension. For example, when arteriosclerotic plaques damage the cerebral blood vessels, the damaged area may trap blood clots (thrombi) or produce circulating blood clots (emboli) that block the flow of blood.

Stroke can also be caused by cerebral hemorrhage (bleeding caused by the rupture of a blood vessel in the brain). When blood leaks into the brain, large areas of nervous tissue may be compressed against the skull, producing widespread or fatal damage. Current estimates suggest that between 40,000 and 50,000 Canadians are hospitalized each year for stroke. Those who survive have a 20 percent chance of having a stroke within two years, and may suffer some degree of permanent physical impairment. Of those who have a stroke 15 percent die, 10 percent recover completely, 25 percent are left with a minor disability, 40 percent are left with a moderate to severe disability, and 10 percent require long-term care because of severe physical impairments from the stroke. It is estimated that over 315,000 Canadians live with the effects of a stroke (Public Health Agency of Canada, 2011). The warning signs of stroke are listed in Table 13.1.

A chief risk of stroke is that more will follow in its wake, ultimately leading to severe disability or death. Researchers have recently discovered that a simple intervention—aspirin—can greatly reduce this risk. Aspirin has immediate benefit for stroke patients by preventing coagulation. Following a stroke, even a few weeks of aspirin's use can reduce the risk of recurrent strokes by as much as a third (Z. Chen et al., 2000). As we saw in the section "What Is Coronary Heart Disease?" aspirin is believed to be helpful in reducing risk of coronary events as well, so this little drug, that has been with us for so long, may prove to be the wonder drug of the century.

TABLE 13.1 | Stroke Warning Signs

The Heart and Stroke Foundation says these are the five warning signs of stroke:

- **Weakness:** Sudden loss of strength or sudden numbness in the face, arm or leg, even if temporary
- **Trouble speaking:** Sudden temporary loss of speech or trouble understanding speech, even if temporary
- **Vision problems:** Sudden loss of vision, particularly in one eye, or double vision, even if temporary
- **Headache:** Sudden severe and unusual headache
- **Dizziness:** Unsteadiness or a sudden fall, especially with any of the above signs

Source: Heart and Stroke Foundation, 2007c.

Risk Factors for Stroke

Risk factors for stroke overlap heavily with those for heart disease. Some factors are hereditary, others result from lifestyle, and still others come from unknown causes. Risk factors include high blood pressure, heart disease, cigarette smoking, a high red blood cell count, and transient ischemic attacks. In addition, psychological distress is related to the likelihood of having a fatal stroke (May et al., 2002). Anger expression also appears to be related to stroke, as it is for coronary heart disease and hypertension; low levels of anger expression appear to be mildly protective (Eng, Fitzmaurice, Kubzansky, Rimm, & Kawachi, 2003).

Each year nearly 15,000 Canadians experience **transient ischemic attacks**—little strokes that produce temporary weakness, clumsiness, or loss of feeling in one side or limb; a temporary dimness or loss of vision, particularly in one eye; or a temporary loss of speech or difficulty in speaking or understanding speech (Heart and Stroke Foundation, 2010).

In addition, the likelihood of a stroke increases with age, and occurs more often in men than in women. However, women are more likely than men to die from a stroke (Heart and Stroke Foundation, 2002). A prior stroke or a family history of stroke also increases the likelihood. Increasingly, health practitioners are recognizing the significance of psychosocial factors in stroke.

Depression and anxiety are predictive of stroke (May et al., 2002). Ethnicity is also a risk factor for stroke. First Nations people and Canadians of African or South Asian descent are also at greater risk for stroke mainly because they are more likely to have high blood pressure and diabetes (Public Health Agency, 2009a).

The numbers of stroke by gender is shown in Figure 13.3. As can be seen, deaths from stroke decreased by 62 percent during the 1980s and 1990s but have been steadily increasing since 1999. The number of deaths of Canadian women is expected to increase until 2015 when the number will plateau, whereas the number of deaths among men is expected to increase until 2025 (Heart and Stroke Foundation, 2003).

Consequences of Stroke

Stroke affects all aspects of one's life: personal, social, vocational, and physical. Not surprisingly, over 77 percent of Canadians who have had a stroke need to restrict their activities because of the impairments suffered from stroke, and over 71 percent require help with their daily activities (Heart and Stroke Foundation, 2003). Although many victims have already reached retirement age, stroke can also attack younger people. Patients who are minimally impaired following a stroke may return to work after a few months, but many patients are unable

FIGURE 13.3 | Number of Stroke Deaths in Canada by Gender, Actual and Projected, 1950–2025

Source: Heart and Stroke Foundation of Canada, *The Growing Burden of Heart Disease and Stroke in Canada 2003*, Ottawa, 2003, 1-896242-30-8 (English), www.cvdinfobase.ca/cvdbook/CVD_En03.pdf.

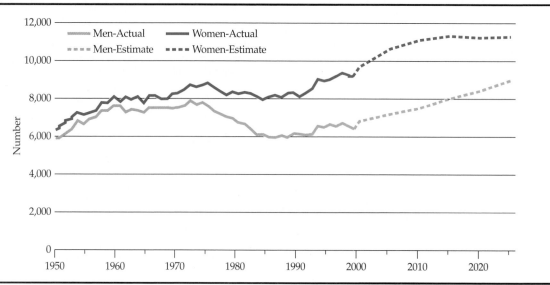

to return to work even part-time. Stroke almost inevitably leads to increased dependence on others, at least for a while; as a consequence, family or other social relationships may be profoundly affected.

Motor Problems   Immediately after a stroke, motor difficulties are common. Because the right side of the brain controls movement in the left half of the body and the left side of the brain controls movement in the right half of the body, motoric impairments occur on the side opposite to the side of the brain that was damaged in the stroke. It is usually difficult or impossible for the patient to move the arm and leg on the affected side; therefore, he or she usually requires help walking, dressing, and performing other physical activities.

Cognitive Problems   The cognitive difficulties that the stroke victim faces depend on which side of the brain was damaged. Patients with left-brain damage may have communication disorders, such as aphasia, which involves difficulty in understanding others and expressing oneself. A stroke patient described a relevant incident:

> One of my first shopping expeditions was to a hardware store, but when I got there I couldn't think of the words, "electric plug," and it took me a while to get the message across. Naturally, I was humiliated and frustrated. I was close to tears at the store, and let them out to Jane [the patient's wife] at home. I was learning day by day the frustrations of a body and mind I could not command. (Dahlberg, 1977, p. 124)

Other problems of left-brain dysfunction include cognitive disturbances, an apparent reduction in intellect, and difficulty in learning new tasks. In particular, cognitive tasks that require the use of short-term memory seem to be particularly affected after a stroke that causes left-brain damage.

Patients with right-brain damage may be unable to process or make use of certain kinds of visual feedback. As a result, such a patient may shave only one side of his face or put makeup on only half her face. The patient may eat only the food on the right side of the plate and ignore the food on the left. Patients may have trouble reading a clock, dialling a phone, or making change. These patients sometimes have difficulty perceiving distances accurately and may bump into objects or walls.

Patients with right-brain damage may also feel that they are going crazy because they cannot understand the words they read or seem to be able to perceive only the last part of each word. Although some stroke patients

seem to have a good idea of how much damage has been done, a fact that is depressing in its own right, others are quite inaccurate in their assessment of how the stroke has changed their cognitive abilities, their memory, and their moods (Hibbard, Gordon, Stein, Grober, & Sliwinski, 1992). These misperceptions lead them to misjudge what they are capable of doing and to inaccurately assess how well they have done.

Emotional Problems   Emotional problems after a stroke are common. Patients with left-brain damage often react to their disorder with anxiety and depression; patients with right-brain damage more commonly seem indifferent to their situation. These differences in emotional response appear to be due to neurological damage (Paradiso, Anderson, Boles Ponto, Tranel, & Robinson, 2011). Right-brain-damaged patients have alexithymia, which involves difficulty in identifying and describing feelings (Spalletta et al., 2001).

As we have seen, depression is a serious problem for stroke patients, and its degree depends on the site of the stroke and its severity. However, psychosocial factors also predict the degree of depression. Depression depends, in part, on the relationship the stroke patient has to the caregiver. Overprotection by a caregiver, a poor relation with a caregiver, and a caregiver who views the caregiving situation negatively all lead to depression on both sides.

Relationship Problems   The stroke patient may have problems with social relationships. Strokes produce symptoms that interfere with effective communication. For example, facial muscles may fail to work properly, producing the appearance of disfigurement. Cognitive impairment leads to memory loss, difficulty in concentrating, and other socially disruptive impairments, such as inappropriate emotional expression. A condition known as *multiinfarct dementia,* which results from the accumulating effects of small strokes, may produce Alzheimer's-like symptoms. Spousal relationships can also be profoundly affected. In addition to lack of control and changes in perception of self, stroke survivors report that problems with sexual desire and sexual functioning significantly alter their spousal relationships (Thompson & Ryan, 2009).

Types of Rehabilitative Interventions

Interventions with stroke patients have typically taken four approaches: psychotherapy, including treatment for depression; cognitive remedial training to restore intellectual functioning; training in specific skills development; and the use of structured, stimulating environments to challenge the stroke patient's capabilities (Krantz & Deckel, 1983). Home visits from volunteers or counsellors can provide help for the confused and frightened stroke patient who is too ill to go to a facility.

Treatment for depression usually takes the form of antidepressants, although in some cases, patients cannot take these medications because they aggravate other medical conditions. Consequently, psychotherapy is employed to help stroke patients learn ways of coping with their altered circumstances. The progress is often slow (Hibbard, Grober, Stein, & Gordon, 1992).

Interventions designed to deal with cognitive problems after stroke address several goals. First, patients must be made aware that they have problems. Often, the stroke patient thinks he or she is performing adequately when this is simply not so. A risk of making patients aware of these problems is the sense of discouragement or failure that may arise. Thus, it is important for patients to see that these deficits are correctable.

Hopefulness regarding the optimism of patients to recover their faculties is based on a new approach called *neurorehabilitation,* which relies on the brain's ability to rebuild itself and learn new tasks. Essentially the idea is to rewire the brain so that other areas of the brain than the area affected by the stroke can come to take on those functions, thus improving patients' ability to move, speak, and articulate clearly. Whereas it was once believed that stroke patients would achieve their maximum recovery within the first six months after stroke, it now appears that these gains can occur over subsequent years (J. E. Allen, 2003). Certain drugs such as antidepressants and cholesterol-lowering drugs appear to promote the growth of new neurons and may consequently be employed in the future to treat stroke (Abbott, 2004).

There are a variety of techniques to help right-brain-damaged stroke patients regain a full visual field (Paolucci, Antonucci, Grasso, & Pizzamiglio, 2001). One method is to spread out an array of money before a patient and ask him or her to pick all of it up. The right-brain-damaged patient will pick up only the money on the right side, ignoring that on the left. When the patient is induced to turn his or her head toward the impaired side, he or she will see the remaining money and can then pick it up as well.

A scanning machine can improve this process further. Patients are first instructed to follow a moving stimulus with their eyes. When the stimulus moves to the left side of the stimulus array, it is out of sight of right-brain-damaged patients unless they turn their heads. Thus, patients quickly learn to turn their heads so that they can pick up all information when the scanner moves into the left side of the visual field. Various tasks that require scanning, such as number cancelling, are then introduced, so the patient can get practice using the entire visual field. Gradually, the patient is led to do tasks without benefit of the artificial scanner. Through these kinds of retraining efforts, many stroke patients are able to regain many of their lost capabilities. Eventually, they can negotiate the world much as they did before the stroke (Paolucci et al., 2001).

Cognitive remediation is a slow process, and skills retraining needs to proceed in an orderly fashion, beginning with easy problems and moving to more difficult ones. As each skill is acquired, practise is essential (W. A. Gordon & Hibbard, 1992).

WHAT IS DIABETES? (L04)

Diabetes is one of the most common chronic illnesses in this country and one of the fastest growing chronic health concerns. It is the sixth leading cause of death in Canada (Statistics Canada, 2008). In 2010, about 6.4 percent of Canadians age 20 and older had diabetes, and an estimated 1 million other cases remain undiagnosed (Ross, Gilmour, & Dasgupta, 2010). What is more troubling is that rates are expected to continue to soar with an estimated 8 percent of Canadians expected to be diagnosed with diabetes by the year 2030. An aging population, rising rates of obesity and unhealthy weight, and physical activity are the main reasons for this expected increase (Ross, Gilmour, & Dasgupta, 2010). People with diabetes are at high risk for hypertension and stroke as well (Roan, 2003). Diabetes costs Canada more than $4 billion a year in medical costs, not including the indirect costs that result from disability and work loss, and the cost is expected to almost double by 2016 as more Canadians are diagnosed with diabetes (Ohinmaa, Jacobs, Simpson, & Johnson, 2004).

Between 2002–3 and 2006–7, the prevalence of diabetes increased by 21 percent, and in 2006–7 alone, over 211,000 new cases were diagnosed (Public Health Agency of Canada, 2009). It is estimated that over 63 percent of people with diabetes also have a diagnosis of hypertension, and people with diabetes are also more likely to have other long-term health complications such as heart disease, chronic kidney disease, stroke, and lower limb amputations (Public Health Agency of

Canada, 2009). In addition, the majority of deaths among people with diabetes are due to heart disease and stroke (Heart and Stroke Foundation, 2003). The incidence of cases of Type II diabetes is increasing so rapidly that it is considered a pandemic, especially among the Aboriginal population in this country (Public Health Agency of Canada, 2003b). The complications of diabetes are pictured in Figure 13.4.

Diabetes is a chronic condition of impaired carbohydrate, protein, and fat metabolism that results from insufficient secretion of insulin or from insulin resistance. The cells of the body need energy to function, and the primary source of energy is glucose, a simple sugar that results from the digestion of foods containing carbohydrates. Glucose circulates in the blood as a potential source of energy for cells that need it.

Insulin is a hormone, produced by the beta cells of the pancreas, which bonds to the receptor sites on the outside of a cell and acts essentially as a key to permit glucose to enter the cells. When there is not enough

FIGURE 13.4 | The Potential Health Complications of Diabetes Are Extensive, Life-Threatening, and Costly

Source: Public Health Agency of Canada, "Diabetes," www.phac-aspc.gc.ca/ccdpc-cpcmc/diabetes-diabete/english/risk/index.html. Reproduced with the permission of the Minister of Public Works and Government Services Canada, 2008.

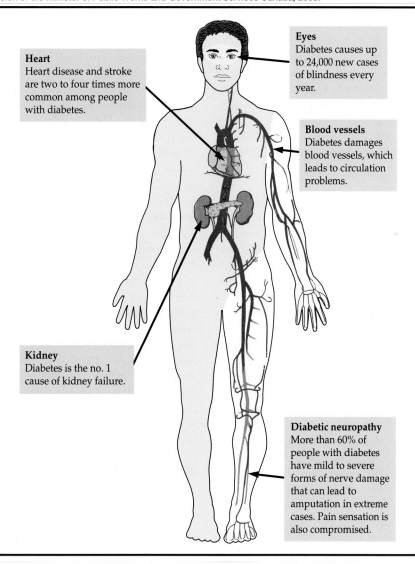

Heart
Heart disease and stroke are two to four times more common among people with diabetes.

Eyes
Diabetes causes up to 24,000 new cases of blindness every year.

Blood vessels
Diabetes damages blood vessels, which leads to circulation problems.

Kidney
Diabetes is the no. 1 cause of kidney failure.

Diabetic neuropathy
More than 60% of people with diabetes have mild to severe forms of nerve damage that can lead to amputation in extreme cases. Pain sensation is also compromised.

insulin produced or when insulin resistance develops (that is, the glucose can no longer be used by the cells), glucose stays in the blood instead of entering the cells, resulting in a condition called hyperglycemia. The body attempts to rid itself of this excess glucose, yet the cells are not receiving the glucose they need and send signals to the hypothalamus that more food is needed.

Types of Diabetes

There are two major types of diabetes, insulin-dependent (or Type I) diabetes and non-insulin-dependent (or Type II) diabetes. They differ in origin, pathology, role of genetics in their development, age of onset, and treatment.

Type I Diabetes   Type I diabetes is characterized by the abrupt onset of symptoms, which result from lack of insulin production by the beta cells of the pancreas. The disorder may result from viral infection or autoimmune reactions, and probably has a genetic contribution as well. In Type I diabetes, the immune system falsely identifies cells in the pancreas as invaders and accordingly destroys these cells, compromising or eliminating their ability to produce insulin. Type I diabetes usually develops relatively early in life, earlier for girls than for boys, between the ages of 5 and 6 or later between 10 and 13.

The most common early symptoms are frequent urination, unusual thirst, excessive drinking of fluids, weight loss, fatigue, weakness, irritability, nausea, uncontrollable craving for food (especially sweets), and fainting. These symptoms are due to the body's attempt to find sources of energy, which prompts it to feed off its own fats and proteins. By-products of these fats then build up in the body, producing symptoms; if the condition is untreated, a coma can result.

Type I diabetes is a serious, life-threatening illness accounting for about 10 percent of all diabetes. It is managed primarily through direct injections of insulin—hence the name insulin-dependent diabetes (Public Health Agency of Canada, 2003b). The individual with Type I diabetes is especially vulnerable to hyperglycemia. When this occurs, the skin is flushed and dry, and the individual feels drowsy and has deep, laboured breathing. Vomiting may occur, and the tongue is dry; feelings of hunger are rare, but thirst is common. Abdominal pain may occur, and a large amount of sugar is detectable in the urine. Hyperglycemia may require medical intervention because coma may result, requiring hospitalization.

Type II Diabetes   Type II (or non-insulin-dependent) diabetes is milder than the insulin-dependent type. Type II diabetes is typically a disorder of middle and old age, striking those primarily over the age of 40. As obesity has become rampant, Type II diabetes, to which obesity is a major contributor, has become more prevalent, especially at earlier ages. Many children and adolescents now have Type II diabetes. This type of diabetes is increasing at astronomical rates.

A good deal is known about the mechanisms that trigger Type II diabetes. Glucose metabolism involves a delicate balance between insulin production and insulin responsiveness. As food is digested, carbohydrates are broken down into glucose. Glucose is absorbed from the intestines into the blood, where it travels to the liver and other organs. Rising levels of glucose in the blood trigger the pancreas to secret insulin into the bloodstream. When this balance goes awry, it sets the stage for Type II diabetes. First, cells in muscle, fat, and liver lose some of their ability to respond fully to insulin, a condition known as insulin resistance. In response to insulin resistance, the pancreas temporarily increases its production of insulin. At this point, insulin-producing cells may give out, with the result that insulin production falls, and the balance between insulin action and insulin secretion becomes disregulated, resulting in Type II diabetes (Alper, 2000). The symptoms include frequent urination; fatigue; dryness of the mouth; impotence; irregular menstruation; loss of sensation; frequent infection of the skin, gums, or urinary system; pain or cramps in legs, feet, or fingers; slow healing of cuts and bruises; and intense itching and drowsiness.

The majority of people with Type II diabetes are overweight (90 percent), and Type II diabetes is more common in men and individuals of low socio-economic status (Ross, Gilmour, & Dasgupta, 2010). Although demographic factors such as education or behavioural factors do explain some of the reason for the social gradient in the incidence of diabetes, they do not fully account for it (Ross, Gilmour, & Dasgupta, 2010). Type II diabetes is primarily a disorder of aging, although increasingly, new cases are being diagnosed in children. More than 23 percent of people 75 or older have diabetes, compared with 2 percent among those 30 to 39 (Public Health Agency of Canada, 2009). Diabetes is also more common in minority communities in Canada. Rates of diabetes are higher among Canadians of African descent compared to Caucasians, and rates are three to five times higher in Aboriginal peoples compared to the general population (Public Health Agency of Canada,

TABLE 13.2 | Risk Factors for Type II Diabetes

You are at risk if:

- You are overweight
- You are over age 65
- You have an apple-shaped figure, that is, you carry most of your weight above the hips
- You get little exercise
- You have high blood pressure
- You have a sibling or parent with diabetes
- You had a baby weighing over 9 pounds at birth
- You are a member of a high-risk ethnic group, which includes Aboriginal, Black Canadians, Latin American, Asian, and Pacific Islanders

Source: http://www.phac-aspc.gc.ca/ccdpc-cpcmc/diabetes-diabete/english/risk/index.html. Reproduced with the permission of the Minister of Public Works and Government Services Canada, 2008.

2003b). Canadians of South Asian descent also have higher rates of diabetes than other Canadians, although their behavioural risk factors, such as diet and activity, are the same or lower than that for Euro-Canadians. It is believed that the interplay of genetics and environmental factors are responsible for this increased risk among South Asian and Aboriginal Canadians (Health Council of Canada, 2007b).

Type II diabetes is on the increase because of an increase in the prevalence of a sedentary lifestyle and obesity, both of which are risk factors for the development of the disorder. According to the World Health Organization, 90 percent of diabetes cases could be prevented by having a healthy diet, staying physically active, and not smoking. Risk factors for Type II diabetes are listed in Table 13.2.

Health Implications of Diabetes

The reason that diabetes is such a major public health problem stems less from the consequences of insufficient insulin production per se than from the complications that may develop. Diabetes is associated with a thickening of the arteries due to the buildup of wastes in the blood. As a consequence, diabetic patients show high rates of coronary heart disease.

Diabetes is the leading cause of blindness among adults, and it accounts for 50 percent of all the patients who require renal dialysis for kidney failure. Diabetes may also be associated with nervous system damage, including pain and loss of sensation. In severe cases, amputations of the extremities, such as toes and feet, are

required. As a consequence of these complications, people with diabetes have a shorter life expectancy than do non-diabetic individuals. Diabetes may also exacerbate other difficulties in psychosocial functioning, contributing to eating disorders (Criego, Crow, Goebel-Fabbri, Kendall, & Parkin, 2009) and sexual dysfunction in both men and women (Bitzer & Alder, 2009; Burke et al., 2007), as well as depression (Pan et al., 2011), among other problems. In addition, a recent study suggests that women with diabetes who also have depression have a greater risk of dying from cardiovascular disease (Pan et al., 2011). Diabetes may produce central nervous system impairment that interferes with memory (Warren, Zammitt, Deary, & Frier, 2007), especially among the elderly (Maggi et al., 2009).

Some of the risk factors for developing diabetes have also been found to heighten the risk of being hospitalized for those with Type 2 diabetes. Analyses of the Canadian Community Health Survey found that among people with diabetes, being a former or current smoker and being physically inactive were associated with a greater likelihood of being hospitalized, even after accounting for differences in health status demographic and socioeconomic characteristics (Ng, McGrail, & Johnson, 2010). Because diabetes is considered to be a condition that can be largely managed through community care, higher rates of hospitalization can be considered an indirect indicator of poor health outcomes.

Diabetes is one component of the so-called deadly quartet, the other three of which are interabdominal body fat, hypertension, and elevated lipids. This cluster of symptoms, also known as the metabolic syndrome, is potentially fatal because it is strongly linked to an increased risk of myocardial infarction and stroke (Weber-Hamann et al., 2002). Hostility may also foster the metabolic syndrome as well (Zhang et al., 2005).

Stress and Diabetes   People with either Type I or Type II diabetes are sensitive to the effects of stress (Gonder-Frederick, Carter, Cox, & Clarke, 1990; Halford, Cuddihy, & Mortimer, 1990). People at high risk for diabetes show abnormal glycemic responsiveness to stress, which, when coupled with the experience of intermittent or long-term stress, may be implicated in the development of the disease (Esposito-Del Puente et al., 1994). Stress also aggravates both Type I and Type II diabetes after the disease is diagnosed (Surwit & Schneider, 1993; Surwit & Williams, 1996). Stress is generally disruptive to the performance of preventive health behaviours and its effect on important diabetes management behaviours is no different. Stress can also adversely affect adherence and diet (Balfour, White, Schiffrin, Dougherty, & Dufresne, 1993). Despite the detrimental effects of stress on self-management behaviours, there is mounting evidence that lack of social support may be a more important predictor of poor diabetes control than stress (Mann, Ponieman, Leventhal, & Halm, 2009).

Just as they appear to be implicated in the development of coronary heart disease and hypertension, anger and hostility may be implicated in higher glucose levels (Vitaliano, Scanlan, Krenz, & Fujimoto, 1996), and an examination of their role in the potential aggravation of diabetes is warranted. Diabetic patients with depression appear to be at enhanced risk for coronary heart disease (Kinder, Kamarck, Baum, & Orchard, 2002). A population-based study of people with diabetes in Saskatchewan found that the rates of depression among newly diagnosed young adults were much higher than those without diabetes, suggesting that depression may be a risk factor for developing diabetes among this group (L. C. Brown, Majumdar, Newman, & Johnson, 2005).

Just as sympathetic nervous system reactivity is implicated in the development of coronary heart disease and hypertension, it likewise appears to be involved in the pathophysiology of Type II diabetes. In particular, a hyperresponsivity to epinephrine, higher levels of circulating catecholamines, and elevated levels of endogenous opioid-peptides are found in many diabetes patients. Thus, theoretically, as is the case with heart disease and hypertension patients, interventions to reduce sympathetic nervous system activity can be useful for modulating hyperglycemia.

Problems in Self-management of Diabetes

> I had to make a decision, continuing my university or working to pay for my insulin pump. . . . I made the switch back to shots. . . . University was much easier on a pump, I had better control and the flexibility needed to live the student life. Better control meant better focus, meaning better grades and better scholarships.

Student with diabetes
Health Council of Canada (2007c)

The key to the successful control of diabetes is active self-management (Auerbach et al., 2001). However, for those without extended health care plans, self-management can be challenging. Indeed, Type II diabetes can be completely prevented by changes in the lifestyle of high-risk individuals (Tuomilehto et al., 2001), and the trajectory of the disease in already diagnosed patients can be greatly

The management of Type I diabetes critically depends on proper monitoring of blood glucose level and regular injections of insulin, yet many adolescents and adults fail to adhere properly to the treatment regimen.

improved by changes in lifestyle. The lifestyle factors most strongly implicated are the need for exercise, weight loss among those that are overweight, stress management, and dietary control. The ideal treatment is patient centred and patient directed, rather than physician directed.

Management of Type I Diabetes   Because very tight control of glucose levels can make a huge difference in the progression of this disease, patients with Type I diabetes need to monitor their glucose levels throughout each day and take immediate action when it is needed.

The treatment goal for diabetes is to keep blood sugar at normal levels. This regulation is typically accomplished through regular insulin injections, dietary control, weight control, and exercise. The number of calories taken in each day must be relatively constant. Food intake must be controlled by a meal plan and not by temptation or appetite. Insulin injections are most often recommended on a regular basis for Type I diabetes, whereas diet, weight control, and exercise figure prominently in the management of both types of diabetes. When blood glucose levels can be actively controlled through such methods, onset and progression of diabetes-related disorders, including eye disease, kidney disease, and nerve disorders, may be significantly reduced (Canadian Diabetes Association, 2008).

Adherence   Unfortunately, adherence to self-management programs appears to be low. For example, the Diabetes in Canada Evaluation (DICE) study examined the charts of over 2,500 patients with Type II diabetes across 10 provinces. Results indicated that nearly one in five Canadians (17 percent) had inadequate control over their blood sugar levels, and another third had levels that were considered suboptimal (Health Council of Canada, 2007b).

Moreover, many of the severe complications that arise from diabetes are not evident for 15 or 20 years after its onset. Therefore, complications do not frighten people into being adherent. They may feel no symptoms and, because the disease does not seem insistent on a day-to-day basis, fail to adhere to their treatment regimen. Many of the errors made by people with diabetes in adhering to their treatment regimen, then, are errors of omission rather than errors of commission. That is, it is relatively unusual for people with diabetes to intentionally relapse but common for them to forget to undertake particular behaviours they are supposed to do regularly (Kirkley & Fisher, 1988).

One of the dilemmas involved in adequate adherence is that diabetic patients often fail to self-monitor their blood glucose level. Instead, like hypertensive patients, they rely on what their blood glucose level "feels like," and they may hold inaccurate beliefs about the need to take medication or monitor their blood glucose levels (Mann et al., 2009). Unfortunately, diabetic patients who fail to monitor their blood glucose are also likely to have poor adherence to medication regimens for other health problems they may have that co-occur with diabetes, such as hypertension (Voorham, Haaijer-Ruskamp, Wolffenbuttel, Stolk, & Denig, 2010).

Effective diabetes management involves multiple aspects of behaviour change, and as we have seen, complex regimens directed to multiple health habits are often difficult to implement. As a result, interventions with people with diabetes often pull together into a single treatment program all the self-regulation techniques that are required. People with diabetes are trained in monitoring blood sugar accurately, using the information as a basis for making changes in behaviour as through self-injection, reinforcing themselves for efforts to improve blood sugar control, managing stress, controlling diet, exercising, and developing social and problem-solving skills to deal with situational pressures to break with their treatment regimen (Schachinger et al., 2005). By seeing the relations among all the components in an organized program of self-regulation, adherence to the separate aspects of the regimen may be improved (R. E. Glasgow et al., 1989). Evidence suggests that intensive treatment interventions are more successful than less intensive programs in promoting long-term weight loss and maintaining adherence to treatment.

Management of Type II Diabetes   People with Type II diabetes are often unaware of the health risks they face. Clearly, education is an important component of intervention.

Dietary intervention involves reducing the sugar and carbohydrate intake of diabetic patients. Obesity especially seems to tax the insulin system, so patients are encouraged to achieve a normal weight. Exercise is encouraged (Von Korff et al., 2005) because it helps use up glucose in the blood and helps reduce weight. Adherence is problematic for people with Type II diabetes as well. Poor adherence seems to be due to more transient situational factors, such as psychological stress and social pressure to eat (Goodall & Halford, 1991). However, people with good self-control skills do a better job achieving glycemic control by virtue of their greater adherence to a treatment regimen (Peyrot, McMurry, & Kruger, 1999). The nature of the diabetes treatment regimen also contributes to poor rates of adherence. Specifically, the chief factors that require self-control, diet and exercise, are lifestyle factors, and, as we noted in Chapter 3, adherence to recommendations to alter lifestyle is very low.

One reason for this fact is that such advice is often not seen as medical but as advisory and discretionary, and patients often fail to follow their regimen or modify it according to their own theories and desires. Another reason is that dietary control and exercise are very difficult health habits to follow regularly. The person attempting to exert rigorous dietary control is constantly besieged by temptations to depart from a preset course, and the person trying to fit exercise into an already busy day may find it easy to forget this activity when other demands seem more pressing or necessary. Voluntarily restricting calories, avoiding desired foods, and engaging in an exercise program may seem like self-punishment, something that many patients are unwilling to do.

Improving Adherence   Nonadherence to treatment programs is also influenced by knowledge and health beliefs. Many diabetic patients simply do not have enough information about glucose utilization and metabolic control of insulin. A patient may simply be told what to do without understanding the rationale for it. Inaccurate medication beliefs, for example believing that you only need to use medication when blood sugar is too high, are linked to poor medication adherence (Mann, Ponieman, Leventhal, & Halm, 2009). Patients who are threatened by their disease show poor metabolic control, and those who have strong feelings of self-efficacy seem to achieve better control (Sander, Odell, & Hood, 2010; Kavanaugh, Gooley, & Wilson, 1993). Consequently, education is vital.

Does social support improve adherence to a diabetes regimen? Generally, support improves adherence, and this appears to be the case for diabetes in most instances. Whether the support comes from family of professional contacts, social support appears to make a difference for improving the self-management of diabetes (Rosland et al., 2008). However, for adolescents with diabetes being part of a social network may compromise self-management behaviours by exposing them to tempting situations and situations which may make them feel singled out (Salamon, Hains, Fleischman, Davies, & Kichler, 2010).

As is true of all chronic diseases, patients with diabetes must play an active role in their own care. Consequently, any intervention that focuses on improving a sense of self-efficacy and the ability to independently regulate one's behaviour has the potential to improve adherence and glycemic control (Macrodimitris & Endler, 2001; G. C. Williams, McGregor, Zeldman, Freedman, & Deci, 2004).

Diabetes Prevention   Increasingly, health psychologists and policy-makers are recognizing that diabetes is a major public health problem. Proactive responses to its increasing incidence are on the rise and include more active efforts to control obesity as the first defence against this common, costly, and rapidly growing disorder (R. E. Glasgow et al., 2002).

Several initiatives have been launched in Canada to address this issue. For example, recall from Chapter 3 the Kahnawake Schools Diabetes Prevention Program, an awareness and prevention program implemented in a Mohawk First Nations community near Montreal. Over the 12 years it has been running, the once increasing rates of new diabetes cases have declined and are now closer to the national average. Funded by Health Canada's Aboriginal Diabetes Initiative, this program is now educating and raising awareness about healthy lifestyle choices in a second generation of children (Health Council of Canada, 2007b). Prevention programs like this are increasingly needed to help slow the pandemic of diabetes in First Nations communities and Canada's Aboriginal peoples.

Interventions to Treat People with Diabetes

A variety of cognitive behavioural interventions have been undertaken with people with diabetes to improve adherence to aspects of their regimen. As a result of ties between stress and diabetes (for example, Herschbach et al., 1997), behavioural investigators have examined the effect of stress management programs on diabetic control. An example of combating stress to control diabetes appears in the Health Psychology in Action box, "Stress Management and the Control of Diabetes."

Weight control improves glycemic control and reduces the need for medication, and so behavioural interventions that help diabetic patients lose weight have been undertaken and appear to show at least some success (Eakin et al., 2010). However, as with most weight-loss programs, following initial success, people often relapse to their poor habits and may gain back much of the weight (Wing, Blair, Marcus, Epstein, & Harvey, 1994).

Self-management is an important focus for all interventions with people with chronic disease but is especially true with diabetes. Recognition of the importance of self-regulation for diabetes self-management has led to novel and simple interventions based on implementation intentions theory. One study found that individuals who formed implementation intentions showed significantly greater self-monitoring of blood glucose over a two-week period compared to those in the control group (Nadkarni, Kucukarslan, Bagozzi, Yates, & Erickson, 2010). Because the diabetes regimen is complex, involves lifestyle change, and implicates multiple risk factors, technical skills to manage the regimen as well as problem-solving skills and active coping methods are needed. Thus, training in self-management skills is a vital part of many interventions with diabetes (Hill-Briggs, 2003).

Stress Management and the Control of Diabetes

Mrs. Goldberg had had Type II diabetes for some time. Her doctor had made the diagnosis 10 years earlier, just after her 40th birthday. She watched her diet, got sufficient exercise, and was able to control her blood glucose with oral medication. During the past several months, however, Mrs. Goldberg's diabetes control had begun to deteriorate. Despite the fact that she continued to follow her diet and exercise regimen, her blood glucose levels became elevated more frequently.

Mrs. Goldberg consulted her physician, who asked her if her lifestyle had changed in any way over the past several months. She told him that her boss had added several new responsibilities to her job and that these made her workday much more stressful. Things were so bad that she was having trouble sleeping at night and dreaded going to work in the morning. Mrs. Goldberg's physician told her that this additional stress might be responsible for her poor diabetes control. Rather than

initially changing her medications, he suggested that she first speak with her boss to see if some of the stress of her job might be relieved. Fortunately, her boss was understanding and allowed Mrs. Goldberg to share her responsibilities with another employee. Within several weeks, she no longer dreaded going to work, and her diabetes control improved significantly.

This case illustrates how a relatively simple change in a patient's environment may have a clinically significant impact on blood glucose control. It underscores the need for the physician to be aware of what is happening in the patient's life in order to determine requirements for treatment. Under the circumstances described, it would have been inappropriate to have altered this patient's medication.

Source: Feinglos & Surwit, 1988, p. 29.

Because of problems involving adherence, a focus on maintenance and relapse prevention is essential.

The fact that stress and social pressure to eat have such major effects on adherence to treatment regimens has led researchers to focus increasingly on social skills and problem-solving skills training in diabetes management (for example, R. E. Glasgow, Toobert, Hampson, & Wilson, 1995). That is, in addition to information about the treatment regimen, diabetic patients often need training in how to maintain the treatment regimen in the face of circumstances that undermine it (Goodall & Halford, 1991). Thus, for example, just as the smoker is trained to resist social pressure to smoke, the person with diabetes is trained in resisting influences to consume foods that would have adverse effects on blood sugar (Toobert & Glasgow, 1991).

A complication of diabetes is the depression that often accompanies it. Especially as symptoms increase and the disease intrudes increasingly on life activities, patients may become depressed (Sacco et al., 2005). Depression reduces self-efficacy, compromises treatment adherence, which leads to poor glucose control. Depression is linked to an enhanced risk of coronary heart disease risk among women diagnosed with diabetes; thus, it represents a particularly problematic complication (Clouse et al., 2003). As a result, depression is

often an object of treatment, as well as a symptom of the disease.

Because diabetes is so clearly linked to other disorders, including cardiovascular disease, stroke, and heart attack, interventions that aim toward multiple risk factors may be especially successful. One study that employed behaviour modification and pharmacological therapy that targeted hyperglycemia, hypertension, elevated lipids, and cardiovascular disease (treated by an aspirin) found substantial reduction not only in diabetes but in cardiovascular events as well (Goede et al., 2003).

Special Problems of Adolescents with Diabetes

The management of diabetes is a particular problem with adolescents (for example, Sander, Odell, & Hood, 2010). To begin with, adolescents often have Type I diabetes, so their disease is severe. They are entangled in issues of independence and developing self-concept; diabetes and the restrictions that it imposes are inconsistent with these developmental tasks. Adolescents may see their parents' limitations on food as efforts to control them and may regard the need to monitor diet or to be conscientious about injections as rules and regulations imposed from the outside. Emotionally stable and conscientious adolescents are more likely to follow the complex regimen that diabetes requires than those who do not have these qualities (Skinner, Hampson, & Fife-Schaw, 2002).

Relations with Family   Problems of managing Type I diabetes among adolescents are not confined to the person with diabetes's own difficulties of accepting the limitations imposed by the disease. Other family members may also react in ways that defeat management efforts. Parents, for example, may treat their newly diagnosed adolescent as a child and restrict activities beyond what is necessary, infantilizing the adolescent and increasing dependence. Alternatively, the parents may try to convince the child that he or she is normal, like everyone else, yet the adolescent quickly learns otherwise.

The family environment can be important to diabetic control and adherence. One study found that family support predicted better adherence and metabolic control among children (Pereira, Berg-Cross, Almeida, & Machado, 2008). Lack of family conflict was also associated with better disease management and quality of life. One reason that family support may improve adherence and metabolic control is that it may enhance self-efficacy to manage diabetes (D. K. King et al., 2010). For example, one study found that although family conflict was associated with poor self-monitoring of glucose, this association was weaker once self-efficacy was taken into account (Sander et al., 2010). Interventions that focus on improving family support may also indirectly improve self-efficacy and therefore better self-management of diabetes.

Studies suggest that when parents are actively involved in diabetes management tasks, such as helping their adolescents monitor blood glucose levels, better metabolic control over the disease can be obtained (B. L. Andersen, Ho, Brackett, Finkelstein, & Laffel, 1997).

Adherence   Increasingly, health psychologists have been involved in the development of interventions to improve adherence and adjustment and control over Type I diabetes. The health psychologist can help with the delineation of problems in achieving control over diabetes (R. E. Glasgow & Anderson, 1995) and with the identification of complicating psychological and social factors not yet identified that may compromise the treatment of diabetes (Talbot, Nouwen, Gingras, Gosselin, & Audet, 1997).

The health psychologist, then, has an important role to play in the management of diabetes, by developing the best format for teaching the complex treatment regimen, ensuring adherence, developing effective means for coping with stress, and helping the diagnosed person with diabetes develop the self-regulatory skills needed to manage the multiple factor treatment program that is required. ●

SUMMARY

 Describe coronary heart disease

- Coronary heart disease is the number two killer in Canada. It is a disease of lifestyle, and risk factors include cigarette smoking, obesity, elevated serum cholesterol, low levels of physical activity, chronic stress, and hostility.

- Coronary proneness is associated with hostility and with hyperreactivity to stressful situations, including a slow return to baseline. These exaggerated cardiovascular responses to stress may be genetically based, related to heightened neuroendocrine reactivity to environmental stressors.

- Efforts to modify excessive reactivity to stress and hostility through training in relaxation and stress management show promise in reducing morbidity and mortality due to CHD.

- Cardiac rehabilitation is designed to help diagnosed CHD patients obtain their optimal physical, medical, psychological, social, emotional, vocational, and economic status. Components of these programs typically include education in CHD, drug treatments, nutritional counselling, supervised exercise, stress management, and, under some circumstances, psychological counselling and/or social support group participation.

- MI patients often have difficulty managing the stress-reduction aspects of their regimens, and sometimes marital relations can be strained as a result of the changes forced on the patient and the spouse by the post-MI rehabilitative regimen.

 Explain hypertension

- Hypertension, or high blood pressure, affects about 19 percent of Canadians. Most hypertension is of unknown origin, although risk factors include family history of hypertension, and increased sodium intake. Low SES individuals from minority groups, such as Aboriginals, South Asians, and those of African or Caribbean descent are particularly vulnerable to the disorder.

- People with hypertension show heightened reactivity to stressful events. Hostility is also implicated.

- Hypertension is typically treated by diuretics or beta-blocking drugs, which may have adverse side effects. Cognitive behavioural treatments, including stress management, have been used to control the disorder and to reduce drug dosages.

- The biggest problems related to the control of hypertension concern high rates of nondiagnosis and nonadherence to therapy. The fact that the disease is symptomless helps explain both problems. Low rates of adherence are also explained by the adverse side effects of drugs.

 Understand stroke

- Stroke results from a disturbance in blood flow to the brain. It may disrupt all aspects of life. Motor difficulties, cognitive impairments, and depression are particular problems associated with stroke.

- Interventions for stroke patients have typically involved psychotherapy, including treatment for depression; cognitive remedial training to restore intellectual functioning; skill building; and structured, stimulating environments to challenge the stroke patient's capabilities.

Describe diabetes

- Diabetes is one of the most common chronic diseases in Canada, and is considered an epidemic among Aboriginal peoples. Insulin-dependent, or Type I, diabetes typically develops in childhood and is more severe than non- insulin-dependent, or Type II, diabetes, which develops typically after age 40. Stress is known to exacerbate glycemic control in both types of diabetes.

- The diabetes self-care regimen is complex, involving testing urine for sugar content, administering insulin, (Type I), eating prescribed foods, eating at regular intervals, and exercising regularly. Adherence to this regimen is poor.

- Interventions can improve adherence, especially if the different components of the regimen are logically linked to each other in a programmatic effort toward effective self-care. Training in diabetes-specific social management skills and problem-solving skills are especially important components.

KEY TERMS

cardiac invalidism   p. 362
cardiac rehabilitation   p. 359
cardiopulmonary resuscitation
    (CPR)   p. 363

coronary heart disease
    (CHD)   p. 350
diabetes   p. 372
hypertension   p. 363

metabolic syndrome   p. 351
stroke   p. 369
transient ischemic attacks   p. 370

Psychoneuroimmunology, AIDS, Cancer, and Arthritis

LEARNING OBJECTIVES

After reading this chapter, students will be able to:

(LO1) Explain psychoneuroimmunology

(LO2) Understand AIDS and its consequences

(LO3) Describe cancer and the psychosocial factors involved

(LO4) Define arthritis

Mei-ling was facing the toughest semester she had ever had. Her father had lost his job, so in addition to trying to provide social support to her parents, she had been forced to take on a part-time job to help pay for her college expenses.

She had scheduled all her courses for the first few hours of the morning so that by 1:30 p.m., she was able to get over to the accountant's office, where she answered phones and billed clients until 6:00 at night. Then she headed back to the dorm to study long into the night.

Her boyfriend, Mark, was complaining that he never saw her anymore. When he was free and wanted to go out to a movie or to a fraternity party, she was always studying, trying to make up for the time she lost while she was working. He hadn't actually said that he was going to start dating other women, but she suspected he might soon reach that point.

And now she faced exams. All of them promised to be challenging, and she would have to rearrange her work hours to accommodate the exam schedule. Her boss was annoyed enough at the fact that she sometimes had to reduce her hours to complete course requirements, and he was not going to appreciate the further complications in her schedule that the exams would create.

Mei-ling made it through her exams, but just barely. Following her last exam, in Spanish, she headed back to her room and collapsed into bed with a temperature of 102, where she stayed, nursing a respiratory flu, for the next 10 days.

In this chapter, we take up the question of immunity, the factors that influence it, the situations that compromise it, and the disorders related to its disregulation. Mei-ling's case is not unusual. Stress and problems in social support are among the most clearly documented conditions that compromise the ability of the body to mount resistance to potential infection. After reviewing the immune system, its functioning and the factors that impact immunity, we will consider three chronic illnesses that reflect compromises in immune functioning. AIDS and cancer which are linked to poor immune functioning, and arthritis, an autoimmune disease in which the immune system goes into overdrive and attacks healthy tissues and cells. For these chronic illnesses, the psychological factors that impact immunity for better or worse are particularly important for disease management.

WHAT IS PSYCHONEURO-IMMUNOLOGY?

(L01)

For many years, the immune system was one of the most poorly understood systems of the human body. However, in the past two decades, research advances in this area have been substantial, leading to the burgeoning field of psychoneuroimmunology.

Psychoneuroimmunology refers to the interactions among behavioural, neuroendocrine, and immunological processes of adaptation (Ader, 1995). In this chapter, we consider developments in this rapidly growing field and then turn in more detail to three disorders believed to be related to immunologic functioning: AIDS, cancer, and arthritis.

The Immune System

As noted in Chapter 2, the immune system is the surveillance system of the body. It is implicated in infection, allergies, cancer, and autoimmune diseases among other disorders. Recall from Chapter 2 that the primary function of the immune system is to distinguish between what is "self" and what is foreign and then to attack and rid the body of foreign invaders.

Profile of the Immune System To understand the relationship of psychosocial factors to the immune system, the distinction between natural and specific immunity is important. Natural immunity is involved in defence against a variety of pathogens. That is, the cells involved in natural immunity do not provide defence against a particular pathogen, but rather against many pathogens. As noted in Chapter 2, the largest group of cells involved in natural immunity is granulocytes, which include neutrophils and macrophages; both are phagocytic cells that engulf target pathogens. Neutrophils and macrophages congregate at the site of an injury or infection and release toxic substances. Macrophages release cytokines that lead to inflammation and fever, among other side effects, and promote wound healing. Natural killer cells are also involved in natural immunity; they recognize non-self material (such as viral infections or cancer cells) and lyse (break up and disintegrate) those cells by releasing toxic substances. Natural killer cells are believed to be important in signalling potential malignancies and in limiting early phases of viral infections.

Specific immunity is slower and, as its name implies, more specific than natural immunity. The lymphocytes involved in specific immunity have receptor sites on their cell surfaces that fit with one, and only one, antigen, and thus they respond to only one kind of invader. When they

FIGURE 14.1 | Interaction between Lymphocytes and Phagocytes

B lymphocytes release antibodies, which bind to pathogens and their products, aiding recognition by phagocytes. Cytokines released by T cells activate the phagocytes to destroy the material they have taken up. In turn, mononuclear phagocytes can present antigen to T cells, thereby activating them.

Source: Reprinted from Roitt, Brostoff, & Male, *Immunology*, 5th Edition, 1998, Mosby International Ltd. With permission from Elsevier.

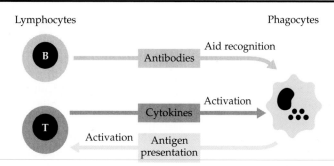

are activated, these antigen-specific cells divide and create a population of cells called the proliferative response.

Essentially, natural and specific immunity work together, such that natural immunity contains an infection or wound rapidly and early on following the invasion of a pathogen, whereas specific immunity involves a delay of up to several days before a full defence can be mounted. Figure 14.1 illustrates the interaction between lymphocytes and phagocytes.

Humoral and Cell-mediated Immunity As explained in Chapter 2, specific immunity is of two types—humoral and cell mediated. Humoral immunity is mediated by B lymphocytes, which provide protection against bacteria, neutralize toxins produced by bacteria, and prevent viral reinfection. Cell-mediated immunity, involving T lymphocytes from the thymus gland, operates at the cellular level. Cytotoxic (T_C) cells respond to specific antigens and kill by producing toxic substances that destroy virally infected cells. Helper T (T_H) cells enhance the functioning of T_C cells, B cells, and macrophages by producing lymphokines. Lymphokines also appear to serve a counterregulatory immune function that suppresses immune activity. Components of the immune system are pictured in Figure 14.2.

FIGURE 14.2 | Components of the Immune System

Source: Reprinted from Roitt, Brostoff, & Male, *Immunology*, 5th Edition, 1998, Mosby International Ltd. With permission from Elsevier.

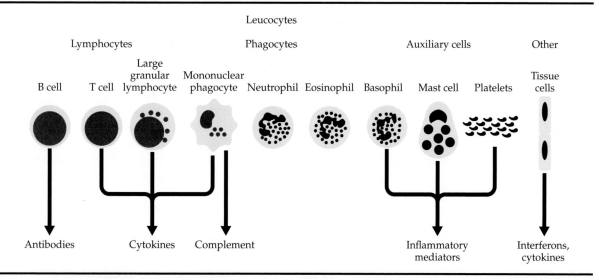

Assessing Immunocompetence

There are many potential indicators of immune functioning. Two general approaches have been used:

1. Measuring the numbers of different kinds of cells in the immune system by looking at blood samples.

2. Assessing the functioning of immune cells.

Examples of the first approach involve counting the numbers of T, B, and NK cells and assessing the amount of circulating lymphokines or antibody levels in the blood.

Assessing the functioning of cells involves examining the activation, proliferation, transformation, and cytotoxicity of cells. Common assessments include the ability of lymphocytes to kill invading cells (lymphocyte cytotoxicity), the ability of lymphocytes to reproduce when artificially stimulated by a chemical (mitogen), and the ability of certain white blood cells to ingest foreign particles (phagocytotic activity). For example, in the mitogenic stimulation technique, it is assumed that the more proliferation that occurs in response to the mitogen, the better cells are functioning.

Another measure of how well the immune system is functioning has to do with the degree to which an individual produces antibodies to a latent virus. All of us carry around viruses that are latent, that is, not active. If our bodies begin to produce antibodies to these inactive viruses (such as Epstein-Barr virus or herpes simplex virus), this is a sign that the immune system is not working well enough to control these latent viruses. Consequently, levels of antibodies to these latent viruses constitute a third type of measure of how well the immune system is functioning.

Producing antibodies to a vaccine is also a measure of immune functioning. When people have received vaccination for particular disorders, the degree to which the body is able to produce antibodies to the vaccine is a sign of good functioning. For example, in studies in which participants received a course of hepatitis B vaccinations, lower antibody response was predicted by a poorer initial T cell proliferation response to mitogenic stimulation and by negative affect (A. L. Marsland, Cohen, Rabin, & Manuck, 2001; see also V. E. Burns, Drayson, Ring, & Carroll, 2002). Subsequent to vaccination, those with higher stress exposure were more likely to show an inadequate antibody titre. Level of antibody titre was also compromised by substance use. Those who coped with stressful life events through emotion-focused coping—that is, by accepting the reality of the situation—were more likely to have an adequate antibody titre one year later.

When indicators such as these suggest that the immune system is working effectively, a state of **immunocompetence** is said to exist. When these indicators suggest that immune functioning may have been disrupted or reduced below a normal level, a state of **immunocompromise** is said to exist.

Another way of studying the effects of stress and psychosocial resources on immune functioning is to examine wound healing. Wounds heal faster when the immune system is functioning more vigorously. Using this method, researchers make a small puncture wound usually in the forearm then examine how quickly the wound heals over and shrinks in people who are under stress or not. Psychological distress impairs the inflammatory response that initiates wound repair (Broadbent, Petrie, Alley, & Booth, 2003; Glaser et al., 1999). Although this method may only indirectly assess the relation of stress to the immune system, it is of critical importance because it demonstrates a relation to health outcomes. For example, stress impairs wound repair due to surgery and thus may prolong the recovery period (Broadbent et al., 2003).

Stress and Immune Functioning

Despite the methodological difficulties of psychoneuroimmunology research, a number of studies suggest that many commonplace stressors can adversely affect the immune system. This research began with animal studies showing that experimentally manipulated stressors altered immunologic functioning and increased susceptibility to disorders under immunologic regulation. Exposures of rats to loud noise, electric shock, and separation from the mother, for example, are all stressful events that produce adverse immunologic effects (Dhabhar, 2009). Research on humans shows similar effects (Segerstrom & Miller, 2004).

Stress and Immunity in Humans   There are more than 300 studies examining the relation of stress to immune functioning in humans (Segerstrom & Miller, 2004). Different kinds of stressors create different demands on the body, so they may be expected to show different effects on the immune system. Human beings likely evolved so that in response to sudden stress, changes in the immune system could take place quickly, leading to wound repair and infection prevention. For example, short-term stressors (of a few minutes' duration) produce a fight-or-flight response and would be expected to elicit

Studies show that exams and other stressful aspects of academic life can adversely compromise immune functioning.

immune responses that anticipate risk of injury and possible entry of infectious agents into the blood stream. Although short-term stressors now rarely involve wounds and the subsequent threat of infection, the system that evolved to deal with these threats is, nonetheless, mobilized in response to short-term stressors. Thus, for example, a short-term stressor, such as being called on in class or having to rapidly compute mental arithmetic in one's head, leads to marked increases in both natural killer cells and large granular lymphocytes. These increases in cell numbers are consistent with the idea that an acutely stressful event causes immune cells to redistribute themselves to fight off infection. In contrast, some measures of specific immunity decrease in response to acute short-term stressors. Recall that specific immunity is quite slow to develop, so specific immunity would be of little, if any, help for combating short-term stressors. Thus, immediate short-term stressors produce a pattern of immune responses involving upregulation of natural immunity accompanied by downregulation of specific immunity (Segerstrom & Miller, 2004).

Brief naturalistic stressors of several days' duration, such as preparing for an examination, show a different pattern. Rather than altering the number or percentage of cells in the blood, short-term stressors mobilize immune functioning, particularly changes in cytokine production, indicating a shift away from cellular immunity toward humoral immunity. Essentially then, real-life, short-term challenges seem to mobilize the immune system to fight off invaders (Segerstrom & Miller, 2004).

Chronically stressful events—including living with a chronic illness or disability; being unemployed; or engaging in long-term, difficult caregiving—are reliably tied to adverse effects on almost all functional measures of the immune system, involving both cellular and humoral downregulation. These effects are stronger among people with pre-existing vulnerabilities, such as old age or disease. Chronic inflammation, which can occur in response to chronically stressful conditions (Robles, Glaser, & Kiecolt-Glaser, 2005), contributes to a wide range of disorders including heart disease (Miller & Blackwell, 2006) and declines in cognitive performance (Marsland et al., 2006).

Thus, different types of stressful events (short term versus a few days versus long term) make different demands on the body that are reflected in different patterns of immune activity, in ways consistent with evolutionary arguments. Intense, short-term stressors recruit cells that may help defend against wounds and infection. Acute stressors of several days' duration upregulate immune functioning in ways likely to ward off threats posed by pathogens. However, chronic stressors seem to affect most measures of immune functioning adversely, ultimately leaving a person vulnerable to diseases (Segerstrom & Miller, 2004).

The body's stress systems appear to partially regulate these effects. As we saw in Chapter 6, stress engages the sympathetic nervous system and the HPA axis, both of which also influence immune functioning (Kudielka & Wüst, 2010). Sympathetic activation in response to stress has immediate effects of increasing immune activity, especially natural killer cell activity. Stress-related changes in hypothalamic adrenocortical functioning have immunosuppressive effects (Miller, Chen, & Zhou, 2007). That is, activation of the HPA axis leads to the release of glucocorticoids such as cortisol; cortisol reduces the number of white blood cells, affects the functioning of lymphocytes, and reduces the release of cytokines, which can reduce the ability of these substances to signal and communicate with other aspects of the immune system. Cortisol can also trigger apoptosis (cell death) of white blood cells. There may also be downward modulation of the immune system by the cerebral cortex, possibly via the release of neuropeptides, such as beta-endorphins (S. M. Levy, Fernstrom, et al., 1991). Self-rated health also predicts levels of circulating cytokines, Possibly, levels of circulating cytokines are a source of people's perceptions of their own health states (Lekander, Elofsson, Neve, Hansson, & Unden, 2004).

Examples of Stress Studies   An example of the kind of study that relates stress to immunologic changes is an investigation of the impact of space flight on astronauts' immune functioning. Eleven astronauts who flew five different space shuttle flights ranging in length from 4 to 16 days were studied before launch and after landing. As expected, space flight was associated with a significant increase in number of circulating white blood cells, and natural killer cells decreased. At landing, catecholamines (epinephrine and norepinephrine) increased substantially as did white blood cells. These effects were stronger for astronauts who had been in space approximately a week, but in those who had experienced long-term flight (about two weeks), the effects were attenuated. This evidence suggests that the stress of space flight and landing produces a sympathetic nervous system response that mediates redistribution of circulating leukocytes, but this response may be attenuated after longer missions. Perhaps the stress of landing is muted by the relief of being at home (Mills, Meck, Waters, D'Aunno, & Ziegler, 2001). Another study of astronauts found that space flight resulted in decreased T-cell immunity and reactivation of the Epstein-Barr virus (a latent virus), consistent with the idea that the immune system was showing the effects of stress (Stowe, Pierson, & Barrett, 2001).

Most studies of stress, however, are literally quite closer to home and involve the effects of natural disasters and other traumas on immune functioning. A study of community responses to Hurricane Andrew damage, for example, revealed substantial changes in the immune systems of those most directly affected, changes that appeared to be due primarily to sleep problems that occurred in the wake of the hurricane (Ironson et al., 1997). In a study with older adults, perceived stress was associated with a lower antibody response to influenza vaccine, but for those with strong social support systems antibody titers were stronger (Moynihan et al., 2004).

Stress involving threats to the self may be especially likely to produce changes in immune functioning. A study by Dickerson and colleagues (2004) had healthy participants write about traumatic experiences in which they had blamed themselves or more neutral experiences. Those who wrote about traumas in which they blamed themselves showed an increase in shame and guilt, coupled with elevations in proinflammatory cytokine activity. These findings suggest that self-related emotions can cause changes in inflammatory processes (Gruenewald, Kemeny, Aziz, & Fahey, 2004).

Anticipatory stress can also compromise immune functioning. In a longitudinal study of patients vulnerable to genital herpes recurrences, Kemeny and her colleagues (1989) found that over a six-month period, the number of stressful events experienced was associated with a decreased percentage of T_H cells. More interesting is the fact that anticipated stressors, those that had not yet occurred but that were expected, also related to decreased percent of T_H cells. The Health Psychology in Action box, "Academic Stress and Immune Functioning," illustrates how academic stress affects immune functioning.

Interestingly, the effects of stress on immune functioning can be somewhat delayed. A study of antibody responses to influenza vaccine suggested that psychological stress just before the vaccine was not related to the response, but in the 10 days following vaccination, stress had shaped long-term antibody responses. These effects may have been mediated by the effect of stress on sleep loss (G. E. Miller et al., 2004).

Health Risks   Is the immune modulation that is produced by psychological stressors sufficient to lead to actual effects on health? The answer seems to be yes.

Research suggests that both children and adults under stress show increased vulnerability to infectious disease, including colds, flus, and herpes virus infections, such as cold sores or genital lesions, chicken pox, mononucleosis, and Epstein-Barr virus (for example, S. Cohen & Herbert, 1996; S. Cohen, Tyrrell, & Smith, 1993), and poor antibody response to vaccines (Miller et al., 2004). Among people who are already ill, such as people with a respiratory infection, stress predicts more severe illness and higher production of cytokines (S. Cohen, Doyle, & Skoner, 1999). Diseases whose onset and course may be influenced by proinflammatory cytokines are also potential health risks associated with stress-related immune changes. These include cardiovascular disease, arthritis, and other major chronic disorders (Kiecolt-Glaser, McGuire, Robles, & Glaser, 2002).

Autoimmune Disorders   In autoimmune diseases, the immune system attacks the body's own tissues, falsely identifying them as invaders (Medzhitov & Janeway, 2002). Autoimmune diseases include more than 80 conditions, and virtually every organ is potentially vulnerable. Some of the most common disorders include Graves' disease, involving excessive production of thyroid hormone; chronic active hepatitis, involving the chronic inflammation of the liver; lupus, which is chronic inflammation of the connective tissue and which can affect multiple organ systems; multiple sclerosis, which involves the destruction of the myelin sheath that surrounds nerves and which produces a range of

Academic Stress and Immune Functioning

Students are a captive population who are often willing and able to participate in research; consequently, much of the groundbreaking work on stress and the immune system has involved coping with the stress of school. Students may take grim satisfaction from studies indicating that, indeed, examinations, public speaking, and other stressful events of academic life can lead to enhanced cardiovascular activity, changes in immunologic parameters, and even illness (for example, Gerritson, Heijnen, Wiegant, Bermond, & Frijda, 1996; R. Glaser et al., 1992; Vedhara & Nott, 1996).

One study conducted by researchers at Carleton University and the University of Ottawa (Lacey et al., 2000), for example, assessed immune parameters in a sample of graduate students at 6 to 8 weeks before an oral exam and then again 1 hour before the exam. The students showed elevated cortisol levels one hour prior to the exam but not weeks before. However, there were detrimental alterations in other markers of immune functioning six to eight weeks before the exam but not one hour before. These findings suggest that anticipation of distal academic stressors is linked to

alterations in immune functioning whereas more immediate stressors are linked to alterations in endocrine functioning.

Several other studies have confirmed these (L. Cohen, Marshall, Cheng, Agarwal & Wei, 2000; R. Glaser et al., 1999). Even five-year-old kindergarten children attending school for the first time showed elevations in cortisol and changes in certain immune measures in response to this stressor (Boyce, Adams, et al., 1995). Moreover, these immune changes may have implications for health.

School-related stress, then, does appear to compromise immune functioning. Are these changes inevitable? If people take care of themselves, can they avoid adverse changes in immunity in response to stress? As noted earlier, Segerstrom and her colleagues (1998) found that students who were optimistic about their ability to manage school-related stress and who made active efforts to cope with it fared better both psychologically and immunologically than those who did not. Good coping, then, may help offset the adverse effects of stress on the immune system.

neurological symptoms; rheumatoid arthritis, in which the immune system attacks and inflames the tissue lining the joints; inflammatory bowel disease (IBD, Crohn's disease or ulcerative colitis), which causes inflammation of the intestines; and Type I diabetes. Nearly 80 percent of people who have these and other autoimmune disorders are women.

Exactly why women are so vulnerable is not yet completely understood. One possibility is that hormonal changes relating to estrogen modulate the occurrence and severity of symptoms. Consistent with this point, many women first develop symptoms of an autoimmune disorder in their twenties, when estrogen levels are high. Another theory is that testosterone may help protect against autoimmune disorders, a hormone that women have in short supply (Angier, 2001). A third theory is that during pregnancy, mother and fetus exchange bodily cells, which can remain in the mother's body for years. Although these cells are very similar to the mother's own, they are not identical and, the theory suggests, the immune system may get confused and at-

tack both the leftover fetal cells and the maternal cells that look similar.

Because autoimmune disorders are a related group of conditions, the likelihood of suffering from one and then contracting another is relatively high. Genetic factors are implicated in autoimmunity (Ueda et al., 2003); one family member may develop lupus, another may develop rheumatoid arthritis, and a third may develop Graves' disease. Individuals with certain types of arthritis are also more prone to getting Crohn's disease, and vice versa, especially if the gene for a particular tissue type is present. Efforts to understand autoimmune diseases have recently been given extra urgency by the fact that immune-related disorders now appear to be implicated in disorders such as atherosclerosis or even diabetes. For example, people with lupus are at risk for premature coronary artery atherosclerosis (Asanuma et al., 2003) and for accelerated atherosclerosis (Ham, 2003; Roman et al., 2003). Thus, increasing attention to autoimmune disorders, their relation to other disorders, and gender differences in them merits additional intention.

Negative Affect and Immune Functioning

Stress may compromise immune functioning, in part, because it increases negative emotions such as depression or anxiety. Depression has been heavily studied as a culprit in the stress-immune relationship (S. Cohen & Herbert, 1996; Robles et al., 2005). A review relating clinical depression to immunity (Blume, Douglas, & Evans, 2011) found depression to be associated with several alterations in cellular immunity—specifically, lowered proliferative response of lymphocytes to mitogens, lowered NK cell activity, and alterations in numbers of white blood cells (see G. E. Miller, Cohen, & Herbert, 1999). These immune effects were stronger among older people and people who were hospitalized, suggesting that already vulnerable people are at special risk.

Moreover, the research suggests a fairly straightforward relationship between depression and immunity such that the more depressed a person is, the more compromise of cellular immunity is likely to be found. Depressive symptoms can be associated with amplified and prolonged inflammatory responses as well, which may explain important links to disease (Robles et al., 2005). The adverse effects of depression on immunity may also be mediated by sleep disturbance that results from depression (for example, Cakirbay et al., 2004).

Stress, Immune Functioning, and Interpersonal Relationships

Both human and animal research suggests the importance of personal relationships to health (S. Cohen & Herbert, 1996). One of the earliest investigations examined bereavement. In a prospective study, Bartrop and associates (1977) studied 26 bereaved individuals and 26 comparison subjects matched for age, sex, and race. A number of immunologic parameters were examined three weeks after bereavement and again six weeks later. At the second time point, the bereaved group showed less responsiveness to mitogenic challenge than did the comparison group. More recent research, however, suggests that impaired immunity in response to bereavement is found largely among those people who become depressed in response to the bereavement (Gerra et al., 2003).

Loneliness also appears to adversely affect immune functioning. Lonely people have poorer health and show more immunocompromise on certain indicators than do people who are not lonely (Pressman et al., 2005). People with insecure attachments to others show lower NK cell cytotoxicity, which may pose potential health risks also (Picardi et al., 2007).

Marital Disruption and Conflict   Marital disruption and conflict have also been tied to adverse changes in immunity. In a seminal study by Kiecolt-Glaser et al. (1987), women who had been separated one year or less showed poorer functioning on some immune parameters than did their matched married counterparts. Among separated and divorced women, recent separation and continued attachment to, or preoccupation with, the ex-husband were associated with poorer immune functioning and with more depression and loneliness. Similar results have been found for men facing separation or divorce (Kiecolt-Glaser & Newton, 2001). Partner violence has also been tied to adverse changes in immune functioning (Garcia-Linares, Sanchez-Lorente, Coe, & Martinez, 2004; Kiecolt-Glaser et al., 2005).

Even short-term marital conflict can have a discernible effect on the immune system. Kiecolt-Glaser and colleagues (1993) assessed the relationship between problem solving and immune functioning in 90 newlywed couples. The couples were asked to spend 30 minutes discussing their marital problems. Those who showed negative or hostile behaviours during the discussion showed impairment on several functional immunologic tests. These results are especially noteworthy because adjustment among newlyweds is generally very high, and the couples had been initially selected because they had good physical and mental health. A subsequent study showed similar effects in couples who had been married, on average, 42 years, suggesting that even in long-term marriages, people are not protected against the adverse immunologic effects of marital conflict (Kiecolt-Glaser et al., 1997). Adverse effects of marital problems and conflict appear to fall more heavily on women than on men (for a review, see Kiecolt-Glaser & Newton, 2001). Positive behaviour during marital conflicts can lead to steeper declines in stress hormones with associated beneficial effects on immunity (Robles, Shaffer, Malarkey, & Kiecolt-Glaser, 2006).

Caregiving   In Chapter 11, we saw how stressful caregiving can be for people who provide care for a friend or family member with a long-term illness, such as AIDS or Alzheimer's disease. Caregiving has been investigated for its impact on the immune system (for example, O'Rourke, Cappeliez, & Neufeld, 2007; Glaser, Sheridan, Malarkey, MacCallum, & Kiecolt-Glaser, 2000; Redwine, Mills, Sada, Dimsdale, Patterson, & Grant, 2004). In one study, the caregivers for Alzheimer's patients were more depressed and showed lower life satisfaction than did a comparison sample. The caregivers had higher EBV antibody titres (an indication of poor immune control of latent virus reactivation) and lower percentages of T cells and T_H cells. These differences did not appear to be related to nutrition, alcohol use, caffeine consumption, or sleep loss.

Other studies have found that the stress of caregiving has adverse effects on wound repair (Kiecolt-Glaser, Marucha, Malarkey, Mercado, & Glaser, 1995), on defects in NK cell function (Esterling et al., 1996), and on reactions to flu vaccine (Segerstrom, Schipper, & Greenberg, 2008). Caregivers who experience emotional distress such as anger or depression may be at particular risk for adverse effects on the immune system (Scanlan, Vitaliano, Zhang, Savage, & Ochs, 2001). Effective coping can, however, mitigate this distress (Engler et al., 2006).

This research suggests that severe and long-term stressors, such as those that result from caregiving, particularly in the elderly, may leave caregivers vulnerable to a range of health-related problems. Moreover, these immune alterations can persist well beyond the end of the stressful situation—that is, after caregiving activities have ceased (Esterling, Kiecolt-Glaser, Bodnar, & Glaser, 1994).

Protective Effects of Social Support   A number of studies now indicate a potentially important role for social support in buffering people against adverse immune change in response to stress. The links between social support and immune functioning are especially strong for older adults, which is especially important as risk for many disorders of the immune system increases with age (Uchino, 2006). In a study of ovarian cancer patients, Lutgendorf and colleagues (2005) found that perceived social support predicted greater NK cell activity. Specifically, individuals with higher levels of social support had greater NK cell activity in tumor-infiltrating lymphocytes. In contrast, individuals with small social networks and who experience loneliness show poor antibody response to influenza vaccination (Pressman et al., 2005).

Coping and Coping Resources as Moderators of the Stress–Immune Functioning Relationship

In Chapter 7, we saw that the impact of stressful events on distress and adverse health outcomes can sometimes be muted by coping methods, such as problem solving, stress management, and relaxation. Research suggests that these resources may also moderate the relation between stress and immune functioning.

Optimism   A number of studies now support the links between optimism and enhanced immune functioning

(see Nes & Segerstrom, 2006 for a review). For example, Segerstrom and colleagues (1998) found that optimism and active coping strategies were protective against stress. In this study, 90 first-year law students, tested at the beginning of law school and again halfway through the first semester, completed questionnaire measures regarding how they coped with the stress of law school, and they had blood drawn for an assessment of immune measures. The optimistic law students and students who used fewer avoidant coping methods showed less increase in distress across the quarter; pessimism, avoidance coping, and mood disturbance, in turn, predicted less NK cell cytotoxicity and fewer numbers of T cells, suggesting that optimism and coping can be important influences on stress-related distress and immune changes.

Self-efficacy/Personal Control   Feelings of self-efficacy and the ability to exercise control over stressful events are associated with less immunocompromise under stress. Such changes could conceivably come about in three ways (Bandura, 1989):

1. Perceived self-efficacy may reduce the experience of stress itself.

2. It may reduce the tendency to develop depression in response to stressful events.

3. It may create some expectancy-based central nervous system modulation of immunologic reactivity.

Evidence shows that, when people are exposed to controllable or uncontrollable stressors, such as noise, those who perceive that they can control the noise show little change in immune parameters. In contrast, those people exposed to uncontrollable stressors are more likely to show adverse effects (Isowa, Ohira, & Murashima, 2006).

Finding benefits in stressful events may improve immune functioning or at least undercut the potential damage that stress may otherwise do. A study by Bower and colleagues (2003) found that women who wrote about positive changes in important personal goals over a month-long period showed increases in natural killer cells cytotoxicity. Potentially then, prioritizing goals and emphasizing relationships, personal growth, and meaning in life may have beneficial biological effects on immune functioning.

Other coping styles may also be related to the stress–immune functioning relationship (S. Cohen & Herbert, 1996). Active methods of coping may be particularly helpful at high stress levels for maintaining immune function while at lower stress levels avoidance coping may be more helpful (Stowell, Kiecolt-Glaser, & Glaser, 2001).

Interventions to Enhance Immunocompetence

A number of investigators have examined whether stress management interventions can mute the impact of stressful events on the immune system. In Chapter 7, we saw that emotional disclosure appears to enhance health and mood in individuals who have suffered a traumatic event. These results may be immunologically mediated. One study examined the effects of written emotional disclosure on wound healing as stress is known to impair the progress of wound healing (Weinman, Ebrecht, Scott, Walburn, & Dyson, 2008). Participants first received a small punch biopsy wound and then wrote about either traumatic experiences or time management. Those who wrote about traumatic or upsetting events had significantly smaller wounds 14 and 21 days after the wound, than did those who wrote about a superficial topic, demonstrating the beneficial effects of disclosure on immunocompetence.

Relaxation   Relaxation may mute the effects of stress on the immune system. In a study of malignant melanoma patients, Fawzy, Kemeny, et al. (1990) found that those patients assigned to a group intervention program that involved relaxation, problem-solving skills, and effective coping strategies showed higher NK activity, higher percentages of NK cells, lower percentages of T_H cells, and higher interferon-augmented NK cell cytotoxic activity than did a comparison group six months after the intervention was completed. They also found that those patients who received the intervention were less likely to have a melanoma recurrence (Fawzy et al., 1993). Similar interventions have shown success with people suffering from herpes simplex virus type 2 (S. Cruess, Antoni, Cruess, et al., 2000). Training in mindfulness meditation has produced demonstrable effects on immune functioning, specifically increasing antibody titres to influenza vaccine (R. J. Davidson et al., 2003). A study using tai chi chih (TCC) as an intervention for older adults reduced the intensity and severity of herpes oster (shingles), suggesting that this may be a useful intervention as well (Irwin, Pike, Cole, & Oxman, 2003).

In one study, healthy volunteers and cancer patients received a 20-minute leg massage to induce relaxation (Noto, Kitajima, Kudo, Okudera, & Hirota, 2010). For both the healthy volunteers and the cancer patients, leg massage increased relaxation and increased indicators of immunocompetence suggesting some enhancement of cellular immunity associated with the relaxation intervention.

A recent study examined the effects of a 45-minute session of Swedish massage on immune functioning in comparison to a light touch control condition (Hyman

Training in relaxation may help people learn how to mute the adverse effects of stress on the immune system.

Rapaport, Schettler, & Bresee, 2010). Significant changes pre- to post-intervention were found for a variety of markers of immune functioning. Massage increased the number of circulating leukocytes and decreased cortisol, and several types of interleukin relative to baseline levels. These results, though preliminary, suggest that massage therapy may be a promising method for managing inflammatory and autoimmune conditions.

Overall, the evidence suggests that these kinds of interventions can have significant effects on the immune system and even on health outcomes (Kiecolt-Glaser et al., 2002; G. E. Miller & Cohen, 2001). Stress management interventions including relaxation show more consistent benefits (G. E. Miller & Cohen, 2001).

WHAT IS AIDS?   (LO2)

A Brief History of AIDS

Exactly when **acquired immune deficiency syndrome (AIDS)** first appeared is unknown. It seems to have begun in Central Africa, perhaps in the early 1970s. It spread rapidly throughout Zaire, Uganda, and other central

African nations, largely because its origins were not understood. A high rate of extramarital sex, little condom use, and a high rate of gonorrhea also facilitated the spread of the AIDS virus in the heterosexual population.

Medical clinics may have inadvertently promoted the spread of AIDS because, in attempting to vaccinate as many people as possible against the common diseases in the area, needles were used over and over again, promoting the exchange of fluids. From Africa, the disease appears to have made its way slowly to Europe and to Haiti, and from Haiti into the United States. The first reported case of AIDS in Canada appeared in 1982. By 2000, over 16,000 people in Canada had AIDS, and over 45,000 people were positive for HIV, with 4,190 new infections in the previous year (Government of Canada, 2006). By 2006, these numbers had increased to over 20,000 cases of AIDS and over 60,000 diagnoses of HIV (Public Health Agency of Canada, 2006b).

A profile of one of the earliest and most notorious carriers of HIV appears in the Focus on Social Issues box, "A Profile of Patient Zero." The current location and prevalence of HIV infection is listed in Figure 14.3.

An estimated 33 million people are living with HIV/AIDS worldwide, with a disproportionate number of these individuals being women, children, and youth (World Health Organization, 2011a). In fact 41 percent

(5 million) of new infections are among young adults, and 60 percent of these are young women, making interventions that target this group especially critical (World Health Organization, 2011b). Approximately two-thirds of these people live in Sub-Saharan Africa; another 22 percent live in Asia and the Pacific (World Health Organization, 2011a). Worldwide, approximately 11 of every 1,000 adults ages 15 to 49 are infected with HIV. Over 60,000 Canadian residents have been diagnosed as being HIV-positive since the first case appeared in 1982, and over 13,000 Canadians have died of AIDS. It is estimated that as many as 15,000 Canadians may be unaware of their infection (Norris, 2006; UNAIDS, 2007).

AIDS researchers are projecting an estimated 120 million deaths from AIDS by the year 2030—more than six times the number who died in the first 20 years of the epidemic—unless major efforts toward primary prevention or major developments in treatment take place (Mathers & Loncar, 2006). Thus far the primary prevention programs appear to be effective, as the number of new HIV infections has globally declined by 19 percent in the past decade, and AIDS related deaths have dropped by 19 percent worldwide between 2004 and 2009 (World Health Organization, 2011a). But despite the large numbers of people who have already died of AIDS, the epidemic is actually still in its early stages and

FIGURE 14.3 | Regional HIV/AIDS Statistics, 2007

(Source: UNAIDS Report on the Global AIDS Epidemic, 2007)

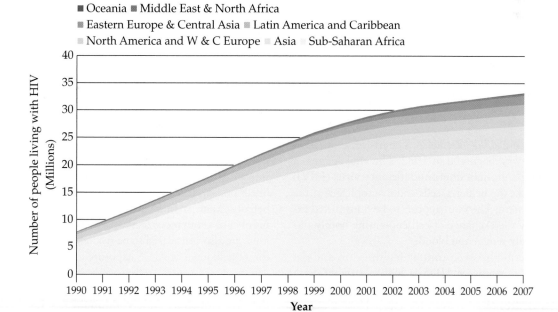

A Profile of Patient Zero?

In the 1970s, a number of seemingly isolated cases of Kaposi's sarcoma and other rare opportunistic infections broke out in the gay community. By the early 1980s, the Centers for Disease Control (CDC) was able to put together these anomalous and seemingly unrelated disorders into a pattern defined as acquired immune deficiency syndrome. As the cluster of disorders associated with this syndrome became clearer, agents from the CDC began to track the cases in an effort to identify common links. They soon became aware that one name was turning up repeatedly as a sexual partner of those now suffering from AIDS, the name of Gaetan Dugas:

> Gaetan Dugas was an attractive, sexually active French-Canadian airline flight attendant. His job and sexual proclivities made him an effective and deadly carrier for spreading the AIDS virus as far and wide as possible.
>
> Gaetan was the man everybody wanted, the ideal for this community, at this time and in this place. His sandy hair fell boyishly over his forehead, his mouth easily curled into an inviting smile, and his laugh could flood color into a room of black and white. He bought his clothes in the trendiest shops of Paris and London. He vacationed in Mexico and on the Caribbean beaches. Americans tumbled for his soft, Quebecois accent and sexual magnetism.
>
> There was no place that the 28-year-old airline steward would rather have the boys fall for him than in

San Francisco. Here, Gaetan could satisfy his voracious sexual appetite with the beautiful California men he liked so much. He returned from every stroll down Castro Street with a pocketful of match covers and napkins that were crowded with addresses and phone numbers. But lovers were like suntans to him: they would be so wonderful, so sexy for a few days, and then fade. At times, Gaetan would study his address book with genuine curiosity, trying to recall who this or that person was.

> He didn't feel like he had cancer at all. That was what the doctor had said after cutting that bump from his face. Gaetan had wanted the small purplish spot removed to satisfy his vanity. The doctor had wanted it for a biopsy. Weeks later, the report came back that he had Kaposi's sarcoma, a bizarre skin cancer that hardly anyone got . . . He was terrified at first, but he consoled himself with the knowledge that you can beat cancer. He had created a life in which he could have everything and everyone he wanted. He'd figure a way around this cancer, too. (Shilts, 1987, pp. 21–22)

When he was finally tracked down by the CDC in 1982, Dugas readily and happily acknowledged his sexual activities, apparently unaware that he had infected dozens of homosexual men. "Including his nights at the baths, he figured he had 250 sexual contacts a year. He'd been involved in gay life for about 10 years, and easily had had 2,500 sexual partners" (p. 83). By the time he learned he

is now being transmitted to every part of the world. Currently, AIDS is the sixth leading cause of death worldwide (World Health Organization, 2008). However, one study suggests that by 2030 it will rank third behind heart disease and stroke (Mathers & Loncar, 2006).

AIDS in Canada

What Are AIDS and HIV Infection?   The first case of AIDS in Canada was diagnosed in 1982. The viral agent is a retrovirus, the **human immunodeficiency virus (HIV),** and it attacks the helper T cells and macrophages of the immune system. The virus appears to be transmitted exclusively by the exchange of cell-containing bodily fluids, especially semen and blood.

The period between contracting the virus and developing symptoms of AIDS is highly variable, with some individuals developing symptoms quite quickly and others free of symptoms for years. Thus, a person

may test HIV-seropositive (HIV+) but be free of AIDS and, during the asymptomatic period, pass on the virus to many other people.

How is HIV transmitted? Among drug users, needle sharing leads to the exchange of bodily fluids, thereby spreading the virus. Among homosexual men, exchange of the virus has been tied to sexual practices, especially anal-receptive sex involving the exchange of semen without a condom. In the heterosexual population, vaginal intercourse is associated with the transmission of AIDS, with women more at risk than men. The likelihood of developing AIDS increases with the number of sexual partners a person has had and with the number of anonymous sexual partners; thus, these behaviours are also considered to be risk related (see Table 14.1 for a breakdown of AIDS exposure categories).

How HIV Infection Progresses   Following transmission, the virus grows very rapidly within the first few weeks of

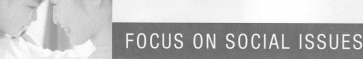
A Profile of Patient Zero? (continued)

was contagious, he had had the disease for almost two years and it had progressed only minimally. Although Dugas was urged to stop having sex by the CDC, he responded: "Of course I'm going to have sex. Nobody's proven to me that you can spread cancer. Somebody gave this to me; I'm not going to give up sex" (p. 138).

Nonetheless, he cooperated by providing as many names and phone numbers of his previous lovers as he could locate. Time after time, these connections led back to small enclaves of AIDS in San Francisco, New York, and other gay communities. "By April, 1982, epidemiologists found that 40 of the first 248 gay men diagnosed could be tied directly to Gaetan Dugas. All had either had sex with him or sex with someone who had. In fact, from just one tryst with Gaetan, 11 early cases could be connected. He was connected to nine of the first 19 cases in L.A., 22 in New York City, and nine in eight other American cities" (p. 147).

CDC officials started talking to the San Francisco city attorneys to see if any laws existed to enable them to take formal action against Dugas. There weren't. "It was around this time that rumours began on Castro Street about a strange guy at the 8th and Howard bathhouse, a blonde with a French accent. He would have sex with you, turn up the lights in the cubicle, and point out his Kaposi's sarcoma lesions. 'I've got gay cancer,' he'd say. 'I'm going to

die and so are you'" (p. 165). Eventually, he became well enough known in the San Francisco gay community that other gay men tried to stop him from having anonymous sex at the bathhouses. Finally, after having AIDS for four years, Gaetan Dugas died in March 1984.

Originally, the CDC speculated that Dugas was *the* person who brought AIDS to North America. As author Randy Shilts summarized Dugas' legacy: "At one time, Gaetan had been what every man wanted from gay life; by the time he died, he had become what every man feared" (p. 439).

Although Dugas' behaviour makes him a good candidate for the title of "patient zero," recent evidence calls the theory of patient zero into question. Findings from a genetic analysis of blood samples from AIDS patients suggest instead that AIDS was brought to North America in 1969 via an infected immigrant from Haiti (Gilbert et al., 2007).

Sources: Randy Shilts, "A Profile of Patient Zero," from *And the Band Played On: People, Politics, and the AIDS Epidemic.* Copyright © 2000 by the author and reprinted by permission of St. Martin's Press, LLC, and Frederick Hill Agency; Gilbert, M. T. P., Rambaut, R., Spira, T., Wlasiuk, G., Pitchenik, A., Worobey, M.(2007). The Emergence of HIV/AIDS in the Americas and Beyond. *Proc Natl Acad Sci USA,* 104:18566–18570.

TABLE 14.1 | Estimated Case Range by Exposure Category and Year, Canada, 2002 and 2005

Following is the distribution of the estimated number of incident HIV infections among Canadian adults and adolescents by exposure category for the years 2002 and 2005.

Exposure Category	2002	2005
Male-to-male sexual contact	900–1,700	1,100–2,000
Male-to-male sexual contact and injection drug use	60–120	70–150
Injection drug use	400–700	350–650
Heterosexual contact with a person at risk or infected	450–850	550–950
Heterosexual contact in a country where HIV is endemic	300–600	400–700
Other*	< 20	< 20
TOTAL	2,100–4,000	2,300–4,500

*Includes recipient of blood transfusion or clotting factor, perinatal, and occupational transmission

Source: Estimated Case Range by Exposure Category and Year, Canada, 2002 and 2005, www.phac-aspc.gc.ca/aids-sida/info/2_e.html. Reproduced with the permission of the Minister of Public Works and Government Services Canada, 2008.

infection and spreads throughout the body. Early symptoms are mild, with swollen glands and mild, flulike symptoms predominating. After three to six weeks, the infection may abate, leading to a long asymptomatic period, during which viral growth is slow and controlled. The amount of virus typically rises gradually, eventually severely compromising the immune system by killing the helper T cells and producing a vulnerability to opportunistic infections that leads to the diagnosis of AIDS.

Early in the disease process, people infected with HIV begin to show abnormalities in their neuroendocrine and cardiovascular responses to stress (for example, Starr et al., 1996). Chronic diarrhea, wasting, skeletal pain, and blindness are also complications. AIDS also eventually leads to neurological involvement. Early symptoms of central nervous system (CNS) impairment are similar to those of depression and include forgetfulness, inability to concentrate, psychomotor retardation, decreased alertness, apathy, withdrawal, diminished interest in work, and loss of sexual desire. In more advanced stages, patients may experience confusion, disorientation, seizures, profound dementia, and coma. CNS disturbance is variable, not appearing until the late stages in some patients but developing early among others.

Antiretroviral Therapy   Highly active antiretroviral therapy (HAART) is a combination of antiretroviral medications that has dramatically improved the health of HIV individuals. So successful have these drug combinations been proven to be that, in some patients, HIV can no longer be discerned in the bloodstream. However, people on protease inhibitors must take these drugs faithfully, often several times a day, or the drugs will fail to work. Yet because the treatments are complex and can disrupt activi-

The possibility that the AIDS virus may move into the adolescent population is substantial, but as yet there are few signs that adolescents have changed their sexual practices in response to the threat of AIDS.

ties, adherence to the drugs is variable, posing a major problem for stemming the progress of the virus (Catz, Kelly, Bogart, Benotsch, & McAuliffe, 2000). In addition, depression, a common condition among people with HIV, is well known to predict non-adherence, and can further threaten adherence with HAART regimens.

To address this issue, a team of researchers from Ottawa developed and tested an intervention program designed to increase psychological readiness for taking HAART with the aim of increasing adherence and reducing depression (Balfour et al., 2006). The psychoeducational intervention was based on several theoretical frameworks, including the health belief model, the theory of planned behaviour, and the transtheoretical model, and targeted individuals who had not yet began HAART. Over the four sessions of the randomized controlled intervention trial, patients explored their beliefs about starting HIV medications, and were educated about the consequences of medication non-adherence. Self-efficacy and motivation were also enhanced through practising medication adherence using jelly beans, and providing feedback about their mock adherence behaviours. Finally, their readiness for change and coping strategies for dealing with barriers to adherence were explored to maximize adherence success. How effective was the intervention? Those in the trial group as compared to the control scored significantly higher on medication readiness, after controlling for baseline scores when compared to the non- treatment group. The intervention was also successful in lowering depression. Although promising, whether the intervention promotes long-term adherence remains to be tested (Balfour et al., 2006).

Adherence to treatment may also be affected by socioeconomic factors, such as housing status. Researchers from the University of Toronto conducted a systematic review of the literature and found that having housing that was affordable and stable was associated with better antiretroviral treatment adherence, use of health and social services, health status, and fewer HIV risk behaviours (Leaver, Bargh, Dunn, & Hwang, 2007). The authors suggested that having a stable home environment enables people with AIDS to meet the demands of the complex treatment regimen, the need for support, monitoring, and a healthy lifestyle that living with this disease requires.

Who Gets AIDS?   Early on in the Canadian AIDS epidemic, the two major at-risk groups were homosexual men and intravenous drug users. While these groups continue to have the largest number of AIDS cases, Aboriginal peoples and other minority populations are increasingly at risk. In fact, this group of Canadians is overrepresented in Canada's AIDS epidemic, representing approximately 7.5 percent of all people with AIDS/HIV in Canada, although they make up only 3.3 percent of the Canadian population. They are also infected at a younger age than non-Aboriginal peoples, with injection drug use as their main risk factor (Public Health Agency of Canada, 2006d).

In all populations, adolescents and young adults are the most at risk because they are the most sexually active group, having more sex with different partners than any other age group. It is estimated that about half of all new infections reported worldwide occur within this group (Public Health Agency of Canada, 2006c). Child and adolescent runaways represent a particularly at-risk group, largely because they sometimes exchange sex for money in order to live. Of particular concern is the fact that AIDS infections are climbing again. The estimated number of new cases of HIV infections among gay and bisexual men increased slightly from 2002 to 2005, after dramatically decreasing prior to 2000 (Public Health Agency of Canada, 2006c).

There is evidence that individuals who have multiple risk factors are at increased risk for AIDS. For example, one Vancouver-based study found that rates of HIV seroconversion were found to be seven times higher among men who had sex with men and who were injection drug users (IDU) compared to men who had sex with men and were not IDU (Weber et al., 2003). Results from a prospective study of young gay and bisexual men in the greater Vancouver region suggest this increased risk is not simply due to a cumulative effect of the combined risk factors, but rather to a synergistic combination of different AIDS risk behaviours (Weber et al., 2003). Men who were not HIV-positive at the beginning of the study were followed over a five-year period, with initial and periodic assessments of sexual behaviour, injection drug use, and HIV status. Among the sample of gay or bisexual men, those who were IDU were more likely to test HIV-positive over the course of the study than non–injection drug users. The profiles of IDU also differed significantly from the men who were not IDU. The IDU group were more likely to be younger, Aboriginal, and economically disadvantaged; more likely to report more casual sexual partners; and more likely to report having female partners. They were also more likely to have unprotected anal intercourse, and more likely to engage in sex trade, engaging in sex for money or drugs. Thus the higher risk for acquiring and transmitting HIV in gay or bisexual men who are IDU is largely due to the increased practice of sexual risk behaviours rather than to IDU alone (Weber et al., 2003).

Nonetheless, the Centre for Infectious Disease Prevention and Control (CIDPC), a branch of the Public Health Agency of Canada, currently reports that the number of AIDS cases is growing faster among women, especially minority women, than for any other group. Between 1985 and 1997, women accounted for 12 percent of adults/adolescents testing positive for HIV—by the period of 1999 to 2002, the proportion had more than doubled to almost 25 percent. By 2005 it had increased slightly again to 25.4 percent. Heterosexual contact and injection drug use are the two main means of exposure for women (Public Health Agency of Canada, 2006c). Among Canadian Aboriginal women, a history of physical abuse or childhood sexual abuse, and having one or both parents who went to residential schools was associated with having AIDS (Shipp, Norton, & Roussil, 1999). Worldwide, women working in the sex trade now represent a common source of the spread of infection (Morisky, Stein, Chiao, Ksobiech, & Malow, 2006).

Providing knowledge about treatments for AIDS is assuming increasing importance, as research advances have brought treatments that prolong the lives of those infected with HIV. Surveys show that the availability of antiretroviral therapeutic agents has relieved psychological distress in the gay community (Rabkin, Ferrando, Lin, Sewell, & McElhiney, 2000). However, optimism regarding AIDS may have indirectly fuelled an increase in risk-related behaviour because the new treatments relieve worries about unsafe sex (Huebner & Gerend, 2001; Vanable, Ostrow, McKirnan, Taywaditep, & Hope, 2000).

Psychosocial Impact of HIV Infection

Thousands of people currently test positive for HIV but have not yet developed AIDS. Most health experts believe that the majority will eventually go on to develop AIDS. Thus, this group of people lives with a major threatening event (HIV+ status) coupled with substantial uncertainty and fear. How do these people cope?

Depression is common with a diagnosis of HIV, and is most likely to occur among those who have little social support, who engage in avoidant coping, and who have more severe symptoms (Heckman et al., 2004). Also, people who test seropositive and learn their serostatus appear to sharply curtail their HIV risk-related behaviour. People seem to cope with the threat of AIDS surprisingly well (for example, Blaney, Millon, Morgan, Eisdorfer, & Szapocznik, 1990), although a subset of people diagnosed with AIDS reacts with extreme depression and thoughts of suicide (Vance, Struzick, & Childs, 2010).

Over the longer term, most people cope with AIDS fairly well. The majority of people diagnosed with AIDS appear to make positive changes in their health behaviours almost immediately after diagnosis. Changing diet in a healthier direction, getting more exercise, quitting or reducing smoking, and reducing or eliminating drug use are among the most common changes people report having made to improve their quality of life and helpfully the course of illness as well (R. L. Collins et al., 2001). Many of these improve psychological well-being, and they may affect course of health as well. Interventions that reduce depression are potentially valuable in the fight against AIDS because depression exacerbates many immune-related disorders (Motivala et al., 2003).

Disclosure   Not disclosing HIV status or simply lying about risk factors, such as the number of partners one has had, is a major barrier to controlling the spread of HIV infection (Kalichman, DiMarco, Austin, Luke, & DiFonzo, 2003). Those less likely to disclose their HIV serostatus to sex partners also appear to be more likely to use cocaine before intercourse, whereas serostatus disclosure is associated with condom use (Sullivan, 2009; Sullivan, Voss, & Li, 2010). Not having disclosed to a partner is associated with low self-efficacy for disclosing, suggesting that self-efficacy interventions might well address the disclosure process as well (Sullivan, 2009). Disclosure may have some surprising benefits. Several studies have shown the positive health consequences of disclosure on health, and in one study, those who had disclosed their HIV+ status to their friends had significantly higher levels of CD4 cells than those who had not (Strachan, Bennett, Russo, & Roy-Byrne, 2007).

Women and HIV   The lives of HIV-infected women, particularly those with symptoms, are often chaotic and unstable. Many of these women have no partners, they may not hold jobs, and many depend on social services to survive. Some of these women have problems with drugs. Many have experienced trauma from sexual or physical abuse (Simoni & Ng, 2002). To an outsider, being HIV+ would seem to be their biggest problem, but in fact, getting food and shelter for the family is often far more salient. Low-income women who are HIV-seropositive experience considerable stress, especially related to family issues (Schrimshaw, 2003), and depressive symptoms that result from stress may exacerbate the course of disease (D. J. Jones, Beach, Forehand, &

Prostitution is one source of the increasing numbers of women who are infected with HIV.

Foster, 2003). Suicide attempts are not uncommon (Cooperman & Simoni, 2005).

Despite problems that women encounter once they have been diagnosed as HIV-seropositive, many women are able to find meaning in their lives, often prompted by the shock of testing positive. A study of low-income, seropositive women (Updegraff, Taylor, Kemeny, & Wyatt, 2002) found that the majority reported positive changes in their lives, including the fact that the HIV diagnosis had gotten them off drugs, gotten them off the street, and enabled them to feel better about themselves. The stigma associated with AIDS and the negative ways in which people respond to those who have HIV infection or AIDS is a problem for those already diagnosed and may act as a deterrent to those not yet tested (Herek, Capitanio, & Widaman, 2003).

Employment and HIV Although many individuals who are seropositive continue to work (Rabkin, McElhiney, Ferrando, Gorp, & Lin, 2004), whether those with HIV are able to continue working depends on several factors. Individuals who experience other AIDS-related illness, are older, and who have worse overall adjustment to AIDS are more likely to be unemployed, whereas individuals with better self-rated health, higher education, and who have lived with AIDS for a shorter period of time tend to remain employed (Fogarty, Zablotska, Rawstorne, Prestage, & Kippax, 2007). Continuing to work early after diagnoses may be particularly beneficial for psychological well-being. One study found that after controlling for illness related variables, employed individuals with HIV reported a significantly higher quality of life than those who were not employed (Blalock et al., 2002).

Interventions to Reduce the Spread of AIDS

Interventions to reduce risk-related behaviour loom large as the best way to control the spread of HIV infection. These interventions centre around practices that involve the exchange of bodily fluids. Refraining from high-risk sex, using a condom, and not sharing needles if one is an injection drug user are the major behaviours on which interventions have focused. Given the diversity of groups at special risk for AIDS—adolescents, injection drug users, men who have sex with men, low-income women, Aboriginal peoples—intensive, community-based interventions aimed at particular at-risk populations seem most likely to be effective. Evidence to date is promising as they appear to be very effective with respect to curbing the number of new incidences of HIV worldwide. Increased access to HIV prevention programs among certain high-risk groups such as injection drug users, men who have sex with men, and sex workers has been instrumental in the global decline of infection rates (World Health Organization, 2011a).

Education Most interventions begin by educating the target population about risky activity, providing knowledge about AIDS and modes of transmission. Studies suggest a high degree of "magical thinking" about AIDS, with people overreacting to casual contact with HIV+ individuals but underreacting to their own sexual risk resulting from casual sex and failure to use a condom.

In addition, people seem to see HIV as socially discriminating, such that the harmfulness of germs depends on the relationship to the person with those germs. Lovers' germs are seen as less threatening than are the germs of people who are disliked or unfamiliar (Nemeroff, 1995). On the whole, gay men are well informed about AIDS, heterosexual adolescents considerably less, and some at-risk groups are very poorly informed (Goldstein et al., 2010). A study of urban female adolescents revealed that about half the participants underestimated the risks entailed in their sexual behaviour (Kershaw, Ethier, Niccolai, Lewis, & Ickovics, 2003). Studies of single, pregnant, inner-city women, likewise, reveal poor knowledge about AIDS, little practice of safe sex, and little knowledge of their partner's current or past behaviour and the ways in which it places them at risk (for example, Hobfoll, Jackson, Lavin, Britton, & Shepherd, 1993). Providing education with respect to HIV and pregnancy is an important educational priority as well (D. A. Murphy, Mann, O'Keefe, & Rotheram-Borus, 1998).

How successful are educational interventions? A review of 27 published studies that provided HIV counselling and testing information found that this type of education was an effective means of secondary prevention for HIV+ individuals, reducing behaviours that might infect others, but was not as effective as a primary prevention strategy for uninfected participants (Albarracín et al., 2003).

Culturally sensitive interventions pitched to a specific target group may fare somewhat better. A study of the effects of a comprehensive AIDS curriculum on the knowledge and attitudes of predominantly Aboriginal students attending a Northern Canadian college demonstrated that providing knowledge could be an effective agent of behaviour change in populations in which the level of information may initially be somewhat low (Moskal, 1991). The students were assigned to an AIDS risk-reduction intervention aimed at increasing their knowledge about AIDS and risky sexual behaviour, or to a control group. In the program, students discussed their personal opinions and values regarding AIDS, and were given information about transmission and prevention of HIV. The students who received the course reported greater knowledge of AIDS prevention and transmission, and more informed attitudes toward low-risk behaviours and those with AIDS compared with students who did not receive the course.

The overwhelming majority of early AIDS cases occurred among gay men. The gay community responded with dramatic and impressive efforts to reduce risk-related behaviours.

Health Beliefs and AIDS Risk-related Behaviour   Knowledge, of course, provides only a basis for effective interventions. In addition to knowledge, one must perceive oneself to be capable of controlling risk-related activity (Forsyth & Carey, 1998). As is true for so many risk-related behaviours, perceptions of self-efficacy with respect to AIDS risk-related behaviour is critical. Gay men who are higher in a sense of self-efficacy are more likely to use condoms (Teng & Mak, 2011), as are university students (Heeren, Jemmott, Mandeya, & Tyler, 2007; see Forsyth & Carey, 1998). Gay men who are high in self-efficacy beliefs have fewer sexual partners and fewer anonymous sexual partners as well (Aspinwall, Kemeny, Taylor, Schneider, & Dudley, 1991; Lin, Simoni, & Zemon, 2005).

The health belief model (see Chapter 3) has shown modest ability to predict the number of sexual partners of Taiwanese immigrants (Lin, Simoni, & Zemon, 2005). It also predicts condom use among HIV infected men (Lance Coleman, 2007). The theory of planned behaviour (see Chapter 3) has been somewhat more informative, in part because social norms are so important to several of the populations at risk for AIDS, especially adolescents (Heeren, Jemmott, Mandeya, & Tyler, 2007).

Targeting Sexual Activity   Interventions to address AIDS risk-related sexual behaviour also need to account for the dynamics of sexuality. Sexual activity is a very personal aspect of life, endowed with private meaning by every individual. Consequently, knowledge of how to practise safe sex and the belief that one is capable of doing so may not translate into behaviour change if spontaneous sexuality is seen as an inherent part of one's personal identity. For example, for many gay men, being gay is associated with the belief that they should be free to do what they want sexually; consequently, modifying sexual activity can represent a threat to identity and lifestyle. In addition, even among men who show high rates of condom use, sexual risk-taking behaviour can vary over time, as personal circumstances change (Mayne et al., 1998).

Past sexual practice is, nonetheless, an important predictor of AIDS risk-related behaviour (Guilamo-Ramos, Jaccard, Pena, & Goldberg, 2005). As people become more sexually experienced, they develop a sexual style that may become integrated into their life more generally. Consistent with this point, people who have had a large number of partners, especially anonymous partners, and who have not used condoms in the past tend to continue these behaviours, perhaps because those behaviours are well integrated into their sexual style (Horvath, Bowen, & Williams, 2006). The Spotlight on Canadian Research box, "Sexual Norms and HIV Prevention," examines the role of social norms in HIV prevention behaviours.

Some interventions have focused on improving skills relating to sexual activity. Sexual encounters, particularly with a new partner, are often rushed, nonverbal, and passionate, conditions not very conducive to a rational discussion of safe-sex practices. To address these issues, health psychologists have developed interventions that involve practice in sexual negotiation skills (for example, L. C. Miller, Bettencourt, DeBro, & Hoffman, 1993). Sexual negotiation skills may be especially important for intervening with adolescents. One of the reasons that young women engage in unsafe sex is the coercive sexual behaviour of their young male

Sexual Norms and HIV Prevention

The increasing rates of HIV infection in young Canadian women are largely due to heterosexual contact with an infected male partner. However, most prevention programs target the female partners, and rarely address the need to include heterosexual males. To address this issue, researchers from Dalhousie University conducted in-depth interviews with heterosexual males in Nova Scotia to explore their perceptions of HIV preventive programming, and possible barriers to HIV prevention strategies such as condom use.

Several themes were revealed, and suggested that masculine sexual norms influenced how open the young men were to receiving education about condom use and HIV prevention. This meant that the young men did not seek out information and instead engaged in risky HIV behaviours rather than reveal their lack of knowledge.

> A lot of males that I know would rather go have sex without a condom because they don't know how to put a condom on.
>
> And they won't learn how to put one on.
> And they won't go ask you how to do it cause that would look kind of weird.

Normative pressures from peers also played a role in the lack of discussion or sharing of information regarding safe sex practices and preventive HIV behaviours.

> Like it's pretty hard to strike a serious conversation with a friend about safe sex and such because they just . . . I mean and I know, I know cause they would rather not talk about it.

The researchers concluded that HIV prevention programs need to consider the powerful effects of male sexual norms on sexual risk taking behaviours when designing effective strategies to better educate young heterosexual males. Without such a consideration, campaigns and programs aimed at education and reduction of HIV risky behaviours are likely to not be effective.

Source: Extracts from Gahagan, J., Rehman, L., Barbour, L., & McWilliam, S. "The preliminary findings of a study exploring the perceptions of a sample of young heterosexual males regarding HIV prevention education programming in Nova Scotia, Canada," *Journal of HIV/AIDS Prevention in Children & Youth, 8(1).* Reprinted by permission of the publisher (Haworth Press, www.haworthpress.com).

partners. Teaching sexual negotiation skills to both young men and women, and especially teaching young women how to resist coercive sexual activity, is therefore important (M. P. Carey, 1999).

Risky sexual activity may be part of a more generally risky experimental lifestyle, involving cigarette smoking, illicit drug and alcohol use, and antisocial activity (Kalichman, Weinhardt, DiFonzo, Austin, & Luke, 2002). Unfortunately, these activities can put temptations or deterrents to condom use in place. For example, one study found that the thought of envisioning a new lover reduced perceptions of risk (Corbin & Fromme, 2002). Debunking the myth that alcohol enhances sexual performance and pleasure may also contribute to reducing the behaviours that facilitate risky sex (Kalichman et al., 2002). Even brief but intensive interventions addressing risk factors and skills may have these beneficial effects (Kalichman et al., 2005; Naar-King et al., 2006).

Cognitive Behavioural Interventions Cognitive behavioural stress management interventions have been employed with some HIV+ groups, including homosexual men and low-income women (N. Schneiderman, 1999). These interventions can decrease distress, buffer the psychological and immunologic consequences of learning about positive serostatus, and improve surveillance of opportunistic infections, such as herpes; in turn, the improved psychological adjustment may retard the progress of the HIV virus, thus contributing to better health.

In a review of behavioural interventions conducted with adolescents, gay and bisexual men, innercity women, college students, and mentally ill adults—all groups at significant risk for AIDS—interventions oriented toward reducing their sexual activity and enhancing their abilities to negotiate condom use with partners were beneficial for reducing risk-related behaviour (Kalichman, Carey, & Johnson, 1996). Another review of behavioural interventions found that only 57 percent were effective, and concluded that interventions based on behavioural theory were needed to improve the efficacy of interventions (Pedlow & Carey, 2003).

Building on these findings, many programs have included not only educational interventions and skills training but also motivational components to try to increase the motivation for at-risk groups to change their risk-related behaviour. Recall that "motivation training" refers to inducing a state of readiness to change, as by helping individuals develop behaviour-change goals, recognize the discrepancy between their goals and their current behaviour, and develop a sense of self-efficacy that they can change. An empathetic, non-judgmental style on the part of the therapist is thought to promote this motivational component. Research suggests that adding a motivational component to education and skills training can enhance the effectiveness of interventions designed to reduce HIV risk-related behaviour (Kalichman et al., 2005).

Targeting IV Drug Use   Interventions with IV drug users need to be targeted toward reducing contact with infected needles as well as toward changing sexual activity. For example, safe injection site programs, such as Vancouver's Insite, provide information about AIDS transmission, offer needle exchange programs, and give instruction on how to sterilize needles, which can reduce risky injection practices among IV drug users (Vancouver Coastal Health, n.d.). Methadone maintenance treatments, coupled with HIV-related education, may help reduce the spread of AIDS by reducing the frequency of injections and shared needle contacts, by reducing health risk behaviours, by increasing use of condoms, and by reducing the number of sexual partners (Margolin, Avants, Warburton, Hawkins, & Shi, 2003). Working with the drug-abusing peer group may result in more success than trying to reach individual drug users (Latkin, Sherman, & Knowlton, 2003).

HIV Prevention Programs   Prevention programs implemented in public schools warn adolescents about the risks of unprotected sexual intercourse and help instill safe-sex practices. Teenagers who are HIV+ sometimes pitch these programs, making the risk graphically clear to the audience. There is some evidence that adolescents try to distance themselves from peers who have HIV in an effort to control the threat that such an encounter produces, so interventions that stress information, motivation, and sexual negotiation skills, as opposed to peer-based interventions, may be more successful in changing adolescent behaviour (Fisher, Fisher, Bryan, & Misovich, 2002).

Interventions in schools have made use of HIV prevention videos that provide training in communication skills and condom use skills. Increasing self-efficacy regarding condom use also improves the likelihood of us-ing them (Longmore, Manning, Giordano, & Rudolph, 2003). There is some evidence that community level HIV prevention programs can be effective for reducing HIV risk behaviours. Researchers from Dalhousie University and the University of Toronto examined the sexual behaviours of bisexual men living in geographical regions with and without prevention programs and found that unprotected sex with men was significantly reduced for men living in areas that had prevention programs (Leaver, Allman, Meyers, & Veugelers, 2004).

Coping with HIV+ Status and AIDS

Now that AIDS is a chronic rather than an acute disease, a number of psychosocial issues raised by chronic illness come to the fore. One such issue is employment. Research suggests that men with HIV who were working at the time of diagnosis continue to work but that those who are unemployed may not return to work. Interventions may be needed to help those who can return to work do so (Rabkin, McElhiney, Ferrando, Van Gorp, & Lin, 2004). People with AIDS must continually cope with the fear and prejudice that they encounter from the general community.

Coping Skills   The chronic burdens associated with HIV infection necessitate coping resources, and those who lack such coping skills are at risk for psychological distress (Penedo et al., 2003). Coping effectiveness training appears to be successful for managing the psychological distress that can be associated with HIV-seropositive status (Chesney, Chambers, Taylor, Johnson, & Folkman, 2003). In one study, a cognitive behavioural stress management program designed to increase positive coping skills and the ability to enlist social support was associated with improvement of psychological wellbeing and quality of life among HIV-seropositive individuals (S. K. Lutgendorf et al., 1998). As has been found with other chronic or advancing diseases, a sense of personal control, or self-efficacy, is important in successful adjustment to AIDS (Benight et al., 1997; Rotheram-Borus, Murphy, Reid, & Coleman, 1996). Not suprisingly though, avoidance coping is associated with higher stress and poorer overall adjustment (Brincks, Feaster, & Mitrani, 2010).

Social Support   Social support is very important to people with AIDS. Men with AIDS who have emotional, practical, and informational support are less depressed (Turner-Cobb et al. 2002), and men with strong partner support are less likely to practise risky sex (Darbes & Lewis, 2005). Informational support appeared to be especially important in buffering the stress associated with AIDS-related symptoms (R. B. Hays, Turner, & Coates, 1992; K. Siegel et al., 1997).

The Internet represents an important resource for people with AIDS. Research suggests that those who use the Internet in conjunction with managing their seropositive status had more HIV disease knowledge, had more active coping skills, engaged in more information-seeking coping, and had more social support than those not using the Internet (Kalichman et al., 2003).

Psychosocial Factors That Affect the Course of AIDS

In recent years, studies have provided evidence that psychosocial factors can influence the rate of immune decline from AIDS (Ironson et al., 2005). Stress itself may foster a more rapid course of illness in people with AIDS and/or foster more opportunistic symptoms or more aggressive opportunistic symptoms (Pereira et al., 2003). Several studies have found that negative beliefs about the self and the future are associated with helper T cell (CD4) decline and onset of AIDS in individuals with HIV (Segerstrom, Taylor, Kemeny, Reed, & Visscher, 1996), and other studies have found that negative expectations about the course of illness can lead to an accelerated course of disease (Reed, Kemeny, Taylor, & Visscher, 1999; Remor, Penedo, Shen, & Schneiderman, 2007).

On the positive side, the ability to find meaning in one's experiences appears to slow declines in CD4 levels and has been related to less likelihood of AIDS-related mortality (Bower et al., 1997). Optimists have been shown to perform more health-promoting behaviours than pessimists, so one recent intervention (Mann, 2001) assigned HIV-infected women to write about positive events that would happen in the future, or they were in a no-writing control group. Among participants who were initially low in optimism, the writing intervention led to increased optimism, a self-reported increase in adherence to medication, and less distress from medication side effects. The results suggest that future-oriented, positive writing intervention may be a useful technique for decreasing distress and increasing medication adherence, especially in pessimistic individuals. Optimism may also help people already infected with HIV withstand additional stressors better (D. Cruess, Antoni, McGregor, et al., 2000).

Research has also linked psychological inhibition to physical illness or a more rapid course of illness, and this relationship also appears to be true for people with HIV. In one investigation, HIV infection advanced more rapidly in men who concealed their homosexual identity relative to men who were openly gay (S. W. Cole, Kemeny, Taylor, Visscher, & Fahey, 1996). Psychological inhibition is known to lead to alterations in sympathetic nervous system activation and immune function, which may have accounted for these differences in physical health. This may also help explain the beneficial effects of disclosure of HIV status on CD4 levels.

Bereavement of a partner can have adverse effects on the immune systems of HIV+ men (Kemeny et al., 1994) and women (Ickovics et al., 2001). For example, Kemeny et al. (1995) found that HIV+ men who had been bereaved by the death of their partner showed a significant increase in immune activation and a significant decrease in proliferative response to mitogenic stimulation. Depression may also play a role in T cell declines (Miller, 2010). Positive affect lowers the risk of AIDS mortality (Moskowitz, 2003).

WHAT IS CANCER?   (L03)

Cancer is a set of more than 100 diseases that have several factors in common. All cancers result from a dysfunction in DNA—that part of the cellular programming that controls cell growth and reproduction. Instead of ensuring the regular, slow production of new cells, this malfunctioning DNA causes excessively rapid cell growth and proliferation (Kiberstis & Marx, 2002). Unlike other cells, cancerous cells provide no benefit to the body. They merely sap it of resources.

In 2007, cancer was the leading cause of death in Canada (Statistics Canada, 2010; see Figure 14.4). Between 1998 and 2007, the incidences of certain cancers—thyroid and liver—have been on the rise, while mortality rates for other cancers—lung and prostate in men, and breast and cervical in women—have declined (Canadian Cancer Society, 2011). The decline in smoking in men combined with the increase in smoking for women accounts for much of this change. The rest of the decline in cancer deaths can be attributed to improvements in screening programs. Nonetheless, it is estimated that 177,800 people were newly diagnosed with

FIGURE 14.4 | Leading Sites of New Cancer Cases and Deaths, Males and Females, 2011 Estimates

(*Source:* Canadian Cancer Society's Steering Committee on Cancer Statistics. Canadian Cancer Statistics, 2011. Toronto, ON.)

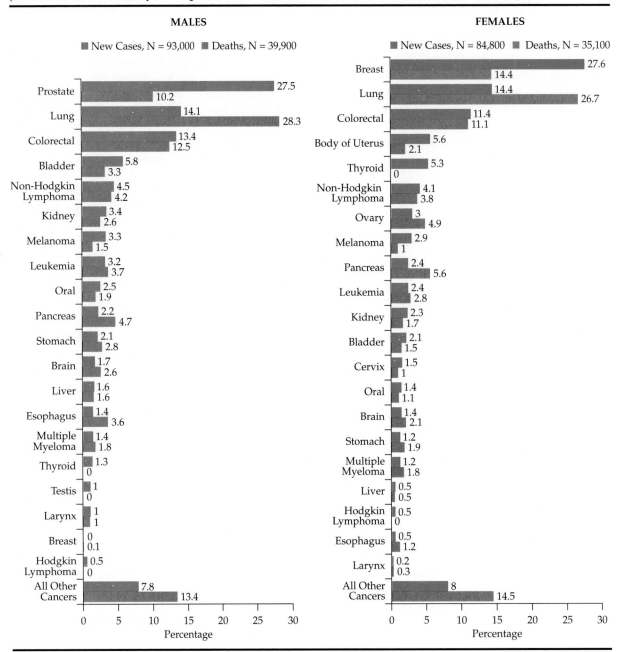

cancer and 75,000 people died from cancer in Canada in 2011 (Canadian Cancer Society, 2011). Deaths from cancer worldwide are expected to rise to 12 million by 2030 (World Health Organization, 2009a).

Because psychosocial factors are so clearly implicated in the causes and course of cancer, the health psychologist has an important role in addressing issues involving etiology and progression of cancer. Moreover, because cancer is a disease with which people often live for many years, interventions to reduce it and to improve coping with it are essential (Holland, 2002). Nonetheless, the five-year survival rate of Canadians diagnosed with an invasive form of cancer is estimated to be about 62 percent of that of Canadians without cancer (Ellison & Wilkins, 2010).

Why Is Cancer Hard to Study?

A number of factors make cancer very difficult to study, in terms of identifying causes and factors that may exacerbate or ameliorate the disease. Many cancers are species specific, and some species are more vulnerable to cancer than others. For example, mice typically contract a lot of cancers, whereas monkeys get very few. Moreover, even a cancer that develops in more than one species may develop in different ways. For example, breast cancer in dogs is very different from breast cancer in humans. As a consequence, it is difficult to use animal models to understand factors that influence the development and course of some human cancers.

Many cancers have long or irregular growth cycles, which contribute to difficulties in studying them. Tumours are measured in terms of their doubling time—that is, the time it takes a tumour to double in size. Doubling time ranges from 23 to 209 days; thus, a tumour may take anywhere from 2 to 17 years to reach a size that can be detected.

There is also high within-species variability such that some subgroups within a species are susceptible to certain cancers, whereas other subgroups are susceptible to different ones. Thus, for example, three individuals all exposed to the same carcinogen may develop different tumours at different times, or one individual may develop a tumour, whereas the others remain tumour free.

Who Gets Cancer? A Complex Profile

Many cancers run in families. To a degree, this tendency occurs because many cancers have a genetic basis. Recent research implicates genetic factors in a subset of colon cancers and breast cancer, discoveries that will help in assessing the risk status of many people. However, family history does not always imply a genetically inherited predisposition to cancer. Many things run in families besides genes, including diet and

other lifestyle factors that influence the development of cancer, and on the whole cancer is more closely tied to lifestyle than to genetics (P. Lichtenstein et al., 2000). Infectious agents are implicated in some cancers. For example, human papillomavirus (HPV) is a cause of cervical cancer (Waller, McCaffery, Forrest, & Wardle, 2004).

Lifestyle factors figure prominently in the development of cancer. According to the World Health Organization (2009), more than 30 percent of cancer could be prevented by modifying or reducing risk factors such as tobacco use, obesity, low intake of fruits and vegetables, physical inactivity, alcohol use, and sexual transmission of the HPV. Because these factors can show regional variability cancer incidence and mortality rates can vary across different regions. In general, cancer incidence and mortality rates are higher in Atlantic Canada and Quebec and lower in British Columbia, although rates can differ by sex and type of cancer. This regional variability can be attributed to differences in cancer risk behaviours such as smoking, as smoking rates are historically higher in Atlantic Canada and Quebec (Canadian Cancer Society, 2011a). Figure 14.5 shows the leading types of cancer for men and women broken down by the provinces and territories in Canada, by incidence.

Married people, especially married men, develop fewer cancers than single people. The sole exception to this pattern is gender-linked cancers, such as prostate or cervical cancer, to which married people are somewhat more vulnerable than single people. These health benefits may derive from having a regular source of social support, regularity in health habits, and as yet unidentified factors.

Dietary factors are also implicated in cancer development. Cancers are more common among people who are chronically malnourished and among those who consume high levels of fats, certain food additives (such as nitrates), and alcohol (National Cancer Institute of Canada, 2005).

Research is beginning to identify interactions among risk factors that may contribute to particular cancers. For example, women who are sedentary and significantly overweight have a higher risk of pancreatic cancer if their diets are also high in starch and starchy foods such as potatoes and rice (Michaud et al., 2002). As researchers increasingly identify risk factors and focus on their co-occurrence, other such relationships may be found.

FIGURE 14.5 | Estimated Incidence Rates for Selected Cancers by Sex and Province, Canada, 2011 (Adjusted to Eliminate Age as a Determining Factor)

(*Source:* Canadian Cancer Society's Steering Committee on Cancer Statistics. Canadian Cancer Statistics, 2011. Toronto, ON)

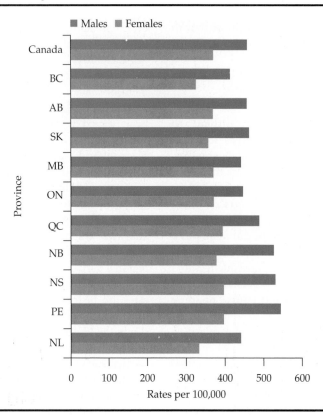

Critical Checkpoint

Behaviour & Cancer: Is There a Link?
Increasingly, new research is uncovering evidence demonstrating the role of the behavioural factors in the development of certain cancers. For example, the link between smoking and lung cancer is well-established. How might current and future knowledge about the modifiable factors linked to cancer development affect people's attitudes about cancer patients, and/or the lifestyle choices that people make if they engage in cancer risk behaviours?

Psychosocial Factors and Cancer

We have already considered many of the factors that initiate and lead to a progression of cancer, including such risk factors as smoking, alcohol consumption, or fatty diet (Chapters 4 and 5), and variables that promote delay behaviour and nonadherence (Chapters 8 and 9). In this chapter, we focus more heavily on the evidence regarding stress and psychosocial factors in the initiation and course of cancer, specifically whether the cancer progresses rapidly or slowly.

Depression and Cancer   Research has found a positive association between depression and cancer (for example, Carney, Jones, Woolson, Noyes, & Doebbeling, 2003; Pinquart & Duberstein, 2010). One suggested mechanism is through altered biological responses to stress (Giese-Davis et al., 2006). Depression can be associated with elevated neural endocrine responses such as cortisol and norepinephrine, which may, in turn, have implications for cancer via their impact on the immune system. Psychological distress more generally has been linked to colorectal cancer mortality (Kojima et al., 2005). However, emerging evidence suggests a modest but reliable link between depression and cancer mortality. A meta-analysis of 76 prospective studies found that depression was associated with higher cancer mortality even after controlling for differences in medical variables (Pinquart & Duberstein, 2010). Despite this sobering finding, there is evidence that changes in depression may also predict cancer survival. Researchers at the University of Calgary examined the depression scores of women with breast cancer over their first year since diagnosis and found that decreasing depression scores were associated with significantly longer cancer survival (Giese-Davis et al., 2011).

At present, evidence suggests only a modest association between psychosocial factors and the development of at least some cancers and questions any general relationship between personality and the development of cancer (Antoni & Lutgendorf, 2007). Moreover, a recent review suggests that there is little research supporting the notion that depression is linked to cancer progression (Satin, Linden, & Phillips, 2009). On the whole, the evidence relating depression to cancer survival is increasingly persuasive and underscores the importance of identifying and intervening in depression early, so as to mute its impact on cancer survival.

Stress and Cancer   Does stress cause cancer? One approach to this question has focused on major life events and their relationship to cancer development. For example, confronting major stressors such as divorce, infidelity, marital quarrelling, financial stress, and the like increases risk for diagnosed cervical cancer (Coker, Bond, Madeleine, Luchok, & Pirisi, 2003). Generally, studies on both animals and humans suggest such a link. A few prospective studies in humans have found evidence of a link between uncontrollable stress and cancer progression (Moreno-Smith et al., 2010). Experiencing stressful events such as divorce, infidelity, marital quarrelling, and financial stress, can increase the risk for cervical cancer (Coker, Bond, Madeleine, Luchok, & Pirisi, 2003).

Avoidant or passive coping is also a risk factor for psychological distress and depression, which may represent another way in which these forms of coping may adversely influence course of disease (Kim, Valdimarsdottir, & Bovbjerg, 2003). Repressive coping appears to be especially common in children with cancer, so this coping style warrants particular consideration in their care (Phipps, Steele, Hall, & Leigh, 2001).

Mechanisms Linking Stress, Coping, and Cancer

How, exactly, might stressful events and cancer be linked? A number of studies implicate the immune and neuroendocrine systems (Antoni & Lutgendorf, 2007). As noted earlier, NK cells are involved in the surveillance and destruction of tumour cells and virally infected cells, and therefore, they are believed to have a role in tumour surveillance in the body. NK cell activity is also believed to be involved in whether or not a carcinogen takes hold after exposure.

Psychological stress appears to adversely affect the ability of NK cells to destroy tumours (for example, Arranz et al., 2010; Lutgendorf et al., 2005), an important finding because NK cell activity appears to be important in survival rates for certain cancers, especially early breast cancer (S. M. Levy, Herberman, Lippman, D'Angelo, & Lee, 1991). Researchers have also begun to explore the pathways by which coping may affect the course of cancer. Repressive and anxiety coping have been linked to autonomic, endocrine, and immunologic disregulation (Giese-Davis et al., 2006). Alterations in biological stress regulatory pathways represent possible mechanisms for these relations (Antoni & Lutgendorf, 2007).

Adjusting to Cancer

Based on current rates, 40 percent of Canadian women and 45 percent of men will eventually develop cancer, and each year cancer causes approximately 75,000 deaths in Canada (Canadian Cancer Society, 2011a). The psychosocial toll of cancer is enormous. Two out of every three families will have a family member who develops cancer, and virtually every member of these families will be affected by the disease. However, 60 percent of cancer victims live at least five years after their diagnosis, thus creating many issues of long-term adjustment. Many of the issues that we explored in Chapters 11 and 12 in the context of chronic, advancing, and terminal illness are especially relevant to the cancer experience. We highlight a few additional issues in this section.

Coping with Physical Limitations   Cancer takes a substantial toll, both physically and psychologically. The physical difficulties usually stem from the pain and discomfort cancer can produce, particularly in the advancing and terminal phases of illness. Fatigue is also a common and debilitating symptom (Curran, Beacham, & Andrykowski, 2004).

Cancer can lead to downregulation of the immune system, which may enhance vulnerability to a variety of other disorders, including respiratory tract infections. These persistent health problems can compromise quality of life (B. L. Andersen, Kiecolt-Glaser, & Glaser, 1994). Fatigue due to illness and treatment is also one of the main complaints of cancer patients (Andrykowski, Curran, & Lightner, 1998).

Treatment-related Problems   Difficulties also arise as a consequence of treatment. Some cancers are treated surgically. Removal of organs can create cosmetic problems, as for patients with breast cancer who may have a breast removed (mastectomy) or for patients with head and neck cancer who may have a portion of this area removed (Vos, Garssen, Visser, Duivenvoorden, & de Haes, 2004). Body image concerns stem not only from concern about appearance following surgery but also from concerns about a sense of wholeness, bodily integrity, and the ability to function normally. Either concern can complicate reactions to treatment (Carver et al., 1998).

In some cases, organs that are vital to bodily functions must be taken over by a prosthesis. For example, a patient whose larynx has been removed must learn to speak with the help of a prosthetic speech device. Side effects due to surgery are also common. A colostomy (prosthetic replacement of the lower colon) produces a loss of bowel control. Men may also receive treatments for prostate cancer that compromise sexual functioning (Steginga & Occhipinti, 2006).

Some cancer patients receive debilitating follow-up treatments. Patients undergoing chemotherapy may expect and experience debilitating nausea and vomiting and may develop anticipatory nausea and vomiting that occurs even before the chemotherapy session begins (for example, Montgomery & Bovbjerg, 2003). As a result, symptoms of nausea, distress, and vomiting can continue to adversely affect quality of life among cancer patients long after the treatment has ended (C. L. Cameron et al., 2001). Because chemotherapy is often administered in the same place by the same person under the same circumstances, patients may develop conditioned nausea to a wide variety of stimuli, including the hospital staff (Bovbjerg, Montgomery, & Raptis, 2005; Bovbjerg, 2006). One chemotherapy nurse remarked that once she saw one of her chemotherapy patients in a supermarket. She said hello, and the patient threw up in the aisle. Fortunately, in recent years, chemotherapies with less virulent side effects have been developed. Patients may also develop conditioned immune suppression in response to repeated pairings of the hospital, staff, and other stimuli with the immunosuppressive effects of chemotherapy (Cameron et al., 2001; Lekander, Furst, Rotstein, Blomgren, & Fredrikson, 1995), which can have adverse effects on the course of cancer.

These physical problems are not only important in their own right, but they can often feed into psychological adjustment problems, increasing the likelihood of cancer-related distress post treatment (Jim, Andrykowski, Munster, & Jacobsen, 2007). Research suggests that stress management skills may contribute to a more positive state of mind following radical treatments (Penedo et al., 2003).

Psychosocial Issues and Cancer

Because of early identification techniques and promising treatments, many people who are diagnosed with cancer live long and fulfilling lives free of disease. Others may have recurrences but nonetheless maintain a high quality of life for 15 or 20 years. Others live with active cancers over the long term, knowing that the disease will ultimately be fatal. All of these trajectories, however, indicate that cancer is now a chronic disease, which poses long-term issues related to psychosocial adjustment.

Intermittent and long-term depression is among the most common difficulties experienced as a result of cancer (Stommel et al., 2004). Depression not only compromises quality of life in its own right, but as discussed previously, it can increase risk for mortality (Pinquart & Duberstein, 2010). Adjustment problems appear to be greatest among women who have a history of life stressors or a lack of social support (L. D. Butler, Koopman, Classen, & Spiegel, 1999). Although cancer patients do not have more psychological distress than people without cancer for the most part, they are more susceptible to depression (van't Spijker, Trijsburg, & Duivenvoorden, 1997). Restriction of usual activities is a common outcome of the disease and its treatment, which can foster depression and other adverse psychosocial responses (Williamson, 2000).

Issues Involving Social Support   Despite the fact that many cancer patients receive considerable emotional support from their families and friends, social support can be problematic. Although cancer patients may desire a significant amount of social support they may only receive this shortly after diagnoses, as social support tends to significantly drop off even within the first year after diagnoses (Arora, Finney Rutten, Gustafson, Moser, & Hawkins, 2007). Effective support is important for several reasons. It improves psychological adjustment to cancer, and it can help patients deal with intrusive thoughts and rumination about the cancer (J. A. Lewis et al., 2001). Support may improve immunologic responses to cancer as well. If there was any doubt of the importance of social support to cancer survival, one investigation (Lai et al., 1999) found that married patients with cancers have significantly better survival than single, separated, divorced, or widowed patients. What's more, there is some evidence that social support buffers stress and increases NK cell activity in cancer patients with impaired immunity (Lutgendorf et al., 2005).

How spouses provide support matters. Hagedoorn and colleagues (2000) found that actively engaging in conversations with the patient about the cancer and finding constructive methods for solving problems were beneficial, whereas hiding one's concerns and overprotecting the patient were less beneficial. Interventions directed to these issues can significantly improve quality of life (Graves, 2003).

Problems concerning a cancer patient's children are relatively common. Young children may show fear or distress over the parent's prognosis (Compas et al., 1994). Older children may find new responsibilities thrust on them and may respond by rebelling. When a mother gets breast cancer this means the daughter is also at risk, and both may be distressed (M. Cohen & Pollack, 2005; Fletcher, Clemow, Peterson, Lemon, Estabrook, & Zapka, 2006).

Marital and Sexual Relationships A strong marital relationship is important in cancer because marital adjustment predicts psychological distress following cancer diagnosis (Banthia et al., 2003). Unfortunately, disturbances in marital relationships after a diagnosis of cancer are not uncommon (Ybema, Kuijer, Buunk, DeJong, & Sanderman, 2001). Having an unsupportive partner may have a lasting negative impact on the cancer patient's quality of life (Manne et al., 2004). Sexual functioning is particularly vulnerable. Body image concerns and concerns about a partner's reactions represent psychosocial vulnerabilities, especially when there has been disfiguring surgery, as in the case of breast cancer (Spencer et al., 1999). Breast-conserving techniques, such as

lumpectomy, lead to moderately better psychological, marital, sexual, and social adjustment than the more extensive mastectomy surgery (Moyer, 1997).

Sexual functioning can be directly affected by treatments, such as surgery or chemotherapy, and indirectly affected by anxiety or depression, which often reduce sexual desire (B. L. Andersen, Woods, & Copeland, 1997). Sexual functioning problems have been particularly evident in patients with gynecologic cancers and prostate cancer and underscore the fact that different types of cancers create different kinds of problems (for example, Moyer & Salovey, 1996).

Psychological Adjustment and Treatment Adverse psychological reactions to cancer can also be severe when the treatments are severe, or if the patient has a poor understanding of the disease and treatment or both. Survivors of childhood leukemia, for example, sometimes show signs of post-traumatic stress disorder (PTSD), which may persist for years following treatment (Somerfield, Curbow, Wingard, Baker, & Fogarty, 1996; Stuber, Christakis, Houskamp, & Kazak, 1996). Nonetheless, one longitudinal study found that most survivors of childhood cancer report relatively good health-related quality of life and overall life satisfaction (Zeltzer et al., 2009). Among adult patients, signs of PTSD appear to be relatively rare, and when present may be attributable to trauma and anxiety disorders that predate cancer diagnoses (Shelby, Golden-Kreutz, & Andersen, 2008). Trying to understand the experience of cancer patients through our understanding of trauma may therefore be misleading (Palmer, Kagee, Coyne, & DeMichele, 2004).

Identifying and attending to psychological distress in response to cancer is an important issue, not only for maintaining quality of life but also because psychological distress may itself be related to prospects for long-term survival. For example, research shows that cancer survivors may show elevated cortisol and alterations in their HPA axis responses to stress subsequent to cancer treatment; this may be due to fear of recurrence, stress associated with cancer treatment and the disease, or a combination (Porter et al., 2003). These hormones may, in turn, exert a regulatory effect on the immune system that may influence the likelihood of a recurrence (see also Luecken & Compas, 2002).

Self-presentation of Cancer Patients Vocational disruption may occur for patients who have chronic discomfort from cancer or its treatments (Somerfield et al., 1996), and job discrimination against cancer patients has been documented. Difficulties in managing social interactions can result from alterations in physical appearance, disrupting social and recreational activity. An ostomy patient, for example, described his fear of revolting others:

> When I smelled an odor on the bus or subway before the colostomy, I used to feel very annoyed. I'd think that the people were awful, that they didn't take a bath, or that they should have gone to the bathroom before traveling. I used to think that they might have odors from what they ate. I used to be terribly annoyed; to me it seemed that they were filthy, dirty. Of course, at the least opportunity I used to change my seat and if I couldn't, it used to go against my grain. So naturally, I believe that the young people feel the same way about me if I smell. (Goffman, 1963, p. 34)

There is now cause for considerable optimism. Many people with active malignant disease live long, active, satisfying, unrestricted lives. The sense of doom that a cancer diagnosis once conveyed no longer casts a shadow over cancer patients. The stigma attached to cancer has largely lifted. Nonetheless, cancer does pose a variety of issues including physical disabilities, family and marital disruptions, sexual difficulty, self-esteem problems, social and recreational disruptions, and psychological distress for which coping and interventions may be needed.

Coping with Cancer

> I needed some emotional support. When you're diagnosed [with breast cancer] I guess some people might isolate themselves, but other people think omigod, I gotta find more ladies like me. I joined [dragon boat racing] recognizing the need for emotional support and the emotional support is huge. I mean, the girls in my group, a certain number of the girls in my group are my best friends.
>
> Breast cancer survivor (Parry, 2008)

Although different people may choose different coping strategies to deal with cancer, not all strategies are equally beneficial. Certain strategies do appear to be helpful in dealing with the problems related to cancer. In a study of 603 cancer patients, Dunkel-Schetter et al. (1992) identified five patterns of coping:

1. Seeking or using social support.
2. Focus on the positive.
3. Distancing.
4. Cognitive escape-avoidance.
5. Behavioural escape-avoidance.

Coping through social support, focusing on the positive, and distancing were all associated with less emotional distress from cancer. Patients high in optimism also experience less psychological distress (Carver et al., 2005).

Patients who cope with their cancer-related problems through cognitive and behavioural escape-avoidant strategies show more emotional distress (for example, Manne, Glassman, & DuHamel, 2000). When spouses cope with their partner's illness using these same avoidance strategies, a patient's distress may also be high (Ben-Zur, Gilbar, & Lev, 2001).

Despite documented psychosocial problems associated with cancer, many people clearly have cancer experiences that they weather quite well from a psychological standpoint, adjusting successfully to major changes in their lives (Reaby & Hort, 1995). With the exception of depression, the psychological distress experienced by cancer patients does not differ from people without cancer and is significantly less than people suffering from psychiatric disorders (van't Spijker et al., 1997). Pain, fatigue, and depression can nonetheless persist and have implications not only for quality of life but also for biological stress regulatory functioning (Bower, Ganz, & Aziz, 2005).

Finding Meaning in Cancer   Indeed, some cancer patients report that their lives have been made better in important ways by the cancer experience, permitting them to experience growth (Widows, Jacobsen, Booth-Jones, & Fields, 2005), and satisfaction in personal relationships that they might not otherwise have achieved (Fromm, Andrykowski, & Hunt, 1996; Jim & Andersen, 2007; Katz, Flasher, Cacciapaglia, & Nelson, 2001). Such growth experiences may mute neuroendocrine stress responses, which may, in turn, have a beneficial effect on the immune system (D. G. Cruess, Antoni, McGregor, et al., 2000).

These positive adaptations to the cancer experience can be enhanced by feelings of control or self-efficacy in response to the cancer experience. People who are able to experience a sense of personal control over their cancer, its treatments, or their daily activities cope more successfully with cancer (Newsom, Knapp, & Schulz, 1996; Fang et al., 2006). Control over emotional reactions and physical symptoms appear to be especially important for psychosocial adjustment (S. C. Thompson et al., 1993).

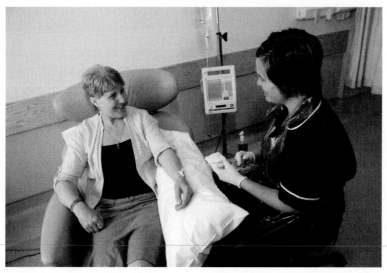

Many cancer patients who receive intravenously administered chemotherapy experience intense nausea and vomiting. Interventions using relaxation and guided imagery can substantially improve these problems.

Interventions

Cognitive Behavioural Interventions   Common cancer-related problems such as depression, stress, pain, appetite control, and side effects associated with chemotherapy, radiation therapy, and other cancer treatments are often the focus of cognitive behavioural interventions (Antoni et al., 2001; Curran, Beacham, & Andrykowski, 2004). Interventions directed to these issues can significantly improve quality of life (Graves, 2003; Tatrow & Montgomery, 2006), and in some cases may also have beneficial immunological effects. In one study of a cognitive behavioural, stress management intervention with women newly diagnosed with breast cancer, the intervention successfully reduced the prevalence of depression and increased the women's ability to find benefits in their experience (Antoni et al., 2001). This intervention also reduced cortisol levels in these women, which may have positive implications for the course of their cancer (D. G. Cruess, Antoni, McGregor, et al., 2000).

Mindfulness-based, stress reduction interventions have also been undertaken with cancer patients. For example, researchers from the University of Calgary employed a mindfulness intervention involving the active cultivation of conscious awareness through relaxation, meditation, and yoga, with daily practice with breast and prostate cancer patients. The intervention not only enhanced quality of life and decreased stress symptoms but also produced a shift in immune profile from one associated with depressive symptoms to a more normal profile (Carlson, Speca, Patel, & Goodey, 2003).

Recent evidence suggests that relaxation techniques may not only reduce stress and improve quality of life, but also have important immune-modulatory effects for those undergoing cancer treatments that may compromise immunity. In one randomized controlled trial, women undergoing multi-modal breast cancer treatment including chemotherapy, radiation therapy, surgery, and hormone therapy received training in relaxation and guided imagery for 37 weeks (Oleg et al., 2009). Compared to those in the control group, those receiving the relaxation and imagery training had higher levels of NK cell activity and activated T cells following chemotherapy and radiation, and relaxation frequency was associated with higher T helper cell counts. Thus, relaxation training may be one way to help counteract the negative immunological effects of standard cancer treatments.

Exercise is also increasingly recommended as a general intervention to improve quality of life following cancer. Researchers from the University of Alberta have conducted a number of reviews of research studies on the effectiveness of exercise as an intervention for cancer patients. In general they have found that physical exercise has a positive effect on quality of life following cancer diagnosis, improving physical and emotional functioning, and reducing fatigue (Courneya & Friedenreich, 1999; 2001; McNeely, Campbell, Rowe, Klassen, Mackey, & Courneya, 2006; Thorsen, Courneya,

Dragon Boat Racing for Breast Cancer Survivors—A Canadian Innovation

Dragon boat racing is a dynamic team sport that originated in ancient China and has been around for more than 2,000 years. It involves 22 people working as a team to paddle a 12- to 18-metre boat down a 250- to 1,000-metre straight course toward a finish line (Parry, 2008). Yet it is only recently that this physically challenging team sport has become a popular way for breast cancer survivors to stay fit and obtain needed social support from others who are all "in the same boat in the race against breast cancer" (Mitchell & Nielsen, 2002).

It all started in 1996 when a sports medicine physician from the University of British Columbia, Dr. Don McKenzie, conducted a small study to test the effects of strenuous upper body physical exercise on the risk for lymphedema, a complication of cancer surgery or treatment, with a group of women treated for breast cancer. Thus, the first breast cancer survivor dragon boat team, "Abreast in a Boat," was formed. Contrary to expectations, participation in dragon boat racing was not found to increase the women's risk for lymphedema (McKenzie, 1998). Although it was expected that the dragon boat team would disband, the women continued to paddle, and anecdotally reported improvements in both their physical and mental well-being as a result of their dragon boat racing experience (McKenzie, 1998). Soon after, word quickly spread throughout breast cancer communities in Canada and the rest of the world about this exciting new leisure activity for breast cancer survivors (Parry, 2008). Today, there are nearly 100 dragon boat racing teams for breast cancer survivors worldwide, with an estimated 50 of these in Canada (T. L. Mitchell, Yakiwchuk, Griffin, Gray, & Fitch, 2007).

Given the growing body of research suggesting the physical and psychological benefits of physical exercise for cancer survivors, and the known benefits of support group involvement for the well-being of cancer patients, it follows that dragon boat racing, which combines exercise with social support, should be beneficial for cancer survivors' quality of life. To date, only a handful of studies have examined the psychosocial benefits of dragon boat racing, and the majority of these have been conducted by Canadian researchers.

One of the first studies to examine the positive influence of dragon boat racing was conducted by Mitchell and Nielson (2002). Their qualitative study of two teams from Ontario explored the meaning, experience, and impact of dragon boat racing for the breast cancer survivors. A number of themes reflecting the positive influence of the dragon boating experience emerged including hope, camaraderie, regaining control, facing the disease, and having fun. In a second study Mitchell (now at Wilfred Laurier University) and a team of researchers, further explored perceptions and experiences with dragon boat racing by conducting interviews with new team members before their first experience of dragon boating and then again after they completed their first season (T. L. Mitchell, Yakiwchuk, et al., 2007). Findings indicated that the dragon boating experience surpassed the women's expectations and provided them with strength, hope, and the ability to regain control over their lives.

Other qualitative investigations have found similar themes suggesting a positive impact of dragon boating for the well-being of breast cancer survivors. For example, researchers from the University of British Colum-

Stevinson, & Fosså, 2008). A particular type of exercise, dragon boat racing, that has been found to be beneficial for women with breast cancer is examined in the Spotlight on Canadian Research box, "Dragon Boat Racing for Breast Cancer Survivors—A Canadian Innovation."

Recall from Chapter 7 that writing interventions involving expressive disclosure can be effective for helping people manage stressful situations. Such interventions are also useful for cancer patients. Writing about benefits derived from cancer has been linked to less physical symptom reporting and fewer medical appointments for cancer-related problems over a three-month period (Low, Stanton, & Danoff-Burg, 2006). Being given an oppor-

tunity to affirm important personal values may account for most of these benefits (Creswell et al., 2007). Written emotional disclosure may be particularly helpful for managing negative feedback received from family members and friends in response to the cancer patients' attempts to express their feelings about cancer (Zakowski, Ramati, Morton, Johnson, & Flanigan, 2004).

Psychotherapeutic Interventions   Psychotherapeutic interventions—including individual psychotherapy, group therapy, family therapy, and cancer support groups—attempt to meet the psychosocial and informational needs of cancer patients.

Dragon Boat Racing for Breast Cancer Survivors—A Canadian Innovation (continued)

bia found that dragon boating provided opportunities for social support, regaining a sense of personal control, and developing a new identity as an athlete, which contributed to positive psychological growth (Sabiston, McDonough, & Crocker, 2007). A researcher from the University of Waterloo similarly found that dragon boat racing contributed to the physical, emotional, social, spiritual, and mental health of the women (Parry, 2008). And dragon boat racing facilitated the development of new coping strategies and finding meaning among women with breast cancer in a study conducted by a researcher from Dalhousie University (Unruh & Elvin, 2004).

In one of the few quantitative investigations of dragon boat racing, six crews were assessed early in the season and again later in the season to examine the effects on quality of life over the season (Culos-Reed, Shields, Brawley, 2005). The team of researchers from the University of Calgary and the University of Waterloo found that the levels of physical and mental quality of life found among the women at the end of season were comparable to those for healthy women of the same age.

Overall, this emerging research is encouraging, and suggests that dragon boat racing may be an effective and enjoyable means for improving the quality of life of women after breast cancer treatment.

Individual Therapy Patients seeking individual therapy after a diagnosis of cancer are most likely to experience:

1. Significant anxiety, depression, or suicidal thoughts.
2. Central nervous system dysfunctions produced by the illness and treatment, such as the inability to concentrate.
3. Specific problems that have arisen as a consequence of the illness, its management, or family dynamics.
4. Previously existing psychological problems that have been exacerbated by cancer.

Individual therapy with cancer patients typically follows a crisis-intervention format rather than an intensive psychotherapy model. That is, therapists working with cancer patients try to focus on the specific issues faced by the patient rather than undertaking a more general, probing, long-term analysis of the patient's psyche. The most common issues arising in individual therapy are fear of recurrence (Vickberg, 2003), pain, or death; fear of loss of organs as a consequence of additional surgeries; interference with valued activities; practical difficulties, such as job discrimination and problems with dating and social relationships; and communication problems with families.

As cancer patients approach death, there is often a spike in psychological distress; thus, end-stage clinical interventions are especially needed at this time (Butler et al., 2003). Psychotherapeutic interventions focus on helping a cancer patient make use of and build personal resources such as optimism and control, as well as social resources such as social support. These psychological resources are most important for mental and physical functioning over the long term (Helgeson, Snyder, & Seltman, 2004).

Family Therapy

As previously noted, cancers almost always have an impact on other family members. Including family members in therapy is important because families can either help or hinder an individual cancer patient's adjustment to illness.

Emotional support from family is highly desired by cancer patients, and it promotes good psychological adjustment (Arora et al., 2007; Northouse, Templin, & Mood, 2001). Not all families are able to communicate freely with each other, and not all offers of support by friends or family members are desired. A mismatch in the type of support wanted and that received by cancer patients may actually increase distress (Reynolds & Perrin, 2004). Cancer patients' distress may be hard for families to bear and accordingly may actually contribute to a loss of social support from the family (Alferi, Carver, Antoni, Weiss, & Duran, 2001). Therefore, family therapy provides an opportunity for family members to share their problems and difficulties in communicating.

Support Groups

A number of cancer service programs have been developed to help the patient adjust to problems posed by a particular cancer. Several of these programs are sponsored by the Canadian Cancer Society, including Reach to Recovery for breast cancer patients and CanSurmount for people with any type of cancer and their caregivers. These programs provide either a one-on-one or a group experience in which individuals can discuss some of their common problems. Reach to Recovery is one of several such groups that has adopted a peer counselling approach, in which a well-adjusted breast cancer patient acts as an adviser to a newly diagnosed patient. This kind of educational and informational support has been found to be valuable in promoting psychological adjustment to cancer (Helgeson & Cohen, 1996).

Self-help groups in which patients share emotional concerns are also available to many cancer patients.). Although the self-help experience currently appeals to a fairly limited portion of the cancer population, it appears to be beneficial for many who try it. On the whole, social support groups appear to be most helpful to women who have more problems, who lack support, or who have fewer personal resources, but they may provide few if any benefits for those who already have high levels of support (L. Cameron et al., 2005; K. L. Taylor et al., 2003). Spending time with well-adjusted people who have had the same disorder can satisfy patients' needs for information and emotional support (Stanton, Danoff-Burg, Cameron, Snider, & Kirk, 1999). The Internet is also a useful tool for cancer patients to receive support from other cancer patients (Owen, Klapow, Roth, & Tucker, 2004). More recently, video conferencing has been used to deliver social support groups to women with breast cancer living in remote rural areas who would otherwise not have access to this type of face-to-face support. Preliminary results suggest that this form of social support delivery is effective at reducing depression and improving well-being (Collie et al., 2007).

In closing our discussion of cancer, we return to the issue of SES disparities and the fact that low-income people are both at greater risk for cancer initially and for a faster course of illness once detected. It is clear that more investigations into how SES exerts these effects and to why SES is related to higher incidence and mortality are vital. In addition, the development of culturally appropriate interventions and research is also needed to identify the needs of these obviously underserved groups (Glanz, Croyle, Chollette, & Pinn, 2003).

WHAT IS ARTHRITIS?   (LO4)

We learned in Chapter 2 about a set of more than 100 different diseases known as autoimmune diseases, in which the body falsely identifies its own tissue as foreign matter and attacks it (The Arthritis Society, 2010). The most prevalent of these autoimmune diseases is arthritis, and we examine it both because of its relationship to immune functioning and because it is one of the most common chronic disorders and causes of disability, ranking among the top ten causes of disability worldwide (The Arthritis Society, 2010).

Arthritis has been with humankind since the beginning of recorded history. Ancient drawings of people with arthritic joints have been found in caves, and early Greek and Roman writers described the pain of arthritis (S. Johnson, 2003). *Arthritis* means inflammation of a joint; it refers to more than 100 diseases that attack the joints or other connective tissues. Nearly 4 million people, or about one in six people in Canada are affected by arthritis and other rheumatic conditions, and two-thirds of Canadians with arthritis are women. Approximately one quarter of Canadians afflicted with arthritis cannot work. Contrary to what most people believe, three out of every five people with arthritis are under the age of 65 (The Arthritis Society, 2010). Among Canada's Aboriginal peoples, 19 percent have arthritis, and rates are even higher among First Nations women, with over 30 percent having some form of arthritis compared to about 17 percent of non-Aboriginal women (Assembly of First Nations, 2007). The rates of arthritis have increased by 50 percent in the past decade, and by 2031 it is estimated that one in seven Canadians will have arthritis (The Arthritis Society, 2010). Although it is rarely fatal, arthritis is one of the most widespread chronic diseases in Canada today. Arthritis costs the Canadian economy nearly $6.4 million in health care and indirect expenses such as lost work days (The Arthritis Society, 2010).

The severity of and prognosis for arthritis depend on the type; the disease ranges from a barely noticeable and occasional problem to a crippling, chronic condition. Nonetheless, people with arthritis report a lower quality of life compared to other Canadians with chronic conditions. This may be partly due to the pain associated with arthritis, as the proportion of people with arthritis reporting pain that is moderate to severe is three times higher those with other chronic conditions (The Arthritis Society, 2005a). And among those with arthritis, Aboriginal people report having more disability than non-Aboriginals. There are five major forms of arthritis: rheumatoid arthritis, osteoarthritis, gout, lupus, and ankylosing spondilitis (arthritis of the spine). We will examine the first four of these types as they are the most prevalent in Canada.

Rheumatoid Arthritis

Rheumatoid arthritis (RA) affects 300,000 Canadians, is three times more common in women than in men (The Arthritis Society, 2005b), and is the most crippling form of arthritis. The disease first strikes primarily the 25- to 50-year-old age group, although it can attack people of any age group, including children. It usually affects the small joints of the hands and feet, as well as the wrists, knees, ankles, and neck. In mild cases, only one or two joints are involved, but sometimes the disease becomes widespread. In severe cases, there may be inflammation of the heart muscle, blood vessels, and tissues just beneath the skin. Rheumatoid arthritis may be brought on by an autoimmune process (Firestein, 2003): Agents of the immune system that are supposed to protect the body instead attack the thin membranes surrounding the joints. This attack leads to inflammation, stiffness, and pain. If not controlled, the bone and surrounding muscle tissue of the joint may be destroyed. Almost half of RA patients recover completely, nearly half remain somewhat arthritic, and about 10 percent are severely disabled.

The main complications of rheumatoid arthritis are pain, limitations in activities, and the need to be dependent on others (van Lankveld et al., 1993). In addition, because rheumatoid arthritis primarily affects older people, its sufferers often have other chronic conditions present as well, such as poor cognitive functioning and poor vision, which may interact with arthritis to produce high levels of disability (Shifren, Park, Bennett, & Morrell, 1999).

Arthritis commonly co-occurs with other chronic conditions, including mood disorder such as depression or anxiety. More than half of Canadians with arthritis also have at least one other chronic health condition, with cardiovascular disease and diabetes among the most common (Health Council of Canada, 2007a). As is the case for co-morbidity with any chronic health condition, comorbidity with arthritis can complicate treatment and further compromise quality of life.

Not surprisingly, one of the most common complications of rheumatoid arthritis is depression (Dickens, McGowan, Clark-Carter, & Creed, 2002). Depression may feed back into the pain process enhancing pain from RA (Zautra & Smith, 2001). Negative affect may increase arthritis disease activity (B. W. Smith & Zautra, 2002). A vicious spiral may be sent into effect: As the disease progresses, greater disability results. Depression can further complicate matters by negatively impacting cognitive performance (Brown, Glass, & Park, 2002). Patients may come to doubt their abilities to manage vital life activities, which can contribute to a high level of depression, which, in turn, exacerbates physical impairment (Neugebauer, Katz, & Pasch, 2003). As the following quote illustrates, arthritis can take a toll on daily functioning and motivation:

> I have a window of about 4–6 hours a day where I feel I can function at all. I now require a couple of hours to motivate myself to complete getting dressed, bathed, eat breakfast before being able to determine what I might be capable of doing each day.
>
> 44-YEAR-OLD WOMAN WITH RA
>
> (SIROIS, 2011)

Cognitive distortions and feelings of helplessness can aggravate depression and other emotional responses to arthritis (for example, Clemmey & Nicassio, 1997; Fifield et al., 2001). The loss of independence associated with not being able to look after oneself due to mobility and pain limitations can be particularly problematic (P. P. Wang, Badley, & Gignac, 2004).

> I can no longer do for myself, i.e., dressing, bathing, housecleaning, sitting to play piano, walking. Energy level is null and I am very depressed. I have trouble sleeping with the pain.
>
> 44-YEAR-OLD WOMAN WITH RA
> (SIROIS, 2011)

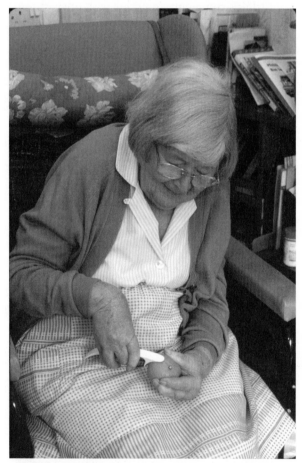

Approximately 1 percent of the population of Canada has rheumatoid arthritis, and it is especially common among women. The frustration of being unable to do things that one used to do and the need to be dependent on others are problems for this group.

Psychosocial Impact of RA   Living with rheumatoid arthritis can have several consequences beyond the immediate pain, fatigue, and loss of independence. The dependence on others can erode social relationships, resulting in a gap in much needed social support (Fyrand, Moum, Finset, & Glennas, 2002). This may occur in part because family members or spouses underestimate the amount of pain, physical limitations, and fatigue experienced by the RA patient, which in turn can lead to problematic support (P. P. Wang, Badley, & Gignac, 2004). Thus, lack of understanding about the nature of RA and its effects can leave patients feeling misunderstood by family and friends.

> Other people think RA is only in the joints. They don't understand that I have no energy & difficulty performing most tasks. My family gets angry with me for forgetting things, much of this is due to my medication.
>
> 40-YEAR-OLD WOMAN WITH RA
> (SIROIS, 2011)

A lack of understanding may be particularly problematic when the person with arthritis does not have any outwards signs of the disease. As was noted in Chapter 11, this can have implications in the employment setting. For example, people often hold stereotypes of arthritis being associated with being wheelchair bound or using assistive devices such as canes and walkers or alternatively as having a mildly arthritic knee or finger that only acts up when there is rain. For individuals with moderate to severe RA that has not progressed to the point of disfigurement or severe immobility, these stereotypes can create misunderstanding and frustration. In addition, the tendency of people to associate arthritis with old age can make living with arthritis especially difficult for younger adults.

> The thing is I am young, so some people think I shouldn't be whining at all about it as they have arthritis in their finger . . . others have said to me 'oh god you are going to be a cripple'—a very close group of friends called me a hypochondriac.
>
> 28-YEAR-OLD WOMAN WITH RA
> (SIROIS, 2011)

Others avoid the misperceptions by learning to cope silently, managing as best they can. This can unfortunately reinforce friends' and family members' beliefs about the manageability of RA and leave the person with RA without support when needed.

Very few people believe how sick I am because I do a very good job of coping with and concealing my illness—this is really isolating for me, especially since I have difficulty asking for help when I do need it.

47-YEAR-OLD WOMAN WITH RA
(SIROIS, 2011)

Yet despite these psychosocial difficulties, many people with RA report that, overall, their relationships have improved as a result of their illness. For example, one longitudinal study of RA patients found that over 70 percent reported experiencing interpersonal benefits such as receiving support from their loved ones as a result of their illness (Danoff-Burg & Revenson, 2005). Moreover, at the 12-month follow-up, interpersonal benefit finding predicted lower disability levels suggesting that perceived support may assist with illness adjustment. Similar results have been found with RA patients in Japan who reported compassion towards others and appreciating things not previously important as the two most common forms of benefit finding (Sato, Yamazaki, Sakita, & Bryce, 2008).

Stress and RA   Stress may play a role both in the development of rheumatoid arthritis and in its aggravation. In particular, disturbances in interpersonal relationships may contribute to the course of the disease (Affleck, Tennen, Urrows, & Higgins, 1994; Zautra, Burleson, Matt, Roth, & Burrows, 1994). Increased reactivity to stress and pain may be increased by the depression felt by RA patients (Zautra & Smith, 2001).

The aggravation of rheumatoid arthritis by stress appears to be mediated by the immune system, inasmuch as those with rheumatoid arthritis show stronger immune responses to stress than do comparison groups (for example, Cutolo & Straub, 2006; Zautra & Smith, 2001). Unfavourable social reactions to people with rheumatoid arthritis may also contribute to disability (McQuade, 2002).

Coping and RA   How individuals cope with the stress and limitations associated with arthritis has implications for their overall quality of life and pain management. For example, efficacious coping, that is coping that is effective for managing arthritis related stress, was associated with psychological thriving, as well as expectations for achieving hoped for possible selves in a large sample of people with arthritis (Sirois & Hirsch, 2011). Conversely, less adaptive coping styles, such as a self-sacrificing defence style, may amplify the effects of pain

on health-related quality of life in people with RA (Bai et al., 2009).

Paradoxically, using positive affect to cope with RA pain may come at a cost. One study found that the negative impact of pain on executive functioning working memory, decision making, and cognitive control—was amplified in patients who were high in positive affect. The authors concluded that trying to stay positive while experiencing pain may put a drain on limited cognitive resources and make self-regulation that much more difficult (Abeare et al., 2010).

Treatment of RA   Treatments to arrest or control the problems of rheumatoid arthritis include medications such as corticosteroids, non-steroidal anti-inflammatory drugs (NSAIDs) including aspirin and ibuprofen, and disease modifying drugs; rest; and supervised exercise. Surgery is rarely needed, and hospitalization is necessary only in extreme cases or for extreme pain or flare-ups. Exercise is strongly recommended for rheumatoid arthritis patients so that they can gain more control over the affected joints (The Arthritis Society, 2005b). Unfortunately, adherence is often low.

Increasingly, psychologists have used cognitive behavioural interventions in the treatment of rheumatoid arthritis. In one study (Hewlett et al., 2011), RA patients were randomized into a cognitive behavioural group treatment that taught skills for managing fatigue, or they received fatigue self-management information in a one-hour didactic session. Results indicated that patients in the cognitive behavioural treatment experienced reduced fatigue severity and improved coping, perceived arthritis severity, and well-being. Strong support from a partner can further improve self-management (Strating, van Schuur, & Suurmeijer, 2006).

Because a chief side effect of rheumatoid arthritis is the sense of helplessness over the inability to control the disease and the pain it causes, any intervention that enhances feelings of self-efficacy should have beneficial effects on psychological adjustment (Schiaffino & Revenson, 1992; C. A. Smith & Wallston, 1992). As one patient in such an intervention put it, "I went from thinking about arthritis as a terrible burden that had been thrust upon me to something I could control and manage. I redefined it for myself. It's no longer a tragedy, it's an inconvenience." As this comment also suggests, optimism can lead people to cope more actively with rheumatoid arthritis, improving adjustment over time (Brenner, Melamed, & Panush, 1994), and result in better relations with family and friends (Danoff-Burg & Revenson, 2005). Nonetheless, as is true for all cognitive behavioural interventions, relapse to old habits is likely; therefore, relapse prevention strategies to preserve both behavioural changes and a sense of self-efficacy and optimism must be an important part of these interventions with rheumatoid arthritis patients (Keefe & Van Horn, 1993).

Overall, cognitive behavioural interventions, including biofeedback, relaxation training, problem-solving skills, and cognitive pain-coping skills training, have been modestly successful in aiding pain management for rheumatoid arthritis patients (Dixon et al., 2007). Interventions such as these appear to be modestly successful in improving both joint pain and psychological functioning, although the interventions appear to be more effective for the patients who have had the illness for a shorter period of time (Astin, Beckner, Soeken, Hochberg, & Berman, 2002). Coordinating these cognitive behavioural interventions with the use of drug therapies to control pain appears to provide the most comprehensive approach at present (Zautra & Manne, 1992).

Juvenile RA   Another form of rheumatoid arthritis is juvenile rheumatoid arthritis. Its causes and symptoms are similar to those of the adult form, but the victims are children between the ages of 2 and 5. Among them, the disease flares up periodically until puberty. The disease is rare and affects girls four times as often as boys. With treatment, most children are managed well and experience few adverse effects. However, there is a juvenile form of rheumatoid disease that can be severely crippling and can lead to extensive psychological and physical problems for its sufferers, including missed school and participation in few social activities (Jordan & McDonagh, 2006). Social support from family members is also important in helping the juvenile rheumatoid arthritis patient adjust successfully to the disorder.

Osteoarthritis

Osteoarthritis is the most common form of arthritis in Canada, affecting an estimated 3 million or one in ten Canadians. Women and men are equally affected, and onset is usually after age 45, although it can occur at any age (The Arthritis Society, 2005c).

The disorder develops when the smooth lining of a joint, known as the articular cartilage, begins to crack or

wear away because of overuse, injury, or other causes. Thus, the disease tends to affect the weight-bearing joints: the hips, knees, and spine. As the cartilage deteriorates, the joint may become inflamed, stiff, and painful. The disease afflicts many elderly people and some athletes. For example, Wayne Gretzky developed osteoarthritis at age 38. As is true for other forms of arthritis, depression may result, and depressive symptoms may in turn elevate pain and distress (Zautra & Smith, 2001). Psychosocial interventions to reduce distress and improve coping have been shown to reduce pain significantly (Dixon et al., 2007).

Weight gain is an issue with osteoarthritis because of the involvement of weight-bearing joints and the implications for mobility. However, the pain and medications needed to manage the illness can make weight management particularly challenging.

> I cannot walk or exercise, which is causing weight gain. I cannot keep up with household chores; cannot shop for family needs. I feel isolated from friends and family due to limitations. Have had to change work restrictions and work load in my employment.
>
> 47-YEAR-OLD WOMAN WITH OSTEOARTHRITIS
> (SIROIS, 2011)

Unfortunately, the emotional distress and isolation due to limitations can lead to inappropriate means of coping such as emotional eating, which further aggravates osteoarthritis by promoting weight gain. There is some evidence, though, that interventions designed to enhance self-efficacy for managing arthritis and more specifically for resisting eating. One study found that self-efficacy for resisting eating predicted better eating behaviours and psychological adjustment among overweight and obese patients with osteoarthritis (Pells et al., 2007).

With proper treatment, osteoarthritis can be managed through self-care. Treatment includes keeping one's weight down and taking aspirin. Exercise is also recommended, although adherence to exercise recommendations is mixed; exercise can initially aggravate the discomfort associated with osteoarthritis, but over time, ameliorate pain and improve physical functioning (Focht, Ewing, Gauvin, & Rejeski, 2002). Occasionally, use of more potent pain relievers, anti-inflammatory drugs, or steroids is needed. In more severe cases, osteoarthritis may lead to the destruction of the cartilage and surgery to replace the whole joint, usually a knee or hip, may be necessary (The Arthritis Society, 2005c).

Those who manage the pain of osteoarthritis through active coping efforts and spontaneous pain control efforts appear to cope better with the disease (P. P. Wang et al., 2004).

Other Forms of Arthritis

Other common or significant forms of arthritis include fibromyalgia (which was discussed in Chapter 11), gout, and lupus. About 500,000 (or 1 in 30) Canadians suffer from **gout,** and it is four times more prevalent in males than in females (The Arthritis Society, 2005d). This condition is caused by a buildup of uric acid in the body due to the kidneys' inability to excrete the acid in the urine. Treatment varies depending on severity and can include NSAIDS, diet, alcohol control, and exercise.

Lupus affects approximately 15,000 Canadians and although it can affect men and children, it is most common among women of child-bearing age (15–45). Lupus is the name given to a group of autoimmune diseases, the most common of which is systemic lupus erythematosus. The symptoms of lupus are caused by an immune system malfunction, which leads to the generation of antibodies that attack healthy tissue in different parts of the body causing them to become inflamed. Because lupus can affect different tissues for different people it is a disease that is very different for each person it affects. However, it can become life-threatening when it attacks the tissues of the body's vital organs. Anti-inflammatory medications or immune suppressants are common treatments. Diet and exercise are also used to help control flares (The Arthritis Society, 2005e).

Summary   Arthritis is the second most prevalent chronic disease in the Canada, and it commonly co-occurs with other chronic conditions. Although it rarely kills its victims, it causes substantial pain and discomfort, creating problems of management. The self-care regimen of arthritis patients centres largely around pain control, dietary control, stress management, and exercise; therefore, the health habits and issues of adherence that we have discussed throughout this book are clearly important in the effective management of arthritis. ●

SUMMARY

 Explain psychoneuroimmunology

- The immune system is the surveillance system of the body; it guards against foreign invaders. It involves a number of complex processes, comprising humoral immunity and cell-mediated immunity.

- Studies suggest that stressors, such as academic exams and stressful interpersonal relationships, can compromise immune functioning.

- Negative emotions, such as depression or anxiety, may also compromise immune functioning. Coping methods may buffer the immune system against adverse changes due to stress.

- Studies have evaluated the potential of conditioned immune responses and interventions such as relaxation and stress management as clinical efforts to augment immune functioning in the face of stress.

 Understand AIDS and its consequences

- Acquired immune deficiency syndrome (AIDS) was first identified in Canada in 1982. It results from the human immunodeficiency virus (HIV) and is marked by the presence of unusual opportunistic infectious diseases that result when the immune system, especially the helper T cells, has been compromised in its functioning.

- Gay men and intravenous, needle-sharing drug users have been the primary risk groups for AIDS in Canada. More recently, Aboriginal peoples are over-represented in the spread of AIDS in Canada, and they are also being infected at younger ages than non-Aboriginal peoples. Heterosexually active adolescents and young adults are also at risk.

- Primary prevention, in the form of condom use and control of number of partners, is a major avenue for controlling the spread of AIDS. Such interventions focus on providing knowledge, increasing perceived self-efficacy to engage in protective behaviour, changing peer norms about sexual practices, and communicating sexual negotiation strategies.

- Many people live with asymptomatic HIV-seropositivity for years. Exercise and active coping may help prolong this state. Drugs such as protease inhibitors now hold promise for enabling people with HIV and AIDS to live longer, healthier lives.

- AIDS itself creates a variety of debilitating physical and psychosocial problems. The main psychosocial tasks faced by people diagnosed with AIDS are dealing psychologically with the likelihood of a shortened life, dealing with negative reactions from others, and developing strategies for maintaining physical and emotional health. A variety of interventions have been developed to aid in these tasks.

 Describe cancer and the psychosocial factors involved

- Cancer is a set of more than 100 diseases marked by malfunctioning DNA and rapid cell growth and proliferation. Research investigations have attempted to relate psychosocial factors to the onset and progression of cancer. Recent evidence implicates depression in particular, in cancer mortality but not its progression.

- Cancer can produce a range of physical and psychosocial problems, including surgical scarring, the need for prostheses, debilitating responses to chemotherapy, avoidance or rejection by the social network, vocational disruption, and adverse psychological responses such as depression. Behavioural and psychotherapeutic interventions are being used successfully to manage these problems, as is exercise.

 Define arthritis

- Arthritis, involving inflammation of the joints, affects about 4 million people in Canada. Rheumatoid arthritis is the most crippling form. Stress appears to exacerbate the disease.

- Interventions involving cognitive behavioural techniques to help people manage pain effectively and increase perceptions of self-efficacy have proven helpful in alleviating some of the discomfort and psychosocial difficulties associated with arthritis.

KEY TERMS

acquired immune deficiency
   syndrome (AIDS) p. 392
gout p. 419
human immunodeficiency virus
   (HIV) p. 394

immunocompetence p. 386
immunocompromise p. 386
lupus p. 419

osteoarthritis p. 418
psychoneuroimmunology p. 384
rheumatoid arthritis (RA) p. 415

part

Toward the Future

CHAPTER
15

Health Psychology:
Challenges for the Future

LEARNING OBJECTIVES

After reading this chapter, students will be able to:

(LO1) Describe the health psychology priorities for the future

(LO2) Know where stress research is headed

(LO3) Understand the future of health services

(LO4) Identify the issues in chronic illness management for the future

(LO5) Describe the health psychology trends for the future

In the past 25 years, health psychology has made dramatic and impressive advances. This last chapter highlights some of the research accomplishments and likely future directions of the field.

WHAT ARE THE HEALTH PSYCHOLOGY PRIORITIES FOR THE FUTURE?

In the future, countries with the best health will be those that do the best job of preventing diabetes.

—DR. DOUG MANUEL, SENIOR SCIENTIST, INSTITUTE FOR CLINICAL EVALUATIVE SCIENCES (CBC NEWS, 2007, MARCH 5)

In recent years, Canadians have made substantial gains in altering their poor health habits. Accordingly, several health promotion areas will continue to be a priority for health psychology. Different public health promotion efforts have meant that many people have successfully stopped smoking, and many have reduced their consumption of high-cholesterol and high-fat foods. Coronary heart disease and other chronic diseases have shown dramatic decreases as a result. Although alcohol consumption patterns remain largely unchanged, exercise has increased. Despite these advances, overweight and obesity are currently endemic and will shortly take over from smoking as the major avoidable contributor to mortality. And diabetes and high blood pressure are on the rise in Canada.

Clearly, most people know that they need to practise good health behaviours, and many have tried to develop or change them on their own. Not everyone is successful, however. Thus, the potential for health psychology to make a contribution to health promotion remains. Increasingly, we will see efforts to identify the most potent and effective elements of behaviour-change programs in order to incorporate them into cost-effective, efficient interventions that reach the largest number of people. The refinement and development of new psychological theories will also be needed to guide how such interventions may be best implemented.

In Canada, a number of interventions and initiatives to promote healthy living have been launched in recent years, and many of these are designed for mass consumption at the community level, the workplace level, and in the schools. One strategy that has been used to effectively advertise these initiatives to Canadians over the past few decades is **social marketing.** Social marketing is defined as "the application of marketing technologies developed in the commercial sector to the solution of social problems where the bottom line is behaviour change,"

and it involves "the analysis, planning, execution, and evaluation of programs designed to influence the voluntary behaviour of target audiences to improve their personal welfare and that of society" (Health Canada, 2005e). Recall from Chapter 3 the ParticipACTION program, one of the best known and earliest social marketing strategies launched in Canada. Through the use of media and other communication tools such as the Internet, social marketing can help raise awareness of health risks, promote the advantages of healthy living, and facilitate attitude and behaviour change (Health Canada, 2005e). With advances in communication technologies in coming years, the tools of social marketing will also likely change. Health psychologists have an opportunity to play a role in helping to adapt these health promotional messages to effectively disseminate them to the Canadian population so that we may reach the goal of modifying the behaviour of the greatest number of people in the most efficient and cost-effective manner.

Focus on Those at Risk

As medical research increasingly identifies genetic and behavioural risk factors for chronic illness, the at-risk role will be increasingly important. Individuals who are identified early as at risk for particular disorders need to learn how to cope with their risk status and how to change their modifiable risk-relevant behaviours. If certain behaviours are identified as putting people at risk, then interventions at the individual or public level can be designed to help modify these behaviours. Psychologists can aid substantially in each of these tasks.

Studies of people who are at risk for particular disorders are very useful in identifying additional risk factors for various chronic disorders. Not everyone who is at risk for an illness will develop it, and by studying which people do and do not, and how they differ in terms of social and environmental factors, researchers can identify the further precipitating or promoting factors of these illnesses.

Prevention

Preventing poor health habits from developing will continue to be a priority for health psychology. As noted earlier, adolescence is a window of vulnerability for most bad health habits, and closing this window is of paramount importance. **Behavioural immunization** programs are already in existence for smoking, drug abuse, and, in some cases, diet or eating disorders. Programs that expose students in Grades 5 and 6 to antismoking or antidrug campaigns before they begin these habits appear to be somewhat successful in keeping some adolescents from undertaking such habits. Media campaigns directed at adolescents and young adults about the dangers of smoking and excessive alcohol use have been implemented in recent years and will likely continue to be implemented as an effective means for reaching these groups.

Focus on the Elderly

The rapid aging of the population means that within the next 10 years, we will have the largest elderly cohort ever seen in Canada. This cohort can be an ill one, plagued with chronic pain, disease, depression, and disability (Ramage-Morin, 2008), or it can be a healthy, active one, with high levels of quality of life (Shields & Martel, 2006). Findings from the Canadian Community Health Survey suggest that health behaviours such as consuming more fruits and vegetables, exercising frequently, minimizing stress levels, and feeling connected to one's community were all factors associated with overall good health among Canada's seniors, even after accounting for socio-economic and health status variables (Shields & Martel, 2006). What's more, these effects appear to be cumulative, with the proportion of seniors with good health increasing as more of these factors were considered. Accordingly, community-based initiatives and individual interventions should focus on helping the elderly achieve the highest level of functioning possible through programs that emphasize diet, exercise, social support, stress management, and other health habits (Public Health Agency of Canada, 2006e).

Refocusing Health Promotion Efforts

In the past, we have stressed mortality more than morbidity. Although the reduction of mortality, especially early mortality, is an important priority, there will always be 10 major causes of death (Becker, 1993). Refocusing our effort toward morbidity is important for a number of reasons.

One obvious reason is cost. Chronic diseases are expensive to treat, particularly when those diseases persist for years, even decades (Yach, Leeder, Bell, & Kistnasamy, 2005). For example, conditions such as rheumatoid arthritis and osteoarthritis have little impact on mortality rates but have a major impact on the functioning and well-being of the population, particularly the elderly population. And for other conditions, such as

The health needs of the elderly will take on increasing importance with the aging of the population. Helping the elderly achieve a high level of functioning through interventions that emphasize diet, exercise, and other health habits is a high priority for the future.

diabetes, which can impact mortality rates as well as increase the risk of other chronic conditions, lifestyle change programs may have a significant impact on health care costs. For example, in 2004 the British Columbia Provincial Health Officer estimated the projected costs of health care for people with diabetes, and how much these costs could potentially be reduced if the rates of diabetes in the province declined as a result of lifestyle changes. The potential savings were estimated to be between $100 and $200 million annually (see Figure 15.1). As a result, in part, of this report, the British Columbia government implemented ActNow BC, a program designed to increase healthy lifestyles among the province's population (www.actnowbc.ca; Health Council of Canada, 2007b). This province-wide strategy, which uses an all-of-government approach, addresses a number of health promotion areas, including physical activity, healthy eating, healthy schools, healthy workplaces, healthy communities, healthy pregnancies, and tobacco control, to reduce the risk factors for

FIGURE 15.1 | Projected Annual Growth in Health Services Costs to British Columbia Ministry of Health for People with Diabetes, with Implementation of Lifestyle Modification Programs, British Columbia 2003–04 to 2015–16

(*Source:* Health Council of Canada (2007b). Why Health Care Renewal Matters: Learning from Canadians with Chronic Health Conditions. Toronto: Health Council. ISBN 978-1-897463-10-9. (Data source: Provincial Health Officers' Annual Report 2004. The Impact of Diabetes on the Health and Well-Being of People in British Columbia.)

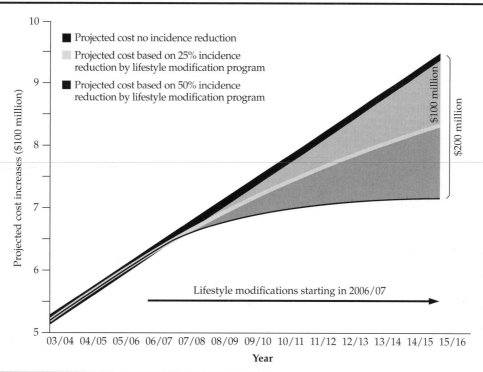

chronic disease (Health Council of Canada, 2007b). Keeping people as healthy as possible for as long as possible can help reduce the burden of chronic illness costs. Moreover, maximizing the number of good years during which an individual is free from the burdens of chronic illness produces a higher quality of life.

Because it is important that interventions address more than one behavioural risk factor at a time, many of these programs are comprehensive, such as ActNow BC, which aspires to be the most comprehensive health promotion program in North America. Although some programs, such as Alberta's Health U, which aims to increase activity levels and healthy eating habits, have been in effect for several years, others have been recently launched. For example, Newfoundland and Labrador launched its Go Healthy Wellness Plan in 2006. Phase I targets healthy eating, physical activity, tobacco control, and injury prevention, and Phase II targets areas such as mental health, child and youth development, environmental

health, and health protection. The effectiveness of these programs for long-term behaviour change and continued maintenance may not be known for some years. Accordingly, finding ways in which these public health promotion efforts can be integrated with individuallevel interventions will be a continuing priority now and in years to come (Public Health Agency of Canada, 2006e).

Promoting Resilience

In addition to continuing to target the behavioural factors that may help to reduce risk, future health promotion efforts should place greater weight on positive factors that may reduce morbidity or delay mortality. For example, although eliminating heart disease and cancer would lengthen lives by several years, increasing social support and a sense of connectedness to one's community may also add years to people's lives (Shields & Martel, 2006), and for men in particular (Wilkins, 2006).

Health psychologists have focused most of their research on risk factors for chronic illnesses and have largely ignored the positive experiences that may keep some people from developing these disorders (Ryff & Singer, 1998), or recovering from illness (Shields & Martel, 2006). Studying how people spontaneously reduce their levels of stress, for example, and how they seek out opportunities for rest, renewal, and relaxation may provide knowledge for effective interventions. Personal resources, such as optimism or a sense of control, may prove to be protective against chronic illness. Can these resources be taught? Research suggests that they can (for example, Mann, 2001). The coming decades may explore these and related possibilities.

Promotion as a Part of Medical Practice

A true philosophy of health promotion cannot be adequately implemented until a focus on health promotion becomes an integral part of medical practice. For example, a survey of Canadians who sought care from a family doctor found that almost half were asked questions about their regular health habits such as eating and exercise. However, about the same proportion reported that they were not usually asked about their health habits or assisted with setting specific goals for their health (Health Council of Canada, 2006). Clearly this is an area for improvement in the future.

One potential venue for encouraging and supporting health behaviour change is complementary and alternative medicine providers. The holistic health focus associated with CAM care and longer consultation times make this an appropriate setting to facilitate healthy lifestyle changes. For example one recent study found that patients reported that receiving care from CAM providers had fostered health behaviour changes including smoking cessation, improved diet, and increasing exercise (Greene, Walsh, Sirois, & McCaffrey, 2009). Consistent with Social Cognitive Theory and Self-determination Theory, one study found that CAM providers play a role in health behaviour change by encouraging and supporting autonomous health behaviour changes and increasing self-efficacy and responsibility for one's health (Williams-Piehota, Sirois, Bann, & Walsh, 2011). Future research should therefore focus on how these and other agents of change might help their patients' engage in important health behaviours.

As noted in Chapter 3, there is as yet no formal diagnostic process for identifying and targeting preventive health behaviours on an individual basis. If the annual physical that many people obtain were to include a simple review of the particular health issues and habits that the individual should focus on, this step would, at the very least, alert each of us to the health goals we should consider and would perhaps prod us in the direction of taking necessary action.

Physicians are high in status and tend to be persuasive when other change agents are not. A young woman who wolfs down a burrito between classes might be given information about the need for a healthy diet and simple steps she can undertake to improve her current diet, such as having a yogourt, fruit, and cereal instead. In the future, we may begin to see practicing physicians integrate prevention into their daily practice with their healthy patients as well as their ill ones. This may be especially important for Canada's growing population of seniors who may need counselling from primary care professionals to help reduce the risk of isolation, falls, reduced physical activity, and compromised nutrition (Public Health Agency of Canada, 2006e).

SES and Health Disparities

One of the most potent risk factors for early disease, disability, and death is low socio-economic status (SES). Recall from Chapter 1 that education, income, and social status are recognized as important social determinants of health in Canada. From birth throughout life, those of us who are born into the lower social classes experience more and more intense stressors of all kinds, which have a cumulative toll on health risks (Steinbrook, 2004a). Lower income and educational and occupational attainment leads to exposure to a broad array of stressors including inadequate housing, violence, danger, lack of vital goods and services, poor sanitation, exposure to environmental pollutants, and numerous other hazards (for example, Ewart & Suchday, 2002; Grzywacz, Almeida, Neupert, & Ettner, 2004). In contrast, people with higher income and educational attainment have a broad array of psychosocial resources and a lower risk of illnesses and disabilities across the life span (Shields & Martel, 2006).

The effect of low SES on poor health is true for both men and women (Chen, Langer, Raphaelson, & Matthews, 2004; McDonough, Williams, House, & Duncan, 1999) and at all age levels, although the effect of SES tends to narrow toward the end of life (Beckett, 2000). Among the many risk factors tied to low socioeconomic status are alcohol consumption, high levels of lipids, obesity, tobacco use, and fewer psychosocial resources such as a sense of mastery, selfesteem, and social support. Each of these has an effect on health. Low

SES is tied to a higher incidence of chronic illness, a heightened risk of low-birth-weight babies and infant mortality, and a heightened risk of accidents among numerous other causes of death and disability. In fact, the overwhelming majority of diseases and disorders show an SES gradient, with poor people experiencing greater risk. For example, people with the lowest household incomes in Canada are almost three times more likely to have diabetes than those with the highest household incomes (Health Council of Canada, 2007b). Even in the case of diseases that lower- and upper-class individuals are equally likely to develop, such as some cancers, mortality is earlier among the more disadvantaged (Leclere, Rogers, & Peters, 1998). Designing interventions targeted specifically to low SES individuals to modify risk factors associated with social class such as smoking, drug use, alcohol consumption, and consumption of an unhealthy diet needs to assume very high priority (for example, Droomers, Schrijivers, & Mackenbach, 2002).

Increasingly, health psychologists are exploring ethnic differences in health, and the picture is bleak. Although just over half of non-reserve Aboriginal peoples self-report good health, the gap between their health status and that of other Canadians successively widens for each older age group. This gap is even more pronounced for women. In addition, a larger portion of Canada's Aboriginal population report having arthritis, hypertension, and asthma than the rest of the nation. Add to this rates of diabetes that are at least twice as high among non-reserve

Aboriginal peoples as those in the Canadian population, and even higher among on reserve populations, and the portrait of Canada's Aboriginal peoples health is a grim one (O'Donnell & Tait, 2003). The life expectancy gap between Aboriginal and non-Aboriginal Canadians is high, with Aboriginal peoples expected to live years less than the average Canadian. There is a seven-year difference for men and a five-year difference for women. Injury rates, which include suicide, are also four times higher among Aboriginal people than for other Canadians (Public Health Agency of Canada, 2004c). Some of these differences in health stem from the fact that Aboriginal peoples are, on average, lower in socio-economic status, so they are disproportionately subject to the stressors that accompany low SES. However, lack of access to traditional medicines, healers, or wellness practices, especially for those living in urban centres, may also play a role (O'Donnell & Tait, 2003).

Social Change to Improve Health

Individual health behaviour changes alone may not substantially improve the health of the general population. What is needed is individual change coupled with social change. Although Canada has a universal access health care system, access to health care is relatively not as good as it could be when compared to other developed nations (Esmail & Walker, 2005). Despite the fact that Canadians enjoy one of the longest life expectancies in the

Stressful living situations with noise, crowding, and crime take a particular toll on vulnerable populations, such as children, the elderly, and the poor. Increasingly, research must focus on interventions to alleviate the impact of these conditions.

world, the burden of chronic disease continues to rise. As our aging population enjoys a longer lifespan, the quality of these extra years may be marred by increasing rates of disease and disability. In addition, there remain great disparities in the conditions in which Canadians live that may further compromise health. For example, many people live in intrinsically unhealthy environments (S. E. Taylor, Repetti, & Seeman, 1997)—that is, environments that threaten safety, undermine the creation of social ties, or are conflictual, abusive, or violent. Social conditions that breed social conflict and lack of control have been tied to the development of coronary heart disease and to indicators of allostatic load, as described in Chapter 6. The hostility and depression that may evolve in people living in these chronically stressful environments appear to have health risks as well.

By contrast, healthy environments provide safety, opportunities for social integration, and the chance to experience a sense of personal control over important life tasks. A successful policy of health promotion needs to address not just individual risk but also the social conditions in which they are embedded (Health Council of Canada, 2006).

Gender and Health

Another significant gap in health care and research concerns gender, and it has only been in recent years that gender has been acknowledged as a key social determinant of health. As one critical article put it, "Women are studied for what distinguishes them from men—their breasts and genitals" (Meyerowitz & Hart, 1993). Thus, for example, breast, ovarian, and other sexual cancers have received substantial attention, but many other disorders have not.

Weak justification for such discrimination has sometimes been based on the fact that women live, on average, seven years longer than men. But women are sick more than men, and their advantage in mortality has been decreasing in recent years (Statistics Canada, 2006a). Despite this, women still outlive men, and as a consequence experience greater disability from chronic health conditions than men do, likely because they are usually older and have no one to assist them once they become ill. The result is that more women are referred to long-term-care facilities or nursing homes once they suffer a chronic illness or serious health condition.

However, the diversity among Canadian women with respect to risk factors for health and access to health care also needs to be recognized when considering the health promotion priorities of the future.

Immigrant women, Aboriginal women, women with disabilities, elderly women, women in low-income households or situations, women in rural or remote areas, and lesbian, bisexual, and transgendered women, all have different health care needs and health risks (Statistics Canada, 2006a). For example, senior women are more likely to have cataracts/glaucoma, back problems, and arthritis than are senior men (Gilmour and Park, 2006). And young Aboriginal women are at greater risk for obesity and the associated health problems than non-Aboriginal women, with poor eating habits as a possible explanation (Garriguet, 2008). Considering these differential risks among Canadian women is therefore essential for designing appropriate health promotion interventions and treatment programs.

In the past, women were not routinely included as research subjects in studies of many major diseases because cyclical variations in hormones were thought to obscure results or because pharmaceutical companies feared lawsuits if experimental drugs have adverse effects on women of childbearing age, harming fetuses or putting future children at risk (S. E. Taylor et al., 2000). Heart disease research has been based largely on men, and women are often ignored in studies of cancers, except for reproductive cancers. Some drugs that are used primarily to treat health problems in women have been tested only on men and male laboratory animals. For example, women with lung cancer respond differently to certain cancer drugs, a fact that goes unnoticed if only men are included in clinical trials (Grady, 2004, April 14).

Women may have different risk factors for major diseases, or existing risk factors may be more or less virulent (Grady, 2004, April 14). For example, women's risk for coronary heart disease increases greatly following menopause, and the symptoms of heart disease can be very different for women than they are for men (Public Health Agency of Canada, 2008b). Until recently, however, research unearthing these important relationships was not even conducted. Without a systematic investigation of women's health and their particular risk factors, as well as changes in both over the life span, women will simply be treated more poorly than men for the same diseases.

Finally, the need to go beyond just medical issues and recognize the importance of social factors in health may be essential to better address the health needs of women. For example, women's health organizations in British Columbia have challenged the government to consider such issues as violence against women as one of its top priorities to help improve the health of women in the future (CBC News, 2007, July 31).

L02 **WHERE IS STRESS RESEARCH HEADED?**

Substantial advances in stress research have been made in the past two decades. Physiological, cognitive, motivational, and behavioural consequences of stress have been identified. Moreover, the biopsychosocial routes by which stress adversely affects bodily functions and increases the likelihood of illness are increasingly well understood. Recent attention to stress and inflammatory processes represents a significant knowledge breakthrough of the past few years.

Occupational stress researchers have identified many of the job characteristics that are tied to stress such as low control, high demands, and little opportunity for social support. As a consequence, promising workplace interventions have been developed to redesign jobs or reduce on-the-job stressors. However, other types of occupational stress, such as job insecurity, may be inevitable consequences of a changing global economy. Transient, unstable, and uncertain employment situations that contribute to this type of stress cannot be easily changed. Designing programs that address this type of stress and equip workers with the coping skills necessary to endure periods of economic decline and the threat of being laid off may be a fruitful area for health psychologists in the future.

Nonetheless, the demographics of stress may be offsetting whatever concessions can or might be made in the workplace. The majority of Canadian families find that both parents must work in order to make ends meet, yet, like all families, the two-career family must absorb an extra month a year of housework, home activities, and child care. Moreover, increasing numbers of adult children have responsibility for their aging parents, and these responsibilities, too, more frequently fall to women than to men.

These trends put the adult Canadian female population under unprecedented degrees of stress, patterns that may be increasing in other countries as well. Additional health and mental health consequences, as well as effective solutions to these dilemmas, have yet to fully emerge.

Advances in Stress Management

Research should focus on those populations at particular risk for stress-related disorders in an attempt to reduce or offset their stressful circumstances. In theory, knowledge of how people adjust successfully to stressful events can be translated into interventions to help those coping unsuccessfully to cope more successfully.

Many important advances in stress research will continue to come from research on the neurophysiology of stress, particularly the links between stress and corticosteroid functioning, temperamental differences in sympathetic nervous system activity, and factors influencing the release of endogenous opioid peptides and their links to the immune system including inflammatory processes. New perspectives on the role of stress in the experience of pain, such as that offered by the neuromatrix theory of pain (Melzack, 2001), provide opportunities for research into the benefits of stress management for managing pain. Through these studies, we may increasingly understand the pathways by which stress exerts adverse effects on health.

Having a social support network is recognized as an important social determinant of health in Canada. The two-job family, coupled with high rates of living alone because of divorce or never marrying, may provide fewer opportunities for building socially supportive networks. The number of single person households in Canada is growing, as is the number of unmarried adults (Milan, Vézina, & Hall, 2007), and these trends are likely to continue in the future. Families have fewer children and are less likely to live in extended families, and they may belong to fewer clubs or have fewer long-term opportunities for social contact. Fostering social support systems and social connectedness among Canadians of all ages to offset the trends that isolate individuals will likely remain a high priority for prevention in the future.

Self-help groups, both real and virtual via the Internet, are increasingly popular ways of providing social support for those who otherwise might lack it. Through these formats, people can discuss a common problem or stressor with each other and try to help each other work it out. With advances in technology, some of the limitations of virtual social support may be overcome. Consider for instance the growing use of video phones, social networking sites and mediums such as text messaging. This and other advances in technology may provide new opportunities for the delivery of Internet-mediated social support in the future.

WHAT IS THE FUTURE OF HEALTH SERVICES? L03

Health care renewal is one of the most important issues facing Canada (Health Council of Canada, 2006). In order to adequately address the health care needs of Canadians and provide quality care, three main goals need to be addressed: improve access to needed health care;

improve the quality of care; and narrow the health inequality gap by addressing the health care needs of Aboriginal peoples and those with low SES (Health Council of Canada, 2006).

Improving Access to Health Care

Canada is still in the midst of a health care provider shortage that began in the mid-1990s. We have one of the poorest physician-to-patient ratios among developed nations, and this is expected to worsen between now and 2015 (Esmail, 2006). According to a recent study of 11 commonwealth countries' access to health care, Canadian residents were more likely than those from all other countries to experience wait times to see a doctor or nurse, difficulty getting after-hours care, and wait times for elective surgery (Schoen & Osborn, 2010). Add to this the nursing shortage and extensive wait times for specialist services, diagnostic tests, cardiac and cancer care, and joint replacement and cataract surgeries, and it becomes clear that improving access to health care in Canada is a critical priority for the future (Health Council of Canada, 2006).

What can be done to solve these access issues? Some suggest that easing the restrictions placed upon foreign physicians and the practice and number of graduating physicians will increase the number of physicians available (Esmail, 2006). But with the greying of Canada's health care providers in coming years, this may not be enough. Other more immediate efforts have focused on increasing the availability of telehealth technologies to underserved areas such as Canada's northern and rural communities (Health Council of Canada, 2006).

Other initiatives to help improve access include the training and integration of physician assistants into the Canadian health care system, an initiative that has begun in Manitoba and Ontario at the time of this writing. And implementation of **interprofessional teams** can also address current problems with health care access, especially for Canadians living in remote areas. Such teams usually consist of three or more physicians and nurses, but can also include nurse practitioners, social workers, or psychologists. Interprofessional teams collaborate to deliver primary care services, and share responsibility for the patients' care (Health Council of Canada, 2006). Such teams may be particularly well positioned to deal with complex and emergency health issues, and for the delivery of chronic illness care and management. Care is often delivered in a manner that reduces the need to travel for either the patient or the family members, and can include the use of telehealth (Health Council of Canada, 2006). In addition to improving access to needed services, the integration of interprofessional teams into Canada's health care system will help realize the goal of providing health promotion and disease prevention services to patients during their first contact with primary care.

Improving the Quality of Care

Although for the most part Canada's health care system delivers quality health care, recent research suggests that it does not always operate as efficiently as it could (Health Council of Canada, 2006). The result can be a failure to maximize the benefits of the care delivered, and in some instances people may actually be harmed. Initiatives to improve patient safety and better organize and manage electronic health records aim to address this issue. In fact, the introduction of portable personal electronic health records is considered by some to be an inevitable next step to address this issue (see the Focus on Social Issues box, "Health and Illness in 2020: A Canadian Perspective"). One study found that 23 percent of Canadians reported that they or a family member had experienced an unintended injury or complication as a result of health care delivery (Health Council of Canada, 2006). Many of these complications resulted from nosocomial infections. Recall from Chapter 8 that these infections can be avoided through strict adherence to handwashing and sanitation guidelines in health care settings. Health psychologists could play a role in addressing this issue by developing interventions and awareness campaigns to remind busy health care personnel to wash their hands and adhere to sanitation guidelines. Because safer care is cheaper care, addressing such threats to quality care will continue to be a priority in the future.

Narrowing the Health Inequality Gap

It has been suggested that the biggest health issue in Canada is inequality (Health Council of Canada, 2006). This is a common problem among industrialized nations and the current trend is unfortunately toward even wider gaps in health status between upper and lower socio-economic groups. Shorter life expectancies, lower birth weights and increased infant mortality, and the high prevalence of health compromising behaviours such as smoking and physical inactivity among low-income Canadians are all health issues that will need to be addressed in the future. With respect to health services, little is known about the wait times and access to health services among low-income groups, despite the high health needs of these Canadians (Health Council of Canada, 2006).

Similar health inequities exist regarding the health status of Canada's Aboriginal population. In 2004, the federal government committed $700 million to transform health care for Aboriginal people. One target goal was to improve the delivery of and access to health services, and to increase the number of community educational programs for diabetes and other chronic health conditions that are prevalent in this population.

WHAT ARE THE ISSUES IN CHRONIC ILLNESS MANAGEMENT FOR THE FUTURE?

> The doctor cannot be expected to supply the magic bullet in chronic health conditions. We have to do our part. In order to do so, people need the simple tools we can all use, and the confidence and guidance to apply them.
>
> HEALTH COUNCIL OF CANADA (2007c)

Because chronic illness has become our major health problem, its physical, vocational, social, and psychological consequences have been increasingly recognized. Although a focus on health promotion and illness prevention may help reduce the incidence of chronic illness in the future, many Canadians currently have or may develop a chronic illness that will require management. A number of key issues will need to be addressed to ensure effective disease management and self-care, and to maximize the quality of life among those who live with one or more chronic illnesses.

Quality-of-life Assessment

A chief goal for health psychologists in the coming years, then, should be to develop programs to assess quality of life for people with a chronic illness and to develop cost-effective interventions to improve quality of life. Such interventions may even be delivered within the context of interprofessional teams as Canada's health care system moves towards a more collaborative model of care. Early assessment to help identify potential problems, such as anxiety or depression, before they fully disrupt the patient's life and bring about additional costs to the health care system will remain an

important priority in the future. Because psychosocial states such as depression and hostility affect both the development and exacerbation of chronic disorders, psychological interventions directed to these important cofactors in illness will be a high priority. Equally important will be interventions that help strengthen qualities such as optimism, perceived control, and resilience that contribute to psychological health and well-being. No intervention that fails to improve psychological functioning is likely to profoundly affect health or survival (B. H. Singer, 2000).

Pain Management

Among the advancements in the treatment of chronic disease is progress in pain management. Recent years have witnessed a shift away from dependence on expensive pharmacologic and invasive surgical pain control techniques to ones that favour cognitive behavioural methods, such as biofeedback or relaxation. This change has brought about a shift in responsibility for pain control from practitioner to co-management between patient and practitioner. The enhanced sense of control provided to the chronic pain patient is a treatment advance in its own right, as research on self-efficacy also underscores. As discussed in Chapter 10, greater emphasis on low cost and accessible pain control options such as using preferred music to control pain may also help reach this goal.

However, current pain and coping research has focused almost exclusively on younger adults and ignored how pain coping strategies may be different for older adults (Lachapelle & Hadjistavropoulos, 2005). Accordingly, research into these possible differences is needed so that pain management efforts can be tailored specifically to Canada's growing senior population.

Adherence

The management of specific chronic disorders contains both accomplishments and gaps in knowledge. One of the chief remaining tasks is to identify the best ways to gain adherence to multiple treatment goals simultaneously. That is, how does one induce a patient to control diet, alter smoking, manage stress, and get exercise all at the same time? How does one maximize compliance with the often aversive or complex regimens used to treat such diseases as hypertension or diabetes? Finding answers to these questions is one of the challenges of the future.

End-of-life Care

The past 20 years have witnessed substantial changes in attitudes toward terminal illness as well. Health psychology research has been both a cause and an effect of these changing attitudes, as clinical health psychologists have turned their attention to the needs of the terminally ill and the gaps in psychological care that still exist.

The appearance of AIDS has added weight to these issues. Following more than a decade of watching thousands of Canada's gay men die in their youth, medical research has now uncovered the promise of longer-term survival in the form of protease inhibitors.

However, the face of AIDS is changing, and it has spread heavily into the poor urban populations of the country, and among Canada's Aboriginal peoples. Women are at special risk, and as a result, a growing population of infants is infected with HIV as well. AIDS is becoming a disease of families, and adequate attention needs to be paid to helping mothers, especially single mothers with HIV, manage their families while coping with their own deteriorating health and to helping the HIV-infected children who will survive their mothers.

With the prevalence of chronic disease increasing and the aging of the population occurring rapidly, ethical issues surrounding death and dying—including aid in dying, living wills, the patient's right to die, family decision making in death and dying, and euthanasia—will increasingly assume importance.

The Aging of the Population

The substantial shift in the population toward the older years poses a challenge for health psychologists to anticipate what the health problems of the coming decades will be. Although the growth of Canada's senior population has been modest until now, starting in 2011 it will accelerate as the baby boomers begin to turn 65. Sometime in the not-too-distant future, we will reach a point where seniors outnumber children aged 15 and under in Canada (see Figure 15.2). What kinds of living situations will these increasing numbers of elderly people have? What kinds of economic resources will they have available to them? How will these resources influence their health habits, their level of health, and their ability to seek treatment? How can we evaluate and monitor care in residential treatment settings, such as nursing homes, to guard against the risks of maltreatment?

For some seniors requiring specialized care because of health issues, a nursing home or long-term-care facility may be inevitable. However, results from a recent survey suggest that being a resident of a nursing home can lead to the development of new problems that will require further interventions. Among residents living in nursing homes in Nova Scotia, 45 percent showed signs of behavioural problems, such as resistance to care, wandering, and physical abuse, which threatened their own and other residents' quality of life (Canadian Institute for Health Information, 2008b).

FIGURE 15.2 | Number of Canadians Aged 65 Years and Over, and Number of Children Aged Less Than 15 Years, 1956–2016

Source: Adapted from Statistics Canada, "Portrait of the Canadian Population in 2006, by Age and Sex, 2006 Census," catalogue no. 97-551-XWE2006001, released on July 17, 2007, www12.statcan.ca/english/census06/analysis/agesex/charts/chart1.htm.

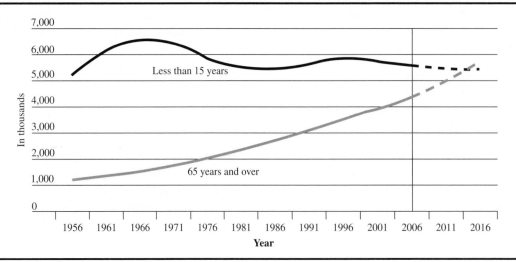

As our population ages, we can expect to see a higher incidence of chronic, but not life-threatening conditions, such as arthritis, osteoporosis, cataracts, glaucoma, hearing losses, incontinence, and blindness. Some effort to control these non-communicable diseases must necessarily focus on prevention. For example, the incidence of deafness is rising, attributable in part to the blasting rock music that teenagers in the 1950s and 1960s (who are now in their fifties, sixties, and seventies) listened to. Because rock music is not getting any quieter and because adolescents now go to rock concerts and use headphones as well, prevention of deafness will take on increasing significance in the coming years. Similarly, rates of vision problems among Canadian seniors are very high (approximately 80 percent), with nearly 30 percent of seniors afflicted with cataracts (W. J. Millar, 2004). Considering that young and middle-aged adults today now spend a great deal of time in front of a computer screen, vision problems can be expected to be a growing concern for the seniors of tomorrow. These are just some examples of the kinds of problems that are created for health psychologists as a result of the shift in age of the population and a shift in leisure-time activities.

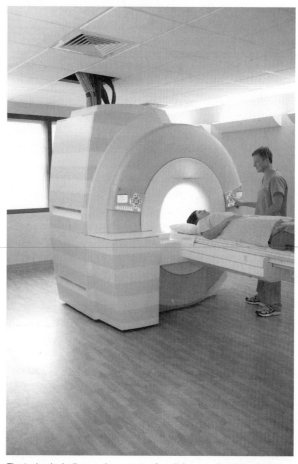

The technologically complex aspects of medicine are often intimidating to patients, but when the purpose of the technology is fully explained and patients are committed to their use, it helps reduce this anxiety.

(L05) WHAT ARE THE HEALTH PSYCHOLOGY TRENDS FOR THE FUTURE?

The Changing Nature of Medical Practice

Health psychology is continually responsive to changes in health trends and medical practice (Nicassio, Meyerowitz, & Kerns, 2004). For example, as the population has aged, the significance of diseases of aging has increased, such as the mortality due to prostate cancer. Changes in the environment also pose challenges for health. For example, the negative effects of air pollution on lung development in children can lead to increased risks for asthma in both childhood and adulthood (Gauderman et al., 2004; Public Health Agency of Canada, 2007b). Climate change can also affect illness patterns. For example, rates of tropical diseases such as diarrheal disorders and malaria, are increasing and heading north (Jack, 2007, April 25). By the year 2020, many of the environmental issues of today will persist and give rise to new health challenges for the future (see the Focus on Social Issues box, "Health and Illness in 2020: A Canadian Perspective").

The face of health psychology may change yet again as patterns of infectious disease have altered. Although the past century has brought substantial control over infectious diseases, they remain a public health problem globally and are still responsible for 13 million deaths each year. For example, the recent outbreak of H1N1 flu in early 2009 resulted in 18,000 deaths worldwide a year later, 428 deaths in Canada, and thousands more infections (Gilmore & Hoffman, 2010). Nonetheless, only 41 percent of Canadians reported being vaccinated for H1N1, suggesting that increasing public awareness of pandemic outbreaks such as H1N1 and the need for preventive health behaviours is one area where health psychology may play a larger role in the future. Moreover, changes in society, technology, and microorganisms themselves are leading to the emergence of new diseases, the re-emergence of diseases that were once successfully controlled, and problems with drug-resistant strains of once successfully controlled disorders (Emerson & Purcell, 2004; Hien, de Jong, & Farrar, 2004). A bigger role in health psychology may emerge from this important and frightening trend.

Health and Illness in 2020: A Canadian Perspective

What will the world be like in the year 2020? And what issues will Canadians face with respect to health, illness, and health care? According to a report prepared on behalf of the Canadian Nurses Association, some of the health concerns of the future are to be expected while others may represent new challenges. These issues will occur against a backdrop of social and environmental changes, many of which are already underway.

In the year 2020, environmental change will have permanently altered the planet, impacting disease patterns. For example, global warming will mean that formerly colder climates will be plagued by diseases of warmer climates, as mosquitoes and other carriers move north. The impact of current environmental issues on health will continue to be felt in 2020. There will be more allergies, asthma, waterborne diseases, environmental sensitivities, and infectious diseases. Ecotoxicity from organic pollutants such as dichloro-diphenyltrichloroethane (DDT) and polychlorinated biphenyls (PCBs) that Canadians have been exposed to for over 50 years will show their long-term effects, perhaps giving rise to a new class of medically unexplained symptoms. Global interconnectedness will mean increased risk for the spread of infectious diseases and the fears of a global flu pandemic may well be realized by 2020.

Population growth due to immigration will continue into 2020, resulting in one in five Canadians being foreign- born, and one in four being a member of a visible minority group, including Aboriginal peoples. At least half of all visible minority persons will be Chinese or South Asian, and three-quarters will be living in Canada's largest urban centres: Montreal, Toronto, and Vancouver. For most, English will be their second language. Canada's Aboriginal population is also expected to increase, with the largest increases expected in Saskatchewan and Manitoba. For example, Saskatchewan's First Nations population is expected to almost double its 11 percent rate from 1996 to 20 percent in 2020.

The increasing cultural diversification of the Canadian population will present several challenges for health promotion and health care. Although the healthy immigrant effect—the tendency for newly arrived immigrants to be in better health than the overall population—will be evident, the usual declines in immigrants' health that follow will also put these new Canadians at risk for the development of chronic illness (Vissandjee, Desmeules, Cao, Abdool & Kawanjian, 2004). Health promotion efforts may have to be increasingly tailored to these diverse populations to help them either maintain the healthy habits of their own culture or adopt new health protective ones. In addition, greater attention will have to be paid to the delivery of culturally sensitive health care, including accommodating English speaking Canadians living in Quebec.

The full impact of Canada's aging population will be felt by 2020, with half of the Canadian population over age 44, and there will be as many seniors in the population as there will be children. This will be most evident in the Atlantic Provinces, Quebec, and British Columbia, suggesting that this is where the competition for health care dollars will be most apparent.

Changing disease patterns will also be evident as a result of the aging population. Arthritis and diabetes will increase along with other non-communicable diseases associated with aging, and there will be an increase in virulent infectious diseases, including the re-emergence of tuberculosis. The health promotion efforts of the present day will result in a decrease of certain diseases related to obesity, inactivity, and poor eating habits in 2020. However, because of the after-effects of today's obesity levels on tomorrow's seniors, there will be a greater need for joint replacements. This may lead to a new "health tourism," with wealthy Canadians who are having difficulty getting certain procedures such as joint replacements in Canada due to long wait times travelling to resorts on the Indian Ocean to get these procedures at a fraction of the cost.

Other expected trends include a continued focus on wellness instead of illness, with more people wanting to participate in their health and expecting the information and resources to do so. Accordingly, self-care, workplace wellness programs, and accessible community-supported activity programs will be the norm. Complementary and alternative health care will continue to grow in popularity and by 2020 will become more integrated within the health care system. Health records will become standardized, with every Canadian having a portable, secure, and accessible electronic health record.

The health care system of 2020 will be very different from how it is now, as it adapts to the demands of Canada's changing population, culture, and patterns of disease. It will be characterized by diversity, interdisciplinary care, and community and consumer involvement, and shaped by the simultaneous progression of the technology and holistic health movements.

Source: Villeneuve & MacDonald, 2006

Impact of Technology Technological advances in medicine have contributed greatly to the enormous costs of contemporary medicine (Reinhardt, 2004), and in the future technology will continue to shape how health care is delivered. These complex aspects of medicine itself also are often daunting for many patients. Explaining the purposes of these technologies and using control-enhancing interventions to enable people to feel like active participants in their treatment can help reduce fear. The growth of medical technology also raises complex questions about how it should be used. Consider transplantation. At present, insufficient numbers of transplantable organs are available; consequently, how to increase the supply of transplantable organs and how to develop priorities as to who should receive transplants have been highly controversial issues (Singh, Katz, Beauchamp, & Hannon, 2002).

The ethics of transplantation seem tame, compared with the host of ethical questions raised by recent technological developments in human reproduction. What are the implications of cloning for humans? It is now technically possible to transplant eggs and even ovaries from aborted female fetuses into women who have been unable to conceive a child on their own (Kolata, 1994). What are the ethics of using one life to create another? What psychosocial issues are raised by these dilemmas? As a science, health psychology must begin to anticipate many of these controversial issues to help provide a blueprint for considering the psychosocial and ethical issues that will arise.

As medical care has grown more technologically complex, it has also, paradoxically, begun to incorporate psychological and spiritual sides of healing, especially those approaches that draw on Eastern healing traditions. Relaxation and other alternative and complementary treatment methods are becoming increasingly popular health care choices among Canadians. Such treatments can be remarkably effective for treating stress-related disorders, including such severely problematic conditions as hypertension.

Comprehensive Intervention Another trend within medicine that affects health psychology is the movement toward **comprehensive intervention models.** These are several models that concentrate and coordinate medical and psychological expertise in welldefined areas of medical practice. One is the pain management program, in which all available treatments for pain have been brought together so that individual regimens can be developed for each patient. A second model is the hospice, in which palliative management technologies and psychotherapeutic technologies are available to the dying patient. Coordinated residential and outpatient rehabilitation programs for coronary heart disease patients, in which multiple health habits are dealt with simultaneously, constitute a third example. Finally, a recent movement toward the integration of complementary therapies with traditional medical care for treating cancer patients heralds a new trend toward **integrative care.** Integrative care combines complementary therapies with conventional treatments to provide holistic treatment that addresses body, mind, and spirit with the aim of increasing patients' sense of control over their health. For example, InspireHealth (formerly known as the Centre for Integrated Healing) in Vancouver is Canada's first and only government-funded integrated cancer care centre, and has been serving cancer patients since 1997. Other integrated care centres continue to appear across the country as this new trend in cancer care echoes the call of researchers to move toward a whole-systems approach to health care (Verhoef, Vanderheyden, & Fonnebo, 2006).

Making use of the mass media, youth prevention projects, educational interventions, public health solutions, and tax solutions to such problems as smoking, lack of exercise, excessive alcohol consumption, and drug abuse, are increasingly being used to help improve the health of Canadians. For example, the Ontario government waived the provincial tax for any bicycles purchased in 2008 as part of an ongoing initiative to increase the activity levels among the population. The coordination of public health management at the institutional and community levels, with individual health management and illness management for those already ill, is represented in Figure 15.3.

Systematic Documentation of Treatment Effectiveness

An important professional goal of health psychology for the future is the continued documentation of the **treatment effectiveness** of health psychology's technologies and interventions. We know that our behavioural, cognitive, and psychotherapeutic technologies work, but we must increasingly find ways to communicate this success to others. This issue has taken on considerable significance in recent years as debate rages over whether and to what degree behavioural and psychological interventions should be covered in managed health care systems.

FIGURE 15.3 | Continuum of Care and Types and Levels of Intervention
Source: D. B. Abrams et al., 1996

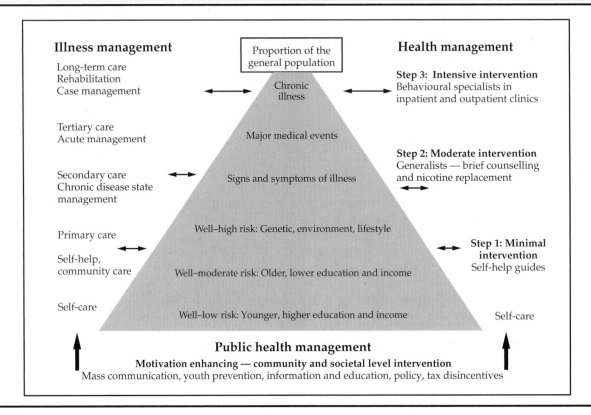

Cost containment pressures have prompted the development of interventions that are time limited, symptom focused, and offered as outpatient services (Sanchez & Turner, 2003), a format that is not always conducive to change through behavioural intervention. Moreover, this has been accompanied by a shift in treatment decision-making power from behavioural health care providers to policy-makers. These changes affect health psychology in several ways. A lack of empirical data regarding treatment outcomes and efficacy represents a striking gap in how behavioural scientists and practitioners present their interventions to policy makers (Sanchez & Turner, 2003). Developing convincing methods of measuring successful psychosocial interventions is of paramount importance.

The potential for health psychology to make major contributions to medicine and medical practice has never been greater. **Evidence-based medicine** is now the criterion for adopting medical standards. Evidence-based medicine refers to the conscientious, explicit,

judicious use of the best scientific evidence for making decisions about the care of individual patients (Timmermans & Angell, 2001). This trend means that, with documentation of the success of health psychology interventions, the potential for empirical contributions to contribute to practice is enhanced.

Systematic Documentation of Cost Effectiveness

As noted earlier, one of the major forces facing health psychology, as well as every other disciplinary contributor to behavioural medicine, is the growing cost of health care services and the accompanying mounting pressure to contain costs (see Figure 15.4). This reality is relevant to health psychologists in several respects. It nudges the field to keep an eye on the bottom line in research and intervention. While effective health psychology interventions are an important goal of the field, their likelihood of being integrated into medical care will be influenced by their **cost effectiveness.**

FIGURE 15.4 | National Health Care Expenditures: Selected Calendar Years, 1975–2003

Source: Canadian Institute for Health Information, Health Care in Canada, 2004, reprinted by permission of Canadian Institute for Health Information.

Total Expenditures on Health Care   We now spend over $100 billion more on health care than in 1975. Even when adjusted for inflation, total (public and private) spending on health care (in constant 1997 dollars) continues to rise.

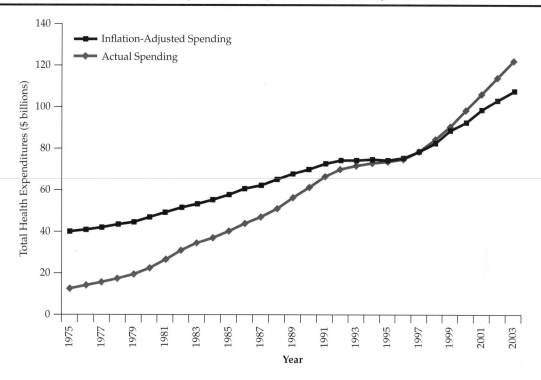

Note: 2002 and 2003 figures cited are forecasts.

Subtly, the pressures of cost containment push the health psychology field in the direction of research that is designed to keep people out of the health care system altogether. On the clinical practice side, interventions include self-help groups, peer counselling, self-management programs, and other inexpensive ways to provide services to those who might otherwise not receive care. Writing about intensely traumatic or stressful events is also a lowcost, easily implemented intervention that has demonstrated beneficial effects (for example, Ullrich & Lutgendorf, 2002). Another example is the stress reduction and pain amelioration benefits that can be achieved by simple, inexpensive techniques of relaxation, such as mindfulness-based stress reduction programs, and other cognitive behavioural interventions.

In addition, health psychology could help develop interventions to save costs. For example, finding ways of identifying and drawing off the two-thirds of patients whose medical complaints are believed to be primarily of psychological origin would save the health care delivery system billions of dollars yearly and would direct these people more appropriately into psychological services (R. M. Kaplan, 1991).

The provision of appropriate psychological services can result in savings to the health care system in a variety of ways. For example, elderly patients who receive mental health care spend fewer days in the hospital, and presurgical counselling has been linked to fewer postsurgery complications and subsequent medical visits (Hunsley, 2002). Numerous studies suggest that psychological interventions can be a cost-effective treatment for a variety of health conditions and issues, including hypertension, heart disease, chronic pain, diabetes, and cancer. Such treatments may also be more cost-effective and safer than many commonly used pharmacological interventions, and can offer greater accessibility to patients living in rural areas. How much can psychological interventions save in health care expenses? A report from the Canadian Psychological Association estimated that for every $1 spent on psychological care there is a $5 saving in medical costs (Hunsley, 2002). Given the rising health care expenditures in Canada over the past three decades (see Figure 15.4), this degree of saving will hopefully convince policy-makers to move toward including coverage for such interventions within Canada's universal health care plan in years to come.

The Future of Health Psychology Theory

A health behaviour change program or pain management strategy is only as good as the theory it is based on. Indeed, the social psychologist Kurt Lewin once said, "There is nothing so practical as a good theory" (1951, p. 169). Given the challenges we face today and in the future as the population ages and disease patterns change, it will be essential to have good health psychology theories to help address these issues. But what constitutes a good theory? It has been suggested that a "good" theory in health psychology is one that will describe how one variable affects another in a way that can guide interventions to change, promote, and maintain people's health (Michie, Rothman, & Sheeran, 2007). Current theories in health psychology have been applied with some success (e.g., the health belief model and the theory of planned behaviour), but may not be nearly as effective as what is required given the current and coming health challenges. Researchers have accordingly suggested that if health psychology is to grow as a field and continue to improve health effectively, then researchers will need to move beyond simply applying theory to developing theory (Michie, Rothman, & Sheeran, 2007). This can also include adapting or building on current theory, such as implementation intentions, by including additional innovative interventions (for example, Knauper et al., 2011).

Several Canadian health psychology researchers have already been active in this endeavour. For example, researchers at the University of Waterloo have developed the Temporal Self-regulation Theory which proposes that understanding individual health related behaviour depends upon how this health behaviour is framed over time (Hall & Fong, 2007). The Compensatory Health beliefs model developed by researchers at McGill University focus on understanding the role of compensatory beliefs for explaining why people fail to bridge the intention-behaviour gap in the context of tempting unhealthy alternative choices (Knauuper, Rabiau, Cohen, & Patriciu, 2004). These are just two examples of health psychology theory development and hopefully other Canadian researchers will continue to answer this call.

Foretelling the future is never an easy task. Some trends, such as the aging of the population, are obvious and have clear implications for the field. Others are not so easily anticipated; thus their implications for health psychology are still elusive. ●

SUMMARY

LO1 **Describe the health psychology priorities for the future**

- Health psychology research and practice have identified the complexity of faulty health habits and how best to modify them. Priorities for the future include the modification of the most consequential risk factors, incorporation of the most potent and effective elements of behaviour-change programs into cost-effective interventions, and the continuing search for the best venue for intervention.

- Health psychology interventions will continue to focus on people at risk for particular disorders, on preventing poor health habits from developing, and on developing effective health promotion interventions with the elderly. Health promotion efforts must consider not only mortality but also the reduction of morbidity and the importance of enhancing overall quality of life.

- As medicine develops a health promotion orientation, the potential for collaborative interventions between psychologists and medical practitioners through the media, the community, and the physician's office may come to be more fully realized.

- An effective health promotion program must involve not only health behaviour change but also social change that makes high-quality health care available to all elements of the population, especially Canada's Aboriginal peoples and those low in socio-economic status (SES).

LO2 **Know where stress research is headed**

- Research on stress will continue to focus on vulnerable populations and on trends in the economy and culture that increase the stress on particular subpopulations, such as children, the elderly, and the poor.

- In the future, many important advances in stress research will likely come from research examining the pathways by which stress exerts adverse effects on health.

LO3 **Understand the future of health services**

- Improving access to needed health care, improving the quality of care delivered, and narrowing the health inequality gap are three priorities that will need to be addressed in order to achieve health care renewal in Canada.

LO4 **Identify the issues in chronic illness management for the future**

- The management of chronic illness will increasingly focus on quality of life and appropriate ways to measure it. The management of terminal illness will increasingly focus on ways of enabling people to die physically and psychologically comfortable deaths. In addition, ethical issues involving aid in dying, living wills, the patient's right to die, family decision making in death and dying, and euthanasia will continue to be prominent.

LO5 **Describe the health psychology trends for the future**

- A target for future work is identification of the health and lifestyle issues that will be created by the aging of the population. Anticipating medical disorders and developing interventions to offset their potential adverse effects should be targets for research now.

- Health psychology needs to be responsive to changes in medical practice, including changes in disease demographics (such as age). The changing face of medicine creates challenges for health psychologists in anticipating the impact of technologically complex interventions and helping prepare patients for them.

- Important goals for health psychology's future are systematic documentation of treatment effectiveness using the criteria of evidence-based medicine, systematic documentation of the cost effectiveness of interventions, and continued efforts to find ways to reduce health costs. The development of new health psychology theories to guide the implementation of health behaviour change interventions is also critical.

KEY TERMS

GLOSSARY

abstinence violation effect A feeling of loss of control that results when one has violated self-imposed rules, such as not to smoke or drink. (p. 75)

acquired immune deficiency syndrome (AIDS) Progressive impairment of the immune system by the human immunodeficiency virus (HIV); a diagnosis of AIDS is made on the basis of the presence of one or more specific opportunistic infections. (p. 392)

acupuncture A technique of healing and pain control, developed in China, in which long, thin needles are inserted into designated areas of the body to reduce discomfort in a target area of the body. (p. 281)

acute disorders Illnesses or other medical problems that occur over a short period of time, that are usually the result of an infectious process, and that are reversible. (p. 11)

acute pain Short-term pain that usually results from a specific injury. (p. 273)

acute stress paradigm A laboratory procedure whereby an individual goes through moderately stressful procedures (such as counting backwards rapidly by 7s), so that stress-related changes in emotions and physiological and/or neuroendocrine processes may be assessed. (p. 168)

addiction The state of physical or psychological dependence on a substance that develops when that substance is used over a period of time. (p. 122)

adherence The degree to which an individual follows a recommended health-related or illness-related recommendation. (p. 249)

adrenal glands Two small glands, located on top of the kidneys, that are part of the endocrine system and secrete several hormones, including cortisol, epinephrine, and norepinephrine, that are involved in responses to stress. (p. 26)

aerobic exercise High-intensity, long-duration, and high-endurance exercise, believed to contribute to cardiovascular fitness and other positive health outcomes. Examples are jogging, bicycling, running, and swimming. (p. 95)

after-effects of stress Performance and attentional decrements that occur after a stressful event has subsided; believed to be produced by the residual physiological, emotional, and cognitive draining in response to stressful events. (p. 165)

alcoholism The state of physical addiction to alcohol that manifests through such symptoms as stereotyped drinking, drinking to maintain blood alcohol at a particular level, increasing frequency and severity of withdrawal, drinking early in the day and in the middle of the night, a sense of loss of control over drinking, or a subjective craving for alcohol. (p. 125)

allostatic load The accumulating adverse effects of stress, in conjunction with pre-existing risks, on biological stress regulatory systems. (p. 162)

angina pectoris Chest pain that occurs because the muscle tissue of the heart is deprived of adequate oxygen or because removal of carbon dioxide and other wastes interferes with the flow of blood and oxygen to the heart. (p. 29)

anorexia nervosa A condition produced by excessive dieting and exercise that yields body weight grossly below optimal level, most common among adolescent girls. (p. 148)

appraisal delay The time between recognizing that a symptom exists and deciding that it is serious. (p. 226)

approach (confrontative, or vigilant) coping style The tendency to cope with stressful events by tackling them directly and attempting to develop solutions; may ultimately be an especially effective method of coping, although it may produce accompanying distress. (p. 192)

assertiveness training Techniques that train people how to be appropriately assertive in social situations; often included as part of health behaviour modification programs, on the assumption that some poor health habits, such as excessive alcohol consumption or smoking, develop in part to control difficulties in being appropriately assertive. (p. 73)

atherosclerosis A major cause of heart disease; caused by the narrowing of the arterial walls due to the formation of plaques that reduce the flow of blood through the arteries and interfere with the passage of nutrients from the capillaries into the cells. (p. 29)

at risk A state of vulnerability to a particular health problem by virtue of heredity, health practices, or family environment. (p. 52)

autoimmunity A condition in which the body produces an immune response against its own tissue constituents. (p. 45)

avoidant (minimizing) coping style The tendency to cope with threatening events by withdrawing, minimizing, or avoiding them; believed to be an effective short-term, though not an effective long-term, response to stress. (p. 192)

behavioural assignments Home practice activities that clients perform on their own as part of an integrated therapeutic intervention for behaviour modification. (p. 72)

behavioural delay The time between deciding to seek treatment and actually doing so. (p. 226)

behavioural immunization Programs designed to inoculate people against adverse health habits by exposing them to mild versions of persuasive communications that try to engage them in a poor health practice and giving them techniques that they can use to respond effectively to these efforts. (p. 425)

behavioural inoculation A concept, developed for smoking interventions and similar in rationale to inoculation against disease, that suggests that exposure to a weak version of a persuasive message may help to develop counterarguments against that message so that a stronger form of that message can be successfully resisted. (p. 144)

behavioural medicine The interdisciplinary field concerned with integrating behavioural science and biomedical science for understanding physical health and illness and for developing and applying knowledge and techniques to prevent, diagnose, treat, and rehabilitate. (p. 7)

benefit finding Acknowledgement of the positive affects of illness in one's life. (p. 313)

biofeedback A method whereby an individual is provided with ongoing, specific information or feedback about how a particular physiological process operates so that he or she can learn how to modify that process. (p. 279)

biomedical model The viewpoint that illness can be explained on the basis of aberrant somatic processes and that psychological and social processes are largely independent of the disease process; the dominant model in medical practice until recently. (p. 8)

biopsychosocial model The view that biological, psychological, and social factors are all involved in any given state of health or illness. (p. 8)

blood pressure The force that blood exerts against vessel walls. (p. 29)

body image The perception and evaluation of one's body, one's physical functioning, and one's appearance. (p. 299)

broad-spectrum cognitive behaviour therapy The use of a broad array of cognitive-behavioural intervention techniques to modify an individual's health behaviour. (p. 73)

buffering hypothesis The hypothesis that coping resources are useful primarily under conditions of high stress and not necessarily under conditions of low stress. (p. 202)

bulimia An eating syndrome characterized by alternating cycles of binge eating and purging through such techniques as vomiting or extreme dieting. (p. 149)

bullying Acts intended to harm, which are repeated over time and often occur in a relationship where there is an imbalance of power. (p. 176)

cardiac invalidism A psychological state that can result after a myocardial infarction or diagnosis of coronary heart disease, consisting of the perception that a patient's abilities and capacities are lower than they actually are; both patients and their spouses are vulnerable to these misperceptions. (p. 362)

cardiac rehabilitation An intervention program designed to help heart patients achieve their optimal physical, medical, psychological, social, emotional, vocational, and economic status after the diagnosis of heart disease or a heart attack. (p. 359)

cardiopulmonary resuscitation (CPR) A method of reviving the functioning of heart and lungs after a loss of consciousness in which the patient's pulse has ceased or lungs have failed to function appropriately. (p. 363)

cardiovascular system The transport system of the body responsible for carrying oxygen and nutrients to the body and carrying away carbon dioxide and other wastes to the kidneys for excretion; composed of the heart, blood vessels, and blood. (p. 28)

catecholamines The neurotransmitters, epinephrine and norepinephrine, that promote sympathetic nervous system activity; released in substantial quantities during stressful times. (p. 25)

cell-mediated immunity Slow acting immune response, involving T lymphocytes, that operates at the cellular level. (p. 43)

cerebellum The part of the hindbrain responsible for the coordination of voluntary muscle movement, the maintenance of balance and equilibrium, and the maintenance of muscle tone and posture. (p. 24)

cerebral cortex The main portion of the brain, responsible for intelligence, memory, and the detection and interpretation of sensation. (p. 24)

chronic benign pain Pain that typically persists for six months or longer and is relatively intractable to treatment. The pain varies in severity and may involve any of a number of muscle groups. Chronic low back pain and myofascial pain syndrome are examples. (p. 274)

chronic illnesses Illnesses that are long lasting, are the main contributors to disability and death, and are usually irreversible. (p. 11)

chronic pain Pain that may begin after an injury but which does not respond to treatment and persists over time. (p. 274)

chronic progressive pain Pain that persists longer than six months and increases in severity over time. Typically, it is associated with malignancies or degenerative disorders, such as skeletal metastatic disease or rheumatoid arthritis. (p. 274)

chronic strain A stressful experience that is a usual but continually stressful aspect of life. (p. 164)

classical conditioning The pairing of a stimulus with an unconditioned reflex, such that over time the new stimulus acquires a conditioned response, evoking the same behaviour; the process by which an automatic response is conditioned to a new stimulus. (p. 69)

clinical breast exam (CBE) A thorough physical examination of the breast by a health care professional to detect changes or abnormalities that could indicate the early signs of breast cancer. (p. 91)

clinical thanatology The clinical practice of counselling people who are dying on the basis of knowledge of reactions to dying. (p. 338)

cognitive behaviour therapy (CBT) The use of principles from learning theory to modify the cognitions and behaviours asso-ciated with a behaviour to be modified; cognitive-behavioural approaches are used to modify poor health habits, such as smoking, poor diet, and alcoholism. (p. 69)

cognitive restructuring A method of modifying internal monologues in stress-producing situations; clients are trained to monitor what they say to themselves in stress-provoking situations and then to modify their cognitions in adaptive ways. (p. 72)

cold pressor test A method for assessing pain tolerance and intensity that involves participants submerging their hands to the wrist in frigid water and keeping them there as long as they can. (p. 280)

complementary and alternative medicine (CAM) A diverse group of healing therapies (e.g., chiropractic, massage therapy, homeopathy, and acupuncture) not currently considered an integral part of conventional medical practice; some therapies are delivered by a health care professional, and others involve self-care. (p. 242)

comprehensive intervention model A model that pools and coordinates the medical and psychological expertise in a well-defined area of medical practice so as to make all available technology and expertise available to a patient; the pain management program is one example of a comprehensive intervention model. (p. 437)

confrontative (vigilant) coping style See **approach (confrontative, or vigilant) coping style.** (p. 192)

contingency contracting A procedure in which an individual forms a contract with another person, such as a therapist, detailing what rewards or punishments are contingent on the performance or nonperformance of a target behaviour. (p. 72)

conversion hysteria The viewpoint, originally advanced by Freud, that specific unconscious conflicts can produce physical disturbances symbolic of the repressed conflict; no longer a dominant viewpoint in health psychology. (p. 7)

coping The process of trying to manage demands that are appraised as taxing or exceeding one's resources. (p. 185)

coping outcomes The beneficial effects that are thought to result from successful coping; these include reducing stress, adjusting more successfully to it, maintaining emotional equilibrium, having satisfying relationships with others, and maintaining a positive self-image. (p. 199)

coping style An individual's preferred method of dealing with stressful situations. (p. 192)

coronary heart disease (CHD) A general term referring to illnesses caused by atherosclerosis, which is the narrowing of the coronary arteries, the vessels that supply the heart with blood. (p. 350)

correlational research Measuring two variables and determining whether they are associated with each other. Studies relating smoking to lung cancer are correlational, for example. (p. 15)

cost containment The effort to reduce or hold down health care costs. (p. 438)

cost effectiveness The formal evaluation of the effectiveness of an intervention relative to its cost and the cost of alternative interventions. (p. 438)

counterirritation A pain control technique that involves inhibiting pain in one part of the body by stimulating or mildly irritating another area, sometimes adjacent to the area in which the pain is experienced. (p. 278)

covert self-control The manipulation and alteration of private events, such as thoughts, through principles of reinforcement and self-instruction. (p. 72)

craving A strong desire to engage in a behaviour or consume a substance, such as alcohol or tobacco, which appears, in part, to occur through the conditioning of physical dependence on environmental cues associated with the behaviour. (p. 122)

creative nonadherence The modification or supplementation of a prescribed treatment regimen on the basis of privately held theories about the disorder or its treatment. (p. 250)

curative care Care designed to cure the patient's disease. (p. 337)

daily hassles Minor daily stressful events; believed to have a cumulative effect in increasing the likelihood of illness. (p. 171)

death education Programs designed to inform people realistically about death and dying, the purpose of which is to reduce the terror connected with and avoidance of the topic. (p. 346)

delay behaviour The act of delaying seeking treatment for recognized symptoms. (p. 226)

denial A defence mechanism involving the inability to recognize or deal with external threatening events; believed to be an early reaction to the diagnosis of a chronic or terminal illness. (p. 297)

depression A neurotic or psychotic mood disorder marked especially by sadness, inactivity, difficulty with thinking and concentration, a significant increase or decrease in appetite and time spent sleeping, feelings of dejection and hopelessness, and sometimes suicidal thoughts or an attempt to commit suicide. (p. 298)

detoxification The process of withdrawing from alcohol, usually conducted in a supervised, medically monitored setting. (p. 127)

diabetes A chronic disorder in which the body is not able to manufacture or use insulin properly. (p. 372)

dietician Trained and licensed individuals who apply principles of nutrition and food management to meal planning for institutions, such as hospitals, or for individuals who need help planning and managing special diets. (p. 18)

dignity therapy A process that aims to address concern or distress experienced in physical, psychosocial, spiritual, and existential domains to help rebuild dignity for a terminally ill patient. It involves interviewing the patient to produce a document that details important issues and anything that they would want remembered about themselves and their lives as death approaches. (p. 339)

direct effects hypothesis The theory that coping resources, such as social support, have beneficial psychological and health effects under conditions of both high stress and low stress. (p. 202)

discriminative stimulus An environmental stimulus that is capable of eliciting a particular behaviour; for example, the sight of food may act as a discriminative stimulus for eating. (p. 71)

dispositional optimism A general expectancy that good things, not bad, will happen in the future. (p. 188)

distraction A pain control method that may involve either focusing on a stimulus irrelevant to the pain experience or reinterpreting the pain experience; redirecting attention to reduce pain. (p. 282)

double-blind experiment An experimental procedure in which neither the researcher nor the patient knows whether the patient received the real treatment or the placebo until precoded records indicating which patient received which are consulted; designed to reduce the possibility that expectations for success will increase evidence for success. (p. 260)

dyadic coping The interplay of the stress experienced and expressed by one partner and the coping reactions of the other. (p. 203)

elderspeak An overly caring and infantilizing communication style that includes using overly familiar terms such as "dear" and "sweetie" to address elderly strangers. (p. 245)

emotional support Indications from other people that one is loved, valued, and cared for; believed to be an important aspect of social support during times of stress. (p. 199)

emotion-focused coping An effort to regulate emotions experienced because of a stressful event; emotion-focused coping skills develop in late childhood or early adolescence. (p. 193)

endocrine system A bodily system of ductless glands that secrete hormones into the blood to stimulate target organs; interacts with nervous system functioning. (p. 26)

endogenous opioid peptides Opiatelike substances produced by the body. (p. 272)

epidemiology The study of the frequency, distribution, and causes of infectious and noninfectious disease in a population, based on an investigation of the physical and social environment. Thus, for example, epidemiologists not only study who has what kind of cancer but also address questions such as why certain cancers are more prevalent in particular geographic areas. (p. 13)

etiology The origins and causes of illness. (p. 4)

euthanasia Ending the life of a person who has a painful terminal illness for the purpose of terminating the individual's suffering. (p. 331)

evidence-based medicine The conscientious, explicit, judicious use of the best scientific evidence for making decisions about the care of individual patients. (p. 438)

expectancy-value theory The theory that suggests that people will choose to engage in behaviours that they expect to succeed in and that have outcomes that they value. (p. 63)

experiment A type of research in which a researcher randomly assigns people to two or more conditions, varies the treatments that people in each condition are given, and then measures the effect on some response. (p. 15)

fear appeals Efforts to change attitudes by arousing fear to induce the motivation to change behaviour; fear appeals are used to try to get people to change poor health habits. (p. 62)

fight-or-flight response A response to threat in which the body is rapidly aroused and motivated via the sympathetic nervous system and the endocrine system to attack or flee a threatening stimulus; the response was first described by Walter Cannon in 1932. (p. 155)

functional somatic syndrome Marked by the symptoms, suffering, and disability it causes rather than by any demonstrable tissue abnormality. (p. 306)

gate control theory Theory for understanding pain, developed by Canadian psychologist Ronald Melzack and British physiologist Patrick Wall, that suggests psychological factors play a significant role in the experience of pain. (p. 269)

general adaptation syndrome Developed by Hans Selye, a profile of how organisms respond to stress; the general adaptation syndrome is characterized by three phases: a nonspecific mobilization phase, which promotes sympathetic nervous system activity; a resistance phase, during which the organism makes efforts to cope with the threat; and an exhaustion phase, which occurs if the organism fails to overcome the threat and depletes its physiological resources. (p. 156)

gout A form of arthritis produced by a buildup of uric acid in the body, producing crystals that become lodged in the joints; the most commonly affected area is the big toe. (p. 419)

grief A response to bereavement involving a feeling of hollowness and sometimes marked by preoccupation with the dead person, expressions of hostility toward others, and guilt over death; may also involve restlessness, inability to concentrate, and other adverse psychological and physical symptoms. (p. 343)

guided imagery A technique of relaxation and pain control in which a person conjures up a picture that is held in mind during a painful or stressful experience. (p. 283)

harm reduction An intervention strategy that focuses on the risks and consequences of substance use rather than on the use itself. (p. 122)

health The absence of disease or infirmity, coupled with a complete state of physical, mental, and social well-being; health psychologists recognize health to be a state that is actively achieved rather than the mere absence of illness. (p. 4)

health behaviours Behaviours undertaken by people to enhance or maintain their health, such as exercise or the consumption of a healthy diet. (p. 53)

health belief model A theory of health behaviours; the model predicts that whether a person practises a particular health habit can be understood by knowing the degree to which the person perceives a personal health threat and the perception that a particular health practice will be effective in reducing that threat. (p. 63)

health habit A health-related behaviour that is firmly established and often performed automatically, such as buckling a seat belt or brushing one's teeth. (p. 53)

health locus of control The perception that one's health is under personal control; is controlled by powerful others, such as physicians; or is determined by external factors, including chance. (p. 54)

health promotion A general philosophy that maintains that health is a personal and collective achievement; the process of enabling people to increase control over and improve their health. Health promotion may occur through individual efforts, through interaction with the medical system, and through a concerted health policy effort. (p. 52)

health psychology The subarea within psychology devoted to understanding psychological influences on health, illness, and responses to those states, as well as the psychological origins and impacts of health policy and health interventions. (p. 3)

health risk assessment An assessment designed to identify employees' specific risks based on current age, family history, and lifestyle factors that provide employers with a general view of their employees' health and areas for improvement. (p. 80)

holistic health A philosophy characterized by the belief that health is a positive state that is actively achieved; usually associated with certain nontraditional health practices. (p. 244)

home care Care for dying patients in the home; the choice of care for the majority of terminally ill patients, though sometimes problematic for family members. (p. 342)

hospice An institution for dying patients that encourages personalized, warm palliative care. (p. 341)

hospice care An alternative to hospital and home care, designed to provide warm, personal comfort for terminally ill patients; may be residential or home-based. (p. 341)

human immunodeficiency virus (HIV) The virus that is implicated in the development of AIDS. (p. 394)

humoral immunity Fast-acting immune response that defends the body against bacterial and viral infections that have not yet invaded the cells; mediated by B lmphocytes. (p. 43)

hypertension Excessively high blood pressure that occurs when the supply of blood through the blood vessels is excessive, putting pressure on the vessel walls; a risk factor for a variety of medical problems, including coronary heart disease. (p. 363)

hypnosis A pain management technique involving relaxation, suggestion, distraction, and the focusing of attention. (p. 281)

hypothalamus The part of the forebrain responsible for regulating water balance and controlling hunger and sexual desire; assists in cardiac functioning, blood pressure regulation, and respiration regulation; has a major role in regulation of the endocrine system, which controls the release of hormones, including those related to stress. (p. 24)

illness delay The time between recognizing that a symptom implies an illness and the decision to seek treatment. (p. 226)

illness representations (schemas) An organized set of beliefs about an illness or a type of illness, including its nature, cause, duration, and consequences. (p. 218)

immunity The body's resistance to injury from invading organisms, acquired from the mother at birth, through disease, or through vaccinations and inoculations. (p. 42)

immunocompetence The degree to which the immune system functions effectively. (p. 386)

immunocompromise The degree to which the immune system responds suboptimally, because of either reduced numbers of cells or reduced functioning. (p. 386)

implementation intentions A specific behavioral intention that highlights the how, when, and where of a behaviour, and also includes "if-then" contingency plans to deal with anticipated barriers to the behaviour. (p. 66)

implicit social support Social support that originates from implicit social networks without being directly targeted at a specific problem. (p. 200)

infant mortality rate The number of infant deaths per thousand infants. (p. 322)

informational support The provision of information to a person going through stress by friends, family, and other people in the individual's social network; believed to help reduce the distressing and health-compromising effects of stress. (p. 199)

integrative care Treatment that combines complementary therapies with conventional treatments to provide holistic treatment that addresses body, mind, and spirit with the aim of increasing patients' sense of control over their health. (p. 437)

interprofessional teams Teams usually consisting of three or more physicians and nurses, and sometimes including nurse practitioners, social workers, or psychologists, who collaborate to deliver primary care services, especially for Canadians living in remote areas, and share responsibility for the patients' care. (p. 432)

invisible support When one receives help from another, but is unaware of it; support that is most likely to benefit a person. (p. 199)

kidney dialysis A procedure in which blood is filtered to remove toxic substances and excess fluid from the blood of patients whose kidneys do not function properly. (p. 37)

lay referral network An informal network of family and friends who help an individual interpret and treat a disorder before the individual seeks formal medical treatment. (p. 219)

life–skills-training approach A smoking-prevention program characterized by the belief that training in self-esteem and coping skills will boost self-image to the point that smoking becomes unnecessary or inconsistent with lifestyle. (p. 145)

lifestyle rebalancing Concerted lifestyle change in a healthy direction, usually including exercise, stress management, and a healthy diet; believed to contribute to relapse prevention after successful modification of a poor health habit, such as smoking or alcohol consumption. (p. 77)

living will A will prepared by a person with a terminal illness, requesting that extraordinary life-sustaining procedures not be used in the event that the person's ability to make this decision is lost. (p. 331)

longitudinal research The repeated observation and measurement of the same individuals over a period of time. (p. 16)

lupus The name given to a group of autoimmune diseases, the most common of which is systemic lupus erythematosus. The symptoms of lupus are caused by an immune system malfunction, which leads to the generation of antibodies that attack healthy tissue in different parts of the body causing them to become inflamed. (p. 419)

lymphatic system The drainage system of the body; believed to be involved in immune functioning. (p. 44)

matching hypothesis The hypothesis that social support is helpful to an individual to the extent that the kind of support offered satisfies the individual's specific needs. (p. 204)

medical delay A delay in treating symptoms, which results from problems within the medical system, such as faulty diagnoses, lost test results, and the like. (p. 226)

medically unexplained physical symptoms (MUPS) See **functional somatic syndromes.** (p. 306)

medical students' disease The relabelling of symptoms of fatigue and exhaustion as a particular illness resulting from learning about that illness; called medical students' disease because overworked medical students are vulnerable to this labelling effect. (p. 216)

medulla Part of the brain that regulates heart rate, constriction of blood vessels, and rate of breathing. (p. 24)

metabolic syndrome A pattern of risk factors for the chronic health problems of diabetes, heart disease, and hypertension, characterized by obesity, a high waist-to-hip ratio, and insulin resistance. Metabolic syndrome is exacerbated by inactivity, overeating, age, and hostility. (p. 351)

mind–body relationship The philosophical position regarding whether the mind and body operate indistinguishably as a single system or whether they act as two separate systems; the view guiding health psychology is that the mind and body are indistinguishable. (p. 4)

mindfulness-based stress reduction (MBSR) Systematic training in meditation to assist people in self-regulating their reactions to stress and any negative emotions that may result. (p. 206)

modelling Learning gained from observing another person performing a target behaviour. (p. 70)

morbidity The number of cases of a disease that exist at a given point in time; it may be expressed as the number of new cases (incidence) or as the total number of existing cases (prevalence). (p. 13)

mortality The number of deaths due to particular causes. (p. 13)

myocardial infarction (MI) A heart attack produced when a clot has developed in a coronary vessel, blocking the flow of blood to the heart. (p. 29)

natural health products (NHP) Therapeutic products, including vitamins, minerals, herbal remedies and teas, and plant products, that can be self-administered or delivered by a complementary and alternative medicine (CAM) practitioner. (p. 220)

negative affectivity A personality variable marked by a pervasive negative mood, including anxiety, depression, and hostility; believed to be implicated in the experience of symptoms, the seeking of medical treatment, and possibly illness. (p. 186)

nervous system The system of the body responsible for the transmission of information from the brain to the rest of the body and from the rest of the body to the brain; it is composed of the central nervous system (the brain and the spinal cord) and the peripheral nervous system (which consists of the remainder of the nerves in the body). (p. 23)

neuromatrix theory An extension to the gate control theory; there is a network of neurons that extends throughout areas of the brain to create the felt representation of a unified physical self, called the body-self neuromatrix, that contributes to the experience of pain and can explain phenomena such as phantom limb pain. (p. 270)

neurotransmitters Chemicals that regulate nervous system functioning. (p. 25)

nociception The perception of pain. (p. 269)

nonadherence The failure to comply fully with treatment recommendations for modification of a health habit or an illness state. (p. 249)

nonspecific immune mechanisms A set of responses to infection or a disorder that is engaged by the presence of a biological invader. (p. 43)

nosocomial infection Infection that results from exposure to disease in the hospital setting. (p. 229)

nurse practitioners Nurses who, in addition to their training in traditional nursing, receive special training in primary care so that they may provide routine medical care for patients. (p. 238)

obesity An excessive accumulation of body fat, believed to contribute to a variety of health disorders, including cardiovascular disease. (p. 104)

occupational therapist Trained and licensed individuals who work with emotionally and/or physically disabled people to determine skill levels and to develop a rehabilitation program to build on and expand these skills. (p. 18)

operant conditioning The pairing of a voluntary, nonautomatic behaviour to a new stimulus through reinforcement or punishment. (p. 70)

osteoarthritis A form of arthritis that results when the articular cartilage begins to crack or wear away because of overuse of a particular joint; may also result from injury or other causes; usually affects the weight-bearing joints and is common among athletes and the elderly. (p. 418)

pain behaviours Behaviours that result in response to pain, such as cutting back on work or taking drugs. (p. 266)

pain control The ability to reduce the experience of pain, report of pain, emotional concern over pain, inability to tolerate pain, or presence of pain-related behaviours. (p. 271)

pain management programs Coordinated, interdisciplinary efforts to modify chronic pain by bringing together neurological, cognitive, behavioural, and psychodynamic expertise concerning pain; such programs aim not only to make pain more manageable but also to modify the lifestyle that has evolved because of the pain. (p. 285)

palliative care Care designed to make the patient comfortable, but not to cure or improve the patient's underlying disease; often part of terminal care. (p. 337)

parasympathetic nervous system The part of the nervous system responsible for vegetative functions, the conservation of energy, and the damping down of the effects of the sympathetic nervous system. (p. 23)

passive smoking Non-smokers' inhaling of smoke as a result of exposure to smokers; believed to cause health problems such as bronchitis, emphysema, and lung cancer. (p. 146)

patient-centred communication A way to improve patient-provider dialogue that enlists the patient directly in decisions about medical care; physicians try to see the disorder and treatment as the patient does in order to enlist the patient's cooperation in the diagnostic and treatment process. (p. 254)

patient education Programs that include coping skills training relative to particular disorders, which have been found to improve functioning for a broad variety of chronic diseases. (p. 316)

perceived stress The perception that an event is stressful independent of its objective characteristics. (p. 172)

perfectionism A tendency to experience frequent cognitions about the attainment of one's own or other's ideal standards. (p. 188)

person–environment fit The degree to which the needs and resources of a person and the needs and resources of an environment complement each other. (p. 155)

pessimism A relatively stable dispositional characteristic to expect negative outcomes in the future. (p. 187)

pessimistic explanatory style A chronic tendency to explain negative events as due to internal, stable, and global qualities of the self and to attribute positive events to external, unstable, and nonglobal factors; believed to contribute to the likelihood of illness. (p. 187)

phagocytosis The process by which phagocytes ingest and attempt to eliminate a foreign invader. (p. 43)

phantom limb pain A phenomena that occurs commonly among amputees whereby an individual experiences pain in a limb that is not there. (p. 270)

physical dependence A state in which the body has adjusted to the use of a substance, incorporating it into the body's normal functioning. (p. 122)

physical rehabilitation A program of activities for chronically ill or disabled persons geared toward helping them use their bodies as much as possible, sense changes in the environment and in themselves so as to make appropriate physical accommodations, learn new physical and management skills if necessary, pursue a treatment regimen, and learn how to control the expenditure of energy. (p. 305)

physician assistants Graduates of 2-year programs who perform routine health care functions, teach patients about their treatment regimens, and record medical information. (p. 238)

physiotherapist Trained and licensed individuals who help people with muscle, nerve, joint, or bone diseases to overcome their disabilities as much as possible. (p. 18)

pituitary gland A gland located at the base of and controlled by the brain that secretes the hormones responsible for growth and organ development. (p. 26)

placebo A medical treatment that produces an effect in a patient because of its therapeutic intent and not its nature. (p. 256)

placebo drinking The consumption of nonalcoholic beverages in social situations in which others are drinking alcohol. (p. 131)

placebo effect The medically beneficial impact of an inert treatment. (p. 256)

platelets Small disks found in vertebrate blood that contribute to blood coagulation. (p. 30)

polymodal nociception The experience of pain that triggers chemical reactions from tissue damage. (p. 269)

pons Link between the hindbrain and the midbrain; it helps control respiration. (p. 24)

possible selves Visions of the self for the future that can help to motivate, organize, and direct an individual's current goals and aspirations. (p. 300)

post-traumatic stress disorder (PTSD) A syndrome that results after exposure to a stressor of extreme magnitude, marked by emotional numbing, the reliving of aspects of the trauma, intense responses to other stressful events, and other symptoms, such as hyperalertness, sleep disturbance, guilt, or impaired memory or concentration. (p. 166)

premature death Death that occurs before the projected age of 79. (p. 325)

primary appraisal The perception of a new or changing environment as beneficial, neutral, or negative in its consequences; believed to be a first step in stress and coping. (p. 158)

primary prevention Measures designed to combat risk factors for illness before an illness has a chance to develop. (p. 53)

problem drinking Uncontrolled drinking that leads to social, psychological, and biomedical problems resulting from alcohol; the problem drinker may show some signs associated with alcoholism, but typically problem drinking is considered to be a pre-alcoholic or a lesser alcoholic syndrome. (p. 125)

problem-focused coping An attempt to do something constructive about the stressful conditions that are harming, threatening, or challenging an individual; problem-focused coping appears to emerge during childhood. (p. 193)

prospective research A research strategy in which people are followed forward in time to examine the relationship between one set of variables and later occurrences. For example, prospective research can enable researchers to identify risk factors for diseases that develop at a later point in time. (p. 16)

prospect theory The theory that different presentations of risk information will change people's perspectives and actions. (p. 62)

psychoactive substances Substances such as alcohol and illicit drugs that, when ingested, impact cognitive and affective processes and alter the way a person behaves. (p. 123)

psychological control The perception that one has at one's disposal a response that will reduce, minimize, eliminate, or offset the adverse effects of an unpleasant event, such as a medical procedure. (p. 191)

psychoneuroimmunology Interactions among behavioural, neuroendocrine, and immunological processes of adaptation. (p. 384)

psychosomatic medicine A field within psychiatry, related to health psychology, that developed in the early 1900s to study and treat particular diseases believed to be caused by emotional conflicts, such as ulcers, hypertension, and asthma. The term is now used more broadly to mean an approach to health-related problems and diseases that examines psychological as well as somatic origins. (p. 7)

quality of life The degree to which a person is able to maximize his or her physical, psychological, vocational, and social functioning; an important indicator of recovery from or adjustment to chronic illness. (p. 294)

qualitative research A research method that can provide a rich understanding of the experiences and factors related to the research question because it includes the individual's voice and perspective. Common forms of qualitative research include interviews, focus groups, case studies, and open-ended questions on surveys. (p. 16)

randomized clinical trial An experimental study of the effects of a variable (e.g., a drug or treatment) administered to human subjects who are randomly selected from a broad population and assigned on a random basis to either an experimental or a control group. The goal is to determine the clinical efficacy and pharmacologic effects of the drug or procedure. (p. 15)

reactivity The predisposition to react physiologically to stress; believed to be genetically based in part; high reactivity is believed to be a risk factor for a range of stress-related diseases. (p. 161)

recurrent acute pain Pain that involves a series of intermittent episodes of pain that are acute in character but chronic inasmuch as the condition persists for more than six months; migraine headaches, temporomandibular disorder (involving the jaw), and trigeminal neuralgia (involving spasms of the facial muscles) are examples. (p. 274)

relapse prevention A set of techniques designed to keep people from relapsing to prior poor health habits after initial successful behaviour modification; includes training in coping skills for high-risk-for-relapse situations and lifestyle rebalancing. (p. 76)

relaxation training Procedures that help people relax; include progressive muscle relaxation and deep breathing; may also include guided imagery and forms of meditation or hypnosis. (p. 73)

renal system Part of the metabolic system; responsible for the regulation of bodily fluids and the elimination of wastes; regulates bodily fluids by removing surplus water, surplus electrolytes, and waste products generated by the metabolism of food. (p. 36)

respiratory system The system of the body responsible for taking in oxygen, excreting carbon dioxide, and regulating the relative composition of the blood. (p. 31)

retrospective research A research strategy whereby people are studied for the relationship of past variables or conditions to current ones. Interviewing people with a particular disease and asking them about their childhood health behaviours or exposure to risks can identify conditions leading to an adult disease, for example. (p. 16)

rheumatoid arthritis (RA) A crippling form of arthritis believed to result from an autoimmune process, usually attacking the small joints of the hands, feet, wrists, knees, ankles, and neck. (p. 415)

role conflict Conflict that occurs when two or more social or occupational roles that an individual occupies produce conflicting standards for behaviour. (p. 179)

secondary appraisal The assessment of one's coping abilities and resources and judgment as to whether they will be sufficient to meet the harm, threat, or challenge of a new or changing event. (p. 158)

secondary gains Benefits of being treated for illness, including the ability to rest, to be freed from unpleasant tasks, and to be taken care of by others. (p. 225)

second-hand smoke See **passive smoking.** (p. 146)

self-concept An integrated set of beliefs about one's personal qualities and attributes. (p. 299)

self-control A state in which an individual desiring to change behaviour learns how to modify the antecedents and the consequences of that target behaviour. (p. 71)

self-efficacy The perception that one is able to perform a particular action. (p. 64)

self-esteem A global evaluation of one's qualities and attributes. (p. 299)

self-help aids Materials that can be used by an individual on his or her own without the aid of a therapist to assist in the modification of a personal habit; often used to combat smoking and other health-related risk factors. (p. 143)

self-management Involvement of the patient in all aspects of a chronic illness and its implications, including medical management, changes in social and vocational roles and coping. (p. 293)

self-monitoring, self-observation Assessing the frequency, antecedents, and consequences of a target behaviour to be modified. (p. 69)

self-reinforcement Systematically rewarding or punishing oneself to increase or decrease the occurrence of a target behaviour. (p. 71)

self-talk Internal monologues; people tell themselves things that may undermine or help them implement appropriate health habits, such as "I can stop smoking" (positive self-talk) or "I'll never be able to do this" (negative self-talk). (p. 72)

sleep apnea An air pipe blockage that disrupts sleep and can compromise health. When apnea occurs, a sleeping person stops breathing, sometimes for as long as three minutes, until he or she suddenly wakes up, gasping for air. Researchers now believe that sleep apnea triggers thousands of nighttime deaths, including heart attacks. (p. 117)

smoking-prevention programs Programs designed to keep people from beginning to smoke, as opposed to programs that attempt to induce people to stop once they have already become smokers. (p. 143)

social cognition models Models which propose that the beliefs that people hold about a particular health behaviour motivate their decision to change that behaviour. (p. 62)

social engineering Social or lifestyle change through legislation; for example, water purification is done through social engineering rather than by individual efforts. (p. 77)

social influence intervention A smoking-prevention intervention that draws on the social learning principles of modelling and behavioural inoculation in inducing people not to smoke; youngsters are exposed to older peer models who deliver antismoking messages after exposure to simulated peer pressure to smoke. (p. 143)

socialization The process by which people learn the norms, rules, and beliefs associated with their family and society; parents and social institutions are usually the major agents of socialization. (p. 56)

social marketing The application of marketing technologies developed in the commercial sector to the solution of social problems where the bottom line is behaviour change; a strategy that has been used to effectively advertise initiatives to promote healthy living to Canadians over the past few decades. (p. 425)

social skills training Techniques that teach people how to relax and interact comfortably in social situations; often a part of health behaviour modification programs, on the assumption that maladaptive health behaviours, such as alcohol consumption or smoking, may develop in part to control social anxiety. (p. 73)

social support Information from other people that one is loved and cared for, esteemed and valued, and part of a network of communication and mutual obligation. (p. 199)

social worker Trained and licensed individuals who help patients and their families deal with problems by providing therapy, making referrals, and engaging in social planning; medical social workers help patients and their families ease transitions between illness and recovery states. (p. 18)

somaticizers People who express distress and conflict through bodily symptoms. (p. 224)

specific immune mechanisms Responses designed to respond to specific invaders; includes cell-mediated and humoral immunity. (p. 43)

stages of dying A theory, developed by Kübler-Ross, that maintains that people go through five temporal stages in adjusting to the prospect of death: denial, anger, bargaining, depression, and acceptance; believed to characterize some but not all dying people. (p. 335)

stimulus-control interventions Interventions designed to modify behaviour that involve the removal of discriminative stimuli that evoke a behaviour targeted for change and the substitution of new discriminative stimuli that will evoke a desired behaviour. (p. 71)

stress Appraising events as harmful, threatening, or challenging and assessing one's capacity to respond to those events; events that are perceived to tax or exceed one's resources are seen as stressful. (p. 155)

stress carriers Individuals who create stress for others without necessarily increasing their own level of stress. (p. 210)

stress eating Eating in response to stress; approximately half the population increases eating in response to stress. (p. 110)

stressful life events Events that force an individual to make changes in his or her life. (p. 169)

stress inoculation The process of identifying stressful events in one's life and learning skills for coping with them, so that when the events come up, one can put those coping skills into effect. (p. 209)

stress management A program for dealing with stress in which people learn how they appraise stressful events, develop skills for coping with stress, and practise putting these skills into effect. (p. 207)

stress moderators Internal and external resources and vulnerabilities that modify how stress is experienced and its effects. (p. 185)

stressors Events perceived to be stressful. (p. 155)

stroke A condition that results from a disturbance in blood flow to the brain, often marked by resulting physical or cognitive impairments and, in the extreme, death. (p. 369)

sudden infant death syndrome (SIDS) A common cause of death among infants, in which an infant simply stops breathing. (p. 323)

support group A group of individuals who meet regularly and usually have a common problem or concern; support groups are believed to help people cope because they provide opportunities to share concerns and exchange information with similar others. (p. 317)

symbolic immortality The sense that one is leaving a lasting impact on the world, as through one's children or one's work, or that one is joining the afterlife and becoming one with God. (p. 338)

sympathetic nervous system The part of the nervous system that mobilizes the body for action. (p. 23)

systems theory The viewpoint that all levels of an organization in any entity are linked to each other hierarchically and that change in any level will bring about change in other levels. (p. 9)

tangible assistance The provision of material support by one person to another, such as services, financial assistance, or goods. (p. 199)

teachable moment The idea that certain times are more effective than others for teaching particular health practices; pregnancy constitutes a teachable moment for getting women to stop smoking. (p. 56)

telehealth A variety of services, including the delivery of advice and information via telephone, as well as consultation, diagnoses, treatment, and family visiting using audiovideo conferencing, that use communication technology to connect people with health services. (p. 238)

tend-and-befriend A theory of responses to stress that maintains that, in addition to fight-or-flight, humans respond to stress with social and nurturant behaviour; these responses may be especially true of women. (p. 157)

terminal care Medical care of the terminally ill. (p. 337)

thalamus The portion of the forebrain responsible for the recognition of sensory stimuli and the relay of sensory impulses to the cerebral cortex. (p. 24)

thanatologists Those who study death and dying. (p. 338)

theory of planned behaviour Derived from the theory of reasoned action, this theoretical viewpoint maintains that a person's behavioural intentions and behaviours can be understood by knowing the person's attitudes about the behaviour, subjective norms regarding the behaviour, and perceived behavioural control over that action. (p. 64)

thermal damage The experience of pain due to temperature exposure. (p. 269)

time management Skills for learning how to use one's time more effectively to accomplish one's goals. (p. 210)

tolerance The process by which the body increasingly adapts to a substance, requiring larger and larger doses of it to obtain the same effects; a frequent characteristic of substance abuse, including alcohol and drug abuse. (p. 122)

transient ischemic attacks Little strokes that produce temporary weakness, clumsiness, or loss of feeling in one side or limb; a temporary dimness or loss of vision, particularly in one eye; or a temporary loss of speech or difficulty in speaking or understanding speech. (p. 370)

transtheoretical model of behaviour change An analysis of the health behaviour change process that draws on the stages and processes people go through in order to bring about successful long-term behaviour change. The stages include precontemplation, contemplation, preparation, action, and maintenance. Successful attitude or behaviour change at each stage depends on the appropriateness of intervention. For example, attitude-change materials help move people from precontemplation to contemplation, whereas relapse-prevention techniques help move people from action to maintenance. (p. 67)

treatment effectiveness Formal documentation of the success of an intervention. (p. 437)

window of vulnerability The fact that, at certain times, people are more vulnerable to particular health problems. For example, early adolescence constitutes a window of vulnerability for beginning smoking, drug use, and alcohol abuse. (p. 57)

withdrawal Unpleasant physical and psychological symptoms that people experience when they stop using a substance on which they have become physically dependent; symptoms include anxiety, craving, hallucinations, nausea, headaches, and shaking. (p. 122)

work–life balance The concept of managing multiple roles simultaneously in one's life; most adults are workers, partners, and parents, and each of these roles entails heavy, and potential stressful, obligations. (p. 181)

worried well Individuals free from illness who are nonetheless concerned about their physical state and frequently and inappropriately use medical services. (p. 224)

REFERENCES

Aaronson, N. K., Calais de Silva, F., Yoshida, O., van Dam, F. S. A. M., Fossa, S. D., Miyakawa, M., et al. (1986). Quality of life assessment in bladder cancer clinical trials: Conceptual, methodological and practical issues. *Progress in Clinical and Biological Research, 22,* 149–170.

Abar, B. W., Turrisi, R., Hillhouse, J., Loken, E., Stapleton, J., & Gunn, H. (2010). Preventing skin cancer in college females: Heterogeneous effects over time. *Health Psychology, 29,* 574–582.

Abbott, A. (2004, May 27). Striking back. *Nature, 429,* 338–339.

Abeare, C. A., Cohen, J. L., Axelrod, B. N., Leisen, J. C. C., Mosley-Williams, A., & Lumley, M. A. (2010). Pain, Executive Functioning, and Affect in Patients With Rheumatoid Arthritis. *The Clinical Journal of Pain, 26*(8), 683–689.

Achtziger, A., Gollwitzer, P. M., & Sheeran, P. (2008). Implementation intentions and shielding goal striving from unwanted thoughts and feelings. *Personality and Social Psychology Bulletin, 34,* 381–393. doi: 10.1177/0146167207311201 34.

Ackerman, K. D., Heyman, R., Rabin, B. S., Anderson, B. P., Houck, P. R., Frank, E., et al. (2002). Stressful life events precede exacerbations of multiple sclerosis. *Psychosomatic Medicine, 64,* 916–920.

Adams, K. F., Schatzkin, A., Harris, T. B., Kipnis, V., Mouw, T., Ballard—Barbash, R., Hollenbeck, A., & Leitzmann, M. F. (2006). Overweight, obesity, and mortality in a large prospective cohort of persons 50 to 71 years old. *The New England Journal of Medicine, 355,* 763–778.

Adelman, R. C., & Verbrugge, L. M. (2000). Death makes news: The social impact of disease on newspaper coverage. *Journal of Health and Social Behavior, 41,* 347–367.

Ader, R. (1995). Historical perspectives on psychoneuroimmunology. In H. Friedman, T. W. Klein, & A. L. Friedman (Eds.), *Psychoneuroimmunology, stress, and infection* (pp. 1–24). Boca Raton, FL: CRC Press.

Adlaf, E. M., Begin, P., & Sawka, E. (Eds.). (2005). *Canadian Addiction Survey (CAS): A national survey of Canadians' use of alcohol and other drugs: Prevalence of use and related harms: Detailed report.* Ottawa: Canadian Centre on Substance Abuse.

Adlaf, E. M., Demers, A. & Gilksman, L. (Eds.). (2005). *Canadian campus survey 2004.* Toronto, Centre for Addictions and Mental Health.

Adler, N. E., Boyce, W. T., Chesney, M. A., Folkman, S., et al. (1993). Socioeconomic inequalities in health: No easy solution. *Journal of the American Medical Association, 269,* 3140–3145.

Adler, N., & Matthews, K. A. (1994). Health and psychology: Why do some people get sick and some stay well? *Annual Review of Psychology, 45,* 229–259.

Affleck, G., Tennen, H., Croog, S., & Levine, S. (1987). Causal attribution, perceived control, and recovery from a heart attack. *Journal of Social and Clinical Psychology, 5,* 339–355.

Affleck, G., Tennen, H., Urrows, S., & Higgins, P. (1994). Person and contextual features of daily stress reactivity: Individual differences in relations of undesirable daily events with mood disturbance and chronic pain intensity. *Journal of Personality and Social Psychology, 66,* 329–340.

Agras, W. S. (1982). Behavioral Medicine in the 1980s: Nonrandom connections. *Journal of Consulting and Clinical Psychology, 50,* 797–803.

Agras, W. S., Berkowitz, R. I., Arnow, B. A., Telch, C. F., Marnell, M., Henderson, et al. (1996). Maintenance following a very-low-calorie diet. *Journal of Consulting and Clinical Psychology, 64,* 610–613.

Agras, W. S., Schneider, J. A., Arnow, B., Raeburn, S. D., & Telch, C. F. (1989). Cognitive-behavioral and response-prevention treatments for bulimia nervosa. *Journal of Consulting and Clinical Psychology, 57,* 215–221.

Agras, W. S., Taylor, C. B., Kraemer, H. C., Southam, M. A., & Schneider, J. A. (1987). Relaxation training for essential hypertension at the worksite: II. The poorly controlled hypertensive. *Psychosomatic Medicine, 49,* 264–273.

Ahluwalia, J. S., Nollen, N., Kaur, H., James, A. S., Mayo, M. S., & Resnicow, K. (2007). Pathway to health: Cluster-randomized trail to increase fruit and vegetable consumption among smokers in public housing. *Health Psychology, 26*(2), 214–221.

Ahmad, F., Cameron J. I., & Stewart D. E. (2005). A tailored intervention to promote breast cancer screening among South Asian immigrant women. *Social Science and Medicine, 60,* 575–586.

Ajzen, I., & Fishbein, M. (1980). *Understanding attitudes and predicting social behaviour.* Englewood Cliffs, NJ: Prentice-Hall.

Ajzen, I., & Madden, T. J. (1986). Prediction of goal-directed behavior: Attitudes, intentions, and perceived behavioral control. *Journal of Experimental Social Psychology, 22,* 453–474.

Akil, H., Mayer, D. J., & Liebeskind, J. C. (1972). Comparaison chez le Rat entre l'analgesie induite par stimulation de la substance grise periaqueducale et l'analgesie morphinique. C. R. *Academy of Science, 274,* 3603–3605.

Akil, H., Mayer, D. J., & Liebeskind, J. C. (1976). Antagonism of stimulation—produced analgesia by naloxone, a narcotic antagonist. *Science, 191,* 961–962.

Al'Absi, M., & Wittmers, L. E., Jr. (2003). Enhanced adrenocortical response to stress in hypertension-prone men and women. *Annals of Behavioral Medicine, 25,* 25–33.

Al'Absi, M., France, C., Harju, A., France, J., & Wittmers, L. (2006). Adrenocortical and nociceptive responses to opioid blockade in hypertension-prone men and women. *Psychosomatic Medicine, 68,* 292–298.

Alati, R., O'Callaghan, M., Najman, J. M., Williams, G. M., Bor, W., & Lawlor, D. A. (2005). Asthma and internalizing behavior problems in adolescence: A longitudinal study. *Psychosomatic Medicine, 67,* 462–470.

Albarracin, D., McNatt, P. S., Klein, C. T. F., Ho, R. M., Mitchell, A. L., & Kumkale, G. C. (2003). Persuasive communications to change actions: An analysis of behavioral and cognitive impact in HIV prevention. *Health Psychology, 22,* 166–177.

Albery, I. P., & Messer, D. (2005). Comparative optimism about health and non-health events in 8- and 9-year old children. *Health Psychology, 24*(3), 316–320.

Albom, M. (1997). *Tuesdays with Morrie.* New York: Doubleday.

Alcoholics Anonymous (2011). Estimates of A.A. Groups and Members. Accessed May 12, 2011 from : http://www.aa.org/subpage.cfm?page=74.

Alderman, B. L., Arent, S. M., Landers, D. M., & Rogers, T. J. (2007). Aerobic exercise intensity and time of stressor administration influence cardiovascular responses to psychological stress. *Psychophysiology, 44,* 759–766.

Alexander, F. (1950). *Psychosomatic medicine.* New York: Norton.

Alexandrov, A., Isakova, G., Maslennikova, G., Shugaeva, E., Prokhorov, A., Olferiev, A., et al. (1988). Prevention of atherosclerosis among 11-year-old schoolchildren in two Moscow administrative districts. *Health Psychology, 7*(Suppl.), 247–252.

Alferi, S. M., Carver, C. S., Antoni, M. H., Weiss, S., & Duran, R. E. (2001). An exploratory study of social support, distress, and life disruption among low-income Hispanic women under treatment for early stage breast cancer. *Health Psychology, 20,* 41–46.

Alhalaiqa, F., Deane, K. H. O., Nawafleh, A. H., Clark, A., & Gray, R. (2011). Adherence therapy for medication non-compliant patients with hypertension: a randomised controlled trial. *J Hum Hypertens.*

Ali, A., Toner, B. B., Stuckless, N., Gallop, R., Diamant, N. E., Gould, M. I., et al. (2000). Emotional abuse, self-blame, and self-silencing in women with irritable bowel syndrome. *Psychosomatic Medicine, 62,* 76–82.

Allen, J. E. (2003, April 7). Stroke therapy sets sights higher, farther. *Los Angeles Times,* pp. F1, F7.

Allen, J., Markovitz, J., Jacobs, D. R., & Knox, S. S. (2001). Social support and health behavior in hostile black and white men and women. *Psychosomatic Medicine, 63,* 609–618.

Allen, K., Blascovich, J., & Mendes, W. B. (2002). Cardiovascular reactivity and the presence of pets, friends, and spouses: The truth about cats and dogs. *Psychosomatic Medicine, 64,* 727–739.

Allen, L. A., Escobar, J. I., Lehrer, P. M., Gara, M. A., & Woolfolk, R. L. (2002). Psychosocial treatments for multiple unexplained physical symptoms: A review of the literature. *Psychosomatic Medicine, 64,* 939–950.

Allgöwer, A., Warldle, J., & Steptoe, A. (2001). Depressive symptoms, social support, and personal health behaviors in young men and women. *Health Psychology, 20,* 223–227.

Aloisi, A. M. (2003). Gonadal Hormones and Sex Differences in Pain Reactivity. *The Clinical Journal of Pain, 19,* 168–174.

Alonso, C., & Coe, C. L. (2001). Disruptions of social relationships accentuate the association between emotional distress and menstrual pain in young women. *Health Psychology, 20,* 411–416.

Alper, J. (2000). New insights into Type II diabetes. *Science, 289,* 37–39.

Alpert, B., Field, T., Goldstein, S., & Perry, S. (1990). Aerobics enhances cardiovascular fitness and agility in preschoolers. *Health Psychology, 9,* 48–56.

Altena, E., Van Der Werf, Y. D., Strijers, R. L. M., & Van Someren, E. J. W. (2008). Sleep loss affects vigilance: effects of chronic insomnia and sleep therapy. *Journal of Sleep Research, 17,* 335–343.

American Psychiatric Assocation. (2000). *Diagnostic and Statistical Manual of Mental Disorders* (4th ed. text revision). Washington, DC: Author.

Amick, B. C., III, McDonough, P., Chang, H., Rodgers, W. H., Pieper, C. F., & Duncan, G. (2002). Relationship between all-cause mortality and cumulative working life course psychosocial and physical exposure in the United States labor market from 1968 to 1992. *Psychosomatic Medicine, 64,* 370–381.

Anda, R., Dong, M., Brown, D., Felitti, V., Giles, W., Perry, G., et al. (2009). The relationship of adverse childhood experiences to a history of premature death of family members. *BMC Public Health, 9,* 106.

Andersen, B. L., Cacioppo, J. T., & Roberts, D. C. (1995). Delay in seeking a cancer diagnosis: Delay stages and psychophysiological comparison processes. *British Journal of Social Psychology, 34,* 33–52.

Andersen, B. L., Ho, J., Brackett, J., Finkelstein, D., & Laffel, L. (1997). Parental involvement in diabetes management tasks: Relationships to blood glucose monitoring adherence and metabolic control in young adolescents with insulin-dependent diabetes mellitus. *Journal of Pediatrics, 130,* 257–265.

Andersen, B. L., Kiecolt-Glaser, J., & Glaser, R. (1994). A biobehavioral model of cancer stress and disease course. *American Psychologist, 49,* 389–404.

Andersen, B. L., Woods, X. A., & Copeland, L. J. (1997). Sexual self-schema and sexual morbidity among gynecologic cancer survivors. *Journal of Consulting and Clinical Psychology, 65,* 1–9.

Andersen, I., Osler, M., Petersen, L., Grønbæk, M., & Prescott, E. (2003). Income and risk of ischaemic heart disease in men and women in a Nordic welfare country. *International Journal of Epidemiology, 32,* 367–374.

Andersen, R. M. (1995). Revisiting the behavioral model and access to medical care: Does it matter? *Journal of Health and Social Behavior, 36,* 1–10.

Anderson, J. W., Liu, C., & Kryscio, R. J. (2008). Blood Pressure Response to Transcendental Meditation: A Meta-analysis. *Am J Hypertens, 21,* 310–316.

Andrade, A. M., Coutinho, S. R., Silva, M. N., Mata, J., Vieira, P. N., Minderico, C. U. S., et al. (2010). The effect of physical activity on weight loss is mediated by eating self-regulation. *Patient education and counseling, 79,* 320–326.

Andrews, J. A., & Duncan, S. C. (1997). Examining the reciprocal relation between academic motivation and substance use: Effects of family relationships, self-esteem, and general deviance. *Journal of Behavioral Medicine, 20,* 523–549.

Andrykowski, M. A., Curran, S. L., & Lightner, R. (1998). Off-treatment fatigue in breast cancer survivors: A controlled comparison. *Journal of Behavioral Medicine, 21,* 1–18.

Aneshensel, C. S., Botticello, A. L., & Yamamoto-Mitani, N. (2004). When caregiving ends: The course of depressive symptoms after bereavement. *Journal of Health and Social Behavior, 45,* 422–440.

Aneshensel, C. S., Pearlin, L. I., & Schuler, R. H. (1993). Stress, role captivity, and the cessation of caregiving. *Journal of Health and Social Behavior, 34,* 54–70.

Angel, R. J., Frisco, M., Angel, J. L., & Chiriboga, D. A. (2003). Financial strain and health among elderly Mexican-origin individuals. *Journal of Health and Social Behavior, 44,* 536–551.

Angier, N. (2001, June 19). Researchers piecing together autoimmune disease puzzle. *The New York Times,* pp. D1, D8.

Anisman, H., Griffiths, J., Matheson, K., Ravindran, A. V., & Merali, Z. (2001). Posttraumatic stress symptoms and salivary cortisol levels. *American Journal of Psychiatry, 158,* 1509–1511.

Annesi, J. J. (2009). Predictors of exercise-induced mood change during a 6-month exercise and nutrition education program with obese women. *Perceptual and Motor Skills, 109,* 931–940. Bartholomew, J. B., Morrison, D., & Ciccolo, J. T. (2005). Effects of Acute Exercise on Mood and Well-Being in Patients with Major Depressive Disorder. *Medicine & Science in Sports & Exercise, 37,* 2032–2037.

Anstey, K. J., & Luszcz, M. A. (2002). Mortality risks varies according to gender and change in depressive status in very old adults. *Psychosomatic Medicine, 64,* 880–888.

Anstey, K. J., Jorm, A. F., Réglade-Meslin, C., Maller, J., Kumar, R., von Sanden, C., Windsor, T. D., Rodgers, B., Wen, W., & Sachdev, P. (2006). Weekly alcohol consumption, brain atrophy, and white matter hyperintensities in a community-based sample aged 60 to 64 years. *Psychosomatic Medicine, 68,* 778–785.

Antoni, M. H., & Lutgendorf, S. (2007). Psychosocial factors and disease progression in cancer. *Current Directions in Psychological Science, 16,* 42–46.

Antoni, M. H., Lehman, J. M., Kilbourne, K. M., Boyers, A. E., Culver, J. L., Alferi, S. M., et al. (2001). Cognitive-behavioral stress management intervention decreases the prevalence of depression and enhances benefit finding among women under treatment of early-stage breast cancer. *Health Psychology, 20,* 20–32.

Appels, A., Bar, F. W., Bar, J., Bruggeman, C., & DeBaets, M. (2000). Inflammation, depressive symptomatology, and coronary artery disease. *Psychosomatic Medicine, 62,* 601–605.

Armitage, C. J. (2005). Can the theory of planned behavior predict the maintenance of physical activity? *Health Psychology, 24,* 235–245.

Armitage, C. J. (2007). Effects of an implementation intention-based intervention on fruit consumption. *Psychology & Health, 22,* 917–928.

Arnst, C. (2004, February 23). Let them eat cake-if they want to. *BusinessWeek,* pp. 110–111.

Arora, N. K., Finney Rutten, L. J., Gustafson, D. H., Moser, R., & Hawkins, R. P. (2007). Perceived helpfulness and impact of social support provided by family, friends, and health care providers to women newly diagnosed with breast cancer. *Psycho-Oncology, 16*(5), 474–486.

Arranz, A., Venihaki, M., Mol, B., Androulidaki, A., Dermitzaki, E., Rassouli, O., et al. (2010). The impact of stress on tumor growth: peripheral CRF mediates tumor-promoting effects of stress. *Molecular Cancer, 9*(1), 261.

Arthur, N. (1998). The effects of stress, depression, and anxiety on postsecondary students' coping strategies. *Journal of College Student Development, 39(1),* 11–22.

Asanuma, Y. et al. (2003). Premature coronary artery atherosclerosis in systematic lupus erythematosus. *New England Journal of Medicine, 349,* 2407–2415, http://www.nejm.org.

Aschbacher, K., Patterson, T. L., von Känel, R., Dimsdale, J. E., Mills, P. J., Adler, K. A., Ancoli-Israel, S., & Grant, I. (2005). Coping processes and hemostatic reactivity to acute stress in dementia caregivers. *Psychosomatic Medicine, 67,* 964–971.

Ashbury, F. D., Cameron, C., Finlan, C., Holmes, R., Villareal, E., Décoste, Y., Kulnies, T., Swoboda-Geen, C., & Kralj, B. (2006). The impact of a quit smoking contest on smoking behaviour in Ontario. *Chronic Diseases in Canada, 27(2),* 77–84.

Ashley, M. J., Victor, J. C., & Brewster, J. (2007). Pharmacists' attitudes, role perceptions and interventions regarding smoking cessation: Findings from four Canadian provinces. *Chronic Disease in Canada, 28(1–2),* 20–28.

Ashton, M. C., Lee, K., & Paunonen, S. V. (2002). What is the central feature of Extraversion? Social attention versus reward sensitivity. *Journal of Personality and Social Psychology, 83,* 245–252.

Aspinwall, L. G., & MacNamara, A. (2005). Taking positive changes seriously: Toward a positive psychology of cancer survivorship and resilience. *Cancer, 104(11 Suppl),* 2549–2556.

Aspinwall, L. G., Kemeny, M. E., Taylor, S. E., Schneider, S. G., & Dudley, J. P. (1991). Psychosocial predictors of gay men's AIDS risk-reduction behavior. *Health Psychology, 10,* 432–444.

Assembly of First Nations. (2007). *Results for adults, youth and children living in first nations communities: First nations regional longitudinal health survey (RHS) 2002/03.* Retrieved July 19, 2007, from http://rhs-ers.ca/english/pdf/rhs2002-03reports/rhs2002-03-technicalreport-afn.pdf.

Astin, J. (1998). Why patients use alternative medicine: Results of a national study. *Journal of the American Medical Association, 279,* 1548–1553.

Astin, J. A., Beckner, W., Soeken, K., Hochberg, M. C., & Berman, B. (2002). Psychological interventions for rheumatoid arthritis: A meta-analysis of randomized controlled trials. *Arthritis and Rheumatism, 47,* 291–302.

Auerbach, S. M., Clore, J. N., Kiesler, D. J., Orr, T., Pegg, P. O., Quick, B. G., et al. (2001). Relation of diabetic patients' health-related control appraisals and physician-patient interpersonal impacts to patients' metabolic control and satisfaction with treatment. *Journal of Behavioral Medicine, 25,* 17–32.

Austenfeld, J. L. & Stanton, A. L. (2004). Coping through emotional approach: A new look at emotion, coping and health-related outcomes. *Journal of Personality, 72(6),* 1335–1363.

Avlund, K., Osler, M., Damsgaard, M. T., Christensen, U., & Schroll, M. (2000). The relations between musculoskeletal diseases and mobility among old people: Are they influenced by socio-economic, psychosocial, and behavioral factors? *International Journal of Behavioral Medicine, 7,* 322–339.

Babyak, M., Blumenthal, J. A., Herman, S., Khatri, P., Doraiswamy, M., Moore, K., et al. (2000). Exercise treatment for major depression: Maintenance of therapeutic benefit at 10 months. *Psychosomatic Medicine, 62,* 633–638.

Bachmann, K. (2002). *Health promotion programs at work: A frivolous cost or a sound investment?* The Conference Board of Canada. Retrieved June 26, 2007, from www.alderweb.com/website/dev_centre/cda/site/resources/pdfs/frivolous_cost_or_sound_investment.pdf.

Badr, H., Carmack, C. L., Kashy, D. A., Cristofanilli, M., & Revenson, T. A. (2010). Dyadic Coping in Metastatic Breast Cancer. *Health Psychology, 29,* 169–180.

Baer, J. S., & Marlatt, G. A. (1991). Maintenance of smoking cessation. *Clinics in Chest Medicine, 12,* 793–800.

Baer, J. S., Kivlahan, D. R., Fromme, K., & Marlatt, G. A. (1991). Secondary prevention of alcohol abuse with college students: A skills-training approach. In N. Heather, W. R. Miller, & J. Greeley (Eds.), *Self-control and the addictive behaviours* (pp. 339–356). New York: Maxwell-McMillan.

Baer, J. S., Marlatt, G. A., Kivlahan, D. R., Fromme, K., Larimer, M. E., & Williams, E. (1992). An experimental test of three methods of alcohol risk reduction with young adults. *Journal of Consulting and Clinical Psychology, 60,* 974–979.

Bai, M., Tomenson, B., Creed, F., Mantis, D., Tsifetaki, N., Voulgari, P., et al. (2009). The role of psychological distress and personality variables in the disablement process in rheumatoid arthritis. *Scandinavian Journal of Rheumatology, 38(6),* 419–430.

Bair, M. J., Robinson, R. L., Eckert, G. J., Stang, P. E., Croghan, T. W., & Kroenke, K. (2004). Impact of pain on depression treatment response in primary care. *Psychosomatic Medicine, 66,* 17–22.

Baker, C. W., Little, T. D., & Brownell, K. D. (2003). Predicting adolescent eating and activity behaviors: The role of social norms and personal agency. *Health Psychology, 22,* 189–198.

Baker, C., Whisman, M. A., & Brownell, K. D. (2000). Studying intergenerational transmission of eating attitudes and behaviors: Methodological and conceptual questions. *Health Psychology, 19,* 376–381.

Baldwin, A. S., Rothman, A. J., Hertel, A. W., Linde, J. A., Jeffery, R. W., Finch, E. A., & Lando, H. A. (2006). Specifying the determinants of the initiation and maintenance of behavior change: An examination of self-efficacy, satisfaction, and smoking cessation. *Health Psychology, 25,* 626–634.

Balfour, L., Kowal, J., Silverman, A, Tasca, G. A., Angel, J. B., Macpherson, P.A., Garber, G., Cooper, C. L., & Cameron, D. W. (2006). A randomized controlled psycho-education intervention trial: Improving psychological readiness for successful HIV medication adherence and reducing depression before initiating HAART. *AIDS Care, 18(7),* 830–838.

Balfour, L., White, D. R., Schiffrin, A., Dougherty, G., & Dufresne, J. (1993). Dietary disinhibition, perceived stress, and glucose control in young, Type I diabetic women. *Health Psychology, 12,* 33–38.

Balneaves, L. G., Truant, T. L. O., Kelly, M., Verhoef, M. J., & Davison, B. J. (2007). Bridging the gap: Decision-making processes of women with breast cancer using complementary and alternative Medicine (CAM). *Supportive Care in Cancer, 15,* 973–983.

Bambauer, K. Z., Aupont, O., Stone, P. H., Locke, S. E., Mullan, M. G., Colagiovanni, J., & McLaughlin, T. J. (2005). The effect of a telephone counseling intervention on self-rated health of cardiac patients. *Psychosomatic Medicine, 67,* 539–545.

Bandura, A. (1969). *Principles of behavior modification.* New York: Holt, Rinehart & Winston.

Bandura, A. (1977). Self-efficacy: Toward a unifying theory of behavioral change. *Psychological Review, 84,* 191–215.

Bandura, A. (1986). *Social foundations of thought and action: A social cognitive theory.* Englewood Cliffs, NJ: Prentice-Hall.

Bandura, A. (1989). Perceived self-efficacy in the exercise of control over AIDS infection. In S. J. Blumenthal, A. Eichler, & G. Weissman (Eds.), *Women and AIDS.* Washington, D.C.: American Psychiatric Press.

Bandura, A. (1991). Self-efficacy mechanism in physiological activation and health-promotion behavior. In J. Madden IV (Ed.), *Neurobiology of learning, emotion, and affect* (pp. 229–269). New York: Raven Press.

Bann, C. M., Sirois, F. M., & Walsh, E. G. (2010). Provider Support in Complementary and Alternative Medicine: Exploring the Role of Patient Empowerment. *The Journal of Alternative and Complementary Medicine, 16(7),* 745–752.

Banthia, R., Malcarne, V. L., Varni, J. W., Ko, C. M., Sadler, G. R., & Greenbergs, H. L. (2003). The effects of dyadic strength and coping styles on psychological distress in couples faced with prostate cancer. *Journal of Behavioral Medicine, 26,* 31–51.

Barefoot, J. C. (1992). Developments in the measurement of hostility. In H. S. Friedman (Ed.), *Hostility, coping, and health* (pp. 13–31). Washington, D.C.: American Psychological Association.

Barefoot, J. C., Maynard, K. E., Beckham, J. C., Brummett, B. H., Hooker, K., & Siegler, I. C. (1998). Trust, health, and longevity. *Journal of Behavioral Medicine, 21,* 517–526.

Bárez, M., Blasco, T., Fernández-Castro, J., & Viladrich, C. (2009). Perceived control and psychological distress in women with breast cancer: a longitudinal study. *Journal of Behavioral Medicine, 32,* 187–196.

Barnes, V. A., Davis, H. C., Murzynowski, J. B. & Treiber, F. A. (2004). Impact of medication on resting and ambulatory blood pressure and heart rate in youth. *Psychosomatic Medicine, 66,* 909–914.

Barnett, R. C., & Marshall, N. L. (1993). Men, family-role quality, job-role quality, and physical health. *Health Psychology, 12,* 48–55.

Barnett, R. C., Raudenbush, S. W., Brennan, R. T., Pleck, J. H., & Marshall, N. L. (1995). Change in job and marital experiences and change in psychological distress: A longitudinal study of dual-earner couples. *Journal of Personality and Social Psychology, 69,* 839–850.

Barraco, D., Valencia, G., Riba, A. L., Nareddy, S., Draus, C. B. S. N., & Schwartz, S. M. (2005). Complementary and alternative medicine (CAM) use patterns and disclosure to physicians in acute coronary syndromes patients. *Complementary Therapies in Medicine, 13(1),* 34–40.

Barry, L. C., Lichtman, J. H., Spertus, J. A., Rumsfeld, J. S., Vaccarino, V., Jones, P. G., Plomondon, M. E., Parashar, S., & Krumholz, H. M. (2007). Patient satisfaction with treatment after acute myocardial infarction: Role of psychological factors. *Psychosomatic Medicine, 69,* 115–123.

Barth, J., Schumacher, M., & Herrmann-Lingen, C. (2004). Depression as a risk factor for mortality in patients with coronary heart disease: A meta-analysis. *Psychosomatic Medicine, 66,* 802–813.

Bartholomew, J. B., Morrison, D., & Ciccolo, J. T. (2005). Effects of Acute Exercise on Mood and Well-Being in Patients with Major Depressive Disorder. *Medicine & Science in Sports & Exercise, 37,* 2032–2037.

Bartlett, G., Blais, R. g., Tamblyn, R., Clermont, R. J., & MacGibbon, B. (2008). Impact of patient communication problems on the risk of preventable adverse events in acute care settings. *Canadian Medical Association Journal, 178,* 1555–1562.

Bartrop, R. W., Lockhurst, E., Lazarus, L., Kiloh, L. G., & Penny, R. (1977). Depressed lymphocyte function after bereavement. *Lancet, 1,* 834–836.

Basch, E. (2010). The Missing Voice of Patients in Drug-Safety Reporting. *New England Journal of Medicine, 362,* 865–869.

Battle, E. K., & Brownell, K. D. (1996). Confronting a rising tide of eating disorders and obesity: Treatment vs. prevention and policy. *Addictive Behaviors, 21,* 755–765.

Baum, A. (1990). Stress, intrusive imagery, and chronic distress. *Health Psychology, 9,* 653–675.

Baum, A. (1994). Behavioral, biological, and environmental interactions in disease processes. In S. Blumenthal, K. Matthews, & S. Weiss (Eds.), *New research frontiers in behavioral medicine: Proceedings of the national conference* (pp. 61–70). Washington, D.C.: NIH Publications.

Baum, A., Cohen, L., & Hall, M. (1993). Control and intrusive memories as possible determinants of chronic stress. *Psychosomatic Medicine, 55,* 274–286.

Baum, A., Friedman, A. L., & Zakowski, S. G. (1997). Stress and genetic testing for disease risk. *Health Psychology, 16,* 8–19.

Baum, A., Grunberg, N. E., & Singer, J. E. (1982). The use of psychological and neuroendocrinological measurements in the study of stress. *Health Psychology, 1,* 217–236.

Bauman, K. E., Koch, G. G., & Fisher, L. A. (1989). Family cigarette smoking and test performance by adolescents. *Health Psychology, 8,* 97–105.

Beal, L. A. (1995). Post-traumatic stress disorder in prisoners of war and combat veterans of the Dieppe Raid: A 50-year follow-up. *The Canadian Journal of Psychiatry, 40(4),* 177–184.

Becker, M. H. (1993). A medical sociologist looks at health promotion. *Journal of Health and Social Behavior, 34,* 1–6.

Beckett, M. (2000). Converging health inequalities in later life—An artifact of mortality selection? *Journal of Health and Social Behavior, 41,* 106–119.

Beckman, H. B., & Frankel, R. M. (1984). The effect of physician behavior on the collection of data. *Annals of Internal Medicine, 101,* 692–696.

Beecher, H. K. (1959). *Measurement of subjective responses.* New York: Oxford University Press.

Belar, C. D. (1997). Clinical health psychology: A specialty for the 21st century. *Health Psychology, 16,* 411–416.

Belloc, N. D., & Breslow, L. (1972). Relationship of physical health status and family practices. *Preventive Medicine, 1,* 409–421.

Benight, C. C., Antoni, M. H., Kilbourn, K., Ironson, G., Kumar, M. A., Fletcher, M. A., et al. (1997). Coping self-efficacy buffers psychological and physiological disturbances in HIV-infected men following a natural disaster. *Health Psychology, 16,* 248–255.

Bennett, K. K., Compas, B. E., Beckjord, E., & Glinder, J. G. (2005). Self-blame among women with newly diagnosed breast cancer. *Journal of Behavioral Medicine, 28,* 313–323.

Bennett, M. P., & Lengacher, C. (2008). Humor and Laughter May Influence Health: III. Laughter and Health Outcomes. *Evidence Based Complementary and Alternative Medicine, 5,* 37–40.

Benotsch, E. G., Christensen, A. J., & McKelvey, L. (1997). Hostility, social support, and ambulatory cardiovascular activity. *Journal of Behavioral Medicine, 20,* 163–182.

Ben-Sira, Z. (1980). Affective and instrumental components in the physician patient relationship: An additional dimension of interaction theory. *Health and Social Behavior, 21,* 170–180.

Ben-Zur, H., Gilbar, O., & Lev, S. (2001). Coping with breast cancer: Patient, spouse, and dyad models. *Psychosomatic Medicine, 62,* 32–39.

Berkley, K. J., Zalcman, S. S., & Simon, V. R. (2006). Sex and gender differences in pain and inflammation: a rapidly maturing field. *American Journal of Physiology Regulatory, Integrative and Comparative Physiology, 291,* R241–R244.

Berlin, A. A., Kop, W. J., & Deuster, P. A. (2006). Depressive mood symptoms and fatigue after exercise withdrawal: The potential role of decreased fitness. *Psychosomatic Medicine, 68,* 224–230.

Bernstein, C. N., & Shanahan, F. (2008). Disorders of a modern lifestyle: reconciling the epidemiology of inflammatory bowel diseases. *Gut, 57(9),* 1185–1191.

Bernstein, C. N., Wajda, A., Svenson, L. W., MacKenzie, A., Koehoorn, M., Jackson, M., Fedorak, R., Israel, D., & Blanchard, J.F. (2006). The epidemiology of inflammatory bowel disease in Canada: A population based study. *The American Journal of Gastroenterology, 101,* 1559–1568.

Bessenoff, G. R. (2006). Can the media affect us? Social comparison, self-discrepancy, and the thin ideal. *Psychology of Women Quarterly, 30(3),* 239–251.

Bigatti, S. M., & Cronan, T. A. (2002). An examination of the physical health, heath care use and psychological well-being of spouses of people with fibromyalgia syndrome. *Health Psychology, 21,* 157–166.

Bishop, G. D., & Converse, S. A. (1986). Illness representations: A prototype approach. *Health Psychology, 5,* 95–114.

Bishop, M., Frain, M. P., & Tschopp, M. K. (2008). Self-Management, Perceived Control, and Subjective Quality of Life in Multiple Sclerosis. *Rehabilitation Counseling Bulletin, 52,* 45-56.

Bishop S. R. (2002). What do we really know about mindfulness-based stress? *Psychosomatic Medicine, 64,* 71–84.

Bishop, S. R, & Warr, D. (2003). Coping, catastrophizing and chronic pain in breast cancer. *Journal of Behavioral Medicine, 26*:265–81.

Bitzer, J., & Alder, J. (2009). Diabetes and female sexual health. *Women's Health, 5,* 629-636.

Bjorntorp, P. (1996). Behavior and metabolic disease. *International Journal of Behavioral Medicine, 3,* 285–302.

Blakeslee, S. (1998, October 13). Placebos prove so powerful even experts are surprised. *The New York Times,* Sect. F, p. 2.

Blalock, A. C., McDaniel, J. S., & Farber, E. W. (2002). Effect of Employment on Quality of Life and Psychological Functioning in Patients With HIV/AIDS. *Psychosomatics, 43(5),* 400-404. doi: 10.1176/appi.psy.43.5.400

Blaney, N. T., Millon, C., Morgan, R., Eisdorfer, C., & Szapocznik, J. (1990). Emotional distress, stress-related disruption and coping among healthy HIV—positive gay males. *Psychology and Health, 4,* 259–273.

Bleil, M. E., McCaffery, J. M., Muldoon, M. F., Sutton-Tyrrell, K., & Manuck, S. B. (2004). Anger-related personality traits and carotid artery atherosclerosis in untreated hypertensive men. *Psychosomatic Medicine, 66,* 633–639.

Blissmer, B., & McAuley, E. (2002). Testing the requirements of stages of physical activity among adults: The comparative effectiveness of stage-matched, mismatched, standard care, and control interventions. *Annals of Behavioral Medicine, 24,* 181–189.

Blomhoff, S., Spetalen, S., Jacobsen, M. B., & Malt, U. F. (2001). Phobic anxiety changes the function of brain–gut axis in irritable bowel syndrome. *Psychosomatic Medicine, 63,* 959–965.

Bluebond-Langner, M. (1977). Meanings of death to children. In H. Feifel (Ed.), *New meanings of death* (pp. 47–66). New York: McGraw-Hill.

Blume, J., Douglas, S. D., & Evans, D. L. (2011). Immune suppression and immune activation in depression. *Brain, Behavior, and Immunity, 25(2),* 221–229.

Blumenthal, J. A., & Emery, C. F. (1988). Rehabilitation of patients following myocardial infarction. *Journal of Consulting and Clinical Psychology, 56,* 374–381.

Bogart, L. M. (2001). Relationship of stereotypic beliefs about physicians to healthcare relevant behaviors and cognitions among African American women. *Journal of Behavioral Medicine, 245,* 573–586.

Bolger, N., & Amarel, D. (2007). Effects of social support visibility on adjustment to stress: Experimental evidence. *Journal of Personality and Social Psychology, 92,* 458–475.

Bolger, N., DeLongis, A., Kessler, R. C., & Schilling, E. A. (1989). Effects of daily stress on negative mood. *Journal of Personality and Social Psychology, 57,* 808–818.

Bolger, N., Zuckerman, A., & Kessler, R. C. (2000). Invisible support and adjustment to stress. *Journal of Personality and Social Psychology, 79,* 953–961.

Bombardier, C., Gorayeb, R., Jordan, J., Brooks, W. B., & Divine, G. (1991). The utility of the psychosomatic system checklist among hospitalized patients. *Journal of Behavioral Medicine, 14,* 369–382.

Bonanno, G. A., et al. (2002). Resilience to loss and chronic grief: A prospective study from preloss to 18-months postloss. *Journal of Personality and Social Psychology, 83,* 1150–1164.

Bonanno, G. A., Galea, S., Bucciareli, A., & Vlahov, D. (2007). What predicts psychological resilience after disaster? The role of demographics, resources, and life stress. *Journal of Consulting and Clinical Psychology, 75(5),* 671–682.

Bonanno, G. A., Keltner, D., Holen, A., & Horowitz, M. J. (1995). When avoiding unpleasant emotions might not be such a bad thing: Verbal-autonomic response dissociation and midlife conjugal bereavement. *Journal of Personality and Social Psychology, 69,* 975–989.

Boon, H. S., Olatunde, F., & Zick, S. M. (2007). Trends in complementary/alternative medicine use by breast cancer survivors: Comparing survey data from 1998 and 2005. *BMC Women's Health, 7,* 1–7.

Booth, A., & Amato, P. (1991). Divorce and psychological stress. *Journal of Health and Social Behavior, 32,* 396–407.

Boscarino, J., & Chang, J. (1999). Higher abnormal leukocyte and lymphocyte counts 20 years after exposure to severe stress: Research and clinical implications. *Psychosomatic Medicine, 61,* 378–386.

Bosma, H., Marmot, M. G., Hemingway, H., Nicholson, A. C., Brunner, E., & Stanfeld, S. A. (1997). Low job control and risk of coronary heart disease in Whitehall II (prospective cohort) study. *British Medical Journal, 314,* 285.

Bostrom, H. (1997). Placebo—The forgotten drug. *Scandinavian Journal of Work and Environmental Health, 23* (Suppl. 3), 53–57.

Botvin, G. J., Dusenbury, L., Baker, E., James-Ortiz, S., Botvin, E. M., & Kerner, J. (1992). Smoking prevention among urban minority youth: Assessing effects on outcome and mediating variables. *Health Psychology, 11,* 290–299.

Boutelle, K. N., Kirschenbaum, D. S., Baker, R. C., & Mitchell, M. E. (1999). How can obese weight controllers minimize weight gain during the high risk holiday season? By self-monitoring very consistently. *Health Psychology, 18,* 364–368.

Bouton, M. E. (2000). A learning theory perspective on lapse, relapse, and the maintenance of behavior change. *Health Psychology, 19,* 57–63.

Bovbjerg, D. H. (2006). The continuing problem of post chemotherapy nausea and vomiting: Contributions of classical conditioning. *Autonomic Neuroscience, 129*(1-2), 92–98.

Bovbjerg, D. H., Montgomery, G. H., & Raptis, G. (2005). Evidence for classically conditioned fatigue response in patients receiving chemotherapy treatment for breast cancer. *Journal of Behavioral Medicine, 28,* 231–237.

Bowen, D. J., Tomoyasu, N., Anderson, M., Carney, M., & Kristal, A. (1992). Effects of expectancies and personalized feedback on fat consumption, taste, and preference. *Journal of Applied Social Psychology, 22,* 1061–1079.

Bower, J. E., Ganz, P. A., & Aziz, N. (2005). Altered cortisol response to psychologic stress in breast cancer survivors with persistent fatigue. *Psychosomatic Medicine, 67,* 277–280.

Bower, J. E., Kemeny, M. E., Taylor, S. E., & Fahey, J. L. (1997). Cognitive processing, discovery of meaning, CD4 decline, and AIDS-related mortality among bereaved HIV-seropositive men. *Journal of Consulting and Clinical Psychology, 66,* 979–986.

Bower, J. E., Kemeny, M. E., Taylor, S. E., & Fahey, J. L. (2003). Finding meaning and its association with natural killer cell cytotoxicity among participants in bereavement-related disclosure intervention. *Annals of Behavioral Medicine, 25,* 146–155.

Bowker, S. L., Pohar, S., Johnson, J. A. (2006). A cross-sectional study of health-related quality of life deficits in individuals with comorbid diabetes and cancer. *Health and Quality of Life Outcomes, 4(17),* 1–9.

Bowlby, J. (1977). The making and breaking of affectional bonds. *British Journal of Psychiatry, 130,* 201–210.

Boyce, W. (2004). *Young people in Canada: Their health and well-being.* Public Health Agency of Canada. Retrieved from www.phac-aspc.gc.ca/media/nr-rp/2004/2004_53bk2_e.html#skipfirst.

Boyce, W. T., Adams, S., Tschann, J. M., Cohen, F., Wara, D., & Gunnar, M. R. (1995). Adrenocortical and behavioral predictors of immune responses to starting school. *Pediatric Research, 38,* 1009–1017.

Boyce, W. T., Alkon, A. Tschann, J. M., Chesney, M. A., & Alpert, B. S. (1995). Dimensions of psychobiologic reactivity: Cardiovascular responses to laboratory stressors in preschool children. *Annals of Behavioral Medicine, 17,* 315–323.

Boyle, S. H., Michalek, J. E., & Suarez, E. C. (2006). Covariation of psychological attributes and incident coronary heart disease in U.S. Air Force veterans of the Vietnam War. *Psychosomatic Medicine, 68,* 844–850.

Boyle, S. H., Williams, R. B., Mark, D. B., Brummett, B. H., Siegler, I. C., Helms, M. J., & Barefoot, J. C. (2004). Hostility as a predictor of survival in patients with coronary artery disease. *Psychosomatic Medicine, 66,* 629–632.

Brabant, S., & Kalich, D. (2008). Who enrolls in college death education courses? A longitudinal study. *Omega, 58,* 1–18.

Bradley, L. A., Young, L. D., Anderson, K. O., Turner, R. A., Agudelo, C. A., McDaniel, L. K., et al. (1987). Effects of psychological therapy on pain behavior of rheumatoid arthritis patients: Treatment outcome and six-month followup. *Arthritis and Rheumatism, 30,* 1105–1114.

Brands, B., Paglia-Boak, A., Sproule, B. A., Leslie, K., & Adlaf, E. M. (2010). Non-medical use of opioid analgesics among Ontario students. *Canadian Family Physician, 56,* 256–262.

Brantley, P. J., Dutton, G. R., Grothe, K. B., Bodenlos, J. S., Howe, J., & Jones, G. N. (2005). Minor life events as predictors of medical utilization in low income African-American family practice patients. *Journal of Behavioral Medicine, 28,* 395–401.

Brantley, P. J., Mosley, T. H., Jr., Bruce, B. K., McKnight, G. T., & Jones, G. N. (1990). Efficacy of behavioral management and patient education on vascular access cleansing compliance in hemodialysis patients. *Health Psychology, 9,* 103–113.

Bray, G. A., & Tartaglia, L. A. (2000). Medicinal strategies in the treatment of obesity. *Nature, 404,* 672–677.

Breivik, H., Collett, B., Ventafridda, V., Cohen, R., & Gallacher, D. (2006). Survey of chronic pain in Europe: Prevalence, impact on daily life, and treatment. *European Journal of Pain, 10,* 287–333.

Brennan, P. L., Schutte, K. K., & Moos, R. H. (2010). Patterns and Predictors of Late-Life Drinking Trajectories: A 10-Year Longitudinal Study. *Psychology of Addictive Behaviors, 24,* 254–264.

Brenner, G. F., Melamed, B. G., & Panush, R. S. (1994). Optimism and coping as determinants of psychosocial adjustment to rheumatoid arthritis. *Journal of Clinical Psychology in Medical Settings, 1,* 115–134.

Brent, D., Melhem, N., Donohoe, M. B., & Walker, M. (2009). The Incidence and Course of Depression in Bereaved Youth 21 Months After the Loss of a Parent to Suicide, Accident, or Sudden Natural Death. *Am J Psychiatry, 166,* 786–794.

Breslin, F. C., Day, D., Tompa, E., Irvin, E., Bhattacharyya, S., Clarke, J., et al. (2007). Non-agricultural Work Injuries Among Youth: A Systematic Review. *American journal of preventive medicine, 32,* 151–162.

Breslow, L., & Enstrom, J. E. (1980). Persistence of health habits and their relationship to mortality. *Preventive Medicine, 9,* 469–483.

Brewer, N. T., Weinstein, N. D, Cuite, C. L., & Herrington, J. E. (2004). Risk perceptions and their relation to risk behavior. *Annals of Behavioral Medicine, 27,* 125–130.

Brincks, A. M., Feaster, D. J., & Mitrani, V. B. (2010). A Multilevel Mediation Model of Stress and Coping for Women with HIV and Their Families. *Family Process, 49*(4), 517–529.

Brissette, I., & Cohen, S. (2002). The contribution of individual differences in hostility to the associations between daily interpersonal conflict, affect, and sleep. *Personality and Social Psychology Bulletin, 28,* 1265–1274.

Brissette, I., Leventhal, H., & Leventhal, E. A. (2003). Observer ratings of health and sickness: Can other people tell us anything about our health that we don't already know? *Health Psychology, 22,* 471–478.

Brissette, I., Scheier, M. F., & Carver, C. S. (2002). The role of optimism and social network development, coping, and psychological adjustment during a life transition. *Journal of Personality and Social Psychology, 82,* 102–111.

Brisson, C., LaFlamme, N., Moisan, J., Milot, A., Masse, B., & Vezina, M. (1999). Effect of family responsibilities and job strain on ambulatory blood pressure among white-collar women. *Psychosomatic Medicine, 61,* 205–213.

Britton, A., & Marmot, M. (2004). Different measures of alcohol consumption and risk of coronary heart disease and all-cause mortality: 11-year follow-up of the Whitehall II Cohort Study. *Addiction, 99,* 109–116.

Broadbent, E., Petrie, K. J., Alley, P. G., & Booth, R. J. (2003). Psychological stress impairs early wound repair following surgery. *Psychosomatic Medicine, 65,* 865–869.

Broadwell, S. D., & Light, K. C. (1999). Family support and cardiovascular responses in married couples during conflict and other interactions. *International Journal of Behavioral Medicine, 6,* 40–63.

Broderick, J. E., Junghaenel, D. U., & Schwartz, J. E. (2005). Written emotional expression produces health benefits in fibromyalgia patients. *Psychosomatic Medicine, 67,* 326–334.

Brody, H. (1997). The doctor as therapeutic agent: A placebo effect research agenda. In A. Harrington (Ed.), *The Placebo Effect* (pp. 77–92). Cambridge MA: Harvard University Press.

Brody, J. E. (2002, January 22). Misunderstood opioids and needless pain. *The New York Times,* p. D8.

Broemeling, A. M., Watson, D., & Black, C. (2005). *Chronic conditions and co—morbidity among residents of British Columbia.* Retrieved February 18, 2008, from www.chspr.ubc.ca/files/publications/2005/chspr05-08.pdf.

Broman, C. L. (1993). Social relationships and health-related behavior. *Journal of Behavioral Medicine, 16,* 335–350.

Bromberger, J. T., & Matthews, K. A. (1996). A longitudinal study of the effects of pessimism, trait anxiety, and life stress on depressive symptoms in middle-aged women. *Psychology and Aging, 11,* 207–213.

Brondolo, E., Rieppi, R., Erickson, S. A., Bagiella, E., Shapiro, P. A., McKinley, P., & Sloan, R. P. (2003). Hostility, interpersonal interactions, and ambulatory blood pressure. *Psychosomatic Medicine, 65,* 1003–1011.

Brosschot, J., Godaert, G., Benschop, R., Olff, M., Ballieux, R., & Heijnen, C. (1998). Experimental stress and immunological reactivity: A closer look at perceived uncontrollability. *Psychosomatic Medicine, 60,* 359–361.

Brown, J. H., & Raven, B. H. (1994). Power and compliance in doctor/patient relationships. *Journal of Health Psychology, 6,* 3–22.

Brown, J. L., & Miller, D. (2002). Couples' Gender Role Preferences and Management of Family Food Preferences. *Journal of nutrition education and behavior, 34,* 215–223.

Brown, J. L., Sheffield, D., Leary, M. R., & Robinson, M. E. (2003). Social support and experimental pain. *Psychosomatic Medicine, 65,* 276–283.

Brown, K. M., Middaugh, S. J., Haythornthwaite, J. A., & Bielory, L. (2001). The effects of stress, anxiety and outdoor temperature on the frequency and severity of Raynaud's attacks: The Raynaud treatment study. *Journal of Behavioral Medicine, 24,* 137–153.

Brown, K. W., & Ryan, R. M. (2003). The benefits of being present: Mindfulness and its role in psychological well-being. *Journal of Personality and Social Psychology, 84,* 822–848.

Brown, L. C., Majumdar, S. R., Newman, S. C., & Johnson, J. A. (2005). History of depression increases risk of type 2 diabetes in younger adults. *Diabetes Care, 28,* 1063–1067.

Brown, M. M., Brown, A. A., & Jason, L. A. (2010). Illness Duration and Coping Style in Chronic Fatigue Syndrome. *Psychological Reports, 106,* 383–393.

Brown, S. C., Glass, J. M., & Park, D. C. (2002). The relationship of pain and depression to cognitive function in rheumatoid arthritis patients. *Pain, 96*(3), 279–284.

Brown, S. L. (1997). Prevalence and effectiveness of self-regulatory techniques used to avoid drunk driving. *Journal of Behavioral Medicine, 20,* 55–66.

Brown, S. L., Nesse, R. M., Vinokur, A. D., & Smith, D. M. (2003). Providing social support may be more beneficial than receiving it: Results from a prospective study of mortality. *Psychological Science, 14,* 320–327.

Browne, A. J. (2007). Clinical encounters between nurses and First Nations women in a western Canadian hospital. *Social Science & Medicine, 64,* 2165–2176.

Brownell, K. D. (1982). Obesity: Understanding and treating a serious, prevalent and refractory disorder. *Journal of Consulting and Clinical Psychology, 50,* 820–840.

Brownell, K. D., & Napolitano, M. A. (1995). Distorting reality for children: Body size proportions of Barbie and Ken dolls. *International Journal of Eating Disorders, 18,* 295–298.

Brownell, K. D., & Wadden, T. A. (1992). Etiology and treatment of obesity: Understanding a serious, prevalent, and refractory disorder. *Journal of Consulting and Clinical Psychology, 60,* 505–517.

Bruce, E. C., & Musselman, D. L. (2005). Depression, alterations in platelet function, and ischemic heart disease. *Psychosomatic Medicine, 67,* S34–S36.

Bruera, E., Neumann, C. M., Mazzocato, C., Stiefel, F., & Sala, R. (2000). Attitudes and beliefs of palliative care physicians regarding communication with terminally ill cancer patients. *Palliative Medicine, 14(4),* 287–298.

Brummett, B. H., Babyak, M. A., Mark, D. B., Clapp-Channing, N. E., Siegler, I. C., & Barefoot, J. C. (2004). Prospective study of perceived stress in cardiac patients. *Annals of Behavioral Medicine, 27,* 22–30.

Brummett, B. H., Babyak, M. A., Sigeler, I. C., Vitaliano, P. P., Ballard, E. L., Gwyther, L. P., & Williams, R. D. (2006). Associations among perceptions of social support, negative affect and quality of sleep in caregivers and noncaregivers. *Health Psychology, 25,* 220–225.

Bryan, A., Fisher, J. D., & Fisher, W. A. (2002). Tests of the mediational role of preparatory safer sexual behavior in the context of the theory or planned behavior. *Health Psychology, 21,* 71–80.

Bryan, A., Ray, L. A., & Cooper, M. L. (2007). Alcohol Use and Protective Sexual Behaviors Among High-Risk Adolescents. *Journal of Studies on Alcohol and Drugs, 68,* 327–335.

Buchwald, D., Herrell, R., Ashton, S., Belcourt, M., Schmaling, K., Sullivan, P., et al. (2001). A twin study of chronic fatigue. *Psychosomatic Medicine, 63,* 936–943.

Buckalew, L. W., & Coffield, K. E. (1982). An investigation of drug expectancy as a function of capsule color and size and preparation form. *Journal of Clinical Psychopharmacology, 2(4),* 245–248.

Buckmaster, A. M., & Gallagher, P. (2010). Experiences of and perspectives on genetic testing for breast/ovarian cancer in and outside of the customary clinical setting. Psychology & Health, 25, 1041–1059.

Budman, S. H. (2000). Behavioral health care dot-com and beyond: Computer-mediated communications in mental health and substance abuse treatment. *American Psychologist, 55,* 1290–1300.

Buglar, M. E., White, K. M., & Robinson, N. G. (2010). The role of self-efficacy in dental patients' brushing and flossing: Testing an extended Health Belief Model. *Patient education and counseling, 78,* 269–272.

Bunde, J., & Martin, R. (2006). Depression and prehospital delay in the context of myocardial infarction. *Psychosomatic Medicine, 68,* 51–57.

Burg, M. M., Barefoot, J., Berkman, L., Catellier, D. J., Czajkowski, S., Saab, P., Huber, M., DeLillo, V., Mitchell, P., Skala, J., & Taylor, C. B. (2005). Low perceived social support and post-myocardial infarction prognosis in the enhancing recovery in coronary heart disease clinical trial: The effects of treatment. *Psychosomatic Medicine, 67,* 879–888.

Burg, M. M., Benedetto, M. C., Rosenberg, R., & Soufer, R. (2003). Presurgical depression predicts medical mortality 6 months after coronary artery bypass graft surgery. *Psychosomatic Medicine, 65,* 111–118.

Burgard, S. A., Brand, J. E., & House, J. S. (2009). Perceived job insecurity and worker health in the United States. *Social Science & Medicine, 69,* 777–785.

Burke, J. P., Jacobson, D. J., McGree, M. E., Nehra, A., Roberts, R. O., Girman, C. J., et al. (2007). Diabetes and Sexual Dysfunction: Results From the Olmsted County Study of Urinary Symptoms and Health Status Among Men. *The Journal of urology, 177,* 1438–1442.

Burns, J. W. (2000). Repression predicts outcome following multidisciplinary treatment of chronic pain. *Health Psychology, 19,* 75–84.

Burns, V. E., Drayson, M., Ring, C., & Carroll, D. (2002). Perceived stress and psychological well-being are associated with antibody status after meningitis C conjugate vaccination. *Psychosomatic Medicine, 64,* 963–970.

Burrel, G., & Granlund, B. (2002). Women's hearts need special treatment. *International Journal of Behavioral Medicine, 9,* 228–242.

Burton, R. P. D. (1998). Global integrative meaning as a mediating factor in the relationship between social roles and psychological distress. *Journal of Health and Social Behavior, 39,* 201–215.

Busato, A., & Kunzi, B. (2010). Differences in the quality of interpersonal care in complementary and conventional medicine. *BMC Complementary and Alternative Medicine, 10*(1), 63.

Buske-Kirschbaum, A., Auer, K. von, Kreiger, S., Weis, S., Rauh, W., & Hellhammer, D. (2003). Blunted cortisol responses to psychosocial stress in asthmatic children: A general feature of atopic disease? *Psychosomatic Medicine, 65,* 806–810.

Bute, B. P., Mathew, J., Blumenthal, J. A., Welsh-Bomer, K., White, W. D., Mark, D., et al. (2003). Female gender is associated with impaired quality of life 1 year after coronary artery bypass surgery. *Psychosomatic Medicine, 65,* 944–951.

Butler, D. (2004, March 18). Slim pickings. *Nature, 428,* 252–254.

Butler, L. D., Koopman, C., Classen, C., & Spiegel, D. (1999). Traumatic stress, life events, and emotional support in women with metastatic breast cancer: Cancer-related traumatic stress symptoms associated with past and current stressors. *Health Psychology, 18,* 555–560.

Butler, L. D., Koopman, C., Cordova M. J., Garlan, R. W., DiMiceli S., & Spiegel, D. (2003). Psychological distress and pain significantly increase before death in metastatic breast cancer patients. *Psychosomatic Medicine, 65,* 416–426.

Buunk, B. (1989). Affiliation and helping within organizations: A critical analysis of the role of social support with regard to occupational stress. In W. Stroebe & M. Hewstone (Eds.), *European review of social psychology* (Vol. 1). Chichester, England: Wiley.

Buunk, B. P., Doosje, B. J., Jans, L. G. J. M., & Hopstaken, L. E. M. (1993). Perceived reciprocity, social support, and stress at work: The role of exchange and communal orientation. *Journal of Personality and Social Psychology, 65,* 801–811.

Byock, I. R. (1991). Final Exit: A wake-up call to hospices. *Hospice Journal, 7,* 51–66.

Cacioppo, J. T., Hawkley, L. C., Crawford, L. E., Ernst, J. M., Burleson, M. H., Kowalewski, R. B., et al. (2002). Loneliness and health: Potential mechanisms. *Psychosomatic Medicine, 64,* 407–417.

Cakirbay, H., Bilici, M., Kavakçi, O., Cebi, A., Güler, M., & Tan, U. (2004). Sleep quality and immune functions in rheumatoid arthritis patients with and without major depression. *International Journal of Neuroscience, 114,* 245–256.

Calhoun, L. G., Cann, A., Tedeschi, R. G., & McMillan, J. (2000). A correlational test of the relationship between posttraumatic growth, religion, and cognitive processing. *Journal of Traumatic Stress, 13,* 521–527.

Calhoun, L. G., Tedeschi, R. G., Cann, A., & Hanks, E. A. (2010). Positive Outcomes Following Bereavement: Paths to Posttraumatic Growth. *Psychologica Belgica, 50,* 125–143.

Cameron, C. L., et al. (2001). Persistent symptoms among survivors of Hodgkin's disease: An explanatory model based on classical conditioning. *Health Psychology, 20,* 71–75.

Cameron, L., Booth, R. J., Schlatter, M., Ziginskas, D., Harman, J. E., & Benson, S. R. C. (2005). Cognitive and affective determinants of decisions to attend a group psychosocial support program for women with breast cancer. *Psychosomatic Medicine, 67,* 584–589.

Cameron, L., Leventhal, E. A., & Leventhal, H. (1993). Symptom representations and affect as determinants of care seeking in a community-dwelling, adult sample population. *Health Psychology, 12,* 171–179.

Cameron, L., Leventhal, E. A., & Leventhal, H. (1995). Seeking medical care in response to symptoms and life stress. *Psychosomatic Medicine, 57,* 1–11.

Cameron, N. (1963). *Personality development and psychology: A dynamic approach.* Boston: Houghton Mifflin.

Cameron, S., Horsburgh, M. E., & Armstrong-Strassen, M. (1994). Job satisfaction, propensity to leave and burnout in RNs and RNA: A multivariate perspective. *The Canadian Journal of Nursing Administration, 7(3),* 43–64.

Campbell, C. M., & Edwards, R. R. (2009). Mind—body interactions in pain: the neurophysiology of anxious and catastrophic pain-related thoughts. *Translational research : the journal of laboratory and clinical medicine, 153,* 97–101.

Campbell, M. K., James, A., Hudson, M. A., Carr, C., Jackson, E., Oates, V., Demissie, S., Farrell, D., & Tessaro, I. (2004). Improving multiple behaviors for colorectal cancer prevention among African American church members. *Health Psychology, 23,* 492–502.

Campbell, R. L., Svenson, L. W., & Jarvis, G. K. (1992). Perceived level of stress among university undergraduate students in Edmonton, Canada. *Perceptual and Motor Skills, 75(2),* 552–554.

Campo, S., & Cameron, K. A. (2006). Differential Effects of Exposure to Social Norms Campaigns: A Cause for Concern. *Health Communication, 19,* 209–219.

Canada Safety Council (2004). *Buckle up basics.* Retrieved June 22, 2008, from www.safety-council.org/info/child/childcar.htm.

Canadian Association of Physician Assistants. (2006). *What is a PA?* Retrieved August 24, 2007, from www.caopa.net/whatsapa.htm.

Canadian Cancer Society. (2005). *Progress in cancer prevention: Modifiable risk factors.* Retrieved from ww.cancer.ca/ccs/internet/standard/0,3182,3172_367655_390750327_langId-en,00.html.

Canadian Cancer Society. (2008a). *Lung cancer statistics.* Retrieved January 20, 2008, from www.cancer.ca/ccs/internet/standard/0,3182,3172_14459_371459_langId-en,00.html.

Canadian Cancer Society. (2008b). *Early detection and screening for breast cancer.* Retrieved from www.cancer.ca/ccs/internet/standard/0,3182,3172_10175_74544430_langId-en,00.html.

Canadian Cancer Society. (2008c). *Early detection for prostate cancer.* Retrieved January 27, 2008, from www.cancer.ca/ccs/internet/standard/0,3182,3172_10175_74550606_langId-en,00.html.

Canadian Cancer Society. (2008d). *Screening for colorectal cancer.* Retrieved January 30, 2008, from www.cancer.ca/ccs/internet/standard/0,3182,3172_10175_74549480_langId-en,00.html.

Canadian Cancer Society. (2009). *Causes of Leukemia.* http:// www.cancer.ca/Canadawide/About%20cancer/Types%20of%20cancer/ Causes%20of%20leukemia.aspx?sc_lang=en.

Canadian Cancer Society. (2011a). Canadian Cancer Statistics, 2011. Canadian Cancer Society's Steering Committee on Cancer Statistics. Toronto, ON.

Retrieved from: http://www.cancer.ca/Canada-wide/About%20cancer/~/media/CCS/Canada%20wide/Files%20List/English%20files%20heading/PDF%20-%20Policy%20-%20Canadian%20Cancer%20Statistics%20-%20English/Canadian%20Cancer%20Statistics%202011%20-%20English.ashx.

Canadian Cancer Society/National Cancer Institute of Canada. (2007). *Canadian cancer statistics.* Retrieved January 30, 2008, from www.cancer.ca/vgn/images/portal/cit_86751114/36/15/1816216925cw_2007stats_en.pdf.

Canadian Council of Motor Transport Administrators. (2001). *National occupant restraint program (NORP) 2010 strategy.* Retrieved July 15, 2007, from www.ccmta.ca/english/committees/rsrp/norp/norp-strategy.cfm.

Canadian Diabetes Association. (2005). *The prevalence and costs of diabetes.* Retrieved July 15, 2007, from www.diabetes.ca/Section_About/prevalence.asp.

Canadian Diabetes Association. (2008). *Type 1 diabetes: the basics.* Retrieved June 30, 2008, from www.diabetes.ca/Section_About/type1.asp.

Canadian Epilepsy Alliance. (2008). *Explaining epilepsy.* Retrieved August 14, 2008, from www.epilepsymatters.com/english/faqexplaining.html.

Canadian Fertility and Andrology Society. (2006). *Human assisted reproduction and live birth rates for Canada.* Retrieved August 10, 2008, from www.cfas.ca/2006_Press_Release.pdf.

Canadian Fitness and Lifestyle Research Institute. (2004). *2004 physical activity monitor and sport.* Retrieved July 10, 2007, from www.cflri.ca/eng/statistics/surveys/pam2004.php.

Canadian Foundation for the Study of Infant Deaths. (2007). *Smoking and SIDS.* Retrieved August 4, 2007, from www.sidscanada.org/smoking.html.

Canadian Foundation for the Study of Infant Deaths. (n.d.). *Sudden infant death syndrome and aboriginals.* Retrieved February 24, 2008, from http://sidscanada.org/aboriginal.html.

Canadian Hospice Palliative Care Association. (2006). *Hospice palliative care fact sheet.* Retrieved August 3, 2007, from www.chpca.net/events/nhpc_week/2006/Factsheet-HospicePalliativeCareinCanada-May2006.pdf.

Canadian Institute for Health Information (2004a). *Improving the health of Canadians, the summary report.* Ottawa: CIHI.

Canadian Institute for Health Information. (2005). *Canada's health care providers.* Retrieved July 29, 2007, from http://secure.cihi.ca/cihiweb/products/HCP_Chartbook05_e.pdf.

Canadian Institute for Health Information. (2006a). *Health personnel trend in Canada, 1995–2004. Health Personnel Database.* Retrieved August 17, 2007, from http://secure.cihi.ca/cihiweb/productsHealth_Personnel_Trend_1995-2004_e.pdf.

Canadian Institute for Health Information. (2006b). *How healthy are rural Canadians? An assessment of their health status and health determinants.* Retrieved February 3, 2008, from http://secure.cihi.ca/cihiweb/products/acknowledgements_rural_canadians_2006_report_e.pdf.

Canadian Institute for Health Information. (2007a). *Drug expenditure in Canada.* Retrieved February 26, 2008, from http://secure.cihi.ca/cihiweb/dispPage.jsp?cw_page=AR_80_E.

Canadian Institute for Health Information. (2007b). *Health care in Canada 2007.* Retrieved September 16, 2007, from http://secure.cihi.ca/cihiweb/products/hcic2007_e.pdf.

Canadian Institute for Health Information. (2008a). *Highlights of 2006–2007 inpatient hospitalizations and emergency department visits.* Retrieved February 24, 2008, from www.icis.ca/cihiweb/en/downloads /DAD_NACRS_Dec11_e.pdf.

Canadian Institute for Health Information. (2008b). *Nearly half of residents in Nova Scotia nursing homes display behavioural problems* Retrieved February 16, 2008, from http://secure.cihi.ca/cihiweb/dispPage.jsp?cw_page=media_20mar2008_e.

Canadian Institutes for Health Information. (2010). National Health Expenditure Database (NHEX) Downloaded May 4, 2011 from: http://secure.cihi.ca/cihiweb/dispPage.jsp?cw_page=statistics_results_source_nhex_e&cw_topic=National%20Health%20Expenditure%20Database%20%28NHEX%29.

Canadian Institute for Health Information. (2011). Summer is peak season for wheel- and water-related injuries. Accessed August 23, 2011 from http://www.cihi.ca/CIHI-ext-portal/internet/en/Document/types+of+care/RELEASE_21JULY11.

Canadian Institute for Health Information/Canadian Nurses Association. (2006). *The regulation and supply of nurse practitioners in Canada: 2006 update.* Retrieved March 1, 2008, from www.cna-nurses.ca/CNA/documents/pdf/publications/Nurse_Practitioner_Workforce_Update_2006_e.pdf.

Canadian Institute for Health Research. (2005). *5 million Canadians affected—Minister Dosanjh attends blood pressure clinic event to mark world hypertension day.* Retrieved August 10, 2007, from www.cihr-irsc.gc.ca/e/28015.html.

Canadian Lung Association. (2007a). *What is COPD?* Retrieved September 14, 2007, from www.lung.ca/diseases-maladies/copd-mpoc/what-quoi/index_e.php.

Canadian Lung Association. (2007b). *TB remains global pandemic: The lung association.* Retrieved February 6, 2008, from www.lung.ca/diseases-maladies/tuberculosis-tuberculose/tbday-jourtb/newsrelease-communique_e.php?print51.

Canadian Mental Health Association. (2005). *Eating disorders.* Retrieved from http://download.cmha.ab.ca/Edmonton/Eating%20Disorders.pdf.

Canadian Mental Health Association. (2007). *Post traumatic stress disorder.* Retrieved July 18, 2007, from www.cmha.ca/bins/content_page.asp?cid=3-94-97.

Canadian Pain Society. (2006). *Establishing acceptable waiting times for treatment of pain in Canada.* Retrieved August 14, 2007, from www.canadianpainsociety.ca/WaitTimes_Report.pdf.

Canadian Paraplegic Association. (2008). *Canadian facts on spinal cord injury.* Retrieved January 27, 2008, from www.canparaplegic.org/en/SCI_Facts_67.html.

Canadian Women's Health Network. (2006). *Women, mental health, mental illness and addiction in Canada: Response to Out of the Shadows at Last.* Retrieved February 5, 2008, from www.cwhn.ca/resources/cwhn/mentalHealth.html.

Cannon, C. P., Braunwald, E., McCabe, C. H., Rader, D. J., Rouleau, J. L., Belder, R., et al. (2004). Intensive versus moderate lipid lowering with statins after acute coronary syndromes. *New England Journal of Medicine, 350,* 1495–1504, http://www.nejm.org.

Cannon, W. B. (1932). *The wisdom of the body.* New York: Norton.

Carels, R. A., Blumenthal, J. A., & Sherwood, A. (1998). Effect of satisfaction with social support on blood pressure in normotensive and borderline hypertensive men and women. *International Journal of Behavioral Medicine, 5,* 76–85.

Carels, R. A., Darby, L., Cacciapaglia, H. M., Konrad, K., Coit, C., Harper, J., Kaplar, M. E., Young, K., Baylen, C. A., & Versland, A. (2007). Using motivational interviewing as a supplement to obesity treatment: A stepped-care approach. *Health Psychology, 26,* 369–374.

Carey, J. (2002, November 11). Waking up a sleeping anticancer gene. *BusinessWeek,* p. 82.

Carey, M. P. (1999). Prevention of HIV infection through changes in sexual behavior. *American Journal of Health Promotion, 14,* 104–111.

Carlson, L. E., & Garland, S. N. (2005). Impact of mindfulness-based stress reduction (MBSR) on sleep, mood, stress and fatigue symptoms in cancer outpatients. *International Journal of Behavioral Medicine, 12,* 278–285.

Carlson, L. E., Speca, M., Patel, K. D., & Faris, P. (2007). One year pre-post intervention follow-up of psychological, immune, endocrine and blood pressure outcomes of mindfulness-based stress reduction (MBSR) in breast and prostate cancer outpatients. *Brain, Behavior, and Immunity, 21(8),* 1038–1049.

Carlson, L. E., Speca, M., Patel, K. D., & Goodey, E. (2003). Mindfulness-based stress reduction in relation to quality of life, mood, symptoms of stress, and immune parameters in breast and prostate cancer outpatients. *Psychosomatic Medicine, 65(4),* 571–581.

Carmin, C. N., Wiegartz, P. S., Hoff, J. A., & Kondos, G. T. (2003). Cardiac anxiety in patients self-referred for electron beam tomography. *Journal of Behavioral Medicine, 26,* 67–80.

Carney, C. P., Jones, L., Woolson, R. F., Noyes, R., & Doebbeling, B. N. (2003). Relationship between depression and pancreatic cancer in the general population. *Psychosomatic Medicine, 65,* 884–888.

Carney, R. M., Freedland, K. E., Stein, P. K., Skala, J. A., Hoffman, P., & Jaffe, A. S. (2000). Change in heart rate and heart rate variability during treatment of depression in patients with coronary heart disease. *Psychosomatic Medicine, 62,* 639–647.

Carney, R. M., Howells, W. B., Blumenthal, J. A., Freedland, K. E., Stein, P. K., Berkman, L. F., Watkins. L. L., Czajkowski, S. M., Steinmeyer, B., Hayano, J., Domitrovich, P. P., Burg, M. M., & Jaffe, A. S. (2007). Heart rate turbulence, depression, and survival after acute myocardial infarction. *Psychosomatic Medicine, 69,* 4–9.

Carr, D., & Friedman, M. A. (2005). Is obesity stigmatizing? Body weight, perceived discrimination, and psychological well-being in the United States. *Journal of Health and Social Behavior, 46,* 244–259.

Carrière, G. (2003). Parent and child factors associated with youth obesity. *Supplement to Health Reports.* Statistics Canada Catalogue 82-003. Retrieved January 27, 2008, from www.statcan.ca/english/freepub/82-003-SIE/ 2003000 / pdf/82-003-SIE2003003.pdf.

Carrière, G. (2004). Use of hospital emergency rooms. *Health Reports, 15(1),* 35–38 (Statistics Canada Catalogue, 82-003). Retrieved March 2, 2008, from www.statcan.ca/english/studies/82-003/archive/2004/16-1-c.pdf.

Carroll, D., Smith, G. D., Shipley, M. J., Steptoe, A., Brunner, E. J., & Marmot, M. G. (2001). Blood pressure reactions to acute psychological stress and future blood pressure status: A 10-year follow-up of men in the Whitehall II study. *Psychosomatic Medicine, 63,* 737–743.

Cartwright, M., Wardle, J., Steggles, M., Simon, A. E., Croker, H., & Jarvis, M. J. (2003). Stress and dietary practices in adolescents. *Health Psychology, 22,* 362–369.

Carver, C. S., Lehman, J. M., & Antoni, M. H. (2003). Dispositional pessimism predicts illness-related disruption of social and recreational activities among breast cancer patients. *Journal of Personality and Social Psychology, 84,* 813–821.

Carver, C. S., Pozo, C., Harris, S. D., Noriega, V., Scheier, M. F., Robinson, D. S., et al. (1993). How coping mediates the effect of optimism on distress: A study of women with early stage breast cancer. *Journal of Personality and Social Psychology, 65,* 375–390.

Carver, C. S., Pozo-Kaderman, C., Price, A. A., Noriega, V., Harris, S. D., Derhagopian, R. P., et al. (1998). Concern about aspects of body image and adjustment to early stage breast cancer. *Psychosomatic Medicine, 60,* 168–174.

Carver, C. S., Scheier, M. F., & Weintraub, J. K. (1989). Assessing coping strategies: A theoretically based approach. *Journal of Personality and Social Psychology, 56,* 267–283.

Carver, C. S., Smith, R. G., Antoni, M. H., Petronis, V. M., Weiss, S., Derhagopian, R. P. (2005). Optimistic personality and psychosocial well-being during treatment predict psychosocial well-being among long-term survivors of breastcancer. *Health Psychology, 24,* 508–516.

Case, R. B., Moss, A. J., Case, N., McDermott, M., & Eberly, S. (1992). Living alone after myocardial infarction: Impact on prognosis. *Journal of the American Medical Association, 267,* 515–519.

Caspi, O., Koithan, M., & Criddle, M. W. (2004). Alternative medicine or "alternative" patients: A qualitative study of patient-oriented decision-making processes with respect to complementary and alternative medicine. *Medical Decision Making, 24,* 64-79.

Cassileth, B. R., Temoshok, L. Frederick, B. E., Walsh, W. P., Hurwitz, S., Guerry, D., et al. (1988). Patient and physician delay in melanoma diagnosis. *Journal of the American Academy of Dermatology, 18,* 591–598.

Castro, C. M., King, A. C., & Brassington, G. S. (2001). Telephone versus mail interventions for maintenance of physical activity in older adults. *Health Psychology, 20,* 438–444.

Castro, C. M., Wilcox, S., O'Sullivan, P., Bauman, K., & King, A. C. (2002). An exercise program for women who are caring for relatives with dementia. *Psychosomatic Medicine, 64,* 458–468.

Catalano, R., Dooley, D., Wilson, C., & Hough, R. (1993). Job loss and alcohol abuse: A test using data from the epidemiologic catchment area. *Journal of Health and Social Behavior, 34,* 215–225.

Catalano, R., Hansen, H., & Hartig, T. (1999). The ecological effect of unemployment on the incidence of very low birthweight in Norway and Sweden. *Journal of Health and Social Behavior, 40,* 422–428.

Catz, S. L., Kelly, J. A., Bogart, L. M., Benotsch, E. G., & McAuliffe, T. L. (2000). Patterns, correlates, and barriers to medication adherence among persons prescribed new treatments for HIV disease. *Health Psychology, 19,* 124–133.

CBC News. (2006, February 28). New nurses facing stress, burnout, survey finds. CBC News. Retrieved August 7, 2007, from www.cbc.ca/health/story/2006/02/28/nurses-burnout060228.html.

CBC News. (2007, March 5). Prevent, manage diabetes better: Report. Retrieved February 18, 2008, from www.cbc.ca/health/story/2007/03/05/diabetesmanage.html.

CBC News. (2007, June 11). The fight for the right to die. *CBC News.* Retrieved July 21, 2007, from www.cbc.ca/news/background/assistedsuicide.

CBC News. (2007, July 31). Violence against women one of top B.C. health priorities: Report. Retrieved September 29, 2007, from www.cbc.ca/canada/-british-columbia/story/2007/07/30/bcwomen.html.

CBC News, (2011, March 29). N.L. to ban smoking in cars with children. *CBC News.* Retrieved July 28, 2011, from www.cbc.ca/news/health/story/2011/03/28/nl-smoking-ban-driving-328.html?ref=rss.

Center for the Advancement of Health. (2003, September). Shouting from the rooftops: Where we reside can affect our lives. *Facts of Life, 8,* 1.

Centre for Addiction and Mental Health. (2007). *About marijuana.* Retrieved January 20, 2008, from www.camh.net/About_Addiction_Mental_Health/Drug _and_Addiction_ Information/about_marijuana.html.

Cepeda-Benito, A. (1993). Meta-analytical review of the efficacy of nicotine chewing gum in smoking treatment programs. *Journal of Consulting and Clinical Psychology, 61,* 822–830.

Cepeda, M. S., Chapman, C. R., Miranda, N., Sanchez, R., Rodriguez, C. H., Restrepo, A. E., et al. (2008). Emotional Disclosure Through Patient Narrative May Improve Pain and Well-Being: Results of a Randomized Controlled Trial in Patients with Cancer Pain. *Journal of Pain and Symptom Management, 35,* 623–631.

Cesana, G., Sega, R., Ferrario, M., Chiodini, P., Corrao, G., & Mancia, G. (2003). Job strain and blood pressure in employed men and women: A pooled analysis of four northern Italian population samples. *Psychosomatic Medicine, 65,* 558–563.

Chabaud, P., Ferrand, C., & Maury, J. (2010). Individual Differences in Undergraduate Student Athletes: The Roles of Perfectionism and Trait Anxiety on Perception of Procrastination Behavior. *Social Behavior and Personality: an international journal, 38,* 1041–1056.

Chambers, C. T., Craig, K. D., & Bennett, S. M. (2002). The impact of maternal behavior on children's pain experiences: An experimental analysis. *Journal of Pediatric Psychology, 27(3),* 293–301.

Champion, V. L., & Springston, J. (1999). Mammography adherence and beliefs in a sample of low-income African American women. *International Journal of Behavioral Medicine, 6,* 228–240.

Champion, V. L., Skinner, C. S., Menon, U., Seshadri, R., Anzalone, D. C., & Rawl, S. M. (2002). Comparisons of tailored mammography interventions at two months postintervention. *Annals of Behavioral Medicine, 24,* 211–218.

Champion, V., Maraj, M., Hui, S., Perkings, A.J., Tierney, W., Menon, U., & Skinner, C. S. (2003). Comparison of tailored interventions to increase mammography screening in nonadherent older women. *Preventive Medicine, 36(2),* 150–158.

Chandola, T., Britton, A., Brunner, E., Hemingway, H., Malik, M., Kumari, M., et al. (2008). Work stress and coronary heart disease: what are the mechanisms? *European Heart Journal, 29,* 640–648.

Chang, C. (2007). Ideal Self-Image Congruency as a Motivator for Smoking: The Moderating Effects of Personality Traits. *Health Communication, 22,* 1–12.

Chang, E. C. (1998). Dispositional optimism and primary and secondary appraisal of a stressor: Controlling for confounding influences and relations to coping and psychological and physical adjustment. *Journal of Personality and Social Psychology, 74,* 1109–1120.

Chang, E. C., Ivezaj, V., Downey, C. A., Kashima, Y., & Morady, A. R. (2008). Complexities of measuring perfectionism: Three popular perfectionism measures and their relations with eating disturbances and health behaviors in a female college student sample. *Eating Behaviors, 9,* 102–110.

Chapman, B. P., Lyness, J. M., & Duberstein, P. (2007). Personality and medical illness burden among older adults in primary care. *Psychosomatic Medicine, 69,* 277–282.

Chapman, C. R., & Gavrin, J. (1999). Suffering: the contributions of persisting pain. *Lancet, 353,* 2233–2237.

Charles, S. T., Gatz, M., Kato, K., & Pedersen, N. L. (2008). Physical Health 25 Years Later: The Predictive Ability of Neuroticism. *Health Psychology, 27,* 369–378.

Charpentier, C., Stout, D., Benoit, A., Poulin, E., & Philip, C. (2011). Availability, accessibility and acceptability of English-Language mental health services for Estrie's English-speaking population: Service user and provider perspectives. *Journal of Eastern Townships Studies, 36,* 27–54.

Chassin, L., Presson, C. C., Pitts, S. C., & Sherman, S. J. (2000). The natural history of cigarette smoking from adolescence to adulthood in a midwestern community sample: Multiple trajectories and their psychosocial correlates. *Health Psychology, 19,* 223–231.

Chassin, L., Presson, C. C., Rose, J. S., & Sherman, S. J. (1996). The natural history of cigarette smoking from adolescence to adulthood: Demographic predictors of continuity and change. *Health Psychology, 15,* 478–484.

Chassin, L., Presson, C. C., Sherman, S. J., & Kim, K. (2002). Long-term psychological sequelae of smoking cessation and relapse. *Health Psychology, 21,* 438–443.

Chen, E., & Schreier, H. M. C. (2008). Does the social environment contribute to asthma? *Immunology and Allergy Clinics of North America,* 28(3), 649–664.

Chen, E., Bloomberg, G. R., Fisher, E. B., Jr., & Strunk, R. C. L. (2003). Predictors of repeat hospitalizations in children with asthma: The role of psychosocial and socioenvironmental factors. *Health Psychology, 22,* 12–18.

Chen, E., Fisher, E. B., Bacharier, L. B., & Strunk, R. C. (2003). Socioeconomic status, stress, and immune markers in adolescents with asthma. *Psychosomatic Medicine, 65,* 984–992.

Chen, E., Hermann, C., Rodgers, D., Oliver-Welker, T., & Strunk, R. C. (2006). Symptom perception in childhood asthma: The role of anxiety and asthma severity. *Health Psychology, 25,* 389–395.

Chen, E., Langer, D. A., Raphaelson, Y. E., & Matthews, K. A. (2004). Socioeconomic Status and Health in Adolescents: The Role of Stress Interpretations. *Child Development,* 75, 1039–1052. doi: 10.1111/j.1467-8624.2004.00724.x.

Chen, E., Matthews, K. A., & Boyce, W. T. (2002). Socioeconomic differences in children's health: How an why do these relationships change with age? *Psychological Bulletin, 128,* 295–329.

Chen, E., Matthews, K. A., Salomon, K., & Ewart, C. K. (2002). Cardiovascular reactivity during social and nonsocial stressors: Do children's personal goals and expressive skills matter? *Health Psychology, 21,* 16–24.

Chen, E., Miller, G. E., Walker, H. A., Arevalo, J. M., Sung, C. Y., & Cole, S. W. (2009). Genome-wide transcriptional profiling linked to social class in asthma. *Thorax,* 64(1), 38–43.

Chen, E., Schreier, H. M. C., Strunk, R. C., & Brauer, M. (2008). Chronic traffic-related air pollution and stress interact to predict biologic and clinical outcomes in asthma. *Environmental Health Perspectives, 116.*

Chen, Y., Johansen, H., Thillaiampalam, S., & Sambell, C. (2005). Asthma. *Health Reports, 16(2),* 43–46 (Statistics Canada Catalogue 82-003). Retrieved August 20, 2007, from www.statcan.ca/english/freepub/82-003-XIE/0020482-003-XIE.pdf.

Chen, Z., Sandercock, P., Pan, P., Counsell, C., Collins, R., Liu, L., et al. (2000). Indications of early aspirin use in acute ischemic stroke: A combined analysis of 40,000 randomized patients from the Chinese acute stroke trial and the international stroke trial. *Stroke, 31,* 1240–1249.

Cheng, C. (2003). Cognitive and motivational processes underlying coping flexibility: A dual-process model. *Journal of Personality and Social Psychology, 84,* 425–438.

Cheng, C., Hui, W., & Lam, S. (2004). Psychosocial factors and perceived severity of functional dyspeptic symptoms: A psychosocial interactionist model. *Psychosomatic Medicine, 66,* 85–91.

Chenier, N. M. (2001). *Substance abuse and public policy.* Retrieved July 15, 2007, from http://dsp-psd.pwgsc.gc.ca/Collection-R/LoPBdP/CIR/942-e.htm#a.%20Alcohol.

Cherny, N. I. (1996). The problem of inadequately relieved suffering. *Journal of Social Issues, 52,* 13–30.

Chesney, M. A., Chambers, D. B., Taylor, J. M., Johnson, L. M., & Folkman, S. (2003). Coping effectiveness training for men living with HIV: Results from a randomized clinical trial testing a group-based intervention. *Psychosomatic Medicine, 65,* 1038–1046.

Chiaramonte, G. R., & Friend, R. (2006). Medical students' and residents' gender bias in the diagnosis, treatment, and interpretation of coronary heart disease symptoms. *Health Psychology, 25,* 255–266.

Chida, Y., & Steptoe, A. (2008). Positive Psychological Well-Being and Mortality: A Quantitative Review of Prospective Observational Studies. *Psychosomatic Medicine, 70,* 741–756.

Chochinov, H. M., Hack, T., Hassard, T., Kristjanson, L. J., McClement, S., & Harlos, M. (2002a). Dignity in the terminally ill: a cross-sectional, cohort study. *Lancet, 360,* 2026–2030.

Chochinov, H. M., Hack, T., Hassard, T., Kristjanson, L. J., McClement, S., & Harlos, M. (2005). Dignity Therapy: A Novel Psychotherapeutic Intervention for Patients Near the End of Life. *Journal of Clinical Oncology, 23*(24), 5520–5525.

Chochinov, H. M., Hack, T., McClement, S., Kristjanson, L., & Harlos, M. (2002b). Dignity in the terminally ill: a developing empirical model. *Social Science and Medicine, 54,* 433–443.

Choi, W. S., Harris, K. J., Okuyemi, K., & Ahluwalia, J. S. (2003). Predictors of smoking initiation among college-bound high school students. *Annals of Behavioral Medicine, 26,* 69–74.

Choinière, R., Lafontaine, P., & Edwards, A. C. (2000). Distribution of cardiovascular disease risk factors by socioeconomic status among Canadian adults. *CMAJ, 162(9),* S13–S24.

Chow, H. P. H. (2007). Psychological well-being and scholastic achievement among university students in a Canadian prairie city. *Social Psychology of Education, 10(4),* 483–493.

Chrisler, J. C., McCreary, D. R., Gill, D. L., & Kamphoff, C. S. (2010). Gender in Sport and Exercise Psychology *Handbook of Gender Research in Psychology* (pp. 563–585): Springer New York.

Christakis, N. A., & Allison, P. D. (2006). Mortality after the hospitalization of a spouse. *The New England Journal of Medicine, 354,* 719–730.

Christenfeld, N., Gerin, W., Linden, W., Sanders, M., Mathur, J., Deich, J. D., et al. (1997). Social support effects on cardiovascular reactivity: Is a stranger as effective as a friend? *Psychosomatic Medicine, 59,* 388–398.

Christensen, A. J., Edwards, D. L., Wiebe, J. S., Benotsch, E. G., McKelvey, L., Andrews, M., et al. (1996). Effect of verbal self-disclosure on natural killer cell activity: Moderating influence of cynical hostility. *Psychosomatic Medicine, 58,* 150–155.

Christensen, A. J., Ehlers, S. L., Raichle, K. A., Bertolatus, J. A., & Lawton, W. J. (2000). Predicting change in depression following renal transplantation: Effect of patient coping preferences. *Health Psychology, 19,* 348–353.

Christensen, A. J., Ehlers, S. L., Wiebe, J. S., Moran, P. J., Raichle, K., Ferneyhough, K., et al. (2002). Patient personality and mortality: A 4-year prospective examination of chronic renal insufficiency. *Health Psychology, 21,* 315–320.

Christensen, A. J., Moran, P. J., Wiebe, J. S., Ehlers, S. L., & Lawton, W. J. (2002). Effect of a behavioral self-regulation intervention on patient adherence in hemodialysis. *Health Psychology, 21,* 393–397.

Christensen, U., Schmidt, L., Budtz-Jørgensen, E., & Avlund, K. (2006). Group Cohesion and Social Support in Exercise Classes: Results From a Danish Intervention Study. *Health Education & Behavior, 33,* 677–689.

Chronic Disease Prevention Alliance of Canada. (2007). *Chronic Disease Prevention Alliance supports healthy weights, healthy children report – and urges action now!* Retrieved June 29, 2007, from www.cdpac.ca/media.php?mid=221.

Ciccone, D. S., & Natelson, B. H. (2003). Comorbid illness in women with chronic fatigue syndrome: A test of the single syndrome hypothesis. *Psychosomatic Medicine, 65,* 268–275.

Ciccone, D. S., Just, N., & Bandilla, E. (1999). A comparison of economic and social reward in patients with chronic nonmalignant back pain. *Psychosomatic Medicine, 61,* 552–563.

Clarke, L. H., Griffin, M., & Team, P. R. (2008). Failing Bodies: Body Image and Multiple Chronic Conditions in Later Life. *Qualitative Health Research, 18,* 1084–1095.

Clarke, V. A., Lovegrove, H., Williams, A., & Macpherson, M. (2000). Unrealistic optimism and the health belief model. *Journal of Behavioral Medicine, 23,* 367–376.

Clarke, V. A., Williams, T., & Arthey, S. (1997). Skin type and optimistic bias in relation to the sun protection and suntanning behaviors of young adults. *Journal of Behavioral Medicine, 20,* 207–222.

Clemmey, P. A., & Nicassio, P. M. (1997). Illness self-schemas in depressed and nondepressed rheumatoid arthritis patients. *Journal of Behavioral Medicine, 20,* 273–290.

Clouse, R. E., Lustman, P. J., Freedland, K. E., Griffith, L. S., McGill, J. B., & Carney, R. M. (2003). Depression and coronary heart disease in women with diabetes. *Psychosomatic Medicine, 65,* 376–383.

Clucas, C., & St Claire, L. (2010). The Effect of Feeling Respected and the Patient Role on Patient Outcomes. *Applied Psychology: Health and Well-Being, 2,* 298–322.

Cody, R., & Lee, C. (1999). Development and evaluation of a pilot program to promote exercise among mothers of preschool children. *International Journal of Behavioral Medicine, 61,* 13–29.

Cohen, F., & Lazarus, R. (1979). Coping with the stresses of illness. In G. C. Stone, F. Cohen, & N. E. Adler (Eds.), *Health psychology: A handbook* (pp. 217–254). San Francisco: Jossey-Bass.

Cohen, F., Kemeny, M. E., Zegans, L. S., Johnson, P., Kearney, K. A., & Stites, D. P. (2007). Immune function declines with unemployment and recovers after stressor termination. *Psychosomatic Medicine, 69,* 225–234.

Cohen, L. M., Dobscha, S. K., Hails, K. C., Pekow, P. S., & Chochinov, H. M. (2002). Depression and suicidal ideation in patients who discontinue the life-support treatment of dialysis. *Psychosomatic Medicine, 64,* 889–896.

Cohen, L., Cohen, R., Blount, R., Schaen, E., & Zaff, J. (1999). Comparative study of distraction versus topical anesthesia for pediatric pain management during immunizations. *Health Psychology, 18,* 591–598.

Cohen, L., Marshall, G. D., Jr., Cheng, L., Agarwal, S. K., & Wei, Q. (2000). DNA repair capacity in healthy medical students during and after exam stress. *Journal of Behavioral Medicine, 23,* 531–544.

Cohen, M., & Pollack, S. (2005). Mothers with breast cancer and their adult daughters: The relationship between mothers' reaction to breast cancer and their daughters' emotional and neuroimmune status. *Psychosomatic Medicine, 67,* 64–71.

Cohen, R. Y., Brownell, K. D., & Felix, M. R. J. (1990). Age and sex differences in health habits and beliefs of schoolchildren. *Health Psychology, 9,* 208–224.

Cohen, S. (1980). Aftereffects of stress on human performance and social behavior: A review of research and theory. *Psychological Bulletin, 88,* 82–108.

Cohen, S., & Herbert, T. B. (1996). Health psychology: Psychological factors and physical disease from the perspective of human psychoneuroimmunology. *Annual Review of Psychology, 47,* 113–142.

Cohen, S., & Hoberman, H. M. (1983). Positive events and social supports as buffers of life change stress. *Journal of Applied Social Psychology, 13,* 99–125.

Cohen, S., & McKay, G. (1984). Social support, stress, and the buffering hypothesis: A theoretical analysis. In A. Baum, S. E. Taylor, & J. Singer (Eds.), *Handbook of psychology and health* (Vol. 4, pp. 253–268). Hillsdale, NJ: Erlbaum.

Cohen, S., & Pressman, S. D. (2006). Positive affect and health. *Current Directions in Psychological Science, 15,* 122–125.

Cohen, S., & Williamson, G. M. (1991). Stress and infectious disease in humans. *Psychological Bulletin, 109,* 5–24.

Cohen, S., & Wills, T. A. (1985). Stress, social support, and the buffering hypothesis. *Psychological Bulletin, 98,* 310–357.

Cohen, S., Alper, C. M., Doyle, W. J., Treanor, J. J., & Turner, R. B. (2006). Positive emotional style predicts resistance to illness after experimental exposure to rhinovirus or influenza A virus. *Psychosomatic Medicine, 68,* 809–815.

Cohen, S., Doyle, W. J., & Baum, A. (2006). Socioeconomic status is associated with stress hormones. *Psychosomatic Medicine, 68,* 414–420.

Cohen, S., Doyle, W., & Skoner, D. (1999). Psychological stress, cytokine production, and severity of upper respiratory illness. *Psychosomatic Medicine, 61,* 175–180.

Cohen, S., Doyle, W. J., Skoner, D. P., Rabin, B. S., & Gwaltney, J. M., Jr. (1997). Social ties and susceptibility to the common cold. *Journal of the American Medical Association, 277,* 1940–1944.

Cohen, S., Doyle, W. J., Turner, R. B., Alper, C. M., & Skoner, D. P. (2003). Emotional style and susceptibility to the common cold. *Psychosomatic Medicine, 65,* 652–657.

Cohen, S., Hamrick, N., Rodriguez, M. S., Feldman, P. J., Rabin, B. S., & Manuck, S. R. (2002). Reactivity and vulnerability to stress-associated risk for upper respiratory illness. *Psychosomatic Medicine, 64,* 302–310.

Cohen, S., Kamarck, T., & Mermelstein, R. (1983). A global measure of perceived stress. *Journal of Health and Social Behavior, 24,* 385–396.

Cohen, S., Kessler, R. C., & Gordon, L. U. (1995). Conceptualizing stress and its relation to disease. In S. Cohen, R. C. Kessler, & L. U. Gordon (Eds.), *Measuring stress: A guide for health and social scientists* (pp. 3–26). New York: Oxford University Press.

Cohen, S., Line, S., Manuck, S. B., Rabin, B. S., Heise, E. R., & Kaplan, J. R. (1997). Chronic social stress, social status, and susceptibility to upper respiratory infection in nonhuman primates. *Psychosomatic Medicine, 59(3),* 222–223.

Cohen, S., Sherrod, D. R., & Clark, M. S. (1986). Social skills and the stress—protective role of social support. *Journal of Personality and Social Psychology, 50,* 963–973.

Cohen, S., Tyrrell, D. A. J., & Smith, A. P. (1993). Negative life events, perceived stress, negative affect, and susceptibility to the common cold. *Journal of Personality and Social Psychology, 64,* 131–140.

Coker, A. L., Bond, S., Madeleine, M. M., Luchok, K., & Pirisi, L. (2003). Psychological stress and cervical neoplasia risk. *Psychosomatic Medicine, 65,* 644–651.

Cole, S. W., Kemeny, M. E., Fahey, J. L., Zack, J. A., & Naliboff, B. D. (2003). Psychological risk factors for HIV pathogenesis: Mediation by the autonomic nervous system. *Biological Psychiatry, 54,* 1444–1456.

Cole, S. W., Kemeny, M. E., Taylor, S. E., Visscher, B. R., & Fahey, J. L. (1996). Accelerated course of human immunodeficiency virus infection in gay men who conceal their homosexual identity. *Psychosomatic Medicine, 58,* 219–231.

College of Physicians and Surgeons of Ontario (2007). *2006 Physician resources in Ontario: Small triumphs, big challenges: College of Physicians and Surgeons of Ontario.*

Colley, R. C., Garriguet, D., Janssen, I., Craig, C. L., Clarke, J., & Tremblay, M. S. (2011). Physical activity of Canadian adults: Accelerometer results from the 2007 to 2009 Canadian Health Measures Survey. *Health Reports,* 22 (1), Statistics Canada, Catalogue no. 82-003-XPE Accessed April 14, 2011 from http://www.statcan.gc.ca/pub/82-003-x/2011001/article/11396-eng.pdf.

Collie, K., Kreshka, M. A., Ferrier, S., Parsons, R., Graddy, K., Avram, S., et al. (2007). Videoconferencing for delivery of breast cancer support groups to women living in rural communities: a pilot study. *Psycho-Oncology, 16*(8), 778–782.

Collijn, D. H., Appels, A., & Nijhuis, F. (1995). Psychosocial risk factors for cardiovascular disease in women: The role of social support. *International Journal of Medicine, 2,* 219–232.

Collin, C. (2006). *Substance abuse and public policy in Canada: V. Alcohol and related harms.* Retrieved July 12, 2007, from www.parl.gc.ca/information/library/PRBpubs/prb0620-e.htm.

Collins, N. L., & Feeney, B. C. (2004). Working models of attachment shape perceptions of social support: Evidence from experimental and observational studies. *Journal of Personality and Social Psychology, 87,* 363–383.

Collins, N. L., Dunkel-Schetter, C., Lobel, M., & Scrimshaw, S. C. M. (1993). Social support in pregnancy. Psychosocial correlates of birth outcomes and postpartum depression. *Journal of Personality and Social Psychology, 6,* 1243–1258.

Collins, R. L., Kanouse, D. E., Gifford, A. L., Senterfitt, J. W., Schuster, M. A., McCaffrey, D. F., et al. (2001). Changes in health-promoting behavior following diagnosis with HIV: Prevalence and correlates in a national probability sample. *Health Psychology, 20,* 351–360.

Collins, R. L., Taylor, S. E., & Skokan, L. A. (1990). A better world or a shattered vision? Changes in perspectives following victimization. *Social Cognition, 8,* 263–285.

Commission for Environmental Cooperation. (2006). *Children's health and the environment in North America: A first report on available indicators and measures.* Retrieved February 18, 2008, from www.cec.org/news/details/index.cfm?varlan=English&ID=2693.

Compas, B. E., Barnez, G. A., Malcarne, V., & Worsham, N. (1991). Perceived control and coping with stress: A developmental perspective. *Journal of Social Issues, 47,* 23–34.

Compas, B. E., Worsham, N. L., Epping-Jordan, J. A. E., Grant, K. E., Mireault, G., Howell, D. C., et al. (1994). When mom or dad has cancer: Markers of psychological distress in cancer patients, spouses, and children. *Health Psychology, 13,* 507–515.

Compas, B. E., Worsham, N. L., Ey, S., & Howell, D. C. (1996). When mom or dad has cancer: II. Coping, cognitive appraisals, and psychological distress in children of cancer patients. *Health Psychology, 15,* 167–175.

Conger, R. D., Lorenz, F. O., Elder, G. H., Jr., Simons, R. L., & Ge, X. (1993). Husband and wife differences in response to undesirable life events. *Journal of Health and Social Behavior, 34,* 71–88.

Conis, E. (2003a, August 4). Chips for some, tofu for others. *Los Angeles Times,* p. F8.

Conn, V. S., Valentine, J. C., & Cooper, H. M. (2002). Interventions to increase physical activity among aging adults: A meta-analysis. *Annals of Behavioral Medicine, 24,* 190–200.

Conrad, P. (2005). The shifting engines of medicalization. *Journal of Health and Social Behavior, 46(1),* 3–14.

Cooper, C. J., & Marshall, J. (1976). Occupational sources of stress: A review of the literature relating to coronary heart disease and mental ill health. *Journal of Occupational Psychology, 49,* 11–28.

Cooper, M. L., Wood, P. K., Orcutt, H. K., & Albino, A. (2003). Personality and the predisposition to engage in risky or problem behaviors during adolescence. *Journal of Personality and Social Psychology, 84,* 390–410.

Cooperman, N. A., & Simoni, J. M. (2005). Suicidal ideation and attempted suicide among women living with HIV/AIDS. *Journal of Behavioral Medicine, 28,* 149–156.

Copeland, A. L., & Carney, C. E. (2003). Smoking expectancies as mediators between dietary restraint and disinhibition and smoking in college women. *Experimental and Clinical Psychopharmacology, 11(3),* 247–251.

Corbière, M., Sullivan, M. J. L., Stanish, W. D., & Adams, H. (2007). Pain and depression in injured workers and their return to work: A longitudinal study. *Canadian Journal of Behavioral Science, 39(1),* 23–31.

Corbin, W. R., & Fromme, K. (2002). Alcohol use and serial monogamy as risks for sexually transmitted diseases in young adults. *Health Psychology, 21,* 229–236.

Cordova, M. J., Cunningham, L. L. C., Carlson, C. R., & Andrykoski, M. A. (2001). Posttraumatic growth following breast cancer: A controlled comparison study. *Health Psychology, 20,* 176–185.

Corle, D. K., et al. (2001). Self-rated quality of life measures: Effect of change to a low-fat, high fiber, fruit and vegetable enriched diet. *Annals of Behavioral Medicine, 23,* 198–207.

Cornelissen, V. A., Verheyden, B., Aubert, A. E., & Fagard, R. H. (2009). Effects of aerobic training intensity on resting, exercise and post-exercise blood pressure, heart rate and heart-rate variability. *J Hum Hypertens, 24,* 175–182.

Cornford, C. S., & Cornford, H. M. (1999). I'm only here because of my family. A study of lay referral networks. *British Journal of General Practice, 49,* 617-620.

Courneya, K. S., & Friedenreich, C. M. (1999). Physical exercise and quality of life following cancer diagnosis: A literature review. *Annals of Behavioral Medicine, 21,* 171–179.

Courneya, K. S., Segal, R. J., Mackey, J. R., Gelmon, K., Reid, R. D., Friedenreich, C. M., Ladha, A. B., Proulx, C., Vallance, J. K., Lane, K., Yasui, Y., & McKenzie, D. C. (2007). Effects of aerobic and resistance exercise in breast cancer patients receiving adjuvant chemotherapy: A multicenter randomized controlled trial. *Journal of Clinical Oncology, 25(28),* 4396–4404.

Cousins, N. (1979). *Anatomy of an illness.* New York: Norton.

Cousins, N. (1989). Belief becomes biology. *Advances,* 6(3), 20–29.

Coutu, M. F., Dupuis, G., D'Antono, B., & Rochon-Goyer, L. (2003). Illness representation and change in dietary habits in hypercholesterolemic patients. *Journal of Behavioral Medicine, 26,* 133–152.

Craig, C. L., Russell, S. J., Cameron, C., & Bauman, A. (2004). Twenty-year trends in physical activity among Canadian adults. *Canadian Journal of Public Health, 95(1),* 59–63.

Cresci, B., Tesi, F., La Ferlita, T., Ricca, V., Ravaldi, C., Rotella, C. M., et al. (2007). Group versus individual cognitive-behavioral treatment for obesity: results after 36 months. *Eating and Weight Disorders, 12,* 147–153.

Creswell, J. D., Lam, S., Stanton, A. L., Taylor, S. E., Bower, J. E., & Sherman, D. K. (2007). Does self-affirmation, cognitive processing, or discovery of meaning explain cancer-related health benefits of expressive writing? *Personality and Social Psychology Bulletin, 33,* 238–250.

Creswell, J. D., Welch, W. T, Taylor, S. E., Sherman, D. K., Gruenewald, T. L., & Mann, T. (2005). Affirmation of personal values buffers neuroendocrine and psychological stress responses. *Psychological Science, 16(11),* 846–851.

Criego, A., Crow, S., Goebel-Fabbri, A. E., Kendall, D., & Parkin, C. (2009). Eating Disorders and Diabetes: Screening and Detection. *Diabetes Spectrum, 22,* 143–146.

Crohn's and Colitis Foundation of Canada. (2008). *What is inflammatory bowel disease (IBD)?* Retrieved February 12, 2008, from www.ccfc.ca/English/info/ibd.html.

Crompton, S. (2010) Life satisfaction of working-age women with disabilities. Component of Statistics Canada Catalogue no. 11-008-X

Crosnoe, R. (2002). Academic and health-related trajectories in adolescence: The intersection of gender and athletics. *Journal of Health and Social Behavior, 43,* 317–335.

Croyle, R. T., & Barger, S. D. (1993). Illness cognition. In S. Maes, H. Leventhal, & M. Johnston (Eds.), *International review of health psychology* (Vol. 2, pp. 29–49). New York: Wiley.

Croyle, R. T., & Ditto, P. H. (1990). Illness cognition and behavior: An experimental approach. *Journal of Behavioral Medicine, 13,* 31–52.

Croyle, R. T., & Hunt, J. R. (1991). Coping with health threat: Social influence processes in reactions to medical test results. *Journal of Personality and Social Psychology, 60,* 382–389.

Croyle, R. T., Loftus, E. F., Barger, S. D., Sun, Y. C., Hart, M., & Gettig, J. (2006). How well do people recall risk factor test results? Accuracy and bias among cholesterol screening participants. *Health Psychology, 25(3),* 425–432.

Cruess, S., Antoni, M., Cruess, D., Fletcher, M., Ironson, G., Kumar, M., et al. (2000). Reduction in herpes simplex virus type 2 antibody titers after cognitive behavioral stress management and relationships with neuroendocrine function, relaxation skills, and social support in HIV-positive men. *Psychosomatic Medicine, 62,* 828–837.

Cruess, D. G., Antoni, M. H., McGregor, B. A., Kilbourn, K. M., Boyers, A. E., Alferi, S. M., et al. (2000). Cognitive-behavioral stress management reduces serum cortisol by enhancing benefit finding among women being treated for early stage breast cancer. *Psychosomatic Medicine, 62,* 304–308.

Culos-Reed, S. N., Shields, C., & Brawley, L. R. (2005). Breast cancer survivors involved in vigorous team physical activity: Psychosocial correlates of maintenance participation. *Psycho-Oncology, 14(7),* 594–605.

Curbow, B., Bowie, J., Garza, M. A., McDonnell, K., Scott, L. B., Coyne, C. A., & Chiappelli, T. (2004). Community-based cancer screening programs in older populations: Making progress but can we do better? *Preventive Medicine, 38,* 676–693.

Curran, S. L., Beacham, A. O., & Andrykowski, M. A. (2004). Ecological momentary assessment of fatigue following breast cancer treatment. *Journal of Behavioral Medicine, 27,* 425–444.

Currie, S. R., Wilson, K. G., & Curran, D. (2002). Clinical significance and predictors of treatment response to cognitive-behavior therapy for insomnia secondary to chronic pain. *Journal of Behavioral Medicine, 25,* 135–153.

Cutolo, M., & Straub, R. H. (2006). Stress as a risk factor in the pathogenesis of rheumatoid arthritis. *Neuroimmunomodulation, 13,* 277–282.

Czaja, S. J., & Rubert, M. P. (2002). Telecommunications technology as an aid to family caregivers of persons with dementia. *Psychosomatic Medicine, 64,* 469–476.

D'Amico, E. J., & Fromme, K. (1997). Health risk behaviors of adolescent and young adult siblings. *Health Psychology, 16,* 426–432.

Dahlberg, C. C. (1977, June). Stroke. *Psychology Today,* 121–128.

Dakof, G. A., & Taylor, S. E. (1990). Victims' perceptions of social support: What is helpful from whom? *Journal of Personality and Social Psychology, 58,* 80–89.

Dalle Grave, R., Calugi, S., Centis, E., El Ghoch, M., & Marchesini, G. (2011). Cognitive-Behavioral Strategies to Increase the Adherence to Exercise in the Management of Obesity. *Journal of Obesity, Article ID 348293,* 11 pages.

Dallman, M. F. et al. (2003). Chronic stress and obesity: A new view of "comfort food." *Proceedings of the National Academy of Sciences, 100,* 11696–11701.

Dalton, W. T., & Kitzmann, K. M. (2011). A Preliminary Investigation of Stimulus Control, Self-Monitoring, and Reinforcement in Lifestyle Interventions for Pediatric Overweight. *American Journal of Lifestyle Medicine.* doi: 10.1177/1559827611402582

Danoff, B., Kramer, S., Irwin, P., & Gottlieb, A. (1983). Assessment of the quality of life in long-term survivors after definitive radiotherapy. *American Journal of Clinical Oncology, 6,* 339–345.

Danoff-Burg, S., & Revenson, T. A. (2005). Benefit-finding among patients with rheumatoid arthritis: Positive effects of interpersonal relationships. *Journal of Behavior Medicine, 28,* 91–103.

Dar, R., Leventhal, E. A., & Leventhal, H. (1993). Schematic processes in pain perception. *Cognitive Therapy and Research, 17,* 341–357.

Darbes, L. A., & Lewis, M. A. (2005). HIV-specific social predicts less sexual risk behavior in gay male couples. *Health Psychology, 24,* 617–622.

Dauvergne, M., & Turner, J. (2010). *Police-reported crime statistics in Canada, 2009.* Ottawa.

David, D. H., & Lyons-Ruth, K. (2005). Differential attachment responses of male and female infants to frightening maternal behavior: Tend or befriend versus fight or flight? *Infant Mental Health Journal, 26,* 1–18.

David, S. J. H., & Michael, J. B. (2000). Twenty years' research on peer victimization and psychosocial maladjustment: A meta-analytic review of cross-sectional studies. *Journal of Child Psychology and Psychiatry, 41,* 441–455.

Davidson, K., Hall, P., & MacGregor, M. Wm. (1996). Gender differences in the relations between interview-derived hostility scores and resting blood pressure. *Journal of Behavioral Medicine, 19,* 185–201.

Davidson, K., MacGregor, M. W., Stuhr, J., & Gidron, Y. (1999). Increasing constructive anger verbal behavior decreases resting blood pressure: A secondary analysis of a randomized controlled hostility intervention. *International Journal of Behavioral Medicine, 6,* 268–278.

Davidson, K. W., Kupfer, D. J., Bigger, J. T., Califf, R. M., Carney, R. M., Coyne, J. C., et al. (2006). Assessment and treatment of depression in patients with cardiovascular disease: National Heart, Lung, and Blood Institute Working Group Report. *Psychosomatic Medicine, 68(5),* 645–650.

Davidson, K. W., Reikmann, N., & Lesperance, F. (2004). Psychological theories of depression: Potential application for the prevention of acute coronary syndrome occurrence. *Psychosomatic Medicine, 66,* 165–173.

Davidson, R. J., Kabat-Zinn, J., Schumacher, J., Rosenkranz, M., Muller, D., Santorelli, S. F., et al. (2003). Alterations in brain and immune function produced by mindfulness meditation. *Psychosomatic Medicine, 65,* 564–570.

Davis, C. G., Lehman, D. R., Wortman, C. B., Silver, R. C., & Thompson, S. C. (1995). The undoing of traumatic life events. *Personality and Social Psychology Bulletin, 21(2),* 109–124.

Davis, C. G., Wohl, M. J. A., & Verberg, N. (2007). Profiles of posttraumatic growth following an unjust lost. *Death Studies, 31(8),* 693–712.

Davis, M., Matthews, K., & McGrath, C. (2000). Hostile attitudes predict elevated vascular resistance during interpersonal stress in men and women. *Psychosomatic Medicine, 62,* 17–25.

Davis, M. C., Matthews, K. A., Meilahn, E. N., & Kiss, J. E. (1995). Are job characteristics related to fibrinogen levels in middle-aged women? *Health Psychology, 14,* 310–318.

Davis, M. C., Twamley, E. W., Hamilton, N. A., & Swan, P. D. (1999). Body fat distribution and hemodynamic stress responses in premenopausal obese women: A preliminary study. *Health Psychology, 18,* 625–633.

de Graaf, R., & Bijl, R. V. (2002). Determinants of mental distress in adults with a severe auditory impairment: Difference between prelingual and postlingual deafness. *Psychosomatic Medicine, 64,* 61–70.

de Groot, M., Anderson, R., Freedland, K. E., Clouse, R. E., & Lustman, P. J. (2001). Association of depression and diabetes complications: A meta—analysis. *Psychosomatic Medicine, 63,* 619–630.

de Jonge, P., Latour, C., & Huyse, F. J. (2003). Implementing psychiatric interventions on a medical ward: Effects on patients' quality of life and length of hospital stay. *Psychosomatic Medicine, 65,* 997–1002.

de Moor, C., Sterner, J., Hall, M., Warneke, C., Gilani, Z., Amato, R., et al. (2002). A pilot study of the side effects of expressive writing on psychological and behavioral adjustment in patients in a phase II trial of vaccine therapy for metastatic renal cell carcinoma. *Health Psychology, 21,* 615–619.

de Moor, J. S., De Moor, C. A., Basen-Engquist, K., Kudelka, A., Bevers, M. W., & Cohen, L. (2006). Optimism, distress, health-related quality of life, and change in cancer antigen 125 among patients with ovarian cancer undergoing chemotherapy. *Psychosomatic Medicine, 68,* 555–562.

Degenhardt, L., Dierker, L., Chiu, W. T., Medina-Mora, M. E., Neumark, Y., Sampson, N., et al. (2010). Evaluating the drug use "gateway" theory using cross-national data: Consistency and associations of the order of initiation of drug use among participants in the WHO World Mental Health Surveys. *Drug and Alcohol Dependence, 108*, 84–97.

Dell, C. A., & Garabedian, K. (2003). *Canadian community epidemiology network on drug use (CCENDU): 2002 National report drug trends and the CCENDU network.* Retrieved July 18, 2007, from www.ccsa.ca/NR/rdonlyres/2982EC4F-53E3-400E-995C-C1822A0F1941/0/CCENDUNational2002e.pdf.

DeLongis, A., Coyne, J. C., Dakof, G., Folkman, S., & Lazarus, R. S. (1982). Relationship of daily hassles, uplifts, and major life events to health status. *Health Psychology, 1*, 119–136.

Denton, M., Prus, S., & Walters, V. (2004). Gender differences in health: A Canadian study of the psychosocial, structural and behavioural determinants of health. *Social Science & Medicine, 58(12)*, 2585–2600.

Deri, C. (2005). Social networks and health service utilization. *Journal of Health Economics, 24*, 1076–1107.

Dersh, J., Polatin, P. B., & Gatchel, R. J. (2002). Chronic pain and psychopathology: Research findings and theoretical considerations. *Psychosomatic Medicine, 64*, 773–786.

Detweiler, J. B., Bedell, B. T., Salovey, P., Pronin, E., & Rothman, A. J. (1999). Message framing and sunscreen use: Gain-framed messages motivate beachgoers. *Health Psychology, 18*, 189–196.

Devine, C. M., Connors, M. M., Sobal, J., & Bisogni, C. A. (2003). Sandwiching it in: Spillover of work onto food choices and family roles in low- and moderate-income urban households. *Social Science and Medicine, 56*, 617–630.

Dew, M. A., Hoch, C. C., Buysse, D. J., Monk, T. H., Begley, A. E., Houck, P. R., Hall, M., Kupfer, D. J., & Reynolds, C. F. (2003). Healthy older adults' sleep predicts all-cause mortality at 4 to 19 years of follow-up. *Psychosomatic Medicine, 65*, 63–73.

De Wit, L., Luppino, F., van Straten, A., Penninx, B., Zitman, F., & Cuijpers, P. (2010). Depression and obesity: A meta-analysis of community-based studies. *Psychiatry research, 178*, 230–235.

Dhabhar, F. S. (2009). Enhancing versus Suppressive Effects of Stress on Immune Function: Implications for Immunoprotection and Immunopathology. *Neuroimmunomodulation, 16(5)*, 300–317.

Di Giorgio, A., Hudson, M., Jerjes, W., & Cleare, A. J. (2005). 24-hour pituitary and adrenal hormone profiles in chronic fatigue syndrome. *Psychosomatic Medicine, 67*, 433–440.

Dial-A-Dietitian. (2007). *Eating guidelines for preventing gallbladder disease.* Retrieved February 2, 2008, from www.dialadietitian.ca/includes/imageserver.asp?id=930.

Dickens, C., McGowan, L., Clark-Carter, D., & Creed, F. (2002). Depression and rheumatoid arthritis: A systematic review of the literature with meta-analysis. *Psychosomatic Medicine, 64*, 52–60.

Dickens, C., McGowan, L., & Dale, S. (2003). Impact of depression on experimental pain perception: A systematic review of the literature with meta-analysis. *Psychosomatic Medicine, 65*, 369–375.

Dickerson, S. S., & Kemeny, M. E. (2004). Acute stressors and cortisol responses: A theoretical integration and synthesis of laboratory research. *Psychological Bulletin, 130*, 355–391.

Dickerson, S. S., Kemeny, M. E., Aziz, N., Kim, K. H., & Fahey, J. L. (2004). Immunological effects of induced shame and guilt. *Psychosomatic Medicine, 66*, 124–131.

Diefenbach, M. A., Leventhal, E. A., Leventhal, H., & Patrick-Miller, L. (1996). Negative affect relates to cross-sectional but not longitudinal symptom reporting: Data from elderly adults. *Health Psychology, 15*, 282–288.

Dienstbier, R. A. (1989). Arousal and physiological toughness: Implications for mental and physical health. *Psychological Review, 96*, 84–100.

Dietz, W. H. (2004). Overweight in childhood and adolescence. *New England Journal of Medicine, 350*, 855–857.

Dietz, W. H., & Gortmaker, S. L. (2001). Preventing obesity in children and adolescents. *Annual Review of Public Health, 22*, 337–353.

Dijkstra, A., & Borland, R. (2003). Residual outcome expectations and relapse in ex-smokers. *Health Psychology, 22*, 340–346.

DiLorenzo, T. A., Schnur, J., Montgomery, G. H., Erblich, J., Winkel, G., & Bovbjerg, D. H. (2006). A model of disease-specific worry in heritable disease: The influence of family history, perceived risk and worry about other illnesses. *Journal of Behavioral Medicine, 29*, 37–49.

DiMatteo, M. R. (2004). Social support and patient adherence to medical treatment: A meta-analysis. *Health Psychology, 23*, 207–218.

DiMatteo, M. R., & DiNicola, D. D. (1982). *Achieving patient compliance: The psychology of the medical practitioner's role.* New York: Pergamon Press.

DiMatteo, M. R., Giordani, P. J., Lepper, H. S., & Croghan, T. W. (2002). Patient adherence and medical treatment outcomes: A meta-analysis. *Medical Care, 40*, 794–811.

DiMatteo, M. R., Lepper, H. S., & Croghan, T. W. (2000). Depression is a risk factor for noncompliance with medical treatment. *Archives of Internal Medicine, 160*, 2101–2107.

DiMatteo, M. R., Sherbourne, C. D., Hays, R. D., Ordway, L., Kravitz, R. L., McGlynn, E. A., et al. (1993). Physicians' characteristics influence patients' adherence to medical treatment: Results from the medical outcomes study. *Health Psychology, 12*, 93–102.

Dishman, R. K., Hales, D. P., Pfeiffer, K. A., Felton, G., Saunders, R., Ward, D. S., Dowda, M. & Pate, R. R. (2006). Physical self-concept and self-esteem mediate cross-sectional relations of physical activity and sport participation with depression symptoms among adolescent girls. *Health Psychology, 25*, 396–407.

Ditto, P. H., & Hawkins, N. A. (2005). Advance directives and cancer decision making near the end of life. *Health Psychology, 24(4 suppl.)*, S63–70.

Ditto, P. H., Druley, J. A., Moore, K. A., Danks, H. J., & Smucker, W. D. (1996). Fates worse than death: The role of valued life activities in health-state evaluations. *Health Psychology, 15*, 332–343.

Ditto, P. H., Munro, G. D., Apanovich, A. M., Scepansky, J. A., & Lockhart, L. K. (2003). Spontaneous skepticism: The interplay of motivation and expectation in response to favorable and unfavorable medical diagnoses. *Personality and Social Psychology Bulletin, 29*, 1120–1132.

Ditzen, B., Neumann, I. D., Bodenmann, G., von Dawans, B., Turner, R. A., Ehlert, U., & Heinrichs, M. (2007). Effects of different kinds of couple interaction on cortisol and heart rate responses to stress in women. *Psychoneuroendocrinology, 32*, 565–574.

Dixon, K. E., Keefe, F. J., Scipio, C. D., Perri, L. M., & Abernethy, A. P. (2007). Psychological interventions for arthritis pain management in adults: A meta-analysis. *Health Psychology, 26*, 241–250.

Dobbins, T. A., Simpson, J. M., Oldenburg, B., Owen, N., & Harris, D. (1998). Who comes to a workplace health risk assessment? *International Journal of Behavioral Medicine, 5*, 323–334.

Dobkin, P. L., Da Costa, D., Abrahamowicz, M., Dritsa, M., Du Berger, R., Fitzcharles, M. A., et al. (2006). Adherence During an Individualized Home Based 12-Week Exercise Program in Women with Fibromyalgia. *The Journal of Rheumatology, 33*, 333–341.

Dobkin, P. L., et al. (2002). Counterbalancing patient demands with evidence: Results from a Pan-Canadian randomized clinical trial of brief supportive—expressive group psychotherapy for women with systemic lupus erythematosus. *Annals of Behavioral Medicine, 24*, 88–99.

Doering, S., Katzlberger, F., Rumpold, G., Roessler, S., Hofstoetter, B., Schatz, D. S., et al. (2000). Videotape preparation of patients before hip replacement surgery reduces stress. *Psychosomatic Medicine, 62*, 365–373.

Doll, J., & Orth, B. (1993). The Fishbein and Ajzen theory of reasoned action applied to contraceptive behavior: Model variants and meaningfulness. *Journal of Applied Social Psychology, 23*, 341–395.

Dominiczak, A. F., & Munroe, P. B. (2010). Genome-Wide Association Studies Will Unlock the Genetic Basis of Hypertension: Pro Side of the Argument. *Hypertension, 56*, 1017–1020.

Donoho, C. J., Weigensberg, M. J., Emken, B. A., Hsu, J.-W., & Spruijt-Metz, D. (2011). Stress and Abdominal Fat: Preliminary Evidence of Moderation by the Cortisol Awakening Response in Hispanic Peripubertal Girls. *Obesity, 19*, 946–952.

Doshi, A., Patrick, K., Sallis, J. F., & Calfas, K. (2003). Evaluation of physical activity web sites for use of behavior change theories. *Annals of Behavioral Medicine, 25*, 105–111.

Downey, G., Silver, R. C., & Wortman, C. B. (1990). Reconsidering the attribution-adjustment relation following a major negative event: Coping with the loss of a child. *Journal of Personality and Social Psychology, 59,* 925–940.

Downing-Matibag, T. M., & Geisinger, B. (2009). Hooking Up and Sexual Risk Taking Among College Students: A Health Belief Model Perspective. *Qualitative Health Research, 19,* 1196–1209.

Dracup, K. (1985). A controlled trial of couples' group counseling in cardiac rehabilitation. *Journal of Cardiopulmonary Rehabilitation, 5,* 436–442.

Dracup, K., & Moser, D. (1991). Treatment-seeking behavior among those with signs and symptoms of acute myocardial infarction. *Heart and Lung, 20,* 570–575.

Droge, D., Arntson, P., & Norton, R. (1986). The social support function in epilepsy self-help groups. *Small Group Behavior, 17,* 139–163.

Droomers, M., Schrijivers, C. T. M., & Mackenbach, J. P. (2002). Why do lower educated people continue smoking? Explanations from the longitudinal GLOBE study. *Health Psychology, 21,* 263–272.

Drossman, D. A., Leserman, J., Li, Z., Keefe, F., Hu, Y. J. B., & Toomey, T. C. (2000). Effects of coping on health outcome among women with gastrointestinal disorders. *Psychosomatic Medicine, 62,* 309–317.

Duarte-Franco, E., & Franco, E. L. (2004). Other gynecologic cancers: Endometrial, ovarian, vulvar and vaginal cancers. *BMC Women's Health 2004, 4 (Suppl 1):* S14. Retrieved July 17, 2007, from www.biomedcentral.com/1472-6874/4/S1/S14.

Duenwald, M. (2002, September 17). Students find another staple of campus life: Stress. *The New York Times,* p. F 5.

Duff, R. S., & Hollingshead, A. B. (1968). *Sickness and society.* New York: Harper & Row.

DuHamel, K. N., Manne, S., Nereo, N., Ostroff, J., Martini, R., Parsons, S., et al. (2004). Cognitive processing among mothers of children undergoing bone marrow/stem cell transplantation. *Psychosomatic Medicine, 66,* 92–103.

Duits, A. A., Boeke, S., Taams, M. A., Passchier, J., & Erdman, R. A. M. (1997). Prediction of quality of life after coronary artery bypass graft surgery: A review and evaluation of multiple, recent studies. *Psychosomatic Medicine, 59,* 257–268.

Dunbar, F. (1943). *Psychosomatic diagnosis.* New York: Hoeber.

Duncan, S. C., Duncan, T. E., Strycker, L. A., & Chaumeton, N. R. (2002). Relations between youth antisocial and prosocial activities. *Journal of Behavioral Medicine, 25,* 425–438.

Duncan, T. E., Duncan, S. C., Beauchamp, N., Wells, J., & Ary, D. V. (2000). Development and evaluation of an interactive CD-ROM refusal skills program to prevent youth substance use: "Refuse to use." *Journal of Behavioral Medicine, 23,* 59–72.

Dunkel-Schetter, C., Feinstein, L. G., Taylor, S. E., & Falke, R. L. (1992). Patterns of coping with cancer. *Health Psychology, 11,* 79–87.

Dusek, J. A., Hibberd, P. L., Buczynski, B., Chang, B.-H., Dusek, K. C., Johnston, J. M., et al. (2008). Stress management versus lifestyle modification on systolic hypertension and medication elimination: a randomized trial. *Journal of Alternative and Complementary Medicine, 14,* 129–138.

Duxbury, T., & Higgins, C. (2001). *The 2001 national work-life conflict study: Report One.* Health Canada, Ottawa.

Dying with Dignity Canada, *The Voice,* 27(1), p. 3, (2011, February), "Youth: A Fountain of Hope" by Anonymous. Accessed October 1, 2011 from http://www.dyingwithdignity.ca/database/rte/files/Feb%202011.pdf.

Eakin, E., Reeves, M., Marshall, A., Dunstan, D., Graves, N., Healy, G., et al. (2010). Living Well with Diabetes: a randomized controlled trial of a telephone-delivered intervention for maintenance of weight loss, physical activity and glycaemic control in adults with type 2 diabetes. *BMC Public Health, 10,* 452.

Earl, L. (2004). Health information and Internet use. *Innovation Analysis Bulletin, 6(3),* 9–10 (Statistics Canada Catalogue 88-003 XIE). Retrieved July 26, 2007, from www.statcan.ca/english/freepub/88-003-XIE/88-003-XIE2004003.pdf.

Edwards, C. J., Syddall, H., Goswami, R., Goswami, P., Dennison, E., Arden, N., et al. (2007). Rheumatoid factor may be an independent risk factor for ischaemic heart disease. *Heart, 93,* 1263–1267.

Edwards, R., Telfair, J., Cecil, H., & Lenoci, J. (2001). Self-efficacy as a predictor of adult adjustment to sickle cell disease: One-year outcomes. *Psychosomatic Medicine, 63,* 850–851.

Edwards, S., Hucklebridge, F., Clow, A., & Evans, P. (2003). Components of the diurnal cortisol cycle in relation to upper respiratory symptoms and perceived stress. *Psychosomatic Medicine, 65,* 320–327.

Egede, L. E. (2005). Effect of comorbid chronic diseases on prevalence and odds of depression in adults with diabetes. *Psychosomatic Medicine, 67,* 46–51.

Eifert, G. H., Hodson, S. E., Tracey, D. R., Seville, J. L., & Gunawardane, K. (1996). Heart-focused anxiety, illness beliefs, and behavioral impairment: Comparing healthy heart-anxious patients with cardiac and surgical inpatients. *Journal of Behavioral Medicine, 19,* 385–400.

Ekkekakis, P., Hall, E. E., VanLanduyt, L. M., & Petruzzello, S. J. (2000). Walking in (affective) circles: Can short walks enhance affect? *Journal of Behavioral Medicine, 23,* 245–275.

Ekstedt, M., Åkerstedt, T., & Söderström, M. (2004). Microarousals during sleep are associated with increased levels of lipids, cortisol, and blood pressure. *Psychosomatic Medicine, 66,* 925–931.

Elder, J. P., Sallis, J. F., Woodruff, S. I., & Wildey, M. B. (1993). Tobacco-refusal skills and tobacco use among high-risk adolescents. *Journal of Behavioral Medicine, 16,* 629–642.

Elgar, K., & Chester, A. (2007). The mental health implications of maternal employment: Working versus at-home mothering identities. *Advances in Mental Health, 6,* 47–55.

Elhai, J. D., Richardson, J. D., & Pedlar, D. J. (2007). Predictors of general medical and psychological treatment use among a national sample of peacekeeping veterans with health problems. *Journal of Anxiety Disorders, 21(4),* 580–589.

Elkins, G., Jensen, M. P., & Patterson, D. R. (2007). Hypnotherapy for the Management of Chronic Pain. *International Journal of Clinical and Experimental Hypnosis, 55(3),* 275–287.

Ellickson, P. L., Bird, C. E., Orlando, M., Klein, D. J., & McCaffrey, D. F. (2003). Social context and adolescent health behavior: Does school-level smoking prevalence affect students' subsequent smoking behavior? *Journal of Health and Social Behavior, 44,* 525–535.

Ellington, L., & Wiebe, D. (1999). Neuroticism, symptom presentation, and medical decision making. *Health Psychology, 18,* 634–643.

Ellison, L. F., & Wilkins, K. (2010, September). Component of Statistics Canada Catalogue no. 82-003-X, *Health Reports.*

Elmore, J. G., & Gigerenzer, G. (2005). Benign breast disease: The risks of communicating risk. *The New England Journal of Medicine, 353,* 297–299.

Elovainio, M., Keltikangas-Järvinen, L., Kivimäki, M., Pulkki, L., Puttonen, S., Heponiemi, T., Juonala, M., Viikari, J. S., & Raitakari, O. T. (2005). Depressive symptoms and carotid artery intima-media thickness in young adults: The cardiovascular risk in young Finns study. *Psychosomatic Medicine, 67,* 561–567.

Emerson, S. U., & Purcell, R. H. (2004). Running like water- The omnipresence of Hepatitis E. *The New England Journal of Medicine, 351,* 2367–2368.

Emery, C. F., Frid, D. J., Engebretson, T. O., Alonzo, A. A., Fish, A., Ferketich, A. K., et al. (2004). Gender differences in quality of life among cardiac patients. *Psychosomatic Medicine, 66,* 190–197.

Emery, C. F., Kiecolt-Glaser, J. K., Glaser, R., Malarkey, W. B., & Frid, D. J. (2005). Exercise accelerates wound healing among healthy older adults: A preliminary investigation. *Journal of Gerontology: Medical Sciences, 60A,* 1432–1436.

Emery, C. F., Schein, R. L., Hauck, E. R., & MacIntyre, N. R. (1998). Psychological and cognitive outcomes of a randomized trial of exercise among patients with chronic obstructive pulmonary disease. *Health Psychology, 17,* 232–240.

Emery, C. F., Shermer, R. L., Hauck, E. R., Hsaio, E. T., & MacIntyre, N. R. (2003). Cognitive and psychological outcomes of exercise in a 1-year follow-up study of patients with chronic obstructive pulmonary disease. *Health Psychology, 22,* 598–604.

Eng, P. M., Fitzmaurice, G., Kubansky, L. D., Rimm, E. B., & Kawachi, I. (2003). Anger in expression and risk of stroke and coronary heart disease among male health professionals. *Psychosomatic Medicine, 65,* 100–110.

Engel, B. T. (1986). Psychosomatic medicine, behavioral medicine, just plain medicine. *Psychosomatic Medicine, 48,* 466–479.

Engler, P., Anderson, B., Herman, D., Bishop, D., Miller, I., Pirraglia, P., Hayaki, J., & Stein, M. (2006). Coping and burden among HIV caregivers. *Psychosomatic Medicine, 68,* 985–992.

Enright, M. F., Resnick, R., DeLeon, P. H., Sciara, A. D., & Tanney, F. (1990). The practice of psychology in hospital settings. *American Psychologist, 45,* 1059–1065.

Epel, E. S., McEwen, B., Seeman, T., Matthews, K., Catellazzo, G., Brownell, K., et al. (2000). Stress and body shape: Stress-induced cortisol secretion is consistently greater among women with central fat. *Psychosomatic Medicine, 62,* 623–632.

Epp, J. (1986). Achieving health for all. *Health Promotion International, 1*(4), 419–428.

Epping-Jordan, J., Williams, R., Pruitt, S., Patterson, T., Grant, I., Wahlgren, D., et al. (1998). Transition to chronic pain in men with low back pain: Predictive relationships among pain intensity, disability, and depressive symptoms. *Health Psychology, 17,* 421–427.

Epstein, E. M., Sloan, D. M., & Marx, B. P. (2005). Getting to the heart of the matter: Written disclosure, gender, and heart rate. *Psychosomatic Medicine, 67,* 413–419.

Epstein, L. H., Paluch, R. A., Roemmich, J. N., & Beecher, M. D. (2007). Family-Based Obesity Treatment, Then and Now: Twenty-Five Years of Pediatric Obesity Treatment. *Health Psychology, 26,* 381–391.

Epstein, L. H., Valoski, A., Wing, R. R., & McCurley, J. (1994). Ten-year outcomes of behavioral family-based treatment for childhood obesity. *Health Psychology, 13,* 373–383.

Epstein, S., & Katz, L. (1992). Coping ability, stress, productive load, and symptoms. *Journal of Personality and Social Psychology, 62,* 813–825.

Erickson, K. I., & Kramer, A. F. (2009). Aerobic exercise effects on cognitive and neural plasticity in older adults. *British Journal of Sports Medicine, 43,* 22–24.

Esmail, N. (2006). *Canada's physician shortage: Effects, projections, and solutions.* Retrieved August 7, 2007, from the Fraser Institute Web site: www.fraserinstitute.org/commerce.web/publication_details.aspx?pubID=3147.

Esmail, N. (2007). Complementary and alternative medicine in Canada: Trends in use and public attitudes, 1997–2006. *Public Policy Sourcers, 87,* 1–53. Retrieved August 24, 2007, from www.fraserinstitute.org/Commerce.web/product_files/Altmedicine.pdf.

Esmail, N., & Walker, M. (2005). How good is Canadian health care? 2005 Report. *Critical Issues Bulletin.* Retrieved August 7, 2007, from the Fraser Institute Web site: www.cimca.ca/reports/How%20Good%20is%20Canadian%20Health%20Care%20(2005)%20Fraser%20Institute.pdf.

Esposito-Del Puente, A., Lillioja, S., Bogardus, C., McCubbin, J. A., Feinglos, M. N., Kuhn, C. M., et al. (1994). Glycemic response to stress is altered in euglycemic Pima Indians. *International Journal of Obesity, 18,* 766–770.

Estabrooks, P. A., Lee, R. E., & Gyurcsik, N. C. (2003). Resources for physical activity participation: Does availability and accessibility differ by neighborhood socioeconomic status? *Annals of Behavioral Medicine, 25,* 100–104.

Esterling, B. A., Kiecolt-Glaser, J. K., & Glaser, R. (1996). Psychosocial modulation of cytokine-induced natural killer cell activity in older adults. *Psychosomatic Medicine, 58,* 264–272.

Esterling, B. A., Kiecolt-Glaser, J. K., Bodnar, J. C., & Glaser, R. (1994). Chronic stress, social support, and persistent alterations in the natural killer cell response to cytokines in older adults. *Health Psychology, 13,* 291–298.

Evans, G. W., & Kantrowitz, E. (2001). *Socioeconomic status and health: The potential role of suboptimal physical environments.* John D. and Catherine T. MacArthur Research Network on Socioeconomic Status and Health. Retrieved from: http://www.macses.ucsf.edu.

Evans, R. I., Dratt, L. M., Raines, B. E., & Rosenberg, S. S. (1988). Social influences on smoking initiation: Importance of distinguishing descriptive versus mediating process variables. *Journal of Applied Social Psychology, 18,* 925–943.

Evans, W. D., Powers, A., Hersey, J., & Renaud, J. (2006). The influence of social environment and social image on adolescent smoking. *Health Psychology, 25*(1), 26–33.

Evenson, B. (2003). Is SARS with us for good? *National Post,* April 5, 2003.

Everson, S. A., Goldberg, D. E., Kaplan, G. A., Cohen, R. D., Pukkala, E., Tuomilehto, J., et al. (1996). Hopelessness and risk of mortality and incidence of myocardial infarction and cancer. *Psychosomatic Medicine, 58,* 113–121.

Ewart, C. K. (1991). Familial transmission of essential hypertension: Genes, environments, and chronic anger. *Annals of Behavioral Medicine, 13,* 40–47.

Ewart, C. K., & Jorgensen, R. S. (2004). Agonistic interpersonal striving: Social—cognitive mechanism of cardiovascular risk in youth? *Health Psychology, 23,* 75–85.

Ewart, C. K., & Suchday, S. (2002). Discovering how urban poverty and violence affect health: Development and validation of a neighborhood stress index. *Health Psychology, 21,* 254–262.

Fagan, J., Galea, S., Ahern, J., Bonner, S., & Vlahov, D. (2003). Relationship of self-reported asthma severity and urgent health care utilization to psychological seguelae of the September 11, 2001, terrorist attacks on the world trade center among New York City area residents. *Psychosomatic Medicine, 65,* 993–996.

Fahrenwald, N. L., Atwood, J. R., Walker, S. N., Johnson, D. R., & Berg, K. (2004). A randomized pilot test of "moms on the move": A physical activity intervention on WIC mothers. *Annals of Behavioral Medicine, 27,* 82–90.

Fang, C. Y., Daly, M. B., Miller, S. M., Zerr, T., Malick, J., & Engstrom, P. (2006). Coping with ovarian cancer risk: The moderating effects of perceived control on coping and adjustment. *British Journal of Health Psychology, 11*(4), 561–580.

Faresjö, Å., Anastasiou, F., Lionis, C., Johansson, S., Wallander, M.-A., & Faresjö, T. (2006). Health-related quality of life of irritable bowel syndrome patients in different cultural settings. *Health and Quality of Life Outcomes, 4,* 1–7.

Fautrel, B., Adam, V., St. Pierre, Y., Joseph, L., Clark, A. E., & Penrod, J. R. (2002). Use of complementary and alternative therapies by patients self-reporting arthritis or rheumatism: Results from a nationwide Canadian survey. *The Journal of Rheumatology, 29,* 2435–2441.

Fawzy, F. I., et al. (1993). Malignant melanoma: Effects of an early structured psychiatric intervention, coping, and affective state on recurrence and survival six years later. *Archives of General Psychiatry, 9,* 681–689.

Fawzy, F. I., Kemeny, M. E., Fawzy, M. W., Elashoff, R., Morton, D., Cousins, N., et al. (1990). A structured psychiatric intervention for cancer patients, II: Changes over time in immunological measures. *Archives of General Psychiatry, 47,* 729–735.

Feather, N. T. (1982). Human values and the prediction of action: An expectancy-valence analysis. In N. T. Feather (Ed.), *Expectations and actions: Expectancy-value models in psychology.* (pp. 263–289). Hillsdale, NJ: Erlbaum.

Feldman, P. E. (1956). The personal element in psychiatric research. *American Journal of Psychiatry, 113,* 52–54.

Feldman, P. J., & Steptoe, A. (2004). How neighborhoods and physical functioning are related: The roles of neighborhood socioeconomic status, perceived neighborhood strain, and individual health risk factors. *Annals of Behavioral Medicine, 27,* 91–99.

Feldman, P., Cohen, S., Doyle, W., Skoner, D., & Gwaltney, J. (1999). The impact of personality on the reporting of unfounded symptoms and illness. *Journal of Personality and Social Psychology, 77,* 370–378.

Feldstein, A. C., Perrin, N., Rosales, A. G., Schneider, J., Rix, M. M., Keels, K., et al. (2009). Effect of a Multimodal Reminder Program on Repeat Mammogram Screening. *American journal of preventive medicine, 37,* 94–101.

Felgoise, S. (2005). History of Behavioral Medicine *Encyclopedia of Cognitive Behavior Therapy* (pp. 209–214).

Felitti, V. J., Anda, R. F., Nordenberg, D., Williamson, D. F., Apitz, A. M., Edwards, V., et al. (1998). Relationship of childhood abuse and household dysfunction to many of the leading causes of death in adults. *American Journal of Preventive Medicine, 14,* 245–258.

Felton, B. J., & Revenson, T. A. (1984). Coping with chronic illness: A study of illness controllability and the influence of coping strategies on psychological adjustment. *Journal of Consulting and Clinical Psychology, 52,* 343–353.

Fernandez, E., & Turk, D. C. (1992). Sensory and affective components of pain: Separation and synthesis. *Psychological Bulletin, 112,* 205–217.

Fichten, C. S., Libman, E., Creti, L., Balles, S., & Sabourin, S. (2004). Long sleepers sleep more and short sleepers sleep less: A comparison of older adults who sleep well. *Behavioral Sleep Medicine, 2,* 2–23.

Fielding, J. E. (1978). Successes of prevention. *Milbank Memorial Fund Quarterly, 56,* 274–302.

Fife, B. L., & Wright, E. R. (2000). The dimensionality of stigma: A comparison of its impact on the self of persons with HIV/AIDS and cancer. *Journal of Health and Social Behavior, 41*, 50–67.

Fifield, J., McQuinlan, J., Tennen, H., Sheehan, T. J., Reisine, S., Hesselbrock, V., et al. (2001). History of affective disorder and the temporal trajectory of fatigue in rheumatoid arthritis. *Annals of Behavioral Medicine, 23*, 34–41.

Fiissel, D. L., & Lafreniere, K. D. (2006). Weight control motives for cigarette smoking: Further consequences of the sexual objectification of women? *Feminism and Psychology, 16(3)*, 327–344.

Findley, J. C., Kerns, R., Weinberg, L. D., & Rosenberg, R. (1998). Self-efficacy as a psychological moderator of chronic fatigue syndrome. *Journal of Behavioral Medicine, 21*, 351–362.

Findley, L. C. (2011). Physical activity among First Nations people off reserve, Métis and Inuit. *Health Reports*, 22 (1), Statistics Canada, Catalogue no. 82-003-XPE. Accessed April 14, 2011 from http://www.statcan.gc.ca/pub/82-003-x/2011001/article/11403-eng.pdf.

Findley, T. (1953). The placebo and the physician. *Medical Clinics of North America, 37*, 1821–1826.

Fink, G. (2011). Stress Controversies: Post-Traumatic Stress Disorder, Hippocampal Volume, Gastroduodenal Ulceration*. Journal of Neuroendocrinology, 23, 107–117.

Fink, P., Toft, T., Hansen, M. S., Ornbol, E., & Olesen, F. (2007). Symptoms and syndromes of bodily distress: An exploratory study of 978 internal medical, neurological, and primary care patients. *Psychosomatic Medicine, 69*, 30–39.

Finkelstein, D., Kubzansky, L, Capitman, J., & Goodman, E. (2007). Socioeconomic differences in adolescent stress: The role of psychological resources. *Journal of Adolescent Health, 40(2)*, 127–134.

Firestein, G. S. (2003, May 15). Evolving concepts of rheumatoid arthritis. N*ature, 423*, 356–361.

Fishbain, D., Cutler, R., Rosomoff, H., & Rosomoff, R. (1998). Do antidepressants have an analgesic effect in psychogenic pain and somatoform pain disorder? A meta-analysis. *Psychosomatic Medicine, 60*, 503–509.

Fishbein, M. (1967). Attitude and the prediction of behavior. In M. Fishbein (Ed.), *Readings in attitude theory and measurement*. New York: Wiley.

Fishbein, M., & Ajzen, I. (1975). *Belief, attitude, intention, and behavior: An introduction to theory and research*. Reading, MA: Addison-Wesley.

Fisher, J. D., Fisher, W. A., Bryan, A. D., & Misovich, S. J. (2002). Information-motivation-behavioral skills model-based HIV risk behavior change intervention for inner-city high school youth. *Health Psychology, 21*, 177–186.

Fisher, L., Soubhi, H., Mansi, O., Paradis, G., Gauvin, L., & Potvin, L. (1998). Family process in health research: Extending a family typology to a new cultural context. *Health Psychology, 17*, 358–366.

Fitzgerald, S. T., Haythornthwaite, J. A., Suchday, S., & Ewart, C. K. (2003). Anger in young black and white workers: Effects of job control, dissatisfaction, and support. *Journal of Behavioral Medicine, 26*, 283–296.

Fitzgerald, T. E., Tennen, H., Affleck, G., & Pransky, G. S. (1993). The relative importance of dispositional optimism and control appraisals in quality of life after coronary artery bypass surgery. *Journal of Behavioral Medicine, 16*, 25–43.

Fitzgibbon, M. L., Stolley, M. R., & Kirschenbaum, D. S. (1993). Obese people who seek treatment have different characteristics than those who do not seek treatment. *Health Psychology, 12*, 342–345.

Flensborg-Madsen, T., Bay von Scholten, M., Flachs, E. M., Mortensen, E. L., Prescott, E., & Tolstrup, J. S. (2011). Tobacco smoking as a risk factor for depression. A 26-year population-based follow-up study. *Journal of Psychiatric Research, 45*, 143–149.

Fletcher, K. E., Clemow, L., Peterson, B. A., Lemon, S. C., Estabrook, B., & Zapka, J. G. (2006). A path analysis of factors associated with distress among first-degree female relatives of women with breast cancer diagnosis. *Health Psychology, 25*, 413–425.

Flett, G. L., Blankstein, K. R., & Martin, T. R. (1995). Procrastination, negative self-evaluation, and stress in depression and anxiety: A review and preliminary model.

In J. R. Ferrari, J. H. Johnson & W. G. McCown (Eds.), *Procrastination, and task avoidance: Theory, research, and treatment* (pp. 137–167). New York: Plenum.

Flett, G. L., Hewitt, P. L., Blankstein, K. R., & Gray, L. (1998). Psychological distress and the frequency of perfectionistic thinking. *Journal of Personality & Social Psychology, 75*, 1363–1381.

Flett, G. L., Madorsky, D., Hewitt, P. L., & Heisel, M. J. (2002). Perfectionism cognitions, rumination, and psychological distress. *Journal of Rational-Emotive & Cognitive Behavior Therapy, 20*, 33–47.

Flink, I. K., Mroczek, M. Z., Sullivan, M. J. L., & Linton, S. J. (2009). Pain in childbirth and postpartum recovery The role of catastrophizing. *European journal of pain (London, England), 13*, 312–316.

Flor, H., Birbaumer, N., & Turk, D. C. (1990). The psychology of chronic pain. *Advances in Behavior Research and Therapy, 12*, 47–84.

Focht, B. C., Ewing, V., Gauvin, L., & Rejeski, W. J. (2002). The unique and transient impact of exercise on pain perception in older, overweight, or obese adults with knee osteoarthritis. *Annals of Behavioral Medicine, 24*, 201–210.

Fogarty, A. S., Zablotska, I., Rawstorne, P., Prestage, G., & Kippax, S. C. (2007). Factors distiguishing employed from unemployed people in the Positive Health Study. *AIDS, 21*, S37–S42.

Fogel, J., Albert, S. M., Schnabel, F., Ditkoff, B. A., & Neuget, A. I. (2002). Internet use and support in women with breast cancer. *Health Psychology, 21*, 398–404.

Folkman, S., & Lazarus, R. S. (1980). An analysis of coping in a middle-aged community sample. *Journal of Health and Social Behavior, 21*, 219–239.

Folkman, S., & Moskowitz, J. T. (2004). Coping: Pitfalls and promise. *Annual Review of Psychology, 55*, 745–774.

Folkman, S., Schaefer, C., & Lazarus, R. S. (1979). Cognitive processes as mediators of stress and coping. In V. Hamilton & D. M. Warburton (Eds.), *Human stress and cognition: An information processing approach* (pp. 265–298). London, England: Wiley.

Foltz, V., St Pierre, Y., Rozenberg, S., Rossignol, M., Bourgeois, P., Joseph, L., Adam, V., Penrod, J. R., Clarke, A. E., & Fautrel, B. (2005). Use of complementary and alternative therapies by patients with self reported chronic back pain: A nationwide survey in Canada. *Joint Bone Spine, 72(6)*, 571–577.

Ford, J. D., Campbell, K. A., Storzbach, D., Binder, L. M., Anger, W. K., & Rohlman, D. S. (2001). Posttraumatic stress symptomatology is associated with unexplained illness attributed to Persian Gulf War military service. *Psychosomatic Medicine, 63*, 842–849.

Fors, E. A., Sexton, H., & Götestam, K. G. (2002). The effect of guided imagery and amitriptyline on daily fibromyalgia pain: a prospective, randomized, controlled trial. *Journal of Psychiatric Research, 36*(3), 179–187.

Forsyth, A. D., & Carey, M. P. (1998). Measuring self-efficacy in the context of HIV risk reduction: Research challenges and recommendations. *Health Psychology, 6*, 559–568.

Foster, G. D., Wadden, T. A., & Vogt, R. A. (1997). Body image in obese women before, during, and after weight loss treatment. *Health Psychology, 16*, 226–229.

Fountoulakis, K. N., Siamouli, M., Magiria, S., & Kaprinis, G. (2008). Late-life depression, religiosity, cerebrovascular disease, cognitive impairment and attitudes towards death in the elderly: Interpreting the data. *Medical hypotheses, 70*, 493–496.

Frankenberg, E., & Jones, N. R. (2004). Self-rated health and mortality: Does the relationship extend to a low income setting? *Journal of Health and Social Behavior, 45*, 441–452.

Frankenhaeuser, M. (1991). The psychophysiology of workload, stress, and health: Comparison between the sexes. *Annals of Behavioral Medicine, 13*, 197–204.

Frankish, C. J., Green, L. W., Ratner, P. A., Chomik, T., & Larsen, C. (1996). *Health impact assessment as a tool for population health promotion and public policy*. Retrieved January 26, 2008, from www.phac-aspc.gc.ca/ph-sp/phdd/impact.

Franko, D. L., Mintz, L. B., Villapiano, M., Green, T. C., Mainelli, D., Folensbee, L., Butler, S. F., Davidson, M. M., Hamilton, E., Little, D., Kearns, M., & Budman, S.H. (2005). Food, mood, and attitude: Reducing risk for eating disorder in college women. *Health Psychology, 24*, 567–578.

Fredrickson, B. L., Maynard, K. E., Helms, M. J., Haney, T. L., Siegler, I. C., & Barefoot, J. C. (2000). Hostility predicts magnitude and duration of blood pressure response to anger. *Journal of Behavioral Medicine, 23*, 229–243.

Fredrickson, B. L., Tugade, M. M., Waugh, C. E. & Larkin, G. R. (2003). What good are positive emotions in crises? A prospective study of resilience and emotions following the terrorist attacks on the United States on September 11th, 2001. *Journal of Personality and Social Psychology, 84,* 365–376.

Freedland, K. E., Rich, M. W., Skala, J. A., Carney, R. M., Davila-Roman, V. G., & Jaffe, A. S. (2003). Prevalence of depression in hospitalized patients with congestive heart failure. *Psychosomatic Medicine, 65,* 119–128.

Freedman, V. A. (1993). Kin and nursing home lengths of stay: A backward recurrence time approach. *Journal of Health and Social Behavior, 34,* 138–152.

Freidson, E. (1960). Client control and medical practice. *American Journal of Sociology, 65,* 374–382.

Friedlander, L. J., Reid, G. J., Shupak, N., & Cribbie, R. (2007). Social support, self-esteem, and stress as predictors of adjustment to university among first-year undergraduates. *Journal of College Student Development, 48(3),* 259–274.

Friedman, H. S., Tucker, J. S., Tomlinson-Keasey, C., Schwartz, J. E., Wingard, D. L., & Criqui, M. H. (1993). Does childhood personality predict longevity? *Journal of Personality and Social Psychology, 65,* 176–185.

Friedman, H. S., & Booth-Kewley, S. (1987). The "disease-prone" personality: A meta-analytic view of the construct. *American Psychologist, 42,* 539–555.

Friedman, H. S., Tucker, J. S., Schwartz, J. E., Martin, L. R., Tomlinson-Keasey, C., Wingard, D. L., et al. (1995a). Childhood conscientiousness and longevity: Health behaviors and cause of death. *Journal of Personality and Social Psychology, 68,* 696–703.

Friedman, H. S., Tucker, J. S., Schwartz, J. E., Tomlinson-Keasey, C., Martin, L. R., Wingard, D. L., et al. (1995b). Psychosocial and behavioral predictors of longevity: The aging and death of the "Termites." *American Psychologist, 50,* 69–78.

Friedrich, M. J. (2008). Exercise May Boost Aging Immune System. *JAMA: The Journal of the American Medical Association, 299,* 160–161.

Fritz, H. L. (2000). Gender-linked personality traits predict mental health and functional status following a first coronary event. *Health Psychology, 19,* 420–428.

Fromm, K., Andrykowski, M. A., & Hunt, J. (1996). Positive and negative psychosocial sequelae of bone marrow transplantation: Implications for quality of life assessment. *Journal of Behavioral Medicine, 19,* 221–240.

Frostholm, L., Fink, P., Christensen, K. S., Toft, T., Oernboel, E., Olesen, F., & Weinman, J. (2005). The patients' illness perceptions and the use of primary health care. *Psychosomatic Medicine, 67,* 997–1005.

Fry, P. S., & Debats, D. L. (2009). Perfectionism and the five-factor personality traits as predictors of mortality in older adults. *Journal of Health Psychology, 14,* 513–524.

Fucito, L. M., & Juliano, L. M. (2009). Depression moderates smoking behavior in response to a sad mood induction. *Psychology of Addictive Behaviors, 23,* 546–551.

Fukuda, H., Ichinose, T., Kusama, T., Yoshidome, A., Anndow, K., Akiyoshi, N., et al. (2008). The Relationship Between Job Stress and Urinary Cytokines in Healthy Nurses: A Cross-Sectional Study. *Biological Research For Nursing, 10,* 183–191.

Fuller, R. K., & Hiller-Strumhofel, S. (1999). Alcoholism treatment in the United States. An overview. *Alcohol research and health. Journal of the National Institute on Alcohol Abuse and Alcoholism 23,* 69–77.

Fuller-Thomson, E., Bottoms, J., Brennenstuhl, S., & Hurd, M. (2011). Is Childhood Physical Abuse Associated With Peptic Ulcer Disease? Findings From a Population-Based Study. *Journal of Interpersonal Violence.*

Fung, T. T., Willett, W. C., Stampfer, M. J., Manson, J. E., & Hu, F. B. (2001). Dietary patterns and the risk of coronary heart disease in women. *Archives of Internal Medicine, 161,* 1857–1862.

Fyrand, L., Moum, T., Finset, A., & Glennas, A. (2002). The impact of disability and disease duration on social support of women with rheumatoid arthritis. *Journal of Behavioral Medicine, 25,* 251–268.

Gaab, J., Hüster, D., Peisen, R., Engert, V., Schad, T., Schürmeyer, T. H., et al. (2002). Low-dose dexamethasone suppression test in chronic fatigue syndrome and health. *Psychosomatic Medicine, 64,* 311–318.

Gahagan, J., Rehman, L., Barbour, L., & McWilliam, S. (2007). The preliminary findings of a study exploring the perceptions of a sample of young heterosexual males regarding HIV prevention education programming in Nova Scotia, Canada. *Journal of HIV/AIDS Prevention in Children & Youth, 8(1),* 135–153.

Gallacher, J. E. J., Yarnell, J. W. G., Sweetnam, P. M., Elwood, P. C., & Stansfeld, S. A. (1999). Anger and incident heart disease in the Caerphilly study. *Psychosomatic Medicine, 61,* 446–453.

Gallo, L. C., & Matthews, K. A. (2006). Adolescents' attachment orientation influences ambulatory blood pressure responses to everyday social interactions. *Psychosomatic Medicine, 68,* 253–261.

Gallo, L. C., Troxel W. M., Kuller, L. H., Sutton-Tyrell, K., Edmundowicz, D., & Matthews, K. A. (2003a). Marital status, marital quality and atherosclerotic burden in postmenopausal women. *Psychosomatic Medicine, 65,* 952–962.

Gallo, L. C., Troxel, W. M., Matthews, K. A., Jansen-McWilliams, L., Kuller, L. H., & Sutton-Tyrell, K. (2003b). Occupation and subclinical carotid artery disease in women: Are clerical workers at greater risk? *Health Psychology, 22,* 19–29.

Garcia-Linares, M. I., Sanchez-Lorente, S., Coe, C. L., & Martinez, M. (2004). Intimate male partner violence impairs immune control over herpes simplex virus type 1 in physically and psychologically abused women. *Psychosomatic Medicine, 66,* 965–972.

Garrett, V. D., Brantley, P. J., Jones, G. N., & McKnight, G. T. (1991). The relation between daily stress and Crohn's disease. *Journal of Behavioral Medicine, 14,* 87–96.

Garriguet, D. (2004). *Overview of Canadians' eating habits, 2004.* Statistics Canada Catalogue 82-620. Retrieved August 2, 2007, from www.statcan.ca/english/research/82-620-MIE/82-620-MIE2006002.pdf.

Garriguet, D. (2008). Obesity and the eating habits of the Aboriginal population. *Health Reports, 19(1),* 21–35 (Statistics Canada Catalogue 82-003). Retrieved March 4, 2008, from www.statcan.ca/english/freepub/82-003-XIE/82-003-XIE2008001.pdf.

Gatchel, R. J., Robinson, R. C., Pulliam, C., & Maddrey, A. M. (2003). Biofeedback with pain patients: evidence for its effectiveness. *Seminars in Pain Medicine, 1(2),* 55-66.

Gauderman, W. J., Avol, E., Gilliland, F., Vora, H., Thomas, D., Berhane, K., McConnell, R., Kuenzli, N., Lurmann, F., Rappaport, E., Margolis, H., Bates, D., & Peters, J. (2004). The effect of air pollution on lung development from 10 to 18 years of age. *The New England Journal of Medicine, 351,* 1057–1067.

Gaughan, M. (2006). The gender structure of adolescent peer influence on drinking. *Journal of Health and Social Behavior, 47(1),* 47–61.

Geers, A. L., Helfer, S. G., Kosbab, K., Weiland, P. E., & Landry, S. J. (2005). Reconsidering the role of personality in placebo effects: Dispositional optimism, situational expectations, and the placebo response. *Journal of Psychosomatic Research, 58,* 121–127.

Geers, A. L., Kosbab, K., Helfer, S. G., Weiland, P. E., & Wellman, J. A. (2007). Further evidence for individual differences in placebo responding: An interactionist perspective. *Journal of Psychosomatic Research, 62,* 563–570.

Gerbert, B., Stone, G., Stulbarg, M., Gullion, D. S., & Greenfield, S. (1988). Agreement among physician assessment methods: Searching for the truth among fallible methods. *Medical Care, 26,* 519–535.

Gerend, M. A., & Maner, J. K. (2011). Fear, anger, fruits, and veggies: Interactive effects of emotion and message framing on health behavior. *Health Psychology.* doi: 10.1037/a0021981.

Gerin, W., & Pickering, T. G. (1995). Association between delayed recovery of blood pressure after acute mental stress and parental history of hypertension. *Journal of Hypertension, 13,* 603–610.

Gerin, W., Davidson, K. W., Christenfeld, N. J. S., Goyal, T., & Schwartz, J. E. (2006). The role of angry rumination and distraction in blood pressure recovery from emotional arousal. *Psychosomatic Medicine, 68,* 64–72.

Germann, J. N., Kirschenbaum, D. S., & Rich, B. H. (2007). Child and Parental Self-Monitoring as Determinants of Success in the Treatment of Morbid Obesity in Low-Income Minority Children. *Journal of Pediatric Psychology, 32,* 111–121.

Gerra, G., Monti, D., Panerai, A. E., Sacerdote, P., Anderlini, R., Avanzini, P., et al. (2003). Long-term immune-endocrine effects of bereavement: relationships with anxiety levels and mood. *Psychiatry research, 121,* 145–158.

Gerrard, M., Gibbons, F. X., Benthin, A. C., & Hessling, R. M. (1996). A longitudinal study of the reciprocal nature of risk behaviors and cognitions in adolescents: What you do shapes what you think, and vice versa. *Health Psychology, 15,* 344–354.

Gerrard, M., Gibbons, F. X., Lane, D. J., & Stock, M. L. (2005). Smoking cessation: Social comparison level predicts success for adult smokers. *Health Psychology, 24(6)*, 623–629.

Gerritson, W., Heijnen, C. J., Wiegant, V. M., Bermond, B., & Frijda, N. H. (1996). Experimental social fear: Immunological, hormonal, and autonomic concomitants. *Psychosomatic Medicine, 58*, 273–286.

Gibbons, F. X., & Eggleston, T. J. (1996). Smoker networks and the "typical smoker": A prospective analysis of smoking cessation. *Health Psychology, 15*, 469–477.

Gibbons, F. X., Gerrard, M., Lane, D. J., Mahler, H. I. M., & Kulik, J. A. (2005). Using UV photography to reduce use of tanning booths: A test of cognitive mediation. *Health Psychology, 24*, 358–363.

Gibson, B. (1997). Suggestions for the creation and implementation of tobacco policy. *Journal of Social Issues, 53*, 187–192.

Gibson, S.J. (2006). Older people's pain. *Pain: Clinical Updates, 14*, 1–4.

Gick, M. L., & Sirois, F. M. (2010). Insecure attachment moderates women's adjustment to inflammatory bowel disease severity. *Rehabilitation Psychology, 55*, 170–179.

Gick, M. L., & Thompson, W. G. (1997). Negative affect and the seeking of medical care in university students with irritable bowel syndrome: a preliminary study. *Journal of Psychosomatic Research, 43(5)*, 535–540.

Gidron, Y., & Davidson, K. (1996). Development and preliminary testing of a brief intervention for modifying CHD-predictive hostility components. *Journal of Behavioral Medicine, 19*, 203–220.

Gidron, Y., Davidson, K., & Bata, I. (1999). The short-term effects of a hostility-reduction intervention on male coronary heart disease patients. *Health Psychology, 18*, 416–420.

Giese-Davis, J., Collie, K., Rancourt, K. M. S., Neri, E., Kraemer, H. C., & Spiegel, D. (2011). Decrease in Depression Symptoms Is Associated With Longer Survival in Patients With Metastatic Breast Cancer: A Secondary Analysis. *Journal of Clinical Oncology, 29(4)*, 413–420.

Giese-Davis, J., Wilhelm, F. H., Conrad, A., Abercrombie, H. C., Sephton, S., Yutsis, M., Neri, E., Taylor, C. B., Kraemer, H. C., & Spiegel, D. (2006). Depression and stress reactivity in metastatic breast cancer. *Psychosomatic Medicine, 68*, 675–683.

Gignac, M. A., Sutton, D., & Badley, E. M. (2007). Arthritis symptoms, the work environment, and the future: Measuring perceived job strain among employed persons with arthritis. *Arthritis and Rheumatism, 57*, 738–747.

Gil, K. M., Carson, J. W., Porter, L. S., Scipio, C., Bediako, S. M., & Orringer, E. (2004). Daily mood and stress predict pain, health care use, and work activity in African American adults with sickle-cell disease. *Health Psychology, 23*, 267–274.

Gill, T. M., Baker, D. I., Gottschalk, M., Peduzzi, P. N., Allore, H., & Byers, A. (2002). A randomized trial of a prehabilitation program to prevent functional decline among frail community-living older persons. *New England Journal of Medicine, 347*, 1068–1074.

Gilmour, H. (2007). Physically active Canadians. *Health Reports, 18(3)*, 45–65. Statistics Canada Catalogue 82-003. Retrieved February 11, 2008, from www.statcan.ca/english/freepub/82-003-XIE/2006008/articles/physically/physicallyactivecanadians-en.pdf.

Gilmore, H. (2008). Depression and risk of heart disease. *Health Reports*, 19 (3), 1-12. Component of Statistics Canada Catalogue no. 82-003-X , Retrieved May 1, 2011 from http://www.statcan.gc.ca/pub/82-003-x/2008003/article/10649-eng.pdf.

Gilmour, H. & Hofmann, N. (2010). H1N1 vaccination • Health matters. *Health Reports, 21(4)*, Statistics Canada, Catalogue no. 82-003-XPE •, December 2010 1

Gilmour, H., & Park, J. (2006). Dependency, chronic conditions and pain in seniors. *Supplement to Health Reports, 16*, 21–31 (Statistics Canada Catalogue 82-003). Retrieved March 4, 2008, from www.statcan.ca/english/freepub/82-003-SIE/2005000/pdf/82-003-SIE20050007443.pdf.

Girdler, S. S., Hinderliter, A. L., Brownley, K. A., Turner, J. R., Sherwood, A., & Light, K. C. (1996). The ability of active versus passive coping tasks to predict future blood pressure levels in normotensive men and women. *International Journal of Behavioral Medicine, 3*, 233–250.

Girdler, S. S., Jamner, L. D., Jarvik, M., Soles, J. R., & Shapiro, D. (1997). Smoking status and nicotine administration differentially modify hemodynamic stress reactivity in men and women. *Psychosomatic Medicine, 59*, 294–306.

Glanz, K., Croyle, R. T., Chollete, V. Y., & Pinn, V. W. (2003). Cancer-related health disparities in women. *American Journal of Public Health, 93*, 292–298.

Glaros, A. G., & Burton, E. (2004). Parafunctional clenching, pain, and effort in temporomandibular disorders. *Journal of Behavioral Medicine, 27*, 91–100.

Glaser, R., Kiecolt-Glaser, J. K., Bonneau, R. H., Malarkey, W., Kennedy, S., & Hughes, J. (1992). Stress-induced modulation of the immune response to recombinant hepatitis B vaccine. *Psychosomatic Medicine, 54*, 22–29.

Glaser, R., Kiecolt-Glaser, J. K., Marucha, P. T., MacCallum, R. C., Laskowski, B. F., & Malarkey, W. B. (1999). Stress-related changes in proinflammatory cytokine production in wounds. *Archives of General Psychiatry, 56*, 450–456.

Glaser, R., Sheridan, J., Malarkey, W. B., MacCallum, R. C., & Kiecolt-Glaser, J. K. (2000). Chronic stress modulates the immune response to a pneumococcal pneumonia vaccine. *Psychosomatic Medicine, 62*, 804–807.

Glasgow, R. E., & Anderson, B. J. (1995). Future directions for research on pediatric chronic disease management: Lessons from diabetes. *Journal of Pediatric Psychology, 20*, 389–402.

Glasgow, R. E., Funnell, M. M., Bonomi, A. E., Davis, C., Beckham, V., & Wagner, E. H. (2002). Self-management aspects of the improving chronic illness care breakthrough series: Implementation with diabetes and heart failure teams. *Annals of Behavioral Medicine, 24*, 80–87.

Glasgow, R. E., Klesges, L. M., Dzewaltowski, D. A., Bull, S. S., & Estabrooks, P. (2004). The future of health behavior change research: What is needed to improve translation of research into health promotion practice? *Annals of Behavioral Medicine, 27*, 3–12.

Glasgow, R. E., Toobert, D. J., Hampson, S. E., & Wilson, W. (1995). Behavioral research on diabetes at the Oregon Research Institute. *Annals of Behavioral Medicine, 17*, 32–40.

Glasgow, R. E., Toobert, D. J., Mitchell, D. L., Donnelly, J. E., & Calder, D. (1989). Nutrition education and social learning interventions for type II diabetes. *Diabetes Care, 12*, 150–152.

Glass, D. C., & Singer, J. E. (1972). *Urban stress*. New York: Academic Press.

Glass, T. A., DeLeon, C. M., Marottoli, R. A., & Berkman, L. F. (1999). *Population based study of social and productive activities as predictors of survival among elderly Americans*. British Medical Journal, 319, 478–483.

Glenn, B., & Burns, J. W. (2003). *Pain self-management in the process and outcome of multidisciplinary treatment of chronic pain: Evaluation of a stage of change model*. Journal of Behavioral Medicine, 26, 417–433.

Gluck, M. E., Geliebter, A., Hung, J., & Yahav, E. (2004). Cortisol, hunger, and desire to binge eat following a cold stress test in obese women with binge eating disorder. *Psychosomatic Medicine, 66*, 876–881.

Glynn, L. M., Christenfeld, N., & Gerin, W. (1999). Gender, social support, and cardiovascular responses to stress. *Psychosomatic Medicine, 61*, 234–242.

Glynn, L. M., Christenfeld, N., & Gerin, W. (2002). The role of rumination in recovery from reactivity: Cardiovascular consequences of emotional states. *Psychosomatic Medicine, 64*, 714–726.

Goatcher, S. (2002). *Health benefits and risks of moderate alcohol consumption: policy background paper*. Retrieved September 7, 2007, from www.aadac.com/documents/policy_alcohol_background_moderate_consumption.pdf.

Goede, P., Vedel, P., Larsen, N., Jensen, G. V. H., Parving, H., & Pedersen, O. (2003). Multifactorial intervention and cardiovascular disease in patients with type 2 diabetes. *New England Journal of Medicine, 348*, 383–393, http://www.nejm.org.

Goffman, E. (1961). *Asylums*. Garden City, NY: Doubleday.

Goffman, E. (1963). *Stigma: Notes on the management of spoiled identity*. Englewood Cliffs, NJ: Prentice-Hall.

Goforth, H. W., Lowery, J., Cutson, T. M., McMillan, E. S., Kenedi, C., & Cohen, M. A. (2009). Impact of Bereavement on Progression of AIDS and HIV Infection: A Review. *Psychosomatics, 50*, 433–439.

Goldberg, J. H., Halpern-Felsher, B. L., & Millstein, S. G. (2002). Beyond invulnerability: The importance of benefits in adolescents' decision to drink alcohol. *Health Psychology, 21*, 477–484.

Goldman, S. L., Whitney-Saltiel, D., Granger, J., & Rodin, J. (1991). Children's representations of "everyday" aspects of health and illness. *Journal of Pediatric Psychology, 16*, 747–766.

Goldring, A. B., Taylor, S. E., Kemeny, M. E., & Anton, P. A. (2002). Impact of health beliefs, quality of life and the physician-patient relationship on the treatment intentions of inflammatory bowel disease patients? *Health Psychology, 21,* 219–228.

Goldsmith, D. J., Lindholm, K. A., & Bute, J. J. (2006). Dilemmas of talking about lifestyle changes among couples coping with a cardiac event. *Social Science & Medicine, 63,* 2079–2090.

Goldstein, M. F., Eckhardt, E. A., Joyner-Creamer, P., Berry, R., Paradise, H., & Cleland, C. M. (2010). What do deaf high school students know about HIV? *AIDS education and prevention, 22,* 523–537.

Gollwitzer, P. M. (1993). Goal achievement: The role of intentions. In W. Stroebe & M. Hewstone (Eds.), *European Review of Social Psychology* (Vol. 4, pp. 141–185). Chichester, England: Wiley.

Gollwitzer, P. M. (1999). Implementation intentions. *American Psychologist, 54,* 493–503.

Gollwitzer, P. M., & Sheeran, P. (2006). Implementation intentions and goal achievement: A meta-analysis of effects and processes. *Advances in Experimental Social Psychology, 38,* 69–119.

Gonder-Frederick, L. A., Carter, W. R., Cox, D. J., & Clarke, W. L. (1990). Environmental stress and blood glucose change in insuring insulin-dependent diabetes mellitus. *Health Psychology, 9,* 503–515.

Gonzalez, C. A., & Riboli, E. (2010). Diet and cancer prevention: Contributions from the European Prospective Investigation into Cancer and Nutrition (EPIC) study. *European journal of cancer (Oxford, England : 1990), 46,* 2555–2562.

Goodall, T. A., & Halford, W. K. (1991). Self-management of diabetes mellitus: A critical review. *Health Psychology, 10,* 1–8.

Goodman, E., McEwan, B. S., Huang, B., Dolan, L. M., & Adler, N. E. (2005). Social inequalities in biomarkers of cardiovascular risk in adolescence. *Psychosomatic Medicine, 67,* 9–15.

Goodwin, R. D., Cox, B. J., & Clara, I. (2006). Neuroticism and physical disorders among adults in the community: Results from the national comorbidity survey. *Journal of Behavioral Medicine, 29(3),* 229–238.

Goodwin, R. D., Kroenke, K., Hoven, C. W., & Spitzer, R. L. (2003). Major depression, physical illness and suicidal ideation in primary care. *Psychosomatic Medicine, 65,* 501–505.

Goodwin, R. D., Lewinsohn, P. M., & Seeley, J. R. (2004). Respiratory symptoms and mental disorders among youth: Results from a prospective, longitudinal study. *Psychosomatic Medicine, 66,* 943–949.

Gopalakrishnan, R., Ross, J., O'Brien, C., & Oslin, D. (2009). Course of late-life depression with alcoholism following combination therapy. *Journal of Studies on Alcohol and Drugs, 70,* 237–241.

Gorbatenko-Roth, K. G., Levin, I. P., Altmaier, E. M., & Doebbling, B. N. (2001). Accuracy of health-related quality of life assessment: What is the benefit of incorporating patients' preferences for domain functioning? *Health Psychology, 20,* 136–140.

Gordon, W. A., & Hibbard, M. R. (1992). Critical issues in cognitive remediation. *Neuropsychology, 6,* 361–370.

Gore, S. A., Brown, D. M., & West, D. S. (2003). The role of postpartum weight retention in obesity among women: A review of the evidence. *Annals of Behavioral Medicine, 26,* 149–159.

Gorman, C. (1999, March 29). Get some sleep. *Time,* 225.

Government of Canada. (2006). HIV and AIDS. *BioBasics.* Retrieved August 19, 2007, from www.biobasics.gc.ca/english/View.asp?x=764.

Government of Canada (2008). *Healthy pregnancy: Healthy Canadians.* Retrieved June 22, 2008, from www.healthycanadians.ca/hp-gs/index_e.html.

Goyal, T. M., Idler, E. L., Krause, T. J., & Contrada, R. J. (2005). Quality of life following cardiac surgery: Impact of the severity and course of depressive symptoms. *Psychosomatic Medicine, 67,* 759–765.

Grabe, H. J., Mahler, J., Witt, S. H., Schulz, A., Appel, K., Spitzer, C., et al. (2011). A risk marker for alcohol dependence on chromosome 2q35 is related to neuroticism in the general population. *Molecular Psychiatry, 16,* 126–128.

Grady, D. (2002, May 23). Hormones may explain difficulty dieters have keeping weight off. *The New York Times,* pp. A1, A24.

Grady, D. (2003, October 24). Women with genetic mutation at high risk for breast cancer, study confirms. *The New York Times,* p. A15.

Grady, D. (2004, April 14). Lung cancer affects sexes differently. *The New York Times,* p. A18.

Graham, J. E., Robles, T. F., Kiecolt-Glaser, J. K., Malarkey, W. B., Bissell, M. G., & Glaser, R. (2006). Hostility and pain are related to inflammation in older adults. *Brain, Behavior, and Immunity, 20,* 389–400.

Graham, R., Kremer, J., & Wheeler, G. (2008). Physical Exercise and Psychological Well-being among People with Chronic Illness and Disability. *Journal of Health Psychology, 13,* 447-458.

Gramling, S. E., Clawson, E. P., & McDonald, M. K. (1996). Perceptual and cognitive abnormality model of hypochondriasis: Amplification and physiological reactivity in women. *Psychosomatic Medicine, 58,* 423–431.

Grant, I., Adler, K. A., Patterson, T. L., Dimsdale, J. E., Zeigler, M. G., & Irwin, M. R. (2002). Health consequences of Alzheimer's caregiving transitions: Effects of placement and bereavement. *Psychosomatic Medicine, 64,* 477–486.

Graugaard, P., & Finset, A. (2000). Trait anxiety and reactions to patient-centered and doctor-centered styles of communication: An experimental study. *Psychosomatic Medicine, 62,* 33–39.

Graves, K. D. (2003). Social cognitive theory and cancer patients' quality of life: A meta-analysis of psychosocial intervention components. *Health Psychology, 22,* 210–219.

Green, J. H. (1978). *Basic clinical physiology* (3rd ed.). New York: Oxford University Press.

Greenberg, E. S., & Grunberg, L. (1995). Work alienation and problem alcohol behavior. *Journal of Health and Social Behavior, 36,* 83–102.

Greene, A. M., Walsh, E. G., Sirois, F. M., & McCaffrey, A. M. (2009). Perceived benefits of complementary and alternative medicine: A whole systems research perspective. *The Open Complementary Medicine Journal, 1,* 35–45.

Greenfield, S., Kaplan, S. H., Ware, J. E., Jr., Yano, E. M., & Frank, H. J. L. (1988). Patients' participation in medical care: Effects on blood sugar control and quality of life in diabetes. *Journal of General Internal Medicine, 3,* 448–457.

Greenglass, E., & Burke, R. J. (2000). Hospital downsizing, individual resources, and occupational stressors in nurses. *Anxiety, Stress and Coping, 13,* 371–390.

Greenglass, E., & Burke, R. J. (2001). Workload and burnout in nurses. *Journal of Community and Applied Social Psychology, 11,* 211–215.

Gregerson, M.B. (2000). The curious 2000-year case of asthma. *Psychosomatic Medicine, 62,* 816–827.

Gregg, M. E. D., Matyas, T. A., & James, J. E. (2005). Association between hemodynamic profile during laboratory stress and ambulatory pulse pressure. *Journal of Behavioral Medicine, 28,* 573–579.

Grembowski, D., Patrick, D., Diehr, P., Durham, M., Beresford, S., Kay, E., et al. (1993). Self-efficacy and health behavior among older adults. *Journal of Health and Social Behavior, 34,* 89–104.

Grewin, K. M., Girdler, S. S., Amico, J., & Light, K. C. (2005). Effects of partner support on resting oxytocin, cortisol, norepinephrine, and blood pressure before and after warm partner contact. *Psychosomatic Medicine, 67,* 531–538.

Griffin, M. J., & Chen, E. (2006). Perceived control and immune and pulmonary outcomes in children with asthma. *Psychosomatic Medicine, 68,* 493–499.

Griva, F., Anagnostopoulos, F., & Madoglou, S. (2009). Mammography Screening and the Theory of Planned Behavior: Suggestions Toward an Extended Model of Prediction. *Women & Health, 49,* 662–681.

Grogan, S., Hartley, L., Conner, M., Fry, G., & Gough, B. (2010). Appearance concerns and smoking in young men and women: Going beyond weight control. *Drugs: Education, Prevention & Policy, 17,* 261–269.

Grossi, E., Dalle Grave, R., Mannucci, E., Molinari, E., Compare, A., Cuzzolaro, M., et al. (2006). Complexity of attrition in the treatment of obesity: clues from a structured telephone interview. *Int J Obes, 30,* 1132–1137.

Groth-Marnat, G., & Fletcher, A. (2000). Influence of neuroticism, catastrophizing, pain, duration, and receipt of compensation on short-term response to nerve block treatment for chronic back pain. *Journal of Behavioral Medicine, 23,* 339–350.

Gruenewald, T. L., Kemeny, M. E., Aziz, N., & Fahey, J. L. (2004). Acute threat to the social self: Shame, social self-esteem, and cortisol activity. *Psychosomatic Medicine, 66,* 915–924.

Grzywacz, J. G., Almeida, D. M., Neupert, S. D., & Ettner, S. L. (2004). Socioeconomic status and health: A micro-level analysis of exposure and vulnerability to daily stressors. *Journal of Health and Social Behavior, 45,* 1–16.

Gu, J., Lau, J. T. F., Chen, X., Liu, C., Liu, J., Chen, H., et al. (2009). Using the Theory of Planned Behavior to investigate condom use behaviors among female injecting drug users who are also sex workers in China. *AIDS Care: Psychological and Socio-medical Aspects of AIDS/HIV, 21*(8), 967–975.

Guerrero, C., & Palmero, F. (2010). Impact of Defensive Hostility in Cardiovascular Disease. *Behavioral Medicine, 36,* 77–84.

Guilamo-Ramos, V., Jaccard, J., Pena, J., & Goldberg, V. (2005). Acculturation—related variables, sexual initiation, and subsequent sexual behavior among Puerto-Rican, Mexican, and Cuban youth. *Health Psychology, 24,* 88–95.

Gump, B. B., & Matthews, K. A. (1998). Vigilance and cardiovascular reactivity to subsequent stressors in men: A preliminary study. *Health Psychology, 17,* 93–96.

Gump, B. B., & Matthews, K. A. (2000). Are vacations good for your health? The 9-year mortality experience after the multiple risk factor intervention trial. *Psychosomatic Medicine, 62,* 608–612.

Gunthert, K. C., Cohen, L. H., & Armeli, S. (1999). The role of neuroticism in daily stress and coping. *Journal of Personality and Social Psychology, 77,* 1087–1100.

Günüşen, N. P., & Üstün, B. (2010). An RCT of coping and support groups to reduce burnout among nurses. *International Nursing Review, 57,* 485–492.

Gupta, A., Kumar, A., & Stewart, D. E. (2002). Cervical cancer screening among South Asian women in Canada: The role of education and acculturation. *Health Care for Women International, 23(2),* 123–134(12).

Gupta, R., Solanki, R. K., & Pathak, V. (2008). Blood pressure is associated with cognitive impairment in young hypertensives. *World Journal of Biological Psychiatry, 9,* 43–50.

Gupta, S. (2002, August 26). Don't ignore heart-attack blues. *Time,* 71.

Gurevich, M., Devins, G. M., Wilson, C., McCready, D., Marmar, C. R., & Rodin, G. M. (2004). Stress responses syndromes in women undergoing mammography: A comparison of women with and without a history of breast cancer. *Psychosomatic Medicine, 66,* 104–112.

Gutiérrez-Maldonado, J., Cabas-Hoyos, K., Gutiérre Martínez, O., Loreto-Quijada, D., & Peñaloza-Salazar, C. (2011). FC09-02 Efficacy of distraction by means of virtual reality in the control and reduction of pain using the cold-pressor test. *European Psychiatry, 26,* 1859–1859.

Guyll, M., & Contrada, R. J. (1998). Trait hostility and ambulatory cardiovascular activity: Responses to social interaction. *Health Psychology, 17,* 30–39.

Guzman, S. J., & Nicassio, P. M. (2003). The contribution of negative and positive illness to depression in patients with end-stage renal disease. *Journal of Behavioral Medicine, 26,* 517–534.

Gwaltney, C. J., Magill, M., Barnett, N. P., Apodaca, T. R., Colby, S. M., & Monti, P. M. (2011). Using daily drinking data to characterize the effects of a brief alcohol intervention in an emergency room. *Addictive Behaviors, 36,* 248–250.

Hacihasanoğlu, R., & Gözüm, S. (2011). The effect of patient education and home monitoring on medication compliance, hypertension management, healthy lifestyle behaviours and BMI in a primary health care setting. *Journal of clinical nursing, 20,* 692–705.

Hagedoorn, M., Kuijer, R. G., Buunk, B. P., DeJong, G., Wobbes, T., & Sanderman, R. (2000). Marital satisfaction in patients with cancer: Does support from intimate partners benefit those who need it the most? *Health Psychology, 19,* 274–282.

Hagedoorn, M., & Molleman, E. (2006). Facial disfiguration in patients with head and neck cancer: The role of social self-efficacy. *Health Psychology, 25,* 643–647. Halford, W. K., Cuddihy, S., & Mortimer, R. H. (1990). Psychological stress and blood glucose regulation in Type I diabetic patients. *Health Psychology, 9,* 516–528.

Hagedoorn, M., Sanderman, R., Bolks, H. N., Tuinstra, J., & Coyne, J. C. (2008). Distress in Couples Coping With Cancer: A Meta-Analysis and Critical Review of Role and Gender Effects. *Psychological Bulletin, 134,* 1–30.

Halding, A.G., Heggdal, K., & Wahl, A. (2011). Experiences of self-blame and stigmatisation for self-infliction among individuals living with COPD. *Scandinavian Journal of Caring Sciences, 25,* 100–107.

Halford, W. K., Cuddihy, S., & Mortimer, R. H. (1990). Psychological stress and blood glucose regulation in Type I diabetic patients. *Health Psychology, 9*(5), 516–528.

Hall, J. A., Epstein, A. M., DeCiantis, M. L., & McNeil, B. J. (1993). Physicians' liking for their patients: More evidence for the role of affect in medical care. *Health Psychology, 12,* 140–146.

Hall, J. A., Irish, J. T., Roter, D. L., Ehrlich, C. M., & Miller, L. H. (1994). Gender in medical encounters: An analysis of physician and patient communication in a primary care setting. *Health Psychology, 13,* 384–392.

Hall, P. A., & Fong, G. T. (2003). The effects of a brief time perspective intervention for increasing physical activity among young adults. *Psychology and Health, 18(6),* 685–706.

Hall, P. A., & Fong, G. T. (2007). Temporal self-regulation theory: A model for individual health behavior. Health Psychology Review, 1, 6–52.

Hall, S., Chochinov, H., Harding, R., Murray, S., Richardson, A., & Higginson, I. (2009). A Phase II randomised controlled trial assessing the feasibility, acceptability and potential effectiveness of Dignity Therapy for older people in care homes: Study protocol. *BMC Geriatrics, 9*(1), 9.

Hall, S., Weinman, J., & Marteau, T. M. (2004). The motivating impact of informing women smokers of a link between smoking and cervical cancer: The role of coherence. *Health Psychology, 23,* 419–424.

Halpern-Felsher, B. L., Millstein, S. G., Ellen, J. M., Adler, N. E., Tschann, J. M., & Biehl, M. (2001). The role of behavioral experience in judging risks. *Health Psychology, 20,* 120–126.

Ham, B. (Ed.). (2003). Health behavior information transfer. *Habit, 6.* Retrieved from: http://www.cfah.org/habit.

Hamburg, D. A., & Adams, J. E. (1967). A perspective on coping behavior: Seeking and utilizing information in major transitions. *Archives of General Psychiatry, 19,* 277–284.

Hamel, M., Zoutman, D., & O'Callaghan, C. (2010). Exposure to hospital roommates as a risk factor for health care-associated infection. *American journal of infection control, 38*(3), 173–181.

Hamilton, L. D., Newman, M. L., Delville, C. L., & Delville, Y. (2008). Physiological stress response of young adults exposed to bullying during adolescence. *Physiology & Behavior, 95,* 617–624.

Hamilton, M. K., Gelwick, B. P., & Meade, C. J. (1984). The definition and prevalence of bulimia. In R. C. Hawkins, W. J. Fremouw, & P. F. Clement (Eds.), *The binge-purge syndrome* (pp. 3–26). New York: Springer.

Hamilton, N. A., Catley, D., & Karlson, C. (2007). Sleep and the affective response to stress and pain. *Health Psychology, 26,* 288–295.

Hamilton, N. A., Karoly, P., & Zautra, A. J. (2005). Health goal cognition and adjustment in women with fibromyalgia. *Journal of Behavioral Medicine, 28,* 455–466.

Hamilton, V. L., Broman, C. L., Hoffman, W. S., & Renner, D. S. (1990). Hard times and vulnerable people: Initial effects of plant closing on autoworkers' mental health. *Journal of Health and Social Behavior, 31,* 123–140.

Hammond, D., Fong, G. T., Borland, R., Cummings, M., McNeil, A., & Driezen, P. (2007). Text and graphic warnings on cigarette packages: Findings from the international tobacco control four country study. *American Journal of Preventive Medicine, 32(3),* 202–209.

Hammond, D., Fong, G. T., McDonald, P. W., Cameron, R.., & Brown, K. S. (2003). Impact of the graphic Canadian warning labels on adult smoking behavior. *Tobacco Control, 12,* 391–395.

Hampson, S. E., Andrews, J. A., Barckley, M., Lichtenstein, E., & Lee, M. E. (2000). Conscientiousness, perceived risk, and risk-reduction behaviors: A preliminary study. *Health Psychology, 19,* 496–500.

Hampson, S. E., Goldberg, L. R., Vogt, T. M.., & Dubanoski, J. P. (2006). Forty years on: Teachers' assessments of children's personality traits predict self-reported health behaviors and outcomes at midlife. *Health Psychology, 25(1),* 57–64.

Hamrick, N., Cohen, S., & Rodriguez, M. S. (2002). Being popular can be healthy or unhealthy: Stress, social network diversity, and incidence of upper respiratory infection. *Health Psychology, 21,* 294–298.

Han, S., & Shavitt, S. (1994). Persuasion and culture: Advertising appeals in individualistic and collectivistic societies. *Journal of Experimental Social Psychology, 30,* 326–350.

Hansen, C. J., Stevens, L. C., & Coast, J. R. (2001). Exercise duration and mood state: How much is enough to feel better? [doi:10.1037/0278-6133.20.4.267]. *Health Psychology, 20,* 267–275.

Harburg, E., Julius, M., Kaciroti, N., Gleiberman, L., & Schork, M. A. (2003). Expressive/suppressive anger-coping responses, gender, and types of mortality: a 17-year follow-up (Tecumseh, Michigan, 1971–1988). *Psychosomatic Medicine, 65,* 588–597.

Harmon, A. (2004, July 21). As gene test menu grows, who gets to choose? *The New York Times*, pp. A1, A15.

Harnish, J. D., Aseltine, R. H., & Gore, S. (2000). Resolution of stressful experiences as an indicator of coping effectiveness in young adults: An event history analysis. *Journal of Health and Social Behavior, 41*, 121–136.

Harrell, J. P. (1980). Psychological factors and hypertension: A status report. *Psychological Bulletin, 87*, 482–501.

Harrington, A. (1997). Introduction. In A. Harrington (Ed.), *The Placebo Effect* (pp. 1–11). Cambridge, MA: Harvard University Press.

Harris, K. F., & Matthews, K. A. (2004). Interactions between autonomic nervous system activity and the endothelial function: A model for the development of cardiovascular disease. *Psychosomatic Medicine, 66*, 153–164.

Harvey, S., Kelloway, E. K., & Duncan-Leiper, L. (2003). Trust in Management as a Buffer of the Relationships Between Overload and Strain. *Journal of Occupational Health Psychology, 8*, 306–315.

Hassinger, H., Semenchuk, E., & O'Brien, W. (1999). Appraisal and coping responses to pain and stress in migraine headache sufferers. *Journal of Behavioral Medicine, 22*, 327–340.

Haug, T. T., Mykletun, A., & Dahl, A. A. (2004). The association between anxiety, depression, and somatic symptoms in a large population: The HUNT-II study. *Psychosomatic Medicine, 66*, 845–851.

Hawkley, L. C., Burleson, M. H., Berntson, G. G., & Cacioppo, J. T. (2003). Loneliness in everyday life: Cardiovascular activity, psychosocial context, and health behaviors. *Journal of Personality and Social Psychology, 85*, 105–120.

Hawryluck, L., Gold, W. L., Robinson, S., Pogorski, S., Galae, S., & Styra, R. (2004). SARS control and psychological effects of quarantine, Toronto, Canada. *Emerging Infectious Disease, 10(7)*, 1206–1212.

Haydon, E., Rehm, J., Fischer, B., Monga, N., & Adlaf, E. (2005). Prescription drug abuse in Canada and the diversion of prescription drugs into the illicit drug market. *Canadian Journal of Public Health, 96*, 459–461.

Hayes, D., & Ross, C. E. (1987). Concern with appearance, health beliefs, and eating habits. *Journal of Health and Social Behavior, 28*, 120–130.

Haynes, R. B., McKibbon, K. A., & Kanani, R. (1996). Systematic review of randomized controlled trials of the effects on patient adherence and outcomes of interventions to assist patients to follow prescriptions for medications. *The Cochrane Library, 2*, 1–26.

Haynes, S. G., Odenkirchen, J., & Heimendinger, J. (1990). Worksite health promotion for cancer control. *Seminars in Oncology, 17*, 463–484.

Hays, J., et al. (2003). Effects of estrogen plus progestin on health-related quality of life. *New England Journal of Medicine, 348*, 1839–1854. Retrieved from: http://www.nejm.org.

Hays, N. P., & Roberts, S. B. (2007). Aspects of Eating Behaviors Disinhibition and Restraint Are Related to Weight Gain and BMI in Women. *Obesity, 16*, 52–58.

Hays, R. B., Turner, H., & Coates, T. J. (1992). Social support, AIDS-related symptoms, and depression among gay men. *Journal of Consulting and Clinical Psychology, 60*, 463–469.

Haythornthwaite, J. A., Lawrence, J. W., & Fauerbach, J. A. (2001). Brief cognitive interventions for burn pain. *Annals of Behavioral Medicine, 23*, 42–49.

Hazuda, H. P., Gerety, M. B., Lee, S., Mulrow, C. D., & Lichtenstein, M. J. (2002). Measuring subclinical disability in older Mexican Americans. *Psychosomatic Medicine, 64*, 520–530.

Hazavehei, S. M., Taghdisi, M. H., & Saidi, M. (2007). Application of the Health Belief Model for Osteoporosis Prevention among Middle School Girl Students, Garmsar, Iran. *Education for Health, 20*.

Health Canada. (1999). *Best practices: Substance abuse treatment and rehabilitation.* Retrieved July 8, 2007, from www.hc-sc.gc.ca/hl-vs/pubs/adp-apd/bp-mp-abuse-abus/index_e.html.

Health Canada. (2002a). *Food for thought: Schools and nutrition.* Retrieved September 26, 2007, from www.hc-sc.gc.ca/fn-an/nutrition/child-enfant/food_thought_schools-reflection_aliments_ecole_e.html.

Heatlh Canada. (2002b).

Health Canada. (2003). *Arthritis in Canada. An ongoing challenge.* Retrieved August 19, 2007, from www.phac-aspc.gc.ca/publicat/ac/pdf/ac_e.pdf.

Health Canada. (2003a). *It's your health: Hepatitis C.* Retrieved August 20, 2007, from www.hc-sc.gc.ca/iyh-vsv/diseases-maladies/hepc_e.html.

Health Canada. (2004a). Measuring up: Results from the national immunization coverage survey, 2002. *Canada Communicable Disease Report; 30(5)*, 37–48. Retrieved August 18, 2007, from www.phac-aspc.gc.ca/publicat/ccdr-rmtc/04pdf/cdr3005.pdf.

Health Canada. (2004b). *What is second-hand smoke? Cigarette smoke: It's toxic.* Retrieved August 3, 2007, from www.hc-sc.gc.ca/hl-vs/tobac-tabac/second/fact-fait/tox_e.html.

Health Canada. (2004c). *Second-hand smoke and children.* Retrieved August 3, 2007, from www.hc-sc.gc.ca/hl-vs/tobac-tabac/second/fact-fait/child-enfant_e.html.

Health Canada. (2005a). *Evaluation strategies in Aboriginal substance abuse programs: A discussion.* Retrieved January 18, 2008, from www.hc-sc.gc.ca/fnih-spni/pubs/ads/literary_examen_review/rev_rech_3_e.html.

Health Canada. (2005b). *Baseline natural health products survey among consumers, March 2005.* Retrieved September 7, 2007, from www.hc-sc.gc.ca/dhp-mps/pubs/natur/eng_cons_survey_e.html.

Health Canada. (2005c). *Canada's health care system.* Retrieved September 7, 2007, from www.hc-sc.gc.ca/hcs-sss/alt_formats/hpb-dgps/pdf/pubs/2005-hcs-sss/2005-hcs-sss_e.pdf.

Health Canada. (2005d). *Sudden infant death syndrome (SIDS).* Retrieved August 24, 2007, from www.hc-sc.gc.ca/hl-vs/babies-bebes/sids-smsn/index_e.html.

Health Canada. (2005e). *Social marketing in health promotion…the Canadian experience.* Retrieved February 26, 2008, from www.hc-sc.gc.ca/ahc-asc/alt-formats/cmcd-dcmc/pdf/marketsoc/experience_e.pdf.

Health Canada. (2006a). *SARS.* Retrieved January 20, 2008, from www.hc-sc.gc.ca/dc-ma/sars-sras/index_e.html.

Health Canada. (2006b). *Preventing skin cancer.* Retrieved February 3, 2008, from www.hc-sc.gc.ca/iyh-vsv/diseases-maladies/cancer_e.html.

Health Canada. (2006c). *Nursing issues: Primary health care nurse practitioners.* Office of Nursing Policy. Retrieved August 20, 2007, from www.hc-sc.gc.ca/hcs-sss/alt_formats/hpb-dgps/pdf/nurs-infirm/2006-np-ip_e.pdf.

Health Canada. (2007a). *Report to the conference of the parties on the implementation of the framework convention on tobacco control.* Retrieved October 4, 2007, from www.hc-sc.gc.ca/hl-vs/pubs/tobac-tabac/cop-cdp/part-section6_e.html.

Health Canada. (2007b). *Canadian tobacco use monitoring survey (CTUMS) 2006.* Retrieved August 3, 2007, from www.hc-sc.gc.ca/hl-vs/tobac-tabac/research-recherche/stat/ctums-esutc_2007_e.html.

Health Canada. (2007c). *Supplementary tables: 2004–2005 youth smoking survey.* Retrieved August 3, 2007, from www.hc-sc.gc.ca/hl-vs/tobac-tabac/research-recherche/stat/survey-sondage_2004-2005_e.html.

Health Canada (2009a). The Risks. Not4Me Youth drug prevention program. Accessed July 12, 2010 from http://www.hc-sc.gc.ca/hc-ps/drugs-drogues/youth-jeunes/risks-risques/index-eng.php.

Health Canada (2009b) retrieved May 1, 2011 from http://www.hc-sc.gc.ca/hc-ps/tobac-tabac/research-recherche/stat/_ctums-esutc_2008/ann-histo-eng.php#tab1.

Health Canada (2010). Do Canadian Adults Meet their Nutrient Requirements through Food Intake Alone? Cat. No.: H164-112/3-2009E-PDF. Accessed April 30, 2011 from http://www.hc-sc.gc.ca/fn-an/surveill/nutrition/commun/art-nutr-adult-eng.php.

Health Council of Canada. (2006). *Health care renewal in Canada: Clearing the road to quality.* February 2006. Retrieved from www.healthcouncilcanada.ca/en/index.php?option=com_content&task=view&id=90&Itemid=92.

Health Council of Canada. (2007a). Canadians' experiences with chronic illness care in 2007. A data supplement to *Why health care renewal matters: Learning from Canadians with chronic health conditions.* Retrieved February 15, 2008, from www.healthcouncilcanada.ca/docs/rpts/2007/outcomes2/Outcomes2ExperiencesFINAL.pdf.

Health Council of Canada. (2007b). *Why health care renewal matters: Lessons from diabetes.* Retrieved March 2, 2008, from www.healthcouncilcanada.ca/docs/rpts/2007/HCC_DiabetesRpt.pdf.

Health Council of Canada. (2007c). *Diabetes and chronic illness care in Canada: Online consultation: Shared stories and ideas.* Retrieved May 29, 2008, from www.healthcouncilcanada.ca/docs/HCC-Consultation_Shared-Stories.pdf.

Heart and Stroke Foundation. (1997). *Women heart disease and stroke in Canada: Issues and Options.* Retrieved March 2, 2008, from www.med.mun.ca/chh-dbc/pdf/womanhrt.pdf.

Heart and Stroke Foundation. (1999). *The changing face of heart disease and stroke in Canada 2000.* Retrieved August 18, 2007, from www.statcan.ca/english/freepub/SubCategory.

Heart and Stroke Foundation. (2001). *Should you drink alcohol to protect yourself.* Retrieved August 10, 2007, from ww2.heartandstroke.ca/Page.asp?PageID=33&ArticleID=167&Src=news&From=SubCategory.

Heart and Stroke Foundation. (2002). *Stroke Statistics.* Retrieved August 18, 2007, from ww2.heartandstroke.ca/Page.asp?PageID=33&ArticleID=1078&Src=news&From=.

Heart and Stroke Foundation of Canada. (2003). *The growing burden of heart disease and stroke in Canada 2003.* Retrieved August 10, 2007, from www.cvdinfobase.ca/cvdbook/CVD_En03.pdf.

Heart and Stroke Foundation. (2007). *Reducing salt intake would eliminate hypertension in one million Canadians.* Retrieved August 18, 2007, from ww2.heartandstroke.ca/Page.asp?PageID=1613&ContentID=26017&ContentTypeID=1.

Heart and Stroke Foundation. (2008). *High blood pressure.* Retrieved June 30, 2008, from ww1.heartandstroke.ca/Page.asp?PageID=33&ArticleID=434&Src=stroke&From=SubCategory.

Heart and Stroke Foundation of Canada. (2010). http://www.heartandstroke.qc.ca/site/c.pkI0L7MMJrE/b.3660197/k.358C/Statistics.htm.

Heart & Stroke Foundation (2011) What is blood cholesterol? Accessed August 23, 2011 from http://www.heartandstroke.com/site/c.ikIQLcMWJtE/b.3484027/k.5C04/High_blood_cholesterol.htm?src=home.

Heart and Stroke Foundation (2011a). STROKE IS URGENT: The Heart and Stroke Foundation 2011 Stroke Report warns stroke awareness is dangerously low among women. Accessed August 24, 2011 from : http://www.heartandstroke.com/site/apps/nlnet/content2.aspx?c=ikIQLcMWJtE&b=3485819&ct=10858207.

Heatherton, T. F., Herman, C. P., & Polivy, J. (1992). Effects of distress on eating: The importance of ego-involvement. *Journal of Personality and Social Psychology, 62,* 801–803.

Hebebrand, J., & Hinney, A. (2009). Environmental and Genetic Risk Factors in Obesity. *Child and Adolescent Psychiatric Clinics of North America, 18,* 83–94.

Hebert, R. S., Schulz, R., Copeland, V. C., & Arnold, R. M. (2009). Preparing Family Caregivers for Death and Bereavement. Insights from Caregivers of Terminally Ill Patients. *Journal of Pain and Symptom Management, 37,* 3–12.

Hebestreit, A., Keimer, K., Hassel, H., Nappo, A., Eiben, G., Fernández, J., et al. (2010). What do children understand? Communicating health behavior in a European multicenter study. *Journal of Public Health, 18,* 391–401.

Heckman, T. G. (2003). The chronic illness quality of life (CIQOL) model: Explaining life satisfaction in people living with HIV disease. *Health Psychology, 22,* 140–147.

Heckman, T. G., Anderson, E. S., Sikkema, K. J., Kochman, A., Kalichman, S. C., & Anderson, T. (2004). Emotional distress in nonmetropolitan persons living with HIV disease enrolled in a telephone-delivered, coping improvement group intervention. *Health Psychology, 23,* 94–100.

Heesch, K. C., Mâsse, L. C., Dunn, A. L., Frankowski, R. F., & Mullen, P. D. (2003). Does adherence to a lifestyle physical activity intervention predict changes in physical activity? *Journal of Behavioral Medicine, 26,* 333–348.

Heim, E., Valach, L., & Schaffner, L. (1997). Coping and psychosocial adaptation: Longitudinal effects over time and stages in breast cancer. *Psychosomatic Medicine, 59,* 408–418.

Heishman, S. J., Kozlowski, L. T., & Henningfield, J. E. (1997). Nicotine addiction: Implications for public health policy. *Journal of Social Issues, 53,* 13–33.

Helgeson, V. S. (1992). Moderators of the relation between perceived control and adjustment to chronic illness. *Journal of Personality and Social Psychology, 63,* 656–666.

Helgeson, V. S. (1993). Implications of agency and communion for patient and spouse adjustment to a first coronary event. *Journal of Personality and Social Psychology, 64,* 807–816.

Helgeson, V. S. (1999). Applicability of cognitive adaptation theory to predicting adjustment to heart disease after coronary angioplasty. *Health Psychology, 18,* 561–569.

Helgeson, V. S. (2003). Cognitive adaptation, psychological adjustment and disease progression among angioplasty patients: 4 years later. *Health Psychology, 22,* 30–38.

Helgeson, V. S., & Cohen, S. (1996). Social support and adjustment to cancer: Reconciling descriptive, correlational, and intervention research. *Health Psychology, 15,* 135–148.

Helgeson, V. S., & Fritz, H. L. (1999). Cognitive adaptation as a predictor of new coronary events after percutaneous transluminal coronary angioplasty. *Psychosomatic Medicine, 61,* 488–495.

Helgeson, V. S., Cohen, S., Schulz, R., & Yasko, J. (2001). Long-term effects of educational and peer discussion group interventions on adjustment to breast cancer. *Health Psychology, 20,* 387–392.

Helgeson, V. S., Escobar, O., Siminerio, L., & Becker, D. (2007). Unmitigated Communion and Health Among Adolescents With and Without Diabetes. *Personality and Social Psychology Bulletin, 33,* 519–536.

Helgeson, V. S., Snyder, P., & Seltman, H. (2004). Psychological and physical adjustment to breast cancer over 4 years: Identifying distinct trajectories of change. *Health Psychology, 23,* 3–15.

Hemenover, S. H. (2003). The good, the bad, and the healthy: Impacts of emotional disclosure of trauma on resilient self-concept and psychological distress. *Personality and Social Psychology Bulletin, 29,* 1236–1244.

Henderson, C. J., Hagger, M. S., & Orbell, S. (2007). Does priming a specific illness schema result in an attentional information-processing bias for specific illness? *Health Psychology, 26,* 165–173.

Henry, J. P., & Cassel, J. C. (1969). Psychosocial factors in essential hypertension: Recent epidemiologic and animal experimental evidence. *American Journal of Epidemiology, 90,* 171–200.

Henson, J. M., Carey, M. P., Carey, K. B., & Maisto, S. A. (2006). Associations among health behaviors and time perspective in young adults: Model testing with bootstrapping replication. *Journal of Behavioral Medicine, 29(2),* 127–137.

Herbst-Damm, K. L., & Kulik, J. A. (2005). Volunteer support, marital status, and the survival times of terminally ill patients. *Health Psychology, 24(2),* 225–229.

Heeren, G. A., Jemmott, J. B., Mandeya, A., & Tyler, J. C. (2007). Theory-based predictors of condom use among university students in the United States and South Africa. *AIDS Educ Prev., 19(1),* 1–12.

Herek, G. M., Capitanio, J. P., & Widaman, K. F. (2003). Stigma, social risk, and health policy: Public attitudes toward HIV surveillance policies and the social construction of illness. *Health Psychology, 22,* 533–540.

Herman, S., Blumenthal, J. A., Babyak, M., Khatri, P., Craighead, W. E., Krishnan, K. R., et al. (2002). Exercise therapy for depression in middle-aged and older adults: Predictors of early dropout and treatment failure. *Health Psychology, 21,* 553–563.

Hermand, D., Mullet, E., & Lavieville, S. (1997). Perception of the combined effects of smoking and alcohol on health. *Journal of Health Psychology, 2,* 481–491.

Hernandez, A., & Sachs-Ericsson, N. (2006). Ethnic differences in pain reports and the moderating role of depression in a community sample of Hispanic and Caucasian participants with serious health problems. *Psychosomatic Medicine, 68,* 121–128.

Herring, M. P., O'Connor, P. J., & Dishman, R. K. (2010). The Effect of Exercise Training on Anxiety Symptoms Among Patients: A Systematic Review. *Arch Intern Med, 170,* 321–331.

Herrmann, C., Brand-Driehorst, S., Kaminsky, B., Leibing, E., Staats, H., & Ruger, U. (1998). Diagnostic groups and depressed mood as predictors of 22-month mortality in medical inpatients. *Psychosomatic Medicine, 60,* 570–577.

Herschbach, P., Duran, G., Waadt, S., Zettler, A., Amm, C., Marten-Mittag, B., et al. (1997). Psychometric properties of the questionnaire on stress in patients with diabetes-revised (QSD-F). *Health Psychology, 16,* 171–174.

Hershey, J. C., Niederdeppe, J., Evans, W. D., Nonnemaker, J., Blahut, S., Holden, D., Messeri, P., & Haviland, M. L. (2005). The theory of "truth": How counterindustry media campaigns affect smoking behavior among teens. *Health Psychology, 24(1),* 22–31.

Herzog, A. R., House, J. D., & Morgan, J. N. (1991). Relation of work and retirement to health and well-being in older age. *Psychology and Aging, 6,* 202–211.

Hewitt, P. L., & Flett, G. L. (1991). Perfectionism in the self and social contexts: Conceptualization, assessment, and association with psychopathology. *Journal of Personality and Social Psychology, 60*, 456–470.

Hewlett, S., Ambler, N., Almeida, C., Cliss, A., Hammond, A., Kitchen, K., et al. (2011). Self-management of fatigue in rheumatoid arthritis: a randomised controlled trial of group cognitive-behavioural therapy. *Annals of the Rheumatic Diseases, 70*(6), 1060–1067. doi: 10.1136/ard.2010.144691

Hibbard, M. R., Gordon, W. A., Stein, P. N., Grober, S., & Sliwinski, M. (1992). Awareness of disability in patients following stroke. *Rehabilitation Psychology, 37*, 103–120.

Hibbard, M. R., Grober, S. E., Stein, P. N., & Gordon, W. A. (1992). Post-stroke depression. In A. Freeman & F. M. Dattilio (Eds.), *Comprehensive casebook of cognitive therapy* (pp. 303–310). New York: Plenum Press.

Hien, T. T., de Jong, M., & Farrar, J. (2004). Avian influenza—A challenge to global health care structures. *The New England Journal of Medicine, 351*, 2363–2365.

Higgins-Biddle, J. C., Babor, T. F., Mullahyl, J., Daniels, J., & McRee, B. (1997). Alcohol screening and brief intervention: Where research meets practice. *Connecticut Medicine, 61*, 565–575.

Hill, S., Dziedzic, K., Thomas, E., Baker, S. R., & Croft, P. (2007). The illness perceptions associated with health and behavioral outcomes in people with musculoskeletal hand problems: Findings from the North Staffordshire Osteoarthritis Project (NorStOP). *Rheumatology, 46*, 944–951.

Hill-Briggs, F. (2003). Problem solving in diabetes self-management: A model of chronic illness self-management behavior. *Annals of Behavior Medicine, 25*, 182–193.

Hillhouse, J., Turrisi, R., Stapleton, J., & Robinson, J. (2008). A randomized controlled trial of an appearance-focused intervention to prevent skin cancer. *Cancer, 113*, 3257–3266.

Hillman, C. H., Erickson, K. I., & Kramer, A. F. (2008). Be smart, exercise your heart: exercise effects on brain and cognition. Nature Reviews Neuroscience, 9, 58–65.

Hinrichs, A. L., Murphy, S. E., Wang, J. C., Saccone, S., Saccone, N., Steinbach, J. H., et al. (in press). Common polymorphisms in FMO1 are associated with nicotine dependence. *Pharmacogenetics and Genomics.*

Hinton, J. M. (1967). *Dying.* Baltimore, MD: Penguin.

Hirayama, T. (1981). Non-smoking wives of heavy smokers have a higher risk of lung cancer: A study from Japan. *British Medical Journal, 282*, 183–185.

Hirsh, A. T., Dillworth, T. M., Ehde, D. M., & Jensen, M. P. (2010). Sex Differences in Pain and Psychological Functioning in Persons With Limb Loss. *The journal of pain : official journal of the American Pain Society, 11*, 79–86.

Hobbis, I. C. A., & Sutton, S. (2005). Are Techniques Used in Cognitive Behaviour Therapy Applicable to Behaviour Change Interventions Based on the Theory of Planned Behaviour? *Journal of Health Psychology, 10*, 7–18. doi: 10.1177/1359105305048549

Hobfoll, S. E. (1989). Conservation of resources: A new attempt at conceptualizing stress. *American Psychologist, 44*, 513–524.

Hobfoll, S. E., Jackson, A. P., Lavin, J., Britton, P. J., & Shepherd, J. B. (1993). Safer sex knowledge, behavior, and attitudes of inner-city women. *Health Psychology, 12*, 481–488.

Hochbaum, G. (1958). Public participation in medical screening programs (DHEW Publication No. 572, Public Health Service). Washington, D.C.: U.S. Government Printing Office.

Hodgson, C., Lindsay, P., & Rubini, F. (2007). Can mass media influence emergency department visits for stroke? *Stroke, 38*, 2115–2122.

Hodis, H. N., et al. (2003). Hormone therapy and the progression of coronary—artery atherosclerosis in postmenopausal women. *New England Journal of Medicine, 349*, 535–545. http://www.nejm.org.

Hogan, B. E., & Linden, W. (2004). Anger response style and blood pressure: At least don't ruminate about it! *Annals of Behavioral Medicine, 27*, 38–49.

Holahan, C. J., & Moos, R. H. (1990). Life stressors, resistance factors, and improved psychological functioning: An extension of the stress resistance paradigm. *Journal of Personality and Social Psychology, 58*, 909–917.

Holahan, C. J., & Moos, R. H. (1991). Life stressors, personal and social resources, and depression: A four-year structural model. *Journal of Abnormal Psychology, 100*, 31–38.

Holahan, C. J., Moos, R. H., Holahan, C. K., & Brennan, P. L. (1997). Social context, coping strategies, and depressive symptoms: An expanded model with cardiac patients. *Journal of Personality and Social Psychology, 72*, 918–928.

Holland, J. C. (2002). History of psycho-oncology: Overcoming attitudinal and conceptual barriers. *Psychosomatic Medicine, 64*, 206–221.

Hollon, S. D., & Beck, A. T. (1986). Cognitive and cognitive-behavioral therapies. In S. L. Garfield & A. E. Bergin (Eds.), *Handbook of psychotherapy and behavior change* (3rd ed., pp. 443–482). New York: Wiley.

Holmes, J. A., & Stevenson, C. A. Z. (1990). Differential effects of avoidant and attentional coping strategies on adaptation to chronic and recent-onset pain. *Health Psychology, 9*, 577–584.

Holmes, T. H., & Rahe, R. H. (1967). The social readjustment rating scale. *Journal of Psychosomatic Research, 11*, 213–218.

Holt-Lunstad, J., Birmingham, W. A., & Light, K. C. (2008). Influence of a "Warm Touch" Support Enhancement Intervention Among Married Couples on Ambulatory Blood Pressure, Oxytocin, Alpha Amylase, and Cortisol. *Psychosomatic Medicine, 70*, 976–985.

Holt-Lunstad, J., Smith, T. B., & Layton, J. B. (2010). Social Relationships and Mortality Risk: A Meta-analytic Review. *PLoS Med, 7*, e1000316.

Holtzman, S., & DeLongis, A. (2007). One day at a time: The impact of daily satisfaction with spouse responses on pain, negative affect and catastrophizing among individuals with rheumatoid arthritis. *Pain, 131(1–2)*, 202–213.

Holtzman, S., Newth, S., & DeLongis, A. (2004). The role of social support in coping with daily pain among patients with rheumatoid arthritis. *Journal of Health Psychology, 9*, 749–767.

Hopman, W. M., Towheed, T., Anastassiades, T., Tenenhouse, A., Poliquin, S., Berger, C., Joseph, L., Brown, J. P., Murray, T. M., Adachi, J. D., Hanley, D. A., Papadimitropoulos, E., & and the CaMos Research Group. (2000). Canadian normative data for the SF-36 health survey. *CMAJ, 163*(3), 265–271.

Hopman, W., Berger, C., Joseph, L., Towheed, T., VandenKerkhof, E., Anastassiades, T., Adachi, J. D., Ioannidis, G., Brown, J. P., Hanley, D. A., Papadimitropoulos, E. A., & the CaMos Research Group. (2006). The natural progression of health-related quality of life: Results of a five-year prospective study of SF-36 scores in a normative population. *Quality of Life Research, 15(3)*, 527–536(10).

Horgan, O., & MacLachlan, M. (2004). Psychosocial adjustment to lower-limb amputation: A review. *Disability and Rehabilitation, 26(14–15)*, 837–850.

Horgen, K. B., & Brownell, K. D. (2002). Comparison of price change and health message interventions in promoting healthy food choices. *Health Psychology, 21*, 505–512.

Horvath, K. J., Bowen, A. M., & Williams, M. L. (2006). Virtual and physical venues as contexts for HIV risk among rural men who have sex with men. *Health Psychology, 25*, 237–242.

Horwitz, A. V., Reinhard, S. C., & Howell-White, S. (1996). Caregiving as reciprocal exchange in families with seriously mentally ill members. *Journal of Health and Social Behavior, 37*, 149–162.

House, J. S., Landis, K. R., & Umberson, D. (1988). Social relationships and health. *Science, 241*, 540–545.

House, W. C., Pendelton, L., & Parker, L. (1986). Patients' versus physicians' attributions of reasons for diabetic patients' noncompliance with diet. *Diabetes Care, 9*, 434.

Houston, B. K., & Vavak, C. R., (1991). Cynical hostility: Developmental factors, psychosocial correlates, and health behaviors. *Health Psychology, 10*, 9–17.

Houston, B. K., Babyak, M. A., Chesney, M. A., Black, G., & Ragland, D. R. (1997). Social dominance and 22-year all-cause mortality in men. *Psychosomatic Medicine, 59*, 5–12.

Howren, M. B., & Suls, J. (2011). The Symptom Perception Hypothesis Revised: Depression and Anxiety Play Different Roles in Concurrent and Retrospective Physical Symptom Reporting. *Journal of Personality and Social Psychology, 100*, 182-195.

Høye, A., & Vaa, T. (2010). Will announcing seat-belt checkpoints reduce the non-use of seat-belts or increase other violations? *Transportation Research Part F: Traffic Psychology and Behaviour, 13*, 233–242.

Hsieh, A. Y., Tripp, D. A., Ji, L.-J., & Sullivan, M. J. L. (2010). Comparisons of Catastrophizing, Pain Attitudes, and Cold-Pressor Pain Experience Between Chinese and European Canadian Young Adults. *The journal of pain : official journal of the American Pain Society, 11,* 1187–1194.

Hu, F. B., Stampfer, M. J., Manson, J. E., Grodstein, F., Colditz, G. A., Speizer, F. E., & Willett, W. C. (2000). Trends in the incidence of coronary heart disease and changes in diet and lifestyle in women. *New England Journal of Medicine, 343,* 530–537.

Huebner, D. M., & Gerend, M. A. (2001). The relation between beliefs about drug treatments for HIV and sexual risk behavior in gay and bisexual men. *Annals of Behavioral Medicine, 23,* 304–312.

Hughes, J. R. (1993). Pharmacotherapy for smoking cessation: Unvalidated assumptions, anomalies, and suggestions for future research. *Journal of Consulting and Clinical Psychology, 61,* 751–760.

Hughes, M. E., & Waite, L. J. (2002). Health in household context: Living arrangements and health in late middle age. *Journal of Health and Social Behavior, 43,* 1–21.

Hughes, T., Schumacher, M., Jacobs-Lawson, J. M., & Arnold, S. (2008). Confronting Death: Perceptions of a Good Death in Adults with Lung Cancer. *American Journal of Hospice and Palliative Medicine, 25,* 39–44.

Huizink, A. C., Robles de Medina, P. G., Mulder, E. J. H., Visser, G. H. A., & Buitelaar, J. K. (2002). Coping in normal pregnancy. *Annals of Behavioral Medicine, 24,* 132–140.

Hulbert, A. (2006, July 16). Confidant crisis: Americans have fewer close friends than before. Is that a problem? *New York Times Magazine,* p. 15.

Hum, A. M., Robinson, L. A., Jackson, A. A., & Ali, K. S. (in press). Physician Communication Regarding Smoking and Adolescent Tobacco Use. *Pediatrics.*

Humbke, K. L., Brown, D. L., Welder, A. N., Fillion, D. T., Dobson, K. S., & Arnett, J. L. (2004). A survey of hospital psychology in Canada. *Canadian Psychology, 45(1),* 31–41.

Humpel, N., Marshall, A. L., Leslie, E., Bauman, A., & Owen, N. (2004). Changes in neighborhood walking are related to changes in perceptions of environmental attributes. *Annals of Behavioral Medicine, 27,* 60–67.

Hunsley, J. (2002). The cost-effectiveness of psychological interventions. *Canadian Psychological Association.* Retrieved September 14, 2007, from www.cpa.ca/documents/Cost-Effectiveness.pdf.

Hunsley, T. (2006). Work-life balance in an aging population. *Horizons, 8(3),* 1–60. Policy Research Initiative, Government of Canada. Retrieved August 14, 2007, from http://policyresearch.gc.ca/page.asp?pagenm=v8n3_art_02.

Huntington Society of Canada. (2008). *What is Huntington disease?* Retrieved from www.huntingtonsociety.ca.

Hunton, J., & Rose, J. M. (2005). Cellular telephones and driving performance: The effects of attentional demands on motor vehicle crash risk. Risk Analysis, 25, 855–866.

Huot, I., Paradis, G., & Ledoux, M. (2004). Effects of the Quebec heart health demonstration project on adult dietary behaviors. *Preventive Medicine, 38(2),* 137–148.

Hyland, M. E., Whalley, B., & Geraghty, A. W. A. (2007). Dispositional predictors of placebo responding: a motivational interpretation of flower essence and gratitude therapy. *Journal of Psychosomatic Research, 62,* 331–340.

Hyman Rapaport, M., Schettler, P., & Bresee, C. (2010). A Preliminary Study of the Effects of a Single Session of Swedish Massage on Hypothalamic–Pituitary–Adrenal and Immune Function in Normal Individuals. *The Journal of Alternative and Complementary Medicine, 16,* 1079–1088.

Ickovics, J. R., Hamburger, M. E., Vlahov, D., Schoenbaum, E. E., Schuman, P., Boland, R. J., et al. (2001). Mortality, CD4 cell count decline, and depressive symptoms among HIV-seropositive women. *Journal of the American Medical Association, 285,* 1466–1474.

Iezzi, T., Archibald, Y., Barnett, P., Klinck, A., & Duckworth, M. (1999). Neurocognitive performance and emotional status in chronic pain patients. *Journal of Behavioral Medicine, 22,* 205–216.

Ingelfinger, J. R. (2004). Pediatric antecedents of adult cardiovascular disease—awareness and intervention. *The New England Journal of Medicine, 350,* 2123–2126, http://www.nejm.org.

Institute of Medicine. (1997). Approaching Death: Improving Care at the End of Life, Committee on Care at the End of Life; Marilyn J. Field and Christine K. Cassel, Editors, Division of Health Care Services, Institute of Medicine, National Academy Press, Washington, D.C.

Interian, A., Gara, M., Díaz-Martínez, A. M., Warman, M. J., Escobar, J. I., Allen, L. A., & Manetti-Cusa, J. (2004) The value of pseudoneurological symptoms for assessing psychopathology in primary care. *Psychosomatic Medicine, 66,* 141–146.

Inweregbu, K., Dave, J., & Pittard, A. (2005). Nosocomial infections. *Continuing Education in Anaesthesia, Critical Care & Pain, 5,* 14–17.

Ironson, B., O'Cleirigh, C., Fletcher, M., Laurenceau, J. P., Balbin, E., Klimas, N., Schneiderman, N., & Solomon, G. (2005). Psychosocial factors predict CD4 and viral load change in men and women with human immunodeficiency virus in the era of highly active antiretroviral treatment. *Psychosomatic Medicine, 67,* 1013–1021.

Ironson, G., Wynings, C., Schneiderman, N., Baum, A., Rodriguez, M., Greenwood, D., et al. (1997). Posttraumatic stress symptoms, intrusive thoughts, loss, and immune function after Hurricane Andrew. *Psychosomatic Medicine, 59,* 128–141.

Irvine, J., Baker, B., Smith, J., Janice, S., Paquette, M., Cairns, J., et al. (1999). Poor adherence to placebo or amiodarone therapy predicts mortality: Results from the CAMIAT study. *Psychosomatic Medicine, 61,* 566–575.

Irwin, M. R., Cole, J. C., & Nicassio, P. M. (2006). Comparative meta-analysis of behavioral interventions for insomnia and their efficacy in middle-aged adults and in older adults 55+ years of age. *Health Psychology, 25,* 3–14.

Irwin, M. R., Pike, J. L., Cole, J. C., & Oxman, M. N. (2003). Effects of a behavioral intervention, tai chi chih, on varicella-zoster virus specific immunity and health functioning in older adults. *Psychosomatic Medicine, 65,* 824–830.

Irwin, M., Mascovich, A., Gillin, J. C., Willoughby, R., Pike, J., & Smith, T. L. (1994). Partial sleep deprivation reduces natural killer cell activity in humans. *Psychosomatic Medicine, 56,* 493–498.

Ishigami, Y., & Klein, R. M. (2009). Is a hands-free phone safer than a handheld phone? Journal of Safety Research, 40, 157–164.

Isowa, T., Ohira, H., & Murashima, S. (2006). Immune, endocrine and cardiovascular responses to controllable and uncontrollable acute stress. *Biological Psychology, 71(2),* 202–213.

Itkowitz, N. I., Kerns, R. D., & Otis, J. D. (2003). Support and coronary heart disease: The importance of significant other responses. *Journal of Behavioral Medicine, 26,* 19–30.

Iversen, A. C., Fear, N. T., Ehlers, A., Hacker Hughes, J., Hull, L., Earnshaw, M., et al. (2008). Risk factors for post-traumatic stress disorder among UK Armed Forces personnel. *Psychological Medicine, 38,* 511–522.

Jachuck, S. J., Brierley, H., Jachuck, S., & Willcox, P. M. (1982). The effect of hypotensive drugs on the quality of life. *Journal of the Royal College of General Practitioners, 32,* 103–105.

Jack, A. (2007, April 25). Climate change bites. *Financial Times,* p. 9.

Jackson, J. L., Passamonti, M., & Kroenke, K. (2007). Outcome and impact of mental disorders in primary care at 5 years. *Psychosomatic Medicine, 69,* 270–276.

Jackson, K. M., & Aiken, L. S. (2000). A psychosocial model of sun protection and sunbathing in young women: The impact of health beliefs, attitudes, norms, and self-efficacy for sun protection. *Health Psychology, 19,* 469–478.

Jacobs, K. W., & Nordan, F. M. (1979). Classification of placebo drugs' effect color. *Perceptual and Motor Skills, 49,* 367–372.

Jacobs, N., Rijsdijk, F., Derom, C., Vlietinck, R., Delespaul, P., Van Os, J., & Myin-Germeys, I. (2006). Genes making one feel blue in the flow of daily life: A momentary assessment study of gene-stress interaction. *Psychosomatic Medicine, 68,* 201–206.

Jacobsen, P. B., Bovbjerg, D. H., Schwartz, M. D., Hudis, C. A., Gilewski, T. A., & Norton, L. (1995). Conditioned emotional distress in women receiving chemotherapy for breast cancer. *Journal of Consulting and Clinical Psychology, 63,* 108–114.

Jacobson, E. (1938). *Progressive relaxation* (2nd ed.). Chicago: University of Chicago Press.

Jacobson, M. F., & Brownell, K. D. (2000). Small taxes on soft drinks and snack foods to promote health. *American Journal of Public Health, 90,* 854–857.

James, J. E. (2004). Critical review of dietary caffeine and blood pressure: A relationship that should be taken more seriously. *Psychosomatic Medicine, 66,* 63–71.

Jameson, M. (2004, January 19). No standing pat. *Los Angeles Times,* p. F7.

Janicki, D. L., Kamarck, T. W., Shiffman, S., Sutton-Tyrrell, K., & Gwaltney, C. J. (2005). Frequency of spousal interaction and 3-year progression of carotid artery intima medial thickness: The Pittsburgh health heart project. *Psychosomatic Medicine, 67,* 889–896.

Janis, I. (1983). *Groupthink: Psychological Studies of Policy Decisions and Fiascoes.* Boston: Houghton Mifflin.

Jann, M. W., & Slade, J. H. (2007). Antidepressant Agents for the Treatment of Chronic Pain and Depression. *Pharmacotherapy, 27,* 1571–1587.

Janszky, I., Ahnve, S., Lundberg, I., & Hemmingsson, T. (2010). Early-Onset Depression, Anxiety, and Risk of Subsequent Coronary Heart Disease: 37-Year Follow-Up of 49,321 Young Swedish Men. *J Am Coll Cardiol, 56,* 31–37.

Jean, L., Thomas, B., Tahiri-Alaoui, A., Shaw, M., & Vaux, D. J. (2007). Heterologous Amyloid Seeding: Revisiting the Role of Acetylcholinesterase in Alzheimer's Disease. PLoS ONE, 2, e652.

Jeffrey, R. W., Kelly, K. M., Rothman, A. J., Sherwood, N. E., & Boutelle, K. N. (2004). The weight loss experience: A descriptive analysis. *Annals of Behavioral Medicine, 27,* 100–106.

Jemmott, J. B., III, Croyle, R. T., & Ditto, P. H. (1988). Commonsense epidemiology: Self-based judgments from laypersons and physicians. *Health Psychology, 7,* 55–73.

Jensen, M. P., Barber, J., Romano, J. M., Molton, I. R., Raichle, K. A., Osborne, T. L., et al. (2009). A Comparison of Self-Hypnosis Versus Progressive Muscle Relaxation in Patients With Multiple Sclerosis and Chronic Pain. *International Journal of Clinical and Experimental Hypnosis, 57*(2), 198–221.

Jha, P. Avoidable global cancer deaths and total deaths from smoking. Nature Reviews: Cancer. Sept. 2009; 9(9):655–664.

Jiang, W., Babyak, M., Krantz, D. S., Waugh, R. A., Coleman, R. E., Hanson, M. M., et al. (1996). Mental stress-induced myocardial ischemia and cardiac events. *Journal of the American Medical Association, 275,* 1651–1656.

Jim, H. S., & Andersen, B. L. (2007). Meaning in life mediates the relationship between social and physical functioning and distress in cancer survivors. *British Journal of Health Psychology, 12*(3), 363–381.

Jim, H., Andrykowski, M., Munster, P., & Jacobsen, P. (2007). Physical symptoms/side effects during breast cancer treatment predict posttreatment distress. *Annals of Behavioral Medicine, 34*(2), 200–208.

Johansen, H., & Miller, W. J. (1999). Health care services: Recent trends. *Health Reports, 11*(3), 91–108 (Statistics Canada Catalogue 82-003 XIE). Retrieved August 15, 2007, from www.statcan.ca/english/freepub/82-003-XIE/0039982-003-XIE.pdf.

Johansson, E., & Lindberg, P. (2000). Low back pain patients in primary care: Subgroups based on the multidimensional pain inventory. *International Journal of Behavioral Medicine, 7,* 340–352.

Johnson, C. G., Levenkron, J. C., Suchman, A. L., & Manchester, R. (1988). Does physician uncertainty affect patient satisfaction? *Journal of General Internal Medicine, 3,* 144–149.

Johnson, J. E., Lauver, D. R., & Nail, L. M. (1989). Process of coping with radiation therapy. *Journal of Consulting and Clinical Psychology, 57,* 358–364.

Johnson, K. C., Miller, A. B., Collishaw, N. E., Palmer, J. R., Hammond, S. K., Salmon, A. G., et al. (2011). Active smoking and secondhand smoke increase breast cancer risk: the report of the Canadian Expert Panel on Tobacco Smoke and Breast Cancer Risk (2009). *Tobacco Control, 20,* e2.

Johnson, M. K. (2004). Further evidence on adolescent employment and substance use: Differences by race and ethnicity. *Journal of Health and Social Behavior, 45*(2), 187–197.

Johnson, R. J., McCaul, K. D., & Klein, W. M. P. (2002). Risk involvement and risk perception among adolescents and young adults. *Journal of Behavioral Medicine, 25,* 67–82.

Johnson, S. (2003). *Arthritis has plagued mankind throughout the ages.* DeWitt Publishing.

Johnston, D. W., Johnston, M., Pollard, B., Kinmonth, A. L., & Mant, D. (2004). Motivation is not enough: Prediction of risk behavior following diagnosis of coronary heart disease from the theory of planned behavior. *Health Psychology, 23,* 533–538.

Jonas, B. S., & Lando, J. F. (2000). Negative affect as a prospective risk factor for hypertension. *Psychosomatic Medicine, 62,* 188–196.

Jones, D. J., Beach, S. R. H., Forehand, R., & Foster, S. E. (2003). Self reported health in HIV-positive African American women: The role of family stress and depressive symptoms. *Journal of Behavioral Medicine, 26,* 577– 599.

Jones, J. L., & Leary, M. R. (1994). Effects of appearance-based admonitions against sun exposure on tanning intentions in young adults. *Health Psychology, 13,* 86–90.

Jonsdottir, I. H. (2000). Neuropeptides and their interaction with exercise and immune function. *Immunology and Cell Biology, 78*(5), 562–570.

Jordan, A., & McDonagh, J. (2006). Juvenile idiopathic arthritis: the paediatric perspective. *Pediatric Radiology, 36*(8), 734–742.

Jorgensen, R. S., Frankowski, J. J., & Carey, M. P. (1999). Sense of coherence, negative life events and appraisal of physical health among university students. *Personality and Individual Differences, 27,* 1079–1089.

Jung, W., & Irwin, M. (1999). Reduction of natural killer cytotoxic activity in major depression: Interaction between depression and cigarette smoking. *Psychosomatic Medicine, 61,* 263–270.

Junghaenel, D. U., Schwartz, J. E., & Broderick, J. E. (2008). Differential efficacy of written emotional disclosure for subgroups of fibromyalgia patients. *British Journal of Health Psychology, 13,* 57–60.

Juster, R. P., McEwen, B. S., & Lupien, S. J. (2010). Allostatic load biomarkers of chronic stress and impact on health and cognition. *Neuroscience & Biobehavioral Reviews, 35,* 2–16.

Kafetsios, K., & Sideridis, G. D. (2006). Attachment, social support and well-being in young and older adults. *Journal of Health Psychology, 11*(6), 863–875.

Kahana, E., Lawrence, R. H., Kahana, B., Kercher, K., Wisniewski, A., Stoller, E., et al. (2002). Long-term impact of preventive proactivity on quality of life of the old-old. *Psychosomatic Medicine, 64,* 382–394.

Kahn, J. R., & Pearlin, L. I. (2006). Financial strain over the life course and health among older adults. *Journal of Health and Social Behavior, 47,* 17–31.

Kahn, R. L. (1981). *Work and health.* New York: Wiley.

Kahn, R. L., & Juster, F. T. (2002). Well-being: Concepts and measures. *Journal of Social Issues, 58,* 627–644.

Kahneman, D., & Tversky, A. (1979). Prospect theory: An analysis of decision under risk. *Econometrica, 47*(2), 263–292.

Kakalacheva, K., Münz, C., & Lünemann, J. D. (2011). Viral triggers of multiple sclerosis. Biochimica et Biophysica Acta (BBA) Molecular Basis of Disease, 1812, 132–140.

Kalaydjian, A., Swendsen, J., Chiu, W.-T., Dierker, L., Degenhardt, L., Glantz, M., et al. (2009). Sociodemographic predictors of transitions across stages of alcohol use, disorders, and remission in the National Comorbidity Survey Replication. *Comprehensive Psychiatry, 50,* 299–306.

Kalichman, S. C., Cain, D., Weinhardt, L., Benotsch, E., Presser, K., Zweben, A., Bjodstrup, B., & Swain, G. R. (2005). Experimental components analysis of brief theory-based HIV/AIDS risk-reduction counseling for sexually transmitted infection patients. *Health Psychology, 24,* 198–208.

Kalichman, S. C., Carey, M. P., & Johnson, B. T. (1996). Prevention of sexually transmitted HIV infection: A meta-analytic review of the behavioral outcome literature. *Annals of Behavioral Medicine, 18,* 6–15.

Kalichman, S. C., Cherry, C., Cain, D., Weinhardt, L. S., Benotsch, E., Pope, H., & Kalichman, M. (2006). Health information on the internet and people living with HIV/AIDS: Information evaluation and coping styles. *Health Psychology, 25,* 205–210.

Kalichman, S. C., DiMarco, M., Austin, J., Luke, W., & DiFonzo, K. (2003). Stress, social support, and HIV-status disclosure to family and friends among HIV-positive men and women. *Journal of Behavioral Medicine, 26,* 315–332.

Kalichman, S. C., Weinhardt, L., DiFonzo, K., Austin, J., & Luke, W. (2002). Sensation seeking and alcohol use as markers of sexual transmission risk behavior in HIV-positive men. *Annals of Behavioral Medicine, 24,* 229–235.

Kamarck, T. W., Muldoon, M. F., Shiffman, S. S., & Sutton-Tyrrell, K. (2007). Experiences of demand and control during daily life are predictors of carotid atherosclerotic progression among healthy men. *Health Psychology, 26,* 324–332.

Kamarck, T. W., Muldoon, M. F., Shiffman, S., Sutton-Tyrell, K., Gwaltney, C., & Janieki, D. L. (2004). Experiences of demand and control in daily life as correlates of subclinical carotid atherosclerosis in a healthy older sample. *Health Psychology, 23,* 24–32.

Kamenou, N. (2008). Reconsidering Work–Life Balance Debates: Challenging Limited Understandings of the 'Life' Component in the Context of Ethnic Minority Women's Experiences. *British Journal of Management, 19,* S99–S109.

Kamijo, T., & Murakami, M. (2009). Regular physical exercise improves physical motor functions and biochemical markers in middle-age and elderly women. *Journal of Physical Activity and Health, 6,* 55–62.

Kanner, A. D., Coyne, J. C., Schaeffer, C., & Lazarus, R. S. (1981). Comparison of two modes of stress measurement: Daily hassles and uplifts versus major life events. *Journal of Behavioral Medicine, 4,* 1–39.

Kaplan, H. I. (1975). Current psychodynamic concepts in psychosomatic medicine. In R. O. Pasnau (Ed.), *Consultation-liaison psychiatry.* New York: Grune & Stratton.

Kaplan, M. S, Chang, C., Newsom, J. T., & McFarland, B. H. (2002). Acculturation status and hypertension among Asian immigrants in Canada. *Journal of Epidemiology and Community Health, 56(6),* 455–456.

Kaplan, R. M. (1991). Health-related quality of life in patient decision making. *Journal of Social Issues, 47,* 69–90.

Kaplan, R. M., & Simon, H. J. (1990). Compliance in medical care: Reconsideration of self-predictions. *Annals of Behavioral Medicine, 12,* 66–71.

Kaplan, R. M., Orleans, C. T., Perkins, K. A., & Pierce, J. P. (1995). Marshaling the evidence for greater regulation and control of tobacco products: A call for action. *Annals of Behavioral Medicine, 17,* 3–14.

Kaplan, R. M., Ries, A. L., Prewitt, L. M., & Eakin, E. (1994). Self-efficacy expectations predict survival for patients with chronic obstructive pulmonary disease. *Health Psychology, 13,* 366–368.

Kaptchuk, T. J., Friedlander, E., Kelley, J. M., Sanchez, M. N., Kokkotou, E., Singer, J. P., et al. (2010). Placebos without Deception: A Randomized Controlled Trial in Irritable Bowel Syndrome. *PLoS ONE, 5,* e15591.

Kaptchuk, T. J., Shaw, J., Kerr, C. E., Conboy, L. A., Kelley, J. M., Csordas, T. J., et al. (2009). "Maybe I made up the whole thing": placebos and patients' experiences in a randomized controlled trial. *Culture, Medicine and Psychiatry, 33,* 382–411.

Kaptein, A. A., Klok, T., Moss-Morris, R., & Brand, P. L. P. (2010). Illness perceptions: impact on self-management and control in asthma. *Current Opinion in Allergy and Clinical Immunology, 10,* 194–199

Karasek, R., Baker, D., Marxer, F., Ahlbom, A., & Theorell, T. (1981). Job decision latitude, job demands, and cardiovascular disease: A prospective study of Swedish men. *American Journal of Public Health, 71,* 694–705.

Karlamangla, A. S., Singer, B. H., & Seeman, T. E. (2006). Reduction in allostatic load in older adults is associated with lower all-cause mortality risk: MacArthur studies of successful aging. *Psychosomatic Medicine, 68,* 500–507.

Karoly, P., & Ruehlman, L. S. (1996). Motivational implications of pain: Chronicity, psychological distress, and work global construal in a national sample of adults. *Health Psychology, 15,* 383–390.

Karoly, P., & Ruehlman, L. S. (2007). Psychosocial Aspects of Pain-Related Life Task Interference: An Exploratory Analysis in a General Population Sample. *Pain Medicine, 8,* 563–572.

Kassam, A., & Patten, S. B. (2006). Major depression, fibromyalgia and labour force participation: A population-based cross-sectional study. *BMC Musculoskeletal Disorders, 7(4),* 1–5.

Kassem, N. O. & Lee, J. W. (2004). Understanding soft drink consumption among male adolescents using the theory of planned behavior. *Journal of Behavioral Medicine, 27,* 273–296.

Katon, W. J., Richardson, L., Lozano, P., & McCauley, E. (2004). The relationship of asthma and anxiety disorder. *Psychosomatic Medicine, 66,* 349–355.

Katz, R. C., Flasher, L., Cacciapaglia, H., & Nelson, S. (2001). The psychological impact of cancer and lupus: A cross validation study that extends the generality of "benefit finding" in patients with chronic disease. *Journal of Behavioral Medicine, 24,* 561–571.

Katzmarzyk, P. T., & Ardern, C. I. (2004). Overweight and obesity mortality trends in Canada, 1985–2000. *Canadian Journal of Public Health, 95(1),* 16–20.

Katzmarzyk, P. T., & Janssen, I. (2004). The economic costs associated with physical inactivity and obesity in Canada: An update. *Canadian Journal of Applied Physiology, 29(1),* 90–115.

Kaufman, M. R. (1970). Practicing good manners and compassion. *Medical Insight, 2,* 56–61.

Kavanaugh, D. J., Gooley, S., & Wilson, P. H. (1993). Prediction of adherence and control in diabetes. *Journal of Behavioral Medicine, 16,* 509–522.

Ke, X., Liu, C., & Li, N. (2010). Social support and Quality of Life: a cross-sectional study on survivors eight months after the 2008 Wenchuan earthquake. *BMC Public Health, 10,* 573.

Keane, T. M., & Wolfe, J. (1990). Comorbidity in post-traumatic stress disorder: An analysis of community and clinical studies. *Journal of Applied Social Psychology, 20,* 1776–1788.

Kearney, M. H., Rosal, M. C., Ockene, J. K., & Churchill, L. C. (2002). Influences on older women's adherence to a low-fat diet in the women's health initiative. *Psychosomatic Medicine, 64,* 450–457.

Keefe, F. J., & Van Horn, Y. (1993). Cognitive-behavioral treatment of rheumatoid arthritis pain. *Arthritis Care and Research, 6,* 213–222.

Keefe, F. J., Lumley, M. A., Buffington, A. L. H., Carson, J. W., Studts, J. L., Edwards, C. L., et al. (2002). Changing face of pain: Evolution of pain research in psychosomatic medicine. *Psychosomatic Medicine, 64,* 921–938.

Kelley, J. M., Lembo, A. J., Ablon, J. S., Villanueva, J. J., Conboy, L. A., Levy, R., et al. (2009). Patient and practitioner influences on the placebo effect in irritable bowel syndrome. *Psychosomatic Medicine, 71,* 789–797.

Kelner, M., & Wellman, B. (1997). Health care and consumer choice: Medical and alternative therapies. *Social Science & Medicine, 45(2),* 203–212.

Kelner, M., Wellman, B., Boon, H., & Welsh, S. (2004). Responses of established healthcare to the professionalization of complementary and alternative medicine in Ontario. *Social Science and Medicine, 59(5),* 915–930.

Keltikangas-Järvinen, L., Pulkki-Råback, L., Puttonen, S., Viikari, J., & Raitakari, O. T. (2006). Childhood hyperactivity as a predictor of carotid artery intima media thickness over a period of 21 years: The cardiovascular risk in young Finns study. *Psychosomatic Medicine, 68,* 509–516.

Kemeny, M. E. (2003). The psychobiology of stress. *Current Directions, 12,* 124–129.

Kemeny, M. E., Cohen, R., Zegans, L. S., & Conant, M. A. (1989). Psychological and immunological predictors of genital herpes recurrence. *Psychosomatic Medicine, 51,* 195–208.

Kemeny, M. E., Weiner, H., Duran, R., Taylor, S. E., et al. (1995). Immune system changes after the death of a partner in HIV-positive gay men. *Psychosomatic Medicine, 57,* 547–554.

Kemeny, M. E., Weiner, H., Taylor, S. E., Schneider, S., Visscher, B., & Fahey, J. L. (1994). Repeated bereavement, depressed mood, and immune parameters in HIV seropositive and seronegative homosexual men. *Health Psychology, 13,* 14–24.

Kenchaiah, S., Evans, J. C., Levy, D., Wilson, P. W. F., Benjamin, E. J., Larson, M. G., et al. (2002). Self-appraised problem solving and pain-relevant social support as predictors of the experience of chronic pain. *Annals of Behavioral Medicine, 24,* 100–105.

Kerns, R. D., Rosenberg, R., & Otis, J. D. (2002). Self-appraised problem solving and pain-relevant social support as predictors of the experience of chronic pain. *Annals of Behavioral Medicine, 24,* 100–105.

Kershaw, T. S., Ethier, K. A., Niccolai, L. M., Lewis J. B., & Ickovics, J. R. (2003). Misperceived risk among female adolescents: Social and psychological factors associated with sexual risk accuracy. *Health Psychology, 22,* 523–532.

Kessels, L. T. E., Ruiter, R. A. C., & Jansma, B. M. (2010). Increased Attention but More Efficient Disengagement: Neuroscientific Evidence for Defensive Processing of Threatening Health Information. *Health Psychology, 29,* 346–354.

Kessler, R. C., & Wethington, E. (1991). The reliability of life event reports in a community survey. *Psychological Medicine, 21,* 723–738.

Kessler, R. C., Kendler, K. S., Heath, A. C., Neale, M. C., & Eaves, L. J. (1992). Social support, depressed mood, and adjustment to stress: A genetic epidemiological investigation. *Journal of Personality and Social Psychology, 62,* 257–272.

Khechine, H., Pascot, D., & Premont, P. (2008). Use of health-related information from the Internet by English-speaking patients. *Health Informatics Journal, 14*(1), 17-28.

Kiberstis, P., & Marx, J. (2002, July 26). The unstable path to cancer. *Science, 297,* 543–569.

Kiecolt-Glaser, J. K., & Newton, T. L. (2001). Marriage and health: His and hers. *Psychological Bulletin, 127,* 472–503.

Kiecolt-Glaser, J. K., Fisher, L., Ogrocki, P., Stout, J. C., Speicher, C. E., & Glaser, R. (1987). Marital quality, marital disruption, and immune function. *Psychosomatic Medicine, 49,* 13–34.

Kiecolt-Glaser, J. K., Glaser, R., Cacioppo, J. T., MacCallum, R. C., Snydersmith, M., Kim, C., et al. (1997). Marital conflict in older adults: Endocrinological and immunological correlates. *Psychosomatic Medicine, 59,* 339–349.

Kiecolt-Glaser, J. K., Loving, T. J., Stowell, J. R., Malarkey, W. B., Lemeshow, S., Dickinson, S. L., & Glaser, R. (2005). Hostile marital interactions, proinflammatory cytokine production, and wound healing. *Archives of General Psychiatry, 62,* 1377–1384.

Kiecolt-Glaser, J. K., Malarkey, W. B., Chee, M. A., Newton, T., Cacioppo, J. T., Mao, H. Y., et al. (1993). Negative behavior during marital conflict is associated with immunological down-regulation. *Psychosomatic Medicine, 55,* 395–409.

Kiecolt-Glaser, J. K., Marucha, P. T., Malarkey, W. B., Mercado, A. M., & Glaser, R. (1995). Slowing of wound healing by psychological stress. *Lancet, 346,* 1194–1196.

Kielcolt-Glaser, J. K., McGuire, L., Robles, T. F., & Glaser, R. (2002). Psychoneuroimmunology and psychosomatic medicine: Back to the future. *Psychosomatic Medicine, 64,* 15–28.

Kiene, S. M., Barta, W. D., Zelenski, J. M., & Cothran, D. L. (2005). Why are you bringing up condoms now? The effect of message content on framing effects of condom use messages. *Health Psychology, 24(3),* 321–326.

Kim, H. S., Sherman, D. K., Ko, D., & Taylor, S. E. (2006). Pursuit of Comfort and Pursuit of Harmony: Culture, Relationships, and Social Support Seeking. *Personality and Social Psychology Bulletin, 32,* 1595–1607.

Kim, Y., Schulz, R., & Carver, C. S. (2007). Benefit finding in the cancer caregiving experience. *Psychosomatic Medicine, 69,* 283–291.

Kim, Y., Valdimarsdottir, H. B., & Bovbjerg, D. H. (2003). Family histories of breast cancer, coping styles, and psychological adjustment. *Journal of Behavioral Medicine, 26,* 225–243.

Kimm, S. Y. S., Glynn, N. W., Kriska, A. M., Barton, B. A., Kronsberg, S. S., Daniels, S. R., et al. (2002). Decline in physical activity in Black girls and White girls during adolescence. *New England Journal of Medicine, 347,* 709–715, http://www.nejm.org.

Kinder, L. S., Carnethon, M. R., Palaniappan, L. P., King, A. C., & Fortmann, S. P. (2004). Depression and the metabolic syndrome in young adults: Findings from the third national health and nutrition examination survey. *Psychosomatic Medicine, 66,* 316–322.

Kinder, L. S., Kamarck, T. W., Baum, A., & Orchard, T. J. (2002). Depressive symptomology and coronary heart disease in type I diabetes mellitus: A study of possible mechanisms. *Health Psychology, 21,* 542–552.

King, A. C., Castro, C., Wilcox, S., Eyler, A. A., Sallis, J. F., & Brownson, R. C. (2000). Personal and environmental factors associated with physical inactivity among different racial-ethnic groups of U.S. middle-aged and older-aged women. *Health Psychology, 19,* 354–364.

King, D. K., Glasgow, R. E., Toobert, D. J., Strycker, L. A., Estabrooks, P. A., Osuna, D., et al. (2010). Self-Efficacy, Problem Solving, and Social-Environmental Support are Associated With Diabetes Self-Management Behaviors. *Diabetes Care.*

King, D. W., King, L. A., Gudanowski, D. M., & Vreven, D. L. (1995). Alternative representations of war zone stressors: Relationships to posttraumatic stress disorder in male and female Vietnam veterans. *Journal of Abnormal Psychology, 104,* 184–196.

King, S., & Laplante, D. P. (2005). The effects of prenatal maternal stress on children's cognitive development: Project Ice Storm. *Stress: The International Journal on the Biology of Stress, 8,* 35–45.

Kirby, E. D., Williams, V. P., Hocking, M. C., Lane, J. D., & Williams, R. B. (2006). Psychosocial benefits of three formats of a standardized behavior stress management program. *Psychosomatic Medicine, 68,* 816–823.

Kirby, J. B. (2002). The influence of parental separation on smoking initiation in adolescents. *Journal of Health and Social Behavior, 43,* 56–71.

Kirkley, B. G., & Fisher, E. B., Jr. (1988). Relapse as a model of nonadherence to dietary treatment of diabetes. *Health Psychology, 7,* 221–230.

Kirkley, B. G., Agras, W. S., & Weiss, J. J. (1985). Nutritional inadequacy in the diets of treated bulimics. *Behavior Therapy, 16,* 287–291.

Kirmayer, L. J., & Young, A. (1998). Culture and somatization: Clinical, epidemiological, and ethnographic perspectives. *Psychosomatic Medicine, 60,* 420–430.

Kirschbaum, C., Klauer, T., Filipp, S., & Hellhammer, D. H. (1995). Sex-specific effects of social support on cortisol and subjective responses to acute psychological stress. *Psychosomatic Medicine, 57,* 23–31.

Kirscht, J. P. (1983). Preventive health behavior: A review of research and issues. *Health Psychology, 2,* 277–301.

Kivimäki, M., Head, J., Ferrie, J. E., Brunner, E., Marmot, M. G., Vahtera, J., & Shipley, M. J. (2006). Why is evidence on job strain and coronary heart disease mixed? An illustration of measurement challenges in the Whitehall II study. *Psychosomatic Medicine, 68,* 398–401.

Kivimäki, M., Kinnunen, M., Pitkänen, T., Vahtera, J., Elovainio, M., & Pulkkinen, L. (2004). Contribution of early and adult factors to socioeconomic variation in blood pressure: Thirty-four-year follow-up study of school children. *Psychosomatic Medicine, 66,* 184–189.

Kivimaki, M., Vahtera, J., Elovainio, M., Lillrank, B., & Kevin, M. V. (2002). Death or illness of a family member, violence, interpersonal conflict, and financial difficulties as predictors of sickness absence: Longitudinal cohort study on psychological and behavioral links. *Psychosomatic Medicine, 64,* 817–825.

Kiviniemi, M. T., Voss-Humke, A. M., & Seifert, A. L. (2007). How do I feel about the behavior? The interplay of affective associations with behaviors and cognitive beliefs as influences on physical activity behavior. *Health Psychology, 26,* 152–158.

Kivlahan, D. R., Marlatt, G. A., Fromme, K., Coppel, D. B., & Williams, E. (1990). Secondary prevention with college drinkers: Evaluation of an alcohol skills training program. *Journal of Consulting and Clinical Psychology, 58,* 805–810.

Klein, W., Lipkus, I., Scholl, S., McQueen, A., Cerully, J., & Harris, P. (2010). Self-affirmation moderates effects of unrealistic optimism and pessimism on reactions to tailored risk feedback. *Psychology and Health, 25,* 1195–1208.

Klepp, K. I., Kelder, S. H., & Perry, C. L. (1995). Alcohol and marijuana use among adolescents: Long-term outcomes of the class of 1989 study. *Annals of Behavioral Medicine, 17,* 19–24.

Kline, K. A., Fekete, E. M., & Sears, C. M. (2008). Hostility, emotional expression, and hemodynamic responses to laboratory stressors: Reactivity attenuating effects of a tendency to express emotion interpersonally. *International Journal of Psychophysiology, 68,* 177–185.

Klonoff, E. A., & Landrine, H. (1992). Sex roles, occupational roles, and symptom-reporting: A test of competing hypotheses on sex differences. *Journal of Behavioral Medicine, 15,* 355–364.

Klonoff, E. A., & Landrine, H. (1999). Acculturation and cigarette smoking among African Americans: Replication and implications for prevention and cessation programs. *Journal of Behavioral Medicine, 22,* 195–204.

Klumb, P., Hoppmann, C., & Staats, M. (2006). Work hours affect spouse's cortisol secretion—for better and for worse. *Psychosomatic Medicine, 68,* 742–746.

Klump, K. L., & Culbert, K. M. (2007). Molecular genetic studies of eating disorders. *Current Directions in Psychological Science, 16,* 37–41.

Knäuper, B., Cheema, S., Rabiau, M., & Borten, O. (2005). Self-set dieting rules: Adherence and prediction of weight loss success. *Appetite, 44,* 283–288.

Knäuper, B., McCollam, A., Rosen-Brown, A., Lacaille, J., Kelso, E., & Roseman, M. (2011). Fruitful plans: Adding targeted mental imagery to implementation intentions increases fruit consumption. *Psychology and Health, 26,* 601–617.

Knäuper, B., Rabiau, M., Cohen, O., & Patriciu, N. (2004). Compensatory health beliefs: Theory and measurement. *Psychology and Health, 19(5),* 607–624.

Knutson, K. L., & Van Cauter, E. (2008). Associations between Sleep Loss and Increased Risk of Obesity and Diabetes. *Annals of the New York Academy of Sciences, 1129,* 287–304.

Kocaman, N., Kutlu, Y., Ozkan, M., & Ozkan, S. (2007). Predictors of psychosocial adjustment in people with physical disease. *Journal of clinical nursing, 16*, 6–16.

Kohler, C. L., Fish, L., & Greene, P. G. (2002). The relationship of perceived self-efficacy to quality of life in chronic obstructive pulmonary disease. *Health Psychology, 21*, 610–614.

Kojima, M., Wakai, K., Tokudome, S., Tamakoshi, K., Toyoshima, H., Watanabe, Y., Hayakawa, N., Suzuki, K., Hashimoto, S., Kawado, M., Suzuki, S., Ito, Y., & Tamakoshi, A. (2005). Perceived psychological stress and colorectal cancer mortality: Findings from the Japan collaborative cohort study. *Psychosomatic Medicine, 67*, 72–77.

Kolata, G. (1994, January 6). Fetal ovary transplant is envisioned. *The New York Times*, p. 8.

Konigsberg, R. D. (2011). *The Truth About Grief: The Myth of Its Five Stages*: Simon & Schuster.

Koo-Loeb, J. H., Costello, N., Light, K., & Girdler, S. S. (2000). Women with eating disorder tendencies display altered cardiovascular, neuroendocrine, and psychosocial profiles. *Psychosomatic Medicine, 62*, 539–548.

Koolhaas, J. M., Bartolomucci, A., Buwalda, B., de Boer, S. F., Flügge, G., Korte, S. M., et al. (2011). Stress revisited: A critical evaluation of the stress concept. *Neuroscience & Biobehavioral Reviews, 35*, 1291–1301.

Kop, W. J., & Gottdiener, J. S. (2005). The role of immune system parameters in the relationship between depression and coronary artery disease. *Psychosomatic Medicine, 67*, S37–S41.

Kopelman, P. G. (2000, April 6). Obesity as a medical problem. *Nature, 404*, 635–643.

Koretz, G. (2003a, May 19). Stub out that cigarette, lady: Smoking narrows the mortality gap. *BusinessWeek*, 25.

Koretz, G. (2003b, November 10). Those heavy Americans. *BusinessWeek*, 34.

Kozak, B., Strelau, J., & Miles, J. N. V. (2005). Genetic determinants of individual differences in coping styles. *Anxiety, Stress and Coping: An International Journal, 18(1)*, 1–15.

Krantz, D. S. (1980). Cognitive processes and recovery from heart attack: A review and theoretical analysis. *Journal of Human Stress, 6*, 27–38.

Krantz, D. S., & Deckel, A. W. (1983). Coping with coronary heart disease and stroke. In T. G. Burish & L. A. Bradley (Eds.), *Coping with chronic disease: Research and applications*. New York: Academic Press, pp. 85–112.

Krause, D., Matz, J., Weidinger, E., Wagner, J., Wildenauer, A., Obermeier, M., et al. (2010). The association of infectious agents and schizophrenia. World Journal of Biological Psychiatry, 11, 739–743.

Krause, N. (2007). Evaluating the Stress-Buffering Function of Meaning in Life Among Older People. *Journal of Aging and Health, 19*, 792–812.

Kreuter, M. W., & McClure, S. M. (2004). The role of culture in health communication. *Annual Review of Public Health, 25*(1), 439–455.

Kreuter, M. W., & Strecher, V. J. (1995). Changing inaccurate perceptions of health risk: Results from a randomized trial. *Health Psychology, 14*, 56–63.

Kristal-Boneh, E., Melamed, S., Bernheim, J., Peled, I., & Green, M. S. (1995). Reduced ambulatory heart rate response to physical work and complaints of fatigue among hypertensive males treated with beta-blockers. *Journal of Behavioral Medicine, 18*, 113–126.

Kristenson, M., Eriksen, H. R., Sluiter, J. K., Starke, D., & Ursin, H. (2004). Psychobiological mechanisms of socioeconomic differences in health. *Social Science & Medicine, 58*, 1511–1522.

Krittayaphong, R., Cascio, W. E., Light, K. C., Sheffield, D., Golden, R. N., Finkel, J. B., et al. (1997). Heart rate variability in patients with coronary artery disease: Differences in patients with higher and lower depression scores. *Psychosomatic Medicine, 59*, 231–235.

Krohne, H. W., & Slangen, K. E. (2005). Influence of social support on adaptation to surgery. *Health Psychology, 24(1)*, 101–105.

Kübler-Ross, E. (1969). *On death and dying*. New York: Macmillan.

Kübler-Ross, E. (1975). *Death: The final stage of growth*. Englewood Cliffs, NJ: Prentice-Hall.

Kubzansky, L. D., Davidson, K. W., & Rozanski, A. (2005). The clinical impact of negative psychological states: Expanded the spectrum of risk for coronary artery disease. *Psychosomatic Medicine, 67*, S10–S14.

Kubzansky, L. D., Sparrow, D., Vokonas, P., & Kawachi, I. (2001). Is the glass half empty or half full? A prospective study of optimism and coronary heart disease in the normative aging study. *Psychosomatic Medicine, 63*, 910–916.

Kubzansky, L. D., Wright, R. J., Cohen, S., Weiss, S., Rosner, B., & Sparrow, D. (2002). Breathing easy: A prospective study of optimism and pulmonary function in the normative aging study. *Annals of Behavioral Medicine, 24*, 345–353.

Kudielka, B. M., & Wüst, S. (2010). Human models in acute and chronic stress: Assessing determinants of individual hypothalamuspituitaryadrenal axis activity and reactivity. *Stress, 13*, 1–14.

Kugler, J., Dimsdale, J. E., Hartley, L. H., & Sherwood, J. (1990). Hospital supervised versus home exercise in cardiac rehabilitation: Effects on aerobic fitness, anxiety, and depression. *Archives of Physical Medicine and Rehabilitation, 71*, 322–325.

Kuklina, E. V., Tong, X., Bansil, P., George, M. G., & Callaghan, W. M. (2011). Trends in pregnancy hospitalizations that included a stroke in the United States from 1994 to 2007. *Stroke*.

Kulik, J. A., & Carlino, P. (1987). The effect of verbal communication and treatment choice on medication compliance in a pediatric setting. *Journal of Behavioral Medicine, 10*, 367–376.

Kulik, J. A., & Mahler, H. I. M. (1987). Effects of preoperative roommate assignment on preoperative anxiety and recovery from coronary-bypass surgery. *Health Psychology, 6*, 525–543.

Kulik, J. A., & Mahler, H. I. M. (1989). Social support and recovery from surgery. *Health Psychology, 8*, 221–238.

Kulik, J. A., & Mahler, H. I. M. (1993). Emotional support as a moderator of adjustment and compliance after coronary artery bypass surgery: A longitudinal study. *Journal of Behavioral Medicine, 16*, 45–64.

Kulik, J. A., Moore, P. J., & Mahler, H. I. M. (1993). Stress and affiliation: Hospital roommate effects on preoperative anxiety and social interaction. *Health Psychology, 12*, 118–124.

Kundermann, B., Spernal, J., Huber, M.T., Krieg, J-C., & Lautenbacher, S. (2004). Sleep deprivation affects thermal pain thresholds but not somatosensory thresholds in healthy volunteers. *Psychosomatic Medicine, 66*, 932–937.

Kurland, A. A. (1957). The drug placebo—its psychodynamic and conditional reflex action. *Behavioral-Science, 2*, 101–110.

Kwaijtaal, M., van der Ven, A. J., van Diest, R., Bruggeman, C. A., Bär, F. W., Calandra, T., Appels, A., & Sweep, F. C. (2007). Exhaustion is association with low macrophage migration inhibitory factor expression in patients with coronary artery disease. *Psychosomatic Medicine, 69*, 68–73.

Lacaille, D., White, M. A., Backman, C. L., & Gignac, M. A. (2007). Problems faced at work due to inflammatory arthritis: New insights gained from understanding patients' perspective. *Arthritis and Rheumatism, 15(7)*, 1269–1279.

Lacey, K., Zaharia, M. D., Griffiths, J., Ravindran, A. V., Merali, Z., & Anisman, H. (2000). A prospective study of neuroendocrine and immune alterations associated with the stress of an oral academic examination among graduate students. *Psychoneuroendocrinology, 25(4)*, 339–356.

LaChapelle, D. (2004). *Chronic pain: A silent epidemic in Canada*. Retrieved August 18, 2007, from University of New Brunswick, *UNB Perspectives: A Newsletter*, from UNB Web site: www.unb.ca/perspectives/view.php?id=225.

Lachapelle, D. L., & Hadjistavropoulos, T. (2005). Age-related differences among adults coping with pain: Evaluation of a developmental life-context model. *Canadian Journal of Behavioural Science, 37(2)*, 123–137.

Lacroix, J. M., Martin, B., Avendano, M., & Goldstein, R. (1991). Symptom schemata in chronic respiratory patients. *Health Psychology, 10*, 268–273.

Lai, H., Lai, S., Krongrad, A., Trapido, E., Page, J. B., & McCoy, C. B. (1999). The effect of marital status on survival in late-stage cancer patients: An analysis based on surveillance, epidemiology, and end results (SEER) data, in the United States. *International Journal of Behavioral Medicine, 6*, 150–176.

Lallukka, T., Martikainen, P., Reunanen, A., Roos, E., Sarlo-Lahteenkorva, S., & Lahelma, E. (2006). Associations between working conditions and angina pectoris symptoms among employed women. *Psychosomatic Medicine, 68*, 348–354.

Lam, T. H., Stewart, M., & Ho, L. M. (2001). Smoking and high-risk sexual behavior among young adults in Hong Kong. *Journal of Behavioral Medicine, 24*, 503–518.

Lamprecht, F., & Sack, M. (2002). Posttraumatic stress disorder revisited. *Psychosomatic Medicine, 64,* 222–237.

Lance Coleman, C. (2007). Health beliefs and high-risk sexual behaviors among HIV-infected African American men. *Applied Nursing Research, 20*(3), 110–115.

Landsbergis, P. A., Schnall, P. L., Deitz, D., Friedman, R., & Pickering, T. (1992). The patterning of psychological attributes and distress by "job strain" and social support in a sample of working men. *Journal of Behavioral Medicine, 15,* 379–414.

Lane, N. E., Leatherdale, S. T., & Ahmed, R. (2011). Use of Nicotine Replacement Therapy Among Canadian Youth: Data From the 2006–2007 National Youth Smoking Survey. *Nicotine & Tobacco Research.* (epub ahead of print)

Lane, R. D., Laukes, C., Marcus, F. I., Chesney, M. A., Sechrest, L., Gear, K., Fort, C. L., Priori, S. G., Schwartz, P. J., & Steptoe, A. (2006). Psychological stress preceding idiopathic ventricular fibrillation. *Psychosomatic Medicine, 67,* 359–365.

Lang, A. R., & Marlatt, G. A. (1982). Problem drinking: A social learning perspective. In R. J. Gatchel, A. Baum, & J. E. Singer (Eds.), *Handbook of psychology and health: Vol. 1. Clinical psychology and behavioral medicine: Overlapping disciplines* (pp. 121–169). Hillsdale, NJ: Erlbaum.

Lange, L. J., & Piette, J. D. (2006). Personal models for diabetes in context and patients' health status. *Journal of Behavioral Medicine, 29,* 239–253.

Lange, T., Perras, B., Fehm, H. L., & Born, J. (2003). Sleep enhances the human antibody response to Hepatitis A vaccination. *Psychosomatic Medicine, 65,* 831–835.

Langens, T. A., & Schuler, J. (2007). Effects of written emotional expression: The role of positive expectancies. *Health Psychology, 26,* 174–182.

Langevin, H. M., Wayne, P. M., Macpherson, H., Schnyer, R., Milley, R. M., Napadow, V., et al. (2011). Paradoxes in acupuncture research: strategies for moving forward. *Evidence-Based Complementary and Alternative Medicine, Article ID 180805.*

Langewitz, W., Eich, P., Kiss, A., & Wossmer, B. (1998). Improving communication skills—A randomized controlled behaviorally oriented intervention study for residents in internal medicine. *Psychosomatic Medicine, 60,* 268–276.

Langston, C. A. (1994). Capitalizing on and coping with daily-life events: Expressive responses to positive events. *Journal of Personality and Social Psychology, 67,* 1112–1125.

Lankford, T. R. (1979). *Integrated science for health students* (2nd ed.). Reston, VA: Reston.

Lantz, P. M., House, J. S., Mero, R. P., & Williams, D. R. (2005). Stress, life events and socioeconomic disparities in health: Results from the Americans' changing lives study. *Journal of Health and Social Behavior, 46,* 274–288.

Laplante, D., P. , Brunet, A., Schmitz, N., Ciampi, A., & King, S. (2008). Project Ice Storm: Prenatal maternal stress affects cognitive and linguistic functioning in 5½-year-old children. *Journal of the American Academy of Child and Adolescent Psychiatry, 47,* 1063–1072.

László, K. D., Pikhart, H., Kopp, M. S., Bobak, M., Pajak, A., Malyutina, S., et al. (2010). Job insecurity and health: A study of 16 European countries. *Social Science & Medicine, 70,* 867–874.

Latkin, C. A., Sherman, S., & Knowlton, A. (2003). HIV prevention among drug users: Outcome of network-oriented peer outreach intervention. *Health Psychology, 22,* 332–339.

Latkin, C. A., Williams, C., Wang, J., & Curry, A. D. (2005). Neighborhood social disorder as a determinant of drug injection behaviors: A structural equation modeling approach. *Health Psychology, 24,* 96–100.

Lau, R. R., Kane, R., Berry, S., Ware, J. E., Jr., & Roy, D. (1980). Channeling health: A review of televised health campaigns. *Health Education Quarterly, 7,* 56–89.

Lauterbach, D., Vora, R., & Rakow, M. (2005). The relationship between posttraumatic stress disorder and self-reported health problems. *Psychosomatic Medicine, 67,* 939–947.

Lauver, D. R., Henriques, J. B., Settersten, L., & Bumann, M. C. (2003). Psychosocial variables, external barriers, and stage of mammography adoption. *Health Psychology, 22,* 649–653.

Laveist, T. A., & Nuru-Jeter, A. (2002). Is doctor–patient race concordance associated with greater satisfaction with care? *Journal of Health and Social Behavior, 43,* 296–306.

Lavie, C. J., & Milani, R. V. (2004). Prevalence of anxiety in coronary patients with improvement following cardiac rehabilitation and exercise training. *The American Journal of Cardiology, 93,* 336–339.

Lavie, C. J., Thomas, R. J., Squires, R. W., Allison, T. G., & Milani, R. V. (2009). Exercise Training and Cardiac Rehabilitation in Primary and Secondary Prevention of Coronary Heart Disease. *Mayo Clinic Proceedings, 84,* 373–383.

Lawes, C. M., Vander, H. S., & Rodgers, A. (2008). Global burden of blood-pressure-related disease, 2001. *Lancet, 371*(9623), 1513–1518.

Lawler, K. A., Younger, J. W., Piferi, R. L., Jobe, R. L., Edmondson, K. A., & Jones, W. H. (2005). The unique effects of forgiveness on health: An exploration of pathways. *Journal of Behavioral Medicine, 28,* 157–167.

Lawlor, D. A., O'Callaghan, M. J., Mamun, A. A., Williams, G. M., Bor, W., & Najman, J. M. (2005). Socioeconomic position, cognitive function, and clustering of cardiovascular risk factors in adolescence: Findings from the Mater University study of pregnancy and its outcomes. *Psychosomatic Medicine, 67,* 862–868.

Lawton, R., Connor, M., & Parker, D. (2007). Beyond cognition: Predicting health risk behaviors from instrumental and affective beliefs. *Health Psychology, 26,* 259–267.

Lazarus, A. A. (1971). *Behavior therapy and beyond.* New York: McGraw-Hill.

Lazarus, R. S. (1968). Emotions and adaptation: Conceptual and empirical relations. In W. Arnold (Ed.), *Nebraska symposium on motivation* (pp. 175–266). Lincoln: University of Nebraska Press.

Lazarus, R. S. (1983). The costs and benefits of denial. In S. Bresnitz (Ed.), *Denial of stress* (pp. 1–30). New York: International Universities Press.

Lazarus, R. S., & Folkman, S. (1984a). Coping and adaptation. In W. D. Gentry (Ed.), *The handbook of behavioral medicine* (pp. 282–325). New York: Guilford Press.

Lazarus, R. S., & Folkman, S. (1984b). *Stress, appraisal, and coping.* New York: Springer.

Lazarus, R. S., & Launier, R. (1978). Stress-related transactions between person and environment. In L. A. Pervin & M. Lewis (Eds.), *Internal and external determinants of behavior, 287*–327. New York: Plenum Press.

Lear, S. A., Humphries, K. H., Kohli, S., Chockalingam, A., Frohlick, J. J., & Birmingham, C. L. (2007). Visceral adipose tissue accumulation differs according to ethnic background: Results of the Multicultural Community Health Assessment Trial (M-CHAT). *American Journal of Clinical Nutrition, 86*(2), 353–359.

Leaver, C. A., Allman, D., Meyers, T., & Veugelers, P. J. (2004). Effectiveness of HIV Prevention in Ontario, Canada: A Multilevel Comparison of Bisexual Men. *Am J Public Health, 94*(7), 1181–1185.

Leaver, C. A., Bargh, G., Dunn, J. R., & Hwang, S. W. (2007). The effects of housing status on health-related outcomes in people living with HIV: A systematic review of the literature. *AIDS and Behavior, 11*(Suppl. 2), 85–100.

Lecci, L., & Cohen, D. J. (2002). Perceptual consequences of an illness-concern induction and its relation to hypochondriacal tendencies. *Health Psychology, 21,* 147–156.

Leclerc, J., Rahn, M., & Linden, W. (2006). Does personality predict blood pressure over a 10-year period? *Personality and Individual Differences, 40,* 1313–1321.

Leclere, F. B., Rogers, R. G., & Peters, K. (1998). Neighborhood social context and racial differences in women's heart disease mortality. *Journal of Health and Social Behavior, 39,* 91–107.

Lee, M. R., Chassin, L., & MacKinnon, D. (2010). The effect of marriage on young adult heavy drinking and its mediators: Results from two methods of adjusting for selection into marriage. *Psychology of Addictive Behaviors, 24,* 712–718.

Lee, R., Rodin, G., Devins, G., & Weiss, M. G. (2001). Illness experience, meaning and help-seeking among Chinese immigrants in Canada with chronic fatigue and weakness. *Anthropology and Medicine, 8*(1), 89–107(19).

Lee, R. T., & Brotheridge, C. M. (2006). When prey turns predatory: Workplace bullying as a predictor of counteraggression/bullying, coping, and well-being. *European Journal of Work and Organizational Psychology, 15,* 352–377.

Lee, S. S., & Ruvkun, G. (2002, July 18). Don't hold your breath. *Nature, 418,* 287–288.

Lehman, B. J., Taylor, S. E., Kiefe, C. I., & Seeman, T. E. (2005). Relation of childhood socioeconomic status and family environment to adult metabolic functioning in the CARDIA study. *Psychosomatic Medicine, 67,* 846–854.

Lehrer, P., Feldman, J., Giardino, N., Song, H. S., & Schmaling, K. (2002). Psychological aspects of asthma. *Journal of Consulting and Clinical Psychology, 70,* 691–711.

Lekander, M., Elofsson, S., Neve, I., Hansson, L., & Unden, A. (2004). Self-rated health is related to levels of circulating cytokines. *Psychosomatic Medicine, 66,* 559–593.

Lekander, M., Furst, C., Rotstein, S., Blomgren, H., & Fredrikson, M. (1995). Anticipatory immune changes in women treated with chemotherapy for ovarian cancer. *International Journal of Behavioral Medicine, 2,* 1–12.

Lenert, L., & Skoczen, S. (2002). The Internet as a research tool: Worth the price of admission? *Annals of Behavioral Medicine, 24,* 251–256.

Lennon, M. C., & Rosenfield, S. (1992). Women and mental health: The interaction of job and family conditions. *Journal of Health and Social Behavior, 33,* 316–327.

LePage, M. L., & Crowther, J. H. (2010). The effects of exercise on body satisfaction and affect. *Body Image, 7,* 124–130.

Lepore, S. J. (1995). Cynicism, social support, and cardiovascular reactivity. *Health Psychology, 14,* 210–216.

Lepore, S. J., & Smyth, J. M. (Eds.). (2002). *The writing cure: How expressive writing promotes health and emotional well-being.* (pp. 3–14). Washington, D.C., US: American Psychological Association.

Lepore, S. J., Helgeson, V. S., Eton, D. T., & Schulz, R. (2003). Improving quality of life in men with prostate cancer: A randomized controlled trial of group education interventions. *Health Psychology, 22,* 443–452.

Lepore, S. J., Miles, H. J., & Levy, J. S. (1997). Relation of chronic and episodic stressors to psychological distress, reactivity, and health problems. *International Journal of Behavioral Medicine, 4,* 39–59.

Lepore, S. J., Ragan, J. D., & Jones, S. (2000). Talking facilitates cognitive—emotional processes of adaptation to an acute stressor. *Journal of Personality and Social Psychology, 78,* 499–508.

Lepore, S. J., Shejwal, B., Kim, B. H., & Evans, G. W. (2010). Associations between chronic community noise exposure and blood pressure at rest and during acute noise and non-noise stressors among urban school children in India. *International Journal of Environmental Research and Public Health, 7,* 3457–3466.

Lerman, C., Gold, K., Audrain, J., Lin, T. H., Boyd, N. R., Orleans, C. T., et al. (1997). Incorporating biomarkers of exposure and genetic susceptibility into smoking cessation treatment: Effects on smoking-related cognitions, emotions, and behavior change. *Health Psychology, 16,* 87–99.

Lerman, C., Shields, P. G., Wileyto, E. P., Audrain, J., Hawk, L. H., Jr., Pinto, A., et al. (2003). Effects of dopamine transporter and receptor polymorphisms of smoking cessation in a bupropion clinical trial. *Health Psychology, 22,* 541–548.

Leserman, J. (2005). Sexual abuse history: Prevalence, health effects, mediators, and psychological treatment. *Psychosomatic Medicine, 67,* 906–915.

Lett, H. S., Blumenthal, J. A., Babyak, M. A., Sherwood, A., Strauman, T., Robins, C., et al. (2004). Depression as a risk factor for coronary artery disease: Evidence, mechanisms, and treatment. *Psychosomatic Medicine, 66,* 305–315.

Lett, H. S., Davidson, J., & Blumenthal, J. A. (2005). Nonpharmacologic treatment for depression in patients with coronary heart disease. *Psychosomatic Medicine, 67,* S58–S62.

Leung, Y. W., Gravely-Witte, S., Macpherson, A., Irvine, J., Stewart, D. E., & Grace, S. L. (2010). Post-traumatic Growth among Cardiac Outpatients. *Journal of Health Psychology, 15,* 1049-1063.

Leveille, S. G., et al. (1998). Preventing disability and managing chronic illness in frail older adults: A randomized trial of community-based partnership with primary care. *Journal of the American Geriatrics Society, 46,* 191–198.

Leventhal, E. A., Easterling, D., Leventhal, H., & Cameron, L. (1995). Conservation of energy, uncertainty reduction, and swift utilization of medical care among the elderly: Study II. *Medical Care, 33,* 988–1000.

Leventhal, E. A., Hansell, S., Diefenbach, M., Leventhal, H., & Glass, D. C. (1996). Negative affect and self-report of physical symptoms: Two longitudinal studies of older adults. *Health Psychology, 15,* 193–199.

Leventhal, H., Diefenbach, M., & Leventhal, E. A. (1992). Illness cognition: Using common sense to understand treatment adherence and affect cognition interactions. *Cognitive Therapy and Research, 16,* 143–163.

Leventhal, H., Weinman, J., Leventhal, E. A., & Phillips, L. A. (2008). Health psychology: The search for pathways between behavior and health. *Annual Reviews (59),* 477–505.

Levine, J. A., Lanningham-Foster, L. M., McCrady, S. K., Krizan, A. C., Olson, L. R., Kane, P. H., Jensen, M. D., & Clark, M. M. (2005). Interindividual variation in posture allocation: Possible role in human obesity. *Science, 30,* 584–586.

Levine, M. N., Guyatt, G. H., Gent, M., De Pauw, S., Goodyear, M. D., Hryniuk, W. M., et al. (1988). Quality of life in stage II breast cancer: An instrument for clinical trials. *Journal of Clinical Oncology, 6,* 1798–1810.

Levitsky, D. A., & DeRosimo, L. (2010). One day of food restriction does not result in an increase in subsequent daily food intake in humans. *Physiology & Behavior, 99,* 495–499.

Levy, B. R. (2003). Mind Matters: Cognitive and Physical Effects of Aging Self-Stereotypes. *The Journals of Gerontology Series B: Psychological Sciences and Social Sciences, 58*(4), P203–P211.

Levy, B. R., Zonderman, A. B., Slade, M. D., & Ferrucci, L. (2009). Age Stereotypes Held Earlier in Life Predict Cardiovascular Events in Later Life. *Psychological Science, 20*(3), 296–298.

Levy, S. M., Fernstrom, J., Herberman, R. B., Whiteside, T., Lee, J., Ward, M., et al. (1991). Persistently low natural killer cell activity and circulating levels of plasma beta endorphin: Risk factors for infectious disease. *Life Sciences, 48,* 107–116.

Levy, S. M., Herberman, R. B., Lippman, M., D'Angelo, T., & Lee, J. (1991, Summer). Immunological and psychosocial predictors of disease recurrence in patients with early-stage breast cancer. *Behavioral Medicine 17,* 67–75.

Levy, S. M., Lee, J. K., Bagley, C., & Lippman, M. (1988). Survival hazards analysis in first recurrent breast cancer patients: Seven-year follow-up. *Psychosomatic Medicine, 50,* 520–528.

Lewandowski, A. S., Palermo, T. M., Stinson, J., Handley, S., & Chambers, C. T. (2010). Systematic Review of Family Functioning in Families of Children and Adolescents With Chronic Pain. *The journal of pain : official journal of the American Pain Society, 11,* 1027–1038.

Lewin, K. (1951). *Field theory in social science: Selected theoretical papers.* New York, NY: Harper & Row.

Lewis, E., Mayer, J. A., Slymen, D., Belch, G., Engelberg, M., Walker, K., Kwon, H., & Elder, J. (2005). Disseminating a sun safety program to zoological parks: The effects of tailoring. *Health Psychology, 24,* 456–462.

Lewis, J. A., Manne, S. L., DuHamel, K. N., Vicksburg, S. M. J., Bovbjerg, D. H., Currie, V. et al. (2001). Social support, intrusive thoughts, and quality of life in breast cancer survivors. *Journal of Behavioral Medicine, 24,* 231–245.

Lewis, M. A., & Rook, K. S. (1999). Social control in personal relationships: Impact on health behaviors and psychological distress. *Health Psychology, 18,* 63–71.

Li, J., Laursen, T. M., Precht, D. H., Olsen, J., & Mortensen, P. D. (2005). Hospitalization for mental illness among parents after the death of a child. *The New England Journal of Medicine, 352,* 1190–1196.

Li, Y., & Ferraro, K. F. (2005). Volunteering and depression in later life: Social benefit or selection processes? *Journal of Health and Social Behavior, 46(1),* 68–84.

Liberman, A., & Chaiken, S. (1992). Defensive processing of personally relevant health messages. *Personality and Social Psychology Bulletin, 18,* 669–679.

Liberman, R. (1962). An analysis of the placebo phenomenon. *Journal of Chronic Diseases, 15,* 761–783.

Lichtenstein, P., Holm, N. V., Verkasalo, P. K., Iliadou, A., Kaprio, J., Koskenvuo, M., et al. (2000). Environmental and heritable factors in the causation of cancer: Analyses of cohorts of twins from Sweden, Denmark, and Finland. *New England Journal of Medicine, 343,* 78–85.

Lieberman, M. D., Jarcho, J. M., Berman, S., Naliboff, B. D., Suyenobu, B. Y., Mandelkern, M., et al. (2004). The neural correlates of placebo effects: A disruption account. *NeuroImage,* May, 447–495.

Lifton, R. J. (1977). The sense of immortality: On death and the continuity of life. In H. Feifel (Ed.), *New meanings of death.* New York: McGraw-Hill.

Lin, P., Simoni, J. M., & Zemon, V. (2005). The health belief model, sexual behaviors, and HIV risk among Taiwanese immigrants. *AIDS Education and Prevention, 17*(5), 469–483.

Lindauer, R. T. L., van Meijel, E. P. M., Jalink, M., Olff, M, Carlier, I. V. E., & Gersons, B. P. R. (2006). Heart rate responsivity to script-driven imagery in posttraumatic stress disorder: Specificity of response and effects of psychotherapy. *Psychosomatic Medicine, 68,* 33–40.

Linde, J. A., Rothman, A. J., Baldwin, A. S., & Jeffery, R. W. (2006). The impact of self-efficacy on behavior change and weight change among overweight participants in a weight loss trial. *Health Psychology, 25,* 282–291.

Linden, W., & Chambers, L. (1994). Clinical effectiveness of non-drug treatment for hypertension: A meta-analysis. *Annals of Behavioral Medicine, 16,* 35–45.

Linden, W., Chambers, L., Maurice, J., & Lenz, J. W. (1993). Sex differences in social support, self-deception, hostility, and ambulatory cardiovascular activity. *Health Psychology, 12,* 376–380.

Lipkus, I. M., McBride, C. M., Pollack, K. I., Lyna, P., & Bepler, G. (2004a). Interpretation of genetic risk feedback among African American smokers with low socioeconomic status. *Health Psychology, 23,* 178–188.

Lipkus, I. M, McBride, C. M., Pollak, K. I., Schwartz-Bloom, R. D., Tilson, E., & Bloom, P. N. (2004b). A randomized trail comparing the effects of self-help materials and proactive telephone counseling on teen smoking cessation. *Health Psychology, 23(4),* 396–406.

Lisspers, J., Sundin, Ö., Öhman, A., Hofman-Bang, C., Rydén, L., & Nygren, Å. (2005). Long-term effects of lifestyle behavior change in coronary artery disease: Effects on recurrent coronary events after percutaneous coronary intervention. *Health Psychology, 24,* 41–48.

Litt, M. D., Kleppinger, A., & Judge, J. O. (2002). Initiation and maintenance of exercise behavior in older women: Predictors from the social learning model. *Journal of Behavioral Medicine, 25,* 83–97.

Liu, Y., Tanaka, H., & The Fukuda Heart Study Group. (2002). Overtime work, insufficient sleep, and risk of non-fatal acute myocardial infarction in Japanese men. *Occupational and Environmental Medicine, 59,* 447–451.

Livneh, H. (2009a). Denial of Chronic Illness and Disability. *Rehabilitation Counseling Bulletin, 52,* 225–236.

Livneh, H. (2009b). Denial of Chronic Illness and Disability: Part II. Research Findings, Measurement Considerations, and Clinical Aspects. *Rehabilitation Counseling Bulletin, 53,* 44–55.

Lobel, M., Dias, L., & Meyer, B. A. (2005). Distress associated with prenatal screening for fetal abnormality. *Journal of Behavioral Medicine, 28,* 65–76.

Lock, M. (1993). *Encounters with aging: Mythologies of menopause in Japan and North America.* Berkeley, CA: University of California Press.

Lock, M. (2002). Symptom reporting at menopause: A review of cross-cultural findings. *Journal of the British Menopause Society, 8(4),* 132–136(5).

Loeber, S., Croissant, B., Nakovics, H., Zimmer, A., Georgi, A., Klein, S., et al. (2007). The Startle Reflex in Alcohol-Dependent Patients: Changes after Cognitive-Behavioral Therapy and Predictive Validity for Drinking Behavior. *Psychotherapy and Psychosomatics, 76,* 385–390.

Logsdon, R. G., Gibbons, L. E., McCurry, S. M., & Teri, L. (2002). Assessing quality of life in older adults with cognitive impairment. *Psychosomatic Medicine, 64,* 510–519.

Longboat, D. M. (2002). *Indigenous perspectives on death and dying.* Retrieved February 17, 2008, from www.cme.utoronto.ca/endoflife/Modules/Indigenous%20Perspectives%20on%20Death%20and%20Dying.pdf.

Longmore, M. A., Manning, W. D., Giordano, P. C., & Rudolph, J. L. (2003). Contraceptive self-efficacy: Does it influence adolescents' contraceptive use? *Journal of Health & Social Behavior, 44,* 45–60.

Lootens, C. M., & Nelson-Gray, R. O. (2010). *Self-Monitoring.* John Wiley & Sons, Inc.

Lorig, K. R., & Holman, H. R. (2003). Self-management education: History, definition, outcomes, and mechanisms. *Annals of Behavioral Medicine, 26,* 1–7.

Lorig, K., Chastain, R. L., Ung, E., Shoor, S., & Holman, H. (1989). Development and evaluation of a scale to measure perceived self-efficacy in people with arthritis. *Arthritis and Rheumatism, 32,* 37–44.

Los Angeles Times. (1993, March 30). Three-hundred-sixty days in row not overwork.

Lovallo, W. R., & Gerin, W. (2003). Psychophysical reactivity: Mechanisms and pathways to cardiovascular disease. *Psychosomatic Medicine, 65,* 36–45.

Lovallo, W. R., Al'Absi, M., Pincomb, G. A., Passey, R. B., Sung, B., & Wilson, M. F. (2000). Caffeine, extended stress, and blood pressure in borderline hypertensive men. *International Journal of Behavioral Medicine, 7,* 183–188.

Low, C. A., Stanton, A. L, & Danoff-Burg, S. (2006). Expressive disclosure and benefit finding among breast cancer patients: Mechanisms for positive health effects. *Health Psychology, 25,* 181–189.

Löwe, B., Grafe, K., Kroenke, K., Zipfel, S., Quentier, A., Wild, B., et al. (2003). Predictors of psychiatric comorbidity in medical outpatients. *Psychosomatic Medicine, 65,* 764–770.

Lowery, D., Fillingim, R. B., & Wright, R. A. (2003). Sex differences and incentive effects on perceptual and cardiovascular responses to cold pressor pain. *Psychosomatic Medicine, 65,* 284–291.

Lubeck, D. P., & Yelin, E. H. (1988). A question of value: Measuring the impact of chronic disease. *The Millbank Quarterly, 66,* 444–464.

Lubman, D. I., Yucel, M., Kettle, J. W. L., Scaffidi, A., MacKenzie, T., Simmons, J. G., et al. (2009). Responsiveness to Drug Cues and Natural Rewards in Opiate Addiction: Associations With Later Heroin Use. *Arch Gen Psychiatry, 66,* 205–212.

Luckow, A., Reifman, A., & McIntosh, D. N. (1998, August). *Gender differences in coping: A meta-analysis.* Poster session presented at the 106th annual convention of the American Psychological Association, San Francisco, CA.

Ludwig, D. S., Pereira, M. A., Kroenke, C. H., Hilner, J. E., Van Horn, L., Slattery, M., & Jacobs, D.R., Jr. (1999). Dietary fiber, weight gain, and cardiovascular disease risk factors in young adults. *Journal of the American Medical Association, 282,* 1539–1546.

Luecken, L. J., & Compas, B. E. (2002). Stress, coping, and immune function in breast cancer. *Annals of Behavioral Medicine, 24,* 336–344.

Luecken, L. J., Rodriguez, A. P., & Applehans, B. M. (2005). Cardiovascular stress responses in young adulthood associated with family-of-origin relationship experiences. *Psychosomatic Medicine, 67,* 514–521.

Luecken, L., Suarez, E., Kuhn, C., Barefoot, J., Blumenthal, J., Siegler, I., & Williams, R. (1997). Stress in employed women: impact of marital status and children at home on neurohormone output and home strain. *Psychosomatic Medicine, 59(4),* 352–359.

Luff, D., & Thomas, K. J. (2000). 'Getting somewhere', feeling cared for: Patients' perspectives on complementary therapies in the NHS. *Complementary Therapies in Medicine, 8,* 253–259.

Lumeng, J. C., Somashekar, D., Appugliese, D., Kaciroti, N., Corwyn, R. F., & Bradley, R. H. (2007). Shorter sleep duration is associated with increased risk for being overweight at ages 9 to 12 years. *Pediatrics, 120(5),* 1020–1029.

Lundahl, B. W., Kunz, C., Brownell, C., Tollefson, D., & Burke, B. L. (2010). A Meta-Analysis of Motivational Interviewing: Twenty-Five Years of Empirical Studies. *Research on Social Work Practice, 20,* 137–160. doi: 10.1177/1049731509347850

Luo, W., Morrison, H., de Groh, M., Waters, C., DesMeules, M., Jones-McLean, E., Ugnat, A. M., Desjardins, S., Lim, M., & Mao, Y. (2007). The burden of adult obesity in Canada. *Chronic Diseases in Canada, 27(4),* 135–144.

Lustman, P. J. (1988). Anxiety disorders in adults with diabetes mellitus. *Psychiatric Clinics of North America, 11,* 419–432.

Lutgendorf, S. K., Anderson, B., Sorosky, J. I., Butler, R. E., & Lubaroff, D. M. (2000). Interleukin-6 and use of social support in gynecologic cancer patients. *International Journal of Behavioral Medicine, 7,* 127–142.

Lutgendorf, S. K., Antoni, M. H., Ironson, G., Starr, K., Costello, N., Zuckerman, M., et al. (1998). Changes in cognitive coping skills and social support during cognitive behavioral stress management intervention and distress outcomes in symptomatic human immunodeficiency virus (HIV)–seropositive gay men. *Psychosomatic Medicine, 60,* 204–214.

Lutgendorf, S. K., Sood, A. K., Anderson, B., McGinn, S., Maiseri, H., Dao, M., et al. (2005). Social Support, Psychological Distress, and Natural Killer Cell Activity in Ovarian Cancer. *Journal of Clinical Oncology, 23*(28), 7105–7113.

Lutsey, P. L., Diez Roux, A. V., Jacobs, D. R., Jr., Burke, G. L., Harman, J., Shea, S., et al. (2008). Associations of Acculturation and Socioeconomic Status With Subclinical Cardiovascular Disease in the Multi-Ethnic Study of Atherosclerosis. *Am J Public Health, 98,* 1963–1970.

Lutz, R. S., Stults-Kolehmainen, M. A., & Bartholomew, J. B. (2010). Exercise caution when stressed: Stages of change and the stress-exercise participation relationship. *Psychology of Sport and Exercise, 11,* 560–567.

Lynch, D. J., Birk, T. J., Weaver, M. T., Gohara, A. F., Leighton, R. F., Repka, F. J., et al. (1992). Adherence to exercise interventions in the treatment of hypercholesterolemia. *Journal of Behavioral Medicine, 15,* 365–378.

Macaulay, A. C., Paradis, G., Potvin, L., Cross, E. J., Saad-Haddad, C., McComber, A., Desrosiers, S., Kirby, R., Montour, L. T., Lamping, D. L., Leduc, N., & Rivard, M. (1997). The Kahnawake schools diabetes prevention project: Intervention, evaluation and baseline results of a diabetes primary prevention program with a Native community in Canada. *Preventive Medicine, 26(6),* 779–790.

Macdonald, R. A. R., Mitchell, L. A., Dillon, T., Serpell, M. G., Davies, J. B., & Ashley, E. A. (2003). An Empirical Investigation of the Anxiolytic and Pain Reducing Effects of Music. *Psychology of Music, 31*(2), 187–203.

Maciejewski, P. K., Zhang, B., Block, S. D., & Prigerson, H. G. (2007). An empirical examination of the stage theory of grief. *Journal of the American Medical Association, 297,* 716–723.

Mackey, E. R., & La Greca, A. M. (2007). Adolescents' Eating, Exercise, and Weight Control Behaviors: Does Peer Crowd Affiliation Play a Role? *Journal of Pediatric Psychology, 32,* 13–23. doi: 10.1093/jpepsy/jsl041

MacLachlan, M., McDonald, D., & Waloch, J. (2004). Mirror treatment of lower limb phantom pain: A case study. *Disability and Rehabilitation, 26(14–15),* 901–904.

Macpherson, A. K., To, T. M., Macarthur, C., Chipman, M. L., Wright, J. G., & Parkin, P. C. (2002). Impact of mandatory helmet legislation on bicycle—related head injuries in children: A population-based study. *Pediatrics, 110(5),* 1–5.

Macrodimitris, S. D., & Endler, N. S. (2001). Coping, control and adjustment in type 2 diabetes. *Health Psychology, 20,* 208–216.

Maddux, J. E., Roberts, M. C., Sledden, E. A., & Wright, L. (1986). Developmental issues in child health psychology. *American Psychologist, 41,* 25–34.

Madlensky, L., Natarajan, L., Flatt, S. W., Faerber, S., Newman, V. A., & Pierce, J. P. (2008). Timing of Dietary Change in Response to a Telephone Counseling Intervention: Evidence From the WHEL Study. *Health Psychology, 27,* 539–547.

Maes, S., Leventhal, H., & DeRidder, D. T. D. (1996). Coping with chronic diseases. In M. Zeidner & N. S. Endler (Eds.), *Handbook of coping: Theory, research, and applications* (pp. 221–251). New York: Wiley.

Maggi, S., Hertzman, C., & Vaillancourt, T. (2007). Changes in smoking behaviors from late childhood to adolescence: Insights from the Canadian National Longitudinal Survey of Children and Youth. *Health Psychology, 26,* 232–240.

Maggi, S., Limongi, F., Noale, M., Romanato, G., Tonin, P., Rozzini, R., et al. (2009). Diabetes as a Risk Factor for Cognitive Decline in Older Patients. *Dementia and Geriatric Cognitive Disorders, 27,* 24–33.

Mago, R., Gomez, J. P., Gupta, N., & Kunkel, E. (2006). Anxiety in medically Ill patients. *Current Psychiatry Reports, 8,* 228-233. Magrone, T., & Jirillo, E. (2010). Polyphenols from red wine are potent modulators of innate and adaptive immune responsiveness. *Proceedings of the Nutrition Society, 69,* 279–285.

Magrone, T., & Jirillo, E. (2011). Potential Application of Dietary Polyphenols from Red Wine to Attaining Healthy Ageing. *Current Topics in Medicinal Chemistry.*

Mahler, H. I. M., & Kulik, J. A. (1998). Effects of preparatory videotapes on self-efficacy beliefs and recovery from coronary bypass surgery. *Annals of Behavioral Medicine, 20,* 39–46.

Mahler, H. I. M., Kulik, J. A., Gerrard, M., & Gibbons, F. X. (2007). Long-term effects of appearance-based interventions on sun protection behaviors. *Health Psychology, 26,* 350–360.

Mahler, H. I. M., Kulik, J. A., Gibbons, F. X., Gerrard, M., & Harrell, J. (2003). Effects of appearance-based interventions on sun protection intentions and self-reported behaviors. *Health Psychology, 22,* 199–209.

Maier, K. J., Waldstein, S. R., & Synowski, S. J. (2003). Relation of cognitive appraisal to cardiovascular reactivity, affect, and task engagement. *Annals of Behavioral Medicine, 26,* 32–41.

Maixner, W., Fillingim, R., Kincaid, S., Sigurdsson, A., Odont, C., & Harris, B. (1997). Relationship between pain sensitivity and resting arterial blood pressure in patients with painful temporomandibular disorders. *Psychosomatic Medicine, 59,* 503–511.

Malloy, K. M., & Milling, L. S. (2010). The effectiveness of virtual reality distraction for pain reduction: A systematic review. *Clinical Psychology Review, 30,* 1011–1018.

Manber, R., Kuo, T. F., Cataldo, N., & Colrain, I. M. (2003). The effects of hormone replacement therapy on sleep-disordered breathing in postmenopausal women: A pilot study. *Journal of Sleep & Sleep Disorders Research, 26,* 163–168.

Mann, D., Ponieman, D., Leventhal, H., & Halm, E. (2009). Predictors of adherence to diabetes medications: the role of disease and medication beliefs. *Journal of Behavioral Medicine, 32,* 278–284.

Mann, T. (2001). Effects of future writing and optimism on health behaviors in HIV-infected women. *Annals of Behavioral Medicine, 23,* 26–33.

Mann, T., Sherman, D., & Updegraff, J. (2004). Dispositional motivations and message framing: A test of the congruency hypothesis in college students. *Health Psychology, 23,* 330–334.

Manne, S. L., & Zautra, A. J. (1990). Couples coping with chronic illness: Women with rheumatoid arthritis and their healthy husbands. *Journal of Behavioral Medicine, 13,* 327–342.

Manne, S. L., Jacobsen, P. B., Gorfinkle, K., Gerstein, F., & Redd, W. H. (1993). Treatment adherence difficulties among children with cancer: The role of parenting style. *Journal of Pediatric Psychology, 18,* 47–62.

Manne, S. L., Jacobsen, P. B., Ming, M. E., Winkel, G., Dessureault, S., & Lessin, S. R. (2010). Tailored Versus Generic Interventions for Skin Cancer Risk Reduction for Family Members of Melanoma Patients. *Health Psychology, 29,* 583–593.

Manne, S. L., Ostroff, J., Winkel, G., Goldstein, L., Fox, K., & Grana, G. (2004). Posttraumatic growth after breast cancer: Patient, partner, and couple perspectives. *Psychosomatic Medicine, 66,* 442–454.

Manne, S., Glassman, M., & Du Hamel, K. (2000). Intrusion, avoidance, and psychological distress among individuals with cancer. *Psychosomatic Medicine, 63,* 658–667.

Manning, B. K., Catley, D., Harris, K. J., Mayo, M. S., & Ahluwalia, J. S. (2005). Stress and quitting among African-American smokers. *Journal of Behavioral Medicine, 28,* 325–333.

Manson, J. E., Colditz, G. A., Stampfer, M. J., Willett, W. C., Rosner, B., Monson, R. R., et al. (1990). A prospective study of obesity and risk of coronary heart disease in women. *New England Journal of Medicine, 322,* 882–888.

Manson, J. E., Hsia, J., Johnson, K. C., Rossouw, J. E., Assaf, A. R., Lasser, N. L., et al. (2003). Estrogen plus progestin and the risk of coronary heart disease. *New England Journal of Medicine, 349,* 523–534, http://www.nejm.org.

Mantler, J., Matejicek, A., Matheson, K., & Anisman, H. (2005). Coping with employment uncertainty: A comparison of employed and unemployed workers. *Journal of Occupational Health Psychology, 10(3),* 200–209.

Marcus, B. H., Dubbert, P. M., Forsyth, L. H., McKenzie, T. L., Stone, E. J., Dunn, A. L., et al. (2000). Physical activity behavior change: Issues in adoption and maintenance. *Health Psychology, 19,* 32–41.

Margolin, A., Avants, S. K., Warburton, L. A., Hawkins, K. A., & Shi, J. (2003). A randomized clinical trial of a manual-guided risk reduction intervention for HIV-positive injection drug users. *Health Psychology, 22,* 223–228.

Markovitz, J. H. (1998). Hostility is associated with increased platelet activation in coronary heart disease. *Psychosomatic Medicine, 60,* 586–591.

Marks, M., Sliwinski, M., & Gordon, W. A. (1993). An examination of the needs of families with a brain injured child. *Journal of Neurorehabilitation, 3,* 1–12.

Markus, H., & Nurius, P. (1986). Possible selves. *American Psychologist, 41(9),* 954–969.

Marlatt, G. A. (1990). Cue exposure and relapse prevention in the treatment of addictive behaviors. *Addictive Behaviors, 15,* 395–399.

Marlatt, G. A., & George, W. H. (1988). Relapse prevention and the maintenance of optimal health. In S. Shumaker, E. Schron, & J. K. Ockene (Eds.), *The adoption and maintenance of behaviors for optimal health.* New York: Springer.

Marlatt, G. A., Baer, J. S., Kivlahan, D. R., Dimeff, L. A., Larimer, M. E., Quigley, L. A., et al. (1998). Screening and brief intervention for high-risk college student drinkers: Results from a 2-year follow-up assessment. *Journal of Consulting and Clinical Psychology, 66,* 604–615.

Marlatt, G. A., Larimer, M. E., Baer, J. S., & Quigley, L. A. (1993). Harm reduction for alcohol problems: Moving beyond the controlled drinking controversy. *Behavior Therapy, 24,* 461–504.

Marquez, D. X., & McAuley, E. (2006). Social cognitive correlates of leisure time physical activity among Latinos. *Journal of Behavioral Medicine, 29,* 281–289.

Marsh, B. (2002, September 10). A primer on fat, some of it good for you. *The New York Times,* p. D7.

Marsh, H. W., Papaioannou, A., Theodorakis, Y. (2006). Causal ordering of physical self-concept and exercise behavior: Reciprocal effects model and the influence of physical education teachers. *Health Psychology, 25,* 316–328.

Marshall, A. L., Bauman, A. E., Owen, N., Booth, M. L., Crawford, D., & Marcus, B. H. (2003). Population-based randomized controlled trial of a stage-targeted physical activity intervention. *Annals of Behavioral Medicine, 25,* 194–202.

Marsland, A. L., Cohen, S., Rabin, B. S., & Manuck, S. B. (2001). Associations between stress, trait negative affect, acute immune reactivity, and antibody response to hepatitis B injection in healthy young adults. *Health Psychology, 20,* 4–11.

Marsland, A. L., Petersen, K. L., Sathanoori, R., Muldoon, M. F., Neumann, S. A., Ryan, C., Flory, J. D., Manuck, S. B. (2006). Interleukin-6 covaries inversely with cognitive performance among middle-aged community volunteers. *Psychosomatic Medicine, 68,* 895–903.

Martin, D., Greenwood, H., & Nisker, J. (2010). Public Perceptions of Ethical Issues Regarding Adult Predictive Genetic Testing. Health Care Analysis, 18, 103–112.

Martin, L. R., Friedman, H. S., Clark, K. M., & Tucker, J. S. (2005). Longevity following the experience of parental divorce. *Social Science & Medicine, 61,* 2177–2189.

Martin, L. R., Friedman, H. S., Tucker, J. S., Tomlinson-Keasey, C., Criqui, M. H., & Schwartz, J. E. (2002). Life course perspective on childhood cheerfulness and its relations to mortality risk. *Personality and Social Psychology Bulletin, 28,* 1155–1165.

Martin, R., & Lemos, K. (2002). From heart attacks to melanoma: Do common sense models of somatization influence symptom interpretation for female victims? *Health Psychology, 21,* 25–32.

Martin, R., Davis, G. M., Baron, R. S., Suls, J., & Blanchard, E. B. (1994). Specificity in social support: Perceptions of helpful and unhelpful provider behaviors among irritable bowel syndrome, headache, and cancer patients. *Health Psychology, 13,* 432–439.

Martin, T. R., Flett, G., Hewitt, P. L., Krames, L., & Szanto, G. (1996). Personality correlates of depression and health symptoms: A test of a self-regulation model. *Journal of Research in Personality, 31,* 264–277.

Martire, L. M., Stephens, M. A. P., Druley, J. A., & Wojno, W. C. (2002). Negative reactions to received spousal care: Predictors and consequences of miscarried support. *Health Psychology, 21,* 167–176.

Maruta, T., Colligan, R. C., Malinchoc, M., & Offord, K. P. (2002). Optimism—pessimism assessed in the 1960s and self-reported health status 30 years later. *Mayo Clinic Proceedings, 77,* 748–753.

Maschke, C. (2011). Cardiovascular effects of environmental noise: Research in Germany. *Noise and Health, 13,* 205–211. doi: 10.4103/1463-1741.80150

Mask, L., & Blanchard, C. M. (in press). The protective role of general self-determination against 'thin ideal' media exposure on women's body image and eating-related concerns. *Journal of Health Psychology.*

Maslach, C. (2003). Job burnout: New directions in research and intervention. *Current Directions, 12,* 189–192.

Mason, J. W., Wang, S., Yehuda, R., Lubin, H., Johnson, D., Bremner, J. D., et al. (2002). Marked lability in urinary cortisol levels in subgroups of combat veterans with posttraumatic stress disorder during an intensive exposure treatment program. *Psychosomatic Medicine, 64,* 238–246.

Masood, S. (2008). The Knowledge About Risk for Breast Cancer: The Patients' Right to Know. *The Breast Journal, 14,* 219–220.

Masuda, A., Munemoto, T., Yamanaka, T., Takei, M., & Tei, C. (2002). Psychological characteristics and immunological functions in patients with postinfectious chronic fatigue syndrome and noninfectious chronic fatigue syndrome. *Journal of Behavioral Medicine, 25,* 477–485.

Matarazzo, J. (1994). Health and behavior: The coming together of science and practice in psychology and medicine after a century of benign neglect. *Journal of Clinical Psychology in Medical Settings, 1,* 7–37.

Matarazzo, J. D. (1980). Behavioral health and behavioral medicine: Frontiers for a new health psychology. *American Psychologist, 35,* 807–817.

Mathers, C. D., & Loncar, D. (2006). Projections of global mortality and burden of disease from 2002 to 2030. *PLoS Medicine, 3(11),* 2011–2030. Retrieved August 10, 2007, from http://medicine.plosjournals.org/archive/1549-1676/3/11/pdf/10.1371_journal.pmed.0030442-S.pdf

Matt, G. E., & Dean, A. (1993). Social support from friends and psychological distress among elderly persons: Moderator effects of age. *Journal of Health and Social Behavior, 34,* 187–200.

Matthews, J. R., Friman, P. C., Barone, V. J., Ross, L. V., & Christophersen, E. R. (1987). Decreasing dangerous infant behaviors through parent instruction. *Journal of Applied Behavior Analysis, 20,* 165–169.

Matthews, K. A., & Rodin, J. (1992). Pregnancy alters blood pressure responses to psychological and physical challenge. *Psychophysiology, 29,* 232–240.

Matthews, K. A., Gump, B. B., & Owens, J. F. (2001). Chronic stress influences cardiovascular and neuroendocrine responses during acute stress and recovery, especially in men. *Health Psychology, 20,* 403–410.

Matthews, K. A., Owens, J. F., Kuller, L. H., Sutton-Tyrrell, K., & Jansen-McWilliams, L. (1998). Are hostility and anxiety associated with carotid atherosclerosis in healthy postmenopausal women? *Psychosomatic Medicine, 60,* 633–638.

Matthews, K. A., Räikkönen, K., Everson, S. A., Flory, J. D., Marco, C. A., Owens, J. F., et al. (2000). Do the daily experiences of healthy men and women vary according to occupational prestige and work strain? *Psychosomatic Medicine, 62,* 346–353.

Matthews, K. A., Räikkönen, K., Sutton-Tyrrell, S., & Kuller, L. H. (2004). Optimistic attitudes protect against progression of carotid atherosclerosis in health middle-aged women. *Psychosomatic Medicine, 66,* 640–644.

Matthews, K. A., Salomon, K., Brady, S. S., & Allen, M. T. (2003). Cardiovascular reactivity to stress predicts future blood pressure in adolescence. *Psychosomatic Medicine, 65,* 410–415.

Matthews, K. A., Schott, L. L., Bromberger, J., Cyranowski, J., Everson-Rose, S. A., & Sowers, M. F. (2007). Associations between depressive symptoms and inflammatory/hemostatic markers in women during the menopausal transition. *Psychosomatic Medicine, 69,* 124–130.

Matthews, K. A., Woodall, K. L., & Allen, M. T. (1993). Cardiovascular reactivity to stress predicts future blood pressure status. *Hypertension, 22,* 479–485.

Matthews, K. A., Woodall, K. L., Kenyon, K., & Jacob, T. (1996). Negative family environment as a predictor of boys' future status on measures of hostile attitudes, interview behavior, and anger expression. *Health Psychology, 15,* 30–37.

Matthews, S. C., Nelesen, R. A., & Dimsdale, J. E. (2005). Depressive symptoms are associated with increased systemic vascular resistance to stress. *Psychosomatic Medicine, 67,* 509–513.

Maunder, R. G., & Hunter, J. J. (2001). Attachment and psychosomatic medicine: Developmental contributions to stress and disease. *Psychosomatic Medicine, 63,* 556–567.

Mausbach, B. T., Dimsdale, J. E., Ziegler, M. G., Mills, P. J., Ancoli-Israel, S., Patterson, T. L., & Grant, I. (2005). Depressive symptoms predict norepinephrine response to a psychological stressor task in Alzheimer's caregivers. *Psychosomatic Medicine, 67,* 638–642.

Maxwell, C. J., Bancej, C. M., & Snider, J. (2001). Predictors of mammography use among Canadian women aged 50–69: Findings from the 1996/97 National Population Health Survey. *Canadian Medical Association Journal, 164(3),* 329–334.

Maxwell, C. J., Onysko, J., Bancej, C. M., Nichol, M., & Rakowski, W. (2006). The distribution and predictive validity of the stages of change for mammography adoption among Canadian women. *Preventive Medicine, 43(3),* 171–177.

Maxwell, T. D., Gatchel, R. J., & Mayer, T. G. (1998). Cognitive predictors of depression in chronic low back pain: Toward an inclusive model. *Journal of Behavioral Medicine, 21,* 131–143.

May, M., McCarron, P., Stansfeld, S., Ben-Schlomo, Y., Gallacher, J., Yarnell, J., et al. (2002). Does psychological distress predict the risk of ischemic stroke and transient ischemic attack? *Stroke, 33,* 7–12.

Mayne, T. J., Acree, M., Chesney, M. A., & Folkman, S. (1998). HIV sexual risk behavior following bereavement in gay men. *Health Psychology, 17*, 403–411.

McAmmond, D. (2000). *Food and nutrition surveillance in Canada: An environmental scan.* Retrieved August 19, 2007, from www.hc-sc.gc.ca/fn-an/surveill/environmental_scan_e.html.

McAuley, E. (1992). The role of efficacy cognitions in the prediction of exercise behavior in middle-aged adults. *Journal of Behavioral Medicine, 15*, 65–88.

McAuley, E., & Courneya, K. S. (1992). Self-efficacy relationships with affective and exertion responses to exercise. *Journal of Applied Social Psychology, 22*, 312–326.

McAuley, E., Jerome, G. J., Marquez, D. X., Elavsky, S., & Blissmer, B. (2003). Exercise self-efficacy in older adults: Social, affective, and behavioral influences. *Annals of Behavioral Medicine, 25,* 1–7.

McBride, C. M., Pollack, K. I., Lyna, P., Lipkus, I. M., Samsa, G. P., & Bepler, G. (2001). Reasons for quitting smoking among low-income African American smokers. *Health Psychology, 20,* 334–340.

McCaffery, J. M., Niaura, R., Todaro, J. F., Swan, G. E., & Carmelli, D. (2003). Depressive symptoms and metabolic risk in adult male twins enrolled in the national heart, lung and blood study. *Psychosomatic Medicine, 65,* 490–497.

McCaffery, J. M., Pogue-Geile, M. F., Muldoon, M. F., Debski, T. T., Wing, R. R., & Manuck, S. B. (2001). The nature of the association between diet and serum lipids in the community: A twin study. *Health Psychology, 20,* 341–350.

McCann, B. S., Bovbjerg, V. E., Curry, S. J., Retzlaff, B. M., Walden, C. E., & Knopp, R. H. (1996). Predicting participation in a dietary intervention to lower cholesterol among individuals with hyperlipidemia. *Health Psychology, 15,* 61–64.

McCarroll, J. E., Ursano, R. J., Fullerton, C. S., Liu, X., & Lundy, A. (2002). Somatic symptoms in Gulf War mortuary workers. *Psychosomatic Medicine, 64,* 29–33.

McCarthy, C. J. (1995). The relationship of cognitive appraisals and stress coping resources to emotion-eliciting events. *Dissertation Abstracts International: Section B: The Sciences & Engineering, 56,* 1746.

McCaul, K. D., Branstetter, A. D., Schroeder, D. M., & Glasgow, R. E. (1996). What is the relationship between breast cancer risk and mammography screening? A meta-analytic review. *Health Psychology, 15,* 423–429.

McCaul, K. D., Glasgow, R. E., & O'Neill, H. K. (1992). The problem of creating habits: Establishing health-protective dental behaviors. *Health Psychology, 11,* 101–110.

McClearn, G., Johansson, B., Berg, S., Pedersen, N., Ahern, F., Petrill, S. A., et al. (1997). Substantial genetic influence on cognitive abilities in twins 80 or more years old. *Science, 276,* 1560–1563.

McClement, S., Chochinov, H. M., Hack, T., Hassard, T., Kristjanson, L. J., & Harlos, M. (2007). Dignity Therapy: Family Member Perspectives. *Journal of Palliative Medicine, 10*(5), 1076–1082.

McCubbin, J., Pilcher, J., & Moore, D. (2010). Blood Pressure Increases During a Simulated Night Shift in Persons at Risk for Hypertension. *International Journal of Behavioral Medicine, 17,* 314–320.

McCullough, M. E., & Laurenceau, J. (2004). Gender and the natural history of self-rated health: A 59-year longitudinal study. *Health Psychology, 23,* 651–655.

McDade, T. W., Hawkley, L. C., & Cacioppo, J. T. (2006). Psychosocial and behavioral predictors of inflammation in middle-aged and older adults: The Chicago health, aging, and social relations study. *Psychosomatic Medicine, 68,* 376–381.

McDonough, P., Williams, D. R., House, J. S., & Duncan, G. J. (1999). Gender and the socioeconomic gradient in mortality. *Journal of Health and Social Behavior, 40,* 17–31.

McEwen, B. S. (1998). Protective and damaging effects of stress mediators. *New England Journal of Medicine, 338,* 171–179.

McEwen, B. S., & Stellar, E. (1993). Stress and the individual: Mechanisms leading to disease. *Archives of Internal Medicine, 153,* 2093–2101.

McFarland, C., & Alvaro, C. (2000). The impact of motivation on temporal comparisons: Coping with traumatic events by perceiving personal growth. *Journal of Personality and Social Psychology, 79,* 327–343.

McGill University Health Centre Journal. (2002). *Changing the face of pain: How Dr. Ronald Melzack abolished a 300-year-old medical theory.* Retrieved August 7, 2007, from www.muhc.ca/media/ensemble/2002feb/pain/.

McGilton, K. S., Boscart, V., Fox, M., Sidani, S., Rochon, E., & Sorin-Peters, R. (2009). A Systematic Review of the Effectiveness of Communication Interventions for Health Care Providers Caring for Patients in Residential Care Settings. *Worldviews on Evidence-Based Nursing, 6,* 149–159.

McGilton, K., Sorin-Peters, R., Sidani, S., Rochon, E., Boscart, V., & Fox, M. (2010). Focus on communication: increasing the opportunity for successful staff–patient interactions. *International Journal of Older People Nursing, 6,* 13–24.

McGinnis, M., Richmond, J. B., Brandt, E. N., Windom, R. E., & Mason, J. O. (1992). Health progress in the United States: Results of the 1990 objectives for the nation. *Journal of the American Medical Association, 268,* 2545–2552.

McGonagle, K. A., & Kessler, R. C. (1990). Chronic stress, acute stress, and depressive symptoms. *American Journal of Community Psychology, 18,* 681–706.

McGregor, D. (1967). *The professional manager.* New York: McGraw-Hill.

McGuire, L., Heffner, K., Glaser, R., Needleman, B., Malarkey, W., Dickinson, S., Lemeshow, S., Cook, C., Muscarella, P., Melvin, W. S., Ellison, E. C., & Kiecolt-Glaser, J. K. (2006). Pain and wound healing in surgical patients. *Annals of Behavioral Medicine, 31,* 165–172.

McGuire, W. J. (1964). Inducing resistance to persuasion: Some contemporary approaches. In L. Berkowitz (Ed.), *Advances in experimental social psychology* (Vol. 1, pp. 192–231). New York: Academic Press.

McGuire, W. J. (1973). Persuasion, resistance and attitude change. In I. de Sola Pool, F. W. Frey, W. Schramm, N. Maccoby, & E. B. Parker (Eds.), *Handbook of communication* (pp. 216–252). Chicago: Rand-McNally.

McIlroy, A. (2006, October 24). Want chronic-pain relief? It helps to be rich. *The Globe and Mail,* pp. A9.

McKenzie, D. C. (1998). Abreast in a boat—A race against breast cancer. *Canadian Medical Association Journal, 159,* 376–378.

McLeod, J. D., Kessler, R. C., & Landis, K. R. (1992). Speed of recovery from major depressive episodes in a community sample of married men and women. *Journal of Abnormal Psychology, 101,* 277–286.

McMahon, C. E. (1975). Placebo effects in Renaissance medicine. *Journal of the American Society of Psychosomatic Dentistry and Medicine, 22,* 3–9.

McNally, J. D., Matheson, D. A., & Bakowsky, V. S. (2006). The epidemiology of self-reported fibromyalgia in Canada. *Chronic Diseases in Canada, 27*(1), 9–16.

McNeely, M. L., Campbell, K. L., Rowe, B. H., Klassen, T. P., Mackey, J. R., & Courneya, K. S. (2006). Effects of exercise on breast cancer patients and survivors: A systematic review and meta-analysis. *CMAJ, 175*(1), 34–41.

McNeil, D. G., Jr. (2002, May 17). With folk medicine on rise, health group is monitoring. *The New York Times,* p. A9.

McPherson, M., Smith-Lovin, L., & Brashears, M. E. (2006). Social isolation in America: Changes in core discussion networks over two decades. *American Sociological Review, 71,* 353–375.

McQuade, D. V. (2002). Negative social perception of hypothetical workers with rheumatoid arthritis. *Journal of Behavioral Medicine, 25,* 205–217.

McQuillen, A. D., Licht, M. H., & Licht, B. G. (2003). Contributions of disease severity and perceptions of primary and secondary control to the prediction of psychological adjustment to Parkinson's disease. *Health Psychology, 22,* 504–512.

Meagher, M., Arnau, R., & Rhudy, J. (2001). Pain and emotion: Effects of affective picture modulation. *Psychosomatic Medicine, 63,* 79–90.

Meana, M., Cho, R., & DesMeules, M. (2003). Chronic pain: The extra burden on Canadian Women. *Women's Health Surveillance Report.* Retrieved August 17, 2007, from www.phac-aspc.gc.ca/publicat/whsr-rssf/pdf/WHSR_Chap_16_e.pdf.

Means-Christensen, A. J., Arnau, R. C., Tonidandel, A. M., Bramson, R., & Meagher, M. W. (2005). An efficient method of identifying major depression and panic disorder in primary care. *Journal of Behavioral Medicine, 28,* 565–573.

Meara, E., White, C., & Cutler, D. M. (2004). Trend in medical spending by age, 1963–2000. *Health Affairs, 23,* 176–183.

Mechanic, D. (1972). Social psychologic factors affecting the presentation of bodily complaints. *New England Journal of Medicine, 286,* 1132–1139.

Mechlin, M. B., Maixner, W., Light, K. C., Fisher, J. M., & Girdler, S. S. (2005). African Americans show alterations in endogenous pain regulatory mechanisms and reduced pain tolerance to experimental pain procedures. *Psychosomatic Medicine, 67,* 948–956.

Medicinenet.com. (2002). *Alcohol abuse.* Retrieved from: http://www.medicinenet.com/script/main/art.asp?articlekey=38054&page=2.

Medzhitov, R., & Janeway Jr., C. A. (2002). Decoding the patterns of self and non-self by the innate immune system. *Science, 296,* 298–316.

Meechan, G., Collins, J., & Petrie, K. J. (2003). The relationship of symptoms and psychological factors to delay in seeking medical care for breast symptoms. *Preventive Medicine, 36,* 374–378.

Meichenbaum, D. H., & Cameron, R. (1974). The clinical potential and pitfalls of modifying what clients say to themselves. In M. J. Mahoney & C. E. Thoresen (Eds.), *Self-control: Power to the person* (pp. 263–290). Monterey, CA: Brooks-Cole.

Meichenbaum, D. H., & Jaremko, M. E. (Eds.). (1983). *Stress reduction and prevention.* New York: Plenum Press.

Meichenbaum, D. H., & Turk, D. (1982). *Stress, coping, and disease: A cognitive—behavioral perspective. In R. W. J. Neufield (Ed.), Psychological stress and psychopathology* (pp. 289–306). New York: McGraw-Hill.

Meisner, B. A. (2011). Physicians' attitudes toward aging, the aged, and the provision of geriatric care: a systematic narrative review. *Critical Public Health.*

Melamed, B. (1995). The interface between physical and mental disorders: The need to dismantle the biopsychosocialneuroimmunological model of disease. *Journal of Clinical Psychology in Medical Setting, 2,* 225–231.

Melamed, S., Shirom, A., Toker, S., Berliner, S. & Shapira, I. (2004). Association of fear of terror with low grade inflammation among apparently healthy employed adults. *Psychosomatic Medicine* 66, pp. 481–491.

Melzack, R. (1975). The McGill Pain Questionnaire: Major properties and scoring methods. *Pain, 1(3),* 277–299.

Melzack, R. (1990). Phantom limbs and the concept of a neuromatrix. *Trends in Neurosciences, 13(3),* 88–92.

Melzack, R. (1992). Phantom limbs. *Scientific American, 266(4),* 120–126.

Melzack, R. (1993). Pain: Past, present, and future. *Canadian Journal of Experimental Psychology, 47,* 615–629.

Melzack, R. (1999). From the gate to the neuromatrix. *Pain, Suppl6,* S121–126.

Melzack, R. (2001). Pain and the neuromatrix in the brain. *Journal of Dental Education, 65(12),* 1378–1382.

Melzack, R., & Wall, P.D. (1965). Pain mechanisms: A new theory. *Science, 150,* 171–179.

Melzack, R., & Wall, P. D. (1982). *The challenge of pain.* New York: Basic Books.

Menaghan, E., Kowaleski-Jones, L., & Mott, F. (1997). The intergenerational costs of parental social stressors: Academic and social difficulties in early adolescence for children of young mothers. *Journal of Health and Social Behavior, 38,* 72–86.

Mercado, A. C., Carroll, L. J., Cassidy, J. D., & Cote, P. (2000). Coping with neck and low back pain in the general population. *Health Psychology, 19,* 333–338.

Merskey, H. (1998). History of pain research and management in Canada. *Pain Research and Management, 3(3),* 164–173.

Messina, C. R., Lane, D. S., Glanz, K., West, D. S., Taylor, V., Frishman, W., et al. (2004). Relationship of social support and social burden to repeated breast cancer screening in the women's health initiative. *Health Psychology, 23,* 582–594.

Meyerowitz, B. E., & Hart, S. (1993, April*). Women and cancer: Have assumptions about women limited our research agenda?* Paper presented at the Women's Psychological and Physical Health Conference, Lawrence, KS.

Mezzacappa, E. S., Kelsey, R. M., Katkin, E. S., & Sloan, R. P. (2001). Vagal rebound and recovery from psychological stress. *Psychosomatic Medicine, 63,* 650–657.

Michaud, D.S., Liu, S., Giovannucci, E., Willett W.C., Colditz, G.A., Fuchs, C.S. (2002). Dietary sugar, glycemic load, and pancreatic cancer risk in a prospective study. J Nat Cancer Inst 94: 1293–1300.

Michie, S., Rothman, J., & Sheeran, P. (2007). Current issues and new direction in psychology and health: Advancing the science of behavior change. *Psychology and Health, 22(3),* 249–253.

Milan, A., Vézina, M., & Wells, C. (2007). *Family portrait: Continuity and change in Canadian families and households in 2006: Findings.* Retrieved February 12, 2008, from http://www12.statcan.ca/english/census06/analysis/famhouse/index.cfm.

Millar, M. G., & Millar, K. (1995). Negative affective consequences of thinking about disease detection behaviors. *Health Psychology, 14,* 141–146.

Millar, W. J. (2004). Vision problems among seniors. *Health Reports,* Vol. 16, No. 1, 45–49, October 2004, Statistics Canada, Catalogue 82-003.

Miller, A. H. (2010). Depression and immunity: A role for T cells? *Brain, Behavior, and Immunity, 24*(1), 1–8

Miller, F. G., & Kaptchuk, T. J. (2008). The power of context: reconceptualizing the placebo effect. *J R Soc Med, 101,* 222–225.

Miller, G.E., & Blackwell, E. (2006). Turning up the heat: Inflammation as a mechanism linking chronic stress, depression, and heart disease. *Current Directions in Psychological Science,* 15, 269–272.

Miller, G. E. & Cohen, S. (2001). Psychological interventions and the immune system: A meta-analytic review and critique. *Health Psychology, 20,* 47–63.

Miller, G. E., Chen, E., & Cole, S. W. (2009). Health psychology: Developing biologically plausible models linking the social world and physical health. *Annual Review of Psychology,* 60, 501–524.

Miller, G. E., Chen, E., & Zhou, E. S. (2007). If it goes up, must it come down? Chronic stress and the hypothalamic-pituitary-adrenocortical axis in humans. *Psychological Bulletins, 133,* 25–45.

Miller, G. E., Cohen, S., & Herbert, T. B. (1999). Pathways linking major depression and immunity in ambulatory female patients. *Psychosomatic Medicine, 61,* 850–860.

Miller, G. E., Cohen, S., & Ritchey, A. K. (2002). Chronic psychological stress and the regulation of pro-inflammatory cytokines: A glucocorticoid-resistance model. *Health Psychology, 21,* 531–541.

Miller, G. E., Cohen, S., Pressman, S., Barkin, A., Rabin, B. S., & Treanor, J. J. (2004). Psychological stress and antibody response to influenza vaccination: When is the critical period for stress, and how does it get inside the body? *Psychosomatic Medicine, 66,* 215–223.

Miller, G. E., Freedland, K. E., Carney, R. M., Stetler, C. A., & Banks, W. A. (2003). Cynical hostility, depressive symptoms and the expression of inflammatory risk markers for coronary heart disease. *Journal of Behavioral Medicine, 26,* 501–516.

Miller, K. A., Siscovick, D. S., Sheppard, L., Shepherd, K., Sullivan, J. H., Anderson, G. L., & Kaufman, J. D. (2007). Long-term exposure to air pollution and incidence or cardiovascular events in women. *The New England Journal of Medicine, 356,* 447–458.

Miller, L. C., Bettencourt, B. A., DeBro, S., & Hoffman, V. (1993). Negotiating safer sex: Interpersonal dynamics. In J. Pryor & G. Reeder (Eds.), *The social psychology of HIV infection* (pp. 85–123). Hillsdale, NJ: Erlbaum.

Miller, N. E. (1989). Placebo factors in types of treatment: Views of a psychologist. In M. Shepherd & N. Sartorius (Eds.), *Non-specific aspects of treatment* (pp. 39–56). Lewiston, NY: Hans Huber.

Miller, N. E. (1992). Some trends from the history to the future of behavioral medicine. *Annals of Behavioral Medicine, 14,* 307–309.

Miller, W. R. & Rollnick, S. (1991). *Motivational interviewing: Preparing people to change addictive behavior.* New York, NY, Guilford Press.

Miller Smedema, S., Catalano, D., & Ebener, D. J. (2010). The Relationship of Coping, Self-Worth, and Subjective Well-Being: A Structural Equation Model. *Rehabilitation Counseling Bulletin, 53,* 131–142.

Mills, P. J., Meck, J. V., Waters, W. W., D'Aunno, D., & Ziegler, M. G. (2001). Peripheral leukocyte subpopulations and catecholamine levels in astronauts as a function of mission duration. *Psychosomatic Medicine, 63,* 886–890.

Miranda, J., Perez-Stable, E. J., Munoz, R. F., Hargreaves, W., & Henke, C. J. (1991). Somatization, psychiatric disorder, and stress in utilization of ambulatory medical services. *Health Psychology, 10,* 46–51.

Mishra, K. D., Gatchel, R. J., & Gardea, M. A. (2000). The relative efficacy of three cognitive-behavioral treatment approaches to temporomandibular disorders. *Journal of Behavioral Medicine, 23,* 293–309.

Mitchell, L. A., MacDonald, R. A. R., & Brodie, E., E. (2006). A comparison of the effects of preferred music, arithmetic and humour on cold pressor pain. *European Journal of Pain 10*(4), 343–351.

Mitchell, L. A., MacDonald, R. A. R., Knussen, C., & Serpell, M. G. (2007). A survey investigation of the effects of music listening on chronic pain. *Psychology of Music, 35*(1), 37–57.

Mitchell, T. L., Yakiwchuk, C. V., Griffin, K. L., Gray, R. E., & Fitch, M. I. (2007). Survivor dragon boating: a vehicle to reclaim and enhance life after treatment for breast cancer. *Health Care for Women International, 28(2),* 122–140.

Mitchell, T., & Nielsen, E. (2002). Living life to the limits: Breast cancer and dragon boating. *Canadian Woman's Studies Journal, 21(3),* 50–57.

Mitchell, T., Griffin, K., Stewart, S., & Loba, P. (2004). 'We will never ever forget…': The Swissair flight 111 disaster and its impact on volunteers and communities. *Journal of Health Psychology, 9(2),* 245–262.

Mittag, W., & Schwarzer, R. (1993). Interaction of employment status and self—efficacy on alcohol consumption: A two-wave study on stressful life transitions. *Psychology and Health, 8,* 77–87.

Mittermaier, C., Dejaco, C., Waldhoer, T., Oefferlbauer-Ernst, A., Miehsler, W., Beier, M., et al. (2004). Impact of depressive mood on relapse in patients with inflammatory bowel disease: A prospective 18-month follow up study. *Psychosomatic Medicine, 66,* 79–84.

Miyashita, M., Morita, T., Sato, K., Hirai, K., Shima, Y., & Uchitomi, Y. (2008). Good Death Inventory: A Measure for Evaluating Good Death from the Bereaved Family Member's Perspective. *Journal of Pain and Symptom Management, 35,* 486–498.

Miyazaki, T., Ishikawa, T., Iimori, H., Miki, A., Wenner, M., Fukunishi, I., et al. (2003). Relationship between perceived social support and immune function. *Stress and Health, 19,* 3–7.

Moholdt, T., Wisløff, U., Nilsen, T. I. L., & Slørdahl, S. A. (2008). Physical activity and mortality in men and women with coronary heart disease: a prospective population-based cohort study in Norway (the HUNT study). *European Journal of Cardiovascular Prevention & Rehabilitation, 15,* 639–645.

Mohr, D. C., Dick, L. P., Russo, D., Pinn, J., Boudewyn, A. C., Likosky, W., et al. (1999). The psychological impact of multiple sclerosis: Exploring the patient's perspective. *Health Psychology, 18,* 376–382.

Mohr, D. C., Goodkin, D. E., Nelson, S., Cox, D., & Weiner, M. (2002). Moderating effects of coping on the relationship between stress and the development of new brain lesions in multiple sclerosis. *Psychosomatic Medicine, 64,* 803–809.

Mohr, D., Bedantham, K., Neylan, T., Metzler, T. J., Best, S., & Marmar, C. R. (2003). The mediating effects of sleep in the relationship between traumatic stress and health symptoms in urban police officers. *Psychosomatic Medicine, 65,* 485–489.

Mohr, D., Hart, S. L., & Goldberg, A. (2003). Effects of treatment for depression on fatigue in multiple sclerosis. *Psychosomatic Medicine, 65,* 542–547.

Mok, H., & Morishita, K. (2002). Depression detection and treatment across cultures: Addressing barriers within elderly populations. *Visions: BC's Mental Health Journal, 15,* 7–8.

Mokdad, A. H., Marks, J. S., Stroup, D. F., & Gerberding, J. L. (2004). Actual cause of death in the United States, 2000. *Journal of the American Medical Society, 291,* 1238–1245.

Moller, J., Hallqvist, J., Diderichsen, F., Theorell, T., Reuterwall, C., & Ahlbom, A. (1999). Do episodes of anger trigger myocardial infarction? A case-crossover analysis in the Stockholm Heart Epidemiology Program (SHEEP). *Psychosomatic Medicine, 61,* 842–849.

Molnar, D., & Sadava, S. (2010). Perfectionism and health: The key role of stress. In G. Flett and P. Fry (chairs) *Perfectionism and Health: A Multidimensional Analysis.* Paper presented at the 22nd annual convention of the Association for Psychological Science, Boston, MA.

Molnar, D. S., Reker, D. L., Culp, N. A., Sadava, S. W., & DeCourville, N. H. (2006). A mediated model of perfectionism, affect, and physical health. *Journal of Research in Personality, 40,* 482–500.

Mommersteeg, P. M. C., Heijnen, C. J., Kavelaars, A., & van Doornen, L. J. P. (2006). Immune and Endocrine Function in Burnout Syndrome. *Psychosomatic Medicine, 68,* 879–886.

Montgomery, G. H., & Bovjerg, D. H. (2003). Expectations of chemotherapy—related nausea: Emotional and experiential predictors. *Annals of Behavioral Medicine, 25,* 48–54.

Montgomery, G. H., DuHamel, K. N., & Redd, W. H. (2000). A meta-analysis of hypnotically induced analgesia: how effective is hypnosis? *International Journal of Clinical and Experimental Hypnosis, 48*(138–153).

Moody, L., McCormick, K., & Williams, A. (1990). Disease and symptom severity, functional status, and quality of life in chronic bronchitis and emphysema (CBE). *Journal of Behavioral Medicine, 13,* 297–306.

Mookadam, F., & Arthur, H. M. (2004). Social Support and Its Relationship to Morbidity and Mortality After Acute Myocardial Infarction: Systematic Overview. *Arch Intern Med, 164,* 1514–1518.

Moore, P. J., Adler, N. E., Williams, D. R., & Jackson, J. S. (2002). Socioeconomic status and health: The role of sleep. *Psychosomatic Medicine, 64,* 337–344.

Moos, R. H. (1988). Life stressors and coping resources influence health and well-being. *Psychological Assessment, 4,* 133–158.

Moos, R. H., Brennan, P. L., & Moos, B. S. (1991). Short-term processes of remission and nonremission among later-life problem drinkers. *Alcoholism: Clinical and Experimental Review, 15,* 948–955.

Moreira, J. M., de Fátima Silva, M., Moleiro, C., Aguiar, P., Andrez, M., Bernardes, S., et al. (2003). Perceived social support as an offshoot of attachment style. Personality and Individual Differences, 34, 485–501.

Morell, V. (1993). Huntington's gene finally found. *Science, 260,* 28–30.

Moreno-Smith, M., Lutgendorf, S. K., & Sood, A. K. (2010). Impact of stress on cancer metastasis. *Future Oncology, 6*(12), 1863–1881.

Morens, D. M., Folkers, G. K., & Fauci, A. S. (2004, July 8). The challenge of emerging and re-emerging infectious diseases. *Nature, 430,* 242–249.

Moretti, M. M., Obsuth, I., Odgers, C. L., & Reebye, P. (2006). Exposure to maternal vs. paternal partner violence, PTSD and aggression in adolescent girls and boys. *Aggressive Behavior, 32(4),* 385–395.

Morin, C. M., Rodrigue, S., & Ivers, H. (2003). Role of stress, arousal, and coping skills in primary insomnia. *Psychosomatic Medicine, 65,* 259–267.

Morisky, D. E., Stein, J. A., Chiao, C., Ksobiech, K., & Malow, R. (2006). Impact of a social influence intervention on condom use and sexually transmitted infections among established-based females sex workers in the Philippines: A multilevel analysis. *Health Psychology, 25,* 595–603.

Morris, R. P. (1961). Effect of the mother on goal-setting behaviour of the asthmatic child. *Annals of Allergy, 19,* 44–54.

Morrongiello, B. A., Corbett, M., & Bellissimo, A. (2008). "Do as I say, not as I do": Family influences on children's safety and risk behaviors. *Health Psychology, 27,* 498–503.

Morton, G. J., Cummings, D. E., Baskin, D. G., Barsh, G. S., & Schwartz, M. W. (2006). Central nervous system control of food intake and body weight. *Nature, 443* (Sept. 21, 2006), 289–295.

Moser, D. K., & Dracup, K. (2004). Role of spousal anxiety and depression in patients' psychosocial recovery after a cardiac event. *Psychosomatic Medicine, 66,* 527–532.

Moser, D. K., Dracup, K., McKinley, S., Yamaski, K., Kim, C., Reigel, B., et al. (2003). An international perspective on gender differences in anxiety early after acute myocardial infarction. *Psychosomatic Medicine, 65,* 511–516.

Moskal, R. J. (1991). Effect of a comprehensive AIDS curriculum on knowledge and attitudinal changes in northern Canadian college students. *Canadian Journal of Counselling, 25(3),* 338–348.

Moskowitz, J. T. (2003). Positive affect predicts lower risk of AIDS mortality. *Psychosomatic Medicine, 65,* 620–626.

Moskowitz, J. T., Epel, E. S., & Acree, M. (2008). Positive affect uniquely predicts lower risk of mortality in people with diabetes. *Health Psychology, 27(1sup)*, S73–S82.

Moss-Morris, R., & Petrie, K. J. (2001). Discriminating between chronic fatigue syndrome and depression: A cognitive analysis. *Psychological Medicine, 31*, 469–479.

Moss-Morris, R., & Spence, M. (2006). To "lump" or to "split" the functional somatic syndromes: Can infectious and emotional risk factors differentiate between the onset of chronic fatigue syndrome and irritable bowl syndrome? *Psychosomatic Medicine, 68*, 463–469.

Moss-Morris, R., Petrie, K. J., & Weinman, J. (1996). Functioning in chronic fatigue syndrome: Do illness perceptions play a regulatory role? *British Journal of Health Psychology, 1*, 15–25.

Motivala, S. J., & Irwin, M. R. (2007). Sleep and immunity: Cytokine pathways linking sleep and health outcomes. *Current Directions in Psychological Science, 16*, 21–25.

Motivala, S. J., Hurwitz, B. E., Llabre, M. M., Klimas, N. G., Fletcher, M. A., Antoni, M. H., et al. (2003). Psychological distress is associated with decreased memory and helper T-cell and B-cell counts in pre-AIDS HIV-seropositive men and women but only in those with low viral load. *Psychosomatic Medicine, 65*, 627–635.

Motl, R. W., Dishman, R. K., Saunders, R. P., Dowda, M., Felton, G., Ward, D. S., et al. (2002). Examining social-cognitive determinants of intention and physical activity among Black and White adolescent girls under structural equation modeling. *Health Psychology, 21*, 459–467.

Motl, R. W., Dishman, R. K., Ward, D. S., Saunders, R. P., Dowda, M., Felton, G., & Pate, R. R. (2005). Comparison of barriers self-efficacy and perceived behavioral control for explaining physical activity across year 1 among adolescent girls. *Health Psychology, 24*, 106–111.

Motl, R. W., Konopack, J. F., McAuley, E., Elavsky, S., Jerome, G. J., & Marquez, D. X. (2005). Depressive symptoms among older adults: Long-term reduction after a physical activity intervention. *Journal of Behavioral Medicine, 28*, 385–394.

Moussavi, S., Chatterji, S., Verdes, E., Tandon, A., Patel, V., & Ustun, B. (2007). Depression, chronic diseases, and decrements in health: results from the World Health Surveys. *The Lancet, 370*, 851–858.

Moyer, A. (1997). Psychosocial outcomes of breast-conserving surgery versus mastectomy: A meta-analytic review. *Health Psychology, 16*, 284–298.

Moyer, A., & Salovey, P. (1996). Psychosocial sequelae of breast cancer and its treatment. *Annals of Behavioral Medicine, 18*, 110–125.

Moynihan, J. A., Larson, M. R., Treanor, J., Duberstein, P. R., Power, A., Shore, B., & Ader, R. (2004). Psychosocial factors and the response to influenza vaccination in older adults. *Psychosomatic Medicine, 66*, 950–953.

Muhonen, T., & Torkelson, E. (2003). The demand-control-support model and health among women and men in similar occupations. *Journal of Behavioral Medicine, 26*, 601–613.

Mullally, W. J., Hall, K., & Goldstein, R. (2009). Efficacy of biofeedback in the treatment of migraine and tension type headaches. *Pain Physician, 12*, 1005–1011.

Mulia, N., Schmidt, L., Bond, J., Jacobs, L., & Korcha, R. (2008). Stress, social support and problem drinking among women in poverty. *Addiction, 103*, 1283–1293.

Multiple Sclerosis Society of Canada. (2006). *Multiple sclerosis is a complex disease.* Retrieved August 14, 2007, from www.mssociety.ca/en/information/default.htm.

Munro, S., Lewin, S., Swart, T., & Volmink, J. (2007). A review of health behaviour theories: how useful are these for developing interventions to promote long-term medication adherence for TB and HIV/AIDS? *BMC Public Health, 7(1)*, 104.

Murphy, D. A., Mann, T., O'Keefe, Z., & Rotheram-Borus, M. (1998). Number of pregnancies, outcome expectancies, and social norms among HIV-infected young women. *Health Psychology, 17*, 470–475.

Murphy, S. L. (2000, July 24). *Deaths: Final data for 1998.* National Vital Statistics Reports (NCHS), pp. 26, 73.

Murray, C. D., Patchick, E., Pettifer, S., Caillette, F., & Howard, T. (2006). Immersive virtual reality as a rehabilitative technology for phantom limb experience: A protocol. *CyberPsychology & Behavior, 9(2)*, 167–170.

Murray, C. D., Pettifer, S., Howard, T., Patchick, E. L., Caillette, F., Kulkarni, J., & Bamford, C. (2007). The treatment of phantom limb pain using immersive virtual reality: Three case studies. *Disability and Rehabilitation, 29(18)*, 1465–1469.

Mutterperl, J. A., & Sanderson, C. A. (2002). Mind over matter: Internalization of the thinness norm as a moderator of responsiveness to norm misperception education in college women. *Health Psychology, 21*, 519–523.

Myers, L. B., & Horswill, M. S. (2006). Social Cognitive Predictors of Sun Protection Intention and Behavior. *Behavioral Medicine 32*, 57–63.

Myers, R. S., & Roth, D. L. (1997). Perceived benefits of and barriers to exercise and stage of exercise adoption in young adults. *Health Psychology, 16*, 277–283.

Naar-King, S., Wright, K., Parsons, J. T., Frey, M., Templin, T., Lam, P., & Murphy, D. (2006). Healthy choices: Motivational enhancement therapy for health risk behaviors in HIV-positive youth. *AIDS Education and Prevention, 18(1)*, 1–11.

Nabalamba, A., & Millar, W. J. (2007). Going to the doctor. *Health Reports, 18(1)*, 23–35 (Statistics Canada Catalogue 82-003). Retrieved February 17, 2008, from www.statcan.ca/english/freepub/82-003-XIE/82-003-XIE2006003.pdf.

Nadkarni, A., Kucukarslan, S. N., Bagozzi, R. P., Yates, J. F., & Erickson, S. R. (2010). A simple and promising tool to improve self-monitoring of blood glucose in patients with diabetes. *Diabetes Research and Clinical Practice, 89*, 30–37.

Naliboff, B. D., Mayer, M., Fass, R., Fitzgerald, L. Z., Chang, L., Bolus, R., et al. (2004). The effect of life stress on symptoms of heartburn. *Psychosomatic Medicine, 66*, 426–434.

Napolitano, M. A., Fotheringham, M., Tate, D., Sciamanna, C., Leslie, E., Owen, N., et al. (2003). Evaluation of an Internet-based physical activity intervention: A preliminary investigation. *Annals of Behavioral Medicine, 25*, 92–99.

Naqvi, T. Z., Naqvi, S. S. A., & Merz, C. N. B. (2005). Gender differences in the link between depression and cardiovascular disease. *Psychosomatic Medicine, 67*, S15–S18.

Nash, J. M., Williams, D. M., Nicholson, R., & Trask, P. C. (2006). The contribution of pain-related anxiety to disability from headache. *Journal of Behavioral Medicine, 29*, 61–67.

Nashold, B. S., & Friedman, H. (1972). Dorsal column stimulation for pain: A preliminary report on thirty patients. *Journal of Neurosurgery, 36*, 590–597.

National Cancer Institute of Canada. (2005). *Progress in cancer prevention: Modifiable risk factors.* Retrieved July 24, 2007, from www.ncic.cancer.ca/ncic/internet/standard/ 0,3621,84658243_ 85787780_399354909_langId-en,00.html.

National Center for Complementary and Alternative Medicine. (2007). *National Center for Complementary and Alternative Medicine: What is CAM?* Retrieved July 16, 2007, from http://nccam.nih.gov/health/whatiscam/#4.

National Institute on Alcohol Abuse and Alcoholism. (2000a). *10th special report to the U.S. Congress on alcohol and health.* Bethesda, MD: Author. Retrieved from: http://silk.nih.gov/silk/niaaa1/publication/10report/10-order.htm.

National Institute on Alcohol Abuse and Alcoholism. (2000b, October). *Alcohol alert: New advances in alcoholism treatment.* Bethesda, MD: Author. Retrieved from: www.niaaa. nih.gov.

Nelsom, D. B., SammelL, M. D., Freeman, E. W., Lin, H., Gracia, C. R., & Schmitz, K. H. (2008). Effect of Physical Activity on Menopausal Symptoms among Urban Women. *Medicine & Science in Sports & Exercise, 40*, 50–58.

Nelson, C., Franks, S., Brose, A., Raven, P., Williamson, J., Shi, X., McGill, J., & Harrell, E. (2005). The influence of hostility and family history of cardiovascular disease on autonomic activation in response to controllable versus non-controllable stress, anger imagery induction, and relaxation imagery. *Journal of Behavioral Medicine, 28*, 213–221.

Nemeroff, C. J. (1995). Magical thinking about illness virulence: Conceptions of germs from "safe" versus "dangerous" others. *Health Psychology, 14*, 147–151.

Nemeroff, C., Bremner, J. D., Foa, E. B., Mayberg, H. S., North, C. S., & Stein, M. B. (2006). Posttraumatic stress disorder: A state-of-the-science review. *Journal of Psychiatric Research, 40*, 1–21.

Nes, L. S., & Segerstrom, S. C. (2006). Dispositional Optimism and Coping: A Meta-Analytic Review. *Personality and Social Psychology Review, 10*(3), 235–251.

Neugebauer, A., Katz, P. P., & Pasch, L. A. (2003). Effect of valued activity disability, social comparisons, and satisfaction with ability on depressive symptoms in rheumatoid arthritis. *Health Psychology, 22*, 253–262.

Neuling, S. J., & Winefield, H. R. (1988). Social support and recovery after surgery for breast cancer: Frequency and correlates of supportive behaviors by family, friends, and surgeon. *Social Science and Medicine, 27*, 385–392.

Neumann, S. A., Waldstein, S. R., Sollers, J. J., Thayer, J. F., & Sorkin, J. D. (2004). Hostility and distraction have differential influences on cardiovascular recovery from anger recall in women. *Health Psychology, 23*, 631–640.

Neumark-Sztainer, D., Wall, M. M., Story, M., & Perry C. L. (2003). Correlates of unhealthy weight-control behaviors among adolescents: Implications for prevention programs. *Health Psychology, 22*, 88–98.

Neuroscience Canada (2010). Annual report 2009. Retrieved May 11, 2011 from http://www.braincanada.ca/files/2009AnnualReport.pdf.

New York Times. (2000 October 3). Passing along the diet-and-binge habit, p. D8.

Newcomb, M. D., Rabow, J., Monte, M., & Hernandez, A. C. R. (1991). Informal drunk driving intervention: Psychosocial correlates among young adult women and men. *Journal of Applied Social Psychology, 21*, 1988–2006.

Newsom, J. T., Knapp, J. E., & Schulz, R. (1996). Longitudinal analysis of specific domains of internal control and depressive symptoms in patients with recurrent cancer. *Health Psychology, 15*, 323–331.

Newton, T. L., & Sanford, J. M. (2003). Conflict structure moderates associations between cardiovascular reactivity and negative marital interaction. *Health Psychology, 22*, 270–278.

Neylan, T. C., et al. (2002). Critical incident exposure and sleep quality in police officers. *Psychosomatic Medicine, 64*, 345–352.

Ng, D. M., & Jeffery, R. W. (2003). Relationships between perceived stress and health behaviors in a sample of working adults. *Health Psychology, 22*, 638–642.

Ng, E., McGrail, K. M., & Johnson, Jeffrey A. (2010). "Hospitalization risk in a type 2 diabetes cohort." *Health Reports.* Component of Statistics Canada Catalogue no. 82-003-X.

Ní Chróinín, D., Syed Farooq, S. F., Burke, M., & Kyne, L. (2011). Patient understanding of discharge diagnoses: Prevalence and predictors. *European Geriatric Medicine, 2*, 74-78.

Ni Mhurchu, C., Aston, L., & Jebb, S. (2010). Effects of worksite health promotion interventions on employee diets: a systematic review. *BMC Public Health, 10*(1), 62.

Niaura, R., Todaro, J. F., Stroud, L., Spiro, A., III, Ward, K. D., & Weiss, S. (2002). Hostility, the metabolic syndrome and incident coronary heart disease. *Health Psychology, 21*, 588–593.

Nicassio, P. M., Meyerowitz, B. E., & Kerns, R. D. (2004). The future of health psychology interventions. *Health Psychology, 23*, 132–137.

Nicassio, P. M., Radojevic, V., Schoenfeld-Smith, K., & Dwyer, K. (1995). The contribution of family cohesion and the pain-coping process to depressive symptoms in fibromyalgia. *Annals of Behavioral Medicine, 17*, 349–356.

Nichol, K. L., Nordin, J., Mullooly, J., Lask, R., Fillbrandt, K., & Iwane, M. (2003). Influenza vaccination and reduction in hospitalizations for cardiac disease and stroke among the elderly. *New England Journal of Medicine, 348*, 1322–1332, http://www.nejm.org.

Nicholson, A., Fuhrer, R., & Marmot, M. (2005). Psychological distress as a predictor of CHD events in men: The effect of persistence and components of risk. *Psychosomatic Medicine, 67*, 522–530.

Nielsen, S. J., & Popkin, B. M. (2003). Patterns and trends in food portion sizes, 1977–1998. *Journal of the American Medical Association, 289*, 450–453.

Nigg, C. R. (2001). Explaining adolescent exercise behavior change: A longitudinal application of the transtheoretical model. *Annals of Behavioral Medicine, 23*, 11–20.

Nixon, K., & McClain, J. A. (2010). Adolescence as a critical window for developing an alcohol use disorder: current findings in neuroscience. *Current Opinion in Psychiatry, 23*, 227–232.

Nolen-Hoeksema, S., McBride, A., & Larson, J. (1997). Rumination and psychological distress among bereaved partners. *Journal of Personality and Social Psychology, 72*, 855–862.

Norman, P., & Brain, K. (2005). An application of an extended health belief model to the prediction of breast self-examination among women with a family history of breast cancer. *British Journal of Health Psychology, 10*, 1–16.

Norman, P., Conner, M., & Bell, R. (1999). The theory of planned behavior and smoking cessation. *Health Psychology, 18*, 89–94.

Norman, S. A., Lumley, M. A., Dooley, J. A., & Diamond, M. P. (2004). For whom does it work? Moderators of the effects of written emotional disclosures in a randomized trial among women with chronic pelvic pain. *Psychosomatic Medicine, 66*, 174–183.

Norris, S. (2006). *HIV/Aids-Past, present and future.* Retrieved September 16, 2007, from www.parl.gc.ca/information/library/PRBpubs/prb0208-e.pdf.

Northcott, H. C., & Wilson, D. M. (2001). *Dying and death in Canada.* Aurora, ON: Garamond Press.

Northouse, L., Templin, T., & Mood, D. (2001). Couples' adjustment to breast disease during the first year following diagnosis. *Journal of Behavioral Medicine, 24*, 115–136.

Noto, Y., Kitajima, M., Kudo, M., Okudera, K., & Hirota, K. (2010). Leg massage therapy promotes psychological relaxation and reinforces the first-line host defense in cancer patients. *Journal of Anesthesia, 24*(6), 827–831.

Novak, S. P., & Clayton, R. R. (2001). The influence of school environment and self-regulation on transitions between stages of cigarette smoking: A multilevel analysis. *Health Psychology, 20*, 196–207.

Novotny, P., Colligan, R. C., Szydlo, D. W., Clark, M. M., Rausch, S., Wampfler, J., et al. (2010). A Pessimistic Explanatory Style Is Prognostic for Poor Lung Cancer Survival. *Journal of Thoracic Oncology, 5*, 326–332.

Nowack, R. (1992). Final ethics: Dutch discover euthanasia abuse. *Journal of NIH Research, 4*, 31–32.

Noyes, R., et al. (2000). Illness fears in the general population. *Psychosomatic Medicine, 62*, 318–325.

Noyes, R., Jr., Stuart, S. P., Langbehn, D. R., Happel, R. L., Longley, S. L., Muller, B. A., et al. (2003). Test of an interpersonal model of hypochondriasis. *Psychosomatic Medicine, 65*, 292–300.

Nurses' Health Study (2004). History. Retrieved August 1, 2004 from http://www.channing.harvard.edu/nhs/history/index.shtml.

O'Brien, A., Fries, E., & Bowen, D. (2000). The effect of accuracy of perceptions of dietary-fat intake on perceived risk and intentions to change. *Journal of Behavioral Medicine, 23*, 465–473.

O'Brien, T. B., DeLongis, A., Pomaki, G., Puterman, E., & Zwicker, A. (2009). Couples Coping with Stress: The Role of Empathic Responding. *European Psychologist, 14*, 18–28.

O'Brien-Pallas, L. (2007). Nursing health human resources in Canada: The time for action was yesterday! Canadian Federation of Nurses Union fact sheet retrieved from www.nursesunions.ca/media.php?mid=104.

O'Carroll, R. E., Ayling, R., O'Reilly, S. M., & North, N. T. (2003). Alexithymia and sense of coherence in patients with total spinal cord transection. *Psychosomatic Medicine, 65*, 151–155.

O'Connor, D. B., Jones, F., Conner, M., McMillan, B., & Ferguson, E. (2008). Effects of daily hassles and eating style on eating behavior. *Health Psychology, 27*(1), S20–S31.

O'Donnell, M. L., Creamer, M., Elliott, P., & Bryant, R. (2007). Tonic and phasic heart rate as predictors of posttraumatic stress disorder. *Psychosomatic Medicine, 69*, 256–261.

O'Donnell, V., & Tait, H. (2003). *Aboriginal peoples survey 2001—initial findings: Well-being of the non-reserve Aboriginal population* (Statistics Canada Catalogue 89-589). Retrieved August 23, 2007, from www.statcan.ca/english/freepub/89-589-XIE/pdf/89-589-XIE03001.pdf.

O'Donovan, A., Lin, J., Dhabhar, F. S., Wolkowitz, O., Tillie, J. M., Blackburn, E., et al. (2009). Pessimism correlates with leukocyte telomere shortness and elevated interleukin-6 in post-menopausal women. *Brain, Behavior, and Immunity, 23,* 446–449.

O'Keefe, D. J., & Jensen, J. D. (2009). The Relative Persuasiveness of Gain-Framed and Loss-Framed Messages for Encouraging Disease Detection Behaviors: A Meta-Analytic Review. *Journal of Communication, 59,* 296–316.

O'Neil, J. (2003, January 21). When aspirin can't help a heart. *The New York Times,* p. D6.

O'Rourke, N. (2004). Psychological resilience and the well-being of widowed woman. *Ageing International, 29(3),* 267–280.

O'Rourke, N., Cappeliez, P., & Neufeld, E. (2007). Recurrent depressive symptomatology and physical health: A 10-year study of informal caregivers of persons with dementia. *Canadian Journal of Psychiatry, 52(7),* 434–441.

Ockene, J. K., Emmons, K. M., Mermelstein, R. J., Perkins, K. A., Bonollo, D. S., Voorhees, C. C., et al. (2000). Relapse and maintenance issues for smoking cessation. *Health Psychology, 19,* 17–31.

Odendaal, J. S. J., & Meintjes, R. A. (2002). Neurophysiological correlates of affiliative behaviour between humans and dogs. *Veterinary Journal, 165,* 296–301.

Ogborne, A. C., Carver, V., & Wiebe, J. (2001). *Harm reduction and injection drug use: An international comparative study of contextual factors influencing the development and implementation of relevant policies and programs.* Retrieved January 19, 2008, from www.phac-aspc.gc.ca/hepc/pubs/hridu-rmudi/index.html.

Ogden, J. (2003). Some problems with social cognition models: A pragmatic and conceptual analysis. *Health Psychology, 22,* 424–428.

Ohinmaa, A., Jacobs, P., Simpson, S. H., & Johnson, J. A. (2004). The projection of prevalence and cost of diabetes in Canada: 2000 to 2016. *Canadian Journal of Diabetes, 28,* 116–123.

Oken, D. (2000). Multiaxial diagnosis and the psychosomatic model of disease. *Psychosomatic Medicine, 62,* 171–175.

Oksuzyan, A., Brønnum-Hansen, H., & Jeune, B. (2010). Gender gap in health expectancy. *European Journal of Ageing, 7,* 213–218.

Oleck, J. (2001, April 23). Dieting: More fun with a buddy? *BusinessWeek,* 16.

Oleg, E., Mary, B. W., Edna, S., Steven, D. H., Antoine, K. A.-S., Andrew, W. H., et al. (2009). Immuno-modulatory effects of relaxation training and guided imagery in women with locally advanced breast cancer undergoing multimodality therapy: A randomised controlled trial. *Breast 18(1),* 17–25.

Oliver, G., Wardle, J., & Gibson, E. L. (2000). Stress and food choice: A laboratory study. *Psychosomatic Medicine, 62,* 853–865.

Oliver, L. N., & Hayes, M. V. (2008). Effects of neighbourhood income on reported body mass index: An eight-year longitudinal study of Canadian children. *BMC Public Health, 8(16),* 1–20.

Olsen, M. B., Krantz, D. S., Kelsey, S. F., Pepine, C. J., Sopko, G., Handberg, E., Rogers, W. J., Gierach, G. L., McClure, C. K., & Merz, C. N. (2005). Hostility scores are associated with increased risk of cardiovascular events in women undergoing coronary angiography: A report from the NHLBI—sponsored WISE study. *Psychosomatic Medicine, 67,* 546–552.

Onen, S. H., Onen, F., Mangeon, J.-P., Abidi, H., Courpron, P., & Schmidt, J. (2005). Alcohol abuse and dependence in elderly emergency department patients. *Archives of gerontology and geriatrics, 41,* 191–200.

Ong, A. D., Bergeman, C. S., Bisconti, T. L., & Wallace, K. A. (2006). Psychological resilience, positive emotions, and successful adaptation to stress in later life. *Journal of Personality and Social Psychology, 91,* 730–749.

Ong, A. D., Zautra, A. J., & Reid, M. C. (2010). Psychological Resilience Predicts Decreases in Pain Catastrophizing Through Positive Emotions. *Psychology and Aging, 25,* 516–523.

Ontario Federation for Cerebral Palsy (2009). *A Guide to Cerebral Palsy.* Retrieved from www.ofcp.on.ca/aboutcp.html.

Ontario Medical Association. (2004). *Exposure to second-hand smoke: Are we protecting our kids?* Retrieved from www.oma.org/Health/tobacco/smoke2004.pdf.

Onysko, J., Maxwell, C., Eliasziw, M., Zhang, J. X., Johansen, H., & Campbell, N. R. C. (2006). Large increases in hypertension diagnosis and treatment in Canada after a healthcare professional education program. *Hypertension, 48,* 853–860.

Orbell, S., & Hagger, M. (2006). "When no means no": Can reactance augment the theory of planned behavior? *Health Psychology, 25,* 586–594.

Organization for Economic Co-operation and Development. (2011). OECD Health Data 2011—Frequently Requested Data. Retrieved July 12, 2011 from http://www.oecd.org/document/16/0,3343,en_2649_34631_2085200_1_1_1_1,00.html.

Ortega-Sanchez, R., Jimenez-Mena, C., Cordoba-Garcia, R., Muñoz-Lopez, J., Garcia-Machado, M. L., & Vilaseca-Canals, J. (2004). The effect of office-based physician's advice on adolescent exercise behavior. *Preventive Medicine, 38,* 219–226.

Oslin, D. W., Sayers, S., Ross, J., Kane, V., Have, T. T., Conigliaro, J., et al. (2003). Disease management for depression and at-risk drinking via telephone in an older population of veterans. *Psychosomatic Medicine, 65,* 931–937.

Osterhaus, S., Lange, A., Linssen, W., & Passchier, J. (1997). A behavioral treatment of young migrainous and nonmigrainous headache patients: Prediction of treatment success. *International Journal of Behavioral Medicine, 4,* 378–396.

Ostir, G. V., Berges, I. M., Markides, K. S., & Ottenbacher, K. J. (2006). Hypertension in older adults and the role of positive emotions. *Psychosomatic Medicine, 68,* 727–733.

Ottawa Charter for Health Promotion. (1986). *First international conference on health promotion.* Retrieved January 18, 2008, from www.who.int/hpr/NPH/docs/ottawa_charter_hp.pdf.

Ots, T. (1990). The angry liver, the anxious heart and the melancholy spleen. *Culture, Medicine and Psychiatry, 14(1),* 21–58.

Owen, J. E., Klapow, J. C., Roth, D. L., & Tucker, D. C. (2004). Use of the Internet for information and support: Disclosure among persons with breast cancer and prostate cancer. *Journal of Behavioral Medicine, 27,* 491–505.

Owens, I. P. F. (2002, September 20). Sex differences in mortality rate. *Science's Compass,* 2008–2009.

Oxlad, M., Stubberfield, J., Stuklis, R., Edwards, J., & Wade, T. D. (2006). Psychological risk factors for increased post-operative length of hospital stay following coronary artery bypass graft surgery. *Journal of Behavioral Medicine, 29,* 179–190.

Pacchetti, C., Mancini, F., Aglieri, R., Fundaro, C., Martignoni, E., & Nappi, G. (2000). Active music therapy in Parkinson's disease: An integrative method for motor and emotional rehabilitation. *Psychosomatic Medicine, 62,* 386–393.

Pacheco-López, G., Engler, H., Niemi, M.-B., & Schedlowski, M. (2006). Expectations and associations that heal: Immunomodulatory placebo effects and its neurobiology. *Brain, Behavior, and Immunity, 20,* 430–446.

Pagato, S., McChargue, D., & Fuqua, R. W. (2003). Effects of a multicomponent intervention on motivation and sun protection behaviors among Midwestern beachgoers. *Health Psychology, 22,* 429–433.

Pakenham, K. I. (1999). Adjustment to multiple sclerosis: Application of a stress and coping model. *Health Psychology, 18,* 383–392.

Pakenham, K. I. (2005). Benefit finding in multiple sclerosis and associations with positive and negative outcomes. *Health Psychology, 24,* 123–132.

Pakenham, K. I. (2008). Making sense of illness or disability. The nature of sense making in multiple sclerosis (MS). *Journal of Health Psychology, 13(1),* 93–105.

Pakenham, K. I., & Cox, S. (2009). The dimensional structure of benefit finding in multiple sclerosis and relations with positive and negative adjustment: A longitudinal study. *Psychology & Health, 24,* 373–393.

Pakhomov, S. V., Jacobsen, S. J., Chute, C. G., & Roger, V. L. (2008). Agreement between patient-reported symptoms and their documentation in the medical record. *The American journal of managed care, 14,* 530–539.

Palmer, S. C., Kagee, A., Coyne, J. C., & DeMichele, A. (2004). Experience of trauma, distress, and posttraumatic stress disorder among breast cancer patients. *Psychosomatic Medicine, 66,* 258–264.

Pampel, F. C., & Rogers, R. G. (2004). Socioeconomic status, smoking, and health: A test of competing theories of cumulative advantage. *Journal of Health and Social Behavior, 45(3),* 306–321.

Pan, A., Lucas, M., Sun, Q., van Dam, R. M., Franco, O. H., Willett, W. C., et al. (2011). Increased Mortality Risk in Women With Depression and Diabetes Mellitus. *Arch Gen Psychiatry, 68,* 42–50.

Pao, M., & Bosk, A. (2011). Anxiety in medically ill children/adolescents. *Depression and Anxiety, 28,* 40–49.

Paolucci, S., Antonucci, G., Grasso, M. G., & Pizzamiglio, L. (2001). The role of unilateral spatial neglect in rehabilitation of right brain–damaged ischemic stroke patients: A matched comparison. *Archives of Physical Medicine and Rehabilitation, 82*, 743–749.

Papies, E. K., & Hamstra, P. (2010). Goal Priming and Eating Behavior: Enhancing Self-Regulation by Environmental Cues. *Health Psychology, 29*, 384–388.

Paradiso, S., Anderson, B. M., Boles Ponto, L. L., Tranel, D., & Robinson, R. G. (2011). Altered Neural Activity and Emotions Following Right Middle Cerebral Artery Stroke. *Journal of stroke and cerebrovascular diseases : the official journal of National Stroke Association, 20*, 94–104.

Park, C. L., & Adler, N. E. (2003). Coping style as a predictor of health and well-being across the first year of medical school. *Health Psychology, 22*, 627–631.

Park, E. R., DePue, J. D., Goldstein, M. G., Niaura, R., Harlow, L. L., Willey, C., Rakowski, W., Prokhorov, A. V., (2003). Assessing the transtheoretical model of change constructs for physicians counseling smokers. *Annals of Behavioral Medicine, 25*, 120–126.

Park, J. (2005). Use of alternative health care. *Health Reports, 16(2)*, 39–42 (Statistics Canada Catalogue 82-003). Retrieved August 24, 2007, from www.statcan.ca/english/freepub/82-003-XIE/0020482-003-XIE.pdf.

Park, J. (2007). Work stress and job performance. *Perspectives*, 5–17. Statistics Canada Catalogue 75-001. Retrieved January 21, 2008, from www.statcan.ca/english/freepub/75-001-XIE/2007112/articles/10466-en.pdf.

Park, J., & Knudson, S. (2007). Medically unexplained physical symptoms. *Health Reports, 18(1)*. Statistics Canada Catalogue 82-003. Retrieved February 17, 2008, from www.statcan.ca/english/freepub/82-003-XIE/2006001/articles/symptoms/findings2.htm.

Parker, J. C., Frank, R. G., Beck, N. C., Smarr, K. L., Buescher, K. L., Phillips, L. R., et al. (1988). Pain management in rheumatoid arthritis patients: A cognitive-behavioral approach. *Arthritis and Rheumatism, 31*, 593–601.

Parkinson Society of Canada. (2003). *Parkinson's: The facts.* Retrieved from www.parkinson.ca/pdf/TheFacts-Eng.pdf.

Parry, D. C. (2008). The contribution of dragon boat racing to women's health and breast cancer survivorship. *Qualitative Health Research, 18(2)*, 222–233.

Parsons, T. (1954). The professions and the social structure. In T. Parsons, (Ed.), *Essays in sociological theory* (pp. 34–49). New York: Free Press.

Pasch, L. A., & Dunkel-Schetter, C. (1997). Fertility problems: Complex issues faced by women and couples. In S. J. Gallant, G. P. Keita, & R. Royak-Schaler (Eds.), *Health care for women: Psychological, social, and behavioral influences* (pp. 187–202). Washington, D.C.: American Psychological Association.

Pasic, J., Levy, W. C., & Sullivan, M.D. (2003). Cytokines in depression and heart failure. *Psychosomatic Medicine, 65*, 181–193.

Patra, J., Popova, S., Rehm, J., Bondy, S., Flint, R., & Giesbrecht, N. (2007). *Economic cost of chronic disease in Canada 1995–2003.* Retrieved February 17, 2007, from www.ocdpa.on.ca/docs/OCDPA_EconomicCosts.pdf.

Patten, S. B. (2005). An analysis of data from two general health surveys found that increased incidence and duration contributed to elevated prevalence of major depression in persons with chronic medical conditions. *Journal of Clinical Epidemiology, 58(2)*, 184–189.

Patten, S. B., Beck, C. A., Kassam, A., Williams, J. V. A., Barbui, C., & Metz, L. (2005). Long-term medical conditions and major depression: Strength of association for specific conditions in the general population. *Canadian Journal of Psychiatry, 50(4)*, 195–202.

Patten, S. B., Beck, C. A., Williams, J. V. A., Barbui, C., & Metz, L. M. (2003). Major depression in multiple sclerosis: A population based perspective. *Neurology, 61(11)*, 1524–1527.

Patterson, D. R., & Jensen, M. P. (2003). Hypnosis and clinical pain. *Psychological Bulletin, 129*, 495–521.

Patton, D., & Adlaf, E. M. (2005). Cannabis use and problems. In *Canadian addiction survey* (chap. 5). Retrieved January 20, 2008, from www.ccsa.ca/NR/rdonlyres/6806130B-C314-4C96-95CC-075D14CD83DE/0/ccsa0040282005.pdf.

Pavalko, E. K., & Woodbury, S. (2000). Social roles as process: Caregiving careers and women's health. *Journal of Health and Social Behavior, 41*, 91–105.

Pavalko, E. K., Elder, G. H., Jr., & Clipp, E. C. (1993). Worklives and longevity: Insights from a life course perspective. *Journal of Health and Social Behavior, 34*, 363–380.

Pavlin, D. J., Sullivan, M. J. L., Freund, P. R., & Roesen, K. (2005). Catastrophizing: A Risk Factor For Postsurgical Pain. *The Clinical Journal of Pain, 21*, 83–90.

Pearlin, L. I., & Schooler, C. (1978). The structure of coping. *Journal of Health and Social Behavior, 19*, 2–21.

Pearson, H. (2004, April 8). Public health: The demon drink. *Nature, 428*, 598–600.

Peck, C. L., & King, N. J. (1982). Increasing patient compliance with prescriptions. *Journal of the American Medical Association, 248*, 2874–2877.

Peckerman, A., LaManca, J. J., Qureishi, B., Dahl, K. A., Golfetti, R., Yamamoto, Y., et al. (2003). Baroreceptor reflex and integrative stress responses in chronic fatigue syndrome. *Psychosomatic Medicine, 65*, 889–895.

Pedlow, C. T., & Carey, M. P. (2003). HIV Sexual Risk-Reduction Interventions for Youth: A Review and Methodological Critique of Randomized Controlled Trials. *Behavior Modification, 27(2)*, 135–190.

Peeters, A., Barendregt, J. J., Willekens, F., Mackenbach, J. P., Mamun, A. A., & Bonneux, L. (2003). Obesity in adulthood and its consequences for life expectancy: A life-table analysis. *Annals of Internal Medicine, 138*, 24–32.

Pelletier, L. G., Dion, S. C., Slovines-D'Angelo, M., & Reid, R. (2004). Why do you regulate what you eat? Relationships between forms of regulation, eating behaviors, sustained dietary behavior change, and psychological adjustment. *Motivation and Emotion, 28(3)*, 245–277.

Pells, J. J., Shelby, R. A., Keefe, F. J., Dixon, K. E., Blumenthal, J. A., Lacaille, L., et al. (2007). Arthritis self-efficacy and self-efficacy for resisting eating: Relationships to pain, disability, and eating behavior in overweight and obese individuals with osteoarthritic knee pain. *Pain.*

Penedo, F. J., Gonzalez, J. S., Davis, C., Dahn, J., Antoni, M. H., Ironson, G., et al. (2003). Coping and psychological distress among symptomatic HIV1 men who have sex with men. *Annals of Behavioral Medicine, 25*, 203–213.

Peng, P., Choiniere, M., Dion, D., Intrater, H., LeFort, S., Lynch, M., et al. (2007). Challenges in accessing multidisciplinary pain treatment facilities in Canada. *Canadian Journal of Anesthesia / Journal canadien d'anesthésie, 54*, 977–984.

Penley, J. A., Tomaka, J., & Wiebe, J. S. (2002). The association of coping to physical and psychological health outcomes: A meta-analytic review. *Journal of Behavioral Medicine, 25*, 551–603.

Pennebaker, J. W. (1980). Perceptual and environmental determinants of coughing. *Basic and Applied Social Psychology, 1*, 83–91.

Pennebaker, J. W. (1997). Writing about emotional experiences as a therapeutic process. *Psychological Science, 8*, 162–166.

Pennebaker, J. W., & Beall, S. (1986). Confronting a traumatic event: Toward an understanding of inhibition and disease. *Journal of Abnormal Psychology, 95*, 274–281.

Pennebaker, J. W., Colder, M., & Sharp, L. K. (1990). Accelerating the coping process. *Journal of Personality and Social Psychology, 58*, 528–537.

Pennebaker, J. W., Hughes, C., & O'Heeron, R. C. (1987). The psychophysiology of confession: Linking inhibitory and psychosomatic processes. *Journal of Personality and Social Psychology, 52*, 781–793.

Penninx, B. W. J. H., van Tilburg, T., Boeke, A. J. P., Deeg, D. J. H., Kriegsman, D. M. W., & van Eijk, J. T. M. (1998). Effects of social support and personal coping resources on depressive symptoms: Different for various chronic diseases? *Health Psychology, 17*, 551–558.

Pepler, D. J., & Craig, W. M. (2000). Making a Difference in Bullying. *LaMarsh Centre for Research on Violence and Conflict Resolution.* Retrieved from http://psycserver.psyc.queensu.ca/craigw/Craig_Pepler_2000_REPORT_Making_a_Difference_in_Bullying.pdf.

Peralta-Ramírez, M. I., Jiménez-Alonso, J., Godoy-García, J. F., & Pérez-García, M. (2004). The effects of daily stress and stressful life events on the clinical symptomology of patients with lupus erythematosus. *Psychosomatic Medicine, 66*, 788–794.

Pereira, D. B., Antoni, M. H., Danielson, A., Simon, T., Efantis-Potter, J., Carver, C. S., Duran, R. E. F., Ironson, G., Klimas, N., & O'Sullivan, M. (2003). Life stress and cervical squamous intraepithelial lesions in women with human papillomavirus and human immunodeficiency virus. *Psychosomatic Medicine, 65,* 427–434.

Pereira, M. G., Berg-Cross, L., Almeida, P., & Machado, J. C. (2008). Impact of family environment and support on adherence, metabolic control, and quality of life in adolescents with diabetes. *International Journal of Behavioural Medicine, 15,* 187–193.

Perez, M. A., Skinner, E. C., & Meyerowitz, B. E. (2002). Sexuality and intimacy following radical prostatectomy: Patient and partner. *Health Psychology, 21,* 288–293.

Pérez-Peña, R., & Glickson, G. (2003, November 29). As obesity rises, so do indignities in health care. *The New York Times,* pp. A1, A13.

Perkins, K. A. (1985). The synergistic effect of smoking and serum cholesterol on coronary heart disease. *Health Psychology, 4,* 337–360.

Perlis, M. L., Sharpe, M., Smith, M. T., Greenblatt, D., & Giles, D. (2001). Behavioral treatment of insomnia: Treatment outcome and the relevance of medical and psychiatric morbidity. *Journal of Behavioral Medicine, 24,* 281–296.

Perlis, M., Aloia, M., Millikan, A., Boehmler, J., Smith, M., Greenblatt, D., et al. (2000). Behavioral treatment of insomnia: A clinical case series study. *Journal of Behavioral Medicine, 23,* 149–161.

Perna, F. M., & McDowell, S. L. (1995). Role of psychological stress in cortisol recovery from exhaustive exercise among elite athletes. *International Journal of Behavioral Medicine, 2,* 13–26.

Perreaux, L. (2007). Passengers file lawsuit against American traveller with TB infection. *Canadian Press.* July 12, 2007. Retrieved February 6, 2008, from www.medbroadcast.com/channel_health_news_details.asp?news_channel_id=1000&channel_id=1044&news_id=12848&relation_id=6661.

Persky, I., Spring, B., Vander Wal, J.S., Pagoto, S., & Hedeker, D. (2005). Adherence across behavioral domains in treatment promoting smoking cessation plus weight control. *Health Psychology, 24,* 153–160.

Pescosolido, B. A., Tuch, S. A., & Martin, J. K. (2001). The profession of medicine and the public: Examining Americans' changing confidence in physician authority from the beginning of the 'health care crisis' to the era of health care reform. *Journal of Health and Social Behavior, 42,* 1–16.

Peters, E., Slovic, P., Hibbard, J. H., & Tusler, M. (2006). Why worry? Worry, risk perceptions, and willingness to act to reduce medical errors. *Health Psychology, 25,* 144–152.

Peters, M., Godaert, G., Ballieux, R., Brosschot, J., Sweep, F., Swinkels, L., et al. (1999). Immune responses to experimental stress: Effects of mental effort and uncontrollability. *Psychosomatic Medicine, 61,* 513–524.

Peterson, C., Seligman, M. E. P., & Vaillant, G. E. (1988). Pessimistic explanatory style is a risk factor for physical illness: A thirty-five-year longitudinal study. *Journal of Personality and Social Psychology, 55,* 23–27.

Peterson, L. & Soldana, L. (1996). Accelerating children's risk for injury: Mother's decisions regarding common safety rules. *Journal of Behavioral Medicine, 19,* 317–332.

Peterson, L., Farmer, J., & Kashani, J. H. (1990). Parental injury prevention endeavors: A function of health beliefs? *Health Psychology, 9,* 177–191.

Peto R., & Lopez A.D. (2001). The future worldwide health effects of current smoking patterns. In: Koop EC, Pearson CE, Schwarz MR, eds. Critical Issues in Global Health. New York: Jossey-Bass; 2001:154–161.

Petrak, F., Hardt, J., Clement, T., Borner, N., Egle, U. T., & Hoffmann, S. O. (2001). Impaired health-related quality of life in inflammatory bowel diseases: Psychosocial impact and coping styles in a national German sample. *Scandinavian Journal of Gastroenterology, 36(4),* 375–382.

Petrie, K. J., & Weinman, J. A. (Eds.). (1997). *Perceptions of health and illness: Current research and applications.* Reading, England: Harwood Academic.

Petrie, K. J., & Wessely, S. (2002). Modern worries, new technology, and medicine. *British Journal of Medicine, 324,* 690–691.

Petrie, K. J., Booth, R. J., Pennebaker, J. W., Davison, K. P., & Thomas, M. G. (1995). Disclosure of trauma and immune response to a hepatitis B vaccination program. *Journal of Consulting and Clinical Psychology, 63,* 787–792.

Petrie, K. J., Buick, D., Weinman, J., & Booth, R. J. (1999). Positive effects of illness reported by myocardial infarction and breast cancer patients. *Journal of Psychosomatic Research, 47,* 537–543.

Petrie, K. J., Fontanilla, I., Thomas, M. G., Booth, R. J., & Pennebaker, J. W. (2004). Effect of written emotional expression on immune function in patients with human immunodeficiency virus: A randomized trial. *Psychosomatic Medicine, 66,* 272–275.

Petrovic, P., Kalso, E., Peterson, K. M., & Ingvar, M. (2002, March 1). Placebo and opioid analgesia – Imaging a shared neuronal network. *Science, 295,* 1737–1740.

Peyrot, M., McMurry, J. F., Jr., & Kruger, D. F. (1999). A biopsychosocial model of glycemic control in diabetes: Stress, coping and regimen adherence. *Journal of Health and Social Behavior, 40,* 141–158.

Pfeifer, J. E., & Brigham, J. C. (Eds.). (1996). Psychological perspectives on euthanasia. *Journal of Social Issues, 52* (entire issue).

Phillips, A. C., Carroll, D., Ring, C., Sweeting, H., & West, P. (2005). Life events and acute cardiovascular reactions to mental stress: A cohort study. *Psychosomatic Medicine, 67,* 384–392.

Phillips-Bute, B., Mathew, J. P., Blumenthal, J. A., Grocott, H. P., Laskowitz, D. T., Jones, R. H., Mark, D. B., & Newman, M. F. (2006). Association of neurocognitive function and quality of life 1 year after coronary artery bypass graft (CABG) surgery. *Psychosomatic Medicine, 68,* 369–375.

Phipps, S., & Steele, R. (2002). Repressive adaptive style in children with chronic illness. *Psychosomatic Medicine, 64,* 34–42.

Phipps, S., Steele, R. G., Hall, K., & Leigh, L. (2001). Repressive adaptation in children with cancer: A replication and extension. *Health Psychology, 20,* 445–451.

Physicians for a Smoke-Free Canada. (2002). *Tobacco and the health of Canadians.* Retrieved August 15, 2007, from www.smoke-free.ca/Health/pscissues_health.htm.

Physicians for a Smoke-Free Canada. (2003). *Filter-tips: A review of cigarette marketing in Canada* (4th ed.). Retrieved August 15, 2007, from www.smokefree.ca/filtertips04/Tobacco%20Act%20Provisions.htm.

Physicians for a Smoke-Free Canada. (2004). *Fact sheet: Canadian tobacco use monitoring survey.* Retrieved August 15, 2007, from www.smoke-free.ca/factsheets/pdf/Quitting%20Behaviours.pdf.

Physicians for a Smoke-Free Canada. (2006). *The Heather Crowe campaign.* Retrieved August 16, 2007, from www.smoke-free.ca/heathercrowe.

Physicians for a Smoke-Free Canada. (2007). *Smoking in Canada: Percentage of Canadians who smoke 1965–2003.* Retrieved August 15, 2007, from www.smoke-free.ca/factsheets/pdf/prevalence.pdf.

Physiotherapists in Canada, 2008. (2009). Canadian Institute for Health Information. http://dsp-psd.pwgsc.gc.ca/collection_2009/icis- cihi/H115-47-2008E.pdf.

Piasecki, T. M. (2006). Relapse to smoking. *Clinical Psychology Review, 26,* 196–215.

Picardi, A., Battisti, F., Tarsitani, L., Baldassari, M., Copertaro, A., Mocchegiani, E., & Biondi, M. (2007). Attachment security and immunity in healthy women. *Psychosomatic Medicine, 69,* 40–46.

Pickering, T. G., Schwartz, J. E., & James, G. D. (1995). Ambulatory blood pressure monitoring for evaluating the relationships between lifestyle, hypertension, and cardiovascular risk. *Clinical and Experimental Pharmacology and Physiology, 22,* 226–231.

Pickett, M. (1993). Cultural awareness in the context of terminal illness. *Cancer Nursing, 16,* 102–106.

Pignone, M. P., Gaynes, B. N., Rushton, J. L., Burchell, C. M., Orleans, C. T., Mulrow, C. D., et al. (2002). Screening for depression in adults: A summary of the evidence for the U.S. preventive services task force. *Annals of Internal Medicine, 136,* 765–776.

Pike, J., Smith, T., Hauger, R., Nicassio, P., Patterson, T., McClintock, J., et al. (1997). Chronic life stress alters sympathetic, neuroendocrine, and immune responsivity to an acute psychological stressor in humans. *Psychosomatic Medicine, 59,* 447–457.

Pinquart, M., & Duberstein, P. R. (2010). Depression and cancer mortality: a meta-analysis. *Psychological Medicine, 40*(11), 1797–1810.

Pitman, D. L., Ottenweller, J. E., & Natelson, B. H. (1988). Plasma corticosterone levels during repeated presentation of two intensities of restraint stress: Chronic stress and habituation. *Physiology and Behavior, 43,* 47–55.

Polivy, J., & Herman, C. P. (1985). Dieting and binging: A causal analysis. *American Psychologist, 40,* 193–201.

Polk, D. E., Cohen, S., Doyle, W. J., Skoner, D. P., & Kirschbaum, C. (2005). State and trait affect as predictors of salivary cortisol in healthy adults. *Psychoneuroendocrinology, 30,* 261–272.

Pollard, T. M., & Schwartz, J. E. (2003). Are changes in blood pressure and total cholesterol related to changes in mood? An 18-month study of men and women. *Health Psychology, 22,* 47–53.

Porter, L. S., Mishel, M., Neelon, V., Belyea, M., Pisano, E., & Soo, M. S. (2003). Cortisol levels and responses to mammography screening in breast cancer survivors: A pilot study. *Psychosomatic Medicine, 65,* 842–848.

Poulin, C. (2006). *Harm reduction policies and programs for youth.* Retrieved from www.ccsa.ca/NR/rdonlyres/D0254373-5F2B-459D-BB79-6EE7C22CC303/0/ccsa113402006.pdf.

Powell, L. H., William, R. L., Matthews, K. A., Meyer, P., Midgley, A. R., Baum, A., et al. (2002). Physiologic markers of chronic stress in premenopausal, middle-aged women. *Psychosomatic Medicine, 64,* 502–509.

Power, M., Bullinger, M., Harper, A., & The World Health Organization Quality of Life Group. (1999). The World Health Organization WHOQOL-100: Tests of the universality of quality of life in 15 different cultural groups worldwide. *Health Psychology, 18,* 495–505.

Pradhan, A. D., Rifai, N., & Ridker, P. (2002). Soluble intercellular adhesion molecule-1, soluble vascular adhesion molecule-1, and the development of symptomatic peripheral arterial disease in men. *Circulation, 106,* 820–825.

Pressman, E., & Orr, W. C. (Eds.). (1997). *Understanding sleep: The evolution and treatment of sleep disorders.* Washington, D.C.: American Psychological Association.

Pressman, S. D., & Cohen, S. (2005). Does positive affect influence health? *Psychological Bulletin, 131,* 925–971.

Pressman, S. D., Cohen, S., Miller, G. E., Barkin, A., Rabin, B. S., & Treanor, J. J. (2005). Loneliness, social network size, and immune response to influenza vaccination in college freshmen. *Health Psychology, 24,* 297–306.

Presti, D. E., Ary, D. V., & Lichtenstein, E. (1992). The context of smoking initiation and maintenance: Findings from interviews with youths. *Journal of Substance Abuse, 4,* 35–45.

Price, D. (2000, June 9). Psychological and neural mechanisms of the affective dimension of pain. *Science, 288,* 1769–1771.

Prickett, C., Lister, E. C., M., Trevithick-Sutton, C., Hirst, M., Vinson, J., Noble, E., & Trevithick, R. (2004). Alcohol: Friend or foe? Alcoholic beverage hormesis for cataract and atherosclerosis is related to plasma antioxidant activity. *Nonlinearity in Biology, Toxicology and Medicine, 2(1),* 353–370(318).

Primack, B. A., Fine, D., Yang, C. K., Wickett, D., & Zickmund, S. (2009). Adolescents' impressions of antismoking media literacy education: qualitative results from a randomized controlled trial. *Health Education Research, 24,* 608–621.

Prochaska, J. J., & Sallis, J.F. (2004). A randomized controlled trial of single versus multiple health behavior change: Promoting physical activity and nutrition among adolescents. *Health Psychology, 23,* 314–318.

Prochaska, J. O. (1994). Strong and weak principles for progressing from precontemplation to action on the basis of 12 problem behaviors. *Health Psychology, 13,* 47–51.

Prochaska, J. O., & DiClemente, C. C. (1984a). Self change processes, self-efficacy, and decisional balance across five stages of smoking cessation. In A. R. Liss (Ed.), *Advances in cancer control: Epidemiology and research.* New York: Liss.

Prochaska, J. O., DiClemente, C. C., & Norcross, J. C. (1992). In search of how people change: Applications to addictive behaviors. *American Psychologist, 47,* 1102–1114.

Prochaska, J. O., Velicer, W. F., Rossi, J. S., Goldstein, M. G., Marcus, B. H., Rakowski, W., et al. (1994). Stages of change and decisional balance for 12 problem behaviors. *Health Psychology, 13,* 39–46.

Province of Nova Scotia. (2008). *Diversity and social inclusion in primary health care.* Retrieved February 17, 2008, from www.gov.ns.ca/health/primaryhealthcare/diversity.htm.

Pruessner, M., Hellhammer, D. H., Pruessner, J. C., & Lupien, S. J. (2003). Self-reported depressive symptoms and stress levels in healthy young men: Associations with the cortisol response to awakening. *Psychosomatic Medicine, 65,* 92–99.

Public Health Agency of Canada. (2002). *What is the population health approach?* Retrieved January 17, 2008, from www.phac-aspc.gc.ca/ph-sp/phdd/approach/index.html.

Public Health Agency of Canada. (2002a). A Report on Mental Illnesses in Canada, Chapter 6, Eating Disorders. Accessed August 23, 2011 from: http://www.phac-aspc.gc.ca/publicat/miic-mmac/chap_6-eng.php.

Public Health Agency of Canada. (2003a). *Centre of chronic disease prevention and control cardiovascular disease.* Retrieved January 29, 2008, from www.phac-aspc.gc.ca/ccdpc-cpcmc/cvd-mcv/index_e.html.

Public Health Agency of Canada. (2003b). *Diabetes: Facts & figures.* Retrieved September 6, 2007, from www.phac-aspc.gc.ca/ccdpc-cpcmc/diabetes-diabete/english/facts/index.html.

Public Health Agency of Canada. (2003c). *What is it? Canada's physical activity guide.* Retrieved July 24, 2007, from www.phac-aspc.gc.ca/pau-uap/paguide/intro.html.

Public Health Agency of Canada. (2004). *Young people in Canada: their health and well-being;* in Chapter 6: Youth Health Risk Behaviours. Retrieved January 28, 2008 from www.phac-aspc.gc.ca/dca-dea/publications/hbsc-2004/-chapter_6_e.html#6-1.

Public Health Agency of Canada. (2004a). *Comprehensive school health: Children Adolescents 7 18 Years.* Retrieved August 18, 2007, from www.phac-aspc.gc.ca/dca-dea/7-18yrs-ans/comphealth_e.html.

Public Health Agency of Canada. (2004b). Youth health risk behaviours. In *Young people in Canada: Their health and well-being* (chap. 6). Retrieved January 19, 2008, from www.phac-aspc.gc.ca/dca-dea/publications/hbsc-2004/chapter_6_e.html.

Public Health Agency of Canada. (2004c). *Reducing health disparities roles of health sector: Recommended policy directions and activities.* Retrieved July 28, 2007, from www.phac-aspc.gc.ca/ph-sp/disparities/dr_policy_e.html.

Public Health Agency of Canada. (2005). *Drug resistant tuberculosis among the foreign-born in Canada.* Retrieved February 11, 2008, from www.phac-aspc.gc.ca/publicat/tbcan02/sr-tb2002_e.html.

Public Health Agency of Canada. (2006a). *What are the different types of complementary and alternative therapies?* Retrieved September 24, 2007, from www.canadian-health-network.ca/servlet/ContentServer?cid=1065630192034&pagename=CHN-RCS%2FCHNResource%2FFAQCHNResourceTemplate&lang=En&parented= 1048540760989&c=CHNResource.

Public Health Agency of Canada. (2006b). *HIV and AIDS in Canada. Surveillance report to June 30, 2006.* Retrieved August 19, 2007, from www.phac-aspc.gc.ca/publicat/aids-sida/haic-vsac0606/pdf/haic-vsac0606.pdf.

Public Health Agency of Canada. (2006c). *HIV/AIDS Epi updates, August 2006.* Retrieved August 19, 2007, from www.phac-aspc.gc.ca/publicat/epiu-aepi/epi-06/pdf/epi06_e.pdf.

Public Health Agency of Canada. (2006d). *Are you at risk of contracting HIV?* Retrieved August 19, 2007, from www.phac-aspc.gc.ca/aids-sida/info/2_e.html.

Public Health Agency of Canada. (2006e). *Health aging in Canada: A new vision, a vital investment.* Retrieved February 18, 2008, from www.phac-aspc.gc.ca/-seniors-aines/pubs/haging_newvision/pdf/vision-brief-bref_e.pdf.

Public Health Agency of Canada. (2007a). *Breast cancer.* Retrieved from www.phac-aspc.gc.ca/ccdpc-cpcmc/bc-cds/index_e.html.

Public Health Agency of Canada. (2007b). *Life and breath: Respiratory disease in Canada.* Retrieved August 14, 2007, from www.phac-aspc.gc.ca/publicat/2007/lbrdc-vsmrc/index-eng.php.

Public Health Agency of Canada. (2008a). *Hepatitis b fact sheet: Bloodborne pathogens section.* Retrieved April 25, 2008, from www.phac-aspc.gc.ca/hcai-iamss/bbp-pts/hepatitis/hep_b_e.html.

Public Health Agency of Canada. (2008b). *What are the symptoms of heart attacks in women?* Retrieved July 14, 2008, from www.phac-aspc.gc.ca/cd-mc/cvd-mcv/women-femmes_03-eng.php.

Public Health Agency of Canada. (2009). PHAC Diabetes surveillance. http://www.phac-aspc.gc.ca/publicat/2009/ndssdic-snsddac-09/pdf/report-2009-eng.pdf.

Public Health Agency of Canada. (2009a). Tracking Heart Disease and Stroke in Canada: Stroke Highlights 2009, Retrieved September 25, 2011 from http://www.phac-aspc.gc.ca/publicat/2009/cvd-avc/pdf/cvd-avs-2009-eng.pdf.

Public Health Agency of Canada. (2010). Sudden Infant Death Syndrome (SIDS) Awareness Month. Accessed April2, 2011 from http://www.hc-sc.gc.ca/ahc-asc/minist/messages/_2010/2010_10_01-b-eng.php.

Public Health Agency of Canada. (2011). Tracking Heart Disease and Stroke in Canada: Stroke Highlights 2011. Retrieved http://www.phac-aspc.gc.ca/cd-mc/cvd-mcv/sh-fs-2011/pdf/StrokeHighlights_EN.pdf.

Puhl, R. M., Schwartz, M. B., & Brownell, K. D. (2005). Impact of perceived consensus on stereotypes about obese people: a new approach for reducing bias. *Health Psychology, 24(5),* 517–525.

Purc-Stephenson, R. J., & Gorey, K. M. (2008). Lower adherence to screening mammography guidelines among ethnic minority women in American: A meta-analytic review. *Preventive Medicine, 46,* 479–488.

Pury, C. L. S., McCubbin, J. A., Helfer, S. G., Galloway, C., & McMullen, L. J. (2004). Elevated resting blood pressure and dampened emotional response. *Psychosomatic Medicine, 66,* 583–587.

Puterman, E., Lin, J., Blackburn, E., O'Donovan, A., Adler, N., & Epel, E. (2010). The Power of Exercise: Buffering the Effect of Chronic Stress on Telomere Length. *PLoS ONE, 5,* e10837.

Quan, H., Fong, A., Coster, C. D., Wang, J., Musto, R., Noseworthy, T. W., & Ghali, W. A. (2006). Variation in health services utilization among ethnic populations. *Canadian Medical Association Journal, 174(6),* 787–791.

Quick, J. C. (1999). Occupational health psychology: Historical roots and future directions. *Health Psychology, 18,* 82–88.

Quillin, J., Bodurtha, J., McClish, D., & Wilson, D. (2011). Genetic Risk, Perceived Risk, and Cancer Worry in Daughters of Breast Cancer Patients. *Journal of Genetic Counseling, 20,* 157–164.

Quillin, J., Bodurtha, J., Siminoff, L., & Smith, T. (2010). Exploring Hereditary Cancer Among Dying Cancer Patients—A Cross-Sectional Study of Hereditary Risk and Perceived Awareness of DNA Testing and Banking. *Journal of Genetic Counseling, 19,* 497–525.

Quinlan, K. B., & McCaul, K. D. (2000). Matched and mismatched interventions with young adult smokers: Testing a stage theory. *Health Psychology, 19,* 165–171.

Quittner, A. L., Espelage, D. L., Opipari, L. C., Carter, B., Eid, N., & Eigen, H. (1998). Role strain in couples with and without a child with a chronic illness: Associations with marital satisfaction, intimacy, and daily mood. *Health Psychology, 17,* 112–124.

Raabe, H.C., et al. (2005). *Euthanasia and physician-assisted suicide: A joint statement by doctors and lawyers 2005.* Retrieved August 3, 2007, from LifeSiteNews.com (www.lifesite.net/ldn/2005_docs/StatementEuthanasiaandPAS.pdf).

Rabiau, M., Knäuper, B., & Miquelon, P. (2006). The eternal quest for optimal balance between maximizing pleasure and minimizing harm: The compensatory health beliefs model. *British Journal of Health Psychology, 11,* 139–153.

Rabin, C., Leventhal, H., & Goodin, S. (2004). Conceptualization of disease timeline predicts posttreatment distress in breast cancer patients. *Health Psychology, 23,* 407–412.

Rabin, C., Ward, S., Leventhal, H., & Schmitz, M. (2001). Explaining retrospective reports of symptoms in patients undergoing chemotherapy: Anxiety, initial symptom experience and posttreatment symptoms. *Health Psychology, 20,* 91–98.

Rabkin, J. G., Ferrando, S. J., Lin, S., Sewell, M., & McElhiney, M. (2000). Psychological effects of HAART: A 2-year study. *Psychosomatic Medicine, 62,* 413–422.

Rabkin, J. G., McElhiney, M., Ferrando, S. J., Van Gorp, W., & Lin, S. H. (2004). Predictors of employment of men with HIV/AIDS: A longitudinal study. *Psychosomatic Medicine, 66,* 72–78.

Radcliffe-Brown, A. R. (1964). *The Andaman Islanders.* New York: Free Press.

Rahe, R. H., Taylor, C. B., Tolles, R. L., Newhall, L. M., Veach, T. L., & Bryson, S. (2002). A novel stress and coping workplace program reduces illness and healthcare utilization. *Psychosomatic Medicine, 64,* 278–286.

Räikkönen, K., & Matthews, K. A. (2008). Do Dispositional Pessimism and Optimism Predict Ambulatory Blood Pressure During Schooldays and Nights in Adolescents? *Journal of Personality, 76,* 605–630.

Räikkönen, K., Matthews, K. A., Flory, J. D., & Owens, J. F. (1999). Effects of hostility on ambulatory blood pressure and mood during daily living in healthy adults. *Health Psychology, 18,* 44–53.

Räikkönen, K., Matthews, K. A., Kondwani, K. A., Bunker, C. H., Melhem, N. M., Ukoli, F. A. M., et al. (2004). Does nondipping of blood pressure at night reflect a trait of blunted cardiovascular responses to daily activities? *Annals of Behavioral Medicine, 27,* 131–137.

Raine, K. D. (2004). *Overweight and obesity in Canada: A population health perspective.* Retrieved February 17, 2008, from www.cihi.ca/cihiweb/dispPage.jsp?cw_page=download_ form_e&cw_sku=OOCPHPPDF&cw_ctt=2&cw_dform=null.

Rakowski, W., Fulton, J. P., & Feldman, J. P. (1993). Women's decision making about mammography: A replication of the relationship between stages of adoption and decisional balance. *Health Psychology, 12,* 209–214.

Ramachandran, V. S., & Rogers-Ramachandran, D. (1996). Synaesthesia in phantom limbs induced with mirrors. *Proceedings of the Royal Society, Biological Sciences, 263(1369),* 377–386.

Ramage-Morin, P. L. (2008). Chronic pain in Canadian seniors. *Health Reports, 19(1).* Statistics Canada Catalogue 82-003.

Ramage-Morin, P. L., & Gilmour, H. (2010). "Chronic pain at ages 12 to 44." *Health Reports.* http://www.statcan.gc.ca/pub/82-003-x/2010004/article/11389-eng.pdf.

Ramirez, A., Wildes, K., Nápoles-Springer, A., Pérez-Stable, E., Talavera, G., & Rios, E. (2009). Physician gender differences in general and cancer-specific prevention attitudes and practices. *Journal of Cancer Education, 24,* 85–93.

Ramírez-Maestre, C., López Martinez, A. E., & Zarazaga, R. E. (2004). Personality characteristics as differential variables of the pain experience. *Journal of Behavioral Medicine, 27,* 147–165.

Rana, J. S., Arsenault, B. J., Després, J.-P., Côté, M., Talmud, P. J., Ninio, E., et al. (2011). Inflammatory biomarkers, physical activity, waist circumference, and risk of future coronary heart disease in healthy men and women. *European Heart Journal, 32,* 336–344.

Raynor, D. A., Pogue-Geile, M. F., Kamarck, T. W., McCaffery, J. M., & Manuck, S. B. (2002). Covariation of psychosocial characteristics associated with cardiovascular disease: Genetic and environmental influences. *Psychosomatic Medicine, 64,* 191–203.

Reaby, L. L., & Hort, L. K. (1995). Postmastectomy attitudes in women who wear external breast prostheses compared to those who have undergone breast reconstruction. *Journal of Behavioral Medicine, 18,* 55–68.

Redman, S., Webb, G. R., Hennrikus, D. J., Gordon, J. J., & Sanson-Fisher, R. W. (1991). The effects of gender on diagnosis of psychological disturbance. *Journal of Behavioral Medicine, 14,* 527–540.

Redwine, L., Dang, J., Hall, M., & Irwin, M. (2003). Disordered sleep, nocturnal cytokines, and immunity in alcoholics. *Psychosomatic Medicine, 65,* 75–85.

Redwine, L., Mills, P. J., Sada, M., Dimsdale, J., Patterson, T., & Grant, I. (2004). Differential immune cell chemotaxis responses to acute psychological stress in Alzheimer caregivers compared to non-caregiver controls. *Psychosomatic Medicine, 66,* 770–775.

Redwine, L., Snow, S., Mills, P., & Irwin, M. (2003). Acute psychological stress: Effects in chemotaxsis and cellular adhesion molecule expression. *Psychosomatic Medicine, 65,* 598–603.

Reed, G. M., Kemeny, M. E., Taylor, S. E., & Visscher, B. R. (1999). Negative HIV-specific expectancies and AIDS-related bereavement as predictors of symptom onset in asymptomatic HIV-positive gay men. *Health Psychology, 18,* 354–363.

Rehm, J., Baliunas, D., Brochu, S., Fischer, B., Gnam, W., Patra, J., Popova, S., Sarnocinska-Hart, A., & Taylor, B. (2006). *The costs of substance abuse in Canada 2002: Highlights.* Retrieved June 30, 2007, from www.ccsa.ca/NR/rdonlyres/18F3415E-2CAC-4D21-86E2-CEE549EC47A9/0/ccsa0113322006.pdf.

Reif, J. S., Dunn, K., Ogilvie, G. K., & Harris, C. K. (1992). Passive smoking and canine lung cancer risk. *American Journal of Epidemiology, 135,* 234–239.

Reilkoff, R. A., Bucala, R., & Herzog, E. L. (2011). Fibrocytes: emerging effector cells in chronic inflammation. Nature Reviews Immunology, advance online publication.

Reinhardt, U. E. (2004, March 12). Health care in the service of science? *Science, 303,* 1613–1614.

Rejeski, W. J., Brawley, L. R., Ambrosius, W. T., Brubaker, P. H., Focht, B. C., Foy, C. G., & Fox, L. D. (2003). Older adults with chronic disease: Benefits of group-mediated counseling in the promotion of physically active lifestyles. *Health Psychology, 22,* 414–423.

Remor, E., Penedo, F. J., Shen, B. J., & Schneiderman, N. (2007). Perceived stress is associated with CD4 cell decline in men and women living with HIV/AIDS in Spain. *AIDS Care: Psychological and Socio-medical Aspects of AIDS/HIV, 19*(2), 215–219.

Repetti, R. L. (1989). Effects of daily workload on subsequent behavior during marital interactions: The role of social withdrawal and spouse support. *Journal of Personality and Social Psychology, 57,* 651–659.

Repetti, R. L. (1993a). The effects of workload and the social environment at work on health. In L. Goldberger & S. Bresnitz (Eds.), *Handbook of stress* (pp. 368–385). New York: Free Press.

Repetti, R. L. (1993b). Short-term effects of occupational stressors on daily mood and health complaints. *Health Psychology, 12,* 125–131.

Repetti, R. L., & Pollina, S. L. (1994). *The effects of daily social and academic failure experiences on school-age children's subsequent interactions with parents.* Unpublished manuscript, University of California, Los Angeles.

Repetti, R. L., Taylor, S. E., & Seeman, T. E. (2002). Risky families: Family social environments and the mental and physical health of offspring. *Psychological Bulletin, 128,* 330–366.

Repetto, P. B., Caldwell, C. H., & Zimmerman, M. A. (2005). A longitudinal study of the relationship between depressive symptoms and cigarette use among African-American adolescents. *Health Psychology, 24,* 209–219.

Resnick, B., Orwig, D., Magaziner, J., & Wynne, C. (2002). The Effect of Social Support on Exercise Behavior in Older Adults. *Clinical Nursing Research, 11,* 52–70.

Resnicow, K., DiIorio, C., Soet, J. E., Borrelli, B., Hecht, J., & Ernst, D. (2002). Motivational interviewing in health promotion: It sounds like something is changing. *Health Psychology, 21,* 444–451.

Resnicow, K., Jackson, A., Blissett, D., Wang, T., McCarty, F., Rahotep, S., Periasamy, S. (2005). Results of the health body healthy spirit trial. *Health Psychology, 24,* 339–348.

Revenson, T. A. (2003). Scenes from a marriage: Examining support, coping, and gender within the context of chronic illness. In J. Suls & K. Wallston (Eds.), *Social Psychological Foundations of Health and Illness* (pp. 530–559). Oxford, England: Blackwell Publishing.

Revicki, D. A., & May, H. J. (1985). Occupational stress, social support, and depression. *Health Psychology, 4,* 61–77.

Reynolds, D. V. (1969). Surgery in the rat during electrical analgesia induced by focal brain stimulation. *Science, 164,* 444–445.

Reynolds, J. R. (1997). The effects of industrial employment conditions on job—related distress. *Journal of Health & Social Behavior, 38,* 105–116.

Reynolds, J. S., & Perrin, N. A. (2004). Mismatches in social support and psychosocial adjustment to breast cancer. *Health Psychology, 23*(4), 425–430.

Reynolds, K. D., Buller, D. B., Yaroch, A. L., Maloy, J. A., & Cutter, G. R. (2006). Mediation of a middle school skin cancer prevention program. *Health Psychology, 25,* 616–625.

Rhee, H., Holditch-Davis, D., & Miles, M. S. (2005). Patterns of physical symptoms and relationships with psychosocial factors in adolescents. *Psychosomatic Medicine, 67,* 1006–1012.

Rhodes, R. E., & Plotnikoff, R. C. (2006). Understanding action control: Predicting physical activity intention-behavior profiles across six months in a Canadian sample. *Health Psychology, 25,* 292–299.

Rhudy, J. L., & Williams, A. E. (2005). Gender differences in pain: Do emotions play a role? *Gender Medicine, 2,* 208–226.

Richards, J. C., Hof, A., & Alvarenga, M. (2000). Serum lipids and their relationships with hostility and angry affect and behaviors in men. *Health Psychology, 19,* 393–398.

Richardson, J. (2004). What patients expect from complementary therapy: A qualitative study. *American Journal of Public Health, 94*(6), 1049–1053.

Richardson, S. A., Goodman, N., Hastorf, A. H., & Dornbusch, S. M. (1961). Cultural uniformity in reaction to physical disabilities. *American Sociological Review, 26,* 241–247.

Rickels, K., Hesbaucher, P. T., Weise, C. C., Gray, B., & Feldman, H. S. (1970). Pills and improvement: A study of placebo response in psychoneurotic outpatients. *Pyschopharmacologia, 16,* 318–328.

Ridker, P. M., Rifai, N., Rose, L., Buring, J. E., & Cook, N. R. (2002). Comparison of c-reactive proteins and low-density lipoprotein cholesterol levels in the prediction of first cardiovascular events. *New England Journal of Medicine, 347,* 1557–1565. http://www.nejm.org.

Rief, W., Hessel, A., & Braehler, E. (2001). Somatization symptoms and hypochondriachal features in the general population. *Psychosomatic Medicine, 63,* 595–602.

Rief, W., & Broadbent, E. (2007). Explaining medically unexplained symptoms-models and mechanisms. *Clinical Psychology Review, 27,* 821-841.

Rief, W., Martin, A., Klaiberg, A., & Brähler, E. (2005). Specific effects of depression, panic, and somatic symptoms on illness behavior. *Psychosomatic Medicine, 67,* 596–601.

Riga, A. (2006, February 16). Business awakes to cost of stress. *The Montreal Gazette.* Retrieved September 24, 2007, from www.canada.com/montrealgazette/story.html?id=eb9c321c-364e-4435-adbc-7b781d041fcb&k=22077.

Riley, D. (1993). *The harm reduction model: Pragmatic approaches to drug use from the area between intolerance and neglect.* Retrieved February 2, 2008, from www.ccsa.ca/pdf/ccsa-004011-1993.pdf.

Rimes, K. A., Salkovskis, P. M., Jones, L., & Lucassen, A. M. (2006). Applying a cognitive-behavioral model of health anxiety in a cancer genetics service. *Health Psychology, 25,* 171–180.

Ritz, T., & Steptoe, A. (2000). Emotion and pulmonary function in asthma: Reactivity in the field and relationship with laboratory induction of emotion. *Psychosomatic Medicine, 62,* 808–815.

Rivenes, A. C., Harvey, S. B., & Mykletun, A. (2009). The relationship between abdominal fat, obesity, and common mental disorders: Results from the HUNT Study. *Journal of Psychosomatic Research, 66,* 269–275.

Roan, S. (2003, March 10). Diabetes study has wide reach. *Los Angeles Times,* p. F3.

Robbins, M. A., Elias, M. F., Elias, P. K., & Budge, M. M. (2005). Blood pressure and cognitive function in an African-American and a Caucasian-American sample: The Maine-Syracuse study. *Psychosomatic Medicine, 67,* 707–714.

Robert, J. G., & Akiko, O. (2006). Evidence-Based Scientific Data Documenting the Treatment and Cost-Effectiveness of Comprehensive Pain Programs for Chronic Nonmalignant Pain. *The journal of pain: official journal of the American Pain Society, 7,* 779–793.

Roberts, A. H., Kewman, D. G., Mercier, L., & Hovell, M. (1993). The power of nonspecific effects in healing: Implications for psychosocial and biological treatments. *Clinical Psychology Review, 13,* 375–391.

Robinson, A., & Cooper, S. (2007). Trusted information sources: The preferred option for complementary and alternative medicine users. *Complementary Health Practice Review, 12,* 120–138.

Robinson, A., & McGrail, M. R. (2004). Disclosure of CAM use to medical practitioners: a review of qualitative and quantitative studies. *Complementary Therapies in Medicine, 12*(2-3), 90–98.

Robinson, R. G. (1986). Post-stroke mood disorder. *Hospital Practice, 21,* 83–89.

Robles, T. F., Glaser, R., & Kiecolt-Glaser, J. K. (2005). Out of balance: A new look at chronic stress, depression, and immunity. *Current Directions in Psychological Science, 14,* 111–115.

Robles, T. F., Shaffer, V. A., Malarkey, W. B., & Kiecolt-Glaser, J. K. (2006). Positive behaviors during marital conflict: Influences on stress hormones. *Journal of Social and Personal Relationships, 23,* 305–325.

Rodin, J., Elias, M., Silberstein, L. R., & Wagner, A. (1988). Combined behavioral and pharmacologic treatment for obesity: Predictors of successful weight maintenance. *Journal of Consulting and Clinical Psychology, 56,* 399–404.

Rodriguez, D., Moss, H. B., & Audrin-McGovern, J. (2005). Developmental heterogeneity in adolescent depressive symptoms: Associations with smoking behavior. *Psychosomatic Medicine, 67,* 200–210.

Rodriguez, D., Romer, D., & Audrin-McGovern, J. (2007). Beliefs about the risks of smoking mediate the relationship between exposure to smoking and smoking. *Psychosomatic Medicine, 69,* 106–113.

Rohrbaugh, M. J., Mehl, M. R., Shoham, V., Reilly, E. S., & Ewy, G. A. (2008). Prognostic significance of spouse we talk in couples coping with heart failure. *Journal of Consulting and Clinical Psychology, 76,* 781–789.

Rojo, L., Conesa, L., Bermudez, O., & Livianos, L. (2006). Influence of stress in the onset of eating disorders: Data from a two-stage epidemiologic controlled study. *Psychosomatic Medicine, 68,* 628–635.

Rollman, B. L., & Shear, M. K. (2003). Depression and medical comorbidity: Red flags for current suicidal ideation in primary care. *Psychosomatic Medicine, 65,* 506–507.

Roman, M. J., Shanker, B. A., Davis, A., Lockshin, M. D., Sammaritano, L., Simantov, R., et al. (2003). Prevalence and correlates of accelerated atherosclerosis in systematic lupus erythematosus. *New England Journal of Medicine, 349,* 2399–2406, http://www.nejm.org.

Rosal, M. C., Ockene, J. K., Yunsheng, M., Hebert, J. R., Ockene, I. S., Merriam, P., & Hurley, T. G. (1998). Coronary artery smoking intervention study (CA-SIS): 5-year follow-up. *Health Psychology, 17,* 476–478.

Rose, J. E. (2010). Stress Alleviation and Reward Enhancement: Two Promising Targets for Relapse Prevention. *Biological psychiatry, 68,* 687–688.

Rose, J. S., Chassin, L., Presson, C. C., & Sherman, S. J. (1996). Prospective predictors of quit attempts and smoking cessation in young adults. *Health Psychology, 15,* 261–268.

Rosenfield, S. (1992). The costs of sharing: Wives' employment and husbands' mental health. *Journal of Health and Social Behavior, 33,* 213–225.

Rosenstock, I. M. (1966). Why people use health services. *Milbank Memorial Fund Quarterly, 44,* 94ff.

Rosenstock, I. M. (1974). Historical origins of the health belief model. *Health Education Monographs, 2,* 328–335.

Rosland, A. M., Kieffer, E., Israel, B., Cofield, M., Palmisano, G., Sinco, B., et al. (2008). When Is Social Support Important? The Association of Family Support and Professional Support with Specific Diabetes Self-management Behaviors. *Journal of General Internal Medicine, 23,* 1992–1999.

Ross, A., & Thomas, S. (2010). The health benefits of yoga and exercise: A review of comparison studies. *The Journal of Alternative and Complementary Medicine, 16,* 3–12.

Ross, C. E., & Bird, C. E. (1994). Sex stratification and health lifestyle: Consequences for men's and women's perceived health. *Journal of Health and Social Behavior, 35,* 161–178.

Ross, H. E., & Young, L. J. (2009). Oxytocin and the neural mechanisms regulating social cognition and affiliative behavior. *Frontiers in Neuroendocrinology, 30,* 534–547.

Ross, N. A., Gilmour, H., & Dasgupta, K. (2010). 14-year diabetes incidence: The role of socio-economic status. *Health Reports, 21,* Statistics Canada, Catalogue no. 82-003-XPE.

Rossy, L. A., Buckelew, S. P., Dorr, N., Hagglund, K. J., Thayer, J. F., McIntosh, M. J., et al. (1999). A meta-analysis of fibromyalgia treatment interventions. *Annals of Behavioral Medicine, 21,* 180–191.

Roth, G. S., Lane, M. A., Ingram, D. K., Mattison, J. A., Elahi, D., Tobin, J. D., et al. (2002, August 2). Biomarkers of caloric restriction may predict longevity in humans. *Science, 297,* 811.

Rotheram-Borus, M. J., Murphy, D. A., Reid, H. M., & Coleman, C. L. (1996). Correlates of emotional distress among HIV1 youths: Health status, stress, and personal resources. *Annals of Behavioral Medicine, 18,* 16–23.

Rothman, A. J. (2000). Toward a theory-based analysis of behavioral maintenance. *Health Psychology, 19,* 64–69.

Rothman, A. J., & Salovey, P. (1997). Shaping perceptions to motivate healthy behavior: The role of message framing. *Psychological Bulletin, 121,* 3–19.

Roy, A. (2002). Family history of suicide and neuroticism: a preliminary study. *Psychiatry research, 110,* 87–90.

Rozanski, A. (2005). Integrating psychological approaches into the behavioral management of cardiac patients. *Psychosomatic Medicine, 67,* S67–S73.

Rubin, G. J., Cleare, A., & Hotopf, M. (2004). Psychological factors in postoperative fatigue. *Psychosomatic Medicine, 66,* 959–964.

Ruiz, J. M., Matthews, K. A., Scheier, M. F., & Schulz, R. (2006). Does who you marry matter for your health? Influence of patients' and spouses' personality on their partners' psychological well-being following coronary artery bypass surgery. *Journal of Personality and Social Psychology, 91,* 255–267.

Rushing, B., Ritter, C., & Burton, R. P. D. (1992). Race differences in the effects of multiple roles on health: Longitudinal evidence from a national sample of older men. *Journal of Health and Social Behavior, 33,* 126–139.

Russek, L. G., & Schwartz, G. E. (1997). Feelings of parental caring can predict health status in midlife: A 35-year follow-up of the Harvard Mastery of Stress study. *Journal of Behavioral Medicine, 20,* 1–13.

Russek, L. G., Schwartz, G. E., Bell, I. R., & Baldwin, C. M. (1998). Positive perceptions of parental caring are associated with reduced psychiatric and somatic symptoms. *Psychosomatic Medicine, 60,* 654–657.

Rutledge, T., & Hogan, B. E. (2002). A quantitative review of prospective evidence linking psychological factors with hypertension development. *Psychosomatic Medicine, 64,* 758–766.

Rutledge, T., & Linden, W. (2003). Defensiveness and 3-year blood pressure levels among young adults: The mediating effect of stress-reactivity. *Annals of Behavioral Medicine, 25(1),* 34–40.

Rutledge, T., Linden, W., & Davies, R. F. (1999). Psychological risk factors may moderate pharmacological treatment effects among ischemic heart disease patients. *Psychosomatic Medicine, 61,* 834–841.

Rutledge, T., Linden, W., & Paul, D. (2000). Cardiovascular recovery from acute laboratory stress: Reliability and concurrent validity. *Psychosomatic Medicine, 62,* 648–654.

Rutledge, T., Matthews, K. A., Lui, L. Y., Stone, K. L., & Cauley, J. A. (2003). Social networks and marital status predict mortality in older women: Prospective evidence from the Study of Osteoporotic Fractures (SOF). *Psychosomatic Medicine, 65,* 688–694.

Rutledge, T., Reis, S. E., Olson, M., Owens, J., Kelsey, S. F., Pepine, C. J., Mankad, S., Rogers, W. J., Bairey-Merz, C. N., Sopko, G., Cornell, C. E., Sharaf, B., & Matthews, K. A. (2004). Social networks are associate with lower mortality rates among women with suspected coronary disease: The national heart, lung, and blood institute sponsored women's ischemia syndrome evaluation study. *Psychosomatic Medicine, 66,* 882–888.

Rutledge, T., Reis, S. E., Olson, M., Owens, J., Kelsey, S. F., Pepine, C. J., Mankad, S., Rogers, W. J., Sopko, G., Cornell, C. E., Sharaf, B., & Merz, C. N. (2006). Depression is associated with cardiac symptoms, mortality risk, and hospitalization among women with suspected coronary disease: The NHLBI-sponsored WISE study. *Psychosomatic Medicine, 68,* 217–223.

Rydén, A., Karlsson, J., Sullivan, M., Torgerson, J. S., & Taft, C. (2003). Coping and distress: What happens after intervention? A 2-year follow-up from the Swedish Obese Subjects (SOS) Study. *Psychosomatic Medicine, 65,* 435–442.

Ryff, C. D., & Singer, B. (1996). Psychological well-being: Meaning, measurement, and implications for psychotherapy research. *Psychotherapy and Psychosomatics, 65,* 14–23.

Ryff, C. D., & Singer, B. (1998). The contours of positive human health. *Psychological Inquiry, 9,* 1–28.

Ryff, C. D., & Singer, B. (2000). Interpersonal flourishing: A positive health agenda for the new millennium. *Personality and Social Psychology Review, 4,* 30–44.

Ryff, C. D., Dienberg-Love, G., Urry, H. L., Muller, D., Rosenkranz, M. A., Friedman, E. M., Davidson, R. J., & Singer, B. (2006). Psychological well-being and ill-being: do they have distinct or mirrored biological correlates? *Psychotherapy and Psychosomatics, 75(2),* 85–95.

Sabiston, C. M., McDonough, M. H., & Crocker, P. R. E. (2007). Psychosocial experiences of breast cancer survivors involved in a dragon boat program: Exploring links to positive psychological growth. *Journal of Sport and Exercise Psychology, 29(4),* 419–438.

Saboonchi, F., & Lundh, L. G. (2003). Perfectionism, anger, somatic health, and positive affect. *Personality and Individual Differences, 35,* 1585–1599.

Sacco, W. P., Wells, K. J., Vaughan, C. A., Friedman, A., Perez, S., & Matthew, R. (2005). Depression in adults with type 2 diabetes: The role of adherence, body mass index, and self-efficacy. *Health Psychology, 24,* 630–634.

Sachs-Ericsson, N., Blazer, D., Plant, E. A., & Arnow, B. (2005). Childhood sexual and physical abuse and the 1-year prevalence of medical problems in the national comorbidity survey. *Health Psychology, 24,* 32–40.

Sadava, S. W., & Pak, A. W. (1994). Problem drinking and close relationships during the third decade of life. *Psychology of Addictive Behaviors, 8,* 251–258.

Safe Kids Canada. (2008). *Child passenger safety updates.* Retrieved January 29, 2008, from www.sickkids.ca/SKCForParents/section.asp?s= Safety%2BInformation%2Bby%2BTopic&sID=10774&ss=Child%2BPassenger%2BSafety&ssID=11330&sss=Updates&sssID=21097.

Safe Kids Canada (2010). Bike Helmet Legislation Chart. Accessed May 3, 2010 from http://www.safekidscanada.ca/Professionals/Advocacy/Documents/26783-BikeHelmetLegislationChart.pdf.

Safer, M. A., Tharps, Q. J., Jackson, T. C., & Leventhal, H. (1979). Determinants of three stages of delay in seeking care at a medical care clinic. *Medical Care, 17,* 11–29.

Salamon, K. S., Hains, A. A., Fleischman, K. M., Davies, W. H., & Kichler, J. (2010). Improving adherence in social situations for adolescents with type 1 diabetes mellitus (T1DM): A pilot study. *Primary care diabetes, 4,* 47–55.

Salmon, J., Owen, N., Crawford, D., Bauman, A., & Sallis, J. F. (2003). Physical activity and sedentary behavior: A population-based study of barriers, enjoyment, and preference. *Health Psychology, 22,* 178–188.

Salomons, T. V., Johnstone, T., Backonja, M.-M., & Davidson, R. J. (2004). Perceived Controllability Modulates the Neural Response to Pain. *J. Neurosci., 24*(32), 7199–7203.

Salovey, P., O'Leary, A., Stretton, M. S., Fishkin, S. A., & Drake, C. A. (1991). Influence of mood on judgments about health and illness. In J. P. Firgas (Ed.), *Emotion and social judgments* (pp. 241–262). New York: Pergamon Press.

Sampalis, J., Boukas, S., Liberman, M., Reid, T., & Dupuis, G. (2001). Impact of waiting time on the quality of life of patients awaiting coronary artery bypass grafting. *CMAJ, 165(4),* 429–433.

Sanchez, L. M., & Turner, S. M. (2003). Practicing psychology in the era of managed care: Implications for practice and training. *American Psychologist, 58,* 116–129.

Sander, E. P., Odell, S., & Hood, K. K. (2010). Diabetes-Specific Family Conflict and Blood Glucose Monitoring in Adolescents With Type 1 Diabetes: Mediational Role of Diabetes Self-Efficacy. *Diabetes Spectrum, 23,* 89–94.

Sanderson, C. A., Darley, J. M., & Messinger, C. S. (2002). "I'm not as thin as you think I am": The development and consequences of feeling discrepant from the thinness norm. *Personality and Social Psychology Bulletin, 28,* 172–183.

Sandgren, A. K., & McCaul, K. D. (2003). Short-term effects of telephone therapy for breast cancer patients. *Health Psychology, 22,* 310–315.

Sanmartin, C., Ng, E., Blackwell, D., Gentleman, J., Martinez, M., & Simile, C. (2004). *Joint Canada/United States survey of health, 2002–03* 9Statistics Canada Catalogue 82M0022XIE). Retrieved from www.statcan.ca:8096/bsolc/english/bsolc?catno=82M0022X.

Santiago, C. D., Wadsworth, M. E., & Stump, J. (2011). Socioeconomic status, neighborhood disadvantage, and poverty-related stress: Prospective effects on psychological syndromes among diverse low-income families. *Journal of Economic Psychology, 32,* 218–230.

Sapolsky, R. M. (1998). *Why zebras don't get ulcers: an updated guide to stress, stress-related disease and, coping.* New York, NY: Freeman.

Sarason, I. G., Sarason, B. R., Pierce, G. R., Shearin, E. N., & Sayers, M. H. (1991). A social learning approach to increasing blood donations. *Journal of Applied Social Psychology, 21,* 896–918.

Sarkar, U., Ali, S., & Whooley, M. A. (2007). Self-efficacy and health status in patients with coronary heart disease: Findings from the heart and soul study. *Psychosomatic Medicine, 69,* 306–312.

Satia-Abouta, J., Patterson, R. E., Kristal, A. R., Teh, C., & Tu, S. P. (2002). Psychosocial predictors of diet and acculturation in Chinese American and Chinese Canadian women. *Ethnicity and Health, 7(1),* 21–39.

Satin, J. R., Linden, W., & Phillips, M. J. (2009). Depression as a predictor of disease progression and mortality in cancer patients. *Cancer, 115*(22), 5349–5361. doi: 10.1002/cncr.24561

Sato, M., Yamazaki, Y., Sakita, M., & Bryce, T. J. (2008). Benefit-finding among people with rheumatoid arthritis in Japan. *Nursing & Health Sciences, 10*(1), 51–58.

Sausen, K. P., Lovallo, W. R., Pincomb, G. A., & Wilson, M. F. (1992). Cardiovascular responses to occupational stress in male medical students: A paradigm for ambulatory monitoring studies. *Health Psychology, 11,* 55–60.

Sauter, S. L., Murphy, L. R., & Hurrell, J. J., Jr. (1990). Prevention of work-related psychological disorders: A national strategy proposed by the National Institute for Occupational Safety and Health (NIOSH). *American Psychologist, 45,* 1146–1158.

Savard, J., Laroche, L., Simard, S., Ivers, H., & Morin, C. M. (2003). Chronic insomnia and immune functioning. *Psychosomatic Medicine, 65,* 211–221.

Saxby, B. K., Harrington, F., McKeith, I. G., Wesnes, K., & Ford, G. A. (2003). Effects of hypertension in attention, memory and executive function in older adults. *Health Psychology, 22,* 587–591.

Sayette, M. A., George FinkAssociate Editors: Bruce, M., Kloet, E. R. d., Robert, R., George, C., Andrew, S., et al. (2007). Alcohol and Stress: Social and Psychological Aspects *Encyclopedia of Stress* (pp. 123–126). New York: Academic Press.

Scanlan, J. M., Vitaliano, P. P., Zhang, J., Savage, M., & Ochs, H. D. (2001). Lymphocyte proliferation is associated with gender, caregiving, and psychosocial variables in older adults. *Journal of Behavioral Medicine, 24,* 537–559.

Schachinger, H., Hegar, K., Hermanns, N., Straumann, M., Keller, U., Fehm-Wolfsdorf, G., Berger, W., & Cox, D. (2005). Randomized controlled clinical trial of blood glucose awareness training (BGAT III) in Switzerland and Germany. *Journal of Behavior Medicine, 28,* 587–594.

Schaefer, J. A., & Moos, R. H. (1992). Life crises and personal growth. In B. N. Carpenter (Ed.), *Personal coping, theory, research, and application* (pp. 149–170). Westport, CT: Praeger.

Schaeffer, J. J. W., Gil, K. M., Burchinal, M., Kramer, K. D., Nash, K. B., Orringer, E., et al. (1999). Depression, disease severity, and sickle cell disease. *Journal of Behavioral Medicine, 22,* 115–126.

Schanowitz, J. Y., & Nicassio, P. M. (2006). Predictors of positive psychosocial functioning of older adults in residential care facilities. *Journal of Behavioral Medicine, 29,* 191–201.

Schapira, K., McClelland, H. A., Griffiths, N. R., & Newells, D. J. (1970). Study of the effects of tablet color in the treatment of anxiety states. *British Medical Journal, 2,* 446–449.

Schechtman, K. B., Ory, M. G., & The FICSIT Group (2001). The effects of exercise on the quality of life of frail older adults: A preplanned meta-analysis of the FICSIT trials. *Annals of Behavioral Medicine, 23,* 186–197.

Scheier, M. F., & Carver, C. S. (1985). Optimism, coping, and health: Assessment and implications of generalized outcome expectancies. *Health Psychology, 4,* 219–247.

Scheier, M. F., Carver, C. S., & Bridges, M.W. (1994). Distinguishing optimism from neuroticism (and trait anxiety, self-mastery, and self-esteem): A re—evaluation of the Life Orientation Test. *Journal of Personality and Social Psychology, 7,* 1063–1078.

Scheier, M. F., Matthews, K. A., Owens, J., Magovern, G. J., Sr., Lefebvre, R. C., Abbott, R. A., et al. (1989). Dispositional optimism and recovery from coronary artery bypass surgery: The beneficial effects on physical and psychological well-being. *Journal of Personality and Social Psychology, 57,* 1024–1040.

Scheier, M. F., Weintraub, J. K., & Carver, C. S. (1986). Coping with stress: Divergent strategies of optimists and pessimists. *Journal of Personality and Social Psychology, 51,* 1257–1264.

Scherrer, J. F., Xian, H., Bucholz, K. K., Eisen, S. E., Lyons, M. J., Goldberg, J., et al. (2003). A twin study of depression symptoms, hypertension, and heart disease in middle-aged men. *Psychosomatic Medicine, 65,* 548–557.

Scheufele, P. M. (2000). Effects of progressive relaxation and classical music on measurements of attention, relaxation, and stress responses. *Journal of Behavioral Medicine, 23,* 207–228.

Schiaffino, K. M., & Revenson, T. A. (1992). The role of perceived self-efficacy, perceived control, and causal attributions in adaptation to rheumatoid arthritis: Distinguishing mediator from moderator effects. *Personality and Social Psychology Bulletin, 18,* 709–718.

Schins, A., Honig, A., Crijns, H., Baur, L., & Hamulyak, K. (2003). Increased coronary events in depressed cardiovascular patients: 5HT2A receptor as missing link? *Psychosomatic Medicine, 65,* 729–737.

Schlehofer, M. M., Thompson, S. C., Ting, S., Ostermann, S., Nierman, A., & Skenderian, J. (2010). Psychological predictors of college students' cell phone use while driving. Accident Analysis & Prevention, 42, 1107–1112.

Schlereth, T., & Birklein, F. (2008). The Sympathetic Nervous System and Pain. *NeuroMolecular Medicine, 10,* 141–147.

Schlotz W, Hellhammer J, Schulz P, Stone AA. (2004). Perceived work overload and chronic worrying predict weekend-weekday differences in the cortisol awakening response. Psychosomatic Medicine. 66(2):207–14.

Schmaling, K. B., Fiedelak, J. I., Katon, W. J., Bader, J. O., & Buchwald, D. S. (2003). Prospective study of the prognosis of unexplained chronic fatigue in a clinic-based cohort. *Psychosomatic Medicine, 65,* 1047–1054.

Schmaling, K. B., Smith, W. R., & Buchwald, D. S. (2000). Significant other responses are associated with fatigue and functional status among patients with chronic fatigue syndrome. *Psychosomatic Medicine, 62,* 444–450.

Schneider, R., Nidich, S., Salerno, J., Sharma, H., Robinson, C., Nidich, R., & Alexander, C. (1998). Lower lipid peroxide levels in practitioners of the Transcendental Meditation program. *Psychosomatic Medicine, 60*(1), 38–41.

Schneiderman, N. (1999). Behavioral medicine and the management of HIV/AIDS. *International Journal of Behavioral Medicine, 6,* 3–12.

Schnoll, R. A., Martinez, E., Tatum, K. L., Glass, M., Bernath, A., Ferris, D., et al. (2011). Increased self-efficacy to quit and perceived control over withdrawal symptoms predict smoking cessation following nicotine dependence treatment. *Addictive Behaviors, 36,* 144-147.

Schoen, C. & Osborn, R. (2010). *The Commonwealth Fund 2010 International Health Policy Survey in Eleven Countries*, accessed June 4, 2011, from <http://www.commonwealthfund.org/Content/Surveys/2010/Nov/2010-International-Survey.aspx>.

Schommer, N. C., Hellhammer, D. H., & Kirschbaum, C. (2003). Dissociation between reactivity of the hypothalamus-pituitary-adrenal axis and the sympathetic-adrenal-medullary system to repeated psychosocial stress. *Psychosomatic Medicine, 65,* 450–460.

Schrimshaw, E. W. (2003). Relatioship-specific unsupportive social interactions and depressive symptoms among women living with HIV/AIDS: Direct and moderating effects. *Journal of Behavioral Medicine, 26,* 297–313.

Schroeder, D. H., & Costa, P. T., Jr. (1984). Influence of life event stress on physical illness: Substantive effects or methodological flaws? *Journal of Personality and Social Psychology, 46,* 853–863.

Schuckit, M. A. (2009). An overview of genetic influences in alcoholism. *Journal of Substance Abuse Treatment, 36,* S5–14.

Schultz, S. E., & Kopec, J. A. (2003). Impact of chronic conditions. *Health Reports, 14(4),* 41–53 (Statistics Canada Catalogue 82-003 XIE). Retrieved August 14, 2007, from www.statcan.ca/english/freepub/82-003-IE/0040282-003-XIE.pdf.

Schulz, R., & Beach, S.R. (1999). Caregiving as a risk factor for mortality: The caregiver health effects study. *Journal of the American Medical Association, 282,* 2215–2219.

Schulz, R., & Decker, S. (1985). Long-term adjustment to physical disability: The role of social support, perceived control, and self-blame. *Journal of Personality and Social Psychology, 48,* 1162–1172.

Schulz, R., O'Brien, A.T., Bookwala, J., & Fleissner, K. (1995). Psychiatric and physical morbidity effects of dementia caregiving: Prevalence, correlates, and causes. *The Gerontologist, 35,* 771–791.

Schum, J. L., Jorgensen, R. S., Verhaeghen, P., Sauro, M., & Thibodeau. (2003). Trait anger, anger expression and ambulatory blood pressure: A meta-analytic review. *Journal of Behavioral Medicine, 26,* 395–416.

Schwartz, A., Hazen, G., Leifer, A., & Heckerling, P. (2008). Life Goals and Health Decisions: What Will People Live (or Die) For? *Medical Decision Making, 28,* 209–219.

Schwartz, C., Meisenhelder, J. B., Ma, Y., & Reed, G. (2003). Altruistic social interest behaviors are associated with better mental health. *Psychosomatic Medicine, 65,* 778–785.

Schwartz, G. E., & Weiss, S. M. (1978). Yale Conference on Behavioral Medicine: A proposed definition and statement of goals. *Journal of Behavioral Medicine, 1,* 3–12.

Schwartz, J. E., Neale, J., Marco, C., Shiffman, S. S., & Stone, A. A. (1999). Does trait coping exist? A momentary assessment approach to the evaluation of traits. *Journal of Personality and Social Psychology, 77,* 360–369.

Schwartz, M. D., Taylor, K. L., & Willard, K. S. (2003). Prospective association between distress and mammography utilization among women with a family history of breast cancer. *Journal of Behavioral Medicine, 26,* 105–117.

Schwarzer, R., & Renner, B. (2000). Social-cognitive predictors of health behavior: Action self-efficacy and coping self-efficacy. *Health Psychology, 19,* 487–495.

Schweinhardt, P., Seminowicz, D. A., Jaeger, E., Duncan, G. H., & Bushnell, M. C. (2009). The anatomy of the mesolimbic reward system: A link between personality and the placebo analgesic response. *Journal of Neuroscience, 29,* 4882–4887.

Seal, N. (2006). Preventing tobacco and drug use among Thai high school students through life skills training. *Nursing & Health Sciences, 8,* 164–168.

Sears, S. R., & Stanton, A. L. (2001). Physician-assisted dying: Review of issues and roles for health psychologists. *Health Psychology, 20,* 302–310.

Sears, S. R., Stanton, A. L., & Danoff-Burg, S. (2003). The yellow brick road and the emerald city: Benefit finding, positive reappraisal coping and posttraumatic growth in women with early-stage breast cancer. *Health Psychology, 22,* 487–497.

Seelman, K. D. (1993). Assistive technology policy: A road to independence for individuals with disabilities. *Journal of Social Issues, 49,* 115–136.

Seeman, T. E., Berkman, L. F., Gulanski, B. I., Robbins, R. J., Greenspan, S. L., Charpentier, P. A., et al. (1995). Self-esteem and neuroendocrine response to challenge: MacArthur studies of successful aging. *Journal of Psychosomatic Research, 39,* 69–84.

Seeman, T. E., Lusignolo, T. M., Albert, M., & Berkman, L. (2001). Social relationships, social support, and patterns of cognitive aging in healthy, high–functioning older adults: MacArthur studies of successful aging. *Health Psychology, 20,* 243–255.

Seeman, T. E., Singer, B. H., Ryff, C. D., Love, G. D., & Levy-Storms, L. (2002). Social relationships, gender, and allostatic load across two age cohorts. *Psychosomatic Medicine, 64,* 395–406.

Segan, C. J., Borland, R., & Greenwood, K. M. (2004). What is the right thing at the right time? Interactions between stages and processes of change among smokers who make a quit attempt. *Health Psychology, 23,* 86–93.

Segerstrom, S. C. (2001). Optimism, goal conflict, and stressor-related immune change. *Journal of Behavioral Medicine, 24,* 441–467.

Segerstrom, S. C. (2006). How does optimism suppress immunity? Evaluation of three affective pathways. *Health Psychology, 25,* 653–657.

Segerstrom, S. C., & Miller, G. E. (2004). Psychological stress and the human immune system: A meta-analytic study of 30 years of inquiry. *Psychological Bulletin, 130,* 601–630.

Segerstrom, S. C., Castañeda, J. O., & Spencer, T. E. (2003). Optimism effects on cellular immunity: Testing the affective and persistence models. *Personality and Individual Differences, 35,* 1615–1624.

Segerstrom, S. C., Schipper, L. J., & Greenberg, R. N. (2008). Caregiving, repetitive thought, and immune response to vaccination in older adults. *Brain, Behavior, and Immunity, 22*(5), 744–752.

Segerstrom, S. C., Taylor, S. E., Kemeny, M. E., & Fahey, J. L. (1998). Optimism is associated with mood, coping, and immune change in response to stress. *Journal of Personality and Social Psychology, 74,* 1646–1655.

Segerstrom, S. C., Taylor, S. E., Kemeny, M. E., Reed, G. M., & Visscher, B. R. (1996). Causal attributions predict rate of immune decline in HIV-seropositive gay men. *Health Psychology, 15,* 485–493.

Selye, H. (1956). *The stress of life.* New York: McGraw-Hill.

Selye, H. (1976). *Stress in health and disease.* Woburn, MA: Butterworth.

Seneff, M. G., Wagner, D. P., Wagner, R. P., Zimmerman, J. E., & Knaus, W. A. (1995). Hospital and 1-year survival of patients admitted to intensive care units with acute exacerbation of chronic obstructive pulmonary disease. *Journal of the American Medical Association, 274,* 1852–1857.

Serido, J., Almeida, D. M., & Wethington, E. (2004). Chronic stress and daily hassles: Unique and interactive relationships with psychological distress. *Journal of Health and Social Behavior, 45,* 17–33.

Severeijns, R., Vlaeyen, J. W. S., van den Hout, M. A., & Picavet, H. S. J. (2004). Pain catastrophizing is associated with health indices in musculoskeletal pain: A cross-sectional study in the Dutch community. *Health Psychology, 23,* 49–57.

Sexton, M., Bross, D., Hebel, J. H., Schumann, B. C., Gerace, T. A., Lasser, N., et al. (1987). Risk-factor changes in wives with husbands at high risk of coronary heart disease (CHD): The spin-off effect. *Journal of Behavioral Medicine, 10,* 251–262.

Shadel, W. G., & Mermelstein, R. J. (1996). Individual differences in self-concept among smokers attempting to quit: Validation and predictive utility of measures of the smoker self-concept and abstainer self-concept. *Annals of Behavioral Medicine, 18,* 151–156.

Shadel, W. G., Niaura, R., & Abrams, D. B. (2004). Who am I? The role of self-conflict in adolescents' responses to cigarette advertising. *Journal of Behavioral Medicine, 27(5),* 463–475.

Shalev, A. Y., Bonne, M., & Eth, S. (1996). Treatment of posttraumatic stress disorder: A review. *Psychosomatic Medicine, 58,* 165–182.

Shaham, Y., J. Singer, and M. Schaeffer. (1992). Stability/Instability of Cognitive Strategies Across Tasks Determine Whether Stress Will Affect Judgmental Processes, Journal of Applied Psychology, 22 (9), 691–713.

Shapiro, A. K. (1960). A contribution to a history of the placebo effect. *Behavioral Science, 5,* 109–135.

Shapiro, D. E., Boggs, S. R., Melamed, B. G., & Graham-Pole, J. (1992). The effect of varied physician affect on recall, anxiety, and perceptions in women at risk for breast cancer: An analogue study. *Health Psychology, 11,* 61–66.

Shapiro, D., Hui, K. K., Oakley, M. E., Pasic, J., & Jamner, L. D. (1997). Reduction in drug requirements for hypertension by means of a cognitive-behavioral intervention. *American Journal of Hypertension, 10,* 9–17.

Sharpe, M., et al. (1994). Why do doctors find some patients difficult to help? *Quarterly Journal of Medicine, 87,* 187–193.

Sharpe, T. R., Smith, M. C., & Barbre, A. R. (1985). Medicine use among the rural elderly. *Journal of Health and Social Behavior, 26,* 113–127.

Shattuck, F. C. (1907). The science and art of medicine in some of their aspects. *Boston Medical and Surgical Journal, 157,* 63–67.

Shaver, J. L. F., Johnston, S. K., Lentz, M. J., & Landis, C. A. (2002). Stress exposure, psychological distress, and physiological stress activation in midlife women with insomnia. *Psychosomatic Medicine, 64,* 793–802.

Sheehy, G. (1974). *Passages.* New York: Dutton.

Sheese, B. E., Brown, E. L., & Graziaon, W. G. (2004). Emotional expression in cyberspace: Searching for moderators of the Pennebaker Disclosure effect via e-mail. *Health Psychology, 23(5),* 457–464.

Sheffield, D., Biles, P., Orom, H., Maixner, W., & Sheps, D. (2000). Race and sex differences in cutaneous pain perception. *Psychosomatic Medicine, 62,* 517–523.

Shelby, R. A., Golden-Kreutz, D. M., & Andersen, B. L. (2008). PTSD diagnoses, subsyndromal symptoms, and comorbidities contribute to impairments for breast cancer survivors. *Journal of Traumatic Stress, 21(2),* 165–172.

Shelton, J. L., & Levy, R. L. (1981). *Behavioral assignments and treatment compliance: A handbook of clinical strategies.* Champaign, IL: Research Press.

Shemesh, E., Yehuda, R., Milo, O., Dinur, I., Rudnick, A., Vered, Z., & Cotter, G. (2004). Posttraumatic stress, nonadherence, and adverse outcomes in survivors of a myocardial infarction. *Psychosomatic Medicine, 66,* 521–526.

Sherbourne, C. D., Hays, R. D., Ordway, L., DiMatteo, M. R., & Kravitz, R. L. (1992). Antecedents of adherence to medical recommendations: Results from the medical outcomes study. *Journal of Behavioral Medicine, 15,* 447–468.

Sherman, D. K., Mann, T. L., & Updegraff, J. A. (2006). Approach/avoidance orientation, message framing, and health behavior: Understanding the congruency effect. *Motivation and Emotion, 30,* 164–168.

Sherwood, A., Hinderliter, A. L., & Light, K. C. (1995). Physiological determinants of hyperreactivity to stress in borderline hypertension. *Hypertension, 25,* 384–390.

Shields, M. (2006a). Overweight and obesity among children and youth. *Health Reports, 17(3),* 27–42. Statistics Canada Catalogue 82-003. Retrieved July 14, 2007, from www.statcan.ca/english/freepub/82-003-XIE/82-003-XIE2005003.pdf.

Shields, M. (2006b). Stress and depression in the employed population. *Health Reports, 17(4),* 11–29.

Shields, M. (2007). Smoking-prevalence, bans and exposure to second-hand smoke. *Health Reports, 18(3).* Statistics Canada Catalogue 82-003. Retrieved from www.statcan.ca/english/freepub/82-003-XIE/2006007/articles/smoking/smoking-en.pdf.

Shields, M., & Martel, L. (2006). Health living among seniors. *Supplement to Health Reports, 16,* 7–20 (Statistics Canada Catalogue 82-003). Retrieved March 1, 2008, from www.statcan.ca/english/freepub/82-003-SIE/2005000/pdf/82-003-SIE20050007445.pdf.

Shields, M., & Tjepkema, M. (2006). Trends in adult obesity. *Health Reports, 17(3),* 53–59. Statistics Canada Catalogue 82-003. Retrieved August 3, 2007, from www.statcan.ca/english/freepub/82-003-XIE/82-003-XIE2005003.pdf.

Shields, M., Tremblay, M. S., Laviolette, M., Craig, C. L., Janssen, I., & Gorber, S. C. (2010). Fitness of Canadian adults: Results from the 2007–2009 Canadian Health Measures Survey. Statistics Canada, Catalogue no. 82-003-XPE • Health Reports, Vol. 21, no. 1.

Shields, M., & Wilkins, K. (2006). *National survey of the work and health of nurses.* Statistics Canada Catalogue 83-003-XIE.

Shields, M., & Wilkins, K. (2009). An update on mammography use in Canada. Statistics Canada, Catalogue no. 82-003-XPE • Health Reports, Vol. 20, no. 3.

Shiffman, S., Balabanis, M. H., Paty, J. A., Engberg, J., Gwaltney, C. J., Liu, K. S., et al. (2000). Dynamic effects of self-efficacy on smoking lapse and relapse. *Health Psychology, 19,* 315–323.

Shiffman, S., Fischer, L. A., Paty, J. A., Gnys, M., Hickcox, M., & Kassel, J. D. (1994). Drinking and smoking: A field study of their association. *Annals of Behavioral Medicine, 16,* 203–209.

Shiffman, S., Hickcox, M., Paty, J. A., Gnys, M., Kassel, J. D., & Richards, T. J. (1996). Progression from a smoking lapse to relapse: Prediction from abstinence violation effects, nicotine dependence, and lapse characteristics. *Journal of Consulting and Clinical Psychology, 64,* 993–1002.

Shifren, K., Park, D. C., Bennett, J. M., & Morrell, R. W. (1999). Do cognitive processes predict mental health in individuals with rheumatoid arthritis? *Journal of Behavioral Medicine, 22,* 529–547.

Shiloh, S., Gerad, L., & Goldman, B. (2006). Patients' information needs and decision-making processes: What can be learned from genetic counselees? *Health Psychology, 25,* 211–219.

Shilts, R. (1987). *And the band played on: Politics, people, and the AIDS epidemic.* New York: St. Martin's Press.

Shimizu, M., & Pelham, B. W. (2004). The unconsciousness cost of good fortune: Implicit and explicit self-esteem, positive life events, and health. *Health Psychology, 23,* 101–105.

Shin, J. Y., Martin, R., & Suls, J. (2010). Meta-analytic evaluation of gender differences and symptom measurement strategies in acute coronary syndromes. *Heart & lung : the journal of critical care, 39,* 283–295.

Shipp, S. J., Norton, L., & Roussil, A. (1999). *It's hard being a woman with HIV: Aboriginal women and HIV/AIDS, final research report.* Kahnawake, Quebec: National Indian and Inuit Community Health Representatives Organization.

Shultz, K. S., Wang, M., & Olson, D. A. (2010). Role overload and underload in relation to occupational stress and health. *Stress and Health, 26,* 99–111.

Sicotte, C., Pineault, R., Tilquin, C., & Contandriopoulos, A. P. (1996). The diluting effect of medical work groups on feedback efficiency in changing physician's practice. *Journal of Behavioral Medicine, 19,* 367–384.

Siegel, K., Karus, D., & Raveis, V. H. (1997). Correlates of change in depressive symptomatology among gay men with AIDS. *Health Psychology, 16,* 230–238.

Siegler, I. C., Costa, P. T., Brummett, B. H., Helms, M. J., Barefoot, J. C., Williams, R. B., et al. (2003). Patterns of change in hostility from college to midlife in the UNC alumni heart study predict high-risk status. *Psychosomatic Medicine, 65,* 738–745.

Siegman, A. W., & Snow, S. C. (1997). The outward expression of anger, the inward experience of anger, and CVR: The role of vocal expression. *Journal of Behavioral Medicine, 20,* 29–46.

Siegman, A. W., Townsend, S. T., Civelek, A. C., & Blumenthal, R. S. (2000). Antagonistic behavior, dominance, hostility, and coronary heart disease. *Psychosomatic Medicine, 62,* 248–257.

Sieverding, M., Matterne, U., & Ciccarello, L. (2010). What role do social norms play in the context of men's cancer screening intention and behavior? Application of an extended theory of planned behavior. . *Health Psychology, 29,* 72–81.

Silver, E. J., Bauman, L. J., & Ireys, H. T. (1995). Relationships of self-esteem and efficacy to psychological distress in mothers of children with chronic physical illnesses. *Health Psychology, 14,* 333–340.

Silver, R. C., Holman, E. A., McIntosh, D. N., Poulin, M., & Gil-Rivas, V. (2002). Nationwide longitudinal study of psychological responses to September 11. *Journal of American Medical Association, 288,* 1235–1244.

Simkin-Silverman, L. R., Wing, R. R., Boraz, M. A., & Kuller, L. H. (2003). Lifestyle intervention can prevent weight gain during menopause: Results from a 5-year randomized clinical trial. *Annals of Behavioral Medicine, 26,* 212–220.

Simkin-Silverman, L., Wing, R. R., Hansen, D. H., Klem, M. L., Pasagian-Macaulay, A., et al. (1995). Prevention of cardiovascular risk factor elevations in healthy premenopausal women. *Preventive Medicine, 24,* 509–571.

Simon, L. S., Judge, T. A., & Halvorsen-Ganepola, M. D. K. (2010). In good company? A multi-study, multi-level investigation of the effects of coworker relationships on employee well-being. *Journal of Vocational Behavior, 76,* 534–546.

Simon, N. (2003, September). Can you hear me now? *Time.* Retrieved from: http://www.time.com/time/archive/preview/0,10987,1005468,00.htm.

Simon, R. W. (1992). Parental role strains, salience of parental identity and gender differences in psychological distress. *Journal of Health and Social Behavior, 33,* 25–35.

Simoni, J. M., & Ng, M. T. (2002). Abuse, health locus of control, and perceived health among HIV-positive women. *Health Psychology, 21,* 89–93.

Simrén, M., Ringström, G., Björnsson, E. S., & Abrahamsson, H. (2004). Treatment with hypnotherapy reduces the sensory and motor component of the gastrocolonic response in irritable bowel syndrome. *Psychosomatic Medicine, 66,* 233–238.

Singer, B. H. (Ed.). (2000). *Future directions for behavioral and social sciences research at the National Institutes of Health.* Washington, D.C.: National Academy of Sciences Press.

Singh, M., Katz, R. C., Beauchamp, K., & Hannon, R. (2002). Effects of anonymous information about potential organ transplant recipients on attitudes toward organ transplantation and the willingness to donate organs. *Journal of Behavioral Medicine, 25,* 469–476.

Sinha, R., Fisch, G., Teague, B., Tamborlane, W. V., Banyas, B., Allen, K., et al. (2002). Prevalence of impaired glucose tolerance among children and adolescents with marked obesity. *New England Journal of Medicine, 346,* 802–810, http://www.nejm.org.

Sirois, F. M. (2004). Procrastination and intentions to perform health behaviors: The role of self-efficacy and the consideration of future consequences. *Personality and Individual Differences, 37,* 115–128.

Sirois, F. M. (2007a). Procrastination and motivations for household safety behaviours: an expectancy-value theory perspective *Psychology of Motivation* (pp. 1–13): Nova Science Publishers, Inc.

Sirois, F. M. (2007b). *Adjustment to arthritis and inflammatory bowel disease: Self-perception, relationships, and well-being over time.* Unpublished data.

Sirois, F. M. (2008). Provider-based complementary and alternative medicine use among three chronic illness groups: Associations with psychosocial factors and concurrent use of conventional health-care services. *Complementary Therapies in Medicine, 16,* 74–81.

Sirois, F. M. (2008, June). What is and what may never be: Possible selves and adjustment to inflammatory bowel disease. In F.M. Sirois (chair), *Guts, gumption, and go-ahead: Psychological adjustment to inflammatory bowel disease.* Paper presented at the 69th Annual Convention of the Canadian Psychological Association, Halifax, NS.

Sirois, F. M. (2009, May). Towards an integrated, person-centered model of the placebo effect. Paper presented at the 2009 North American Research Conference on Complementary & Integrative Medicine, Minneapolis, MN.

Sirois, F. M. (2010a, May). Blame it on time: Time-related perfectionism, health, and well-being. In G. Flett and P. Fry (chairs) *Perfectionism and Health: A Multidimensional Analysis.* Paper presented at the 22nd annual convention of the Association for Psychological Science, Boston, MA.

Sirois, F. M. (2010b, May). "I would be foolish to stop something that has helped" Reasons for continuing use of complementary and alternative medicine (CAM). Paper presented at the 5th International Congress on Complementary Medicine Research (ICCMR), Tromso, Norway.

Sirois, F. M. (Date TBD).

Sirois, F. M., & Gick, M. L. (2002). An investigation of the health beliefs and motivations of complementary medicine clients. *Social Science and Medicine, 55,* 1025–1037.

Sirois, F. M. , & Hirsch, J. K. (2011). Self perceptions and adjustment to chronic illness: Past, present and future selves. In F. M. Sirois (chair) *Self-perceptions, Health and Well-being: A Temporal Perspective.* Paper presented at the 72nd Annual Convention of the Canadian Psychological Association, Toronto, ON.

Sirois F. M., & Purc-Stephenson, R. (2006). The same….but different: Factors associated with in-person and on-line support group use across three chronic illness groups. [Abstract]. *Canadian Psychology, 47,* 81.

Sirois, F. M., & Purc-Stephenson, R. (2008a). Consumer decision factors for initial and long-term use of complementary and alternative medicine. *Complementary Health Practice Review, 13,* 3–19.

Sirois, F. M., & Purc-Stephenson, R. (2008b). When one door closes, another door opens: Physician availability and motivations to consult complementary and alternative medicine providers. *Complementary Therapies in Clinical Practice, 14*(4), 228–236.

Sirois, F. M., & Pychyl, T. A. (2002, August). Academic procrastination: Costs to health and well-being. In J. R. Ferrari & T. A. Pychyl (chairs) *Academic procrastination: A common event that's not commonly understood,* Symposium presented at the 110th Annual Convention of the American Psychological Association, Chicago, Illinois.

Sirois, F. M., & Tosti, N. (2011 online). *Lost in the moment? An investigation of procrastination, mindfulness, and well-being.* Invited submission for a special issue of the *Journal of Rational-Emotive & Cognitive-Behavior Therapy.*

Sirois, F. M., Davis, C. G., & Morgan, M. (2006). "Learning to live with what you can't rise above": Control beliefs, symptom control, and adjustment to tinnitus. *Health Psychology, 25,* 119–123.

Sirois, F. M., Melia-Gordon, M. L., & Pychyl, T. A. (2003). "I'll look after my health, later": An investigation of procrastination and health. *Personality and Individual Differences, 35,* 1167–1184.

Skala, J. A., & Freedlan, K. E. (2004). Death take a raincheck. *Psychosomatic Medicine, 66,* 382–386.

Skinner, N., & Brewer, N. (2002). The dynamics of threat and challenge appraisals prior to stressful achievement events. *Journal of Personality and Social Psychology, 83,* 678–692.

Skinner, T. C., Hampson, S. E., & Fife-Schaw, C. (2002). Personality, personal model beliefs, and self-care in adolescents and young adults with type 1 diabetes. *Health Psychology, 21,* 61–70.

Slaughter, V. (2005). Young children's understanding of death. *Australian Psychologist, 40,* 179–186.

Sloan, R. P., Shapiro, P. A., Bagiella, E., Myers, M. M., & Gorman, J. M. (1999). Cardiac autonomic control buffers blood pressure variability responses to challenge: A psychophysiologic model of coronary artery disease. *Psychosomatic Medicine, 61,* 58–68.

Smalec, J. L., & Klingle, R. S. (2000). Bulimia interventions via interpersonal influence: The role of threat and efficacy in persuading bulimics to seek help. *Journal of Behavioral Medicine, 23,* 37–57.

Smith, B. W., & Zautra, A. J. (2002). The role of personality in exposure and reactivity to interpersonal stress in relation to arthritis disease activity and negative effects in women. *Health Psychology, 21,* 81–88.

Smith, C. A., & Wallston, K. A. (1992). Adaptation in patients with chronic rheumatoid arthritis: Application of a general model. *Health Psychology, 11,* 151–162.

Smith, G. (2004). Asian-American deaths near the harvest moon festival. *Psychosomatic Medicine, 66,* 378–381.

Smith, G. (2006). The five elements and Chinese-American mortality. *Health Psychology, 25,* 124–129.

Smith, G. R., Williamson, G. M., Miller, L. S., & Schulz, R. (2011). Depression and quality of informal care: A longitudinal investigation of caregiving stressors. *Psychology and Aging.*

Smith, J. A., Lumley, M. A., & Longo, D. J. (2002). Contrasting emotional approach coping with passive coping for chronic myofascial pain. *Annals of Behavioral Medicine, 24,* 326–335.

Smith, L., Adler, N., & Tschann, J. (1999). Underreporting sensitive behaviors: The case of young women's willingness to report abortion. *Health Psychology, 18,* 37–43.

Smith, T. W., & Gallo, L. C. (1999). Hostility and cardiovascular reactivity during marital interaction. *Psychosomatic Medicine, 61,* 436–445.

Smith, T. W., & Ruiz, J. M. (2002). Psychosocial influences on the development and course of coronary heart disease: Current status and implications for research and practice. *Journal of Consulting and Clinical Psychology, 70,* 548–568.

Smith, T. W., Peck, J. R., Milano, R. A., & Ward, J. R. (1988). Cognitive distortion in rheumatoid arthritis: Relation to depression and disability. *Journal of Consulting and Clinical Psychology, 56,* 412–416.

Smith, T. W., Ruiz, J. M., & Uchino, B. N. (2000). Vigilance, active coping, and cardiovascular reactivity during social interaction in young men. *Health Psychology, 19,* 382–392.

Smith, T. W., Ruiz, J. M., & Uchino, B. N. (2004). Mental activation of supportive ties, hostility, and cardiovascular reactivity to laboratory stress in young men and women. *Health Psychology, 23,* 476–485.

Smyth, J. M., Soefer, M. H., Hurewitz, A., & Stone, A. A. (1999). The effect of tape-recorded relaxation training on well-being, symptoms and peak expiratory flow rate in adult asthmatics: A pilot study. *Psychology and Health, 14,* 487–501.

Sobel, H. (1981). Toward a behavioral thanatology in clinical care. In H. Sobel (Ed.), *Behavioral therapy in terminal care: A humanistic approach* (pp. 3–38). Cambridge, MA: Ballinger.

Society of Obstetricians and Gynaecologists of Canada, (2009), Overview of HPV, http://www.hpvinfo.ca/hpvinfo/adults/overview.aspx.

Solano, L., Donati, V., Pecci, F., Persichetti, S., & Colaci, A. (2003). Postoperative course after papilloma resection: Effects of written disclosure of the experience in subjects with different alexithymia levels. *Psychosomatic Medicine, 65,* 477–484.

Somerfield, M. R., Curbow, B., Wingard, J. R., Baker, F., & Fogarty, L. A. (1996). Coping with the physical and psychosocial sequelae of bone marrow transplantation among long-term survivors. *Journal of Behavioral Medicine, 19,* 163–184.

Sorkin, D. H., Rook, K. S., & Lu, J. (2002). Loneliness, lack of emotional support, lack of companionship and the likelihood of having a heart condition in an elderly sample. *Annals of Behavioral Medicine, 24,* 290–298.

Sorrentino, E. A. (1992). Hospice care: A unique clinical experience for MSN students. *American Journal of Hospice and Palliative Care, 9,* 29–33.

Spalletta, G., Pasini, A., Costa, A., De Angelis, D., Ramundo, N., Paolucci, S., & Cartagirone, C. (2001). Alexithymic features in stroke: Effects of laterality and gender. *Psychosomatic Medicine, 63,* 944–950.

Speca, M., Carlson, L.E., Goodey, E., & Angen, M. (2000).A randomized, wait-list controlled clinical trial: The effect of a mindfulness meditation-based stress reduction program on mood and symptoms of stress in cancer outpatients. *Psychosomatic Medicine, 62*(5), 613–622.

Speisman, J., Lazarus, R. S., Mordkoff, A., & Davidson, L. (1964). Experimental reduction of stress based on ego defense theory. *Journal of Abnormal and Social Psychology, 68,* 367–380.

Spencer, S. M., Lehman, J. M., Wynings, C., Arena, P., Carver, C. S., Antoni, M. H., et al. (1999). Concerns about breast cancer and relations to psychosocial well-being in a multiethnic sample of early-stage patients. *Health Psychology, 18,* 159–168.

Spiegel, D., & Bloom, J. R. (1983). Group therapy and hypnosis reduce metastatic breast carcinoma pain. *Psychosomatic Medicine, 45,* 333–339.

Spiegel, K., Tasali, E., Penev, P., & Van Cauter, E. (2004). Brief communication: Sleep curtailment in healthy young men is associated with decreased leptin levels, elevated ghrelin levels, and increased hunger and appetite. *Annals of Internal Medicine, 141,* 846–850.

Spinetta, J. J., Spinetta, P. D., Kung, F., & Schwartz, D. B. (1976). *Emotional aspects of childhood cancer and leukemia: A handbook for parents.* San Diego, CA: Leukemia Society of America.

Spinney, L. (2006). Eat your cake and have it. *Nature, 441* (June 15, 2006), 807–809.

Spitzer, R. L., Yanovski, S., Wadden, T., Wing, R., Marcus, M. D., Stunkard, A., Devlin, M., et al. (1993). Binge eating disorder: Its further validation in a multisite study. *International Journal of Eating Disorders, 13,* 137–153.

Sprangers, M., Bartels, M., Veenhoven, R., Baas, F., Martin, N., Mosing, M., et al. (2010). Which patient will feel down, which will be happy? The need to study the genetic disposition of emotional states. *Quality of Life Research, 19,* 1429–1437.

Spruill, T. (2010). Chronic Psychosocial Stress and Hypertension. *Current Hypertension Reports, 12,* 10–16.

Stajduhar, K. I., Martin, W. L., Barwich, D., & Fyles, G. (2008). Factors Influencing Family Caregivers' Ability to Cope With Providing End-of-Life Cancer Care at Home. *Cancer Nursing, 31,* 77–85.

Stampfer, M. J., Hu, F. B., Manson, J. E., Rimm, E. B., & Willett, W. C. (2000). Primary prevention of coronary heart disease in women through diet and lifestyle. *New England Journal of Medicine, 343,* 16–22.

Stanford, E. A., Chambers, C. T., Craig, K. D., McGrath, P. J., Cassidy, K. L. (2005). "Ow!": Spontaneous verbal pain expression among young children during immunization. *Clinical Journal of Pain, 21(6),* 499–502.

Stansfeld, S. A., Bosma, H., Hemingway, H., & Marmot, M. G. (1998). Psychosocial work characteristics and social support as predictors of SF-36 health functioning: The Whitehall II study. *Psychosomatic Medicine, 60,* 247–255.

Stansfeld, S. A., Fuhrer, R., Shipley, M. J., & Marmot, M. G. (2002). Psychological distress as a risk factor for coronary heart disease in the Whitehall II Study. *International Journal of Epidemiology, 31,* 248–255.

Stanton, A. L., Danoff-Burg, S., Cameron, C. L., & Ellis, A. P. (1994). Coping through emotional approach: Problems of conceptualizaton and confounding. *Journal of Personality & Social Psychology, 66,* 350–362.

Stanton, A. L., Danoff-Burg, S., Cameron, C. L., Snider, P. R., & Kirk, S. B. (1999). Social comparison and adjustment to breast cancer: An experimental examination of upward affiliation and downward evaluation. *Health Psychology, 18,* 151–158.

Stanton, A. L., Danoff-Burg, S., Sworowski, L. A., Collins, C. A., Branstetter, A. D., Rodriguez-Hanley, A., Kirk, S. B., & Austenfeld, J. L. (2002). Randomized, controlled trial of written emotional expression and benefit finding in breast cancer patients. *Journal of Clinical Oncology, 20,* 4160–4168.

Stanton, A. L., Kirk, S. B., Cameron, C. L., & Danoff-Burg, S. (2000). Coping through emotional approach: Scale construction and validation. *Journal of Personality and Social Psychology, 78,* 1150–1169.

Stanton, A. L., Revenson, T. A., & Tennen, H. (2007). Health psychology: Psychological adjustment to chronic disease. Annual Review of Psychology, 58(1), 565–592.

Starkman, M. N., Giordani, B., Berent, S., Schork, M. A., & Schteingart, D. E. (2001). Elevated cortisol levels in Cushing's Disease are associated with cognitive decrements. *Psychosomatic Medicine, 63,* 985–993.

St-Arnaud, J., Beaudet, M. P., & Tully, P. (2005). Life expectancy. *Health Report, 17(1),* 43–49 (Statistics Canada Catalogue 82-003). Retrieved August 3, 2007, from www.statcan.ca/english/freepub/82-003-XIE/0010582-003-XIE.pdf.

Starr, K. R., Antoni, M. H., Hurwitz, B. E., Rodriguez, M. S., Ironson, G., Fletcher, M. A., et al. (1996). Patterns of immune, neuroendocrine, and cardiovascular stress responses in asymptomatic HIV seropositive and seronegative men. *International Journal of Behavioral Medicine, 3,* 135–162.

Statistics Canada. (1999). Health status of children. *Health Reports, 11(3),* 25–34 (Statistics Canada Catalogue 82-003). Retrieved September 10, 2007, from www.statcan.ca/english/freepub/82-003-XIE/0039982-003-XIE.pdf.

Statistics Canada. (2001a). The health divide: How the sexes differ. *The Daily.* Retrieved September 21, 2007, from www.statcan.ca/Daily/English/010426/d010426a.htm.

Statistics Canada. (2001b). Death-shifting trends. *Health Report, 12(3),* 41–46 (Statistics Canada Catalogue 82-003). Retrieved September 10, 2007, from www.statcan.ca/english/freepub/82-003-XIE/0030082-003-XIE.pdf.

Statistics Canada. (2004, November 9). Study: Infant mortality among First Nations and non-First Nations people in British Columbia. *The Daily.* Retrieved September 10, 2007, from www.statcan.ca/Daily/English/041109/d041109c.htm.

Statistics Canada. (2004a). *Deaths, by selected grouped causes and sex, Canada, provinces and territories, annual.* Retrieved February 10, 2008, from www.statcan.ca/english/freepub/84F0209XIE/2004000/related.htm.

Statistics Canada. (2006a). *Women in Canada: A gender-based statistical report (5th ed.)* (Statistics Canada Catalogue 89-503). Retrieved February 18, 2008, from www.statcan.ca/english/freepub/89-503-XIE/0010589-503-XIE.pdf.

Statistics Canada. (2007). *Causes of death.* (Statistics Canada Catalogue 84-208-XIE.) Retrieved July 18, 2008, from www.statcan.ca/bsolc/english/bsolc?catno =84-208-X.

Statistics Canada. (2008). *Leading causes of death in Canada, 2000 to 2004.* (Statistics Canada Catalogue 84-215-X).

Statistics Canada. (2010). Statistics Canada, CANSIM, table 105-0501 and Catalogue no. 82-221-X. http://www40.statcan.gc.ca/l01/cst01/health53a-eng.htm.

Statistics Canada (2010a). Life expectancy. Retrieved April 6, 2011 from http://www.statcan.gc.ca/pub/82-229-x/2009001/demo/lif-eng.htm.

Statistics Canada. (2010b). *Leading Causes of deaths in Canada, 2007,* CANSIM Table 102–0561. Ranking and number of deaths for the 10 leading causes, Canada 2000 and 2007. Retrieved May 14, 2011 from http://www.statcan.gc.ca/pub/84-215-x/2010001/table-tableau/tbl001-eng.htm.

Statistics Canada (2011). Bicycle Helmet Use, 2009. Accessed August 23, 2011 from http://www.statcan.gc.ca/pub/82-625-x/2010002/article/11274-eng.htm.

Statistics Canada. (2011a). Smoking, 2010. Retrieved August 23, 2011 from http://www.statcan.gc.ca/pub/82-625-x/2011001/article/11468-eng.htm.

Statistics Canada (2011b). Fruit and vegetable consumption, 2009. Accessed May 10, 2011 from http://www.statcan.gc.ca/pub/82-625-x/2010002/article/11259-eng.htm.

Statistics Canada. (2011c). Exposure to second-hand smoke at home, 2010. Accessed August 24, 2011 from http://www.statcan.gc.ca/pub/82-625-x/2011001/article/11460-eng.htm.

Stauder, A., & Kovacs, M. (2003). Anxiety symptoms in allergic patients: Identification and risk factors. *Psychosomatic Medicine, 65,* 816–823.

Steel, P. (2007). The nature of procrastination. *Psychological Bulletin, 133,* 65–94.

Steffen, P. R., Smith, T. B., Larson, M., & Butler, L. (2006). Acculturation to western society as a risk factor for high blood pressure: A meta-analytic review. *Psychosomatic Medicine, 68,* 386–397.

Steginga, S. K., & Occhipinti, S. (2006). Dispositional optimism as a predictor of men's decision-related distress after localized prostate cancer. *Health Psychology, 25,* 135–143.

Stein, N., Folkman, S., Trabasso, T., & Richards, T. A. (1997). Appraisal and goal processes as predictors of psychological well-being in bereaved caregivers. *Journal of Personality and Social Psychology, 72,* 872–884.

Stein, P. N., Gordon, W. A., Hibbard, M. R., & Sliwinski, M. J. (1992). An examination of depression in the spouses of stroke patients. *Rehabilitation Psychology, 37,* 121–130.

Steinbrook, R. (2004a). Disparities in health care-from politics to policy. *New England Journal of Medicine, 350,* 1486–1488, http://www.nejm.org.

Steinhauser, K. E., Clipp, E. C., McNeilly, M., Christakis, N. A., McIntyre, L. M., & Tulsky, J. A. (2000). In Search of a Good Death: Observations of Patients, Families, and Providers. *Annals of Internal Medicine, 132,* 825–832.

Stephens, M. A. P., Druley, J. A., & Zautra, A. J. (2002). Older adults' recovery from surgery for osteoarthritis of the knee: Psychological resources and constraints as predictors of outcomes. *Health Psychology, 21,* 377–383.

Steptoe, A. (2008). Psychophysiological Stress Reactivity and Hypertension. *Hypertension, 52,* 220-221. doi: 10.1161/hypertensionaha.108.115477.

Steptoe, A., & Marmot, M. (2003). Burden of psychosocial adversity and vulnerability in middle age: Associations with biobehavioral risk factors and quality of life. *Psychosomatic Medicine, 65,* 1029–1037.

Steptoe, A., Brydon, L., Kunz-Ebrecht, S. (2005). Changes in financial strain over three years, ambulatory blood pressure, and cortisol responses to awakening. *Psychosomatic Medicine, 67,* 281–287.

Steptoe, A., Doherty, S., Kerry, S., Rink, E., & Hilton, S. (2000). Sociodemographic and psychological predictors of changes in dietary fat consumption in adults with high blood cholesterol following counseling in primary care. *Health Psychology, 19,* 411–419.

Steptoe, A., Kerry, S., Rink, E., & Hilton, S. (2001). The impact of behavioral counseling on stage of change in fat intake, physical activity, and cigarette smoking in adults at increased risk coronary heart disease. *American Journal of Public Health, 91,* 265–269.

Steptoe, A., Kunz-Ebrecht, S., Owen, N., Feldman, P. J., Rumley, A., Lowe, G. D. O., et al. (2003). Influence of socioeconomic status and job control on plasma fibrinogen responses to acute mental stress. *Psychosomatic Medicine, 65,* 137–144.

Steptoe, A., Roy, M. P., & Evans, O. (1996). Psychosocial influences on ambulatory blood pressure over working and non-working days. *Journal of Psychophysiology, 10,* 218–227.

Steptoe, A., Siegrist, J., Kirschbaum, C., & Marmot, M. (2004). Effort-reward imbalance, overcommitment, and measures of cortisol and blood pressure over the working day. *Psychosomatic Medicine, 66,* 323–329.

Stetson, B. A., Rahn, J. M., Dubbert, P. M., Wilner, B. I., & Mercury, M. G. (1997). Prospective evaluation of the effects of stress on exercise adherence in community-residing women. *Health Psychology, 16,* 515–520.

Steven, D., Fitch, M., Dhaliwal, H., Kirk-Gardner, R., Sevean, P., Jamieson, J., & Woodbeck, H. (2004). Knowledge, attitudes, beliefs, and practices regarding breast and cervical cancer screening in selected ethnocultural groups in Northwestern Ontario. *Oncology Nursing Forum, 31(2),* 305–311.

Stevenson, K. (2002). Health information on the net. *Canadian Social Trends,* 7–10 (Statistics Canada Catalogue 11-008). Retrieved August 15, 2007, from www.statcan.ca/english/freepub/11-008-XIE/2002002/articles/6346.pdf.

Stevinson, C., Faugh, W., Steed, H., Tonkin, K., Ladha, A. B., Vallance, J. K., Capstick, V., Schepansky, A., & Courneya, K. S. (2007). Associations between physical activity and quality of life in ovarian cancer survivors. *Gynecologic Oncology, 106(1),* 244–250.

Stewart, D. E., Abbey, S. E., Shnek, Z. M., Irvine, J., & Grace, S. L. (2004). Gender differences in health information needs and decisional preferences in patients recovering from an acute ischemic coronary event. *Psychosomatic Medicine, 66,* 42–48.

Stewart, M. A. (1995). Effective physician-patient communication and health outcomes: a review. *Canadian Medical Association Journal, 152*(9), 1423–1433.

Stewart, M., Brown, J. B., Donner, A., McWhinney, I. R., Oates, J., Weston, W. W., et al. (2000). The impact of patient-centered care on outcomes. *Journal of Family Practice, 49*(9), 796–804.

Stewart-Williams, S. (2004). The placebo puzzle: Putting together the pieces. *Health Psychology, 23,* 198–206.

Stice, E., Presnell, K., & Spangler, D. (2002). Risk factors for binge eating onset in adolescent girls: A 2-year prospective investigation. *Health Psychology, 21,* 131–138.

Stilley, C. S., Sereika, S., Muldoon, M. F., Ryan, C. M., & Dunbar-Jacob, J. (2004). Psychological and cognitive function: Predictors of adherence with cholesterol lowering treatment. *Annals of Behavioral Medicine, 27,* 117–124.

Stinson, D. A., Logel, C., Zanna, M. P., Holmes, J. G., Cameron, J. J., Wood, J. V., et al. (2008). The cost of lower self-esteem: Testing a self- and social-bonds model of health. *Journal of Personality and Social Psychology, 94,* 412–428.

Stoelb, B. L., Molton, I. R., Jensen, M. P., & Patterson, D. R. (2009). The efficacy of hypnotic analgesia in adults: A review of the literature. *Contemporary Hypnosis, 26*(1), 24–39.

Stolberg, S. G. (1999a, April 25). Sham surgery returns as a research tool. *The New York Times,* p. 3.

Stolberg, S. G. (1999b, September 23). Study finds shortcomings in care for chronically ill. *The New York Times,* p. A21.

Stommel, M., Kurtz, M. E., Kurtz, J. C., Given, C. W., & Given, B. A. (2004). A longitudinal analysis of the course of depressive symptomology in geriatric patients with cancer of the breast, colon, lung, or prostate. *Health Psychology, 23,* 564–573.

Stone, A. A., & Neale, J. M. (1984). New measure of daily coping: Development and preliminary results. *Journal of Personality & Social Psychology, 46,* 892–906.

Stone, A. A., Kennedy-Moore, E., & Neale, J. M. (1995). Association between daily coping and end-of-day mood. *Health Psychology, 14,* 341–349.

Stone, A. A., Mezzacappa, E. S., Donatone, B. A., & Gonder, M. (1999). Psychosocial stress and social support are associated with prostate-specific antigen levels in men: Results from a community screening program. *Health Psychology, 18,* 482–486.

Stoney, C. M., & Finney, M. L. (2000). Social support and stress: Influences on lipid reactivity. *International Journal of Behavioral Medicine, 7,* 111–126.

Stoney, C. M., Owens, J. F., Guzick, D. S., & Matthews, K. A. (1997). A natural experiment on the effects of ovarian hormones on cardiovascular risk factors and stress reactivity: Bilateral salpingo oophorectomy versus hysterectomy only. *Health Psychology, 16,* 349–358.

Stoney, C., Niaura, R., Bausserman, L., & Matacin, M. (1999). Lipid reactivity to stress: I. Comparison of chronic and acute stress responses in middle-aged airline pilots. *Health Psychology, 18,* 241–250.

Storch, J. L. (2007). Divisions of labour in health care: Pragmatics and ethics. *Humane Medicine Health Care, 10*(4).

Storer, J. H., Frate, D. M., Johnson, S. A., & Greenberg, A. M. (1987). When the cure seems worse than the disease: Helping families adapt to hypertension treatment. *Family Relations, 36,* 311–315.

Stotts, A. L., DiClemente, C. C., Carbonari, J. P., & Mullen, P. D. (2000). Postpartum return to smoking: Staging a "suspended" behavior. *Health Psychology, 19,* 324–332.

Stout, D., Charpentier, C., Chiasson, M., & Fillion, E. (2009). Culture, language, and self-assessments of future health: Anglophones and Frnacophones in Quebec's Eastern Townships. *Journal of the Eastern Townships Studies, 34,* 7–30.

Stout, M. A. (1984). A cognitive-behavioral study of self-reported stress factors in migraine headache. *Psychopathology, 17,* 290–296.

Stowe, R. P., Pierson, D. L., & Barrett, A. D. T. (2001). Elevated stress hormone levels relate to Epstein-Barr virus reactivation in astronauts. *Psychosomatic Medicine, 63,* 891–895.

Stowell, J. R., Kiecolt-Glaser, J. K., & Glaser, R. (2001). Perceived stress and cellular immunity: When coping counts. *Journal of Behavioral Medicine, 24,* 323–339.

Strachan, E. D., Bennett, W. R. M., Russo, J., & Roy-Byrne, P. P. (2007). Disclosure of HIV status and sexual orientation independently predicts increased absolute CD4 cell counts over time for psychiatric patients. *Psychosomatic Medicine, 69,* 74–80.

Stranges, S., Cappuccio, F. P., Kandala N. B., Miller, M. A., Taggart, F. M., Kumari, M., Ferrie, J. E., Shipley, M. J., Brunner, E. J., & Marmot, M. G. (2007). Cross-sectional versus prospective associations of sleep duration with changes in relative weight and body fat distribution: The Whitehall II study. *American Journal of Epidemiology, 167*(3), 321–329.

Strating, M. M. H., van Schurr, W. H., & Suurmeijer, T. P. B. M. (2006). Contribution of partner support in self-management of rheumatoid arthritis patients. An application of the theory of planned behavior. *Journal of Behavioral Medicine, 29,* 51–60.

Strayer, D. L., Drews, F. A., & Crouch, D. J. (2006). A comparison of the cell phone driver and the drunk driver. Human Factors: The Journal of the Human Factors and Ergonomics Society, 48, 381–391.

Striegel-Moore, R. H., & Bulik, C. M. (2007). Risk factors for eating disorders. *American Psychologist, 62,* 181–198.

Striegel-Moore, R. H., Silberstein, L. R., Frensch, P., & Rodin, J. (1989). A prospective study of disordered eating among college students. *International Journal of Eating Disorders, 8,* 499–511.

Strike, P. C., & Steptoe, A. (2005). Behavioral and emotional triggers of acute coronary syndromes: A systematic review and critique. *Psychosomatic Medicine, 67,* 179–186.

Stroebe, M., Gergen, M. M., Gergen, K. J., & Stroebe, W. (1992). Broken hearts or broken bonds: Love and death in historical perspective. *American Psychologist, 47,* 1205–1212.

Stroebe, W., & Stroebe, M. S. (1987). *Bereavement and health: The psychological and physical consequences of partner loss.* New York: Cambridge University Press.

Stroke Survivors Association of Ottawa. (2005). *Over the long term: John.* Retrieved August 28, 2007, from www.strokesurvivors.ca/index.php?nav=john.

Strube, M. J., Smith, J. A., Rothbaum, R., & Sotelo, A. (1991). Measurement of health care attitudes in cystic fibrosis patients and their parents. *Journal of Applied Social Psychology, 21,* 397–408.

Stuber, M. L., Christakis, D. A., Houskamp, B., & Kazak, A. E. (1996). Post trauma symptoms in childhood leukemia survivors and their parents. *Journal of Consulting and Clinical Psychology, 37,* 254–261.

Suarez, E. C. (2003). Joint effect of hostility and severity of depressive symptoms on plasma interleukin-6 concentration. *Psychosomatic Medicine, 65,* 523–527.

Suarez, E. C. (2004). C-reactive protein is associated with psychological risk factors of cardiovascular disease in apparently healthy adults. *Psychosomatic Medicine, 66,* 684–691.

Suarez, E. C., Krishnan, R. R., & Lewis, J. G. (2003). The relation of severity of depressive symptoms in monocyte-associated proinflammatory cytokines and chemokines in apparently healthy men. *Psychosomatic Medicine, 65,* 362–368.

Suarez, E. C., Shiller, A. D., Kuhn, C. M., Schanberg, S., Williams, R. B., Jr., & Zimmermann, E. A. (1997). The relationship between hostility and B-adrenergic receptor physiology in healthy young males. *Psychosomatic Medicine, 59,* 481–487.

Suhr, J. A., Stewart, J. C., & France, C. R. (2004). The relationship between blood pressure and cognitive performance in the Third National Health and Nutrition Examination Survey (NHANES III). *Psychosomatic Medicine, 66,* 291–297.

Sullivan, K. (2009). Male Self-Disclosure of HIV Infection to Sex Partners: A Hawaii-Based Sample. *Journal of the Association of Nurses in AIDS care, 20*(6), 442–457.

Sullivan, K., Voss, J., & Li, D. (2010). Female Disclosure of HIV-Positive Serostatus to Sex Partners: A Two-City Study. *Women & Health, 50*(6), 506–526.

Sullivan, M. J., & Adams, H. (2010). Psychosocial treatment techniques to augment the impact of physiotherapy interventions for low back pain. *Physiotherapy Canada, 62,* 180–189.

Sullivan, M. J. L., & Stanish, W. D. (2003). Psychologically Based Occupational Rehabilitation: The Pain-Disability Prevention Program. *The Clinical Journal of Pain, 19,* 97–104.

Sullivan, M. J. L., Bishop, S. R., & Pivik, J. (1995). The pain catastrophizing scale: Development and validation. *Psychological Assessment, 7*(4), 524–532.

Sullivan, M. J. L., Martel, M. O., Tripp, D. A., Savard, A., & Crombez, G. (2006). Catastrophic thinking and heightened perception of pain in others. *Pain, 123,* 37–44.

Suls, J., & Bunde, J. (2005). Anger, Anxiety, and Depression as Risk Factors for Cardiovascular Disease: The Problems and Implications of Overlapping Affective Dispositions. *Psychological Bulletin, 131,* 260–300.

Suls, J., & Green, P. (2003). Pluralistic ignorance and college student perceptions of gender-specific alcohol norms. *Health Psychology, 22,* 479–486.

Suls, J., & Rittenhouse, J. D. (1990). Models of linkages between personality and disease. In H. S. Friedman (Ed.), *Personality and Disease* (pp. 38–63). New York: Wiley.

Suls, J., & Rothman, A. (2004). Evolution of the biopsychosocial model: Prospects and challenges for health psychology. *Health Psychology, 23,* 119–125.

Suls, J., & Wan, C. K. (1993). The relationship between trait hostility and cardiovascular reactivity: A quantitative review and analysis. *Psychophysiology, 30,* 1–12.

Surwit, R. S., & Schneider, M. S. (1993). Role of stress in the etiology and treatment of diabetes mellitus. *Psychosomatic Medicine, 55,* 380–393.

Surwit, R. S., & Williams, P. G. (1996). Animal models provide insight into psychosomatic factors in diabetes. *Psychosomatic Medicine, 58,* 582–589.

Surwit, R. S., Schneider, M. S., & Feinglos, M. N. (1992). Stress and diabetes mellitus. *Diabetes Care, 15,* 1413–1422.

Sutherland, G., Andersen, M. B., & Morris, T. (2005). Relaxation and health–related quality of life in multiple sclerosis: The example of autogenic training. *Journal of Behavioral Medicine, 28,* 249–256.

Suzuki, R., Iwasaki, M., Kasuga, Y., Yokoyama, S., Onuma, H., Nishimura, H., et al. (2010). Leisure-time physical activity and breast cancer risk by hormone receptor status: effective life periods and exercise intensity. *Cancer Causes and Control, 21,* 1787–1798.

Suzuki, R., Iwasaki, M., Yamamoto, S., Inoue, M., Sasazuki, S., Sawada, N., et al. (2011). Leisure-time physical activity and breast cancer risk defined by estrogen and progesterone receptor status—The Japan Public Health Center-based Prospective Study. *Preventive Medicine, 52,* 227–233.

Swindle, R. E., Jr., & Moos, R. H. (1992). Life domains in stressors, coping, and adjustment. In W. B. Walsh, R. Price, & K. B. Crak (Eds.), *Person environment psychology: Models and perspectives* (pp. 1–33). New York: Erlbaum.

Talbot, F., Nouwen, A., Gingras, J., Gosselin, M., & Audet, J. (1997). The assessment of diabetes-related cognitive and social factors: The multidimensional diabetes questionnaire. *Journal of Behavioral Medicine, 20,* 291–312.

Tam, L., Bagozzi, R. P., & Spanjol, J. (2010). When planning is not enough: The self-regulatory effect of implementation intentions on changing snacking habits. *Health Psychology, 29,* 284–292.

Tamres, L., Janicki, D., & Helgeson, V. S. (2002). Sex differences in coping b-ehavior: A meta-analytic review. *Personality and Social Psychology Review, 6,* 2–30.

Tatrow, K., & Montgomery, G. H. (2006). Cognitive behavioral therapy techniques for distress and pain in breast cancer patients: A meta-analysis. *Journal of Behavioral Medicine, 29,* 17–27.

Taylor, A. H., & Fox, K. R. (2005). Effectiveness of a primary care exercise referral intervention for changing physical self-perceptions over nine months. *Health Psychology, 24,* 11–21.

Taylor, C. B., Bandura, A., Ewart, C. K., Miller, N. H., & DeBusk, R. F. (1985). Exercise testing to enhance wives' confidence in their husbands' cardiac capability soon after clinically uncomplicated acute myocardial infarction. *American Journal of Cardiology, 55,* 635–638.

Taylor, J., & Turner, R. J. (2001). A longitudinal study of the role and significance of mattering to others for depressive symptoms. *Journal of Health and Social Behavior, 42,* 310–325.

Taylor, K. L., Lamdan, R. M., Siegel, J. E., Shelby, R., Moran-Klimi, K., & Hrywna, M. (2003). Psychological adjustment among African American patients: One-year follow-up results of a randomized psychoeducational group intervention. *Health Psychology, 22,* 316–323.

Taylor, S. E. (1983). Adjustment to threatening events: A theory of cognitive adaptation. *American Psychologist, 41,* 1161–1173.

Taylor, S. E. (1989). *Positive illusions: Creative self-deception and the healthy mind.* New York: Basic Books.

Taylor, S. E. (1998). *Optimism/pessimism.* Retrieved January 27, 2008, from www.macses.ucsf.edu/Research/Psychosocial/notebook/optimism.html.

Taylor, S. E. (2002). *The tending instinct: How nurturing is essential to who we are and how we live.* New York: Holt.

Taylor, S. E. (2007). Social support. In H.S. Friedman & R.C. Silver (Eds.), *Foundations of Health Psychology* (pp. 145–171). New York: Oxford University Press.

Taylor, S. E., & Aspinwall, L. G. (1990). Psychological aspects of chronic illness. In G. R. VandenBos & P. T. Costa, Jr. (Eds.), *Psychological aspects of serious illness.* Washington, D.C.: American Psychological Association.

Taylor, S. E., & Brown, J. D. (1988). Illusion and well-being: A social psychological perspective on mental health. *Psychological Bulletin, 103,* 193–210.

Taylor, S. E., & Stanton, A. (2007). Coping resources, coping processes, and mental health. *Annual Review of Clinical Psychology, 3,* 129–153.

Taylor, S. E., Gonzaga, G. C., Klein, L. C., Hu, P., Greendale, G. A., & Seeman, T. E. (2006). Relation of oxytocin to psychological stress responses and hypothalamic-pituitary-adrenocortical axis activity in older women. *Psychosomatic Medicine, 68,* 238–245.

Taylor, S. E., Helgeson, V. S., Reed, G. M., & Skokan, L. A. (1991). Self-generated feelings of control and adjustment to physical illness. *Journal of Social Issues, 47,* 91–109.

Taylor, S. E., Kemeny, M. E., Reed, G. M., Bower, J. E., & Gruenewald, T. L. (2000). Psychological resources, positive illusions, and health. *American P-sychologist, 55,* 99–109.

Taylor, S. E., Klein, L. C., Lewis, B. P., Gruenewald, T. L., Gurung, R. A. R., & Updegraff, J. A. (2000). Biobehavioral responses to stress in females: Tend-and-befriend, not fight-or-flight. *Psychological Review, 107,* 411–429.

Taylor, S. E., Lichtman, R. R., & Wood, J. V. (1984a). Attributions, beliefs about control, and adjustment to breast cancer. *Journal of Personality and Social Psychology, 46,* 489–502.

Taylor, S. E., Repetti, R. L., & Seeman, T. (1997). Health psychology: What is an unhealthy environment and how does it get under the skin? *Annual Review of Psychology, 48,* 411–447.

Taylor, S. E., Welch, W. T., Kim, H. S., & Sherman, D. K. (2007). Cultural Differences in the Impact of Social Support on Psychological and Biological Stress Responses. *Psychological Science, 18,* 831–837.

Teixeira, P. J., Going, S. B., Houtkooper, L. B., Cussler, E. C., Martin, C. J., Metcalfe, L. L., et al. (2002). Weight loss readiness in middle-aged women: Psychosocial predictors of success for behavioral weight reduction. *Journal of Behavioral Medicine, 25,* 499–523.

Telch, C. F., & Agras, W. S. (1996). Do emotional states influence binge eating in the obese? *International Journal of Eating Disorders, 20,* 271–279.

Tempelaar, R., de Haes, J. C. J. M., de Ruiter, J. H., Bakker, D., van den Heuvel, W. J. A., & van Nieuwenhuijzen, M. G. (1989). The social experiences of cancer patients under treatment: A comparative study. *Social Science and Medicine, 29,* 635–642.

Teng, Y., & Mak, W. W. S. (2011). The Role of Planning and Self-Efficacy in Condom Use Among Men Who Have Sex With Men: An Application of the Health Action Process Approach Model. *Health Psychology, 30*(1), 119–128.

Tennen, H., Affleck, G., & Zautra, A. (2006). Depression history and coping with chronic pain: A daily process analysis. *Health Psychology, 25,* 370–379.

Tennen, H., Affleck, G., Urrows, S., Higgins, P., & Mendola, R. (1992). Perceiving control, construing benefits, and daily processes in rheumatoid arthritis. *Canadian Journal of Behavioral Science, 24,* 186–203.

Teno, J. M., Fisher, E. S., Hamel, M. B., Coppola, K., & Dawson, N. V. (2002). Medical care inconsistent with patients' treatment goals: Association with 1-year medicare resource use and survival. *Journal of the American Geriatrics Society, 50,* 496–500.

The Arthritis Society. (2005a). *Fast facts: What is arthritis?* Retrieved July 28, 2007, from www.arthritis.ca/toolbox/media%20centre/statistics/what%20is-%20-arthritis/default.asp?s=1.

The Arthritis Society. (2005b). *Rheumatoid arthritis.* Retrieved July 28, 2007, from www.arthritis.ca/types%20of%20arthritis/ra/default.asp?s=1#{78100F57-A913-11D4-BCC5-00D0B7474671}.

The Arthritis Society. (2005c). *Osteoarthritis.* Retrieved July 28, 2007, from www.arthritis.ca/types%20of%20arthritis/osteoarthritis/default.asp?s=1#{5C-B4540E-AB9A-11D4-BCC6-00D0B7474671}.

The Arthritis Society. (2005d). *Gout.* Retrieved July 28, 2007, from www.arthritis.ca/types%20of%20arthritis/gout/default.asp?s=1#{9BE6C51D-AA24-11D4-BCC6-00D0B7474671}.

The Arthritis Society. (2005e). *Lupus.* Retrieved February 19, 2008, from www.arthritis.ca/types%20of%20arthritis/lupus/default.asp?s=1.

The Arthritis Society. (2010). Annual Report, 2010. http://www.arthritis.ca/local/files/pdf%20documents/About%20TAS/Eng_Annual%20report.pdf.

Theorell, T., Blomkvist, V., Lindh, G., & Evengard, B. (1999). Critical life events, infections, and symptoms during the year preceding chronic fatigue syndrome (CFS): An examination of CFS patients and subjects with a nonspecific life crisis. *Psychosomatic Medicine, 61,* 304–310.

Thieme, K., Turk, D. C., & Flor, H. (2004). Comorbid depression and anxiety in fibromyalgia syndrome: Relationship to somatic and psychosocial variables. *Psychosomatic Medicine, 66,* 837–844.

Thoits, P. A. (1994). Stressors and problem-solving: The individual as psychological activist. *Journal of Health and Social Behavior, 35,* 143–159.

Thoits, P. A., Harvey, M. R., Hohmann, A. A., & Fletcher, B. (2000). Similar-other support for men undergoing coronary artery bypass surgery. *Health Psychology, 19,* 264–273.

Thompson, H. S., & Ryan, A. (2009). The impact of stroke consequences on spousal relationships from the perspective of the person with stroke. *Journal of clinical nursing, 18,* 1803–1811.

Thompson, J. K., & Heinberg, L. J. (1999). The media's influence on body image disturbance and eating disorders: We've reviled them, now can we rehabilitate them? *Journal of Social Issues, 55,* 339–353.

Thompson, S. C. (1981). Will it hurt less if I can control it? A complex answer to a simple question. *Psychological Bulletin, 90,* 89–101.

Thompson, S. C., & Spacapan, S. (1991). Perceptions of control in vulnerable populations. *Journal of Social Issues, 47,* 1–22.

Thompson, S. C., Nanni, C., & Schwankovsky, L. (1990). Patient-oriented interventions to improve communication in a medical office visit. *Health Psychology, 9,* 390–404.

Thompson, S. C., Sobolew-Shubin, A., Galbraith, M. E., Schwankovsky, L., & Cruzen, D. (1993). Maintaining perceptions of control: Finding perceived control in low-control circumstances. *Journal of Personality and Social Psychology, 64,* 293–304.

Thomsen, D. K., Mehlsen, M. Y., Hokland, M., Viidik, A., Olesen, F., Avlund, K., et al. (2004). Negative thoughts and health: Associations among rumination, immunity, and health care utilization in an young and elderly sample. *Psychosomatic Medicine, 66,* 363–371.

Thoresen, C. E., & Mahoney, M. J. (1974). *Behavioral self-control.* New York: Holt.

Thorsen, L., Courneya, K., Stevinson, C., & Fosså, S. (2008). A systematic review of physical activity in prostate cancer survivors: outcomes, prevalence, and determinants. *Supportive Care in Cancer,* 16(9), 987–997.

Thornton, B., Gibbons, F. X., & Gerrard, M. (2002). Risk perception and prototype perception: Independent processes predicting risk behaviors. *Personality and Social Psychology Bulletin, 28,* 986–999.

Tibben, A., Timman, R., Bannink, E. C., & Duivenvoorden, H. J. (1997). Three-year follow-up after presymptomatic testing for Huntington's disease in tested individuals and partners. *Health Psychology, 16,* 20–35.

Timberlake, D. S., Haberstick, B. C., Lessem, J. M., Smolen, A., Ehringer, M., Hewitt, J. K., & Hopfer, C. (2006). An association between the DAT1 polymorphism and smoking behavior in young adults from the National Longitudinal Study of Adolescent Health. *Health Psychology, 25,* 190–197.

Time. (1970, November 2). The malpractice mess, pp. 36, 39.

Time. (1996, October 7). Notebook: The bad news, p. 30.

Timko, C., Finney, J. W., Moos, R. H., & Moos, B. S. (1995). Short-term treatment careers and outcomes of previously untreated alcoholics. *Journal of Studies on Alcohol, 56,* 597–610.

Timko, C., Stovel, K. W., Moos, R. H., & Miller, J. J., III. (1992). A longitudinal study of risk and resistance factors among children with juvenile rheumatic disease. *Journal of Clinical Child Psychology, 21,* 132–142.

Timman, R., Roos, R., Maat-Kievit, A., & Tibben, A. (2004). Adverse effects of predictive testing for Huntington Disease underestimated: Long-term effects 7–10 years after the test. *Health Psychology, 23,* 189–197.

Timmermans, S., & Angell, A. (2001). Evidence-based medicine, clinical uncertainty, and learning to doctor. *Journal of Health and Social Behavior, 42,* 342–359.

Tjepkema, M. (2005). *Adult obesity in Canada: Measured height and weight.* Statistics Canada Catalogue 82-620. Retrieved July 16, 2007, from www.statcan.ca/english/research/82-620-MIE/2005001/pdf/aobesity.pdf.

Tobe, S. W., Kiss, A., Sainsbury, S., Jesin, M., Geerts, R., & Baker, B. (2007). The impact of job strain and marital cohesion on ambulatory blood pressure during 1 year: the double exposure study. *American Journal of Hypertension, 20* (2), 148–153.

Tobe, S. W., Kiss, A., Szalai, J. P., Perkins, N., Tsigoulis, M., & Baker, B. (2005). Impact of job and marital strain on ambulatory blood pressure results from the double exposure study. *American Journal of Hypertension, 18 (8),* 1046–1051.

Toh, S., Hernández-Díaz, S., Logan, R., Rossouw, J. E., & Hernán, M. A. (2010). Coronary Heart Disease in Postmenopausal Recipients of Estrogen Plus Progestin Therapy: Does the Increased Risk Ever Disappear? *Annals of Internal Medicine, 152,* 211–217.

Tolma, E. L., Reininger, B. M., Evans, A., & Ureda, J. (2006). Examining the Theory of Planned Behavior and the Construct of Self-Efficacy to Predict Mammography Intention. *Health Education & Behavior, 33,* 233–251.

Tomich, P. L., & Helgeson, V. S. (2004). Is finding something good in the bad always good? Benefit finding among women with breast cancer. *Health Psychology, 23,* 16–23.

Tonkin, R. S. (2002). Marijuana use in adolescence. *Paediatric Child Health, 7(2),* 73–75.

Toobert, D. J., & Glasgow, R. E. (1991). Problem solving and diabetes self-care. *Journal of Behavioral Medicine, 14,* 71–86.

Topol, E. J. (2004). Intensive strain therapy—A sea change in cardiovascular prevention. *New England Journal of Medicine, 350,* 1562–1564, http://www.nejm.org.

Tourangeau, A. E., Cummings, G., Cranley, L. A., Ferron, E. M., & Harvey, S. (2010). Determinants of hospital nurse intention to remain employed: broadening our understanding. *Journal of Advanced Nursing, 66,* 22–32.

Toynbee, P. (1977). *Patients.* New York: Harcourt Brace.

Traffic Injury Research Foundation. (2007). *What's New: Opinion Poll.* Retrieved August 7, 2007, from www.trafficinjuryresearch.com/index.cfm.

Transport Canada (2008). Observational Survey of Cell Phone use by Drivers of Light Duty Vehicles 2006–2007. Road Safety and Motor Vehicle Regulation Directorate. Fact Sheet TP 2436E RS-2008-02, Retrieved May 10, 2010 from: http://www.tc.gc.ca/eng/roadsafety/tp-tp2436-rs200802-menu-139.htm.

Transport Canada. (2004). *Results of Transport Canada's surveys of seat belt use in Canada 2002–2003.* Retrieved August 21, 2007, from www.tc.gc.ca/roadsafety/tp2436/rs200405/menu.htm.

Treiber, F. A., Kamarck, T., Schneiderman, N., Sheffield, D., Kapuku, G., & Taylor, T. (2003). Cardiovascular reactivity and development of preclinical and clinical disease states. *Psychosomatic Medicine, 65,* 46–62.

Tremblay, M. S., Shields, M., Laviolette, M., Craig, C. L., Janssen,I., & Gorber, S. C. (2010). Fitness of Canadian children and youth: Results from the 2007–2009 Canadian Health Measures Survey. Statistics Canada, Catalogue no. 82-003-XPE • Health Reports, Vol. 21, no. 1.

Treue, W. (1958). *Doctor at court* (translated from the German by Frances Fawcett). London: Weidenfeld and Nicolson.

Trikas, P., Vlachonikolis, I., Fragkiadakis, N., Vasilakis, S., Manousos, O., & Paritsis, N. (1999). Core mental state in irritable bowel syndrome. *Psychosomatic Medicine, 61,* 781–788.

Trinh, K. V., Phillips, S. D., Ho, E., & Damsma, K. (2004). Acupuncture for the alleviation of lateral epicondyle pain: A systematic review. *Rheumatology, 43(9),* 1085–1090.

Tripp, D. A., Vandenkherkoff, L., & MacAlister, M. (2006). The Southeastern Ontario Chronic Pain Survey: Prevalence and determinants of pain and pain-related disability in urban and rural settings. *Pain Research Management, 11,* 225–233.

Tuckey, M. R., Dollard, M. F., Hosking, P. J., & Winefield, A. H. (2009). Workplace bullying: The role of psychosocial work environment factors. *International Journal of Stress Management, 16,* 215–232.

Tugade, M. M., & Fredrickson, B. L. (2004). Resilient individuals use positive emotions to bounce back from negative emotional experiences. *Journal of Personality and Social Psychology, 86,* 320–333.

Tuomilehto, J., Geboers, J., Salonen, J. T., Nissinen, A., Kuulasmaa, K., & Puska, P. (1986). Decline in cardiovascular mortality in North Karelia and other parts of Finland. *British Medical Journal, 293,* 1068–1071.

Tuomilehto, J., Lindstrom, J., Eriksson, J. G., Valle, T. T., Hamalainen, H., Ilanne-Parikka, P., et al. (2001). Prevention of Type 2 diabetes mellitus by changes in lifestyle among subjects with impaired glucose tolerance. *New England Journal of Medicine, 344,* 1343–1350.

Tuomisto, M. T. (1997). Intra-arterial blood pressure and heart rate reactivity to behavioral stress in normotensive, borderline, and mild hypertensive men. *Health Psychology, 16,* 554–565.

Turbin, M. S., Jessor, R., Costa, F. M., Dong, Q., Zhang, H., & Wang, C. (2006). Protective and risk factors in health-enhancing behavior among adolescents in China and the United States: Does social context matter? *Health Psychology, 25,* 445–454.

Turcotte, M., & Schellenberg, G. (2007). *A portrait of seniors in Canada: 2006* (Statistics Canada Catalogue 89–519). Retrieved February 11, 2008, from www.statcan.ca/english/freepub/89-519-XIE/89-519-XIE2006001.pdf.

Turk, D. C. (1994). Perspectives on chronic pain: The role of psychological factors. *Current Directions in Psychological Science, 3,* 45–48.

Turk, D. C., & Feldman, C. S. (1992a). Facilitating the use of noninvasive pain management strategies with the terminally ill. In D. C. Turk & C. S. Feldman (Eds.), *Non-invasive approaches to pain management in the terminally ill* (pp. 1–25). New York: Haworth Press.

Turk, D. C., & Feldman, C. S. (1992b). Noninvasive approaches to pain control in terminal illness: The contribution of psychological variables. In D. C. Turk & C. S. Feldman (Eds.), *Non-invasive approaches to pain management in the terminally ill* (pp. 193–214). New York: Haworth Press.

Turk, D. C., & Meichenbaum, D. (1991). Adherence to self-care regimens: The patient's perspective. In R. H. Rozensky, J. J. Sweet, & S. M. Tovian (Eds.), *Handbook of clinical psychology in medical settings* (pp. 249–266). New York: Plenum Press.

Turk, D. C., & Rudy, T. E. (1991). Neglected topics in the treatment of chronic pain patients—Relapse, noncompliance, and adherence enhancement. *Pain, 44,* 5–28.

Turk, D. C., Wack, J. T., & Kerns, R. D. (1995). An empirical examination of the "pain-behavior" construct. *Journal of Behavioral Medicine, 8,* 119–130.

Turner, R. J., & Avison, W. R. (1992). Innovations in the measurement of life stress: Crisis theory and the significance of event resolution. *Journal of Health and Social Behavior, 33,* 36–50.

Turner, R. J., & Lloyd, D. A. (1999). The stress process and the social distribution of depression. *Journal of Health and Social Behavior, 40,* 374–404.

Turner-Cobb, J. M., Gore-Felton, C., Marouf, F., Koopman, C., Kim, P., Israelski, D., & Spiegel, D. (2002). Coping, social support, and attachment style as psychosocial correlates of adjustment in men and women with HIV/AIDS. *Journal of Behavioral Medicine, 25,* 337–353.

Turner-Cobb, J. M., Sephton, S. E., Koopman, C., Blake-Mortimer, J., & Spiegel, D. (2000). Social support and salivary cortisol in women with metastatic breast cancer. *Psychosomatic Medicine, 62,* 337–345.

Turrisi, R., Wiersma, K. A., & Hughes, K. K. (2000). Binge-drinking-related consequences in college students: Role of drinking beliefs and mother–teen communications. *Psychology of Addictive Behaviors, 14,* 342–355.

Turton, S., & Carol, C. (2005). Tend and befriend versus fight or flight: Gender differences in behavioral response to stress among university students. *Journal of Applied Behavioural Research, 10,* 209–232.

U.S. Department of Health, Education, and Welfare and U.S. Public Health Service, Centers for Disease Control and Prevention. (1964). *Smoking and health: Report of the advisory committee to the surgeon general of the Public Health Service* (Publication No. PHS-1103). Washington, D.C.: U.S. Government Printing Office.

Uchino, B. (2006). Social Support and Health: A Review of Physiological Processes Potentially Underlying Links to Disease Outcomes. *Journal of Behavioral Medicine, 29*(4), 377–387.

Uchino, B. N., & Garvey, T. S. (1997). The availability of social support reduces cardiovascular reactivity to acute psychological stress. *Journal of Behavioral Medicine, 20,* 15–27.

Ueda, H., et al. (2003, May 29). Association of the T-cell regulatory gene CTLA-4 with susceptibility to autoimmune disease. *Nature, 423,* 506–511.

Uliaszek, A. A., Zinbarg, R. E., Mineka, S., Craske, M. G., Sutton, J. M., Griffith, J. W., et al. (2010). The role of neuroticism and extraversion in the stress–anxiety and stress–depression relationships. *Anxiety, Stress & Coping: An International Journal, 23,* 363–381.

Ullman, T. A., & Itzkowitz, S. H. (2011). Intestinal Inflammation and Cancer. Gastroenterology, 140, 1807-1816.e1801.

Ullrich, P. M., & Lutgendorf, S. K. (2002). Journaling about stressful events: Effects of cognitive processing and emotional expression. *Annals of Behavioral Medicine, 24,* 244–250.

Uman, L. S., Chambers, C. T., McGrath, P. J., & Kisely, S. (2006). Psychological intervention for needle-related procedural pain and distress in children and adolescents. *Cochrane Database of Systematic Reviews, 18(4),* CD005179.

Umberson, D., Williams, K., Powers, D. A., Liu, H., & Needham, B. (2006). You make me sick: Marital quality and health over the life course. *Journal of Health and Social Behavior, 47,* 1–16.

Umberson, D., Wortman, C. B., & Kessler, R. C. (1992). Widowhood and depression: Explaining long-term gender differences in vulnerability. *Journal of Health and Social Behavior, 33,* 10–24.

UNAIDS. (2007). AIDS epidemic update : December 2007. Joint United Nations Programme on HIV/AIDS (UNAIDS) and World Health Organization (WHO) 2007. Retrieved September 25, 2011 from http://data.unaids.org/pub/epislides/2007/2007_epiupdate_en.pdf.

Underhill, C., & McKeown, L. (2008). Getting a second opinion: Health information and the Internet. *Health Reports, 19(1),* 65–69 (Statistics Canada Catalogue 82-003). Retrieved February 17, 2008, from www.statcan.ca/english/freepub/82-003-XIE/82-003-XIE2008001.pdf.

Unger, J. B., Hamilton, J. E., & Sussman, S. (2004). A family member's job loss as a risk factor for smoking among adolescents. *Health Psychology, 23(3),* 308–313.

United Nations. (2011). World Drug Report, 2010. United Nations Publication, Sales No. E.10.XI.13. Accessed May 5, 2011 from:http://www.unodc.org/documents/wdr/WDR_ 2010/World_Drug_Report_2010_lo-res.pdf.

Uno, D., Uchino, B. N., & Smith, T. W. (2002). Relationship quality moderates the effect of social support given by close friends on cardiovascular reactivity in women. *International Journal of Behavioral Medicine, 9,* 243–262.

Unruh, A. M., & Elvin, N. (2004). In the eye of the dragon: Women's experiences of breast cancer and the occupation of dragon boat racing. *Canadian Journal of Occupational Therapy, 71(3),* 138–149.

Updegraff, J. A., Taylor, S. E., Kemeny, M. E., & Wyatt, G. E. (2002). Positive and negative effects of HIV infection in women with low socioeconomic resources. *Personality and Social Psychology Bulletin, 28,* 382–394.

Vaccarino, V., Badimon, L., Corti, R., de Wit, C., Dorobantu, M., Hall, A., et al. (2011). Ischaemic heart disease in women: are there sex differences in pathophysiology and risk factors? *Cardiovascular Research, 90,* 9–17.

Vahtera, J., Kivimäki, M., Väänänen, A., Linna, A., Pentti, J., Helenius, H., & Elovainio, M. (2006). Sex differences in health effects of family death or illness: Are women more vulnerable than men? *Psychosomatic Medicine, 68,* 283–291.

Valdimarsdottir, H. B., Zakowski, S. G., Gerin, W., Mamakos, J., Pickering, T., & Bovbjerg, D. H. (2002). Heightened psychobiological reactivity to laboratory stressors in healthy women at familial risk for breast cancer. *Journal of Behavioral Medicine, 25,* 51–65.

Valentiner, D. P., Holahan, C. J., & Moos, R. H. (1994). Social support, appraisals of event controllability, and coping: An integrative model. *Journal of Personality and Social Psychology, 66,* 1094–1102.

van der Wal, M. F., de Wit, C. A. M., & Hirasing, R. A. (2003). Psychosocial health among young victims and offenders of direct and indirect bullying. *Pediatrics, 111,* 1312–1317. doi: 10.1542/peds.111.6.1312

van Dulmen, A. M., Fennis, J. F. M., & Bleijenberg, G. (1996). Cognitive-behavioral group therapy for irritable bowel syndrome: Effects and long-term follow-up. *Psychosomatic Medicine, 58,* 508–514.

Van Houdenhove, B. (1986). Prevalence and psychodynamic interpretation of pre-morbid hyperactivity in patients with chronic pain. *Psychotherapy and Psychosomatics, 45,* 195–200.

van Lankveld, W., Naring, G., van der Staak, C., van't Pad Bosch, P., & van de Putte, L. (1993). Stress caused by rheumatoid arthritis: Relation among subjective stressors of the disease, disease status, and well-being. *Journal of Behavioral Medicine, 16,* 309–322.

van Melle, J. P., de Jonge, P., Spijkerman, T. A., Tijssen, J. G., Ormel, J., van Veldhuisen, D. J., van den Brink, R. H., & van den Berg, M. P. (2004). Prognostic association of depression following myocardial infarction with mortality and cardiovascular events: a meta-analysis. *Psychosomatic Medicine, 66,* 814–822.

van't Spijker, A., Trijsburg, R. W., & Duivenvoorden, H. J. (1997). Psychological sequelae of cancer diagnosis: A meta-analytic review of 58 studies after 1980. *Psychosomatic Medicine, 59,* 280–293.

Van Zundert, R. M. P., Engels, R. C. M. E., & Kuntsche, E. (2011). Contextual correlates of adolescents' self-efficacy after smoking cessation. *Psychology of Addictive Behaviors.*

Vanable, P. A., Ostrow, D. G., McKirnan, D. J., Taywaditep, K. J., & Hope, B. A. (2000). Impact of combination therapies on HIV risk perceptions and sexual risk among HIV-positive and HIV-negative gay and bisexual men. *Health Psychology, 19,* 134–145.

Vance, D. E., Struzick, T., & Childs, G. (2010). Challenges of Depression and Suicidal Ideation Associated With Aging With HIV/AIDS: Implications for Social Work. *Journal of Gerontological Social Work, 53*(2), 159–175.

Vancouver Coastal Health. (n.d.). *Saving lives: Vancouver's supervised injection site.* Retrieved February 7, 2008, from www.vch.ca/sis/docs/insite_brochure.pdf.

Vanderploeg, R., Panaccione, R., Ghosh, S., & Rioux, K. (2010). Influences of intestinal bacteria in human inflammatory bowel disease. *Infectious Disease Clinics of North America, 24*(4), 977–993.

Varni, J. W., Burwinkle, T. M., Rapoff, M. A., Kamps, J. L., & Olson, N. (2004). The PedsQL in pediatric asthma: Reliability and validity of the Pediatric Quality of Life Inventory Generic Core Scales and Asthma Module. *Journal of Behavioral Medicine, 27,* 297–318.

Vedhara, K., & Nott, K. (1996). The assessment of the emotional and immunological consequences of examination stress. *Journal of Behavioral Medicine, 19,* 467–478.

Vella, E. J., Kamarck, T. W., & Shiffman, S. (2008). Hostility moderates the effects of social support and intimacy on blood pressure in daily social interactions. *Health Psychology, 27,* S155–S162.

Vendrig, A. (1999). Prognostic factors and treatment-related changes associated with return to working: The multimodal treatment of chronic back pain. *Journal of Behavioral Medicine, 22,* 217–232.

Verhoef, M. J., Vanderheyden, L. C., Dryden, T., Mallory, D., & Ware, M. A. (2006). Evaluating complementary and alternative medicine interventions: in search of appropriate patient-centered outcome measures. *BMC Complementary and Alternative Medicine, 6*(1), 38.

Verhoef, M. J., Vanderheyden, L. C., & Fonnebo, V. (2006). A whole systems research approach to cancer care: Why do we need it and how do we get started? *Integrative Cancer Therapies, 5,* 287–292.

Verkooijen, K. T., Nielsen, G. A., & Kremers, S. P. J. (2009). Leisure time physical activity motives and smoking in adolescence. *Psychology of Sport and Exercise, 10,* 559–564.

Vernon, S. W., Gritz, E. R., Peterson, S. K., Amos, C. I., Perz, C. A., Baile, W. F., & Lynch, P. M. (1997). Correlates of psychologic distress in colorectal cancer patients undergoing genetic testing for hereditary colon cancer. *Health Psychology, 16,* 73–86.

Veugelers, P. J., & Fitzgerald, A. L. (2005). Effectiveness of school programs in preventing child obesity: A multilevel comparison. *American Journal of Public Health, 95*(3), 432–435.

Vickberg, S. M. J. (2003). The concerns about recurrence scale (CARS): A systematic measure of women's fears about the possibility of breast cancer recurrence. *Annals of Behavioral Medicine, 25,* 16–24.

Vickers, K. S., Patten, C. A., Lane, K., Clark, M. M., Croghan, I. T., Schroeder, D. R., & Hurt, R. D. (2003). Depressed versus nondepressed young adult tobacco users: Differences in coping style, weight concerns, and exercise level. *Health Psychology, 22,* 498–503.

Vila, G., Porche, L. & Mouren-Simeoni, M. (1999). An 18-month longitudinal study of posttraumatic disorders in children who were taken hostage in their school. *Psychosomatic Medicine, 61,* 746–754.

Visintainer, M. A., Volpicelli, T. R., & Seligman, M. E. P. (1982). Tumor rejection in rats after inescapable or escapable electric shock. *Science, 216,* 437–439.

Vissandjee, B., Desmeules, M., Cao, Z., Abdool, S., & Kazanjian, A. (2004). Integrating ethnicity and migration as determinants of Canadian women's health. *BMC Women's Health, 4*(Suppl 1), S32.

Vitaliano, P. P., Maiuro, R. D., Russo, J., Katon, W., DeWolfe, D., & Hall, G. (1990). Coping profiles associated with psychiatric, physical health, work, and family problems. *Health Psychology, 9,* 348–376.

Vitaliano, P. P., Scanlan, J. M., Krenz, C., & Fujimoto, W. (1996). Insulin and glucose: Relationships with hassles, anger, and hostility in nondiabetic older adults. *Psychosomatic Medicine, 58,* 489–499.

Vitaliano, P. P., Scanlan, J. M., Zhang, J., Savage, M. V., Hirsch, I. B., & Siegler, I. C. (2002). A path model of chronic stress, the metabolic syndrome, and coronary heart disease. *Psychosomatic Medicine, 64,* 418–435.

Vittinghoff, E., Shlipak, M. G., Varosy, P. D., Furberg, C. D., Ireland, C. C., Khan, S. S., et al. (2003). Risk factors and secondary prevention in women with heart disease: The heart and estrogen/progestin replacement study. *Annals of Internal Medicine, 138,* 81–89.

von Kaenel, R., Dimsdale, J. E., Patterson, T. L., & Grant, I. (2003). Acute procoagulant stress response as a dynamic measure of allostatic load in Alzheimer caregivers. *Annals of Behavioral Medicine, 26,* 42–48.

von Kaenel, R., Mills, P. J., Fainman, C., & Dimsdale, J. E. (2001). Effects of psychobiological stress and psychiatric disorders on blood coagulation and fibrinolysis: A biobehavioral pathway to coronary artery disease? *Psychosomatic Medicine, 63,* 531–544.

Von Korff, M., Katon, W., Lin, E. H. B., Simon, G., Ludman, E., Ciechanowski, P., Rutter, C., & Bush, T. (2005). Potentially modifiable factors associated with disability among people with diabetes. *Psychosomatic Medicine, 67,* 233–240.

Voorham, J., Haaijer-Ruskamp, F. M., Wolffenbuttel, B. H. R., Stolk, R. P., & Denig, P. (2010). Medication Adherence Affects Treatment Modifications in Patients With Type 2 Diabetes. *Clinical therapeutics, 33,* 121–134.

Vos, P. J., Garssen, B., Visser, A. P., Duivenvoorden, H. J., & de Haes, C. J. M. (2004). Early stage breast cancer: Explaining level of psychosocial adjustment using structural equation modeling. *Journal of Behavioral Medicine, 27,* 557–580.

Voth, J., & Sirois, F. M. (2009). The role of self-blame and responsibility in adjustment to inflammatory bowel disease. *Rehabilitation Psychology, 54,* 99–108.

Vowles, K. E., Zvolensky, M. J., Gross, R. T., & Sperry, J. A. (2004). Pain-related anxiety in the prediction of chronic low-back pain distress. *Journal of Behavioral Medicine, 27,* 77–89.

Wager, T. D., Rilling, J. K., Smith, E. E., Sokolik, A., Casey, K. L., Davidson, R. J., et al. (2004, February 20). Placebo-induced changes in fMRI in the anticipation and experience of pain. *Science, 303,* 1162–1167.

Wagner, K. D., Ritt-Olson, A., Chou, C.-P., Pokhrel, P., Duan, L., Baezconde-Garbanati, L., et al. (2010). Associations between family structure, family functioning, and substance use among Hispanic/Latino adolescents. *Psychology of Addictive Behaviors, 24,* 98–108.

Wagner, P. J., & Curran, P. (1984). Health beliefs and physician identified "worried well." *Health Psychology, 3,* 459–474.

Waldron, I., Weiss, C. C., & Hughes, M. E. (1998). Interacting effects of multiple roles on women's health. *Journal of Health and Social Behavior, 39,* 216–236.

Waldstein, S. R., & Burns, H. O. (2003). Interactive relation of insulin and gender to cardiovascular reactivity in healthy young adults. *Annals of Behavioral Medicine, 25,* 163–171.

Walji, R., Boon, H., Barnes, J., Austin, Z., Welsh, S., & Baker, G. R. (2010). Consumers of natural health products: natural-born pharmacovigilantes? *BMC Complementary and Alternative Medicine, 10*(1), 8.

Waller, J., McCaffery, K. J., Forrest, S., Wardle, J. (2004). Human papillomavirus and cervical cancer: Issues for biobehavioral and psychosocial research. *Annals of Behavioral Medicine, 27(1),* 68–79.

Wallston, K. A., Wallston, B. S., & DeVellis, R. (1978). Development of the Multidimensional Health Locus of Control (MHLC) Scale. *Health Education Monographs, 6,* 161–170.

Wang, F., Wild, T. C., Kipp, W., Kuhle, S., & Veugelers, P. J. (2009). The influence of childhood obesity on the development of self-esteem. Statistics Canada, Catalogue no. 82-003-XPE • Health Reports, Vol. 20, no. 2.

Wang, J., & Li, M. D. (2009). Common and Unique Biological Pathways Associated with Smoking Initiation/Progression, Nicotine Dependence, and Smoking Cessation. *Neuropsychopharmacology, 35,* 702–719.

Wang, J. C., Grucza, R., Cruchaga, C., Hinrichs, A. L., Bertelsen, S., Budde, J. P., et al. (2008). Genetic variation in the CHRNA5 gene affects mRNA levels and is associated with risk for alcohol dependence. *Mol Psychiatry, 14,* 501–510.

Wang, P. P., Badley, E. M., & Gignac, M. (2004). Activity limitation, coping efficacy and self-perceived physical independence in people with disability. *Disability and Rehabilitation, 26*(18), 785–793.

Wang, S. S., Houshyar, S., & Prinstein, M. J. (2006). Adolescent girls' and boys' weight-related health behaviors and cognitions: associations with reputation- and preference-based peer status. *Health Psychology, 25*(5), 658–663.

Warburton, D. E. R., Nicol, C. W., & Bredin, S. S. D. (2006). Health benefits of physical activity: The evidence. *CMAJ, 174(6),* 801–809.

Ward, S., & Leventhal, H. (1993). *Explaining retrospective reports of side effects: Anxiety, initial side effect experience, and post-treatment side effects.* Series paper from the School of Nursing, University of Wisconsin, Madison.

Wardle, J., & Gibson, E. L. (2007). Diet and Stress, Non-Psychiatric. *Encyclopedia of Stress,* (pp. 797–805). New York: Academic Press.

Wardle, J., & Steptoe, A. (2003). Socioeconomic differences in attitudes and beliefs about healthy lifestyles. *Journal of Epidemiology and Community Health, 27,* 440–443.

Wardle, J., Robb, K. A., Johnson, F., Griffith, J., Brunner, E., Power, C., & Towee, M. (2004). Socioeconomic variation in attitudes to eating and weight in female adolescents. *Health Psychology, 23,* 275–282.

Wardle, J., Williamson, S., McCaffery, K., Sutton, S., Taylor, T., Edwards, R., et al. (2003). Increasing attendance at colorectal cancer screening: Testing the efficacy of a mailed, psychoeducational intervention in a community sample of older adults. *Health Psychology, 22,* 99–105.

Wareham, S., Fowler, K., & Pike, A. (2007). Determinants of depression severity and duration in Canadian adults: The moderating effects of gender and social support. *Journal of Applied Social Psychology, 37,* 2951–2979.

Warren, R., Zammitt, N., Deary, I., & Frier, B. (2007). The effects of acute hypoglycaemia on memory acquisition and recall and prospective memory in type 1 diabetes. *Diabetologia, 50,* 178–185.

Watkins, L. L., Grossman, P., Krishnan, R., & Sherwood, A. (1998). Anxiety and vagal control of heart rate. *Psychosomatic Medicine, 60,* 498–502.

Watson, D., & Clark, L. A. (1984). Negative affectivity: The disposition to experience aversive emotional states. *Psychological Bulletin, 96,* 465–490.

Watson, D., & Pennebaker, J. W. (1989). Health complaints, stress, and distress: Exploring the central role of negative affectivity. *Psychological Review, 96,* 234–264.

Waxler-Morrison, N., Anderson, J. M., Richardson, E., & Chambers, N. A. (2005). *Cross-cultural caring: A handbook for health professionals* (2nd ed.). Vancouver, BC: UBC Press.

Weber, A. E., Craib, K. J. P., Chan, K., Martindale, S., Miller, M. L., Cook, D., Schechter, M. T., & Hogg, R. S. (2003). Determinants of HIV serconversion in an era of increasing HIV infection among young gay and bisexual men. *AIDS, 17(5),* 774–777.

Weber-Hamann, B., Hentschel, F., Kniest, A., Deuschle, M., Colla, M., Lederbogen, F., et al. (2002). Hypercortisolemic depression is associated with increased intra-abdominal fat. *Psychosomatic Medicine, 64,* 274–277.

Weidner, G., Boughal, T., Connor, S. L., Pieper, C., & Mendell, N. R. (1997). Relationship of job strain to standard coronary risk factors and psychological characteristics in women and men of the family heart study. *Health Psychology, 16,* 239–247.

Weidner, G., Rice, T., Knox, S. S., Ellison, C., Province, M. A., Rao, D. C., et al. (2000). Familial resemblance for hostility: The National Heart, Lung, and Blood Institute Family Heart Study. *Psychosomatic Medicine, 62,* 197–204.

Weinman, J., Ebrecht, M., Scott, S., Walburn, J., & Dyson, M. (2008). Enhanced wound healing after emotional disclosure intervention. *British Journal of Health Psychology, 13*(1), 95–102.

Weinman, J., Petrie, K. J., Moss-Morris, R., & Horne, R. (1996). The illness perception questionnaire: A new method for assessing the cognitive representation of illness. *Psychology and Health, 11,* 431–445.

Weinstein, N. D., Kwitel, A., McCaul, K. D., Magnan, R. E., Gerrard, M., & Gibbons, F. X. (2007). Risk perceptions: Assessment and relationship to influenza vaccination. *Health Psychology, 26,* 146–151.

Weinstein, N. D., Rothman, A. J., & Sutton, S. R. (1998). Stage theories of health behavior: Conceptual and methodological issues. *Health Psychology, 17,* 290–299.

Weintraub, A. (2004, January 26). "I can't sleep." *BusinessWeek, 67–70, 72, 74.*

Weisman, A. D. (1972). *On death and dying.* New York: Behavioral Publications.

Weisman, A. D. (1977). The psychiatrist and the inexorable. In H. Feifel (Ed.), *New meanings of death* (pp. 107–122). New York: McGraw-Hill.

Weiss, R. S., & Richards, T. A. (1997). A scale for predicting quality of recovery following the death of a partner. *Journal of Personality and Social Psychology, 72,* 885–891.

Welch-McCaffrey, S. (1985). Cancer, anxiety, and quality of life. *Cancer Nursing, 8,* 151–158.

Wenninger, K., Weiss, C., Wahn, U., & Staab, D. (2003). Body image in cystic fibrosis—Development of a brief diagnostic scale. *Journal of Behavioral Medicine, 26,* 81–94.

Westmaas, J. L., Wild, T. C., Ferrence, R. (2002). Effects of gender in social control of smoking cessation. *Health Psychology, 21,* 368–376.

Wetter, D. W., Kenford, S. L., Welsch, S. K., Smith, S. S., Fouladi, R. T., Fiore, M. C., et al.. (2004). Prevalence and predictors of transitions in smoking behavior among college students. *Health Psychology, 23,* 168–177.

Whalen, C. K., Jamner, L. D., Henker, B., & Delfino, R. J. (2001). Smoking and moods in adolescents with depressive and aggressive dispositions: Evidence from surveys and electronic diaries. *Health Psychology, 20,* 99–111.

Whisman, M. A., & Kwon, P. (1993). Life stress and dysphoria: The role of self-esteem and hopelessness. *Journal of Personality and Social Psychology, 65,* 1054–1060.

Whittam, E. H. (1993). Terminal care of the dying child: Psychosocial implications of care. *Cancer, 71,* 3450–3462.

Wichstrom, L. (1994). Predictors of Norwegian adolescents' sunbathing and use of sunscreen. *Health Psychology, 13,* 412–420.

Wickrama, K. A. S., Conger, R. D., & Lorenz, F. O. (1995). Work, marriage, lifestyle, and changes in men's physical health. *Journal of Behavioral Medicine, 18,* 97–112.

Wickrama, K. A. S., Conger, R. D., Wallace, L. E., & Elder, G. H., Jr. (2003). Linking early social risks to impaired physical health during the transition to adulthood. *Journal of Health and Social Behavior, 44,* 61–74.

Widows, M. R., Jacobsen, P. B., & Fields, K. K. (2000). Relation of psychological vulnerability factors to posttraumatic stress disorder symptomatology in bone marrow transplant recipients. *Psychosomatic Medicine, 62,* 873–882.

Widows, M., Jacobsen, P., Booth-Jones, M., & Fields, K. K. (2005). Predictors of posttraumatic growth following bone marrow transplantation for cancer. *Health Psychology, 24,* 266–273.

Wilcox, S., & Stefanick, M. L. (1999). Knowledge and perceived risk of major diseases in middle-aged and older women. *Health Psychology, 18,* 346–353.

Wilcox, S., & Storandt, M. (1996). Relations among age, exercise, and psychological variables in a community sample of women. *Health Psychology, 15,* 110–113.

Wilcox, S., Evenson, K. R., Aragaki, A., Wassertheil-Smoller, S., Mouton, C. P., & Loevinger, B. L. (2003). The effects of widowhood on physical and mental health, health behaviors, and health outcomes: The women's health initiative. *Health Psychology, 22,* 513–522.

Wilkins, K. (2005). Predictors of death in seniors. *Supplements to Health Reports, 16,* 57–67. Statistics Canada Catalogue 82-003. Retrieved February 10, 2008, from www.statcan.ca/english/freepub/82-003-SIE/2005000/pdf/82-003-SIE20050007447.pdf.

Wilkins, K. (2006). Predictors of death in seniors. *Health Reports, 16,* 57–69 (Statistics Canada Catalogue 82-003). Retrieved August 24, 2007, from www.statcan.ca/english/freepub/82-003-SIE/2005000/pdf/82-003-SIE20050007447.pdf.

Wilkins, K., & Park, E. (2004). "Injuries." *Health Reports, 15(3),* 43–48. Statistics Canada, Catalogue 82-003. Retrieved from www.statcan.ca/english/studies/82-003/archive/2004/15-3-d.pdf.

Wilkins, K., Campbell, Norman R. C., Joffres, M. R., McAlister, F. A., Nichol, M., Quach, S., Johansen, H. L., and Tremblay, M. S. (2010, February). "Blood pressure in Canadian adults." *Health Reports.* Component of Statistics Canada Catalogue no. 82-003-X.

Wilkins, K., Shields, M., & Rotermann, M. (2009). *Smokers' use of acute care hospitals—A prospective study.* Statistics Canada, Catalogue no. 82-003-XPE • Health Reports, Vol. 20, no. 4, December 2009.

Williams, C. J. (2001, April 24). Entertained into social change. *Los Angeles Times,* pp. A1, A6–A7.

Williams, D. R. (2002). Racial/ethnic variations in women's health: The social embeddedness of health. *American Journal of Public Health, 92*(4), 588–597.

Williams, D. R. (2003). The health of men: Structured inequalities and opportunities. *American Journal of Public Health, 93,* 724–731.

Williams, E. D., Steptoe, A., Chambers, J. C., & Kooner, J. S. (2011). Ethnic and Gender Differences in the Relationship Between Hostility and Metabolic and Autonomic Risk Factors for Coronary Heart Disease. *Psychosomatic Medicine, 73,* 53–58.

Williams, G. C., McGregor, H. A., Zeldman, A., Freedman, Z. R., & Deci, E. L. (2004). Testing a self-determination theory process model for promoting glycemic control through diabetes self-management. *Health Psychology, 23,* 58–66.

Williams, J. E., Mosley Jr, T. H., Kop, W. J., Couper, D. J., Welch, V. L., & Rosamond, W. D. (2010). Vital Exhaustion as a Risk Factor for Adverse Cardiac Events (from the Atherosclerosis Risk In Communities [ARIC] Study). *The American Journal of Cardiology, 105,* 1661–1665.

Williams, K. N., Herman, R., Gajewski, B., & Wilson, K. (2009). Elderspeak Communication: Impact on Dementia Care. *American Journal of Alzheimer's Disease and Other Dementias, 24*(1), 11–20.

Williams, M. A., Fleg, J. L., Ades, P. A., Chaitman, B. R., Miller, N. H., Mohiuddin, S. M., Ockene, I. S., Taylor, C. B., & Wenger, N. K. (2002). Secondary Prevention of Coronary Heart Disease in the Elderly (With Emphasis on Patients ≥75 Years of Age). *Circulation, 105*(14), 1735-1743.

Williams, P. D., Williams, A. R., Graff, J. C., Hanson, S., Stanton, Hafeman, C., et al. (2002). Interrelationships among variables affecting wall siblings and mothers in families of children with chronic illness or disability. *Journal of Behavioral Medicine, 25,* 411–424.

Williams, P. G., Colder, C. R., Lane, J. D., McCaskill, C. C., Feinglos, M. N., & Surwit, R. S. (2002). Examination of the neuroticism-symptom reporting relationship in individuals with type-2 diabetes. *Personality and Social Psychology Bulletin, 28,* 1015–1025.

Williams, R. B. (1984). An untrusting heart. *The Sciences, 24,* 31–36.

Williams, S., & Kohout, J. L. (1999). Psychologists in medical schools in 1997. *American Psychologist, 54,* 272–276.

Williamson, G. M. (2000). Extending the activity restriction model of depressed affect: Evidence from a sample of breast cancer patients. *Health Psychology, 19,* 339–347.

Williamson, G. M., Shaffer, D. R., & Schulz, R. (1998). Activity restriction and prior relationship history as contributors to mental health outcomes among middle-aged and older spousal caregivers. *Health Psychology, 17,* 152–162.

Williams-Piehota, P., Sirois, F. M., Bann, C., Isenberg, K., & Walsh, E. G. (2011). Agents of change: What role do CAM providers play in health behavior change? *Alternative Therapies in Health and Medicine, 17,* 22–31.

Willows, N. D. (2005). Determinants of healthy eating in Aboriginal peoples in Canada: The current state of knowledge and research gaps. *Canadian Journal of Public Health, 96,* 32–37.

Wills, T. A., Gibbons, F. X., Gerrard, M., & Brody, G. H. (2000). Protection and vulnerability processes relevant for early onset of substance use: A test among African American children. *Health Psychology, 19,* 253–263.

Wills, T. A., Pierce, J. P., & Evans, R. I. (1996). Large-scale environmental risk factors for substance use. *American Behavioral Scientist, 39,* 808–822.

Wills, T. A., Sandy, J. M., & Yaeger, A. M. (2002). Stress and smoking in adolescence: A test of directional hypotheses. *Health Psychology, 21,* 122–130.

Wilson, D. K., & Ampey-Thornhill, G. (2001). The role of gender and family support on dietary compliance in an African American adolescent hypertension prevention study. *Annals of Behavioral Medicine, 23,* 59–67.

Wilson, D. M., Northcott, H. C., Truman, C. D., Anderson, M. C., Fainsinger, R. L., & Stingl, M. J. (2001). Location of death in Canada: A comparison of 20th-century hospital and nonhospital locations of death and corresponding population trends. *Evaluation and the Health Professions, 24*(4), 385–403.

Wilson, G. T., Grilo, C. M., & Vitousek, K. M. (2007). Psychological treatment of eating disorders. *American Psychologist, 62,* 199–216.

Wilson, K., & Brookfield, D. (2009). Effect of Goal Setting on Motivation and Adherence in a Six-Week Exercise Program. *International Journal of Sport and Exercise Psychology, 7,* 89–100.

Wilson, K. G., Chochinov, H. W., McPherson, C. J., Graham, M., Allard, P. Chary, S., Gagnon, P. R., Macmillan, K., DeLuca, M., O'Shea, F., Kuhl, D., Fainsinger, R. L., Karam, A. M., & Clinch, J. J. (2007). Desire for euthanasia or physician-assisted suicide in palliative cancer care. *Health Psychology, 26*(3), 314–323.

Wilson, R. (1963). The social structure of a general hospital. *Annals of the American Academy of Political and Social Science, 346,* 67–76.

Wilson, R. S., Beck, T. L., Bienias, J. L., & Bennett, D. A. (2007). Terminal cognitive decline: Accelerated loss of cognition in the last years of life. *Psychosomatic Medicine, 69,* 131–137.

Wilson, R. S., Krueger, K. R., Gu, L., Bienias, J. L, Mendes de Leon, C. F., & Evans, D. A. (2005). Neuroticism, extraversion, and mortality in a defined population of older persons. *Psychosomatic Medicine, 67,* 841–845.

Wing, R. R. (2000). Cross-cutting themes in maintenance of behavior change. *Health Psychology, 19,* 84–88.

Wing, R. R., & Jeffery, R. W. (1999). Benefits of recruiting participants with friends and increasing social support for weight loss and maintenance. *Journal of Consulting and Clinical Psychology, 67,* 132–138.

Wing, R. R., Blair, E., Marcus, M., Epstein, L. H., & Harvey, J. (1994). Yearlong weight loss treatment for obese patients with Type II diabetes: Does including an intermittent very-low-calorie diet improve outcome? *American Journal of Medicine, 97,* 354–362.

Wing, R. R., Matthews, K. A., Kuller, L. H., Meilahn, E. N., & Plantinga, P. L. (1991). Weight gain at the time of menopause. *Archives of Internal Medicine, 151,* 97–102.

Wirtz, P. H., Ehlert, U., Emini, L., Rüdisüli, K., Groessbauer, S., Gaab, J., Elsenbruch, S., & Von Kanel, R. (2006). Anticipatory cognitive stress appraisal and the acute procoagulant stress response in men. *Psychosomatic Medicine, 68,* 851–858.

Wirtz, P. H., Von Kanel, R., Schnorpfeil, P., Ehlert, U., Frey, K., & Fischer, J. E. (2003). Reduced glucocorticoid sensitivity of monocyte interleukin-6 production in male industrial employees who are vitally exhausted. *Psychosomatic Medicine, 65,* 672–678.

Wittchen, H. U., Hoch, E., Klotsche, J., & Muehlig, S. (2011). Smoking cessation in primary care–a randomized controlled trial of bupropione, nicotine replacements, CBT and a minimal intervention. *International Journal of Methods in Psychiatric Research, 20,* 28–39.

Witte, K., & Allen, M. (2000). A meta-analysis of fear appeals: Implications for effective public health campaigns. *Health Education & Behavior, 27*(5), 591–615.

Wolfe, B., & Sirois, F. M. (2008, June). Understanding the coping strategies of patients with inflammatory bowel disease: Passive coping or secondary control? In F.M. Sirois (chair), *Guts, gumption, and go-ahead: Psychological adjustment to inflammatory bowel disease.* Paper presented at the 69th Annual Convention of the Canadian Psychological Association, Halifax, NS.

Wolpe, J. (1958). *Psychotherapy by reciprocal inhibition.* Stanford, CA: Stanford University Press.

World Health Organization. (1948). *Constitution of the World Health Organization.* Geneva, Switzerland: World Health Organization Basic Documents.

World Health Organization. (2002). *Active ageing: A policy framework.* Retrieved January 23, 2008, from http://whqlibdoc.who.int/hq/2002/WHO_NMH_NPH_02.8.pdf.

World Health Organization. (2004, October 11). *World Health Organization supports global effort to relieve chronic pain.* Retrieved February 18, 2008, from www.who.int/mediacentre/news/releases/2004/pr70/en/index.html.

World Health Organization. (2006a). *What is asthma?* Retrieved February 3, 2008, from www.who.int/mediacentre/factsheets/fs307/en.

World Health Organization. (2006b). *Obesity and overweight.* Retrieved April 25, 2007, from www.who.int/mediacentre/factsheets/fs311/en.

World Health Organization. (2007). *World Health Day: Road safety is no accident!* Retrieved April 25, 2007, from www.who.int/mediacentre/news/releases/2004/pr24/en.

World Health Organization (2008), Future trends in global mortality: Major shifts in cause of death patterns. World Health Statistics 2008, retrieved April 29, 2011 from http://www.who.int/whosis/whostat/EN_WHS08_Full.pdf.

World Health Organization. (2008a). *Screening for breast cancer.* Retrieved February 11, 2008, from www.who.int/cancer/detection/breastcancer/en/index.html.

World Health Organization. (2009). Cardiovascular diseases (CVDs). Fact sheet N°317, Updated September 2009 http://www.who.int/mediacentre/factsheets/fs317/en/index.html.

World Health Organization. (2009a). Cancer, Fact sheet N°297. Retrieved June 3, 2011 from http://www.who.int/mediacentre/factsheets/fs297/en/.

World Health Organization. (2009b). Intervention on Diet & Physical Activity: What Works and What Doesn't. Summary Report. Retrieved from http://www.who.int/dietphysicalactivity/summary-report-09.pdf.

World Health Organization. (2010). Lexicon of alcohol and drug terms published by the World Health Organization. Accessed July 10, 2010 from http://www.who.int/substance_abuse/terminology/who_lexicon/.

World Health Organization. (2011). Global Health Observatory (GHO): Noncommunicable diseases (NCD). Accessed May 29, 2011 from http://www.who.int/gho/ncd/en/index.html.

World Health Organization. (2011a). Global health sector strategy on HIV/AIDS 2011-2015. Retrieved April 23, 2011 from http://whqlibdoc.who.int/publications/2011/ 9789241501651_eng.pdf.

World Health Organization. (2011b). Opportunity in Crisis: Preventing HIV from early adolescence to young adulthood. Retrieved June 15, 2011 from: http://www.who.int/hiv/pub/oic_report_en.pdf.

World Health Organization. (2011c). World Health Statistics. Retrieved April 7, 2011 from http://www.who.int/whosis/whostat/EN_WHS2011_Full.pdf.

Wright, R. J., Finn, P., Contreras, J. P., Cohen, S., Wright, R. O., Staudenmayer, J., et al. (2004). Chronic caregiver stress and IgE expression, allergen-induced proliferation, and cytokine profiles in a birth cohort predisposed to atopy. *The Journal of allergy and clinical immunology, 113,* 1051–1057.

Wroe, A. L. (2001). Intentional and unintentional nonadherence: A study of decision making. *Journal of Behavioral Medicine, 25,* 355–372.

Wrosch, C., Schulz, R., & Heckhausen, J. (2002). Health stresses and depressive symptomatology in the elderly: The importance of health engagement control strategies. *Health Psychology, 21,* 340–348.

Wrosch, C., Schulz, R., Miller, G. E., Lupien, S., & Dunne, E. (2007). Physical health problems, depressive mood, and cortisol secretion in old age: Buffer effects of health engagement control strategies. *Health Psychology, 26,* 341–349.

Wulfert, E., & Wan, C. K. (1993). Condom use: A self-efficacy model. *Health Psychology, 12,* 346–353.

Wulsin, L. R., & Singal, B. M. (2003). Do depressive symptoms increase the risk for the onset of coronary disease? Systemic quantitative review. *Psychosomatic Medicine, 65,* 201–210.

Wulsin, L. R., Vaillant, G. E., & Wells, V. E. (1999). A systematic review of the mortality of depression. *Psychosomatic Medicine, 61,* 6–17.

Wyckam, R. G. (1997). Regulating the market of tobacco products and controlling smoking in Canada. *Canadian Journal of Administrative Sciences, 14(2),* 141–165.

Yach, D., Leeder, S. R., Bell, J., & Kistnasamy, B. (2005). Global chronic diseases. *Sciences, 307,* 317.

Yamada, Y., Izawa, H., Ichihara, S., Takatsu, F., Ishihara, H., Hirayama, H., et al. (2002). Prediction of the risk of myocardial infarction from polymorphisms in candidate genes. *New England Journal of Medicine, 347,* 1916–1923, http://www.nejm.org.

Yap, S., Yang, Z., Wang, J., Bacon, S. L., & Campbell, T. S. (2006). Waist circumference, not body mass index is associated with blood pressure in a sample of young Chinese adults. *Journal of Human Hypertension, 20,* 904–906.

Yarnold, P., Michelson, E., Thompson, D., & Adams, S. (1998). Predicting patient satisfaction: A study of two emergency departments. *Journal of Behavioral Medicine, 21,* 545–563.

Yazdanbakhsh, M., Kremsner, P. G., & van Ree, R. (2002, April 19). Allergy, parasites, and the hygiene hypothesis. *Science, 296,* 490–494.

Ybema, J. F., Kuijer, R. G., Buunk, B. P., DeJong, G. M., & Sanderman, R. (2001). Depression and perceptions of inequity among couples facing cancer. *Personality and Social Psychology Bulletin, 27,* 3–13.

Young, D. R., He, X., Genkinger, J., Sapun, M., Mabry, I., & Jehn, M. (2004). Health status among urban African American women: Associations among well-being, perceived stress, and demographic factors. *Journal of Behavioral Medicine, 27,* 63–76.

Young Casey, C., Greenberg, M. A., Nicassio, P. M., Harpin, R. E., & Hubbard, D. (2008). Transition from acute to chronic pain and disability: A model including cognitive, affective, and trauma factors. *Pain, 134,* 69–79.

Youth Smoking Survey (2010). Smoking Profile for Canada, 2008/2009. Retrieved July 8, 2010 from http://www.yss.uwaterloo.ca/index.cfm?section=5&page=288.

Yvonne, N., & Alexandra, M. (2007). Efficacy of biofeedback for migraine: A meta-analysis. *Pain, 128(1),* 111–127.

Zabinsky, M. F., Calfas, K. J., Gehrman, C. A., Wilfley, D. E., & Sallis, J. F. (2001). Effects of a physical activity intervention on body image in university seniors: Project GRAD. *Annals of Behavioral Medicine, 23,* 247–252.

Zakowski, S. G., Hall, M. H., Klein, L. C., & Baum, A. (2001). Appraised control, coping, and stress in a community sample: A test of the goodness-of-fit hypothesis. *Annals of Behavioral Medicine, 23,* 158–165.

Zakowski, S. G., Ramati, A., Morton, C., Johnson, P., & Flanigan, R. (2004). Written emotional disclosure buffers the effects of social constraints on distress among cancer patients. *Health Psychology, 23(6),* 555–563.

Zanjani, F. A. K., Schaie, W. K., & Willis, S. L. (2006). Age Group and Health Status Effects on Health Behavior Change. *Behavioral Medicine 32,* 36–46.

Zautra, A. J., & Manne, S. L. (1992). Coping with rheumatoid arthritis: A review of a decade of research. *Annals of Behavioral Medicine, 14,* 31–39.

Zautra, A. J., & Smith, B. W. (2001). Depression and reactivity to stress in older women with rheumatoid arthritis and osteoarthritis. *Psychosomatic Medicine, 63,* 687–696.

Zautra, A. J., Burleson, M. H., Matt, K. S., Roth, S., & Burrows, L. (1994). Interpersonal stress, depression, and disease activity in rheumatoid arthritis and osteoarthritis patients. *Health Psychology, 13,* 139–148.

Zautra, A. J., Fasman, R.., Reich, J. W., Harakas, P., Johnson, L. M., Olmsted, M. E., & Davis, M. C. (2005). Fibromyalgia: Evidence for deficits in positive affect regulation. *Psychosomatic Medicine, 67,* 147–155.

Zautra, A. J., Maxwell, B. M., & Reich, J. W. (1989). Relation among physical impairment, distress, and well-being in older adults. *Journal of Behavioral Medicine, 12,* 543–557.

Zelinski, E. M., Crimmins, E., Reynolds, S., & Seeman, T. (1998). Do medical conditions affect cognition in older adults? *Health Psychology, 17,* 504–512.

Zellner, D. A., Loaiza, S., Gonzalez, Z., Pita, J., Morales, J., Pecora, D., et al. (2006). Food selection changes under stress. *Physiology & Behavior, 87,* 789–793.

Zeltzer, L. K., Recklitis, C., Buchbinder, D., Zebrack, B., Casillas, J., Tsao, J. C. I., et al. (2009). Psychological Status in Childhood Cancer Survivors: A Report From the Childhood Cancer Survivor Study. *Journal of Clinical Oncology, 27*(14), 2396–2404.

Zhang, J., Niaura, R., Todaro, J. F., McCaffery, J. M., Shen, B., Spiro III, A., & Ward, D. (2005). Suppressed hostility predicted hypertension incidence among middle-aged men: The normative aging study. *Journal of Behavioral Medicine, 28,* 443–454.

Zhu, S. H., Sun, J., Hawkins, S., Pierce, J., & Cummins, S. (2003). A population study of low-rate smokers: Quitting history and instability over time. *Health Psychology, 22,* 245–252.

Zielgelstein, R. C., Kim, S. Y., Kao, D., Fauerbach, J. A., Thombs, B. D., McCann, U., Colburn, J., & Bush, D. E. (2005). Can doctors and nurses recognize depression in patients hospitalized with an acute myocardial infarction in the absence of formal screening? *Psychosomatic Medicine, 67,* 393–397.

Zimbardo, P. G. (1969). The human choice: Individuation, reason, and order versus deindividuation, impulse, and chaos. In W. J. Arnold & D. Levine (Eds.), *Nebraska symposium on motivation.* Lincoln: University of Nebraska Press.

Zola, I. K. (1966). Culture and symptoms—An analysis of patients' presenting complaints. *American Sociological Review, 31,* 615–630.

Zoutman, D. E., Ford, B. D., Bryce, E., Gourdeau, M., Hebert, G., Henderson, E., & Paton, S. (2003). The state of infection surveillance and control in Canadian acute care hospitals: Global issues in surgical infections and surveillance. *American Journal of Infection Control, 31(5),* 266–273.

PHOTO CREDITS

NAME INDEX

Kaptein, A.A., 304
Karasek, R., 179
Karlamanga, A.S., 163
Karlson, C., 116
Karlsson, J., 107
Karmarck, T., 172
Karoly, P., 274, 276, 308
Kashani, J.H., 88
Kashima, Y., 188
Kashy, D.A., 204
Kassam, A., 298, 306
Kassem, N.O., 65
Katkin, E.S., 357
Kato, K., 187
Katon, W.J., 298, 306
Katz, L., 171
Katz, P.P., 415
Katz, R.C., 313
Katzmarzyk, P.T., 105, 115
Kaufman, M.R., 246
Kavanaugh, D.J., 378
Kavelaars, A., 233
Kawachi, I., 190, 370
Kazak, A.E., 409
Ke, X., 202
Keane, T.M., 167
Kearney, M.H., 76, 103
Keefe, F.J., 265, 418
Kelder, S.H., 82
Kelley, J.M., 257, 258
Kelloway, E.K., 179
Kelly, J.A., 396
Kelly, K.M., 113
Kelly, M., 243
Kelner, M., 240, 243
Kelsey, R.M., 357
Keltikanagas-Järvinen, L., 356
Keltner, D., 343
Kemeny, M.E., 63, 155, 157, 163, 200, 305, 330, 388, 392, 398, 400, 403
Kenchaiah, S., 106
Kendall, D., 375
Kendler, K.S., 202
Kennedy-Moore, E., 194
Kenyon, K., 355
Kerns, R., 307
Kerns, R.D., 266, 283, 362
Kerry, S., 100, 102
Kershaw, T.S., 399
Kessels, L.T.E., 61
Kessler, R.C., 171, 172, 176*n*, 199, 202, 203, 205, 344
Kevin, M.V., 180
Kewman, D.G., 257
Khechine, H., 220
Kiberstis, P., 403
Kichler, J., 378
Kiecolt-Glaser, J.K., 356, 387, 388, 390, 391, 392, 408
Kiecolt-Glaser, R., 96, 204, 312
Kiefe, C.L., 351
Kiene, S.M., 62
Kim, B.H., 164
Kim, H.S., 200
Kim, K., 142
Kim, Y., 312, 407
Kimm, S.Y.S., 98
Kinder, L.S., 353, 376
King, A., 210
King, A.C., 98, 99, 353
King, D.K., 380
King, D.W., 166
King, L.A., 166
King, N.J., 253
King, S., 175
Kinmonth, A.L., 360
Kipp, W., 108
Kippax, S.C., 399
Kirby, E.D., 207
Kirby, J.B., 138
Kirk, S.B., 194, 414
Kirkley, B.G., 150, 376
Kirmayer, L.J., 216
Kirschenbaum, C., 165, 168, 178, 187, 201
Kirschenbaum, D.S., 110, 111
Kirscht, J.P., 66, 251*n*
Kisely, S., 285
Kiss, A., 254
Kiss, J.E., 179
Kitajima, M., 392
Kitzmann, K.M., 71
Kivimäki, M, 178, 179, 180, 364
Kiviniemi, M.T., 66, 98
Kivlahan, D.R., 131
Klaiberg, A., 224
Klapow, J.C., 414
Klassen, T.P., 411
Klauer, T., 168
Kleges, L.M., 84
Klein, D.J., 139
Klein, L.C., 157, 193
Klein, R.M., 90
Klein, W.M.P., 55, 66
Kleinman, 198*n*
Klepp, K.I., 82
Kleppinger, A., 99
Klinck, A., 285
Kline, K.A., 356
Klingle, R.S., 150
Klok, T., 304
Klonoff, E.A., 79, 222
Klotsche, J., 140
Klumb, P., 182
Klump, K.L., 148
Knapp, J.E., 313
Knaüper, B., 66, 113
Knäuper, B., 110
Knaus, W.A., 332
Knowlton, A., 402
Knox, S.S., 356
Knudson, S., 306, 307
Knussen, C., 280
Knutson, K.L., 116
Kocaman, N., 303
Koch, G.G., 134
Kohler, C.L., 304
Kohout, J.L., 19
Koithan, M., 220
Kojima, M., 172, 407
Kondos, G.T., 215
Konigsberg, R.D., 335, 336
Konopack, J.F., 97
Koolhaas, J.M., 163
Koo-Loeb, J.H., 148
Kooner, J.S., 355
Koopman, C., 167, 202, 408
Kop, W.J., 98, 350, 352
Kopec, J.A., 291
Kopelman, P.G., 104, 105
Korcha, R., 126
Koretz, G., 109, 136
Kosbab, K., 258
Kovacs, M., 298
Kowaleski-Jones, L., 182
Kozak, B., 185
Kozlowski, L.T., 145
Kraemer, H.C., 317
Kramer, A.F., 60, 96, 99
Kramer, S., 313
Krames, L., 188
Krantz, D.S., 308, 372
Krause, D., 45, 193
Krause, N., 192
Krause, T.J., 361
Kravitz, R.L., 251
Kremer, J., 301
Kremers, S.P.J., 135
Kremsner, P.G., 32
Krenz, C., 376
Kreuter, M.W., 61, 66
Krieg, J.-C., 116
Kripke, 117
Krishnan, R., 358
Krishnan, R.R., 357
Kristal, A., 102
Kristal, A.R., 366
Kristal-Boneh, E., 368
Kristenson, M., 172
Kristjanson, L.J., 339
Krittayaphong, R., 361
Kroenke, K., 224, 299
Krohne, H.W., 201
Kruger, D.F., 376
Kryscio, R.J., 367
Ksobiech, K., 397
Kubansky, L.D., 370
Kübler-Ross, E., 335, 336, 344, 345, 347
Kubzansky, L., 188, 190
Kubzansky, L.D., 358
Kucukarslan, S.N., 378
Kudielka, B.M., 387
Kudo, M., 392
Kugler, J., 360
Kuhle, S., 108
Kuijer, R.G., 409
Kuklina, E.V., 106
Kulik, J.A., 95, 235, 254, 342
Kuller, L.H., 115, 353, 356
Kumar, A., 93
Kundermann, B., 116
Kunkel, E., 315
Kuntsche, E., 142
Kunz, C., 73
Kunz-Ebrecht, S., 177, 179
Kunzi, B., 243, 244
Kuo, T.F., 116
Kurland, A.A., 256
Kutlu, Y., 303
Kwaijtaal, M., 358
Kwon, P., 191
Kyne, L., 247

La Greca, A.M., 56
Lacaille, D., 310*n*
Lacey, K., 389
LaChapelle, D., 264
Lacroix, J.M., 316
Laffel, L., 380
Lafontaine, P., 351
Lafreniere, K.D., 138
Lai, H., 409
Lallukka, T., 353
Lam, S., 194, 303
Lam, T.H., 121
LaManca, J.J., 306
Lamprecht, F., 166
Lance Coleman, C., 400
Landers, D.M., 96
Landis, C.A., 161
Landis, K.R., 205
Lando, J.F., 364
Landrine, H., 79, 222
Landry, S.J., 258
Landsbergis, P.A., 179
Lane, D.J., 95, 143
Lane, J.D., 207
Lane, N.E., 140
Lane, R.D., 351
Lang, A.R., 131
Lange, A., 274
Lange, L.J., 218
Lange, T., 116
Langens, T.A., 207
Langevin, H.M., 282
Langewitz, W., 254
Langston, C.A., 198
Lankford, T.R., 31*n*, 36*n*, 38*n*

SUBJECT INDEX

abdominal fat, 108–109
Aboriginal peoples
  colorectal cancer, 93–94
  death, view of, 344
  diabetes, 27, 374–375
  health risks and habits, 60
  infant mortality rates, 322–323
  patient stereotypes, 246
  sudden infant death syndrome
    (SIDS), 323
  youth health risks and
    habits, 60
abstinence violation effect, 75
academic stress, 389
acceptance, 336
access to health care, 241f
  and health behaviours, 54–55
  wait times, 241
accidents. *See* injuries
acculturation, 366
achieving self, 301
acquired immune deficiency
    syndrome (AIDS), 38, 44, 253
  adherence, 396
  in Canada, 394–397
  coping with AIDS, 402–403
  deaths from, 393
  educational interventions, 399
  estimated case range by exposure
    category and year, 395f
  health beliefs, 400
  highly active antiretroviral therapy
    (HAART), 396
  history of AIDS, 392–394
  human immunodeficiency virus
    (HIV). *See* human immunode-
    ficiency virus (HIV)
  interventions targeting sexual
    activity, 400–401
  interventions to reduce spread
    of AIDS, 399–402
  IV drug users, 402
  major at-risk groups, 396–397
  patient zero, theory
    of, 394–395
  psychosocial factors, 403
  risk factors, 397
  risk-related behaviour, 400
  social support, 402–403
  statistics, 393–394, 393f
acquired immunity, 43
action stage, 67–68
active aging, 59
acupuncture, 281–282
acute disorders, 11
acute glomerular nephritis, 37
acute illness, 218

acute pain, 273–275
  vs. chronic pain, 274–275
  recurrent acute pain, 274
acute stress, 351
acute stress paradigm, 168
addiction
  see also alcoholism; smoking
  defined, 122
  and pharmacological control of
    pain, 278
  relapse, 75–77, 76f
adherence, 249
  see also non-adherence
  acquired immune deficiency
    syndrome (AIDS), 396
  barriers to, 253–254
  causes of, 250–252
  diabetes, 377, 378, 380
  exercise programs, 360
  hypertension, 368–369
  improving, 255
  measuring, 250
  physical rehabilitation, 309
  and presentation of treatment,
    252–253
  treatment regimens and care,
    251–252, 251t
adolescents
  see also children; young adults
  and acquired immune deficiency
    syndrome (AIDS), 397
  diabetes, 379–380
  and exercise, 98
  health behaviours, 56–58
  influence on adult health, 58
  injuries, 324
  marijuana use, 125
  and multiple roles, 182
  peer influence, 138
  and smoking, 137–139, 137f
  socialization, 56
  and stress, 182
  stress, and eating, 102
  and substance abuse, 122
  sunscreen use, 95
  teachable moments, 56–57
  window of vulnerability, 57–58
adoption studies, 39
adrenal glands, 26–27, 27f
adrenocorticotropic hormone
    (ACTH), 26, 160
adult survivors, 343–344
adults. *See* middle age; seniors;
    young adults
advance directives, 331–332
advancing illness. *See* terminal illness
aerobic exercise, 95

after-effects of stress, 165–167
age
  and health behaviours, 54
  health services, use of, 221
agency, 354
aging. *See* seniors
aid in dying, 331, 332
AIDS. *See* acquired immune
    deficiency syndrome (AIDS)
alcohol abuse. *See* alcoholism
alcohol consumption
  see also alcoholism; problem drinking
  and the elderly, 60
  modest alcohol consumption,
    133–134
  red wine, 133
  social origins of, 126
  and stress, 126
  window of vulnerability, 126
Alcoholics Anonymous (AA), 71,
    79, 129
alcoholism, 34, 124–134
  see also addiction; alcohol consumption
  associated behaviours, 126
  classical conditioning, 69–70, 70f
  cognitive behaviour therapy
    (CBT), 74
  cognitive behavioural treatments,
    128–129
  and depression, 126
  detoxification, 127
  drinking and driving, 133
  evaluation of treatment
    programs, 130
  minimal interventions, 130
  modelling, 71
  and moderate drinking, 130
  origins of, 126
  patterns, 125–126
  placebo drinking, 131–132
  preventive approaches, 130–133
  relapse prevention, 130
  scope of the problem, 124–125
  treatment, 126–130
  university students, and drinking,
    131–132, 131t, 132f
  window of vulnerability, 126
Alexander, Franz, 7
allied health professional fields,
    17, 18t
allostatic load, 162–163
alternative medicine. *See*
    complementary and alternative
    medicine (CAM)
Alzheimer's disease, 25
Alzheimer's disease, 44–45
ambiguity, 179

ambiguous events, 163
ambulatory monitoring, 365
amenorrhea, 38
Andaman Islanders, 344–345
anemia, 30
aneurysms, 29
anger, 336, 355, 365–366, 376
  see also hostility
angina pectoris, 29
anorexia nervosa, 148–149
anoxia, 32
anticipatory grief, 338
anticipatory stress, 388
antimicrobial substances, 43
antiretroviral therapy, 396
anxiety
  and chronic illness, 297–298
  and chronic pain, 277
  and coronary heart disease (CHD),
    357, 358
  and immune functioning, 390
  and modelling, 71
  and placebo effects, 258
  stress eating, 110
appetite-suppressing drugs, 111
"apples," 109
appraisal delay, 226
approach (confrontative or vigilant)
    coping style, 192–193
appropriate death, 338
arteriosclerosis, 29
arthritis, 310, 414–419
  co-occurrence with other chronic
    conditions, 415
  gout, 419
  lupus, 419
  osteoarthritis, 418–419
  other forms of, 419
  prevalence, 414–415
  rheumatoid arthritis, 389, 415–417
artificial immunity, 43
Asian-Canadians, 366
asphyxia, 32
aspirin, 360
assertiveness training, 73, 129, 210
assisted suicide, 333
asthma, 32
at risk, 52
  acquired immune deficiency
    syndrome (AIDS), 396–397
  benefits of focusing on at-risk
    people, 58
  ethical issues in working with
    at-risk populations, 59
  health behaviours, 58–59
  interventions, 58–59
  problems of focusing on risk, 58